THE OXFORD HAN

ORGANIZED
CRIME

THE OXFORD HANDBOOKS IN CRIMINOLOGY AND CRIMINAL JUSTICE

GENERAL EDITOR: MICHAEL TONRY

THE OXFORD HANDBOOKS IN CRIMINOLOGY AND CRIMINAL JUSTICE offer authoritative, comprehensive, and critical overviews of the state of the art of criminology and criminal justice. Each volume focuses on a major area of each discipline, is edited by a distinguished group of specialists, and contains specially commissioned, original essays from leading international scholars in their respective fields. Guided by the general editorship of Michael Tonry, the series will provide an invaluable reference for scholars, students, and policy makers seeking to understand a wide range of research and policies in criminology and criminal justice.

OTHER TITLES IN THIS SERIES:

GENDER, SEX, AND CRIME
Rosemary Gartner and Bill McCarthy

POLICE AND POLICING
Michael D. Reisig and Robert J. Kane

ETHNICITY, CRIME, AND IMMIGRATION
Sandra Bucerius and Michael Tonry

CRIMINOLOGICAL THEORY
Francis T. Cullen and Pamela Wilcox

JUVENILE CRIME AND JUVENILE JUSTICE
Barry C. Feld and Donna M. Bishop

CRIME AND CRIMINAL JUSTICE
Michael Tonry

CRIME PREVENTION
Brandon C. Welsh and David P. Farrington

SENTENCING AND CORRECTIONS
Joan Petersilia and Kevin R. Reitz

CRIME AND PUBLIC POLICY
Michael Tonry

THE OXFORD HANDBOOK OF

ORGANIZED CRIME

Edited by

LETIZIA PAOLI

OXFORD

UNIVERSITY PRESS

OXFORD
UNIVERSITY PRESS

Oxford University Press is a department of the University of Oxford. It furthers
the University's objective of excellence in research, scholarship, and education
by publishing worldwide. Oxford is a registered trade mark of Oxford University
Press in the UK and certain other countries.

Published in the United States of America by Oxford University Press
198 Madison Avenue, New York, NY 10016, United States of America.

© Oxford University Press 2014

First issued as an Oxford University Press paperback, 2019

Library of Congress Cataloging-in-Publication Data
The Oxford handbook of organized crime / edited by Letizia Paoli.
pages cm. — (The Oxford handbooks in criminology and criminal justice)
Includes bibliographical references and index.
ISBN 978–0–19–973044–5 (hardcover : alk. paper); 978–0–19–094732–3 (paperback : alk. paper)
1. Organized crime. 2. Criminology. I. Paoli, Letizia.
HV6441.O94 2014
364.106—dc23
2013020568

CONTENTS

PART I CONCEPT, THEORIES, HISTORY, AND RESEARCH METHODS

PART II ACTORS AND INTERACTIONS

PART III MARKETS AND ACTIVITIES

PART IV POLICIES TO CONTROL ORGANIZED CRIME

LIST OF CONTRIBUTORS

Jay S. Albanese is professor in the Wilder School of Government & Public Affairs at Virginia Commonwealth University, US.

Georgios A. Antonopoulos is professor of criminology in the School of Social Sciences and Law at Teesside University, UK.

Julie Ayling is a research fellow in the Regulatory Institutions Network at the Australian National University.

Margaret Beare is professor in the Osgoode Hall Law School and former director of the Jack and Mae Nathanson Centre for the Study of Organized Crime and Corruption at York University, Canada.

Tim Boekhout van Solinge is assistant professor of criminology at Utrecht University and coordinator of the Criminology Course of the Dutch Study Centre of the Public Ministry.

Martin Bouchard is associate professor in the School of Criminology at Simon Fraser University, Canada.

Roderic Broadhurst is professor of criminology in the Australian National University's College of Arts and Social Sciences.

Ko-Lin Chin is a distinguished professor at the Rutgers School of Criminal Justice, US.

Kim-Kwang Raymond Choo is senior lecturer in the School of Information Technology and Mathematical Sciences at the University of South Australia.

Scott H. Decker is foundation professor in the School of Criminology and Criminal Justice at Arizona State University, US.

Elizabeth Dondlinger Wyman received her J.D. from New York University Law School in 2010.

Nicholas Farrelly is a research fellow at the School of International, Political and Strategic Studies at Australian National University.

Andrew Feinstein was an ANC member of parliament in South Africa's first democratic elections in 1994 and is now a co-director of the organization Corruption Watch, UK.

Cyrille Fijnaut is professor emeritus of international and comparative criminal law at the Law School of Tilburg University, The Netherlands.

Peter Grabosky is professor emeritus, Regulatory Institutions Network, College of Asia and the Pacific, Australian National University.

Peter Hill is an independent researcher. Formerly a British Academy Postdoctoral Fellow in the Department of Sociology at University of Oxford, UK.

Dick Hobbs is professor of sociology at University of Essex and at University of Western Sidney Australia.

Paul Holden is a South African historian and writer focusing on corruption and governance issues. He is the author of two books on the arms trade, *The Arms Deal in Your Pocket* and *The Devil in the Detail: How the Arms Deal Changed Everything.*

James B. Jacobs is the Chief Justice Warren E. Burger Professor of Constitutional Law and the Courts and Director director of the Center for Research in Crime and Justice at New York University Law School, US.

Susanne Karstedt is professor of criminology and criminal justice at the University of Leeds, UK.

Michael Kilchling is a senior researcher at the Max Planck Institute for Foreign and International Criminal Law, Germany.

Edward R. Kleemans is full professor at the VU School of Criminology, Faculty of Law, VU University Amsterdam, The Netherlands.

Antonio La Spina is professor in the School of Government and Faculty of Political Science of the LUISS University "Guido Carli", Rome, Italy.

Michael Levi is professor of criminology in the School of Social Sciences at Cardiff University, Wales, UK.

Monica Medel is a graduate student in the Teresa Lozano Long Institute of Latin American Studies at the University of Texas, US. She previously spent fifteen years as a reporter covering drug trafficking in Mexico.

Carlo Morselli is assistant professor at the School of Criminology, Université de Montréal, Canada.

Letizia Paoli is professor in the Leuven Institute of Criminology at the University of Leuven, Belgium.

David C. Pyrooz is assistant professor in the College of Criminal Justice at Sam Houston State University, US.

Peter Reuter is professor in the School of Public Affairs and in the Department of Criminology at the University of Maryland, US.

Dina Siegel is professor of criminology at the Willem Pompe Institute for Criminal Law and Criminology at Utrecht University, The Netherlands.

Toine Spapens is professor of criminology at Tilburg Law School, The Netherlands.

Monika Smit is a researcher at WODC (Research and Documentation Centre), The Netherlands Ministry of Security and Justice and at Free University Amsterdam.

Francisco E. Thoumi is a Senior Member Colombian Academy of economic Sciences and Member of the International Narcotics Control Board.

Henk van de Bunt is professor of criminology at the Faculty of Law of the Erasmus Rotterdam University, The Netherlands and director of the Interdisciplinary Graduate School of Social Security.

Tom Vander Beken is professor of criminology at Ghent University Law School, Belgium.

Federico Varese is professor of criminology in the Department of Sociology at University of Oxford and Senior Research Fellow at Nuffield College, Oxford, UK.

Vadim Volkov is vice-rector for international affairs, professor at the Department of Political Science and Sociology, and head of the Research Institute for the Rule of Law at the European University at St. Petersburg, Russia.

Phil Williams is professor in the Matthew B. Ridgway Center for International Security Studies at the University of Pittsburgh, US.

Michael Woodiwiss is senior lecturer in History at the University of the West of England, UK.

Damián Zaitch is associate professor of criminology at Willem Pompe Institute for Criminal Law and Criminology at Utrecht University, US.

THE OXFORD HANDBOOK OF

ORGANIZED CRIME

INTRODUCTION

LETIZIA PAOLI

WITH two spectacular bomb attacks in 1992, the Sicilian mafia organization Cosa Nostra murdered two prominent anti-mafia judges, Giovanni Falcone and Paolo Borsellino, the former's wife, and eight members of their police escorts. The following year, it placed bombs in three of Italy's main cities, killing more innocent people and destroying historical buildings. Although these events appear to be of modest proportions vis-à-vis the death toll produced by other criminal organizations in other nations (in Mexico alone, 100,000 people are estimated to have died between 2006 and 2012 in the "war" staged by drug cartels; Miroff & Booth 2012), they sent huge shock waves throughout Europe and the international community. Both European policy-makers and the public worried about the Sicilian mafia's excessive power and its presumed ability to expand all over Europe. Together with the epochal fall of the Berlin Wall in 1989 and the collapse of the Soviet Union two years later, Cosa Nostra's "excellent cadavers" (Stille 1995) played a prominent role in putting organized crime high on the crime control agenda of the European Union, the United Nations, and most European governments. In this political and public debate, organized crime was initially identified with criminal organizations, even though much looser definitions of organized crime were finally adopted in the law books and in international treaties (see Paoli and Vander Beken in this volume for details).

Media and political entrepreneurs also played an important part in that process, increasing both the fascination with and worry about criminal organizations of Italian and other origin—as they had also done in the 1960s and 1970s when the Italian American mafia came to be identified as a crime control priority in the United States (Woodiwiss 2001; see also Beare and Woodiwiss in this volume). It was also thanks to the great success of the book and movie trilogy *The Godfather* that the Italian (American) mafia came to be seen worldwide as the archetype of criminal organizations.

The same mix of factors—spectacular or long-lasting bursts of violence by criminal organizations as well as the savvy action of moral entrepreneurs and media—have also more recently drawn public and policy attention to the problem of organized crime in other contexts, in both the developed and developing world: from Latin America to Australia, from Canada to China. In the United States, too, the Obama administration published a "Strategy to Combat Transnational Organized Crime" in 2011, after three decades of neglect of the topic (White House 2011).

To enhance the fight against organized crime, policy-makers all over the world have granted special investigative powers to their law enforcement agencies. In several countries, they have also engaged in institutional reforms, setting up new police agencies and/or centralizing competences from local units to a nationwide police agency, as happened, for example, in the United Kingdom with the establishment of the Serious Organised Crime Agency in 2005 (which fused with other agencies to become the National Crime Agency in 2013). There have also been numerous regional and international initiatives, meant to foster police and justice cooperation in the fight against organized crime, and many of these have had large international support. As of March 2014, there were 179 parties to the UN Convention against Transnational Organized Crime of 2000, the overwhelming majority of the world's nation-states (for more details, see the essays written in the fourth part of the handbook).

I. Organized Crime: Two Main Notions and Types

Despite—or perhaps because of—the great public and policy interest, organized crime remains a fuzzy and contested umbrella concept. As explained in more detail in Paoli and Vander Beken (in this volume), the understanding of organized crime has since the 1920s shifted back and forth between two rivaling notions: (a) a set of stable organizations illegal per se or whose members systematically engage in crime; and (b) a set of serious criminal activities, particularly the provision of illegal goods and services, mostly carried out for monetary gain. The general public, the media, and most policy-makers primarily use the expression "organized crime" to refer to criminal organizations, such as the Sicilian and American Cosa Nostra, the Japanese Yakuza, Colombian and Mexican drug cartels, and other large-scale criminal groups around the world thought to have a hierarchical and lasting structure. Particularly in countries with no direct experience of such large-scale crime groups, however, scholars, law enforcement officials, and some policy-makers relate organized crime to trafficking in illegal drugs and human beings, gambling, and the provision of other goods and services that are fully criminalized or heavily restricted. To fit both notions and maximize the range of problems covered, broad, lowest-common denominator definitions of organized crime have finally been adopted at the international level and in many countries as well. Torn between the two rivaling notions, some policy-makers and law enforcement agencies use the term "organized crime" in both senses within the same text—not to the benefit of clarity. In its 2013 Serious and Organized Crime Threat

Assessment, for example, Europol, the European Union's police intelligence agency, speaks both of "organized crime groups" and "serious and organized crime areas of activities" (Europol 2013, p. 42).

In the collective imaginary and even in the understanding of many policy-makers and some law enforcement officers, criminal organizations and criminal profit-making activities seem to go hand in hand. Famously, the Kefauver Committee, the first U.S. congressional body to deal with the problem of organized crime after World War II, claimed that "there is a nationwide crime syndicate known as the Mafia, whose tentacles are found in many large cities....Its leaders are usually found in control of the most lucrative rackets of their cities" (U.S. Senate 1951, p. 131). In reality, however, the picture is more complicated, as there is no necessary link between large-scale criminal organizations à la the mafia and the criminal money-making activities they are presumed to control, as a growing body of literature, as is well documented in this handbook.

Large, stable, structured criminal organizations operate in a number of countries, engaging in a plurality of money-making activities and usually also claiming some sort of control over the political, economic, and social life of their home areas of settlement. Contrary to popular perceptions, however, these organizations are a rarity. They consolidated and have survived in contexts in which government structures are weak or the latter's representatives are willing to enter into pacts with the bosses of criminal organizations. The oldest and most established among them, such as the Chinese Triads, Japanese Yakuza, and the two main Southern Italian mafia organizations, Cosa Nostra and 'Ndrangheta, for example, go back to the 18th and 19th centuries (Chin, Hill, and Paoli in this volume). These mafia-type organizations all emerged in contexts in which the local government authorities were not able to guarantee even a minimum of security, and the residents had to protect their property, women, and their own lives by themselves. Large-scale criminal groups posing as proto-states were also active in several parts of pre-modern Europe (Fijnaut in this volume), but most of them were swept away by the consolidation of modern government structures—a counterfactual proof of mafia-type organizations' dependence on the weakness of government authorities. The American Cosa Nostra rose in the early 20th century when the U.S. government still had limited authority in the Italian ethnic community, and some of its representatives preferred to come to terms with, rather than prosecute, Cosa Nostra bosses and other criminal entrepreneurs fostered by Prohibition (Albanese, this volume). Other large-scale organizations, such as the Colombian and Mexican drug trafficking cartels, developed more recently to feed the U.S. and European appetite for illegal drugs, but they, too, assumed their current shape because of the weakness and corruption of their home governments (Thoumi and Medel, and Thoumi in this volume).

Whereas large-scale criminal organizations are rather rare, illegal money-making activities occur everywhere. Many of them consist of the production and sale of goods and services that are still demanded by the public, despite the fact of having been tout court prohibited or highly restricted since the early 20th century onward. As an illegal market emerges to feed this demand, these activities are often referred to as illegal market activities. In addition, there are predatory (or extortionary) money-making activities, which produce no value added and merely entail an involuntary transfer of property by force or deceit. In their basic variants, some of these activities, such as theft or fraud, are probably as old as mankind. Many more variants have been made possible by technological progress, including the entirely new branch of cybercrime. If the stolen or counterfeited products are sold, illegal markets for these products may also emerge (for these activities, see the essays of the third part of the volume).

Regardless of the type, illegal money-making activities can hardly be stopped in their entirety by democratic governments committed to the rule of law. That theft and fraud have presumably occurred since the beginning of mankind testifies to the impossibility of uprooting such problems in any political context. As long as governments are not willing to resort to authoritarian border and law enforcement methods or to disrupt legitimate trade by, say, inspecting every container crossing their national borders, they will also not be able to stop illegal market flows. Contemporary governments have even less leverage than their predecessors over illegal—and legal—market flows as a result of economic globalization. The diminution of state-enforced restrictions on exchanges across borders—the core trait of globalization—has accelerated the interconnections between previously separate domestic, legal and illegal, markets and increased the mobility of goods, capital, and human beings. For illegal organizations and other entrepreneurs, it has become easier than ever to move drugs and other illegal products from producing to consuming countries, to repatriate profits, to establish business partnerships with foreign counterparts and even to operate in foreign countries themselves.

If the prospects of controlling global illegal market flows are rather bleak, government authorities, even in democratic societies, are not powerless vis-à-vis organized crime activities. In particular, government action can heavily impact the size, organization, and operating methods of the groups—or "enterprises"—that engage in predatory activities or produce, or trade in, illegal products. In countries with an effective government, in fact, large-scale criminal organizations are not allowed to consolidate, and that is why the great majority of illegal exchanges (voluntary or otherwise) in Western countries are carried out by numerous, relatively small and often ephemeral enterprises minimizing the use of violence in order to avoid attracting law enforcement attention. In other words, "disorganized crime" (Reuter 1983)—rather than organized crime understood in terms of large-scale stable criminal organizations—predominates in Western countries, reflecting the local governments' capability to enforce their prohibitions (see Bouchard and Morselli in this volume).

II. Policy Dilemmas

The suppression of large-scale criminal organizations, the enforcement of prohibitions on specific goods and services and, more generally, the control of any form of crime, organized or not, do not come without a cost. First, these interventions involve the disbursement of considerable financial and human resources that could have been used elsewhere. Second, they restrict the rights of the defendants, convicts, and sometimes even of the public at large. Third, through the criminalization of specific goods and services, they also create opportunities for corruption and violence, because the criminals involved aim to obtain the covert support of government officials or the control of legitimate businesses, or because they resort to violence or the threat of violence to solve conflicts that obviously cannot be brought to court. Fourth, these policy interventions occasionally prompt the offenders and/or the final customers to engage in very harmful practices. One of the latter is body-packing, that is, swallowing cocaine or heroin balls to smuggle them across borders. The injection of diluted, impure drugs can also be considered an unintended consequence of drug prohibition, as users often start injecting to maximize the drug effects given the latter's high costs and have no control on quality because the drugs are criminalized. In other cases, an effective policy intervention in a specific country or local area may merely spread the problem elsewhere. The latter effect is known as the "balloon-effect" in the field of drug policy. This refers to the fact that the illegal drug industry—is like a balloon: when it is "squeezed" or curbed in one location, it tends to "bulge" or reemerge in another location (e.g., Friesendorf 2007). Whereas some studies have shown that police interventions in city contexts can effectively reduce crime and not just displace it (e.g., Braga and Weisburd 2010), it seems unlikely that such effects can be replicated across cities and regions, especially for the wholesale phase of many illegal market activities.

The U.S. war on drugs of the past three decades, for example, may have helped keep the U.S. drug market relatively "disorganized" but has failed to reach its main goal of reducing drugs availability (Reuter and Trautman 2009). Through its interdiction, moreover, it has helped spread the problem of drug production and trafficking to a number of Latin American countries, has created endless opportunities for corruption and violence in both the United States and abroad, and has unintentionally contributed to the destabilization of several, already weak Central American and, more recently, West African countries (e.g., OAS 2013). Of the world's eight most murderous countries, seven lie on the cocaine-trafficking route from the Andes to the United States and Europe. Honduras, for example, a small Central American country of 8 million people, records each year more than 7,000 murders. In the European Union, with a population of 500 million, the figure is under 6,000 (*Economist* 2013). Even in the United States itself, the U.S. war on drugs has produced huge social and financial costs: it is enough to say that drug convictions account for almost half of American prisoners in federal prisons and 17% of those under state jurisdiction (Carson and Golinelli 2013, p. 3). Of the adults on probation and parole, 25% and 33%, respectively, also had a drug charge as their most serious offense (Maruschak and Bonczar 2013, pp. 17 and 19). While no country can legitimately aspire to host large-scale, powerful criminal organizations or a large number of drug addicts, preventing such developments needs to be traded off with the costs and unintended consequences of the policies adopted to reach such goals and the goals of more generic crime control and health policies. The case of gambling is particularly enticing: this activity was once considered a quintessential activity of the Italian American mafia and other U.S. crime groups (e.g., Reuter 1983). However, its progressive decriminalization and regulation have subtracted sources of revenues for illegal players and opened up the market for legitimate businesses, with no major rise in gambling addiction (Spapens in this volume).

Policy interventions to control whatever form of organized crime should, in other words, be inspired by the realization of the governments' limits and potential for harm. They should also be checked—both ex ante and ex post, that is, prior to and after enactment—for their appropriateness and effectiveness. Ex post, special attention should be given to the policy's unintended consequences, as these are difficult to fully anticipate in advance. Alas, whereas legal scholars and policy analysts usually scrutinize proposed bills and other policy documents for their respect of basic human rights principles and other constitutional norms, much less research has so far been carried out on the effects, including the unintended consequences, of the policy measures adopted. Such research is often not supported by government agencies: these seem often not to be interested in knowing ex post if the policies they adopted out of faith or ideology or in reaction to an emergency are really working.

The evaluation of organized crime control measures is also hampered by the imprecise knowledge we still have of the many phenomena related to the umbrella concept of organized crime. As we have no precise measure of the extent of many organized crime problems, it is impossible to say if an intervention has led to a 10% reduction of those problems. The evaluation of organized crime control measures is also hindered by the umbrella concept of organized crime itself. No single researcher or even team of researchers has the capability to assess the impact of policies targeting such a broad spectrum of problems ranging from Cosa Nostra– or mafia-type organizations to human trafficking, from thieves' and youth gangs to money laundering, from illegal drug trafficking to cybercrime in a national or, even worse, international context. The policy assessment, as the study of the underlying organized crime phenomena, can only be done case by case. In other words, organized crime might well have been a catchy umbrella concept to raise the public's and policy-makers' attentions but because of its imprecision, conflicting definitions, and multiple referents, it is not an adequate research or policy-making concept.

Despite these uncertainties, the overall goal of organized crime control policies should be clear: envisaging interventions that can reduce the total harms resulting from both the organized crime phenomena and the policies aiming to control these phenomena, drawing from the realization that both organized crime actors and activities *and* the related policies cause harms and that bad policies may even inadvertently create opportunities for organized crime.

III. The Structure of the Handbook

Reflecting the dual understanding and two main types of organized crime, the two longest parts—the second and third—of this handbook are devoted to "Actors and

Interactions" and "Markets and Activities," respectively. The second part, "Actors and Interactions," consists of 12 chapters. The first seven of them are devoted to some of the most infamous criminal organizations in the world: the Italian mafia (Letizia Paoli), the Italian-American mafia (Jay Albanese), the Russian mafia (Vadim Volkov), organized crime in Colombia (Francisco Thoumi), Mexican drug cartels (Monica Medel and Francisco Thoumi), the Triads and other forms of Chinese organized crime (Ko-Lin Chin), the Japanese Yakuza (Peter Hill), and West African organized crime (Phil Williams). Each of these chapters briefly reconstructs the history, analyzes the internal structure and activities, and assesses the economic and political power and future prospects of the selected organization (or set of organizations).

The following chapter, written by Scott H. Decker and David C. Pyrooz, considers the extent to which urban and youth gangs can be considered a form of organized crime. Martin Bouchard and Carlo Morselli's chapter is devoted to the opportunistic structures of organized crime: these are no-name, ephemeral criminal groups and cliques that, as we said above, are primarily responsible for illegal market and predatory activities in the developed world. Further moving away from the traditional referents of organized crime, Susanne Karstedt's chapter examines under which conditions state authorities engage in organizing crime and thus become an actor or even a form of organized crime.

This part of the handbook ends with a chapter written by Henk van de Bunt, Dina Siegel, and Damián Zaitch on interactions and, more precisely, the embeddedness of organized actors and activities in wider gender, occupational, and ethnic relationships. This chapter thus also deals with the role of women in organized crime groups and activities.

The nine chapters of the third part of the handbook examine the criminal activities most frequently associated with organized crime. This part begins with a chapter on the sale of "protection" and extortion, quintessential activities of mafia-type criminal organizations (Federico Varese). The following five chapters focus on the provision of illegal goods and services and the resulting illegal markets and more specifically drug trafficking (Peter Reuter), human smuggling, human trafficking, and exploitation in the sex industry (Edward R. Kleemans and Monika Smits), illegal gambling (Toine Spapens), money laundering (Michael Levi), and arms trafficking (Andrew Feinstein and Paul Holden). The remaining three chapters of this part are devoted to predatory activities: organized fraud (Michael Levi), cybercrime (Kim-Kwang Raymond Choo and Peter Grabosky), and the illegal exploitation of natural resources (Tim Boekhout van Solinge).

These nine chapters are built on a similar model. They each examine the patterns of an organized crime activity since its criminalization, single out the most effected countries, and if appropriate, discuss the socioeconomic, cultural, and institutional factors promoting the countries' involvement. They also analyze the actors participating in the selected illegal market, predatory or extortionary activities, estimate, if possible, the actors' revenues, provide information on the victims and harms they suffer and, finally, consider the efforts made to control these activities.

The two core parts of the handbook are preceded by an introductory first part on the concept of organized crime, related theories, history, and research methods. Letizia Paoli and Tom Vander Beken reconstruct the different meanings given to the expression "organized crime" in the scientific and public debate since its invention in the early 20th century. Edward R. Kleemans reviews the principal explanatory theories of organized crime. In a historical perspective, Cyrille Fijnaut points to the many criminal groups that were active in Asia, Europe, and the United States prior to the invention of the expression organized crime and analyzes the groups' structure, activities as well as the reasons for their emergence and dissolution. In the final chapter of the first part, Dick Hobbs and Georgios A. Antonopoulos present the principal research methods used to study organized crime, assessing the pros and cons of each method and indicating representative studies for each of them.

The fourth and final part of the handbook is devoted to the policies to control organized crime. Consisting of five chapters, this part is largely organized on the basis of a geographic criterion. Four chapters cover, respectively, organized crime control polices in the United States of America (James B. Jacobs and Elizabeth A. Dondlinger), at the European Union level (Cyrille Fijnaut), in Australia and New Zealand (Julie Ayling and Roderic Broadhurst), and in Asia, with examples from India, China, and the Golden Triangle (Roderic Broadhurst and Nicholas Farrelly). An ad hoc chapter, written by Antonio La Spina, is devoted to the fight against the mafia in Italy, as this country has often been considered a model, or at least a source of inspiration, in the control of organized crime. Deviating from the geographic criterion, the fourth part ends with an assessment of finance-oriented strategies of organized crime control (Michael Kilchling). Since the 1990s, in fact, these strategies have become the second main pillar in the worldwide control of organized crime, next to the traditional criminal prosecution of the offenders.

Acknowledgements

As to be expected, putting together a large edited volume such as this handbook has entailed a lot of work. This work has been compensated by the privilege of collaborating, and having inspiring exchanges, with the contributors of this handbook. In my view, these are the most authoritative scholars researching the different manifestations of organized crime and the related control policies—and in the meanwhile a number of them have also become my friends. I am really grateful to all the handbook contributors for their first-class contributions, brilliant reflections and occasional jokes, readiness to consider and implement my suggestions and, last but not least, their patience.

I am also deeply indebted to Michel Tonry for his unfailing trust and support from the commission of the handbook up to the end of the lengthy production process.

My final thoughts go to the victims of organized crime and of badly conceived organized crime control policies, to all of whom I devote this handbook. Some of these victims, like the two Sicilian judges mentioned at the outset of this introduction, are veritable heroes: representatives of the government and judiciary who paid with their lives for their determination to fulfill their duty in the best way possible, regardless of the threats and corrupt offers received. Equally heroic are the many members of local communities all over the world that find the courage to stand up against the impositions of bullying criminal organizations or report evidence on criminal activities—and for this reason become targets of organized crime violence. There are also those who die just because they happen to live or be in the "wrong" place: for example, the many victims of the current drug wars in Mexico and other Central American states. Other victims do not lose their lives but suffer serious harms to their physical and psychological integrity and material interests, such the victims of human trafficking. Still others are victims of thefts, fraud, or extortions. Others, more indirectly but sometimes throughout their lives, suffer harms to their material interests because the presence of organized crime groups or the concentration of criminal activities discourages investment in their areas of residence and they thus cannot find a (good) job. For the same reasons, legitimate businesses also suffer economic harms. They, as well as the government authorities, are also harmed in their functional integrity, whenever they are infiltrated, or their representatives are corrupted, by criminals. As the chapter of Tim Boekhout van Solinge aptly shows, the environment can also be harmed, in its forests, soil, underground natural resources, and wildlife.

There are also many victims of misconceived organized crime control policies. Among them, the largest group is probably made up of those sent to prison for the mere possession of drugs. Of the 223,000 prisoners serving time for drug offenses in a U.S. state prison as of December 2012, 25% (or 55,000, slightly less than the entire prison population of France, a country of 62 million people; Walmsley 2012) had been convicted for mere drug possession (Carson and Golinelli 2013, p. 3). Other victims of organized crime policies include the thousands of Mexicans who have died since 2006, when the then President Felipe Calderon unintentionally triggered a drug war, by sending battalions of poorly trained soldiers into the streets to fight powerful crime organizations.

Hopefully, a better knowledge of the many different manifestations of organized crime—to which this handbook is intended to contribute—and, on this basis, the adoption of more appropriate, realistic, and effective control policies will reduce the numbers of all types of victims and improve their lot.

REFERENCES

Braga, Anthony and David Weisburd, 2010. *Policing Problem Places: Crime Hot Spots and Effective Prevention*. Oxford: Oxford University Press.

Carson, E. Ann and Daniela Golinelli. 2013. *Prisoners in 2012: Trends in Admissions and Releases, 1991-2012*. Washington, DC: US Dept. of Justice Bureau of Justice Statistics, Dec. 2013, NCJ243920. http://www.bjs.gov/content/pub/pdf/p12tar9112.pdf

Economist, The. 2013. "Towards a ceasefire: Experiments in legalisation are showing what a post-war approach to drug control could look like." February 23. Available at: http://www.

economist.com/news/international/21572184-experiments-legalisation-are-showing-what
-post-war-approach-drug-control-could-look.

Europol. 2013. *SOCTA 2013: EU Serious and Organised Crime Threat Assessment.* 's-Gravenzande: Deventer.

Friesendorf, C. 2007. *U.S. Foreign Policy and the War on Drugs: Displacing the Cocaine and Heroin Industry.* London: Routledge.

Maruschak, Laura M. and Thomas P. Bonczar. 2013. "Probation and Parole in the United States, 2012." Washington, DC: U.S. Dept of Justice Bureau of Justice Statistics, December 2013, NCJ 243826.

Miroff, Nick and William Booth. 2012. "Mexico's drug war is at a stalemate as Calderon's presidency ends." *Washington Post.* November 27. Available at: http://www.washingtonpost. com/world/the_americas/calderon-finishes-his-six-year-drug-war-at-stalemate/2012/ 11/26/82c90a94-31eb-11e2-92f0-496af208bf23_story_1.html.

OAS, Organization of American States. 2013. *The Drug Problem in the Americas.* Washington, DC: OAS.

Reuter, Peter. 1983. *Disorganized Crime: The Economics of the Visible Hand.* Cambridge: MIT Press.

Reuter, Peter and Franz Trautman, eds. 2009. *A Report on Global Illicit Drugs Markets 1998–2007.* Luxembourg: European Communities.

Stille, Alexander. 1995. *Excellent Cadavers: The Mafia and the Death of the First Italian Republic.* London: Jonathan Cape.

U.S. Senate. 1951. *Third Interim Report of the Special Committee to Investigate Organized Crime in Interstate Commerce (Kefavuer Committee).* 81st Cong., 2d sess. Washington, D.C.: U.S. Government Printing Office.

Walmsley, Roy. 2012. *World Prison Population List.* Ninth edition. Essex: International Centre for Prison Studies, April.

White House. 2011. "Strategy to Address Transnational Organized Crime: Addressing Converging Threats to National Security." July. http://www.justice.gov/criminal/ocgs/ org-crime/docs/08-30-11-toc-strategy.pdf

Woodiwiss, Michael. 2001. *Organized Crime and American Power.* Toronto: University of Toronto Press.

PART I

CONCEPT, THEORIES, HISTORY, AND RESEARCH METHODS

CHAPTER 1

···

ORGANIZED CRIME

A Contested Concept

···

LETIZIA PAOLI AND TOM VANDER BEKEN

THE concept of organized crime has had a winding history, with many partially contradictory meanings attached to it since the expression began to be used in the United States more than a hundred years ago.[1] Throughout this span of time, the term *organized crime* has had moments of veritable policy success—from the 1950s to the early 1970s in the United States and during the 1990s in Europe—as it has been used to indicate different criminal phenomena regarded as serious social problems. Whereas the term *organized crime* still has strong evocative power, which undoubtedly explains its political success, the many different criminal actors and activities that have been subsumed under this label make it a vague umbrella concept that cannot be used, without specification, as a basis for empirical analyses, theory-building, or policymaking.

The essay proceeds as follows. In section I of this chapter, we single out the main shifts in meanings, territorial scope and scientific and political legitimacy of the concept *organized crime*. With sections II, III, and IV, we reconstruct its historical trajectory, starting in the United States where it was used almost exclusively until the 1970s and then following its rapid spread in Europe since the late 1980s. In section V, we consider the growing emphasis placed on the transnational nature of organized crime from the early 1990s onward, particularly by the United Nations (UN). In the last section, we discuss the future of the concept of organized crime, drawing from its incipient decline in Europe and the recent interest in the topic in Asia and Oceania.

I. THE SHIFTS IN MEANINGS, TERRITORIAL SCOPE, AND LEGITIMACY

···

The meanings of organized crime have changed considerably and repeatedly over time: according to Levi, this expression is now like a psychiatrist's Rorschach blot, whose "attraction as well as…weakness is that one can read almost anything into it" (2002, p. 887; see also von Lampe 2001; Finckenauer 2005; and Varese 2010). Basically, the understanding of organized crime has shifted back and forth between two rival notions: (1) a set of stable organizations illegal per se or whose members systematically engage in crime, and (2) a set of serious criminal activities mostly carried out for monetary gain. Depending on time and place, some authors as well as national and international policy and law enforcement agencies have emphasized the "Who," that is, the individual offenders and their variable partnerships, whereas others have given more relevance to the "What," that is, the criminal activities conducted. The "Who" and "What" distinction goes back to Smith (1991). More recently Hagan (2006, p. 134) introduced the distinction between *Organized Crime* (capitalized) to refer to criminal organizations and *organized crime* (lower case) to refer to criminal activities that require a degree of organization. Roughly speaking, the evolution of the organized crime debate worldwide over the past one hundred years can be synthesized in a shift from "What" to "Who" and a reverting tide from "Who" to "What," with an increasing merger of the two; however, not all countries, as we will see below, fall neatly into this scheme.

The two basic and rival notions of organized crime have been used not only interchangeably, but also simultaneously. From the 1950s onward, in fact, the assumption spread in the United States that criminal organizations were responsible for most serious criminal activities for gain. However, starting with Reuter's seminal book *Disorganized Crime* (1983), numerous researchers (e.g., van Duyne 1997; Naylor 2003; van Duyne and Levi 2005) have proven this assumption to be wrong (see also Paoli 2002b and Kleemans's essay titled Theoretical Perspectives on Organized Crime and Bouchard and Morselli's essay titled Opportunistic Structures of Organized Crime), so much so that most academics now have to choose between one of the two rival notions of organized crime. Policymaking and law enforcement agencies worldwide also increasingly realize that stable, large-scale criminal organizations are far from monopolizing profit-making criminal activities (e.g., Europol 2003). Rather than discarding the pair "criminal organizations" and "profit-making criminal activities," they have increasingly watered down the definition of criminal organizations so as to include also networks, gangs, cells and any group composed of at least three people working together for some time (e.g., United Nations General Assembly 2000a; White House 2011; Serious Organised Crime Agency 2012; BKA annual; see below). For some agencies (e.g., Serious Organised Crime Agency 2012) and scholars (e.g. Felson 2009, p. 159–160), organized crime seems to mean little more than co-offending by more than two perpetrators (see Finckenauer 2005, pp. 76–78; Calderoni 2012, p. 1373).

The supposed territorial scope of organized crime has also changed. Originally, organized crime was equated with racketeering, another vague notion at the core of which there is extortion, an activity necessarily territorially based and usually carried out only on a local basis. Since the 1990s, instead, many researchers (e.g., Williams and Florez 1994; Siegel, van de Bunt, and Zaitch 2003) and an even larger number of government agencies and international organizations, ranging from the European Union to the United Nations (United Nations 1994; Council of the European Union 1997a; United

Nations General Assembly 2000a; White House 2011), have emphasized the transnational nature of organized crime.

The policy and scientific legitimacy and relevance of the organized crime concept have also varied considerably over time. Except for the United States and Italy, most other nations did not regard organized crime as a serious domestic problem until the late 1980s. Whereas media accounts of organized crime and mafias have always fascinated the general public, most scholars shunned the topic until the early 1990s. Only since that period has organized crime become an accepted policy and scientific concept virtually throughout the world.

Since the 1990s, the majority of governments, at least in the developed world, and many international organizations, including the UN, have adopted bills, decrees, action plans, or international treaties specifically targeting organized crime, often foreseeing extensive new prosecutorial powers to law enforcement agencies—as the United States had already done in the 1960s and 1970s. The fight against organized crime has also been used to justify far-reaching criminal justice reforms in several countries, particularly in Europe (see Fijnaut and Paoli 2004). In turn, international organizations, such as the European Union bureaucracy (e.g., Council 1997 and 2003; see Fijnaut's essay titled European Union Organized Crime Control Policies), have been keen, since the early 1990s, to emphasize the transnational dimension of the organized crime threat in order to increase their competencies and powers and/or to harmonize and extend criminal laws and law enforcement procedural powers across their Member States. This harmonization has also been the main goal of the 2000 UN Convention against Transnational Organized Crime (McClean 2007).

Despite some persisting resistance (e.g., Cornils and Greve 2004), organized crime has also become a legitimate scientific research topic, attracting considerable attention from criminologists and other social scientists during the 1990s and the early 21st century, particularly in Europe. The concept of organized crime might have already reached its apex of popularity, however. As shown below, again particularly in Europe, both policymakers and researchers have begun to replace it with alternative concepts.

A. The American Debate: From "What" to "Who"

Despite uncertainties about the time and place of its coinage, organized crime is—originally—an American concept. The exact term *organized crime* was probably first used in the 1896 annual report of the New York Society for the Prevention of Crime, which employed it to refer to gambling and prostitution operations that were protected by public officials (Woodiwiss 2003, p. 5; see von Lampe 2001; Woodiwiss 2001).

Commentators and academics began to make serious efforts to define and discuss organized crime in the 1920s and 1930s, when Prohibition greatly enhanced the development of North American illegal markets. Several meanings were then attached to the term *organized crime*, but it was still rarely used to signify separate associations of gangsters. Most often organized crime was made synonymous with racketeering, another loose expression that usually referred to extortion, predatory activities, and the provision of a variety of illegal goods and services, ranging from illegal drugs and liquor to gambling and counterfeit documents (Smith 1975, pp. 66–81; Woodiwiss 2003, p. 7). Even Thrasher, whose 1927 book *The Gang* (1963, p. 286) constitutes the first full-scale treatment of organized crime, made it clear that "organized crime must not be visualized as a vast edifice of hard and fast structures" and stressed its links with the upper world by highlighting the "indispensable functions" for professional criminals played by "certain specialized persons or groups," including doctors, lawyers, politicians, and corrupt officials (ibid.).

The first US government attempt to study organized crime was conducted between 1929 and 1931 under the auspices of the National Commission on Law Observance and Enforcement chaired by George Wickersham. In their report to the commission on the costs of crime, two of the commission's consultants dealt extensively with organized crime, structuring their data "around categories based on criminal law, not categories based on criminals. *What* was more important than *Who*" (Smith 1991, p. 142).

The understanding of organized crime as a set of criminal entrepreneurial activities with the frequent involvement of legal businesses and government representatives was abandoned after World War II. From the late 1940s on, conceptualizations of the problem focused on foreign career criminals who allegedly constituted well-structured and powerful criminal organizations representing a threat to the integrity of American society and politics. As opposed to previous analyses, the role played by politicians, public officials, professionals, and other representatives of the "respectable classes" was largely played down or ignored (Woodiwiss 2003, pp. 14–15).

The new organization-based approach, which was dubbed the "alien conspiracy" theory by its critics due to its emphasis on foreign criminals, was most clearly enunciated by the US Senate Special Committee to Investigate Organized Crime in Interstate Commerce, which was active from 1950 to 1951 under the chairmanship of Sen. Estes Kefauver. Despite the scarcity of empirical proof, the committee set out the terms of an Italian mafia-centered view of organized crime that remained the US official standpoint for almost three decades. This identified organized crime with a nationwide, centralized criminal organization dominating the most profitable illegal markets, which allegedly derived from an analogous parallel Sicilian organization and largely consisted of migrants of Italian (and specifically Sicilian) origin. In its *Third Interim Report*, the Kefauver Committee famously concluded: "There is a nationwide crime syndicate known as the Mafia, whose tentacles are found in many large cities. It has international ramifications which appear most clearly in connection with the narcotics traffic. Its leaders are usually found in control of the most lucrative rackets of their cities" (US Senate 1951, p. 131).

By stressing the Mafia's control of US illegal markets, Kefauver and his colleagues effectively demonstrated the need for increased federal involvement in the enforcement of the gambling and drug laws. Seen from this perspective, it is perhaps no coincidence that the Federal Narcotics Bureau (a forerunner of the contemporary Drug Enforcement

Administration) was the major "moral entrepreneur" of the new organization-based understanding of organized crime (Smith 1975, pp. 138–141).

The merger of the two concepts of organized crime and mafia was fully accomplished in 1963 when Joe Valachi testified before the Senate Permanent Subcommittee on Investigations. By recalling his experiences as a low-ranking member of an Italian-American mafia association called (La) Cosa Nostra, Valachi gave a new name to the menacing criminal organization singled out by the Kefauver Committee and provided many details about its internal composition and illegal activities (US Senate 1963). Thanks to extensive television coverage, Valachi's views were popularized among the American public (Smith 1975, pp. 222–242; see also Albanese's essay titled The Italian-American Mafia).

The mafia-centered concept of organized crime that consolidated during the 1950s and 1960s was to no small degree the result of a focus on New York City. Despite its tremendous impact on public perception, it soon proved unsuitable for devising valid law enforcement strategies for the entire United States. After rejecting a proposal to outlaw membership in Cosa Nostra,[2] Congress passed the Racketeer Influenced and Corrupted Organizations (RICO) Act in 1970, which embodied an extremely broad underlying concept of organized crime (Atkinson 1978; see also Blakey 2006 and Douglass and Layne 2011). Likewise, many state commissions on organized crime, established in response to the national debate, at best paid lip-service to the concept of Cosa Nostra as an all-encompassing criminal organization. Instead, they defined organized crime in much broader terms to include less structured gangs and illicit enterprises (von Lampe 1998, pp. 97–99).

However, the myth of a powerful and centralized mafia organization representing a threat to America's political, economic, and legal systems long continued to be resorted to whenever police budgets had to be raised or new legislation increasing federal jurisdiction had to be passed. New legislation gave federal law enforcement and intelligence agencies an unprecedented array of powers, such as installing wiretapping and eavesdropping devices, resorting to informants, and seizing the financial assets of their targets. It also authorized special grand juries, the detention of recalcitrant witnesses, and increased sentences for dangerous adult special offenders (Block and Chambliss 1981, pp. 191–215; Woodiwiss and Hobbs 2009; see also Jacobs and Dondlinger's essay titled Organized Crime Control in the United States of America).

The mafia-centered view of organized crime also continued to dominate the public perception of the problem, both in the United States and internationally. Since the 1960s, hundreds of books have been written on the topic and dozens of movies have been made. Some of these—above all, Mario Puzo's The Godfather (1969) and its film adaptation by Francis Ford Coppola (1972)—have been so successful that they have profoundly shaped the general understanding of organized crime and the mafia in the United States and elsewhere. For many people, the Italian-American mafia, which is de facto identified with organized crime, is and behaves as is recounted in these romanticized novels and films (see Finckenauer 2005).

Such an interpretation received scientific systematization from Donald Cressey (1969). In his view, La Cosa Nostra constituted a hierarchical and "rationally designed" organization, very close to Max Weber's ideal type of legal-rational bureaucracy and, therefore, capable of operating in contemporary America.

II. THE AMERICAN DEBATE II: THE MERGER OF "WHO" AND "WHAT"

The identification of the mafia with organized crime—and thus the idea of an alien conspiracy polluting the economic and social life of the country—has been rejected by the majority of American social scientists since the 1960s. These have alternatively accused the mafia-centered view of organized crime of being ideological, serving personal political interests, and lacking in accuracy and empirical evidence (Moore 1974; Smith 1975). Some scholars, however, overreacted; up to the early 1980s, they categorically denied the existence of the Italian-American mafia as a structured and longstanding criminal organization (see, among others, Hawkins 1969).

Scientific attention was redirected from "Who" back to "What" and upon the most visible and noncontroversial aspect of organized crime: the supply of illegal products and services. To eradicate ethnic stereotypes of crime and direct attention to the marketplace, several authors have put forward the expression "illicit" or "illegal enterprise" as a substitute for the ethnically loaded term *organized crime*. As Smith (1975, p. 335), one of the earliest proponents of the new approach, expressed it, "illicit enterprise is the extension of legitimate market activities into areas normally proscribed—i.e., beyond existing limits of law—for the pursuit of profit and in response to a latent illicit demand" (see also Haller 1990 and Yeager 2012).

More often, however, organized crime itself has been equated with the provision of illegal goods and services. Hence, according to Block and Chambliss, "organized crime [should] be defined as (or perhaps better limited to) those illegal activities involving the management and coordination of racketeering and vice" (1981, p. 13). Organized crime has, thus, become a synonym for illegal enterprise. That is, the involvement in criminal market activities has become nowadays the basic requirement of virtually all definitions of organized crime in the US scientific and official discourse, and this view is shared by both supporters of the mafia-centered understanding of organized crime and its critics (see Hagan 1983).

A negative side-effect of this partial consensus has been that the term *organized crime* is intermittently used to refer to both sets of criminal organizations and sets of activities. In the definition quoted above, Block and Chambliss clearly present organized crime as a set of activities. The identification of organized crime with a set of organizations is instead fostered by supporters of the US official standpoint and a few independent scholars, including critics of the official understanding of organized crime. According to Reuter (1983, p. 175), for example, "organized crime consists of organizations that have durability, hierarchy and involvement in a multiplicity of criminal activities.... The Mafia provides the most enduring and significant form of organized crime" (see also Finckenauer 2005). Unsurprisingly, the frequent confusion between offender and offense often leads to circular reasoning (Maltz 1976). In 1986, for example, the (second) President's Commission on Organized Crime (1986, p. 11) concluded that drug trafficking was "the single most serious organized crime problem in the United States and the largest source of income for organized crime."

When it became evident in the early 1980s that "the histories of American organized crime have been ordinarily drawn too narrowly in that they have focused nearly exclusively on the Mafia or La Cosa Nostra" (President's Commission 1986, p. 176), the strategy pursued by American government institutions was to broaden the definition of organized crime to include other criminal organizations involved full-time in the supply of illegal commodities in demand by the general populace. In its 1986 report, the President's Commission on Organized Crime (1986), for example, listed a host of other organized crime entities in addition to Cosa Nostra, including outlaw motorcycle and prison gangs, Colombian cartels, the Japanese Yakuza, and Russian groups. Potter (1994, p. 7) aptly described the new official consensus as the "pluralist" revision of the alien conspiracy interpretation.

While organized crime disappeared from the US policy agenda during the 1990s and at the dawn of the current century (see Finklea 2010), interest has resurged since 2008. In that year, the US Department of Justice (2008) released the "Law Enforcement Strategy to Combat International Organized Crime" and the Attorney General reconvened the Organized Crime Council, which had not met for the previous fifteen years. In 2009, the Justice Department also established the International Organized Crime Intelligence and Operations Center (Picarelli 2011). In 2011, the Obama administration announced its new "Strategy to Combat Transnational Organized Crime" (White House 2011). In both strategies, organized crime is still understood as a set of criminal organizations primarily interested in pursuing gain with crime: "organized crime refers to those self-perpetuating associations of individuals who operate internationally for the purpose of obtaining power, influence, monetary and/or commercial gains, wholly or in part by illegal means, while protecting their activities through a pattern of corruption and/or violence" (US Department of Justice 2008, p. 2; White House 2011).

In line with international research and policy developments, however, US policymakers now adopt a looser understanding of organized crime. They write: "there is no single structure under which transnational criminals operate; they vary from hierarchies to clans, networks, cells, and may evolve to other structures" (ibid.). The focus on the transnational (or international) nature of organized crime is also new and reflects changes in the international policy context (see below) as well as in the underlying phenomenon, but it is also reminiscent of the old habit of US policy-makers' of considering organized crime as a threat coming from abroad. Moreover, as in other jurisdictions, the initial focus on criminal organizations gives way to a listing of illegal market activities under the assumption that transnational organized crime is responsible for them (White House 2011; see infra).

III. The Debate in Europe: Prevalent Focus on "What" with Few Exceptions

Together with Spain, where organized crime is often equated with terrorist groups (de la Cuesta 2004), Italy is the only country in Europe that has remained faithful to an understanding of organized crime in terms of criminal organizations. True, until the early 1980s the authors of the first studies on the mafia denied the corporate dimension of the mafia phenomenon (e.g., Hess 1973 and Arlacchi 1988)—i.e., they stated that single individuals behaved according to mafia subcultural codes and exercised power on a local basis but that no formal mafia organization existed—with some of them being inspired by the illegal enterprise paradigm in vogue in the United States. Since the late 1980s, however, a consensus has emerged in Italy—among policymakers, law enforcement agencies, the public, and the scholars—that organized crime consists of criminal organizations, which, in that context, primarily means Southern Italian mafia organizations. The key conceptual reference is the article 416bis of the Italian Criminal Code, which was adopted in 1982 and that introduced the offense of *associazione a delinquere di tipo mafioso* (mafia-type criminal organization), thus bringing for the first time the sociological concept of mafia into the criminal code (Turone 1995; see also Mitsilegas 2003, p. 57). Accordingly, a mafia-type delinquent organization consists of three or more persons

> who belong use of the power of intimidation afforded by the associative bond and the state of subjugation and criminal silence (*omertà*) which derives from such a bond to commit crimes, to acquire directly or indirectly the management or control of economic activities, concessions, authorizations or public contracts and services, to gain unjust profits or advantages for themselves or for others or to prevent or obstruct the free exercise of the vote and to obtain votes for themselves or others during elections. (Codice penale 2013).

In Italy, both policymakers (e.g., Forgione 2009) and (academic and nonacademic) observers (e.g., Massari and Becucci 2001; Saviano 2008) also tend to believe that Italian mafia groups constitute the archetype of organized crime as reflected by the Italian expressions "new" or "ethnic mafias."

With the exception of Italy and Spain, the "illegal enterprise" approach has since the 1970s acquired a dominant position in the scientific debate in Europe and has since the late 1980s been dominant in the policy debate as well, with a resulting focus on criminal activities for gain. As early as the mid-1970s (1975), Hans-Jürgen Kerner and John Mack talked about a "crime industry," and, in an earlier report written in German, Kerner subscribed even more explicitly to the view of organized crime as an enterprise (1973). The emphasis on illegal market activities has remained unchallenged ever since. Thus, for example, according to Hobbs (1994, pp. 444–445) "the master context for professional and organized crime is the marketplace... [and] the marketplace can be seen to define and shape professional and organized criminal activity." Likewise, the Dutch scholar van Duyne points out that organized crime results from illegal market dynamics: "What is organized crime without organizing some kind of criminal trade; without selling and buying of forbidden goods and services in an organizational context? The answer is simply nothing" (1997, p. 203). More recently, scholars such as Naylor (2003), van Duyne, Maljevic, and van Dijck (2006), Edwards and Levi (2008), and Levi (2012) have suggested getting rid altogether of the expression *organized crime* and focusing instead on the organization of crime for gain.

The loose understanding of organized crime in terms of profit-making criminal activities has allowed organized crime to become a successful policy term even in European countries that had no mafia problems. Concern for organized crime first spread in the late 1980s to Germany and the Netherlands and then, to various degrees, to other European states (van Duyne and Vander Beken 2009). Given its vagueness and elasticity, the term *organized crime* could be used to express the fear that the Italian mafia groups could invade the rest of Europe—a fear that reached its peak in the early 1990s after the murders of Judges Falcone and Borsellino by the Sicilian Cosa Nostra—but also refer to profit-making criminal activities and entrepreneurs close to home or to the real and imagined threats coming from the East after the 1989 fall of the Iron Curtain and the 1991 implosion of the Soviet Union.

With few partial exceptions (e.g., for the Netherlands, Fijnaut et al. 1998; and, for Spain, de la Cuesta 2004), the official (or semi-official) definitions of organized crime adopted in Europe draw from the illegal enterprise paradigm. The definition adopted by German state ministers of the interior and justice in 1986, which has been very influential (e.g., van Duyne 1997) and has been adopted also by other governments (e.g., Belgium [College van Procureurs-generaal bij de Hoven van Beroep 2006]), for example states:

> Organized crime constitutes the planned commission of criminal offenses to acquire profit or power. Such criminal offenses have to be, each or in their entirety, of a major significance and be carried out by more than two participants who cooperate within a division of labor for a long or undetermined time-span using a) commercial or commercial-like structures, b) violence or other means of intimidation, or c) influence on politics, media, public administration, justice, and legitimate economy. (BKA, annual)

The influence of the illegal enterprise paradigm on the understanding of organized crime in Germany and elsewhere is well illustrated by the following statement, made by Korneck, an experienced Frankfurt prosecutor:

> Experts who work not only theoretically but also practically maintain that organized crime implies the activities of persons who commit serious offences in an enduring co-operation founded on the principle of the division of labor with the aim of maximizing profits. If you omit the reference to "serious offences," you are left with the description of an activity that in Germany and in the entire Western world is usually described as entrepreneurial activity. (Raith 1989, p. 268)

Analogous, market-oriented definitions of organized crime have been adopted in the United Kingdom. The most recent one is bafflingly simple: "Organised crime is defined as those involved, normally working with others, in continuing serious criminal activities for substantial profit, whether based in the UK or elsewhere" (Serious Organised Crime Agency 2012; see Paoli and Fijnaut 2004. pp. 36–37 for earlier definitions).

The UK approach not only resembles the German one, but also shares the important characteristic of not providing a legal definition. The concept of organized crime too vague to be transformed into a full-fledged legal category and policymakers and practitioners do not welcome a legal definition for fear of creating legal controversy that might unduly complicate criminal trials (see Levi 2004).

Once the European Union began to deal with the issue in the early 1990s, it turned out to be impossible to adopt a uniform definition of organized crime, given the divergent assessment of the underlying problems and the different legal systems of the European Member States (at that time 12 states, now 27; see van der Heijden 1996). As a result, the EU developed in 1997 a mere grid with 11 characteristics. Accordingly, there is organized crime if the criminal groups involved have at least six of the following characteristics, of which 1, 3, 5, and 11 were considered mandatory:

1. Collaboration of more than two people;
2. each with their own appointed tasks;
3. for a prolonged or indefinite period of time (this criterion refers to the stability and (potential) durability of the group);
4. using some form of discipline and control;
5. suspected of the commission of serious criminal offenses;
6. operating on an international level;
7. using violence or other means suitable for intimidation;
8. using commercial or businesslike structures;
9. engaged in money laundering;
10. exerting influence on politics, the media, public administration, judicial authorities, or the economy;
11. motivated by the pursuit of profit and/or power (Council of the European Union 1997b).

Despite its vagueness, this grid-like definition of organized crime served as a basis for a flurry of high-level policy initiatives. At times the need to fight organized crime more effectively was presented as one of the main reasons for the advancement of policymaking on justice and home affairs within the EU. Due to its ambiguity, organized crime has not become a full-fledged legal category. However, the EU has repeatedly tried to "approximate"—i.e., harmonize—the Member States' legal definition of the offense of membership in a criminal organization, which is the closest legal category (see Calderoni 2012), as well as to increase police and prosecutorial powers and foster international law enforcement cooperation (see Fijnaut's essay titled European Union Organized Crime Control Policies).

On the basis of the grid, Europol, the EU criminal intelligence agency, started to produce the first organized crime situation reports.[3] In some of its reports, Europol (e.g., 2006 and 2007) proposed typologies of organized crime groups and, following the shift from mere "Organized Crime Situation Reports" to "Organized Crime Threat Assessments" in 2006, it attempted to assess—with inadequate means and much criticized results (Edwards and Levi 2008; van Duyne and Vander Beken 2009; Zoutendijk 2010)—organized crime threats. More recently, Europol as well as the German Federal Police Office (BKA, annual) and the Serious Organised Crime Agency (2006) in the United Kingdom arranged their organized crime reports around criminal activities—with limited attention to the actors themselves. The policy definitions of organized crime have been so watered down that policymakers and law enforcement officials seem to assume, at least implicitly, that all offenders engaging in profit-making criminal activities fulfill the definitional requirements and thus belong to organized crime.

IV. GOING INTERNATIONAL: TRANSNATIONAL ORGANIZED CRIME

Since the late 1980s, the transnational nature of organized crime has been emphasized so much so that the expression *transnational organized crime* has become fixed. Already during that decade, the Council of Europe, the Western European states that had signed the 1985 Schengen Agreement on the abolishment of border controls, and the European Communities (the predecessor of the European Union) started to talk about cross-border crime and addressed typical transnational criminal activities, such as drug trafficking and money laundering (Paoli and Fijnaut 2009). During the 1990s, the UN fully institutionalized the expression *transnational organized crime*, stressing the seriousness of the related problems and the need for an encompassing policy approach. In 1994, the UN convened a World Ministerial Conference on Organised Transnational Crime in Naples in which this "new dimension of more 'traditional' forms of organized crime" was singled out as "one of the major threats that Governments have to deal with in order to ensure their stability, the safety of their people, the preservation of the whole fabric of society and the viability and further development of their economies" (United Nations General Assembly 1994, p. 2).

The concept of transnational organized crime serves the UN and other international organizations well as it allows them to justify their intervention in this area at the same time as it spreads the responsibility of the problem over many countries, thus avoiding the politically dangerous stigmatization of a few. However, the emphasis on the transnational dimension of organized crime can be misleading, as it obscures the strong local roots and spheres of activity of most forms of organized crime. In Hobbs's words (1998, p. 419), "organized crime is not experienced globally or transnationally for these are abstract fields devoid of relations" (see also Beare 2003, p. xxi). Some of the longest-standing and most notorious criminal organizations, such as the Italian mafia groups or the Chinese Triads, could develop and can even today continue to reproduce themselves only within very specific sociocultural contexts (see Paoli's essay titled The Italian Mafia and Chin's essay titled Chinese Organized Crime). Even in typically transnational illegal types of trade, such as drug trafficking, transnationality usually refers exclusively to the transportation of commodities, communication between exporters and importers, and the eventual laundering of profits (Paoli and Fijnaut 2009). Crucial phases, such as production and processing, wholesale and retail distribution, and final consumption of the drugs take place locally.

At the World Ministerial Conference in Naples, the new emphasis on the complexity and borderlessness of transnational organized crime was exploited to foster increased and more effective international cooperation. Countries were called to adopt many of the measures pioneered by the United States and Italy in their fight against mafia-type organized crime, neglecting the fact that this form of organized crime was not present in most UN Member States and was far from controlling illegal markets and exhausting organized crime *qua* enterprise crime even in the two aforementioned countries.

The policy goals outlined by the World Ministerial Conference were actively pursued with the drafting and ratification of the UN Convention against Transnational Organized Crime, which was opened for signature in December 2000, came into force in September 2003 and, as of September 2012, was ratified by 147 countries (United Nations 2012). When it comes to the crucial task of legally defining organized crime, however, this international agreement has adopted "a minimum common denominator definition" (Paoli 2002a: 208), with no strict criteria in terms of number of members and group structure. Article 2, paragraph (a) of the Convention states: "'Organized criminal group' shall mean a structured group of three or more persons, existing for a period of time and acting in concert with the aim of committing one or more serious crimes or offences established in accordance with this Convention, in order to obtain, directly or indirectly a financial or other material benefit" (United Nations General Assembly 2000a: 25). To dispel any doubts regarding the broadness of this definition, in the interpretative notes for the official records, enclosed in the convention, the Ad Hoc Committee for the Elaboration of the Convention states: "the term 'structured group' is to be used in a broad sense so as to include both groups with hierarchical or other elaborate structure and non-hierarchical groups where the roles of the members need not be formally defined" (United Nations General Assembly 2000b, p. 2; see also McClean 2007; Obokata 2010). This means that the incisive investigative methods and other legislative and institutional changes recommended by the World Ministerial Conference of 1994 and now to a large extent included in the Convention can be also applied to cliques, gangs, and networks that are very far removed from the stereotypes dominating the media and political discourse (see Levi 2012, p. 597).[4]

V. Conclusions: The Future of the Concept *Organized Crime*

In Europe, this policy-making pattern is reaching full completion, as EU policymakers are shifting emphasis from "organized" crime to a combination of organized and "serious" crime. As early as 2002, Eurojust, the EU's judicial cooperation unit, was set up by the Council of the European Union (2002), "with a view to reinforcing the fight against serious crime." In 2009, Europol's mission was enlarged to support law enforcement agencies of EU Member States "in preventing and combating organised crime, terrorism and other forms of serious crime affecting two or more Member States" (Council of the European Union 2009, p. 37; de Moor and Vermeulen 2010). The third EU multiannual program for justice and home affairs, the so-called Stockholm Programme, which was adopted in 2009 and extends until 2014, also called for the "protection against serious and organized crime" and for a selection of criminal activities to be tackled as a priority at the EU level (Council of the European Union 2010). Dorn (2009) interprets these policy changes as signs of the "end of organized crime in the EU." Cynics might say that, once an entire instrumentation was established at the EU level and in the EU Member States for the fight against organized crime, policymakers broadened as much as possible its scope of application by substituting organized crime with the even vaguer concept of serious crime, which does not require the participation of three persons and is thus also applicable to lone offenders. More benign observers would interpret the shift to serious crime as an implicit recognition of the considerable differences in the manifestations of organized crime across the EU and their resulting harm, anticipating a possible admission that not all forms of organized crime are equally serious (Dorn 2009).

Several scholars also increasingly prefer to use alternative, more specific, albeit partially overlapping, concepts. Those focusing on criminal actors speak of illegal enterprises and networks (for a review, see Bouchard and Morselli's essay titled Opportunistic Structures of Organized Crime), criminal groups (Morselli, Turcotte, and Tenti 2011) or mafias (Varese 2011). Scholars emphasizing criminal activities refer to organized crimes (Cornish and Clarke 2002), profit-driven crime (Naylor 2003), criminal entrepreneurship (Gottschalk 2009), or the organization of serious crimes for gain (Edwards and Levi 2008; Levi 2012).

Despite all the weaknesses of the concept of organized crime, it is far too soon to speak of its decline at the international level. As mentioned earlier, in the United States, policy interest in the topic has recently revived. Despite the shift within the EU bureaucracy, some European countries still emphasize the threat of organized crime (e.g., Cabinet Office 2011). In a number of countries outside Europe and North America concern is also growing about organized crime, and ad hoc bills have been recently passed to control it more effectively. This concern and the resulting police initiatives have sometimes been triggered by the implementation of the UN Convention against Transnational Organized Crime (see Obokata 2010), but they have mostly been fostered by the growing concern for local criminal phenomena and organizations, some of which have a long history. In Australia, for example, the public and policy attention has focused since the turn of the 21st century on outlaw motorcycle gangs. In a number of other countries criminal organizations sometimes going back to the 17th century, such as the thuggees in India and the Triads in China, traditionally embody the local conceptions of organized crime (see Ayling and Broadhurst's essay titled Organized Crime Control in Australia and New Zealand and Broadhurst and Farrelly's essay titled Organized Crime Control in Asia: Examples from India, China and the Golden Triangle). In these countries as well, we can identify the same policy-making pattern that we have seen in both the United States and Europe: New legislative provisions usually entailing heavier sentences for the culprits and/or more incisive powers for law enforcement agencies are justified with the threat coming from one or more allegedly powerful and well-structured criminal organizations; the provisions adopted are crafted in such a way that they are applicable to a much broader range of offenders, including those who merely cooperate with each other in the commission of criminal activities (see, for Australia, Ayling 2011).

These developments show that organized crime remains a catchy label to signify popular anxieties and foster legislative and institutional changes. Moreover, it is engrained in numerous policy documents, including some key international treaties, and therefore, despite all its ambiguities, it is not likely to lose its policy and, consequently, its scientific relevance soon.

NOTES

1. For a list of definitions, see http://www.organized-crime.de/OCDEF.htm. Other criminological concepts, such as white-collar, political and professional crime, entail similar definitional problems (see Hagan 2006).
2. See U.S. Senate Bill 2187, 89th Congress and U.S. Senate Bill 678, 90th Congress.
3. From 1996 to 2005, the Council of Europe—another European supranational organization larger than the EU and comprising 47 European states—also produced annual reports with regards to organized crime. The reports' definition of organized crime and data collection methods, were comparable to those of Europol's (e.g., Council of Europe 1998).
4. A similar path has been followed by the European Union: see Paoli and Fijnaut (2004) and Calderoni (2012).

REFERENCES

Arlacchi, Pino [1983] 1988. *Mafia Business. The Mafia Ethic and the Spirit of Capitalism.* Oxford: Oxford University Press.

Atkinson, J. 1978. Racketeer Influenced and Corrupt Organizations, 18 U.S.C. §§ 1961–68: Broadest of the Federal Criminal Statutes. *Journal of Criminal Law and Criminology* 69:1–18.

Ayling, Julie. 2011. "Criminalizing Organizations: Towards Deliberative Lawmaking." *Law & Policy* 33(2): 149–178.

Beare, Margaret E. 2003. "Introduction." In *Critical Reflections on Transnational Organized Crime, Money Laundering and Corruption*, edited by Margaret E. Beare, xi–xxix. Toronto: University of Toronto Press.

BKA, Bundeskriminalamt. Annual. *Lagebild Organisierte Kriminalität Bundesrepublik Deutschland.* Wiesbaden: BKA.

Blakey, G. Robert. 2006. "RICO: The Genesis of an Idea." *Trends in Organized Crime* 9:8–34.

Block, Alan, and William Chambliss. 1981. *Organizing Crime.* New York: Elsevier.

Cabinet Office. 2011. *The National Security Strategy of the United Kingdom: Security in an Interdependent World.* London: Cabinet Office.

Calderoni, Francesco. 2012. "A Definition That Does Not Work: The Impact of the EU Framework Decision on the Fight against Organized Crime." *Common Market Law Review* 49:1365–1394.

College van Procureurs-generaal bij de Hoven van Beroep. 2006. Omzendbrief COL 19.

Cornils, Karin, and Vagn Greve. 2004. "Denmark on the Road to Organised Crime." In *Organised Crime in Europe: Concepts, Patterns and Policies in the European Union and Beyond*, edited by Cyrille Fijnaut and Letizia Paoli, 853–878. Dordrecht: Springer.

Cornish, Derek B., and Roland V. Clarke. 2002. "Analyzing Organized Crimes." In *Rational Choice and Criminal Behavior: Recent Research and Future Challenges*, edited by Alex R. Piquero and Stephen G. Tibbetts, 41–64. New York: Garland.

Council of Europe. 1998. *Report on the Organised Crime Situation in Council of Europe Member States*. http://www.coe.int/t/dghl/cooperation/economiccrime/organisedcrime/Report1996E.pdf

Council of the European Union. 1997a. "Action Plan to Combat Organized Crime Adopted by the Council on 28 April 1997." *Official Journal of the European Communities*, 15.8.1997, C 251:1–16.

——. 1997b. Doc. 6204/2/97. Enfopol 35 rev. 2, adopted by the Council on 21 April 1997.

——. 2002. "Council Decision of 28 February 2002 Setting Up Eurojust with a View to Reinforcing the Fight against Serious Crime." (2002/187/JHA). *Official Journal of the European Communities* L 63:1–13.

——. 2009. "Council Decision of 6 April 2009 Establishing the European Police Office (Europol)." (2009/371/JHA). *Official Journal of the European Union* 15.5.2009 L 121:37–66.

——. 2010. "The Stockholm Programme: An Open and Secure Europe Serving and Protecting Citizens." *Official Journal of the European Union*, C 115, 04/05/2010: 0001–0038.

Cressey, Donald. 1969. *Theft of the Nation*. New York: Harper and Row.

de la Cuesta, José L. 2004. "Organised Crime Control Policies in Spain: A 'Disorganised' Criminal Policy for 'Organised' Crime." In *Organised Crime in Europe: Concepts, Patterns and Policies in the European Union and Beyond*, edited by Cyrille Fijnaut and Letizia Paoli, 795–822. Dordrecht: Springer.

de Moor, Alexandra, and Gert Vermeulen. 2010. "Shaping the Competence of Europol: An FBI Perspective." In *EU and International Crime Control*, edited by Marc Cools et al., 63–94. Gofs Research Paper Series 4. Antwerp: Maklu.

Dorn, Nicholas. 2009. "The End of Organised Crime in the European Union." *Crime Law and Social Change* 51:283–295

Douglass, Sean M., and Tyler Layne. 2011. "Racketeer Influenced and Corrupt Organizations." *American Criminal Law Review* 48(2):1075–1127.

Edwards, Adam and Michael Levi. 2008. "Researching the Organization of Serious Crimes." *Criminology and Criminal Justice* 8:363–388.

Europol. 2003. *2003 European Union Organised Crime Report*. Luxembourg: Office for the Official Publications of the European Communities.

——. 2006. *EU Organised Crime Threat Assessment 2006*. The Hague: Europol.

——. 2007. *EU Organised Crime Threat Assessment 2007*. The Hague: Europol.

Felson, Marcus. 2009. "The Natural History of Extended Co-offending." *Trends in Organized Crime* 12:159–165.

Fijnaut, Cyrille, Frank Bovenkerk, Gerben Bruinsma, and Henk van de Bunt. 1998. *Organized Crime in the Netherlands*. The Hague: Kluwer Law International.

Fijnaut, Cyrille, and Letizia Paoli, eds. 2004. *Organised Crime in Europe: Concepts, Patterns and Policies in the European Union and Beyond*. Dordrecht: Springer.

Finklea, M. 2010. "Organized Crime in the United States: Trends and Issues for Congress, Congressional Research Service." Available at: http://www.fas.org/sgp/crs/misc/R40525.pdf

Finckenauer, James O. 2005. "Problems of Definition: What Is Organized Crime?" *Trends in Organized Crime* 12:63–83.

Forgione, Francesco. 2009. *Mafia Export: Come 'Ndrangheta, Cosa Nostra e Camorra hanno colonizzato il mondo*. Baldini: Castoldi Dalai.

Gottschalk, Petter. 2009. *Entrepreneurship and Organized Crime: Entrepreneurs in Illegal Business*. Cheltenham, UK: Edward Elgar.

Hagan, Frank. E. 1983. "The Organized Crime Continuum: A Further Specification of a New Conceptual Model." *Criminal Justice Review* 8 (Spring): 52–57.

———. 2006. " 'Organized Crime' and 'organized crime': Indeterminate Problems of Definitions." *Trends in Organized Crime* 9(4): 127–137.

Haller, Mark. 1990. "Illegal Enterprise: A Theoretical and Historical Interpretation." *Criminology* 28(2): 207–235.

Hawkins, G. 1969. "God and the Mafia." *Public Interest* 14 (Winter): 24–51.

Hess, Henner. 1973. *Mafia and Mafiosi: The Structure of Power*. Farnborough: Saxon House.

Hobbs, Dick 1994. "Professional and Organized Crime in Britain." In *The Oxford Handbook of Criminology*, edited by Mike Maguire, Rodney Morgan, and Robert Reiner, 441–468. 2d ed. Oxford: Clarendon.

———. 1998. "Going Down the Glocal: The Local Context of Organized Crime." *Howard Journal* 37(4): 407–422.

Kerner, Hans-Jürgen. 1973. *Professionelles und Organisiertes Verbrechen:. Versuch einer Bestandsaufnahme und Bericht über neuere Entwicklungstendenzen in der Bundesrepublik Deutschland und in den Niederlanden*. Wiesbaden: BKA.

Kerner, Hans-Jürgen, and John Mack. 1975. *The Crime Industry*. Lexington, MA: Lexington Books.

Levi, Michael. 2002. "Organized Crime." In *The Oxford Handbook of Criminology*, edited by Mike Maguire, Rodney Morgan, and Robert Reiner, 878–913. 3d ed. Oxford: Clarendon.

———. 2004. "The Making of the United Kingdom's Organised Crime Control Policies." In *Organised Crime in Europe: Concepts, Patterns and Policies in the European Union and Beyond*, edited by Cyrille Fijnaut and Letizia Paoli, 823–852. Dordrecht: Springer.

———. 2012. "The Organization of Serious Crime for Gain." *The Oxford Handbook of Criminology*, edited by Mike Maguire, Rodney Morgan, and Robert Reiner, 595–622. Oxford: Oxford University Press.

Maltz, M. 1976. "On Defining Organized Crime: The Development of a Definition and Typology." *Crime and Delinquency* 3:338–346.

Massari Monica and Stefano Becucci, eds. 2001. *Mafie nostre, mafie loro: Criminalità organizzata italiana e straniera al Centro Nord*. Milan: Comunità.

McClean, David. 2007. *Transnational Organized Crime: A Commentary on the UN Convention and Its Protocols*. Oxford: Oxford University Press.

Mitsilegas, Valsamis. 2003. "From National to Global, from Empirical to Legal: The Ambivalent Concept of Transnational Organized Crime." In *Critical Reflections on Transnational Organized Crime, Money Laundering and Corruption*, edited by Margaret Beare, 55–87. Toronto: University of Toronto Press.

Moore, William. 1974. *The Kefauver Committee and the Politics of Crime, 1950–1962*. Columbia: University of Missouri Press.

Morselli, Carlo, Mathilde Turcotte, and Valentina Tenti. 2011. "The Mobility of Criminal Groups." *Global Crime* 12(3): 165–188.

Naylor, Robin. 2003. "Toward a General Theory of Profit-Driven Crimes." *British Journal of Criminology* 43:81–101.

Obokata, Tom. 2010. *Transnational Organised Crime in International Law*. Oxford: Hart.

Paoli, Letizia. 2002a. "The Implementation of the UN Convention against Transnational Organized Crime: Concepts and Actors." In *The Containment of Transnational Organized Crime: Comments on the UN Convention of December 2000*, edited by Hans-Jörg Albrecht and Cyrille Fijnaut, 207–233. Freiburg: iuscrim.

——. 2002b. "The Paradoxes of Organized Crime." *Crime, Law and Social Change* 37 (1): 51–97.

Paoli, Letizia and Cyrille Fijnaut. 2004. "Introduction to Part I: The History of the Concept." In *Organised Crime in Europe: Concepts, Patterns and Policies in the European Union and Beyond*, edited by Cyrille Fijnaut and Letizia Paoli, 21–46. Dordrecht: Springer.

——. 2009. "Transnational Organised Crime." In *Max Planck Encyclopedia of Public International Law*, edited by Rüdiger Wolfrum. Oxford: Oxford University Press.

Picarelli, John T. 2011. "Responding to Transnational Organized Crime: Supporting Research, Improving Practice." *NIJ Journal*, 268(October): 4–9.

Potter, Gary. 1994. *Criminal Organizations. Vice, Racketeering, and Politics in an American City*. Prospect Heights, IL: Waveland.

President's Commission on Organized Crime. 1986. *The Impact: Organized Crime Today*. Report to the President and the Attorney General. Washington, DC: US Government Printing Office.

Puzo, Mario. 1969. *The Godfather*. New York: Putnam.

Raith, Werner. 1989. *Mafia: Ziel Deutschland: Vom Verfall der politischen Kultur zur Organisierten Kriminalität*. Cologne: Kösler.

Reuter, Peter. 1983. *Disorganized Crime: The Economics of the Visible Hand*. Cambridge, MA: MIT Press.

Saviano, Roberto. 2008. *Gomorrah: Italy's Other Mafia*. New York: Macmillan.

Siegel, Dina, Henk van de Bunt, and Damián Zaitch, eds. 2003. *Global Organized Crime: Trends and Developments*. Dordrecht: Kluwer.

Smith, Dwight, Jr. 1975. *The Mafia Mystique*. New York: Basic Books.

——. 1991. "Wickersham to Sutherland to Katzenbach: Evolving an 'Official' Definition for Organized Crime." *Crime, Law and Social Change* 16(2): 138–142.

SOCA, Serious Organised Crime Agency. 2006. The United Kingdom Threat Assessment of Serious Organised Crime. London: SOCA.

Serious Organised Crime Agency. 2012. "Organised Crime Groups." http://www.soca.gov.uk/threats/organised-crime-groups.

Thrasher, Frederik 1963. *The Gang: A Study of 1,313 Gangs in Chicago*. Chicago: University of Chicago Press.

Turone, Giuliano. 1995. *Il delitto di associazione mafiosa*. Milan: Giuffrè.

United Nations. 1994. *Background Release* (17 November). World Ministerial Conference on Organized Transnational Crime, Naples, Italy, 21–23 November.

——. 2012. Treaty Collection: 12. United Nations Convention against Transnational Organized Crime.

United Nations General Assembly. 1994. *Report of the World Ministerial Conference on Organized Transnational Crime*. A/49/748, 2 December.

——. 2000a. *Report of the Ad Hoc Committee on the Elaboration of a Convention against Transnational Organized Crime on the Work of Its First to Eleventh Session*. A/55/383. 2 November.

——. 2000b. *Report of the Ad Hoc Committee on the Elaboration of a Convention against Transnational Organized Crime on the Work of Its First to Eleventh Session. Addendum: Interpretative Notes for the Official Records (travaux préparatoires) of the Negotiation of the United Nations Convention against Transnational Organized Crime and the Protocols Thereto*. A/55/383/Add.1. 3 November.

US Department of Justice. 2008. *Overview of the Law Enforcement Strategy to Combat International Organized Crime*. Washington, DC: US Government Printing Office. http://www.justice.gov/ag/speeches/2008/ioc-strategy-public-overview.pdf.

US Senate. 1951. *Third Interim Report of the Special Committee to Investigate Organized Crime in Interstate Commerce (Kefauver Committee)*. 81st Cong., 2d sess. Washington, DC: US Government Printing Office.

US Senate, Committee on Government Operations. 1963. *Hearings of Joseph Valachi before the Permanent Subcommittee on Investigations of the Committee on Government Operations*. Washington, DC: US Government Printing Office.

Varese, Federico. 2010. "Introduction." In *Organized Crime. Critical Concepts in Criminology*, edited by Federico Varese, 1–35. London: Routledge.

——. 2011. *Mafias on the Move: How Organized Crime Conquers New Territories*. Princeton, NJ: Princeton University Press.

van der Heijden, Toon. 1996. "Measuring Organized Crime in Western Europe." http://www.ncjrs.gov/policing/mea313.htm.

van Duyne, Petrus. 1997. "Organized Crime, Corruption, and Power." *Crime, Law, and Social Change* 26:201–238.

van Duyne, Petrus, and Mike Levi. 2005. *Drugs and Money: Managing the Drug Trade and Crime-Money in Europe*. London: Routledge.

van Duyne, Petrus, Almir Maljevic, and Maarten van Dijck, 2006. *The Organisation of Crime for Profit: Conduct, Law and Measurement*. Nijmegen: Wolf.

van Duyne, Petrus, and Tom Vander Beken, 2009. "The Incantations of the EU Organised Crime Policy Making." *Crime Law and Social Change* 51:261–81.

von Lampe, Klaus. 1998. *Organized Crime: Begriff und Theorie organisierter Kriminalität in den USA*. Frankfurt: Peter Lang.

——. 2001. "Not a Process of Enlightenment: The Conceptual History of Organized Crime in Germany and the United States of America." *Forum on Crime and Society* 1(2): 99–116.

Yeager, Matthew G. 2012. "Fifty Years of Research on Illegal Enterprise: An Interview with Mark Haller." *Trends in Organized Crime* 15:1–12.

White House. 2011. "Strategy to Combat Transnational Organized Crime." July. http://www.justice.gov/criminal/ocgs/org-crime/docs/08-30-11-toc-strategy.pdf.

Williams, Phil, and Carl Florez 1994. "Transnational Criminal Organizations and Drug Trafficking." *Bulletin on Narcotics* 46(2): 9–24.

Woodiwiss, Michael 2001. *Organized Crime and American Power*. Toronto: University of Toronto Press.

——. 2003. "Transnational Organized Crime: The Strange Career of an American Concept." In *Critical Reflections on Transnational Organized Crime, Money Laundering and Corruption*, edited by Margaret Beare, 3–34. Toronto: University of Toronto Press.

Woodiwiss, Michael, and Dick Hobbs. 2009. "Organized Evil and the Atlantic Alliance: Moral Panics and the Rhetoric of Organized Crime Policing in America and Britain." *British Journal of Criminology* 49(1): 106–128.

Zoutendijk, Andries J. 2010. "Organised Crime Threat Assessments: A Critical Review." *Crime, Law and Social Change* 54(1): 63–86.

CHAPTER 2

··

THEORETICAL PERSPECTIVES ON ORGANIZED CRIME

··

EDWARD R. KLEEMANS

THEORY is not the opposite of empirical research. On the contrary, theories and theoretical perspectives shape the ways in which we are able to describe and analyze empirical realities. Theories are "spotlights," and all observation is theory-driven (e.g., Popper 1959, 1972). All knowledge is provisional and conjectural, and science progresses through a continuing interaction between theory and empirical research. However, a basic problem in organized crime research is that theories and theoretical perspectives are underdeveloped. A related problem is that the empirical phenomena that are the subject of research are ill-defined: Some researchers focus on long-established organized crime groups and the control of these groups over certain territories or economic sectors (protection and racketeering); some concentrate on complex, transnational illegal activities, such as drug trafficking, human trafficking, or fraud; and others restrict themselves to very local illegal markets, such as local drug dealing or gambling—topics that can all be captured by the broad umbrella term *organized crime*. Therefore, the history of organized crime research is not only the history of shifting theoretical perspectives, but it is also the history of oscillating empirical phenomena that are at the forefront of public and scientific discussion: from the long-established dominance of Mafia groups in certain rural Italian areas and the threat of powerful Italian-American Mafia families in New York (e.g., Cressey 1969) to the emergence of transnational organized crime in the 1970s and 1980s, involving large-scale drug trafficking, human trafficking, human smuggling, and international fraud (e.g., Kleemans 2007). During all these periods, scientists have also continued studying various local markets of illegal products and services, ranging from drugs and prostitution to gambling, numbers, and loan sharking (e.g., Reuter 1983). These local illegal markets are also the most accessible research topics, whereas different phenomena mostly require (privileged) access to criminal justice sources, including the results of police investigations and statements of "defectors."

In this essay, six theoretical approaches will be discussed. The first perspective involves the "alien conspiracy theory," stating that organized crime is the result of an alien conspiracy of outsiders that threatens open, democratic societies (section I). The second perspective, the bureaucracy model, focuses upon the way in which groups are organized and presupposes that criminal organizations are quite similar to formal bureaucracies (section II). The third perspective, illegal enterprise theory, is part of the fierce criticism toward the bureaucracy model. Enterprise theory states that illegal activities are quite similar to legal activities and that illegal entrepreneurs (and illegal enterprises) may be best viewed as calculating individuals (or enterprises) operating in illegal markets in a similar way as in legal markets (section III). All three perspectives have a long history in research and appear on a regular basis in public debate. Three more specific and contemporary perspectives will be discussed as well: protection theory (section IV), the social network approach (section V), and the logistic or situational approach toward organized crime (section VI). Furthermore, we will review three emerging issues in organized crime theory (section VII). Finally, we will draw conclusions about theoretical and empirical progress in organized crime research (section VIII).

I. Alien Conspiracy Model

The "alien conspiracy" model is central to the history of the organized crime debate in the United States. This model was not developed by scientists but by policymakers in the course of public debate. It has evolved particularly around the dominance of Italian-American Mafia groups in society. The involvement of American citizens of Italian descent in organized crime is well documented, from bootlegging and other criminal activities during the Great Depression to the postwar involvement of Italian-American Mafia families in New York and other major North American cities. In 1951, after public hearings that were televised nationwide in the United States, the Kefauver Committee concluded that organized crime in the United States was largely under the control of an alien conspiracy known as the "Mafia." Alien conspiracy theory assumes that Italian immigrants imported the problem of organized crime from Italy during the immigration waves at the end of the nineteenth century and the beginning of the twentieth century. As a result, an "invisible hand" of a centrally led "alien conspiracy" was threatening open, democratic societies, such as the United States, by taking over democratic institutions by means of corruption and violence. The central idea is that organized crime is not a part of society and shaped by society itself; rather, it is a problem of "outsiders" that threaten society. Often the "alien conspiracy" is accompanied by threatening characteristics of organized crime that can also be found in other theoretical perspectives: bureaucracy as its predominant organizational form, pursuit of monopolies and cartels, ethnic homogeneity, and the undermining of democracy through corruption (for a critical review, see e.g., Potter 1994).

The "alien conspiracy" perspective dominated the organized crime debate in the United States until the 1980s, but it has also been prominent in many other countries. In various countries, particularly in public debate, specific immigrant groups have been blamed for constituting the main problem of organized crime or the central players in specific criminal activities, from Chinese and Turkish offenders as central players in heroin trafficking to Russian groups in protection rackets. When the Soviet Union imploded and travel restrictions between eastern and western Europe faded away, worries emerged in many European countries that they would be flooded by Russian and eastern European organized crime groups. Furthermore, ethnicity is often considered to be a key defining characteristic of organized crime groups. Hence, organized crime is defined as a problem of "outsiders," while the involvement of "insiders" and the ways societies create and promote organized crime opportunities themselves is neglected.

II. Bureaucracy Model

The bureaucracy model of organized crime became widely known by the public confessions of Mafia defectors, such as Joe Valachi, during interrogations by members of US Senate committees in the 1960s and the scientific work of Donald Cressey for the Federal Task Force on Organized Crime. In his frequently cited book *Theft of the Nation* (Cressey 1969), Donald Cressey describes organized crime as a more or less formal bureaucracy: pyramid-shaped, with a strict hierarchy, a clear division of tasks, codes of conduct, and internal and external sanctions. Basically, organized crime is viewed as a distinct organization and equated with a specific organizational form. This bureaucracy model of organized crime is very popular in criminal justice circles and turns up regularly in the media and in public debate, with frequent reference to godfathers being in charge and lieutenants controlling certain specialized divisions.

During the 1970s, many scientists fiercely criticized this conception of organized crime (e.g., Albini 1971; Ianni and Reuss-Ianni 1972; Smith 1975). Some critics took an entirely different theoretical position, based upon the enterprise model, while others confronted the model with findings from original empirical research (e.g., Ianni and Reuss-Ianni 1972). Yet, the general pattern was the same: The bureaucracy model was constantly "debunked" as naive and at odds with the facts. With the benefit of hindsight, one may conclude that the bureaucracy model of organized crime, for many forms of organized crime and for many illegal market activities, is indeed the exception rather than the rule. Yet, the discussion lost track of empirical realities. Cressey described Italian-American Mafia families during a specific time period. Perhaps he overemphasized certain structural features and the level of organization, but fierce critics sometimes seem to focus too much on local illegal markets in developed countries with a "strong state." Meanwhile, they neglect the fact that some large criminal organizations do exist and have existed for a long period of time, even before major illegal markets, such as drug markets, developed. Examples are the Sicilian Mafia, the Japanese Yakuza, the Hong Kong Triads, and the Russian Mafia. However, authors describing these phenomena often do not conceptualize these as formal bureaucracies (e.g., Paoli 2002, 2003; Varese 2011). For example, Paoli (2003) interprets Mafia groups as brotherhoods, similar to primordial societies of generalized exchange, that are tied together by status or fraternization contracts. Through initiation rituals, recruits are bound to become brothers of other members and show altruistic behavior without expecting short-term reward. These status and fraternization contracts guarantee extraordinary flexibility, as Mafia bosses dispose of the capacities of members (and even their lives) to reach their goals. It also explains the fact that Mafia groups are multifunctional entities, which are used by members to achieve a variety of goals.

III. Illegal Enterprise

Illegal enterprise theory emphasizes the—sometimes remarkable—similarities between illegal activities and legal activities. Offenders are viewed as normal, rational, profit-oriented entrepreneurs who are involved in activities that, though illegal, are driven by the same laws of supply and demand as legal activities. Some products and services have been criminalized by governments, such as drugs, prostitution, numbers, and loansharking, yet are still in high demand by some parts of the population; other products and services are subject to high taxes (e.g., cigarettes, oil, and alcohol) or restrictions (e.g., import or export restrictions, quota, and licenses). According to economists, restrictions on supply do not eradicate demand; instead, they only alter market conditions for illegal entrepreneurs. Several authors have used concepts from economics to explain behavior in illegal markets (e.g., Schelling 1965; Block and Chambliss 1981; Reuter 1983; Moore 1987; Haller 1990; van Duyne 1993). Others have extended this line of reasoning to opportunities for illegal activities that are created by differences between countries, regulations, and local policies. Passas (1999) uses the term *criminogenic asymmetries*, referring to profits generated by taking advantage of differences in regulations and policies between countries.

Though not the first application of the illegal enterprise perspective (e.g., Schelling 1965), the best-known book is Peter Reuter's *Disorganized Crime* (Reuter 1983). Illegality presents several problems to offenders as contracts are not enforceable (as in legal business), illegal activities have to be concealed, people can be arrested, and assets can be seized at any time. Due to these constraints of illegality, Reuter predicts that most criminal enterprises will be small and short-lived. Reuter also uses several concepts borrowed from industrial economics (transaction costs and property rights theory) and concludes that, in illegal markets, small is beautiful. It is interesting to note that Reuter's work is cited in various contexts, though Reuter originally focused upon very specific local illegal markets, including gambling, numbers, and loansharking. Research on opportunistic structures of organized crime is reviewed in Bouchard and Morselli's Opportunistic Structures of Organized Crime.

Central to enterprise theory are the similarities between legal and illegal activities. It is, therefore, not surprising that some authors focus on the thin line between legal activities and illegal activities and between "illegal entrepreneurs" and fraudulent and criminal "legal entrepreneurs." Furthermore, the rationality assumptions of economic theory sometimes drive authors in the direction of overemphasizing personal characteristics of illegal entrepreneurs (e.g., van Duyne 1993). Illegal activities and adaptation are explained by rational behavior, and success or failure is viewed as the result of intelligence and resourcefulness (or the lack thereof). In public debate, concepts from illegal enterprise theory appear regularly in discussions relating to questions such as how different organized crime is from fraudulent or illegal "normal" economic activities, how successful governments can be in prohibiting or restricting certain illegal products and services (as these are in high demand), and how smart "the enemy" actually is: very intelligent and well-organized (according to some) or disorganized and inept (to others)?

IV. Protection Theory

Protection theory is mainly based on the historical manifestation of Mafia control over specific territories (e.g., Mafia control in Sicily since the late nineteenth century) and over specific licit economic sectors, such as the building industry in Italy and the dominance of Italian-American Mafia families in New York, in the building sector, the waste disposal industry, the Fulton Fish Market, the unions, and the harbor, among others (e.g., Gambetta 1993; Jacobs 1999; Jacobs and Peters 2003; Paoli 2003). Mafia groups gained control, acting as "alternative governments," and made profits by taking over two traditional state monopolies: the use of violence and taxation. In the international literature, these illegal operations on legal markets are also referred to as "racketeering." These manifestations of Mafia control were often paralleled by "weak states," Sicily being the main historical example of absent state control (Paoli 2003). Other authors refer to periods of rapid transition, the Soviet Union constituting the main recent illustration of rapid change and evaporating centralized state control that presented opportunities for Mafia groups (Varese 2001).

One specific interpretation of these phenomena is that Mafia groups actually render a service (private protection) that is not provided by the state. In the absence of state protection of property rights and economic transactions, Mafia groups step into this business of selling private protection and ensuring economic transactions. According to this view, Mafia groups actually respond to a demand for "private protection" and provide a "service." Diego Gambetta, in his book *The Sicilian Mafia* (Gambetta 1993), states that the Mafia is a specific economic enterprise which produces, promotes, and sells private protection and protects property rights and economic transactions, both legal and illegal. The Mafia, in short, renders the basic services that the state is unable to provide. Several authors have used similar ideas and have applied them to similar phenomena, such as the Hong Kong Triads, the Russian Mafia, and the Japanese Yakuza (for a review, see Protection and Extortion by Federico Varese). Many of these authors borrow from theories from political science (e.g., public choice) and economics (monopoly, cartel formation) (for a review, see e.g., von Lampe 2006). They also share a "benign" interpretation of the Mafia as responding to a "demand" for protection instead of seizing upon opportunities for extortion and abuse of power.

One of the strong aspects of protection theory is that it presents an explanation for both the dominance and the endurance of certain Mafia groups. One cannot imagine that the longevity of Mafia dominance in certain regions could do without the implicit or explicit support of large parts of the population, the government, and economic actors. The explanation is simple: Mafia groups respond to a demand for "private protection" and render a service. A weak aspect of protection theory is that the analogy between Mafia groups and states is ill-conceived: States generally neither guarantee illegal transactions in illegal markets nor illegal operations in legal markets. Furthermore, the idea of a demand for "private protection" presupposes that market mechanisms regulate the behavior of Mafia groups and citizens. However, the empirical reality of protection money, extortion, violence, and killings could also favor an alternative interpretation in terms of abuse of opportunities and abuse of power.

One of the fiercest critics of the interpretation of Gambetta (1993) is Paoli (2003). According to Paoli, Mafia groups can best be viewed as multifunctional organizations, founded on premodern status and fraternization contracts. They have historically been used by their members to achieve a plurality of goals and to accomplish a variety of functions. Paoli credits Gambetta for having rediscovered the political dimension of southern Italian Mafia organizations that had been neglected in the studies conceptualizing Mafia groups as illicit enterprises. For Paoli as well, the provision of protection and, more generally, the exercise of political functions remain typifying activities of Mafia organizations. She describes Mafia groups as political communities that are not fully institutionalized. As such, they are ready to impose their dominion with violence, even when there is no demand in the surrounding society, thus contradicting Gambetta's "benign" interpretation of Mafia protection services. Hence, Paoli agrees with Gambetta that Mafia groups "tax" local productive activities, yet she disagrees with his "benign" interpretation that this is a price for a rendered service. Nevertheless, one of the strongest aspects of protection theory is that it highlights situations that are conducive to the emergence of Mafia control, which is a dominant theme in the study of organized crime (see Protection and Extortion by Federico Varese).

V. Social Embeddedness, Social Capital, and Criminal Networks

Organized crime does not operate within a social vacuum but interacts with its social environment; consequently, we should have a thorough understanding of social ties and social interactions if we want to explain it (e.g., Albini 1971; Ianni and Reuss-Ianni 1972; Chambliss 1978; Kleemans and van de Bunt 1999; Morselli 2009). Social ties are important, as offenders operate in relatively hostile and uncertain environments, primarily as a result of the illegality of their activities. Though several authors stress the similarities between legal and illegal activities (see section III), illegality does make a difference. Illegality implies that contracts are not enforceable (as in licit business), illegal activities have to be concealed, people can be arrested, and assets can be seized at any time. The world of organized crime might be characterized as a kind of "jungle": The financial stakes are high, yet the rules and mechanisms that regulate transactions in the licit world are absent: entering into contracts, paying debts via the official banking system, and—in case of disagreement—the availability of mediation or the courts. Hence, cooperation in the world of organized crime is not easy to come by, and curbing distrust between offenders is a continually recurring problem.

Granovetter (1985) puts forward the idea that, in normal economic transactions, problems of distrust are mitigated by the fact that these transactions are "embedded" within networks of personal relations. Several sociologists have elaborated upon this idea of "embeddedness" (e.g., Coleman 1990; Burt 1992, 2005; Buskens and Raub 2013). These insights from the emerging field of "economic sociology" might enrich the study of organized crime. Time and again we find that family, friends, and acquaintances work together and provide each other with introductions to third parties (Kleemans and van de Bunt 1999). Offenders may find new opportunities through the use of their acquaintances' resources, such as money, knowledge, and contacts. Social relations might also dissolve problems of cooperation in an environment dominated by distrust, suspicion, and deceit. Cooperation becomes easier if relevant parties have information about each other and if they have invested time and energy in relationships (producing a "shadow of the past"). Furthermore, it helps if offenders know they will probably meet again in the future, providing a "shadow of the future" (see e.g., Buskens and Raub 2013).

General ideas about the structure of social relations can also be applied to organized crime research (e.g., Kleemans and van de Bunt 1999; Kleemans 2007). Social relations do not happen at random but often obey the laws of social and geographical distance (Feld 1981): The closer people live, the more daily activities they have in common, and the less social distance exists between them, the more probable it is that ties will be forged between them. This produces a clustering of people based on factors such as geographical distance, ethnicity, education, age, etc. The same kind of clustering exists within criminal networks. People who have grown up together or who live in the same neighborhood may, at a later date, become companions in crime, whereas people sharing a similar ethnic background may also become members of the same criminal group.

Different parts of these networks, however, might be poorly connected as a result of geographical and/or social barriers between different countries, between different ethnic groups, and between the underworld and the licit world. These barriers produce "structural holes" in networks that are difficult to bridge (Burt 1992; Kleemans 2007). For example, the main drug consumer markets are the United States and Europe, but there are few connections between South American cocaine producers and European or US drug importers. The illegal nature of criminal activities presupposes a high degree of mutual trust. Therefore, those offenders who are able to bridge these structural holes have all kinds of strategic opportunities to make a profit. Case studies on transnational organized crime show that offenders in such strategic positions often operate at an international or inter-ethnic level or somewhere between the underworld and the licit world: they provide "bridges" between people in different countries, between people from different ethnic backgrounds, and between criminal networks and the licit world (Kleemans 2007). These offenders are the ones who make the necessary connections between networks that would otherwise remain apart. Because of the importance of trust in such activities, these connections are often forged through family ties or other strong social bonds. An example of how this works is a case involving trafficking cocaine from South America via the Caribbean to the Netherlands (Kleemans and van de Bunt 1999). The most vital link between the various countries was a man from the Netherlands Antilles who was a "broker" between Colombian suppliers and European buyers. His sister was married to a Colombian who occupied a fairly high position in a cocaine organization, which was mainly based upon family ties. The Antillean lived in the Netherlands for a while, resulting in connections with Antilleans in the Netherlands who bought the cocaine and distributed it. Another old acquaintance was a native Dutchman who shipped—with the assistance of friends—the cocaine to the Netherlands. Hence, "structural" holes at a macro level are bridged by social relations at a micro level.

The idea of social embeddedness has been applied by many authors on organized crime (for reviews, see e.g., Morselli 2009; Carrington 2011). Although many authors refer to ideas of social embeddedness and resource pooling, theoretical perspectives vary. Some depart from traditional sociology and assume that social structure and culture are quite dominant in determining individuals' courses of action, leaving little room for "agency" (for a critical review, see e.g., Tremblay 1993). Conversely, others take an individualistic, rational choice position and assume that individuals use other people's resources in a strategic way (e.g., Morselli 2005, 2009).

A very specific application is the more technical use of social network analysis. Based upon data on contacts between offenders, such as wiretapping data, researchers have tried to reconstruct criminal networks (for a review, see Carrington 2011). Most of these studies focus on the frequency of contacts, with a few exceptions of studies that focus on the context of relationships and the content of wiretapped communication (Natarajan 2006; Campana 2011; Varese 2011). A central theme in this kind of research is that researchers "seek rather than assume structure" (for a review, see Opportunistic Structures of Organized Crime by Bouchard and Morselli).

One of the key theoretical improvements of the social embeddedness literature on organized crime is that the traditional question of hierarchical models, such as the bureaucracy model, has been changed. Instead of asking the question, "Who is in charge?" different questions are posed, such as: "Who is dependent on whom? And for what reason?" Answers to these questions are found in social relationships between offenders and their resources, such as money, knowledge, and contacts. This theoretical perspective opens up ways for describing different modes of cooperation instead of superimposing one specific model on different criminal groups and different criminal activities. It seeks rather than assumes structure. It also explains two key findings on criminal networks: their flexibility and their resilience against arrests and seizures. If there are many connections between offenders, some offenders may be more important than others, yet nobody is really irreplaceable. As a consequence, offenders may seek different alliances, and criminal networks may evolve over time. Kleemans and van de Bunt (1999) use the term *social snowball effect* to describe how offenders get involved in organized crime and how their careers develop: Offenders get in touch with criminal networks through social relations, and—as they go along—their dependency on other people's resources (such as money, knowledge, and contacts) gradually declines. Subsequently, they choose their own ways: They generate new criminal groups by attracting people from their own social environment and the story begins all over again. The nature of criminal networks also explains resilience. In networks, nobody is really irreplaceable; even important persons, such as investors, organizers, and facilitators, can be substituted by others. Perhaps this is the main reason why criminal networks often seem to suffer little damage from arrests or seizures: links may be lost, but the chain is easily repaired.

Other improvements of the social embeddedness perspective are several theoretical concepts that can be used to describe strategic positions in criminal networks in a more detailed way. One category of concepts refers to the fact that not only the quantity of contacts and the density of networks are important, but also the quality of contacts and the strategic positioning of certain individuals between parts of networks. One concept refers to "brokers" who bridge "structural holes" in criminal networks, providing them with all kinds of strategic options (Morselli 2005). Social network analysis may capture this concept in a more technical way as "betweenness centrality" (Carrington 2011). Another important innovation from this different way of looking at criminal cooperation is the concept "facilitator." Hierarchical models focus upon "bosses and lieutenants," while this different approach also highlights more peripheral players, "facilitators," who are important players for many offenders as they provide crucial services for many groups of offenders (Kleemans 2007, pp. 178–180). Examples are money exchangers and money launderers, document forgers, and financial and legal advisers. Many offenders face the same problems. They need to change money (into different, larger denominations and into different currencies) or transfer or launder money. They also need financial or legal advice or forged documents (particularly in cases of human smuggling and fraud). People who provide these services are in high demand and render these services to different offenders and different groups. Hence, the concept "facilitator" highlights the salience of these service providers in criminal networks, whereas hierarchical models often overlook these service providers as peripheral to criminal organizations.

An important criticism is that the social embeddedness perspective is quite a broad church. Though many authors agree that it has become part of the "mainstream" of organized crime research, this mainstream consists of many different perspectives, ranging from sociological writings on the breeding ground for organized crime to in-depth descriptions of criminal networks and the technical use of social network analysis. A second criticism is that the technical use of social network analysis, though "seeking rather than assuming structure," also falls prey to the historical preoccupation of organized crime research with structure. Although the social embeddedness perspective opens up questions on seeking suitable co-offenders and the dynamics of criminal cooperation, technical social network analysis often remains static instead of dynamic, and—for reasons of convenience—gives more weight to the frequency of (observed) contacts than the content of these contacts (with a few exceptions, e.g., Natarajan 2006; Campana 2011; Varese 2011). Furthermore, one may question whether or not the use of wiretapping data is an adequate way of catching the most important persons and the most important communication within criminal networks.

VI. Logistic or Situational Approach toward Organized Crime

Mainstream criminology traditionally focuses upon offenders instead of criminal events and criminal activities. Furthermore, Steffensmeier and Ulmer (2005, pp. 293–311) state that traditional theories focus too much on "losers" and "bottom-barrel thieves and hustlers." The prevailing line of reasoning is roughly that something is wrong about offenders who continue along the path of crime, either in a biological sense (for example, a lack of self-control) or in a social sense (for example, a lack of conventional ties or stakes in conformity). However, organized crime research shows, first, that some offenders are quite normal in many respects, though they are involved in serious forms of crime; and, second, that not all crimes are the same or just symptoms of latent characteristics such as low self-control (Gottfredson and Hirschi 1990). Each type of crime imposes different requirements and can be analyzed from a situational perspective. It is interesting to note that this situational perspective already had a history in the study of the logistics of organized crime (Sieber and Bögel 1993) even before the situational approach was transplanted from the study of ordinary crime to that of organized crime (Cornish and Clarke 2002).

An interesting aspect of situational analysis is that it changes our perspective from the motivations of offenders to the opportunities and constraints arising from the environment. Several authors have applied this situational approach to organized crime, with a specific focus upon opportunities for crime prevention (for a review, see Bullock et al. 2010; von Lampe 2011). Situational analysis is "crime specific." It is not focused upon organized crime in general, instead, it concentrates, for example, on cocaine smuggling or preferably even more specific activities or events, such as passengers smuggling swallowed "balloons" of cocaine on transnational flights. Cornish and Clarke (2002) state that the problem analysis starts with unpacking the sets of "crime scripts" involved, as these will reveal the opportunity structures that enable the activities involved. In this way, barriers for the commission of organized crime can be discovered and developed, similar to the "twenty-five techniques of situational crime prevention," that are aimed at increasing the effort, increasing the risks, reducing the rewards, reducing provocations, or removing excuses. Examples of this approach involve drugs smuggling, contraband cigarettes, sex trafficking, organized timber theft, mortgage fraud, and infiltration in the public construction industry (Bullock et al. 2010).

The situational approach conceptualizes organized criminal activity as sets of criminal events. It has enriched the organized crime literature with concepts such as "opportunity structures," "crime scripts," and "offender convergence settings." Offender convergence settings are locations where offenders may find co-offenders and which allow criminal cooperation to persist even when the particular persons vary (Felson 2006, pp. 97–99; Kleemans and van de Bunt 2008).

Central to the situational approach is a general disbelief that criminal groups and criminal organizations are that important in explaining organized crime. Instead of focusing upon criminal groups, the focus lies on criminal activities and opportunity structures. However, von Lampe (2011) comments that the situational model does not seem to fit properly for organized crime activities. Perhaps it is true that much street crime can be prevented, if motivated offenders, suitable targets, and the absence of capable guardians do not converge in time and space. However, offenders in organized crime, in the first place, seem to be more resourceful in a way that makes them less dependent on any given opportunity structure in time and space. Second, a "target" in terms of the "crime triangle" (motivated offender, suitable target, absence of a capable guardian) is often lacking as the basis of the activities lies in cooperation. Third, the mechanisms assumed to generate preventive effects within a situation, most notably the discouraging effects of the presence of others, do not seem to work under all circumstances. Hence, applying the situational crime prevention model to organized crime seems to stretch several concepts beyond the point where their explanatory power is strongest: ordinary, predatory crimes at a specific point in time and space.

VII. Emerging Theoretical Issues

Science makes progress through interaction between theory and sound empirical research. Over the last decades, several new theoretical issues have emerged as a result of concrete empirical research. We will elaborate upon three important issues: criminal careers in organized crime; the relationship between ethnicity and organized crime; and transit crime, Mafia transplantation and adaptation of traditional Mafia groups.

A. Criminal Careers in Organized Crime

Traditional research on criminal careers has mainly focused on juveniles, adolescents, and high-volume crime. Although much empirical progress has been made in developmental and life-course criminology (e.g., Piquero, Farrington, and Blumstein 2003; Farrington 2005), this research tradition tends to ignore certain kinds of offenders, particularly adult offenders, and certain types of crime, particularly organized crime and white-collar crime. Certain basic findings and received wisdoms, however, have been challenged by research into criminal careers in organized crime. Among these is the validity of the age-crime curve, which affirms that, in general, the prevalence of offending rises steeply in the early teenage years and reaches a peak between the ages of 15 and 17, followed by a decline over the rest of the life course. Also being challenged is the supposed dominance of individual differences (risk factors) in explaining persistence in offending for a very small group of offenders ("life-course-persistent offenders" as opposed to the majority of "adolescence-limited offenders"; e.g., Moffitt 1993, 2006).

Several reasons are advanced why criminal careers in organized crime may be different from high-volume crime. Various crimes, such as property crime and violent crime, are simply open to everyone. Yet, the situation is somewhat more complex in organized crime, in particular in cases of cross-border crime, or "transit crime" (Kleemans and de Poot 2008). The first distinct feature is the greater importance of social relations in organized crime, providing access to suppliers, co-offenders, and profitable criminal opportunities. As more co-offenders are generally required for the successful commission of these crimes, seeking and finding suitable co-offenders is important (see e.g., Reiss 1988; Tremblay 1993; Waring and Weisburd 2002; Warr 2002; Levi 2008). Reliance on co-offenders from within one's own social circle is not always sufficient as they may not possess the necessary capabilities. Contacts with the legal world are also salient for transport, money transactions, and shielding activities from the authorities. Trust is also important as the financial stakes are high and the rules and mechanisms that make transactions in the legal world so much easier are absent (Reuter 1983; Potter 1994; Gambetta 2000; von Lampe and Johansen 2004). For this reason, existing social ties are used or illegal business relationships have to be built up. The second distinct feature of organized crime is the transnational character of many of these criminal activities. Many types of organized crime are based on international smuggling activities. Not all offenders have access to these transnational contacts and some only later on in life. A third common feature is that the crimes committed are logistically considerably more complex than high-volume crime (e.g., Sieber and Bögel 1993; Cornish and Clarke 2002).

These differences between organized crime and street crime may explain several interesting findings that challenge basic findings from developmental and life-course criminology. First, juveniles are almost absent in organized crime, and most offenders are quite old, in their 30s, 40s, 50s, or even older. Second, many offenders get involved in organized crime only at a later age. Late starters are not exceptional, as in traditional research on criminal careers, but instead make up a substantial group of offenders (Kleemans and de Poot 2008). This finding of a substantial presence of "late starters" is robust across several different criminal activities (drugs, fraud, and other activities) and different roles in criminal groups (van Koppen et al. 2010). Kleemans and de Poot (2008) explain these findings by the "social opportunity structure"—social ties providing access to profitable criminal opportunities. Some offenders lack these social ties at a younger age, which explains why some offenders become involved in organized crime only at a later age. It also explains the interesting phenomenon of "late starters"—people without any appreciable criminal history—and legally employed people switching careers. According to Kleemans and de Poot (2008), four different involvement mechanisms may explain the start of a criminal career: social ties, work ties, leisure activities and sidelines, and life events (most notably life events causing financial setbacks). Other authors have also analyzed criminal careers in organized crime (e.g., Steffensmeier and Ulmer 2005) and highlight, among others, "zigzag patterns" in criminal careers and "moonlighting" of people between legal and illegal business. Furthermore, Morselli (2005) has put forward the idea that "brokers do better" and that advancements in criminal careers can be explained by deliberate choices people make in investing in certain relationships.

Studies on criminal careers in organized crime pose several challenges for criminal career research. First, these studies might refocus attention to social context and co-offenders promoting certain pathways in crime. Co-offending is still an understudied aspect in criminal career research. Second, these findings challenge the traditional boundaries between legality and illegality. Social ties cross boundaries between legality and illegality as do some people's activities at particular times in their lives. Third, the studies on organized crime careers suggest that criminal career research should focus not only on adolescence, but also on later stages in life, as important changes in criminal careers occur with age. Fourth, studying these stages in life should go beyond a preoccupation with desistance. Steffensmeier and Ulmer (2005) state that desistance cannot be explained by stakes in conformity alone; another important factor is the lack of (or presence of) profitable criminal opportunities. One could argue that this is particularly salient during stages in life when making money is more important than in adolescence. It could also provide an answer to the question of why successful offenders in organized crime never seem to "retire" but, rather, continue along the path of crime.

B. Questioning the Link between Ethnicity and Organized Crime

In many textbooks, organized crime is divided along ethnic lines. Ethnicity is assumed to be the key to determining group membership, distinguishing between, for instance, Italian organized crime, Chinese organized crime, Russian organized crime, and so forth, and it is the primary focus of many "ethnic" explanations of organized crime phenomena (for a review, see e.g., Bovenkerk 1998; Bovenkerk, Siegel, and Zaitch 2003). This "ethnic" conception of organized crime is vulnerable to three sets of criticism (Soudijn and Kleemans 2009). First, ethnicity is often linked to generalizations regarding the structure of criminal cooperation, often related with claims of links with well-known pyramid-shaped organizations in the countries of origin, most notably the Sicilian Mafia, Chinese Triads, Japanese Yakuza, and Russian *vory v zakone*. Second, ethnic homogeneity and ethnic closure of criminal groups are overemphasized, whereas ethnic heterogeneity and interethnic cooperation are neglected. Third, ideas of "ethnic specialization" tend to identify particular ethnic groups with particular criminal activities.

However, empirical research reveals that criminal cooperation is built not so much on ethnicity as on social relationships between several individuals. People cooperate because they are family or because they originate from the same village. Often this means that they have the same ethnicity, because ethnicity affects social relations. Yet it does not preclude the involvement of people from other ethnic backgrounds. To a certain extent, this relationship between ethnicity and organized crime is a "spurious" relationship as it can be explained by the logic of social relations (Kleemans and van de Bunt 1999).

This new way of looking at ethnicity explains the existence of ethnically heterogeneous criminal groups next to ethnically homogeneous groups. The literature presents several empirical examples of crime groups consisting of, or having substantial interactions with, individuals of various ethnic backgrounds (e.g., Block 1979; Potter and Jenkins 1984; Adler 1985; Albanese 1996; Bovenkerk, Siegel, and Zaitch 2003). It also explains interethnic cooperation. Organized crime often involves transnational activities, such as drug trafficking, smuggling or trafficking of illegal immigrants, arms trafficking, and other transnational illegal activities such as money laundering. These transnational activities add new dimensions to the relationships between ethnicity and crime because offenders benefit from contacts between different nations and different ethnic groups.

Interesting lines of research have followed the transatlantic links of certain ethnic groups. Transnational social bonds, created by migration, can be a breeding ground for transnational criminal cooperation. This may explain why certain migration patterns may create particular comparative advantages for specific ethnic groups in transnational drug trafficking or human smuggling (Kleemans and van de Bunt 1999; Kleemans 2007, 2009). Paoli and Reuter (2008), in an article on drug trafficking and ethnic minorities in Europe, show how ethnicity can be transformed from a "trait" into a product of social position, social ties, and opportunity structures. They state that examination of the existing research literature, together with a careful reading of the official data, indicates that certain sectors of the drug market are dominated by a small number of specific immigrant groups. Yet, marked contrasts are apparent between the presence of certain ethnic groups at the retail level of open drugs settings and the presence of other groups in closed settings. The same applies to the production and trafficking of specific kinds of drugs. According to Paoli and Reuter, Turkish and Albanian ethnic groups largely control the importation, high-level trafficking, and open-air retailing of heroin, whereas Colombian groups dominate the importation of cocaine. However, there are other major sectors of the drug market, most notably those for cannabis and synthetic drugs, in which native populations seem to be more important. In their explanation, the authors go beyond ethnicity. Although referring to cultural differences, they also explicitly consider how distinct structures of opportunity available to members of different ethnic groups may account for this configuration.

Another interesting line of research relates to comparing different criminal activities that are carried out by specific ethnic groups (e.g., Chinese). Instead of focusing upon typical "Chinese" characteristics and reproducing an ethnic conception of organized crime, such analysis reveals not only similarities between Chinese offenders and Chinese groups, but also differences that are related to the specific activities that are carried out. Zhang and Chin (2002) took a comparative view on organized crime groups in the human smuggling business and the heroin market and characterized Chinese criminal groups as "temporary business alliances." Soudijn and Kleemans (2009) compared Chinese human smuggling with the involvement of Chinese offenders in trafficking in precursors (the basic chemical ingredients for synthetic drugs). Such comparisons highlight similarities and differences and enable researchers to go beyond ethnicity by adding explanations based on social relations, social networks, and situational aspects of certain criminal activities.

A last interesting line of research involves the symbolic and instrumental use of "ethnic stereotypes" (Bovenkerk, Siegel, and Zaitch 2003). A Russian self-employed prostitute may benefit from stereotypes of Russian organized crime: by pretending to have connections with the Russian Mafia, she may be able to keep pimps and bodyguards at a distance. Similar to this, Colombians in the cocaine business may benefit from stereotypes of Colombian cocaine traffickers, whereas bodyguards and blackmailers profit from the violent reputation of certain ethnic groups.

C. Transit Crime, Mafia Transplantation, and Adaptation of Traditional Mafia Groups

A third emerging theoretical issue relates to the juxtaposition of traditional Mafia groups and their dominance over certain territories and certain economic sectors ("racketeering") and the emergence of transnational criminal activities, also referred to as "transit crime" (Kleemans 2007). These two different ways of making money, "taxation" versus international illegal trade, require different things from criminal groups.

One theoretical question relates to the fact that traditional Mafia groups, most notably the Sicilian Mafia, have faced difficulties in their attempts to get involved in transnational drug trafficking. Paoli (2003) describes how their strength (status and fraternization contracts) limits their acquisition of resources to compete in international illegal markets and how they pay high costs for their territorial control and political power. It limits international expansion, and profits are largely reinvested locally. Furthermore, according to Paoli, these groups are marginalized from transnational business, whereas bosses, even when they have to go into hiding, stay in the region to ensure their control over local activities. Zhang and Chin (2003) propose a "structural deficiency" perspective to explain why traditional Chinese crime syndicates have not seized upon the opportunities of transnational criminal activities. As these syndicates and their traditional racketeering activities—such as gambling, prostitution, or loansharking—are geographically constrained, they are not well suited to fluid transnational market conditions.

A second theoretical question relates to how Mafias move or how Mafia groups may relocate in other territories and other countries. In a seminal paper, Federico Varese (Varese 2006) compares the (successful and unsuccessful) movement of 'Ndrangheta groups to two different places: a small skiing resort versus a medium-sized town in northern Italy. Varese concludes that certain features of the economy, the presence of significant sectors of the economy that are not protected by the state, and a local rather than an export orientation generate a demand for protection and that successful transplantation occurs in the presence of such a demand. Varese extended his theoretical and empirical work to various examples of "Mafias on the Move," in which Mafia groups managed to move their core business abroad in specific circumstances (Varese 2011). One of his conclusions is that supply of protection (by Mafia groups) in itself is not sufficient for Mafias to become entrenched in new territory, whereas a local "demand" from sectors of the society is always present in cases of successful "transplantation" (see also: Protection and Extortion by Federico Varese). Campana (2011) builds upon Varese's work in his in-depth study—using wiretapped conversations—of a Camorra group with branches in Italy, Scotland (Aberdeen), and the Netherlands (Amsterdam). He concludes that they act as a monopolist in the protection racket in their territory of origin, but that a protection racket is a difficult business to move or expand (cf. Reuter 1983; Gambetta 1993). The Camorra group did not expand its core business and is still highly dependent on its territory of origin, where the vast majority of the members live. Nevertheless, they diversified their activities by using Amsterdam as a "hub" in international drug trafficking and by making investments in Aberdeen in the food and catering sector, in the construction industry, and in real estate. Hence, Mafia groups may change their modus operandi across territories: brooking no competition in their territory of origin, while behaving just like any other actor in other places.

A third theoretical question concerns "transit crime" (Kleemans 2007, pp. 176–178). Despite the major emphasis in the literature on "racketeering" and protection, many profitable criminal activities boil down to international smuggling activities—drug trafficking, smuggling illegal immigrants, human trafficking for sexual exploitation, arms trafficking, trafficking in stolen vehicles, and other transnational illegal activities such as money laundering and evasion of taxes (cigarette smuggling, European Community fraud, for example). Profitability is the major reason why "transit crime" seems to be the main activity of many organized crime groups. This is true for drugs production and import and export; yet, handsome profits can also be made by smuggling illegal immigrants and highly taxed goods (such as cigarettes, alcohol, and oil) and from VAT fraud and EU fraud (see e.g., van Duyne 1993). Furthermore, in many developed countries, the opportunities for organized crime groups to get control of certain regions or economic sectors have always been quite low, while the opportunity structure for transit crime is excellent. More generally, Fijnaut and Paoli state that, in most western European countries, the ability of traditional organized crime groups to infiltrate the legitimate economy and corrupt civil and political institutions has been grossly overstated, with the exception of Italy and Turkey (Fijnaut and Paoli 2004, pp. 614–616). Transit crime does not require corruption. In fact, it may benefit from reliable government and an excellent infrastructure for the transportation of legal (and illegal) goods, a transit country such as the Netherlands being a prime example. This means that foreign criminal groups have better opportunities to operate in these open, developed economies than in isolated areas that are dominated by locally based criminal groups.

VIII. Conclusion

Advances in criminological theory emerge from posing new questions and providing new answers. These advances may roughly take on four different forms. First, the search for the Holy Grail of an overarching "theory of crime." In criminology, examples of such endeavors are the "general theory of crime" of Gottfredson and Hirschi (1990) and the "control balance theory" of Tittle (1995). Organized crime theory lacks such general theories, perhaps because many authors realize that no theory could ever encompass the diversity of different criminal groups and the diversity of different criminal activities that are often labeled as "organized crime."

A second route to theoretical advancement is "signaling knowledge problems," for which existing theoretical perspectives do not provide satisfactory answers. The history of organized crime research is full of such "knowledge problems" that open ways for new theoretical questions and new theoretical perspectives. Illegal enterprise theory may be viewed as a reaction against the bureaucracy model, whereas the social capital and social network perspective may be interpreted as an answer to unexplained questions of illegal enterprise theory.

A third route is the transplantation of theories from other disciplines with similar research questions. Examples are theories from economics (including new institutional economics), organization theory, political science, and psychology (see also von Lampe 2006). One advantage is that these theories already have a history in another discipline and have been elaborated in different research settings. A disadvantage is that these disciplines often have a very one-dimensional vision of reality, for instance, explaining all activities as "economic" activities (economics) or as events explained primarily by individual differences (psychology and biology) or "interests and power relations" (political science).

A fourth route to theoretical advancement is the least ambitious, yet the most practical one: the continuous interaction between theory and empirical research. The history of organized crime research is a history both of shifting theoretical perspectives and of oscillating empirical phenomena that are at the forefront of public and scientific discussion: from the long-established dominance of Mafia groups in certain rural Italian areas and the threat of powerful Italian-American Mafia families in New York to the emergence of transnational organized crime in the 1970s and 1980s, involving large-scale drug trafficking, human trafficking, human smuggling, and international fraud.

Sound empirical research has put traditional theoretical perspectives under attack and has opened up ways for theoretical advancements. It has also generated particular promising lines of research on criminal careers in organized crime, the relationship between ethnicity and organized crime, and the relationships among transit crime, racketeering, and questions of Mafia transplantation and adaptation.

Finally, organized crime theory and research may also enrich traditional criminology by expanding criminology's empirical and theoretical domain. Criminologists too often ignore issues of co-offending and complex criminal activities as these are difficult to capture in empirical research. Co-offending and complex criminal activities are very close to the core of organized crime research, and there is no reason why criminologists should ignore such issues.

REFERENCES

Adler, Patricia A. 1985. *Wheeling and Dealing: An Ethnography of an Upper-level Drug Dealing and Smuggling Community.* New York: Colombia University Press.

Albanese, Jay A. 1996. *Organized Crime in America.* Cincinnati: Anderson.

Albini, Joseph L. 1971. *The American Mafia: Genesis of a Legend.* New York: Appleton.

Block, Alan A. 1979. "The Snowman Cometh: Coke in Progressive New York." *Criminology* 17(1): 75–99.

Block, Alan A., and William J. Chambliss. 1981. *Organizing Crime.* New York: Elsevier.

Bovenkerk, Frank. 1998. "Organized Crime and Ethnic Minorities: Is There a Link?" *Transnational Organized Crime* 4(3–4): 109–126.

Bovenkerk, Frank, Dina Siegel, and Damián Zaitch. 2003. "Organized Crime and Ethnic Reputation Manipulation." *Crime, Law, and Social Change* 39(1): 23–28.

Bullock, Karen, Clarke, Ron V., and Laycock, Gloria, eds. 2010. *Situational Prevention of Organised Crimes.* Cullompton, UK: Willan.

Burt, Ronald S. 1992. *Structural Holes.* Cambridge, MA: Harvard University Press.

Burt, Ronald S. 2005. *Brokerage and Closure: An Introduction to Social Capital.* Oxford: Oxford University Press.

Buskens, Vincent, and Raub Werner. 2013. "Rational Choice Research on Social Dilemmas: Embeddedness Effects on Trust." In *Handbook of Rational Choice Research,* edited by Wittek, Rafael, Snijders, Tom A. B. and Nee, Victor, 113-150. Stanford, CA: Stanford University Press.

Campana, Paolo. 2011. "Eavesdropping on the Mob: The Functional Diversification of Mafia Activities across Territories." *European Journal of Criminology* 8(3): 213–228.

Carrington, Peter. 2011. "Crime and Social Network Analysis." In *SAGE Handbook of Social Network Analysis,* edited by Scott, John and Carrington, Peter J., 236–255. London: SAGE.

Chambliss, William J. 1978. *On the Take: From Petty Crooks to Presidents.* Bloomington: Indiana University Press.

Coleman, James S. 1990. *Foundations of Social Theory.* Cambridge, MA: Harvard University Press.

Cornish, Derek B., and Clarke, Ronald V. 2002. "Analyzing Organized Crimes." In *Rational Choice and Criminal Behavior: Recent Research and Future Challenges,* edited by Piquero, Alex R. and Tibbetts, Stephen G. 41–64. New York: Garland.

Cressey, Donald R. 1969. *Theft of the Nation: The Structure and Operations of Organized Crime in America.* New York: Harper and Row.

Farrington, David P. 2005. *Integrated Developmental and Life-Course Theories of Offending.* Advances in Criminological Theory 14. New Brunswick, NJ: Transaction.

Feld, Scott L. 1981. "The Focused Organization of Social Ties." *American Journal of Sociology* 86(5): 1015–1035.

Felson, Marcus. 2006. *Crime and Nature.* Thousand Oaks, CA: Sage.

Fijnaut, Cyrille, and Paoli, Letizia. 2004. *Organised Crime in Europe: Concepts, Patterns and Control Policies in the European Union and Beyond.* Dordrecht: Springer.

Gambetta, Diego. 1993. *The Sicilian Mafia.* Cambridge, MA: Harvard University Press.

Gambetta, Diego. 2000. *Trust: Making and Breaking Cooperative Relations.* Available at: http://www.nuffield.ox.ac.uk/users/gambetta/Trust_making%20and%20breaking%20cooperative%20relations.pdf.

Gottfredson, Michael R., and Travis Hirschi. 1990. *A General Theory of Crime.* Stanford, CA: Stanford University Press.

Granovetter, Mark. 1985. "Economic Action and Social Structure: The Problem of Embeddedness." *American Journal of Sociology* 91:481–510.

Haller, Mark H. 1990. "Illegal Enterprise: A Theoretical and Historical Interpretation." *Criminology* 28:207–235.

Ianni, Francis A. J., and Reuss-Ianni, Elizabeth. 1972. *A Family Business: Kinship and Social Control in Organized Crime.* London: Routledge and Kegan Paul.

Jacobs, James B. 1999. *Gotham Unbound: How New York City Was Liberated from the Grip of Organized Crime.* New York: New York University Press.

Jacobs, James B., and Peters, Ellen. 2003. "Labor Racketeering: The Mafia and the Unions." In *Crime and Justice,* edited by Tonry, Michael, 229–282. Crime and Justice. A Review of Research 30. Chicago: University of Chicago Press.

Kleemans, Edward R. 2007. "Organized Crime, Transit Crime, and Racketeering." In *Crime and Justice in the Netherlands,* edited by Tonry, Michael and Bijleveld, Catrien, 163–215. Crime and Justice 35. Chicago: University of Chicago Press.

Kleemans, Edward R. 2009. "Human Smuggling and Human Trafficking." In *Oxford Handbook on Crime and Public Policy,* edited by Tonry, Michael, 409–427. Oxford: Oxford University Press.

Kleemans, Edward R., and de Poot, Christianne J. 2008. "Criminal Careers in Organized Crime and Social Opportunity Structure." *European Journal of Criminology* 5(1): 69–98.

Kleemans, Edward R., and van de Bunt., Henk G. 1999. "The Social Embeddedness of Organized Crime." *Transnational Organized Crime* 5(1): 19–36.

Kleemans, Edward R., and van de Bunt, Henk G. 2008. "Organised Crime, Occupations and Opportunity." *Global Crime* 9(3): 185–197.

Levi, Michael. 2008. "Organized Fraud and Organizing Frauds: Unpacking Research on Networks and Organization." *Criminology & Criminal Justice* 8(4): 389–419.

Moffitt, Terrie E. 1993. "Adolescence-Limited and Life-Course-Persistent Anti-social Behavior: A Developmental Taxonomy." *Psychological Review* 100:674–701.

Moffitt, Terrie E. 2006. "A Review of Research on the Taxonomy of Life-Course Persistent and Adolescence-Limited Offending." In *Taking Stock: The Status of Criminological Theory,* edited by Cullen, Francis T. , Wright, John Paul , and Coleman, M., 277–312. Advances in Criminological Theory 15. New Brunswick, NJ: Transaction.

Moore, Mark H. 1987. "Organized Crime as a Business Enterprise." In *Major Issues in Organized Crime Control,* edited by Edelhertz, H., 51–63. Washington, DC: US Government Printing Office.

Morselli, Carlo. 2005. *Contacts, Opportunities, and Criminal Enterprise*. Toronto: University of Toronto Press.

Morselli, Carlo. 2009. *Inside Criminal Networks*. New York: Springer.

Natarajan, Mangai. 2006. "Understanding the Structure of a Large Heroin Distribution Network: A Quantitative Analysis of Qualitative Data." *Journal of Quantitative Criminology* 22(2): 171–192.

Paoli, Letizia. 2002. "The Paradoxes of Organized Crime." *Crime, Law and Social Change* 37(1): 51–97.

Paoli, Letizia. 2003. *Mafia Brotherhoods: Organized Crime, Italian Style*. New York: Oxford University Press.

Paoli, Letizia, and Reuter, Peter. 2008. "Drug Trafficking and Ethnic Minorities in Europe." *European Journal of Criminology* 5(1): 13–37.

Passas, Nikos. 1999. "Globalization, Criminogenic Asymmetries and Economic Crime." *European Journal of Law Reform* 1(4): 399–423.

Piquero, Alex R., Farrington, David P., and Blumstein, Alfred. 2003. "The Criminal Career Paradigm: Background and Recent Developments." In *Crime and Justice*, edited by Tonry, Michael, 137–183. Crime and Justice. A Review of Research 30. Chicago: University of Chicago Press.

Popper, Karl R. 1959. *The Logic of Scientific Discovery*. New York: Basic Books.

Popper, Karl R. 1972. *Objective Knowledge: An Evolutionary Approach*. Oxford: Clarendon.

Potter, Gary W. 1994. *Criminal Organizations: Vice, Racketeering, and Politics in an American City*. Prospect Heights, IL: Waveland.

Potter, Gary W., & Philip Jenkins. 1985. *The City and the Syndicate: Organizing Crime in Philadelphia*. Lexington, MA: Ginn Custom Publishing.

Reiss, Albert J., Jr. 1988. "Co-offending and Criminal Careers." In *Crime and Justice*, edited by Tonry, Michael and Morris, Norval, 117–170. Crime and Justice. A Review of Research 10. Chicago: University of Chicago Press.

Reuter, Peter. 1983. *Disorganized Crime: The Economics of the Visible Hand*. Cambridge, MA: MIT Press.

Schelling, Thomas. 1965. "Economics and Criminal Enterprise." *Public Interest* 7:61–78.

Sieber, Ulrich, and Bögel, Marion. 1993. *Logistik der Organisierten Kriminalität*. Wiesbaden: Bundeskriminalamt.

Smith, Dwight C., Jr. 1975. *The Mafia Mystique*. New York: Basic Books.

Soudijn, Melvin, and Kleemans, Edward R. 2009. "Chinese Organized Crime and Situational Context: A Comparison of Human Smuggling and Synthetic Drugs Trafficking." *Crime, Law and Social Change* 52(5): 457–474.

Steffensmeier, Darrell, and Ulmer, Jeffery T. 2005. *Confessions of a Dying Thief: Understanding Criminal Careers and Criminal Enterprise*. New Brunswick, NJ: Transaction Aldine.

Tittle, Charles R. 1995. *Control Balance: Toward a General Theory of Deviance*. Boulder, CO: Westview.

Tremblay, Pierre. 1993. "Searching for Suitable Co-offenders." In *Routine Activity and Rational Choice*, edited by Clarke, Ronald V. and Felson, Marcus, 17–36. Advances in Criminological Theory 5. New Brunswick, NJ: Transaction.

van Duyne, Petrus C. 1993. "Organized Crime Markets in a Turbulent Europe." *European Journal on Criminal Policy and Research* 1(3): 10–30.

van Koppen, M. Vere, de Poot, Christianne J., Kleemans, Edward R., and Nieuwbeerta, Paul. 2010. "Criminal Trajectories in Organized Crime." *British Journal of Criminology* 50(1): 102–123.

Varese, Federico. 2001. *The Russian Mafia*. Oxford: Oxford University Press.

Varese, Federico. 2006. "How Mafias Migrate." *Law and Society Review* 40(2): 411–444.

Varese, Federico. 2011. *Mafias on the Move*. Princeton, NJ: Princeton University Press.

von Lampe, Klaus. 2006. "The Interdisciplinary Dimensions of the Study of Organized Crime." *Trends in Organized Crime* 9(3): 77–95.

von Lampe, Klaus. 2011. "The Application of the Framework of Situational Crime Prevention to 'Organized Crime.'" *Criminology & Criminal Justice* 11(2): 145–163.

von Lampe, Klaus, and Per Ole Johansen. 2004. "Organized Crime and Trust: On the Conceptualization and Empirical Relevance of Trust in the Context of Criminal Networks." *Global Crime* 6(2): 159–184.

Waring, Elin, and Weisburd, David. 2002. *Crime and Social Organization*. Advances in Criminological Theory 10. New Brunswick, NJ: Transaction.

Warr, Mark. 2002. *Companions in Crime: The Social Aspects of Criminal Conduct*. Cambridge: Cambridge University Press.

Zhang, Sheldon, and Chin, Ko-Lin. 2002. "Enter the Dragon: Inside Chinese Human Smuggling Organizations." *Criminology* 40(4): 737–767.

Zhang, Sheldon, and Chin, Ko-Lin. 2003. "The Declining Significance of Triad Societies in Transnational Illegal Activities: A Structural Deficiency Perspective." *British Journal of Criminology* 43(3): 469–488.

CHAPTER 3

....

SEARCHING FOR ORGANIZED CRIME IN HISTORY

....

CYRILLE FIJNAUT

I. INTRODUCTION

....

AMERICAN criminological research has traditionally dominated the international literature on organized crime, a fact that has undoubtedly led to the preponderance of books
and papers charting the history of organized crime in the United States, in particular
the history of La Cosa Nostra since the 1920s and—by association—of the Italian Mafia
from the second half the 19th century onward. In turn, the close connection between
historical criminological research and the history of the American and Italian Mafia has
not only diverted attention away from the history of organized crime in other regions
of the world, but also prevented non-criminological investigations of that history from
contributing to historical criminology. The fact that organized crime is today usually
described as a worldwide problem gives us a good reason to rectify the bias toward the
American and Italian Mafia in historical criminology (Ryan and Rush 1997; Albanese
et al. 2003; United Nations Office on Drugs and Crime 2010). It is not an easy matter to
write a concise history of worldwide organized crime, however. A number of complicating factors make this a difficult task.

One problem is that, even today, researchers and others disagree on what may or
should be referred to as organized crime. Does organized crime consist mainly of large,
hierarchically structured criminal groups that play key roles in local black and legitimate
markets or are they relatively small groups of criminals, each one serving as a link in a
network—possibly a transnational one—whose aim is to earn a large amount of money
by illegally producing, moving, and distributing goods, people, services, and capital? Or
is this an artificial or false contrast? And are hierarchically structured criminal groups

just as capable of playing a key role in an international network as relatively small ones? Or—and this is another important issue in the debate—are individuals and organizations actually immaterial in this context, and should we be focusing instead on their illegal activities (Bynum 1987; Aniskiewicz 1994; Brodeur 1997)?

The second problem is that, although organized crime and how to contain it are hot topics in both political and academic circles, there has, in fact, been very little original empirical research into this form of crime for reasons ranging from an absence of theoretical and societal relevance to a lack of financial resources or of access to primary sources (Chambliss 1975; Marx 1984; Fijnaut 1997). Two comments must be made in this connection. To begin with, the rare studies that have been carried out are not always available in an international language (English, French, German, or Spanish). Second, the existing research is very unevenly divided, geographically speaking. For example, a relatively large body of literature on organized crime exists in western Europe (Italy, Germany, the Netherlands) and the United States, but very little on organized crime in Africa, South America, Asia, and eastern Europe. The reason is simple: There are not enough researchers in these regions of the world qualified to carry out the necessary studies.

The third problem is that a fairly broad definition makes it hard to study organized crime as a phenomenon separate from political terrorism, white-collar crime, and street crime. Consider, for example, the parallels with political terrorism. Terrorist groups are known to use the same extortion practices as criminal organizations; indeed, such groups can even grow into formidable criminal organizations themselves when put under pressure by mass arrests and/or successful pacification strategies (Briquet and Favarel-Garrigues 2010). As for the resemblance between organized crime and white-collar crime, it should be noted that legitimate businesses can also engage in systematic corruption in order to build up or defend a monopoly in a particular market. The difference between the two sorts of crime is not always as stark as we sometimes imagine (Passas 1999). In fact, perhaps the only real difference is that organized criminals are prepared to use violence and intimidation against deserters, individuals, and businesses that refuse to accept their fate and against any authorities that threaten to take action against them (Fijnaut et al. 1998).

Given these problems, it makes good sense to define organized crime in accordance with Article 2 of the United Nations Convention against Transnational Organized Crime (2000), which describes an organized criminal group as

> a structured group of three or more persons, existing for a period of time and acting in concert with the aim of committing one or more serious crimes or offences established in accordance with this Convention, in order to obtain, directly or indirectly, a financial or other material benefit.

Although this general definition has many disadvantages (Fijnaut and Albrecht 2002), its great value is that it covers both the many definitions of organized crime proposed in the past and present and the many phenomena that have been, or are, classified as such.

That makes it a suitable starting point for a history of organized crime that looks beyond its evolution in a particular country, on a particular continent, or in a particular time period, or that does not focus only on certain aspects, criminal activities, or criminal groups.

In this attempt to produce a more evenly balanced history of worldwide organized crime, we consider how organized criminal groups have evolved in three different regions of the world. It must be said at the outset that this account is subject to necessary restrictions, not only because there is so little international literature on the history of organized crime in many of the countries covered here, but also because a more detailed history would be well beyond the remit of this article.

We begin by surveying the lengthy history of organized crime in Southeast Asia. The emphasis on organized crime in China and Japan should come as no surprise: Most of the research available on this topic focuses on these two countries. The essay then goes on to describe the form of banditry that developed in western Europe and, in particular, in the German Empire, the Low Countries, and Italy starting in the 17th century. Because these bandit groups were closely interwoven with the urban underworld, they can be considered the precursors of the organized crime groups that operate there today. The history of organized crime in Italy has already featured prominently in the international literature and so our emphasis will be on the history of criminal groups in northwestern Europe—a history that has been neglected in the literature so far.

The essay then positions the histories of organized crime in Southeast Asia and western Europe within the more general worldwide history of organized crime by looking at the evolution of organized crime in the United States. It reveals how, since the end of the 19th century, the history of organized crime in western Europe has been bound up with the history of organized crime (and the battle against it) in the United States in many respects: not only did organized crime itself become more international, but so did the academic literature on such crime and the policy measures intended to combat it. It is also important to discuss the overlap between the two histories because the provisions of the UN Convention, which aims to combat organized crime by taking action at the national level and through international cooperation, were patterned largely on earlier policy developed in the United States and western Europe.

II. The History of Organized Crime in Southeast Asia

Anyone who studies the history of organized crime in Asia will inevitably conclude that it is a very difficult topic to research. The main problem is that many different groups and individuals are associated in some way or another with organized crime as we now define it, but they cannot be regarded as the precursors of today's criminal groups because we lack comparative research—at least in the international literature—exploring the relationship between criminal practices.

At one end of the spectrum are the tribes and clans that populated certain regions of Asia (Uzbekistan, Kazakhstan, etc.) and survived by means of extreme violence (plundering whole villages and robbing travelers) in a world torn apart by political, ethnic, and religious strife (Redo 2004, pp. 57–72).

At the other end are the outlaws that went about robbing individuals and businesses in their own communities. One example is the bandit groups operating in India until the late 19th century who customarily strangled their victims (Sleeman 1934). The bandits that operated in the then Dutch East Indies in around 1900 used more diverse methods, but they were just as parasitical in their communities as their Indian counterparts.

In the middle of the spectrum are such figures as the *jagos* in the Dutch East Indies, who were not guilty of criminal violence themselves but did have the power to protect people and businesses against robbery and other crimes for a fee. That is why the local media often compared these "brokers" to the Italian Mafia (van Till 2006, pp. 18–27, 215–220).

Despite this parallel, academic researchers have so far counted only the hierarchically structured groups of 17th-century Japan and China as the precursors of today's organized crime in Asia. That is why they are the focus of following section.

A. Distant Predecessors (17th Century and Earlier)

It is not difficult to understand why the Japanese bandit groups of the 17th century are considered the distant predecessors of organized criminal groups in Japan today. They specialized in running games of chance and, in that sense, closely resemble the organized crime syndicates known as the Yakuza, which also play an important role in the gambling sector (*ya-ku-za* stands for the numbers 8-9-3, a losing hand in Oicho-Kabu, a game similar to blackjack). But this is not the only sector in which the *yamaguchi-gumi*, the *sumiyoshi-rengo*, the *inagawa-kai,* and so on still operate. In the second half of the 19th century, these groups were increasingly embroiled in the Japanese nationalists' battle for political power. They also played a growing role in the modernization of the Japanese economy, for example, by illegally organizing construction workers and longshoremen. The original gangs gradually expanded in this way into the present-day crime syndicates (Kaplan and Dubro 1986, pp. 3–40; Hill 2003, pp. 36–42).

Organized crime groups in China, specifically the Triads, grew out of 18th-century secret societies founded by enterprising individuals from the lower social orders, mainly in southern China. Their official purpose—to organize mutual assistance among their members—was a direct response to the enormous political and economic challenges that China faced at that time. Lacking an effective government, these societies were meant to protect their members against the widespread disasters that often befell the poor in uncertain times. This type of mutual assistance was nothing new: Similar fraternal societies had been founded in China as far back as the 17th century to ensure survival in turbulent times.

Like these fraternal societies, the secret societies of the 18th century were not as altruistic as their social aims suggest. For one thing, they played a key role in provoking and settling political conflicts. It is well known that they sided with the opponents of the Qing dynasty (1645–1911) and favored a return to the Ming dynasty (1368–1644). They also committed robbery and extortion on a vast scale. From the very beginning, in other words, their economic underpinnings consisted of crime. It is therefore unsurprising that they—like the lawless groups that emerged in 17th-century Japan—gradually developed into crime syndicates (Booth 1990, pp. 9–14; Murray 1994, pp. 5–88; Haar 1998, pp. 17–23, 324–344).

What we do not know is precisely how this process unfolded up to the start of the 20th century. It is clear, however, that throughout this period the Triads continued to be entangled in many different political conflicts, and that they were sometimes harshly repressed. They managed to survive, nonetheless, and, despite everything, succeeded not only in infiltrating legitimate sectors of the economy (transport, entertainment), but also in maintaining their protection racket and their role in the opium trade. It should be noted that the Triads remained active not only in China, but also across Southeast Asia, where they fanned out during the 19th-century Chinese diaspora, developing political and criminal activities in Vietnam and elsewhere alongside those in China (Booth 1990, pp. 61–71; Haar 1998, pp. 23–27, 244–351; Paoli, Greenfield, and Reuter 2009, pp. 16–25).

At the end of the 19th century, the Triads frequently chose the side of revolutionaries such as Sun Yat-sen and took part in numerous rebellions. In this way, they helped bring about the fall of the empire in 1911. They were richly rewarded by the new republican government for their role in the revolution: They received official recognition (up to a point) and were given ample leeway to continue expanding. They became so powerful that civil servants and military officers essentially had to be members of a Triad to succeed in their careers. Merchants and traders also understood that membership of a Triad would be very good for business. As a result, Morgan explains, "It [*the Triad Society, CF*] accordingly degenerated all the more easily into the far-flung criminal organizations that the twentieth century learned to know so well" (Morgan 1989, pp. 3–5, 26–27).

B. The Expansion of the Underworld after the First World War

Organized crime expanded rapidly in China between the two world wars. The best known example is the rise of lawless gangs in the politically and administratively divided city of Shanghai. Immigrants from across China flocked to this metropolis to seek their fortune after the First World War. Gradually, a gigantic network known as the Green gang developed, which was composed of numerous small and large gangs and engaged in every conceivable type of criminal activity. It has been estimated that the city had approximately 100,000 gangsters in the 1920s, or 3 percent of its population (Martin 1996, p. 35).

Initially, they committed robberies and kidnappings and were involved in illegal arms trafficking and the black labor market. After the legal trade in opium was prohibited (in 1919), the criminal organizations of the Green gang network began to focus more on illegal drug trafficking, both in China and elsewhere. They even founded official industry associations to represent their sizeable interests in this area. The Triads—in the traditional sense of the word—envied this development but could do little or nothing to stop it. A number of their leaders ultimately sided with the Green gang (Martin 1996, pp. 182–189).

The success of the Green gang network in Shanghai naturally depended to some degree on the city's jurisdiction problems,[1] which made it almost impossible for the authorities to present a united front against criminal activities. The main reason for its success, however, was that the Green gang had the "protection" of the police force (or at least of influential members of the force); it also maintained close ties with political factions, with influential businessmen, and with the foreign powers that had carved out concessions in the city. For a long time it managed to survive the vicissitudes of political life in the city by concluding secret alliances with rival parties. At times it sided with one party against another, and, at other times, it remained well above the fray. It also cooperated in every conceivable way with political groups, engaging in everything from physical combat to spying on the opposition.

It is not surprising, then, that the Green gang's best-known leader in the 1930s, Du Yuesheng, saw an opportunity to build a prominent position in the city's banking, shipping, and food supply sectors. Given this background, it is equally unsurprising that contemporaries were apt to compare the Green gang's operations with those of the Mafia in the United States, and that they regarded Du Yuesheng as the Chinese counterpart of Chicago's Al Capone. Indeed, such comparisons were taken a step further: Where prohibition was said to have led to the rise of crime syndicates in the United States, the end of the legal opium trade was thought to have fueled the rise of the Green gang in Shanghai (Martin 1996).

The upsurge in organized crime between the two world wars was not restricted to Shanghai on the mainland. According to police sources, Hong Kong—long a base of operations for Triads involved in extortion, organized labor, and the opium trade—became completely "Triadized" between 1914 and 1939, with more than 300 such groups established there during this time. The Triads, in turn, grouped themselves into seven or eight different cartels. Each cartel operated in a particular section of the city and coordinated the activities of the member Triads in the various economic sectors from its "headquarters" (Booth 1990, pp. 40–47; Chu 2000, pp. 14–22). This way they prevented the Triads from battling one another over control of their markets. It is clear that the overall power structure in Hong Kong resembled that of the Green gang in Shanghai.

It should be noted, however, that a considerable number of Hong Kong cartel members did not belong to the Triad hard core. Of the 10,000 members of a particular cartel, only about 30 percent qualified as such. The rest joined mainly because the cartel had the power to mediate in such matters as social security and employment. The Triads' significant role in the community also explains their frequent clashes with the labor unions at this time, and also the fact that the unions sometimes adopted the Triads' methods to help them survive such conflicts. The Japanese occupation forced the Triads to choose sides. Some collaborated successfully with the occupiers, while others backed the Chinese government. Many Triads simply waited until the dust settled (Morgan 1989, pp. 64–73).

The Yakuza, on the other hand, secured greater scope for their operations during the Second World War, certainly in Japan. They not only tightened their grip on prostitution and the restaurant business, particularly in the big cities, but also came to monopolize the production and distribution of synthetic drugs, especially the amphetamines that helped boost the army's "fighting spirit." After the war, they continued making money operating protection rackets. They increasingly resembled the crime syndicates active in the United States, particularly in gaining a relative measure of protection through their close relationship with politicians and the authorities (especially the police). That is why researchers have remarked on the similarity between the postwar Yakuza and the "true" Mafia—in other words, the American Mafia, La Cosa Nostra (Kaplan and Dubro 1986, pp. 36–69; Hill 2003, pp. 42–45).

The gangs operating in Indonesia, or at least in Jakarta, did not undergo the same evolution before and after the Second World War—a significant point in this context. In the 1920s, for example, Dutch businessmen contracted these gangs to keep order on their plantations, but other gangs chose to side with the nationalist revolutionaries and fought—sometimes literally, in the nationalist militias—alongside them against the Dutch. It is no surprise that various gang leaders joined the nationalist movements during the Japanese occupation, but their support did not yield them the same power after the War as the Yakuza in Japan or the Triads in Hong Kong. In fact, the new Indonesian rulers, in particular leaders in the army, wanted nothing to do with the militias that had grown out of the gangs; they considered them a rival armed force that had to be destroyed (Martin 1996, pp. 224–226).

C. Branching Out in Asia and to Europe and the Americas

The Triads that had already fanned out across Southeast Asia before the Second World War continued to make inroads in other parts of the world after the end of the war. This was true not only of the Triads based on mainland China, but also of those that developed in Hong Kong in the first half of the 20th century. After the end of the Japanese occupation in 1945, they had every opportunity to recapture their old glory in the city's legitimate and black markets, capitalizing on the weakened position of Britain's postwar colonial administrators. They quickly regained control not only of the labor market and ports, but also of opium trafficking and prostitution in the city.

The Communist victories over the Nationalist army at the end of the 1940s brought a new wave of Triads to Hong Kong, and a pitched battle for control soon erupted between the newcomers and the established groups. The new Triads that had abandoned the Chinese mainland established themselves in Hong Kong under new names, such as the 14k Triad, and in some cases under a nationalist banner. The violent confrontations between the old and the new groups proved difficult to settle, and the stubborn rivalry between them led to constant difficulties. Triads were torn apart by internal differences of opinion; the members would regroup into new Triads or form separate factions within existing ones. Even insiders had trouble following the twists and turns of the Hong Kong Triad society in the 1950s (Morgan 1989, pp. 83–92; Booth 1990, pp. 49–61; Reif 1984).

One thing was obvious, however: The Triads not only led to considerable violence in the city, but also severely disrupted social and economic life. Ultimately, many Triads made their money by operating protection rackets; their victims included larger enterprises in the building trade, the entertainment industry, and even market and street vendors. They also controlled a significant portion of the illegal gambling market and were very active in loansharking. They were, of course, able to develop and run their criminal operations thanks to their close relationship with the authorities. According to estimates, for example, some 30 percent of all Chinese police officers in Hong Kong were members of a Triad in the early 1970s. The corrupting influence of the Triads on the police was only reined in in the 1980s after a series of lengthy and elaborate undercover operations (Morgan 1989, pp. 86–92; Booth 1990, pp. 48–61, 90–102).

In the meantime, the Triads—both on the mainland and in Hong Kong—found new ways to make money. In the 1960s, they began to exploit the overall globalization of transport, monetary transactions, and communication to sell their goods and services on international markets. There is sufficient evidence that they once again made extensive use of their ties with Chinese communities overseas and sent their own people into those communities to build up a base of operations. They began by getting involved in international heroin trafficking between Southeast Asia, North America, western Europe, South America, and Australia (Robertson 1977). We know, for example, that they routed the supply of heroin to western Europe through key contacts in Amsterdam, becoming embroiled in an enormous police corruption scandal there (Punch 1985, pp. 40–120). Second, they began to play a role in human trafficking to the same continents. Descriptions of their involvement in this global form of transnational crime suggest that the Triads did not, in fact, dominate, much less monopolize, these illegal markets. This particular category of global crime always involves many different parties, for all sorts of reasons, one being its geographical and logistical complexity. Even the Triads cannot organize it entirely on their own (Booth 1990, pp. 107–132; Chin 1999; Chu 2000, pp. 107–120; Faligot 2001).

Some recent studies give us a good idea of the complexity of Chinese organized crime today. The studies focus on organized crime in American Chinatowns, for example, Chin's examination of Chinese gangs in New York and other large American cities (Chin 1990, 1996). Not only are these gangs involved in all sorts of crime, but they also maintain dynamic relationships with mainstream interest groups in Chinese communities. Equally revealing is the study by Zhang on human trafficking between China and the United States (Zhang 2008). Zhang shows that this particular form of human trafficking is not run by hierarchical organizations that control operations from start to finish, but rather by loosely organized, horizontal networks of individuals and gangs active along various smuggling routes from China to the United States. In fact, it has always been this way, as revealed in McIllwain's (2004) study of Chinese criminal groups in New York between 1890 and 1910. Not only were these groups heavily involved in extortion, but they also played a key role in black markets, i.e., prostitution, gambling, and drug trafficking.

We have already pointed out that, at around the time of the Second World War, the Yakuza came to resemble what was then regarded as the "true" Mafia in their activities. The resemblance did not stop there, however. Under the influence of wartime conditions, the syndicates also adapted their gang culture to that of American gangsters—or at least the image of the Mafia propagated by Hollywood. Yakuza members not only began to dress like American gangsters but also imitated their violent methods. This became very obvious around 1960, when the Yakuza syndicates battled one another for various markets. The struggle erupted into what can only be termed gang warfare. Armed with new special powers, the police attempted to subdue the violence, but their efforts were less than successful. They did manage to take out a number of smaller gangs, but this only succeeded in making the big syndicates more powerful. The *yamaguchi-gumi*—the largest of around ten syndicates that formed the backbone of the Yakuza network around 1980—had a national network of 587 gangs at the time, with a total membership of more than 13,000 (Kaplan and Dubro 1986, pp. 89–123, 134–140, 181–185).

Despite increasingly severe government crackdowns, the Yakuza have made an almost unimaginable fortune in recent decades in gambling, prostitution, drug trafficking, and extortion. They have also used black market money to gain a firmer foothold in legitimate markets. They are, for example, active not only in the building and transport trades, but also in the real estate market, the financial sector, and the school system (Hill 2003, pp. 92–136).

It should also be noted that the Yakuza became increasingly active in the international market in the second half of the 20th century. To some extent, they focused on their own region, Southeast Asia. Their activities there included trafficking in synthetic drugs from Korea and later the Philippines and in women from the same countries as well as Taiwan and Thailand. They built relationships with gangs operating in the relevant black markets in these countries and with the Triads in China, in particular when it came to heroin trafficking and distribution. The Yakuza did not limit their international network to Southeast Asia, however. Starting in the 1970s, they also established relationships with criminal groups in South America, North America, and Europe. Their main reason was to supply the Japanese market with drugs, arms, and pornography. Another reason, however, was that it was attractive for the Yakuza to follow Japanese businesses and tourism to other continents. On the one hand, it gave them the opportunity to make money in foreign Japanese communities from drug trafficking and prostitution. On the other, Japan's worldwide economic expansion gave the Yakuza the chance to extort money from Japanese businesses abroad (Kaplan and Dubro 1986, pp. 189–270).

III. The History of Organized Crime in Western Europe

Undoubtedly, all sorts of criminal groups were active across Europe until the 19th century, and these groups ranged from the Balkans to the United Kingdom and France (Hobsbawm 1972; Chesney 1979, pp. 32–98; Henry 1984). Those examined most closely are the bandits and brigands that operated in German-speaking regions, the Low Countries, and southern Italy from the second half of the 17th century to the first decades of the 19th century. Below, we look first at the history of banditry as it flourished in northwestern Europe until the early 19th century, when it died out for a number of different reasons. We then discuss the transformation of banditry in southern Italy in the mid-19th century, which served as the starting point for the Mafia as it now exists.

A. The Rise of Banditry in Northwestern Europe

It is impossible to say how many criminal groups were active in the 17th and 18th centuries in the regions that now make up Germany and the Netherlands. For one thing, not all of the groups can be traced. For another, most of them were not strictly organized hierarchies; rather, they consisted of a permanent core of experienced criminals with a large circle of reliable accomplices and helpers (tipsters and informers, fences, conveyors, publicans, skippers, and so on). By definition, then, it is impossible to say how many groups there were; their internal and external networks were much too flexible and dynamic.

In the majority of cases, the most we can do is paint a picture of some of the key figures who, along with their cliques, served as main nodes in the criminal networks. Most of the groups did not even have a clear leader. Their hard core and helpers operated in fluid groups and usually worked on a project-like basis when it came to more serious crimes. The more established groups did have a certain internal division of roles, in the sense that various key figures specialized in particular forms of theft or violence and also knew precisely which specialists they needed to call in for certain jobs. In that respect, they resembled the professional criminal networks of the 1980s described by McIntosh in such minute detail. But by far the biggest advantage of this flexible organization was that it considerably reduced the risk of being caught by the authorities (McIntosh 1975; Krausnick 1978, pp. 102–144; McIntosh 1982, pp. 98–132; Küther 1987, pp. 60–80, 147–148; Egmond 2004, pp. 82–87).

One interesting point is that the groups were able to operate on differing geographical levels. Some were active mainly at the local level and were completely embedded in their communities. Others were more mobile in nature and active at regional or interregional levels (Küther 1987, pp. 38–51). The Grote Nederlandse Bende, active in the Low Countries between 1790 and 1799, consisted of a network of local and regional robber bands that spanned the relevant areas of northwestern Europe. The bands first operated mainly in what is now Flanders (Belgium). They then shifted to what is today the Meuse-Rhine region, near the cities of Maastricht (Netherlands), Liège (Belgium), and Aachen (Germany) and the northern and southern Rhineland. They subsequently moved into the provinces of North Holland and South Holland (Netherlands) and finally into what is today the Dutch province of Noord-Brabant (Krausnick 1978, pp. 32–84; Egmond 1986, pp. 12–15, 30–43). Taken as a whole, their territory ranged from northern France through Brabant and Holland and across to Kassel, Augsburg, and Konstanz in the German Empire.

Remarkably, this complex criminal network was extremely hierarchical in structure. At the very top were the leaders, who carried a crowbar as a symbol of their power and were surrounded by tipsters and informants. Next in line were the experienced members and below them came the younger members, called up to join raids on a case-by-case basis (Küther 1987, p. 33). Be that as it may, these vast robber bands show that transnational criminal groups are certainly not a recent phenomenon. They have, in fact, been around for centuries and have long presented local and national authorities with a tricky legal and organizational problem, right up to the present day (Spapens and Fijnaut 2005): how to fight them effectively across national borders.

It would be a mistake to think that these outlaws operated only in rural areas. Research has shown that much of their criminal activity took place in towns or cities. No defensive walls or city gates could keep them out. After all, cities were an ideal place not only to commit theft or robbery, but also to sell contraband goods on the black market, for example through fences. In fact, Egmond has argued that northwestern Europe in the 17th and 18th centuries already had something resembling an international urban underworld. The fact that this criminal underworld had local idiosyncrasies, differing from city to city and region to region, does nothing to undermine her argument. The brigands in the southern Netherlands, for example, had closer ties to rural communities and were more military in nature than the criminal groups in the north of the country, where the cities served as "natural" crime magnets and havens. When necessary, however, the inhabitants of these two worlds knew where to find one another, regardless of their differences (Egmond 1994, pp. 243–247; Egmond 2004, pp. 83, 95–99).

The crimes committed by these outlaws ran the gamut from offenses against property to violence. They included simple theft (for example, clothing or cattle) and lesser types of fraud, but also extortion, robbery, burglary, and hold-ups. The latter crimes were perpetrated by the more professional groups, which worked with a large measure of precision but also employed brute force. Their actions naturally intimidated the local population. They bound, tortured, raped, and murdered their victims. They set homes, farms, and country estates on fire. They intimidated and blackmailed prosperous citizens (van den Eerenbeemt 1970, pp. 1–12, 74–80; Küther 1987, pp. 30–31).

It was difficult to prevent such crimes or track down the perpetrators because the groups had their own subculture, including their own vocabulary, internal sanctions for misbehavior, and even special initiation ceremonies for newcomers. Such means and methods—meant to maintain secrecy about who was involved in which criminal operations and how—made it very difficult for the authorities to repress them. In fact, one important element of their subculture was the severe punishment meted out to members who cooperated with law enforcement or judicial authorities. The sanctions ranged from expulsion to liquidation (Egmond 2004, pp. 88–92; Lange 2004, pp. 133–140). Nonetheless, bandit groups sometimes received broad support from their communities. They were able to organize or increase such support themselves by leaving ordinary people alone and attacking the authorities, monks and priests, noblemen, and other powerful figures in local communities (Krausnick 1978, pp. 10–15, 29–32; Küther 1987, pp. 117–118).

This final point raises the usual question as to the origins and composition of these bandit groups. First of all, undoubtedly circumstances of dire poverty—the outcome of crops occasionally failing across an entire region—contributed to their rise. After all, the groups offered their members a modicum of protection against the disasters that devastated local populations. It is hardly surprising, then, that the groups of bandits operating across vast stretches of Germany consisted mainly of people from the social and economic margins of society, i.e., not only vagrants, beggars and those of their ilk, but also impoverished farmers, shepherds, and craftsmen (Grosz 1893, pp. 147–188; Lange 2004, pp. 114–118).

The many wars were the second factor fueling the rise and survival of bandit groups. That is not only because soldiers had to forage for their own provisions before and after a battle, but also because large numbers of them remained in the regions where they had fought and either joined existing groups of brigands there or founded new groups to provide for themselves. That is why the brigand groups in the southern Netherlands were more like military organizations than their northern counterparts; during the Eighty Years' War (1468–1648), the Duchy of Brabant served as the frontline between the Spanish forces and the Dutch rebels (van den Eerenbeemt 1970, pp. 1–12, 43–57; Egmond 1994, pp. 93–116; Fritz 2003, pp. 14–29; Adriaenssen 2007, pp. 127–224).

The third important factor behind the far-flung criminal network in northwestern Europe in the 17th and 18th centuries was social exclusion. More specifically, the thousands upon thousands of Jews and gypsies who had been expelled from eastern and southern Europe in the 17th and 18th centuries ended up settling in northwestern Europe. Some of these outcasts founded criminal groups to support themselves by illegal means; others joined mixed, multiethnic groups. Interesting in this regard is that the Jewish groups were generally small and consisted only of men, whereas the gypsy groups encompassed entire clans. This important distinction can be traced to the home base of the two groups. The Jewish groups were more likely than their gypsy counterparts to have their base in a town or city; when the men were away on business, the women and children remained behind (Egmond 1994, pp. 117–168, 240–241; Egmond 2004, pp. 99–101).

Looking ahead to the following section, which covers banditry in 19th-century southern Italy, mention should be made of Blok's detailed study of the bandit groups that operated in the Dutch area of the Meuse-Rhine region between 1730 and 1778 (Blok 1991). Blok is the only researcher who has examined not only this particular criminal network, but also the Sicilian Mafia (Blok 1988). Many of the bandits and brigands in what is now the Meuse-Rhine region were called *bokkenrijders* (literally "goat-riders") by the local population, the goats symbolizing the devils that members supposedly rode through the region. Most of them were local inhabitants. Some were itinerant crafts-men, in particular, flayers, and could, therefore, move about unnoticed when commit-ting their crimes. Others were innkeepers, couriers, or cartwrights and, thus, came to know everything that went on in the region. A small number of them had a military background and were, therefore, experienced at planning and carrying out attacks.

The goat-riders targeted a wide range of different properties, from houses and farms to monasteries, presbyteries, churches, and beyond. Their raids were not for criminal gain alone; they had also rejected the political status quo to some extent. For example, they did not simply rob churches and monasteries of valuables and money, but also com-mitted all sorts of sacrilege, such as parodying the consecration and distributing hosts to their brothers-in-arms. Further evidence can be found in the oath that newcomers were obliged to swear before they were allowed to take part in a foray. The references to Roman Catholicism are obvious. The criminals had to stand before a table bearing two lighted candles, a crucifix, and a statuette of the Virgin and, raising their hand with thumb and forefingers extended, renounce God and all the saints and submit to the devil as the source of all aid. They had to swear that, if apprehended, they would rather be tortured to death than betray a comrade. The purpose of the oath is clear: It marked the transition from mainstream society to a special, secret brotherhood in which mutual loyalty was paramount (Blok 1991).

B. The Demise of Banditry in Northwestern Europe

The authorities regarded the lawless bands as subversive for their secret, violent, and blasphemous nature, and that is probably why they pursued them so relentlessly throughout the 18th century. Blok writes that, in the region he studied, a total of six hun-dred bandits were prosecuted in three successive waves between 1741 and 1778, and that more than half of them were sentenced to death and executed. The punishments grew increasingly severe as time passed: of the 244 individuals apprehended in the 1770s, 236 were condemned to death by hanging. Blok concludes that this merciless repres-sion may well have rooted out banditry in this region. The groups were simply unable to recover from the fatal consequences of successive campaigns of repression.

If that is true, then their extermination constituted an overture to the wholesale disap-pearance of the bandit network in northwestern Europe at the start of the 19th century. At that point, criminal groups in several regions of northwestern Europe came under attack, with civil militias and armies being called in to hunt down their members, and with draconian punishments being meted out to those captured (capital and corporal punishment and imprisonment) (Fritz 2003, pp. 72–122). But the early actions discussed by Blok did not have the anticipated results in many areas for all sorts of reasons, mainly because they were too incidental and small-scale in nature.

Thus, historians tend to ascribe the disappearance of banditry in northwestern Europe to the changes that took place in the law enforcement and justice systems during the French Revolution and the era of Napoleon. Consisting of numerous small, separate jurisdictions, hopelessly divided and therefore powerless, these systems were replaced by a dense, effective, centrally controlled network of law enforcement officers and judges (van den Eerenbeemt 1970, pp. 123–132; Krausnick 1978, pp. 144–163; Küther 1984; Küther 1987, pp. 127–144; Boehncke and Sarkowicz, 1991, Vol. 1, pp. 9–20). Not only did the French introduce a centrally controlled public prosecutor and military-style police force (the gendarmerie), but they also systematically built up a uniform civilian police corps in towns and rural areas by appointing chief constables and rural constables. This stable combination of professional institutions and public services—with roots in the local community but a uniform structure that eased transnational cooperation—was too much for the groups. They were systematically tracked down and prosecuted, and the punishment meted out to their members was severe. Many of them were condemned to death or to corporal punishment and/or imprisonment. Ruthless repression rooted out the bandits. In November 1803, the notorious Schinderhannes, who had long terrorized the Rhineland with his robber band, went to the guillotine in Mainz with 20 of his accomplices (Pfister 1812; Franke 1984).

The second reason for the demise of the criminal groups in northwestern Europe was the emergence of poverty relief measures, in particular assistance for beggars and vagrants. These included foundations to assist beggars, rural housing estates built for the poor, reform schools, public nursing homes, and unemployment relief work. Such policies must have been instrumental in preventing a resurgence of banditry (Küther 1987, pp. 123–127; Depreeuw 1988, pp. 242–310; Fritz 2003, pp. 205–295).

Third, after Napoleon's defeat, the Congress of Vienna brought many decades of armed peace to the region's superpowers, which had waged long and frequent wars against one another. This cut off an important source of new members, i.e. incessant warfare and its disastrous consequences for local populations.

The foregoing analysis appears to contradict the account set out by Friedrich Christian Avé-Lallemant in his book *Das deutsche Gaunertum* (1858). Close reading, however, makes clear that he, too, attributed the virtual disappearance of these bandits largely to the efforts of the French-style gendarmerie (Avé-Lallemant 1858, Vol. 1, pp. 87–88, 94–95; Vol. 2, pp. 267–269, 283–286). He echoes an observation noted by other German authors of his day, such as the illustrious head of Berlin's crime investigation service, Wilhelm Stieber. In his well-known instruction manual for criminal investigators, he claims that the introduction of an effective urban police corps reduced the criminal network to little more than fractured groups operating in remote areas (Stieber 1860, pp. 88–90). It is interesting that only a few of these authors also recognized that the bandit groups had not been beaten in Italy but survived in the Camorra and the Mafia. Hans Kurella attributed this to the fragmented state of society there and to the government's lack of authority (Kurella 1893, p. 229). His interpretation is one that is generally shared nowadays: the status of organized crime is regarded today as a yardstick for the strength or weakness of government.

Avé-Lallemant (1858, pp. 11–14) believed that the bandits of bygone days had, in fact, been replaced by a modern *Gaunertum*—a less visible but equally dangerous class of criminals who came from every walk of life, from manual laborers to shopkeepers and scientists. And once again, he was not alone in his conviction. Many in France (e.g., Fregier 1940), for example, believed that society was being threatened, directly and indirectly, by the *classes dangereuses*. Such ideas gained credence in the second half of the 19th century in Germany, where the existence of an urban underworld, populated by all sorts of criminals—vagabonds, whores, pimps, thieves, fences, swindlers, murderers—was widely accepted (Roscher 1912, pp. 186–209; Roth 1997, pp. 249–288, 348–410).

C. The Steady Growth of Criminal Groups in Southern Italy

Whereas banditry had more or less disappeared in Germany and the Netherlands by the mid-19th century, the opposite was true of Italy. It was mentioned above that a number of German authors had already pointed out this contrast. In the following, we will draw on several contemporary studies to explain why, according to these authors, lawless groups in southern Italy, and especially the Sicilian Mafia, did not disappear in the first half of the 19th century, but instead amassed power during that period and managed to increase it in the decades thereafter. Their ascendency continued until the 1920s, when Mussolini not only intervened and drove the Mafia into a corner in Italy, but also sent hundreds of *mafiosi* fleeing to the United States. Our review of Mussolini's policy also allows us to consider, briefly, how organized crime has evolved in the United States since the end of the 19th century. That knowledge will help us understand the complex relationship that has developed between northwestern Europe and the United States since the 1930s with respect to organized crime, which is the topic of Section V.

Although accounts of the recent history of the Italian Mafia are found in numerous publications, its roots in the 18th and 19th centuries are less clear than the history of German and Dutch banditry. Various reasons can be cited for this paucity. The first is that, unlike for the bandits in northwestern Europe, very few detailed studies of specific Italian Mafia groups or of the Mafia in particular regions exist (among the few exceptions, see Arlacchi 1983; Pezzino 1990; and Lupo 1999). Second, the studies that have been published are based on differing sources and written from differing perspectives. Third, the early history of the Sicilian Mafia has been examined in much greater detail than that of the Camorra (Naples and environs), the 'Ndrangheta (Calabria), and the Sacra Corona Unita (Apulia). Fourth, conclusions drawn in the 1970s have been refuted—or at least seriously challenged—by later research. One good example is an earlier conviction that the Mafia is largely a manifestation of a violent culture and should not be equated with an organization that deliberately and systematically perpetrates violent crimes. Statements by key *pentitti* (i.e., Mafia defectors) have indicated otherwise, and that idea has now been abandoned for the most part. Be that as it may, for reasons of space we will confine ourselves in the following to the history of the Sicilian Mafia.

Let us begin by considering Fulvetti's relatively recent survey of research on the Italian Mafia (Fulvetti 2004, pp. 51–66). It is clear from this survey that the present Sicilian Mafia descended from armed groups founded by Sicilian landowners in the distant past to protect their property. These groups turned to banditry after 1812 (when the Sicilian Parliament abolished feudalism and they were disbanded) and engaged in every possible form of theft and violence (Hess 1973, pp. 18–21; Gambetta 1993, pp. 75–99). This transformation—the Italian version of the history of banditry in northwestern Europe in around 1800—was made possible for two closely related reasons.

The first reason is the political vacuum that arose in Sicily at the end of the French era. The House of Bourbon, which reclaimed power in 1815, was incapable of establishing an effective, modern system of government on the island, and power, therefore, remained largely in the hands of the traditional administrative, economic, and social elites. The second reason is closely bound up with the first. The power vacuum made it impossible to build an effective system of law enforcement and justice capable of maintaining public order and safety, and the authorities, therefore, remained helpless in the face of the bandit groups. That does not mean, however, that the groups were entirely free to do as they pleased. For their own reasons, they joined forces with representatives of the local elite, who were prepared to support them in exchange for protection. In other words, after 1815, various organizations, associations and partnerships arose that foreshadowed the *coscas* or "Mafia families" operating in the first half of the 20th century. After all, one of the typical features of these "families" was that they were based on alliances between members of the social elite and criminals from the lower social orders. That is why the leader of a family was called a *uomo di rispetto* ("man of honor") and the villains he collaborated with the *bassi mafiosi*, the footmen of the Mafia (Hess 1973, pp. 80–82; Blok 1988, pp. 89–102; Matard-Bonucci 1994, pp. 52–57; Riall 1998, pp. 30–61; Dickie 2004, pp. 47–54).

The 1848 revolution did not put an end to these criminal organizations; neither did the unification of Italy in 1860 under Garibaldi. In both instances, the new governments were not powerful enough to use state reform to wrest the "monopoly on violence" from the Mafia, in part due to repeated rebellions against the new order both in Palermo and in the countryside. The highest authorities in Sicily admitted as much. In 1865, the prefect of Palermo sent a letter to the minister of the interior claiming that, time and again, the island's ruling classes had entered into agreements with criminals when they felt the need to use violence and intimidation to protect their interests (Riall 1998, pp. 183–185; Dickie 2004, pp. 59–61). It should be noted that such collaboration was not equally well organized across the island at that time. The closest alliances could be found, most obviously, in and around Palermo, the most prosperous and, therefore, most lucrative part of Sicily. In around 1870, various separate Mafia-like *coscas* demanded control of certain sections of the city and its suburbs, and they began to extort money from all within their territory in exchange for "protection."

In the years thereafter, similar illegal power blocs developed in other Sicilian towns. Here too, the Mafia gained control of more and more sources of income thanks to its control of private violence. In the countryside, gangs were still given leeway to rob, kidnap, or commit other crimes as long as their activities served—or in any event did not encroach on—the interests of their powerful patrons. In addition, they were frequently called in to "mediate" conflicts between landowners and rural laborers, usually through the *gabellottos*, or land agents, who were themselves simply *mafiosi* (Hess 1973, pp. 38–39, 56–58; Blok 1988, pp. 121–131; Duggan 1989, pp. 85–91; Matard-Bonucci 1994, pp. 61–79; Lupo 1999, pp. 140–167; Riall 1998, pp. 138–197; Paoli 2003, pp. 33–39; Schneider and Schneider 2003, pp. 25–39; Dickie 2004, pp. 21–33).

In view of the above, it is not surprising that countless sources put Sicily under the control of "the" Mafia prior to the First World War. Mafia-like groups were indeed in control in numerous places, and anyone who tried to stop them—individuals as well as associations or enterprises—were made to toe the line with threats and violence. That is not to say that the groups themselves lived in mutual harmony. On the contrary, they clashed—sometimes violently—with another over power and, therefore, income in many places. And it was not only those directly involved who were affected by such conflicts. Blok's study of the Mafia in the Genuardo region shows that the battles between Mafia families over certain sources of income and/or social status was not only waged by the members themselves, but also created deep rifts in local communities. In other words, the families basically controlled entire populations (Blok 1988, pp. 161–181). On the other hand, separate Mafia families were also capable of cooperating closely at local, regional, and interregional levels when they shared the same interests (Hess 1973, pp. 88–92).

What this description tells us is that certain late-19th-century German authors had, in fact, correctly attributed the rise of criminal groups in Italy—in striking contrast to the demise of such groups in Germany and the Netherlands—to the country's failure to establish an effective central government. It would be fitting here to also consider the remarks made by Cesare Lombroso (1895, pp. 539–558) in the same period concerning both the Sicilian Mafia and the Neapolitan Camorra. If we compare his comments to the descriptions of the Mafia in present-day publications, we see that he too had correctly identified a number of their features: their organizational structure, composition and division of tasks, political alliances, involvement in extortion, standards and values, specific vocabulary, and so on. He also noted the initiation rituals that marked a new member's accession to the Mafia. Camorra newcomers had to swear, over and over (sometimes on a set of crossed swords), that they would never betray other members to the police, and indeed would love their fellow members as they would those who constantly put their lives at risk. Newcomers were sometimes even asked to murder their best friend in order to prove their loyalty to the gang.

Given this description of the Camorra as a violent secret society, Lombroso's conclusion, namely, that the Camorra and the Mafia were, in fact, alternative versions of the type of banditry that existed or had existed elsewhere in Europe, such as Germany, was not so surprising. Although he did not refer explicitly to the rituals practiced by some of the criminal groups that operated on the German-Dutch border at the end of the 18th century, the resemblance to the Camorra ritual is naturally striking. The parallel is even stronger if we recall the ritual customary among the Sicilian Mafia since the 19th century in which a newcomer had to hold a holy card in his hand, smear it with blood from his index finger, and allow another member to burn it on his hand while incanting: as this saint burns, so will burn he who betrays *cosa nostra*. The oath is thus literally "burned into" the novice (Gambetta 1993, pp. 146–155; Dickie 2004, pp. 34–38; Fijnaut 2009).

This parallel brings us to Mussolini's decision in 1924 to bring Sicily under the control of the Italian state once and for all and to appoint a new prefect, Cesare Mori, to break the Mafia's grip on the island (Falcionelli 1936, pp. 221–230; Duggan 1989, pp. 121–163, 222–243; Dickie 2004, pp. 172–191). Many of the dictatorial methods that Mori used in the years thereafter to reestablish the fascist state's monopoly on violence in Sicily resembled those applied in the late 18th and early 19th centuries to destroy banditry in the German states and the Netherlands: the establishment of a special law enforcement unit across the entire island, use of informants and the arrest of suspects, raids on hide-outs, intimidating mass trials, long prison sentences, and so on.

Mori eventually clashed with top-ranking military officers and leading politicians who questioned the success of his operations, and, in 1929, he was unexpectedly (at least for outsiders) relieved of his duties (Duggan 1989, pp. 245–257). Historians agree that, although the Mafia continued to offer pockets of resistance across Sicily, it had been decimated in vast areas of the island. Blok, however, notes that Mori's military operations did not spell the end of the Mafia because the social and economic context in which it had flourished survived largely intact. That became clear when Mussolini's regime collapsed in 1943 and the Mafia—with the support of the Allied forces—recovered its lost power (Blok 1988, pp. 182–212). One irony in this story is that La Cosa Nostra ultimately emerged stronger than ever on the other side of the Atlantic. It has been said that Mori's campaign against the Sicilian Mafia sent some five hundred *mafiosi* fleeing to the United States, where they joined the ranks of the many Italian criminals who had settled in the "New World" since the end of the 19th century (Hess 1973, pp. 170–176; Matard-Bonucci 1994, pp. 143–162).

IV. The Evolution of Italian Organized Crime in the United States

A. The Image of the Italian Mafia about 1900

In our introduction, we mentioned that historians of organized crime tend to devote a disproportionately large amount of attention to the evolution of La Cosa Nostra in the United States and that—certainly in a publication covering the international history of organized crime—a more balanced view is required. Many explanations can be given for this unilateral approach to the origins of organized crime (see the Introduction), but one that we have not mentioned yet is that the history of La Cosa Nostra also long dominated research into organized crime in the United States undertaken by American historians. That is certainly understandable, given the mass exodus of Italians to the country at the end of the 19th century and the prominent role that a number of Italian criminals played, and continue to play, in organized crime there. On the other hand, the one-sided emphasis on La Cosa Nostra can also be attributed to the popular image of the Italian Mafia's role in organized crime since the late 19th century (Reppetto 2004, pp. 18–35).

That image was formed largely by stories in the press concerning the origins and organization of extortion practices in the early 20th century, specifically in Chicago, which were attributed to the Black Hand (Ianni and Reuss-Ianni 1972, pp. 43–54; Nelli 1976, pp. 69–100; Woodiwiss 2001, pp. 94–101; Lombardo 2010). These mainly took the form of threatening letters sent to wealthy individuals, including criminal gang bosses, demanding that a certain amount of money should be handed over on a particular date and in a particular manner. If the money was not forthcoming, then a terrible fate—murder, arson, etc.—would befall the victim or victims. The criminals made good on their threats often enough to be credible, and they, consequently, achieved their aims: Their victims paid up or moved, lived in fear for many years, and so on. The newspapers claimed that these practices had been brought to the United States by members of the Sicilian Mafia and the Neapolitan Camorra, that it was generally *mafiosi* who were guilty of these specific crimes, and that the victims also included Italians. The Black Hand did, undoubtedly, hold sway in Italian communities, but Lombardo (2010) has shown beyond dispute that the perpetrators of this particular brand of extortion were not limited to Italian criminals, and that the victims included members of very different communities.

Other studies have shown that neither the Sicilian Mafia nor the Neapolitan Camorra deliberately built up La Cosa Nostra in the United States as a sort of overseas branch of their Italian operations (Critchley 2009). Undoubtedly, many Italians who immigrated to the United States in the late 19th century included *mafiosi*, and some of them continued their careers in crime in their new home, particularly in counterfeiting and other criminal activities that they had carried out in Italy. It is also obvious that Italian criminals maintained contact with friends and family back home after settling in the United States, and—if convenient—continued to cooperate with criminals, *mafiosi* and others, who had remained in Italy.

It is not true, however, that the Mafia or Camorra was transplanted as such to the United States. Of course, that does not mean that the Mafia groups that evolved in New York and elsewhere in the first decades of the 20th century did not bear a certain resemblance to the *coscas* of the Sicilian Mafia, for example. Not only was their internal organization similar to that of these basic units, but so were their initiation rituals. It is also important to note that membership of a Mafia family in Italy could be an important advantage to someone aspiring to join one of the American crime families, although it was certainly no requirement for taking part in their activities. Eventually, the families recruited many of their members from young Italians who had shown their criminal acumen in the streets of New York, for example in a juvenile gang.

Long before 1920 (the year in which Prohibition was introduced), however, numerous criminal gangs were active in "syndicate crime" (prostitution, gambling, and drug trafficking) that had no ties with the American Italian community. Italian criminals naturally played a prominent role in syndicate crime in places like Chicago, as noted by criminologist John Landesco in his 1929 report for the Illinois Association for Criminal Justice (Landesco 1968, pp. 845–905). Nonetheless, other immigrant communities had their own criminal gangs, which operated similarly on a smaller or larger scale (Nelli 1976, pp. 101–140). Indeed, many criminal gangs in the United States had both the infrastructure and the manpower to organize the illegal production and distribution of alcohol in 1920. In that sense, Prohibition was nothing more than a new and tremendous opportunity—not only for the Italian gangs but equally for the Chinese, Jewish, and Irish gangs—to operate successfully in an illegal market and make a lot of money doing so.

We mentioned above that Chinese organized crime groups had begun to infiltrate the United States in the late 19th century and engaged not only in extortion, but also in prostitution, gambling, and drug trafficking. In the first edition of his renowned study *The Gangs of New York*, Asbury described in colorful detail which gangs operated these criminal activities in Chinatown in that period and on what scale as well as how the police at times helped bring violent conflicts between rival Chinese gangs to a peaceful resolution (Asbury 1990, pp. 299–324).

As for the Jewish gangs, a study by Fried (1993, pp. 1–43, 90–91) shows that, around 1910, many hundreds of Jewish women worked as prostitutes in New York and, indeed, preferred earning their keep in this dubious fashion to slaving in the sweatshops and factories of Manhattan. This phenomenon was not restricted to New York; the Jewish communities of Chicago, Cleveland, and Detroit had similar black markets.

The same goes for the Irish gangs. They too played an important role in the evolution of organized crime in the United States. Durney (2000, pp. 11–51) describes how the mass immigration of the Irish in the mid-19th century led to the emergence of very large and extremely violent gangs; some even required candidates to have committed a murder before they were accepted as members. Like their Italian, Chinese, and Jewish counterparts, the Irish gangs were involved not only in all sorts of traditional crimes of violence and theft, but also in organizing prostitution rings and in racketeering, particularly among longshoremen.

Gangs also became more multicultural in composition in the early 20th century, with Jewish gangsters, for example, joining Italian gangs and vice versa. Members also came from ethnic groups other than Italian, Jewish, Chinese, or Japanese; in Philadelphia, for example, Polish criminals joined gangs involved in the illegal distribution of alcohol (Nelli 1976, pp. 101–140, 168–170).

B. Prohibition and Organized Crime

Once the Eighteenth Amendment to the US Constitution establishing Prohibition was adopted in 1919 and the National Prohibition Act (also known as the Volstead Act) came into force in 1920, Prohibition indeed became an important stimulus for organized crime in the United States—but its role should not be overestimated (Kerr 1985, pp. 139–210). It did not, in any event, cause organized crime to be concentrated in the hands of a few gangs or syndicates or shift that concentration of power mainly to the Italian gangs. Prohibition inarguably encouraged the rise of large, extremely violent crime syndicates in certain cities, for example Chicago's Torrio-Capone syndicate, active not only in black markets, but also in racketeering in numerous legitimate businesses sectors (Landesco 1968, pp. 923–997). Competition between criminal gangs at local, regional, and national levels did not end during Prohibition, however, and the Italian gangs were no exception. Indeed, in 1930 and 1931, rivalry between opposing Italian gangs in New York and other cities led to the so-called Castellammarese War between the Maranzano and Masseria gangs (Reppetto 2004, pp. 91–110).

We must also bear in mind that, in certain regions of the United States, Jewish criminals were at least as successful in serious crime as their Italian counterparts, especially in the liquor trade. The most notorious example was the Purple gang in Detroit (Kavieff 2000), but Jewish criminal groups also flourished in Boston and environs. New York's Rothstein gang set an unprecedented record for intrigue and violence in the 1920s with its illegal gambling operations and criminal involvement in organized labor and real estate. And we must not ignore the Irish gangsters, many of whom were given a new lease on life by Prohibition. Their extensive syndicates quickly began supplying liquor to speakeasies and bribing law enforcement, judicial, and administrative officials to turn a blind eye to their lucrative activities. New York's Irish bootleggers eventually played as important a role in the liquor trade as the Italian smugglers (Durney 2000, pp. 52–96). As it turns out, the influx of *mafiosi* who had fled Sicily in the 1920s during Mori's anti-Mafia campaign did not have a defining impact on the evolution of organized crime in the United States. Consider, for example, that almost all the key figures in the Castellammarese War already lived in the United States before Prohibition (Foote Whyte 1955, pp. 111–115; Nelli 1976, pp. 159–176; Katcher 1994; Critchley 2009, pp. 140–197, 207–210, 235–237; Kavieff 2000).

Prohibition promoted racketeering not only in the liquor trade, but also in numerous legitimate markets, for example textiles, construction, and food supply in New York and Chicago—a famous example being the protection racket in Manhattan's Fulton Fish Market (Nelli 1976, pp. 241–253)—but it did not spark a revolutionary change in this area. Criminal gangs had been using racketeering to generate income in many legitimate business sectors long before the Volstead Act came into force. We need only remember that, starting in the late 19th century, businesses called in both Italian and Jewish gangsters to intimidate strikers and beat down labor unrest. As we know, the labor unions responded by deploying their own thugs to protect themselves and their workers (Woodiwiss 2001, pp. 124–141, 148–164). At first they did so only occasionally, but during the mass strikes of 1909 they hired an army of gangsters to protect strikers and picket lines.

In the cities, the unintentional result of this strategy was that the gangs gradually gained control of unions in various sectors and, consequently, of business activity in those sectors, for example, by making the relevant businesses part of their cartels. Between 1910 and 1920, criminal infiltration into the construction and the hotel industry, for example, gained momentum in Chicago and elsewhere. Previously, around 1900, Irish and, somewhat later, Italian gangs seized control of the longshoremen (and their unions) in New York and other places, with all that that implied. This illegal monopoly—which the gangs reinforced by appointing their own people as union officials and intimidating any unionists who opposed them—allowed them to rob the longshoremen blind, both directly (for example, by paying them low wages) and indirectly (by plundering their pension funds), but it also gave them an opportunity to steal (or have others steal) massive amounts of goods from ports (MacDougall 1933; Nelli 1976, pp. 107–111; Fried 1993, pp. 32–36; Durney 2000, pp. 137–147; Jacobs 2006, pp. 24–34).

C. Sutherland Explains the Rise of Organized Crime

Organized crime flourished in the United States in the early decades of the 20th century because criminal gangs exploited opportunities arising from social, economic, criminal, and political circumstances to consolidate their hold on legitimate and illegal markets. That is not the whole story, however. The gangs also succeeded in gaining unlawful control of these markets because their attempts to amass more influence and, therefore, more income had the support of the authorities in their various manifestations.

First of all, there is ample evidence that the political parties—or in any event, powerful politicians—cooperated closely and regularly with influential criminals at municipal and state levels from the 19th century onward (Landesco 1968, pp. 999–1021; Asbury 1990, pp. 247–271; Reppetto 2004, pp. 54–74). They joined forces with them not only to augment their personal income or the coffers of their party by illegal means, but also to drum up votes. Criminals, in turn, had every interest in corrupting politicians; it allowed them to influence legislation in areas in which they had major illegal interests and to work the enforcement system to their advantage, for example, when it came to issuing or withdrawing licenses and permits.

Al Capone, for example, financed both the Republican and the Democratic election campaigns for mayor of Chicago in 1927. He was not the first to use such tactics, however: His predecessor, Johnny Torrio, had done the same years before in a bid to protect his illegal activities against the authorities (Foote Whyte 1955, pp. 159–193; Landesco 1968, pp. 909–919; Nelli 1976, pp. 111–115, 190–192). Similar collusion took place in New York in the 1920s and 1930s, with local Democrats cooperating regularly with leading crime figures in order to retain control of Tammany Hall (Repetto 2004, pp. 75–90). The close ties between them became obvious at the 1932 Democratic National Convention in Chicago, when "Lucky" Luciano shared a suite with Al Marinelli, one of the Big Apple's leading Democrats, at the Drake Hotel. Addressing this issue, criminologist Edwin Sutherland stated the following in his renowned *Principles of Criminology* (1934, p. 188):

> Large and strong criminal organizations cannot develop if the government is strongly organized.... The disorganization of the present American governments, however, is different from the early types of governmental disorganization. Modern law enforcement agencies cooperate with criminal organizations because they are under the control of politicians who are either criminals in the usual sense of the word, grafters, and bribe-takers (specialized forms of criminals), or have sympathetic relations because of common membership in the underworld.

Second, corruption—mainly in the police force, but also in the courts and in city hall—had grown to endemic proportions by around 1900. As a result, criminal gangs in various American cities had free rein for many years to organize their illegal activities in black or legitimate markets (Foote Whyte 1955, pp. 115–146). Or, as Sutherland has noted (1934, pp. 189–190):

> Protection against arrest and conviction is a necessary part of organized crime.... The techniques of fixing crimes are much more important than the techniques of executing crimes.... The police, the prosecutor and the judge can be severe with the friendless and unorganized criminals, who have no money and no political connections, and thus the favors granted to organized criminals are not apparent.

Because organized crime was entrenched in so many ways and in so many different domains of American society, said Sutherland, it could not be expected to disappear suddenly if Prohibition were to be repealed. When Prohibition was, indeed, repealed in 1932–1933, following the Wickersham Commission's critical 1931 *Report on the Enforcement of the Prohibition Laws of the United States*, researchers such as Sutherland and Foote Whyte were in any event very skeptical on this point (National Commission on Law Observance and Enforcement 1931). In 1934, Sutherland wrote (pp. 191–193) that the gangs that had played a key role in the illegal liquor trade during Prohibition were still very active in the prostitution racket and the white slave trade as well as in illegal gambling. They were, therefore, far from disappearing from American society.

Sociologist William Foote Whyte shared his views. In his landmark study *Street Corner Society: The Social Structure of an Italian Slum*, he wrote that when Prohibition came to an end, Chicago gangsters turned en masse to illegal gambling, everything from casinos and slot machines to numbers rackets and horse and dog racing. That also gave them considerable influence over the taverns, stores, barber shops, and other establishments that took bets and served as the "legitimate" branches of their crime syndicates. The gangsters invested their earnings from illegal gambling in mainstream businesses, thereby tightening their grip on the community (Foote Whyte 1955, pp. 142–146).

Chicago was not alone in this respect. The New York gangsters did not abandon the liquor trade altogether; some acquired stakes in important production and distribution companies before the repeal of Prohibition and continued to make money in the legitimate market (Nelli 1976, pp. 220–237).

D. Devising and Implementing Effective Policy, Step by Step

American policymakers did not expect organized crime to disappear with the end of Prohibition. They were well aware that it would remain a major problem in all its manifestations and that it would not be easy to defeat. That reality had naturally been amply demonstrated in Chicago, where it took years to put Al Capone behind bars. In fact, the chosen strategy was an unusual one: In October 1931, Capone was sentenced to 11 years imprisonment and a fine not for his direct and indirect involvement in organized crime as such, but for large-scale tax evasion (Bergreen 1996, pp. 485–489).

Given the key role that Capone played in Italian organized crime in Chicago in the 1920s, it is not surprising that so much has been published about the government's attempts to sideline him (Kobler 1992, pp. 316–346; Bergreen 1996, pp. 440–492; Woodiwiss 2001, pp. 194–198; Reppetto 2004, pp. 111–131; Eig 2010, pp. 303–367). However, nothing can match the documents produced by the Intelligence Unit of the Bureau of Internal Revenue, in which the agents involved recount their campaign against Capone. The documents were released by the Internal Revenue Service in February 2008. In inimitable style, one of the agents wrote in 1931 that "[t]he course of the investigation into the hidden sources of income of the 'big fellows' was a tortuous trail through the crooked ramifications of underworld intrigue." They also made no secret of the reason for that "tortuous trail": It had proved almost impossible to find anyone to testify against Capone. The authors go on to describe Capone's brand of organized crime in Chicago between 1924 and 1931, i.e., the many murders, large-scale gambling operations, illegal distribution of beer, and so on (Internal Revenue Service).

Organized crime was therefore at the top of the agenda at a 1934 conference on crime organized by the then Attorney General of the United States, Homer Stille Cummings. Cummings himself suggested that crime formed a "graver menace to the Nation than could possibly have been true only a few decades ago"; he made it clear that he was referring to gangsters and racketeers, although some continued to glorify them. Another speaker, John J. Bennett Jr., the Attorney General of the State of New York, fleshed out Cummings's reference. In his view, "[c]ommercial racketeering in the United States is one of the revolting forms of modern organized crime" (Cummings 1936, p. 46), and he stressed how urgent it was to use the force of law against it. He suggested broadening the scope of the criminal code, protecting witnesses, and more closely regulating business. His proposals had the backing of another speaker, criminologist John Landesco, who blamed some of the problems on anti-trust legislation, which he claimed went too far and caused instability in markets, leading businesses to hire gangsters to discipline competitors who refused to stick to agreements. Eventually, however, those gangsters muscled in and took over ownership of the same businesses (Cummings 1936, pp. 7, 46–52, 430–432).

Some doubt was registered at the conference as to whether Congress would, in fact, be prepared to introduce an effective action program against organized crime. In the summer and autumn of 1933, a Subcommittee of the Committee of Commerce launched an investigation into "so-called rackets," but the hearings did not produce vigorous proposals (US Senate 1933). Nonetheless, given the seriousness of the situation, a number of speakers urged that such measures be taken. A New York judge, for example, proposed the following (US Senate 1933, pp. 13–35): establish an American version of Scotland Yard to investigate racketeering; amend anti-trust legislation to make it easier to catch racketeers who violated the law; clean up the unions by tying the establishment of a union and the appointment of union officials to permits and by encouraging organized labor and business owners to cooperate more closely on fighting racketeering. The judge, Jonah Goldstein, knew all too well what he was talking about, and unsurprisingly, he had the support of other New York judges, such as the United States Attorney Eastern District of New York, Howard Ameli (US Senate 1933, pp. 94–100):

> Drastic measures are necessary to protect the public from the operations of the gangsters and the racketeers who are able, at times, to "beat the rap" and to go "unwhipped by justice" because of legal technicalities and also by reason of the racketeers' ability and willingness to pay for silence.

It should be noted that the above-mentioned reports do not cite La Cosa Nostra as the biggest problem in organized crime. Nonetheless, the impression is that, out on the streets, it was mainly the Italian Mafia that posed the biggest threat to American society.

Evidence can be found in the fact that the American authorities did everything possible in the 1930s to eliminate the key figures of La Cosa Nostra in the big cities. The first was Al Capone, as we have seen. The second was "Lucky" Luciano. Originally from Sicily, Luciano had managed to turn the war between large Italian crime families in around 1930 to his advantage, and he ruled the entire Italian organized crime scene in New York with a heavy hand thereafter. He was targeted by legendary special prosecutor Thomas E. Dewey, who was appointed Chief Assistant US Attorney for the Southern District of New York in 1931 to look into organized crime in the city. Dewey became the embodiment of the "war" that New York's mayor, Fiorello H. La Guardia, had declared on organized crime in 1933 (Block 1999, pp. 63–89).

Dewey prosecuted Luciano in April 1936 for running a large-scale prostitution ring in the city—with some 200 bordellos and 3,000 prostitutes—basing his case mainly on testimonies by prostitutes, pimps, and porters as well as police observations and testimonies by protected witnesses. He was successful, obtaining Luciano's conviction and a sentence of 30 to 50 years imprisonment on June 7, 1936. Luciano served only part of that sentence, however. In 1946, he was paroled on the condition that he depart the United States and return to Sicily. As is well known, this "exit strategy" was Luciano's reward for presumably helping to keep the Germans away from the US coast and drive them out of Italy. This "favor" cost Dewey his political career (Nelli 1976, pp. 239–241; Campbell

1977; Stolberg 1995, pp. 116–161; Block 1999, pp. 141–148; Reppetto 2004, pp. 162–180; Donati 2010, pp. 125–205; Newark 2010, pp. 94–178).

The notion that La Cosa Nostra constituted the biggest criminal threat to American society, not only in Chicago and New York, but also across the country, was borne out in the early 1950s by the much-publicized Kefauver Committee hearings. This Senate committee, chaired by Estes Kefauver, was installed in 1950 to investigate the role of organized crime in interstate commerce. After considering a wide range of sources, the committee published its conclusion the following year, stating that the crime syndicates in the big cities not only monopolized illegal markets—in particular gambling—but also engaged in racketeering in a variety of economic sectors (US Senate 1951). The committee reached the following shocking conclusion (US Senate, p. 2):

> There is a sinister criminal organization known as the Mafia operating throughout the country with ties to other nations in the opinion of the committee. The Mafia is the direct descendant of a criminal organization of the same name originating in the island of Sicily. In this country, the Mafia has also been known as The Black Hand and the Unione Siciliano. The membership of the Mafia today is not confined to persons of Sicilian origin. The Mafia is a loose-knit organization specializing in the sale and distribution of narcotics, the conduct of various gambling enterprises, prostitution and other rackets based on extortion and violence. The Mafia is the binder which ties together two major criminal syndicates as well as numerous other criminal groups throughout the country. The power of the Mafia is based on a ruthless enforcement of its edicts and its own law of vengeance, to which have been creditably attributed hundreds of murders throughout the country.

The committee's conclusion was immediately controversial and remained so in subsequent decades. Some claimed that the committee lacked sound empirical evidence because it had based its findings on police statements, newspaper articles, and reports by the crime commissions but not on any systematic investigation of its own. Others contested the way the committee had presented various matters, for example, its description of the Black Hand (as shown in the detailed investigation referred to above—Lombardo 2010). In addition, Kefauver's attempts to exploit the issue of organized crime politically stirred up controversy regarding the investigation's underpinnings and implications (Moore 1974; Wade 1996).

Nonetheless, Kefauver's depiction of organized crime, while the source of much commotion, was not his invention alone. It clearly had the support of every major branch of the US government. We see that, first of all, in the report on the national conference on organized crime organized by Attorney General J. Howard McGrath on February 15, 1950. State governors, mayors, police commissioners, and prosecutors—speaking either in their own name or on behalf of their association—used the same words as the Kefauver Committee to describe the enormous threat that organized crime posed to the United States (Department of Justice 1950). Other evidence can be found in various studies by renowned legal experts into the problem of organized crime, carried out at the initiative of the American Bar Association and under the auspices of its Commission on Organized Crime (e.g., Ploscowe 1952). The studies show that legal professionals and the judiciary also wanted the United States to come to grips with a problem that was undermining its democratic principles and economic system. Kefauver was certainly not alone in his convictions.

It is, therefore, not surprising that Kefauver's opinions are echoed in reports issued by subsequent important committees. There were, to begin with, the reports by various Senate committees convening in the late 1950s and early 1960s under Senator John McClellan's leadership. These committees investigated racketeering among labor unions, such as the Teamsters, and the role of organized crime in illegal drug trafficking (Jacobs 2006, pp. 13–15). The first series of investigations shot to international fame in 1960, after Robert Kennedy published *The Enemy Within*, a book in which he described labor racketeering in somewhat apocalyptic terms and criticized the Department of Justice, including the Federal Bureau of Investigation and its director, J. Edgar Hoover, for letting matters slide (Kennedy 1960; Schlesinger 1996, pp. 137–169). The second series of investigations gained worldwide renown thanks to mobster Joseph Valachi's disclosures concerning La Cosa Nostra in New York and other cities and how it was run by a national ruling committee known as "The Commission" (Maas 1968; Kenney and Finckenauer 1995, pp. 236–242).

Second, there was *The Challenge of Crime in a Free Society*, a 1968 report by the President's Commission on Law Enforcement and Administration of Justice, installed in 1965 under the leadership of then Attorney General Nicholas Katzenbach. The first line of the chapter on organized crime left no doubt as to the problem (President's Commission on Law Enforcement and Administration 1968, p. 437): "Organized crime is a society that seeks to operate outside the control of the American people and their governments." A few paragraphs later, the report describes what is meant by "organized crime" (President's Commission on Law Enforcement and Administration 1968, p. 448): "Today the hard core of organized crime in the United States consists of 24 groups operating as criminal cartels in large cities across the Nation." The commission argued that a national strategy was needed to ward off the enormous threat of the Mafia (President's Commission on Law Enforcement and Administration 1968, pp. 465–486). It favored giving law enforcement and justice officials broader powers, setting up special investigation units in cities and states, increasing federal aid for local and regional initiatives (for example, by establishing a computerized database), and expanding the Justice Department's Organized Crime and Racketeering Section (Smith 1991; Calder and Lynch 2008).

These proposals were in line with plans that Kennedy—to Hoover's great displeasure—had already drawn up during his term as Attorney General (1961–1964), most of which were implemented only in 1968 and thereafter (Schlesinger 1996, pp. 269–285; Jacobs 2006, pp. 16–22). A succession of laws introduced such tactics as electronic surveillance, witness protection, and specific methods for tackling racketeering in businesses. In parallel actions, special strike forces operating under the supervision of the Department of Justice were set up in a large number of cities, and steps were taken to improve cooperation between federal, state, and local law enforcement. For various reasons, however, it took until the 1980s before the authorities actually deployed the entire set of repressive measures to take down La Cosa Nostra. No one today questions the success of this offensive. In New York, two further factors played an important role: first of all, the cooperation of witnesses such as Salvatore Gravano and Salvatore Vitale and, second, the use of administrative measures, for example, the refusal or withdrawal of permits and licenses as means of cleaning up the waste disposal, textile, and construction industries (Jacobs, Panarella, and Worthington 1994, pp. 8–18; Jacobs, Friedland, and Radick, 1999).

Finally, it should be noted that the depiction of organized crime in *The Challenge of Crime in a Free Society* was based largely on the views of renowned criminologist Donald Cressey, as expounded in his 1969 book *Theft of the Nation*. As a result, he found himself at the center of a heated academic and journalistic debate concerning the nature of organized crime in the United States. Critics objected not only to the commission's depiction of La Cosa Nostra as a kind of alien conspiracy attempting to gain control of the United States within its own borders, but also to its failure to appreciate the other forms of serious organized crime in the country (Smith 1975; Kenney and Finckenauer 1995, pp. 242–255).

That depiction was corrected by the President's Commission on Organized Crime, led by US Court of Appeals Judge Irving Kaufman, which published its report *The Impact: Organized Crime Today* in 1986. The report looked beyond La Cosa Nostra in any event, paying at least some attention to Chinese organized crime, motorcycle gangs, the Yakuza, and to Columbian and Irish organized crime. This shift in focus was echoed in the academic literature on organized crime in the United States (e.g., Kleinknecht 1996; Finckenauer and Waring 1998).

V. THE CONNECTIONS BETWEEN NORTHWESTERN EUROPE AND THE UNITED STATES

Previously, in our historical survey of organized crime in Southeast Asia, we indicated that both the Italian Mafia and the American La Cosa Nostra had served as benchmarks for appraising the state of organized crime in other countries. In fact, the two also functioned as role models for criminal gangs in Southeast Asia, at least in Japan. Their members even began to imitate the behavior (or what they thought to be the behavior) of American gangsters. But things did not end there. As we mentioned above, after the Second World War the Yakuza systematically extended their field of operations to the United States, following in the footsteps of Chinese gangsters, who had begun their migration some 50 years earlier, at the end of the 19th century.

By contrast, no evidence exists that any German or Dutch criminal groups shifted operations to the United States in the 19th century or first half of the 20th century. We know of some individual Dutch criminals who crossed the Atlantic to avoid prison or after serving time, but that is obviously not the same as a gang extending its network to North America. Even in the case of the Italian Mafia, no evidence exists that the Sicilian Mafia or the Camorra transplanted operations directly to the United States, as we have seen. Of course, many Italian immigrants to the United States were acquainted with the criminal practices of these groups in one way or another.

We do not know whether the same can also be said of the Irish and Jewish organized crime groups that became active in the United States in the 19th century. In their cases, historians tend to look no further than their operations within the territory of the United States and not at their possible involvement in crime in their countries of origin. So far, this is unexplored territory in historical research.

An entirely different matter is how historians and criminologists in northwestern Europe, particularly in Germany and the Netherlands, viewed the evolution of organized crime in the United States in the 20th century, and what role the American policy on organized crime played in policymaking in such countries as Germany and the Netherlands and later in the European Union. These questions, which are certainly as important as questions concerning the relationship between organized crime and criminals on the two continents, will be addressed below in as much as the present situation allows.

The same questions obviously apply for the connections between Southeast Asia and the United States. Since we lack accessible literature exploring possible interactions between these two regions, however, we are unable to address these questions in the present publication, and will have to leave that to researchers who master the Chinese and Japanese languages.

A. German Research on Organized Crime in the United States

German crime historians and criminologists publishing in the late 19th and early 20th centuries largely ignored the development of the Italian Mafia and the evolution of the American La Cosa Nostra when reviewing serious or professional crime in their own country. One possible explanation is that these authors, while recognizing persistent—and sometimes major—problems of vagrancy, beggary, and so forth, did not find evidence of the kind of banditry common in the 18th century. Another explanation is that authors of the day had been influenced by bio-anthropological criminology, which focused on individual criminals and not on group crime (Heindl 1929; Wulffen 1926). Nonetheless, many Germans—and certainly many German politicians—believed that a dangerous criminal underworld had gradually materialized in the cities. Although this idea was widely shared, however, no one investigated that underworld as such.

It is not at all clear, then, why, in around 1930, a number of young German-speaking researchers traveled to the United States to study crime—specifically organized crime—and the American government's campaign against it. Was it because they were interested in the American situation for theoretical or perhaps ideological reasons, as in Franz Exner's case? Or were they intrigued by reports that had reached Europe about the rise of serious crime across the Atlantic, as may have been the case for Roland Graszberger, who taught at the University of Vienna and was awarded a grant by the Rockefeller Foundation to study the situation first-hand? What we do know is that the author of two German-language books on serious organized crime in the United States, Hans von Hentig, did not go willingly. He fled to the United States after the Nazis removed him from his post at the University of Bonn in 1935. In the United States, he was invited by Colorado University and the governor of the state of Colorado to participate in an extensive research project, the Colorado Crime Survey, and so he began to study the phenomenon of *Der Gangster* (the title of his renowned book, published in 1959).

1. *Graszberger's Pioneering Study (1933)*

Franz Exner, professor at the University of Munich, did not go into detail about organized crime in the United States in his travel report. After briefly discussing the problems of kidnappings and hold-ups, he pointed out that Prohibition had been an important stimulus for the development of gangs, and that the repeal of Prohibition had not brought the gangs to an end. On the contrary, they had simply gone in search of other domains in which they could apply their violent methods to make money (Exner 1935, p. 11).

Roland Graszberger (1933), on the other hand, did provide a detailed description of the illegal markets in which the gangsters had been successful, i.e. prostitution, illegal drug trafficking, and gambling. He also discussed the widespread phenomenon of racketeering, the systematic extortion by criminal gangs of legitimate businesses in every conceivable sector of the economy, from textiles to food supply and from steel manufacturing to cleaning and construction. Graszberger even identified the violent methods employed by the gangs, ranging from intimidation to arson and murder. In his view, racketeering was essentially the violent monopolization of power in economic life.

The question that we must pose within the context of this article is: did Graszberger also link the problem of organized crime to the rise of bandit groups in Europe? The answer is that he did not. Or rather, he did not compare the earlier bandit groups in Germany with gangster society in the United States, and he also did not explore whether German criminals who moved to the United States in the course of the 19th and 20th centuries had continued their life of crime there. The latter is perhaps more peculiar than it seems. After all, why ask that question about Italian criminals who immigrated to the United States and not about Germans, Austrians, and other nationalities who fled the Old World? Or was the question more obvious in the case of Italian criminals than for other nationalities because Italy had not exterminated banditry the way other western European countries largely had at the start of the 19th century?

Whatever the case, what is relevant for us is that Graszberger described American organized crime as essentially an extension of more traditional forms of violent crime against individuals, such as robbery, burglary, or extortion. Therefore, he did not think it strange that the members of organized crime gangs were themselves frequently individuals with a criminal past; they had already built their careers in the criminal world, as burglars, robbers, or gunmen in a racket. While he did not say in so many words that the same course of events had taken, or could take, place in Europe, he certainly did not exclude the possibility given the right conditions. Those conditions went beyond a lack of awareness/non-interiorization of the law, which, in his view, meant placing individual self-interest above the general good of society, to include a similar absence of stability in economic and private life (Graszberger 1933, pp. 79, 97–108, 142–197, 298–299).

It is also important to note Graszberger's observation that, although those involved in organized crime came from many different backgrounds (Irish, Dutch, Jewish, and so on), Italian criminals, nonetheless, played a dominant role in this type of crime. He was not able to explain why that was the case, but he did not believe it was related to Mussolini's war on the bandits of southern Italy because most of the Italians who played such a large role in the illegal liquor trade had in fact immigrated to the United States before the First World War. He also did not rule out the notion that the Italian migrants had been forced to enter the illegal market because industrialization in the United States had deprived them of the heavy physical labor that they had been accustomed to at home, although he was not certain about this theory. However, despite this emphasis on Italian gangsters active in the United States, Graszberger did not specifically refer to the Mafia as such in southern Italy.

2. Hentig's Comparative Analysis (1959)

Writing more than 20 years later, Hans von Hentig specifically contrasted developments in the United States to those in Europe and, in particular, Italy, in his book *Der Gangster*. First of all, he made it perfectly clear in his analysis of the situation that the bandit groups that had roamed Germany and the Netherlands (Röling 1933) in the 18th century could be regarded, in the functional sense, as the precursors of organized criminals in the United States. This observation led him to conclude that such criminal groups had a chance of succeeding only in nations with weak governments. They were doomed to failure in strong nations because the latter were better organized, had more resources, and higher morale—characteristics that would always triumph over criminal groups. In essence, he was repeating what his former colleagues in Germany (e.g., Kurella) had always claimed.

Based on this principle, Hentig then discussed how such gang-related crimes as extortion, burglary, hold-ups, kidnappings, threats, physical abuse, and murder were traditional methods of acquiring money and status by direct, immediate, and simple means. When old-fashioned gangs developed into rackets, the gangsters no longer attacked people or property directly; instead, they used intimidation and violence to levy an indirect "tax" on the supply of goods and services—prostitution, gambling, liquor and food, drugs, transport, hospitality, and so forth—that were much in demand in legitimate and black markets. To succeed in racketeering, gangs had to do three things. First, they had to create an efficient and powerful organization by requiring strict discipline and high morale of all those in their ranks who were involved in such practices. Second, they had to do everything possible to undermine the forces of government ranged against them, for example, by engaging in clandestine activities, corrupting politicians and public servants, infiltrating key institutions, threatening witnesses, money-laundering their ill-gotten gains, and so on. Third, they had to gain control of the labor unions in order to muscle in on the relevant business sectors (Hentig, 1959, pp. 74–83, 109–138).

After this explanation, Hentig did not get around to answering a very obvious question, that is, whether the United States was strong enough at that point to frustrate the undermining impact of the crime syndicates. Unlike Graszberger, he neither asked nor answered the question of whether the traditional bandit groups had already developed, or could or would develop, into rackets in Europe or Italy. In that respect, Hentig never really completed his account of the gangster.

With respect to the origins of what was then the gangland hard core, Von Hentig was much less inclined than Graszberger to identify the "Italians" as the dominant force. He argued—and as we saw earlier, his argument has been substantiated by a considerable body of research in recent years—that it was not by any means Italians alone, but also the Irish and the Jews who had become a huge problem in this connection. He attributed this to the burden of history that had brought these three groups to the United States. "The Irish," he wrote, "have spent centuries fighting poverty and oppression. The Sicilians have had rebellion against repression and exploitation coursing through their veins since time immemorial. The Jews have only been able to defend themselves by forming a phalanx against their persecutors." In his opinion, the traditional pugnacity of these immigrants had been revived by the struggle to survive in their adopted country (Hentig 1959, pp. 4–5, 9–18, 84–176).

In conclusion, we must emphasize that the studies published by Graszberger and Hentig, while important in themselves, did not lead directly to a closer examination of organized crime by German-speaking criminologists in Europe. Why that is so is unclear. It seems obvious, however, that the first and foremost reason is the decline of criminology in Germany during the Second World War. Another important factor may have been that the German-speaking regions of Europe did not regard organized crime (as described by Graszberger and Hentig) as a relevant social problem in the 1950s.

B. Sidelong References to Organized Crime in the Netherlands

There were no Dutch criminologists who went to the United States in the 1930s to study organized crime there first-hand. This does not mean that no one in the Netherlands was interested in what was happening on the other side of the Atlantic. The interest was there, but it did not inspire researchers to study the development of organized crime in the Netherlands. At most, there were a few sidelong references to American publications.

The first was in Cornelia Schreven's study of a series of burglaries committed between 1939 and 1947 by a criminal gang in the city of Groningen. Schreven did draw on publications covering the various successive forms of organized crime (the 18th-century bandit groups, the Mafia and the Camorra, and the American rackets)—basing herself in particular on Walter Reckless's introduction to criminology, *The Crime Problem* (1950, pp. 142–187)—but made no reference to those publications in the empirical portion of her study. In that section, she referred mainly to Frederic Thrasher's book *The Gang: A Study of 1313 Gangs in Chicago*, which examined the organization, composition, function, and so on of more traditional gangs (Schreven 1957, pp. 131–144).

The second reference was in the dissertation that Willem Nagel wrote in 1949, based on his study of crime in the municipality of Oss (southern Netherlands, near the city of 's-Hertogenbosch) in the 1930s. Like Schreven, he made minor reference to American research on organized crime. He did so because the crimes committed in Oss in the 1920s and 1930s had taken the terrifying form of hold-ups that were every bit as violent as the raids committed by robber bands in 18th-century Germany and the Low Countries. The resemblance was heightened by the fact that these criminals belonged to three cliques, which, in turn, represented the hard core of a fairly large gang, one that long succeeded in operating outside the law in the region more or less unpunished.

In interpreting what had taken place in Oss and environs, Nagel too referred to Thrasher's study of gangs and concluded that the criminal groups active in Oss had a number of things in common with the Chicago gangs, for example, the fact that young gang members imitated the behavior of the older ones. Basing himself in part on von Hentig's 1948 book *The Criminal and His Victim*, Nagel also concluded that the Oss gangs and American gangsters shared one major similarity: both, he wrote, displayed a typical "sustained tone of rebellion." Remarkably, Nagel emphasized that the gangs that had emerged in Oss in no way resembled the banditry that had spread throughout Italy (Nagel 1949, pp. 342, 348, 353, 411).

One point worth noting is that Nagel's research in the Netherlands produced no follow-up. After the Second World War, criminology there focused overwhelmingly on the criminal as an individual and not at all on organized crime in any form (Fijnaut 1989b). In addition, organized crime was not regarded as a problem meriting further study in the postwar Netherlands. It was mainly viewed as an exotic phenomenon, something that occurred in the United States, China, Japan, and southern Italy but not in the Netherlands (Fijnaut 1985).

C. The Impact of American Policy on Western European Policymaking

In the 1960s, however, an important change occurred in how Germany and the Netherlands defined the problem of crime. Undoubtedly, the inspiration came from the United States in the form of the report *The Challenge of Crime in a Free Society*, published in 1968 by the President's Commission on Law Enforcement and Administration of Justice. The alarming message of this report—that organized crime posed a serious threat to an orderly society—drew considerable attention in the Netherlands and Germany. A top-ranking Dutch police officer wrote in 1969 that there was every reason to take the American report to heart in that respect because, although the problem of organized crime had not yet grown to American proportions in the Netherlands, it could certainly move in that direction. Therefore, it behooved Dutch law enforcement officials to take steps that would prevent such a trend (Fijnaut 2011, pp. 296–297).

His views were not only echoed in the years thereafter by other Dutch police officials, but also, starting in the 1970s, increasingly defended by leading German police chiefs, such as Wolfgang Sielaff, head of the Hamburg criminal investigation division. Although organized crime in the United States had developed in ways unknown in Germany in the previous 70 years, Sielaff wrote, this was certainly no reason to remain idle and allow serious crime to take such extremes forms. On the contrary, there was every reason to avoid the American situation and take systematic action against existing crime in the worlds of prostitution, gambling, drugs, human trafficking extortion, and so on (Fijnaut et al. 1998, pp. 7–23; Sielaff 1983). His arguments garnered widespread support in German police circles (Lenhard 1989).

The growing alarm about serious crime among police officials, which was echoed by journalists (Behr 1985; Middelburg 1988; Lindlau 1989), introduced the term *organized crime* in Germany and the Netherlands, which was coined in the United States and until then had never been used in Europe. This does not mean that everyone in these countries or in other parts of western Europe, for example, the United Kingdom, agreed on the meaning of the term, let alone on the actual nature and scale of the problem and how that compared with the problem in the United States (Albini 1975; Mack 1970; Mack and Kerner 1975).

To resolve these disagreements, the New York State Organized Crime Task Force was invited to the Netherlands in October 1990 to discuss the differences and similarities between organized crime in the United States and in the Netherlands with Dutch police officials, public prosecutors, mayors, and criminologists (Fijnaut 1990; Fijnaut and Jacobs 1991). The results of this conference made it clear that there were certain parallels between the two countries, for example with respect to illegal drug trafficking, but that there were also major differences, such as the control that criminal gangs exercised over legitimate sectors of the economy, the degree of government corruption, and the negative role of the labor unions. These insights were also highlighted in the reports produced by the Fijnaut research group for a Dutch parliamentary committee, which had ordered an inquiry into the use of special investigation methods for combating organized crime in 1994–1996 (Fijnaut et al. 1998).

Regardless of the conceptual differences within and between the member states of the European Union and the discrepancy between the problems encountered in western Europe and the United States, since 1985 organized crime has become one of the issues that the member states are taking pains to address in their crime policies. And, as I made clear in my article "European Union Organized Crime Control Policies," the issue became even more pressing around 1990 for two reasons. The first is that the murders of Italian prosecuting magistrates Giovanni Falcone and Paolo Borsellini in May and July 1992 had intensified the fear of organized crime, and specifically the Italian Mafia, in the European Union. The second reason is that the collapse of the Soviet Union had raised fears of Russian organized crime spreading throughout Europe (Joutsen 1993;

Handelman 1995; Varese 2001; Volkov 2002). As a result, the European heads of government took the first steps toward formulating an all-around, vigorous response to what was regarded as a major challenge for the European Union.

Viewing this development from a comparative historical perspective, we can say that in 1992, immediately following the Soviet Union's collapse, the European Union found itself in a similar situation to that of the United States in the 1920s, when Prohibition helped fuel the continued rise of organized crime. In that situation, it was virtually impossible to avoid developing a coherent and effective national policy aimed at controlling organized crime.

VI. Conclusion

The foregoing explanation shows that organized crime as it exists today originated in many different locations around the world. It naturally developed in many more places than covered in this essay, but the few places discussed here offer readers an idea of the circumstances that led to particular forms of organized crime and allowed them to evolve. All things considered, it appears that organized crime tends to flourish in divided, conflict-riddled communities in which government is weak and/or corrupt almost as a matter of course and, therefore, becomes part of the problem rather than part of the solution. Unsurprisingly, our historical review shows that organized crime can be tackled effectively only by unified, decisive, incorruptible government. That was true in around 1800, when the authorities repressed the bandit groups in northwestern Europe, and it was true in the late 20th century, when the US government took action against La Cosa Nostra.

The history of organized crime presented above also demonstrates that the internationalization, or globalization, of organized crime has not been a straightforward process; rather, it took place and, indeed, is still taking place along a variety of different paths. First of all, it takes the form of criminals who abandon their homes for demographic and/or economic reasons and settle in other parts of the world. The second form is related to the first: It consists of groups who run criminal operations in other parts of the world from their traditional home base, sometimes with the help of members (or former members) of their gangs or of other gangs in the foreign location. The third form is when up-and-coming criminal gangs imitate the behavior of notorious gangs elsewhere in the world. These three forms of globalization can also occur simultaneously, of course, and be mutually reinforcing.

What we must naturally bear in mind is that organized crime is not always transnational in nature—not by any means. Extortion in black or legitimate markets is usually a very local affair. It is only when organized crime involves the supply of illegal workers and contraband goods that it very quickly transmutes into a transborder affair, at least with respect to the transport of such workers or goods and the related flow of money. In terms of production and distribution, however, it is usually also local in nature, whether the crime involves human trafficking, drug trafficking, or the illegal arms trade. That is why the fight against organized crime primarily comes down to forceful action on the part of local and national governments. Without such action, organized crime cannot be tackled effectively at the local level and international cooperation will also fail. Indeed, successful international cooperation in combating organized crime requires strong local government.

The latter observation leads naturally to the suggestion that a balanced approach to the international history of organized crime should also cover the internationalization of policy meant to combat it. We have already mentioned that the policy pursued in western Europe, and certainly in Germany and the Netherlands, has been heavily influenced by the policy developed in a piecemeal fashion in the United States, and that the United Nations policy on this point rests largely on policymaking in these two regions of the world. It is naturally important to consider how the globalization of policy has proceeded so far and, in particular, which images of organized crime have had a hand in this process as well as the role played by conventions meant to combat the traffic in women, drug trafficking, the illegal arms trade, and other criminal activities (Andreas and Nadelmann 2006; Woodiwiss and Hobbs 2009; Fijnaut 2010; see Beare and Woodiwiss's article, "U.S. Organized Crime Control Policies Exported Abroad").

A final comment concerns the interesting topic of how research on organized crime and the globalization of organized crime became internationalized. This topic not only concerns the internationalization of such research itself, but also what role that process has played in the image of organized crime worldwide and in past and present policymaking in national and transnational contexts. Another question in this connection is how to ensure that research keeps pace with the internationalization of organized crime and policy introduced to combat it. It is clear that more must be done than merely founding scientific societies and promoting academic publications. Such initiatives can serve as a means only to discuss and disseminate research results. However, to encourage research in the first place and improve the quality of what is produced, more funding must be made available worldwide to support it. Another urgent concern is how this research should be organized. Perhaps the best solution is to set up multinational research groups that analyze specific situations and developments in the same manner based on common definitions of the problem.

NOTES

1. Since the end of the First Opium War in 1842, the British had a settlement in Shanghai, which was soon followed by American and French settlements. In 1854, a united municipal council was created to serve all three settlements, but, in 1862, the French concession dropped out of the arrangement. The following year the British and American settlements formally united to become the Shanghai International Settlement. This was run autonomously by the Western powers, although it formally remained Chinese sovereign territory. After the Chinese-Japanese War in 1894–1895, Japan also obtained its own settlement in Shanghai (Shanghai 1973; Martin 1996, pp. 10–18, 27–35, 53–54, 64–69; Haar 1998, pp. 351–360).

REFERENCES

Adriaenssen, Leo. 2007. *Staatsvormend Geweld: Overleven aan de Frontlinies in de Meierij van Den Bosch*. Tilburg: Stichting Zuidelijk Historisch Contact.

Albanese, Jay, Dilip Das, and Arvind Verma, eds. 2003. *Organized Crime*. Upper Saddle River, NJ: Prentice Hall.

Albini, Joseph. 1975. "Mafia as Method: A Comparison between Great Britain and USA: Regarding the Existence and Structure of Types of Organised Crime." *International Journal of Criminology and Penology* 3:295–305.

Andreas, Peter, and Ethan Nadelmann. 2006. *Policing the Globe: Criminalization and Crime Control in International Relations*. Oxford: Oxford University Press.

Aniskiewicz, Rick. 1994. "Metatheoretical Issues in the Study of Organized Crime." *Journal of Contemporary Criminal Justice* 10(4): 314–324.

Arlacchi, Pino. 1983. *Mafia, Peasants and Great Estates: Society in Traditional Calabria*. Cambridge: Cambridge University Press.

Asbury, Herbert. 1990. *The Gangs of New York: An Informal History of the Underworld*. New York: Paragon House.

Avé-Lallemant, Friedrich. 1858. *Das Deutsche Gaunertum in seiner sozialpolitischen, literarischen und linguistischen Ausbildung zu seinem heutigen Bestande*. 2 vols. Wiesbaden, Germany: Verlag Ralph Suchier.

Behr, Hans-Georg. 1985. *Organisiertes Verbrechen*. Düsseldorf: ECON Verlag.

Bergreen, Laurence. 1996. *Capone: The Man and the Mafia*. New York: Touchstone.

Block, Alan. 1999. *East Side, West Side: Organizing Crime in New York, 1930–1950*. New Brunswick, NJ: Transaction.

Blok, Anton. 1988. *The Mafia of a Sicilian Village, 1860–1960: A Study of Violent Peasant Entrepreneurs*. Cambridge, UK: Polity.

Blok, Anton. 1991. *De Bokkerijders: Roversbenden en geheime Genootschappen in de Landen van Overmaas, 1730–1774*. Amsterdam: Prometeus.

Boehncke, Heiner, and Hans Sarkowicz. 1991. *Die Deutschen Räuberbanden: Originaldokumen ten Herausgegeben und Kommentiert*. 3 vols. Frankfurt: Eichborn Verlag.

Booth, Martin. 1990. *The Triads: The Chinese Criminal Society*. London: Grafton Books.

Briquet, Jean-Louis, and Gilles Favarel-Garrigues, eds. 2010. *Organized Crime and States: The Hidden Face of Politics*. New York: Palgrave Macmillan.

Brodeur, Jean-Paul. 1997. "Organized Crime: Trends in the Literature." *International Annals of Criminology* 35 (1–2): 89–129.

Bynum, Timothy, ed. 1987. *Organized Crime in America: Concepts and Controversies*. Monsey, NY: Willow Tree Press.

Calder, James, and William Lynch. 2008. "From Apalachin to the Buffalo Project: Obstacles on the Path to Effective Federal Responses to Organized Crime, 1957–1967." *Trends in Organized Crime* 11:207–269.

Campbell, Rodney. 1977. *The Luciano Project*. New York: McGraw-Hill.

Chambliss, William. 1975. "On the Paucity of Original Research on Organized Crime: A Footnote to Galligher and Cain." *The American Sociologist* 10:36–39.

Chesney, Kellow. 1979. *The Victorian Underworld*. Harmondsworth, UK: Pelican Books.

Chin, Ko-Lin. 1990. *Chinese Subculture and Criminality: Non-traditional Crime Groups in America*. Westport, CT: Greenwood.

Chin, Ko-Lin. 1996. *Chinatown Gangs: Extortion, Enterprise and Ethnicity*. New York: Oxford University Press.

Chin, Ko-Lin. 1999. *Smuggled Chinese: Clandestine Immigration to the United States*. Philadelphia: Temple University Press.

Chu, Yiu-Kong. 2000. *The Triads as Business*. London: Routledge.

Cressey, Donald. 1969. *Theft of the Nation: The Structure and Operations of Organized Crime in America*. New York: Harper & Row.

Critchley, David 2009. *The Origin of Organized Crime in America: The New York City Mafia, 1891–1931*. New York: Routledge.

Cummings, Homer Stille. 1936. *Proceedings of the Attorney General's Conference on Crime, 1934*. Washington, DC: Department of Justice.

Department of Justice. *Attorney General's Conference on Organized Crime*. 1950. Washington, DC: Department of Justice.

Depreeuw, Wim. 1988. *Landloperij, Bedelarij en Thuisloosheid: Een socio-historische Analyse van Repressie, Bijstand en Instellingen*. Antwerp: Kluwer.

Dickie, John. 2004. *Cosa Nostra: History of the Sicilian Mafia*. London: Hodder & Stoughton.

Donati, William. 2010. *Lucky Luciano: The Rise and Fall of a Mob Boss*. Jefferson, NC: McFarland & Company.

Duggan, Christopher. 1989. *Fascism and the Mafia*. New Haven, CT: Yale University Press.

Durney, James. 2000. *The Mob: The History of Irish Gangsters in America*. Naas, Ireland: Leinster Leader.

Egmond, Florike. 1986. *Banditisme in de Franse Tijd: Profiel van de Grote Nederlandse Bende, 1790–1799*. Zutphen: De Bataafsche Leeuw.

Egmond, Florike. 1994. *Op het Verkeerde Pad: Georganiseerde Misdaad in de noordelijke Nederlanden*. Amsterdam: Uitgeverij Bert Bakker.

Egmond, Florike. 2004. "Multiple Underworlds in the Dutch Republic of the Seventeenth and Eighteenth Centuries." In *Organised Crime in Europe: Concepts, Patterns and Control Policies in the European Union and Beyond*, edited by Cyrille Fijnaut and Letizia Paoli, 77–108. Dordrecht: Springer.

Eig, Jonathan. 2010. *Get Capone: The Secret Plot That Captured America's Most Wanted Gangster*. New York: Simon & Schuster.

Exner, Franz. 1935. *Kriminalistischer Bericht über eine Reise nach Amerika*. Berlin: Walter de Gruyter.

Falcionelli, Albert. 1936. *Les sociétés secrètes italiennes: Les Carbonari, La Camorra, La Mafia*. Paris: Payot.

Faligot, Roger. 2001. *La mafia chinoise en Europe*. Paris: Calmann-Lévy.

Fijnaut, Cyrille. 1985. "Georganiseerde Misdaad: Een onderzoeksgerichte Terreinverkenning." *Justitiële Verkenningen* 11 (9): 5–42.

Fijnaut, Cyrille. 1989a. "De Reorganisatie van de Nederlandse Politie en de Organisatie van de Misdaad in de Loop van de 19ᵉ en 20ᵉ Eeuw." In *Georganiseerde Misdaad en Strafrechtelijk Politiebeleid*, edited by Cyrille Fijnaut, 22–30. Lochem: J. van de Brink.

Fijnaut, Cyrille. 1990. "Organized Crime: A Comparison between the United States and Western Europe." *British Journal of Criminology* 30(3): 321–340.

Fijnaut, Cyrille. 1997. "Empirical Criminological Research on Organized Crime: The State of Affairs in Europe." In *L'évolution de la criminalité organisée*, 47–60. Paris: La Documentation Française.

Fijnaut, Cyrille. 2009. "Lombroso's Kijk op de Italiaanse Maffia." *Justitiële Verkenningen* 35 (3): 47–58.

Fijnaut, Cyrille. 2010. "Introduction of the New York Double Strategy to Control Organized Crime in the Netherlands and the European Union." *European Journal of Crime, Criminal Law and Criminal Justice* 18 (4): 43–65.

Fijnaut, Cyrille. 2011. "Hubertus Johannes Heijboer, 1921–2002: Een Grote Vriend van Leuven." In *Deviante Wetenschap: Het Domein van de Criminologie, Liber Amicorum Johan Goethals,* edited by Ivo Aertsen et al., 281–305. Leuven, Belgium: Acco.

Fijnaut, Cyrille, ed. 1989b. *Georganiseerde Misdaad en Strafrechtelijk Politiebeleid.* Lochem: J. van den Brink.

Fijnaut, Cyrille, and Hans-Jörg Albrecht, eds. 2002. *The Containment of Transnational Organized Crime: Comments on the UN Convention of December 2000.* Freiburg, Germany: Max Planck Institut für ausländisches und internationales Strafrecht.

Fijnaut, Cyrille, Frank Bovenkerk, Gerben Bruinsma, and Henk van de Bunt. 1998. *Organized Crime in the Netherlands.* The Hague: Kluwer Law International.

Fijnaut, Cyrille, and James Jacobs, eds. 1991. *Organized Crime and Its Containment: A Transatlantic Initiative.* Deventer: Kluwer.

Finckenauer, James, and Elin Waring. 1998. *Russian Mafia in America: Immigration, Culture and Crime.* Boston: Northeastern University Press.

Foote Whyte, William. 1955. *Street Corner Society: The Social Structure of an Italian Slum.* Chicago: University of Chicago Press.

Franke, Manfred. 1984. *Schinderhannes: Das kurze, wilde Leben des Johannes Bückler, neu erzählt nach Alten Protokollen, Briefen und Zeitungsberichten.* Düsseldorf: Claassen.

Fregier, Honore-Antoine. 1940. *Des classes dangereuses de la population dans les grandes villes et des moyens de les rendre meilleures.* 2 vols. Paris: Bailliere.

Fried, Albert. 1993. *The Rise and Fall of the Jewish Gangster in America.* New York: Columbia University Press.

Fritz, Gerhard. 2003. *Räuberbanden und Polizeistreifen: Der Kampf zwischen Kriminalität und Staatsgewalt im Südwesten des Alten Reichs zwischen 1648 und 1806.* Remshalden, Germany: Verlag Manfred Hannecke.

Fulvetti, Gianluca. 2004. "The Mafia and 'the Problem of the Mafia': Organised Crime in Italy, 1820–1970." In *Organised Crime in Europe: Concepts, Patterns and Control Policies in the European Union and Beyond,* edited by Cyrille Fijnaut and Letizia Paoli, 47–76. Dordrecht: Springer.

Gambetta, Diego. 1993. *The Sicilian Mafia: The Business of Private Protection.* Cambridge, MA: Harvard University Press.

Graszberger, Roland. 1933. *Gewerbs- und Berufsverbrechertum in den Vereinigten Staaten von Amerika.* Vienna: Verlag von Julius Springer.

Grosz, Hans. 1893. *Handbuch für Untersuchungsrichter, Polizeibeamte, Gendarmen u.s.w.* Graz, Austria: Verlag von Leuschner & Lubensky.

Haar, Barend ter. 1998. *Ritual and Mythology of the Chinese Triads: Creating an Identity.* Leiden: Brill.

Handelman, Stephen.1995. *Comrade Criminal: Russia's New Mafiya.* New Haven, CT: Yale University Press.

Heindl, Robert. 1929. *Der Berufsverbrecher: Ein Beitrag zur Strafrechtsreform.* Berlin: Verlag Kurt Metzner.

Henry, Gilles. 1984. *Cartouche.* Paris: Tallandier.

Hentig, Hans von. 1959. *Der Gangster: Eine kriminal-psychologische Studie.* Berlin: Springer-Verlag.

Hess, Henner. 1973. *Mafia & Mafiosi: The Structure of Power*. Westmead, UK: Saxon House.

Hill, Peter. 2003. *The Japanese Mafia: Yakuza, Law, and the State*. Oxford: Oxford University Press.

Hobsbawm, Eric. 1972. *Bandits*. Harmondsworth, UK: Penguin Books.

Ianni, Francis, and Elizabeth Reuss-Ianni. 1972. *A Family Business*. London: Routledge and Kegan Paul.

Internal Revenue Service. *Historical Documents Relating to Alphonse (Al) Capone, Chicago* http://www.irs.gov/foia/article/.

Jacobs, James. 2006. *Mobsters, Unions and Feds: The Mafia and the American Labor Movement*. New York: New York University Press.

Jacobs, James, Christopher Panarella, and Jay Worthington. 1994. *Busting the Mob: United States v. Cosa Nostra*. New York: New York University Press.

Jacobs, James, Coleen Friel, and Robert Radick. 1999. *Gotham Unbound: How New York City Was Liberated from the Grip of Organized Crime*. New York: New York University Press.

Joutsen, Matti. 1993. "The Potential for Growth of Organized Crime in Central and Eastern Europe." *European Journal on Criminal Policy and Research* 1 (3): 77–86.

Kaplan, David, and Alec Dubro. 1986. *Yakuza: The Explosive Account of Japan's Criminal Underworld*. Reading, MA: Addison-Wesley.

Katcher, Leo. 1994. *The Big Bankroll: The Life and Times of Arnold Rothstein*. New York: Da Capo.

Kavieff, Paul. 2000. *The Purple Gang: Organized Crime in Detroit, 1910–1945*. New York: Barricade Books.

Kennedy, Robert. 1960. *The Enemy Within*. New York: Harper & Row.

Kenney, Dennis, and James Finckenauer. 1995. *Organized Crime in America*. Belmont, CA: Wadsworth.

Kerr, Austin. 1985. *Organized for Prohibition: A New History of the Anti-Saloon League*. New Haven, CT: Yale University Press.

Kleinknecht, William. 1996. *The New Ethnic Mobs: The Changing Face of Organized Crime in America*. New York: The Free Press.

Kobler, John. 1992. *Capone: The Life and World of Al Capone*. New York: Da Capo.

Krausnick, Michael.1978. *Von Räubern und Gendarmen: Berichte und Geschichten aus der Zeit der groszen Räuberbanden*. Würzburg, Germany: Arena.

Kurella, Hans. 1893. *Naturgeschichte des Verbrechens*. Stuttgart, Germany: Verlag von Ferdinand Enke.

Küther, Carsten. 1984. "Räuber, Volk und Obrigkeit: Zur Wirkungsweise und Funktion staatlicher Strafverfolgung im 18. Jahrhundert." In *Räuber, Volk und Obrigkeit: Studien zur Geschichte der Kriminalität in Deutschland seit dem 18. Jahrhundert*, edited by Heinz Reif, 17–42. Frankfurt: Suhrkamp.

Küther, Carsten. 1987. *Räuber und Gauner in Deutschland*. Göttingen, Germany: Vandenhoeck & Ruprecht.

Landesco, John. 1968. "Organized Crime in Chicago." In *The Illinois Crime Survey, Conducted by the Illinois Association for Criminal Justice*, 815–1090. Montclair, NJ: Patterson Smith.

Lange, Katrin. 2004. "'Many a Lord Is Guilty, Indeed for Many a Poor Man's Dishonest Deed': Gangs of Robbers in Early Modern Germany." In *Organised Crime in Europe: Concepts, Patterns and Control Policies in the European Union and Beyond*, edited by Cyrille Fijnaut and Letizia Paoli, 109–150. Dordrecht: Springer.

Lenhard, Karl-Heinz. 1989. "Es ist fünf vor zwölf: Zur organisierten Kriminalität und ihrer wirksamen Bekämpfung." *Kriminalistik* 43 (4): 194–199.

Lindlau, Dagobert. 1989. *Der Mob: Recherchen zum Organisierten Verbrechen.* Munich: Deutscher Taschenbuch Verlag.

Lombardo, Robert. 2010. *The Black Hand: Terror by Letter in Chicago.* Urbana: University of Illinois Press.

Lombroso, Cesare. 1895. *L'Homme criminel: Étude anthropologique et psychiatrique.* 2 vols. Paris: Librairie Félix Alcan.

Lupo, Salvatore. 1999. *Histoire de la Mafia des origines à nos jours.* Paris: Flammarion.

Maas, Peter. 1968. *The Valachi Papers.* New York: G. P. Putnam's Sons.

MacDougall, Ernest D., ed. 1933. *Crime for Profit. A Symposium on Mercenary Crime.* Boston: Stratford.

Mack, John. 1970. "Does the Mafia Exist?" *New Society*, 9 (7): 194–195.

Mack, John, and Hans-Jürgen Kerner. 1975. *The Crime Industry.* Farnborough, UK: Saxon House.

McIllwain, Jeffrey. 2004. *Organizing Crime in Chinatown: Race and Racketeering in New York City, 1890–1910.* Jefferson, NC: McFarland & Company.

McIntosh, Mary. 1975. *The Organisation of Crime.* London: Macmillan.

McIntosh, Mary. 1982. "Changes in the Organization of Thieving." In *Images of Deviance*, edited by Stanley Cohen, 98–134. Harmondsworth, UK: Penguin Books.

Martin, Brian. 1996. *The Shanghai Green Gang: Politics and Organized Crime, 1919–1937.* Berkeley: University of California Press.

Marx, Gary. 1984. "Notes on the Discovery, Collection and Assessment of Hidden and Dirty Data." In *Studies in the Sociology of Social Problems*, edited by Joseph Schneider and John Kitsuse, 78–113. Norwood, NJ: Ablex.

Matard-Bonucci, Marie-Anne. 1994. *Histoire de la Mafia.* Paris: Éditions Complexe.

Middelburg, Bart. 1988. *De Mafia in Amsterdam.* Amsterdam: De Arbeiderspers.

Moore, William. 1974. *The Kefauver Committee and the Politics of Crime, 1950–1952.* Columbia: University of Missouri Press.

Morgan, W. P. 1989. *Triad Societies in Hong Kong.* Hong Kong: Government Press (third impression).

Murray, Dian. 1994. *The Origins of the Tiandihui: The Chinese Triads in Legend and History.* Stanford, CA: Stanford University Press.

Nagel, Willem. 1949. *De Criminaliteit van Oss.* The Hague: D. Daamen's Uitgeversmaatschappij.

National Commission on Law Observance and Enforcement. 1931. *Report on the Enforcement of the Prohibition Laws of the United States.* Washington, DC: US Government Printing Office.

Nelli, Humbert. 1976. *The Business of Crime: Italians and Syndicate Crime in the United States.* New York: Oxford University Press.

Newark, Tim. 2010. *Lucky Luciano: The Real and the Fake Gangster.* New York: Thomas Dunne Books.

Paoli, Letizia. 2003. *Mafia Brotherhoods: Organized Crime, Italian Style.* Oxford: Oxford University Press.

Paoli, Letizia, Victoria Greenfield, and Peter Reuter. 2009. *The World Heroin Market: Can Supply Be Cut?* Oxford: Oxford University Press.

Passas, Nikos, ed. 1999. *Transnational Crime.* Aldershot, UK: Dartmouth.

Pezzino, Paolo. 1990. *Una certa reciprocità di favori: Mafia e modernizzazione violenta nella Sicilia postunitaria.* Milan: Angeli.

Pfister. 1812. *Aktenmässige Geschichte der Räuberbanden an den beiden Ufern des Mains im Spessart und im Odenwalde*. Heidelberg, Germany: Gottlieb Braun.

Ploscowe, Morris, ed. 1952. *Organized Crime and Law Enforcement*. 2 vols. New York: Grosby.

President's Commission on Law Enforcement and Administration of Justice. 1968. *The Challenge of Crime in a Free Society*. New York: Avon.

President's Commission on Organized Crime. 1986. *The Impact: Organized Crime Today*. Washington, DC: US Government Printing Office.

Punch, Maurice. 1985. *Conduct Unbecoming: The Social Construction of Police Deviance and Control*. London: Tavistock.

Reckless, Walter. 1950. *The Crime Problem*. New York: Appleton-Century-Crofts.

Redo, Slawomir. 2004. *Organized Crime and Its Control in Central Asia*. Huntsville, AL: Office of International Criminal Justice.

Reif, Heinz, ed. 1984. *Räuber, Volk und Obrigkeit: Studien zur Geschichte der Kriminalität in Deutschland seit dem 18. Jahrhundert*. Frankfurt: Suhrkamp.

Reppetto, Thomas. 2004. *American Mafia: A History of Its Rise to Power*. New York: Holt.

Riall, Lucy. 1998. *Sicily and the Unification of Italy: Liberal Policy and Local Power, 1859–1866*. Oxford: Clarendon.

Robertson, Frank. 1977. *Triangle of Death: The Inside Story of the Triads—the Chinese Mafia*. London: Routledge & Kegan Paul.

Röling, Bernard. 1933. *De Wetgeving tegen zoogenaamde Beroeps- en Gewoontemisdadigers*. The Hague: Martinus Nijhoff.

Roscher, Gustav. 1912. *Groszstadtpolizei: Ein praktisches Handbuch der Deutschen Polizei*. Hamburg: Otto Meiszners Verlag.

Roth, Andreas. 1997. *Kriminalitätsbekämpfung in Deutschen Groszstädten, 1850–1914*. Berlin: Erich Schmidt Verlag.

Ryan, Patrick, and George Rush, eds. 1997. *Understanding Organized Crime in Global Perspective*. Thousand Oaks, CA: SAGE.

Schlesinger, Arthur. 1996. *Robert Kennedy and His Times*. New York: Ballantine.

Schneider, Jane and Peter Schneider. 2003. *Reversible Destiny: Mafia, Antimafia and the Struggle for Palermo*. Berkeley: University of California Press.

Schreven, Cornelia. 1957. *Diefstal in Groepsformatie Gepleegd: Een empirisch Onderzoek met een criminologische Beschouwing*. The Hague: Martinus Nijhoff.

Sielaff, Wolfgang. 1983. "Bis zur Bestechung leitender Polizeibeamter? Erscheinungsformen und Bekämpfung der organisierter Kriminalität in Hamburg." *Kriminalistik* 37 (8): 417–422.

Sleeman, James. 1934. *La secte secrète des Thugs: Le culte de l'assassinat aux Indes*. Paris: Payot.

Smith, Dwight. 1975. *The Mafia Mystique*. New York: Basic Books.

Smith, Dwight. 1991. "Wickersham to Sutherland to Katzenbach: Evolving an 'Official' Definition for Organized Crime." *Crime, Law and Social Change* 15:135–154.

Spapens, Toine, and Cyrille Fijnaut. 2005. *Criminaliteit en Rechtshandhaving in de Euregio Maas-Rijn*. Antwerp: Intersentia.

"Shanghai." 1973. In *Grote Winkler Prins: Encyclopedie in Twintig Delen*, Vol. 17, edited by J. F. Staal, Albert J. Wiggers, et al., 411–412. Amsterdam: Elsevier.

Stieber, Wilhelm. 1860. *Praktisches Lehrbuch der Criminal-Polizei*. Berlin: Verlag von A. Hahn.

Stolberg, Mary. 1995. *Fighting Organized Crime: Politics, Justice and the Legacy of Thomas E. Dewey*. Boston: Northeastern University Press.

Sutherland, Edwin. 1934. *Principles of Criminology*. Chicago: J.B. Lippencott.

van Till, Margreet. 2006. *Batavia bij Nacht: Bloei en Ondergang van het Indonesisch Roverswezen in Batavia en Ommelanden, 1869–1942*. Amsterdam: Aksant.

United Nations Office on Drugs and Crime. 2010. *The Globalization of Crime: A Transnational Organized Crime Threat Assessment*. Vienna: United Nations Office on Drugs and Crime.

US Senate. 1933. *Investigation of So-Called 'Rackets': Hearings before a Subcommittee of the Committee on Commerce*. Washington, DC: US Government Printing Office.

US Senate. 1951. *Third Interim Report of the Special Committee to Investigate Organized Crime in Interstate Commerce*. New York: Arco.

van den Eerenbeemt, Harry. 1970. *Van Mensenjacht en Overheidsmacht: Criminogene Groepsvorming en Afweer in de Meierij van s'-Hertogenbosch, 1795–1810*. Tilburg: Stichting Zuidelijk Historisch Contact.

Varese, Federico. 2001. *The Russian Mafia: Private Protection in a New Market Economy*. Oxford: Oxford University Press.

Volkov, Vadim. 2002. *Violent Entrepreneurs: The Use of Force in the Making of Russian Capitalism*. Ithaca, NY: Cornell University Press.

Wade, David. 1996. "The Conclusion That a Sinister Conspiracy of Foreign Origin Controls Organized Crime: The Influence of Nativism in the Kefauver Committee Investigation." *Northern Illinois University Law Review* 16 (2): 371–409.

Woodiwiss, Michael. 2001. *Organized Crime and American Power*. Toronto: University of Toronto Press.

Woodiwiss, Michael, and Dick Hobbs. 2009. "Organized Evil and the Atlantic Alliance. Moral Panics and the Rhetoric of Organized Crime Policing in America and Britain." *British Journal of Criminology* 49:106–128.

Wulffen, Erich. 1926. *Kriminalpsychologie: Psychologie des Täters*. Berlin: dr. P. Langenscheidt.

Zhang, Sheldon. 2008. *Chinese Human Smuggling Organizations: Families, Social Networks and Cultural Imperatives*. Stanford, CA: Stanford University Press.

CHAPTER 4

···

HOW TO RESEARCH ORGANIZED CRIME

···

DICK HOBBS AND GEORGIOS A. ANTONOPOULOS

I. INTRODUCTION

···

THE purpose of this essay is to provide an overview of the methods and approaches used in researching organized crime and organized crime-related issues. Section II focuses on official data and accounts (including interviews with public officials). Section III deals with quantitative and economic analyses, section IV with historical/archival research, and section V with network analyses. Section VI focuses on ethnographic studies, and section VII on interviewing offenders, consumers/clients, and victims of organized crime.

One of the major issues with research on organized crime concerns exactly the ambiguity around the term "organized crime" (Levi 2004), and the subsequent lack of any definitional consensus (Finckenauer 2005), rendering the researcher vulnerable to shifts in politically motivated renditions of a constantly shifting cluster of often disparate activities. Most of the activities that become designated as "organized crime" are conducted discreetly, and it is often only after the criminal justice system has processed and categorized them that researchers are unleashed to turn transgression into academic product.

The researcher who wants to access active organized criminals directly must recognize that there are seldom any obvious benefits for participants—distributing questionnaires to them or asking them to sign consent forms are less than well-thought approaches,[1] while victims, customers, and clients are often reluctant to talk to researchers. Even nongovernment organizations (NGOs) that directly or indirectly work with organized crime issues (e.g., trafficking for sexual exploitation) and manage systematized databases are reluctant to share their data and information with researchers (see Lehti and Aromaa 2006).

Most organized crime policies have been implemented without the "impediment" of empirical research,[2] and the reality of a nonmonopolistic, fragmented marketplace (Reuter 1983) has proved less amenable to policy, career, and institutional imperialism than criminal conspiracies that mirrored the impending threats suggested by the Cold War or the academic benediction of racial prejudice (Cressey 1969). It was post–World War II United States that located the "emotional kick" (Levi 1998) of organized crime, and it was the United States that advanced the utility of the concept as a political tool. After the collapse of the Soviet bloc, "transnational organized crime" (see Williams and Savona 1995) replaced Cold War narratives and has been embraced by Cold War "warriors" from the security services. The sources informing this genre emanate from national and international enforcement agencies that are shrouded from public view by concerns over security and should be approached with some skepticism (Naylor 1995; Hobbs 1998), as its findings are particularly vulnerable to the whims of political expediency. For instance, in 1993, the United Kingdom's National Criminal Intelligence Service (NCIS) held a conference at which the audience was told by a representative of the Metropolitan Police that, "in five years-time there is no doubt that the major threat confronting the inner cities of the United Kingdom will come from central, eastern European and Russian countries" (Kirby 1993, p. 3). However, Russia became an economic partner when it joined the G8 group in 1998 and the 2000 *UK Threat Assessment* stated that "the UK is not facing an "invasion" by a "red mafiya" (cited in Woodiwiss and Hobbs 2009, p. 120).

Law enforcement agencies seek out criminal hierarchies that mirror the organizational hierarchies of policing (Reuter 1986),[3] and early NCIS threat assessments based entirely on police "research" located the threat among Triads, Yardies, Russians, Colombians, Italians, and Turks (NCIS 1993a, 1993b) and contributed to the generation of a powerful alien conspiracy, while ignoring independent research. The United Kingdom, along with the rest of the European Union (EU), found an ideal enemy in East European organized crime, and the securitization of the organized crime "threat" made it even more difficult for researchers to gain access to data, as nonstate actors now constituted the key threat to Western interests (Gachevska 2009). Transnational organized crime emerged as the prime threat within the European security agenda (see Raine and Cilluffo 1994), as confirmed by the EU Organised Crime Threat Assessment (OCTA), which is formulated from the individual threat assessments of member states (see Vander Beken and Verfaille 2010), underlying the relatively lowly status of research in this field and the dominance and political nature of police work.

Finally, comparative research into organized crime is difficult (Paoli et al. 2009), and cross-border research teams may experience variable access to data. For instance, in the Netherlands, the police are considerably more open to academic researchers than are police in other countries (Kleemans 2007). In addition, not all states recognize organized crime, and therefore not all produce official documentation for analysis, while for other countries, organized crime is a recently constructed phenomenon, and as a consequence longitudinal data are extremely limited. The size of the files, the criteria for selection on behalf of law enforcement, different legal definitions and variations in administrative and legal protocols, and incompatible systems of data management produce such variations that comparative research findings can be rendered virtually meaningless (AOC 2006).

II. Official Data and Accounts

Official data include statistical records, annual reports on organized crime, government and parliamentary commission reports, official surveys, pretrial reports, trial transcripts, case files, and databases from various law enforcement agencies such as the police, customs, and federal agencies. Interviews with law enforcement agents and other public servants may also constitute the basis of research on organized crime and related issues. Official data and accounts have led to the production of valuable studies, many of which are considered classic. Hess (1973), for instance, used official archives, trial transcripts, and police reports, in his analysis of the Mafia, while Blok (1974) also referred to official archives to supplement interviews and conversations gathered during his 2½ years living in a Sicilian village. Catanzaro's (1992) study based on official documents and court files showed how in the absence of competent state agents, landowners turned to local "Men of Respect" (Catanzaro 1992), while Gambetta's (1993) study of "an industry of private protection" (Gambetta 1993, p. 155) is based on interviews and parliamentary and trial sources. Paoli's (2003) study of the structure and culture of the Sicilian Mafia and the Calabrian *Ndrangheta* was based primarily on statements by *pentiti* (former Mafia "members" cooperating with the authorities) and presents Mafia members as complex individuals engaged in a "plurality of business activities" (Paoli 2003, p. 174).

Many European studies on illegal markets relied extensively on law enforcement data. For instance, with regard to cigarette smuggling, van Duyne (2003) and van Dijck (2007) in the Netherlands used Dutch Customs' case files, whereas von Lampe (2007) used data from the German Customs Service database and criminal files documenting investigations conducted by the German customs into cigarette smuggling in the 1990s. Soudijn (2006) examined Dutch court files covering the period 1996–2003 and was concerned primarily with the smuggling of Chinese migrants from the Netherlands. Official data have also been used for the analysis of financial crime and money laundering (van Duyne 2007).

Data from WODC (Dutch Ministry of Justice Research and Documentation Centre) offer detailed insights about links between and among offenders, the relationships between legal and illegal spheres, and organized criminals' careers trajectories (van Koppen et al. 2010), the role of social opportunity structures in organized criminals careers (Kleemans and de Poot 2008), and on occupations, work relations, work settings, and their connections with organized crime activities (Kleemans and van de Bunt 2008). Antonopoulos and Papanicolaou (2009) used pretrial reports to triangulate accounts they obtained from car thieves, and documentary trawls through legal records and other official data are vital tools that can provide key pieces to the organized crime jigsaw, particularly in reconstructions of financially complex, embedded corporate deviation (Levi 1981; Passas 1996) or cases that cross international and legal jurisdictions (van Duyne and Levi 2005).

The relationship between academic researchers and law enforcement officials is crucial in a field where so much valuable data (regardless of its form) are controlled and consequently filtered by state agencies, and engaging with the law enforcement project does place a huge question mark on the critical faculties of academic researchers. Organized crime, as mentioned earlier, is a political construct that serves a particular set of functions for the state, and a key problem in understanding the collage of collaborations that constitute our understanding of organized crime is the reluctance of commentators to consider the embedded complexity of the relationships that such collaborations entail. For law enforcements agents, this complexity is confronted and pragmatically overcome by the presentation of criminal activity in the form of cases constructed with a view to being presented in a court of law in order to gain a successful conviction; these packages of law enforcement–ciphered information are what are regularly offered to academics and go on to form the basis of much organized crime research.

Official data are the result of law enforcement activity, which in turn is the result of resource restrictions, the competency of agents, organizational priorities, and wider political priorities (see Kinzig 2004). By the time third parties such as academics get to examine case files, details irrelevant to the prospect of successful prosecution, such as any unsightly manifestations of individual incompetence, organizational failures, or malpractice on behalf of agents, have been removed. Similarly, paperwork relating to relationships between the accused and individuals not connected with the specificities of a particular case or whose relevance to the interactions implicit to the allegations being made by law enforcement of behalf of the state are marginal, unverifiable, or unlikely to be provable in law will also be excluded, along with details of those whose guilt has been renegotiated as a result of the provision of information.

The construction of a case is ultimately a rhetorical device used to present a façade of competence of behalf of the criminal justice system, and the result is often the projection of a community of the guilty, clusters of individuals whose representation is restricted solely to their alleged involvement in a named criminal act or set of acts. Such a projection limits the scope of an individual's identity to that of the one-dimensional "criminal" and feeds the notion of an underworld of exclusively deviant intent, driven by economic motivation, yet drained of cultural context.

III. Quantitative and Economic Analyses

In this section, four types of research studies are discussed. The first is the counting exercises of government departments, law enforcement agencies, NGOs, and international organizations. The exercises can be, for instance, on the number of victims of trafficking for sexual and labor exploitation (and their characteristics) such as those of the British Home Office (Kelly and Regan 2000), the International Organisation for Migration (e.g., IOM 2000), and the US Department of State (2011). Although these estimates are often given credibility among law enforcement and political circles and, to an extent, can be potentially useful as a starting point for further, empirical research, they are produced on the basis of a vague methodology that is either not mentioned, hardly explained, or can be seriously challenged (Di Nicola and Cauduro 2007).

The second type of studies consists of surveys such as, for instance, those commissioned and/or funded by the British Home Office. By using a survey instrument that drew heavily on victimization and commercial victimization surveys, Tilley and Hopkins (2008) attempted to measure the extent of organized crime against legal businesses across three high-crime residential areas in England. They found that organized crime is responsible for only a small part of the victimization legal businesses experience. Gottschalk (2009) collected data from 1,919 participants aged 16 and over and found that although the majority of respondents (84 percent) believed that organized crime was a problem in the United Kingdom, only a third (32 percent) thought it was a problem in their local area. However, apart from rather "shallow" (although wide) data, the issue of truthfulness of participant responses, and the fact that surveys "miss out" institutionalized or "hidden" populations, there are two additional methodological issues with research studies on organized crime based on surveys. First, a definition of organized crime is usually imposed on respondents by the researchers and the responses may not always be fully informed by the definition they are asked to use. Moreover, in the case of victimization by organized crime, participants are often not aware that their victimization was a product of "organized" crime as opposed to "conventional" crime. Yet, again, we must remind ourselves that organized crime is an exceptionally artificial construct.

The third type of quantitative and economic studies consists of those primarily by Reuter (e.g., Reuter 1983, 1985) and others on the economics of illegal markets. The economic information used and analyzed originates primarily from official reports (e.g., UNODC's World Drug Reports), surveys, official databases (e.g., STRIDE[4] and NIBRS[5]), and even interviews. Caulkins and Pacula (2006) offer a description of the marijuana market and acquisition patterns on the basis of the 2001 National Household Survey on Drug Abuse, whereas Caulkins et al. (2009) conducted an economic analysis of drug purchase and resale "cycles" from qualitative interviews with 65 imprisoned drug dealers in the United Kingdom. There is also a notable case, Levitt and Venkatesh's (2000) study, which used a unique dataset consisting of detailed and monthly updated financial information maintained by the leader of a drug-selling gang in the United States over a 4-year period. More integrated and wide ranging studies, such as Paoli et al.'s (2009) study of the global heroin market, include a meticulous synthesis of economic data, and accounts and data from other disciplines.

Studies have also focused on specific economic-related aspects or outcomes of illegal markets. Reuter and Caulkins (2004), for example, examine variability in the price and purity of cocaine and heroin through the use of data gathered over a 14-year period by STRIDE containing a temporally consistent and large amount of transaction-level data from throughout the United States. Kilmer et al.'s (2010) study attempts at providing an account of how marijuana legalization in the state of California could influence drug trafficking organizations' revenues and violence in Mexico on the basis of gross revenues from export and distribution to wholesale markets near the border between California and Mexico. In addition, economic studies can allow a comparison between some economic aspects of illegal markets and their legal counterparts. For example, Strumpf (2003) found that illegal and legal bookmakers charge about the same for their services. Finally, economic studies are particularly useful in paying attention to the demand side of illegal markets, such as Cameron and Williams' (2001) work on the price elasticity of demand for cannabis, as well as the cross-elasticity among cannabis, alcohol, and cigarette markets.

Economic studies on organized crime and specifically its entrepreneurial manifestations offer important and interesting insights about aspects of these manifestations, determine whether a problematic phenomenon improves or gets worse, and assist in making relevant and more structured policy recommendations (see Reuter and Greenfield 2001). However, economic studies are burdened by the inherent difficulty of estimating (or making estimations about) markets that are illegal and hidden, and datasets such as STRIDE used by Reuter and Caulkins (2004) do not involve a representative and random sample of all transactions taking place in a geographic area and are not constructed with research in mind but are purely administrative datasets heavily affected by law enforcement practices. Even with the extremely interesting data used by Levitt and Venkatesh (2000), it is difficult for one to generalize to the overall drug-selling scene based on the finances of *one* gang.

The fourth type of quantitative study on organized crime relates to penetration indexes such as this by the Italian National Institute of Statistics (ISTAT) or the indexes designed by van Dijk (2007) and Calderoni (2011). Van Dijk (2007) constructed a Composite Organised Crime Index (COCI) combining rates of unsolved murders, data on the perceived prevalence of organized crime (especially racketeering), grand corruption, money laundering, and the extent of the informal economy, drawing on official statistics, the World Economic Forum's annual surveys among chief executive officers of big companies, and the Merchant International Group's assessments of investment risks in a large number of countries, in an attempt to develop a model of the effect of organized crime on legal business and national wealth. Calderoni's (2011) index, which measures the presence of mafias at the provincial level in Italy, combined data on mafia-type associations, mafia murders, city councils dissolved for infiltration by organized crime, and asset confiscation from organized crime for the period 1983–2009.

Indexes of that nature assist toward an exploration of the interrelations between organized crime and other variables (e.g., rule of law, economic development, etc.) (van Dijk 2007) or the disconfirmation of well-consolidated myths. Calderoni's (2011) index, for instance, showed that mafias are not a typically southern Italy but rather a national phenomenon. The limitations of these indexes, on the other hand, are that they are "affected by the unequal distribution of the variables analysed" (Calderoni 2011, p. 59) along, for example, geographical areas, and they are, as we continue to stress, heavily affected by the political stance and consequent practices of law enforcement agencies.

IV. Historical/Archival Studies

Historical/archival studies offer the opportunity to analyze with the benefit of hindsight and, with minimal personal risk, organized criminality. The best of these studies remind us that crime can only be understood by comprehending the socioeconomic context in which it is enacted (Chambliss 1978, p. 2), and historical research using police and judicial reports, economic evidence, pamphlets, cultural products, memoirs, and biographies suggests that "organized crime" has been a malleable concept.

Historical studies have revealed how the establishment and maintenance of British colonies were carried out by pirates (Browning and Gerrassi 1980), who were licensed to plunder Britain's commercial competitors before being rewarded by entry to elite Elizabethan society (Sherry 1986). Historical research should also be credited with highlighting the crucial role of the market and the collaborative efforts required for activities such as smuggling and poaching (Munsche 1981). Hobsbawm (1972) used both national and regional documents, poems, and ballads to develop his tripartite model of banditry, and his notion of "social banditry" remains valuable particularly when considering public attitudes toward organized crime. By the eighteenth century, nascent forms of organized crime were firmly embedded in British society, not only where regimentation of the emerging working class was at its most ineffective (Stedman Jones 1971) but also in coastal, rural, and provincial areas (Styles 1980). Dealers in stolen goods, "fences" (McMullan 1984), should be regarded as vital to the corrupt environment that became integral to urbanism, requiring "some degree of a division of labour, an intelligence and information system, and a sophisticated network for distributing the goods in question" (Sharpe 1999, p. 151).

Scholars of US history have indicated that activities associated with the concept of organized crime, although never being labeled as such, including corruption, political insurrection, and violence, went hand-in-hand with the exploitation of natural resources and were responsible for the establishment of many of America's major industrial and commercial empires (Myers 1936; Bell 1953; Block and Chambliss 1981). As a catalyst for the perception of organized crime as a social phenomenon, the prohibition of alcohol, which lasted from 1920 to 1933, has proved to be a rich seam of analysis for historians (see Block 1983, pp. 130–141).[6] For instance, Haller (1971) used newspaper archives, and the archives of local religious and government bodies, as well as Internal Revenue Service (IRS) files, federal documents, law reports, and other documentary sources to develop his analysis of crime and vice during Prohibition, uncovering an ever-changing series of partnerships in illicit goods and services. Importantly, historians stressed that the repeal of Prohibition enabled collaborations from across the political and economic spectrum to penetrate every aspect of American life (Haller 1985; Critchley 2009).

Overall, historical research or a historiography of organized crime has proved to be more than just valuable details and random pieces of information put in a chronological order about things that occurred in the past in relation to various manifestations of organized crime. First, historical research points to the impact of changes in the law on criminal collaborations (Munsche 1981). Second, it reminds contemporary commentators that rapid changes in criminal trends are not the exclusive prerogative of the modern world (Lloyd Baker 1889, p. 23); elements of criminal organization involved in either predatory or entrepreneurial activities have been features of society for many centuries (Sharpe 1999), and long before the term "organized crime" was to emerge as a key prop of law enforcement rhetoric. Egmond's (1993) research, for instance, revealed that first bandits in the Netherlands were active since 1612 and that ethnically based collectivities were involved in organized criminal activities long before the modern organized crime–related expressed concern.

Third, the historiography of organized crime allows the researcher to seriously challenge well-established assumptions about organized crime by emphasizing—through its retrospective nature—the multiple causality between organized crime–related and other phenomena. McMullan (1982), for example, in providing an account of the "underworld" in sixteenth- and seventeenth-century London, investigates not only how this "underworld" manifested itself but also its link with city ecology, economy, and formal social control of the time.

Fourth, historical research on organized crime can shed light on the mutating and less than rigid entities involved and, by diverting focus on human agency, highlights that organized criminals are indeed very normal people (see Jacobs 2007). Retired organized criminals' published memoirs and biographies, for instance, although subjective and possibly slightly altered for the purpose of publication, can provide intriguing information about an individual's incentives for involvement in organized crime, development of personality and personality traits (see Bovenkerk 2000), critical life events, or background for specific and relevant decisions such as breaking the mob's code of silence (see Firestone 1993).

On the other hand, archival sources are not originally designed to reconstruct organizational or cultural features of crime (McMullen 1984); they do not essentially provide neutral information about an organized crime–related activity but are a product of the emergent political, economic, social, and administrative environments as well as of the actors and processes involved in the production of the source. For example, the disadvantage of criminal justice archive research is that, as the product of the powerful, data are usually skewed away from the crimes of elites and toward the activities of groups of poor and low-level property criminals (Sharpe 1999). In addition, archival sources often romanticize or glamorize organized criminals and their activities, especially if these sources are *popular* cultural artifacts. For instance, pre-Industrial Revolution English ballads used to cast highway robbers in a positive and heroic mode (Brandon 2010). Finally, regardless of the type of historical/archival source, there are a number of issues,

including *authenticity, credibility, representativeness,* and *meaning,* that play an important role in assessing the value of the source used (Scott 1990) and that are often very
difficult, if not impossible, to test or guarantee.

V. Network Analyses

Network analyses are based on the idea that social transactions are "embedded" within fluid and dynamic networks of personal relations (Granovetter 1973;
Wasserman and Faust 1994). The term "network" as an *analytic concept* has existed
since the 1950s and has influenced accounts of classic and influential works on
organized crime in subsequent decades. Lupsha (1983), for instance, applied a network analysis to an organized crime group trafficking drugs in New York. However,
according to Scott (1991), *modern* network analysis developed much later after a synthesis of three schools of thought and approaches: (a) the sociometric analysis using
graph theory; (b) the exploration of the patterns of interpersonal relations (Harvard
School); and (c) the investigation of the structure of relations from an anthropological point of view (Manchester School). By incorporating terms and perspectives that
have been used in investigating criminal organizational systems (Morselli 2009),
modern network analysis has been applied to organized crime, too, although it is still
in an embryonic stage (see Carrington 2011).

Network analyses attempt to reconstruct criminal networks and are based on data on
contacts between and among offenders and other important actors in a network. Such
data include wiretap records from the authorities such as these used in the studies by
Natarajan (2000, 2006) on drug trafficking in New York and Campana (2011) on the
diverse operations of a Neapolitan Camorra group (*La Torre clan*), case files generated
from law enforcement agencies such as the study by Malm et al. (2008) on social network
and distance correlates of criminal associates in illicit drug production in Vancouver,
or even biographical/autobiographical accounts such as in the study by Morselli (2001)
based on the autobiography of an illegal entrepreneur, Howard Marks.

In the past decade or so, criminal network analysis has, in von Lampe's (2009, p. 94)
words, "grown into a sophisticated scientific endeavour, bringing a new level of methodological rigour to the study of organised crime." This was primarily done through
Morselli's (2003, 2005, 2009) and others' (Natarajan 2006; Campana 2011; Varese 2011)
intriguing ways of looking at structures of criminal networks, their differential development, as well as their exploitation opportunities. In some studies, network analysis
has been particularly effective and valuable in addressing questions in relation to, for
example, how individuals from the legitimate sphere, the "upperworld," relate to criminal business (Morselli and Giguere 2006), how criminal risk is managed (Morselli
et al. 2007), and vulnerabilities or strengths in criminal networks (Morselli 2010). In
the majority of network analyses, the focus is on the frequency of contacts; however,
there are a few exceptions, such as the studies by Natarajan (2006) and Campana (2011),

which focus on the content of recorded communication and the context of the actors' relationships (see the essay by Kleemans, this volume).

Network-based methodologies in general can be useful as an essentially descriptive tool dealing with "overlapping and interrelated social relationships" (Potter 1994, p. 116; see McIllwain 1999) and can stand in direct opposition to the monolithic hierarchical structures that tended to dominate traditional studies and media accounts. Networks analyses introduce some "life" and natural dynamism to the "frozen and rigid understanding" of criminal collaborations and allow for some independence from the popular organised crime imagery that revolves around the "alien" nature of organized crime and the aforementioned hierarchical structures (Klerks 2001, p. 62), although with exceptions. Natarajan (2000), for instance, in her study of the organization of a cocaine trafficking group, did find a hierarchical structure was involved. Simultaneously, however, network analyses allow for the description of different types of cooperation that exist within the two poles of the structural continuum ("hierarchical and tight organisations" on one side and "loose networks" on the other) without assuming, and consequently being predisposed toward, any specific structure (see essay by Bouchard and Morselli, this volume).

Network analysis can also be very useful in providing frameworks beyond "commonsensical" or longstanding ones. For example, Savoie-Gargiso and Morselli's (2009) study on the roles, interactions, and resource exchange processes in a prostitution network in a large Canadian city reveals that prostitutes are not mere exploited subordinates to pimps by simply providing sexual services to clients but that they also occupy roles and contribute resources that "make them vital participants in the overall structure of order."

However, network analyses do have some serious limitations. As Malm et al. (2008, p. 84) explicitly put it,

> It is impossible to collect all of the possible nodes (individuals) and edges (ties between individuals) in a network without surveying the individuals involved. However, the hidden, illicit nature of criminal networks makes surveying participants difficult.

In addition, in general, the chaotic sets of personal and business affiliations featuring both settled and transient relationships, and fluid and unpredictable interchanges between transactions and activities, are not suitable for the sociometric analysis concerned with the density and centrality of relations favored by police and police scientists (Sparrow 1991; Coles 2001). What is hidden from our view are the organizational decisions, assumptions, and prior knowledge that impact upon selection, sampling, and interpretation of data that is the result of the actions of control agents although they represent real criminal activity or criminal trends. Creating theoretical frameworks based solely on such data can give the impression of a stable, "mappable" community, rather than a volatile market-based series of fluid and mutating collaborations (Hobbs 2013).

The patterns of relationality suggested by police-generated data are not designed to present nuanced elaborations of criminal cultures, and by disregarding all aspects of the offenders' lifeworld other than aspects of criminality relating to a specific police case, the variables of relationality on which formal network analysis are founded are restricted. As any product of the state derived from largely unaccountable agencies concerned with justifying their own budgets, case files need to be carefully handled, and should always carry a disclaimer that "the content of this file are the fruits of police activity" (see Kitsuse and Cicourel 1963).

VI. Ethnography

What Block (1991) calls the "serious crime community" constitutes a hidden population par excellence and is an ideal area for ethnographers. Ianni and Reuss-Ianni's (1972) research concerned with one of the five Italian mafia families in New York should be regarded as an example of how a qualitative study of that nature can tease out the cultural realities of organized criminality. Based on years of overt fieldwork at family gatherings and private dinners, as well as interviews with informants, the study, among other things, discusses the importance of family lineage, intermarriage, and kinship relationships.

Adler's study of upper level drug dealers and smugglers exposed a culture that is "secretive, deceitful, mistrustful, and paranoid" (Adler 1985, p. 110), where life was lived as a party (see Shover and Honaker 1992). Chambliss (1978) entered the field to examine how organized crime touches every strata of American society and is closely linked to the legitimate political economy, while Hobbs' (1995) work is based on intensive fieldwork with active professional criminals at work and at play and is complemented by interviews that track "career trajectories." Siegel (2005) conducted ethnographic research with the Russian community in the Netherlands, and Zaitch (2002) looked at Colombian participation in the cocaine trade in the Netherlands, which, like Bourgois' (1995) ethnography of crack dealing in Spanish Harlem, is embedded in the everyday realities of urban life. Williams' two ethnographies of the crack trade (1989, 1992) also show how valuable ethnography can be in demystifying criminality among minority groups, examining the entrepreneurial culture that pervades inner-city youth (see Mieczkowski 1990), while Dunlap et al.'s (1994) case study of a female crack dealer establishes that the role of women in the drug trade has close parallels with their role in the legitimate economy. The variable of gender has also been highlighted in Bovenkerk's (1995) ethnographic study with a Dutch female intermediate in the drug business. Finally, ethnographic research has also offered useful insights into organized criminals' identities and, specifically, how organized criminals exploit, construct, and manipulate identities (e.g., ethnic identity) in a variety of ways according to "audiences" (Bovenkerk et al. 2003).

A special reference needs to be made to ethnographic research on organized crime–related issues that does not use the "conventional" ethnographic method. Cauduro et al. (2009), for instance, conducted a virtual ethnography that involved the researchers collecting information from specialized online forums in which clients of trafficked prostituted women leave comments or discuss relevant issues.

Ethnographic research on organized crime offers unique opportunities for exploration, often on an informal level. Innovative ethnographic studies such as virtual ethnographies allow researchers to relatively easily reveal and research hidden populations, and the research subjects themselves to be freed from any possible inhibitions they may have in talking in person to a researcher about their practices.

However, ethnographic research normally requires immersion in the field, emotional investment, and the possession of certain skills allowing adaptation to the cultural milieu of the research. Social researchers have commented or reflected on the role of these variables and social positions of "race," ethnicity, class, age, and gender as well as social capital (personal contacts, linguistic familiarity, perceived status, etc.; see Hobbs 1988) that play a role in the construction of social relations between the researcher and the researched, and consequently affect the research process as a whole. For instance, Antonopoulos (2008) discusses the process of him as a *Greek* conducting ethnographic research with retired *Kurdish* cigarette smugglers and pays particular attention to the significance of the "compatibility" between his and his participants' ethnicity, a result of historical background with social extensions.

The validity of ethnographic research is an issue that also warrants some attention. There can be no guarantee whatsoever that the information given is an accurate representation of the activities and links between actors. There may be instances in which participants do not remember or exaggerate and glorify their deeds, instances in which issues are concealed from the researcher or instances in which there are unclear accounts. There may be instances in which the participants report what they think the researcher would like to hear, and immersion into the field can result in the researcher not being able to be "objective" toward participants in the sense of retaining a neutral, uncaring, distant standpoint (see Bourgois 1995). However, we would strongly argue that this is not a problem but an aspect of research, indeed of social life that should be celebrated. We would also argue that the so-called ungeneralizable nature of ethnographic research, due to the difficulty in replication, is a tradeoff with the depth of data that are acquired from an ethnographic study (albeit not from a brief encounter with the field masquerading as an ethnography). We would add that the problem of generalizability is common to organized crime research, as the phenomenon is a contested concept varying considerably across time as well as national boundaries and legislative regimes.

Ethnographic research involves interacting with "individuals with unpredictable agendas" (Rawlinson 2008, p. 14) who can make the field a dangerous place for the researcher. For instance, Ken Pryce, the author of an ethnography of hustling culture in Bristol (Pryce 1979), was murdered when he turned his attention to Caribbean organized crime. During the course of the research, researchers obtain "dirty knowledge" or even participate in the construction of this "dirty knowledge" (Ferrell 1998, p. 24), and ethnographers have no privileged relations with their research participants; their craft relies on social skills that seldom adhere to the ethics of criminological research orthodoxy, let alone legal protocols (Hobbs 1988).

VII. Interviewing Offenders, Consumers/Clients, and Victims[7]

Zhang and Chin (2004) formally and informally interviewed 129 Chinese human smugglers ("snakeheads") in New York, Los Angeles, and Fuzhou (China) by soliciting participants from their personal contact pool and by using a snowball sampling technique to identify more participants. Antonopoulos et al. (2011) examined the counterfeit CD/DVD market in a provincial city of Greece on the basis of interviews with Nigerian active sellers who were identified by simply being approached in a public space. The sampling method when dealing with active "organized criminals" largely depends—among other things—on the nature of the activity concerned. For instance, human or drug traffickers are much more difficult to approach and recruit than are street-sellers of goods like DVDs who almost exclusively adopt an entrepreneurial identity and are tolerated by the public and often by the authorities themselves.

Because of the practical difficulties of work of that nature with active organized criminals, especially when the activity concerned is dangerous, violent, or clearly criminal, a large number of researchers have attempted to interview different sets of considerably more "approachable" (although not necessarily willing) participants such as incarcerated offenders. For example, Reuter and Haaga (1989) and Decker and Townsend Chapman (2008) conducted retrospective interviews with traffickers who were incarcerated in several US federal prisons. Both studies offered numerous insights into drug trafficking, and the interviewees were able to provide a "longitudinal" representation of the drug smuggling business, present a mosaic of the actors involved in the business and career trajectories, as well as reflect on the several strategies and practices to balance risks and rewards and avoid detection. Similarly, Pearson and Hobbs (2001) conducted interviews with incarcerated drug dealers in Britain who were involved in aspects of the middle market in drugs and focused on some of the less than sophisticated internal organization of drug markets, the role of ethnicity and family, regional variations and cross-regional drug networks, as well as the role of violence. Despite the fact that these institutionalized interviewees would be defined by Polsky (1967) as "inmates" rather than as "offenders," the advantage to this method is that active offenders' attention is easily diverted during the interviews (Akerstrom 1985) and that, in prison interviews, researchers "access a wider range of geographies than would be typically available outside of institutions" (Copes and Hochstetler 2010, p. 63).

Interviews with consumers (or potential consumers) of commodities and services offered by organized crime, the *demand* side, are also useful. For example, Wiltshire et al. (2001) examined the behavior and attitudes related to smoking and contraband tobacco products among smokers in two socioeconomically deprived areas in Edinburgh by interviewing 100 smokers randomly selected from general practitioners' lists from health centers. Eisend and Schuchert-Güler (2006)—by in-depth interviewing of buyers of counterfeit products—attempted to gain insight into the determinants for purchasing counterfeit products and the underlying mechanisms of these determinants. These studies highlight the fact that instead of organized criminals predating on "innocent members of the public," they often offer commodities and services to willing customers who readily legitimize their behavior. They also highlight the forces of demand for specific commodities in a market culture and that forms of organized crime have to be seen as an integral part of the general social, historical, legal, and economic contexts. For instance, (contraband) cigarettes constitute a commodity for which there is a very large, receptive market, which involves "voluntary transfers" and "an implicit notion of fair market value" (Naylor 2003, p. 85) and is, therefore, received well by large parts of the population (see Whiltshire et al. 2001).

Finally, with regard to interviewing, a number of studies have been the product of interviews with victims of organized crime, exposing the sometimes arbitrary perpetrator/victim dichotomy, and ultimately questioning stereotypical images of "victimhood." Research on human trafficking and smuggling is a good example of the latter. Eastern European women (among other) are largely perceived to be falling prey to human traffickers who exploit them. Siegel and Yeşilgöz (2003, p. 75), however, in their interviews with prostituted women from Russia, discovered that "the 'victims' do not look upon their work as criminal or a 'bad job'. On the contrary, in their view, it is a valued, well-paid and very satisfactory activity." Staring (2003), in the context of his research on migrant smuggling, conducted interviews with more than 300 undocumented migrants in the Netherlands on their motives for migration and the logistics of their migratory process. What he found was that human smugglers do facilitate the irregular migratory process and become "service providers" (Ruggiero 1997) to migrants; however, they are less "responsible" for this irregular migration process than commonly assumed, especially for the migrants embedded in transnational networks in the country of destination.

It should be noted also that there have been pieces of research based on interviews with more than one set of participants (including offenders, consumers/clients, "victims"). For instance, Dorn et al.'s (1992) research on drug traffickers and trafficking, and the relevant law enforcement strategies, was based on interviews with imprisoned drug traffickers, drug users, active drug traffickers, key individuals in local communities, law enforcement officers, and, in some cases, their informants. Ruggiero and Khan's (2006) study on drug use and trafficking within British South Asian communities drew on interviews with 123 individuals in and out of prison, key individuals with working knowledge of drug use and distribution in the British South Asian community, as well as law enforcement agencies in Britain and Pakistan.

As reflected on by almost all researchers who have conducted interviews with organized criminals (and this applies to customers/clients and victims of organized crime), such interviews have numerous limitations. Similar to ethnographic research, there are issues of generalizability, and one can never be absolutely certain about validity, although "cross-checking" and "member checking" can significantly contribute toward eliminating untruthful accounts. In addition, there is the issue of representativeness of the sample. In many instances (e.g., Zhang and Chin 2004), researchers use a snowballing sampling method to identify participants, thus limiting the sample to the researcher's own personal network, and in consequence the scope of the findings. In relation to this point, Zhang and Chin (2004, p. 3) suggest that a main finding of their study "about the absence of a substantiated connection between traditional organised crime groups and the human smuggling trade could be an artefact of the limited access—researchers were able to tap into only the part-time, moon-lighting 'non-criminals.'"

VIII. Conclusion

Organized crime should be regarded skeptically, which can be a difficult task for those branches of the academic community wedded to the law enforcement project. Sociological research, as opposed to much of its criminological counterpart, has traditionally insisted on levels of objectivity that are difficult to adhere to, if socially constructed concepts such as organized crime are accepted unquestioned. The problem is even more pronounced if we accept that the forces responsible for creating organized crime are also the gatekeepers to the data that confirm its very existence. As a receptacle for a mutating series of illegal enterprises, organized crime does offer opportunities for the analysis of global governance by crime (Findlay 2008), the flexibility of crime groups defined by ethnicity (Varese 2006), and an understanding of the embeddedness of illegal entrepreneurship (Kleemans and van de Bunt 2002). But it is essential that care is taken that the organized crime label does not lead the researcher to afford the category of transgression an empirical reality beyond the amalgam of political expediency, institution building, police work, and illegal trading, vice, and extortion that constitute the multivariant parts of the whole. Organized crime is a relatively difficult topic on which one can conduct research, however, as is evident much interesting research from a variety of disciplines has been conducted, although one of the major issues that appears through its absence is the presence of comparative studies. Despite the definitional, practical, and ethical issues involved, the studies briefly presented here suggest that researching organized crime is not at all an impossible endeavor even when the primary source of information is active offenders, offenders whose activities highlight some essential truths of the predatory marketplace in which we all live. However, we must also beware of simplifying the complexity of this market, for the very term "organized crime" imposes a sense of order on clusters of unruly disjointed episodes, in flagrant disregard of Matza's warning that "coherence will be imposed on an actual disorder and a forgery thus produced" (1969, p. 1).

Notes

1. Although online survey has worked with clients (see Lombardi and Fonio 2009).
2. See Hobbs (2013, chapters 2 and 3).

3. For an overview of how a national organized crime problem was created without a research base, see Woodiwiss and Hobbs (2009), Hobbs and Hobbs (2012), and Hobbs (2013).

4. *System to Retrieve Information From Drug Evidence*: This is a DEA (Drug Enforcement Administration) data system that has existed since the early 1980s in the United States and possessed information on drug transactions made by enforcement agencies at the local, state, and federal levels. The primary purpose of the database has been to catalogue and inventory all drug acquisitions made by agents so as to have information readily available for court processing of drug offenders. The particular system's data include the date of the drug acquisition, location, nature of the acquisition (seizure or purchase), weight, purity, chemical nature of the drug, and price (Kilmer et al. 2009).

5. *National Incident-Based Reporting System*: This is a reporting system used by law enforcement agencies in the United States that focuses on drug seizures at the local level and possesses information—among other—on the type of drug-related arrest, the suspected drug type, estimated quantity levels, the age, gender, "race," and ethnicity of the arrestee (Kilmer et al. 2009).

6. For a wonderful evocation of Chicago's urban frontier engorged with immigration, poverty, and a corrupt political machine, see Landesco (1927).

7. The definitional issues particularly with "victims" must, of course, be always kept with the reader.

REFERENCES

Adler, Patricia. 1985. *Wheeling and Dealing: An Ethnography of an Upper Level Drug Dealing and Smuggling Community*. New York: Columbia University Press.

Akerstrom, Malin. 1985. *Crooks and Squares*. New Brunswick, NJ: Transaction.

Antonopoulos, Georgios A. 2008. "Interviewing Retired Cigarette Smugglers." *Trends in Organised Crime* 11: 70–81.

Antonopoulos, Georgios A. and Georgios Papanicolaou. 2009. "Gone in 50 Seconds: The Social Organisation and Political Economy of the Stolen Cars Market in Greece." In *Crime, Money and Criminal Mobility in Europe*, edited by P.C. van Duyne, S. Donati, J. Harvey, A. Maljevic, and K. von Lampe. Nijmegen: Wolf Legal.

Antonopoulos, Georgios A., Dick Hobbs and Rob Hornsby. 2011. "A Soundtrack to (Illegal) Entrepreneurship: The Counterfeit CD/DVD Market in a Greek Provincial City." *British Journal of Criminology* 51(5): 804–822.

Assessing Organized Crime (AOC). 2006. *Assessing Organised Crime by a New Common European Approach*. Brussels: European Commission.

Bell, Daniel. 1953. "Crime as an American Way of Life." *The Antioch Review* 13: 131–154.

Blok, Anton. 1974. *The Mafia of a Sicilian Village, 1860–1960*. New York: Harper.

Block, Alan. 1983. *East Side-West Side: Organizing Crime in New York 1930–1950*. Newark, NJ: Transaction.

Block, Alan. 1991. *The Business of Crime*. Boulder, CO: Westview Press.

Block, Alan and William Chambliss. 1981. *Organizing Crime*. New York: Elsevier.

Bourgois, Philippe. 1995. *In Search of Respect*. Cambridge: Cambridge University Press.

Bovenkerk, Frank. 1995. *La Bella Bettien*. Amsterdam: Meulenhoff.

Bovenkerk, Frank. 2000. "'Wanted Mafia Boss'—Essay on the Personology of Organised Crime." *Crime, Law Social Change* 33(3): 225–242.

Bovenkerk, Frank, Dina Siegel and Damian Zaitch. 2003. "Organised Crime and Ethnic Reputation Manipulation." *Crime, Law Social Change* 39: 23–38.

Brandon, David. 2010. *Stand and Deliver: A History of Highway Robbery*. London: The History Press.

Browning, Frank and John Gerassi. 1980. *The American Way of Crime*. New York: G.P. Putnam and Sons.

Calderoni, Francesco. 2011. "Where Is the Mafia in Italy? Measuring the Presence of the Mafia Across Italian Provinces." *Global Crime* 12(1): 41–69.

Cameron, Lisa, and Jenny Williams. 2001. "Cannabis, Alcohol and Cigarettes: Substitutes or Complements?" *Economic Record* 77(236): 19–34.

Campana, Paolo. 2011. "Eavesdropping on the Mob: The Functional Diversification of Mafia Activities Across Territories." *European Journal of Criminology* 8(3): 213–228.

Carrington, Peter J. 2011. "Crime and Social Network Analysis." In *Sage Handbook of Social Network Analysis*, edited by J. Scott and P. J. Carrington. London: Sage.

Catanzaro, Raimondo. 1992. *Men of Respect*. New York: Free Press.

Cauduro, Andrea, Andrea Di Nicola, Chiara Fonio, Andrea Nuvoloni, A., and Paolo Ruspini. 2009. "Innocent When You Dream: Clients and Trafficked Women in Italy." In *Prostitution and Trafficking: Focus on Clients*, edited by A. Di Nicola, A. Cauduro, M. Lombardi, and P. Ruspini. New York: Springer.

Caulkins, Jonathan P., and Rosalie Pacula. 2006. "Marijuana Markets: Inferences from Reports by the Household Population." *Journal of Drug Issues* 36(1): 173–200.

Caulkins, Jonathan P., Benjamin Gurga, and Christopher Little. 2009. "Economic Analysis of Drug Transaction 'Cycles' Described by Incarcerated UK Drug Dealers." *Global Crime* 10(1–2): 94–112.

Chambliss, William. 1978. *On the Take*. Bloomington: Indiana University Press.

Coles, Nigel. 2001. "It's Not *What* You Know, It's *Who* You Know That Counts: Analysing Serious Crime Groups as Social Networks." *British Journal of Criminology* 41: 580–594.

Copes, Heith, and Andy Hochstetler. 2010. "Interviewing the Incarcerated: Promises and Pitfalls." In *Offenders on Offending: Learning About Crime from Criminals*, edited by W. Bernasco. Cullompton, UK: Willan.

Cressey, Donald. 1969. *Theft of the Nation*. New York: Harper and Row.

Critchley, David. 2009. *The Origin of Organised Crime in America: The New York City Mafia, 1891–1931*. New York: Routledge.

Decker, Scott H., and Margaret Townsend Chapman. 2008. *Drug Smugglers on Drug Smuggling*. Philadelphia, PA: Temple University Press.

Di Nicola, Andrea and Andrea Cauduro. 2007. "Review of Official Statistics on Trafficking in Human Beings for Sexual Exploitation and Their Validity in the 25 EU Member States from Official Statistics to Estimates of the Phenomenon." In *Measuring Human Trafficking*, edited by E. Savona., and S. Stefanizzi. New York: Springer.

Dorn, Nicholas, Karim Murji, and Nigel South. 1992. *Traffickers*. London: Routledge.

Dunlap, Eloise, Bruce Johnson, and Ali Manwar. 1994. "A Successful Female Crack Dealer: Case Study of a Deviant Career." *Deviant Behaviour* 15: 1–25.

Egmond, Florike. 1993. *Underworlds. Organised Crime in the Netherlands, 1650–1800*. Cambridge, MA: Polity Press.

Eisend, Martin, and Pakize Schuchert-Güler. 2006. "Explaining Counterfeit Purchases: A Review and Preview." *Academy of Marketing Science Review* 10(12). http://www.amsreview. org/articles/eisend12-2006.pdf.

Ferrell, Jeff. 1998. "Criminological Verstehen: Inside the Immediacy of Crime." In *Ethnography at the Edge,* edited by J. Ferrell, and M. S. Hamm. Boston: Northeastern University Press.

Finckenauer, James O. 2005. "Problems of Definition: What Is Organised Crime?" *Trends in Organised Crime* 8: 63–83.

Findlay, Mark. 2008. *Governing Through Globalised Crime.* Cullhompton, UK: Willan.

Firestone, Thomas A. 1993. "Mafia Memoirs: What They Tell Us About Organised Crime." *Journal of Contemporary Criminal Justice* 9(3): 197–220.

Gachevska, Katerina. 2009. "Building the New Europe: Soft Security and Organised Crime in EU Enlargement." Unpublished PhD Thesis, Wolverhampton University.

Gambetta, Diego. 1993. *The Sicilian Mafia: The Business of Private Protection.* Cambridge, MA: Harvard University Press.

Gottschalk, Eva. 2009. *Public Perception on Organised Crime—Results from an Opinion Poll.* London: Home Office/Mori. http://webarchive.nationalarchives.gov.uk/20100413151441/ http://www.crimereduction.homeoffice.gov.uk/organisedcrime/organisedcrime017.pdf.

Granovetter, Mark. 1973. "The Strengths of Weak Ties." *American Journal of Sociology* 78(6): 1360–1380.

Haller, Mark. 1971. "Organised Crime in Urban Society: Chicago in the Twentieth Century." *Journal of Social History* 5(2): 210–234.

Haller, Mark. 1985. "Bootleggers as Businessmen: From City Slums to City Builders." In *Law, Alcohol, and Order: Perspectives on National Prohibition,* edited by D. Kyvig. Westport, CT: Greenwood.

Hess, Henner. 1973. *Mafia and Mafiosi: The Structure of Power.* Lexington, MA: D.C. Heath.

Hobbs, Dick. 1988. *Doing the Business.* Oxford: Oxford University Press.

Hobbs, Dick. 1995. *Bad Business.* Oxford: Oxford University Press.

Hobbs, Dick. 1998. "Going Down the Glocal: The Local Context of Organised Crime." *The Howard Journal* 37(4): 407–422.

Hobbs, Dick. 2013. *Lush Life.* Oxford: Oxford University Press.

Hobbs, Dick, and Sue Hobbs. 2012. "A Bog of Conspiracy: The Institutional Evolution of Organised Crime in the UK." In *The Handbook of Transnational Organized Crime,* edited by F. Allum and S. Gilmour. London: Routledge.

Hobsbawm, Eric. 1972. *Bandits.* London: Pelican.

Ianni, Francis, and Elizabeth Reuss-Ianni. 1972. *A Family Business: Kinship and Social Control in Organized Crime.* New York: Russell Sage Foundation.

International Organization for Migration (IOM). 2000. *Migrant Trafficking and Human Smuggling in Europe.* Geneva: IOM.

Jacobs, Adam. 2007. "What Criminology Can Learn From Comparative Historical Sociology." Presentation at the annual meeting of the American Society of Criminology, Atlanta, GA, November 14.

Kelly, Liz, and Linda Regan. 2000. *Stopping Traffic: Exploring the Extent of, and Responses to, Trafficking in Women for Sexual Exploitation in the UK.* London: Home Office.

Kilmer, Beau, Rosalie Pacula, Stijn Hoorens, Priscillia Hunt. 2009. *Study on Policy Relevant Information and Data in the Field of Drug Supply Reduction and Drug-Related Crime in the EU and Third Countries.* Cambridge, UK: RAND Europe.

Kilmer, Beau, Jonathan Caulkins, Brittany Bond, and Peter Reuter. 2010. *Drug Trafficking Revenues and Violence in Mexico: Would Legalising Marijuana in California Help?* Santa Monica, CA: RAND.

Kinzig, Jörg. 2004. *Die rechtliche Bewältigung von Erscheinungsformen organisierter Kriminalität.* Berlin: Duncker and Humblot.

Kirby, Terry. 1993. "Russian Gangs Pose Threat to British Cities." *The Independent.* (May 25).

Kitsuse, John, and Aaron Cicourel. 1963. "A Note on the Use of Official Statistics." *Social Problems* 11(2): 131–139.

Kleemans, Edward. 2007. "Organised Crime, Transit Crime and Racketeering." In *Crime and Justice in the Netherlands,* edited by M. Tonry, and C. Bijleveld. Chicago: University of Chicago Press.

Kleemans, Edward, and Christianne de Poot. 2008. "Criminal Careers in Organised Crime, and Social Opportunity Structure." *European Journal of Criminology* 5(1): 69–98.

Kleemans, Edward, and Henk van de Bunt. 2002. "The Social Embeddedness of Organised Crime." *Transnational Organised Crime* 5(1): 19–36.

Kleemans, Edward, and Henk van de Bunt. 2008. "Organised Crime, Occupations and Opportunity." *Global Crime* 9(3): 185–197.

Klerks, Peter. 2001. "The Network Paradigm Applied to Criminal Organizations: Theoretical Nitpicking or a Relevant Doctrine for Investigators?" *Connections,* 24(3): 53–65.

Landesco, John. 1927. *Organised Crime in Chicago.* Chicago: University of Chicago Press.

Lehti, Martti, and Kauko Aromaa. 2006. "Trafficking for Sexual Exploitation." In *Crime and Justice: A Review of Research,* Vol. 34. edited by M. Tonryed. Chicago: University of Chicago Press.

Levi, Mike. 1981. *The Phantom Capitalists.* Aldershot: Gower.

Levi, Mike. 1998. "Perspectives on Organised Crime: An Overview." *The Howard Journal of Criminal Justice* 37(4): 335–345.

Levi, Mike. 2004. "The Making of the UK's Organised Crime Control Policies." In *Organised Crime in Europe: Concepts, Patterns and Control Policies in the European Union and Beyond,* edited by C. Fijnaut, and L. Paoli. Dordrecht: Springer.

Levitt, Steven, and Sudhir A. Venkatesh. 2000. "An Economic Analysis of a Drug-Selling Gang's Finances." *Quarterly Journal of Economics* 115(3): 755–789.

Lloyd Baker, Thomas. 1889. *War With Crime.* London: Longmans.

Lombardi, Marco, and Fonio, Chiara. 2009. "An Internet Survey to Understand Clients." In *Prostitution and Trafficking: Focus on Clients,* edited by A. Di Nicola, A. Cauduro, M. Lombardi, and P. Ruspini. New York: Springer.

Lupsha, Peter. 1983. "Networks vs Networking: Analysis of an Organised Crime Group." In *Career Criminals,* edited by G. Waldo. Beverly Hills, CA: Sage.

Malm, Aili, Bryan Kinney, and Nahanni Pollard. 2008. "Social Network and Distance Correlates of Criminal Associates Involved in Illicit Drug Production." *Security Journal* 21: 77–94.

Matza, David. 1969. *Becoming Deviant.* Englewood Cliffs, NJ: Prentice Hall.

McIllwain, Jeffrey. 1999. "Organised Crime: A Social Network Approach." *Crime, Law and Social Change* 32(4): 301–323.

McMullan, John. 1982. "Criminal Organisation in Sixteenth and Seventeenth Century London." *Social Problems* 29: 311–323.

McMullan, John. 1984. *The Canting Crew: London's Criminal Underworld, 1550–1700.* New Brunswick, NJ: Rutgers University Press.

Mieczkowski, Tom. 1990. "Crack Distribution in Detroit." *Contemporary Drug Problems* 17(1): 19–30.

Morselli, Carlo. 2001. "Structuring Mr. Nice: Entrepreneurial Opportunities and Brokerage Positioning in the Cannabis Trade." *Crime, Law and Social Change* 35(3): 203–244.

Morselli, Carlo. 2003. "Career Opportunities and Network-Based Privileges in the Cosa Nostra." *Crime, Law and Social Change* 39(4): 383–418.

Morselli, Carlo. 2005. *Contacts, Opportunities, and Criminal Enterprise.* Toronto: University of Toronto Press.

Morselli, Carlo. 2009. *Inside Criminal Networks.* New York: Springer.

Morselli, Carlo. 2010. "Assessing Vulnerable and Strategic Positions in a Criminal Network." *Journal of Contemporary Criminal Justice* 26: 382–392.

Morselli, Carlo, and Cynthia Giguere. 2006. "Legitimate Strengths in Criminal Networks." *Crime, Law and Social Change* 45(3): 185–200.

Morselli, Carlo, Cynthia Giguere, and Katia Petit 2007. "The Efficiency/Security Trade-off in Criminal Networks." *Social Networks* 29: 143–153.

Munsche, Peter. 1981. *Gentlemen and Poachers.* Cambridge: Cambridge University Press.

Myers, Gustavus. 1936. *History of Great American Fortunes.* New York: Modern Library.

Natarajan, Mangai. 2000. "Understanding the Structure of a Drug Trafficking Organization: A Conversational Analysis." In *Illegal Drug Markets: From Research to Policy, Crime Prevention Studies*, Vol. 11, edited by M. Natarajan, and M. Hough. Monsey, NY: Criminal Justice Press.

Natarajan, Mangai. 2006. "Understanding the Structure of a Large Heroin Distribution Network: A Quantitative Analysis of Qualitative Data." *Journal of Quantitative Criminology* 22: 171–192.

Naylor, R. Thomas. 1995. "From Cold War to Crime War." *Transnational Organised Crime* 1(4): 37–56.

Naylor, R. Thomas. 2003. "Towards a General Theory of Profit-Driven Crimes." *British Journal of Criminology* 43: 81–101.

National Criminal Intelligence Service. (NCIS). 1993a. *An Outline Assessment of the Threat and Impact by Organised/Enterprise Crime Upon United Kingdom Interests.* London: NCIS.

National Criminal Intelligence Service. (NCIS). 1993b. *Organised Crime Conference: A Threat Assessment.* London: NCIS.

Paoli, Letizia. 2003. *Mafia Brotherhoods.* New York: Oxford University Press.

Paoli, Letizia, Victoria Greenfield, and Peter Reuter. 2009. *The World Heroin Market: Can the Supply Be Cut?* New York: Oxford University Press.

Passas, Nikos. 1996. "The Genesis of the BCCI Scandal." *Journal of Law and Society* 23: 57–72.

Pearson, Geoff, and Dick Hobbs. 2001. *Middle Market Drug Distribution. Home Office Research Study* 227. London: Home Office.

Polsky, Ned. 1967. *Hustlers, Beats and Others.* New York: Aldine.

Potter, Gary. 1994. *Criminal Organisations.* Chicago: Waveland Press.

Pryce, Ken. 1979. *Endless pressure: a study of West Indian life-styles in Bristol.* Harmondsworth: Penguin.

Raine, Linnea, and Cilluffo, Frank. 1994. *Global Organised Crime: The New Empire of Evil.* Washington, DC: Center for Strategic and International Studies.

Rawlinson, Paddy. 2008. "Look Who's Talking: Interviewing Russian Criminals." *Trends in Organised Crime* 11: 12–20.

Reuter, Peter. 1983. *Disorganised Crime: The Economics of the Visible Hand*. Cambridge, MA: MIT Press.

Reuter, Peter. 1985. *The Organisation of Illegal Market: An Economic Analysis*. Washington, DC: The National Institute of Justice.

Reuter, Peter. 1986. *Methodological and Institutional Problems in Organised Crime Research*. Washington, DC: The Rand Corporation.

Reuter, Peter, and Jonathan Caulkins. 2004. "Illegal Lemons: Price Dispersion in Cocaine and Heroin Markets." *Bulletin on Narcotics* LVI(1–2): 141–165.

Reuter, Peter, and Victoria Greenfield. 2001. "Measuring Global Drug Markets." *World Economics* 2(4): 159–173.

Reuter, Peter, and John Haaga. 1989. *The Organisation of High-Level Drug Markets: An Exploratory Study*. Santa Monica, CA: RAND.

Ruggiero, Vincenzo. 1997. "Criminals and Service Providers: Cross-National Dirty Economies." *Crime, Law and Social Change* 28: 27–38.

Ruggiero, Vincenzo, and Kazim Khan. 2006. "British South Asian Communities and Drug Supply Networks in the UK: A Qualitative Study." *International Journal on Drug Policy* 17(6): 473–483.

Savoie-Gargiso, Isa, and Carlo Morselli. 2009. "Lady's Man: The Pimp and His Place Among Prostitutes." Presentation at the 9th European Society of Criminology conference, Ljubljana, Slovenia, September 9–12.

Scott, John. 1990. *A Matter of Record*. Cambridge. MA: Polity Press.

Scott, John. 1991. *Social Network Analysis: A Handbook*. London: Sage.

Sharpe, James. 1999. *Crime in Early Modern England 1550–1750*. London: Longman.

Sherry, Frank. 1986. *Raiders and Rebels*, New York: Hearst Marine Books.

Shover, Neal, and David Honaker. 1992. "The Socially Bounded Decision Making of Persistent Property Offenders." *The Howard Journal* 31: 276–293.

Siegel, Dina. 2005. *Russische Bizniz*. Amsterdam: Meulenhoff.

Siegel, Dina, and Yücel Yeşilgöz. 2003. "Nathashas and Turkish Men: New Trends in Women Trafficking and Prostitution." In *Global Organised Crime: Trends and Developments*, edited by D. Siegel, H. van de Bunt, and D. Zaitch. Dordrecht: Kluwer.

Soudijn, Melvin J.R. 2006. *Chinese Human Smuggling in Transit*. The Hague: BJU.

Sparrow, Malcolm. 1991. "Network Vulnerabilities and Strategic Intelligence in Law Enforcement." *International Journal of Intelligence and Counterintelligence* 5(3): 255–274.

Staring, Richard. 2003. "Smuggling Aliens Towards the Netherlands: The Role of Human Smugglers and Transnational Networks." In *Global Organised Crime: Trends and Developments*, edited by D. Siegel, H. van de Bunt, and D. Zaitch. Dordrecht: Kluwer.

Stedman-Jones, Gareth. 1971. *Outcast London*. Oxford: Oxford University Press.

Strumpf, Koleman. 2003. *Illegal Sport Bookmakers*. http://rgco.org/articles/illegal_sports_bookmakers.pdf.

Styles, John. 1980. "Our Traitorous Moneymakers." In *An Ungovernable People*, edited by J. Brewer, and J. Styles. London: Hutchinson.

Tilley, Nick, and Matt Hopkins. 2008. "Organised Crime and Local Businesses." *Criminology and Criminal Justice* 8(4): 443–459.

US Department of State. 2011. *Trafficking in Persons Report 2011*. Washington, DC: US Department of State.

Vander Beken, Tom, and Kristof Verfaillie. 2010. "Assessing European Futures in an Age of Reflexive Security." *Policing and Society* 20(2): 187–203.

van Dijck, Maarten. 2007. "Cigarette Shuffle: Organising Tobacco Tax Evasion in the Netherlands." In *Crime Business and Crime Money in Europe,* edited by P.C. van Duyne, A. Maljevic, M. van Dijck, K. von Lampe, and J. Harvey. Nijmegen: Wolf Legal.

van Dijk, Jan. 2007. "Mafia Markers: Assessing Organised Crime and Its Impact Upon Societies." *Trends in Organised Crime* 10(4): 39–56.

van Duyne, Petrus. 2003. "Organizing Cigarette Smuggling and Policy Making, Ending Up in Smoke." *Crime, Law and Social Change* 39: 285–317.

van Duyne, Petrus. 2007. "Criminal Finances and State of the Art: Case for Concern." In *Crime Business and Crime Money in Europe,* edited by P.C. van Duyne, A. Maljevic, M. van Dijck, K. von Lampe, and J. Harvey. Nijmegen: Wolf Legal.

van Duyne, Petrus, and Mike Levi. 2005. *Drugs and Money: Managing The Drug Trade and Crime Money in Europe*. London: Routledge.

van Koppen, Vere, Christianne de Poot, Edward Kleemans., and Paul Nieuwbeerta. 2010. "Criminal Trajectories in Organised Crime." *British Journal of Criminology* 50: 102–123.

Varese, Federico. 2006. "How Mafias Migrate." *Law and Society Review* 40(2): 411–444.

Varese, Federico. 2011. *Mafias on the Move*. Princeton, NJ: Princeton University Press.

von Lampe, Klaus. 2009. "Human Capital and Social Capital in Criminal Networks." *Trends in Organised Crime* 12(2): 93–100.

Wasserman, Stanley, and Katherine Faust. 1994. *Social Network Analysis: Methods and Applications*. Cambridge, MA: Cambridge University Press.

Williams, Phil, and Ernesto Savona. 1995. *The United Nations and Transnational Organised Crime*. Oxford: Frank Cass Publishers.

Williams, Terry. 1992. *Crack House*. Reading, MA: Addison-Wesley.

Williams, Terry. 1989. *The Cocaine Kids*. Reading, MA: Addison-Wesley.

Wiltshire, Susan, Angus Bancroft, Amanda Amos, and Odette Parry. 2001. "'They're Doing People a Service': Qualitative Study of Smoking, Smuggling, and Social Deprivation." *British Medical Journal* 323: 203–207.

Woodiwiss, Michael, and Dick Hobbs. 2009. "Organised Evil and the Atlantic Alliance: Moral Panics and the Rhetoric of Organised Crime Policing in America and Britain." *British Journal of Criminology* 49(1): 106–128.

Zaitch, Damián. 2002. *Trafficking Cocaine: Colombian Drug Entrepreneurs in the Netherlands*. The Hague: Kluwer.

Zhang, Sheldon, and Chin, Ko-Lin. 2004. *Characteristics of Chinese Human Smugglers*. Washington, DC: US Department of Justice.

PART II

ACTORS AND INTERACTIONS

CHAPTER 5

....

THE ITALIAN MAFIA

....

LETIZIA PAOLI

TOGETHER with its Italian American counterpart, the Italian "mafia" is often seen as the ultimate epitome of organized crime and, more specifically, of the understanding of organized crime as a set of large-scale, stable organizations that are illegal per se or whose members systematically engage in crime (for more information on this and the rivaling notion of organized crime as a set of profit-making criminal activities, see Paoli and Vander Beken in this volume).

Unlike most other developed countries, in fact, Italy hosts a few large-scale, century-old criminal organizations that not only engage in profit-making criminal activities but also exercise quasi-political functions in their areas of settlement, heavily influencing the local economic and political life. Given their size, longevity, organizational and cultural complexity and multifunctionality, these criminal organizations—in short mafias—are fundamentally different from the ephemeral and mostly small-scale enterprises that continually form and disband in the illegal markets of developed countries, including Italy itself, hoping to earn fast money with the production or distribution of prohibited goods and services.

In the first section, I briefly reconstruct the history of the concept "mafia," singling out the main meanings that have over the decades been attached to it. In the next section, I present the main criminal organizations currently regarded as mafias in Italy. Then, I discuss what in my view are, from an analytical point of view, the four distinguishing characteristics of mafia organizations in Italy and mafia-type organizations elsewhere:

1. The organizations' longevity
2. Their organizational and cultural complexity
3. Their claim to exercise a political dominion over their areas of settlement—a claim that has over the decades been at least partially recognized by the local population and parts of the official government
4. Their resulting ability to control legitimate markets

I argue that the Sicilian Cosa Nostra and the Calabrian 'Ndrangheta meet all four characteristics, whereas several groups of the Camorra, which are based in Naples and its surroundings, meet the latter two. In the last section, I conclude by briefly summarizing government and societal anti-mafia action from the early 1990s onward and consider how mafia groups have reacted to it.

I. A Brief History of the Concept "Mafia"

Mafia is a word of uncertain origin that, starting from the mid-nineteenth century, began to be used by government officials in Sicily as a synonym of the *associazione di malfattori* (that is, association of evildoers), which was then the main offense of criminal organization. In the decades after Italy's Unification in 1861, the term "mafia" and the offense of criminal organization were applied to very different social manifestations, ranging from movements of political opposition to peasant revolts, from union unrest to terrorist groups (e.g., Pezzino 1987). Starting from the late nineteenth century, however, the term "mafia" began to be restricted to those groups and even single individuals active in Sicily that systematically resorted to violence and the threat of violence, in order to control the political and economic life of their towns and villages and whose power was usually accepted by the local population and even considered more legitimate than that of the far-away, oppressive central government. Government officials presented these groups as the embodiment of the offense of criminal organization, denying them any cultural legitimation. As Cesare Mori, the "Iron Prefect" in charge of mafia repression in the 1920s, wrote, "whatever form it takes and however it acts, the mafia, by its very nature, constitutes . . . the typical configuration of the criminal organization"(1993, p. 32).

Whereas the indiscriminate methods used by Prefect Mori during the Fascist regime have long been abandoned, the official understanding of the mafia as a criminal organization has not been questioned since then. Such an understanding was consolidated in 1982, when the Italian Parliament introduced the offense of *associazione a delinquere di tipo mafioso* (art. 416bis of the Italian Penal Code), thus fully transforming the meta-juridical concept of mafia into the juridical category of an ad hoc mafia-type criminal organization (see Paoli and Vander Beken in this volume for the definition).

Next to the official conceptualization of the mafia as a criminal organization, two rivaling notions emerged. From the late nineteenth century onward, media and novelists have presented the mafia as a well-organized and powerful secret society, albeit with different and changing assessments of its legitimacy. This conceptualization found great impulse in the publication—first in 1908–1909 in installments on a Palermitan newspaper and successively as a book—of William Galt's (Natoli 1993) novel *I Beati Paoli*, which obtained great success in Sicily. A secret sect administering justice in a situation of weakness and corruption of public authorities, a sort of collective Robin Hood, the *Beati Paoli* came to be seen—both in the popular imagination and in the ideology of mafia groups—as a proto-manifestation of the mafia (Eco 1993). The understanding of the mafia as a powerful secret society has remained popular until present times—it is enough to recall the enormous success of Francis Ford Coppola's trilogy *The Godfather* as proof—but since World War II, media, novelists and film-makers have largely denied or at least questioned mafia legitimacy, in line with the official understanding of the mafia.

Since the late nineteenth century, the understanding of mafia as a criminal organization was challenged by the "Sicilianist" movement with a fair degree of success. This was a cultural and political movement that was promoted by Sicily's ruling strata and developed in order to oppose what was perceived as an indiscriminate criminalization of all Sicilians by the Italian law enforcement apparatus and Italian public opinion as a whole (Marino 1988). In the eyes of the *sicilianisti*, the mafia was merely an attitude, the product of a particularly fierce Sicilian reaction to the foreign powers that had dominated the island for centuries. For example, the Sicilian ethnographer Giuseppe Pitrè, who contributed enormously to the promotion of this ideology, defined the mafia as follows:

> The mafia is neither a sect, nor an association, it has no regulations nor statutes. The mafioso is not a thief, nor a bandit;... the mafioso is simply a courageous and skillful man, who cannot bear a fly being on his nose; and in this sense, being a mafioso is necessary, indeed, indispensable. The mafia is the awareness of one's own being, an exaggerated concept of individual strength... (1993, p. 292).

The Sicilianist view of the mafia deeply influenced the social scientists carrying out the first field studies in Sicily between the 1960s and the early 1980s. For them the mafia was simply a subcultural attitude as well as a form of behavior and power. That is, they asserted, there were *mafiosi*, single individuals, who embodied determined subcultural values and exercised specific functions within their communities, but no mafia organization existed as such (e.g., Hess 1973). Even as late as 1983, Pino Arlacchi's successful book, *La Mafia Imprenditrice* (*Mafia Business*), opened with the following statement: "Social research into the question of the mafia has probably now reached the point where we can say that the mafia, as the term is *commonly* understood, does not exist" (1988, p. 3, emphasis in the original).

Until the 1980s, the noncorporate view of the mafia also influenced the public understanding of the mafia, even within parts of the judiciary (Di Lello 1994). It was powerfully challenged during the 1980s, when judicial investigations, most prominently the first Palermo "maxi-trial" (Tribunale di Palermo 1985), started to provide clear and solid proof of the existence of well-structured mafia groups. Whereas the existence of such groups is currently no longer questioned, the many anti-mafia organizations that have sprung up in different parts of Italy still promote a wider understanding of the term "mafia," de facto encompassing all forms of organized illegal behavior aiming at achieving private gains to the detriment of the public good as well as the people colluding with mafia organizations (e.g., Libera 2013). To point to the latter broad set of people, the expression "mafia bourgeoisie" is frequently used (e.g., Santino 1994). While acknowledging this broader understanding of the concept of mafia, we will focus on Italian mafia organizations, or mafias, from the next section on.

II. MAFIA ORGANIZATIONS IN ITALY

Three organizations or better sets of organizations are nowadays primarily referred to as mafia in Italy. The first and most prominent is the Sicilian *Cosa Nostra* ("our thing"), a confederation of about 150 groups, mostly located in the western part of Sicily, more specifically the provinces of Palermo (the region's capital), Trapani, and Agrigento (Ministero dell'Interno 2012b, pp. 28–70).

The second organization is called 'Ndrangheta and is also a confederation of about 150 groups. These all originate from the southernmost tip of the Italian peninsula, the region Calabria, mostly from the provinces of Reggio Calabria and Vibo Valentia. In the dialect of Greek origin that is still widespread in Calabria, the word "'Ndrangheta" means "society of the men of honor" and still has a decidedly positive connotation (Marino 1988, p. 16). Unlike Cosa Nostra, the 'Ndrangheta also includes groups located outside its home region, most specifically in Northern Italy and particularly in the regions of Lombardy, Piedmont, and Liguria, as well as in several foreign countries, most prominently Germany, Canada, and Australia. Recent investigations have shown that the Canadian and Australian offshoots still recognize the authority of the 'Ndrangheta groups located in the Reggio Calabria province and their bodies of coordination (DDA Reggio Calabria 2010, pp. 558–2081; see also Tribunale ordinario di Milano 2010).[1]

The number of formal members of the 'Ndrangheta is currently estimated by law enforcement officials to be at least 10,000 (Commissione Antimafia XVI 2010, p. 5). Five hundred of them, organized in about 25 groups, are active in Lombardy (ibid. p. 12). No exact estimate is known for Cosa Nostra but, according to the same and other sources (ibid.; Ministero dell'Interno 2012b, p. 16), their number should be considerably less, perhaps as low as 2,000, down from 3,000 in the mid-1990s. In fact, Cosa Nostra has traditionally been much more selective in its recruitment policies than the 'Ndrangheta, and it has also been more seriously hit by law enforcement action and seen its popular legitimacy more seriously challenged than its Calabrian counterparts (Paoli 2003, pp. 90–91, 2007).

Unlike the first two organizations, the third, the Camorra, does not even constitute a confederation but rather consists of a multiplicity of independent criminal groups and gangs that are located in the province of Naples, the capital of the region Campania, and the surrounding areas, particularly the Caserta province north of Naples. Although they are collectively named as Camorra, these gangs and groups have different characteristics and modus operandi and often enter into violent conflict with each other. Some of them are well-established family businesses that, much like Sicilian and Calabrian mafia groups, claim to exercise a political dominion over their neighborhoods or towns and systematically infiltrate local government institutions, repeatedly enjoying the protection of high-level national politicians as well. One of them is the "cartel" of mafia-type Camorra groups, the Casalesi, active in the Caserta province, which has been very effective in setting up legitimate businesses with crime proceeds and in gaining control of several local economic sectors (see Saviano 2008). Some of these mafia-type Camorra groups have emissaries and operations in Italy's Center-North (primarily neighboring Latium but also Piedmont, Emilia Romagna, and Tuscany), several EU Member States, above all Spain, South America, and also the United States (Europol 2013, pp. 12 and 17).

Other Camorra groups are less lasting formations that have developed around a charismatic chief, usually a successful gangster, and primarily aim at profit making through illegal businesses, most frequently illegal drug trafficking, although they may also be able to exercise some control on local legal activities and public life. Finally, there are also loose gangs of juvenile and adult offenders, which—according to police sources—rather belong to the sphere of common crime than to that of organized crime. The composition of many Camorra gangs and the alliances among them are so unstable that law enforcement agencies often have difficulties, with the exception of few more stable groups, in finding evidence of the offense of mafia-type criminal organization (Ministero dell'Interno 2012b, pp. 130–137).

A few other criminal coalitions and gangs located in eastern and southern Sicily and in northern Calabria, such as the Stidda in the Agrigento and Caltanissetta provinces, are also occasionally referred to as mafia. Their internal cohesion and political and economic resources are much lower than those of Cosa Nostra or 'Ndrangheta groups, although the Stidda groups have from time to time been able to threaten Cosa Nostra's supremacy in local settings, due to the larger number of members and their readiness to use violence (Ministero dell'Interno 2002).

Until the beginning of the present century, crime groups located in another southern Italian region, Apulia (the "heel" of the Italian "boot"), were also referred to as mafia and their members charged and convicted with the offense of mafia-type criminal organization. In particular, the Sacra Corona Unita, a consortium of about ten to fifteen criminal groups from southern Apulia, was sometimes presented as Italy's fourth mafia. Since its founding in 1983, the Sacra Corona Unita imitated the 'Ndrangheta's structure and rituals (Massari 1998), but its cohesion, stability, economic capabilities, and political power were always much lower. After the defection of some of its leaders and the arrest of most of its members at the beginning of the current century, the Sacra Corona Unita no longer exists as a single viable organization (Ministero dell'Interno 2002, pp. 57–64). In southern Apulia and the rest of the region, a variety of crime groups are currently active, which primarily engage in the smuggling of humans and other products across the sea strait separating Apulia from Albania and Greece but occasionally also commit more typical mafia crimes, such as extortions (Europol 2013, pp. 13–14).

The expressions "organized crime" and "mafie" are also increasingly used to refer to foreign criminals operating in Italy (e.g., Ministero dell'Interno 2002). Since the early 1980s, Italy has indeed undergone a process of internationalization and ethnicization of its illegal markets. This trend, which started in other western European countries in the

1950s, took place very rapidly in Italy from the mid-1980s on, when Italy also became the destination of considerable migration flows. As a result, today in Italy's large cities as well as Frankfurt, London, or Amsterdam, illicit goods and services are offered and exchanged by a multiethnic variety of people. Next to *mafiosi* and local criminals, one finds illicit entrepreneurs coming from different parts of the world. A few of these "ethnic" criminals—in particular, those of Chinese descent—aim to exercise a sort of political power within their own communities (Suchan 2001)—much like the Sicilian and Calabrian *mafiosi* in their strongholds. However, most foreign criminal groups and actors as well as the non-mafia Italian criminal entrepreneurs make no claim to exercise a political authority. They merely content themselves with making fast money by trading in illegal products. Their internal composition is also much different than that of southern Italian mafia groups. Most foreign crime groups and gangs active in Italy as well as their numerous Italian counterparts do not have the longevity and organizational complexity of southern Italian mafia organizations. Some of them are family businesses or groups cemented by profit-making or by shared revolutionary or ideological goals; many more are small, loose gangs, founded on ties of friendship and locality (Ministero dell'Interno 2012b, pp. 239–275; Paoli 2002).

III. Longevity

As already mentioned, longevity and organizational and cultural complexities constitute the first two defining characteristics of mafia organizations—and both are fully met by Cosa Nostra and the 'Ndrangheta.

As for longevity, historical research has since the 1980s demonstrated that antecedents of the contemporary Sicilian and Calabrian mafia groups have existed since the 1880s, if not before (e.g., Pezzino 1987; see also Paoli 2003, pp. 33–40). In Calabria, in particular, the biological families at the core of some large 'Ndrangheta groups have held positions of power in their cities and villages over the past 100 years (Ciconte 1992; Gratteri & Nicaso 2010). Unaware of being wiretapped, for example, a member of one of these groups in 2009 boasted, "we are the past, the present and the future" (Commissione Antimafia XVI 2010, p. 39). Due to their roots in pre-modern times, Cosa Nostra and the 'Ndrangheta still detain some key, pre-modern features—most prominently the reliance on "status and fraternization contracts" and their resulting "patrimonialistic" multifunctionality (see infra)—which have helped them survive "without" and increasingly "against, the state" (Paoli 2002) but which currently constrain their competitiveness on global illegal markets.

The same continuity cannot be ascertained in the case of the Camorra. True, in order to strengthen their internal cohesion and legitimacy, many contemporary Camorra groups also resort to the symbols and rituals of the nineteenth-century Camorra. This was an organization sharing several cultural and organizational similarities with its Sicilian and Calabrian counterparts, although it distinguished itself through its concentration in the city of Naples, and its plebeian background. Unlike Cosa Nostra and the 'Ndrangheta, however, the contemporary Campanian crime groups do not directly derive from their nineteenth-century forerunner. As Isaia Sales puts it, "if camorra means a criminal organization that ruled over Naples' popular and plebeian strata, we can safely say that it started and ended in the nineteenth-century" (Sales 2001, p. 468; see also Sales 1993).

IV. ORGANIZATIONAL AND CULTURAL COMPLEXITY

Cosa Nostra and 'Ndrangheta's internal structure and cultural apparatus of legitimation have few parallels in the world of crime for their complexity and sophistication, beyond the other so-called mafia-type criminal organizations (Paoli 2002; i.e., Chinese Triads, Japanese Yakuza, Italian-American Cosa Nostra, and the Russian vory v zakone; see the chapters of Chin, Hills, Albanese, and Volkov, respectively). As already said, both Cosa Nostra and 'Ndrangheta are confederations of about 150 groups. These are often called families but are clearly distinct from the members' biological families, particularly in Cosa Nostra. In the 'Ndrangheta, male relatives are still regarded as an asset for mafia bosses, who often try to have as many relatives as possible affiliated with the mafia group. However, because of the larger size of 'Ndrangheta groups, these also have a much more complicated internal structure than their Sicilian counterparts, which are often composed of fewer than ten members. In the 'Ndrangheta, some mafia groups—or *locali* (i.e., "places") in the 'Ndrangheta slang—are composed of up to 100 to 200 people and, therefore, in order to protect the mafia bosses, an internal ranking system has developed, coupled with a subdivision between a higher and a lower section in each mafia group—and only the older, higher-ranking members have access to the former (Paoli 2003, pp. 40–51; DDA Reggio Calabria 2010, pp. 442–556).

In both mafia organizations, the single groups have their own ruling bodies—the distinguishing trait of organization according to Weber (1978, p. 48). The organization rules foresee that these ruling positions have to be entrusted each year through democratic elections, even though they often end up being occupied sometimes for decades by the most powerful mafia members (Paoli 2003, pp. 40–46). Starting from the 1950s, moreover, superordinate bodies of coordination were set up—first in Cosa Nostra and, during the 1990s, in the 'Ndrangheta as well. Composed of the most important family chiefs, they are known as "commissions." Although these bodies have often been romanticized, they cannot be compared to the board of directors of a company, as the mafia commissions have historically been rarely in charge of the planning or coordination of profit-making activities, rather, they were set up primarily to mediate conflicts within the two organizations and regulate the use of violence against mafia members of other units and high-level government officials, so as to avoid unnecessarily attracting law enforcement attention (ibid., pp. 51–64). According to law enforcement sources, the two Cosa Nostra commissions—coordinating the families of the Palermo province and those of the whole region—have been disbanded since the turn of the century, as it had become too dangerous to bring the most important representatives of mafia groups to a single place at any one time and most of them were imprisoned. In contrast, the 'Ndrangheta's commission seems to have gained authority in recent times (DDA Reggio Calabria 2010, pp. 149–441).

The unity of the two confederations does not depend on the coordinating commissions, however. Rather, it is guaranteed by the sharing of common cultural codes and a single organizational formula. According to a model very frequent in pre-modern societies, in fact, the Cosa Nostra and the 'Ndrangheta are "segmentary societies" (Smith 1974, p. 98), that is, they depend on the solidarity deriving from the replication of corporate and cultural forms—a fact that is also highlighted by mafia defectors (e.g., Paoli 2003, pp. 51–52).

Cosa Nostra and 'Ndrangheta also have a sophisticated cultural apparatus, consisting of symbols, rituals, and a set of rules, comparable to the normative order of a simple society (Paoli 2003, pp. 120–140). Two are the subcultural codes inspiriting this apparatus: honor and *omertà*. Traditionally widespread in many pre-modern Mediterranean societies, the code of honor basically requires a man to defend his person and property, including his women (!), by himself, that is, without resorting to law enforcement authorities. The concept of *omertà* is partially overlapping with honor but additionally emphasizes the duty to keep secret the internal affairs—and in Sicily even the existence—of the mafia organization (ibid., pp. 72–75 and 108–112).

The most powerful ritual of both organizations is the initiation ceremony, through which "status and fraternization contracts" (Weber 1978, p. 672) are imposed on new members. That is, the members are required to assume a new identity permanently—to become a "man of honor," to subordinate their previous allegiances, and even life to the mafia membership—and to consider the other members as "brothers" and share what anthropologists call a regime of "generalized reciprocity" with them (Sahlins 1972, pp. 193–200). This regime presupposes altruistic behavior without expecting any short-term reward. As a nineteenth-century observer already noted, "essential character" of mafia groups lies in "mutual aid without limits and without measure, and even in crimes" (Lestingi 1884, p. 453). Because of the expectation of generalized reciprocity, I termed both Cosa Nostra and 'Ndrangheta "mafia brotherhoods" in a previous work (Paoli 2003). Following Collins (2011), who also draws on Weber, mafia groups can be referred to also as "patrimonial alliances." Status and fraternization contracts distinguish mafia groups from contemporary bureaucratic organizations but were typical of European associational, and even city life until the eighteenth century (see Clawson 1989, p. 15, and Weber 1978, chapter 6).

Whereas the status and fraternization contracts underlying mafia memberships look and are old-fashioned, they can be very effective in guaranteeing the cohesion of an illegal group and the members' subordination to their bosses as well as fostering trust and collaboration among the single members and thus helping each of them to achieve their own goals. There is, however, a major constraint associated with them: namely, mafia status and fraternization contracts can be effectively imposed only on persons who are already socialized to a certain mafia subculture and are thus willing to interiorize the mafia group expectations and values. This constraint has first of all limited the pool of suitable candidates for both organizations, which in fact only recruit people of Sicilian or Calabrian descent. Second, the mafia "honor and brotherhood" ideology is increasingly challenged by the growing amount of time and energy mafia members have since the 1970s invested in making money as a result of the modernization process that has taken place in southern Italy since the 1960s and made wealth a precondition for being recognized as honorable (Paoli 2003, pp. 89–100). Third, in Sicily, the Corleonesi—that is, the mafia bosses from the town of Corleone that gained power over the whole Cosa Nostra during the 1980s and remained dominant until Bernardo Provenzano's arrest in 2006—also contributed to further weakening mafia ideology, by ruthlessly killing dozens of mafia members, violating many of Cosa Nostra's rules and thus unwillingly increasing the number of defectors (Stille 1995).

V. Political Dominion

Cosa Nostra and the 'Ndrangheta share another important characteristic, along with several mafia-type Camorra groups. Unlike most other contemporary organized crime groups, these southern Italian organizations do not content themselves with producing and selling illegal goods and services. Though these activities have acquired a growing relevance over the past 30 years, neither the trade in illegal products nor the maximization of profits has been their primary goal in the past or the present (Paoli 2003, pp. 141–164; Europol, 2013, pp. 5–9).

As a matter of fact, it is hardly possible to identify a single goal: Cosa Nostra, the 'Ndrangheta, and the mafia-type Camorra groups are multifunctional organizations; and throughout their history have always engaged, sometimes simultaneously, in power- and profit-oriented activities. In particular, as opposed to the criminal enterprises populating today's illegal markets, the exercise of political domination has always been very important for the ruling bodies of Cosa Nostra and the 'Ndrangheta and mafia-type Camorra groups. These bodies claim, above all, an absolute power over their members. They control every aspect of their members' lives, and they aim to exercise a similar power over the communities where their members reside. A few years ago a mafia defector explained mafia groups' claim to exercise a political dominion in the following way:

> You must remember that the families [i.e., the groups] have their own businesses and that these involve everything going on in the families' territory. For example, a family in Rome would be interested in all the activities there, whether they had to do with politics, public works, extortions, drug deals, etc.... In practice, the family is sovereign, it controls everything happening on its territory (Commissione Antimafia XI 1993, p. 516).

It is important to stress that mafia power had for a long time a higher degree of effectiveness and legitimacy than that of the government. In western Sicily and in southern Calabria mafia groups successfully policed the general population, settling conflicts, recovering stolen goods, and enforcing property rights. Even government institutions, though formally condemning mafia violence and occasionally repressing it, usually came to terms with the representatives of mafia power; in the territories under their control, the maintenance of public order fell, de facto, to the mafia leaders. As the Parliamentary Anti-Mafia Commission (Commissione Antimafia XI 1993, p. 54) finally acknowledged in 1993,

> In practice, the relationships between [government] institutions and mafia took place for many years in the form of relationships between two distinct sovereignties: neither would attack the other as long as each remained within its own boundaries... an attack (by State forces) would be made only in response to an attack by Cosa Nostra, after which they would go back to being good neighbors again.

Even after World War II, mafia bosses particularly in Sicily were considered respectable and suitable partners by many politicians from the dominant Christian Democracy party and were highly appreciated for the voting blocs they could mobilize. According to an estimate based on judicial investigations, 40% to 75% of Christian Democrat members of parliament and about 40% of all those elected in western Sicily between 1950 and 1992 were openly supported by Cosa Nostra (Arlacchi 1995, pp. 15–17; see also Lupo 1996). Giulio Andreotti, one of the most important Italian politicians in the postwar period (he was a member of parliament from 1948 until 2013, prime minister seven times, and a government minister countless times), well symbolizes these "evil pacts." In 2004, Andreotti was found guilty by Italy's Supreme Court of abetting Cosa Nostra until 1980, although he could not be convicted due to the statute of limitation (Corte Suprema di Cassazione 2004). Especially in Sicily, many "men of honor" were themselves actively involved in political life and held important political positions at the city, regional, and even national levels. One of them, Vito Ciancimino, even became mayor of Palermo in 1968 (Ciancimino and La Licata 2010), after being responsible for public works in the administration of another Christian Democrat politician with very close ties to the mafia, Salvo Lima. Thanks to such high-level political patronage, two other "men of honor," the cousins Salvo, were among the wealthiest persons in Sicily, after having obtained the private concession to collect taxes in Sicily with very favorable conditions (Santino 1997).

Even today, although many mafia rules are no longer systematically enforced, mafia groups exercise a certain "sovereignty" through a generalized system of extortion. As a state would do, they tax the main productive activities carried out within their territory. Moreover, whenever *mafiosi* are asked to mediate conflicts, guarantee property rights, and enforce rules compatible with their own legal order, such as those concerning female honor, that is, virginity, they do not hesitate to intervene (Paoli 2003, pp. 154–172). Despite the growing relevance of profit-making activities, contemporary "men of honor" still take these duties seriously. Giovanni Brusca, a high-level Cosa Nostra member who became a mafia witness after his arrest in 1994, recounts that he "helped lots of people recover their cars." If the stolen vehicle had already been taken apart, his men would steal another that was the same model and color, in order to satisfy whoever had asked for Cosa Nostra's help (Lodato 1999, p. 73).

Although ever larger strata of the southern Italian population are increasingly critical of mafia power and ideology, mafia bosses still have few difficulties in finding hidden allies among politicians eager to obtain mafia groups' electoral support. It is enough to say that since the adoption of an ad hoc bill in 1991, over 200 city councils were dismissed, a few two or three times, for being "polluted" or conditioned by mafia groups (Ciccarello 2012; Mete 2010). Proving the latter's persistent influence, 25 such councils were dismissed in 2012 alone, including for the first time a regional capital, Reggio Calabria (Ciccarello 2012). The 'Ndrangheta's control of southern Calabria's political life is, in fact, still particularly strong, not least because of its groups' size. Making up 10% to 20% of the local population, mafia members, their relatives and associates can easily control up to 40% of the votes in many small and medium-sized southern Calabrian municipalities (Arlacchi 1988, pp. 137–140; Commissione Antimafia XVI 2010). In Caserta province, too, the control of the Casalesi clan of the public administration has long been pervasive. As admitted even by the Italian Ministry of the Interior, "the public administration of the territory has aimed to meet camorra's interests at the same time as the corrupt local policy-makers, thanks to their links with criminality, have consolidated their decision-making power and satisfied their personal ambitions" (Ministero dell'Interno 2012b, p. 166).

Mafia groups' political power is not only local. Numerous investigations in the three affected regions have repeatedly demonstrated that even regional and national politicians continue to accept, or even seek, mafia electoral support in exchange for various favors. The former president of the region Sicily, Totò Cuffaro, is serving a seven-year prison sentence for having abetted Cosa Nostra (Corte Suprema di Cassazione 2011). Even a minister and a vice-minister in the latest Berlusconi cabinet from 2008 to 2012 were suspected of abetting mafia groups. Whereas the minister was finally acquitted, the vice minister, Nicola Cosentino, was arrested in March 2013, when he lost his parliamentary immunity, and is facing trial (Del Porto & Sannino 2013). As a matter of fact, even Berlusconi himself has been suspected of complicity with Cosa Nostra, but has never been formally charged (Viviano 1997, 2002).

Whereas mafia groups usually prefer colluding with politicians, some of them and particularly those of the Cosa Nostra have repeatedly directed their military power against government officials or representatives who had become a danger for the groups themselves or no longer respected corrupt agreements. In particular between the late 1970s and the early 1990s, Cosa Nostra assassinated dozens of policemen, prosecutors, judges, and politicians. Cosa Nostra's challenge to state power reached a climax in 1992–1993. In 1992, Cosa Nostra murdered the Palermitan judges Giovanni Falcone and Paolo Borsellino in two spectacular bomb explosions. In 1993, in an effort to demonstrate the national power of the mafia, it organized a series of terrorist bombings in Rome, Florence, and Milan (Stille 1995). Since then mafia groups have realized that such "excellent cadavers," drawing the attention of the public and of law enforcement, are not in their own best interests and have generally abstained from them. In Calabria, however, 'Ndrangheta groups have since 2005 intimidated numerous local politicians, prosecutors, and judges through repeated minatory letters, phone calls and damages to the latter's cars and properties (MInistero dell'Interno 2012b, pp. 71–79).

VI. The Control of Markets

Thanks to their political and military power, mafia groups have frequently been able to gain control of legal markets in their strongholds. Only in its simplest form does extortion merely entail the (forced) transfer of money, the so-called *pizzo*. Often it also involves a payment in kind, the purchase of unnecessary protection services or goods at a higher price or mafiosi's forced participation in a company or public contract. Threats are sometimes only implicit. As Europol (2013, p. 6) notes, "the power is so strong, that if a Mafioso sells a particular brand of coffee to local bars at a higher price he doesn't need to 'threaten' anyone to buy it; his mere presence is enough to guarantee a full purchase."

From the 1950s onward, mafia members—first in Sicily and then in Calabria and Campania as well—set up building companies to gain subcontracts for the clearance of major public works sites and progressively raised their ambitions in the following decades. In the 1980s building companies close to mafia groups were able to secure a large share of the public work contracts in the three regions, by entering in corrupt agreements with government and national building company representatives. In western Sicily, for example, a sort of "duopoly" was established in the late 1980s: the public works market was subject to the complete top-down control of two strong forces—Cosa Nostra and the *comitati d'affari,* that is, cliques of corrupt government and national building company representatives (e.g., Tribunale di Palermo 1991, and other judicial sources discussed in Paoli 2003).

Thanks to better controls, mafia groups' grip on large building projects seems to have declined since then (Ministero dell'Interno 2012b, pp. 327–340; see also La Spina in this volume). However, the groups' reach has diversified considerably and covers all kinds of services for the public administration, from garbage collection and disposal to health sector procurements (e.g., DDA Calabria 2010). Through a combination of violence and the abundant financial resources gained with illegal activities, some mafia groups have also been able to establish control over local market sectors. Starting in the 1970s, mafia groups in specific parts of Sicily and Campania have controlled the local supply of cement. In the 1990s, a series of 'Ndrangheta groups monopolized the meat sector in Reggio Calabria (Paoli 2003, p. 153; see also DDA Reggio Calabria 2010, pp. 2083–2580). Throughout the past two decades the Polverino clan ran a monopoly in the production and sometimes even distribution of several food products in different areas of the Naples province (Ministero dell'Interno 2012b, p. 144). Thanks to the proceeds of these activities and drug trafficking, the bosses of this mafia-type Camorra group were able to accumulate large wealth, and assets worth over 1 billion euros were seized from them on a single occasion in 2011 (Europol 2013, pp. 12–13). Mafia groups are also discovering new sectors, such as that of alternative energy. In 2013 one of the largest Italian wind energy entrepreneurs was identified as a "straw-man" of an important Cosa Nostra boss and all his companies and properties, allegedly worth over 1.3 billion euros, were seized (Palazzolo 2013).

A peculiarity of the Camorra groups is the distribution of a wide range of counterfeited products, which are partially manufactured in the Naples and Caserta provinces and partially imported from China. Camorra groups are also proficient in the counterfeiting of currencies, which they then sell to crime groups all over Europe (Ministero dell'Interno 2012b: 131; Europol 2013, p. 17). Because of the groups' numerous criminal activities and international reach, the Obama administration has identified "the Camorra" (falsely understood as a single organization) as one of the four most threatening organized crime groups from a U.S. perspective (U.S. Department of Treasury 2012).

Mafia's control over legal and illegal markets should not be exaggerated, however. In 2008, Eurispes (2008), an Italian research center, estimated the yearly revenues of the 'Ndrangheta groups to be 36 and 44 billion euros, respectively, with the latter figure corresponding to 2.9% of the Italian Gross Domestic Product (GDP) in 2007. According to Arlacchi, even the lower figure of 36 billion is implausible because it would be higher than the entire Calabrian GDP, and the Ndrangheta's revenues are unlikely to be higher than 1.8 billion euros (*Narcomafie* 2005). The truth is that nobody has the data to estimate even roughly the revenues raised through multiple criminal activities by multiple criminal groups, such as those comprising the 'Ndrangheta or other mafia organizations. However, the Eurispes estimates are not only implausible but also irresponsible, because they are not even based on a recognizable methodology or entail serious methodological mistakes, such as attributing all the revenues of drug selling to mafia groups. In the same way, Confedesercenti estimated that mafia groups' economic activities generated revenues of €137 billion and profits of €104 billion in 2010 (SOS Impresa 2012, pp. 9–10). Despite their abysmal methodological bases, these figures become "mythical numbers" (Reuter 1984) and are referred to constantly by journalists, policy-makers and even law enforcement officials (e.g., Commissione Antimafia XVI 2010, p. 5; Kluver 2007).

Despite their power, mafia groups have not been able to guarantee themselves a monopoly in any sector of the legal or even the illegal economy outside of southern Italy. Let's consider the frequently cited case of the 'Ndrangheta's involvement in cocaine trafficking. It is a fact that 'Ndrangheta groups have since the 1990s been very successful in importing and trafficking large amounts of cocaine—not least thanks to mafiosi who moved to Colombia (*Repubblica* 2013). However, these groups too are just some of the many players active in the European wholesale drugs market. Research done in Belgium (Paoli et al. 2013) and the Netherlands (Kleemans and van de Bunt 2007), where the two largest entry points for Colombian cocaine are located, provides no empirical support for the claim frequently heard in Italy that the 'Ndrangheta has "a de facto monopoly on the import of Colombian cocaine into Europe" (Commissione Antimafia XV 2008, p. 19).

Other studies show that, when mafia groups move to Northern Italy or abroad, they rarely seek to exercise a political dominion and often merely engage in profit-making legal and illegal activities, even if they seek alliances with local entrepreneurs (Campana 2011)—a point admitted even by Europol (2013, p. 8). Outside their strongholds and 'Ndrangheta's older settlements in Canada and Australia, southern Italian mafia groups have rarely developed ties with politicians or government officials. However, the dismissal of five city councils in Italy's Centre North, three of them in 2012, demonstrates that they can do so and is a worrying signal (Ciccarello 2012; Mete 2010).

Even the investment of crime proceeds in foreign properties or companies is too often mistaken for control of local market sectors. The very size of these investments is sometimes exaggerated in the Italian debate. For example, in 2004 it was emphatically reported that an 'Ndrangheta family had bought an entire neighborhood in Brussels with drug money (*Repubblica* 2004). Subsequent investigations made by the Belgian police proved that the claim had no empirical basis (KPLD 2011, p. 22). Moreover, the mere fact that mafia groups invest crime proceeds in foreign countries does not automatically imply that the groups are also able to exert some sort of undue control on a specific economic sector.

In the case of Cosa Nostra, its power is not unchallenged even within its strongholds. Given the extreme rigidity of their recruitment policies, in fact, Cosa Nostra families often find themselves in a minority position with their local competitors and are hence unable to control the entire underworld. This difficulty was admitted already in the 1990s by the high-ranking Cosa Nostra member-turned-state witness, Brusca:

> Many believe that Cosa Nostra heads all criminal activities. That in Palermo or in Sicily every illegal activity is controlled by the mafiosi. People believe that prostitution and burglaries, bank robberies, and car thefts are all entries in the budget of the Mafia Inc. Those that I have just listed are external activities, known about, tolerated, and controlled by men of honor. But they are separate worlds, which only rarely come into contact with each other. In some cases, there might be some collaboration, but this is only in very special cases (Lodato 1999, p. 67).

Whatever the uncertainties about the extent of mafia groups' wealth and the reach of their economic power, there are no doubts that southern Italian citizens and companies pay a high price for mafia groups' control of the local economy. Campania, Calabria, and Sicily are the poorest regions of the country, have a GDP per capita that is about half of that recorded in the richest regions in the North and, with the exception of Sicily, have been most seriously hit by the current global financial crisis (Giannola 2013). According to an analysis made by Censis (2009, pp. 42–47), at least 30% of southern Italian companies are negatively affected by mafia-type organized crime, for example, because they have to pay higher business costs or face restrictions in business choices concerning suppliers, workers, and customers. Southern Italian companies also face indirect costs. According to a Bank of Italy study, companies located in mafia groups' strongholds pay interest rates up to 30% higher than those located in non-mafia areas (Bonaccorsi di Patti

2009). In another Bank of Italy study, the onset of mafia-type organized crime in the two southern Italian regions of Basilicata and Apulia, which were considered immune to it until the 1970s, was reported to have resulted in reduced growth of 15% in GDP per capita in 30 years, largely due to lower private investments (Pinotti 2010).

VII. The Comeback of Anti-Mafia?

The murders of judges Falcone and Borsellino in 1992 represent a turning-point in the century-long relation between mafia groups and the larger society. In fact, they set in motion an unprecedented reaction by law enforcement agencies and a broad portion of the southern Italian population.

The law enforcement reaction profited from both the great improvement in knowledge about Cosa Nostra and investigative methods achieved with the first Palermo maxi-trial and a series of new acts passed in 1991 and 1992. In addition to the bill allowing the dismissal of city councils, these acts established a new police agency specialized in the fight against mafia-type organized crime, the Direzione Investigativa Antimafia (DIA) and an agency favoring information exchanges among the sections of the local prosecutors' offices specialized in mafia cases, the Direzione Nazionale Antimafia (DNA). They also created a witness protection program and set up a very harsh prison regime for the heads of mafia groups (known as 41bis in Italy; see Paoli 2007, and La Spina in this volume for a review).

For a few years after 1992–1993, law enforcement action was very intense and effective, as recognized even by the then leader of Cosa Nostra, Bernardo Provenzano, in a wiretapped conversation (Ministero dell'Interno 2001, p. 10). Almost all Sicilian mafia bosses, some of whom had been on the run for decades, were arrested, along with hundreds of their associates. It is enough to say that DIA (2013) alone issued over 9,436 arrest warrants between 1992 and 2011, and 1,897 of them affected people associated with Cosa Nostra or other Sicilian crime groups. Remembering the earlier estimate of 2,000 Cosa Nostra "made" members, the DIA figure implies that the chances of being arrested have become very high, especially if one recalls that three other police agencies are involved in anti-mafia action in Italy.

Whereas the pressure initially focused on Cosa Nostra, it progressively extended to Camorra and 'Ndrangheta groups as well. Over the 20-year period, for example, DIA (2013) also issued 2,799 and 2,582 arrest warrants against Camorra and 'Ndrangheta members, respectively. Mafia members were not only arrested but also convicted and given long prison sentences. As of June 2013, for example, 6,758 Italian citizens were imprisoned for the offense of mafia-type criminal organizations (art. 416bis of the Italian Penal Code) (Ministero della Giustizia 2013), and 645 of them were subject, as of December 2009, to the special incarceration regime for mafia members (Ministero della Giustizia 2011).

The financial drain has also been unprecedented. Again, DIA (2013) alone seized assets worth 11 billion euros from the three sets of mafia groups over the 1992–2011 period and confiscated 1.8 billion. For the first time moreover, prosecutors did not only charge mafia members but also their political protectors. Whereas the most prominent trials against Andreotti and Corrado Carnevale, the former president of a section of Italy's Supreme Court, largely backfired, several other lower-level politicians and government officials have been brought to trial accused of favoring mafia groups and some of them have been convicted—such as the already-mentioned former president of the Region Sicily, Cuffaro and Marcello Dell'Utri, formerly Berlusconi's right-hand man (Ziniti 2013).

Many of these high-level investigations have been made possible by the contributions of former mafia members turned witnesses (known as *pentiti* in Italy). At its peak in 1996, 1,214 *pentiti* were under the state protection program; after a 35% decline in the following years due to many polemics concerning *pentiti's* judicial contributions and the adoption of restrictive amendments to the witness protection program, the *pentiti's* number started growing again, reaching 1,093 in 2011 (Ministero dell'Interno 2012a). The *pentiti's* boom in the 1990s and their recent growth suggest that the choice to defect is not only the result of a cost-benefit assessment at the moment of a *mafioso's* arrest but also reflects the long-term delegitimation process undergone by mafia groups (Arlacchi 2010; Paoli 2003, pp. 94–100). Significantly, in recent years, several female relatives of mafia bosses have decided to break with their past and family and filed for protection (Abbate 2013).

Cosa Nostra, the 'Ndrangheta, and Camorra groups have responded in several ways to the intensification of anti-mafia repression. While Cosa Nostra gave up the open challenge to state sovereignty pursued in the early 1990s, all three sets of mafia groups have radically reduced the level of homicidal violence. Between the peak years of 1991 and 2011, in fact, mafia murders decreased by 93% and 97% in Calabria and Sicily, respectively, and by 88% even in Campania, despite the anarchy typical of Camorra groups (see Table 5.1).

More generally, mafia groups have also tended to focus on entrepreneurial activities that do not raise much social alarm, such as extortions, usury, manipulation of public tenders and, to the extent possible, drug trafficking. In Sicily, changes were also recorded in the very organization of extortions. According to the DIA, all producers, and not just the large companies as in the past, are now asked to pay a contribution to Cosa Nostra, but contributions are kept low to prevent popular resentment from reaching critical dimensions (Ministero dell'Interno 2006, pp. 20–21).

The societal reaction to the 1992 murders is part of a broad long-term process of delegitimation of mafia subculture and values, which started after the Second World War. This was initially promoted by small, primarily Sicilian, elites but gained for the first time popular support after the murder of General Dalla Chiesa in Palermo in 1982. After a period of retreat in the 1980s, the anti-mafia movement strongly expanded from the 1990s onward, mobilizing large numbers of people in Sicily and, to a lower extent, also in other southern Italian regions, involving new actors such as the Italian, and above all the Sicilian, Employers' Association and the Catholic Church, which had previously remained silent, and leading to the establishment of numerous anti-mafia and anti-racket associations (see Libera 2013 and Santino 2000 for a history and a general overview). As a result of this slow but probably inexorable delegitimaztion process, traditional mafia

Table 5.1 Recorded Murders and Mafia Murders in Campania, Calabria, and Sicily—1990–2011

	Campania		Calabria		Sicily	
	Murders	Mafia Murders	Murders	Mafia Murders	Murders	Mafia Murders
1990	347	201	326	141	428	150
1991	378	232	277	165	481	253
1992	290	181	151	46	399	200
1993	197	86	126	43	252	85
1994	165	65	121	42	249	90
1995	228	113	95	24	223	88
1996	204	94	103	30	180	66
1997	185	103	100	32	131	34
1998	199	107	85	28	140	35
1999	151	65	82	26	116	28
2000	163	73	84	34	86	13
2001	127	57	88	28	82	20
2002	109	47	61	17	70	11
2003	125	70	69	26	61	10
2004	178	99	76	18	65	8
2005	128	67	69	23	70	11
2006	140	67	61	19	62	15
2007	152	85	59	16	72	12
2008	111	59	76	22	49	12
2009	104	49	64	11	63	19
2010	62	18	60	24	60	10
2011	61	27	59	11	59	8
Difference 1991–2011	−84%	−88%	−79%	−93%	−88%	97%

Source: Istat, annual and I.stat 2013.

values of honor and *omertà* no longer find public supporters, and even the children of mafia bosses publicly declare today to be against the mafia (Arlacchi 2010, p. 268).

However, other typical Italian values and institutions, such as the family and patronage ties, remain broadly accepted and constitute the shared cultural background of *mafiosi* and considerable parts of the Italian society as well as the basis for corrupt agreements between *mafiosi* and politicians and particularistic exchanges between the latter and considerable parts of the southern Italian electorate. In regions affected by chronic unemployment and sharply hit by the post-2008 economic crisis, a career in the mafia or crime also looks attractive to many youngsters with poor education and few hopes of finding a job in the legal economy, and who thus provide an inexhaustible reserve army of criminal manpower. Especially in the Naples area, members of the Camorra groups—with their lavish mansions, flashy lifestyles, and exorbitant expenses—are still role models for many youngsters from marginalized neighborhoods (Europol 2013, p. 12).

Despite the recent law enforcement successes in the fight against mafia groups, therefore, the road ahead is still a long one, and it would be a terrible mistake to claim premature victory.

NOTE

1. In contrast, the Italian American (La) Cosa Nostra, which stemmed from its Sicilian counterpart, became fully independent as early as the 1930s, even though some members of the two organizations have occasionally continued to conduct business together and help each other over the decades (see Albanese's chapter in this volume for an account of the Italian American mafia). A Sicilian Cosa Nostra group, the Cuntrera Caruana, operated primarily from Venezuela and Canada between the 1970s and the 1990s (Blickman 1997), when it was largely disbanded by law enforcement action. With that exception, no other Sicilian mafia group is known to have moved its home seat outside the island, even though single *mafiosi* have migrated temporarily or permanently (Europol 2013, p. 10).

BIBLIOGRAPHY

Abbate, Lirio. 2013. Fimmine ribelli: Come le donne salveranno il paese dalla 'ndrangheta. Milan: Rizzoli.

Arlacchi, Pino. [1983] 1988. *Mafia Business: The Mafia Ethic and the Spirit of Capitalism.* Oxford: Oxford University Press.

Arlacchi, Pino. 1995. *Il processo. Giulio Andreotti sotto accusa a Palermo.* Milan: Rizzoli.

Arlacchi, Pino. 2010. Postfazione: L'occasione perduta a *Gli uomini del disonore: La mafia siciliana nella vita del grande pentito Antonino Calderone.* Milan: Il Saggiatore: 263–299.

Blickman, Tom. 1997. The Rothschilds of the Mafia on Aruba. *Transnational Organized Crime,* 3(2), 50–89.

Bonaccorsi di Patti, Emilia. 2009. Weak Institutions and Credit Availability: The Impact of Crime on Bank Loans. Occasional Paper No. 52/2009, Banca d'Italia.

Campana, Pietro. 2011. Eavesdropping on the Mob: The Functional Diversification of Mafia Activities across Territories. *European Journal of Criminology.* 8(3), 1–16.

Censis. 2009. *Il condizionamento delle mafie sull'economia, sulla società e sulle istituzioni del Mezzogiorno.* Roma: Censis.

Ciancimino, Massimo and Francesco La Licata. 2010. *Don Vito. Le relazione segrete tra Stato e mafia nel racconto di un testimone d'eccezione.* Milan: Feltrinelli.

Ciccarello, Elisa. 2012. Mafia, governo Monti ha sciolto 25 comuni: "Con Cancellieri niente mediazioni." *Il fatto quotidiano.* December 7. Available at: http://www.ilfattoquotidiano. it/2012/12/07/mafia-governo-monti-ha-sciolto-25-comuni-cantone-con-cancellieri-niente-mediazioni/438429/

Ciconte, Enzo. 1992. '*Ndrangheta dall'Unità a oggi.* Rome: Laterza.

Clawson, Mary A. 1989. *Constructing Brotherhood: Class, Gender, and Fraternalism.* Princeton, N.J.: Princeton University Press.

Collins, Randall. 2011. Patrimonial Alliances and Failures of State Penetration: A Historical Dynamic of Crime, Corruption, Gangs, and Mafias. *The Annals of the American Academy of Political and Social Science* 636: 16–31.

Commissione Antimafia XI, Commissione parlamentare d'inchiesta sul fenomeno della mafia e sulle altre associazioni similari. 1992. Audizione del collaboratore di giustizia Leonardo Messina. December 4, XI Legislature. Rome: Camera dei Deputati.

Commissione Antimafia XI. 1993. Relazione sui rapporti tra mafia e politica con note integrative, doc. XXIII, no. 2, XI Legislature. Rome: Camera dei Deputati.

Commissione Antimafia XV, Commissione parlamentare d'inchiesta sul fenomeno della criminalità organizzata mafiosa o similare. 2008. Relazione annuale sulla 'Ndrangheta. Doc. XXIII, n. 3, XV legislature.

Commissione Antimafia XVI, Commissione parlamentare d'inchiesta sul fenomeno della mafia e sulle altre associazioni criminali, anche straniere. 2010. Audizione del Procuratore Distrettuale Antimafia di Reggio Calabria, dottor Giuseppe Pignatone. September 21. XVI legislature. http://www.parlamento.it/service/PDF/PDFServer/DF/231982.pdf.

Corte Suprema di Cassazione. 2004. Sentenza n. 9691/2004.

Corte Suprema di Cassazione. 2011. Sentenza 19 aprile 2011 n. 15583.

DDA Reggio Calabria, Procura della Repubblica presso il Tribunale di Reggio Calabria, Direzione Distrettuale Antimafia. 2010. Decreto di fermo di indiziato di delitto—artt. 384 e segg. c.p.p.—nei confronti di A. A.M. + 156.

Del Porto, Dario and Cochita Sannino. 2013. Cosentino va in carcere—"Non partecipo al processo." *La Repubblica Napoli*, March 15. http://napoli.repubblica.it/cronaca/2013/03/15/news/cosentino_ultime_ore_oggi_pomeriggio_l_arresto-54589256/

Di Lello, Giuseppe. 1994. *Giudici*. Palermo: Sellerio.

DIA, Direzione Investigativa Antimafia. 2013. Valori dei sequestri e delle confische dal 1992—2011 and dati complessivi ordinanze di custodia cautelare. http://www.interno.gov.it/dip_ps/dia/page/rilevazioni_statistiche.html.

Eco, Umberto. [1971] 1993. "Beati Paoli" e l'ideologia del romanzo "popolare." Introduction to L. Natoli (W. Galt). *I Beati Paoli*. Reprint, Palermo: Flaccovio.

Eurispes. 2008. *'Ndrangheta Holding—Dossier 2008*. Rome: Eurispes.

Europol, 2013. Threat Assessment: Italian Organized Crime. June.

Gambetta, Diego. 1993. *The Sicilian Mafia: The Business of Private Protection*. Cambridge: Harvard University Press.

Giannola, Adriano. 2013. Il rilancio dell'economia meridionale. Slides presented on May 13 at the workshop "Il rilancio dell'economia meridionale." *Naples*. http://lnx.svimez.info/images/INTERVENTI/PRESIDENTE/2013_05_09_napoli_slides.pdf. Accessed July 5 2013.

Gratteri, Nicola and Antonio Nicaso. 2010. *Fratelli di sangue: storie, boss e affari della 'ndrangheta, la mafia più potente del mondo*. Milan: Oscar Mondadori.

Hess, Henner. [1970] 1973. *Mafia and Mafiosi: The Structure of Power*. Farnborough: Saxon House.

I.stat. 2003. Delitti denunciati dalle forze di polizia all'autorità giudiziaria. http://dati.istat.it/Index.aspx?DataSetCode=DCCV_DELITTIPS

Istat. Annual. *Statistische giudiziarie penali*. Rome: Istat.

Kleemans, Edward and Henk van de Bunt. 2007. *Georganiseerde criminaliteit in Nederland*. The Hague: Boom.

KLPD, National Crime Squad. 2011. *The 'Ndrangheta in the Netherlands: The Nature, Criminal Activities, and Modi Operandi on Dutch Territory*. N.p.: KLPD—National Crime Squad.

Kluver, Henning. 2007. Saviano: la Germania si svegli la mafia è una holding europea. *La Repubblica*. August 21: 27. http://ricerca.repubblica.it/repubblica/archivio/repubblica/2007/08/21/saviano-la-germania-si-svegli-la-mafia.html?ref=search.

Libera. 2013. Chi siamo. http://www.libera.it/flex/cm/pages/ServeBLOB.php/L/IT/IDPagina/41

Lodato, Saverio. 1999. *Ho ucciso Giovanni Falcone. La confessione di Giovanni Brusca*. Milan: Mondadori.

Lupo, Salvatore. 1996. *Andreotti, la mafia, la storia d'Italia*. Rome: Donzelli.

Marino, Giuseppe C. 1988. *L'ideologia sicilianista*. Palermo: Flaccovio.

Marino, Paolo. 1988. *Per la storia della 'Ndrànghita*. Rome: Dipartimento di studi glottoantropologici dell'Università di Roma La Sapienza.

Mete, Vittorio. [2010]. Decreti di scioglimento dei consigli comunali per province ed anni (maggio 1991—settembre 2009). http://www.avvisopubblico.it/categorie/dati_statistiche/allegati/comuni-sciolti-per-mafia_anni-1991-2009.pdf

Ministero dell'Interno. 2001. Relazione semestrale sull'attività svolta e i risultati conseguiti dalla Direzione Investigativa Antimafia nel secondo semestre del 2000.

Ministero dell'Interno. 2002. Relazione semestrale sull'attività svolta e i risultati conseguiti dalla Direzione Investigativa Antimafia nel primo semestre del 2002.

Ministero dell'Interno. 2006. Relazione semestrale sull'attività svolta e i risultati conseguiti dalla Direzione Investigativa Antimafia nel secondo semestre del 2005.

Ministero dell'Interno. 2012a. Relazione al Parlamento sulle speciali misure di protezione, sulla loro efficacia e sulle modalità generali di applicazione — 1 luglio—31 dicembre 2011.

Ministero dell'Interno. 2012b. Relazione semestrale sull'attività svolta e i risultati conseguiti dalla Direzione Investigativa Antimafia—gennaio—giugno 2012.

Ministero della Giustizia. 2011. Anno giudiziario 2010: relazione del Ministero—Dipartimento dell'amministrazione penitenziaria. Rome: Ministero della Giustizia.

Ministero della Giustizia. 2013. Detenuti presenti per tipologia di reato. Situazione al 30 Giugno 2013. http://www.giustizia.it/giustizia/it/mg_1_14_1.wp?facetNode_1=0_2&previsiousPage=mg_1_14&contentId=SST935038

Mori, Cesare. [1932] 1993. *Con la mafia ai ferri corti*. Reprint, Naples: Flavio Pagano.

Narcomafie. 2005. 'Ndrangheta, Arlacchi contesta l'Eurispes. November 10. http://www.narcomafie.it/tag/pino-arlacchi/

Natoli, Luigi, under the pseudonym of William Galt. [1908–9] 1993. *I Beati Paoli*. Reprint, Palermo: Flaccovio.

Palazzolo, Salvo. 2013. Confisca miliardaria al re dell'eolico. *La Repubblica*. April 4: 20. http://ricerca.repubblica.it/repubblica/archivio/repubblica/2013/04/04/confisca-miliardaria-al-re-delleolico.html?ref=search

Paoli, Letizia. 2002. The Paradoxes of Organised Crime. *Crime, Law and Social Change*, 37(1), 51–97.

Paoli, Letizia. 2003. *Mafia Brotherhoods: Organized Crime, Italian Style*. New York: Oxford University Press.

Paoli, Letizia. 2007. Mafia and Organised Crime: The Unacknowledged Successes of Law Enforcement. *West European Politics*, 30 (4), 854–880.

Paoli, Letizia, Victoria A. Greenfield and Andries Zoutendijk. 2013. The Harm of Cocaine Trafficking. Applying a New Framework for Assessment. *Journal of Drug Issues* 43 (4), 407–436.

Pezzino, Paolo. 1987. Stato violenza società. Nascita e sviluppo del paradigma mafioso. In *La Sicilia*, edited by Maurice Aymard and Giuseppe Giarrizzo. Turin: Einaudi.

Pinotti, Paolo. 2012. The Economic Costs of Organized Crime: Evidence from Southern Italy. Banca d'Italia Working Paper 868.

Pitrè, Giuseppe. [1889] 1993. *Usi e costumi, credenze e pregiudizi del popolo siciliano*. Reprint, Catania: Clio.

Repubblica, La. 2004. A Bruxelles un intero quartiere comprato dalla 'ndrangheta. http://www.repubblica.it/2004/c/sezioni/cronaca/narcotra/narcotra/narcotra.html.

Repubblica, La. 2013. Colombia, arrestato Roberto Pannunzi, il "Pablo Escobar" della 'ndrangheta. July 6. http://www.repubblica.it/cronaca/2013/07/06/news/colombia_arrestato_roberto_pannunzi_il_boss_della_ndrangheta-62481776/?ref=HREC1-5

Reuter, Peter. 1984. The (continued) vitality of mythical numbers. *Public Interest* 75 (Spring), 135–147.

Sahlins, M. D. 1972. Stone Age Economics. Chicago: Aldine Atherton.

Sales, Isaia. 2001. 'Camorra': In *Appendice 2000*, edited by Enciclopedia Treccani. Rome: Treccani, 468–469.

Santino, Umberto. 1993. *La camorra. Le camorre.* Rome: Editori Riuniti.

Santino, Umberto. 1994. *La borghesia mafiosa. Materiali di un percorso di analisi.* Palermo: Centro siciliano di documentazione Giuseppe Impastato.

Santino, Umberto. 2000. *Storia del movimento antimafia. Dalla lotta di classe all'impegno civile.* Rome: Editori Riuniti.

Santino, Umberto. 1997. *L'alleanza e il compromesso. Mafia e politica dai tempi di Lima e Andreotti ai giorni nostri.* Soveria Mannelli: Rubbettino.

Saviano, Roberto. [2006] 2008. *Gomorrah. A Personal Journey into the Violent International Empire of Naples' Organized Crime System.* New York: Picador.

Sahlins, Marshall. 1972. *Stone Age Economics.* Aldine Atherton: Chicago.

Smith, M. G. 1974. *Corporations and Society.* [London]: Duckworth.

SOS Impresa. 2012. Il bilancio della mafia SpA—Audizione in Commissione Parlamentare Antimafia: June 13. Online available: http://www.sosimpresa.it/userFiles/File/Documenti6/13_06_2012_audizione_in_commissione_antimafia.pdf.

Stille, Alexander. 1995. *Excellent Cadavers: The Mafia and the Death of the First Italian Republic.* London: Jonathan Cape.

Suchan, Pietro. 2001. "La criminalità organizzata cinese in Toscana," in Monica Massari and Stefano Becucci, eds. *Mafie nostre, mafie loro. Criminalità organizzata italiana e straniera al Centro Nord.* Edited by Monica Massari and Stefano Becucci Milan, Comunità.

Tribunale di Palermo. 1985. Ordinanza-sentenza di rinvio a giudizio nei confronti di Abbate Giovanni + 706. November 8. Republished as 1986. *Mafia: L'atto di accusa dei giudici di Palermo.* Edited by Corrado Stajano Rome: Editori Riuniti.

Tribunale Ordinario di Milano. 1991. Ordinanza di custodia cautelare in carcere nei confronti di Morici Serafino + 4. July 9.

Tribunale Ordinario di Milano. 2001. Ordinanza di applicazione di misura coercitiva nei confronti di A.F. + 159. N. 43733/06 R.G.N.R.

U.S. Department of Treasury. 2012. Treasury Sanctions Members of the Camorra. August 1. http://www.treasury.gov/press-center/press-releases/Pages/tg1666.aspx.

Viviano, Francesco. 1997. Mafia, il giudicie archivia l'inchiesta su Berlusconi. *La Repubblica.* April 1: 12. http://ricerca.repubblica.it/repubblica/archivio/repubblica/1997/04/01/mafia-il-giudice-archivia-inchiesta-su.html?ref=search

Viviano, Francesco. 2002. Stragi mafiose il gip archivia. *La Repubblica.it.* April 5: http://www.repubblica.it/online/politica/falcone/archiviato/archiviato.html?ref=search.

Weber, Max. [1922] 1978. *Economy and Society,* edited by Günther Roth and Claus Wittich. Berkeley: University of California Press.

Ziniti, Alessandra. 2013. Dell'Utri, condanna a 7 anni per concorso esterno alla mafia. Il Pg: rischio fuga, arréstatelo. *La Repubblica,* March 26: 10. http://ricerca.repubblica.it/repubblica/archivio/repubblica/2013/03/26/dellutri-condanna-anni-per-concorso-esterno-alla.html?ref=search

CHAPTER 6

....

THE ITALIAN-AMERICAN MAFIA

....

JAY S. ALBANESE

THE Mafia in America became a concern that paralleled the immigration wave from Italy during the late 1800s. It was closely associated with victimization within Italian communities in northeastern US cities. National interest in Italian-American organized crime grew after the Prohibition era, and it was ultimately followed by powerful new federal laws to infiltrate organized crime groups, numerous criminal informants coming forward to testify, and many significant convictions, which has weakened the influence of Italian-American groups in American organized crime. The activities of these organized crime groups have remained strikingly similar over the years, although changes in opportunity and criminal markets have impacted Mafia operations, which continue today.

I. "Mafia" in America

....

"Mafia" in the United States can be traced to the murder of David Hennessey in 1890. Hennessey was superintendent of Police in New Orleans when he was shot and seriously wounded on his front doorstep. His deathbed statement was said to be either "Sicilians have done for me" or "Dagoes," which was interpreted as indicating an Italian connection with his death. Although no connection between a Mafia and this shooting was ever established, many in North America assumed that some sort of Mafia existed in Italy (or Sicily), and that some of its members were probably included in the mass of immigrants from southern Italy during the 1880s. As a result, a common explanation given for violent crime was lax immigration controls, which permitted entry to North America of numerous ex-convicts and criminals escaping from Italian justice (Pitkin and Cordasco 1977, pp. 22–30). It was also claimed at that time that many murders of Italians in New Orleans remained unsolved—fueling belief in a Mafia. However, few suspicious Italian deaths have been documented during this period (Albini 1971, chap. 5; Nelli 1981, chap. 3; Smith

1990, p. 32). Local feelings were very much anti-immigrant at this time, however, so it is not surprising that Hennessey's shooting stirred anti-Italian feelings, and in some ways, the assertion of an imported Italian criminals is similar to allegations made against more recent immigrant groups to the United States, such as Cubans, Mexicans, and Asians, that are viewed as disproportionately criminal (Knobel 1997).

A number of subsequent historical investigations have been undertaken to examine more closely the nature of Mafia in Italy. Book-length historical investigations involved examination of old police reports, trial transcripts, official inquiries, newspaper accounts, and interviews. There is disagreement about the extent and scope of organization, but a general consensus exists that there existed the Mafioso type, who emerged to enforce contracts for landowners and businesses that a weak government could not carry out. Furthermore, these Mafiosi often organized locally and formed continuing criminal enterprises in support of extortion and related activities (Albini 1971; Arlacchi 1986, 1993; Blok 1996; Hess 1986, 1998; Paoli 2003; Walston 1986).

II. City Gangs and Prohibition

After the Hennessey shooting in 1890, public interest in a Mafia quickly faded in the United States. In fact, during the 25-year period from 1918 to 1943 the word *Mafia* appeared in the *New York Times* only four times.

During the early 1900s, concerns were expressed about organized crime in the United States, but not about Mafia. John Landesco's work for the Illinois Crime Survey in 1929 examined "Crime in Chicago" and found crime "organized on a scale and with resources unprecedented in the history of Chicago." He found the "leading gangsters were practically immune from punishment," and that organized crime had corrupted local politicians (Landesco 1968, p. 277). The report identified gangsters by name, including: Giacomo "Big Jim" Colosimo, who ran the rackets up until his murder in 1920, followed by John Torrio, who organized a boot-legging syndicate from 1920 to 1924, followed by Al Capone, who consolidated all forms of commercialized vice and gambling in Chicago during the late 1920s (Landesco 1968; Bergeen 1994).

Ironically, concern about these "gangsters" was seen as a local phenomenon rather than a problem of national significance. Keep in mind that this was the era of Prohibition (the period between 1920 and 1933 in the United States when the laws, passed pursuant to the Eighteenth Amendment to the US Constitution [1920], prohibited the making or selling of alcoholic liquors). Prohibition is probably more responsible than any single event for the emergence of strong organized crime groups. Organized crime developed around the underground market created by the void left between public demand for alcoholic beverages (and the other vices of gambling and prostitution) and the prohibition of them.

Illegal alcohol manufacturing, smuggling, and operation of speakeasies were predominant forms of organized crime during this period as Prohibition took effect in

January 1920. Brewers of alcoholic beverages had a choice in 1920: shut down, convert their equipment to make legal one-half percent liquor, or do business as usual by becoming partners with questionable people who would market their product. Organized crime groups slowly evolved into more sophisticated criminal enterprises, which was necessary due to competition from other criminal entrepreneurs, and to evade law enforcement and bribe public officials when necessary. Gang warfare was common, as mostly first- or second-generation immigrants attempted to make their fortune. In Chicago, Giacomo "Big Jim" Colosimo was murdered by Johnny Torrio's people before Prohibition was six months old. Torrio was later shot five times, but he lived because his assassin ran out of bullets. He left for New York to become a mentor to the up-and-coming Lucky Luciano. Hymie Weis controlled part of Chicago's vices with Al Capone as his primary competitor. Weis was killed by Al Capone's gang in 1926 (Browning and Gerassi 1980; Morgan 1985). Given the profits from the Prohibition era, the Chicago "Outfit" (the term used to describe the Italian-American organized crime group there) was a powerful force in Chicago crime and politics for the next 50 years (Russo 2003).

In New York, the story was similar. Arnold Rothstein organized the vices there, and he mentored such infamous figures as Frank Costello and Jack "Legs" Diamond. An attempt on the life of Frank Costello failed. Legs Diamond was shot and recovered, only to be challenged by Dutch Schultz. Rothstein himself was ultimately murdered in 1928, a crime blamed on Legs Diamond. Dutch Schultz was later murdered by Charles "Lucky" Luciano in 1935 (Peterson 1983; Jacobs 1990; Feder and Joesten 1972).

It may be difficult to remember who murdered whom during this period, but the general point is clear: Organized crime in the early 1900s was centered on the vices (especially alcohol), involved a great deal of corruption to maintain a degree of immunity from law enforcement, and the competition to control these vices was violent, at least in selected large cities. This violence, and the reign of these gangs, declined somewhat as the Great Depression took hold in 1930, law enforcement slowly became professionalized and more effective, and Prohibition came to an end in December 1933 (Monaco and Bascom 1991; Ness 1957). The Great Depression took much of their customers' income, and the repeal of Prohibition dried up the huge illegal alcohol market. In spite of these setbacks, however, many organized crime groups maintained themselves largely on the illicit profits to be made through illegal gambling, which also supported loansharking.

It is important to note that not all this activity occurred within Italian-American groups; evidence of interethnic criminal activity throughout the history of organized crime in America is ample. A historical study of the early-20th- century illicit drug trade in New York found major players with Jewish backgrounds but also "notable is the evidence of interethnic cooperation" among New York's criminals. This included involvement of Italians, Greeks, Irish, and blacks, who did not always work within their own ethnics group. Instead, these criminals were "in reality criminal justice entrepreneurs" whose criminal careers were not within a particular organization but were involved in a "web of small but efficient organizations" (Block 1979, p. 95). A historical examination of early opium smuggling networks in California concluded that the operations were "a multiethnic endeavor involving actors with various ethnic origins" (McIllwain 1998).

More recent studies have produced similar findings. An ethnography of the underground drug market by Patricia Adler in "Southwest County" found the market to be "largely competitive" rather than "visibly structured." She found participants "entered the market, transacted their deals, [and] shifted from one type of activity to another," responding to the demands of the market rather than through ethnic structures (Adler 1985, p. 80). A study of illegal gambling and loansharking in New York found economic considerations dictated entry and exit from the illicit marketplace. The criminal enterprises were "not monopolies in the classic sense or subject to control by some external organization" (Reuter 1983, p. 175; Reuter and Rubinstein 1983, p. 52). Like other investigations of organized crime groups, local criminal market forces and opportunities led to operations that extended beyond ethnic ties in producing ongoing criminal enterprises (Block 1978; Lombardo 2002).

III. Raising National Concern

It was not until 1950 that the Mafia made a dramatic return to the headlines in the United States. Senator Estes Kefauver chaired the Special Senate Committee to Investigate Organized Crime in the United States (Kefauver Committee). The committee held public hearings in major cities across the country over the course of a year. Kefauver's investigation received much attention because television carried live coverage of the hearings (at a time when television was new and viewers had few channels from which to choose). A number of law enforcement officials testified, as did a number of individuals with criminal records, but no objective information was produced about the true nature of organized crime in the United States, and no convictions resulted. However, the Kefauver Committee concluded: "There is a sinister criminal organization known as the Mafia operating throughout the country with ties in other nations in the opinion of the committee" (US Senate 1951). These high-profile hearings served to shift the nature of public concern about organized crime in America from a local issue of city gangs to a national issue (Moore 1974; Bell 1953; Turkus and Feder, 1951).

A second event during the 1950s further raised alarm about the nature of Italian-American organized crime in the United States. On November 19, 1957, the New York Times reported on the front page, "65 Hoodlums Seized in a Raid and Run Out of Upstate Village." Sixty-five Italian-Americans, some with criminal records, were gathered at the home of Joseph Barbara in Apalachin, New York. A New York State Police officer had set up a roadblock on the only route away from the house because a large number of unknown guests were visiting a man about whom the officer had long been suspicious. The police had no evidence to bring against the men as they left or against those who were found later inexplicably in the woods adjoining the Barbara property. Police learned the names, addresses, and stated occupations of 58 men and were able to determine whether any were wanted by police as well as those who possessed valid driver's licenses and pistol permits. Police also searched each vehicle, but they found nothing incriminating. So the police had to let them go. Subsequently, a lengthy investigation of this incident was held and those present were called to testify at investigative hearings, but no convictions for criminal conduct ever resulted. Like the Kefauver hearings, therefore, the Apalachin incident served to revive public interest in the Mafia without offering any new information (New York State 1958; Smith 1990; *United States v. Buffalino et al.* 285 F. 2d 408 [2d Cir. 1960]).

IV. "Cosa Nostra" In America

Only a few years later, in September 1963, Joseph Valachi appeared before the US Senate Subcommittee on Investigations and testified to the existence of an organization made up of Italian Americans in the United States. Valachi was an admitted lower-level criminal associated with the Genovese crime "family" in New York City. His testimony, together with more detailed information obtained by federal investigators during months of interviews with Valachi, constituted the first time someone had ever admitted "belonging to or openly talk about a huge criminal conspiracy in this country, indeed an entire subculture of evil…the Cosa Nostra" (Maas 1969, p. 1). In addition to providing his view of the structure of organized crime in the United States, Valachi also discussed the processes by which this structure engaged in crime in a systematic manner.

Valachi had been incarcerated on a drug charge, and he believed he was marked to be killed in prison by his "boss," Vito Genovese. To prevent that from happening, he killed a fellow inmate who turned out to be an uninvolved bystander. To escape the death penalty for his crime, and feeling betrayed by his organization, Valachi agreed to cooperate with federal investigators.

The two major subjects covered by Valachi in his televised testimony before the US Senate were:

1. A power struggle among Italian-American gangs that took place during the early 1930s, called the Castellammarese War.
2. The existence of a structured organization whose principal activity is to pursue crime, called the Cosa Nostra.

Valachi's version of events was accepted, even though law enforcement officials admitted they had not heard of a "Cosa Nostra" prior to his testimony, and his account of the Cosa Nostra became the basis for the conclusions drawn about organized crime by the President's Crime Commission and by others (President's Commission on Law Enforcement and Administration of Justice 1967; Cressey 1969).

The importance of Valachi's testimony lay in the fact that he was the first "insider" to come forward, that he described a more formal structure than was previously known, and that he described "families" of Cosa Nostra existed in more US cities than had been known before. Valachi also described the organizational structure as consisting of "the individual bosses of the individual families, and then we had an underboss, and then we had what we call a caporegima which is a lieutenant, and then we have what we call soldiers" (US Senate 1963, p. 80). When it came to specifying the role of the organization in the lives of its members, however, the Cosa Nostra appears less organized (US Senate 1963, pp. 116,194).

> SENATOR JAVITS: Now, what he (Vito Genovese) got out of it then, your actions and these of other members of the family, was to kill off or otherwise deal with people who were bothering him; is that right?
> MR. VALACHI: Anybody bothering him, naturally he has the soldiers.
> SENATOR JAVITS: That is the function of the family?
> MR. VALACHI: Right.
> SENATOR JAVITS: That is mutual protection?
> MR. VALACHI: Right.
> SENATOR JAVITS: Otherwise, everybody operates by himself. They may take partners but that is their option.
> MR. VALACHI: Right.

As described by Valachi, the Cosa Nostra was a loose association of criminals of Italian-American origin and, since then, much of the discussion about Italian-American organized crime has centered around the degree to which the Cosa Nostra is structured (i.e., formally or informally).

When the President's Crime Commission Task Force on Organized Crime issued its report in 1967, it reconciled the "Mafia" versus "Cosa Nostra" terminology by indicating that the organization had changed its name from Mafia to Cosa Nostra (President's Commission 1967, p. 6). There is no evidence that this assertion is true, and it has never been repeated since. However, the President's Crime Commission made the first systematic effort to describe the activities of Cosa Nostra. The 1967 Task Force Report on Organized Crime (TFR) was emphatic in its claim that "law enforcement officers agree almost unanimously that gambling is the largest source of revenue" for organized crime (President's Commission 1967, p. 2). The TFR concluded that loansharking "is the second largest source of revenue for organized crime" and is funded by gambling profits (President's Commission 1967, p. 3). Interestingly, only two paragraphs in the entire TFR were devoted to narcotics. It was found that narcotics are "imported by organized crime" and sold by independent pushers, not Cosa Nostra. Heroin was the only drug mentioned by name in the report. It was also concluded that prostitution and bootlegging "play a small and declining role in organized crime operations" and little attention was given these in the report.

The TFR discussed the infiltration of legitimate business and how organized criminals invest illegal profits to establish a "legal source of funds." One additional form of organized criminal behavior addressed was labor racketeering. The infiltration of labor unions was seen as a way to "enhance other illegal activities," such as "stealing from union funds and extorting money by threats of possible labor strife" (President's Commission 1967, p. 5). Most Cosa Nostra groups in the United States have been linked to labor racketeering as a way to extort or embezzle union dues and worker pension funds. In some cases, threats or violence have been used to infiltrate union affairs. In other cases, union elections were rigged to gain control over union finances or reluctant employers were forced to accept union workers using violence or bribery. These efforts were made easy by the apathy of union workers toward the governance of their labor unions (Jacobs 2007).

The social science community did not play a major role at this time because most of the serious academic work on Mafia-related organized crime did not begin until the 1970s. Sociologist Gordon Hawkins disputed Valachi's claims and the conclusions of the government's reports because of the lack of evidence provided to support the assertions (1969, p. 50). On the other hand, sociologist Donald Cressey was granted access to interview Valachi and wrote a book, *Theft of the Nation* (1969), that repeated Valachi's account of the structure of organized crime in the United States. An ethnographic study in which an anthropologist lived with an Italian-American family involved in organized crime provided the first detailed insight into how family ties, cultural traditions, and criminal opportunities combined to result in ongoing organized crime activity in family context (Ianni and Reuss-Ianni 1972).

The recommendations of the 1967 President's Crime Commission report on organized crime were significant in that they led to passage of three new laws, which permitted the use of wiretap evidence in criminal trials; provided new prosecution tools, including a racketeering law with more severe penalties (to prosecute ongoing criminal enterprises rather than only individuals), and also witness immunity and the witness protection program; and finally the Bank Secrecy Act, which addressed money laundering for the first time. These laws were enacted in 1968 and 1970, but they were not used extensively in practice until the 1980s[1] (see "Organized Crime Control in the United States of America" by James B. Jacobs).

In 1980, the emergence of Jimmy Fratianno, another criminal turned government informant, became more significant than Valachi because, unlike Valachi, Fratianno was said to be (1) a high-ranking member of an organized criminal group, and (2) his testimony resulted in the conviction of a number of suspected organized criminals (Albanese 2011). This occurred just as the new organized crime laws passed a decade earlier were being applied to a growing number of organized crime cases.

V. The American anti-Mafia Effort and Its Results

The case of *United States v. Frank Tieri* took place in Manhattan in 1980 and, after a month-long trial, Tieri was convicted of racketeering and conspiracy and was, according to court records, the first person ever proven to be "boss" of a Cosa Nostra "family."

Frank Tieri was originally indicted on charges of racketeering, conspiracy, bankruptcy fraud, and income tax evasion under the Racketeer Influenced and Corrupt Organization Act (RICO) provisions enacted in 1970. This statute is particularly important to the *Tieri* case because the "enterprise" he was alleged to have illegally operated or received income from was the Cosa Nostra.

The significance of this case, therefore, was its attempt to prove in court the existence of the Cosa Nostra as a continuing illegal enterprise, that Tieri was the "boss" of one of its families, and that he committed various organized crimes in that capacity (*United States v. Tieri*, trial Transcript, 80 S.D. N.Y. Cr. 381 [1980], pp. 218–12183). The most important aspect of the *Tieri* case was the government's effort to prove the existence of Cosa Nostra. This effort was based on the testimony of Fratianno.

MR. ACKERMAN: Now, directing your attention to late 1947, early 1946, did you become a member of any organization?

MR. FRATIANNO: Yes, sir.

MR. ACKERMAN: What is the name of that organization?

MR. FRATIANNO: La Cosa Nostra.

MR. ACKERMAN: How long have you been a member of La Cosa Nostra?

MR. FRATIANNO: Thirty-two years, sir.

MR. ACKERMAN: Would you tell the jury what La Cosa Nostra is?

MR. FRATIANNO: Well, I would say it is a secret organization, sir.

MR. ACKERMAN: What does it do, primarily?

MR. FRATIANNO: Well, it engages in different businesses, illegal activities.

MR. ACKERMAN: What kinds of illegal activities?

MR. FRATIANNO: I'd say shylocking, bookmaking, taking bets on horses, football games, baseball games, labor racketeering, all sorts of illegal activity...

MR. ACKERMAN: Mr. Fratianno, would you please tell the jury what requirements there are for one to become a member of La Cosa Nostra?

MR. FRATIANNO: Well, you are more or less proposed by somebody. Sometimes you do something significant. Then there is times when you have a brother or a father in it, and you get in that way. There's different ways, sir.

MR. ACKERMAN: Is there any kind of background requirement that's necessary?

MR. FRATIANNO: You have to be Italian, sir.

MR. ACKERMAN: Would you please tell the jury where La Cosa Nostra is located?

MR. FRATIANNO: Well, it is located in different parts of the United States, sir, most of the big cities.

MR. ACKERMAN: How is this national organization broken down with respect to the big cities?

MR. FRATIANNO: It is broken down into families, sir.

MR. ACKERMAN: Now, I am going to put up a map of the United States which has been marked as Government's Exhibit 4 for identification. Mr. Fratianno, starting from the West Coast, could you tell the jury where there are families, and which cities have families of La Cosa Nostra? (*United States v. Tieri* [1980], p. 863).

Fratianno went on to testify that "families" of La Cosa Nostra existed in 25 cities, including San Francisco, San Jose, Los Angeles, Denver, Dallas, Kansas City (Missouri),

Chicago, Detroit, Cleveland, Buffalo, St. Louis, Pittsburgh, Steubenville (Ohio), Milwaukee, Philadelphia, Pittston (Pennsylvania), New Orleans, Tampa, an unknown city in Connecticut, Providence, and five families in New York City. He also testified that he met Frank Tieri in 1976 when Tieri was boss of one of the New York City "families."

Also in 1980, the director of the FBI's organized crime operations testified before the Senate Permanent Subcommittee on Investigations and said that there existed 26 "active" families of Cosa Nostra in the United States. Interestingly, he claimed there were Cosa Nostra families in Tucson (Arizona), Rockford (Illinois), Madison (Wisconsin), and Elizabeth-Newark (New Jersey), all places that Fratianno did not acknowledge. Further, he did not acknowledge that any families existed in Steubenville, Ohio, or in Connecticut, or that there was an active group in Dallas, as Fratianno had testified (US Senate 1980, pp. 114–16). So there is some disagreement about the size and scope of the Cosa Nostra, although there is consensus that it is largest and most influential in several northeastern U.S. cities. A "commission" made up of the heads of several Cosa Nostra families exists to resolve interfamily conflicts, although its size and membership is not entirely clear. At the Tieri trial, Fratianno testified about the organization of LCN "families," describing each "family" with a hierarchy of "soldier" up to "boss," and the families were regulated by a six-member commission of six family bosses (of the five New York City families and Chicago) (*United States v. Tieri* 1980). When the FBI unit chief testified before the Senate the same year, he arrived at a different formulation.

> At that time [when the commission was allegedly formed in 1931], there were seven members on the Mafia Commission, the La Cosa Nostra Commission... Currently, there are nine. It is made up of the five bosses of the New York families, the boss in Philadelphia, the boss in Buffalo, the boss in Detroit, and the boss in Chicago (US Senate 1980, p. 88).

This confusion over the existence and size of the "commission" was further amplified when Fratianno's 1981 biography offers still a *third* version of the commission structure. In it, the commission is said to be composed of 10 Cosa Nostra bosses, and he says that he was told of the family and commission structure by someone else in 1947 (Demaris 1981, pp. 20–22). This is an issue because Fratianno claims he was the one-time "boss" of the Los Angeles "family," so presumably he would have first-hand knowledge of such a crucial fact. Therefore, there is broad agreement about the existence of a commission, although there is some disagreement about its size and membership.

Nevertheless, the *Tieri* trial was the first of series of major organized crime cases in the United States. The 1980s to the present will be remembered as a period when the US Justice Department took new initiatives to prosecute large numbers of reputed organized crime figures around the country. The alleged leaders of 16 of the 24 Mafia groups identified by the government were indicted by 1986. Nearly 5,000 federal organized crime indictments were issued by grand juries in 1985 alone (Powell et al. 1986). By 1988, the FBI reported that 19 bosses, 13 underbosses, and 43 "captains" had been convicted

(Jacobs 1994, p. 4). The year 2003 marked the first time in history that all five leaders of the New York City families of Cosa Nostra were in jail at the same time.

Although few still debated the existence of a Mafia in the United States, the issue was finally rendered moot in a 1986 trial, when the defendants in the "Commission" trial (i.e., the alleged "bosses" of the New York City crime "families") conceded that the "Mafia exists and has members." Furthermore, the defense claimed, "there is a commission" which is mentioned in wiretapped conversations of the defendants (Magnuson 1986, pp. 16–17). Testimony from Sicilian informer Tommaso Buscetta corroborated this claim. He stated that he was told by Joseph Bonanno in 1957 that "it was very advisable" to set up a commission in Sicily "to resolve disputes" among criminal groups (Lubash 1985, p. B3). If this testimony is true, it appears that the organization of criminal groups in Sicily, through establishment of a commission, may have been modeled after that in America rather than the common belief that a Mafia organization was imported to America from Sicily. Similar to both Valachi's and Fratianno's earlier testimony, the role of the commission, according to the defendants in the "commission" trial, is only to approve new members and to avoid conflicts between the groups. The prosecution argued, however, that the defendants participated in "the ruling council of La Cosa Nostra, or the 'Mafia' which directed criminal activity." The criminal charges included bid-rigging of concrete prices, extortion, and murder. The charges were ultimately proven, and the defendants were each sentenced to 100 years in prison (Lubash 1986, p. 1; Oreskes 1986, p. B29).

This dramatic increase in prosecutions was not the result of new laws, but simply due to efforts to devote more resources to the problem and pursue the leaders rather than concentrate on the arrest of lower-level figures. In the 1980s, more than 700 federal wiretaps were authorized, more than twice the number during the 1970s (McShane 2003, p. 25). In a similar way, the use of the racketeering law (RICO) provided for extended sentences and also large fines and forfeitures for offenders shown to engage in a pattern of ongoing criminal activity (Albanese 2011, p. 297; Jacobs, Panarella, and Worthington 1994). In addition, undercover agents and government informants were employed in organized crime investigations more often and for longer periods of time than ever before (Feuer 2001; Garcia and Levin 2009; Pistone 1989; Wansley and Stowers 1989).

The significance of this investigation and prosecution effort is difficult to capture, but the leaders of many Cosa Nostra groups were convicted and sentenced to long terms, including John Gotti in New York, Nicky Scarfo in Philadelphia, and Gennaro Angiulo in Boston, among many others. Most of the convictions of hundreds of organized crime figures were Italian Americans associated with the Cosa Nostra (Albanese 2011; Cox 1992; Friel and Gunther 1992; O'Neill and Lehr 1989; Cummings and Volkman 1999; McPhee, 2002; McShane 2003). Many of these cases were racketeering convictions that involved the infiltration of legitimate or illegitimate businesses through bribery and extortion. Prison sentences averaged more than 20 years per offender whose average age was nearly 60 (Albanese 2011, pp. 158–166). Given an average sentence of 20 years, an entirely new leadership emerged among many Italian-American organized crime groups.

VI. The Modern Mafia in America

Most of the Cosa Nostra cases over the last 30 years occurred in New York City, but other parts of the USA were affected as well, including New England, New Jersey, Chicago, Las Vegas, Pittsburgh, Philadelphia, and elsewhere. One outcome is that Italian-American organized crime groups are nowhere near the size and influence of years past. Some estimates place the number of sworn members of Cosa Nostra or Mafia members at less than 1,000, and observers see Mafia-linked crime as a declining presence in the overall picture of organized crime (Reuter 1995; El-Ghobashy and Gardiner 2011). In some cities, such as Cleveland, Los Angeles, and Tampa, Cosa Nostra families are said to be nearly gone (McShane 2007). In South Florida (Miami), the FBI has stated that Russian-based organized crime is now a more serious problem there than the Cosa Nostra (Weaver 2011; see Associated Press 2011; Finckenauer 2001; Lindberg 2001). According to Ronald Goldstock, former director of the New York State Organized Crime Task Force, "The shrinking of Italian-American neighborhoods results in a lack of gangs, which means that there are no minor leagues to supply the majors anymore. And it used to be that only some children of mobsters would go legitimate, but now most of them are going legitimate" (Goldberg 1999, p. 25). It is likely that the sustained and successful prosecution effort over the past 30 years has played a major role in these decisions, and that generational changes in Cosa Nostra leadership have been hastened by the government's prosecution effort.[2] The result has been the emergence of younger leaders, who often lack the Italian family traditions of loyalty and secrecy and who are unwilling to serve prison time to protect others or the group, resulting in many becoming informants.

The decline in the scope and influence of Italian-American organized crime in the United States is also illustrated by examining trends in US convictions in court. Table 6.1 indicates that convictions of traditional Italian-American organized crime in the United States have been declining in recent years, while prosecutions of emerging, non-Italian groups has been increasing (Transactional Records Clearinghouse 2011).

In addition to successful prosecutions across the United States, the Cosa Nostra has also suffered from market forces, which have reduced the profitability of long-standing criminal activities. For example, the dominance of Cosa Nostra in running illegal gambling enterprises has been impacted by the growth of legal gambling in the United States.

Table 6.1 Organized Crime Prosecutions in the United States

Convictions (U.S.)	1995	2000	2005	2010	Trend
Traditional Cosa Nostra groups	579	329	276	135	−444
Emerging OC groups	3	139	184	261	+258

Source: Transactional Records Clearinghouse 2011.

Nearly all US states now have lotteries, and half the states have legal casino gambling (Albanese 1995; Gambling in America 2005; Humphrey 2012). Therefore, the growth of legal gambling in many different forms has shrunk the organized crime market, which now is dominated by sports gambling. The decline of gambling revenue to organized crime correspondingly reduces its ability to engage in loansharking, which historically was supported by gambling profits (President's Commission 1967; US Department of Justice 2010).

The Cosa Nostra has never been a central player in the narcotics trade with the exception of the so-called Pizza Connection case in New York, which found that Sicilian Mafia figures had conspired with American Mafia figures to import heroin through pizza parlors in the United States. Tons of morphine were smuggled from Turkey to Sicily, processed there into heroin, and then smuggled through US airports (Alexander 1988; Blumenthal 1988; Sterling 1990; Reuter 1995). Despite this notable exception, narcotics trafficking has been dominated by non-Mafia organized crime groups.

While a series of successful prosecutions ("mob trials") against Cosa Nostra families has weakened its influence (and indirectly enhanced the domain of other organized crime groups), their underlying organized crime activity persists. This is evidenced by significant cases that continue to be made against Cosa Nostra members and associates involving many suspects each year (Anastasia 2007). For example, 120 members from seven Cosa Nostra groups were arrested in 2011 in the largest coordinated arrest in FBI history. The charges involved drug trafficking, arson, loansharking, illegal gambling, witness tampering, labor racketeering, extortion, and murder, primarily in the New York City metropolitan area (Rashbaum 2011; US Department of Justice 2011). These arrests were followed by formal charges lodged against 13 members and associates of the Philadelphia Cosa Nostra group Nostra, including its current leadership, and involving racketeering, extortion, loansharking, illegal gambling, and witness tampering (Markon 2011). These cases illustrate that Cosa Nostra groups continue to engage primarily in the activities for which they are best known: not only illegal gambling, loansharking, extortion of businesses, but also infiltration of enterprises (especially labor unions, garbage hauling, and the construction industry) in exchange for a "percentage" of the business or regular pay-offs (Haller 1987; Jacobs 2007; Jacobs and Cooperman 2011; US Department of Justice 2010).

Evidence exists also of a shift by some Cosa Nostra figures toward "safer" (i.e., better insulated from detection), but more complex scams, involving organized crime infiltration into legitimate business to finance illicit business and to launder illegally obtained profits. For example, the New Jersey Commission of Investigation found that more than 30 individuals connected to organized crime were involved in the garbage and recycling industry by using "front" companies to appear legitimate or by becoming owners of real estate or equipment leased to waste companies (Baxter 2011; Cowan and Century 2002). In another case, the son of jailed Philadelphia mob leader Nicodemo Scarfo was charged in 2011 with operating a criminal enterprise set up to siphon millions of dollars from FirstPlus Financial, the Texas-based company. It is alleged that Scarfo and others orchestrated a series of business deals in which FirstPlus bought or invested in companies in Philadelphia and New Jersey, but those companies were shell companies that performed little or no work. The arrangement permitted Scarfo and Pelullo to take more than $12 million out of FirstPlus, which ultimately filed for bankruptcy (Meyerowitz 2011). Sociologist Mary McIntosh has suggested the "technology" or sophistication of organized criminal activity responds to law enforcement effectiveness. Once law enforcement strategy becomes more effective, as the mob trials indicate, "we can expect the criminal technology to reach rapidly the same level of efficiency in order to maintain acceptable levels of success" (McIntosh 1975, p. 72).

This sophistication may take the form of greater dealings in the financing of criminal activities rather than in the operation of criminal enterprises, and operators may be content to finance or extort other illicit entrepreneurs for a percentage of the profits. Illegal profits can then be laundered through legally owned businesses. For example, an investment firm in New York sold worthless stocks to unwitting investors. Cosa Nostra figures became aware of the situation and exploited it by demanding extortion to "protect" the scam, and that money was invested in other businesses (El-Ghobashy and Gardiner 2011; Glaberson 2003; Weiss 2003). In 2011, charges were brought against organized crime and union officials on charges that they conspired to extort Christmas "tribute" money from dockworkers in exchange for better jobs and wages (Strunsky and Rizzo 2011; Strunsky 2010). These cases illustrate criminal activity involving financial manipulation rather than the operation of traditional criminal enterprises.

The continuing arrests of Cosa Nostra suspects in recent years illustrates that, although the size and influence of Cosa Nostra has declined in the United States, it has not vanished. Ongoing organized criminal activity continues to attract a portion of those living in ethnic communities, especially in the northeastern United States. The significant US prosecution effort has emboldened newer, non-Italian groups, which now attract more attention from authorities as these groups expand their reach. However, significant cases continue to be made against Cosa Nostra groups after 30 years of prosecution success against them.

Notes

1. The three major laws passed between 1968 and 1970 were: Title III of The Omnibus Crime Control and Safe Streets Act of 1968; 18 U.S.C. §§ 2510-22; Organized Crime Control Act (OCCA) (P.L. 91-452, 84 Stat. 922 - 1970); The Bank Secrecy Act, 31 CFR 103 (1970).
2. Joseph Bonanno (original leader of the Bonanno crime group) died in 2002 and his son, Bill, died in 2008. Vincent "The Chin" Gigante (boss of Genovese crime group) died in 2005. John Gotti (Gambino crime group) died in prison in 2002 as did Anthony "Tony Ducks" Corallo (Lucchese crime group) in 2000. Carmine "Junior" Persico (Colombo crime group) is serving a life sentence as are many other bosses and supervisors of Cosa Nostra groups (Albanese 2011; Davis 1983; DeStefano 2007).

REFERENCES

Adler, Patricia A. 1985. *Wheeling and Dealing: An Ethnography of an Upper-Level Drug Dealing and Smuggling Community*. New York: Columbia University Press.

Albanese, Jay. 1995. "Casino Gambling and Organized Crime: More Than Reshuffling the Deck." In *Contemporary Issues in Organized Crime*, edited by Jay Albanese, 1–17. Monsey, NY: Willow Tree.

Albanese, Jay S. 2011. *Organized Crime in Our Times*. 6th ed. Burlington, MA: Elsevier.

Albini, Joseph L. 1971. *The American Mafia: Genesis of a Legend*. New York: Irvington.

Alexander, Shana. 1988. *The Pizza Connection: Lawyers, Money, Drugs, Mafia*. New York: Weidenfeld & Nicolson.

Anastasia, George. 2007. "Mob Case Snare 3 Reputed Leaders." *Philadelphia Inquirer* (December 19).

Arlacchi, Pino. 1986. *Mafia Business: The Mafia Ethic and the Spirit of Capitalism*. London: Verso.

Arlacchi, Pino. 1993. *Men of Dishonor: Inside the Sicilian Mafia*. New York: William Morrow.

Associated Press. 2011. "Mob Infiltration Persists at New Jersey Ports" (February 13).

Baxter, Christopher. 2011. "Report: Organized Criminals Infiltrating NJ Garbage, Recycling Industry Due to Failing Regulatory System." *NJ.com* (December 6).

Blok, Anton. 1996. *The Mafia of a Sicilian Village, 1860–1960*. Prospect Heights, IL: Waveland Press.

Blumenthal, Ralph. 1988. *Last Days of the Sicilians: The FBI Assault on the Pizza Connection*. New York: Times Books.

Bell, Daniel. 1953. "Crime as an American Way of Life." *Antioch Review* 13 (June): 131.

Bergeen, Laurence. 1994. *Capone: The Man and the Era*. New York: Simon & Schuster.

Block, Alan A. 1978. "History and the Study of Organized Crime." *Urban Life* 6: 455–474

Block, Alan A. 1979. "The Snowman Cometh: Coke in Progressive New York." *Criminology 17* (May): 75–99.

Browning, F., and J. Gerassi. 1980. *The American Way of Crime*. New York: G.P. Putnam & Sons.

Cowan, Rich and Douglas Century. 2002. *Takedown: The Fall of the Last Mafia Empire*. New York: G.P. Putnam's Sons.

Cox, Donald. 1992. *Mafia Wipeout: How the Feds Put Away an Entire Mob Family*. New York: SPI Books.

Cressey, Donald R. 1969. *Theft of the Nation*. New York: Harper & Row.

Cummings, John, and Ernest, Volkman. 1990. *Goombata: The Improbable Rise and Fall of John Gotti and His Gang*. Boston: Little, Brown.

Davis, John H. 1983. *Mafia Dynasty: The Rise and Fall of the Gambino Crime Family*. New York: HarperCollins.

Demaris, Ovid. 1981. *The Last Mafioso*. New York: Bantam.

DeStefano, Anthony M. 2007. *The King of the Godfathers*. New York: Pinnacle Books.

El-Ghobashy, Tamer and Gardiner, Sean. 2011. "Is the Mob Done or Bouncing Back?" *Wall Street Journal* (January 21).

Feder, Sid, and Joesten, Joachim. 1972. *The Luciano Story*. New York: Award Books.

Feuer, Alan. 2001. "A Mafia Informer Helps Investigators Charge 45." *New York Times* (April 26).

Finckenauer, James O. 2001. *La Cosa Nostra in the United States*. Washington, DC: National Institute of Justice International Center.

Friel, Frank, and John Gunther. 1992. *Breaking the Mob*. New York: Warner Books.

Gambling in America. 2005. *An Overview—Historical Review*. http://www.libraryindex.com/pages/1560/Gambling-in-America-An-Overview-HISTORICAL-REVIEW.html.

Garcia, Jack, and Michael, Levin. 2009. *Making Jack Falcone: An Undercover FBI Agent Takes Down a Mafia Family*. New York: Pocket Books.

Glaberson, William. 2003. "Old Mobs Never Die, and Cliched but Brutal Methods Refuse to Fade Away." *New York Times* (January 26).

Goldberg, Jeffrey. 1999. "The Don Is Done." *New York Times* (January 31).

Haller, Mark H. 1987. "Loansharking in American Cities: Historical Analysis of a Marginal Enterprise." In *Crime and Criminal Law: Major Historical Interpretations*, edited by Kermit L. Hall, New York: Garland. pp. 17–34.

Hawkins, Gordon. 1969. "God and the Mafia," *The Public Interest 14*: 50.

Hess, Henner. 1986. "The Traditional Sicilian Mafia: Organized Crime and Repressive Crime." In *Organized Crime: A Global Perspective*, edited by R. Kelly, 113–133. Totowa, NJ: Rowman & Littlefield.

Hess, Henner 1998. *Mafia & Mafiosi: Origin, Power and Myth*. New York: New York University Press.

Humphrey, Chuck. 2012. *Gambling Law US*. http://www.gambling-law-us.com.

Ianni, Francis A. J., and Elizabeth, Reuss-Ianni. 1972. *A Family Business: Kinship and Social Control in Organized Crime*. New York: Russell Sage Foundation.

Jacobs, James. 2007. *Mobsters, Unions, and Feds: The Mafia and the American Labor Movement*. New York: New York University Press.

Jacobs, James R., and Kerry T., Cooperman. 2011. *Breaking the Devil's Pact: The Battle to Free the Teamsters from the Mob*. New York: New York University Press.

Jacobs, James B., Christopher, Panarella, and Jay, Worthington. 1994. *Busting the Mob: United States v. Cosa Nostra*. New York: New York University Press.

Jacobs, Timothy. 1990. *The Gangsters*. New York: Mallard Press.

Knobel, Dale T. 1997. *America for the American: The Nativist Movement in the US*. New York: Macmillan.

Landesco, John. 1968. *Organized Crime in Chicago: Part III of the Illinois Crime Survey, 1929*. Chicago: University of Chicago Press.

Lindberg, Richard C. 2001. *The Mafia in America: Traditional Organized Crime in Transition*. http://www.search-international.com/Articles/crime/mafiaamerican.htm.

Lombardo, Robert M. 2002. "The Black Hand: Terror by Letter in Chicago." *Journal of Contemporary Criminal Justice 18*: 394–409.

Lubash, Arnold H. 1985. "Mafia Member Testifies on Sicily 'Commission.'" *New York Times* (November 1).

Lubash, Arnold H. 1986. "Persico Asks Jury Not to Be Duped by Mafia Label." *New York Times* (September 19).

Maas, Peter. 1969. *The Valachi Papers*. New York: Bantam.

Magnuson, Ed. 1986. "Hitting the Mafia." *Time* (September 29).

Markon, Jerry. 2011. "13 Charged as Federal Officials Round Up Alleged East Coast Mafia." *Washington Post* (May 23).

McIllwain, Jeffrey Scott. 1998. "An Equal Opportunity Employer: Opium Smuggling Networks in and around San Diego during the Early Twentieth Century." *Transnational Organized Crime 4* (Summer): 31–54.

McIntosh, Mary. 1975. *The Organisation of Crime*. London: Macmillan.

McPhee, Michele. 2002. "Fuhgeddaboud the Old Mob: After Gotti, Mafia Ordered to Clean House." *New York Daily News* (July 7).

McShane, Larry. 2003. "All Five NYC Family Heads Simultaneously behind Bars for First Time." *Associated Press* (January 25).

McShane, Larry. 2007. "Italian Mobsters in Widespread Decline." *Associated Press* (October 27).

Meyerowitz, Steven. 2011. "Mafia Financial Fraud?" *Financial Fraud Law* (December 20).

Monaco, Richard and Lionel Bascom. 1991. *Rubouts: Mob Murders in America*. New York: Avon Books.

Moore, William H. 1974. *The Kefauver Committee and the Politics of Crime, 1950–1952*. Columbia: University of Missouri Press.

Morgan, John. 1985. *Prince of Crime*. New York: Stein & Day.

Nelli, Humbert S. 1981. *The Business of Crime: Italians and Syndicate Crime in the United States*. Chicago: University of Chicago Press.

Ness, Eliot, and Oscar, Fraley. 1957. *The Untouchables*. New York: Pocket Books.

New York State Joint Legislative Committee on Government Operations. 1958. *Interim Report on the Gangland Meeting at Apalachin, Part III*. Legislative Document No. 25.

O'Neill, Gerard, and Dick, Lehr. 1989. *The Underboss: The Rise and Fall of a Mafia Family*. New York: St. Martin's.

Oreskes, Michael. 1986. "Commission Trial Illustrates Changes in Attitude on Mafia." *New York Times* (September 20).

Paoli, Letizia. 2003. *Mafia Brotherhoods*. New York: Oxford University Press.

Peterson, Virgil. 1983. *The Mob: 200 Years of Organized Crime in New York*. Ottawa, IL: Green Hill.

Pistone, Joseph D. 1989. *Donnie Brasco: My Undercover Life in the Mafia*. New York: Signet.

Pitkin, Thomas M., and Francesco Cordasco. 1977. *The Black Hand: A Chapter in Ethnic Crime*. Totowa, NJ: Littlefield Adams.

Powell, Stewart, Steven, Emerson, Kelly Orr, Dan Collins, and Barbara, Quick. 1986. "Busting the Mob." *US News & World Report* (February 3).

President's Commission on Law Enforcement and Administration of Justice. 1967. *Task Force Report: Organized Crime*. Washington, DC: US Government Printing Office.

Rashbaum, William K. 2011. "FBI and Police Arrest More than 100 in Mob Sweep." *New York Times* (January 20).

Reuter, Peter. 1995. "The Decline of the American Mafia." *The Public Interest* 120 (Summer): 89–99.

Reuter, Peter, and Jonathan, Rubinstein. 1983. "Illegal Gambling and Organized Crime." *Society* 20 (July–August): 52.

Russo, Gus. 2003. *The Outfit: The Role of Chicago's Underworld in the Shaping of Modern America*. New York: Bloombury.

Smith, Dwight C. 1990. *The Mafia Mystique*. Lanham, MD: University Press of America.

Sterling, Claire. 1990. *Octopus: The Long Reach of the International Sicilian Mafia*. New York: W.W. Norton.

Strunsky, Steve. 2010. "NJ Waterfront Commission Holds First Hearing on Mob Influence at Docks." *Star-Ledger* (Newark) (October 14).

Strunsky, Steve, and Sal, Rizzo. 2011. "Three Indicted in NJ in Ongoing Ports Probe." *Star-Ledger* (Newark). (February 8).

Transactional Records Clearinghouse 2011. *On-Line Data Source for US Federal Prosecution Statistical Information*. trac.syr.edu.

Turkus, Burton B., and Sid Feder. 1951. *Murder, Inc*. New York: Manor Books.

US Department of Justice. 2008. *Overview of the Law Enforcement Strategy to Combat International Organized Crime.* Washington, DC: U.S. Department of Justice. http://www.justice.gov/ag/speeches/2008/ioc-strategy-public-overview.pdf (accessed January 31, 2011).

US Department of Justice. 2010. *Rhode Island Woman and Son Sentenced for Interstate Extortion Related to Organized Crime.* Washington, DC: US Department of Justice, Offiice of Public Affairs. December 17.

US Department of Justice. 2011. *Mafia Takedown: Largest Coordinated Arrest in FBI History.* Washington, DC: Federal Bureau of Investigation. http://www.justice.gov. January 20.

US Senate Committee on Governmental Affairs Permanent Subcommittee on Investigations. 1980. *Organized Crime and the Use of Violence: Hearings Part I.* 86th Congress, 2nd session. Washington, DC: US Government Printing Office.

US Senate Committee on Government Operations Permanent Subcommittee on Investigations. 1963. *Organized Crime and Illicit Traffic in Narcotics: Hearings Part I.* 88th Congress, 1st session. Washington, DC: US Government Printing Office.

US Senate Special Committee to Investigate Organized Crime in Interstate Commerce. 1951. *Third Interim Report.* Washington, DC: US Government Printing Office.

Walston, James. 1986. "See Naples and Die: Organized Crime in Campania." In *Organized Crime: A Global Perspective,* edited by R. Kelly, 134–158. Totowa, NJ: Rowman & Littlefield.

Wansley, Larry, and Carlton, Stowers. 1989. *FBI Undercover.* New York: Pocket Books.

Weaver, Jay. 2011. "Russian Mob Eclipses Italian Mafia in South Florida, FBI Says." *Miami Herald* (May 31).

Weiss, Gary. 2003. *Born to Steal: When the Mafia Hit Wall Street.* New York: Warner Books.

CHAPTER 7

THE RUSSIAN MAFIA: RISE AND EXTINCTION

VADIM VOLKOV

I. INTRODUCTION

ON August 22, 2007, a special police regiment secretly arrived in Saint Petersburg from Moscow and arrested Vladimir Barsukov, also known as Vladimir Kumarin. By the time of his arrest, Kumarin had outgrown the title of leader of the *Tambovskaya* organized criminal group and earned a reputation as the "night-time governor" of Saint Petersburg, which reflected his status as the chief informal power broker in the city. His company also controlled the petrol trade in the region and owned real estate in the downtown district. The trial, conducted by the Kuibyshevskii district court of Saint Petersburg, was moved to Moscow to avoid pressure from the support network that Kumarin had set up over time. On November 12, 2009, Russia's most powerful criminal boss was sentenced to 14 years in prison.

The historical significance of this episode should be acknowledged. Kumarin's trial was the first of its kind, similar to the trials of Alphonse Capone or Salvatore Luciano in the United States. The Russian state demonstrated its capacity to use formal law against leaders of organized crime of such caliber. Before that, the mafia leaders ended their careers either by being assassinated by rivals or by dying in prison while under investigation. The conviction of Kumarin reflected the process of extinction of the Russian mafia that began after 2000. Another indication of the decline was the death of the *vor v zakone* (thief-in-law) Vyatcheslav Ivan'kov in Moscow on July 28 2009, after an attempt on his life. Although they belonged to different criminal subcultures, both of these men were legends of the criminal world of the 1990s. No successors of comparable status are likely to appear. The "golden age" of the Russian mafia is clearly passed; the mafia turned out to be a one-generation phenomenon.

There are three equally significant questions about the Russian mafia. First, why did it emerge and what were its origins? Second, why did it proliferate so quickly and become so powerful in the new market economy? Third, why did Russian organized crime become extinct almost as quickly as it proliferated? To be sure, criminals and criminal networks existed long before Russia's transition to a market economy in the 1990s and continue to operate to this day. These questions should be viewed from the perspective of sociology rather than of criminology, which means they are not about individuals and groups breaking the law but rather about actors and institutions that emerge, evolve, and disappear under certain historical conditions. Implied in these questions is the process whereby the mafia had become an important and visible actor in the transitional economy and society, exerting economic and cultural influence, after which its importance and visibility declined. Explaining this cycle will help to understand both common features of organized crime and its particular regional and historical variation.

The case of the Russian mafia of the 1990s fits best into the framework of understanding organized crime as both a nonstate governing agency (or a political community) and a form of protection industry (Gambetta 1993; Schelling 1984; Paoli 2003). The distinguishing feature of an organized criminal group or a mafia family is that it recruits members and creates an organizational structure to be able to use violence and coercion in a controlled way to govern other peoples' behavior. Members of such groups may occasionally engage in conventional crime, such as swindling or robbery, but the group itself normally regulates conventional crime rather than directly taking part in it. The ability to govern is then used for generating income by imposing exchange relations with clients in illicit as well as in legal businesses, either through direct extortion or through providing more sophisticated services, such as protection, the regulation of market entry, mediation, contract enforcement, and the like—in these cases the income takes the form of a regular tax legitimated by the claim to provide utility to clients. Acting as governing or managing structures in the criminal realm, such groups should be distinguished from conventional crime. When the mafia is said to engage in drug trafficking or car theft, this does not mean that its members actually transport drugs or steal cars. Likewise, when organized crime is said to participate in the construction business, this does not mean that its members manage or work at construction sites. In both cases the mafia conducts some kind of regulation and in some cases acts as investor. It creates opportunities for running a business, "sanctions" it, controls risks, redistributes incomes, regulates ownership, and settles conflicts.

As some scholars have emphasized, this type of organized crime displays a strong structural isomorphism in relation to the state (Blok 1974; Tilly 1986). Being engaged in essentially the same business and using somewhat similar means, organized crime is the state's major competitor that capitalizes on its weakness. Moreover, state policies of prohibiting certain goods and services, thus creating illegal and therefore unregulated markets, have often inadvertently played into the hands of organized crime, increasing demand for its services. Alcohol and drug prohibitions as well as bans on prostitution are classic stories of states constituting organized crime. Likewise, ineffective regulation by the state and imperfect laws create institutional bottlenecks and thereby opportunities for private ordering and enforcement of property rights by nonstate agencies, including organized crime. Studies of Japanese mafia participation in real estate foreclosure, bankruptcy adjudication, and debt recovery are examples of organized crime profiting from inadequate state regulation (Hill 2003; Milhaupt and West 1999).

II. THE ORIGINS OF POST-SOVIET ORGANIZED CRIME

The reforms that were intended to introduce market principles into the Russian economy started in 1988 while the Soviet Union was still in place. The law "On Cooperatives" admitted elements of private entrepreneurship; the law "On the Freedom of Trade" allowed privately imported or produced goods to be traded at market prices. In 1992, soon after the breakup of the Soviet Union and the disempowerment of the Communist Party, the reformist government dismantled the system of planned economy, released price controls, and launched a swift privatization of economic enterprises. In these very years 1988–1992, the power of the Russian mafia started to grow exponentially, as hundreds of organized criminal groups emerged to capture benefits in the changing economic environment.

For private business enterprises to operate in the long run, property rights, including ownership, control, and rules of exchange, have to be clearly defined. Even more important is reliable protection of these rights and enforcement of rules. Owners of assets who make contracts have to be confident that all parties will respect the terms of contract. For all the importance of honesty and business reputations, there must be a reliable system of enforcement of contracts and of adjudication in case of a failure to fulfill obligations. If private businesspeople were to exchange goods or to invest money, uncertainties and risks, including those caused by the predatory behavior of others, must be reduced. Hence, the fundamental importance of rules, laws, courts, and enforcement mechanisms for any free market economy.

All of this may sound self-evident, if not trivial. But all of this was not even considered by the Russian government in 1992, as it launched the privatization of the economy and market reforms. The major effort of the Russian government during the initial years of reforms was dedicated to destroying the remains of the communist state, to removing price controls, and to rapid privatization. The market, it was believed, would emerge by itself as soon as the communist system was destroyed. The policy of market reforms in Russia in the 1990s focused on freedom and privatization while failing to acknowledge the importance of strong state institutions that guard freedom and private property. If the market was to work in an orderly fashion, hundreds of new laws, efficient courts, legal specialists, professional police, and risk management and consulting agencies had to be there. The Russian government, however, had neither the will nor sufficient financial resources to invest in institution building.

This needs to be stressed, because the price of such a naïve approach to market reforms was the rise of organized crime that not only profited from the power vacuum by looting the economy, but in its own way did what the Russian state failed to do. To understand why the mafia was so successful, one must also outline the objective conditions in which new private businessmen found themselves in the 1990s and which made them vulnerable to organized crime.

A. The Crisis of the State and of the Law

Successive surveys of Russian entrepreneurs indicate that, throughout the 1990s, low contractual discipline and a low reliability of business partners remained the most acute problems. Business failures and a shortage of cash led to the proliferation of mutual debts between enterprises. The emergence of hundreds of new financial institutions in the early 1990s was accompanied by the progressive growth of unpaid debt. According to the author's estimates, the total value of unpaid debts equaled 3.609 trillion rubles (US$1.64 billion) at the beginning of 1994, 8 trillion rubles (US$1.75 billion) in 1995, and 44 trillion rubles (US$7.9 billion) in 1996. Many banks operated at high risk, with their own reserves much lower than those required by existing norms. The situation was further complicated by the hyperinflation in 1992–1994 (average annual inflation exceeded 1,000 percent), which devalued outstanding debts not tied to stable currencies and increased losses caused by failure to repay them in time.

Since 1992, state arbitration courts (*arbitrazh*) have been responsible for handling commercial disputes. According to the law, arbitration courts are to hear cases no later than two months after the appeal. In practice, however, the majority of cases in 1993–1997 were processed much more slowly than prescribed, three to four months on average, with thousands of cases stalled for more than one year. A court verdict did not necessarily lead to an immediate triumph of justice, because enforcement remained even more problematic. According to the claims made by the Minister of Justice Valentin Kovalev (1995), only half of all court decisions involving property disputes were enforced. The minister also underscored an alarming tendency to reduce the number of appeals to arbitration courts in property disputes and explained it as the litigants' preference for out-of-court settlements. Experts estimated the enforcement rate for 1997 even lower, at 32 percent (Skoblikov 1999, p. 30).

The excessively high rate of taxes and unpredictable manner of their collection by state tax inspectors also created incentives for businessmen to avoid the official justice system, to move into the shadow economy sector and, consequently, turn to shadow arbitration. Interviews with businessmen consistently showed that if all formal taxes were accurately paid, the resulting tax rate would be up to 90 percent of profits. The costs of legal economic activity in Russia in the 1990s were prohibitively high. That is why many businessmen either did not register their firms at all or heavily distorted their actual activities in formal records. According to different estimates, the shadow economy in the mid-1990s constituted between 20 percent and 45 percent of the gross domestic product (GDP) (Kosals 1998, p. 59).

B. The Social Origins of Organized Crime

Compared with mafias in other countries, the distinguishing feature of post-Soviet organized crime has been its composite nature and multiple origins. Some of its segments were explicitly criminal, while others had little previous connection with crime or were even affiliated with state law enforcement. In part, this was due to the peculiar conditions of the crisis and disintegration of the Soviet state that could no longer support and control professionals in the use of force. Nor could it offer careers to young people with military or sports backgrounds. Criminal subcultures of the 1990s included the "blue" ones (*sinie*), the "sportsmen" (*sportsmeny*), the "Afghans" (*afgantsy*), and the "Caucasians" (*kavkaztsy*).

One distinct brand of post-Soviet organized crime originated as early as the 1930s in the Soviet prisons and labor camps and survived until the end of the USSR. Its members are known as *blatnye* or *vory* ("thieves"). They rejected any occupation except crime, abstained from penal labor and collaboration with state authorities, served many prison terms, spoke prison jargon, wore tattoos (which earned them the brand name *sinie*, the "blue" ones), and observed their own normative code. All of this brought them in sharp conflict with the communist authorities, and in order to survive in the harsh conditions of Stalinist labor camps, they created a distinct organization and subculture.

The elite of this underworld is known as *vory v zakone*, "thieves-in-law" or "thieves professing the code." The term refers to their special privileges: the exercise of the criminal common law, the issuing of orders, and the management of the communal fund (*obshchak*) to which all criminals had to donate money to support those who were serving prison terms. The status of thief-in-law was usually granted to those who had an elaborate record of criminal activities and earned respect in prison. High disciplined and the availability of violent aides ready to carry out the orders of *vory* enabled them to informally govern inmates in prisons and camps. Their authority, however, rested more on personal charisma and fanatic devotion to their own idea of freedom or *vorovskaya ideya* ("thieves' idea"). The idea of thieves' freedom included autonomy from any external authority and self-entitlement to all kinds of theft. It directly challenged the communist ideology with its commitment to compulsory labor and service to the state.

Sports societies and martial arts clubs also spawned hundreds of racketeering groups in the 1990s. The ability to use and sustain violence, discipline, joint sports careers, and countrywide networks acquired through participation in regular tournaments made boxers, wrestlers, karate masters, and the like fit for violent entrepreneurship. Thus, the authoritative criminal leader Otar Kvantrishvili (assassinated in 1994) coordinated protection rackets in Moscow by setting up a front organization called the Foundation for the Social Support of Sportsmen, which helped to launder criminal incomes. The leader of the *Solntsevskaya* criminal group, Sergei Mikhailov (nickname "Mikhas"), who was tried and acquitted by a Swiss court, had the title "master of sports" in Greco-Roman wrestling. Ethnic gangs combined martial arts virtues with absolute loyalty to their traditional clan structures, seeking opportunities to migrate from depression-stricken ethnic peripheries of the Caucasian regions like Chechnya and Dagestan to the large cities that were centers of private commerce.

More violent groups were formed by Afghan war participants and later by mercenaries who fought in the conflicts in Abkhasia and Transdniestria. Combat fraternities were rich in the same resources as sportsmen and professional criminals: heightened solidarity, geographically extended networks, and proficiency in the use of violence. Among the most prominent leaders of this origin were Anton Malevsky, the leader of the *Izmailovskaya* criminal group who served in the special forces during the war in Afghanistan, and the former paratrooper Sergei Lalakin, the leader of the *Podolskaya* criminal group. The following quote from the interview conducted by the author of this text with Roman, a mid-ranking member of a criminal group and a former soldier, illustrates the commercial use of networks for conducting shadow business operations (in this case, alcohol imports).

> These were wholly Afghan channels. You see, it is very easy for me to work in the country, because as a result of my war trips I have acquired a wide circle of acquaintances in different places, including even here in the tax police. They recommended to me the right people for the business (Roman, born 1969, interviewed in April 1998).

In Ekaterinburg, former participants of the Afghan war formed a criminal group known as *Afgantsy* (the "Afghans"). The group specialized in protection services, insurance business, wholesale trade, and swindling.

Most criminal groups in Russia were named after the city districts where they were initially formed, such as Izmailovo, or towns, such as Podol'sk or Kazan', or after the name of their leaders, like *Malyshevskaya* (after Alexander Malyshev). In the beginning, they imposed their protection over a particular delineated territory. Later, as they developed interregional and international operations, their profile and sphere of influence came to correlate with those sectors of business that they controlled, and the territory as such became much less relevant.

The typical structure of a criminal group was hierarchical and included the leader (*lider, glavar'*), two or three deputy leaders (*avtoritety*), brigade leaders (*brigadiry*) in charge of basic operational units, and brigades, which in turn included five to eight soldiers (*boitsy*). Those groups that infiltrated legitimate business also included commercial and political advisors, a role close to that performed in the Italian American mafia by the *consigliere* ("advisor").

III. From Protection Rackets to Enforcement Partnership

While the official estimates may lump together various kinds of coordinated criminal activities in the general pool of crime, diluting the mafia groups that specialize in regulating and taxing private business, whether criminal or legal, the explosive growth of crime is evident. The Table 7.1 presents the official law enforcement estimates.

Further exposition will focus on the drivers of the criminal mobilization that this data reflects—those groups that managed to integrate into the market economy and thus expand their sources of income, recruiting more and more ambitious youth from the provinces to exploit commercial opportunities. The latter can be best described as a succession of three main forms of economic control: protection rackets, enforcement partnership, and stock ownership (corporate control).

A. Extortion and Protection Rackets

The first years of economic reforms saw the spread of direct and brutal extortion from private businessmen. Initially, criminal groups did not even care to offer protection, demanding regular payments under the threat of violence. They were also quick to discover the effectiveness of framing an assault as a protection offer. Their tactics were flexible enough to accommodate both outright brutal extortion and a protection racket clothed in the rhetoric of partnership. In the language of the participants, this was referred to as *poluchat'* (literally, "to collect"). Because the number of racketeering groups grew rapidly in the early 1990s, they had to protect their clients from one another, even if they did not initially intend to. So they discovered a new method of entrepreneurship—selling protection. The reasoning of a businessman, recorded by the author, illustrates how criminal groups infiltrated private business at that time:

> Q: Did you experience assaults or protection offers from racketeers?
> A: Yes, such cases occurred. Like this happened to one of our directors-general. Business was up, and he bought a new apartment and a new car, and instantly these guys came to demand money. By coincidence, just shortly before that, one of our new Kamaz trucks had been stolen. And we said to them, Okay, you will be our protection if you help to find the stolen car. Obviously, they did not manage to find it, they came again, we repeated our condition, and that was it, they left.
> Q: Do you think protection is beneficial for businessmen?
> A: I think that, in principle, this is a suitable option. Like in that case, if the guys helped to find the car, it was worth working with them, maybe even making a kind of agreement. But when all they can do is demand money.... This is not serious.... A serious racket will not engage in petty extortion. (Alexander, owner of a construction company, Moscow, interviewed in March 1998.)

A survey of the retail sector in three Russian cities conducted in 1996 showed that private protection had become routine. Over 40 percent of retail trade shop owners in Moscow, Smolensk, and Ulyanovsk admitted frequent "contact with racketeers." The study also revealed that shopkeepers believed that private protection served as a substitute for state-provided police protection and, to a lesser extent, for state-provided courts (Frye and Zhuravskaya 2000). In the case of small retail trade, the protection service consisted mainly of physical protection, and payments were collected in cash, normally a fixed monthly fee of US$200 to $300.

B. Enforcement Partnership

As the number and size of private companies grew and their business models became increasingly complex, criminal groups had to adapt their operations to the changing conditions. The more advanced and better organized criminal groups imposed more sophisticated partnerships with businessmen. In their own language, this was referred to as a "roof" (*krysha*) or "enforcement partnership" (*silovoe partnerstvo*).

"Enforcement partnership" is a translation of the Russian *silovoe partnerstvo*, a phrase used by an *avtoritet*, a crime group leader, when he tried to explain to the author the role of his group in relation to business enterprises. The respondent, Vitalii, described how they monitored business opportunities for their clients, backed formal contracts with their guarantees, concluded informal settlement agreements, recovered debts, and provided physical protection. "We are *silovye partnery*," noted the *avtoritet* (literally meaning "partners providing force"). That particular group, whose leader gave two interviews to the author, was formed in Leningrad around 1986 by sportsmen (wrestlers and boxers). They were part of the larger *Malyshevskoe* criminal society named after Alexander Malyshev (under arrest in Spain since 2007). They started their business by setting up illegal alcohol sales during dry hours (after 7 p.m.), then running prostitution rackets, but after 1991 switched to protecting businessmen in the retail trade. "Earlier on we had a businessman who conducted charter trips to Sweden to import goods. We met him at the border and convoyed to Leningrad. But these were low profits, mainly in kind," said Vitalii. Later the group took control of a wholesale outlet, several retail stores, two food processing factories, and acquired shares in construction companies.

Enforcement partnership was not voluntary for ordinary businessmen, however thoroughly its coercive nature was covered by the façade of friendship. Members of criminal groups imposed their protection upon clients in the form of offering a partnership or suggesting to "work together." The widespread presence of crime compelled businessmen to look for ways of shielding against it. Often violent entrepreneurs forced businessmen to work with them by covertly creating dangers or transaction problems for them. Their ability to use force and their criminal reputations made it hard for businessmen to deny or exit from such a partnership.

The editor of *Forbes-Russia* magazine, Paul Khlebnikov (assassinated in 2004), traced the business career of the would-be oligarch Boris Berezovsky back to his cooperation with the Chechen protection rackets coordinated by Magomet Ismailov, who was appointed as the manager for security of Berezovsky's car trading company Logovaz. In an interview given to Khlebnikov, the Chechen paramilitary leader Khozh-Akhmet Nukhaev stated that "Logovaz was always under the Chechens." He also described the practice of enforcement partnership: "If a businessman wanted to seriously develop his business, he had to take a partner. We showed that we could help them with their business, that we could solve many questions" (Khlebnikov 2001, p. 62).

So what did enforcement partners actually do? The most mundane form of their activity was the monitoring of transactions, which consisted of collecting information about prospective contractors, meeting their enforcement partners, exchanging guarantees, and supervising the fulfillment of obligations. If complications arose, enforcement partners would agree on a form of compensation and then ensure that "their" businessmen follow the agreed-on scheme. From the interview with a mid-ranking member of a Petersburg criminal group:

Q: What did you do actually?

A: Well, we had a large warehouse, for example, and we checked potential customers [i.e., those who loaned goods for retail trade], collected information about them, went to see their offices, found ways to arrange the whole thing so that they could not cheat. On the whole, we worked as an ordinary security service. Or when those businessmen could not pay back on time, we met other businessmen's partners, so to speak. We asked them [the "partners"]: do you vouch for him? And they did, or conversely, if our businessman could not repay, we worked out a payment schedule, calculated when he could repay and gave our guarantees.

Expert and interview sources indicate that the majority of high-value business agreements could only be concluded on the condition that enforcement partners, be they criminal groups or legal security services, participated and provided mutual guarantees. The ability to control other people's behavior by means of threats and coercion and thus to guarantee transactions is what constituted the specific utility of enforcement partners in the given business environment. This capacity gave them leverage over their clients as well.

Over time, those criminal groups that were more successful in imposing their partnership on growing businesses would also increase their organizational and financial capacity. The *Podol'skaya* organized criminal group (OCG) in Moscow, for example, is known for setting up the financial pyramid "Vlastelina" that embezzled US$303 million worth of private investors' money in 1993–1994. Sergei Popov, who is considered by the law enforcement experts to be one of the leaders (*avtoritet*) of the *Podolɜskaya* criminal group, moved into legal business after being released from prison in 1993. The criminal group established a partnership with the food imports company *Soyzkontrakt*, set up by the businessmen Lev Goldstein and Mikhail Liubovich. Popov admitted in a printed interview that he joined *Soyzkontrakt* in 1993 and used his influence and connections in "certain circles": "Frozen poultry was at that time much more interesting for us than the aluminum business," he said in an interview for *Forbes* (Sazonov 2008). The former vice president of *Soyzkontrakt*, Nikolai Kovarsky, explained that Popov and his men had influence over the commercial seaport in Saint Petersburg, through which the company brought in frozen food, making sure that all payments were duly made and "resolving problems" with competitors. "This was a kind of parallel institution that performed a serious job of guaranteeing transactions"

(Sazonov 2008). In 1995, the company had a 30 percent share of the frozen poultry market in Russia, with the turnover exceeding US$1 billion.

IV. The Shadow Arbitration and Notional Contracts

Effective regulation and mediation, as well as governing orders, are more efficient if they refer to a certain accepted normative order—that is, rest on a set of rules rather than on bare force. The power of the Russian mafia cannot be explained without an account of the informal notions of justice that legitimated the use of violence and tax claims. During the 1990s, conflicts and property disputes were adjudicated by members of organized crime with reference to the "notions" (*ponyatiya*). To this day, this word remains in wide circulation in Russian society and denotes ways of justification and judgment alternative to formal law. The notions can be traced back to the informal justice procedures worked out by the elite of the professional criminals, thieves-in-law, to regulate the life of criminal communities and inmates in the Soviet Union. Since their inception in the 1930s, "thieves' notions" (*vorovskie ponyatiya*) have had the following main features:

a. They were created and used as an alternative to state laws.
b. They were unwritten and not codified.
c. The exercise of notional justice rested on the specific competence and authority of individuals who acted as judges.
d. The jurisdictional domain of thieves' notions was originally limited to the community of professional criminals.

In the ensuing legal void following the breakup of the Soviet order, notional justice was revived and spread beyond its original jurisdiction. Flexible enough, it was adapted to regulate commercial relations in the new market economy. Thieves-in-law naturally claimed their preeminence in exercising notional justice when applied to new market relations. For a decade, notions became an informal legal order alternative to state law and justice.

State court proceedings and enforcement are limited by procedural norms and depend on the resources and capacity of a legal system that was slow and ineffective in those years. In contrast to that, informal adjudication in accordance with notional justice was done quickly, without paperwork or excessive formalities. Any kind of written agreements or proof, as well as oral agreements made in the presence of a witness, were accepted. What could be counted as proof was decided individually by thieves-in-law or other criminal authorities whom conflicting sides would accept as a mediator. They judged in accordance with an internal sense of justice. The most important advantage of shadow arbitration was its effective enforcement. This capacity stemmed not only from the availability of private enforcers unconstrained by legal procedures but also from a more flexible approach to enforcement itself. Thus, when it came to the repayment of debt, the restitution procedure took into account the property of any close relatives and even friends that could serve as collateral and be confiscated in favor of the creditor, if his claims were regarded as justified by the judge.

In the 1990s, regardless of whether they had the title of thief-in-law, leaders of criminal groups could exercise notional justice, given that they commanded sufficient respect and force. According to notions, members of criminal groups ("bandits") and their words had priority over those of businessmen whom they claimed to protect. In case of contradicting claims, members of criminal groups enjoyed higher trustworthiness. But according to notions, any oral word counted, and criminal judges could make one "answer for one's words." The notions forbade unjustified and excessive use of force or unjustified expropriation of somebody's property. Such instances were referred to as *bespredel* (arbitrary behavior) and were condemned and punished. In reality, a member of organized crime could confiscate assets or extort money from a businessman, but this had to be justified in some way. It was not uncommon that members of organized crime would compel businessmen to write IOU notes under duress and then these could be used to transfer money or valuables.

As notional justice became more widespread, businessmen conducted their affairs with a view to possible adjudication according to the notions. The author's interviews with businessmen revealed the widespread practice of writing "notional agreements" or "notional contracts" (*ponyatiinye soglasheniya*). It was especially widespread in the 1990s and early 2000s but has survived to this day. Notional contracts are handwritten or printed agreements or descriptions of rights and duties composed in a free but clear form. They are drawn up in addition to formal legal papers and corporate documents. Notional contracts cannot be recognized by Russian courts; they are tailored for shadow arbitration as described earlier. Notional contracts are most convenient for those who do not expect to appeal to the Russian state justice system and who have an independent enforcement capacity.

The notional arbitration practice resembled that of common law. In comparison with the Russian official justice system of the 1990s that relied on the civic law tradition, it was much more flexible, accessible, and quick. In combination with the assertive methods of selling criminal protection, notional justice had significant advantages over its official counterpart. The control over arbitration practice and the right to interpret and apply notions further strengthened the domination of criminal groups in the commercial sphere.

V. THE EXTINCTION OF THE RUSSIAN MAFIA

The swift decline of organized crime is no less of an important research problem than its initial proliferation. There are three structural causes of the extinction of the Russian mafia: the competitive pressure from the growing private security industry, the consolidation of the state and of its law enforcement, and the capitalization of the protection tribute causing the change in the mafia business pattern and subculture.

A. The Competitive Pressure in the Market of Protection

In the early 1990s, the Russian "power ministries" (*silovye ministerstva*), the organizations that held the coercive resources of the state and were responsible for the maintenance of the public monopoly of violence, underwent significant reductions. In 1989, 83,500 employees were dismissed from the Russian Interior Ministry (MVD), including 37,000 commissioned officers. More than 30,000 left the service in 1990 (Shelly 1995, p. 56). According to a rough expert estimate, during 1991–1996, up to 200,000 employees were leaving the MVD each year, of which a quarter were dismissed for violations of the law (Dolgova 1997, p. 48). More than 20,000 officers of the Committee for State Security (KGB) left or were discharged between September 1991 and June 1992. In 1992, President Yeltsin ordered that the 137,000-strong central apparatus of the former KGB be reduced to 75,000 (a 46 percent reduction) during the process of restructuring. While a substantial proportion of the former staff of the central apparatus was transferred in 1992–1993 to the newly established state security organizations, such as the Federal Security Service (FSB), and to regional FSB directorates, 11,000 had to leave the state security permanently (Volkov 2002, p. 133).

Consequently, state police and security cadres moved to the private sector, making use of the 1992 Law on Private Protection and Detective Activity and setting up private protection companies and corporate security services. By 1998, the private security sector employed 156,169 licensed personnel, of whom 35,351 (22.6 percent) came from the MVD, 12,414 (7.9 percent) from the KGB-FSB, and 1,223 (0.8 percent) from other security and law enforcement organizations (Volkov 2000). The number of private security agencies grew dramatically in the mid-1990s, and this growth continues to this day, reflecting a high demand for security. The dynamics of the sector are represented by Table 7.1 and the figure.

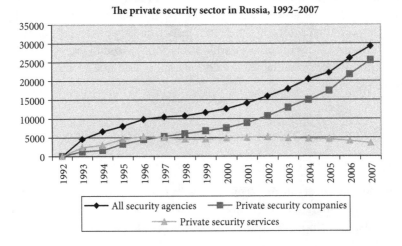

The private security sector in Russia, 1992–2007

Table 7.1 Number of Organized Criminal Groups Revealed by Law Enforcement Agencies

Types of criminal groups	1992	1993	1994	1995	1996	1997
Overall number of revealed organized criminal formations	4,300	5,691	12,849	14,050	12,684	12,500
Overall number of participants	24,100	27,630	50,572	57,545	59,389	60,000
Criminal groups with ties:						
International	n/a	307	461	363	176	222
Interregional	n/a	1011	1258	1065	589	354
Corrupt	n/a	801	1037	857	424	n/a

Source: Dolgova (1997, p. 258).

The regulation of the private security sector gave priority to former law enforcement and security employees, and the latter used their connections and resources in the state services to advance commercial interests. The competence and resources of private security agencies were higher than those of criminal groups. The sector grew steadily: by 2002 the number of private security companies (the main agents in the protection market) reached 10,000, then doubled in 2006, reaching 25,533 in 2007 (the total number of agencies, including corporate security services, was 29,290 in 2007). The growth of legal and professional private security meant that private business had a choice and that organized criminal groups could no longer expand their protection services the way they did in the first half of the 1990s. The competitive pressure from the private security sector forced criminal groups to adapt.

B. The Strengthening of the State

Another clear trend that started around 1998 but became more pronounced from 2000 when Vladimir Putin was elected president was the consolidation and the strengthening of the state (Taylor 2011; Volkov 2008). These policies included the centralization of executive power, the improvement of the fiscal apparatus, and the increase in the capacity of state law enforcement and security. Putin's policies of state building could not have been implemented without systematic appointments of representatives of state security services and law enforcement to key positions in the executive branch of government. The appointments reflected the personal networks of Putin in the Foreign Intelligence Service as well as a broader corporate solidarity of state security cadres from the time when they were part of the KGB. Five of seven presidential envoys in the federal districts came from the military (three from security services, one from the militia, and one from the army). A number of Putin's associates were appointed to the administration of the president. The top management of all major force-wielding agencies, such as the Interior Ministry, the Procuracy, the Tax Police, the Ministry of Defense, and the Federal Customs Service, saw a thorough reshuffling, and people with state security backgrounds were appointed as new ministers. A number of Putin's security cadres were also appointed as governors of regions. The sociologist Olga Kryshtanovskaya estimated that about 77 percent of state officials in 2004 had a military or state security background. Other sources put this figure at the level of one-third (Taylor 2011).

Putin's promotion was not the sole reason for the vertical advancement of security cadres. They were actively involved in private protection and arbitration throughout the 1990s. Internal corporate solidarity, professional skills in the management of information and force became a strong comparative advantage and allowed them to position themselves strategically in the new market economy. With Putin's ascent to power, the state security cadres converted their expanded informal influence into positions in the formal executive power structures. The initial success of the strengthening of executive power and in extending it to Russia's regions was to a large extent due to the organizational culture and discipline of security cadres. Besides that, they took control over protection payments and financial flows. In cooperation with legal security companies the state police and security gradually drove criminal groups out of the protection markets. Some criminal leaders invested in legal business and moved away from violent entrepreneurship. Those who continued ended up in prison. State police or security officers replaced the bandits, but their manner of action was still closer to the bandits' than that of state officials.

When the new policies of strengthening the state and public institutions were put into effect after the 1998 financial crisis and the subsequent change of the government in 1999, the official justice system became more resourceful and efficient. Arbitration courts became much more active, and the institution of bailiffs received public funds for its activities. The tax reform in 2000 led to a radical decrease in tax rates (13 percent flat personal income tax and 24 percent profit tax). The demand for a functioning legal system increased, and the state arbitration system was in a better position to meet it. The figure from the Supreme Arbitration Court of the Russian Federation shows the exponential growth of the activity of state arbitration courts after 2002.

Cases processed by Russian arbitration courts (thousands)

Source: The Supreme Arbitration Court of the Russian Federation.

Legal businessmen began to use the state arbitration system more actively. Once the official justice system regained its power, criminal leaders found themselves in a disadvantageous position, as their powers to resolve commercial disputes diminished. This changed the balance and led to a gradual decrease in the influence of criminal leaders and to the breakdown of enforcement partnerships. Their opportunities to advance their property claims through notional justice within Russia have narrowed.

C. The Change of the Mafia Business Pattern

In the mid-1990s, the need to secure gains from illegal protection business and multiple embezzlement schemes led some criminal groups to adopt a new strategy of converting enforcement partnership into legal ownership. The pattern of criminal influence on the transitional market economy in Russia evolved from the simple racket (*poluchatэ*, "to collect"), which then progressed into the control of financial accounts and transactions (*kontrolirovat'*, "to control"), and finally into the holding of shares of those businesses that were under the protection of OCGs (*byt'v dole*, "to hold a share"). If initially leading members of OCGs positioned themselves as "bandits" (as explicitly violent and criminal types) to earn *avtoritet* (i.e., a reputation as tough enforcers), later in the 1990s they restyled themselves as "businessmen." This change mainly concerned the façade, the way they presented themselves in public and especially in international business circles, when the Russian mafia learned to use offshore companies and foreign banks for accumulating profits. Within Russian business circles, their identity and reputation remained well known and were duly taken into account. Two cases can illustrate the process in question.

D. The Case of OCG Uralmash

The *Uralmash* criminal group evolved from a local racketeering group in the industrial city of Ekaterinburg into an influential regional business group. The core of the group consisted of sportsmen who trained in the 1980s in the athletic clubs sponsored by the machine-building plant *Uralmash* (the group took its name from the plant and the city district). Boxers Sergei Terentiev and Sergei Kurdiumov, wrestler Sergei Vorobiev, skier Alexander Khabarov, and former shadow dealers (*tesekhoviki*) brothers Sergei and Konstantin Tsyganov were among the founding members of the OCG. One of the members of *Uralmash* asserted in an interview with the author that the group survived due to its economic success when they realized that they should use their influence in the legal business world. "Others, especially *sinie* [the "blue ones," another name for traditional criminals], turned out to be unprepared for the new realities. They only knew how to milk [the business], and it did not occur to them that one should invest."

According to police data, *Uralmash* established over 200 companies and 12 banks and obtained shares in an additional 90 companies. Its major investments went into the copper processing holding *Evropa*, the major regional oil processing facilities *Uralnefteproduct*, mobile phone and paging companies *Uralwestcom* and *Continental-Link*, car trades, and beer production. In 1995, *Uralmash* supported Eduard Rossel' in his successful election campaign for the post of regional governor. Rossel', in turn, stated in a public interview that, to his knowledge, *Uralmash* members no longer had any problems with the law. He admitted that what really mattered to him were the investments and other contributions that the members of the group made to the regional economy. "I gave them the order to invest in the building industry of the region" (cited in *Nezavisimaya Gazeta* 1999).

In the 2000s, state law enforcement started investigations into the criminal activities of the members of *Uralmash*. As a result, several leaders, including Alexander Khabarov and Sergei Vorobiev, were arrested. Later, Khabarov was found dead in his prison cell. After that, the influence of *Uralmash* in the region diminished.

E. The Case of the Tambovskaya Criminal Group

The *Tambovskaya* group received its name from the Russian town of Tambov (to the south of Moscow), where several of its founding members, including its leader Vladimir Kumarin, were born. In the early 1990s, they were one of many racketeering groups in Saint Petersburg. In 1994, Kumarin decided to move into legal business, choosing the fuel trade as the main sphere of interest. The leadership of *Tambovskaya* OCG capitalized on the problems the city was experiencing with fuel supplies. Saint Petersburg depended on the large Siberian oil company *Surgutneftegaz* that controlled depots and retail fuel trade in the city. The results were shortages of fuel and randomly increasing prices. In an agreement with the city authorities, the leaders of *Tambovskaya* criminal group invested their money and influence in the development of the fuel trade and took over the existing storage and trade facilities, driving *Surgutneftegaz* out of the retail market by using strong-arm tactics. Together with the city administration and several associated businessmen, they established the Petersburg Fuel Company (PTK), a holding structure that controlled a number of subsidiaries.

By 1998, PTK dominated the petrol trade in the region and acquired an exclusive contract to refuel 80% of the public transport in the city. Kumarin adopted his mother's maiden name "Barsukov" and appointed himself vice president of PTK, while the company's president, Yurii Antonov, became the deputy governor of Saint Petersburg. The city government had a 14.5% share in PTK, while the rest remained with the top management. To this day, PTK remains a major brand in the city. In 2007, its holdings included 149 petrol stations in the Northwestern District of Russia, three fuel storage facilities, the "Petersburg City Bank," the large, centrally located boutique store "Grand-Palace," and a business center. According to expert estimates, the total value of assets associated with PTK is up to US$1.5 billion (data collected by the Agency for Journalistic Investigations). Later, Kumarin-Barsukov had to leave the post of vice president because of a series of assassinations related to the *Tambovskaya* OCG and the public campaign in the press against its members. However,

Kumarin-Barsukov never ceded control over PTK and other assets, being referred to as the "night-time governor" of Saint Petersburg, which meant that he remained actively involved in informal regulation and dispute settlement. On August 23 2007, he was arrested, put on trial in Moscow, convicted, and sentenced to 14 years in prison.

The internal conflicts and external competitive pressures forced the mafia groups to adapt: some leaders emigrated, some restyled themselves as businessmen, others joined regional legislatures in an effort to strengthen their political protection. The mafia style of conducting business started to disappear: protection tribute and enforcement partnerships ceased to be the dominant ways of generating incomes, giving way to direct investments and corporate raiding. The market and the logic of capital accumulation changed organized crime from within, forcing its leaders to dissolve their private armies—whose members became street criminals and were dealt with by the strengthening state police force. A great many leaders of organized crime emigrated and established businesses in Israel and Spain (two favorite destinations). In 2007, the Spanish wing of the *Tambovskaya* and *Malyshevskaya* criminal groups were arrested by Spanish law enforcement and are still awaiting trial. Some enclaves of crime-dominated small towns in Russia remained well into the 2000s. Many mid-ranking leaders are still active in business, keeping a low profile. Having disappeared from urban life, Russian mafia characters have found their due place in the movie industry and on television screens.

VI. CONCLUSION

The trajectory of Russian organized crime tells us about the decisive role of the dynamics of the state in the proliferation and extinction of this type of crime. Yet, the causation is not straightforward. It is not as if state law enforcement first failed to combat the mafia and after a while decisively crushed it. The inability of the state to provide a governing order resulted in alternative private organizations taking over this function and turning it into a kind of commercial activity, into violent entrepreneurship. But the Russian mafia of the 1990s was clearly a multiplicity of private governing agencies of various origins that seized the opportunity as the Soviet socialist state weakened and collapsed. Only one segment among these agencies was of criminal origin—people who were closely connected with prison society and subculture. Others came from many other spheres of society where they had previously learned the skills of using violence and building an organization. Terms such as violent entrepreneurship, shadow arbitration, private governance, and private protection reflect well the nature of these groups that were referred to collectively as the Russian mafia. Later on, the changing conditions, such as competitive pressure from the private security sector, the availability of state arbitration, the growing opportunities for capital accumulation, and the strengthening of state law enforcement resulted in the closure of commercial opportunities for criminal groups and in their swift decline. As the state claimed the right to regulate markets and demonstrated the capacity to use the law against organized crime, the scope of activity of criminal groups was reduced to traditional spheres, such as the drug trade or gambling.

REFERENCES

Blok, Anton. 1974. *The Mafia of a Sicilian Village*. Prospect Heights: Waveland Press.

Dolgova, Azalia. 1997. *Prestupnost', Statistika, Zakon [Crime, Statistics and Law]*. Moscow: Kriminologicheskaya Assotsiatsiya.

Frye, Timothy, and Zhuravskaya, Ekaterina. 2000. "Rackets, Regulation, and the Rule of Law." *Journal of Law, Economics, and Organization* 16(October): 478–502.

Gambetta, Diego. 1993. *The Sicilian Mafia: The Business of Private Protection*. Boston: Harvard University Press.

Hill, Peter. 2003. "Heisei Yakuza: Burst Bubble and Botaiho." *Social Science Japan Journal* 6(1): 1–18.

Khlebnikov, Paul. 2001. *Razgovor s Varvarom [A Conversation With a Barbarian]*. Moscow: Detective Press.

Kosals, Leonid. 1998. "Tenevaia Ekonomika kak Osobennost' Rossiiskogo Kapitalisma" [Shadow Economy as a Feature of Russian Capitalism]. *Voprosy Ekonomiki* 10: 59–80.

Kovalev, Valentin. 1995. "Problema s Zakonom," *Pravda* July 19: 5.

Milhaupt, Curt, and West, Mark. "The Dark Side of Private Ordering." http://www.isnie.org/ISNIE99/Papers/milhaupt.pdf.

Nezavisimaya Gazeta. 1999, June 11.

Paoli, Letizia. 2003. *Mafia Brotherhoods: Organized Crime Italian Style*. Oxford: Oxford University Press.

Sazonov, Alexander. 2008. "Prervannyi Polyot." *Forbes* http://www.forbes.ru/forbes/issue/2008-07/7622-prervannyi-polet.

Schelling, Thomas. 1984. "What Is the Business of Organized Crime." In *Choice and Consequences*. Cambridge, MA: Harvard University Press.

Skoblikov, Piotr. 1999. *Vzyskanie Dolgov i Kriminal [The Collection of Debts and Crime]*. Moscow: Yurist.

Taylor, Brian. 2011. *State Building in Putin's Russia: Policing and Coercion after Communism*. Cambridge: Cambridge University Press.

Tilly, Charles. 1986. "War Making and State Making as Organized Crime." In *Bringing the State Back*, edited by Peter Evans, Theda Skocpol, and Dieter Rushchemeyer. Cambridge, MA: Cambridge University Press.

Volkov, Vadim. 2002. *Violent Entrepreneurs: The Use of Force in the Making of Russian Capitalism*. Ithaca, NY: Cornell University Press.

Volkov, Vadim. 2008. "State Failure and State Building in Russia 1992–2004." In *Persistent State Weakness in a Global Age*, edited by Denisa Kostovicova and Vesna Boijicic-Dzelilovic. London: Ashgate.

CHAPTER 8

··

ORGANIZED CRIME IN COLOMBIA

The Actors Running the Illegal Drug Industry

··

FRANCISCO E. THOUMI

I. ORGANIZED CRIME, INFORMALITY, VIOLENCE, CORRUPTION, COMMON CRIME, AND GOVERNABILITY

TODAY, organized crime in Colombia is a multidimensional activity that reflects a deep governability problem. Since about 1980, the country has been the main illegal cocaine producer, and since the 1990s, the main illegal coca grower. It is less known that it is a main producer of counterfeited US dollars (Stone 2006), euros, and passports; a principal exporter of Latin American prostitutes to Europe; the leading country in the world in the number of displaced citizens[1] and warring children; and a leader in extortive kidnappings and assassins for hire (*sicarios*) who are also exported.[2] White collar and cybercrime and widespread corruption have also become a feature of the society. The existence and resiliency of violent left wing subversive guerrillas and right wing paramilitary groups and the persistence of high levels of violence add complexity to the picture.[3] Most of those engaged in these crimes and activities are organized crime members according to the standard definition of the Palermo Convention. However, almost all research and most of the attention have been focused on the illegal drug industry, which has been a catalyst for the development of organized crime, although this also took advantage of a very propitious structural and institutional environment.

II. THE STRUCTURAL AND INSTITUTIONAL CONTEXT

Because of its geography, the Colombian state has always had great difficulties establishing the rule of law over its territory.[4] The country was formed as a collection of regions with little communication and trade exchanges among them. These isolated regions developed strong local identities and for a long time were highly self-sufficient. International trade, the main source of state revenues for centuries, was very little, and the central government was very poor and unable to develop the infrastructure to integrate the country. Urbanization concentrated government expenditures in urban areas, a trend that accentuated the weak or nonexisting state presence in large parts of the territory. Still today, there are large parts of the country isolated from national markets. Regional heterogeneity resulted in cultural diversity. Local loyalties are strong and the conformation of a national identity has been slow and incomplete (Bushnell 1993; Safford and Palacios 2002).

Throughout history, contraband has been a main activity in border regions, particularly along the coasts (González-Plazas 2008). During the nineteenth century, the country experienced many violent episodes and civil wars, and in many regions, bandit organizations flourished. In the twentieth century, many policies encouraged the development of illegal economic activities. Colombia had an exchange control regime from 1931 to 1991 that made it illegal to hold foreign currencies and required exporters to deliver all their revenues to the central bank that sold foreign exchange to importers and Colombians traveling abroad. A black market of foreign exchange flourished. After World War II until 1991, the government followed an import substitution industrialization strategy with very high import taxes, import quotas, other import restrictions, subsidized credit, and other forms of market intervention. Contraband became an accepted business practice, and corruption was a common business instrument.[5]

Other factors contributed to the government's difficulty in establishing the rule of law. The political party system developed around traditional with a decentralized structure. Local leaders were quite autonomous, and in many regions, party loyalty substituted for state loyalty and the parties became the mediators between the central state and the citizenry. During the 1940s and 1950s, Colombia experienced *La Violencia*, a confrontation between the two parties that killed at least 2% of the population. Victims of this power struggle were almost exclusively rural, and *La Violencia* induced large population displacements and large de facto rural land expropriations. The party in power frequently used the police and the armed forces to fight peasant groups affiliated with the opposition, which further weakened the state's legitimacy. Peace was achieved by a "National Front" agreement by the upper-class leaders of the two parties that alternated the presidency and distributed all public jobs evenly between the two parties from 1958 to 1974, an agreement extended informally until 1986. This led to the depoliticization of the parties, which became electoral machines whose main goal was to distribute the government bounty but achieved little beyond that.

La Violencia and the population explosion of the 1950s and 1960s generated rural–rural migrations and a large expansion of the rural frontier that took place with little or no state presence and support. Most settlers were armed, and many were displaced by rural violence in other regions. These settlements were violent and unstable. In many cases, guerrilla organizations were welcome because they imposed order in the existing power vacuum. Violence-induced migration, be that to rural or urban areas, tends to destroy the social capital of the migrants and to produce social anomy.

After La Violencia, some groups of armed peasants who had a deep distrust of the government refused to give up their weapons and moved to isolated, hard-to-reach areas where they could live without the state. These became known as "independent republics" (González Arias 1992) that were the roots of the Revolutionary Armed Forces of Colombia (FARC), a Marxist guerrilla associated with the Soviet Communist Party that was formally created in 1964 and remains active today. Frustration with and distrust of the government also led to the establishment of other guerrilla groups: the National Liberation Army (ELN) with ties to Cuba; the M-19 movement, an urban group that formed after the apparent presidential electoral fraud of 1970; the Quintín Lame guerrillas, who were rooted in the native American communities; and other minor guerrilla groups.

The weak central state presence in many regions and the outright lack of its presence in many newly settled areas created uncertainty and instability and encouraged the formation of local criminal bands and guerrilla groups who extorted landlords. In response, the government authorized the establishment of self-defense organizations sponsored by local landlords and businessmen (decree 3398 of 1965 and law 48 of 1968) (Americas Watch 1991). Various governments (central or local) since then have enacted legislation to regulate private security firms and self-defense organizations, privatizing essential security forces. These groups have contributed to the development of a strong illegal paramilitary movement that has become symbiotic with some of the local political and economic establishments that have used them to expand their land holdings displacing peasants (Duncan 2006; Rangel 2005). Guerrillas and paramilitary groups have controlled many municipal and some departmental governments and have been privately plundered and used to fund their organizations.

Not surprisingly, Colombia has a very large informal economy that is a principal obstacle to the enforcement of economic laws and facilitates the growth of illegal economic activities. Schneider and Klinglmair (2004, p. 10) estimate that the informal economy in 1999–2000 accounted for 39.1% of the gross domestic product. Perry et al. (2007) found that between 1992 and 2005 Colombian independent workers increased their share in total employment by 17.3% and estimate that informal independent workers plus informal wage earners accounted for 66.8% of those employed in 2006. These are workers who do not comply with many legal requirements and formally operate outside the law.

All of these factors made Colombia a structurally and institutionally vulnerable society that was ready to respond to the increased world demand for marijuana in the 1960s and cocaine in the 1970s.

III. ILLEGAL DRUGS: THEIR HISTORICAL ROOTS THROUGH THE 1960S

A. Old Coca

Coca is a stimulant and an anorectic that allows those who chew it to work longer hours without feeling fatigue. During the colonial era, the quick mixing of the Spanish with the natives (*mestizaje*) weakened native customs, and coca chewing became limited to a small portion of the native population, while high alcohol consumption was an important drug issue (Mora de Tovar 1988). In the nineteenth century, attempts to compete in the international coca market were unsuccessful (López Restrepo 2000).

The colonial government's monopoly on alcohol and tobacco (*Estanco*) was an important source of fiscal revenues. Today, these are important revenue sources for departmental governments. Coca use in Colombia was limited to a few areas and was not a significant policy issue, although until the mid-twentieth century, there were cases in which large landlords (*hacendados*) paid part of their peons' salary in coca leaves (Henmann 1978).

In the 1930s and 1940s, health officials led a movement against coca on the grounds that coca chewing had very harmful effects on the natives' health (Bejarano 1952). The consensus against coca chewing was so widespread that the commitment to eliminate such practice in the 25 years after the ratification of Single Convention on Narcotic Drugs of 1961 was not an issue (Thoumi 2010).

B. Marijuana

There are almost no references to marijuana use before the twentieth century, although it was used in a few isolated Indian tribes. Colonial attempts to grow hemp for industrial use were unsuccessful (López Restrepo 2000). Its recreational use was introduced in the port cities in the early twentieth century (Camacho Guizado 1988), and by 1925, marijuana was grown and used in limited circles along the Caribbean Coast (Ruiz Hernández (1979). In 1930, all marijuana uses were prohibited, and more repressive decrees were issued in the late 1940s by a government that simultaneously promoted hemp as an industrial raw material, apparently without knowing that it was marijuana (Salazar 1998; López Restrepo 2000). At the time, marijuana was grown and consumers were prosecuted in Barranquilla, other coastal cities, and the coffee-growing region (Sáenz Rovner 2007, p. 211).

Marijuana consumption started to grow in the 1950s among middle- and upper-class youth, and small exports to Florida ports using banana boats were frequent (Sáenz Rover 2007, pp. 213–7). Marijuana consumption continued to grow in the 1960s, mainly among young people who had visited the United States (Thoumi 1995, p. 126).

C. Cocaine and Opiates

Before the 1970s, Colombia produced small amounts of cocaine and heroin to satisfy the demand of local artists and bohemians and to export to the US market. In what is likely the first seizure abroad of Colombian drugs, two brothers from Medellin's elite were captured in late 1956 in Havana with 800 grams of heroin (Sáenz Rovner 2008). They apparently had been smuggling cocaine and heroin for almost two decades.

IV. Drugs From the 1970s to the Present

A. Marijuana: A Pioneer Industry

The serious Colombian participation in the illegal drug business started in the early 1970s when marijuana plantings were developed in the Sierra Nevada de Santa Marta on the Caribbean Coast to supply the American market. It appears that Americans came to the region seeking places to grow marijuana, and Colombians from that region who had extensive smuggling experience began to participate in it. *Marihuana* was well known in that region and was traditionally consumed by members of the Aruhaco tribe. Also, in the 1950s, there was a hemp fiber plant under contract with the US Department of Agriculture that operated until 1961 (Partridge 1975, p. 160).

The large Colombian migration to the United States in the 1960s facilitated the development of distribution networks and the substitution of Colombian for American exporters. Marijuana plantings spread to a few other recently settled areas distant from the main urban centers, and a marijuana export boom took place. Beginning in 1975, Mexico started to fumigate marijuana with paraquat in what was called Operation Condor. This accelerated the growth of the plantings in Colombia but also the growth of marijuana on public lands and indoor hydroponic plants in the United States. The development of US domestic cannabis production as well as the manual cannabis eradication campaign that was implemented by the Turbay administration (1978–1982) under pressure from the United States cut short the marijuana boom in Colombia.

Aerial marijuana spraying was generalized during the Betancur government (1982–1986) and became sporadic during the Barco presidency (1986–1990) (Tokatlian 2003; González-Plazas 2006). By the early 1990s, Colombia had become a marginal actor in the marijuana trade (US Department of State 1992).

B. Coca and Cocaine

1. *The Early Developments*

Marijuana was profitable but difficult to smuggle because of its high volume and weight per unit of value.[6] Coca was easy to grow and was not produced in Europe or the United States. It had much greater value-to-weight and -volume ratios, and its refining is so simple that labs are called "kitchens." There are several ways to produce cocaine in a three-step process, and all chemicals used have substitutes. CICAD-OAS (2005) summarizes this process. First, because of leaf volume, coca has to be processed into coca paste in the growing fields where coca leaves are put in a plastic-lined pit or in plastic drums. An alkaline material such as sodium carbonate, water, and an organic solvent such as kerosene are added to allow the extraction of the cocaine alkaloid into the solvent that is separated from the water and leaves. The cocaine alkaloids are further extracted into a solution to which an alkaline material is added. A precipitate forms that can be filtered and dried to produce coca paste. Second, to produce cocaine base, coca paste is dissolved into an acid solution and combined with diluted potassium permanganate that is filtered to eliminate other alkaloids and contaminants. Ammonia water is added to form another cocaine base. Since coca paste can be easily transported, this process can take place anywhere. Third, acetone or ether is then added to dissolve the cocaine base, and the solution is filtered to remove undesirable material. Hydrochloric acid is added, forming cocaine hydrochloride that is dried to get cocaine.

Before the illegal cocaine boom, coca production in Colombia was insignificant. Colombia's involvement in the illegal cocaine trade began with importing coca paste from Bolivia and Peru in small quantities to be refined and exported to the United States (Arango 1988). By the late 1970s, coca plantings had appeared as a backward linkage of the cocaine refining industry. These plantings were concentrated in recently settled areas distant from the main urban concentrations, with token or no state presence, where many settlers had arrived because of the population explosion of the 1950s and 1960s or had been displaced by the rural violence that had plagued the country. By 1983, the government's attack on the trafficking organizations and their routes made it difficult for peasants to find buyers, which led to a decline in coca prices. This resulted in high violence levels in the main coca-growing area as many debts went unpaid. In 1984, the government pressed its eradication campaign. These two factors led to a decline in coca plantings, but the industry adjusted itself after 1985 and plantings moved to harder-to-reach areas. By 1991, the country was the third largest coca producer (Thoumi 1995, chap. 3).

2. *The Medellin and Cali Cartels*

The transition from small-scale to large businesses with sophisticated international criminal organizations was rapid. The high profits generated by the business acted as seed capital to develop large organizations. Available data (Kalmanovitz 1990) suggest that by 1976, there were substantial trafficking organizations with substantial revenues. The large number of Colombian immigrants in the United States facilitated the development of distribution and money-laundering networks. By 1978, Carlos Lehder controlled and owned most of a small island in the Bahamas, on which he had an airport to send the larger shipments of cocaine in small airplanes to the United States (Gugliotta and Leen 1990; Kirkpatrick and Abrahams 1991). This innovation changed the scale and structure of the business. The development of large-scale smuggling methods increased potential gains and induced the formation of "cartels" or export syndicates that coordinated the cocaine industry.[7] They bought coca paste and cocaine base in Bolivia and Peru through emissaries, had the drugs shipped back to Colombia, established laboratories to refine cocaine or subcontracted that process, organized exports, and the wholesale in the United States to minimize risks. One strategy was to pool exports from several producers and traffickers, making several shipments to scatter risks (Thoumi 1995, chap. 3).

The development of distribution networks in the United States was also facilitated by the proclivity of Colombians to use violence against other smuggling organizations (Gugliotta and Leen 1990). Violence was also instrumental in preventing the competition from possible export syndicates from Bolivia and Peru.

The large profits required sophisticated money-laundering systems. Rapid wealth acquisition, furthermore, made it impossible for successful exporters not to be noticed, which created their need for a social support network to protect their business, illegal profits, and accumulated capital. The illegal drug industry included peasants, chemists, various types of suppliers, purchasers and intermediaries, pilots, lawyers, financial and tax advisers, enforcers, bodyguards, and straw men and smugglers to launder profits. Some were directly part of the cartels, but many were loosely tied to them and sold their services for a fee. The social support network included politicians, police, guerrillas, paramilitaries, individual army members, public employees, bankers, loyal relatives, friends, childhood friends, and others. This social support network provided protection to the illegal industry, mostly at a price, and constituted the main channel through which the illegal industry penetrated and corrupted social organisms. To develop these networks, traffickers like Pablo Escobar built a large residential neighborhood in Medellin where more than 1,000 homes were given away to poor families. Today, it is called "Barrio Pablo Escobar." He also built about 50 soccer fields in the city. Many politicians have been linked to the Cali and Medellin cartels.[8]

During the, 1980s Colombians dominated cocaine production and exports to the United States and Europe. In Colombia, there were several export syndicates; those from Medellin and Cali were preeminent. Other significant groups developed in Bogotá and the Caribbean Coast. Smaller syndicates remained in the shadow of the two main ones. These varied from relatively large to "mom-and-pop" organizations that exported small quantities. The size of the cartels is impossible to determine with certainty, but Zabludoff (1997), using US intelligence data, estimated that the managerial core of the 10 largest Colombian cartels was made up of about 500 people. These also employed 5,000 people, counting laboratory employees, transport personnel, money launderers, and order and contract enforcers. One should add to these 1,000 specialized "freelancers": pilots, chemists, lawyers, assassins for hire, financial advisers, and the like. Some of these are permanently employed, but many work only part-time for the illegal industry. The drug industry also used the services of about 10,000 technical and nonqualified personnel. These were also employed on both a permanent and a part-time basis and included guards and bodyguards, "mules," radio operators, messengers, heavy equipment operators, surveillance teams, "Smurfs," and others. Additionally, there is an indeterminate number of people who serve in airlines, airplane and communications equipment maintenance, banks and other financial institutions, chemical input suppliers, and the like. Frequent captures of "mules" carrying small amounts suggest that the number of small organizations could be in the hundreds.

The two cartels followed different strategies. Pablo Escobar and Carlos Lehder sought political power directly. In the early 1980s, Lehder formed a fascist-like party and Escobar was elected as a member of the House of Representatives. Their main goal was to change the extradition treaty with the United States signed in 1978. The Cali cartel followed a low-profile strategy of "purchasing" politicians support while remaining behind the scenes. The two cartels developed armed groups to protect their assets and to influence politics and society. The Medellin cartel used them as a terrorist instrument to fight extradition. It killed a large number of politicians, journalists, law enforcement personnel, and others who opposed the illegal drugs industry. There are no good data on the specific drug-related homicides. Political and criminal violence have been tightly linked, and crime has been politicized in an environment in which the state has lost the monopoly of power and private security has become a leading industry (Gutiérrez Sanín and Jaramillo 2004).[9] A conflict between the two cartels over the control of New York's market led to violent acts between them, including setting bombs in some of their leaders' residences in Colombia. At the beginning, the large cocaine exporters from Medellin and Cali sold to independent distributors at the US port of entry, but with time they sent "cells" to distribute in smaller quantities in the main US markets, and their direct competition led to conflicts. The Medellin cartel developed gangs of young *sicarios* used to kill enemies or rivals, to settle accounts with business partners, or to eliminate competitors (Salazar 1990), and the Cali cartel followed suit. These gangs have been a feature of Colombian society since then.

The government reacted to "narcoterrorism" and, after a period of confrontation, negotiated an agreement with Escobar by which he turned himself in to be jailed in a prison he had built. He continued running his business from jail and escaped when the government tried to move him to a true prison. This led to a massive government operation against the cartel, and by December 2, 1993, when Escobar was killed trying to escape from a safe house, most of the Medellin cartel had been destroyed. The Cali cartel that had had confrontations with the Medellin group collaborated with the government, providing intelligence on Escobar.[10]

The Medellin syndicate had purchased large plots of rural land and, to protect them against guerrilla organizations, developed links with the military and organized its own armed branch, which became one of the roots of a widespread paramilitary movement (Reyes 1997). This group fought the national police, which was trying to destroy the cartel.

The Cali trafficking organization invested mainly in urban areas and developed strong links with Cali police and local politicians. The demise of the Medellin cartel benefited the Cali syndicate that became preeminent, but after the scandal caused by the disclosure of the cartel's funding of Ernesto Samper's presidential election in 1994, the government had to turn against the Cali cartel and succeeded in eliminating and jailing its leaders (Lee and Thoumi 1999).

3. The Fragmentation of the Industry and the Growth of Coca

The success against the two large cartels "democratized" the industry and led to the emergence of many small *cartelitos* and a few mid-sized ones. Some of the branches of the large cartels continued operating as independent smaller organizations, and other sought the opportunity to enter the business (Garzón 2010). The *sicarios'* drug-related demand declined and they diversified into extorting and other criminal activities. Guerrilla and paramilitary groups also sought other revenue sources. In an attempt to solve the long-running guerrilla problem, a new constitution enacted in 1991 sought to democratize the political system and established mechanisms to transfer funds from the central government to local governments. For the first time, poor municipalities in isolated regions had significant revenues. These did not have administrative capabilities and became bounties for guerrilla and paramilitary organizations. These changes created a premium on territorial control by guerrilla paramilitary groups and have become a main source of widespread government corruption (Reyes Posada 1997; Thoumi 2009; López Hernández 2010).

At the same time, coca plantings expanded. Small trafficking organizations had strong incentives to purchase coca paste locally, traffic from Peru became difficult because of the interdiction efforts against illegal flights to Colombia by the Peruvian government, a fungus infestation in that country, and the opening of the Colombian economy from 1990 spanned a rural crisis in parts of the country from where peasants willing to grow coca migrated to unsettled areas. In 1997, Colombia became the largest producer of coca in the world. This development increased the complexity of the "drug issue."

In the 1980s, there had been some large coca plantings, but by the 1990s, almost all were small peasant-size cultivations. This fragmentation was reinforced when the government began to aerially spray plantings. In some rural areas, coca became the main source of employment, strengthened the guerrilla groups, and raised peasant issues in the policy agenda. Paramilitary groups also participated in this process. Guerrillas and the paramilitary were heavily involved in the drug industry, although guerrillas were mainly involved in coca planting protection and coca paste production, while the paramilitary were mostly into the more advanced stages of the trafficking chain.

4. *Other Changes in the 1990s*

Other factors induced changes in the illegal industry during the 1990s. The cocaine demand in the United States was saturated and prices fell sharply, which induced a search for new markets and products. Links were established between Colombian and European criminal organizations (Clawson and Lee III 1996, pp. 62–90; Krauthausen 1998). In the early 1990s, vigorous US interdiction efforts in the Caribbean induced Colombian traffickers to seek alternative routes, and they developed links with Mexican trafficker organizations. At first, Colombians consigned the cocaine to the Mexicans, who in exchange for a fee smuggled it to the United States to deliver it to Colombian networks. Later, Mexicans began to be paid in kind a proportion of the cocaine and began to use their distribution networks in the West Coast, taking advantage of the large Mexican immigrant population. The Colombians lost market share in the United States but deflected the focus of American antidrug foreign policy toward Mexico.

When traffickers invested in land in guerrilla-controlled areas, such as in the Middle Magdalena Valley, the guerrillas tried to apply the same extortion and kidnapping taxation methods used on traditional landowners. These tactics led drug traffickers to create paramilitary groups that took advantage of the legal right to form self-defense community groups to protect the traffickers' investments and allowed them to expand them, displacing or killing peasants and social reform sympathizers.

The importance of weapons as a control instrument in the industry changed the structure of the illegal industry. Traffickers who developed a symbiotic relationship with the paramilitary groups became more powerful and subordinated smaller groups. They, however, did not reach the importance of the earlier cartels. The largest one was the North Valley syndicate based in Cartago, where "for several years, the vacuum left by the big *capos* was filled by some of the emerging *capos* in the Urdinola and Henao clans, and there was an attempt to maintain levels of hierarchy in the organization. Disagreements persisted, however, and the crime organization ended up fragmenting" (Garzón 2010, p. 39).

President Samper (1994–1998) spent almost all his energy responding to the drug-funding accusations and failed to confront the growing social and political problems of the country. During his administration, guerrillas and paramilitary gained power and control over larger areas of the country. By 1998, when President Pastrana took over, it was clear that the armed groups were a main threat to national security. He followed a two-pronged approach: on the one hand, peace negotiations with FARC and, on the other hand, strengthening the military to control the territory and to attack the drug industry.

To implement these policies, Pastrana requested help from the United States. In late 1998, "Plan Colombia" was created with significant US funding. Originally, the US and Colombian goals diverged. For the United States, "Plan Colombia" was an antidrug program. For the Colombian government, it was mainly an anti-FARC program, but the US limited the application of its funds to antidrug measures. After 9/11, FARC and paramilitary groups were declared terrorist organizations in the United States, which allowed the use of those funds against FARC. One of the main goals of "Plan Colombia" was to modernize the country's armed forces so that they could control the national territory. This process took at least four years to achieve results and allowed the following Uribe administration to harvest them (Veillette 2005).

Pastrana granted a "distention" zone to FARC where peace discussions could take place. This zone was 42,000 square kilometers in size,[11] included large coca-growing areas, and was out of bounds to the Colombian police and armed forces. Contrary to the granting rules, FARC substituted local governments and imposed its own laws and a primitive justice system.

FARC used this area to deepen its participation in the illegal drug industry. It imposed price controls on coca and gradually substituted for the intermediaries in the drug business. It also built landing strips for planes carrying cocaine. It taxed coca peasants and controlled the manufacturing and local marketing of illicit drugs.

The "Peace Process" with FARC was limited to talks that did not lead to an agenda of issues to be discussed. FARC stretched out these talks while it gained military strength and made a few successful attacks on government forces outside the distention zone. After more than 3 years of frustrations, Pastrana cancelled the "distention" zone in early 2002 (Thoumi 2009a, p. 219).

5. Drugs and Crime During the Uribe Administration (2002–2010)

The failure of the negotiations with FARC and the discouragement of most Colombians were capitalized by Álvaro Uribe, who ran for president and was elected in 2002 on a hard-hand platform against FARC. Uribe's "democratic security" platform sought to guarantee citizens the right to move freely around the country without fear of kidnapping or extortion. His antidrug policies focused mainly on eradicating illegal crops to undermine FARC finances and on extraditing traffickers to the United States.

In late 2003, the Uribe administration, benefitting from Pastrana's modernization of the military, formulated "Plan Patriota" with an aim to establish control and state presence over large parts of the territory. This action was also designed to go after FARC, which retreated into inhospitable jungle areas hard for the government to penetrate. Since then, FARC has been on the defensive. However, although the government has won substantive battles, it has not been able to eliminate the guerrilla group.

In 2004, Uribe started negotiations with paramilitary groups that had important links to members of the government's coalition. A bill on "Peace, Justice and Reparation" was introduced in Congress, and a safe haven for paramilitary leaders was established in the town of Ralito where negotiations could take place. These resulted in a massive demobilization of some 37,000 paramilitary, most of whom had to be reinserted in civil society. The strong link between drug trafficking and paramilitary groups conspired to allow both groups to accumulate large amounts of land. They purchased large ranches, but a significant proportion was obtained by threatening small owners. Paramilitary groups frequently accused peasants of supporting guerrillas to force them from their lands.[12] Colombia today has more than 3 million displaced peasants resulting from a land concentration process in the hands of paramilitary and drug trafficking lords.

The strength of the paramilitary and drug industry links with the political establishment became evident in the debates in Congress that weakened the reparation aspects of what became the "Peace and Justice" law. Many elected officials openly opposed measures to confiscate land that had been acquired by threatening, displacing, or killing the previous owners. The Ralito episode also was used by some drug traffickers to "purchase" paramilitary groups and pass as paramilitary commanders to qualify for the expected benefits of the negotiation and cleanse their record and assets.[13]

Aerial spraying of coca fields was first tried in the early 1980s, but it was stopped. This practice was revived during the Samper administration, was reinforced by Pastrana, and became massive with Uribe. The official data are dramatic and contradictory: in each of the eight years of the Uribe government, Colombia eradicated more coca than what it was estimated to produce. Also, cocaine seizures increased sharply from around 80 metric tons of cocaine in 2001 to around 210 tons a year in 2005–2008, that is, one-third of the potential production. Indeed, the data on eradication, cocaine seizures, and world cocaine demand are contradictory. If the eradication data are valid, there is not enough coca to produce the cocaine claimed to have been produced. If cocaine seizures are valid, there is not enough cocaine to satisfy the world demand. The two main data source agencies, The United Nations Office on Drugs and Crime (UNODC) and the US State Department, live comfortably with these contradictions.[14]

The intense aerial spraying had important consequences. First, plantings moved and spread across the country. Second, coca plots became smaller to avoid detection and to make spraying difficult. Third, peasants have devised methods of protecting their plants such as heavily pruning plants immediately after being sprayed to prevent the herbicide from reaching the plants' roots. Fourth, spraying aggravates the displacement problems and increases the supply of labor available to illegal armed groups (Duncan 2006).

Alternative development programs have also been implemented, but they have not been as important as eradication and, as is commonly the case with these projects, they have been difficult to implement and sustain (Vargas Meza 2010).

Extradition has been the other antidrug policy anchor. In the 1980s, this was the main trigger of narcoterrorism, and "We prefer a tomb in Colombia than jail in the US" became a drug traffickers' slogan. At that time, extradition was widely perceived as an affront on the country's sovereignty, and the narcoterrorist response made it widely unpopular. Before Uribe, every extradition was an important event. During the Uribe administration, the number of extraditions exploded as more than 1,100 drug traffickers including many paramilitary were extradited, over 10 times more than the number extradited before his presidency.[15]

Extraditions have become controversial. First, criminals can be extradited only for crimes against foreign interests like drug trafficking. This means that those extradited evade accusations of human rights crimes in Colombia and the requirement of reparation to their victims (López Hernández 2010). Second, this protects politicians and others who supported their criminal activities in Colombia. Third, they have learned to plea bargain with the US government. Many extradited criminals negotiate sentences, permanent resident visas for their relatives, turn in a large share of their assets, and leave enough for their family to live comfortably in the United States (Téllez and Lesmes 2006; Reyes 2007)

The intensified repression made possible by the Ralito negotiations (2003–2005) disrupted the drug industry's organization. Many of the main traffickers were detained and extradited. Mid-level traffickers fought to replace them. As a result of these negotiations, the government established a social reinsertion program, but many of the low-level paramilitary personnel who participated in it found that their only skills were in crime and violence and formed new "emerging bands" (Duncan 2006).

The demise of large paramilitary groups, the weakening of the guerrillas, and the fragmentation of the drug industry also produced a cadre of new criminal organizations. The best known are the euphemistically called "collection agencies" that have developed in several cities. These are criminal networks that link the drug-exporting organizations down through the hit men bands, common criminals, gangs, and even the small neighborhood groups of young people (Garzón 2010, p. 42). They extort local business; they are car thieves, burglars, and stick-up artists; and they perform hired killings, steal from gasoline and oil pipes, and control local drug sales. These "agencies" invest in urban licit and illicit businesses that provide a front to hide their own main sources of income. Not surprisingly, in Medellin the homicide rate increased sharply after "Don Berna," the head of the "Envigado Office," the main agency, was extradited on May 13, 2008. The internal struggle for succession and control of the local crime resulted in a homicide rate of 83 per 100,000 residents in 2010, more than double the national average (SEMANA 2011).[16]

The fragmentation also opened opportunities for former paramilitary, guerrillas, and common criminals to form "emerging bands" without a political agenda but with a lot of criminal skills. Some have gone into areas left by the paramilitary and guerrillas and seek control of coca and cocaine-producing areas and trafficking corridors. Others operate in urban areas (Garzón 2010).

There are also reports of small "boutique" syndicates specializing in smaller drug exports and money-laundering operations. These are formed by mostly educated, multilingual, and worldly individuals who have learned to operate with a low profile and have links with international trafficking organizations.[17]

To summarize, the illegal drug industry has become increasingly intertwined with the social fabric, the polity, and the economy of many regions. It adapted to every government policy and evolved into diversified organized crime organizations, and its structure has become increasingly complex.

V. Reasons for Crime and Policy Failure

A. Organized Crime and Illegal Drugs: Do They Have Any Causes?

As noted, the concentration of the coca-cocaine in a few countries cannot be explained by an external demand.[18] The point is quite simple: If a particular product that is easy to produce and can be produced in many countries is declared illegal globally and its production and trafficking are concentrated in one or a few countries, it will do so where it is easier to do illegal things! This means that the competitive advantage of Colombia in the cocaine industry is rooted in its illegality, not in its profitability. Illegal cocaine demand is a great incentive to produce cocaine in the world, but its production is concentrated in Colombia because it is illegal and Colombia has developed a competitive advantage in illegal activities that is based on the country's structure and institutions.

Illegal economic activities are not Newtonian phenomena that have a cause such that "if X then Y." They are the result of evolutionary processes in which factors such as social exclusion, poverty, inequality, unemployment, economic crisis, and corruption contribute to their development. None of those factors, however, are causes: there are innumerable examples of the existence of all those factors in countries where there is no organized crime or large criminal economic. Illegal economic activities have very few necessary factors. Some are related to the "production function"—that is, the appropriate land to grow coca, sufficient knowledge of chemistry to refine cocaine, and access to the necessary inputs. Land, of course, cannot be moved, but the other factors are easy to obtain. The main necessary factor, however, is a strong conflict between the law or formal norms and the social norms accepted as legitimate by a group or various social groups.

It can be argued that some illegal activities are not planned but are simply the result of opportunistic behavior. In this case, the individual might be tempted but also had to be willing. Illegal economic activities beyond petty crime require, however, a plan, the participation of a group, and the development of a support network of people who are willing and who consider it appropriate to break the law. To have a coca-cocaine and poppy-heroin industry and to export those products, it is necessary to have complex illegal organizations that can grow only in countries in which there are groups whose social or informal behavior rules and norms differ substantially from those formulated by the government that prohibit drug production and trafficking.

In a society in which the rule of law prevails, crime is limited to that committed by a few "bad apples," or individuals whose behavior is deviant in the society. In this case, common police and judicial system law enforcement efforts can keep crime levels low. But if a significant part of the society does not accept the formal rules as legitimate, if many individuals are comfortable breaking those laws, and if breaking laws is justified because the legal system is or appears to be controlled by particular groups that benefit from it, then the society becomes fertile ground for the development of illegal economic activities.

There are, however, countries where there is a gap between formal and informal behavior norms that do not have a significant organized crime problem, like Nepal where the Buddhist monks and the government clash on fundamental issues and the monks are not engaged in crime. For the illicit drug industry to develop, one of two other conditions is necessary. First, the informal social norms of behavior should allow individuals to disregard the effect of their actions on other people; that is, the negative effects that drugs may have on society at large should not be an obstacle for an individual to engage in illicit production or trafficking. These are situations of anomie when individuals feel totally disconnected and alienated from the society and disregard its rules.

Second, a society may have marginalized groups whose norms do not comply with the mainstream, and law breaking is justified to achieve a higher cause: national freedom, overturning an "evil" regime, fighting infidels, or simply protecting the well-being of one's family. If through time the gap between norms results in increased illegal behaviors and impunity, and social controls break down, a strong selfish individualistic culture develops and the probability to produce cocaine and heroin increases. Individuals or social groups could feel justified producing drugs because they can be a weapon to achieve their goals.

It is important to point out that there are no sufficient factors for crime, and it is possible for a society to have all contributing and necessary factors and *to not have organized crime understood as the presence of large-scale criminal organizations.* These societies are simply vulnerable and may fall prey to organized crime and illegal economic growth at any time. Societies are like bodies. They either have high or low defenses against various illnesses. These cannot be completely prevented, but the main policy against them should be to raise the weak defenses.

The lack of sufficient factors creates an identification problem. For example, organized crime may grow when there is an economic crisis. This crisis could be perceived as the cause of the organized crime growth when in reality it has been only a triggering factor. The real necessary factor is the conflict between norms, which legitimizes lawbreaking among some citizens.

B. The Ineffectiveness of Policies

Antidrug policies in Colombia are extremely diverse: attacking kingpins, extraditing them, eradicating and fumigating illegal plantings, interdicting chemical precursors and drugs, raising sentences, passing anti-money-laundering legislation, reforming the justice systems, etc. The antidrug policy arsenal is focused on attacking contributing and minor necessary factors like precursor control or poverty, but most policies do not deal with the underlining norms conflict or governance and governability issues. The point is that the illegal industry and organized crime are symptomatic of unresolved social conflicts—as long as they persist, crime and drugs will continue to be a feature of those societies. This is why the "war on drugs" is now 40 years old and there are no signs that the "drug problem" is being solved. The challenge for Colombia is not to legalize drugs but to "legalize Colombia," that is, to build a nation under the rule of law. This surely is a mighty challenge!

ACKNOWLEDGMENT

The author thanks Letizia Paoli for constructive comments on an earlier draft of the essay.

NOTES

1. The United Nations High Commissioner for Refugees estimates that in December 2010, Colombia had 3.6 million refugees (http://www.unhcr.org/pages/49e492ad6.html).
2. Most references to these activities are journalistic; see, for example, http://www.semana.com/noticias-nacion/crimen-exportacion/119996.aspx.
3. The homicide rate is currently "only" 35 per 100,000 inhabitants, a figure much lower than those in the high 60s of a decade ago. This compares with the current "very high" Mexican figure (15), the "high" US figure (5), and the European average of around 1.
4. See Yunis (2003) and Thoumi (2003, 2009b) for deeper and more detailed discussions of these issues.
5. A good history of the Colombian nineteenth and twentieth centuries is Bushnell (1993). Berquist (1978) is a good analysis of the nineteenth-century civil wars and the role played by coffee. Kalmanovitz (1988) provides a good look at the *La Violencia* period of the mid-twentieth century. Thoumi (1995, 2003) studied the development of the illegal drug industry. The recent development of paramilitary, drug-trafficking organizations and their links with the guerrillas and parts of the state and the concentration of land in the hands of violent groups has been the subject of several excellent works such as Reyes (2009), Duncan (2006), and López Hernández (2010).
6. There are no good data on marijuana prices, but whatever they would be, they pale when compared with the wholesale cocaine prices in the United States in the late 1970s ($70,000 per kilo) and early 1980s ($60,000 per kilo) (Kalmanovitz 1990; Sarmiento 1990). Since then, the cocaine price declined dramatically to today's wholesale of about $15,000 per kilo, which, taking inflation into consideration, is less than 10% of the price of 30 years ago.
7. The word *cartel* is used in very different way from the traditional use in economics because these syndicates could not control production or fix prices.
8. The American Embassy in Bogota has suspected that many high-level politicians have been close to the main traffickers. The National Security Archive Colombian project at George Washington University has made public declassified documents that *confirms* this (nsarchive@gwu.edu).
9. During the 1980s, the homicide rate exploded in the country. The homicide rate increased from about 16.8 per 100,000 inhabitants in 1973–1975 to 62.8 per 100,000 inhabitants in 1988. In the early 1970s, 2.5% of all deaths were homicides, a high figure for most countries, but in 1987, it was 8.1%; that is, one in twelve deaths was a homicide (Thoumi 1995, pp. 72–3).
10. Bowden (2001) gives a detailed story of the government's chase of Escobar.
11. Slightly larger than Switzerland.
12. Reyes (2009) presents a comprehensive and compelling record of this process.
13. There are several excellent works on the paramilitary–drugs–politics symbiosis in Colombia and the Uribe administration. See Duncan (2006), Reyes (2009), Garzón (2010), Romero (2007), and López Hernández (2010).
14. This can be verified in various yearly issues of the *World Drug Report* of the UNODC and the US Department of State *International Narcotics Strategy Report*.
15. See http://www.eltiempo.com/archivo/documento/CMS-7681890.
16. There many journalistic references on the Internet to the increase in violence in Medellin. The link of this to "Don Berna's" extradition was confirmed by the city's police head in an interview with the author on October 21, 2011, in Medellin.

17. There are no real data about these, but in interviews of personnel in the Prosecutor General ("Fiscal") office, the police, and the military with the author from 2006 through 2011, they always refer to these as a new threat.

18. This section is adapted from Thoumi (2009b).

REFERENCES

Americas Watch. 1991. *The 'Drug War' in Colombia: The Neglected Tragedy of Political Violence.* Washington, DC: Americas Watch.

Arango, Mario. 1988. *Impacto del Narcotráfico en Antioquia*, 3rd ed. Medellín: J. M. Arango.

Bejarano, Jorge E. 1952. *Nuevos Capítulos Sobre el Cocaísmo en Colombia.* Bogotá.

Berquist, Charles W. 1978. *Coffee and Conflict in Colombia, 1886-1910.* Durham, NC: Duke University Press.

Bowdem, Mark. 2001. *Killing Pablo.* New York: Atlantic Monthly Press.

Bushnell, David. 1993. *The Making of Modern Colombia. A Nation in Spite of Itself.* Berkeley: University of California Press.

Camacho Guizado, Álvaro. 1988. *Droga y Sociedad en Colombia: El Poder y el Estigma.* Bogotá: CIDSE Universidad del Valle—Fondo Editorial CEREC.

CICAD-OAS (Inter-American Drug Abuse Control Commission of the Organization of American States). 2005. *The Toxicology of Selected Substances Used in the Production and Refining of Cocaine and Heroin: A Tier-Two Assessment* Washington, DC: CICAD-OAS.

Clawson, Patrick L., and Lee Rensselaer III. 1996. *The Andean Cocaine Industry.* New York: St. Martin's Press.

Duncan, Gustavo. 2006. *Los Señores de la Guerra. De Paramilitares, Mafiosos y Autodefensas en Colombia.* Bogotá: Planeta Editorial.

Garzón, Juan Carlos. 2010. *Mafia & Co. The Criminal Networks in Mexico, Brazil and Colombia.* Baltimore: The Johns Hopkins University Press for the Woodrow Wilson Center for International Scholars.

González-Arias, José Jairo. 1992. *El Estigma de las Repúblicas Independientes 1955-1965.* Bogotá: CINEP.

González-Plazas, Santiago. 2006. *El Programa de Erradicación de Cultivos Ilícitos Mediante Aspersión Aérea de Glifosato: Hacia la Clarificación de la Política y su Debate.* Bogotá: Centro de Estudios y Observatorio de Drogas y Delitos—CEODD, Universidad del Rosario.

—— 2008. *Pasado y Presente del Contrabando en la Guajira. Aproximaciones al Fenómeno de Ilegalidad en la Región,* Bogotá: Centro de Estudios y Observatorio de Drogas y Delitos— CEODD, Universidad del Rosario.

Gugliotta, Guy, and Jeff Leen. 1990. *Kings of Cocaine.* New York: Harper.

Gutiérrez Sanín, Francisco, and Ana Maria Jaramillo. 2004. "Crime, (Counter-) insurgency and the Privatization of Security—The Case of Medellin, Colombia." *Environment & Urbanization,* 16: 2.

Henman, Anthony. 1978. *Mama Coca.* London: Hassle Free Press.

Kalmanovitz, Salomón. 1988. *Economía y Nación. Una Breve Historia de Colombia*, 3rd ed. Bogotá: Siglo XXI Editores.

Kalmanovitz, Salomón. 1990. "La Economía del Narcotráfico en Colombia." *Economía Colombiana* 226–227: 18–28.

Kirkpatrick, Sidney D., and Peter Abrahams. 1991. *Turning the Tide. One Man Against the Medellin Cartel*. Dutton, UK: Penguin Books.

Krauthausen, Ciro. 1998. *Padrinos y Mercaderes: Crimen Organizado en Italia y Colombia*. Bogotá: Planeta Colombiana Editorial.

López Hernández, Claudia, ed. 2010. *Y Refundaron la Patria. De Cómo Mafiosos y Políticos Reconfirguraron el Estado Colombiano*. Bogotá: Random House Mondadori.

López Restrepo, Andrés. 2000. "De la Prohibición a la Guerra: El Narcotráfico Colombiano en el Siglo XX." In Instituto de Estudios Políticos y Relaciones Internacionales, *Colombia: Cambio de Siglo. Balances y Perspectivas*. Bogotá: Planeta, 69–112.

Mora de Tovar, Gilma. 1988. *Aguardiente y Conflictos Sociales en la Nueva Granada Siglo XVIII*. Bogotá: Universidad Nacional de Colombia.

Partridge, William L. 1975. "Cannabis and Cultural Groups in a Colombian Municipio." In *Cannabis and Culture*, edited by Vera Rubin. The Hague: Mouton, pp. 147–72.

Perry, Guillermo, Arias, Omar S., Fajnzylber, Pablo, Maloney, William. F., Mason, Andrew D., & Saavedra-Chanduvi, Jaime. 2007. *Informality: Exit and Exclusion*. The World Bank.

Rangel, Alfredo, ed. 2005. *El Podre Paramilitar*. Bogotá: Planeta Editorial.

Rensselaer W., Lee, III, and Francisco E. Thoumi. 1999. "Did the Traffickers Subvert Democracy in Colombia." *Trends in Organized Crime* 5(2): 59–84.

Reyes, Gerardo. 2007. *Nuestro Hombre en la D.E.A.* Bogotá: Editorial Planeta.

Reyes Posada, Alejandro. 1997. "Compras de Tierras por Narcotraficantes." In *Drogas Ilícitas en Colombia. Su Impacto Económico, Político y Social*, edited by F. Thoumi. Bogotá: Ariel, PNUD and DNE.

Posada, Alejandro. 2009. *Guerreros y Campesinos. El Despojo de la Tierra en Colombia*. Bogotá: Editorial Norma.

Romero, Mauricio, ed. 2007. *Parapolitica: La Ruta de la Expansión Paramilitar y los Acuerdos Políticos*. Bogotá: Intermedio Editores.

Ruiz Hernández, Hernando. 1979. "Implicaciones Sociales y Económicas de la Producción de la Marihuana," in Asociación Nacional de Instituciones Financieras (ANIF), *Marihuana: Legalización o Represión*. Bogotá: Biblioteca ANIF de Economía.

Sáenz Rovner, Eduardo. 2007. "La Prehistoria de la Marihuana en Colombia: Consumo y Cultivos Entre los Años 30 y 60." *Cuadernos de Economía* XXVI(47): 205–22.

Sáenz Rovner, Eduardo. 2008. *The Cuban Connection: Drug Trafficking, Smuggling, and Gambling in Cuba From the 1920s to the Revolution*. Chapel Hill: The University of North Carolina Press.

Salazar, Alonso. 1990. *No Nacimos Pa' Semilla*. Bogotá: Corporación Región and CINEP.

Salazar, Alonso. 1998. *La Cola del Lagarto*. Medellín: Corporación Región.

Safford, Frank, and Marco Palacios. 2002. *Colombia: Fragmented Land, Divided Society*. New York: Oxford University Press.

Sarmiento, Eduardo. 1990. "Economía del Narcotráfico." In *Narcotráfico en Colombia: Dimensiones Políticas, Económicas, Jurídicas e Internacionales*, edited by C. G. Arrieta et al. Bogotá: Tercer Mundo Editores-Ediciones Uniandes.

Schneider, F., and R. Klinglmair. 2004. "Shadow Economies Around the World: What Do We Know?" Department of Economics, Johannes Kepler University of Linz, Working Paper 0403.

SEMANA. 2011. Medellín: Gama de Favoritos en el Partidor Para la Alcaldía. SEMANA. (February 14).

Stone, Alexander. 2006. "Illegal Tender, Counterfeit Dollars and Colombian Crime." *Harvard International Review*. (May 6).

Téllez, Edgar, and Jorge Lesmes. 2006. *Pacto en la Sombra. Los Tratos Secretos de Estados Unidos con el narcotráfico*. Bogotá: Editorial Planeta.

Thoumi, Francisco E. 1995. *Political Economy and Illegal Drugs in Colombia*. Boulder, CO: Lynne Rienner.

Thoumi, Francisco E. 2003. *Illegal Drugs, Economy and Society in the Andes*. Baltimore, MD: The Johns Hopkins University Press for the Woodrow Wilson International Center for Scholars.

Thoumi, Francisco E. 2009. "From War Lords to Warlords: Illegal Drugs and the 'Unintended' Consequences of Drug Policies in Colombia." In *Governments of the Shadows. Parapolitics and Criminal Sovereignty*, edited by Eric Wilson. New York: Pluto Press.

Thoumi, Francisco E. 2009b. "Necessary, Sufficient and Contributory Factors Generating Illegal Economic Activity, and Specifically Drug-Related Activity, in Colombia." *Iberoamericana* 35: 105–26.

Thoumi, Francisco E. 2010. "The International Drug Control Regime as a Straight Jacket: Are There Any Policy Options?" *Trends in Organized Crime*, 13(1): 75–86.

Tokatlian, Juan Gabriel. 2003. *The United States and Illegal Crops in Colombia: The Tragic Mistake of Futile Fumigation*. Center for Latin American Studies, University of California, Berkeley. Working Paper No. 3. (June).

Vargas Meza, Ricardo. 2010. *Desarrollo Alternativo en Colombia y Participación Social: Propuestas Hacia un Cambio de Estrategias*. Bogotá: Diálogo Interagencial en Colombia.

US Department of State, Bureau of International Narcotics and Law Enforcement Affairs (INL). 1992. *International Narcotics Control Strategy Report*. Washington, DC: US Department of State.

Veillette, Connie. 2005. *Plan Colombia: A Progress Report*. Washington, DC: Foreign Affairs, Defense, and Trade Division, Congressional Research Service, Library of Congress. (February 17).

Yunis, Emilio. 2003. *¿Por Qué Somos Así? ¿Qué pasó en Colombia? Análisis del Mestizaje*. Bogotá: Editorial Temis.

Zabludoff, Sidney. 1997. "Colombian Narcotics Organizations as Business Enterprises." *Transnational Organized Crime* 3(2): 20–49.

CHAPTER 9

....

MEXICAN DRUG "CARTELS"

....

MONICA MEDEL AND FRANCISCO E. THOUMI[1]

I. INTRODUCTION

....

THE illegal drugs industry has been present in Mexico for over a century, during which it has become intertwined with the social and power mainstream. Its history constitutes a fascinating case of social control gone awry coupled with the unintended consequences of policy decisions by a powerful neighbor, the United States. The beginnings of the smuggling organizations can be traced to as early as the US Prohibition era, which outlawed alcohol in the 1920s and early 1930s and saw the emergence of the first organized criminal groups that gained enough notoriety to be named in the press (Astorga 2005). These groups established hubs strategically located along Mexico's border with the United States, particularly in cities such as Tijuana and Ciudad Juárez, which, 70 years later, would become the epicenters of Mexican drug-related violence. Washington had began prohibiting the production, distribution, and use of certain narcotics as far back as 1900, bans that helped fuel a market for controlled substances in that country. Alcohol was only illegal temporarily, but Mexico's availability of marijuana and opium poppies, as well as its close proximity to US soil, provided incentives for Mexican gangs to start producing these substances on larger scales and shipping them north of the Rio Grande. By the late 1930s, drug production and trafficking, based on Mexican poppy and marijuana, was thriving in much of the Mexican northwest, especially in the states of Sinaloa, Durango, Chihuahua, and Baja California, which remain today's main producers and smuggling routes.

Since the beginning, drug leaders have been tied to power structures.[2] Some started their illicit careers with the experience they gathered as former police officers, such as the pioneer Arturo Vaca (Astorga 2005) in the 1930s, and more recently, Miguel Angel Félix-Gallardo, the Guadalajara drug organization kingpin (Lupsha 1992; Astorga

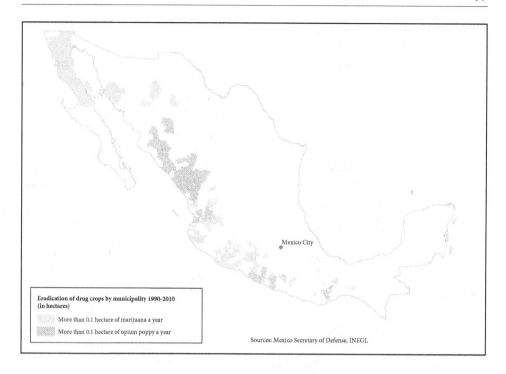

Eradication of drug crops by municipality 1990-2010 (in hectares)

More than 0.1 hectare of marijuana a year

More than 0.1 hectare of opium poppy a year

Sources: Mexico Secretary of Defense, INEGI.

2005), which became Mexico's top smuggling syndicate in the 1980s. Other complex drug organizations emerged from the ranks of deserters from the Mexican Army Special Forces, like the Zetas, a gang that split from the Golfo cartel. But many others have conformed to the control pattern established by the Institutional Revolutionary Party (PRI), which "regulated" the drug smuggling industry while in power from 1929 to 2000. "Dating back at least as far as 1960s, according to most sources, drug producers and traffickers have been the most rewarding, if not the primary, targets of police and politician's extortions" (Paoli, Greenfield, and Reuter 2009, p. 291). For decades during PRI rule, governors, senators, and other high authorities maintained close ties to drug groups. Some were denounced as open collaborators in the press, others directly accused in court of working with, or protecting the activities of, certain groups, often while ensuring authorities targeted rivals. Often, also, entire police agencies have been disbanded after scandals involving corruption and ties with drug trafficking, the most notorious one the Mexican Federal Directorate of Security, which was shutdown in 1985 following the murder of DEA agent Enrique Camarena at the hands of the Guadalajara cartel. But the well-oiled machinery built by the PRI began to crack in the late 1980s, when the party lost governor's races in some northern states. A lack of institutional PRI control created fierce territorial rivalries that fueled drug violence in those areas, and killings increased even more when US anti-narcotics efforts began targeting Mexico more than ever. Soon, the associated violence increased, but it had still not reached the unprecedented levels seen after

2006. That year, President Felipe Calderón declared an all-out war on drugs that saw narcos-related homicides skyrocket.

Mexico's proximity to the United States contributes to the country's involvement in illegal drugs, but it does not explain its evolution. The PRI built an all-powerful bureaucracy and instituted a federated system with many local police forces overlapping in their tasks and weakened law enforcement accountability.[3] Under the PRI, reports have even circulated of police commanders who allegedly paid government officials to be assigned to profitable posts along the border and other strategic drug regions (Andreas 1998, p. 163). Without a large enough or sufficiently trustworthy federal police force to combat drug trafficking, it seemed logical for authorities to call on the military. Unfortunately, the move did little to stem corruption.

In the last few decades, complete battalions have been disbanded for taking bribes from, or openly working for and protecting, drug organizations. Even General Jesús Gutiérrez-Rebollo, the drug czar who was the pride of the Mexican government in the late 1990s, fell into disgrace and was arrested on charges of protecting Amado Carrillo's drug organization, headquartered in Ciudad Juárez (PGR 2000). More recently, the Mexican army has been described by Washington as "reluctant to act on good intelligence and conduct operations against high-level targets" and as suffering from risk aversion, while the head of the federal police for the Calderon administration, Genaro Garcia-Luna, was said to "be counted as a net loser," according to secret cables released by WikiLeaks and cited by newspapers and crime analysis websites.[4]

A weak central state, coupled with powerful local caudillos including state governors, used corruption as an instrument to exert control over the country's territory. Civil society was also very weak and anomie was common among the population. The PRI exerted such tight control over civic organizations that the few that were allowed to exist were co-opted by party machinery, especially trade unions and guilds. Also, the lack of a real political opposition derived from the nonexistence of viable national parties other than the PRI until the 1980s, combined with PRI practices of buying votes and doling out favors, which allowed the party to consolidate a tremendous amount of power.

These created fertile grounds for the development of the illegal drugs industry: "complex illegal organizations can grow only in countries where there are groups whose social or informal behavior rules and norms differ substantially from the formal rules and norms formulated by the government, which prohibit drug production and trafficking" (Thoumi 2009, pp. 106-107).

This combination of factors remained strong until the mid-1980s. The Colombian success against the large Medellín and Cali cartels opened opportunities for Mexican organizations and the beginning of the PRI's loss of political power in the 1980s culminated with Mexico's passage from a single-party political regime to a multiparty system in 2000. The Mexican trafficking organizations reacted to these changes, introduced new trafficking technologies, and displaced the Colombian organizations in many American markets.

The following sections trace the history of the opium and heroin industries going back to their origins in the late 19th century, the development of illegal plantings and smuggling networks, the incentives created by World War II to advance these developments, the rise of the Mexican cartels that started in the 1930s and gained importance in the 1960s and 1970s, the development of links between the dominant party and the illegal industry and the changes induced by external pressures on modernization that led the government to attack the illegal industry, and the response of the trafficking organizations to the government´s actions. The new millennium brought stronger changes due to the state party's loss of political power and the growing globalization of the Mexican economy. These developments resulted in a larger and more sophisticated illegal industry that gained control of local and state governments and induced a crackdown by the Calderón government that has led to very high violence levels. The essay ends with a few conclusions.

II. The Early History

Mexico has produced what today are illegal drugs for a long time. The roots of the industry are in Sinaloa, where at the end of the 19th century native marijuana and opium poppy were introduced by Chinese immigrants. These substances did not have medicinal, cultural, or ritualistic uses in mainstream society. Marijuana was grown and exported to the United States beginning in the late 1800s and opium in the early 20th century (Toro 1995, p. 7).

Prohibitions of narcotics at the municipal and state levels started in 1878. Opium and morphine sales required a medical prescription for the first time in the Americas in the late 1870s in Mexico City (Astorga 2005, p. 19).

Opium had been originally imported from the United States, Europe, and Asia (Astorga 2005, p. 22). This crop took to the country well. From the 19th century through the 1920s, opium, laudanum, and morphine were consumed as medicines, although the press reported opium dens in Mazatlán and Culiacán, suicides, and morphine-overdose deaths. By the early 1900s, heroin was offered as a cough syrup component, while a diluted extract of peyote was a recommended heart tonic. By the early 1920s, coca tonics were advertised to fight anemia, rickets, and paralysis and as rejuvenating potions (Astorga 2005, p. 25).

After the US Opium Exclusion Act of 1909 outlawed opium imports for smoking, Mexico turned into a drug exporting nation. The following US legislation, the Harrison Narcotic Act of 1914 and the Narcotic Drug Import and Export Act of 1922, "created a profitable market for narcotics in the United States" and along with the prohibition of alcohol "provided an incentive for Mexicans (and others) to ship drugs into the US and take advantage of the high prices" (Werner 2001).

At the time, Mexico lacked a federal narcotics law and "Mexican exports of opium and heroin for US consumption flourished in the 1910s and 1920s. Something similar happened with Mexican exports of marijuana, as more and more states in the United States regulated its use, production and sale [....] Thus, a significant contraband along the US-Mexican border emerged after 1910" (Werner 2001, p. 173).

Opium poppy fields developed in Sinaloa, and opium dens spread from Sinaloa and Sonora to many other areas, including Guadalajara and Mexico City. Because of the country's proximity to the illegal US narcotics market, following passage of the Harrison Act, Washington targeted Mexico to establish international drug smuggling controls. In 1916, Mexican president Carranza prohibited opium imports. Most groups smuggling opium into the United States used two primary routes: Mexicali and Tijuana, both in Baja California. Opium arrived by ship from Asia mainly in Acapulco, Mazatlán, and Ensenada, from where it went overland to Baja California. The new laws appeared to specifically target Cornel Esteban Cantu, who headed the military forces in Baja California and who US Customs officials argued controlled the drug trade in the region, conspiring with American citizens to move copious amounts of opium into the United States (Astorga 2003b). Cantu had built a personal fiefdom by levying and collecting taxes. To further attack Cantu and other smugglers, Carranza banned all opium trade in Baja California in 1917.

The frequent raids by US authorities into Mexican territory in pursuit of drug offenders when Americans were involved also helped prompt Carranza to take decisive steps against opium smuggling (Toro 1995, p. 9). At a time when the Mexican Revolution was raging, and with memories of the US-Mexican war still fresh, a move to solidify Mexican sovereignty along the border with the powerful United States seemed prudent.

In 1920, Mexico's government banned the cultivation and sale of marijuana and, three years later, President Obregón barred opium, cocaine, and heroin imports and imposed harsher punishment for the cultivation of their source plants and their manufacturing. With these measures Mexico became a de facto signatory to the 1912 Hague Convention restricting opium and cocaine, despite not formally adhering to the convention until 1925 (Walker 1981, p. 49). In 1926, Mexico's Health Code added opium to the ban on marijuana cultivation and trade and, the following year, President Calles barred the export of both drugs. These attempts to regulate drugs indicate that Mexico was facing a growing narcotics production and smuggling problem. The United States was also pressuring it to improve its anti-narcotics effort as Mexican immigrants began to be identified as marijuana smugglers (Marez 2004, p. 107).

Despite the new laws, production and export of opium and marijuana flourished in Mexico and, in the 1920s and 1930s, the country supplied about 15 percent of the American opium market (Ruiz Cabañas 1989, p. 53). Some medium-sized Mexican traffickers gained notoriety. Enrique Fernandez-Puerta built a small empire smuggling alcohol to the United States during Prohibition. His power and influence grew in Juárez after local authorities proved willing to shelter his activities and associates. He had close ties to the governor of Chihuahua, made large charity contributions, and built schools. Arturo Vaca, a former anti-narcotics police chief, is also mentioned in press reports as the owner of sizeable drug seizures. Newspaper accounts as early as 1937 describe authorities making off with some of the drug shipments they successfully captured.[5] Drug production and trafficking thrived in Sinaloa, Durango, Chihuahua, and Baja California.

III. The World War II Effect

World War II disrupted traditional heroin routes from Asia and through Europe and increased the need for morphine to treat wounded soldiers. This time "the United States did not hesitate to ask Mexican authorities to allow for legal production of marijuana and opium poppy plants in 1940. Indian hemp (marijuana) was required to manufacture ropes, and morphine was needed for medical purposes" (Toro 1995, p. 11). By 1943, opium had become Sinaloa's largest cash crop (Craig 1989, p. 72) and poppy fields appeared in other states in the Sierra Madre Mountains. Marijuana crops emerged in Puebla, Morelos, Guerrero, San Luis Potosí, Tlaxcala, and even Mexico City. Press reports detailed vast marijuana fields in Nuevo León, Coahuila, and Tamaulipas, all on the border with the United States, and in Veracruz, on the Gulf of Mexico.

After the end of World War II, Mexico launched a major US-backed campaign to keep heroin production and drug trafficking at bay (Werner 2001, p. 174), but authorities could not hold back the industry forever. By 1947, US deputy customs secretary John W. Buckley asserted that Mexican traffickers used planes to smuggle opium into the United States. Then, Harry Anslinger, the renowned commissioner of the Federal Bureau of Narcotics, declared Mexico the main US opium supplier, adding that many government officials were involved in drug production and smuggling (Walker 1996, p. 113). Mexico City's newspapers described Culiacán as "the headquarters of opium smugglers" and the state's governor, Pablo Macias-Valenzuela, as a trafficker ringleader (Astorga 2005, p. 73).

In 1948, not long after Anslinger's comments and certainly under US pressure, President Miguel Aleman began the "Great Campaign" to eradicate drug crops in the whole country. Since then, the military has been involved in anti-drug programs. Traffickers adapted to these efforts by developing more consolidated and professional opium and marijuana production networks that prepared them to respond to the American drug demand increase of the 1960s. By the late 1950s, the term *drug dealer* appeared for the first time in the Mexican press and, by 1970, trafficking pioneers Pedro Aviles and Ernesto Fonseca-Carrillo (the "godfather" of the Mexican drug cartels) were well known. Fonseca-Carrillo was first identified as the head of the Guadalajara cartel, where he worked alongside Miguel Angel Félix-Gallardo and Rafael Caro-Quintero, his eventual successors. Fonseca-Carrillo is the uncle of Amado Carrillo, the "Lord of the Skies," who, by the end of the 1980s, was flying cocaine from South America to Miami and other US points.[6]

IV. The Rise of Mexico's Cartels

Since the 1930s, Mexico had been the main source of imported marijuana in the United States. By the early 1970s, it had become its biggest supplier of marijuana and heroin (Reuter and Ronfeldt 1992). Mexico had also become a transit route for cocaine.

By 1975, opium and marijuana plantations were spreading throughout the country almost at will all the way to the Yucatán Peninsula on the Caribbean coast. Poppy fields reached into Oaxaca and Chiapas, which borders Guatemala. The attorney general's office (PGR), reported that authorities eradicated 25,000 hectares of poppy between 1970 and 1976, compared to only 4,370 between 1963 and 1970 (Astorga 2005, p. 119). By 1975, a hectare of poppy generated 5 to 6 kilograms of opium gum that could be transformed into one kilogram of heroin. Technological advances and genetic modification eventually allowed poppy crops to sport more bulbs per plant, increasing productivity. Marijuana eradication and seizures reached 13,300 hectares eradicated and 3,800 tons in the period 1970-1976 (Astorga, 2005, pp. 120–121).

Washington's concerns materialized in "Operation Intercept," a search-and-seizure anti-drug initiative that virtually closed the US border with Mexico for 20 days in 1969. The United States sought joint law enforcement activities with Mexican police, but Mexico refused the offer and launched its own extensive aerial spraying campaign (Toro 1995, p. 17). In January 1977, the country started a major US-backed anti-narcotics offensive ("Operation Condor"), a massive action involving 10,000 troops. The operation was headed by army general José Hernandez-Toledo and Carlos Aguilar-Garza, a PGR official who, in 1984, was arrested with 6 kilograms of heroin and cocaine in Tamaulipas. In 1989, he was captured in Texas and extradited. He was assassinated in 1993 (Gootenberg 1999, p. 187).

The campaign used the military to eradicate drug plantations, reinforce police interdiction efforts against narcotics smuggling, and disrupt trafficking organizations in Sinaloa, Durango, and Chihuahua, the "Golden Triangle" of narcotics production. The eradication results were positive and crime rates that had been rising in all three states fell slightly as a relative calm took hold among rival smuggling gangs. From 1975 to 1977, soldiers destroyed an average of more than 7,000 hectares of marijuana and about 13,500 of opium poppy plantations a year (Toro 1995, pp. 18–21). Operation Condor redefined the US-Mexico relationship in that Mexico adopted Washington's war on drugs: "Mexico began to accept helicopters, specialized aircraft, spare parts, pilot training, and other forms of US technical assistance in large quantities." In exchange, the Mexican government "agreed to formalize the presence of US police agents in Mexico who had been gathering intelligence information for decades with or without previous notification of Mexican authorities." Then, in 1983, "under US pressure, President Miguel de la Madrid greatly increased Mexican military participation in the battle against drug activity" (Dominguez and Fernandez de Castro 2001, p.42). He also declared drug trafficking a threat to "national security" in 1988, soon after the United States began issuing annual certifications of cooperation and achievement to countries around the globe as a condition for aid and assistance. Although Mexico was sometimes threatened with being decertified, that action never happened, despite its growing drug business.

Operation Condor had unintended consequences: the displacement of crops and traffickers to other regions in Mexico, the large-scale exodus of peasants to cities, human rights violations, and the use of harmful chemicals (Paraquat) (Turner et al. 1978).

Operation Condor pushed less daring and smaller traffickers out of business, ensuring that only the largest and best-organized groups survived. These became more powerful and influential, armed themselves, and increased the use of violence (Toro 1995, p. 17).

V. Mexico's Cartels Fight Back

Mexican drug syndicates responded to the decline in crop profits caused by Operation Condor by moving into cocaine transportation to the United States. The heroin business declined after Operation Condor, and interdiction initiatives severely limited the availability of Mexican opium in the United States (Resa Nestares 2003, p. 55). The crackdown on production and smuggling also affected marijuana. Another key factor in that decline was a strong rejection by US consumers of Mexican marijuana after word spread throughout America that Mexican authorities were using Paraquat to eradicate marijuana crops (Anderson 1981; Baum 1996; Resa Nestares 2003). As marijuana sales sagged, Mexican cartels moved into cocaine, triggering a profound revamping of the structures of most smuggling gangs. Even though marijuana export levels recovered fully by 1984, the value of Mexican marijuana began to slide after 1991 and has never fully recovered, as increasing competition in the United States has continued to hold prices down.[7]

In late 1984, authorities destroyed a huge marijuana processing center hidden in El Bufalo ranch in the remote desert of Chihuahua. The area was used to store thousands of tons of marijuana while Operation Condor was being conducted, with those who controlled the area apparently hoping to wait it out until the end of the crackdown. This action was so costly for the traffickers that analysts believe it prompted a decision by the Mexican drug organizations to hit back. In February 1985, undercover DEA operative Enrique Camarena and a Mexican pilot were kidnapped. Both were tortured and murdered to send a message to the Mexican and American authorities: a warning of what could happen if anti-drug operations were not scaled back (Los Angeles Times 1989). Until this event, targeting a US government official had been a line Mexican smugglers weren't willing to cross.[8] US officials believed Mexican police authorities were involved in the agent's kidnapping as he worked to prove that Guadalajara had become a key drug trafficking center. When Mexican investigations into the slayings stalled, DEA director Francis Mullen declared that guards from the Mexican Federal Directorate of Security had let the main suspect in Camarena's kidnapping escape, that the directorate was corrupt, and that its agents protected drug gangs in exchange for sizeable bribes (Los Angeles Times 1985).

Caro-Quintero, the head of the Guadalajara cartel, had a romantic relationship with the niece of the governor of Jalisco, where Guadalajara is located. He was captured in Costa Rica in April 1985 and returned to Mexico to face charges for Camarena's murder and as the leader of one of Mexico's largest and richest drug production and smuggling organizations. After his capture, authorities released a list of the country's top drug kingpins, and they acknowledged that some law enforcement officials had links to the illegal organizations while maintaining that the relationship between the cartels and corrupt officials was that of a few rotten apples and that it had not spread across the law enforcement institutions (Proceso 1985). Despite those assurances, in 1985 Mexico shut down the Federal Directorate of Security (DFS), the national police force assigned to preserve the country's internal stability, which had faced the bulk of allegations of official corruption and of protecting drug traffickers.[9]

Fonseca-Carrillo was arrested a short time after the list was released. More fortunate was Félix-Gallardo. A former police officer who became a member of the board of a local bank, he had close ties to a former Sinaloa governor and was frequently mentioned in the social pages of local newspapers. He remained free until 1989, despite more than a dozen arrest warrants issued against him since 1971 (Astorga 2005, p. 145). The capture of the Guadalajara cartel's main leaders forced the group to reorganize, and low-ranking associates moved up to higher positions. This reorganization divided the group's territory into smaller fiefs that formed an alliance under a makeshift umbrella organization known as "The Federation." Among its members were the Arellano-Félix family, which controlled the city of Tijuana, and lucrative routes into neighboring San Diego and much of Southern California; the Carrillo-Fuentes group, based in Ciudad Juárez, across the border from El Paso; and the Amezcua-Contreras organization, the largest illegal importer of ephedrine—a key component of amphetamine-type drugs—into Mexico and on to US territory. The DEA (1996) characterized those organizations as "major Mexican trafficking groups" and concluded that they "operated within a fluid, flexible, and elastic system." The DEA reported at the time that alliances among the groups held, but that "shifts or shake-ups in the hierarchy occur with the divergence of interests and eruptions of internecine violence. But while the precise roles of specific groups and individual organization members often blur, there is an overarching structure within which drug trafficking operates, namely 'The Federation.'" El Golfo cartel, the other large organization based in Matamoros, shunned the coalition. This group developed in the 1980s under the leadership of Juan Garcia-Abrego, who was captured in 1996 and later extradited to the United States. By the end of the millennium, a young and ambitious hit man named Osiel Cardenas Guillen had risen through the ranks of El Golfo cartel to become the group's leader.

The Federation would last until the early 2000s, but, in the mid-1990s, it was already beginning to crack. The most notorious problem arose with the slaying of the archbishop of Guadalajara, Juan J. Posadas, during a shootout in the parking lot of the city's airport in 1993. Posadas was allegedly mistakenly identified as a rival drug lord and was caught in the crossfire between gangs. These bands should have been cooperating as mandated by the alliance. Instead, members of the Tijuana cartel, headed by the Arellano-Félix brothers, and operatives loyal to Joaquin "El Chapo" Guzman-Loera tried to kill one another. Over the next decade, loyalties would crumble further, with every group working in its own interest, occasionally forging alliances in order to defeat a common rival or gain new territories and routes to smuggle drugs to the United States (DEA 1996).

Although at first, in the late 1980s, the amounts moved unilaterally by the Mexicans were minimal, after more aggressive and effective interdiction measures in the Caribbean by the United States, primary cocaine routes began to pass through Central America and Mexico, and ships replaced planes as the most common form of transport (Reuter 1988, pp. 233–252). Early in the 1990s, the Guadalajara cartel was one of the first Mexican trafficking groups to work with the Colombian cocaine Mafias (DEA 1996). "At first, Colombians smuggled their cocaine to Mexico and consigned it to Mexicans, who in exchange of a fee smuggled it to the United States, where they returned it to the Colombians. Later, Mexicans began to be paid in kind a share of the cocaine. For Mexicans this change was welcomed, because it was relatively easy for them to develop distribution networks on the West Coast among the large Mexican migrant population" (Thoumi 2003, p. 100). The killing of Pablo Escobar, the head of the Medellín cartel on December 2, 1993, and the capture of the leaders of the Cali cartel in Colombia fragmented the Colombian trafficking industry into smaller groups that preferred to follow low-profile operations. For them it was convenient to sell the cocaine in Mexico and avoid confronting US law enforcement efforts. The combination of US and Colombian policy decisions to crack down on Colombian cartels, coming at the same time the traditional Caribbean route was blocked to smugglers, proved fruitful for Mexican drug organizations. And they only got more powerful in the coming years as they finally broke free from the yoke of the PRI. Cases of institutional protection of drug trafficking under the PRI regime abound. Besides the DFS case, another major example was the downfall in 1997 of the head of the National Institute to Combat Drugs, General Jesús Gutiérrez-Rebollo. The Mexican antidrug czar was sentenced to 40 years in prison for protecting and receiving money from the Juárez cartel. Meanwhile, PRI governors had for decades been accused in the press, denounced by lawmakers, and even prosecuted for protecting some drug organizations in their states, often while targeting others. For example, the governor of Quintana Roo, where Cancún is located, was arrested in 2001 and charged with providing assistance to drug traffickers and laundering narco profits for the Juárez cartel. In 1997, the governors of Sonora and Morelos were linked to drug cartels (*New York Times* 1997). Also, a few years later, the governor of Tamaulipas was accused of aiding the Golfo cartel (El Universal 2004). This system, however, which was dismantled at the turn of the new millennium, made possible the flow of drugs to American soil with minimum violence.

VI. The New Millennium

In June 2000, the PRI was defeated and Vicente Fox, the head of the center left National Action Party (PAN), was elected president. Fox vastly improved the image of Mexico's presidency simply by winning as a member of a party other than PRI. He also restructured the government administration, dismantling at least part of the unwieldy PRI bureaucratic system.

Under the PRI regime, illegal drug producers and traffickers had long exchanged bribes for protection from authorities (Astorga 2005). Smuggling syndicates understood that, as long as they kept making protection payments, authorities would generally leave them alone. The Fox government changed that, first involuntarily, by simply replacing the previous PRI bureaucracy, which had had deep contacts within drug organizations, with officials from PAN. The president also sought to clean up the ranks of anti-drug authorities and erase longstanding ties between all levels of government and drug cartels. Drug gangs responded with increased levels of violence and, anxious to restore order, the government began to rely more heavily on the military through "Operation Safe Mexico." Decades of relative calm built on corruption disintegrated and the result was a blood bath that heightened the worries of the government even more. Mexican authorities claimed that rising violence proved they were winning the war against drug smugglers and that the major cartels were being forced to endure violent internal shake-ups and outside challenges just to continue operating.[10] But authorities began "employing the current, desperate measures... such as the increased use of the armed forces, in an attempt to recover the relative control and containment of the drug trafficking business that had previously operated for decades" (Astorga 2005, p.162).

For a while, the strategy worked. The Fox administration captured Benjamin Arellano-Félix, the operations chief of the blood-thirsty Tijuana gang. Around the same time in 2002, the group's fearsome enforcer, Ramon Arellano-Félix, was shot and killed, crippling the family business. Authorities also collared Osiel Cardenas-Guillen, the head of the Golfo cartel, the following year. While Fox claimed these were historic victories, a void at the top unleashed a war for territory that centered on Nuevo Laredo, part of the area under control of the Golfo cartel and the main drug entrance into Texas. Drug-related killings became so frequent in the summer of 2005 that the army had to permanently occupy the city, a move that did not succeed in bringing down the murder rate, but at least it kept the surrounding region from sliding into chaos.

In a spectacular operation in October 2002, the Mexican army sent a whole battalion (600 soldiers) to their barracks in Guamuchil, Sinaloa, to investigate all the troops for links to drug trafficking. This battalion's main focus had been to battle drug smuggling, but "Certain important parts of the battalion protected the planting and cultivation of drugs," Defense Minister Ricardo Clemente Vega said later. In November 2002, army generals Arturo Acosta and Francisco Quiros were sentenced to prison for protecting the Juárez cartel.

VII. Drug Kingpin CEOs

Globalization transformed Mexico's business world and had a major impact on drug trafficking. Businesses that began as family firms evolved into professional and sophisticated operations. Drug groups today produce heroin and marijuana, move record levels of cocaine, and have also diversified into synthetic drugs production.

Mexico is a major source of marijuana and heroin for the United States.[11] The 2003 Narcotics Control Strategy Report (INCSR) identified it as the source of between 30 to 40 percent of the US heroin market, and, by 2005, it acknowledged Mexico as "the second principal supplier of heroin" for American consumers (INCSR 2005). And, even though the INCSR does not mention precise figures, it has identified Mexico every year as the largest foreign source of marijuana sold in the United States for the last decade. Mexico does not produce cocaine, but US authorities estimate that most of the cocaine consumed in the United States is smuggled via Mexico. The figures went from 55 percent in the 2000 INCSR Report to 95 percent in the 2011 INCSR Report. For years, the Mexican attorney general's office barely acknowledged that the country's drug gangs had links to cocaine cartels in other regions of the world, but, in an interview with a Colombian newspaper in March 2007, Luis Hernando Gomez ("Rasguño"), a top leader of the Colombian Norte del Valle cartel, claimed that Mexicans "today…impose the conditions. They are practically managing the business. They are very smart: if you send them 1,000 kilos, 400 are for them and they charge 20 percent for smuggling it to Guadalajara or Mexico City, and the investment is charged totally on us" (El Tiempo 2007). Mexican drug organizations also expanded their links to cocaine producers in Peru since the 1990s. Large cocaine seizures destined to Mexico have been made in Peru since 1995 (IPS 2006). By 2006, Carlos Olivo, the head of Peru's National Anti-drug Directorate, acknowledged that Mexican cartels had sent members "with millions of dollars to invest jointly with the Colombians in cocaine production in Peru. The Colombians contributed added know-how and had even sent their own chemists to the jungle to install labs close to the coca fields."[12] By 2008, Peruvian president Alan Garcia asked for help from Mexican police to fight Mexican cartels in his country (Televisa 2008). Since then, media reports quoting DEA agents in South America have mentioned growing links and the expanding operations of Mexican drug organizations in other Latin American countries, and even in Europe (Reuters 2007, 2008; Weintraub and Wood 2010; National Public Radio 2011; British Broadcasting Corporation 2012).

The use of violence by Mexican trafficking organizations has blocked competition: "Mexican drug kingpins are very violent and territorial. This prevents other organizations from settling in. Although Mexicans tolerate the presence of representatives from other groups, they allow them to move in only to do business, not to exploit territories."[13]

As drugs like methamphetamine became popular in cities and towns across America, Mexican smuggling syndicates learned very quickly that it and other synthetics can be produced virtually anywhere at extremely low costs. The main market for Mexican amphetamine type stimulants is the United States. In 2006, Mexico seized a record 20 tons of ephedrine and nearly 13 tons of pseudoephedrine the following year, according to data from the Attorney General's Office or PGR (the acronym in Spanish for its full name, Procuraduria General de la Republica) (PGR 2009). "These drug lords recognized the synthetic drugs market as an alternative. You have no risk in the transport, you don't need large areas of cultivation, your costs in bribes decrease; you don't need to put at risk a large amount of infrastructure such as planes, ships, vehicles. In a little room of two by two meters, you can 'cook' synthetic drugs with an extraordinary profit."[14]

After the major arrests and resulting violence of the early 2000s, Mexican drug trafficking groups entered a new transitional phase. According to the Mexican attorney general's office, various groups formed a sort of administration board under the umbrella of the Juárez cartel, though external disputes eventually caused that alliance to collapse.[15] The Sinaloa cartel, headed by Joaquín "el Chapo" Guzmán-Loera, emerged as the most powerful and influential. Guzmán-Loera became the most wanted and richest criminal in Mexico, making *Forbes* magazine's top millionaires list for the first time in 2009 (Forbes 2009). Guzmán pioneered building tunnels under the US-Mexico border to smuggle cocaine and heroin into the United States and weapons into Mexico. He was arrested in Guatemala in 1993 and imprisoned in Mexico until 2001, when bribed prison guards allowed him to escape, allegedly in a laundry truck. Despite being on the run since then, he has proven extremely effective at running and even boosting his drug business while avoiding capture.

The Sinaloa cartel operates by means of a complex power structure. Guzman-Loera is the boss and worked closely with Ismael "El Mayo" Zambada and, until his death, Ignacio "Nacho" Coronel. Both were in charge of important territories and smuggling routes. Below Guzman-Loera and his top deputies, regional bosses control certain areas. Other top cartel leaders are in charge of finance, logistics, transportation, and security (SSP 2007).

Armed security branches of Mexican drug trafficking organizations developed after the PRI lost the presidential election in 2000. In a bold response to the military's increased role in antidrug operations, Osiel Cardenas-Guillen, head of the Golfo cartel, co-opted a division of the Mexican army's best-trained Special Forces unit (GAFE). Some members of GAFE resigned, but others simply defected and became part of the Golfo cartel, which also enrolled civilians in its armed wing that became known as the Zetas (Ravelo 2006, pp. 253–259). This group has become a main source of drug trafficking associated violence.

Defection from the armed forces is a huge problem. In January 2008, Mexico's deputy defense minister, Tomás Angeles Dauahare,[16] acknowledged that more than 100,000 soldiers had defected since 2000, an unknown number of them to join drug organizations. (EFE 2008; *La Jornada* 2008) The Zetas are fierce and ruthless. Battles among rival gangs became brutal. Torture and mutilation are common. Previous feuds had involved the members of the trafficking groups but with the Zetas, policemen, local security officials, journalists, judges, and other civilians became targets. The Sinaloa cartel responded by forming its own militia, not using Mexican army officials but instead recruiting members of the Chachos, Los Negros, and Los Texas gangs in Mexico (Notimex 2009; *Time* 2009), and banding together with US gangs like the Texas Mexican Mafia (TMM) and Mara Salvatrucha (MS-13) (TDPS 2010, pp. 22, 30). The latter two gangs operate in Texas, and TMM is structured according to a paramilitary model, reports the 2010 Texas Gang Threat Assessment produced by the Texas Department of Public Safety.

The new structures distinguished themselves from the traditional family managerial style ones. Among the latter was Los Valencia, which had long controlled drug production and smuggling in Michoacán, and the Diaz-Parada group, which produced and transported marijuana in Oaxaca (SSP 2007). Both organizations began to buckle in the face of unprecedented violence, and they lost importance. Currently, all of Mexico's thriving drug gangs rely on business management tactics, necessary to overcome the pressure exerted by Mexican authorities. Family-style gangs' centralized decision making made them vulnerable when authorities, or rival drug gang members, killed or captured a group's kingpin because often no one was capable of stepping up and replacing him. The business management style is more likely to create decentralized administration and decision-making boards in which each member has well-determined territories and the full group meets only to make the biggest decisions. That style has shielded them from catastrophe when top leaders are killed or captured and allowed them to maintain consistent and stable control over large portions of territory suitable for production and smuggling routes.[17]

VIII. The Calderón Crackdown

When President Calderón of the PAN took office in December 2006, he vowed to continue the battle against drug trafficking and developed a cooperation program with the United States that later included the Merida Initiative, a $1.4 billion bilateral security pact that focused on law enforcement, and through which Mexico received equipment and training. The plan was approved by the US Congress in 2008 (US Senate Caucus on International Narcotics Control 2011 pp. 35–38). Calderón also launched joint army-police operations to fight smugglers. Twelve thousand policemen and 45,000 troops were deployed, resulting in thousands of drug-related arrests and seizures. The crackdown reached some of the cartels' leaders: on December 16, 2009, Arturo Beltran-Leyva, one of Mexico's most-powerful traffickers, was killed in Cuernavaca, near Mexico City, and Ignacio Coronel, the head of the Sinaloa cartel's synthetic drug operations met a similar fate on July 30, 2010. Nazario Moreno Gonzalez, the leader and one of the founders of La Familia Michoacana, was shot to death by federal police on December 10, 2010. Between December 2006 and December 2008, 184 offenders were extradited to the United States. Calderón's battle reinforced interdiction and eradication programs, fought kidnapping, organized crime, and corruption. "Operation Cleanup," which was started in October 2008, targeted corruption and led to many arrests of government officials, including the deputy attorney general in charge of fighting drug trafficking, the head of Interpol Mexico, and top leaders in the government's intelligence apparatus, anti-narcotics office, and the heads of police forces and security networks (Mexico's Presidency 2008; WikiLeaks en La Jornada).

But amid complaints about corruption and human rights abuses against members of the army fighting the war on drugs, the Calderón administration began relying more and more on the Special Forces of the navy for its most-important operations, leaving the army aside. Trained by US advisers in counterinsurgency tactics, Mexican navy teams were responsible for one of the most resounding successes in President Calderón's offensive: the quasi dismantling of the Beltran-Leyva organization (BLO).

The BLO, based in Sinaloa state and with operations on the Caribbean and Pacific coasts of Mexico as well as in the state of Sonora and the center of Mexico, is a scission of the Sinaloa drug organization. The BLO allied itself with Zetas hit men against the Sinaloa organization and was headed by Arturo Beltran Leyva, who was killed by Mexican navy commandos in a raid in Cuernavaca (south of Mexico City) on December 16, 2009 (Reuters 2009). In May 2008, the administration of George W. Bush recognized the BLO as a major drug organization, thus subjecting it to sanctions under the Foreign Narcotics Kingpin Designation Act ("Kingpin Act") (US Embassy 2008). According to secret US diplomatic cables released by WikiLeaks, Washington praised Mexican marines in their emerging role in the counternarcotics war and admitted having a close relationship with the navy. "Our ties with the military have never been closer in terms of not only equipment transfers and training, but also the kinds of intelligence exchanges that are essential to making inroads against organized crime," said John Feeley, the deputy chief of mission for the US embassy in Mexico City, in a cable dated January 19, 2010 (WikiLeaks en La Jornada). Other secret cables published by WikiLeaks, meanwhile, leave no doubt about Washington's lack of confidence in the Mexican army. One such cable reveals how US ambassador to Mexico Carlos Pascual said that information on the whereabouts of key Beltran-Leyva leaders was first provided by the DEA to the Mexican army, "whose refusal to move quickly reflected a risk aversion that cost the institution a major counter-narcotics victory" (McClatchy Newspapers 2010).

This change seems to be part of a new strategy President Barack Obama has embraced in Washington's support for Mexico's war on drugs. It is embodied in "Beyond Merida," an initiative launched in the spring of 2010 and designed to enhance the Merida Initiative (Olson and Wilson 2010). Besides narrowly focusing on weakening the drug organizations and giving resources and training for doing so to the Mexican government, the new strategy has a wider scope, which includes strengthening non-army military training, civilian law enforcement, intelligence, and the criminal justice system in efforts at "building a 21st century border to secure communities while encouraging economic trade and growth; and building communities resilient to participating the drug trade or drug consumption" (Felbab-Brown 2010, p. 6).

Meanwhile, the crackdown launched by President Calderón disrupted the illegal business, which became fragmented and responded with increased violence that reached very high levels mainly in the border towns. From December 2006 to September 2011, about 47,500 people were killed in drug-related violence (Mexican Presidency 2010; PGR 2012) (See Chart 9.1). Also, in February 2013, the government announced there had been 26,121 people reported missing during the six years of the Calderón administration (CNN 2013). The revelation came after newspaper reports, citing leaked government information, revealed figures on the number of people who were "disappeared" during Calderón's tenure (*Washington Post* 2012; *Propuesta Cívica* 2012.) They ranged from a

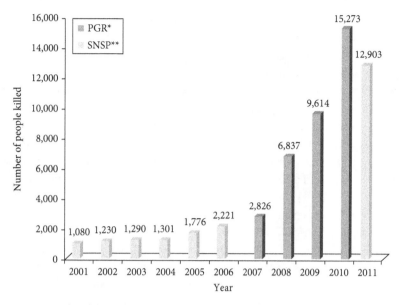

CHART 9.1. Drug—Related Killings 2001–2011

* Data from the Mexican Attorney's General Office (PGR). The 2011 data only runs to September.

** Mexican National Public Security Secretary (SNSP), database released by the Mexican Presidency.

little more than 20,000 to nearly 26,000 victims who vanished. The government has since created an investigative task force to search for the missing people (Los Angeles Times 2013).

The fragmentation resulted in seven main trafficking groups: Beltran-Leyva, La Familia Michoacana, Golfo, Juárez, Sinaloa, Tijuana, and Zetas (United Nations Office on Drugs and Crime 2010. p. 236). While the most recent crackdowns have severely affected the Beltran-Leyva and La Familia organizations, the government offensive against drug organizations has failed to inflict mortal wounds upon the Sinaloa gang. Violence, which used to be a by-product of the activities of drug gangs, has also changed in recent years, coinciding with the PRI's loss of power. Currently, it is used as a tool: first, among the groups that fight for control of trafficking corridors, smuggling locations, and domestic markets; second, as a system to settle old scores: a way to regulate the coexistence among these groups; and third, against law enforcers and critics (journalists and other writers).

Violent methods are frequently very cruel and symbolic, done in a grisly manner and timed to have maximum effect on society (Weintraub and Wood 2010, p. 20). La Familia claims to kill for moral reasons only those who deserve to die. The organization that "espouses a bizarre ideology combining aspects of evangelical Christianity with revolutionary populism, provides the most extreme example" of the use of violence to expand its criminal activities to other areas besides mere drug smuggling, "'taxing' businesses in the areas they control and engaging in very public displays of violence to soften resistance" (United Nations Office of Drugs and Crime 2010, p. 238).

Mexicans have also corrupted officials on the north side of the border. In April 2008, Margarita Crispin, a former border inspector in El Paso, received a 20-year prison sentence for helping smuggle marijuana into the United States (Federal Bureau of Investigation 2009). Since then, scores of US Customs and Border Protection officials have been charged with drug smuggling and accepting bribes from Mexican traffickers (*New York Times* 2009; *Los Angeles Times* 2011).

The Mexican traffickers widespread operations in the United States became clear in October 2009 when a Mexican-American operation aimed at La Familia Michoacana led to massive captures on both sides of the border: "In all, authorities have arrested nearly 1,200 suspected La Familia members or associates in recent months as part of 'Project Coronado,' the 44-month multi-agency effort to dismantle the organization's methamphetamine and cocaine distribution network in the United States" (Department of Justice 2009; *Los Angeles Times* 2009).

The defeat of the PAN in the presidential elections of 2012 brought reports of a possible change in Calderón's strategy to battle drug organizations, which by the end of his administration faced harsh, widespread criticism due to such high levels of violence that it helped unleash. President-elect Enrique Peña Nieto, of the PRI, revealed in a *New York Times* op-ed on July 2, 2012, his plan to combat drug trafficking. In place of an all-out war, he announced the creation of the 40,000-strong National Gendarmerie, a new police force assigned to focus exclusively on rural areas, as well as the expansion of the federal police by "at least 35,000 officers." (*New York Times* 2012). Peña Nieto also vowed to increase spending on national security and the fight against organized crime, offering no ceasefire to drug traffickers but also promising a reexamination of the current antidrug policies to improve efficacy and efficiency. "To those concerned about a return to old ways, fear not...I reject the practices of the past, in the same way I seek to move forward from the political gridlock of the present," he wrote. "I will continue the fight, but the strategy must change."

Less than a year later, however, Peña Nieto sent troops to Michoacán, the same state where Calderón first deployed the army in his crackdown against drug trafficking. (*Los Angeles Times* 2012)

IX. Conclusions

The history of the illegal drugs industry in Mexico is a classic case of social controls gone awry. It has been closely linked to the prohibitions established in the United States. But PRI used corruption functionally and allowed the development of support networks for drug smugglers that sheltered the gangs since their infancy with a total disregard for the law.

Mexican drug violence is not new, but the extreme cruelty and the expansion in activities have been a consequence of the rearrangements of drug organizations after the PRI's downfall and the capture of some of the main cartel's heads. The emergence of new leaderships proved to be a bloody one as was the efforts of leaders to defend their territories from other organizations, to move into areas controlled by other gangs, or to battle the attempts to quash them of the army and the police. This struggle was made all the more deadly by an unending supply of heavy weaponry smuggled south from the United States since the expiration of the assault ban there. The Federal Assault Weapons Ban (AWB) was enacted by President Bill Clinton in 1994 and prohibited "the manufacture, transfer and possession" by civilians of assault weapons. The result was a de facto ban on 18 military-style assault weapons (Koper 2004, p. 1). But the ban gave Congress the ability to renew it after a decade. Lawmakers decided not to do so, and the ban expired in 2004. Mexican authorities blame the expiration of the ban for the increased smuggling of weapons by and for drug organizations from the United States. "Since the ban expired in 2004, we have seen that the firepower of criminal groups in Mexico has grown," said President Calderón (PGR 2009).

The Mexican military, which had been believed not to be as corrupt as the country's police corps, proved to be vulnerable. The growing military involvement in the offensive against drugs, in retrospect, was undermined by military personnel who crossed to the other side and became hired killers. The government's switch to using Special Forces from the navy for more delicate operations instead of the army appears only to confirm this point. At the same time, it shows a switch in Washington's support for Mexico's war on drugs under Barack Obama's administration in comparison with the support provided during the period when George W. Bush served in the White House.

Crackdowns of all kinds have historically failed to quell the drug business in Mexico, even though they tended to placate Washington. Instead, they have allowed Mexican cartels to take advantage of the opportunity to reorganize and become stronger, more violent, more complex, and diversified. The consequences of the latest antidrug campaign in Mexico remain to be seen, but if history is any guide, one should expect further adaptations and survival of the illegal industry. However, the new strategy for cooperation in security, Beyond Merida, a more multifaceted and improved Merida Initiative, certainly represents a ray of hope in this gloomy picture, with its focus not only on law enforcement, but also on building strong and resilient communities and a more effective border. Peña Nieto's National Development Plan 2013–2018 focuses on restoring order, security, and justice while guaranteeing respect for human rights (Mexican Government 2013). It also seeks an improved and more-global strategy with a chief goal of reducing lawlessness and its high costs for the population and the country.

NOTES

1. The authors thank Letizia Paoli for her comments on an earlier draft.
2. The first documented case of this close relationship between the power structures and drug organizations is Cornel Esteban Cantu, who established his own fiefdom in Baja California as the top military authority in the region and who was considered by US officials as the comptroller of the drug trade in the region in the 1910s (Astorga 2003a).

3. Mexico has more than 2,000 municipal police forces plus federal and state police forces, and other specialized corps.

4. A complete version of the WikiLeaks cables was published on December 6, 2010, by Insight Crime, a website that specializes in analyzing organized crime in Latin America and the Caribbean. http://insightcrime.org/insight-latest-news/item/314-wikileaks-us-gave-intel-that-led-to-cartel-leaders-death.

5. *El Universal Grafico*, a series of articles on drug trafficking between November 1937 and January 1938, cited in Astorga 2005 (pp. 40–43).

6. Medel's interviews with Mexico's former deputy attorney general for drug crimes, José L. Santiago-Vasconcelos, between 2002 and 2007.

7. Resa Nestares (2003, pp. 89–90) estimates that the value of Mexican marijuana exports to the United States dropped from one billion dollars in 1975 to 300 million dollars in 1981.

8. US Immigration and Customs Enforcement (ICE) special agent Jaime Zapata was shot dead on January 16, 2011, while a second agent was wounded after being assaulted on a federal highway in northern Mexico, according to a statement released by the agency, http://www.ice.gov/news/releases/1102/110216washingtondc.htm

9. Even though the DFS closed its doors officially and was replaced by the Dirección General de Investigación y Seguridad Nacional, the truth is that the police force also faced allegations of being involved in repression of students, culminating in massacres in the late 1960s and early 1970s, a period dubbed Mexico's "dirty war."

10. Medel's interviews with Santiago-Vasconcelos, cited.

11. According to the United Nations Office on Drugs and Crime (UNODC) 2010 World Drug Report, "since 2003, Mexico has been the world's third largest source of opium" (p. 20).

12. Olivo's comments appeared in the previously mentioned story by news agency IPS from Lima, Peru, on August 24, 2006.

13. Medel's interview with Santiago-Vasconcelos, cited.

14. Santiago-Vasconcelos, *El Universal*, June 2, 2008.

15. Medel's interview with Santiago-Vasconcelos, cited.

16. General Dauahare spent 11 months in a high-security prison for alleged links to organized crime, until he was released in April 2013 due to lack of evidence against him.

17. Medel's interviews with Santiago-Vasconcelos, cited.

REFERENCES

Anderson, P. 1981. *High in America: The True History behind NORML and the Politics of Marijuana.* New York: Viking.

Andreas, Peter 1998. "The Political Economy of Narco-corruption in Mexico." *Current History* (April): 160–165.

Astorga, Luis. 2003a. "Mexico, Colombia and Illegal Drugs: Variations on the Same Topic." Paper Presented at the VIII Annual History Professorship Ernesto Restrepo-Tirado in Bogotà, Colombia, Dedicated to the "Colombian Drug Trafficking Historical Analysis."

Astorga, Luis. 2003b. *Drogas sin fronteras.* Mexico City: Editorial Grijalbo.

Astorga, Luis. 2005. *El Siglo de las drogas: El narcotráfico, del Porfiriato al nuevo milenio.* Mexico City: Random House Mondadori.

Baum, D. 1996. *Smoke and Mirrors: The War on Drugs and the Politics of Failure*. New York: Little, Brown.

British Broadcasting Corporation. 2012. "Guatemala President Orders Army to Join Drugs Fight" (January 15). http://www.bbc.co.uk/news/world-latin-america-16570292

Colegio Nacional (Mexico). 1960. *Estadísticas económicas del Porfiriato: Comercio exterior de Mexico, 1877–1911*. Mexico City: El Colegio de Mexico.

CNN. 2013. "México reports more than 26,000 missing" (February 27). http://www.cnn.com/2013/02/26/world/americas/mexico-disappeared

Craig, Richard. 1989. "US Narcotics Policy toward Mexico: Consequences for the Bilateral Relationship." In *The Drug Connection in US-Mexican Relations*, edited by Guadalupe Gonzalez and Marta Tienda, 71–92. San Diego: University of California Press.

Domínguez, Jorge, and Rafael Fernández de Castro. 2001. *The United States and Mexico: Between Partnership and Conflict*. New York: Routledge.

Drug Enforcement Administration (DEA). 1996. *Methamphetamine Situation in the United States Report*. Washington, DC: Drug Enforcement Administration.

EFE. 2008. *"Reconoce Sedena que narco ha reclutado ex militares"* (January 22).

El Tiempo. 2007. "'Rasguño' habló, en exclusiva, con El Tiempo el pasado 22 de marzo de 2007" (July 19). http://www.eltiempo.com/archivo/documento/CMS-3645628

El Universal. 2004. "Hay pruebas sobre nexos de priistas con narco: PAN" (October 21). http://www2.eluniversal.com.mx/pls/impreso/noticia.html?id_nota=55220&tabla=estados

Federal Bureau of Investigation (FBI). 2009. "Abuse of Trust: The Case of the Crooked Border Official" (June 8). http://www.fbi.gov/news/stories/2009/june/border060809

Felbab-Brown, Vanda. 2010. *Stemming the Violence in Mexico, but Breaking the Cartels*, The CIP Report (September).

Forbes. 2009. "The World's Billionaires: #701 Joaquin Guzman Loera" (March 11). http://www.forbes.com/lists/2009/10/billionaires-2009-richest-people_Joaquin-Guzman-Loera_FSoY.html

Gootenberg, Paul. 1999. *Cocaine: Global Histories*. New York: Routledge.

Insight Crime. 2010. "WikiLeaks: US Gave Intel That Lead to Cartel Leader's Death." http://insightcrime.org/insight-latest-news/item/314-wikileaks-us-gave-intel-that-led-to-cartel-leaders-death

Koper, Christopher S. 2004. *An Updated Assessment of the Federal Assault Weapons Ban: Impacts on Gun Markets and Gun Violence, 1994–2003*. Report to the National Institute of Justice, United States Department of Justice. Philadelphia: Jerry Lee Center of Criminology, University of Pennsylvania.

La Jornada. 2008. "Han desertado 17 mil militares en sólo un año" (January 23). http://www.jornada.unam.mx/2008/01/23/index.php?section=politica&article=007n2pol

Los Angeles Times. 1985. "US Charges Mexico Let Suspect Flee: DEA Chief Also Says Federal Police Aided Kidnapping Fugitive" (February 25).

Los Angeles Times. 1989. *"Drug Lord Convicted in Camarena's 1985 Murder: Narcotics: He Draws a Prison Term of 40 Years: A Mexican Judge Sentences His 'Enforcer' and 23 Others in the US Drug Agent's Killing"* (December 13).

Los Angeles Times. 2009. "Probe of Mexican drug cartels leads to hundreds of U.S. arrests" (October 23). http://articles.latimes.com/2009/oct/23/nation/na-cartel-raids23

Los Angeles Times. 2011. "Border Agency Rapid's Growth, Accompanied by Rise in Corruption" (October 16). http://www.latimes.com/news/local/la-me-border-corrupt-20111017,0,1949024,full.story

Los Angeles Times. 2012. "Mexico launches military push to restore order in Michoacan state" (May 21). http://www.latimes.com/news/world/worldnow/la-fg-wn-mexico-military-push-20130521, 0,5735016.story

Los Angeles Times. 2013. "Mexico creates task force to search for the missing" (May 27). http://www.latimes.com/news/nationworld/world/la-fg-mexico-numbers-20130528,0,614114.story

Lupsha, Peter A. 1992. "Drugs Lords and Narco-Corruption: The Players Change but the Game Continues." In *War on Drugs: Studies in the Failure of US Narcotics Policy*, edited by Alfred W. McCoy and Alan A. Block, 177–196. Boulder, CO: Westview.

Marez, Curtis. 2004. *Drug Wars: The Political Economy of Narcotics*. Minneapolis: University of Minnesota Press.

McClatchy Newspapers.. Dec. 4, 2010. "WikiLeaks: US cables give grim view of Mexico drug war." http://www.mcclatchydc.com/2010/12/04/104741/us-cables-give-grim-snapshot-of.html

Medel, Monica. 2007. "Narcos Mexicanos, nuevos reyes de la droga en América" Reuters (July 17).

Mexico Government. 2013. "National Development Plan." http://pnd.gob.mx/

Mexican Presidency. 2008. "Reitera el presidente Calderón el firme compromiso del gobierno federal para combatir a la delincuencia organizada" (November 27). http://www.presidencia.gob.mx/2008/11/reitera-el-presidente-calderon-el-firme-compromiso-del-gobierno-federal-para-combatir-a-la-delincuencia-organizada/

Mexican Presidency. 2011. "Base de datos de fallecimientos" (January). http://www.presidencia.gob.mx/base-de-datos-de-fallecimientos/.

Miroff, Nick, and William Booth. 2010. "DEA intelligence Aids Mexican Marines in Drug War." *Washington Post* (December 4).

National Public Radio. 2011. "Mexican Cartels Spread Violence to Central America" (May 30). http://www.npr.org/2011/05/30/136690257/mexican-cartels-spread-violence-to-central-america

New York Times. 1997. "Drug Ties Taint 2 Mexican Governors" (February 23). http://www.nytimes.com/1997/02/23/world/drug-ties-taint-2-mexican-governors.html?scp=2&sq=Manlio+Fabio+Beltrones&st=cse&pagewanted=all

New York Times. 2009. "War without Borders: Hired by Customs, but Working for Mexican Cartels" (December 17). http://www.nytimes.com/2009/12/18/us/18corrupt.html?pagewanted=all

New York Times. 2012. "Mexico's Next Chapter" (July 2). http://www.nytimes.com/2012/07/03/opinion/mexicos-next-chapter.html?_r=2&

Notimex. 2009. "Recaptura de 'El Chapo,' prioridad para México y EU" (January 19). http://www.eluniversal.com.mx/notas/570217.html.

Olson, Eric L., and Christopher E. Wilson. 2010. *Beyond Merida: The Evolving Approach to Security Cooperation*. Working Paper Series on US-Mexico Security Cooperation. Washington, DC: Woodrow Wilson International Center for Scholars, Mexico Institute.

Páez, Ángel. 2006. "Invasión de mafias mexicanas" Inter Press Service (August 24). http://ips-noticias.net/nota.asp?idnews=38483

PGR (Attorney General's Office). 2000. Statement No. 510/00. Available on Internet at http://www.pgr.gob.mx/cmsocial/bol00/sep/b51000.html

PGR. 2009. "Press Conference by Presidents Barack Obama and Felipe Calderón in Mexico City" (April 16). http://www.presidencia.gob.mx/2009/04/sesion-de-preguntas-y-respuestas-en-el-mensaje-que-ofrecieron-el-presidente-calderon-y-el-presidente-de-los-estados-unidos-de-norteamerica-barack-obama/

PGR. 2009. "Resultados de la política mexicana contra la delincuencia organizacion" (June 9). http://www.pgr.gob.mx/prensa/2007/docs08/hoja_ruta_results_politicmex.pdf

PGR. 2012. "Base de datos por fallecimientos por presunta rivalidad delincuencial" (January). http://www.pgr.gob.mx/temas&20relevantes/estadistica/estadisticas.asp

Proceso. 1985. "En Estados Unidos se promueven presiones económicas y la Procuraduría niega que México sea trampolín de droga" (February 23).

Propuesta Cívica. 2012. "Derecho a saber. Base de datos de personas desaparecidas en México de 2006 a 2012" (December 5). http://propuestacivica.org.mx/desaparecidos.html

Ravelo, Ricardo. 2006. *Los capos: Las Narco-Rutas de Mexico.* Mexico City: Random House Mondadori.

Resa Nestares, Carlos. 2003. "El valor de las exportaciones mexicanas de drogas ilegales, 1961–2000." Coleccion Documentos, Universidad Autonoma de Madrid.

Reuter, Peter. 1988. "Quantity Illusions and Paradoxes of Drug Interdiction: Federal Intervention into Vice Policy." *Law and Contemporary Problems 51* (1): 233–252.

Reuter, Peter, and David Ronfeldt. 1992. "Quest for Integrity: The Mexican-US Drug Issue in the 1980's." *A Rand Note.* Santa Monica, CA: RAND.

Reuter, Peter, Letizia Paoli, and Victoria Greenfield. 2009. *The World Heroin Market: Can Supply Be Cut?* Oxford: Oxford University Press.

Reuters. 2008. "Mexican Drug Gang Tentacles Reach Europe, Africa" (December 23).

Reuters. 2009. "Factbox: Mexican Drug Lord Arturo Beltran Leyva" (December 17). http://in.reuters.com/article/2009/12/17/idININdia-44796420091217

Ruiz Cabañas, Miguel. 1989. "Mexico's Changing Illicit Drug Supply Role." In *The Drug Connection in US-Mexican Relations,* edited by Guadalupe Gonzalez and Marta Tienda, 43–70. San Diego: University of California Press.

Secretaría de Seguridad Pública (SSP) de Mexico. 2007. "Radiografía de las Organizaciones de Narcotraficantes" (April 19). Document made available to Monica Medel by the PGR in 2007.

Televisa. 2008. "Alan García pide apoyo de policía mexicana" (November 27). http://www2.esmas.com/noticierostelevisa/internacional/026794/alan-garcia-pide-apoyo-policia-mexicana

Texas Department of Public Safety. 2010. "Texas Gang Threat Assessment 2010" (September 1).

The Economist. 2010. "Organised Crime in Mexico: Under the Volcano" (October 14).

Thoumi, Francisco. 2003. *Illegal Drugs, Economy, and Society in the Andes.* Baltimore: Johns Hopkins University Press.

Thoumi, Francisco. 2009. "Necessary, Sufficient and Contributory Factors Generating Illegal Economic Activity, and Specifically Drug-Related Activity, in Colombia."

Time. 2009. "Joaquin Guzman Loera: Billionaire Drug Lord" (March 13). http://www.time.com/time/world/article/0,8599,1884982,00.html

Toro, Maria Celia. 1995. *Mexico's War on Drugs.* Boulder, CO: Lynne Rienner.

Turner, Carlton, Ping Cheng, Lolita Torres, and Mahmoud Elsohly. 1978. *Detection and Analysis of Paraquat in Confiscated Marijuana Samples.* Vienna: United Nations Office on Drugs and Crime.

United Nations Office on Drugs and Crime (UNODC). 2010. *World Drug Report 2010.*

US Department of Justice. 2000. *International Narcotics Control Strategy Report 2000.* http://www.state.gov/j/inl/rls/nrcrpt/2000/888.htm

US Department of Justice. 2009. "More Than 300 Alleged La Familia Cartel Members and Associated Arrested in Two-Day Nationwide Takedown" (October 22). http://www.justice.gov/opa/pr/2009/October/09-ag-1135.html

US Department of State. 2002. *International Narcotics Control Strategy Report 2002*. http:// www.state.gov/j/inl/rls/nrcrpt/2002/html/17941.htm

US Department of State. 2003. *International Narcotics Control Strategy Report 2003*. http:// www.state.gov/j/inl/rls/nrcrpt/2003/vol1/html/29833.htm

US Department of State. 2005. *International Narcotics Control Strategy Report 2005*. http:// www.state.gov/j/inl/rls/nrcrpt/2005/vol1/html/42364.htm

US Department of State. 2008. *International Narcotics Control Strategy Report 2008*. http:// www.state.gov/j/inl/rls/nrcrpt/2008/vol1/html/100777.htm

US Department of State. 2009. *International Narcotics Control Strategy Report 2009*. http:// www.state.gov/j/inl/rls/nrcrpt/2009/vol1/116522.htm

US Department of State. 2011. *International Narcotics Control Strategy Report 2011*. http://www. state.gov/j/inl/rls/nrcrpt/2011/vol1/index.htm

US Embassy in Mexico. 2008. Press Releases 08: "President Bush Designates Beltran Leyva and His Organization under Kingpin Act" (May 30).

US Senate Caucus on International Narcotics Control. 2011. "US and Mexican Responses to Mexican Drug Trafficking Organizations" (May).

Walker, William O. 1981. *Drug Control in the Americas*. Albuquerque: University of New Mexico Press.

———. 1996. *Drugs in the Western Hemisphere: An Odyssey of Cultures in Conflict*. Wilmington, DC: Scholarly Resources.

Washington Post. 2012. "Mexico's crime wave has left about 25,000 missing, government documents show" (November 29). http://articles.washingtonpost.com/2012-11-29/ world/35584943_1_mexico-city-mexican-government-human-rights

Weintraub, Sidney, and Duncan Wood. 2010. *Cooperative Mexican-US Antinarcotics Efforts*. Washington, DC: Center for Strategic and International Studies.

Werner, Michael S. 2001. *Concise Encyclopedia of Mexico*. Chicago: Fitzroy Dearborn.

WikiLeaks en La Jornada. "Existe descoordinación entre agencias de seguridad. Cable 10MEXICO83."http://wikileaks.jornada.com.mx/cables/narcotrafico/existe-descoordinacion-entre-agencias-de-seguridad-cable-10mexico83/

CHAPTER 10

CHINESE ORGANIZED CRIME

KO-LIN CHIN

IN 1985, shortly after a three-day public hearing on Asian organized crime was conducted in New York City by members of the President's Commission on Organized Crime, a police chief in California predicted that "Asian organized crime will end up being the number one organized crime problem in North America in the next five years," and "will make the Sicilian Mafia look like a bunch of Sunday school kids (Chin 1990, p. 4). During the following 25 years, even though the police chief's comments proved to be exaggerated, the alleged engagement of Asian organized crime groups, especially groups formed by Chinese, in transnational criminal activities, such as heroin trafficking, human smuggling, and sex trafficking, has, indeed, drawn the attention of the international law enforcement community (Finckenauer and Chin 2007; Zhang and Chin 2008). With the emergence of China as a key player in global political and economic arenas, coupled with the return of Hong Kong and Macau to China, the stage was set for a dramatic increase in social and economic interactions among Chinese people around the world. It followed that Chinese organized crime groups would take advantage of the many legitimate and illegitimate opportunities created by rapid economic growth in China and the development of a global network of Chinese who were now in touch with each other (Seagrave 1996; Lintner 2002; Lo 2009).

Before we continue to discuss Chinese organized crime, it is important to point out that no monolithic, worldwide criminal organization called the Chinese Mafia, with headquarters somewhere in Asia, exists. In fact, there are many Chinese organized crime groups, including Hong Kong-based triads, Taiwan-based organized gangs and *jiaotou* (street corner or local) groups, China-based Mafia-like gangs, and US-based tongs and street gangs. We will briefly introduce these groups in the first section before we move on to the history, structure, and activities of these groups in the following sections.

I. An Overview of Chinese Organized Crime Groups and Networks

To the law enforcement community and the mass media in the United States and Europe, many Chinese organized crime groups and networks are often lumped together and called "triad" or "Chinese Mafia" with little regard to the varied historical, cultural, social, and economic conditions that gave rise to the different types of crime groups and networks. In Table 10.1, we provide a list of Chinese organized crime groups and networks and compare their geographical, structural, and group characteristics.

A. Hong Kong–based Triads

Triad societies in Hong Kong are alleged to be some of the largest, most dangerous, and best organized crime groups in the world (Black 1992). They evolved from patriotic secret societies (called Hung societies) formed three centuries ago to fight against the oppressive and corrupt Qing dynasty. When the Qing dynasty (1644–1911) collapsed in 1911 and the Republic of China was established, some of these triad societies became involved in criminal activities (Booth 1999). The word *triad* means the unity of three essential elements of existence—heaven, earth, and humanity (Morgan 1960). In the early 1990s, roughly 160,000 triad members could be found in Hong Kong, belonging to some 50 factions. Nowadays, only 14 out of the 50 triad societies remain active and, of these, Sun Yee On, Wo Shing Wo, and 14K are the most powerful organizations (Chu 2000).

B. Taiwan-based Organized Gangs and Jiaotou Groups

Organized gangs are bigger and better organized than the *jiaotou* groups and members are mostly offspring of mainland Chinese who followed Chiang Kai-shek to Taiwan in 1949 (Kaplan 1992). Some of the most powerful organized gangs in Taiwan are the Bamboo United, the Four Seas, and the Celestial Alliance (Chin 2003). *Jiaotou* groups are territorial in nature and members are mainly Taiwanese. The groups are relatively small, with membership ranging from 20 to 50 individuals (Chin 2003).

C. China-based Mafia-like Gangs

According to Chinese authorities, the most powerful and best-organized criminal organizations in China have not yet reached the status of underworld organizations like the Italian Mafia, the Japanese Yakuza, or the Hong Kong triads (Xia 2006). As a

Table 10.1 Chinese organized crime groups and networks

Type of group or network	Where it is based	Key example	Size (number of members)	Ranks	Main activities
Triad	Hong Kong and Macau	14K, Sun Yee On, Wo Shing Wo	Thousands	Red Pole, 49, Blue Lantern	A variety of legal and illegal activities
Organized gang	Taiwan	Bamboo United, Four Seas, Celestial Alliance	Thousands	Top leader, subgroup leader, follower	A variety of legal and illegal activities
Jiaotou	Taiwan	Nyo Pu, Fang Ming Kwan	Dozens	Leader, follower	Gambling, prostitution, engage in politics
Mafia-style gang	China	Liu Yong Group, Chen Kai Group	Dozens	Leader, core member, peripheral member	Gambling, prostitution, and legal businesses
Tong	United States, Southeast Asia, and Europe	On Leong, Hip Sing, Tung On	Thousands, but only core members are engaged in crime	President, vice president, secretary, treasurer, auditor, elders, etc.	Gambling, extortion, community politics
Street gang	United States	Ghost Shadows, Flying Dragons, Tung On	Hundreds	Gang leader, street leader, follower	Extortion, gambling, violence
Heroin trafficking network	The Golden Triangle	The Wa, the Kokang, Chinese drug entrepreneurs	No formal membership	No formalized role	Producing, trafficking, distributing heroin
Human smuggling network	Fuzhou, China	The snakeheads	No formal membership	No formalized role	Smuggling Chinese
Human trafficking network	Shenzhen, China	The chickenheads	No formal membership	No formalized role	Prostitution

result, Chinese authorities describe the most advanced criminal organizations in China as "organizations with underworld characteristics" (or Mafia-like gangs) to differentiate them from other loosely knit and less influential criminal organizations such as criminal gangs (some degree of structure) and crime groups (no structure) (Chin and Godson 2006). The Standing Committee of the National People's Congress in 2002 stated that an organization with underworld characteristics would possess the following characteristics: (1) The formation of a relatively stable organization, with a large number of gang members and clearly identified organizers, leaders, and a reliable core group; (2) The pursuit of economic gains through organized crime or other illegal means, with sufficient economic strength to support its activities; (3) The repeated commission of organized crimes through violence, threat, or other means, such as riding roughshod over people's rights or cruelly injuring or killing them; and (4) By committing illegal or criminal activities, or by being harbored [protected] by government officials, it dominates people in a given area, has illegal control, or imposes a major influence in a certain region or trade, which seriously disrupts both the economic order and the people's daily activities (Chin and Godson 2006). Chinese authorities estimated that, in 2004, about 4,200 mafia-like gangs were operating in China (Xia 2006).

D. US-based Tongs and Street Gangs

The word *tong* means simply "hall" or "gathering place." In the United States, the tongs, like the family and district associations, provided many needed services, such as job referrals and housing assistance, to Chinese immigrants who could not otherwise obtain them. The tongs also acted as power brokers in mediating individual and group conflicts within the community. Most tong members are gainfully employed or have their own businesses. Historically, tongs have been active in operating or providing protection for opium use and dealing, gambling, and brothels (U.S. Senate [1877] 1978; McIllwain 2003). U.S. authorities generally consider tongs such as the On Leong, the Hip Sing, and the Tung On to be organized crime groups that are heavily involved in many illegal activities and are the force behind the street gangs. Many street gangs exist in the Chinatowns of North America; American authorities also consider these street gangs as organized crime groups because of their reputation for violence, their heavy involvement in money-generating local and transnational crimes, and their close affiliation with the tongs (Chin 1996).

E. Other Groups and Networks

Chinese organized crime groups are also active in Macau, Singapore, Malaysia, Indonesia, Thailand, and in certain western European countries such as the United Kingdom and the Netherlands. However, due to limits of space, we will focus on the groups that are active only in Hong Kong, Taiwan, China, and the United States.

Moreover, Chinese groups or networks also specialize in transnational crime, such as heroin trafficking, human smuggling, and human trafficking, and we must not confuse these groups or networks with the better-known groups, such as the triads, gangs, and tongs, that are often reported in the media and targeted by law enforcement authorities.

According to Chin (2009) and Chin and Zhang (2007), people of diverse backgrounds participate in the business of heroin trafficking and distribution. Some of the drug traffickers are poorly educated, with few employable skills or alternatives to make a living comparable to their aspirations. In general, drug traffickers do not belong to street gangs, organized crime groups, or terrorist organizations. Most are simply bold risk takers who work with family members or form alliances with friends or other social contacts whom they come to trust (Zhang and Chin 2008). Heroin and methamphetamine production in the Golden Triangle is under the control of two families—the Bao and the Wei—and the two families do not function like an organized crime group nor are they affiliated with any of the above-mentioned Chinese organized crime groups (Chin 2009).

Every year, tens of thousands of people from China are smuggled to the United States, Europe, and other parts of the world by human smugglers known as big snakeheads. These big snakeheads are assisted by little snakeheads (recruiters), guides, crews, transporters, enforcers, debt collectors, support personnel, and corrupt officials. According to Chin (1999) and Zhang (2008), contrary to widely held conceptions about Chinese organized crime, individuals who are engaged in human smuggling are predominantly ordinary citizens whose familial networks and fortuitous social contacts have enabled them to pool resources to transport human cargo around the world. They come from diverse backgrounds and form temporary alliances to carry out smuggling operations. Before her downfall, Cheng Chui-ping or Sister Ping, also known as the "Mother of All Snakeheads," was a major actor in human smuggling, but she was a motherly figure in her 40s with no underworld background (Zhang 2007; Keefe 2009).

A study conducted by Finckenauer and Chin (2010) suggested that members of various Chinese organized crime groups are not involved in the transnational movement of Chinese women for commercial sex, either as individuals or as groups. Instead, the Chinese sex industry in Asia and the West is dominated by enterprising individuals known as chickenheads (male pimps), agents (coordinators), mommies (female intermediaries), escort agency owners, brothel keepers, fake husbands, and jockeys (car drivers). Some of the facilitators of the Chinese sex trade are actually big business owners who are well protected by government authorities.

II. History

More than three centuries ago, Chinese secret societies were formed in China to overthrow the Qing dynasty and restore the Ming dynasty. The Qing dynasty was established by alien Manchu warriors (non-Han Chinese) after they dethroned the Ming (Han Chinese) emperor. Some secret society members emigrated to Southeast Asia and North America and started new branches of their societies there. Chinese secret societies were not just patriotic societies; they also provided mutual aid in times of weak government, much like Italian mafia groups (Murray 1994). Chinese secret society members (mainly the Hung and the Qing societies) around the world supported Sun Yat-sen, the leader of the revolution that in 1912 finally overthrew the Qing dynasty and led to the establishment of the Republic of China (Chin 1990).

The political party that Sun Yat-sen founded—the Kuomintang (KMT)—ruled China between 1912 and 1949, and, during this period, many KMT officials were believed to be corrupt because of close ties with secret societies that began to dominate the illicit businesses of gambling, prostitution, and drugs, especially in the foreign concessions of Shanghai (Wakeman 1995; Martin 1996). During that time period, some members of secret societies moved to Hong Kong, a British colony, and began to establish the triad societies there by mobilizing peddlers and workers from both the private and the public sectors. Following the defeat of the KMT by the Chinese Communist Party (CCP) in 1949, secret society members who served in the Kuomintang army followed the leader, Chiang Kai-shek, to Taiwan (Kaplan 1992).

After the CCP came to power, a crackdown was launched on all vice activities and many secret society members were imprisoned or executed. Some fled to Hong Kong, Taiwan, Southeast Asia, North America, Europe, or other parts of the world, and they immediately changed the nature of Chinese organized crime in the countries where they had landed. When China was engulfed in a series of political movements and power struggles between 1949 and 1978, the triads in Hong Kong, Macau, and western Europe, the organized gangs and *jiaotou* groups in Taiwan, and the tongs and street gangs in North America became the dominant groups in the Chinese underworld.

After China began to adopt an open-door policy and to engage in economic reform in the early 1980s, organized crime groups in Hong Kong, Taiwan, and North America also began to show up in China to take advantage of the many money-generating activities there (Chin 2003). Soon, however, indigenous Mafia-like gangs also began to develop, and they surpassed the power of the triads from Hong Kong and the organized gangs from Taiwan (Xia 2006).

In sum, the development and transformation of Chinese organized crime groups were closely related to the history and politics of China and the migration and settlement of its people. These groups, many of them initially formed not to commit crime but to achieve a political or a social goal, must be understood both within the sociopolitical and economic contexts of China, Hong Kong, and Taiwan and within the historical fact of the out-migration of Chinese to many parts of the world.

III. STRUCTURE AND CULTURE

Triad societies in Hong Kong are large criminal organizations with thousands of members; they are the opposite of a monolithic organization with one leadership structure. Rather, most of the Hong Kong–based triads are made up of many subgroups that function more or less like as independent entities with their own name, turf, leadership structure, and niches in the legitimate and illegitimate markets. Intragroup violence is common (Chu 2007). These subgroups are loosely linked by one or more influential leaders who are considered to be the spiritual leaders of the loosely knit organization. According to Chu (2007, p. 87): "The triads' organizational structure has become flexible and decentralized. The traditional rank system has been largely reduced to three—Red Pole, 49, and Blue Lanterns. The initiation ceremony had been simplified." The Red Pole is a leader, the 49s are ordinary members, and the Blue Lanterns are new recruits who are yet to be initiated. Under the traditional system, there existed an ultimate leader and a group leader above the Red Pole and an adviser and a liaison officer between the Red Pole and the ordinary members (Chin 1990).

A typical organized gang in Taiwan has a headquarters to oversee the activities of several branches. The headquarters has a master, an associate master, an enforcer, and a bodyguard and confidant of the master. Within each branch, there is a branch master, associate branch master, branch enforcer, confidant of the branch master, and ordinary members. The *jiaotou* groups, on the other hand, are loosely structured. There are only two roles within a *jiaotou* group: the big boss and little brothers.

Mafia-like gangs in China are relatively small; most of these gangs have 25 to 100 members. These gangs are led by a leader, who relies on several core members to carry out his orders. As mentioned above, to be considered a Mafia-like gang, the gang has to be sheltered or protected by one or more government officials; it is common for many of these gangs to have police officers as their "protective umbrella" or to be core members who act as enforcers for their gangs (Chin and Godson 2006). In the so-called No. 1 Underworld Case of 1998, Liang Xiaoming, a police officer as well as a crime boss in Changchun City, Jilin Province, was arrested for murder, assault, robbery, extortion, prostitution, and gambling (He 2003). The political-criminal nexus in China is primarily between gangsters and low- and mid-level government officials from the criminal justice system, i.e., police officers, prosecutors, and judges. High-level political leaders from the executive branch and party apparatus rarely act as a protective umbrella for underworld figures, except in the Liu Yong case in which the mayor and deputy mayor of Shenyang, a major city in northeastern China, were both convicted for taking bribes from Liu Yong, an underworld boss (Ouyang 2004). High-ranking administrators and party officials are more likely to be affiliated with, and corrupted by, seemingly legitimate businesspeople.

Tongs in North America also have thousands of members. For example, the On Leong has chapters in Boston, Philadelphia, Pittsburgh, Providence, Cleveland, St. Louis, Detroit, Minneapolis, Washington, D.C, Baltimore, Miami, Houston, New Orleans, Richmond, and Atlanta. In the United States, there are 30,000 to 40,000 On Leong members (Chin 1990). However, unlike triads and organized gangs, most tong members are gainfully employed or have their own businesses and rarely engage in criminal activities. The tongs are also legitimately registered community-based organizations. However, a handful of tong leaders who make decisions and control the groups' daily affairs will have connections with street gangs and may be involved in illegal activities. Most tong headquarters have a president, a vice president, a secretary, a treasurer, an auditor, and several elders and public relations administrators. Those tong leaders who are associated with their respective street gangs are called *ah kung* (grandfather) or *shuk foo* (uncle) by the gangs (Chin 1996).

Most tong-affiliated street gangs in the United States will have one or two primary leaders who are close to certain officers or members of the affiliated tong. These principal leaders control the various factions of the gang. Each faction has a big brother and one or more street-level clique leaders who are known as second or third brother. Each street-level leader is in charge of several *majais* (little horses) or ordinary members.

Triads, organized gangs, Mafia-like gangs, tongs, and street gangs are neither vertically nor horizontally integrated, and, therefore, it would be a mistake to assume that these groups are routinely involved in coordinated, worldwide criminal conspiracies. Despite the lack of structural integration, however, members of these groups know, consult with, and even cooperate with one another sporadically in carrying out certain legal and illegal activities. They can easily communicate with one another because members all share subcultural norms and values. Among the Chinese, members of this subculture are called Dark Society Elements, and the shady world in which they dwell is called the Dark Society or *jianghu* (literally, "rivers and lakes") (Chin 1990). Snakeheads, drug traffickers, and sex venue operators are, in general, not considered to be part of this subculture.

IV. ACTIVITIES

Chinese organized crime groups around the globe are involved in a variety of criminal activities, especially extortion, gambling, loan sharking, debt collection, and prostitution (Chin 1990, 1996, 2003; Finckenauer and Chin 2007). They also have a reputation for violence and in fact, often engage in violent activities. Almost all the groups are active in the extortion (or protection) and gambling businesses. Occasionally, members of these groups are also involved in the drug trade, but they are not key players in the drug trade and they participate in this activity as individuals rather than as representatives of their groups (Chin 1996). It is important to note that many opportunistic and enterprising businesspeople grouped in loose networks are involved in the drug trade and they are not members of any of the above-mentioned groups (Jelsma, Kramer, and Vervest 2005; Chin and Zhang 2007; Chin 2009).

Triad societies in Hong Kong are involved in a variety of activities, including drugs, pirated VCD/DVD trade in the street, speculative activities in the stock market, money laundering, vehicle theft and smuggling, prostitution, extortion, loan sharking, illegal gambling, and so on, but members are not required to get permission from their organization to conduct these businesses. According to Chu (2007, p. 88), "these are personal investments and individual members will not transfer part of their profits to the Society."

Like most organized crime groups around the world, those in Taiwan are often involved in extorting money from business owners or in providing protection to businessmen for a price. In Taiwan, a strong demand exists for gambling and prostitution, but it is illegal to operate gambling or prostitution establishments. As a result, it is common for organized gangs and *jiaotou* groups to either operate these businesses themselves or to be hired by these establishments. In Taiwan, a well-established underground banking system exists in which ordinary people as well as desperate businessmen may borrow money when they cannot get a loan from legitimate banks. Whenever these underground bankers have difficulty collecting money from their clients, they can turn to gangsters for help. Consequently, organized crime figures are often involved in debt collection. Financial disputes are rarely settled in court because the process is time-consuming and costly and people have little faith in the system. As a result, informal means have emerged to meet the needs of a financial environment requiring a conflict resolution procedure. Powerful crime figures often act as arbitrators in a variety of business disputes. A leader of the Four Seas gang was believed to be murdered because he got involved in a major financial dispute and mishandled the situation badly. It follows that violence is an integral part of all these lucrative activities (Chin 2003). Moreover, members of organized gangs and *jiaotou* groups are very active in politics and play a key role in all local and national elections. Many of them run for public office and become elected lawmakers, representatives, or government officials. For example, a leader of the Heavenly Alliance once served as a lawmaker for many years. Gang leaders in southern Taiwan were elected as county mayors or speakers of local councils. At one point, the minister of justice pointed out that one-third of the city and county councilors in Taiwan were gangsters (Chin 2003).

Mafia-like gangs in China are mainly involved in robbery, extortion, gambling, prostitution, and loansharking. These gangs are also engaged in assault, kidnapping, and murder to achieve their goals. They are also active in the distribution of the so-called emerging drugs (i.e., ketamine powder, ecstasy, amphetamine), but not heroin because they do not want to antagonize the authorities who are protecting them (Chin and Godson 2006). Like organized crime groups elsewhere, Mafia-style gangs in China are also becoming more active in the legitimate business sectors, and wholesale, real estate, and transportation are some of their favorite businesses (Li 2009). For example, Li Qiang, one of the mob bosses arrested in a recent crackdown on organized crime in Chongqing, was alleged to be a key figure in the local transportation industry (Li 2009). Again, like organized crime in Taiwan, Mafia-style gangs in China are making a concerted effort to enter politics by running for office in areas where local officials are elected by the public. Li, the above-mentioned gangster, was a representative of the city's people's congress before his arrest (Li 2009), and Liu Yong, a godfather of Shenyang, was also a city representative before he was sentenced to death (Ouyang 2004).

The tongs as a group are mainly active in gambling, even though they also used to be engaged in the opium and sex businesses (Dillon 1962). Some tong members are also engaged in heroin trafficking or human smuggling, but these are their individual businesses and are not sanctioned by their organizations. For example, Sister Ping, a key figure in the smuggling of Chinese citizens to the United States, was a core member of the Fukien District Association, but her smuggling business was not related to her association (Chin 1999). Even though the tongs are not very active in criminal activities, their close affiliation with violent street gangs often brings them within the radar of law enforcement authorities (Chin 1996).

Extortion of business owners is the bread and butter of Chinese street gangs (Chin 1990). A police officer in New York City disclosed that a leader of the Flying Dragons received $3,400 a week from a gambling house in Chinatown. Another gang leader told a reporter in the mid-1970s that his gang made $10,000 a week from extortion (Chin 1996). The gangs are also active in protecting the gambling and sex establishments in their territories, transporting illegal aliens and collecting smuggling fees for the smugglers, and engaging in home-invasion robbery. For example, according to court materials in a murder case involving the Fuk Ching gang, Ah Chu, a human smuggler, paid a member of the Fuk Ching $500 a head to pick up five illegal Chinese immigrants near the Mexican border (Chin 1999). These gangs are also often involved in serious violence within or between gangs. For instance, in the Golden Dragon Massacre, five people were killed and 11 wounded when three gang members opened fire on customers thought to be rival gang members inside the Golden Dragon Restaurant in San Francisco's Chinatown. Some gang leaders and a small group of followers may work with certain business owners to transport hundreds of kilograms of heroin from Southeast Asia to the United States (Chin 1996).

The networks, on the other hand, are more likely to engage in transnational criminal activities such as human smuggling, sex trafficking, or drug trafficking. These networks are also more likely to specialize in one type of transnational crime, so there is little overlapping among these networks and their activities. It is relatively unlikely for a human smuggling organization to be involved in drug trafficking or for a drug-manufacturing group to participate in the trafficking of women for commercial sex (Finckenauer and Chin 2007).

V. The Link

Hong Kong–based triads and Taiwan-based organized gangs are close to one another in general, and both sets are loosely associated with Mafia-like gangs in China. However, it is not true that these three sets of groups are working together to commit crime on a regular basis. Even though the Chinese authorities often blame the Hong Kong–based triads and the Taiwan-based organized gangs for helping to transform local gangs into Mafia-like gangs, no evidence exists to support the assertion that organized crime groups from overseas play a role in the development of local groups in China (Chin 2003).

Taiwan-based *jiaotou* groups are close to the Japanese Yakuza, but the relationship is mostly symbolic. For example, the *jiatou* groups and the Yakuza often send a delegation to the other party's funerals to show respect to the deceased leaders. No evidence exists to suggest that the *jiaotou* groups and the Yakuza are engaged in joint criminal ventures (Kaplan and Dubro 2003).

U.S.-based tongs and street gangs do not have much interaction with Chinese crime groups in Asia, and they rarely travel to Asia to commit crime. However, the tongs that were once very close to the Kuomintang Party in Taiwan are now beginning to develop good relationships with the Chinese Communist Party in China. Among the street gangs, the Fuk Ching is close to the human smugglers in Asia and in the United States and occasionally gets hired by the smugglers to transport illegal migrants or to collect smuggling fees (Chin 1999).

In general, the relationship between Chinese organized crime groups and organized crime groups of other ethnic origins is weak or almost nonexistent. However, the Chinese human smugglers rely on other ethnic groups in transit and destination countries to move their human cargo on a regular basis (Chin 1999; Soudijn 2006; Zhang 2008), and the Chinese drug producers and traffickers often work with other ethnic groups to transport or market their commodities (Chin 1996, 2009). For example, when Chinese human smugglers move their human cargo to the United States via Mexico, they often seek the help of Mexican smugglers.

Most Chinese organized crime groups are deeply embedded in their respective societies and often maintain strong relationships with a variety of civil and state institutions. Some of the leaders of these groups are well-known businessmen, or politicians, or both, and, even though the police and other politicians and businesspeople are aware of their organized crime background, they treat them with respect and are eager to be associated with them for bribes, votes, protection, or for help in solving personal problems. For example, before his death in 2007, Chen Chi-li, the leader of the United Bamboo gang, was one of the most influential figures in Taiwan.

VI. CONTROL

The existence and activities of Chinese organized crime groups are a major concern for law enforcement authorities in many countries or regions. In Hong Kong, the Organized Crime and Triad Bureau (OCTB) of the Hong Kong Police Force is the leading agency in the investigations of triad activities, while the Independent Commission against Corruption (ICAC) is responsible for the prevention of triad infiltration into government sectors (Finckenauer and Chin 2007). Although the authorities in Hong Kong have not been able to eliminate the triads, they have prevented them from expanding and have minimized the triads' harm to society by targeting the source of triad criminal income and by sending undercover agents to penetrate different triad societies (Chu 2007).

In Taiwan, the Criminal Investigation Division (CID) of the National Police Administration (NPA) and the Ministry of Justice Investigation Bureau (MJIB) are the two agencies most active in dealing with organized gangs and *jiaotou* groups. During the past 25 years, three major gang crackdowns were conducted by the Taiwan government (Operation Cleansweep in 1984, Operation Thunderbolt in 1988, and Operation Chih-ping in 1996), and, as a result, many influential gang leaders are now living in China and certain Southeast Asian countries instead of Taiwan. More recently, because of these crackdowns and massive arrests, many gang and *jiaotou* leaders have started running for public office and have become politicians (or have transformed themselves into successful businessmen) as a way to protect themselves from the authorities (Chin 2003).

In response to the rising crime rates after the open-door policy was adopted by China in the late 1970s, the authorities launched the so-called *yanda* (strike hard) campaign in August 1983, which lasted until January 1987. During the three-year campaign, 197,000 crime groups were dismantled. The government conducted a similar campaign in 1996 after learning that crime rates in the 1990s were eight times higher than in the 1980s. Unlike the wide-ranging 1983 strike-hard campaign, the 1996 operation specifically focused on violent crime groups and Mafia-style gangs. According to He (2003), more than 900 Mafia-like gangs and 5,000 gang members were rounded up during the 1996 campaign. Again, between 1998 and 2003, many powerful Mafia-style gangs across China were dismantled by the authorities, and the leaders of these gangs sentenced to death by the authorities (Chin and Godson 2006). In 2009, authorities in Chongqing, a provincial-level municipality with more than 30 million people, launched a major crackdown against organized crime in their jurisdiction (Li 2009). Hundreds of gang leaders, gang members, and government officials belonging to nine gangs were arrested, and many of them received the death penalty.

In the United States, federal agencies such as the Federal Bureau of Investigation (FBI), the Department of Homeland Security (DHS), the Drug Enforcement Administration (DEA), and the Bureau of Alcohol, Tobacco, Firearms and Explosives (ATF), along with local state police or police departments, are involved in the investigation of Chinese organized crime groups and networks (Chin 1996). Even though a number of key indictments of Chinese tongs and street gangs were handed down in the 1980s, the assaults on Chinese organized crime in America picked up steam to a significant degree after the *Golden Venture* (a smuggling ship) arrived in New York in 1993 with almost 300 illegal Chinese immigrants on board. In the aftermath, almost all the major Chinese tongs and gangs across the United States were indicted jointly as racketeering enterprises under the Racketeer-Influenced and Corrupt Organization Act (RICO) (Chin 1999). The power of the tongs and the gangs diminished significantly after all these indictments resulted in a guilty verdict or plea.

VII. The Future

Chinese-organized crime groups will continue to multiply along with the growing global power of China and the increase in the number of Chinese communities around the world. China began to flex its economic muscle in the new millennium, and large numbers of PRC nationals can be observed as either business entrepreneurs or tourists in almost every corner of the world. The intermingling between Chinese diasporas living overseas for many generations and the newly arrived PRC nationals in the various major urban centers of Asia, Europe, and North America enables the current generation of ethnic Chinese to revitalize old, and establish new, Chinatowns in these urban centers and allows them to position themselves to be competitive in transnational business activities. It is against this backdrop that we must understand the emergence of a new generation of Chinese who are involved in transnational crimes such as drug trafficking, human smuggling, sex trafficking, and money laundering. These transnational criminal activities can be easily carried out by a network of overseas Chinese and PRC nationals, very often with the help of, or in cooperation with, non-Chinese local people in the host countries (Smith 1997; Lintner and Black 2009; Chouvy 2010). The existence of a rapidly expanding global Chinese business network, the ease in traveling back and forth between China and the various host societies, and the trust and secrecy based on a common dialect or hometown allow the Chinese in the global village to circumvent the laws and regulations of the host communities. Most of these networks are based on family or district, and, while they are not set up to commit crime, the existing networks can be used by individuals to occasionally become involved in crime whenever and wherever an opportunity arises. Most people who are involved in transnational crime are not professional criminals with prior criminal records; rather, they are otherwise legitimate businesspeople who are also opportunists and risk takers (Zhang and Chin 2002, 2003).

These emerging crime networks are vertically structured, fluid, and opportunistic. Because these networks do not have a turf, a name, a leader, or sworn members, it is extremely difficult for local law enforcement authorities to understand or penetrate these networks. As a result, for the sake of convenience, the local authorities simply lump all these networks together and call them the "Chinese Mafia," the "Chinese triad," or the "Chinese crime syndicate." And while many well-established Chinese crime groups have been in existence for many years, confusing the newly established criminal networks with the traditional Chinese organized crime syndicates impedes our understanding of the problem and hinders our ability to effectively deal with transnational crime involving ethnic Chinese.

References

Black, David. 1992. *Triad Takeover: A Terrifying Account of the Spread of Triad Crime in the West*. London: Sidgwick and Jackson.

Booth, Martin. 1999. *The Dragon Syndicates: The Global Phenomenon of the Triads*. New York: Carroll and Graf.

Chin, Ko-lin. 1990. *Chinese Subculture and Criminality: Non-traditional Crime Groups in America*. Westport, CT: Greenwood.

——. 1996. *Chinatown Gangs*. New York: Oxford University Press.

——. 1999. *Smuggled Chinese: Clandestine Immigration to the United States*. Philadelphia, PA: Temple University Press.

——. 2003. *Heijin: Organized Crime, Business, and Politics in Taiwan*. Armonk, NY: M.E. Sharpe.

——. 2009. *The Golden Triangle: Inside Southeast Asia's Drug Trade*. Ithaca, NY: Cornell University Press.

Chin, Ko-lin, and Roy Godson. 2006. "Organized Crime and the Political-Criminal Nexus in China." *Trends in Organized Crime* 9(3) (Spring): 5–44.

Chin, Ko-lin, and Sheldon Zhang. 2007. *The Chinese Connection: Cross-Border Drug Trafficking between Myanmar and China.* Final report submitted to the National Institute of Justice for Grant #2004-IJ-CX-0023.

Chouvy, Pierre-Arnaud. 2010. *Opium: Uncovering the Politics of the Poppy.* Cambridge, MA: Harvard University Press.

Chu, Yiu Kong. 2000. *Triads as Business.* London: Routledge.

——. 2007. Hong Kong Gangs. Appendix D-3. In *Asian Transnational Organized Crime,* by James O. Kinckenauer and Ko-lin Chin, 87–95. New York: Nova Science.

Dillon, Richard. 1962. *The Hatchet Men: The Story of the Tong Wars in San Francisco's Chinatown.* New York: Coward-McCann.

Finckenauer, James O., and Ko-lin Chin. 2007. *Asian Transnational Organized Crime.* New York: Nova Science.

——. 2010. *Researching and Rethinking Sex Trafficking: The Movement of Chinese Women to Asia and the United States for Commercial Sex.* Final report submitted to National Institute of Justice for Grant #2006-IJ-CX-0008.

He, Bingsong. 2003 (in Chinese). *Understanding Organized Crime Activities.* Beijing: China Judicial Press.

Jelsma, Martin, Tom Kramer, and Pietje Vervest, eds. 2005. *Trouble in the Triangle: Opium and Conflict in Burma.* Chiang Mai, Thailand: Silkworm Books.

Kaplan, David. 1992. *Fires of the Dragon: Politics, Murder, and the Kuomintang,* New York: Atheneum.

Kaplan, David, and Alec Dubro. 2003. *Yakuza: Japan's Criminal Underworld.* Berkeley: University of California Press.

Keefe, Patrick. 2009. *The Snakehead.* New York: Doubleday.

Li, Xuezhu. 2009 (in Chinese). *Organized Crime in China.* Hong Kong: Caida.

Lintner, Bertil. 2002. *Blood Brothers: The Criminal Underworld of Asia.* New York: Palgrave.

Lintner, Bertil, and Michael Black. 2009. *Merchants of Madness: The Methamphetamine Explosion in the Golden Triangle.* Chiang Mai: Thailand: Silkworm Books.

Lo, Sonny Shiu-hing. 2009. *The Politics of Cross-Border Crime in Greater China.* Armonk, NY: M.E. Sharpe.

Martin, Brian. 1996. *The Shanghai Green Gang.* Berkeley: University of California Press.

McIllwain, Jeffrey. 2003. *Organizing Crime in Chinatown: Race and Racketeering in New York, 1890–1910.* Jefferson, NC: McFarland.

Morgan, J. P. 1960. *Triad Societies in Hong Kong.* Hong Kong: Government Printer.

Murray, Dian. 1994. *The Origins of the Tiandihui: The Chinese Triads in Legend and History.* Stanford, CA: Stanford University Press.

Ouyang, Yifei. 2004 (in Chinese). *Underworld: The Fall of Liu Yong Black Society.* Urumqi, China: Xinjiang People's Publishing.

Seagrave, Sterling. 1996. *Lords of the Rim: The Invisible Empire of the Overseas Chinese.* New York: G.P. Putnam's Sons.

Smith, Paul, ed. 1997. *Human Smuggling.* Washington, DC: Center for Strategic and International Studies.

Soudijn, Melvin. 2006. *Chinese Human Smuggling in Transit.* The Hague: BJU Legal.

US Senate. [1877] 1978. *Report of the Joint Special Committee to Investigate Chinese Immigration.* Reprint. New York: Arno.

Wakeman, Frederic. 1995. *Policing Shanghai, 1927–1937.* Berkeley: University of California Press.

Xia, Ming. 2006. "Assessing and Explaining the Resurgence of China's Criminal Underworld." *Global Crime* 7(2): 151–175.

Zhang, Sheldon. 2008. *Chinese Human Smuggling Organizations.* Stanford, CA: Stanford University Press.

Zhang, Sheldon, and Ko-lin Chin. 2002. "Enter the Dragon: Inside Chinese Human Smuggling Organizations." *Criminology* 40(4): 737–768.

——. 2003. "The Declining Significance of Triad Societies in Transnational Illegal Activities." *British Journal of Criminology* 43(3): 463–482.

——. 2007. *Smuggling and Trafficking in Human Beings.* Westport, CT: Praeger.

——. 2008. "Snakeheads, Mules, and Protective Umbrellas: A Review of Current Research on Chinese Organized Crime." *Crime, Law and Social Change* 50(3): 177–195.

CHAPTER 11

....

THE JAPANESE YAKUZA

....

PETER HILL

I. Historical Development

....

THE modern yakuza have two distinct antecendents: gamblers (*bakuto*) and itinerant peddlars (*tekiya*). Whilst these trades remain within the contemporary yakuza's portfolio of interests, they are now of marginal economic significance. These traditions still inform yakuza cultural identity. Yakuza traditions of chivalry (*ninkyō*) derive from a mythologized link to *machi-yakko*. These were gangs of urban vigilantes that formed in 17th-century Japan to protect their neighborhoods from renegade samurai. Folk heroes such as Banzuiin Chōbei (1622–1657) earned a reputation for "protecting the weak and crushing the strong." This remains a rationalization for the existence of yakuza today (de Vos 1973, pp. 286–287; Ino 1993, pp. 44–49).

As the power of the state declined in the first half of the 19th century, gambling gangs flourished. Some became powerful, well-armed organizations with reputations as community benefactors. Prominent bosses also played a role as mediators in local disputes (Botsman 2005, pp.1272–1278; Siniawer 2008, pp. 20–22). Some played a military role during the Meiji revolution (1868). Shimizu no Jirōchō, a prominent boss, led 480 armed gamblers and secured local highways and cities (Iwai 1963, p. 45; Tamura 1981, p. 225). Similar yakuza paramilitaries operated in northern Japan (Siniawer 2008, p. 25).

However, once it had established effective control, the Meiji state suppressed yakuza with anti-gambling measures. Some gamblers responded by supporting anti-government movements. With the introduction of limited representative democracy, yakuza played a role as suppliers of political violence. During the turbulent period following the Russian Revolution, government figures created a 200,000 strong national alliance of yakuza to act as a weapon against labor unrest. This fractious, uncontrollable outfit failed to live up to its creators' expectations (Iwai 1963, p. 46; Siniawer 2008, pp. 110–116).

Following repression in the 1930s and during the years of World War II, the yakuza thrived in the immediate aftermath of the war. Severe scarcity of resources and a collapse of state capacity created ideal conditions for black markets. Yakuza gangs quickly established control over these markets. Such was the impotence of the police at this time that, by 1946, *tekiya* bosses were officially granted jurisdiction over the Tokyo markets.[1]

The Korean War, and the resulting demand for military equipment, energized Japan's economic recovery. Construction and shipping booms followed, providing new opportunities to gangsters. Yakuza groups operating as labor brokers controlled the supply of day laborers to both these sectors. Economic growth revived the hospitality industry. Bars, restaurants, sexual services, pinball (pachinko), and show-business talent agencies all had close links to the yakuza. These conditions led to a rapid growth in yakuza membership to over 184,000 by 1963 (Hanzai Hakusho 1989). It also encouraged gang conflict as groups fought for control over entertainment districts.

In the mid-1960s, the police systematically targeted yakuza leadership. Legal changes facilitated the prosecution of gambling bosses. This action was partially effective; gang membership declined and some large syndicates disbanded. However, those groups with diverse sources of income survived while traditional gamblers suffered.

When the bosses were released from prison, they restructured their gangs to insulate the elite from prosecution. Gangs also diversified into poorly policed crimes such as corporate extortion, off-shore gambling trips, fake political and social movements, and finance and drug (amphetamine) dealing. The most innovative syndicates, the Yamaguchi-gumi, the Inagawa-kai, and the Sumiyoshi-kai, rapidly expanded into national organizations.

The Yamaguchi-gumi, based in western Japan, was the most aggressive in this respect. Even a nationwide succession war following the death of Taoka Kazuo, its third boss, in the early 1980s could not stop its seemingly inevitable progress toward effective monopolization of Japanese organized crime by the end of the 20th century.

II. Yakuza Organization

As of December 2010, the police had identified 78,600 members of designated violent groups (bōryokudan—the official term for yakuza), and this number has remained reasonably stable over the last two decades. We can be reasonably confident of these statistics; the police have historically kept detailed records of yakuza membership. It has, however, become harder for them to do so as gang affiliation becomes less visible.

Of the 22 designated bōryokudan groups, the big three syndicates are by far the largest organizations by making up 72 percent of the total numbers. Only two other gangs exceed 1,000 initiated members, and the median size of all 22 groups is 280. The big three are also by far the most significant in terms of their geographical extent, having branches throughout Japan. The primacy of the Yamaguchi-gumi is even more marked when it is observed that many bosses of the smaller groups, including the Inagawa-kai, have alliances or brotherhood links with senior Yamaguchi-gumi members.

Gangs are based on fictive family ties of father-son (*oyabun-kobun*) and brother-brother (*kyōdai*) relationships. These are cemented through formal ceremonies involving the exchange of sake cups and other Shintō rituals. For important ceremonies, professional quality videos are made for distribution to allied gangs and other non-yakuza associates as demonstration of the authority of the members. Extracts of these ceremonies have been posted on YouTube.[2]

Under the *oyabun*, the *wakagashira* (young head) or underboss typically coordinates the gang's various operations. Under him are the other *kobun* of the organization known collectively as *wakashu*. Older, senior members of the organization will have a brother-brother rather than a father-son relationship with the boss. A rational bureaucratic structure with functional roles (see Stark 1981) parallels this organic emotional relationship. Within large syndicates this becomes highly formalized with large numbers of executive roles, subcommittees, and meetings.

Within large syndicates we see a quasi-feudal organizational structure. In 2007, the Yamaguchi-gumi head family comprised 93 members. Of these, one was the *kumi-chō* (gang leader), 25 were part of the senior executive cadre, and the remaining 67 were *chokkei kumi-chō* (leaders of powerful subgroups with a direct *oyabun-kobun* relationship to the syndicate boss). Senior executives of these second-level groups are, similarly, bosses of third-level groups, and so on (Hill 2003, p. 69).

Once a month, a meeting is held attended by all members of the head family at which the decisions of the top executive and other relevant information are announced. Control is also exercised through regional blocks consisting of different subgroups within the same geographical area. These are overseen by a designated senior member whose job is to ensure that instructions from the headquarters are relayed to the grass roots of the syndicate and that intrablock disputes between different subgroups are resolved amicably.

The Sumiyoshi-kai traditionally existed as a looser confederation of gangs but has since reorganized to provide for more central control.

It is important to note that the economic activities of large syndicates are primarily conducted at the subgroup level. Traditionally in the Tokyo gangs a boss grants a territory or business to one of his subordinates. The Yamaguchi-gumi's more aggressive business model entails *kobun* making money any way they can (provided it does not violate the syndicate's code of practice or upset gang harmony). At the same time, underlings are required to help out in supporting the activities of their boss and take turns manning the gang office. Members typically pay monthly dues (*jōnōkin*). Advancement within the organization depends on one's ability to make a contribution; money is a key metric by which that is measured.

Although monthly Yamaguchi-gumi *jōnōkin* payments have varied, in 2004, executives were expected to pay 1 million yen ($9,100)[3] and *chokkei kumi-chō* 800,000 ($7,300) yen plus an additional 300,000 yen ($2,700) for the central reserve fund. This equates to a total annual income for the Yamaguchi-gumi headquarters of 1.27 billion yen ($11.5 m). During Watanabe's leadership there were a number of supplementary expenses such as the purchase of the gang headquarters and establishment of a corporate identity. For bosses not earning at least 50 million yen ($450 000) a year, this is a real burden (Mizoguchi 2007, pp. 100–101).

III. Recruitment and Training

What sort of people become yakuza? One common perception is that yakuza are drawn overwhelmingly from three groups, juvenile biker gangs (*bosōzoku*), the descendants of outcastes (*burakumin*), and ethnic Koreans resident in Japan.

No hard data is available to verify this. The issue of *burakumin* is sensitive and the police do not officially compile relevant statistics (not least for fear of inciting claims of discrimination). Estimates vary but agreement is broad that these three groups are disproportionately represented amid yakuza ranks.

During fieldwork I have encountered yakuza backgrounds as diverse as wrestler, police officer, boxer, loan-shark, debt-collector, legitimate businessman, pachinko worker, and university graduate. Up and coming yakuza are constantly scouting for potential talent; it is one way to bolster their own position. Successful gang bosses are frequently charismatic individuals capable of attracting followers. Suitable candidates include those who demonstrate toughness by standing up to yakuza and men with successful illegal businesses. Some people join to stop yakuza bothering them: others just like fighting.

A period of training is required prior to formal initiation. Trainees typically live in the gang office where they carry out menial household chores, run errands, and learn correct yakuza etiquette and behavior. In common with other traditional Japanese trades, they are expected to learn by observation rather than explicit instruction. Mistakes incur physical punishment. The training period used to last for up to three years but has generally contracted (in some cases to six months). This inevitably generates complaints from older yakuza about declining standards.

IV. Yakuza Culture

Until recently, yakuza made little effort to conceal their identities. Advantages accrue to exhibiting reliable markers of gang membership; if you can convincingly demonstrate gangster status without resorting to costly displays of violence each time you meet someone new, business is much easier.[4] Yakuza have developed a number of collective brand images that facilitate identification: *jingi, irezumi,* and *yubetsume.*

Jingi refers to the traditional greetings that yakuza would give when meeting other yakuza for the first time. This consisted of a highly stylized formal account of their gang lineage given in a forward crouch. By the 1970s this was dying out; gangsters now signal membership with name cards and a lapel pin bearing their gang crest. These are easier for non-yakuza to fake, but imposters hoping to free-ride on established yakuza reputations risk severe repercussions if discovered.

Not all yakuza have tattoos (*irezumi*), but they are common. Police research in the 1970s, showed 70 percent of all yakuza had tattoos (Mugishima et al. 1971, pp. 137–139). Yakuza full body tattoos are costly to acquire. Not only is the process painful, time-consuming and expensive, but also it is very damaging to the health; by destroying the sweat glands, the body is less able to get rid of toxins. According to a senior Yamaguchi-gumi retiree, this fact, combined with a heavy intake of alcohol, makes liver disease the cause of roughly one-third of all yakuza deaths (Gotō 2010, p. 233). While displaying yakuza status now incurs greater costs, the perception among young yakuza recruits that tattoos are cool remains.

While finger amputation (*yubitsume*) is generally performed as a punishment, apology, or demonstration of commitment, the absence of one or more fingertips is a recognizable yakuza trademark. Police data from the mid-1990s suggested that one-third of all yakuza were missing at least one finger tip (Yonezato et al. 1994, p. 43). *Yubitsume* is more common in western Japan than in the Tokyo area and is declining generally as bosses increasingly impose fines in its place.

Other clues to yakuza status, including clothing, speech, a style of walking (cutting the air with your shoulders), and hair-styles, are all semiotically significant. For a fuller picture of yakuza self-presentation and social norms, watching Japanese gangster films is informative. This is one way in which gangsters themselves learn how they are expected to look (Gambetta 1993, pp. 134–136).

Many yakuza films explore endurance, loyalty, and the conflict between obligation and emotion in that the heroes are men of traditional honor at odds with a modern, slightly foreign, Japan. Films produced by Tōei Studio starring Takakura Ken and Tsurata Kōji are classics of this genre. *Jingi Naki Tatakai* (Battles without Honor and Humanity, 1973), based on the experiences of a postwar boss from Hiroshima, provides a grittier account of yakuza life. Kitano Takeshi portrays a more stylized contemporary yakuza world (Schilling 2003).

Yakuza must attend numerous ceremonies. Weddings, funerals, office openings, succession ceremonies, initiation rites, and jail release celebrations are all important. Though a considerable drain of both time and money, these events serve to demonstrate gang cohesion, prestige, power, and the importance of networks and hierarchy; participants are expected to dress in expensive clothes and arrive in suitable cars with the appropriate retinue. Cash gifts are also required. Recently, some events have become less public as the police have put pressure on halls to refuse yakuza custom; yakuza themselves have adopted a lower profile (Yamadaira 2001, pp. 12–13).

These ceremonies inevitably conclude with drinking sessions. Alcohol plays a big part in yakuza life. While yakuza are, undoubtedly, hedonists, this is not the only explanation; successful yakuza must maintain extensive social networks and ensure excellent channels of information, and alcohol facilitates this.

V. Yakuza Business

Yakuza sources of income, known as *shinogi*, range from unambiguously illegal activities to venture capital. They are highly sensitive to legal and market conditions; arguably the yakuza are the most dynamic, flexible feature of the Japanese economy.

In 1989, the police published estimates for total yakuza income of 1.3 trillion yen ($11.8 bn) (Keisatsu-chō 1989, p. 46). This was an underestimate; it excluded the sums that derive from yakuza links with big business, which was considered too politically sensitive to mention (Hill 2003, p. 93). Attempts to package yakuza revenue streams into one tidy figure are problematic. It is easier to look at yakuza involvement in particular industries.[5]

Gambling, the traditional bakuto business, is now of marginal economic significance to yakuza. One analysis of the underground economy estimates that, in 2000, gambling/bookmaking accounted for 7 percent of illegal yakuza income, down from 21 percent in 1989 (Kadokura 2003, p. 7). Gambling violations accounted for 3.5 percent of all yakuza arrests in 2009. Gambling falls into three broad categories: organizing card and dice games (including foreign gambling trips), making books on racing and other sporting events, and pachinko (electronic pinball).

Illegal gambling runs from small stake dicing operations in the quarters of day laborers in Tokyo and Osaka to plush underground casinos offering roulette and baccarat. In Nagoya, 27 Yamaguchi-gumi run casinos were recently identified, each earning at least 100 million yen ($900 000) per month (Mizoguchi 2008, p. 63). In the early 2000s, roughly 300 online casino booths offering streamed baccarat, blackjack, and roulette appeared. These yielded 300,000 yen ($2,700) per month per store for the yakuza groups that protected them before being closed down by the police (Mizoguchi 2010, pp. 125–126).

The government operates a monopoly on legal gambling on cycle, horse, and boat racing. Yakuza undercut the state with parallel bookmaking operations. Yakuza also keep books on baseball, soccer, mixed martial arts, and sumo (which has traditional links to yakuza).

Japan's vast pachinko industry has a yearly turnover of around 30 trillion yen ($270 bn) (Kadokura 2003, pp. 26–27). To avoid violating gambling laws, pachinko players win token prizes that they can then exchange for cash at separate establishments. The prizes would then be bought back indirectly by the pachinko parlor. Traditionally, the exchange business was run by yakuza. In the early 1990s, police estimated that the exchange business was worth 60 billion yen ($480 m) per year to Tokyo gangs (Hinago 1992, p. 201). In recent decades, police have squeezed yakuza out of the exchange business by setting up public welfare bodies to run it. Despite police regulation, some pachinko parlors still pay for yakuza protection (Yamaguchi-gumi interviewee Osaka 2003).

Illegal drug use in Japan predominantly involves methamphetamine; 77 percent of all drug-related arrests in 2008 were for methamphetamine. Cannabis, which has become more popular in the last decade, accounted for most of the rest at 19 percent (NPA 2009).

Large yakuza syndicates officially shun drugs. However, the arrest statistics suggest otherwise: of the 26,503 arrests of yakuza (including associate members) in 2009, 6,153 (23 percent) were for violation of the amphetamine control law (which represents about half of all amphetamine arrests, NPA 2009). In the late 1980s, the police estimated that about 85 percent of all yakuza gangs were involved in the trade, including 300 at the wholesale level (Tamura 1988). Tamura's research shows that, while yakuza groups dominated the wholesale trade, among street-level dealers the ratio of yakuza to non-yakuza was equal.

The origin of amphetamine has shifted from South Korea to Taiwan to North Korea. China now seems to be the predominant source country, though there is strong evidence to suggest that the drug is still produced by North Korea and then shipped through China to avoid international censure (Perl 2007).

VI. Protection

Many yakuza activities can most usefully be analyzed as a species of protection. Protection and extra-legal fixing, available to both legitimate and underworld businesses, is not necessarily extortion imposed on unwilling victims; in many cases, it is a good that individuals genuinely desire. This does not, however, make it a "good thing"; frequently yakuza ties enable protectees to behave in socially undesirable ways.[6]

The *tekiya* business of stallholders is a case of internalized protection. Although *tekiya* have been purged from many traditional Japanese festivals, this process is not complete. Other street vendors, such as fast-food stalls and the Israeli jewelry hawkers, are consumers of *tekiya* protection.

Another longstanding mainstay of yakuza protection is the hospitality (*mizushōbai*) sector, which ranges from restaurants, night-clubs, hostess bars, and snack joints to sexual service establishments. *Mizushōbai* has traditional links with the yakuza; many wives and girlfriends work in, or own, bars. In the 1980s and 1990s, roughly two-thirds of bars, clubs, and restaurants were paying for protection; costs varied from a few tens of thousands to a million yen per month (Hill 2003, pp. 94–96). Yakuza protection can be useful in resolving disputes with drunken and unruly customers more effectively than the police; it is not in the protector's interests for customers to be scared away.

Yakuza protection also operates in the sex industry.[7] Japan's prostitution prevention law applies only to sexual intercourse. Consequently, a large industry legally offers various other sexual services that supplements the illegal market for sex. Gangs import foreign sex workers (sometimes by tricking them into indentured servitude) and help control them afterward. Yakuza can, for example, prevent a popular girl from being poached by a rival business (Hill 2005, p. 11). The police exercise considerable administrative control over mizushōbai industries.[8] Direct yakuza ownership is, therefore, difficult for licensed premises.

Construction is another industry with close yakuza links. Traditionally, yakuza controlled the *tehaishi* business supplying day laborers to small construction companies at the bottom of the subcontracting chain; they thereby had a stranglehold on projects. Whilst some yakuza have owned construction companies,[9] to get a license as a general contractor is increasingly hard for them. The standard protection fee in construction projects is 3 percent. Yakuza protection does not just prevent yakuza predation, it can also help deter unprotected competitors from bidding for projects or police bid-rigging collusion among firms. Efforts to eradicate yakuza from construction is difficult; this business is also central to Japanese machine politics.

Construction generates rubble, and yakuza can facilitate its cheap disposal alongside other forms of industrial waste. Yakuza additionally provide disincentives to complain about such environmental crimes. The use of yakuza to combat protests by the victims of mercury poisoning in Minamata in the 1960s is a well-known example.[10]

The Minamata case is significant because the protests were conducted at the polluting company's annual general meetings and demonstrated how sensitive such events were. This led to the growth of a niche scam conducted by general meeting specialists (*sōkaiya*). Essentially this business has two sides: Predatory *sōkaiya* extort money from companies by threatening to disrupt AGMs with embarrassing information of corporate malfeasance, incompetence, or personal indiscretions of senior executives while protective *sōkaiya* neutralize would-be extortionists. This business initially lacked yakuza involvement but, once firms started hiring protection, *sōkaiya* needed to follow suit.

Sōkaiya numbers rose throughout the 1970s. By the early 1980s, more than 6,000 professional *sōkaiya* had been identified by the police, and 30 percent of them were yakuza. In response, the corporate code was revised in 1982 instituting a minimum threshold below which attendance at a company's AGM was not permitted. Moreover, it became illegal for companies to give money to *sōkaiya* (Szymkowiak 1996, pp. 70, 145–147).

While this ostensibly led to a reduction in the number of *sōkaiya*, this was largely cosmetic; low-level *sōkaiya* transformed themselves into analysts, fake political groups, or *burakumin*-liberation movements. Payments were disguised as subscriptions to newsletters or artwork rental (Szymkowiak 1996, p. 147).

The existence of *sōkaiya* seems strange; surely shareholders have a right to hold the managers of their company to account. The Japanese institutional environment differs from the United States or Europe. The logic runs: Information is less freely available in Japan; those who have it are less able to exploit it by shorting the market or profitably launching a class action lawsuit; victims of AGM disruption see a fall in their share price; thus, it is cost effective to keep paying *sōkaiya* (West 1999).

West demonstrates how institutional factors play a significant role in creating opportunities for yakuza. In an important paper with Milhaupt (2000), he further explains how the lack of efficient legal mechanisms for conflict resolution creates demand for a "dark side of private ordering." In particular, slow, costly civil litigation and police reluctance to intervene in civil affairs have encouraged a culture in which yakuza resolution is accepted as a necessary evil. This has engendered a category of yakuza protection known as violent intervention in civil affairs (*minji kainyū bōryoku* or *minbō*).[11]

Debt collection is one example. Even when the debt is legal (not owed to a loan-shark), the machinery for recovering debt through the courts is so cumbersome that many consider it preferable to rely on yakuza despite hefty commissions. Another type of extra-legal fixing is bankruptcy management. Yakuza specialists buy out key creditors of a failed firm at a significant discount. The courts can take many years to resolve a bankruptcy and pay creditors; it can be cost effective to sell out to yakuza, especially if you know that they are already involved.

Minbō increased throughout the 1980s. In some cases, yakuza operated on behalf of others; in others, yakuza actively engineered civil disputes as a pretext for compensation. *Minbō* adversely affects ordinary people in ways that yakuza had, supposedly, traditionally eschewed but, frequently, no laws were broken. Because yakuza trademarks are readily identifiable, when a yakuza complains about damages he has incurred and demands compensation, a threat has implicitly been made. Until the threat is articulated explicitly, or actual damage incurred, no crime has been committed.

During the 1980s, Japan experienced a decade long real estate and stock market speculative bubble. This presented numerous *minbō* opportunities to yakuza. The most significant of these was land-sharking (*jiage*). Japanese law gives strong protections to tenants and, thus, making it difficult for owners to develop property. Yakuza coerced tenants to relinquish their rights, thereby creating plots of developable land. Yakuza typically charged real estate developers a 3 percent commission on the final value of the land. Given stratospheric prices in urban centers during the 1980s, *jiage* became the biggest single source of income for yakuza in this period. Inagawa-kai boss Ishii Susumu, for example, set up a number of companies, just one of which had a turnover of 12.2 billion yen ($81 m) in 1987 in only two years after he had set it up. Ishii's *jiage* profits went into Japan's frothy stock market.

Ishii's financial dealings were complex. They included selling bogus investments and colluding with prominent securities firms to ramp up his own portfolio (Hill 2003, pp. 182–183).

Many yakuza enthusiastically embraced the bubble. Often they would speculate in land and then use that as collateral to borrow money to invest in the stock market. Some took this a step further. The Itoman case is a good example. Itō Suemitsu was a bubble-era property developer who became the protectee of Yamaguchi-gumi underboss, Takumi Masaru. Itō sold the Itoman Corporation (no relation) equal rights to his large development in Ginza for 46.5 billion yen ($423 m). Having been made a director of Itoman, Itō then made dummy or inflated purchases to transfer an estimated 500 to 600 billion yen ($4.5–$5.5 bn) to the underworld (Hill 2003, p. 183).

VII. The Violent Groups Countermeasures Law

Minbō generated increasing public antipathy to the yakuza during the 1980s. Anxiety was exacerbated by a number of gang wars in which unrelated people were killed.

Simultaneously, a scandal-prone government was unpopular at home and subject to international criticism for its ineffective countermeasures taken against organized crime. The government needed to take action.

In 1991, the Violent Group Members' Unjust Activities Prevention Law (its unwieldy Japanese title usually abbreviated to bōtaihō), was passed into law and took effect the following year. The bōtahō empowers regional public safety commissions (PSC) to designate gangs that satisfy certain criteria as violent groups (Bōryokudan). If members of designated Bōryokudan engage in *minbō*-type activities or make "violent demands" (demands that are threatening because they are made under the shadow of the gang's reputation), then the victims of this activity can report it to the police or PSC. The PSC can then issue an administrative order forbidding actions in question. If this order is not obeyed, a fine, and or imprisonment, ensues.

The law also provides for regional centers to promote bōryokudan eradication (largely staffed by retired police officers), compulsory closure of gang offices during periods of intergang conflict, and administrative orders preventing the public display of gang emblems if the public object to them.[12]

In response, yakuza took steps to conceal their activities by creating organizations such as companies, right-wing political groups, fake *burakumin*-liberation groups, and religious bodies. The number of business associates (*kigyō shatei*) increased. The law was subsequently revised to cover "semi-violent demands" made by such yakuza fronts.

In addition, gang signs and emblems were removed from offices and branch offices were instructed on how to behave. Many gangs reduced the level of cooperation extended to the police.

Assessing this law's effect is hard; its introduction coincided with the collapse of Japan's economic bubble, which hit the yakuza hard. Land-sharking, for example, was no longer a viable business. Yakuza had borrowed heavily to invest in risky portfolios that were now worth a fraction of their outstanding debts. For example, of the 6.4 trillion yen ($58 bn) of bad debts in the Jūsen (savings and loans) industry, roughly 40 percent was thought to be held by yakuza (Hill 2003, pp. 186–187).

The aftermath of the bubble witnessed attacks on bank executives who were responsible for resolving debts. Some banks made use of yakuza to resolve debt problems, for instance, employing them to collect debts from other gangs and getting yakuza loss-cutters (*songiri-ya*) to negotiate reduced repayments.

In a reversal of *jiage*, yakuza could profit from getting a sublease in a building owned by a distressed company. By demonstrating yakuza occupation, they depressed the value of the building yet further. They, or their associates, would then be able to purchase it cheaply, vacate, and then sell at a profit. Alternatively, the owner might pay them to leave. Parking an armored truck used to distribute right-wing propaganda or turning up at an auction to intimidate potential bidders were similar tactics.

Economic hardship encouraged market demand for small consumer loans. The Goryō-kai, a Yamaguchi-gumi subgroup, was one organization that exploited this. Their network of loansharks known as the TO group consisted of 1,000 employees with an annual turnover of 100 billion yen ($0.9 bn). At least 10 borrowers committed suicide when they could no longer pay the interest. When Kajiyama Susumu, the mastermind, was arrested in 2003, 5.8 billion yen ($48 m) was seized in Swiss banks and $600,000 in Las Vegas accounts. Kajiyama was later jailed for two and a half years and fined 30 million yen. Some of the TO group's customers have launched a class action law suit for the return of their interest payments but, given that most of their money has disappeared, it is unlikely they will see much of it returned.

Many illegal moneylenders (*yamikin*) are active in Japan. Those that are not themselves yakuza require protection. Even large, legal loan companies maintain connections to the yakuza.

The increasing presence of yakuza business in the financial world constitutes a significant development during this period. To stimulate growth in the high-tech and Internet sectors, the authorities adopted a loose regulatory framework for the Jasdaq over the counter market and the TSE Mothers and OSE Hercules markets. They were, therefore, ideal investment opportunities for yakuza money. At the same time, there was a shortage of venture capital for Internet start-ups. Japanese banks weren't interested. Livedoor, set up by high-profile IT entrepreneur Horie Takafumi, provides one example. Backed by yakuza money, Horie conducted an aggressive strategy of acquisitions; nine years after being founded in 1996, Livedoor consisted of 40 companies and had a capitalization of roughly 1 trillion yen ($9 bn). The stock price was inflated artificially by fraudulent bookkeeping to show profits rather than losses.

Similarly, Ryōzanpaku, a company owned by a former Yamaguchi-gumi executive and acting *kigyō-shatei*, systematically ramped up the value of shares in P-map by shuffling them between 20 yakuza conspirators before selling them. Ryōzanpaku also acquired ICF, an Internet firm, and transferred a number of worthless Ryōzanpaku subsidiaries to ICF. With the connivance of a certified public accountant, Toyotomi then falsified ICF's performance in order to sell it off. From these complicated transactions Ryōzanpaku is said to have made 4 billion yen ($40 m) (Arimori 2008, pp. 36–40, 44). Some certified public accountancy firms, including ones with former prosecutors and senior police officers on the board, have come under the wing of different organized crime groups. This helps conceal fraudulent activity. Foreign firms have also been caught up in yakuza-related scams. In 2008, Lehman Brothers Japan was duped in a 35.2 billion yen ($352 m) fraud conducted by companies high-jacked by yakuza finance.

Part of the reason that these scams are hard to detect is that they are often fronted by yakuza protectees with impeccable credentials; they are graduates of the world's elite universities and top-ranked financial institutions. Yakuza investment is not always predatory; yakuza operate as private equity firms involved in the complete spectrum of Japan's corporate world. In some cases, they are content to have a stake, in others they want control. In sectors such as private detective agencies, the business is directly useful to related yakuza activities. One Tokyo-based financial intelligence analyst estimates that 4.5 percent of companies listed on the Tokyo and Osaka stock exchanges are "seriously tainted by organized crime." The equivalent rate in the Mothers market is 15 percent (private correspondence 2009).

For several years the Financial Services Agency, National Police Agency, and Tokyo Stock Exchange have operated a joint committee to share information. This has yielded some results; recently, several yakuza-related real estate companies have gone bust as the FSA has quietly put pressure on banks to deny them further funding. This has not been reported in the press (private correspondence 2009).

VIII. Organized Crime Countermeasures? Yakuza and the Police

Given the depth and breadth of yakuza penetration of the economy, the obvious question is what are the police doing about this? Are they corrupt, inept, fatalistic, or a combination of these? Kaplan and Dubro (2003, pp. 144–149) provide a good overview of entrenched, widespread corruption in the Osaka police in the early 1980s. More recently, Adelstein mentions a police officer who is known to be a Yamaguchi-gumi informant but is tolerated by his colleagues because his information about the activities of other gangs is so good (Adelstein 2009, p. 306). Mizoguchi, citing a source in the sexual services industry in Aichi prefecture, says that the market rate for police information about forthcoming raids and other relevant activities is 100,000 to 200,000 yen (Mizoguchi 2008, p. 64).

Evidence also exists of police ineptitude (the investigation into the Aum Supreme Truth Cult is one non-yakuza example). The inadvertent uploading to the Internet of over 1 gigabyte of information related to the Gotō-gumi (a prominent Yamaguchi-gumi subgroup) in 2007 by a young police officer while making use of a file-sharing program to download pornography does not inspire confidence either. This included names of front companies and associates as well as the names of many of Gotō's celebrity mistresses (one of Japan's largest talent agencies is a Gotō-gumi front) (Mizoguchi 2008, p. 200).

The standard characterization of the police-yakuza relationship is, however, one of accommodation. The view that the yakuza's existence is tolerated (or even welcomed) by the police because they act as agents of social control is widespread among the Japanese public and in the English-language literature (van Wolferen 1989, pp. 100–105; Kaplan and Dubro 2003, pp. 148–151 are popular examples). Essentially, the argument runs as follows: The police are far more concerned with disorganized street crime than they are with organized criminality, which traditionally has involved the protection or management of supposedly victimless, consensual commercial transactions such as gambling, sexual services, and money lending. Yakuza exercise a policing role in two distinct ways. First, gangs collectively have an interest in avoiding activities that upset the police; therefore, they discourage members from such behavior. Second, gangs want to maximize the patronage enjoyed by the various entertainment businesses under their protection; street hoodlums scare customers away so yakuza have an interest in guarding against them.

In this standard model, yakuza adopt a cooperative stance vis-à-vis the police and accept limits on their behavior as the price to pay for toleration. They provide information to the police about other crimes and expellees (who may become rogue lone wolf criminals); they may surrender gang members to the police to take responsibility for gang activities (sometimes the confessor will not be guilty but will be covering for a senior member[13]) or allow guns to be found. Ames, in his 1981 ethnography of the Japanese police, presents a more nuanced picture of the relationship between the police and the yakuza: Both sides recognize that open hostility would be counterproductive but the apparent cordiality between the two is a façade.

While there is something in this analysis, we should note: First, the police have not been neutral. Much of the yakuza's evolution in the postwar era has been driven by changes in the law and the parameters of what the police have been prepared to tolerate. Second, the level of cooperation has differed widely (the Yamaguchi-gumi being less amenable than Tokyo-based syndicates). Third, yakuza-police relations have deteriorated over the years, particularly since the introduction of the bōtaihō and its subsequent upgrades. One indicator of this deterioration was the discovery by Nagoya detectives of their personal details, including family photographs, in a Kōdō-kai gang office in 2007. Thus, they are being watched.

To a certain extent, the pragmatic policing of organized crime derived from police weakness; following Japan's surrender in 1945, the police needed all the help they could get, and today they are one of the most powerful institutions in Japan. Despite this change, they are unable to put the yakuza out of business. This is demonstrated by the limited regulatory nature of the bōtaihō.

While it is unrealistic to expect the eradication of the yakuza, given their dynamism and deep penetration of society, much could be done to limit their ability to operate with apparent impunity in vast swathes of the legitimate economy. Useful steps in this direction would include: a RICO-style law, plea bargaining and an informant-protection program, wider admissibility of wire-tapping evidence, and the ability to conduct undercover operations. A law criminalizing membership in yakuza associations would not be particularly useful without these other provisions. Whether they actually see the light of day is a matter of political will.

IX. Yakuza and the Political Elite

Yakuza have long played a role in Japanese politics. The extent to which they continue to do so and the way in which this connection operates constitute the holy grail of yakuza studies. Is yakuza-elite symbiosis systemic at the governmental level or does it amount to ad hoc opportunistic individual patronage?

In the immediate postwar period, yakuza "became an integral part of a conservative nexus that was a reincarnation of the prewar nationalist version [of violent political support groups]" (Siniawer 2008, p. 150). With a widely held fear of communist revolution, conservative politicians linked up with right-wing extremists and yakuza to form anti-communist organizations similar to the *ingaidan* of prewar politics.

Extremists such as Kodama Yoshiō and Sasakawa Ryōichi are crucial here as they served as fixers (*kuromaku*) who operated behind the scenes and as financiers. Kodama and Sasakawa funded the establishment of the Liberal Party, which then merged to form the Liberal Democratic Party and which effectively monopolized power over the second half of the 20th century.

The role of yakuza in politics has changed and has become increasingly obscure over this period. In 1952, yakuza were called upon by senior conservative politicians to protect the Diet building against left-wing protestors trying to prevent the passage of the Subversive Activities Bill (Iwai 1963, p. 693). Similarly, yakuza were involved in violent parliamentary scuffles as socialists tried to block the passage of a revised security treaty between the United States and Japan. When, after the treaty was ratified, rioting threatened to disrupt a planned visit by US president Dwight Eisenhower, yakuza were involved in fighting the protestors. Many believe that, at the instigation of Prime Minister Kishi, Kodama set up a composite force of yakuza and right-wing groups to combat the thousands of left-wing students and activists (Siniawer 2008, pp. 166–168).

Throughout the 1950s and 1960s, yakuza-politician links were not greatly concealed. The Lockheed scandal in the mid-1970s involving Kodama and senior politicians engendered public disgust with politicians; yakuza links became embarrassing. In undertaking researching in the late 1970s, Stark observed a clique made up of local politicians, business interests, bureaucrats and, at the center, the local gang boss. All the members made use of the clique to further their own personal interests. Yakuza involvement enhanced the clique's effectiveness as the gang "has the organization, the coercive forces, and expertise in illegal dealings to make the social network a self-regulating, self-enforcing and self-sustaining clique" (1981, p. 198).

While political links with yakuza became harder to spot in the late 20th century, this is not to say that they had disappeared. In 1987, two of the most important politicians in Japan, Takeshita Noboru and Kanemaru Shin, contacted Ishii of the Inagawa-kai and asked him to silence a small right-wing organization that was undermining Takeshita's campaign to become prime minister. Ishii also helped Kanemaru deal with an intransigent colleague and combat right-wing criticism of Kanemaru's visit to North Korea. Kanemaru later entertained Ishii at a swanky restaurant, where he praised his "chivalry." These revelations led, ultimately, to the resignation of the two politicians. A photograph taken of Mori Yasuhirō (prime minister from 2000 to 2001) drinking with yakuza similarly scuppered Mori's political future.

Gotō Tadamasa, formerly a senior executive in the Yamaguchi-gumi, published his autobiography in 2010 following his expulsion from the syndicate. He discusses helping politicians in terms of assisting at election time. He mobilized his men to put up posters and encouraged his contacts in the construction industry to give their support. Itoyama

Eitarō, a former parliamentarian and self-styled fixer between the upper- and under-worlds, claimed in 1999 that yakuza would make unsolicited visits to politicians during election time and give them large cash donations with the tacit understanding that the money would be not only returned if they were elected, but also doubled (*Washington Post* 1999).

In 2009, the LDP's stranglehold on power was broken with the election of a DPJ (Democratic Party of Japan) government. The Yamaguchi-gumi headquarters had already instructed its branches to support the DPJ; the gang leadership was frustrated with the increasingly harsh legal environment with which they were confronted (Mizoguchi 2007, pp. 247–248). This dissatisfaction is evidence that remaining yakuza-politician links are individual rather than systemic. Senior-level relationships persist; in 2008, a financial analyst who closely monitors yakuza investment informed me that six cabinet ministers in a recent LDP government had yakuza links, and these individuals were just the ones he knew about.

What of politicians who have vigorously opposed yakuza? In 2002, Ishii Kōki, a DPJ parliamentarian and outspoken corruption-buster, was stabbed to death outside his home. Itō Hakusui, a right-wing extremist, later surrendered himself and confessed to the crime. Although the assailant claimed to be working alone, it is unlikely that yakuza were not involved in this murder.

X. Yakuza Relations in the Noughties

Within the yakuza world, strains surrounding the use of violence are constant. Whilst the yakuza would be irrelevant without violence, its use incurs significant costs in terms of increased police countermeasures, the risk of retaliation, and the opportunity cost of lost earnings during gang warfare. Ideally, from a gangster's point of view, others will be so scared that violence does not even have to be threatened. When, however, your disputant is a similarly scary gangster, you have a problem.

Historically, the Tokyo gangs have been much better at resolving disputes peacefully than was the case in the Yamaguchi-gumi's heartland of western Japan. In Tokyo this was arranged through the Kantō Hatsuka-kai, an association consisting of the main groups. At a monthly meeting, disputes are discussed and reconciliations brokered. Responsibility for emergency conciliation duties is carried out on a rotating basis. The Tokyo police have been very anxious that this system not be destabilized by a more aggressive Western model.

Despite a long-standing agreement between the Inagawa-kai and Yamaguchi-gumi that the latter would not set up gang offices in the Tokyo area, Yamaguchi-gumi sub-groups have been moving in for several decades. This was somewhat at odds with the conservative leadership of the fifth boss of the Yamaguchi-gumi, Watanabe. He tried to impose peaceful coexistence with other yakuza groups, reinforced by "sakazuki diplomacy" in which senior executives of the syndicate forged brotherhood bonds with bosses of other organizations or acted as their guarantors at succession ceremonies. Such diplomacy was, however, contrary to the syndicate's culture. Attempts to restrict the business activities of gang members while at the same time demanding onerous membership payments generated resentment against the leadership.

Antipathy toward Watanabe was exacerbated by other factors: He showed consistent favoritism to the members of his own subgroup; he was suspected of complicity in the murder of a widely respected subordinate; he considered his own position over the interests of ordinary members (this became increasingly clear as employer responsibility cases started to take effect).

In frustration, a group of senior executives forced Watanabe out in a bloodless coup in July 2005. The key figures in this coup were Tsukasa Shinobu, leader of the Nagoya based Kōdō-kai, and his deputy, Takayama Kiyoshi. Having ousted Watanabe, Tsukasa split up his rival's power base and rearranged the syndicate's executive committee to reflect the new balance of power.

Evidence that the new leadership would be more proactive came in September 2005 when the Kokusui-kai left the Kantō Hatsuka-kai and joined the Yamaguchi-gumi, finally giving the syndicate a formal presence in the heart of Tokyo. A number of other gangs have been drawn close under the Yamaguchi-gumi folds through brotherhood relationships. They are effectively satrapies. Most significantly, the Inagawa-kai is controlled by a faction very close to the Yamaguchi-gumi. This leaves only the Sumiyoshi-kai as a significant independent gang (Adelstein and Norbaksh 2010).

XI. Yakuza and Globalization

Since the 1990s, fears have been widespread in Japan concerning foreign criminal gangs running riot in Japan. With the rapidly growing number of foreign residents in a country where notions of cultural identity are predicated on ethnic homogeneity, such an attitude is understandable. While noting that most foreigners in Japan are entirely legitimate, it is clear that foreign criminal elements are operating in the country. What is their relationship with the yakuza?

Despite the panic over a supposed process of ethnic hybridization within organized crime in Japan, the core businesses discussed above are still the province of the yakuza. Foreign organized crime groups are generally either cooperating with yakuza or engaged in activities unrelated to the yakuza economy. While cases have been reported of yakuza making use of foreign groups to strengthen their position vis-à-vis other yakuza gangs, foreign gangs are not able to establish themselves as protective agencies outside of the narrow confines of their own communities (Hill 2005; Friman 2004).

In many cases, the illegal activities of foreign gangs center on property crimes. Police figures show a number of Chinese and Korean gangs that engage in serial burglary. Koreans, in particular, have a concentrated spree before returning home. Vietnamese groups run systematic shoplifting operations and steal motorbikes for the Vietnamese market. Vehicle theft is undertaken by informal Brazilian groups too. Pakistani middle-men act as agents for the used-car market for the Middle East and Africa (NPA 2009). Property crime does not really impact the yakuza, except to the extent that vehicle theft for the overseas second-hand market is something that occurs at the lower end of the yakuza chain.

Trafficking in women for the sex industry is something requiring cooperation with local agents in the source countries. This sort of relationship is frequently necessary with drug importation too. In the drugs trade, Iranians and other foreigners are involved at the lower level but are thought to be largely working within the yakuza framework or catering to their own ethnic communities. At the higher end of foreign criminality, Chinese groups are involved in issuing fake cards and skimming credit card details; at least some of these work in cooperation with yakuza.

At the same time as non-Japanese have come to Japan, Japanese have increasingly gone abroad to work, study, and play. While it has been hard recently for known yakuza to get entry permits to the mainland USA, they have little trouble moving around Asia. Yakuza money also travels overseas; this has become increasingly important as legal provisions for asset seizure have increased since the introduction of the law on counter-measures against organized crime (sōtaihō) in 1999.

XII. Whither the Yakuza? Mid-term Projections

Over the last half century, the legal regime has become harsher and more rigorously enforced. In addition to the new laws, sentencing patterns have become more severe. Significantly, civil employer responsibility laws have been successfully applied to yakuza groups and formally recognized in a revision of the bōtaihō. In response, yakuza have concealed their activities more effectively by operating behind fronts such as legitimate companies and fake political organizations. This trend will continue.

Another change with profound implications for the yakuza is fundamental legal reform with the aim of creating a legal system that is easy and efficient to use. In particular, speeding up civil litigation by increasing the number of lawyers and judges will ultimately reduce the scope for yakuza to operate as informal dispute resolution agents. These reforms also attempt to increase transparency, which is, of course, bad for the yakuza.

In recent decades, the Japanese have experienced a jump in socioeconomic inequality. This phenomenon has hit the yakuza too; an elite has developed sophisticated financial scams while a lumpen-yakuza rump have suffered as their traditional sources of income have shrunk. Those at the bottom are caught in a vice; in addition to economic contraction and more aggressive policing, they face demands from their elite bosses to avoid activities that might cause the leadership trouble (and, with employer responsibility, these activities constitute a broad category).

One possibility is that these two categories will no longer find it beneficial to remain under the same umbrella. This would result in small specialist firms engaging in high-end financial crime and bringing in precisely targeted violence when necessary, on the one side, and a rump of gangsters who are less able and who are freed from the restraining influence of the head office, on the other. We can already see a system of retroactive expulsion of members to side-step employer responsibility litigation. Senior yakuza are also contingency planning for laws banning outright membership in bōryokudan groups.

The yakuza have proved themselves to be highly resilient, and they constitute one of the most dynamic aspects of Japanese society. While the challenges they face are growing, given their penetration of the economic mainstream and the continued existence of members of Japan's political and business elite who quietly employ their services, any predictions of their impending demise would be premature.

Notes

1. For more detailed analysis of this period, see Wildes 1948; Dower 2000; Whiting 1999; and Aldous 1997.
2. See for example http://www.youtube.com/watch?v=M_b5jZG6JtQ.
3. All dollar values are given at the average exchange rate for the relevant year.
4. For a detailed discussion of the importance of signaling within extra-legal spheres, see Gambetta 2009.
5. For a more detailed analysis of yakuza shinogi, see Hill 2003.
6. Gambetta (1993) is highly relevant.
7. Any figures for the scale of this sector must be treated with caution. Iwanaga (2002 p. 12) estimates that the turnover of legal and illegal sex-related industries in Japan are somewhere between 3.6 and 4 trillion yen.
8. See Adelstein 2009 for a discussion of police and yakuza roles in the Japanese sex industry.
9. An excellent first-hand account of the hand-to-mouth existence of one such yakuza-construction outfit is given in Miyazaki 2005.
10. See Szymkowiak 1996, pp. 98–104.
11. See also Haley 1991.
12. For a more detailed analysis of this law, see Hill 2003.
13. *Migawari* (body swapping) is typically rewarded by promotion and big cash payments after release from prison. Maintenance will be paid to wives and dependants during incarceration. Harsher sentencing has made *migawari* increasingly untenable.

Bibliography

Adelstein, Jake. 2009. *Tokyo Vice: An American Reporter on the Police Beat in Japan.* New York: Pantheon Books.

Adelstein, Jake, and Sarah Noorbaksh. 2010. "Friendly Fire: Inagawa-kai Faces Yamaguchi-gumi Takeover." *Jane's Intelligence Review* (May): 44–48.

Aldous, Christopher. 1997. *The Police in Occupation Japan: Control, Corruption and Resistance to Reform*. London: Routledge.

Arimori, Takashi, and Group K. 2008. *Jitsuroku Angura Manee* [The True Record of Underground Money]. Tokyo: Kōdansha Plusalpha Shinsho.

Botsman, Daniel V. 2005. *Punishment and Power in the Making of Modern Japan*. Princeton, NJ: Princeton University Press.

de Vos, George A. 1973. *Socialization for Achievement: Essays on the Cultural Psychology of the Japanese*. Berkeley: University of California Press.

Dower, John. 2000. *Embracing Defeat: Japan in the Aftermath of World War II*. London: Penguin.

Friman, Richard. 2004. "The Great Escape? Globalization, Immigrant Entrepreneurship and the Criminal Economy." *Review of International Political Economy* 11(1) (February): 98–131.

Gambetta, Diego. 1993. *The Sicilian Mafia: The Business of Private Protection*. Cambridge MA: Harvard University Press.

Gambetta, Diego. 2009. *Codes of the Underworld: How Criminals Communicate*. Princeton, NJ: Princeton University Press.

Gotō, Tadamasa. 2010. *Habakarinagara*. Tokyo: Takarajima-sha.

Haley, John Owen. 1991. *Authority Without Power: Law and the Japanese Paradox*. Oxford: Oxford University Press.

Hanzai Hakusho (White Papers on Crime) (passim) Tokyo: Ôkura-shō Insatsukyoku.

Hill, Peter. 2003. *The Japanese Mafia: Yakuza, Law and the State*. Oxford: Oxford University Press.

Hill, Peter. 2005. "Kabuki-chō Gangsters: Ethnic Succession in Japanese Organised Crime?" *British Academy Review* 2005(8): 9–12.

Hinago, Atsushi. 1992. "No to Ienai Pachinko-nin." [The Pachinko Owners Who Can't Say No]. In *Yakuza to Iu Ikikata: Kore ga Shinogi Ya!*, edited by Kyoji Asakure et al., Tokyo: Takarajima.

Iwanaga, Fumio. 2002. *Fūzoku Shihon-ron* [On Sexual Services]. Tokyo: OS Shuppan.

Ino, Kenji. 1993. *Yakuza to Nihonjin* [Yakuza and the Japanese]. Tokyo: Gendai Shokan.

Iwai, Hiroaki. 1963. *Byōri Shūdan no Kōzō* [The Structure of Pathological Groups]. Tokyo: Seishin Shobō.

Kadokura, Takashi. 2003. *Nihon Chika-Keizai Hakusho* [Whitepaper on Japan's Underground Economy]. Tokyo: Shodensha.

Kaplan, David and Dubro, Alec. 2003. *Yakuza: Japan's Criminal Underworld*. Berkeley: University of California Press.

Keisatsu-chō (passim), Keisatsu Hakusho [Police White Papers]. Tokyo: Ôkura-shō Insatsukyoku.

Milhaupt, Curtis and West, Mark. 2000. "The Dark Side of Private Ordering: An Institutional and Empirical Analysis of Organized Crime." *University of Chicago Law Review*, 67/1. pp. 41–98.

Miyazaki, Manabu. 2005. *Toppamono: Outlaw, Radical, Suspect—My Life in Japan's Underworld*. Tokyo: Kotan.

Mizoguchi, Atsushi. 2007. *Tsukasa Shinobu Kumi-chō to Takayama Kiyoshi Wakagashira no Rokudaime Yamaguchi-gumi* [The Sixth-Generation Yamaguchi-gumi of Tsukasa Shinobu Kumi-chō and Takayama Kiyoshi Wakagashira]. Tokyo: Take Shobō.

Mizoguchi, Atsushi. 2008. *Yamaguchi-gumi Kōdō-kai o Kyodai Saseta Aichi-ken Kei* [The Aichi Prefectural Police who have Made the Yamaguchi-gumi Kōdō-kai Gigantic]. In *Heisei Taboo Taizen*, edited by Ichinomiya Yoshinari. Tokyo: Takarajima, pp. 58–67.

Mizoguchi, Atsushi. 2010. *Roku-daime Yamaguchi-gumi: Kyūjō Kakumei no Shōsha* [The Sixth-Generation Yamaguchi-gumi: The Palace Coup's Victor]. Tokyo: Takeshobo.

Mugishima, F., Hoshino, K., and Kiyonaga, K. 1971. "Bōryokudan-in no Yubitsume to Irezumi." *Keisatsu Kagaku Kenkyû-jo Hōkoku* 12/2 (Dec).

NPA (National Police Agency Organised Crime Countermeasures Bureau). 2009. *Heisei 20 nen no Soshiki Hanzai no Jōsei* [The Organized Crime Situation in 2008] (http://www.npa.go.jp).

Perl, Raphael. 2007. *Drug Trafficking and North Korea: Issues for US Policy*. CRS Report to Congress RL32167.

Siniawer, Eiko Maruko. 2008. *Ruffians, Yakuza, Nationalists: The Violent Politics of Modern Japan. 1860–1960*. Ithaca, NY: Cornell University Press.

Stark, David. 1981. "The Yakuza: Japanese Crime Incorporated." Ph.D. dissertation, University of Michigan, Department of Anthropology.

Schilling, Mark. 2003. *The Yakuza Movie Book: A Guide to Japanese Gangster Books*. Berkeley, CA: Stone Bridge Press.

Szymkowiak, Kenneth. 1996. "Necessary Evil: Extortion, Organized Crime and Japanese Corporations." Unpublished Ph.D. Thesis, University of Hawaii.

Tamura, Eitarō. 1981. *Yakuza no Seikatsu* [The Yakuza's Way of Life]. Tokyo: Oyamakaku Shuppan.

Tamura, Masayuki. 1988. "Kukuseizai no Ryūtsū Kibō o Suite-suru." *Keisatsu-gaku Ronshū* 41(10). Tokyo: Take Shobō.

Van Wolferen, Karel. 1989. *The Enigma of Japanese Power*. London: Macmillan.

Washington Post. April 11 1999. "A New Mob Mentality in Japan: Families Profit by Going Mainstream." (Mary Jordan and Kevin Sullivan).

West, Mark. (1999). "Information, Institutions, and Extortion in Japan and the United States: Making Sense of Sōkaiya Racketeers." *Northwestern University Law Review*, 93/3.

Whiting, Robert. 1999. *Tokyo Underworld: The Fast Times and Hard Life of an American Gangster in Japan*. New York: Vintage.

Wildes, Harry. 1948. "Underground Politics in Post-war Japan." *American Political Science Review* 42(6). pp. 1149–1162.

Yamadaira, Shigeki. 2001. *21 Seiki no Yakuza Kiso Chishiki* [Basic Information on the 21st-Century Yakuza]. Tokyo: Tokuma Shoten.

Yonezato, Seiji, Tamura, M., Hoshino, K., Uchiyama, A., and Kurusu, H. (1994). "Bōryokudan-in no Ridatsu oyobi Shakai Fukki o Shinsoku-suru Yōin ni Kan-suru Kenkyû." *Keisatsu Kagaku Kenkyû-jo Hōkoku*, 35/2 (Dec).

CHAPTER **12**

....

NIGERIAN CRIMINAL
ORGANIZATIONS*

....

PHIL WILLIAMS

I. INTRODUCTION

....

NIGERIAN criminal organizations and networks are unique in both their ubiquity and the diverse nature of their activities. Drug trafficking in Indonesia, extensive fraudulent activities in the countries of the European Union, trafficking of women to Europe for prostitution, and advance fee fraud in the United States and Australia are just a few manifestations of the Nigerian global criminal presence. Criminals from Nigeria and to a lesser degree elsewhere in West Africa are active in every country with criminal opportunities to be exploited. As one observer has noted, "powerful and sophisticated criminal syndicates based in Nigeria have extensive networks reaching into the Western Hemisphere, Europe, Russia and the newly independent states, Southeast and Southwest Asia, Australia, and other countries in Africa. In fact, Nigerian criminal groups are more pervasive around the globe than those of any other nation, with...large numbers of Nigerians thought to be engaged in illegal activities in some 60 countries."[1] Moreover, this presence seems to be expanding rather than diminishing. Recent reports note that Nigerian criminal organizations, which have long controlled a significant portion of the prostitution in southern Italy, have extended their activities into France and the Czech Republic. Sirasco, the French criminal intelligence service, for example, identified and analyzed 36 Nigerian prostitution rings between 2006 and 2010.[2] A Czech media report in June 2011 noted that the police had seen a "noticeable increase in Nigerian prostitutes who arrived in the Czech Republic on the basis of tourist visas furnished in Spain and Italy."[3]

Reports also suggest that Nigerian drug traffickers have been recruiting Bulgarian and Polish couriers, have begun to diversify into methamphetamine production, and have a significant presence in Brazil, with 199 Nigerians imprisoned in Sao Paulo.[4] Indeed, some Nigerian drug traffickers have graduated from their initial role as couriers to become managers of drug transshipments. Many remain as low-level couriers and traffickers, however, and have a presence in countries as diverse as India, Indonesia, and Italy, while, in January 2012 it was reported that 1,000 Nigerian youths have been detained in China for drug offenses.[5] In terms of financial fraud, Nigerian criminals have long had a leadership role, devising and implementing schemes widely imitated by others including various forms of identity theft. Nigerian criminals, sometimes with the active collusion of members of the political and military elites, engage in the theft, diversion, and illegal export of oil (which is formally a government monopoly) from the Niger Delta, a process that is often described as oil bunkering. Estimates suggest that 55 million barrels of oil a year—about one tenth of Nigerian oil production—are lost to theft and smuggling (Africa Economic Development Institute). There has also been an increase in piracy off the coast of West Africa much of which appears to be organized from Nigeria (Smith 2011).

Against this background, this analysis looks at the political, social, and economic context from which Nigerian criminal organizations emerged (and which continues to sustain them today), seeks to explain how they established a global presence, and explores the range of organizational structures they adopt and their various activities. There is something of a puzzle here. The rise of Nigerian organized crime, and particularly Nigerian involvement in drug trafficking, is not as readily explicable as, for example, the burgeoning of Russian organized crime in the 1990s after the collapse of the Soviet Union or the role of Colombian and Mexican drug trafficking organizations. Apart from some cannabis cultivation, Nigeria was not a major drug producer. Nor was Nigeria an obvious transshipment point for the movement of either cocaine or heroin. Despite lacking obvious advantages, Nigerian organized crime has become deeply entrenched within Nigeria, at the regional level in West Africa, and at the global level. This can be understood in terms of a mix of the incentives and pressures for criminal activity, the availability of opportunities, and the resources or capacity to exploit these opportunities, both at the national level and the global level.

II. The Context

The rise of organized crime in particular countries is often attributed to the weakness of the state or inadequacies of governance. Nigeria fits perfectly into this model. Nigeria is a post-colonial state characterized by weak institutions, a weak civil society, multiple tribal groups and power centers, and high levels of corruption (Smith 2007). Nigeria is Africa's most populous country, with more than 250 ethnic groups. The Hausa and Fulani make up 29 percent of the population, the Yoruba 21 percent, the Igbo (Ibo) 18 percent, and the Ijaw 10 percent, with a plethora of other groups providing the remaining 22 percent.

(Central Intelligence Agency 2011) In these circumstances, it is not surprising that the Nigerian state, which became independent of British rule in 1960, quickly became the prize of politics, with the spoils distributed by patrons to their political and tribal clients. "The authors of Nigeria's draft constitution in 1976 even defined political power as 'the opportunity to acquire riches and prestige, to be in a position to hand out benefits in the form of jobs, contracts gifts of money etc. to relations and political allies.'"6 Given the predominance of such sentiments, it is not surprising that the public good has routinely been subordinated to parochial and narrow interests, whether personal, familial, or tribal (Reno 2000, 433–459). Such a system has appropriately been characterized as the "predatory" or "vampire" or "mafia" state that, according to one scholar, is "a mafia-like bazaar, where anyone with an official designation can pillage at will…Their over-arching obsession is to amass personal wealth…"7 While the predatory state has been manifest in a significant number of African countries, Nigeria was particularly badly hurt by this phenomenon. The Nigerian state, under successive military regimes, became little more than a series of glorified criminal enterprises. State officials were highly corrupt and initiated various criminal activities for personal enrichment. This process reached its apogee under General Abacha, who ruled the country from 1993 until his death in 1998, and appropriated at least $3 billion, much of which was deposited in 139 bank accounts in Britain, Switzerland, Luxemburg, Lichtenstein, and the United States (Transparency International 2004b).

Democratic elections and over a decade of civilian government have had some impact on the most egregious cases of corruption but have not succeeded in creating a state that is either law-abiding or responsive to the needs of its citizens. Even with democratic procedures in place, the state is still seen as the prize of politics—with the spoils to be distributed by those in office (Ebbe 1999, 4:29–59). Election victories provide control of state resources that can then be used for personal, family, ethnic, or tribal gain. Without a distinction between public and private goods, leadership and ownership become virtually synonymous. The situation was so bad in 2003 that the Director of the State Security Service (SSS) warned that members of the political elite "often perpetrate lawlessness and political chaos."8 Subsequent bribery scandals and judicial misconduct have made it hard to convict criminals including corrupt state governors (Transparency International 2004a).

The problem in Nigeria, however, transcends corruption. It is not simply that the political elite are corrupt; the political elite are part of what Roy Godson termed the political-criminal nexus (Godson 2003). Indeed, in Nigeria it appears that some members of the political elite are not simply the protectors of organized crime; they also provide much of the leadership. Obi Ebbe, for example, has suggested that the political elite control much of the higher-level prostitution in the country (Ebbe 1999). Moreover, political and administrative elites use their positions to provide stamps and official documents that are integral to the infamous 419 frauds that are now perpetrated primarily through emails.

There is an important trickle-down effect from all this: if members of the political elite are getting rich through crime and corruption, the incentives for ordinary citizens to observe laws are minimal. Elite criminality helps to create "a culture and of impunity, destroying the rule of law and creating a class of overlords who need secrecy to keep their dark deeds hidden in dark places."[9] This culture also encourages ordinary citizens to engage in "clandestine economic transactions in the parallel or informal economy to keep their incomes and assets out of reach of the state. These are survival mechanisms…They involve hoarding, exchange of goods above the official price, smuggling, illegal currency deals, bribery, and corruption."[10] In this climate citizens see state institutions and representatives as "enemies to be evaded, cheated and defeated if possible but never as partners in development."[11] Such sentiments are intensified by the poor management of the Nigerian economy, resulting in what one commentator described as "the strange paradox" in which Nigeria is "the only nation on earth among the top ten oil producing countries classified as poor."[12] As urbanization failed to bring expected opportunities, and an enormous youth bulge contributed to high unemployment levels, therefore, the migration to illicit activities became self-perpetuating. In effect, success in organized crime bred emulation while legal opportunities remained highly constricted and offered little attraction to offset the lure of criminality. As a 2008 U.S. report noted, "abysmal economic conditions for the vast majority of Nigerians contribute significantly to the continuation and expansion of drug trafficking, widespread corruption and other criminal acts in Nigeria."[13] Indeed, not only does organized crime offer considerable opportunities for many people, it also involves few risks. A corrupt environment is highly conducive to organized crime as it facilitates the purchase of impunity. Moreover, the criminal justice and law enforcement systems in Nigeria have major shortcomings, flaws, and deficiencies. When the exploitative nature of the Nigerian state and deeply entrenched corruption are combined with a culture of impunity and the widespread poverty and limited opportunities for a young and rapidly expanding population, criminal activities and involvement in criminal organizations look extremely attractive as alternative career paths.

If Nigeria has provided almost the perfect environment for the growth of domestic organized crime, the country has also become a safe haven for Nigerian transnational criminal organizations. The trigger for this can be found in the early 1980s. Even prior to this, however, Nigerians had become involved in the global drug trade. In the 1960s, Nigerians were moving cannabis grown in Nigeria to Britain (Ellis 2009, 171–196). There are also indications that some of the military regimes condoned drug trafficking (although others imposed very harsh penalties). It was the economic shocks of the early 1980s though that led to the massive growth of Nigerian organized crime as both a domestic and transnational phenomenon. Increased oil prices in the 1970s were a massive boon to the economy and led to "considerable investment in infrastructure, education, and other public services" as a result of which Nigeria expanded the number of graduates and the number of Nigerians attending universities overseas. Both groups "had high expectations of the future."[14] The collapse in oil prices in the early 1980s had a profound impact creating massive economic dislocation and acting as a key trigger for the growth of Nigerian organized crime. "Public and publicly guaranteed external debt increased from $4.3 billion to $11.2 billion, while foreign exchange reserves were almost exhausted, from $10 billion to $1.23 billion, all between 1981 and 1983."[15] One result of this was that many Nigerians were "impelled to spread throughout the region and further afield in search of economic opportunity, and to seek out a livelihood, if necessary by any means."[16] Many young Nigerians overseas, who were suddenly without financial support, turned to drug trafficking as a coping mechanism while domestically many sought to fulfill their expectation by throwing themselves into financial frauds (Swart 2007). What seems to have started as short-term expediencies proved highly lucrative, offering tempting long-term career opportunities which otherwise were unavailable. Partly because of market forces and partly because of elite corruption, Nigerian citizens became losers in globalization—and compensated by moving from the global legal economy to the global illicit economy. Indeed, one of the paradoxes of Nigerian organized crime is that it reflects both failure and success: at the domestic level Nigerian organized crime is a manifestation of an unsuccessful postcolonial economy and society with a culture of corruption and a record of poor economic management; at the global level, Nigerian organized crime is a manifestation of very successful exploitation of globalization and the opportunities it provides.

Resources and capacity are essential to opportunity exploitation. In this connection, the Nigerian elite has traditionally been very well educated, English-speaking, and cosmopolitan in outlook. This provided an important set of resources for drug trafficking, financial fraud, and other criminal activities. Furthermore, "Nigeria's position as a historic trading crossroads... has given Nigerian international criminal syndicates a legacy of moving capital and commodities on a global scale."[17] Because of Nigeria's importance in international trade, many Nigerians have been comfortable doing business—whether licit or criminal—in other countries. Moreover, if Nigeria has long been an important trading nation with an entrepreneurial tradition, it bears emphasis that criminal entrepreneurialism draws on the same drivers of creativity and energy as legal business. In addition, the Nigerian diaspora, which was created by several distinct waves of emigration, fuelled partly by the size of the population, but also by the brutal civil war from 1967 to 1970 and the repression of a series of military governments which ruled from 1966 to 1979 and 1983 to 1998, has provided an extensive overseas presence or transnational émigré network. The Nigerian diaspora—like many others—has contained significant criminal components which feed off the expatriate communities, seeking recruits, cover and support, and using language and dialect as defensive mechanisms against law enforcement. These factors ensured that, from the early 1980s onward, Nigerian criminal organizations became one of the country's major exports. And their diversity and sophistication made them a serious challenge to law enforcement in countries in which they established a presence.

III. STRUCTURE OF NIGERIAN CRIMINAL ORGANIZATIONS

Nigerian criminals are not wedded to any particular organizational form. Consequently, their organizations are "highly fluid in personnel and in methods of operation" ranging "from independent entrepreneurs to highly organized syndicates. These groups are able to change and adapt, as needed, both in the nature of the criminal activities they pursue, and in the members they employ. This flexibility allows them to remain in operation and to insulate themselves from law enforcement."[18] Some groups appear to specialize while others have multiple lines of activity.

At least some of the drug trafficking organizations appear to be well structured with a clear if not formal hierarchy. The core leadership is provided by major organizers, based predominantly in Lagos, who are linked with significant numbers of criminal operations elsewhere in the world. These crime barons are often among the elite and include people in government, who benefit from the criminal activities that they coordinate or support. The barons are also among the major beneficiaries of the proceeds of crime that come back to Nigeria and are often—although not invariably—protected from seizure by poor implementation of Nigeria's money laundering laws. According to Ellis, crime barons have to be able to purchase drugs cheaply at the source, have good contacts in the receiving or market country, and have a substantial supply of capital (Ellis 2009). They often operate through a second tier of people known as strikers who typically work for several barons, have good logistic expertise and connections, and are able to negotiate deals and recruit couriers (Ellis 2009). The couriers themselves are the cannon fodder of the trade and, when caught, are rarely able to provide much information about the people who hired them. As one commentary has observed, "the heads of drug syndicates have accumulated millions of dollars in profit, operate with relative immunity from arrest, and preside over large organizations with thousands of their poor countrymen as drug couriers who incur virtually all the risk for very little in compensation."[19] How large these drug trafficking organizations actually are is uncertain and it seems likely that they vary considerably in size.

It is clear when the focus moves beyond drugs that many Nigerian criminal organizations are relatively small, and are based around bonds created by family membership, tribal affinity, or personal friendship. Often these groups operate within a larger network that resembles trade associations rather than traditional mafia hierarchies. The fluid network provides support, structure, and potential connections that can be activated when it is convenient or beneficial to those involved. Indeed, some observers have discerned a form of organization that is project-based in which individuals come together for a particular criminal venture (UNODC 2005). On other occasions, however, criminal entrepreneurs will take on apprentices and develop longer-term relationships, mixing these with short-term employees as necessary. This apprenticeship system "tends to create very strong associations between specific families, lineages, or ethnic groups and particular trades, in regard to both legitimate and illicit types of business."[20] Moreover, even though project-based organizations dissolve "upon completion of a given project" this does not undermine security, loyalty, or trust because of the strength of the association and the cultural pressures that arise from village, clan or ethnic group as well as "the use of religious and black magic rituals threatening supernatural punishment in the event of betrayal."[21] Even though some are more enduring than others, therefore, most Nigerian criminal organizations appear to be held together by similar forms of social glue.

In the final analysis, perhaps the best way to think about Nigerian criminal organizations is in terms of multiple levels of organization and activity, with a capacity to switch structures, activities and even membership easily and seamlessly. For law enforcement this makes Nigerian criminal organizations a very elusive target. Moreover, the high-level organizers—often based in Nigeria itself—are very difficult to link to the low-level operatives. Typically, couriers know little about their employers, as there is no sustained relationship apart from some kind tribal, ethnic, or geographic affiliation. At the same time, "the practice of recruiting through networks of kinship, typically based on a village or other region of origin, means that the organization of a smuggling or other criminal network may be facilitated by cultural codes known to the perpetrators, but more or less impenetrable to outsiders, including law enforcement officers."[22] Furthermore, the multiple Nigerian dialects can be difficult to interpret and provide a built-in risk management tool for criminals seeking to thwart law enforcement investigations outside Nigeria. While wire-tapping and other forms of electronic surveillance are important tools for law enforcement in many countries, they have only limited effectiveness against Nigerian criminal organizations.

IV. Modus Operandi and Activities of Nigerian Criminal Organizations

In some instances, Nigerian criminal organizations appear to be highly specialized, whether in financial fraud, drug trafficking or human trafficking; in other instances they combine several criminal activities at one time. They also have a capacity to move easily and seamlessly from one type of criminal activity to another, according to available opportunities and the expertise they can bring to bear. This seems to be consistent with organized crime in West Africa where "long-term specialization in a particular field or commodity is rather rare. An entrepreneur who has been successful in one field of operation may move into another field if the opportunity presents itself, including into legitimate commerce. For example, an entrepreneur who has been successful in the drug trade may invest his or her profits in a legitimate business, not purely as a form of camouflage, but simply in pursuit of a commercial logic."[23] This mix of structures and activities not only provides Nigerian criminal organizations with a capacity for rapid adaptation and makes them extremely difficult to penetrate (a difficulty that is increased by the diversity of Nigerian languages and dialects), but it also renders their trajectory extremely hard for law enforcement to anticipate. This is made even more difficult by organizational structures. As one Dutch observer noted, "there is no clear hierarchical structure, as in the case of the mafia. They have a cellular structure, with about 10–12 members in each cell."[24] Moreover, the cell structure itself can be dynamic with members sometimes having no specific role. "They are interchangeable. One time a gang member is the errand boy, another time he is the boss. That is their strength. And they are inventive. Every time, they seek a different way."[25] Other commentaries have suggested that in Nigeria itself, the groups are even smaller with 3 to 5 people, corresponding to the notion of a master and several apprentices (UNODC 2005).

The other difficulty for law enforcement is that Nigerian criminals have an impressive ability to function in various legal and regulatory environments. Although Nigerians are not the only criminal groups with such ability, they have developed a global ubiquity that is unrivaled let alone unsurpassed. In South Africa, Nigerian drug traffickers transformed the market from one revolving around marijuana and mandrax to one in which cocaine and heroin loomed much larger. Nigerian traffickers have also been identified in Paraguay, Brazil, and Venezuela, all of which they use for cocaine trafficking. In the heroin trade, Thailand was traditionally one of their major bases for acquiring heroin produced in Burma, but in 2002 reports suggested the traffickers were moving to Cambodia (UNODC 2002). This kind of jurisdictional arbitrage is typical of many organized crime groups but does help to explain why Nigerian drug traffickers have been so difficult to combat and why they are able to control much of the heroin trade in countries such as Indonesia where they have faced little or no competition either from indigenous organized crime or other transnational drug trafficking organizations (AIPA 2009; Muna). By 2006, Nigerian drug traffickers were also involved in the opium and heroin trade from Afghanistan (Farah 2006). Although this is an area where they face considerable competition from more powerful organizations, there have been frequent reports of Nigerians trafficking heroin from Kazakhstan into China (UNODC 2011). Moreover, in 2009 Nigerian traffickers were the most frequently arrested foreigners for drug offenses in Pakistan, where they were seeking supplies (UNODC 2011).

Nigerian traffickers seem particularly adept in dealing with enforcement efforts in market countries. In the United States and Europe for example, Nigerian traffickers have used a shot-gun or swamping strategy, where so many "swallowers and stuffers" arrive on one flight that even if some are apprehended by customs and law enforcement others get through unscathed. Sometimes, though, the arrests reach double figures. For example, in December 2006, 28 of the 32 drug couriers arrested on a flight into Schiphol were Nigerian (UNODC 2007). In July 2007, 16 couriers were arrested in the weekly flight between the Gambia and the Netherlands—most were Nigerians with residency in Spain, although a few were living in Italy and Greece (UNODC 2007). Indeed, according to UNODC, 44 percent of all West Africans arrested at European airports in 2006 had Nigerian passports (UNODC 2007). In addition to using their own citizens, Nigerian organizers have also used citizens of other countries and have even used children, elderly, and disabled people as couriers. Larger shipments have also been sent in containers and mail services. Nigerian traffickers were also pioneers in using West Africa as a hub for the transshipment of cocaine from Latin America to Europe—something that might have encouraged Colombian and Mexican organizations to follow suit in using the region, especially Guinea-Bissau and Guinea as a useful way-station en route to Europe (Cockayne and Williams 2009).

These loose networks work through trust and allow Nigerian traffickers to maintain a low profile and coexist with more powerful trafficking organizations. Because they generally deal in relatively small quantities, they do not challenge major criminal groups—and can even facilitate the transactions of these more powerful entities on occasion. "Rather than contesting markets already well served by local trafficking groups, these networks are highly adaptive, addressing markets overlooked by others or working in cooperation with established organizations."[26] Other West Africans are not always so careful and in September 2008, six West Africans were killed, sparking considerable speculation that they were selling drugs without permission of the local Italian groups or had not paid for a drug transaction (Kamara 2008). For the most part, however, Nigerians seem to have avoided this kind of backlash and have become important players in drug markets in various countries throughout Europe.

Wherever they operate Nigerian drug traffickers are very flexible and innovative. They adapt rapidly to their environment and are adept at exploiting opportunities and weaknesses in their host society. They are also extremely adept at using false identities, and there is an organized system for obtained forged and counterfeit documents from Nigeria itself—many of which are sent by courier service. Nigerian criminals often have false passports and use false addresses (especially in residences where there is an outside mailbox) as part of fraud schemes that require multiple identities. Indeed, Nigerian criminal organizations pioneered what are known as 419 (after the Nigerian legal code) or advance fee frauds. Typically these frauds involve an offer to collaborate with the chosen recipient in transferring money out of a particularly country and into his bank account—for which he will be amply rewarded with a significant share of the funds. Once the person responds to the communication and expresses an interest, some kind of problem arises and a request is made for advance money in order to expedite the transfer process. In those cases where an advance is made the target is either solicited for further advances or the communication ceases.

Some observers suggest that the origins of these frauds can be found in "abuses of the administrative requirements for importing goods" into Nigeria in the 1970s and early 1980s.[27] The Nigerian oil boom "created massive financial opportunities for Nigerians with access to government contracts and their foreign partners who were able to provide the goods and services required. There were many cases of one or other party using the system dishonestly—or, more damningly, of both colluding."[28] Others see the origin in a simple confidence trick involving the sale of chemicals and dyed notes which were ostensibly bank notes. The chemicals and notes were sold as a package often using one or two real notes to show how the process worked. Whatever the precise origin, Nigerian advance fee fraud has been transformed from a domestic or regional activity to a global phenomenon. Those involved include groups of individuals who have come together specifically to carry out the fraud, particular individuals who are acting alone, and even families for whom advance fee fraud is not only a way of life and a means of subsistence but also a profession. According to a Nigerian student, whose family had been involved in advanced fee fraud for more than 15 years, the business supported several dozen of his family members. He also noted that there was some specialization and division of labor. "We have the letter writers and the people who create the official documentation, the people who talk to our clients on the phone, the people who arrange travel and meetings and tours of government offices in Africa, Canada, Japan, and the United States."[29] The ubiquity of 419 frauds is reflected in the existence of groups such as the anti-419 coalition and the prevalence of web sites and newspaper advertisements warning about the scams. According to the US State Department, "AFF criminals include university-educated professionals who are the best in the world for nonviolent spectacular crimes. AFF letters first surfaced in the mid-1980s around the time of the collapse of world oil prices, which is Nigeria's main foreign exchange earner. Some Nigerians turned to crime in order to survive. Fraudulent schemes such as AFF succeeded in Nigeria, because Nigerian criminals took advantage of the fact that Nigerians speak English, the international language of business, and the country's vast oil wealth and natural gas reserves—ranked 13th in the world—offer lucrative business opportunities that attract many foreign companies and individuals."[30]

The fraud itself has retained its essential simplicity while also morphing in terms of form and content. In terms of form (and mirroring communication changes in the licit business world), 419 fraud has evolved from letters through faxes to emails. This transition has reduced transaction costs and massively enlarged the victim set. The content of these communications still revolves around the very simple scheme described above but has several variations. In some cases the offer is presented as a licit transaction and in other cases as illicit, a stratagem that, in effect, creates a conspiracy between the sender and the recipient. In either case, however, the offer appeals to the greed of the target, who is initially asked to send some of his financial details and subsequently inveigled into sending money. On some occasions, the targeted businessman has actually traveled to Nigeria to meet his partner, often ending up badly beaten or extorted (Smith, Holmes, and Kaufmann 1999). In other instances, the businessman who has lost his money is approached once again, this time with a promise that for a fee the person initiating the contact will be able to recapture the funds (Smith, Holmes, and Kaufmann 1999). Rather than being "twice shy," the businessman, acting out of desperation or frustration, is drawn into a second scam and sends good money after bad. Another variant involves the senders acknowledging that many offers like this are fraudulent but that this particular one is legitimate in an effort to defuse suspicion by noting, at the outset, that such suspicion is understandable.

The content of 419 offers has also become more sophisticated, sometimes in subtle and sometimes in obvious ways. Facilitated by email, the senders can more readily present the offer as coming from a country other than Nigeria—a strategy that, it is hoped, will give the offer greater credence. South Africa, Zimbabwe, Ghana, Saudi Arabia and Somalia, and even Britain, have been among the countries in which the proffered funds are supposedly hidden. According to one report, sources for the letters include Sierra Leone, Ghana, Congo, Liberia, Togo, Ivory Coast, Benin, Burkina Faso, South Africa, Taiwan, and even Canada, Oman, and Vietnam.[31] Moreover, in a recent innovation more of the communications purport "to be coming from accountants, lawyers, or bankers" who "pretend to be acting as fiduciaries for the real dignitary in need of help."[32] In addition, there appears to be a growing tendency to feed off current or recent events such as the war in Iraq or the uprisings in the Middle East.

Nigerian fraudsters have been very active in Spain and in 2005, in one single case on the Costa del Sol, 320 Nigerians were detained. Although this might have had a temporary effect, by 2008 Nigerian criminals were once again extensively involved in fraud schemes in the country. In April 2008, 87 Nigerian were arrested for involvement in these activities (BBC News 2008). Two months later, in June, Spanish police arrested 52 people – mostly Nigerians – in connection with an Internet fraud scheme believed to have yielded about 40 million Euros from victims in the United States and Europe who were sent emails or letters informing them that they had been selected to participate in a Spanish lottery. Subsequently, the targets were informed that they had won between 600,000 and 3 million Euros and were requested to pay administrative costs to obtain their winnings (AFP 2008). Law enforcement successes, however, only reflect the tip of the iceberg and do no more than marginally dent what has become an expanding business linked to identity theft and various kinds of Internet fraud (Ultrascan-agi.com 2009).

Nigerian criminals have also played an increasingly important role in the global sex trade and trafficking in women to Europe. This expanded considerably in the 1990s as "prospects for employment in Nigeria deteriorated."[33] Moreover, there was a self-perpetuating quality to the trafficking business as "the organizers ... are often women, sometimes former prostitutes themselves, who have succeeded in making money and graduating to the status of madams."[34] Italy became the favored destination, but Holland, Britain, and France also witnessed an upsurge in the problem. Threats against family members back in Nigeria are also used to keep them in line. The women come primarily but not exclusively from Edo state (UNICRI 2003). For their part, the trafficking groups tend to be very atomistic. Nevertheless, the manner in which Nigerian mamas (or madams) and prostitutes are allowed to operate unhindered suggests that there has been some kind of agreement with Italian criminal organizations or that traditional Italian mafia groups are not particularly interested in prostitution and consequently have left the market open.

If Italy has been the favored destination for women and girls, Britain has provided a market for young boys, and in 2008 the U.S. State Department's Trafficking in Persons Report identified "an increasing trend" in "the trafficking of African boys and girls from Lagos to the U.K.'s urban centers including London, Birmingham and Manchester, for domestic servitude and forced labor in restaurants and shops. Some of the victims are Nigerian, while others are trafficked from other African countries through Lagos."[35]

It is evident from all this that Nigerian criminals combine flexibility of methods with an ability to operate in several criminal markets. And partly because Nigerian criminals are not as overtly violent as many other criminal groups, they do not draw the same level of attention and enforcement as, for example, groups from the Balkans and the former Soviet Union. As a result of both domestic factors and their ability to operate in multiple countries Nigerian criminal organizations are not going away any time soon.

V. The Current and Future Status of Nigerian Organized Crime

Organized crime and corruption has become deeply embedded in the economy, society, and politics of Nigeria and is unlikely to diminish even though Nigeria has taken some important initiatives to combat organized crime. The Nigerian Drug Law Enforcement Agency has become an important regional leader in West Africa, while Nigeria passed laws to combat corruption in both 2000 and 2003 (Opara 2006). In addition in 2002, the government established the Economic and Financial Crimes Commission (EFCC) to investigate financial crimes. Implementation of these laws, however, has remained problematic, while the EFCC has faced considerable political obstacles as it targeted members of the elite (Zebley 2011). And although law enforcement agencies have improved considerably over the last decade or so, they remain "underfunded" and lack "the sophistication, education, training and other basic incentives as well as encouragement required to effectively check crime."[36] Indeed, "funding for Nigerian law enforcement agencies and key anticrime agencies remains insufficient and erratic in disbursement" giving an impression of lack of commitment.[37] In addition, political corruption is often matched by corruption in law enforcement agencies. And even in those cases where policing is effective, problems in the judiciary provide further opportunities for criminals to avoid justice. As the U.S. State Department's Annual International Narcotics Control Strategy Report noted in March 2008: "Attempts...to arrest and prosecute major traffickers and their associates often fail in Nigeria's courts, which are subject to intimidation and corruption. Asset seizures from narcotics traffickers and money launderers, while permitted under Nigerian law, have never been systematically utilized as an enforcement tool, but some convicted traffickers have had their assets forfeited over the years. The number of major traffickers penalized remains small."[38] The 2011 report was a little more optimistic, noting that corruption and judicial inefficiency remained major impediments to effective prosecutions. (U.S. Department of State 2011).

In other words, the impediments to the continued growth of organized crime are weak. At the same time, those trends facilitating expansion remain powerful. Given the population growth and the high levels of unemployment—even among university graduates—it seems likely that during the next two decades Nigeria's domestic and transnational crime problem will continue its upward trajectory. The return to civilian government has done little to reduce Nigerian organized crime, while the economy continues to exhibit major structural weaknesses. With a burgeoning population amidst growing impoverishment, crime will be an increasingly attractive career path for young Nigerians. Nigerian population growth will also strengthen the global presence of Nigerian criminal organizations. Unfortunately, a somber prognosis of this kind is as compelling and inescapable as it is dismaying.

NOTES

* The author would like to thank Letizia Paoli for her comments on an earlier draft of this chapter and Matthew Clark for his assistance with the research.

1. Peter Chalk, "Countering Nigerian organized crime," *Janes Intelligence Review* (1 September 2003).

2. Christophe Cornevin, ""Strategic Police Officers Countering the Mafias," published as "France Has Set Up Special Unit To Counter International Organized Crime," Paris, *Le Figaro*, March 12, 2011, Open Source Center, EUP20110314029004.

3. Chris Johnstone, "Czechs Recruited by Roma Gangs for 'Slave' Labor in UK" published as "Czech Organized Crime Squad Reports New Trends in Human Trafficking," Prague, *Czechposition.com*, June 28, 2011, Open Source Center, EUP20110628081021.

4. Alana Rizzo, "East European Mafia and Other International Groups Infiltrated in Brazil Control the Lucrative Drug Trafficking Market" published as "Brazilian Daily: International Crime Groups Control Drug Market," *Correio Braziliense Online*, August 1, 2011, Open Source Center, FEA20110808020690.

5. Mustafa Abubakar, 2012. "1,000 Nigerian youths jailed in China for drug offences-Minister." http://www.dailytrust.com.ng/index.php?option=com_content&view=article&id=152875:1000-nigerian-youths-jailed-in-china-for-drug-offences-minister&catid=1:news&Itemid=2.

6. Quoted in Phil Williams and Doug Brooks, "Captured, criminal and contested states: Organised crime and Africa in the 21st century," *South African Journal of International Affairs*, Volume 6, Issue 2, 1999.

7. George B.N. Ayittey, *Africa in Chaos* (New York: St Martin's Griffin, 1999) p. 151.

8. "Conduct of Politicians," *Daily Champion*, October 22, 2003, available from *allAfrica.com*.

9. Sufuyan Ojeifo, "Commonwealth Group Ties Reprieve for Nigeria to Information Access," *Vanguard*, October 12, 2003, available from *allAfrica.com*.

10. George B. N. Ayittey, *Africa in Chaos* (New York: St Martin's Griffin, 1999) p. 217.

11. Claude Ake quoted in Ayittey, *Africa in Chaos* (New York: St Martin's Griffin, 1999) p. 217.

12. Rogers Edor Ochela, "Nigeria: Blundering at 48," *The Daily Sun*, October 10, 2008. http://www.eslnetworld.com/webpages/opinion/2008/oct/10/opinion-10-10-2008-002.htm.

13. US. Department of State, *International Narcotics Control Strategy Report*, March 2008, p. 601. http://www.state.gov.

14. Teemo Peters, quoted in Lisette Swart "Look, Another E-Mail Promising the Earth," published as "Report Analyzes Activities of Nigerian Criminals in Netherlands," Rotterdam NRC *Handelsblad* (Internet Version-WWW) November 21, 2007, Open Source Center, EUP20071121024003.

15. Budina, N., G. Pang, and S. van Wijnbergen. 2007. *Nigeria's Growth Record: Dutch Disease or Debt Overhang?* Working Paper 4256. Washington, DC: World Bank.

16. UNODC. 2005. *Transnational Organized Crime in the West African Region*, p. 5 http://www.unodc.org/pdf/transnational_crime_west-africa-05.pdf.

17. Ellen Brennan-Galvin, "Crime and Violence in an Urbanizing World" *Journal of International Affairs*, Fall 2002, Vol. 56 Issue 1, pp. 123–146 at p. 141.

18. "Schemes, Scams, Frauds," *Nigerian Scams* (2000), http://www.crimes-of-persuasion.com/Crimes/Business/nigerian.htm.

19. Gary W. Potter and Bankole Thompson, "African Organized Crime," http://www.foureaux.sites.uol.com.br/crimeorganizado/african.pdf.

20. United Nations Office on Drugs and Crime (UNODC), *Transnational Organized Crime in the West African Region* (New York, United Nations, 2005) p. 15.

21. Antonio L. Mazzitelli, "The Challenges of Drugs, Organized Crime and Terrorism in West and Central Africa," *Real Instituto Elcano*, April 6, 2006, p. 9.

22. United Nations Office on Drugs and Crime (UNODC), *Transnational Organized Crime in the West African Region* (New York, United Nations, 2005) p. 16.

23. United Nations Office on Drugs and Crime (UNODC), *Transnational Organized Crime in the West African Region* (New York, United Nations, 2005) p. 18.

24. Lisette Swart "Look, Another E-Mail Promising the Earth," published as "Report Analyzes Activities of Nigerian Criminals in Netherlands," Rotterdam NRC *Handelsblad* (Internet Version-WWW) November 21, 2007, Open Source Center, EUP20071121024003.

25. Ibid.

26. UNODC 2008. *Drug Trafficking as a Security Threat in West Africa*. pp. 23–24. http://www.unodc.org/documents/data-and-analysis/Studies/Drug-Trafficking-WestAfrica-English.pdf.

27. UNODC. 2005. *Transnational Organized Crime in the West African Region*, p. 24. http://www.unodc.org/pdf/transnational_crime_west-africa-05.pdf.

28. UNODC. 2005. *Transnational Organized Crime in the West African Region*, p. 24. http://www.unodc.org/pdf/transnational_crime_west-africa-05.pdf.

29. Delio, Michelle. 2002. "Meet the Nigerian E-Mail Grifters," *Wired News* (July 17) http://www.wired.com/news/culture/0,1284,53818,00.html.

30. Vaknin, Sam. 2005. "Nigerian Scams—Begging Your Trust in Africa." (May 25) http://www.globalpolitician.com/2766-nigeria.

31. Vaknin, Sam. 2005. "Nigerian Scams—Begging Your Trust in Africa." (May 25) http://www.globalpolitician.com/2766-nigeria.

32. Vaknin, Sam. 2005. "Nigerian Scams—Begging Your Trust in Africa." (May 25) http://www.globalpolitician.com/2766-nigeria.

33. UNODC. 2005. *Transnational Organized Crime in the West African Region*, p. 27. http://www.unodc.org/pdf/transnational_crime_west-africa-05.pdf.

34. UNODC. 2005. *Transnational Organized Crime in the West African Region*, p. 27. http://www.unodc.org/pdf/transnational_crime_west-africa-05.pdf.

35. US Department of State, *Trafficking in Persons Report 2008*, p. 197. http://www.state.gov/j/tip/rls/tiprpt/2008/index.htm.

36. Iheji Chukwueme,. 2003. "Task of Policing Enugu." *Daily Champion* (October 30) *allAfrica.com*.

37. U.S. Department of State 2008 *International Narcotics Control Strategy Report*. p. 604 http://www.state.gov/j/inl/rls/nrcrpt/2008/index.htm

38. U.S. Department of State 2008 *International Narcotics Control Strategy Report*. p. 602. http://www.state.gov/j/inl/rls/nrcrpt/2008/index.htm

Bibliography

AFP. 2008. "Spain arrests Nigerians, others over fraud network." (June 12) http://home.rmci.net/alphae/419coal/news2008.htm.

Africa Economic Development Institute. "Nigeria and Oil Smuggling." http://africaecon.org/index.php/africa_business_reports/read/73.

AIPA. 2009. "Country Report of Indonesia." Paper presented at the 6th Meeting of the AIPA Fact-Finding Committee (AIFOCOM) to Combat the Drug Menace, Chiang Rai, Thailand,

May 10–14. http://www.aipasecretariat.org/wp-content/uploads/2010/09/9-Country-Report-Indonesia-Final-Report.pdf.

Ayittey, George B. N. 1999. *Africa in Chaos*. New York: St Martin's Griffin.

BBC News. 2008. "Spain holds lottery scam suspects." (April 17) http://news.bbc.co.uk/2/hi/7353003.stm.

Brennan-Galvin, Ellen. 2002. "Crime and Violence in an Urbanizing World." *Journal of International Affairs* 56(Fall): 123–146.

Budina, N., G. Pang, and S. van Wijnbergen. 2007. *Nigeria's Growth Record: Dutch Disease or Debt Overhang?* Working Paper 4256. Washington, DC: World Bank.

Central Intelligence Agency. 2011. "Nigeria." In *World Factbook*. (July 5) https://www.cia.gov/library/publications/the-world-factbook/geos/ni.html.

Chalk, Peter. 2003. "Countering Nigerian Organized Crime." *Janes Intelligence Review* (September 1).

Cockayne, James and Phil Williams. 2009. "The Invisible Tide: Towards an International Strategy to Deal with Drug Trafficking Through West Africa." http://www.uneca.org/coda/unodc/TheInvisibleTide_JamesCockayne.pdf.

Cornevin, Christophe. 2011. "Strategic Police Officers Countering the Mafias" published as "France Has Set Up Special Unit To Counter International Organized Crime." *Le Figaro* (March 12) Open Source Center, EUP20110314029004.

Crimes-of-Persuasion.com. 2000. "Schemes, Scams, Frauds." *Nigerian Scams* http://www.crimes-of-persuasion.com/Crimes/Business/nigerian.htm.

Daily Champion. 2003. "Conduct of Politicians." (October 22) *allAfrica.com*.

Ebbe, Obi N. I. 1999. "The Political-Criminal Nexus: The Nigerian Case." *Trends in Organized Crime* 4(Spring): 29–59.

Ellis, Stephen. 2009. "West Africa's International Drug Trade." *African Affairs*, 108(431): 171–196.

Farah, Douglas. 2006. "Nigerian gangs spread to Afghanistan in heroin trade." (December 19) http://www.douglasfarah.com/article/20/nigerian-gangs-spread-to-afghanistan-in-heroin-trade.

Godson, Roy. 2003. *Menace to Society: Political-Criminal Collaboration around the World*. Piscataway, NJ: Transaction.

Johnstone, Chris. 2011. "Czechs Recruited by Roma Gangs for "Slave" Labor in UK" published as "Czech Organized Crime Squad Reports New Trends in Human Trafficking." *Czechposition.com* (June 28) Open Source Center, EUP20110628081021.

Kamara, Murtala Mohamed. 2008. "6 West Africans killed in Italy" Africa News.com (September 21) http://www.africanews.com/site/list_messages/20614.

Mazzitelli, Antonio L. 2006. "The Challenges of Drugs, Organised Crime and Terrorism in West and Central Africa." *Real Instituto Elcano* (April 6) http://www.realinstitutoelcano.org/wps/portal/rielcano_eng/Content?WCM_GLOBAL_CONTEXT=/elcano/Elcano_in/Zonas_in/ARI%2043-2006.

Muna, Riefqi. "Securitization of Transnational Crime: Small Arms and Light Weapons & Drug Trafficking in Indonesia." http://www.rsis-ntsasia.org/resources/publications/research-papers/transnational-crime/Riefqi.pdf.

Ochela, Rogers Edor. 2008. "Nigeria: Blundering at 48." *The Daily Sun* (October 10) http://www.eslnetworld.com/webpages/opinion/2008/oct/10/opinion-10-10-2008-002.htm.

Ojeifo, Sufuyan. 2003. "Commonwealth Group Ties Reprieve for Nigeria to Information Access." *Vanguard* (October 12) *allAfrica.com*.

Opara, Ijeoma I. 2006. *Nigerian Anti-Corruption Initiatives*. Bepress Legal Series no. 1392. Houston: Texas Southern University, Thurgood Marshall School of Law.

Potter, Gary W. and Bankole Thompson. 1999. "African Organized Crime." foureaux.sites.uol. com.br/crimeorganizado/african.pdf.

Reno, William. 2000. "Clandestine Economies, Violence and States in Africa." *Journal of International Affairs* 53(Spring): 433–459.

Rizzo, Alana. 2011. "East European Mafia and Other International Groups Infiltrated in Brazil Control the Lucrative Drug Trafficking Market" published as "Brazilian Daily: International Crime Groups Control Drug Market." *Correio Braziliense Online* (August 1) Open Source Center, FEA20110808020690.

Smith, Daniel Jordan. 2007. *A Culture of Corruption: Everyday Deception and Popular Discontent in Nigeria.* Princeton, NJ: Princeton University Press.

Smith, M. J. 2011. "W. African Piracy Surge Points to Organized Gang." AFP (August 2) http:// www.google.com/hostednews/afp/article/ALeqM5gNkFpHpDcqvIjMOF6M_LKhSqSLw? docId=CNG.5279263134ca22f6eb101cc7b093b284.491.

Smith, Russell G., Michael N. Holmes, and Philip Kaufmann. 1999. *Nigerian Advance Fee Fraud.* Trends and Issues no. 121. Canberra, Australia: Australian Institute of Criminology.

Swart, Lisette. 2007. "Look, Another E-Mail Promising the Earth," published as "Report Analyzes Activities of Nigerian Criminals in Netherlands," Rotterdam NRC *Handelsblad.* (November 21) Open Source Center, EUP20071121024003.

Transparency International. 2004a. *Global Corruption Report 2004.* http://www.transparency. org/publications/gcr/gcr_2004.

——. 2004b. *National Integrity Systems: Transparency International Country Study Report: Nigeria 2004.* http://info.worldbank.org/etools/ANTIC/docs/Resources/Country%20 Profiles/Nigeria/TransparencyInternational_NIS_Nigeria.pdf.

UNICRI. 2003. *Programme of Action against Trafficking in Minors and Young Women from Nigeria into Italy for the Purpose of Sexual Exploitation: Report of Field Survey in Edo State, Nigeria.* http://www.unicri.it./Nigeria_research.pdf.

UNODC. 2002 *Summary Report of the Illicit Drug Situation in Cambodia 2002* http://www. unodc.un.or.th/material/document/2003_2.pdf.

UNODC. 2005. *Transnational Organized Crime in the West African Region.* http://www.unodc. org/pdf/transnational_crime_west-africa-05.pdf.

——. 2007. *Cocaine Trafficking in Western Africa, Situation Report.* http://www.unodc.org/doc-uments/data-and-analysis/Cocaine-trafficking-Africa-en.pdf.

——. 2008. *Drug Trafficking as a Security Threat in West Africa.* http://www.unodc.org/docu-ments/data-and-analysis/Studies/Drug-Trafficking-WestAfrica-English.pdf.

——. 2011. *The Global Afghan Opium Trade: A Threat Assessment.* http://www.unodc.org/docu-ments/data-and-analysis/Studies/Global_Afghan_Opium_Trade_2011-web.pdf.

Ultrascan-agi.com. 2009. *419 Advance Fee Fraud Statistics 2009.* http://www.ultrascan-agi. com/public_html/html/pdf_files/419_Advance_Fee_Fraud_Statistics_2009.pdf.

——. 2008b. *Trafficking in Persons Report 2008.* http://www.state.gov/j/tip/rls/tiprpt/2008/ index.htm.

——. 2011. *International Narcotics Control Strategy Report.* http://www.state.gov/j/inl/rls/ nrcrpt/2011/index.htm.

Williams, Phil, and Doug Brooks. 1999. "Captured, Criminal and Contested States: Organised Crime and Africa in the 21st century." *South African Journal of International Affairs* 6(2).

Zebley, Julia. 2011. "Nigeria anti-corruption agency ineffective: HRW." (August 25) http://jurist. org/paperchase/2011/08/nigeria-anti-corruption-agency-ineffective-hrw.php.

CHAPTER 13

....

GANGS

Another Form of Organized Crime?

....

SCOTT H. DECKER AND DAVID C. PYROOZ

I. INTRODUCTION

A key task for social scientists is to understand how individuals organize themselves. Whether in kinship groups, occupational groups, or as individuals united in a group by a symbolic purpose, social organization has been a central focus of the social sciences for centuries. Groups vary in motive and purpose; some are conventional and legitimate, others are unconventional and deviant. It is the latter that are of interest to criminologists. Paramount to any group, whether formal or informal, criminal or lawful, is organization—the degree to which a group cohesively and efficiently coordinates and carries out activities in a structured context. The roles of cohesion, coordination, and structure in youthful play groups, athletic leagues, professional associations, governments, and criminal associations are important, as they are indicative of the ability of groups to accomplish tasks. For criminal associations, these characteristics take on added significance since the tasks undertaken involve law violation.

One type of criminal association—gangs, particularly street gangs—has been the subject of scholarly attention for nearly a century. Street gangs are street-oriented groups, made up generally of youth, that exhibit persistence across time and for whom illegal activity constitutes a part of group identity (Klein and Maxson 2006). It is argued that this type of criminal association is "qualitatively different" from other criminal and delinquent groups (Klein and Maxson 2006, p. 195) in that they have a group process that accelerates criminal involvement. From their earliest conceptualization (Thrasher 1927), the study of gangs has attempted to place them in the broader context of other groups, particularly groups involved in crime. In this context it is important not to confuse an association of criminals with a criminal association (Morselli 2009). Instead, it is important to understand gangs relative to other groups involved in crime, particularly those engaged in transnational crime, which may include drug smuggling, human trafficking, and terrorism. The structure, processes, cultural orientations, and activities of these groups and networks constitute useful backdrops against which to compare gangs. These concepts play a role in understanding other crime groups, particularly more organized forms of crime groups—thus, their relevance to this essay.

The topic of gang organization has received considerable attention. Felson (2006) identified the "Big Gang Theory"—descriptions of gangs which claim that they have the capacity to exact revenge and retaliation in a manner similar to Mafia-like organizations. Howell (2007, pp. 40–41) described this as one of the key myths about gangs:

> The myth of formal organization, that gangs were becoming large, powerful criminal organizations—much like highly structured corporations—became widely accepted... [However] very few youth gangs meet the essential criteria for classification as "organized crime."

This is the case when organized crime is defined as a Mafia-like formal organization.[1] Nevertheless, most gangs and some gang activity display a certain level and type of organization. This has important implications for how we think about gangs in the context of other criminal groups and social organization in general. Further, this has implications for understanding the social influence of the group on member behavior (McGloin and Decker 2010; Short 1989). Several studies have demonstrated this influence, holding that greater gang organization is associated with increased delinquency and victimization of gang members (Bjerregaard 2002; Decker, Katz, and Webb 2008; Esbensen et al. 2001; Sheley et al. 1995). Understanding the nature of gang organization can be advanced by a comparison with the nature and degree of organization of other crime groups.

This essay places gangs in the context of other organized crime groups, including transnational organized crime, drug smuggling networks, human trafficking and smuggling operations, and terrorist groups.[2] We do this by emphasizing the similarities and differences between gangs and other organized crime groups. This essay focuses on several key issues that make gangs distinctive at the same time that they share common characteristics with these other groups. We begin with an examination of the evolution of gangs, paying particular attention to the context in which they evolved. We follow this with a discussion of the structural, cultural, and behavioral aspects of gang organization. Here we are able to draw contrasts between the crimes committed by gang members and those committed by members of other organized crime groups. We then assess the extent to which gangs have relationships with other organized crime groups (exclusive of other gangs) and how far-ranging those relationships are. Efforts to curb gang activity are assessed next. The essay concludes with a discussion of the future nature of gangs as a form of criminal organization.

II. History and Scope of Gangs in the United States

Howell and Moore (2010) offer the most recent history of gangs in the United States. Their analysis notes the central role played by immigration, social disadvantage, and urbanization in the emergence of gangs in the United States. Gangs are not new; youth gangs have been present in the United States since at least the 19th century, and their growth corresponds to the waves of immigration that have taken place in the United States. The gangs of the late 19th century were composed primarily of new immigrant groups, as popularized in the movie *Gangs of New York* (see Asbury 1928). The next generation of American gangs emerged in the 1920s. Most of the youth gang members of the 1920s were disorganized groups consisting of recent immigrants, typically the children of Italian, Polish, German, and Irish immigrants. These gangs also faded without substantial involvement on the part of the criminal justice system or social service agencies. The next cycle of gangs emerged in the 1960s. In many ways, these gangs represented a distinct break with the gangs of the 1890s or the 1920s as significant numbers of racial and ethnic minorities were involved. However, the economic and demographic parallels between gang involvement in the 1960s and earlier gangs suggest the importance of underlying economic causes of gang membership. Gang members in the 1960s were predominantly African American, with an emerging presence of Hispanic gang members, and that fact remains consistent with contemporary patterns of minority overrepresentation in gangs (National Youth Gang Center 2009). Intergenerational gangs emerged for the first time in large numbers during this cycle of gangs. More recent research has documented higher rates of gang activity in US cities characterized by greater economic disadvantage and racial and ethnic heterogeneity (Pyrooz, Fox, and Decker 2010).

Miller published the first estimate of the magnitude of the nation's gang problem in 1975 (Miller 1975). He estimated that there were between 760 and 2,700 gangs and 28,500 to 81,500 gang members in the six gang cities he identified. The largest concentration of gangs was in California; indeed, more than 30 percent of all US gangs were located in that state. In 1988, the National Youth Gang Suppression and Intervention Program surveyed 98 cities or localities and found that 76 percent had organized gangs or gang activities. *Chronic* gang problem cities often had a long history of serious gang problems, and *emerging* problem gang cities were often smaller cities that had recognized, and had begun to deal with, a usually less serious but often acute gang problem since 1980. Thirty-five of the jurisdictions in their study provided estimates of the number of gangs (1,439) and gang members (120,636).

In 1991, Curry, Ball, and Fox (1994) reported that 95 percent of police departments in cities with populations over 200,000 reported the presence of gangs, crews, posses, or drug organizations engaged in criminal activity. They estimated that there were 4,881 gangs, 249,324 gang members, and 46,359 gang incidents. In 1991, Klein (1995) identified

261 cities with gang crime problems. In the following year, Klein extended his list of problem gang cities to approximately 800. By 1995, Klein concluded that there were between 800 and 1,100 US cities with gang crime problems and more than 9,000 gangs and at least 400,000 gang members in any given year. In 1995, the National Youth Gang Center conducted its first assessment of the national gang problem by surveying 1,499 law enforcement agencies throughout the United States. The numbers produced by that assessment were larger than those of any prior one-year survey, finding a total of 23,388 youth gangs and 664,906 gang members. In the most recent assessment, gathered from the 2007 survey, law enforcement estimates indicate that there were 27,000 gangs and 788,000 gang members.

These figures document the dramatic increase in gangs and gang members beginning in the late 1980s and increasing steadily to current levels. Tied to the growth of gangs is what attracts scrutiny from myriad sources: violence. For example, between 2002 and 2006, gangs were associated with about 25 percent of homicides in US cities with populations greater than 200,000 (Decker and Pyrooz 2010). While there are many instrumental homicides in this group, the majority have an expressive function that includes retaliation and homicides with a more emotional basis. These numbers suggest that gang membership and gang crime are no longer isolated in a small number of neighborhoods or cities and that they penetrate into most aspects or institutions of American life. For these reasons, researchers are interested in identifying group mechanisms, including organization, structure, culture, and process, that are responsible for producing gang violence.

III. Gangs and Organization

The literature on gang organization can be organized into two camps, one arguing for higher levels of organization and the other arguing that gangs are not well organized (Decker and Van Winkle 1995). Two perspectives from this debate include the instrumental-rational (organized) and informal-diffuse (disorganized). These perspectives developed originally out of the debate surrounding the extent to which gangs controlled the increasingly violent street drug markets in the late 1980s and early 1990s in the United States. Hagedorn (1994), for example, framed the argument around whether gangs were organized drug distributors or gang members were "freelance" drug dealers. Morselli (2009) suggested that gang members participate in a number of different crime groups, including their own gang. Thus, to speak of a gang member being exclusively involved in crime with their gang is a misnomer. For example, an individual may be a member of gang "A" but still participate in drug dealing activities with an informal network. Nevertheless, the research on gang organization has since grown outside of the drug arena to examine areas such as the penetration of gangs into community organization (Venkatesh 1997) and the ability of gangs to organize homicide (Decker and Curry 2002).

The instrumental-rational perspective, as described by Decker and Curry (2000, p. 474), holds that gangs "have a vertical structure, enforce discipline among their members, and are quite successful in defining and achieving group values." Additional indications of an instrumental-rational gang include age-graded levels of membership, leadership roles, regularly attended meetings, coordinated drug sales, written rules and codes of conduct, expansion in legitimate business operations, and ties and influence in the political process (Decker et al. 1998). Examples of these descriptions can be found in the research of Mieczkowski (1986), Padilla (1992), Sanchez-Janikowski (1991), Skolnick et al. (1990), Taylor (1990), Venkatesh (1997), and Venkatesh and Levitt (2000). The pro-totypical example of an instrumental-rational gang can be found in Venkatesh's research in a Chicago public housing development. Venkatesh portrayed the "Black Kings" gang as possessing an inordinate degree of power to influence community affairs. The gang was able to persuade the neighborhood "Council" (nominated leaders of buildings) away from petitioning for greater police patrol in favor of the gang acting as security, which bolstered the operations of the gang's hierarchically structured drug distribution ring. The gang was so well organized that each "constituent [gang] set was tied to the overall organization through trademark and fiduciary responsibilities" (Venkatesh and Levitt 2000, p. 428). Examples of this sort support the claim of gang "corporatization" (Taylor 1990)—i.e., the transition of gang functions from socially oriented to economically oriented process outcomes. To date, however, additional evidence in support of this perspective remains sparse.

The informal-diffuse perspective, as described by Decker and Curry (2000, p. 474), holds that gangs "are diffuse, self-interested and self-motivated aggregations of individuals, most of whom sell drugs for themselves." Informal-diffuse gangs fit the image of the "Big Gang Theory" outlined above but not the reality of the organizational parameters. Leadership is functional and situational, levels of membership are transitory, formal gang meetings are rare or unheard of, codes of conduct are limited to secrecy and loyalty, and, most importantly, gang members distribute drugs for individual as opposed to collective purposes. While gang members are involved in crime—especially drug sales—at substantial levels, their criminality is adaptive and does not reflect loyalty to the gang. Leadership is "transient and versatile" and reflects an adaptive character (Morselli 2009). Examples of these descriptions can be found in the research of Decker and Curry (2000, 2002), Decker et al. (2008), Decker and Van Winkle (1995, 1996), Fagan (1989), Fleisher (1995, 1998), Hagedorn (1988; 1994,), Huff (1996), McGloin (2005), and Waldorf (1993). Decker et al. (1998, p. 413) found that the Gangster Disciples of Chicago were the only gang to adequately fit the instrumental-rational description out of the four gangs identified by the police as the most organized gangs in Chicago and San Diego. However, an interview on drug sales with Gangster Disciples revealed the lack of organization in drug dealing and financial matters: "I never seen the money that I made go into the organization," and "Please, not me. If I'm gonna stand up here and sit up here then use mine [profit] for their benefit, I don't think so. I ain't no sucker." Even in one of the most organized gangs in one of the most organized gang cities, gang members rarely invested their profits in gang enterprises; instead, they used the profits for their own purposes. As a whole, the research indicates that it was far more common for gang members to "freelance" as drug dealers, and that the social networks of gangs are organized only to the extent that they fill structural holes as drug suppliers (Decker et al. 1998; Hagedorn 1994). In addition, these gangs fulfill a variety of symbolic functions, such as friendship, revenge, and peer affiliation, that are largely independent of instrumental concerns such as making money. This function and the role of a gang "turf" help to distinguish gangs from many of the other criminal groups discussed in this volume.

Evidence in favor of the informal-diffuse perspective exceeds that of the instrumental-rational perspective in terms of quantity and breadth. It is noteworthy that the evidence in favor of the instrumental-rational perspective was found (1) only in ethnographic research, and (2) only from research carried out in large cities with longstanding gang problems, such as Chicago, Detroit, Los Angeles, and New York. Selection bias could be facilitating the image of organized gangs in these studies as researchers focus on atypical gangs in areas of traditional gang cities with an extended gang history (Coughlin and Venkatesh 2003). But as Thrasher (1927) asserted, and Klein and Maxson (2006) confirmed, gangs vary. So it is perhaps more useful to conceptualize gangs along a normal distribution of organization, with informal-diffuse at one end and instrumental-rational at the other. A point is reached, however, when a gang becomes so organized and institutionalized that it departs from "street gang" criteria and enters into the definitional parameters of an "organized crime group" (the focus of the next section of this essay). Understanding whether variation in the location along the organizational continuum translates into effects on gang member behavior remains relevant not only for criminology, but also for social and peer influence literatures.

A good deal of research has examined the effect of gang organization on gang member criminal behavior using survey research designs (Bjerregaard 2002; Decker et al. 2008; Esbensen et al. 2001; Sheley et al. 1995). Bjerregaard (2002) and Esbensen et al. (2001) reported on this relationship indirectly—the former based on a sample of 1,663 mostly black and Hispanic inner-city high school students (17 percent "current" gang prevalence) in California, Illinois, Louisiana, and New Jersey; the latter based on a sample of 5,935 middle school students (17 percent "ever" gang prevalence) in 11 demographically diverse, urban, rural, and suburban cities. Both studies used restrictive definitions of gang membership—gang organization being one criteria[3] —to examine how refining categories of gang membership affected delinquent outcomes, including theft, arrest, and firearms involvement (Bjerregaard 2002) as well as and demographic, attitudinal, and behavioral characteristics (Esbensen et al. 2001). The findings suggest that membership in more organized gangs corresponds with greater involvement in serious delinquency, albeit loosely.

Sheley et al. (1995) and Decker et al. (2008) carried out a more direct test of the relationship between gang organization and delinquency. Their studies explored the effect of gang organization on gang member delinquency and victimization. Specifically, they examined whether increases in gang organization corresponded with increases in offending by, or victimization of, gang members. Sheley et al. (1995) surveyed incarcerated youth in six reform schools, three in California, one in Illinois, one in Louisiana, and one in New Jersey. Subjects in structured gangs reported that their gang engaged in more drug sales, robberies, and gun carrying than unstructured gangs. Further, subjects in structured gangs engaged in more gun carrying than those in unstructured gangs, net of their gang's delinquency patterns.

Decker et al. (2008) surveyed recently arrested juveniles in Arizona correctional facilities. They created an index of gang organization that included gang leadership, regular meetings, rules, punishments for rule breaking, unique insignia (e.g., colors, signs, symbols), member responsibilities, and shared money. Gang members from more organized gangs were more likely to experience violent victimizations. They also found that increased gang organization was positively associated with the violent offending and drug selling patterns of gangs. Thus, they concluded that the "more organized the gang, even at low levels of organization, the more likely it is that members will be involved in violent offenses, drug sales, and violent victimizations" (p. 169). What this tells us is that greater organization is associated with great involvement in illegal activities. It is useful, then, to compare and contrast gangs with other criminal groups to shed light on similarities and differences, especially with regard to structure and organization.

Most accounts of gang organization stem from research based in the United States. It is well known, however, that gangs are not found only in the United States. Evidence suggests that gangs can be identified throughout North America, Central America, South America, Europe, Asia, Africa, and Australia (see Decker and Pyrooz 2010 on gang violence; see also Covey 2010). While it is difficult to generalize, the diversity of structural characteristics found among street gangs in the United States is found in other jurisdictions as well. As documented in the "Eurogang Paradox" (Klein et al. 2001), European criminologists denied the existence of gangs in Europe in large part because the organizational structure of "troublesome youth groups" did not conform to beliefs about the structure of gangs in America. The perception of American gangs was that they were formal organizations, with hierarchical structures, and an established system of leaders and discipline. The reality, as we have demonstrated, is that American gangs had little of this kind of structure, and that their European counterparts had a good deal in common with them. European gangs, in particular, appear to be more diffuse, less dependent on turf, and less organized around profit-making ventures than their American counterparts (Esbensen and Weerman 2005). A consequence of this reality is that we know much less about the organizational properties—both quantitatively and qualitatively—of European streets gangs than we would like.

IV. Gangs in Relation to Other Criminal Groups

There is little research that links gangs to other organized crime groups, despite public and media allegations to the contrary. As Morselli (2009) noted, high levels of violence are often mistakenly confounded with high levels of organization by the media (and often law enforcement), though the two can vary independently. We believe that there are four key areas in which gangs can be distinguished from other criminal associations. These include: (1) *differences in goals,* with symbolic ends as opposed to economic ends, being more important to street gangs, (2) *organizational structure* that is looser, reflecting the age structure of gangs, (3) *fluctuating levels of cooperation, leadership, and structure* in sporadic profit-making activities in contrast to organized crime groups, terrorists, and smugglers, where the constant presence of profit making leads to as much organization as is necessary to complete the crime without cueing law enforcement, and (4) the importance of a particular *turf, territory, or place* to gangs.

Curry (ND) examined potential links between gangs, on the one hand, and terrorist groups and organized crime groups, on the other hand. He observed a number of similarities between gangs and terrorist groups, including the fact that most members of both groups are male, that violence is a common offense to both groups, that solidarity and elements of collective behavior are at work in both groups, and that the violence used by both groups often represents a form of "self-help," that is, an attempt to rectify a wrong. But Curry was quick to point out the many differences, including the profit motive for gangs that is largely absent for terrorist groups, the cross-national connections held by terror groups, the diversity in offending types that characterizes gang offending, and the commitment to ideology among terror groups, a commitment generally lacking among gang members. Varese (2006) noted that organized crime groups reinvest the profits of their criminal enterprise to further the group, a behavior largely absent from gangs (see the quote above from a member of the Gangster Disciples). The similarities noted by Curry are not because gangs resemble highly structured efficient organizations, but because terrorists tend to be less structured than is publicly believed (Sageman 2008). Varese (2006) observed that there is a major division of opinion among scholars of organized crime, with some who see organized crime groups in ways that are consistent with networking theory and others who describe them in terms consistent with hierarchical theory. For gangs, it seems to be neither, that is, gangs reflect greater fluidity and a more dynamic structure over time. Thus gangs can be seen as structures with affiliational ties that coalesce over specific activities.

Curry (ND) does describe two notable occasions when gang and terrorist activities did intersect. The first is the well-chronicled attempt by Libya to engage members of the El Rukn street gang in Chicago to participate in acts of terror, including bombing buildings and taking down an airliner (Sadovi 2002). The plot was easily uncovered as El Rukn gang members made their contacts with the Libyans from a telephone in a federal prison,[4] demonstrating the (in)capability of street gangs to participate in large-scale conspiracies. El Rukn members who did not plead guilty and turn state's evidence were convicted and received federal prison time. The second incident involved Jose Padilla, a Latin Disciple gang member from Chicago who was charged with a federal conspiracy to use a radioactive bomb. He was convicted of a lesser charge in federal court after several years. Both of these cases illustrate the reasons why gangs are not viewed by organized crime groups as good co-conspirators, namely they attract a lot of attention from the police and tend not to be good at clandestine operations. These characteristics also are linked to the lack of discipline that exists in such a loosely organized and highly dynamic structure. Because discipline is a key element of successful organized crime activity, gangs have rarely been chosen as partners by traditional organized crime groups. The lack of discipline is what distinguishes gang members who sell drugs from OC groups who also sell drugs (Decker and Pyrooz, 2012).

Many co-offending groups that engage in transnational organized crime, drug smuggling, human trafficking and smuggling, or terrorism have access to information and technology that allows them to operate independently of larger organizational structures. Small, loosely organized groups that are largely self-contained are also better able to avoid detection by law enforcement. These are the examples of networking theory so brilliantly described by Varese (2006) that act as a series of loosely connected nodes (individuals, organizations, firms, and information-sharing tools) that depend on expertise rather than hierarchy to function. Dishman (2005, p. 237) characterized the transformation in crime as the "leaderless nexus," a product of the decentralization that has characterized functions carried out in an age in which information, not labor, is the key to achieving instrumental goals. In this view, crime has evolved from a state where it demanded large numbers of more or less well-controlled individuals to execute to a situation where a small number of equals can execute criminal acts successfully. This model has come to characterize both terrorist groups and criminal syndicates, often blurring the longstanding difference between the two groups. Historically, these groups could be distinguished by the primary goal: for terrorist groups financial profits were secondary to political ends, while for criminal syndicates profits were the primary goal.

In their examination of the relationship between terrorism and criminality, Hutchinson and O'Malley (2007) argued that the goals of transnational organized crime groups and terrorist groups will remain sufficiently distinct as to preclude cooperation. They depict modern forms of crime in a manner similar to Dishman, that is, as acts carried out by more "ephemeral-sporadic" groups, particularly terrorist groups that are opportunistic in seeking out criminal activities that further their own agendas, agendas where profits are secondary or tertiary to political goals. Evidence of this can be found in the analysis by Sverdlick (2005) of the intersection of terrorist and organized crime groups in the "Tri-Border" area of Argentina, Brazil, and Paraguay. In this case study activities of the two groups blended in ways that made it difficult to distinguish organized crime from terror activity. Other analyses of the relationship between transnational organized crime and terrorist groups draw a clearer distinction between the two. In a report prepared for Foreign Affairs Canada/UN Office on Drugs and Crime, Dandurand and Chin (2004) found that the intersection between terror and organized crime groups was slim, and, where such convergence did exist, it was likely to produce a hybrid group, not an enhanced version of either type.

Shelley and Picarelli (2005), however, suggested that there is convergence between transnational organized crime groups and terrorist groups when their motives (particularly profit) intersect. Despite this, Dishman (2001) maintains that the motives of the two groups remain distinct as do the structures capable of achieving each group's largely distinct goals. As Schmid (1996) has documented, organized crime groups lack the political motivation that drives terror groups, seek to avoid public scrutiny, and engage in highly targeted, instrumentally focused activities. Terror groups seek publicity for their cause and act largely from expressive motivations. Sageman (2008) argues that terror groups are far less organized than is the popular—or government—view. He described Middle Eastern terror groups as "leaderless jihad," and he characterized them as groups whose membership typically belongs for a period of a few years, who engage in other crimes along with terror, and who are, in the main, not strongly bonded to their group.

Drug smuggling is a highly profitable activity. Because of the great profits to be reaped, it is often assumed that drug smuggling must be a highly organized activity. However, just as the high levels of violence are mistakenly assumed to reflect high levels of gang organization, drug smuggling generally lacks the formal, corporate organizational structure ascribed to it. Williams (1998) argued that international drug smuggling was horizontally organized, with small groups of individuals well known to each other responsible for most of the functions. A study of cocaine smuggling from Colombia to the Netherlands by Zaitch (2002) documented the role of ethnicity and kinship relations in a business that depended on informal trust and established relationships more so than formal agreements. Similarly, Decker and Chapman (2008) identified discrete cells of smugglers largely disconnected from each other from coca processing to delivery of a finished product to the United States. The work of Morselli (2009) reflected a similar picture of organization. The organizational structure of these groups was flatter, more informal, and less hierarchical than has often been depicted. Dishman (2001) outlined the gulf between terrorists and transnational crime organizations, indicating that motivations and expressive goals form the basis for terrorist groups (narco-terrorists in Colombia) in distancing themselves from organized crime groups.

Recent research on human trafficking and smuggling (Aronowitz 2001; Zhang 2007, 2008; Turner and Kelly 2009) described these groups as small networks of individuals that function largely without a hierarchy or system of internal discipline. Aronowitz (2001) and Turner and Kelly (2009) each underscore the role of local culture and historical practices in the smuggling and trafficking of humans. Zhang's exhaustive ethnographic work described flattened organizations, with little role differentiation and few recognized leaders. The structure of such groups was "amorphous" (p. 108), where even "snakeheads" who formerly exerted strong control over group members lack effective control. Such groups function largely based on "trust," despite the large profits and international scope involved in the enterprise. They are loosely affiliated and function more on the basis of personal relationships and experiences than formal role definitions (Zhang 2007). These "temporary business alliances" (Zhang 2007, p. 124) include individuals who also engage in other business activities—legitimate and illegal. Zhang offered this description of such groups:

These smuggling organizations are made up of loosely affiliated individuals with diverse backgrounds, and the relationships among core members are mostly horizontal, with no clear structure of leadership (2008, p.131).

One could easily substitute a description of American street gangs from Klein and Maxson (2006), illustrating the convergence in organizational characteristics of such crime groups.

Recent research and theory on group offending emphasizes the patterns of interactions between individuals in these groups and the utility of pooling their skills. The work of Morselli (2009) is most notable in this context. In an examination of the organizational structure of various criminal groups (street gangs, drug distribution networks such as Hells Angels, and organized crime), Morselli concluded that these criminal networks were decentralized and with flat structures that reflected a "flexible order" that suggests an adaptable set of relations. This structure enabled the group to more effectively complete tasks while avoiding detection by the criminal justice system. These loosely confederated networks are the antithesis of vertically structured hierarchical crime groups. They are also the antithesis of gangs, which are characterized by undisciplined behavior, diverse offending patterns, and lack of discipline among their members.

V. The Future of Gangs

Gangs are unlikely to vanish in the near future. As long as it remains human nature to seek association with similarly situated and like-minded others, particularly in the face of social and economic disadvantages, gangs will maintain a continued presence in communities. Developments in the last two decades have enhanced the status and impact of gangs; namely globalization and technological advances. No longer is it the case that activities and events remain situated in a local context. To the contrary, from the seemingly benign (e.g., drug use) to the publicly violent (e.g., gang initiations), behaviors are transformed from actions witnessed by a handful of people to images and recordings posted on the Internet and broadcast around the world. This matter is enhanced in the gang context, in contrast to other types of criminal organizations, since gangs are composed of youth where access and knowledge of web-based applications is practically second nature. For example, anyone familiar with YouTube (www.youtube.com) can simply query "gang fight" and well over 50,000 video clips are available for viewing. Further, websites and social networking pages (e.g., Facebook, MySpace) are devoted to specific gangs, as well as communication devices and applications (e.g., cell phones, twitter), that provide the capability to mobilize people and direct their movements in a very short period of time (see Papachristos 2005). How technology factors into the organization of the group remains to be seen as limited research has focused on the intersection where gangs meet technology. In turn, technological advances have implications for globalization and gangs.

Gangs are by no means limited to the United States. While gangs have been present across the world for decades, globalization has played an important role in exacerbating levels of gang activity. Globalization receives more attention in conversations about economics and business, but migration and cultural diffusion have had important implications for the development of gangs in countries outside of the United States. As mentioned above, technology has been instrumental in this regard. From movies to magazines to (especially) music, aspects of gang culture are evident in popular culture. How else would we find the Crips gang in the Netherlands or the Latin Kings gang in Spain? It is unlikely that gang members are immigrating to other countries for the purposes of gang expansion. One could cite the case of Salvadoran gang members in Los Angeles organizing and developing ties in El Salvador or other Latin American countries as an exception (Decker and Pyrooz 2010; Jutersonke, Muggah, and Rodgers 2009), but this occurred only because they were deported from the United States for committing crimes. Instead, Maxson (1998) reported that the diffusion of gangs outside of inner-city areas in the United States was due more to diffusion of culture than coordinated efforts of gang members; however, when families escape the inner city, gang membership is often a source of identity for the accompanying teenager. Gang culture spreads in a manner similar to other aspects of youth culture, and the Internet is only likely to exacerbate the expansion of gang culture.

Migration has affected the global gang scene in other ways, however, most notably in terms of the immigration of groups into marginalized settings (see Decker, van Gemert, and Pyrooz 2009). Immigrant groups seeking opportunity in a new land, whether it is Germany, Canada, Italy, or the United States, often encounter a native culture that clashes with the customs of the home country. Immigrant youth experience conflict in both the household and the surrounding environment, such as school and neighborhood, especially when immigrant youth are located at the lower end of social stratification. This double marginalization occurs in the household when youth attempt to blend into native culture and in school when youth attempt to retain aspects of the "old" culture. When coupled with socioeconomic marginalization, this constitutes a natural recipe for gang emergence. The history of gangs in the United States is as much a history of immigration (Adamson 2000; Decker et al. 2009; Howell and Moore 2010; Thrasher 1927). The intersection where immigration, social marginalization, and concentrated disadvantage come together influences the nature of the gang, including criminal activities, group processes, and gang structure and organization. Identifying these influences is an important area for future study.

VI. Conclusion

Street gangs are generally unattractive partners for terrorist groups or organized crime groups, such as transnational organized crime groups or groups engaged in drug or human smuggling. Gangs engage in cafeteria-style offending; they rarely specialize in one specific offense but rather commit a variety of offenses including (but not limited to) drug sales, robbery, assault, burglary, auto theft, intimidation, and homicide. As a consequence of this generalist approach to crime, little specific expertise is developed in any one crime type. This makes gang members a bad match for groups that specialize in a particular type of crime or, who, in the course of their own offending, need to collaborate with groups with a specific expertise.

Another notable characteristic of gangs in this regard is their orientation to the street. This is a defining characteristic of American gangs and one that makes them bad partners for most offending ventures. The street orientation of American gangs gives them a high degree of visibility to neighborhood residents, to rival gangs, and especially to the police. Since most gang crime is street crime (auto theft, robbery, assault, homicide, drug sales), gang members are very visible as they engage in crime. The expressive motivation of much gang crime—retaliation, marking territory, expressing dominance—requires that it have a highly visible and public character. For more organized crime groups or groups for whom the commission of offenses is most effectively completed in clandestine settings, this is an unattractive characteristic for a potential partner to have. Organized crime groups have an instrumental focus to their offending, it is the profit that matters and not the statement. It is quite difficult to imagine a transnational organized crime group identifying its crimes in the way that street gangs "brand" their activities. The prospective involvement of the El Rukn gang members with the Libyan government is a good example of how the visibility of gang members to the police detracts from their utility to more organized or focused crime groups. Groups that engage in crime and have a more organized structure, whether they are terrorist groups or organized crime groups, would eschew partnering with groups whose members are on rosters of known offenders kept by the police. Similarly, gang members fail to develop the technology to specialize in one form of crime. This too makes gangs inefficient partners for Mafia groups, who need surreptitious specialists, not highly visible generalists.

A related attribute that makes gang members less desirable partners in criminal activities that are highly focused or for which clandestine activities are important is the general lack of discipline that characterizes the control that gangs have over gang members. Varese (2006) and others noted that a key defining characteristic of Russian organized groups operating in Italy is the ability to punish or discipline members. Generally, the presence of regulatory mechanisms that identify and sanction behavior inappropriate to the group is an identifying feature of more organized groups. Clearly, such mechanisms are evident in organized crime groups such as the Italian Mafia, Russian Mafia, and some terror groups such as FARC. However, these mechanisms are largely absent from American street gangs and from most criminal groups engaging in drug trafficking or human smuggling, such as the Hells Angels (Morselli 2009). As a consequence, the behavior of gang members is generally not easily directed or effectively controlled by the larger gang. This is evident in a variety of criminal behaviors that range from drug sales to homicide. The pattern of drug sales that typically play out on the street beyond the control of the gang is a solid example of the inability of gangs to structure the revenue-generating activities of their members (Decker and van Winkle 1996; Hagedorn 1994). There also is evidence from the expressive violence of gang members that their activities are not disciplined or controlled well by their gangs. Decker and Curry (2002) documented that most gang homicides take place within rather than between gangs. If gangs were effective structures for the control of the behavior of their members, this could hardly be the case. After all, survival is a key feature to group longevity, refraining from killing one's fellow gang members is a positive attribute for group survival.

Yet, while gangs may not be attractive partners for organized crime groups or meet the criteria to be defined as formal criminal organizations (at least in terms of the United States), it is important to note that it is incorrect to refer to gangs as simply associations of criminals. This would confound gangs with co-offending groups, which is inaccurate conceptually and empirically. In arguing for the distinction between gangs and co-offending groups, Warr (2002) held that gangs are institutionalized co-offending groups. By definition, gangs exhibit some degree of durability over time and maintain a collective identity (Klein and Maxson 2006). Some gangs persist across decades, regenerating with age-graded membership and withstanding conflict internal and external to the gang. Other gangs dissolve after police intervention or when the members graduate from school, get jobs, or begin families. As we have demonstrated in this essay, there are many organizational similarities between gangs and other organized crime groups, enough so to consider them criminal associations as opposed to associations of criminals.

NOTES

1. However, as Paoli 2002 and Varese 2006 have shown, most organized crime groups do not display the level of organization found in Mafia groups. Definitions in the United States (Shelley and Picarelli 2005) tend to depict such groups as far more structured than most European research.

2. While we do not specifically examine them here, evidence exists that many religious cults have similar organizational structures to organized crime groups, including gangs (Barker 2006).

3. Bjerregaard (2002) had youth report whether they were in a gang, then if that gang was "just a bunch of guys" or an "organized gang." Based on the findings, youth were placed in four categories: (1) youth not in gangs, (2) youth not in gangs but who hung around with "a bunch of guys," (3) youth in gangs that were a "bunch of guys" (i.e., not an organized gang), and (4) youth in gangs that were organized. These four categories were then compared independently of one another. Esbensen et al.'s (2001) method of partitioning began by self-nominated gang membership, then diverged across to the delinquency of the gang, the organization of the gang, and the individual centrality within the gang. This resulted in a total of six categories: (1) youth never in gangs, (2) youth formerly in gangs, (3) youth currently in gangs, (4) youth in delinquent gangs, (5) youth in organized (initiations, leaders, and symbols/colors), delinquent gangs, and (6) youth with high centrality in organized, delinquent gangs.

4. All telephone conversations in state and federal prisons are monitored and recorded.

REFERENCES

Adamson, Christopher. 2000. "Defensive Localism in White and Black: A Comparative History of European-American and African-American Youth Gangs." *Ethnic and Racial Studies* 23:272–298.

Aronowitz, Alexis A. 2001. "Smuggling and Trafficking in Human Beings: The Phenomenon, the Markets That Drive It and the Organisations That Promote It." *European Journal on Criminal Policy and Research* 9:163–195.

Asbury, Herbert. 1928. *The Gangs of New York*. New York: Capricorn.

Barker, Eileen. 2006. "We've Got to Draw the Line Somewhere: An Exploration of Boundaries That Define Locations of Religious Identity." *Social Compass* 53: 201–213.

Bjerregaard, Beth. 2002. "Self-definitions of Gang Membership and Involvement in Delinquent Activities." *Youth and Society*, 34: 31–54.

Coughlin, Brenda C., and Venkatesh, Sudhir. 2003. "The Urban Street Gang after 1970." *Annual Review of Sociology* 29:41–64.

Covey, Herbert C. 2010. *Street Gangs throughout the World*. 2d ed. Springfield, IL: Charles C. Thomas.

Curry, G. David. N.d. "*Gangs, Crime and Terrorism*." Unpublished manuscript. St. Louis: University of Missouri.

Curry, G. David, Ball, Richard A., and Fox, James F. 1994. *Gang Crime and Law Enforcement Recordkeeping*. Research in Brief. Washington, DC: National Institute of Justice.

Dandurand, Yvon, and Chin, Vivienne. 2004. "Links between Terrorism and Other Forms of Crime." A Report Submitted to Foreign Affairs Canada and the United Nations Office on Drugs and Crime. Vancouver, BC: International Centre for Criminal Law Reform and Criminal Justice Policy.

Decker, Scott H., Bynum, Tim, and Weisel, Deborah. 1998. "A Tale of Two Cities: Gangs as Organized Crime Groups." *Justice Quarterly* 15:395–425.

Decker, Scott H., and Chapman, Margaret T. 2008. *Drug Smugglers on Drug Smuggling: Lessons from the Inside*. Philadelphia: Temple University Press.

Decker, Scott H., and Curry, G. David. 2000. "Addressing a Key Feature of Gang Membership: Measuring the Involvement of Young Members." *Journal of Criminal Justice* 28:473–482.

Decker, Scott H., and Curry, G. David. 2002. "Gangs, Gang Homicides, and Gang Loyalty: Organized Crimes or Disorganized Criminals." *Journal of Criminal Justice* 30:343–352.

Decker, Scott H., Katz, Charles M., and Webb, Vincent J. 2008. "Understanding the Black Box of Gang Organization: Implications for Involvement in Violent Crime, Drug Sales, and Violent Victimization." *Crime and Delinquency* 54:153–172.

Decker, Scott H., and Pyrooz, David C. 2010. "Gang Violence Worldwide: Context, Culture, and Country." In Small Arms Survey, by Scott H. Decker and David C. Pyrooz, 128–155. Cambridge: Cambridge University Press.

Decker, Scott H. and Pyrooz, David C. 2012. "Gangs, Terrorism and Radicalization." *Journal of Security Studies* 4:151-166.

Decker, Scott H., van Gemert, Frank, and Pyrooz, David C. 2009. "Gangs, Migration, and Crime: The Changing Landscape in Europe and the United States." *Journal of International Migration and Integration* 10:393–408.

Decker, Scott H., and van Winkle, Barrik. 1995. "'Slinging dope': The Role of Gangs and Gang Members in Drug Sales." *Justice Quarterly* 11:583–604.

Decker, Scott H., and van Winkle, Barrik. 1996. *Life in the Gangs: Family, Friends, and Violence*. New York: Cambridge University Press.

Dishman, Chris. 2001. "Terrorism, Crime and Transformation." *Studies in Conflict and Terrorism* 24:43–58.

Dishman, Chris. 2005. "The Leaderless Nexus: When Crime and Terror Converge." *Studies in Conflict and Terrorism* 28:237–252.

Esbensen, Finn-Aage, and Weerman, Frank M. 2005. "Youth Gangs and Troublesome Youth Groups in the United States and the Netherlands: A Cross-national Comparison." *European Journal of Criminology* 2:5–37.

Esbensen, Finn-Aage, Winfree, L. Thomas Jr., He, Ni, and Taylor, Terrance J. 2001. "Youth Gangs and Definitional Issues: When Is a Gang a Gang, and Why Does It Matter?" *Crime and Delinquency* 47:105–130.

Fagan, Jeffrey. 1989. "The Social Organization of Drug Dealing and Drug Use among Urban Gangs." *Criminology* 27:633–670.

Felson, Marcus. 2006. *Crime and Nature*. Thousand Oaks, CA: SAGE.

Fleisher, Mark. 1995. *Beggars and Thieves: Lives of Urban Street Criminals*. Madison: University of Wisconsin Press.

Fleisher, Mark S. 1998. *Dead End Kids: Gang Girls and the Boys They Know*. Madison: University of Wisconsin Press.

Hagedorn, John M. 1988. *People and Folks: Gangs, Crime and the Underclass in a Rustbelt City*. Chicago: Lakeview Press.

Hagedorn, John M. 1994. "Neighborhoods, Markets, and Gang Drug Organization." *Journal of Research in Crime and Delinquency* 31:264–294.

Howell, James C. 2007. "Menacing or Mimicking? Realities of Youth Gangs." *Juvenile and Family Court Journal* 58(2): 39–50.

Howell, James C., and Moore, John. 2010. *History of Street Gangs in the United States*. National Gang Center Bulletin. Washington, DC: Office of Juvenile Justice and Delinquency Prevention.

Huff, C. Ronald. 1996. *Gangs in America*. 2d ed. Thousand Oaks, CA: SAGE.

Hutchinson, Steven, and O'Malley, Pat. 2007. "A Crime-Terror Nexus? Thinking on Some of the Links between Terrorism and Criminality." *Studies in Conflict and Terrorism* 30:1095–1107.

Jutersonke, Oliver, Muggah, Robert, and Rodgers, Dennis. 2009. "Gangs, Urban Violence, and Security in Central America." *Security Dialogue* 40:373–397.

Klein, Malcolm W. 1995. *The American Street Gang: Its Nature, Prevalence, and Control*. New York: Oxford University Press.

Klein, Malcolm, Kerner, Hans-Jergen, Maxson, Cheryl L., and Weitekamp, Elmar G. M. 2001. *The Eurogang Paradox: Street Gangs and Youth Groups in the US and Europe*. Dordrecht: Kluwer.

Klein, Malcolm W., and Maxson, Cheryl L. 2006. *Street Gang Patterns and Policies*. New York: Oxford University Press.

Maxson, Cheryl L. 1998. *Gang Members on the Move*. Washington, DC: U.S. Department of Justice, Office of Juvenile Justice and Delinquency Prevention.

McGloin, Jean. 2005. "Policy and Intervention Considerations of a Network Analysis of Street Gangs." *Criminology and Public Policy* 4:607–636.

McGloin, Jean, and Decker, Scott H. 2010. "Theories of Gang Behavior and Public Policy." In *Criminology and Public Policy: Putting Theory to Work*, edited by Barlow, H. D. and Decker, S. H., 150–165. Philadelphia: Temple University Press.

Mieczkowski, Thomas. 1986. "'Geeking Up' and 'Throwing Down': Heroin Street Life in Detroit." *Criminology* 24:645–666.

Miller, Walter. 1975. *Violence by Youth Gangs and Youth Groups as a Problem in Major American Cities.* Washington, DC: US Department of Justice, National Institute for Juvenile Justice and Delinquency Prevention.

Morselli, Carlos. 2009. *Inside Criminal Networks.* New York: Springer.

National Youth Gang Center. 2009. *National Youth Gang Survey Analysis.* http://www.nationalgangcenter.gov/Survey-Analysis

Padilla, Felix. 1992. *The Gang as an American Enterprise.* New Brunswick, NJ: Rutgers University Press.

Paoli, Letizia. 2002. "The Paradox of Organized Crime." *Crime, Law and Social Change* 37:51–97.

Papachristos, Andrew V. 2005. "Gang World." *Foreign Policy* (March–April), 48–55.

Pyrooz, David C., Fox, Andrew M., and Decker, Scott H. 2010. "Racial and Ethnic Heterogeneity, Economic Disadvantage, and Gangs: A Macro-level Study of Gang Membership in Urban America." *Justice Quarterly* 27:867–892.

Sadovi, Carlos. 2002. "El Rukns Had Early Terror Ties: It's Not the First Time Gangs Have Been Linked to Terrorism." *Chicago Sun Times,* June 11.

Sanchez-Jankowski, Martin. 1991. *Islands in the Street: Gangs and American Urban Society.* Berkeley: University of California Press.

Sageman, Marc. 2008. *Leaderless Jihad: Terror Networks in the Twenty-First Century.* Philadelphia: University of Pennsylvania Press.

Schmid, Alex P. 1996. "The Links between Transnational Organized Crime and Terrorist Crimes." *Transnational Organized Crime* 2:40–82.

Sheley, Joseph F., Zhang, Joshua, Brody, Charles J., and Wright, James D. 1995. "Gang Organization, Gang Criminal Activity, and Individual Gang Members' Criminal Behavior." *Social Science Quarterly* 76:53–68.

Shelley, Louise I. and Picarelli, John T. 2005. "Methods and Motives: Exploring Links between Transnational Organized Crime and International Terrorism." *Trends in Organized Crime* 9:52–67.

Short, James F., Jr. 1989. "Exploring Integration of Theoretical Levels of Explanations: Notes on Gang Delinquency." In *Theoretical Integration in the Study of Deviance and Crime: Problems and Prospects,* edited by Messner, Steven F., Krohn, Marvin D., and Thornberry, Terance P., 243–261. Albany: State University of New York Press.

Skolnick, Jerome, Correl, T., Navarro, E., and Rabb, R. 1990. "The Social Structure of Street Drug Dealing." Unpublished report to the Office of the Attorney General of the State of California.

Sverdlick, Ana R. 2005. "Terrorists and Organized Crime Entrepreneurs in the 'Triple Frontier' among Argentina, Brazil, and Paraguay." *Trends in Organized Crime* 9: 84–93.

Taylor, Carl. 1990. *Dangerous Society.* East Lansing: Michigan State University Press.

Thrasher, Frederick M. 1927. *The Gang: A Study of 1,313 Gangs in Chicago.* Chicago: University of Chicago Press.

Turner, Jackie, and Kelly, Liz. 2009. "Trade Secrets: Interactions between Diasporas and Crime Groups in the Constitution of the Human Trafficking Chain." *British Journal of Criminology* 49:184–201.

Varese, Federico. 2006. "The Structure of Criminal Connections: The Russian-Italian Mafia." *Oxford Legal Studies.* Research paper No. 21/2006.

Venkatesh, Sudhir. 1997. "The Social Organization of Street Gang Activity in an Urban Ghetto." *American Journal of Sociology* 103:82–111.

Venkatesh, Sudhir A., and Levitt, Steven D. 2000. "Are We a Family or a Business?" History and Disjuncture in the Urban American Street Gang." *Theory and Society* 29:427–462.

Waldorf, Dan. 1993. "When the Crips Invaded San Francisco: Gang Migration." *Journal of Gang Research* 1:11–16.

Warr, Mark. 2002. *Companions in Crime.* Cambridge: Cambridge University Press.

Williams, Phil. 1998. "The Nature of Drug-Trafficking Networks." *Current History* (April): 154–159.

Zaitch, Damian. 2002. *Trafficking Cocaine: Colombian Drug Entrepreneurs in the Netherlands.* The Hague: Kluwer.

Zhang, Sheldon X. 2007. *Smuggling and Trafficking in Human Beings: All Roads Lead to America.* Westport, CT: Praeger-Greenwood.

Zhang, Sheldon X. 2008. *Chinese Human Smuggling Organizations—Families, Social Networks, and Cultural Imperatives.* Palo Alto, CA: Stanford University Press.

CHAPTER 14

....

OPPORTUNISTIC STRUCTURES OF ORGANIZED CRIME

....

MARTIN BOUCHARD AND CARLO MORSELLI

I. INTRODUCTION

....

ORGANIZED crime researchers have often referred to the mass of small and ephemeral groups that form in any given criminal market as opportunistic operators and less organized (or disorganized) forms of criminal operations. Indeed, such groups have been excluded, at times, from the organized crime category. In this essay, we demonstrate that such opportunistic structures are not independent of the organized crime phenomenon, but, on the contrary, they constitute the typical configuration in organized crime.

The first part of the essay will provide the conceptual outline that details why organized crime cannot be restricted only to sophisticated and reputed formal criminal organizations. This point is already well established in past research. The second will review the size of criminal organizations as reported in published organized crime research, which will demonstrate that opportunistic criminal groups are the predominate form of organized crime. The third section turns to past research using network applications in areas related to organized crime and develops the basic elements for a framework that allows us to capture the structural features of illegal markets that are made up primarily of what many perceive to be disorganized groups of criminal entrepreneurs. What the network approach offers is a framework for assessing structure where most see disorder. We conclude by exploring the implications of the prevalence of opportunistic and network structures of organized crime on policies and practices aimed at containing or controlling this phenomenon.

II. Organizational Size and the Consequences of Illegality

Since the work of Reuter (1983) on the organization of illegal markets, the consequences of illegality and the effects on the size of illegal businesses are well known. Offenders face a series of risky and uncertain market conditions that tend to limit the number of partners and employees involved in specific organizations. "Small is beautiful" appears to be the norm by which illegal entrepreneurs operate their businesses. Small groups are considered to be safer, easier, and more efficient than larger organizations (Reuter and Haaga 1989; Adler 1993; Desroches 2005). This is probably what Eck and Gersh (2000, p. 265) had in mind when they asserted that large organizations are scarcely needed in drug markets since "drug trafficking on the small scale may be too easy and too lucrative."

The natural barriers to growth imposed by the context of illegality are substantial. Paoli et al. (2009, p. 204) divide these reasons into two sets: (1) those deriving from the fact that criminal enterprises have to operate without the benefit of the state (e.g., non-enforcement of contracts and property rights, a lack of secured loan mechanisms, the difficulty in imposing and commercializing a brand), and (2) those deriving from the fact that they also operate against the state (e.g., the constant risk of detection, arrest, and incarceration). The latter are of particular importance for this essay as they emphasize the main choice-structuring properties that illegal entrepreneurs need to address when it comes to establishing firm or group size.

The first source of threat to the illegal enterprise lies in the number of partners and employees that will be part of a venture. Certain activities require minimal sizes to be conducted efficiently, but offenders are generally wary of adding more members than necessary to a criminal enterprise, mainly because each additional member is another potential target for the police. It follows that the larger the organization, the more vulnerable it is to infiltration by law enforcement (Moore 1977). Furthermore, trust is usually lower in larger groups. Consequently, risks of defection increase with size. For economists this represents the increasing operating costs of criminal organizations: "...there exists a certain threshold beyond which recruitment of a new member generates additional costs greater than the gain which could be expected" (Kopp 2004, p. 29).

The second source of threat, the size of the clientele and the number of transactions, is related to the size of an organization. The more customers and the more transactions carried out, the greater the chance of being apprehended. Clients often exercise a lower level of trust than direct partners or group members, and they are vulnerable to being used by police as a way of entering the organization. Reuter summarizes the role of customers as a source of threat to the organization in the following manner: "They [customers] are many in number, have small loyalty to the enterprise, and take few precautions against police surveillance because they face little risk from the police" (Reuter 1985,

p. 20). An indication is that the risk of being arrested was shown to be 10 to 20 times higher for dealers than for users of drugs in North America (MacCoun and Reuter 2001; Bouchard and Tremblay 2005).

Other arguments also support the idea that criminal organizations are bound to remain small. Hagedorn (1994), for example, drew on contingency theory to describe how organizations adapt to their environment. Because illegal firms operate in uncertain and unstable worlds, they are more likely to remain small, flexible, and loosely structured. In his study of Milwaukee gangs, Hagedorn (1994) observed how organizational size varied in accordance with the level of law enforcement presence in a given neighborhood.

Such variations between risks and the size of criminal organizations have recently been revisited at the macro level by Paoli, Greenfield, and Reuter (2009) in the context of the international heroin trade. Paoli et al. provide an explicit proposition that variations in effective illegality (the level of law enforcement actually experienced by traffickers in a given region) have a direct impact on the size of criminal organizations. The greater the scope of effective illegality, the smaller the size of organizations. One implication is that much of the argument about the size of criminal organizations is directed at countries with strict and consistent enforcement, and other rules apply in countries with lax enforcement or weak government where large and sophisticated organizations closer to the popular organized crime imagery may grow and prosper.

III. The Size of Criminal Organizations: A Brief Review

Empirical evidence is substantial that opportunistic and small criminal groups are the predominant form of operating unit in organized crime. We compiled a list of past studies that reported the size distribution of the criminal groups and organizations encountered in their research endeavors (Table 14.1). To be sure, we also reviewed ethnographic studies that reported size data (e.g., Reuter and Haaga 1989; Adler 1993; Zaitch 2002; Desroches, 2005; Decker and Chapman 2008)—all of them consistent with the general results presented here.

All of the studies presented in Table 14.1, as well as ethnographic studies, maintained that the majority of criminal organizations are small, with most consisting of less than 10 participants. This pattern emerges across time, space, and markets. The oldest study in the list provides the largest sample of units. Thrasher's (1963) seminal study was not only important as one of the first large-scale street gang studies in the United States, but also because the size of the gangs were documented. Interestingly, the size distribution he provides for gangs in Chicago in the 1920s resembles those found in more recent studies (e.g., Klein and Maxson 2006). Of the almost 1,000 gangs from Thrasher's study, 26 percent had 10 members or less and 90 percent had 50 members or less.[1] Thrasher

Table 14.1 Selected Studies Reporting the Size Distribution of Criminal Organizations

Study	Data/methods	Type of crime analyzed/setting	Size of organization
Thrasher (1963)	N = 895 gangs, ethnographic work	Any illegal activities, Chicago, USA	*Number of members per gang* 3–5: 4.1% 6–10: 22.1% 11–15: 21.5% 16–20: 16.7% 21–50: 25.7% 51–100: 5.7% 101+: 4.2% *Mean*: 11 to 20 members
Block (1979)	N = 22 "combinations"	Drug dealing, New York City, USA	*Number of dealers per group* 3: 45.5% 4: 22.7% 5: 9.1% 6: 4.5% 7: 4.5% 8: 4.5% 9: 4.5% 17: 4.5% *Mean*: 4.9 dealers
Reuter (1983)	N = 53 banks, police records	Numbers industry, New York City, USA	*Number of controllers per bank* 1: 22.6% 2–10: 58.5% 11–20: 11.3% 21+: 7.5% *Mean*: 7.6 controllers
Eck and Gersh (2000)	N = 557 organizations, police data	Drug dealing organizations, Maryland, USA	*Number of dealers per organization* 1: 39.9% 2–5: 24.2% 6–10: 14.4% 11–15: 8.3% 16–20: 5.6% 21+: 7.7% *Mean*: 2–5 dealers
Bouchard (2006)	Inmate interviews (N = 117)	Drug traffickers and retailers, Quebec (province)	*Number of dealers per group* 1: 17.9% 2–5: 44.4% 6–10: 15.4% 11–15: 7.7% 16–20: 0.9% 21+: 13.7% *Mean*: 4.6 dealers
Bouchard (2008)	Interview data, N = 36 grow operations for 20 offenders	Cannabis cultivation, Quebec (province)	*Number of offenders per cultivation site* 2: 19.4% 3: 41.7% 4: 22.2% 5: 8.3% 6: 2.8% 7: 2.8% 13: 2.8% *Mean*: 3.7 offenders

(Continued)

Table 14.1 (Continued)

Study	Data/methods	Type of crime analyzed/setting	Size of organization
Bouchard and Nguyen (2010)	High School Survey (N = 167 growers, 13–17 years old)	Cannabis cultivation, Quebec, Canada	*Number of offenders per cultivation site* 1: 8.4% 2: 22.8% 3–4: 35.9% 5–6: 18.0% 7–9: 6.6% 10–15: 1.8% 16+: 6.6% *Mean*: 3–4 offenders

described the few gangs that to larger sizes as having undergone a process of "conventionalization," meaning that they adopt a more elaborate structure that goes beyond the inner circle structure of other gangs in which "what is said by one of the group can be heard by all" (Thrasher 1963, p. 318). Thrasher added that, in many cases, larger gangs were formed by merging two or more gangs.

Block (1979) also provided data on group size for a similar time period. Drawing on historical files, he analyzed the (Jewish-based) cocaine groups ("combinations") in New York City that were active between 1910 and 1917. As many as 22 different combinations were found in the Jewish community at the time, with the largest having 17 members and the smallest 3 members, with an average of five for the sample. More contemporary studies of illegal markets found very similar results. Reuter's (1983) study of the bookmaking, numbers, and loansharking industries in New York City is the most well known of the group. Although Reuter had enough data on any of those markets to properly conclude that no one organization (or even the top four) had more than 35 percent of the market share, the one market for which he obtained and provided the most details was the numbers industry. In Table 14.1, we use the number of controllers (brokers acting between banks and collectors) as a proxy for group size and reproduce the size distribution for the 53 numbers banks for which Reuter analyzed records (Reuter 1983, p. 64). He found that the largest organization had 33 controllers who were involved at one time or another during the period of observation, and that the majority (55 percent) of banks had between 2 and 10 controllers.

Similar distributions were found in more recent illegal drug market studies. Analyzing a sample of incarcerated dealers in Quebec, Bouchard (2006) also found that a majority (60 percent) of dealers were active in organizations of 2 to 10 members (60 percent), but that 13.7 percent had more than 20 members, including one organization for which a respondent reported more than 100 members. In an analysis of 557 drug dealing cases collected from police files in Baltimore, Eck and Gersh (2000) found that 35 percent of groups consisted of 2 to 10 offenders, and only 7.1 percent (although a respectable 43 organizations) had more than 20 members. Eck and Gersh (2000) argued that "large organizations do not dominate the market, but grow out of it" (p. 264). In other words, it is a competitive market for everyone, but some organizations that are larger than usual still manage to survive. A few case studies of street gangs (Sanchez-Jankowski 1991; Levitt and Venkatesh 2000), biker gangs (Tremblay et al. 1989; Morselli 2009; Tremblay, Bouchard, and Petit 2009), and Mafia groups (Morselli 2003; Paoli 2008) certainly confirm that organizations that are larger than usual exist in almost every setting. However, they remain the exception rather than the rule, and they rarely manage to dominate an illegal market, except on a limited territorial base (e.g., Paoli 2003).

An important point made by Reuter and others is that these small criminal groups are ephemeral. Offenders get together for one importation or a few transactions, and then they split up. The nature of the business makes this more salient than in most conventional markets, although it should be emphasized that most legal businesses do not survive for lengthy periods. For example, Bouchard and Dion (2009) compared the survival rates of flower and hydroponic shops in Quebec and found that close to 30 percent of flower shops did not survive two years in business, compared to just over 20 percent for hydroponic shops (which, they argued, benefited from a booming cannabis industry). Even crimes designed for long term collaboration, like cannabis cultivation or commercial prostitution do not seem to have much stability. Analyzing commercial prostitution establishments (massage studios, escort services) in Montreal in the 1980s, Leguerrier (1989) found that the majority lasted only last 6 to 18 months. Bouchard and Nguyen (2011) provide five years of data for one offender involved in full-time commercial cannabis cultivation. This particular grower was successively involved in 10 grow houses and worked with 16 different co-offenders in that short time period. She was often forced out of a house because of a real or perceived increased risk of burglary/police detection and out of a business partnership because of the lack of trust or reliability of partners.

It should be noted that, although relationships are rarely exclusive and there is constant movement in partnerships, dealers interviewed in most drug market studies reported the existence of long-lasting business partnerships (e.g., Reuter and Haaga 1989; Adler 1993; Desroches 2005). As argued by Morselli (2001), it also makes sense that offenders will "try to keep a good thing going" (p. 208) if they are lucky or good enough to have found one. The bottom line is, of course, that such partnerships are typically hard to find.

The degree of organization also varies from one group to another. Studies examining taxonomies of drug groups described a wide-ranging spectrum of organizational complexity, from very loose and changing partnerships, to corporate-like organizational structures (Adler 1993; Dorn and South 1990; Natarajan and Belanger 1998; Curtis and Wendel 2000). "Corporations" or "professionals" are often described as the entrepreneurial groups that take advantage of the most interesting opportunities at key time periods in different drug markets (Bouchard and Nguyen 2011; Mieczkowski 1992; Rengert 1996; Dorn, Oette, and White 1998; Curtis and Wendel 2000; Tremblay 2010). Two comments are in order here. First, the more organized groups are typically the largest in size (Eck and Gersh 2000), and the fact remains that those organizations are few in numbers in any given setting. Second, rarely do studies actually measure organizational complexity. Bouchard and Spindler (2010) recently proposed a scale of gang organization in which gangs and groups self-reported the presence or absence of nine items (from the presence of a hierarchy to the existence of initiation rituals). The more organizational features found for a group, the more it resembled what we normally refer to as a formal organization. As with Decker et al. (2008), the authors found that the majority of groups had few of those organizational features (1 to 2 out of 9 for the full sample).

For some, the fact that a majority of organizations lack sophisticated internal organization or are small in size is not what is so remarkable. After all, the majority of organizations in legitimate markets are also considered small (e.g., Granovetter 1984). Instead, the most important difference with respect to the size distribution of legal organizations lies in the scope of the distribution. Whereas legal firms profit from standard mechanisms of growth available to them, illegal firms do not. If firm size in legal markets can go from one to 50,000 employees and more, this is less common for illegal firms. Although the scope of the size distribution is shorter in illegal settings, chances are that the size distribution of legal and illegal firms has the same functional form. Legal enterprises, when ranked according to their size, generally follow the same pattern: a large number of small firms in the upper tail and a very long tail composed of a few very large firms (Granovetter 1984). The size distribution of firms found in studies in Table 14.1 is similar: A majority of groups of 2 to 5 persons, and a small minority of very large groups of 60, 80, or more than 100 offenders. This might be enough to add criminal organizations to the list of distributions that follow a power law function in which the frequency of very large units is very small compared to the majority (see also Eck and Gersh 2000).

From this review of past research emerges an important question: how do we define the boundaries of criminal organizations? The authors of those studies, as well as the offenders they studied, clearly have a different view of what constitutes the proper unit of analysis for organizational size. This is an important definitional issue that may explain why some studies report the existence of solo dealers, while others report three members for the same dealer as they also count the main supplier as part of the co-offending group, and perhaps his girlfriend who provides the money and drug stash at her mother's place. Some will prefer to keep the unit of analysis as close to the event as possible (e.g., the drug transaction) while other researchers will be interested in the larger pool of co-offenders necessary to get to that transaction and that emerge before, during, and after the main event (Tremblay 1993). This point is especially important for members of potentially larger organizations. Consider Levitt and Venkatesh's (2000) sizeable drug-selling gang. If asked about size, would members of this gang count every member at every level or would they only consider members that he knows were involved in the drug selling activities? For example, a typical employee in a fast-food restaurant (e.g., McDonalds) will most probably identify to the other 30 individuals working at the same establishment, rather than the 1.5 million employees working in the 31,000 McDonald's establishments worldwide.[2] If so, would a full-patched member of the Hells Angels' Montreal chapter count only his fellow chapter members or would he add all other members who are part of Hells Angels chapters across Quebec and the rest of the world? Would he include his main supplier working under/over him and members of lower-level criminal groups? Such questions are not easily answered by researchers and offenders alike (see Tremblay, Bouchard, and Petit 2009). The solution is not necessarily to choose one over the other but for authors to be as clear as possible on their operational definitions of organizational size when conducting research on criminal groups and reporting their findings.

Despite a wide diversity in methods, samples, types of crimes, and settings, the overall conclusions of those studies are similar: The typical configuration of organized crime is opportunistic. We consider those groups as opportunistic based on the fact that they generally (1) lack history or reputation, (2) are small at the operative level, and (3) lack sophisticated internal organization. In addition, one could also argue that they are minimally ambitious and lack political associations as opposed to what has been found in weak states (Williams and Godson 2002). Importantly, however, these opportunistic groups are part of a more extensive network of contacts that, at times, may be confused with a traditional organization. Below we examine the network perspective and how it provides analytical solutions to many of the issues raised above.

IV. The Importance of a Network Perspective on Organized Crime

Whereas many researchers have focused on the criminal group, firm, or organization as their unit of analysis, a growing number of studies have incorporated a network framework that transcends these units of collective behavior. A network approach allows us to identify structure where many see disorder and is designed around three basic premises underlying criminal network operations and structuring (Morselli 2009). First, a criminal network is a social network at constant risk (a network without a net). Second, flexibility is the principal feature guiding criminal networks. Third, a multitude of positions and key players are needed to assure the emergence and continuity of criminal networks. Most of these reflect participants who are positioned beyond the traditional boss or kingpin designation. Such participants are often found along the periphery of the network and may be represented by a number of increasingly familiar terms in organized crime and in the criminal market.

Von Lampe (2009) describes the network method as a bottom-up approach. This approach is essentially data driven, and a distinction must be made between network methods and network models. As Carrington (2011) emphasizes, the application of social network techniques and theory to organized crime or criminal market data does not necessarily lead to the adoption of a network model. For example, in as much as much research has dispelled the myth of the formal criminal organization and most research in this area has confirmed the presence of loosely structured action groups, this does not exclude the possibility that some demonstrations based on network analytical techniques may confirm that formal, hierarchical criminal groups are indeed in place. Such structures have been documented in research on Mafia families (e.g. Paoli 2003; Morselli 2005) and on outlaw motorcycle gangs such as the Hells Angels (Morselli 2009).

In most cases, criminal network groups or firms are generally formed for opportunistic incentives and are typically action-based. In illegal drug market settings, van Duyne and Levi (2005) referred to them as criminal trading networks and compared them to their noncriminal trade counterparts that "organize by doing." Groups in these networks are action-oriented and organized around their core business ventures. Members of such groups are generally made aware of their organizational status by the law enforcement agencies that target them. According to van Duyne and Levi, no contradiction exists between the illegal network, with its short-term relationships and shifting coalitions, and the existence of continuous enterprises as organizational entities. Small action-oriented network organizations do not exclude the existence of large organizational-oriented criminal networks, which can be maintained for wholesale transport operations by keeping the component parts of the network separate.

Some may argue that such loosely structured networks are found in areas and markets that are more competitive and consisting of small and ephemeral action groups. But, as with early research by Hess (1973), Albini (1971), and Ianni and Reuss-Ianni (1973), network dynamics have been found to be the key governing force even in studies that involved reputed criminal organizations and gangs (Morselli 2003; Morselli 2009; Papachristos 2009; Descormiers and Morselli 2010). An even more striking demonstration is offered by research by Kenney (2007) on the Colombian cocaine trade, which tells us that flexibility is the norm even when we focus on the more notorious (or stereotypical) criminal organizations or cartels. Kenney's fieldwork with law enforcement, intelligence officials, and former drug traffickers found that, contrary to the popular view, cocaine trafficking in Colombia has never been dominated by one or more criminal organizations exerting monopoly control. Instead, the trade is more fluid and diffuse. Cocaine trafficking in Colombia, in short, is flat and not vertical. This pattern is typical of criminal markets and organized crime in general.

The network approach is also consistent with the resource-sharing model (Haller 1990) that has considerably influenced research in organized crime. This model is based on the premise that at the heart of group formations in criminal markets is the need for participants to cooperate with others so as to meet the tasks needed to execute any crime script. Such resource sharing includes all elements of the crime script, ranging from the preparation and movement of the illicit product or service to the financing of various segments and the insulation of the criminal operation. This approach shares the same outlook as the network view in that it also allows us to see that it is not because members of criminal organizations are present in a criminal venture that the venture or the wider crime process surrounding it is controlled by that criminal organization. Even when members of criminal organizations are present in a criminal venture, they are not usually the main participants (although they are typically the main targets). Beyond members of criminal organizations, a multitude of actors take part in, and facilitate, criminal ventures (transporters, corrupted officials, investors, lawyers, accountants).

For example, a three-city (Turin, Barcelona, and Amsterdam) survey on ecstasy markets demonstrated that operations required a network that consisted of participants who assured the transaction of the product across links in the distribution chain (production, export/import, wholesale, retail, and consumer purchases) and all participants involved in the logistics surrounding this chain (chemists, drivers, luggage handlers, airport stewardesses, and cleaners) (Abele 2003). Other examples of such resource allocation were offered by Lyman and Potter (2000), who extended the argument to the diversity and importance of a multitude of participants who act beyond the scenes and without whom the "the organized crime unit could not flourish" (p. 11): middlemen, financiers, smugglers, chemists, pilots, bankers, attorneys, and enforcers; law enforcement officers, judges, prosecutors, mayors, bankers, attorneys, accountants, and elected and appointed political persons at all levels of government. What the network method offers is a framework in which all these participants may be included at the same time.

The bottom line is that organized crime (or a criminal market) is largely a resource pooling process that is built around individuals who are connected (or socially embedded) with each other in various ways beyond co-membership in a criminal organization. The network allows us to capture the convergence of this mix of individuals in a common framework.

Studies on the structure and form of criminal networks that are in place to operate in a criminal market for a given time span may be divided along those that seek insights into the personal network qualifications of offenders and groups (an egocentric analysis, in social network terms) and those that seek a more general assessment of criminal networks beyond any given actor (a sociometric analysis, in social network terms). Across such research, key patterns have been identified and the benefits of brokerage (i.e., the ability of offenders to strategically position themselves between disconnected others) have emerged in a variety of criminal settings. In a study of predatory and market offenders, Morselli and Tremblay (2004) found a straightforward brokerage effect on criminal earnings (higher brokerage, higher criminal earnings). This was particularly true for offenders who participated in criminal markets. Morselli (2005) conducted two case studies on the evolution of individual criminal networks across lengthy careers in international cannabis smuggling and Cosa Nostra racketeering and found that brokerage was highest during the peak levels of success in each criminal career. Although not as explicitly focused on the brokerage effect, past research has recognized that such a networking pattern constituted an important feature in organized crime. Coles (2001), Klerks (2001), and Williams (1998) reviewed past research on brokerage and concluded that the presence of multiple brokers in a criminal network is more likely in groups that indicate a higher degree of sophistication or organization. The value of brokers has also been a consistent finding in studies of illegal drug trafficking (Pearson and Hobbs 2001; Zaitch 2002; Desroches 2005; Natarajan 2006; Bouchard and Nguyen 2010; Malm and Bichler 2011;), human smuggling (Zhang and Chin 2002; Kleemans and van de Bunt 2003;), ringing networks (Bruinsma and Bernasco 2004), and general criminal enterprise settings (Haller 1990; Finckenauer and Waring 1998). Finally, Morselli (2009) also found similar brokerage patterns in case studies of investigative operations against criminal networks. Brokers are essential in criminal networks and organized crime because they have an edge in opportunistic settings. In and out of crime, brokerage capital is strategic capital that offers greater flexibility for the participant in that position and for others surrounding him/her. Brokers, in short, keep a network in motion.

The brokerage component is also related to the level of competition in a criminal setting. Past research establishes that criminal markets are hostile settings in that they demand intense competition from participants and result in important economic disparities. Criminal network research has helped us understand the factors accounting for an offender's status as *haves* or *have-nots*. In the Morselli and Tremblay (2004) research, the more successful offenders were also the most personally organized. Such offenders were not part of fixed and easily identifiable organizations. They were, instead, higher earners who operated autonomously and who were best positioned to access and seize opportunities.

In short, network research on the structure of organized crime has demonstrated that we cannot simply assume the presence of criminal organizations that centralize the actions of participants in criminal markets. Instead, across different periods of time and a wide range of cultural areas, researchers have made the organizational or structural features of criminal groups the direct focus of their work and have become more concerned with how and why which criminal operations are centralized to varying extents.

V. Conclusions

In this essay, we argue that small organizations are the typical configuration of organized crime in the majority of industrialized countries. We also argue that a key development in realizing the prominence of small groups in organized crime is the development and application of social network analysis not only to a variety of crime activities, such as drug trafficking (Malm and Bichler 2011; Natarajan 2006), but also to specific individuals involved in reputed criminal organizations such as La Cosa Nostra (Morselli 2003). Doing so made it possible to see that small groups are, in fact, sampled from a larger network of offenders loosely collaborating on specific ongoing criminal activities, none of which require the full participation of all network members. In other words, such small groups are the typical form of organized crime because this is the form most efficiently adapted to the socio-legal context in which they operate.

A network view also allowed us to see that it is not because members of a reputed criminal organization are present in a criminal venture that the wider crime process surrounding the venture is controlled by that criminal organization. Even when members of criminal organizations are present in a criminal venture, they are not usually the main participants (but they are typically the main targets or focus of analysis). Beyond members of criminal organizations, a multitude of actors take part in criminal ventures (transporters, corrupted officials, investors, lawyers, accountants). Organized crime is essentially a resource pooling process that is built around individuals who are socially embedded in various ways beyond co-membership in a criminal organization. The network approach provides the tools necessary to understand and illustrate the mechanisms underlying this process.

Although weak in recognition, organizational form, and opportunities for impunity, the myriad of opportunistic groups forming the landscape of organized crime are, nevertheless, the most difficult to contain from a law-enforcement and policy outlook. Their massive presence in criminal markets consequently makes these markets more resilient than if the more stereotypical structures of organized crime prevailed (Bouchard 2007). Small organizations and the criminal networks in which they are embedded are resilient because of their flexible, self-organizing, and adaptive makeup. They disperse when disrupted (Morselli and Petit 2007). The more vulnerable participants in criminal networks are those that are most visible (high degree of centrality), while the least vulnerable are those that are positioned as brokers (Morselli 2010). Leadership or principal coordinator status shifts between participants (Morselli 2009). They centralize when allowed to function in a state of impunity (Williams and Godson 2002). Criminal networks, in short, are resilient because participants and groups are generally opportunistic and adapted to the socio-legal environment in which they are embedded.

ACKNOWLEDGMENTS

The authors would like to thank Letizia Paoli and Wei Wang for comments made on an earlier version of this paper.

NOTES

1. No systematic comparisons should be made with the size distribution pattern found in Thrasher's gang study and other studies presented in Table 14.1. All other studies were focused on organizational size in a specific criminal activity, as opposed to the size of the larger pool of co-offenders who may or may not belong to a "gang."
2. http://www.mcdonalds.ca/ca/en/contact_us/faq.html.

REFERENCES

Abele, Gruppo. 2003. *Synthetic Drugs Trafficking in Three European Cities: Major Trends and the Involvement of Organized Crime*. Turin, Italy: Gruppo Abele.

Adler, Patricia A. 1993. *Wheeling and Dealing: An Ethnography of an Upper-level Drug Dealing and Smuggling Community*. 2d ed. New York: Columbia University Press.

Albini, Joseph L. 1971. *The American Mafia: Genesis of a Legend*. New York: Appleton Century Crofts.

Block, Alan. 1979. "The Snowman Cometh: Coke in Progressive New York." *Criminology* 17:75–99.

Bouchard, Martin. 2006. "Segmentation et structure des risques d'arrestation dans les marchés de drogues illégales." PhD dissertation, School of Criminology, University of Montreal.

Bouchard, Martin. 2007. "On the Resilience of Illegal Drug Markets." *Global Crime* 8:325–344.

Bouchard, Martin. 2008. "Towards a Realistic Method to Estimate the Size of Cannabis Cultivation Industry in Developed Countries." *Contemporary Drug Problems* 35:291–320.

Bouchard, Martin, and Claude Dion. 2009. "Growers and Facilitators: Probing the Role of Entrepreneurs in the Development of the Cannabis Cultivation Industry." *Journal of Small Business and Entrepreneurship* 22:25–38.

Bouchard, Martin, and Holly Nguyen. 2010. "Is It Who You Know, or How Many That Counts? Criminal Networks and Cost Avoidance in a Sample of Young Offenders." *Justice Quarterly* 27:130–158.

Bouchard, Martin, and Holly Nguyen. 2011. "Professional or Amateurs? Revisiting the Notion of Professional Crime in the Context of Cannabis Cultivation." In *World Wide Weed: Global Trends in Cannabis Cultivation and Its Control*, edited by Tom Decorte, Gary Potter, and Martin Bouchard, 109–126. London: Ashgate.

Bouchard, Martin, and Andrea Spindler. 2010. "Groups, Gangs, and Delinquency: Does Organization Matter?" *Journal of Criminal Justice* 38:921–933.

Bouchard, Martin, and Pierre Tremblay. 2005. "Risks of Arrest across Markets: A Capture-Recapture Analysis of 'Hidden' Dealer and User Populations." *Journal of Drug Issues* 34:733–754.

Bruinsma, Gerben, and Wim Bernasco. 2004. "Criminal Groups and Transnational Illegal Markets: A More Detailed Examination on the Basis of Social Network Theory." *Crime, Law & Social Change* 41:79–94.

Carrington, Peter. 2011. "Crime and Social Network Analysis." In *SAGE Handbook of Social Network Analysis*, edited by John Scott and Peter J. Carrington, 236–255. London: SAGE.

Coles, Nigel. 2001. "It's Not What You Know—It's Who You Know That Counts: Analysing Serious Crime Groups as Social Networks." *British Journal of Criminology* 41:580–594.

Curtis, Ric, and Travis Wendel. 2000. "Toward the Development of a Typology of Illegal Drug Markets." In *Illegal Drug Markets: From Research to Prevention Policy*, edited by Mangai Natarajan and Mike Hough, 121–152. Monsey, NY: Criminal Justice Press.

Decker, Scott H., and Margaret Chapman. 2008. *Drug Smugglers on Drug Smuggling: Lessons from the Inside*. Philadelphia: Temple University Press.

Decker, Scott H., Charles M. Katz, and Vincent J. Webb. 2008. "Understanding the Black Box of Gang Organization: Implications for Involvement in Violent Crime, Drug Sales, and Violent Victimization." *Crime & Delinquency* 54:153–172.

Descormiers, Karine, and Carlo Morselli. 2010. "Analyse de la structure sociale des conflits et des alliances intergangs sur le territoire montréalais." *Criminologie* 43:57–89.

Desroches, Frederick J. 2005. *The Crime That Pays: Drug Trafficking and Organized Crime in Canada*. Toronto: Canadian Scholars Press.

Dorn, Nicholas, Lutz Oette, and Simone White. 1998. "Drugs Importation and the Bifurcation of Risk." *British Journal of Criminology* 38:537–560.

Dorn, Nicholas, and Nigel South. 1990. "Drug Markets and Law Enforcement." *British Journal of Criminology* 30:171–188.

Eck, John, and Jeffrey S. Gersh. 2000. "Drug Trafficking as a Cottage Industry." In *Illegal Drug Markets: From Research to Prevention Policy*, edited by Mangai Natarajan and Mike Hough, 241–271. Monsey, NY: Criminal Justice Press.

Finckenauer, James O., and Elin Waring. 1998. *Russian Mafia in America: Immigration, Culture, and Crime.* Boston: Northeastern University Press.

Granovetter, Mark. 1984. "Small Is Bountiful: Labor Markets and Establishment Size." *American Sociological Review* 49:323–334.

Hagedorn, John. 1994. "Neighborhoods, Markets, and Gang Drug Organization." *Journal of Research in Crime and Delinquency* 31:264–294.

Haller, Mark H. 1990. "Illegal Enterprise: A Theoretical and Historical Interpretation." *Criminology* 28:207–235.

Hess, Henner. 1973. *Mafia and Mafiosi: The Structure of Power.* Farnborough, UK: Saxon House.

Ianni, Francis A. J., and Elizabeth Reuss-Ianni. 1973. *A Family Business: Kinship and Social Control in Organized Crime.* New York: New American Library.

Kenney, Michael. 2007. "The Architecture of Drug Trafficking: Network Forms of Organization in the Colombian Cocaine Trade." *Global Crime* 8:233–859.

Kleemans, Edward R., and H. G. van de Bunt. 2003. "The Social Organisation of Human Trafficking." In *Global Organized Crime: Trends and Developments*, edited by Dina Siegel, Henk van de Bunt, and Damian Zaitch, 97–104. Boston: Kluwer Academic.

Klein, Malcolm, and Cheryl Maxson. 2006. *Street Gang Patterns and Policies.* New York: Oxford University Press.

Klerks, Peter. 2001. "The Network Paradigm Applied to Criminal Organizations." *Connections* 4:53–65.

Kopp, Pierre. 2004. *Political Economy of Illegal Drugs.* New York: Routledge.

Leguerrier, Yves. 1989. "Les entreprises de prostitution commerciales: Les commerces ephémères des marchés illicites." *Criminologie* 22:35–63.

Levitt, Steven, and Sudhir Alladi Venkatesh. 2000. "An Economic Analysis of a Drug-Selling Gang's Finances." *Quarterly Journal of Economics* 115:755–789.

Lyman, Michael D., and Gary W. Potter. 2000. *Organized Crime.* Upper Saddle River, NJ: Prentice Hall.

MacCoun, Robert J., and Peter Reuter. 2001. *Drug War Heresies: Learning from Other Vices, Times, and Places.* New York: Cambridge University Press.

Malm, Aili, and Gisela Bichler. 2011. "Networks of Collaborating Criminals: Assessing the Structural Vulnerability of Drug Markets." *Journal of Research in Crime and Delinquency* 48:271–297.

Mieczkowski, Tom. 1992. "Crack Dealing on the Street: The Crew System and the Crack House." *Justice Quarterly* 9:151–163.

Moore, Mark H. 1977. *Buy and Bust.* Lexington, MA: Lexington Books.

Morselli, Carlo. 2001. "Structuring Mr. Nice: Entrepreneurial Opportunities and Brokerage Positioning in the Cannabis Trade." *Crime, Law, and Social Change* 35:203–244.

———. 2003. "Career Opportunities and Network-Based Privileges in the Cosa Nostra." *Crime, Law, and Social Change* 39:383–418.

———. 2005. *Contacts, Opportunities, and Criminal Enterprise.* Toronto: University of Toronto Press.

———. 2009. "Hells Angels in Springtime." *Trends in Organized Crime* 12:145–158.

———. 2010. "Assessing Vulnerable and Strategic Positions in a Criminal Network." *Journal of Contemporary Criminal Justice* 26:382–392.

Morselli, Carlo, and Katia Petit. 2007. "Law-Enforcement Disruption of a Drug Importation Network." *Global Crime* 8:109–130.

Morselli, Carlo, and Pierre Tremblay. 2004. "Criminal Achievement, Offender Networks, and the Benefits of Low Self-control." *Criminology* 42:773–804.

Natarajan, Mangai. 2006. "Understanding the Structure of a Large Heroin Distribution Network: A Quantitative Analysis of Qualitative Data." *Journal of Quantitative Criminology* 22:171–192.

Natarajan, Mangai, R., and Mathieu Belanger. 1998. "Varieties of Upper-level Drug Dealing Organizations: A Typology of Cases Prosecuted in New York City." *Journal of Drug Issues* 28:1005–1026.

Paoli, Letizia. 2003. *Mafia Brotherhoods: Organized Crime, Italian Style*. New York: Oxford.

Paoli, Letizia. 2008. "The Decline of the Italian Mafia." In *Organized Crime: Culture, Markets and Policies*, edited by Dina Siegel and Hans Nelen, 15–28. New York: Springer.

Paoli, Letizia, Victoria Greenfield, and Peter Reuter. 2009. *The World Heroin Market: Can Supply Be Cut?* New York: Oxford University Press.

Papachristos, Andrew V. 2009. "Murder by Structure: Dominance Relations and the Social Structure of Gang Homicide in Chicago." *American Journal of Sociology* 115:74–128.

Pearson, Geoffrey, and Dick Hobbs. 2001. *Middle Market Drug Distribution*. London: Home Office Research, Development and Statistics Directorate.

Rengert, George F. 1996. *The Geography of Illegal Drugs*. Boulder, CO: West View Press.

Reuter, Peter. 1983. *Disorganized Crime: The Economics of the Visible Hand*. Cambridge, MA: MIT Press.

——. 1985. *The Organisation of Illegal Markets: An Economic Analysis*. Washington, DC: National Institute of Justice, US Department of Justice.

Reuter, Peter, and John Haaga. 1989. *The Organization of High-Level Drug Markets: An Exploratory Study*. Santa Monica: RAND.

Sanchez-Jankowski, Martin. 1991. *Islands in the Streets: Gangs and American Urban Society*. California: University of California Press.

Thrasher, Frederic. 1963. *The Gang*. Chicago: University of Chicago Press.

Tremblay, Pierre. 1993. "Searching for a Suitable Co-offender." In *Routine Activity and Rational Choice: Advances in Criminological Theory*, edited by Ronald V. Clarke, and Marcus Felson, 17–36. New Brunswick, NJ: Transaction.

Tremblay, Pierre. 2010. *Le délinquant idéal: Performance, discipline, solidarité*. Montreal: Édition Liber.

Tremblay, Pierre, Martin Bouchard, and Sévrine Petit. 2009. "The Size and Influence of a Criminal Organization: A Criminal Achievement Perspective." *Global Crime* 10:24–40.

Tremblay, Pierre, Sylvie Laisne, Gilbert Cordeau, Brian MacLean, and Angela Shewshuck. 1989. "Carrières criminelles collectives: Évolution d'une population délinquante (Groupes de Motards)." *Criminologie* 22:65–94.

van Duyne, Petrus C., and Michael Levi. 2005. *Drugs and Money: Managing the Drug Trade and Crime-Money in Europe*. New York: Routledge.

von Lampe, Klaus. 2009. "Human Capital and Social Capital in Criminal Networks: Introduction to the Special Issue on the 7th Blankensee Colloquium." *Trends in Organized Crime* 12:93–100.

Williams, Joseph. 1998. "Agency and Brokerage of Real Assets in Competitive Equilibrium." *Review of Financial Studies* 11:239–280.

Williams, Phil, and Roy Godson. 2002. "Anticipating Organized and Transnational Crime." *Crime, Law, and Social Change* 37:311–355.

Zaitch, Damian. 2002. "Bosses, Brokers, and Helpers: Labour and Business Relations amongst Colombian Cocaine Traffickers." *Amsterdam Sociologisch Tijdschift* 29:502–529.

Zhang, Sheldon, and Ko-Lin Chin. 2002. "Enter the Dragon: Inside Chinese Human Smuggling Organizations." *Criminology* 40:737–768.

CHAPTER 15

··

ORGANIZING CRIME

The State as Agent

··

SUSANNE KARSTEDT·

I. THE STATE AND ORGANIZED CRIME: VICTIM AND PERPETRATOR

GLOBALLY and regionally organized crime is deemed as a major threat to the economy, the polity and the citizenry of countries (Edwards and Levi 2008; Karstedt 2012a). The United Office on Drugs and Crime (UNDOC) as well as Europol regularly publish their threat assessments of a range of organized crime activities (e.g., Europol 2008, 2009, 2010, 2011, 2013; UNODC 2010). The state as actor on its own account or even only as facilitator of organized crime is conspicuously absent from all of these reports. To the contrary, the state is seen as a victim of organized crime with its economy, society, and even polity being affected by "infiltration" and "influence" from organized crime groups. The EU Organized Crime Threat Assessment 2009 identifies types of "influence" from organized crime mainly by manipulating the legal system or by impacting on local communities (Europol 2009). Surveys of European citizens show that it is a widely held belief among them that organized crime infiltrates the economy and society, which in many cases does not at all reflect the actual presence of organized crime in a particular country (Karstedt 2012a, pp. 106–107). In particular democracies have been seen as vulnerable to the threat of organized crime groups manipulating and funding election campaigns, paying politicians, intruding the very center of government (e.g., Block and Griffin 1997) or even bringing down governments that organized crime groups see as a threat to their activities (Stille 1995). Only a few are as cautious in this kind of threat assessment as van Duyne (1997, p. 201), whose careful analysis comes to the conclusion that "organized criminals may want to enjoy the profits of their business rather than subvert societies."

This image of the state and its institutions as victims of organized crime is in stark contrast to those of the state itself as a form of organized crime or as an actor in organized crime. Famously, Charles Tilly (1997) described the "making" of the modern state as organized crime. Mancur Olson (1993) framed the emergence of the modern state as a process of transforming "roving bandits" into "stationary bandits." Both cast the process of state making as a solution to problems of ensuring security and protection, in exchange for a "tax." Historical analyses of the Sicilian Mafia demonstrate in which ways a weak state and feudal order gave rise to and were complemented by the Mafia and organized crime capable of delivering the level of security and protection that the state could not provide (Hess 1998). Other authors see governments as being promoted by organized crime but also as adopting practices of organized criminals, for example, Lane (2004) in his analysis of the Berlusconi government in Italy. The terminology of the state as "banditry" is not confined to the academic sphere. In China, after the death of Mao, the "Gang of Four," including his wife, were charged and prosecuted by the successor government, and the language of organized crime, conspiracy, and banditry was widely used in official statements.

Perhaps the most influential definition of the state as an organized crime actor, which had a lasting impact until today, originates from the Nuremberg International Military Tribunal (IMT) and its constituting charter, the Charter of London in 1945. In the Nuremberg Trial 1945–1946 and the follow-up trials until 1948, the elite of the Nazi state and its organizations were charged. At the time, it was of utmost importance for the Allies to address the concerted and organized ways in which this regime had committed its heinous crimes epitomized by the Holocaust. The Charter provided in its Article 6 for conspiracy to commit these crimes, and made membership in a criminal organization punishable in its Article 9. According to Telford Taylor (1992), who worked for the U.S. prosecution in Nuremberg, these provisions were inspired not only by the nature of the Nazi state and the crimes that had been committed by the regime but also by the prosecution of organized crime and recent experiences in the United States. When the IMT delivered its judgment on October 1, 1946, it explicitly referred to the linkages between the concept of "criminal organization" and the Anglo American law of conspiracy: "A criminal organization is analogous to a criminal conspiracy in that the essence of both is cooperation for criminal purposes. There must be a group bound together and organized for common purpose" (quoted in Meierhenrich 2006, p. 346).

The innovative and, at the time, highly controversial concepts of "criminal organization" and "conspiracy" laid the groundwork for further decisive developments of international criminal law, when the International Criminal Tribunal for Yugoslavia (ICTY; and Rwanda [ICTR]) introduced the concept of "joint criminal enterprise" into international jurisprudence, again as a legal transplant from the United States. Like the IMT in Nuremberg, both tribunals acknowledged the "logic of collective action" in the commission of these crimes of the state, from command and superior responsibility of those who gave orders, to substantive crimes as defined by the Convention on the Prevention and Punishment of the Crime of Genocide (Genocide Convention) in its Article III: conspiracy and complicity, as well as incitement of genocide (Meierhenrich 2006, p. 342).

The notion of "enterprise" was a transplant from the U.S. Racketeer Influenced and Corrupt Organizations Act (RICO), which had been enacted as part of the Organized Crime Control Act in 1970. Such a (criminal) enterprise includes "any individual, partnership, corporation, association, or other legal entity, and any union or group of individuals associated in fact although not a legal entity" (quoted in Meierhenrich 2006, p. 345). The act mainly targeted organized crime at the time, and accordingly those who transplanted it into international law were cognizant of the conceptual links that they made between state and organized crime. The role of the state in actually organizing these crimes, and its institutions and organizations in committing them, is particularly obvious in the "big cases" of genocide and widespread crimes against humanity. State policy is a core "element" of these crimes and decisive for starting, carrying out, and ending them (Schabas 2008, p. 955). It is therefore in the area of international criminal law, where the state itself most distinctly emerges as an organized crime actor.

As much as international crimes epitomize these state crimes as organized crime, and the state as an organized crime actor, state crimes are a group of crimes of considerable variety. They include military violence, human rights violations, tax evasion by politicians, torture, illegal domestic surveillance, illegal police violence, corruption/bribery, and cover-ups of all of these (Ross 2010, p. 5). They all fit into the two definitions of state organized crime by Chambliss, namely as "acts defined by law as criminal and committed by state officials in pursuit of their jobs as representatives of the state" (Chambliss 1989, p. 184), and as "...behaviour that violates international agreements and principles established in the courts and treaties of international bodies" (Chambliss 1995, p. 9). State agencies particularly prone to state criminality if acting within a climate of encouragement from governments are criminal justice agencies, the police, and the military (Karstedt 2014; Ross 2010). State crime therefore is ubiquitous and affects advanced industrialized democracies as well as nondemocratic regimes even though it might take different forms in the former and might be more pervasive in the latter (Karstedt 2014). However, given the power that the modern state is capable of exerting over its citizens (and abroad), state crimes are crimes of extraordinarily serious nature, as they have the potential of affecting large groups of victims and causing great harm in terms of life, health, and economic and social well-being.

As states, its institutions, and organizations are "organized actors" by definition, they seem to be organized crime actors by default. However, we have to be careful not to identify state crime with organized crime or making state crime and organized crime synonymous. Organized crime and criminal enterprise need the criminal purpose, and this purpose is a precondition for the state to become an organized crime actor. It is decisive to explore the nature of contemporary states, its institutions and organizations and their composition in order to understand the types, preconditions, and causes of organized state crime. States provide the "eco-system" for its own entities and units to engage in organized crime activities (Felson 2009) and for the type of organized relationships that foster organized criminal activity by governments and state representatives. Some conceptual quandaries therefore need to be addressed and forms of organized state crime to be discussed before exploring the type of structural conditions and social relationships that constitute such an eco-system. This exploration will be framed by two paradoxes: the paradox of the state as its own guardian and the paradox of state strength and weakness.

II. Conceptual Quandaries: State Crime as Organized Crime

As Edwards and Levi (2008, p. 363) famously note, the problem of organized crime is the concept of "organized crime" itself, and the same could be easily said about state crime. Conceptual problems thus seem to mount when linking both concepts, and it might be useful to start with an exploration into the nature and characteristics of the modern states and its "elective affinities" (Weber) with organized crime.

In his seminal article "War Making and State Making as Organised Crime," Charles Tilly (1997) describes the birth of modern states within an environment of security dilemmas and anarchy that prevailed at the dawn of modernity during the Middle Ages and the feudal regimes dominating most of Europe at the time. Security dilemmas occur when "large numbers of individuals...make decisions about their personal security that are contingent on their expectations about the decisions of others" (Kasfir 2004, p. 59). If they expect that others prepare and threaten their security, they will turn to preparations and threatening behavior themselves or even consider preemptive violent action. They might also consider and prepare other means to prevent other individuals or groups from an attack, such as, for example, through destroying their basis of subsistence, cutting them off from vital revenues and other actions that might prevent violent attacks. Consequently, in security dilemmas, the search for security is often linked to attempts to acquire material gains that advantage one's own group and disadvantage the "others". The dynamics of security dilemmas paradoxically decrease the security of all actors involved as well as collective security, when actors prepare to enhance their own individual security, and take to more or less violent and predatory means to achieve this.

Tilly argues that the nascent modern states addressed these security dilemmas through classic "protection rackets" as they emerged as centralized authorities from a situation of domestic and external anarchy. The dispersal of power and/or dilution of power from a central authority to a number of smaller units neither produces groups of uniform size nor spreads power evenly. More powerful groups will not only be a greater threat to others but are simultaneously more credible and reliable as providers of security. Those groups and actors that can offer long-term security will be most successful with their racketeering. In classic "protection racket" mode, the nascent states threaten smaller groups and units, and simultaneously offer "protection" in exchange for a "tax" or other forms of payment. They strategically exploit fear among those for material gains, and protection rackets rely on the two strong and mutual motivations of fear and greed. Tax collection sets a strong incentive for enlarging territories of control, and groups and nascent states become competitors, increasingly threatening each other. In this process, states and governments as well as their agencies and institutions thus emerge as criminal actors themselves. As Tilly (1997, p. 167) notes, "To the extent that the threats against which a given government protects its citizens are imaginary or a consequence of its own activities, the government has organized a protection racket." Just like in classic organized crime protection rackets, as the nascent states accumulate more power, they become strong enough to provide protection, and equally strong enough to issue credible threats against their subjects, confiscate their wealth, or exploit them otherwise. As we will see, the "birth" of the modern state has much in common with its demise and failing in the contemporary world order.

Tilly's account is notable for its focus on the *modus operandi* as the constitutive element of elective affinity between state making and organized crime, and on the "eco-system," in which this is operative (see Edwards and Levi 2008). As I have pointed out elsewhere (Karstedt 2011a), this is exactly the environment of security dilemmas that contemporary failed states create for their citizens. Consequently, opportunities and conditions conducive to organized crime thrive. Sung (2004) found that extortion and racketeering were related to institutional failure and severe deficiencies in the judiciary and the rule of law. States that rank highest in the Failed States Index[1] equally top the rankings of organized crime (Karstedt 2012a, p. 102–104; Composite Organized-Crime Index, van Dijk 2008, pp. 162–167). However, Tilly's account also points to the "paradox of state strength and weakness" (Karstedt 2014, p. 130), which gives rise to state crimes generally and organized state crime activity specifically. State formation and consolidation, in particular the monopoly on violence that the modern state holds, provides security for some and insecurity for others; it creates states strong enough to protect property rights of citizens and to confiscate their assets; its institutions facilitate accountability and are equally powerful enough to impede accountability of officials and state organizations, and cover up their illegal activities. All these paradoxes coalesce in the commission of all types of state crimes.

Contemporary scholarship does not conceptualize the state as the monolithic Leviathan, but as an ensemble and structure of institutions (Levi 2006). Institutions are the "humanly devised constraints that structure political, economic and social interaction," combining informal constraints and formal rules (North 1991, p. 97). They thus facilitate cooperation; however, they also represent power structures (Moe 2005). The political process and the institutional structure give rise to differentials in power and influence within the state and civil society by advantaging some and disadvantaging others. Both cooperation and the search for power define the operation of different state institutions, and state crime, in particular illegal violence by state institutions, is instrumental in increasing and consolidating the power of the state or specific institutions. States do not coincide with governments, though most authors who write on state crime rarely make a difference between the two (an exception is Kauzlarich, Mullins, and Matthews 2003). "Major shifts in the personnel, policies or even form of government can change while the state remains stable" (Levi 2006, p. 6);

this applies to the state within the international sphere as well as to its institutional design. States and their governments both establish the type of institutional and "social relations" (Edwards and Levi 2008, pp. 366, 378–381), which are conducive to organized state crime in providing networks and structural links, power imbalances and vacuums, as well as incentives. Even the most autocratic of contemporary states is a space of competition for power and influence among different institutions, and far from providing unambiguous lines of command. Consequently, even the most large-scale of state crimes, the Holocaust seems to have been "improvised" rather than meticulously organized (Kershaw 1992).[2] Modern states operate and are governed through a range of agencies and mechanisms that span from the local to the global with various nodes of connections and lines of command (see, e.g., Doig 2011 for the United Kingdom), thus offering a complex web of relationships for organized crime activity and a range of motivations and incentives for different groups of state representatives. Kauzlarich and his colleagues propose "a differentiation between crimes committed by the state in the interest of the state itself and crimes committed by the state in the interest of a ruling class" (2003, p. 242), a more restricted conceptualization than the pluralistic model outlined here would suggest.

How is state crime defined in this context, and in which ways is it a distinctly organized crime activity? Since Chambliss' (1989, 1995) initial definitions of "state crime," its conceptualization has been enhanced and broadened, as it became ever more closely linked to the international human rights regime (Friedrichs 2009/2010; Green and Ward 2000, 2004). In principle, two major approaches are presently shaping the definition and realm of state crime. Chambliss represents the legalistic approach as he uses legal definitions of crime, in both national and international law. Green and Ward (2000, 2004) represent a human rights–based approach that builds on the concept of "state deviancy" rather than a strictly legal definition of state crime. This includes a range of socially injurious activities of the state and violations of human rights or failure to implement and monitor them within the boundaries of state responsibility. Most authors today subscribe to a broader and human rights–based conceptualization of state crime (e.g., Rothe and Friedrichs 2006; Rothe et al. 2009). This position is best captured by the definition given by Kramer, Michalowski, and Rothe (2005, p. 56):

> State crime is any action that violates public international law, international criminal law, or domestic law when these actions are committed by individuals acting in official or covert capacity as agents of the state pursuant to expressed or implied orders of the state, or resulting from state failure to exercise due diligence over the actions of its agents.

The definition covers a range of actions under the overarching category of state crime (see Karstedt 2014). Michalowski (2010, p. 17) distinguishes between three general variants of state crime—*juridical, deviance, and social injury*. The more limited juridical conceptualization generates a list of traditional crimes that are associated with state activity, its agencies and representatives: military violence; crimes against humanity; human rights violations; tax evasion by politicians; torture and forced disappearances at the hands of the criminal justice system; illegal domestic and international surveillance; illegal police violence; corruption/bribery; illegal actions against other state institutions, such as by the executive and branches of government against parliament; and cover-ups, illegal influence on and obstruction of the judiciary (see Ross 2010, p. 5). Grabosky (2013) complements this list with "state-sponsored cybercrime" including large-scale industrial espionage, attacks on the cyber space of other countries, as the one on Estonia by Russian agents. State crimes that in particular are identified with organized crime include drug manufacture and trafficking, illicit arms transfers, and counterfeiting by agents of the state, as alleged for the Democratic People's Republic of Korea (North Korea; Perl 2007). Violations of human rights are committed by complicit states and their organizations in trans-border actions, as in the case of unlawful extradition and detention of terrorist suspects from the United States via European countries (Council of Europe, Committee on Legal Affairs and Human Rights 2006).

The definition of state crime by Kramer, Michalowski, and Rothe (2005) makes the principle of action by states and their agents and representatives a core requirement of the definition of "state crime." State crime is thus defined by the actors rather than by the action itself. However, state crimes are often committed as "state-sponsored crime" (Grabosky 2013, p. 24), and agents of the state obfuscate the relationship between those who instigate and those who commit the actual crimes. Many violations of public international law and failures to honor treaty obligations involve those other than state actors as representatives of the state. Mass atrocity crimes are presently often committed by nonstate actors like militias and insurgent groups; these groups can hardly be generally categorized as state actors and their actions thus as state crimes (see, e.g., Friedrichs 2009/2010; Karstedt 2013a). Militias who in fact operate as agents of the state in ethnic and civil conflicts are "officially" independent; Guatemala's protracted civil war (Rothenberg 2012; Sanford 2004) and the mass atrocities in Darfur (Hagan and Rymond-Richmond 2009; Hagan and Kaiser 2011) are exemplary cases. As both the trial of former president Milosevic before the International Criminal Tribunal for former Yugoslavia and of Charles Taylor before the Special Court for Sierra Leone have demonstrated, lines of command or action and even only encouragement are difficult to discern in the case of cross-border activities and involvement of higher levels of government (Osiel 2009). In addition to the complex links in which organized state crime evolves, most definitions of state crime include "inaction" and failure to act, such as negligence of oversight over representatives of state institutions or organizations linked to it. In these cases, failures to act are often indicative of factual tacit agreement and acknowledgement (e.g., Kauzlarich, Mullins, and Matthews 2003). Widespread corruption in the state bureaucracy or in police forces is a clear sign of failure to act and acknowledgment and even complicity at the highest levels (Klockars, Kutnjak Ivkovic, and Haberfeld 2004).

A number of authors therefore have suggested a *continuum* of state involvement and complicity in state organized crime. Grabosky (2013, p. 24) constructs a continuum of "hybrid organizational form" of state and state-sponsored crime according to "state-private interaction." It starts with states turning a blind eye to the activity, tacit encouragement of state and nonstate crime actors, active sponsorship by the state, and moves on from loose cooperation between state authorities and other actors to closer formal or informal collaboration between state and nonstate actors. Grabosky (pp. 24–25) lists cases such as the collaboration between the Russian government and the "patriotic hackers" who allegedly attacked government servers in Estonia; the North Korean Army training hackers to commit fraud; and the U.S. National Security Agency engaging private consultants in collecting and analyzing communications intelligence. The actual degree of state involvement in these cases remains obfuscated, thus giving rise to conspiracy theories for which evidence will hardly ever be available.

Kauzlarich and his colleagues' (2003, p. 247) "continuum of state complicity" is based on two dimensions: omission of control and oversight, and commission of harms and crimes, and implicit and explicit illegal and criminal action. Their continuum thus includes four discrete types from "omission–implicit" to "commission–explicit." While implicit omission generates harmful, but not illegal outcomes, the other three categories include illegal and criminal organized action, like lack of bureaucratic oversight, tacit encouragement of corporate crimes and environmental destruction, and finally mass atrocities and genocide as "explicit commission." Failure to stop mass atrocities and war crimes committed by state agencies and collaborating militias indeed constitutes organized state crime, and a liability of those in command according to public international law. In addition, Kauzlarich and his colleagues distinguish between the state as institutional pattern that facilitates these types of state-organized crime and collaborative illegal practices, and governments and powerful elites that use the state as an instrument in pursuit of power, and their own economic and political interests (see also Friedrich 1996, pp. 128–135).

The different forms of collaborative relationships in state-organized crime thus mirror the diversity of patterns of collaboration in organized crime enterprises and groups. We find more networked rather than hierarchical command relationships, though the latter might be more important for contemporary state violence. Networks between different state institutions, or collaboration between state- and nonstate actors as well as trans-border and transnational cooperation are found equally for the commission of state crimes and the range of organized crime activities, and will vary according to the type of illegal activity that state representatives and their allies engage in; just like their counterparts in organized crime, these will often be developed ad-hoc rather than representing long-term relationships (Edwards and Levi 2008; Paoli 2003; see Choo and Grabosky 2014, this volume).

What is the purpose and motivation of such criminal organization and cooperation by representatives of the state and within its institutions? Prevalent in the definitions of organized crime has been the purpose of monetary and economic gains, and the use of violence. However, as Grabosky (2013, p. 20) reminds us with regard to cybercrime, this is a too narrow conceptualization, and much of organized cyber-crime has other purposes. State crime has been predominantly conceptualized as the pursuit of power with illegal means (see, e.g., Friedrich 2009/2010; Kauzlarich, Mullins and Matthews 2003), either by the state itself, by its different institutions or by powerful groups capturing state institutions for their own interests. Even if we concede that the pursuit of power is a major motivation particularly for violent state crimes and for committing atrocity crimes, other purposes or different types of power need to be included. Actual and imagined security threats are a major trigger of repression and unlawful violence by state agencies, and security interests are a strong motivation (Grabosky 2013; Kalyvas 2004, 2006; Karstedt 2013a). Economic gains are a prevalent motive in widespread corruption or in the capture of state institutions for illegal exploitation by powerful groups. Repressive and illegal state violence and crimes against humanity epitomize organized state crime, and violence and corruption are presumably the most prevalent state crimes globally.

Contemporary organized criminal activity by state and nonstate, that is, "traditional" organized crime actors thus have more in common than they differ in terms of the variety of structural patterns, broad range of purposes, and fluidity of relationships through which they operate. As van Duyne (1997, p. 201) notes, it is realistic to assume "the usually disunited and often disorganized composition" for both state-organized and other organized crime. In which ways does the "Underworld" of state organized crime depend on the "Upperworld" (Felson 2006, quoted in Edwards and Levi 2008, p. 378) of state institutions and governments?

III. The Paradox of State and Crime: The Leviathan as Guardian

Felson's routine activity approach and its triangle of motivated offenders, suitable targets, and incapable guardians have recently been adopted for organized crime (Edwards and Levi, 2008; Felson 2009). Are states capable guardians? What sets state crime apart from all other types of crime are two paradoxes: the "paradox of state and crime," and the "paradox of state strength and weakness." Modern states have the capacity to provide security to their citizens and equally to decrease the security of certain groups. They have the capacity to legally protect the property and rights of citizens and to confiscate their wealth illegally (Levi 2006, p. 9). Thus states are the *guardians* of laws and rights and simultaneously "the Behemoth against which rights (and laws. S.K.) need to be defended" by citizens (Ishay 2004, p. 363). How are states and their agents made accountable for the crimes committed and brought to justice if they have the power to grant amnesties and ensure impunity for high- as well as low-ranking perpetrators of major crimes against humanity, committed in the name of the state, and in fulfilling tasks implemented and assigned by state agencies?

Powerful states and governments are built on strong institutions of law and justice and thus capable of monitoring compliance with the rule of law by their agents as well as citizens. Simultaneously, they muster the power to override, ignore, and circumvent their own laws as they and their agents think fit (Doig 2011; Ross and Rothe 2008). The monopoly on force that modern Western states possess is an advantage in fighting crime and implementing the rule of law but simultaneously offers the opportunities for states, governments, and their agents to commit the most atrocious crimes. It is this paradox that defines the problem of the state as guardian against its own crimes. States and governments hardly "police themselves" and prosecute their own agencies. Jorgensen (2009) found that impunity for crimes against humanity and state violence prevail where states are also incapable of controlling other forms of state crime like corruption (see also Karstedt 2014 for European states).

As the state itself turns out to be a mostly incapable guardian, how can states, governments, and their agents be policed, and from where do capable guardians come? State crime is not pervasive in many, if not most of, contemporary states. States with strong institutions that are capable of controlling each other and are made accountable have comparative advantages in guarding against organized state crime by their agents, and state crime should be considerably lower in those countries. Independence of the judiciary is as vital for controlling state crime as it is for controlling organized crime (van Dijk 2008, chapter 7). Karstedt (2014, pp. 133–137) has shown for European states that unlawful state violence mostly committed by criminal justice agencies is significantly lower where the rule of law, other institutions of democratic oversight, and civil society engagement are stronger and well developed. However, capable guardians should be more often located outside rather than inside the state and government machinery, notably within civil society and the international human rights regime. Strength of civil society institutions like freedom of the press and political and social integration and inclusiveness have a significant impact on the level of organized state violence, both globally (Jorgensen 2009) and in Europe (Karstedt 2014). Domestic within-state controls need to be supplemented by international suprastate controls where sovereign states can be held internationally accountable for their domestic practices.

The contemporary human rights regime and its global and regional supranational institutions aim at guarding individual human rights against violation by illegal practices of states, governments, and their agents and at providing protection for citizens. The European Convention on Human Rights and the International Covenant on Civil and Political Rights provide for retrospective punishment of "any act or omission which, at the time when it was committed, was criminal according the general principles of law recognized by civilized nations." This provision has turned out to be decisive in prosecuting state crimes where states and governments hardly or not at all police and prosecute their own agents. It laid the legal foundations for transitional justice procedures in Europe and worldwide to deal with state crimes of past regimes and bring perpetrators to justice (Drumbl 2009; Karstedt 2012b; Sikkink 2011). It is now widely accepted that international crimes imply an "aggravated responsibility" of the state on whose behalf the perpetrators have acted (Cassese 2008). State responsibility is acknowledged as a category in customary international law and has been enshrined in the jurisprudence of the ICTY and ICTR for the crime of genocide and its prosecution (Jorgensen 2000; Meierhenrich 2006; Schabas 2008). State crime is thus acknowledged as organized and collective activity in international criminal law with the guardianship of the international community established in regional and international human rights regimes.

Guardianship by both civil society and the international human rights regime seem to be reasonably effective. We have abundant anecdotal evidence on the control of state crime by the media and whistle-blowers from the Watergate affair in the United States in the 1970s, up to Edward Snowdon and his disclosures about the surveillance practices of the National Security Agency in 2013. More systematic evidence is available for the impact of regional and international human rights regimes. Kathryn Sikkink (2011) showed for Latin America that state violence was significantly reduced since the 1980s when the Latin American human rights regime was established and its institutions started to work. Indeed, Latin America is the only global region where unlawful state violence decreased over the past decades, even if still remaining at high levels (Karstedt 2014). Europe provides the other exemplary case of the impact of regional and international human rights instruments on the level of state-organized violence. After half a century of massive state violence, culminating in genocide, Europe established its regional human rights regime as early as in the 1950s. European states adopted a supranational legal and normative order that was crucially based on the principles of human rights and less on conventions of sovereignty. These principles were strengthened after the end of the Cold War, with new membership criteria, instruments, and programs for democratic and legal reform, aid in the Central and Eastern European countries, and the promotion of international and transitional justice procedures. With the European Convention for the Prevention of Torture and Inhuman or Degrading Treatment or Punishment, and the European Committee for the Prevention of Torture (1987/ 1989) the EU created normative and procedural instruments that had a powerful impact on criminal justice institutions. Presently, Europe is the global region with the lowest level of illegal state violence, and East and Central European states have continuously and successfully reduced the level of such violent state crimes, mainly committed by and within criminal justice agencies (Karstedt 2014).

IV. The Paradox of State Strength and Weakness: Institutional and Control Balance

The Janus-face of contemporary states and their institutions and governments shows itself in their capacities to protect the lives, rights, and properties of citizens and equally violate, confiscate, and destroy them. Strong states make good as well as incapacitated guardians against organized state crime within their realm. Weak or failing states in contrast nearly always turn out to be incapable guardians of the security, rights, and property of their citizens. Among the 20 most failing states according to the Failed States Index (2005–2009), all with the exception of three ranked among the 25 percent of countries where illegal state violence was highest (Karstedt 2013b); in this group corruption also reached highest levels (Karstedt 2011a). In order to unravel this paradox of state strength and weakness, we have to disaggregate the machinery of the state and government into the different institutions that constitute it and to analyze the balance of controls and accountability through which these institutions are connected. A shown above, this will include the institutions of civil society and their relations to state and government.

Where states fail in controlling one type of organized state crime—corruption—they also fail in controlling organized state violence, as the strong correlation between the two types demonstrates: where unlawful state violence is high, so is the level of corruption (Karstedt 2014, p. 147). This applies to European countries as well as worldwide (Jorgensen 2009). If state strength, complemented by civil society weakness, is responsible for unlawful state violence and if state weakness complemented by strong and vested interest groups is the driving factor behind high levels of corruption, how are these two "institutional imbalances" (Karstedt 2010) linked?

Criminologist Charles Tittle (1995) identifies two types of control imbalances, a "control deficit" and a "control surplus," where both are conducive to different types of deviant and criminal behavior. If state agencies and actors have a massive control surplus, as they would have in repressive and authoritarian regimes, we assume that levels of illegal state violence are high. Such a control surplus of the state is achieved by reducing the control level of other actors, either of other institutions, like the judiciary, or of civil society actors. In order to reduce the control level of the latter, strategies of spreading fear through political terror, disappearances, and cutting off the targeted individuals or groups of victims from all support and communication in society are prevalent (Karstedt 2011b). State-organized violence itself is seminal in creating the situation in which it can be excessively used, thus starting vicious cycles of state violence. In generating such a control surplus actors on all levels of the state hierarchy become involved in encouraging, permitting and legitimizing the use of violence and illegal force. Authoritarian regimes certainly are more conducive to such massive use of illegal force. However, as Caldeira and Holston (1999) point out, in transitions to democracy, and in "disjunctive" democracies like Brazil, beneath the cover of the electoral democratic state institutional spaces open up where unlawful violence thrives on the control surplus of confined organizational cultures, in particular in the criminal justice system.

In contrast, pervasive corruption occurs where the state and its institutions have a deficit in controlling powerful groups that are capable of capturing these institutions and use them for their own benefit and vested interests rather than the common good (Hellman, Jones, and Kaufmann 2000). Capture affects a range of institutions and all levels of the state hierarchy. Starting at the lower levels, police exchange their powers against bribes, and low-level bureaucrats offer services only in exchange for payment and favors. At the highest level, government officials abuse their positions of power in issuing government contracts, and they are in a position to influence prosecutions and courts thus curbing the independence of the judiciary. Consequently, changes in these institutions that shield them from undue influence by politicians and higher level bureaucrats can reduce such control imbalances, as demonstrated by a surge in high level corruption cases in the courts of France and Italy at the beginning of the 1990s.

As the empirical relationship between the two most prevalent types of organized state crime—illegal violence and corruption—suggests, control deficits and surpluses are coexistent. They are located in different state institutions and agencies and vary according to the extent of control, guardianship, and accountability that these institutions can exert and the power they have to fulfill their tasks. Control imbalances that generate violent as well as predatory state crime should be found where power differentials within society, as, for example, between elites and other social groups and between civil society actors and the state are significant. Such differences in power and high levels of inequality are conducive to capture of the state and its institutions by powerful groups. Inequality therefore is a predictor of both state violence and corruption (Karstedt 2011b).

Institutional imbalance and weakness are root causes of violent and predatory state crime. State violence and corruption are increasing where the state is incapable of implementing rule of law principles and enforcing these against its own agencies as well as against powerful groups. External and internal human rights monitoring requires a balance of control and institutions within the institutional ensemble and between the state and civil society in order to effectively enforce within-state controls and domestic compliance with human rights obligations. It can be equally assumed for corruption that powerful groups are not only capable of capturing state agencies for their own interests but that they also are capable of interfering with rule of law procedures and monitoring agencies. Likewise, organizational cultures, such as within the police and at lower ranks of state agencies, create a pervasive climate of institutional capture by the professionals who govern it (Klockars, Kutnjak, and Haberfeld 2004). Within such institutional contexts, cooperation and networks emerge that are the seedbed of organized state crime, both violent and predatory.

Failed states epitomize the weakness of state and government, the weakness of its institutions, and severe imbalances between its institutions. As the power of state institutions and governments unravels, power and authority are dispersed and diluted, thus creating an anarchic environment in which different groups and institutions can take advantage of dissolving state power and strive for unmitigated and unrestricted power for themselves. The weakness of the failing state thus gives rise to organized state crime mainly in the pursuit and consolidation of power but is also driven by profit and monetary motives, as well as security needs. Its institutions are defined by a progressive deterioration of public services; its security apparatus increasingly operates as a "state within state," and protective of itself, including the police and the armed forces; powerful groups compete for and achieve the capture of state and economic institutions for exploitation (Karstedt 2011a). In this context of state weakness and loss of power, all types of organized state crimes thrive, often in cooperation with organized crime groups (Nordstrom 2007).

Failed states provide a fertile ground for classic "protection rackets" by state agents, different groups and organized crime alike, thus giving rise to organized state crime that combines all characteristic features of organized crime. As a result, failed states have highest levels of one-sided violence by state agencies as well as by nonstate actors (Human Security Report Project 2012), including mass atrocities that can amount to genocide and politicide with the involvement of state agents and government.

Paradoxically, where the state and its institutions are weakest, repressive state crime reaches extremely high levels. Particularly the security forces collude with organized crime and engage in their criminal activities in pursuit of power in the most violent ways, including massive human rights abuses. Violence becomes predatory at the hands of competing groups and state agents. Notably, Esty and his colleagues in their second report on Failed States (1998) found that genocide and politicide are more often the consequence of state failure rather than its starting points.

V. Controlling State-Organized Crime

"The Underworld depends on the Upperworld. We need to specify how; then we can begin to do something about it" (Marcus Felson, quoted in Edwards and Levi 2008, p. 378). In the upper world of politics, power, and elite groups, we find no less motivation, incentives, and opportunities to engage in organized crime activities than within other settings or social structures that are conducive to more traditional organized crime activity. Contemporary organized crime and state-organized crime have much in common in terms of the nature of collaborative relationships and networks, the "joint criminal enterprise" in which they engage, and the settings in which they thrive. The machinery and institutional settings of contemporary states constitute the "ecosystem" (Felson) of state-organized crime, and its basic structures are found in democratic and nondemocratic regimes alike. Modern states and governments are characterized by paradoxes: they are simultaneously strong enough to protect the rights of citizens and to violate them; the means by which they increase security of one group of citizens decreases the security of others; they are the guardians of rights, and implement them, and simultaneously these need to be defended against them. However, democracies have comparative advantages in their capabilities of guardianship against state crime, in particular mechanisms of institutional accountability, independence of institutions, and active civil societies. This does not prohibit or deter representatives of democratic states and governments from engaging in and with organized crime activities (van Duyne 1997), but may act as a pattern of containment and an instrument of restriction.

Given the paradox of the state as guardian against its own crimes, capable guardians will be strong and independent institutions, situated within the state machinery itself, outside in civil society or in supranational regimes and its bodies. The importance of strong institutions is emphasized by the extreme of the failed state and its utmost institutional weakness and imbalances. Both, state-organized predatory violence and violent predation thrive in the ecosystem of failed states. This institutional perspective provides a synthesis between a routine activity and structural approach to the control of state-organized crime (see Edwards and Levi 2008). The institutional setting of the polity channels motives and incentives in the pursuit of power and gains for different social groups. It also establishes guardianship and capacities to regulate, audit, monitor, and police illegal activities by representative of the states. In sum, the institutional setting and structures constitute the "ecosystem" for state-organized crime. Such a perspective neither falls into the trap of moralistic accounts of a morally and politically decayed political landscape nor into the abyss of conspiracy theories that are so prevalent in narratives of state crime.

On all accounts and counts, state-organized violence globally has had millions of victims in the past decades since World War II alone. Presently, the most serious state-sponsored and state-organized violence decreases globally, and so do the numbers of victims of all state-sponsored violence (see Karstedt 2012b). As global regions, Europe and recently Latin America have been successful in controlling unlawful violence by the state and crimes against humanity (Sikkink 2011; Karstedt 2014). There can be little doubt however that the threat from state-organized and state-sponsored unlawful violence dwarfs the threat of infiltration of states and governments from organized crime groups. The state is rather an actor in organized crime than its victim.

Notes

* I am grateful to the Regulatory Institutions Network, Australian National University, and the Institute of Criminology, University of Cambridge for Visiting Fellowships in 2013. I have a lot of gratitude for Lucy Strang, Brussels, and Johanna Schönhöfer, University of Leeds, for assisting in the research.

1. The Failed State Index (FSI) is a composite index comprising 12 dimensions, each ranking from 0 (low) to 10 (high), with a maximum of 120 assigned to total failure (for a detailed account of the construction of the Failed States Index, see Karstedt 2011a). Fund for Peace: Failed State Index; http://ffp.statesindex.org/.
2. The Nazi-state of Germany is exemplary of an autocratic state with organizations and institutions competing for power, and continuously involved in power struggles. This turned out to be advantageous for the defendants at the IMT, who denied having command or any other responsibility for the crimes that the regime had committed. U.S. Prosecutor Justice Jackson famously commented that he had never seen a government like this where obviously no one had responsibility for anything (Taylor 1992).

References

Block, Alan, and Griffin, Sean P. 1997. "The Teamsters, the White House, the Labour Department." *Crime, Law and Social Change* 26(3): 1–30.
Caldeira, Teresa, and Holston, James. 1999. "Democracy and Violence in Brazil." *Comparative Studies in Society and History* 41(4): 691–729.
Cassese, A. 2008. *International Criminal Law*. Oxford: Oxford University Press.
Chambliss, William J. 1989. "State-Organized Crime." *Criminology* 27(2): 183–208.
Chambliss, William J. 1995. "Commentary by William Chambliss." *Society of Social Problems Newsletter* 26(2): 9.
Choo, Kim-Kwang Raymond, and Peter Grabosky. 2014. "Cyber Crime." In *The Oxford Handbook of Organized Crime*, edited by Letizia Paoli. New York: Oxford University Press.

Council of Europe, Committee on Legal Affairs and Human Rights. 2006. *Alleged Secret Detentions and Unlawful Inter-state Transfers Involving Council of Europe Member States.* Strasbourg: Council of Europe, Parliamentary Assembly.

Doig, Alan. 2011. *State Crime.* Oxford, New York: Willan.

Drumbl, Mark A. 2009. "International Criminal Law: Taking Stock of a Busy Decade." *Melbourne Journal of International Law* 10: 38–45.

Edwards, Adam, and Michael Levi. 2008. "Researching the Organization of Serious Crimes." *Criminology and Criminal Justice* 8(4): 363–388.

Esty, Daniel C., Jack A. Goldstone, Ted R. Gurr, Barbara Harff, Marc Levy, Geoffrey D. Dabelko, and Pamela T. Surko. 1998. *State Failure Task Force Report.* Phase II Findings. Working Papers. 31 July 1998. University of Maryland.

Europol. 2008. OCTA 2008. *EU Organised Crime Threat Assessment.* The Hague.

Europol. 2009. OCTA 2009. *EU Organised Crime Threat Assessment.* The Hague.

Europol. 2011. OCTA 2011. *EU Organised Crime Threat Assessment.* The Hague.

Europol. 2013. SOCTA 2009. *EU Serious and Organised Crime Threat Assessment.* The Hague.

Felson, Marcus. 2009. "The Natural History of Extended Co-offending." *Trends in Organized Crime* 12(2): 159–165.

Friedrichs, David O. 1996. *Trusted Criminals: White Collar Crime in Contemporary Society.* Belmont CA: Wadsworth.

Friedrichs, David O. 2009/2010. "On Resisting State Crime: Conceptual and Contextual Issues." *Social Justice* 36(3): 4–27.

Fund for Peace. 2006–2012. *Failed State Index.* http://ffp.statesindex.org/.

Green, Penny, and Tony Ward. 2000. "State Crime, Human Rights and the Limits of Criminology." *Social Justice* 27(1): 101–115.

Green, Penny, and Tony Ward. 2004. *State Crime: Governments, Violence and Corruption.* London: Pluto Press.

Grabosky, Peter. 2013. "Organized Cybercrime and National Security." In *Information Society and Cybercrime: Challenges for Criminology and Criminal Justice,* edited by the Korean Institute of Criminology and International Society of Criminology, Seoul.

Hagan, John, and Joshua Kaiser. 2011. "The Displaced and Dispossessed of Darfur: Explaining the Sources of a Continuing State-Led Genocide." *British Journal of Sociology* 62(1): 1–25.

Hagan, John, and Wynona Rymond-Richmond. 2009. *Darfur and the Crime of Genocide.* Cambridge: Cambridge University Press.

Hellman, Joel S., Geraint Jones, and Daniel Kaufmann. 2000. "Seize the State, Seize the Day": State Capture, Corruption and the Influence of Transition. Policy Research Working Paper 2444, The World Bank, Washington.

Hess, Henner. 1998. *Mafia & Mafiosi: Origin, Power and Myth.* New York: New York University Press.

Human Security Report Project. 2012. *Human Security Report 2012.* Simon Fraser University. Vancouver, Canada.

Ishay, Micheline R. 2004. "What Are Human Rights? Six Historical Controversies." *Journal of Human Rights* 3(3): 359–371.

Jorgensen, Nina (2000): *The Responsibility of States for International Crimes.* Oxford: Oxford University Press.

Jorgensen, Nick. 2009. "Impunity and Oversight: When Do Governments Police Themselves." *Journal of Human Rights,* 8: 385–404.

Kalyvas, Stathis N. 2004. "The Paradox of Terrorism in Civil Wars." *The Journal of Ethics* 8(1): 97–138.

Kalyvas, Stathis N. 2006. *The Logic of Violence in Civil War*. Cambridge: Cambridge University Press.

Karstedt, Susanne. 2010. "New Institutionalism in Criminology: Approaches, Theories and Themes." In *The Sage Handbook of Criminological Theory*, edited by Eugene McLaughlin, and Tim Newburn. London: Sage.

Karstedt, Susanne. 2011a. "Exit: The State. Globalisation, State Failure and Crime." In *Comparative Criminal Justice and Globalization*, edited by David Nelken. Dartmouth: Ashgate.

Karstedt, Susanne. 2011b. "Our Sense of Justice: Values, Justice and Punishment." In *A Sparking Discipline. The Contribution of Criminology to Social Justice and Sustainable Development*, edited by Stephan Parmentier, Lode Walgrave, Ivo Aertsen, Jeroen Maesschalck and Letizia Paoli. Leuven: Leuven University Press.

Karstedt, Susanne. 2012a. "Organised Crime, Democracy and Democratization: How Vulnerable Are Democracies?" In *Organised Crime. Dark Sides of Globalization*, edited by Caroline Robertson-von-Trotha. Baden: Nomos.

Karstedt, Susanne. 2012b. "Globalization, Mass Atrocities and Genocide." In *Globalization and the Challenge to Criminology*, edited by Frances Pakes. London: Routledge.

Karstedt, Susanne. 2013a. "Contextualizing Mass Atrocity Crimes: Moving Towards a Relational Approach." *Annual Review of Law and Social Sciences* 9: 383–404.

Karstedt, Susanne. 2013b. "Does Democracy Matter for Criminologists? Situating Crime in the Institutional Context of the Polity." Presidential Panel: Situating Crime in Macro-Social and Historical Context. American Society of Criminology Annual Meeting, Atlanta, November 2013.

Karstedt, Susanne. 2014. "State Crime. The European Experience." In *The Routledge Handbook of European Criminology*, edited by Sophie Body-Gendrot, Mike Hough, Klara Kerezsi, and René Lévy. Oxford: Routledge.

Kasfir, Nelson. 2004. "Domestic Anarchy, Security Dilemmas, and Violent Predation: Causes of Failure." In *When States Fail. Causes and Consequences*, edited by Robert I. Rotberg. Princeton: Princeton University Press.

Kauzlarich, David, Christopher Mullins, and Rick Matthews. 2003. "A Complicity Continuum of State Crime." *Contemporary Justice Review: Issues in Criminal, Social and Restorative Justice* 6(3): 241–254.

Kershaw, Ian. 1992. "Improvised Genocide? The Emergence of the 'Final Solution' in the Warthegau." *Transactions of the Royal Historical Society*, 6th series, 2: 51–78.

Klockars, Carl B., Sanja Kutnjak Ivkovic, and Maria R. Haberfeld, eds. 2004. *The Contours of Police Integrity*. Thousand Oaks, London: Sage.

Kramer, Ronald, Raymond Michalowski, and Dawn Rothe. 2005. "'The Supreme International Crime': How the U.S. War in Iraq Threatens the Rule of Law." *Social Justice* 32(2): 52–81.

Lane, David. 2004. *Berlusconi's Shadow. Crime, Justice and the Pursuit of Power*. London, New York: Allen Lane.

Levi, Margaret. 2006. "Presidential Address: Why We Need a New Theory of Government." *Perspectives on Politics* 4(1): 5–19.

Meierhenrich, Jens. 2006. "Conspiracy in International Law." *Annual Review of Law and Social Sciences* 2: 341–357.

Michalowski, Raymond. (2010). "In Search of 'State and Crime' in State Crime Studies." In *State Crime in the Global Age*, edited by William J. Chambliss, Raymond Michalowski, and Ronald C. Kramer. Cullompton: Willan.

Moe, Terry M. 2005. "Power and Political Institutions." *Perspectives on Politics* 3(2): 215–233.

Nordstrom, Carolyn. 2007. *Global Outlaws*. Berkeley: University of California Press.

North, Douglass C. 1991. "Institutions." *Journal of Economic Perspectives* 5(1): 97–112.

Olson, Mancur. 1993. "Dictatorship, Democracy, and Development." *The American Political Science Review* 87(3): 567–576.

Osiel, Mark. 2009. *Making Sense of Mass Atrocity*. Cambridge: Cambridge University Press.

Paoli, Letizia. 2003. *Mafia Brotherhoods. Organized Crime, Italian Style*. New York: Oxford University Press.

Perl, Raphael. 2007. "Drug Trafficking and North Korea: Issues for U.S. Policy." Congressional Research Service, Washington, DC. http://www.fas.org/sgp/crs/row/RL32167.pdf.

Ross, Jeffrey Ian. 2010. "Introduction: Protecting Democracy by Controlling State Crime in Advanced Industrialized Countries." In *Varieties of State Crime and its Control*, edited by Jeffrey Ian Ross. Boulder, London: Lynne Rienner.

Ross, Jeffrey I., and Dawn Rothe. 2008. "Ironies of Controlling State Crime." *International Journal of Law, Crime and Justice* 36: 196–210.

Rothe, Dawn, Jeffrey, Ross C. Mullins, David Friedrichs, Raymond Michalowski, Gregg Barak, David Kauzlarich, and Ronald C. Kramer. 2009. "That Was Then, This Is Now, What About Tomorrow? Future Directions in State Crime Studies." *Critical Criminology* 17: 3–13.

Rothe, Dawn, and David O. Friedrichs. 2006. "The State of the Criminology of Crimes of the State." *Social Justice* 33(1): 147–161.

Rothenberg, Daniel. ed. 2012. *Memory of Silence. The Guatemalan Truth Commission Report*. New York: Palgrave Macmillan.

Sanford, Victoria. 2004. *Buried Secrets. Truth and Human Rights in Guatemala*. New York/London: Palgrave Macmillan.

Schabas, William A. 2008. "State Policy as an Element of International Crimes." *Journal of Criminal Law and Criminology* 98(3): 953–982.

Sikkink, Kathryn. 2011. *The Justice Cascade*. New York: W.W. Norton.

Stille, Alexander. 1995. *Excellent Cadavers. The Mafia and the Death of the First Italian Republic*. New York: Pantheon.

Sung, Hun-en. 2004. "State Failure, Economic Failure, and Predatory Organized Crime: A Comparative Analysis." *Journal of Research in Crime and Delinquency* 41(1): 111–129.

Taylor, Telford. 1992. *The Anatomy of the Nuremberg Trials. A Personal Memoir*. New York: Alfred A. Knopf.

Tilly, Charles (1997): "War Making and State Making as Organised Crime" in Charles Tilly *Roads from the Past to the Future*. 165–192. Lanham: Rowman & Littlefield.

Tittle, Charles. 1995. *Control Balance: Toward a General Theory of Deviance*. Boulder, CO: Westview.

UNODC (United Nations Office on Drugs and Crime). 2010. *The Globalization of Crime. A Transnational Organized Crime Threat Assessment*. Vienna.

Van Dijk, Jan. 2008. *The World of Crime*. Los Angeles/London: Sage.

Van Duyne, Petrus C. 1997. "Organized Crime, Corruption and Power." *Crime, Law and Social Change* 26(3): 201–238.

CHAPTER 16

....

THE SOCIAL EMBEDDEDNESS
OF ORGANIZED CRIME

....

HENK VAN DE BUNT, DINA SIEGEL, AND DAMIÁN ZAITCH

I. INTRODUCTION

ORGANIZED crime groups are often portrayed as entities that derive their strength from strong internal cohesion and an ability to conceal their illegal activities from the outside world. Criminal organizations such as the Italian and Russian mafias, the Japanese Yakuza, and the Chinese Triads are often conceived of as secret societies, with their own sacred rituals (Paoli 2008), secret codes of communication (Gambetta 2009), and verbal agreements about leadership, finances, and social control (Siegel 2005). These representations of organized crime groups strongly resemble the secret societies studied and analyzed by Georg Simmel, who focused on the internal dynamics and interrelationships within these societies.

At the same time, organized crime is a thoroughly social phenomenon. Between organized crime and the legitimate societal context, there are usually all sorts of "interfaces," and the relationships between legality and illegality are by no means necessarily antagonistic or aimed at avoiding one another. Instead of operating in a social vacuum, organized crime has a habit of interacting with its social environment. This contribution aims to develop the perspective of the social embeddedness of organized crime. We will first discuss the concept of "social embeddedness" in general terms and then apply this perspective to the areas of gender, occupation, and ethnic minorities.

II. Social Embeddedness of Organized Crime

The concept of embeddedness originated in the field of economics. It was first used many years ago by Polanyi (1944), who argued that economic behavior cannot be explained without taking into account the social and cultural framework within which this behavior is situated. Three decades later, this idea was again taken up by Granovetter (1973, 1985). Since then, there has been growing attention in the social sciences to the role of social context and social relations in the economic sphere. Explanations for economic behavior are not only sought in "physical capital" but also in terms of "social capital" (Bourdieu 1985). The insights of economic sociology can also help us better understand organized crime (Coles 2001).

Let us start with the concrete example of a network of Dutch cocaine traffickers.[1] These traffickers imported cocaine from Colombia in containers by hiding the drugs inside frozen fruit juice. Over a period of many months, dozens of kilos of cocaine were smuggled into the Netherlands. The idea was hatched in a bar where the Dutch owner of a thriving patisserie business ("the baker") got to talking to several other visitors, who listened with great interest to his stories about his legal trade contacts with Colombia. The baker happened to be a regular importer of frozen fruit juices. After several friendly meetings, the baker and his new "friends" (who already had drug trafficking experience) decided to cooperate in importing cocaine by using the baker's trade routes as well as his Columbian contacts.

This use of an existing trade channel is an illustration of almost literal embeddedness. The trafficking of cocaine was embedded in a legitimate structure and can therefore be called "structural" embeddedness. Structural embeddedness should be distinguished from "relational" embeddedness (Granovetter 1992). Relational embeddedness refers to the concrete social relations and contacts between individuals in a certain context or network. In our case, the conversations between the baker and his future partners in crime started out as ordinary small talk in a bar. Structural embeddedness relates to the institutional aspects of the network: the bar, the trade route, and the bakery.

Social embeddedness means that existing relations and structures are not only the breeding ground for criminal activities, but also determine the form these activities can take. Without the presence of the bar as a social meeting place, the baker would never have come into contact with criminals, and without these contacts with his bar friends, he would never have become a financier of cocaine trafficking.

The structural side of social embeddedness can be analyzed on different levels. The example of the baker illustrates embeddedness on a micro level, with a criminal operation revolving around a specific trade contact and a local bar. However, embeddedness can also be analyzed at the meso/macro level. Criminal activities can be structurally embedded in places (airports, seaports), branches of industry (transport, prostitution, catering), occupations, social communities (neighborhoods, ethnic groups), prevailing gender relations, and public administration.

For example, in nations lacking an effective political structure, so-called failed states, organized crime is bound to be embedded in society in ways that differ from countries where the power of the state is effective and experienced as legitimate. In failed states, the members of criminal groups will take advantage of the absence of formal state power by focusing on duties neglected by the state, such as offering protection (Gambetta 1988). In modern Western states with an adequate infrastructure (a high level of services, a functioning road system, a high education level), organized crime will seek to take advantage of the opportunities offered by this infrastructure. The port of Rotterdam, for example, the largest European seaport, lends itself to smuggling activities. It is also the reason why organized criminality in the Netherlands (a trading nation par excellence) has all the characteristics of "transit criminality". Crime proceeds are generated not from extortion or territorial control, but from the trade in illegal goods.[2]

The relational side of social embeddedness refers to the fact that criminal cooperation does not exist in a social vacuum. Criminal activities cannot be separated from the social relations between the participants and the institutional environments in which their interactions take place. These relationships usually involve more aspects than just committing crimes. "Partners in crime" are first and foremost partners who are bound by relatively strong social ties. Criminal cooperation is usually embedded in existing friendly, familial, or work-related relationships. Collaborating in illicit operations relies heavily on mutual trust. For example, drug smugglers who get "ripped off" are not in a position to ask for police protection and neither are wealthy criminals able to initiate civil action when someone runs off with their money (Reuter 1983; Paoli 2002, p. 64; Zaitch 2005). Everything comes down to trust because there is little to no protection from opportunistic behavior. This is why criminal cooperatives are often characterized by strong internal relationships. Criminals prefer working with family members or friends in order to ensure the smooth running of their operations.

Relational embeddedness also implies the existence of social ties between criminals and persons who do not participate in criminal cooperatives but belong to the same ethnic group, neighborhood, occupation, etc. Social embeddedness of, for instance, a Nigerian criminal gang in a Nigerian community in Amsterdam means that there is an exchange of contacts: the gang members are related to local residents, with whom they maintain all sorts of friendly and economic relations. This relational embeddedness has two faces (Potillo 1998). On the one hand, the criminals can benefit from the resources of the community or local neighborhood. Local residents may act as receivers of stolen goods or contribute to the concealment of criminal activities. This is where we see the strength of social ties: strong relations can contribute to the continued existence of criminal groups (Van de Bunt and Kleemans 2007). On the other hand, strong ties can also have a limiting effect. The fully socially embedded perpetrator is the "local hero," a "respected" criminal with mostly strong ties to his own social environment. Such a person, who is by definition limited in the further expansion of his criminal activities, exemplifies the opposite of what Granovetter (1973) describes as the strength of weak ties: individuals with mostly superficial contacts may find it easier to discover new business opportunities, including criminal activities. Our baker, for instance, just happened to come into contact with people from a totally different background who put new ideas into his head: the frozen fruit juice for his bakery could also be used for cocaine smuggling. The case of the baker demonstrates an example of the strength of weak social ties.

III. Women in Organized Crime

This section focuses on the embeddedness of organized crime with regard to gender relations. Similar to kinship, friendship, and ethnicity, gender relationships can create a fertile ground for organized crime activities, ranging from the marginal involvement of women in specific activities to women occupying leading positions in international drug rings or human trafficking networks. Gender relationships reveal themselves to be valuable channels through which criminal networks can be expanded and new opportunities in illicit markets can be created.

A. Historical Sources on Gender Networks in Criminal Activities

The subject of women and crime has always fascinated criminologists (Adler 1975; Chesney-Lind 1986, 1997; Daly 1994; Chesney-Lind and Pasko 2004), but in the past 20 years, the role of women in organized crime has come particularly to the fore. The publication in 2007 of *Women and the Mafia. Female Roles in Organized Crime Structures*, edited by Giovanni Fiandaca, provided an impressive collection of essays on the history of women in the Mafia as well as comparative contributions from Latin America, Europe, and the United States. Similar to previous attempts to describe the role of women in criminal organizations (Siebert 1996; Longrigg 1998), the criminological and anthropological literature on the subject is largely based on media reports, fragments of biographies (usually of the male partners of female criminals), police files, and court proceedings.

The prevalent explanations for the involvement of women in organized crime are founded on analyses of family/gender role divisions and/or the specific structure of particular crime organizations, such as the Colombian or Mexican cartels (Campbell 2009; Carey and Cisneros 2011). Another frequently used argument in the literature explains the supposedly growing involvement of women in crime by pointing to the emancipation of women both in society in general as well as within criminal groups (Siebert 1996). Explanations such as these leave many questions unanswered, such as whether the involvement of women in organized crime activities can also be linked to their ethnic origin. For instance, why is it that Nigerian female criminals appear to be more daring and more actively involved in criminal networks than their European counterparts?

A brief search of the historical sources reveals that the supposedly passive attitude of women involved in criminal organizations does not reflect the historical truth. All over Europe and the United States we can find examples of female criminal leaders in various periods of history. Sheyndl Bljuvshtein, nicknamed Sonka Zolotaya Rutchka (Sonka, the golden hand), was one of the most admired female criminals in Russian history, despite her extremely violent actions in major Russian cities in the nineteenth century (Siegel 2005; Gilinsky 2007). Agata Galiffi, also known as "the mafia flower" or "the lady boss of all bosses," was a legendary crime boss in 1930s Argentina, who stood at the head of a criminal organization operating in Rosario, Buenos Aires, and Tucuman (Goris 1999; Rossi 2007, p. 153). We can also find examples of female criminal leaders in the Jewish underworld of New York's Lower East Side in the 1930s (Block 1977). After World War II, Yoshika Matsuda, who led the large Kanto Matsuda-gumi gang in Tokyo, and Nami Odagiri, the godmother of the Ryugaki gang in Osaka, were prominent figures in the Japanese underworld (Otomo 2007, p. 210). Their relationships with male criminals, varying from marriage and blood ties to purely business relations, provided these women with access to criminal opportunities and catapulted them to the top of criminal organizations.

B. From Recruiters to "Madams"

Despite past and present examples of women reaching the top of criminal organizations, the majority of women involved in criminal activities either occupy marginal roles or act as partners in crime with their male companions or relatives. Generally speaking, there are three categories of women involved in organized crime: "supporters," "partners in crime," and "madams." Women can be classified as *supporters* when they are subordinate to the leader of a criminal group and either under threat or "voluntarily" participate in criminal activities, for instance as drug couriers or recruiters of potential victims of women trafficking. Female offenders can be called *partners in crime* when they have a relationship with a man and cooperate with him, in principle on the basis of equality, by performing certain tasks and activities. The category "partners in crime" consists of women who voluntarily take part in the criminal activities of their partners (spouses, boyfriends, or business partners). The role of female partners can vary from a fifty-fifty division of work and profit to a managing role with the male partners occupying themselves solely with the task of providing protection through violence and intimidation. The relationships between the partners can vary from intimate to symbolic or "businesslike" (Siegel and De Blank 2010). The *madams* of the last category are female offenders who are themselves in charge of coordinating criminal activities.

In some parts of the world, women in criminal groups remain in marginal positions (Sicily, Eastern Europe), while in other regions they actively participate in criminal activities and sometimes climb to the top of criminal organizations (Latin America, West Africa). Their positions and involvement in criminal enterprises mirror the gender relationships in the broader society where women occupy a wide range of functions and roles (from housewife to top executive or politician).

The relational embeddedness of organized crime in society is also manifested in the intermediary role women sometimes play by building connections to the legitimate world on behalf of their criminal spouses. The mistresses and wives of crime bosses are often actresses, models or popular singers who are constantly invited to appear at functions, parties, television shows, and charitable events. A well-known example of the "glamorous wife" is that of Ceca, the wife of the late Serbian crime boss Željko Ražnatović, alias Arkan. In this context, the role of women in organized crime shows the embeddedness of gender relationships in the broader society and demonstrates the embeddedness argument with regard to gender: organized crime is not exclusively a man's world.

C. Taking Over Men's Positions

When the husbands are in prison, their spouses sometimes take over the role of criminal entrepreneur, and in this position they are not averse to using threats of physical violence. This kind of behavior is well documented in the literature on the wives of Italian Mafiosi. As a result of the intensified fight against the mafia and of the use of *pentiti*,[3] many mafia members have been imprisoned, and their wives and daughters had no choice but to look after their affairs.[4] Here we see family businesses in which everyone fulfils their own task. In the case of Italy, enhanced law enforcement actions against the Cosa Nostra and the 'Ndrangheta in the late 1990s to early 2000s led to the rapid emergence of women in the criminal arena. A great many male members of these criminal organizations were arrested and convicted to long prison sentences (Paoli 2008). As a result, the sisters, wives, and mothers of these imprisoned Mafiosi emerged to take over their activities. Some of these women have become major criminal figures and leaders of criminal clans.[5] Nevertheless, by and large, the Cosa Nostra and the 'Ndrangheta are still male organizations, even though women are increasingly participating in running illegal businesses. In this respect, the gender relations in organized crime replicate the dominant gender relations in broader society.

D. Embeddedness in the Sex Industry

In contrast to the women in the Italian mafia who take on the duties of their imprisoned husbands and sons, Nigerian and Ghanaian female traffickers take the initiative themselves: they set up contacts, plan operations, and use every opportunity to make money. Here we find another example of the embeddedness of organized crime in gender relationships. Since the mid-1980s, African women have managed to obtain leading roles in criminal organizations engaged in large-scale human trafficking and they have left their male competitors behind. The phenomenon of female women traffickers can be explained by socioeconomic developments in the position of women in their native countries on the one hand, and by the opportunities for making money in Europe on the other hand. Economic necessity forced women from various parts of Africa to go and look for opportunities in Europe. They came to Europe in the 1980s as seasonal laborers looking for work in the tomato fields in Italy or as prostitutes with previous experience in their own countries. These women discovered that there was a great demand for African girls. Working as prostitutes themselves, they started recruiting other girls and were able to convince male sponsors to invest in the extremely lucrative sex industry (Monzini 2005, p. 117; Siegel 2007). By using their social ties and the existing structures (the local sex industry, trade channels from Nigeria to Western Europe), some of these prostitutes were able to settle as "madams" in Europe. These women forge relationships with local actors in the sex industry such as pimps, brothel owners, other Nigerian madams, local drivers, and bodyguards. They take advantage of the existing sex industry facilities to guarantee their women protection, a place to work, and a regular supply of clients.

Today, Nigerian female criminals have become associated with women trafficking. They are in charge of fully fledged criminal organizations: they give orders to subordinates, coordinate the trafficking, control the prostitutes, and manage the finances. The networks they lead can vary from small groups with only a few members to sizable, internationally operating organizations (Monzini 2005; Siegel 2009).

Organized crime was and still is dominated by men, the same as it is in the outside world. Every now and then, remarkable women will make it to the top. They will always be remembered because they are exceptional. As a rule, however, women play a subservient role, even when they replace their partners when they are in prison. The above-mentioned examples of the Sicilian mafia and the 'Ndrangheta reflect the traditional gender relations in Italian society. But there are also women who are successful in seizing opportunities in new markets. Thanks to their knowledge, skills, and experience acquired in previous occupations, they are able to develop into "madams."

IV. Occupational Embeddedness

In this section we focus on occupations, work relations, and work settings that can serve as a breeding ground for organized crime activities. There are various ways in which organized crime is embedded in occupations, as each occupation provides different opportunities to commit and conceal criminal activities.

A. Occupations as Opportunity Structures

In some cases, the link between organized crime and occupations is easily explained: certain occupations provide their practitioners with ideal opportunities to engage in organized crime, as demonstrated by the example of the baker (section 2) who discovered that his licit activities provided a golden opportunity to smuggle drugs. Benson, Madensen, and Eck explain how certain occupations provide opportunity structures to commit crimes (2009, p. 108 ff). They distinguish between three aspects of the opportunity structure: nodes, paths, and edges. *Nodes* refer to the social contacts established during the course of a career. In addition to their position in a work-related social network, the practitioners of certain occupations have also gained valuable knowledge on how to follow established procedures and where to find the right people to achieve certain goals (*paths*). In the exercise of his profession, an actor may also run into so-called *edges*, the gray areas that offer opportunities to commit crimes. This usually involves activities insufficiently supervised by others.

By offering a combination of nodes, paths, and edges, some occupations provide excellent opportunities for organized crime activities, particularly in relation to the provision of illegal goods and services. For instance, knowledge of international shipping routes, international road transport, import and export routines, and the social contacts established on these routes are as useful to criminal entrepreneurs as they are to legitimate businessmen. Some of these businessmen may be inclined to use the opportunity structure to make a complete transition from legal to illegal business dealings. Others may use the opportunities to double their income by continuing to perform legal activities while also using the legal trade channels as a cover-up for illegal activities. In this gray area, part-time criminals can smuggle relatively small amounts of drugs in containers full of legitimate commodities.

Occupations involving mobility, transport, or logistics can be a fertile breeding ground for transnational smuggling activities. These occupations not only provide opportunities for smuggling but also for the concealment of illegal activities. For instance, someone with legitimate reasons to travel frequently rarely evokes suspicion. This is not just about the occupations per se but rather about their intersections with legitimate activities such as the transport of goods, the transhipment of goods in ports and airports, the crossing of European Union borders, and so on. Seaports, customs offices, and transport firms are places where we may expect to find such "structural" embeddedness of organized crime.

B. Embeddedness as a Strategy

In the Western world, there are basically two types of organized crime (Paoli 2002). In the United States and Italy, there are criminal groups who try to bring specific sectors or territories under their dominion through corruption or threats of violence or by infiltrating local elites. They offer "regulation" or "protection" in exchange for money, but what they are really engaged in is extortion. The second type of organized crime is aimed at the provision of illegal goods and services; these perpetrators derive their position and income from catering to existing societal needs. Both these forms of organized crime are embedded in different types of occupations. In the previous subsection, we discussed the embeddedness of organized crime groups engaged in the provision of illegal goods and services, more specifically in smuggling activities.

In the literature on the "Italian American" type of organized crime, we find completely different forms of embeddedness, namely in government institutions (customs, police), societal institutions (politics, trade unions), and branches of industry such as the construction industry, the clothing industry, the waste disposal industry, etc. (Massari 2003). Time and again, embeddedness is employed as a strategy to weaken these institutions from within. In the absence of effective social control, criminal organizations are often able to insert their own regulatory mechanisms. In these cases organized crime manipulated its social environment to fit the needs of organized crime. Embeddedness has, as it were, become a means to establish dominion over businesses or government agencies. This strategy is accomplished by influencing ("buying") auditors, lorry drivers, internal security personnel, property developers, aldermen, etc. By colluding with or corrupting these functionaries criminal organizations are able to manage the social environment. An example of this is the role of organized crime in the awarding of public tenders. In some parts of Southern Italy no government contract is awarded without mafia groups having a say in the matter and taking a percentage of the money as a "fee" (Savona 2010). These groups play a decisive role in the cartel agreements between companies (Gambetta and Reuter 1995; Paoli 2003). They are so deeply embedded in the business world that they can claim this role. Without such a far-reaching embeddedness it would be impossible for criminal groups to play this role. In other parts of Western Europe organized crime is not embedded in its social environment to such a far-reaching extent. Cartels do exist in Western Europe, for instance in the construction industry in the Netherlands, as was revealed in 2002 by the findings of a parliamentary inquiry in the Netherlands. Thousands of construction firms were shown to be involved in illegal price and market fixing, but it was concluded that organized crime did not play any role in the arrangement and enforcement of the cartel's agreements (Van de Bunt 2008b). As mentioned above, social embeddedness determines the form of criminality. But what comes first: the embeddedness determining the form or the form of criminality determining the embeddedness? One thing is certain: organized crime in most West European countries appears to be primarily focused on illegal trade and this requires a different kind of embeddedness than that of criminal groups deriving their profits from extortion and dominion.

V. Ethnic Embeddedness

A final example of social embeddedness can be found in cases in which ethnic minorities (whether first-generation immigrants or their second- or third-generation descendents) are involved in organized crime. The link between organized crime and ethnic minorities has been extensively researched and theorized (Ianni and Reuss-Ianni 1972; Ruggiero 1996; Bovenkerk 2001; Paoli and Reuter 2008). Research on the links between ethnic minorities or immigrant groups and organized crime include a vast range of studies.[6] These studies, together with other contributions on specific activities and characteristics[7] explore and discuss how ethnic minorities or immigrant groups use violence, secrecy, trust, kinship, ethnicity, cultural codes, reputations, or economic and political resources when they engage in organized crime activities.

Despite the variety of methodologies followed and arguments put forward on the above-mentioned issues, all authors show, sometimes implicitly, that criminal activities of these ethnic minorities do not take place in a social vacuum or in a parallel, underground, secretive, or "external" reality. On the contrary, researchers offer plenty of evidence that the (illegal) activities and transactions of these groups are socially embedded in various ways. In fact, the notion of social embeddedness has been, particularly in the field of economic sociology, extensively researched, theorized, and applied to immigrant groups and "ethnic enclaves" to understand the nature of informal markets and the different ways in which immigrants are incorporated or assimilated into local arrangements (Portes and Sensenbrenner 1993; Portes 1995; Waldinger 1995).

When we analyze the ways in which ethnic minorities involved in organized crime embed their activities in broader social arrangements, we find that they maintain, establish, cultivate, or negotiate material and symbolic ties (1) with their own (national, ethnic, language) communities (both locally and overseas), (2) with local, mainstream "native" actors or groups, and (3) with other immigrant groups (locally and abroad).

A. Social Embeddedness in Communities

Part of the strength of ethnic minorities in organized crime activities lies in the fact that they are able to mobilize internal resources and relations, both material and symbolic, that grant them a comparative advantage to successfully conduct their (illegal) transactions.

The use of kinship, family, and locality ties, more than ethnicity per se, has consistently been found across all ethnic minorities and immigrant groups, providing a fertile ground for "bounded solidarity," enforceable trust, cooperation, loyalty, and secrecy needed to protect and enforce illegal operations.[8] This form of social embeddedness can take several forms across groups, from an "instrumental," pragmatic use of blood and artificial kinship by, for instance, Colombians (Zaitch 2002) to stronger "ethnic" lines based on tribal affiliation, as in the case of Nigerians (Carling 2006; Oboh 2011), or relying on large extended families, as in the case of Albanians or Kurds (Bovenkerk and Yesilgöz 2007; Arsovska 2009).

Many ethnic minorities successfully involved in illegal transactions are able to hide, disguise, or mix them within a wider range of illegal or informal but mainly legal activities and businesses of the group. Commercial or political diasporas, particularly transnational ethnic enclaves or trading, middlemen minorities, have played a central role in hosting cross-border (illegal) production, smuggling and distribution of (illegal) goods and services, as it has been for example the case of Cubans in Florida (Saenz Rovner

2008), Jews in Antwerp (Siegel 2008), Nigerians in China (Oboh 2011), or Chinese in American Chinatowns (Chin 2000). The symbiotic and parasitical use of own "ethnic" businesses is widespread and includes in many countries the use of restaurants, bars, discotheques, telephone and internet businesses, informal money transfer offices (underground banking), travel agencies, export-import companies, etc.

This is also true for large old and new immigrant groups mainly consisting of migratory blue-collar workers who do not form commercial diasporas and do not develop own ethnic entrepreneurship, but instead are incorporated in the formal and informal economy as industrial or service workers. In these cases, usually involving both first and second generation immigrants, a large number of visible immigrants (mostly experiencing social deprivation) host/embed illegal transactions conducted by a rather small group, often around local, street-level, visible illegal markets. This kind of social embeddedness includes cases such as cocaine trafficking and smuggling by Mexicans in California (Campbell 2009), heroin trafficking by Turks in the Netherlands (Bovenkerk and Yesilgöz 2007), advanced fees scams by Nigerians in Britain (Carling 2006), street drug retail by North Africans in France (Lalam 2004), or extortion by Italians and Irish in Chicago during the days of Prohibition (Bovenkerk 2001).

Another important source of social embeddedness of illegal transactions by ethnic minorities belongs to the realm of geopolitics. Cases of this kind involve at least two types of (overlapping) immigrant groups. First, we have immigrants who come from production or transit areas from where illegal goods (drugs, etc.), services (prostitution), or people (human smuggling and trafficking) originate. Their comparative advantage lies in their privileged access to key actors, commodities, and resources, including corruption. We can think here of Colombians (cocaine production), Albanians and Turks (Balkan Route), Mexicans and Antilleans (cocaine transit), or Nigerians (prostitution, fraud, cocaine transit). A second group of immigrants whose involvement in crime can be explained by geopolitical factors come from border areas, peripheral regions, often economically depressed and a site of lawlessness, rebelliousness, war, banditry, and piracy (Bovenkerk 2001, p. 116). These regions usually show strong autonomy from central political powers, they are in the hands of outlaw (but locally legitimate) power brokers or are located in fragile or failed states. Classic examples cover very different regions of the world including Sicily, Corsica, Malta, the Rif Mountains in Morocco, the South-East Asian Golden Triangle, the Yunnan province (China), Ireland, Galicia (Spain), the Kashmir region (India and Pakistan), Kurdistan (Turkey and Iraq), Sierra Leone, Chechnya, Somalia, El Salvador, the Balkans, or Baluchistan (Pakistan).[9] In some cases, ethnic minorities originating from these areas enjoy political protection from own local leaders (warlords, dictators, local Mafiosi, corrupt politicians, secret services, etc.) and their illegal activities serve their political interests and purposes. Some examples involve Sicilian or Corsican Mafiosi, Lao heroin traffickers, Moroccan hashish entrepreneurs, or Balkan arms traders. In other cases, migrant groups are precisely engaged in political conflicts—or war—against the central government or neighboring countries, and they can use the illegal profits to further support their cause, as in the case of Irish, Chechnyan, Kurdish, or Kashmiri migrants (Bovenkerk 2001; Bovenkerk et al. 2003). In still other cases, migrants involved in crime originate in lawless regions or fragile states, as it is the case of many Salvadorian gangs (*maras*) operating in the United States and Central America, or Somali human smugglers active in Europe.

B. Social Embeddedness in Other (Foreign) Groups or Networks

Immigrants engaged in cross border crime not only rely on their own ethnic, national or language group to facilitate illegal business, but they also establish "weaker" but very fruitful ties (Granovetter 1973) with other illegal entrepreneurs either from abroad or belonging to other minorities. First, all reviewed research indicates that organized crime is strongly interethnic and intraethnic and that part of the competitive advantage of some groups lies in their network of international contacts and their capacity to mobilize them.[10] This is, for example, the case of Nigerian entrepreneurs, with contacts (and mobility) stretching from China and Britain to South Africa and Brazil (Oboh 2011). The same can be argued about Dutch illegal entrepreneurs: neither large in numbers nor with high profiles (no violent reputation), they have been (historically) able to reach and trade with all sorts of commercial diasporas and posts all over the world (Fijnaut et al. 1998).

It has also been argued by many authors that "brokerage" is an essential feature of organized crime. Blok (1974) describes how Sicilian Mafiosi were in fact successful "power brokers" between different social groups, while others have emphasized the key role played by some individuals and minority groups (even entire ethnic enclaves) as intermediates or "trade brokers" in illegal transactions (Bovenkerk 1995; Zaitch 2002; Morselli 2005). La Bella Bettien, for example, was a Dutch female broker who managed in the late 1980s to function as intermediary between Colombian and Italian drug entrepreneurs based in the Netherlands (Bovenkerk 1995). Cases of "ethnic" brokerage involve some immigrant groups living in transit countries, such as Nigerians in Brazil, Colombians in the Dutch Antilles, or Russians in Poland.

Next to engaging with other local or foreign groups as business partners or brokers, ethnic minorities involved in organized crime also heavily rely on them as (international) service providers, facilitators, and customers. Among goods and services provided/sold by legal and illegal foreign entrepreneurs we can mention arms, waste disposal, chemical precursors, contract killers, investment opportunities, or illegal workers (Ruggiero 2000; Passas 2003). Examples include Colombians in the Netherlands contracting professional killers from Yugoslavia (Zaitch 2002), Chinese in Europe smuggling immigrants from all over Asia, Russians in South Spain providing business opportunities to British or Dutch criminals, etc. Other cases can also be found when examining international women trafficking and smuggling networks: Albanian traffickers moving Moldavian or Romanian women to Italy or the Netherlands, Turkish criminals exploiting Bulgarian women in Rotterdam, Nigerian "madams" smuggling women from Ghana or Liberia to Europe, etc. (Carling 2006; Siegel 2007; Becucci 2008; Arsovska 2009).

C. Social Embeddedness in Local Actors, Structures, and Arrangements

A third form of social embeddedness takes place when ethnic minorities involved in organized crime establish parasitic and symbiotic relations (Passas 2003) with local actors and structures (both legal and illegal) from mainstream society. In fact, it can be argued that "ethnic" organized crime has better chances to succeed in contexts where it is able to use local economic infrastructure, receive social acceptance, enjoy some kind of political protection, profit from local technological resources (mainly communication), and/or culturally adapt to the demands of the local context.

The strong links with mainstream economic activity and actors are well documented by all existing research on organized crime and include the use of local import businesses, hotels, restaurants, bars, airports, seaports, transport companies, or financial businesses. Zaitch (2002) found not only Dutch Colombian "mixed couples" in the cocaine business in the Netherlands but also many other "Colombian ties" with the port of Rotterdam or Schiphol airport. As Bovenkerk (2001, p. 119) explains, organized crime minorities flourish around "the ports with well-known underworld traditions such as Marseilles, Hamburg, Odessa, Alexandria, Shanghai, Sydney and New York." Local markets and businesses that use or depend on migrant labor (construction industry, job contractor companies, prostitution, intensive agriculture) or are cash intensive (gambling industry, hotels, catering business) have traditionally been linked in one way or the other with "ethnic" organized crime.

Reviewing the conditions under which transplanted "mafias" can succeed, Federico Varese argues that "the response of the local population (both criminal and law-abiding) to the newly arrived mafia is key to the success, or otherwise, of transplantation" (Varese 2006, p. 419). He analyzes how the local demand for protection works in the cases of the 'Ndrangheta in Verona and the Russian Solntsevo crime group in Budapest.

In many countries, another important dimension in the social embeddedness of ethnic organized crime is the political one: to what extent are these organizations able to enjoy protection (or at least indifference) from local state actors, including politicians, policemen, judges, prosecutors, customs officers, control authorities, etc. While criminal groups might be looking for protection, impunity, security, intelligence, information, money, or assistance, state actors (both politicians and law enforcement agents) are usually interested in money for personal or political purposes, services, favors, information, intelligence, violence, or votes (Godson 2003, p. 9). Social embeddedness in political structures can take the form of passive or active corruption, collaboration, collusion, co-optation, or funding (Passas 2003). The so-called political-criminal nexus (Godson 2003) seems to work differently in various contexts, but in general we can argue that political embeddedness is stronger or even only available for native, powerful mainstream organized crime. However, in many countries particular ethnic minorities may constitute an electoral force due to demographics or economic power, and enjoy political protection for their illegal businesses and activities. Historical cases include Italians in New York, Indian immigrants in Suriname, or Lebanese immigrants in Argentina.

Another way in which immigrant groups involved in organized crime establish a strong link with their environment is through the use and development of particular technological resources. The range of information and communication technologies daily used to conduct illegal transactions includes mobile phones, email, faxes, the Internet (websites and blogging), and social networks. Despite all kinds of measures, illegal entrepreneurs seem to use phones and the Internet in a rather open way, and it is not surprising that law enforcement tries to follow and catch criminals by intercepting their communications. They also leave traces when they use computers for buying commodities, advertising and distributing forbidden goods and services, or engaging in banking operations. Ethnic minorities might use some specific forms of communication (prepaid phones, the Internet, telephone booths, certain websites or social forums for migrants, underground banking systems, etc.).

A final form of embeddedness is found in the realm of the symbolic and the cultural performances of immigrant groups. Far from being culturally or ethnically fixed, immigrant or minority groups are constantly changing and negotiating cultural meanings and practices around crime. Much like trustful individuals who become suspicious in new places, previously peaceful entrepreneurs may feel the need to resort to violence in unfamiliar social contexts (Zaitch 2002, p. 262). Organized crime, if it is to be successful, has to mutate, readapt, and reshape not only at a material level but also in cultural terms. A good example is provided by Zaitch in his study on Colombian drug entrepreneurs in the Netherlands: a newly arrived trafficker who used to carry (and use) a gun in Colombia, continues to carry a knife in the Netherlands. He is immediately told by his own Colombian partners that in the Netherlands you do not carry weapons on the street (Zaitch 2002, p. 270). We can see this as a case of successful "assimilation" of foreign crime into local practices.

To sum up, from the research and literature discussed here on ethnic minorities and organized crime, two central arguments emerge. First, we claim that the way in which ethnic minorities engage (or fail to engage) in organized crime activities is to a large extent shaped by the nature of their social embeddedness, consisting of social ties (relational embeddedness) with local and overseas groups and arrangements such as own communities, native groups and infrastructure, foreign entrepreneurs, etc. (structural embeddedness). This means that their degree of success in any given organized crime related activity or illegal market largely reflects (and depends on) the way in which these groups are able to establish links with their local and global environments, at economic, political, cultural, and technological levels.

Second, it can also be argued that ethnic minorities involved in organized crime activities constantly change and (re)adapt their ways of "conducting business," as their social ties with others (persons, groups, markets, both local and global) also change, develop, and greatly vary according to local contexts. Far from reflecting fixed cultural codes or "accumulated" forms of social capital, illegal transactions at the local level by ethnic minorities are deeply embedded in diverse and changing environments.

VI. CONCLUSION

Social embeddedness refers to the intertwinement of organized crime with the social environments at micro as well as macro levels. These environments provide fertile grounds for crime groups. Old and new environments offer opportunities to commit and conceal crimes. Crime will take on the shape of its social environment. For instance, the gender relations existing in society reflect the ways in which women are represented in crime groups. The social environment determines the form and nature of organized crime and vice versa: organized crime can determine the shape of its environment: criminal ethnic groups can undermine and contaminate the position of ethnic communities; mafia groups are able to control and corrupt their entire social environment. The many examples mentioned above also point to the fact that the relations between the environment and organized crime are constantly changing. By expanding existing networks or by switching to other networks through the use of social ties, criminal groups are able to access new markets and discover new opportunities for criminal activities.

NOTES

1. The example is based on a real case from a research project on organized crime that involved the analysis of 120 police files of large-scale investigations into organized crime (Van de Bunt and Kleemans 2007).
2. The social embeddedness of many organized crime activities is well documented (see Albini 1971; Ianni and Reuss-Ianni 1972; Chambliss 1978; Finckenauer and Waring; Kleemans and Van de Bunt 1999; Van de Bunt and Kleemans 2007; Varese 2001; Zhang and Chin 2002; Morselli 2005; and Natarajan 2006).
3. This term is used for Italian Mafiosi who cooperate with the authorities.
4. Letizia Paoli, Ernesto Savona, and Anton Blok called attention to this phenomenon in their presentations at the CIROC seminar about the Italian Mafia on 20 December 2006 in Amsterdam.
5. "Donna Gemma" or "Pupetta," Assunta Maresca, Erminia Giuliano of the Camorra (Allum, 2007) and Rita DiGiovine of the 'Ndrangheta (Ingrasci, 2007) have become well-known female crime bosses.
6. On Chinese in the United States (Chin 1999; Zhang and Chin 2002; McIllwain 2004); Albanians in Europe (Arsovska 2009); foreign ethnic minorities in Italy (Becucci 2008); South-Italians in North Italy (Paoli 2003; Varese 2006); Turks and Kurds in Europe (Bovenkerk and Yesilgöz 2007); Russians in the Netherlands (Siegel 2005) and in the United States (Finckenauer and Waring 1998); Colombians in the Netherlands (Zaitch 2002) and in New York (Cajas 2004); African Americans in the United States (Ianni 1974; Griffin 2003); Nigerians in Europe (Carling 2006; Siegel 2007; Oboh 2011), just to name a few.
7. On activities: Van de Port (2001), Paoli and Reuter (2008), and Van de Bunt (2008a). On characteristics: Kleemans and Van de Bunt (1999), Von Lampe and Johansen (2004), Bovenkerk et al. (2003), and Zaitch (2005).

8. See Blok (1974), Bovenkerk (2001), Zaitch (2002), Kleemans (2007), and Bovenkerk and Yesilgöz (2007).
9. For the relation between organized violence, illegal entrepreneurship, peripheral autonomous regions, and failed states, see Blok (1974), Bovenkerk (2001), and Koonings and Kruijt (2004).
10. See Kleemans and Van de Bunt (1999), Zaitch (2002), Paoli (2002), Dorn et al. (2005), Kleemans (2007), Paoli and Reuter (2008), and Van de Bunt (2008a).

References

Adler, Freda. 1975. *Sisters in Crime: The Rise of the New Female Criminal*. New York: McGraw-Hill.
Albini, Joseph L. 1971. *The American Mafia: Genesis of a Legend*. New York: Appleton.
Allum, Felia. 2007. "Doing It for Themselves or Standing in for Their Men? Women in the Neapolitan Camorra (1950–2003)." In *Women and the Mafia. Female Roles in Organized Crime Structures*, edited by Giovanni Fiandaca. New York: Springer.
Arsovska, Jana. 2009. "Understanding a 'Culture of Violence and Crime': The Role of Cultural Codes in the Evolution of Ethnic Albanian Organised Crime Groups." Ph.D. Dissertation. Leuven: Katholieke Universiteit Leuven.
Becucci, Stefano. 2008. "New Players in an Old Game: The Sex Market in Italy." In *Organized Crime: Culture, Markets and Policies*, edited by Dina Siegel and Hans Nelen. New York: Springer Science and Business Media.
Benson, Michael L., Tamara D. Madensen, and John E. Eck. 2009. *White-Collar Crime from an Opportunity Perspective*. New York: Springer.
Block, Alan. 1977. "Aw! Your Mother's in The Mafia: Women Criminals in Progressive New York." *Contemporary Crises* 1(1): 5–22.
Blok, Anton. 1974. *The Mafia of a Sicilian Village, 1860–1960*. Prospect Heights: Waveland Press.
Bourdieu, Pierre. 1985. "The Forms of Capital." In *Handbook of Theory and Research for the Sociology of Education*, edited by John G. Richardson. New York: Greenwood.
Bovenkerk, Frank. 1995. *La Bella Bettien*. Amsterdam: Meulenhoff.
Bovenkerk, Frank. 2001. "Organized Crime and Ethnic Minorities: Is There a Link?" In *Combating Transnational Crime: Concepts, Activities, and Responses*, edited by Phil Williams and Dimitri Vlassis. London: Frank Cass Publishers.
Bovenkerk, Frank, Dina Siegel, and Damián Zaitch. 2003. "Organized Crime and Ethnic Reputation Manipulation." *Crime, Law and Social Change* 39(1): 23–38.
Bovenkerk, Frank, and Yücel Yesilgöz. 2007. *The Turkish Mafia*. Preston: Milo Books.
Cajas, Juan. 2004. *El truquito y la maroma. Cocaína, traquetos y pistolocos en Nueva York*. Mexico City: M.A. Porrúa.
Campbell, Howard. 2009. *Drug War Zone. Frontline Dispatches from the Streets of El Paso and Juárez*. Austin: University of Texas Press.
Carey, Elaine, and José Carlos Cisneros Guzman. 2011. "The Daughters of La Nacha: Profiles of Women Traffickers." *NACLA Report on the Americas* 44(3): 23–25.
Carling, Jørgen. 2006. *Migration, Human Smuggling and Trafficking from Nigeria to Europe*. Oslo: International Peace Research Institute.
Chambliss, William J. 1978. *On the Take: From Petty Crooks to Presidents*. Bloomington: Indiana University Press.
Chesney-Lind, Meda. 1986. "Women and Crime: The Female Offender." *Signs* 12(1): 78–96.

Chesney-Lind, Meda. 1997. *The Female Offender*. Thousand Oaks: Sage.

Chesney-Lind, Meda, and Lisa Pasko, eds. 2004. *Girls, Women, and Crime*. Thousand Oaks: Sage.

Chin, Ko-Lin. 1999. Smuggled Chinese: Clandestine Immigration to the United States. Philadelphia: Temple University Press.

Chin, Ko-Lin. 2000. *Chinatown Gangs. Extortion, Enterprise & Ethnicity*. Oxford: Oxford University Press.

Coles, Nigel. 2001. "It's Not What You Know – It's Who You Know That Counts. Analysis Serious Crime Groups as Social Networks." *British Journal of Criminology* 41(4): 580–594.

Daly, Kathleen. 1994. *Gender, Crime, and Punishment*. New Haven: Yale University Press.

Dorn, Nicholas, Michael Levi, and Leslie King. 2005. *Literature Review on Upper Level Drug Trafficking. Home Office Online Report 22/05*. London: Home Office.

Fijnaut, Cyrille, Frank Bovenkerk, Gerben Bruinsma, and Henk van de Bunt. 1998. *Organised Crime in the Netherlands*. The Hague/London/Boston: Kluwer Law International.

Finckenauer, James, and Elin Waring. 1998. *Russian Mafia in America: Immigration, Culture, and Crime*. Boston: Northeastern University Press.

Gambetta, Diego. 1998. *Trust: Making and Breaking Cooperative Relations*. Oxford: Basil Blackwell.

Gambetta, Diego. 2009. *Codes of the Underworld. How Criminals Communicate*. Princeton/Oxford: Princeton University Press.

Gambetta, Diego, and Peter Reuter. 1995. "Conspiracy among the Many: The Mafia in Legitimate Industries." In *The Economics of Organized Crime*, edited by Gianluca Fiorentini and Sam Peltzman. New York: Cambridge University Press.

Gilinsky, Yakov. 2007. "Women in Organized Crime in Russia." In *Women and the Mafia. Female Roles in Organized Crime Structures*, edited by Giovanni Fiandaca. New York: Springer.

Godson, Roy, ed. 2003. *Menace to Society: Political-Criminal Collaboration around the World*. New Brunswick: Transaction Publishers.

Goris, Esther. 1999. *Agata Galiffi, la flor de la mafia*. Buenos Aires: Editorial Sudamericana.

Granovetter, Mark. 1973. "The Strength of Weak Ties." *American Journal of Sociology* 78(6): 1360–1380.

Granovetter, Mark. 1985. "Economic Action and Social Structure: The Problem of Embeddedness." *American Journal of Sociology* 91(3): 481–510.

Granovetter, Mark. 1992. "Problems of Explanation in Economic Sociology." In *Networks and Organizations: Structure, Form, and Action*, edited by Nitin Nohria and Robert G. Eccles. Boston: Harvard Business School.

Griffin, Sean P. 2003. *Philadelphia's 'Black Mafia': A Social and Political History*. Dordrecht: Kluwer Academic Publishers.

Ianni, Francis. 1974. *Black Mafia: Ethnic Succession in Organized Crime*. New York: Simon & Schuster.

Ianni, Francis, and Elizabeth Reuss-Ianni. 1972. *A Family Business: Kinship and Social Control in Organized Crime*. London: Routledge and Kegan Paul.

Ingrasci, Ombretta. 2007. "Women in the 'Ndrangheta: The Serraino-Di Giovine Case." In *Women and the Mafia. Female Roles in Organized Crime Structures*, edited by Giovanni Fiandaca. New York: Springer.

Kleemans, Edward R. 2007. "Organized Crime, Transit Crime, and Racketeering." In *Crime and Justice in the Netherlands. Crime and Justice. A Review of Research, vol. 35*, edited by Michael Tonry and Catrien Bijleveld. Chicago: University of Chicago Press.

Kleemans, Edward R., and Henk G. van de Bunt. 1999. "The Social Embeddedness of Organized Crime." *Transnational Organized Crime* 5(1): 19–36.

Koonings, Kees, and Dirk Kruijt, eds. 2004. Armed Actors. *Organised Violence and State Failure in Latin America*. London: Zed Books.

Lalam, Nacer. 2004. "How Organized Is Organized Crime in France?" In *Organized Crime in Europe: Concepts, Patterns and Control Policies in the European Union and beyond*, edited by Cyrille Fijnaut and Letizia Paoli. Dordrecht: Springer.

Longrigg, Clare. 1998. *Mafia Women*. London: Vintage.

Massari, Mónica, ed. 2003. *Illegal Trafficking of Waste in Italy and Spain*. Rome: Gruppo Abele.

McIllwain, Jeffrey. 2004. *Organizing Crime in Chinatown: Race and Racketeering in New York City, 1890–1910*. Jefferson: McFarland.

Monzini, Paola. 2005. *Sex Traffic. Prostitution, Crime, Exploitation*. London/New York: Zed Books.

Morselli, Carlo. 2005. *Contacts, Opportunities, and Criminal Enterprise*. Toronto: University of Toronto Press.

Natarajan, Mangai. 2006. "Understanding the Structure of a Large Heroin Distribution Network: A Quantitative Analysis of Qualitative Data." *Journal of Quantitative Criminology* 22(2): 171–192.

Oboh, Jude. 2011. "Cocaine Strikers. The Role of Nigerians in International Cocaine Trafficking." Unpublished MA Thesis. Utrecht: Willem Pompe Institute.

Otomo, Ryu. 2007. "Women in Organized Crime in Japan." In *Women and the Mafia. Female Roles in Organized Crime Structures*, edited by Giovanni Fiandaca. New York: Springer.

Paoli, Letizia. 2002. "The Paradoxes of Organized Crime." *Crime, Law and Social Change* 37(1): 51–97.

Paoli, Letizia. 2008. *Mafia Brotherhoods: Organized Crime, Italian Style*. New York: Oxford University Press.

Paoli, Letizia, and Peter Reuter. 2008. "Drug Trafficking and Ethnic Minorities in Western Europe." *European Journal of Criminology* 5(1): 13–37.

Passas, Nikos. 2003. "Cross-Border Crime and the Interface between Legal and Illegal Actors." *Security Journal* 16(1): 19–38.

Patillo, Mary E. 1998. "Sweet Mothers and Gangbangers: Managing Crime in a Black Middle-Class Neighbourhood." *Social Forces* 76 (3): 747–774.

Polanyi, Karl. 1944. The Great Transformation. *The Political and Economic Origins of Our Time*. Boston: Beacon Press.

Portes, Alejandro, ed. 1995. *The Economic Sociology of Immigration. Essays on Networks, Ethnicity and Entrepreneurship*. New York: Russell Sage Foundation.

Portes, Alejandro, and Julia Sensenbrenner. 1993. "Embeddedness and Immigration: Notes on the Social Determinants of Economic Action." *American Journal of Sociology* 98(6): 1320–1350.

Reuter, Peter. 1983. *Disorganized Crime: Illegal Markets and the Mafia*. Cambridge, MA: MIT Press.

Rossi, Adriana. 2007. "Woman in Organized Crime in Argentina." In *Women and the Mafia. Female Roles in Organized Crime Structures*, edited by Giovanni Fiandaca. New York: Springer.

Ruggiero, Vincenzo. 1996. *Organized and Corporate Crime in Europe*. Aldershot: Dartmouth.

Ruggiero, Vincenzo. 2000. *Crime and Markets. Essays in Anti-Criminology*. Oxford: Oxford University Press.

Saenz Rovner, Eduardo. 2008. *The Cuban Connection: Drug Trafficking, Smuggling and Gambling in Cuba from the 1920s to the Revolution*. Chapel Hill: The University of North Carolina Press.

Savona, Ernesto. 2010. "Infiltration by Italian Organised Crime (Mafia, N'drangheta and Camorra) of the Public Construction Industry." In *Situational Prevention of Organised Crimes*, edited by Karen Bullock, Ronald V. Clarke, and Nick Tilley. Devon: Willan Publishing.

Siebert, Renate. 1996. *Secrets of Life and Death, Women and the Mafia.* London: Verso.

Siegel, Dina. 2005. *Russische Bizniz.* Amsterdam: Meulenhoff.

Siegel, Dina. 2007. "Nigeriaanse madams in de mensenhandel in Nederland." *Justitiële Verkenningen* 33(7): 39–49.

Siegel, Dina. 2008. *The Mazzel Ritual. Culture, Customs and Crime in the Diamonds Trade.* New York: Springer.

Siegel, Dina, and Sylvia de Blank. 2010. "Women who Traffic Women: The Role of Women in Human Trafficking Networks – Dutch Cases." *Global Crime* 11(4): 436–447.

Van de Bunt, Henk G. 2008a. "The Role of Hawala Bankers in the Transfer of Proceeds from Organized Crime." In *Organized Crime: Culture, Markets and Policies*, edited by Dina Siegel and Hans Nelen. New York: Springer Science and Business Media.

Van de Bunt, Henk G. 2008b. "Rekeningen vereffenen in de bouw." *Tijdschrift voor Criminologie* 50(2): 130–147.

Van de Bunt, Henk G., and Edward R. Kleemans. 2007. *Georganiseerde criminaliteit in Nederland.* Den Haag: Bju.

Van de Port, Mattijs. 2001. *Geliquideerd. Criminele afrekeningen in Nederland.* Amsterdam: Meulenhoff.

Varese, Federico. 2001. *The Russian Mafia: Private Protection in a New Market Economy.* Oxford: Oxford University Press.

Varese, Federico. 2006. "How Mafias Migrate: The Case of the 'Ndrangheta in Northern Italy." *Law & Society Review* 40(2): 411–444.

Von Lampe, Klaus, and Per Ole Johansen. 2004. "Organized Crime and Trust: On the Conceptualization and Empirical Relevance of Trust in the Context of Criminal Networks." *Global Crime* 6(2): 159–184.

Waldinger, Roger. 1995. "The 'Other Side' of Embeddedness: A Case-study of the Interplay of Economy and Ethnicity." *Ethnic and Racial Studies* 18(3): 555–580.

Zaitch, Damián. 2002. *Trafficking Cocaine. Colombian Drug Entrepreneurs in the Netherlands.* The Hague: Kluwer Law International.

Zaitch, Damián. 2005. "The Ambiguity of Violence, Secrecy and Trust among Colombian Drug Entrepreneurs." *Journal of Drug Issues* 35(1): 201–228.

Zhang, Sheldon, and Ko-Lin Chin. 2002. "Enter the Dragon: Inside Chinese Human Smuggling Operations." *Criminology* 40(4): 737–767.

PART III

MARKETS AND ACTIVITIES

CHAPTER 17

....

PROTECTION AND EXTORTION[1]

....

FEDERICO VARESE

I. INTRODUCTION

SINCE the 1980s, a number of academic studies have claimed that the Sicilian Mafia, the 'Ndrangheta, the Italian American Mafia, the Hong Kong Triads, the Russian Mafia, and the Japanese Yakuza are criminal organizations specializing in the supply of protection.[2] Two authors advanced similar claims in the nineteenth and early twentieth centuries, respectively: Leopoldo Franchetti, an Italian aristocrat who published a report on Sicily in 1876—*Condizioni politiche ed amministrative della Sicilia*; and John Landesco, an American ethnographer employed by the Chicago Crime Commission who published in 1929 *Organized Crime in Chicago* as part of the 1,100-page *Illinois Crime Survey*. In section 2, I review some of the evidence they offer on the nature of Mafia protection, specialization of protectors, and the origins of Mafias.[3] In section 3, I discuss whether Mafias are instead engaged in extorting their victims. Section 4 presents evidence of the negative effects of Mafia protection on the economy, before concluding in section 5.

II. MAFIA PROTECTION

Is Mafia protection real, or is it just protection from an imaginary threat? Or, to put it as Landesco did, "What, if any, is the function of the racketeer? [...] is he parasite or does he perform a service"?[4] For instance, Salvatore Lupo, a preeminent historian of the Sicilian Mafia, gives voice to the view that Mafiosi protect others only from imaginary dangers. He offers the following illustration: "The *santoni*, who promise the Palermo coach drivers to retrieve their stolen coaches in exchange for sums of money that they 'claim has been claimed by the *picciotti*' had already made a prior deal with them to split the ransom."[5] On the other hand, there is compelling evidence suggesting that the criminal organizations listed above are able to provide a genuine service, not just protection against a threat they themselves create. For instance, Filippo Sabetti, in his extensive study of Villalba, a Sicilian village of less than 2,000 inhabitants and the birthplace of Mafia boss Calogero Vizzini (1877–1954), showed how the local *cosca* protected farmers against bandits and the police. By the end of the nineteenth century, it had become clear that public security was not being provided by officers of the Italian state and villagers were left unprotected. The local parish priest encouraged Don Calogero to organize "a group of two armed individuals to escort, at a price, villagers taking their wheat to the mill in the territory of Torsa".[6] Sabetti maintains that, as this service proved effective, Vizzini and his group gained respect and esteem to point that the villagers were now turning to him for help with other problems.[7]

Mafia protection often takes the form of aggression, such as harassment or elimination of business competitors, a set of activities that is often confused with wholesale extortion. For instance, Antonio Calderone recalls in his memoirs that in the mid-50s, his Catania-based *cosca* decided to help the Costanzos, a construction company under their protection: "The goal was to do the Costanzo brothers a favor. A bomb was placed in the chimney of the Rendos' offices [the main competitors of the Constanzos in the construction industry in Catania in the 1980s]; after that, the usual phone call asking for money was made."[8] While the behavior of the *cosca* must have appeared utterly predatory to the Rendos, the Mafia had no intention of supplying them with any service and the "usual phone calls" were only a trick to extort money—Calderone and his accomplices were in fact *protecting* the Costanzo against competition.[9]

Throughout their history, Mafias have also intimidated workers and trade unionists for the benefit of employers. Varese (2001, p. 71) refers to an instance that occurred in Russia in 1997, when a local gang intervened to stop a workers' strike in the town of Vorkuta, a city not far from the Arctic Circle. The beneficiary of such action was the company that owned the Vorgashurskaya coalmine. The new Russian Mafia was following in the footsteps of its Italian, American, and Japanese counterparts, as extensively documented by several studies.[10] Mafias have also offered protection against extortion,[11] protection against theft and police harassment,[12] protection of property rights,[13] protection in relation to credit obtained informally and the retrieval of loans,[14] protection of thieves,[15] and the settlement of a variety of disputes.[16]

A type of protection that was highlighted by both Franchetti and Landesco is the enforcement of cartel agreements. During his trip to Sicily, Franchetti came across a society of millers (La Società dei Mulini) that was said to be under the protection of "powerful Mafiosi." The function of the society was to keep the price of flour high by limiting output. Members paid a fee to join and then agreed not to compete, thereby reaping the benefit of reduced competition. The Mafiosi ensured compliance.[17] Landesco also noted a similar activity undertaken by racketeers in Chicago in the 1920s. Businessmen—he writes—hire gangsters in order to "stabilize the market," in breach of antitrust laws and practices. This involves punishing "outlaw" firms that try to undercut the cartel agreement and charge a lower price than the one collectively agreed to by the business association, invade territories that do not belong to them, and "steal" customers.[18] Peter

Reuter and Diego Gambetta, independently and in a joint essay, have expanded on these early observations.[19] Gambetta and Reuter (1995) specify the conditions under which racketeers are able to penetrate legitimate markets and offers services of cartel enforcement: Mafia-backed cartels tend to emerge when demand is inelastic and there is little product differentiation, firms are numerous, and barriers to enter are low. In their works, they also document how American and Sicilian mobsters organize and police cartels in industries such as construction, transport, street-hawkers, garbage collection, taxi drivers, and concrete contractors. There is evidence that the Mafia enforces cartel agreements in illegal markets as well, for instance, in bookmaking in the United States and in tobacco smuggling and purse snatching in southern Italy. The money paid to the racketeer amounts to a fee for a service.[20] Other scholars have confirmed the involvement of Mafias in cartel enforcement in Hong Kong and Northern Italy.[21]

In connection to the protection of illegal cartel agreements, occasionally the "victims" search for the enforcer: "The racketeer does not always impose himself upon an industry or an association–writes Landesco. He is often invited in because his services are welcome," although the racketeer's domination is not "easy to shake."[22] Nelli (1976) also notes that, "rather than criminals forcing themselves on their victims, it was often the harried businessman faced with the constant threat of cut-throat competition, who turned to underworld elements and invited their help in dealing with excessive competition or with troublesome labor problems."[23] Similarly, in her study of Mafia-backed cartel agreements in the Macaroni business in Depression-era Chicago, Barbara Alexander found that Gennaro Calabrese was hired by the businessmen to enforce the illegal deal.[24] In the case of Sicily, Gambetta and Reuter report that Angelo Siino—a building contractor in Palermo—invited Cosa Nostra to coordinate the bids for public works in Palermo in the 1980s.[25]

It appears that mobsters do not overcharge their "victims." For instance, in the mid-1980s the Italian American Cosa Nostra took no more than $400,000 annually in fees to organize the Long Island carting industry, while the profits accruing to the carters were estimated to be over $10 million. The Mafia-run concrete cartel in New York City levied only 2 percent of the contract price for its services in fixing prices.[26] In the case of Sicily, the Mafia "charged" only 5 percent of the value of each contract for organizing bid rigging in construction, 3 percent going directly to the organization and 2 percent to pay politicians.[27] Those who made a killing were the Mafia-backed entrepreneurs.

A concern for avoiding overcharging is apparent also in the case of the Calabrese Mafia, the 'Ndrangheta. The Anti-Mafia Parliamentary Commission of 2000 reports the words of the Prefect of Catanzaro, Francesco Stranges. The Prefect notes that the sum of money regularly demanded from entrepreneurs by the 'Ndrangheta is often small: "The Mafiosi, since they are not very greedy, practice extortion at an acceptable level, hence it is difficult to find individuals willing to testify in these cases."[28] Members of this crime group have themselves expressed concern when rates of extraction were high. In one instance, the head of the San Luca family, which is considered the repository of certified values and rules of the 'Ndrangheta, was alarmed by the excessive demands that the head of the Locri family was imposing on the latter's victims. He was overheard saying: "Do you know why I came here [to meet you]? Totò, be careful that when the human race, the people go against you, you will lose what you have achieved in thirty years! You just lose it! When you start destroying the shutter of this guy, burn the car of the other, the people will rebel!"[29] A rational racketeer would raise the price until it becomes hard to collect the money and/or the high price invites a competitor in his territory.[30] It seems that the San Luca boss had understood this point without consulting any economics of protection textbook.

Are Mafiosi specialized in offering protection, or do they also carry out other jobs? Observers of organized crime often take the involvement of a known mobster in a given enterprise as proof that this is his main activity, thereby confusing the commodity protected with the business of protection. On the contrary, John Landesco offers an example where a business partner is indeed a protector in disguise. The cleaning and drying sector in Chicago in the 1920s was run by an Association that was threatening a Mr. Morris Becker, an independent operator who had refused to abide by the rules of the cartel. Thus, Mr. Becker turned to Al Capone and made him a partner in his company. The businessman went on to boast to a local paper: "I have no need of the police or the Employers' Association now. I have now the best protection in the world." Although formally a "partner," clearly Al Capone's job was to protect Mr. Backer against the threats of his competitors.[31] This story also highlights another feature of Mafia protection, namely that of producing *negative externalities*: if most people are using Mafia protection in a given market, those who are unprotected will become the target of additional crime and harassment, thereby creating a strong incentive for them to also enlist the help of mobsters, as Mr. Becker did.[32] The equilibrium outcome is a Pareto-inferior one where everybody buys criminal protection (in other words, buying protection is a dominant strategy for each businessman in a n-person Prisoner's Dilemma game). While it is in everybody's individual interest to associate oneself with mobsters, the collective outcome is worse for all entrepreneurs.

More complicated permutations of these dynamics still suggest that the job of producer of goods and services, and the job of protector, remain different. During the Great Depression in the United States, banks were reluctant to lend money to the small garment-makers of New York City, a sector of the economy with low technological requirements, easy entry, and a high turnover. At this point, American mobsters had amassed capital thanks to the profits they made from Prohibition, and, as narrated by Lucky Luciano himself, they started to finance operators in this highly volatile and risky industry. "[W]e gave the companies that worked with us the money to help them buyin' goods and all the stuff they needed to operate with. Then, if one of our manufacturers got into us for dough that he could not pay back, and the guy had what looked like a good business, then we would become partners."[33] On the surface, it appears that the Mafiosi had evolved from protectors to financiers. Yet it was the Mafia's ability to use violence that allowed them to make this transition: they were better than legitimate banks at collecting debts. As remarked recently by Dixit, when cost of entry into an industry is low, so is cost of *exit* and absconding with the bank's loan. The Mafia was more efficient at finding such absconders than a legitimate bank.[34] In addition, Mafiosi with a long-time horizon have an incentive to support an industry they are involved in. The distinguishing feature of a Mafioso is to be able to offer protection to others and, if necessary, to himself, against cheats and competitors.[35] Surely, Mafiosi also invest their own money in profitable enterprises. For instance, Campana (2011) has coded the conversations of the members of the Camorra clan La Torre, wiretapped by police in a period of seven months in 1998–1999. He finds that the task "protection" is discussed in 30.7 percent of the conversations, while "business investments in the legal and illegal economy" are discussed in 18 percent of the conversations. He concludes that protection remains their main source of income.

To what extent are the origins of Mafias related to their ability to offer protection? Franchetti notes that the Italian state was not a credible and effective enforcer of justice and law in Sicily in the nineteenth century. Lack of trust in the ability of the state to enforce deals and promises spread to the general population, reducing interpersonal trust as well. Upward mobile Sicilians, who wanted to make the most of the newly arrived market for land, thus turned to individuals who had started to offer a substitute for state security, namely selective protection to their clients. As these early Mafia groups (*cosche*) were laying claims on sectors of the local economy, they came into conflict with each other, suggesting that they were trying to be the exclusive provider of protection in a given domain.[36]

Building on Franchetti, Diego Gambetta (1993) explains the origin of the Sicilian Mafia as a response to a late and rapid transition to the market economy in the early nineteenth century, in the presence of a state that failed to clearly define and protect the newly granted property rights, pervasive distrust, widespread banditry, and a supply of individuals trained in the use of violence who became suddenly unemployed. The armed guards (*campieri*) formerly at the service of the feudal lords were now out of work. In addition, the Bourbon army had disbanded after the unification of Italy and its soldiers were in search of a purpose. At this point in history, some members of the violent classes turned to banditry. The lethal combination of a demand for the protection of property and property rights, the presence of a threat from banditry and disputes with other owners, low levels of trust, and a supply of disbanded soldiers and unemployed field guards ready to offer protection, gave rise to the Sicilian Mafia in the early to mid-nineteenth century.[37]

This perspective—we can call it "property rights theory of Mafia emergence"—has been applied to other cases, such as Japan and post-Soviet Russia.[38] Japan made a rapid transition from an agrarian, feudal society to a modern, industrialized economy in the Meiji period, which is traditionally dated from 1868 to 1911. During the Meiji period, the country saw the end of feudalism, the spread of property ownership (mainly in land), the enactment of legal reforms—including land reform (1873–1876), a written constitution (1889), and a French-style civil code (1898)—and a process of centralization of government. As a consequence of the spread of ownership, disputes increased, both between individuals and the state (mainly over the levels of taxation) and between individual owners. The state, however, failed to provide mechanisms for dispute resolution that were quick and efficient. At the same time, the transition to the market produced a crisis for the large and economically useless warrior class, leading to a series of Samurai rebellions, including the Saga (1874) and Akizuki (1876) and culminating in the Satsuma rebellion of 1877. While some of them turned to raiding, attacking villages and other locations to gain supplies, other Samurai began selling their services of protection to these same villages. A supply of people trained in violence started to offer services of dispute resolution and protection outside the scope of the state, giving rise to the modern yakuza.[39]

Russia underwent a similar process. From 1986 onward, the country witnessed a rapid spread of property rights that was not matched by the establishment of adequate formal enforcement mechanisms by the state. This generated a demand for non-state sources of protection. Such a demand coincided with the presence of individuals who had acquired violent skills and found themselves unemployed. In the Russian case, these individuals were former Red Army soldiers, Afghan veterans, unemployed sportsmen, and ex-prisoners. The Russian Mafia emerged at this historical juncture, and many groups adopted similar norms and rituals.[40] Generalizing the "property-rights theory of Mafia emergence," one can conclude that Mafias emerge in societies undergoing a sudden and late transition to the market economy, lacking a legal structure that reliably protect property rights or settle business disputes, and has a supply of people trained in violence that become unemployed at this specific juncture. Thus, new property owners develop a *demand* for protection that the state is incapable of fulfilling, while at the same time a *supply* of people trained in violence is present in this very particular market.

Is a demand for protection enough to generate a supply? In an enlightening comparative remark, Landesco notes how "violence in connection to labor disputes is almost unknown in England" in the 1920s, despite the presence of significant labor activism, in contrast to the situation in the Unites States in the same years. He concludes that it is the "availability of gunmen willing to undertake the work" that marks the difference between the United States and the United Kingdom.[41] Thus, assuming that demand is constant, the presence of a supply makes the difference.[42] Indeed, no Mafia emerged in other parts of Southern Italy where the state was equally ineffective at protecting property rights and settling disputes.

The "property rights theory of Mafia emergence" remains a convincing perspective on the origins of Mafias. Yet it has also proved to be a special case. Mafias have emerged in the absence of a wholesale transition to the market economy, as in the case of the Italian American Mafia in the United States in the first part of the twentieth century and the 'Ndrangheta groups in the north of Italy from at least the 1970s. In a new study, Varese (2011) offers a detailed account of these two instances and a more general framework for Mafia emergence.[43]

How can we account for the birth of the Italian American Mafia at a time when the United States was a well-functioning market economy? Mafiosi arrived in New York City starting from the very end of the nineteenth century and to a higher degree in the early part of the twentieth century. The push factor was the unintended consequence of prosecution in Italy along with the attempt of Mafiosi in Sicily to avoid internal punishment (some arrived as part of the generalized migration to North America, in search of

a better life). In the nineteenth century, the most profitable markets were already protected by a combination of corrupt police officers and local politicians. Italians in the
United States did congregate in crime groups and even performed admission rituals,
but they involved themselves in ordinary crimes, such as counterfeiting, horse theft, and
crude extortion.

In the first decade of the twentieth century, something changed: leaders of the
Progressive Movement to reform city politics were successful in curbing grand corruption and removing police protection from illegal markets such as prostitution,
gambling, and late-night drinking. These three markets, together with labor relations,
were suddenly left unprotected. The unintended consequences of police reform gave
Italian criminals a golden opportunity to become entrenched as suppliers of services
of dispute resolution and protection in place of the corrupt police officers. In addition,
the Progressive Movement succeeded in banning alcohol consumption and manufacturing in 1920. Thus, another vast unprotected market was created shortly after the
reform of the police. Mafiosi stepped in to protect truckloads entering the city from
the New Jersey coastline ("Rum Row") and large stills in upstate New York. They were
also instrumental in the creation of spaces where suppliers could meet distributors and
prices could be set. The Italian Mafiosi were independent of either suppliers or distributors, offering their services to both.[44] During and after Prohibition, the Italians
continued their involvement in other illegal markets, such as prostitution and gambling.[45] Rather than a wholesale transition to the market or lack of trust in the state,
the Italian American Mafia emerged because of the existence of a set of unprotected
illegal markets. Prohibition created an even bigger market that by definition could not
be regulated in a legitimate way.

Mafia groups have also expanded to territories that did not undergo a sudden transition to the market economy, such the north of Italy, where `Ndrangheta families have
been operating since at least the 1970s. Varese (2011, pp. 31–52) presents a detailed study
of a region outside Turin (Val Susa) that experienced a sudden economic boom in
the construction sector. Local entrepreneurs lacked a vast enough workforce to meet
the new demand for second homes and were keen to corner the profitable market by
excluding competitors. Thus, a demand for illegal services in the labor market and cartel
enforcement developed. Some members of the `Ndrangheta had been forced to move to
the north by court orders and were able to provide a docile and nonunionized workforce
to construction firms and enforce cartels of both local and Calabrese companies in this
lucrative market. Violence was used to force some firms out of the booming construction sector. Over time, individuals who were favorable toward the Mafia penetrated
politics. Initial high levels of trust did not prevent transplantation, as predicted by the
"property rights theory of Mafia emergence." Thus, Mafias may well emerge within
functioning market economies and for reasons other than to ensure the protection of
property rights or lack of trust. A sudden boom in a local market that is not governed by
the state can lead to a demand for criminal protection, even in countries where property
rights are clearly defined, trust is high, and courts work relatively well at settling legitimate disputes among market actors. Economic transformations that are not properly

governed by legitimate authorities can give rise to a demand for criminal protection. In the presence of a suitable supply, a Mafia may emerge.

The body of work discussed here has come to some key conclusions: there is compelling evidence that Mafia protection is a genuine commodity in many instances, that protectors tend to specialize, and that when major economic transformations—such as a boom in a local market or a generalized transition to the market economy—are not governed by local and national authorities, they give rise to a demand for protection and, if a supply of people trained in violence is present, a Mafia is likely to emerge.

III. Mafia Extortion

What should we make, then, of the fact that many astute observers of the criminal organizations discussed so far have concluded that such groups simply offer protection against a danger they themselves create? Part of the answer might lie in the way the concept is used. Extortion is normally defined in the social sciences as the forced extraction of resources for services that are promised but *not* provided.[46] If an agent forces somebody to pay for a service and fails to deliver anything whatsoever, I would consider that an instance of extortion. However, this definition is not universally adopted. Instead, commentators and scholars alike often interpret extortion to mean (1) overcharging for a service, (2) the imposition of a service (indeed, in most legislation "extortion" is defined as obtaining something of value through coercion, regardless of whether the extortionist delivers something in return[47]), (3) a service of poor quality. I will argue next that items 1 through 3 often accurately describe mafias' behavior, but it does not follow that their protection is bogus.[48]

Mafias (and states) may well overcharge for their services because protection is a natural monopoly. One cannot obey two competing systems of taxation or, to put it as did T. C. Shelling, "I cannot take half the bookies' earnings if you took it before I got there."[49] Since protectors are monopolists, they can charge a monopoly price, which is likely to be more than it costs them to produce the good. Over time and under certain circumstances, the cost of protection might be reduced. For instance, as the protector is firmly established as the monopolist in a given area and external threats are reduced, he can reduce the price he forced his subjects to pay. The main point is that overcharging for a service differs analytically from extortion. Although in ordinary parlance an extortionary price often refers to an exorbitant price, in this context such a perspective is meaningless. As pointed out by the economic historian Fredric Lane in reference to early modern states in Western Europe, the service supplied by the protection-producing enterprises was often of poor quality and overpriced, but it was still a service rendered.[50]

Mafias (and states) also tend to force their protection on their victims, notwithstanding the instances discussed earlier, but such an imposition does not imply that the protection is bogus, as already noted by Franchetti: "The distinction between a damage avoided and a benefit gained is to a point artificial. [In most cases] the line that separates them is impossible to determine, or rather it does not exist in human feeling. When evildoers intrude on and dominate most social relationships, [...] the very act that saves one from their hostility can also bring their friendship with its associated advantages."[51] A story told by Pete Salerno, a Mafioso turned state-witness, further illustrates this point. Pete and Figgy (Anthony Ficarotta), working for the Genovese Family in New York City, started off forcing their protection on stall holders, assuring them that, if needed, they could take care of their problems. They had no intention to actually do anything. After a while, the victims started to demand what they had been paid for: "The fruit guy wants what has been paying for—protection." Now they felt compelled to do something, "or they would revolt—stop paying" (Abadinsky 1983, pp. 150–1). What had started as an imposition of a service and possibly wholesale extortion, turned into genuine protection.[52]

Mafias (and states) can offer a service of poor quality, or one that is partial at best. Varese (2011, pp. 110–3) reports that some kiosk owners in the Russian city of Perm in the 1990s paid a racket that was not able to reduce police harassment. Nor did it provide any help against petty thieves. The same study shows, however, that police "protection" in that context was indeed worse. Often, the Mafia is compared with an ideal state able to solve every single crime effectively and swiftly, while the reality is often far from the ideal. For instance, Italy suffers from chronic delays in settling civil disputes. In that country, it takes on average 1,210 days to enforce a contract, compared with 394 days in Germany, 389 days in the United Kingdom, and 331 days in France (the OECD countries average is 518; legal fees in Italy are also among the highest in Europe).[53] It seems odd to expect Mafia protection to be anything but just marginally more efficient than the state's.

An additional source of confusion involves the perspective of the observer. What is extortion—and the consequent possible financial ruin—for one victim of the Mafia might well amount to genuine criminal protection for another Mafia protégé. This is exemplified by the story narrated by Antonio Calderone discussed earlier. What were extortionary demands for the Rendos amounted to protection against competition for the Costanzos. In his autobiography, Joe Bonanno (1983, p. 79) put it as follows: "What is seen as extortion from the outsider is viewed as self-protection by the insider."[54] There might also be a tendency to overemphasize extortion as opposed to protection because of the type of evidence that filters out from the underworld. Gambetta has noted that "a possible informational bias [...] may exaggerate the importance of extortion as opposed to those transactions in which the likelihood of being cheated is truly reduced thanks to protection. They are more likely to hear about the former simply because dealers are more likely to talk to the police in this case than in the latter."[55]

Yet Mafia extortion exists. For instance, film crews in Palermo, Hong Kong, and Moscow have been victims of such harassment.[56] The shooting of movies is particularly susceptible to extortion because crews work on tight schedules and cannot afford even the smallest delay in production. As they also tend to be from outside, they have no long-term connection with local men of honor.[57] Varese (1996, pp. 133–4) categorizes the crime groups he encountered in Russia in the 1990s into three types: predatory, extortionary, and protective. The first of these generally imposed ever larger taxes on its subject businesses with fatal results for the tax payer; the second type typically extracted small taxes in return for bogus protection; in the third class, there were genuinely protective groups, actively sought out by firms that would do research in order to identify such a strong and reliable protector.[58] From a dynamic point of view, one can expect that extortionary groups turn into protective ones if they want to survive in a competitive environment. Indeed, Varese (1996) suggests that, over time, it is likely that the purely extortionary groups will disappear and only the protective will survive. At the same time, under certain conditions, Mafiosi can stop offering protection and become just predatory extortionists. One such factor is the time-horizon of the protector: the shorter it is, the more likely he will harass customers, raise the price of extortion, and fail to supply any service.[59] If customers know that the protector "life expectancy" is short, they will be more reluctant to pay protection, and a greater degree of coercion will be needed.

In conclusion, under certain conditions protectors can turn into pure predatory agents. Police pressure and a reduced time horizon are normally invoked as the reason for such a transformation. A fruitful discussion of Mafia extortion must, however, do away with common misunderstandings of the nature of extortion, which is often confused with overcharging for a poor service and with imposing a service. While Mafias (and states) do both, it does not follow that their activities are purely predatory.

IV. Mafia Protection Is a Social Bad

Mafia protection remains a social evil. In the economic sphere, it promotes inefficiency and reduces competition. For instance, Lavezzi (2008) finds that regions of Italy with high Mafia density perform worse than other regions in the south where the presence of the Mafia is not pervasive.[60] Pinotti (2012) examines the postwar economic development of two regions in southern Italy exposed to Mafia activity after the 1970s. Applying synthetic control methods to estimate their counterfactual economic performance in the absence of organized crime, the study concludes that the presence of Mafia lowers GDP per capita by 16 percent, at the same time as murders increase sharply relative to the synthetic control.[61] Both Lavezzi (2008) and Pinotti (2012) find that the public sector is large in Mafia regions and that private capital is substituted with less productive public investment.

Is crime higher in Mafia regions? To my knowledge, there are no analytical studies, at least for the case of Italy. The reason for the dearth of studies might be due to underreporting: in a territory where organized crime is pervasive, people might not turn to the police if they are the victims of theft and use the Mafia instead. Thus, reported (low) crime rates might be misleading. Theoretically, two competing hypotheses could be formulated: on the one hand, the Mafia should be willing to protect thieves as well, thereby promoting ordinary crimes. It could also be that it allows some crime to go unpunished in order to keep demand for its services as high as possible. On the other hand, the Mafia might not want widespread petty crime in its areas, as this might attract unwanted police attention. This hypothesis would suggest that there is less crime in Mafia territories. Both hypotheses are in need of empirical testing.[62] In any case, Mafia protection is provided without consideration for justice, fairness or the well-being of society at large. In the world the Mafia runs there is no such a thing as a "right" to the protection one has paid for. Mafiosi can ask for more favors or more money and turn against their dutifully paying clients, and there is no higher authority a victim can appeal to. Ultimately, St Augustine's warning about states is even more poignant for Mafias: "without justice, what is government but a great robbery?"

V. Conclusion

Since the 1980s, a variety of studies have suggested that Mafia organizations are able to supply protection against competition and the enforcement of cartel agreements to selected businesspeople. They can also harass workers and trade unionists for the benefit of entrepreneurs; provide protection against theft and police harassment; protection in relation to credit obtained informally and the retrieval of loans; and the settlement of a variety of disputes. The Mafia also offers protection services to entrepreneurs of illegal commodities, such as thieves, prostitutes, pimps, loan sharks, and drug dealers. Yet, a widespread opinion underestimates these activities while emphasizing extortion as the key activity of Mafia groups. Such an emphasis might be due to conceptual confusion. Some equate extortion to (1) overcharging for a service; (2) imposition of a service; (3) a service of poor quality. Mafias do (1), (2) and (3), but it does not follow that their protection is bogus. Yet, under certain conditions, Mafia groups do engage in extortion. This normally occurs when their time horizon is short and they are under pressure from either the police or fellow racketeers.

Mafia protection is a social bad. Economists have been able to quantify its negative economic effect. One study has shown that two regions in the South of Italy have lost 16 percent of their GDP due to this phenomenon. Mafia protection, even when genuine, is provided without any consideration for fairness, justice, and rights. A world run by organized crime is not only poor and dangerous but also deeply unjust. Observers and policymakers routinely fail to recognize that Mafias can serve powerful and entrenched interests in a democracy, and this is because they offer something of value. Until this alliance of economic and criminal interest is severed, it will be hard to win the fight against the Mafia.

Notes

1. I am grateful to Alison O'Connor and Paolo Campana for their comments on an earlier version of this essay.

2. See Graebner Anderson 1979; Reuter 1984, 1987; Sabetti 2002 (first ed. 1984); Tilly 1985; Gambetta 1988a, 1988b, 1993; Chu 2000; Varese 1994, 2001, 2011; Alexander 1997; Skaperdas 2001; and Hill 2003. See also Fiandaca and Costantino 1994. For recent reflections on this body of scholarship, see Gambetta 2011, Santoro 2011, and Sabetti 2011. Santoro (2011) offers a conceptual map of the differences among some of these scholars.

3. As for definitions, I take a *Mafia* to be a set of Mafia groups that share the same rituals and rules. For instance, a number of Mafia families operate in Sicily and the "Sicilian Mafia" is the collective entity of which they are a part. At different points in the history of each Mafia, different arrangements regulate (or fail to regulate) the relations between Mafia groups. The relations between groups are often dependent on clever institution builders and historical circumstances. Thus, the Sicilian Mafia, the Calabrese `Ndrangheta, the Russian Mafia, the Italian American Mafia, the Japanese Yakuza, and the Hong Kong triads can be collectively referred to as *Mafias*. Clearly, this characterization excludes many other forms of organized crime. See e.g. Hobbs 2001.

4. Landesco [1929] 1968, p. 150.

5. Lupo 2009, p. 139. Cf, however, Lupo 2009, p. 16.

6. Sabetti 2002, p. 103.

7. Sabetti 2002, p. 104. See also Sabetti 2011, pp. 10–11 and 13.

8. Arlacchi 1993, p. 53.

9. See Varese 2010, pp. 17–18; Varese 2011, pp. 204n12. For other instances where the Mafia offers protection against competition, see Chu 2000, pp. 53–76; Varese 2001, pp. 115–17. For a discussion of aggressive protection, see Lane 1942, p. 388.

10. Bell [1953] 1988, p. 131; Block 1983, p. 43; Gambetta 1993, pp. 93–94, 197; Lupo 1996, p. 199; Chu 2000, pp. 71–72, 153–4. See also Jacobs 2006.

11. Arlacchi 1993, pp. 110–1; Gambetta 1993, pp. 174–9; *New York Times* 29/VIII/1999.

12. Gambetta 1993, pp. 171–74, 190; Chu 2000, pp. 43–53; Varese 2001, pp. 69–72, 112–113, 119.

13. Salvatore Contorno, quoted in Gambetta 1993, p. 171.

14. Varese 2001, pp. 110–2.

15. See, e.g., Gambetta 1993, pp. 190–2.

16. Reuter 1995, p. 90; Chu 2000, pp. 77–80; Varese 2001, pp. 102–105, 117.

17. Franchetti [1876] 2000, p. 9. See also Reuter and Gambetta 1995, pp. 120–1.

18. Landesco [1929] 1968, pp. 152 and 154. See also Alexander 1997.

19. See, e.g., Reuter 1984; Gambetta 1993; Gambetta and Reuter 1995. See also Jacobs, Friel, and Raddick 1999.

20. Gambetta and Reuter 1995, p. 116. See also Reuter 1983, pp. 42–4; 1984 and 1987; Gambetta 1993, pp.195–235.

21. See, respectively, Chu 2000 and Varese 2011, pp. 42–43.

22. Landesco [1929] 1968, pp. 152 and 154.

23. Nelli 1976, p. 243.

24. Alexander 1997, p. 144.

25. Gambetta and Reuter 1995, p. 125.

26. Gambetta and Reuter 1995, p. 133. See also Cowan 2003.

27. Gambetta and Reuter 1995, p. 133.

28. Quoted in Varese 2011, p. 208.

29. Quoted in Varese 2011, p. 208.

30. See the remarks by Lane (1942, p. 389fn10; 1958, p. 405) in reference to the early modern states.

31. Landesco [1929] 1968, p. 158.
32. Landesco [1929] 1968, p. 158. The theoretical argument on negative externalities and protection can be found in Lane 1958; Nozick 1974; Gambetta 1993; Bandiera 2003, p. 219; Varese 2010, among others.
33. Gosh and Hammer 1975, pp. 77–9. This is cited also in Reuter and Gambetta 1995, p. 127 and mentioned in Repetto 2004, p. 163.
34. Dixit 2011.
35. Gambetta 1988a, p. 355.
36. Franchetti [1876] 2000, p. 11. See also the discussion in Gambetta (1988b, p. 165).
37. Gambetta 1993. See also Bandiera 2003. Sabetti 2002 offers a historically rich account of this process.
38. For an application to China, see Wang 2011.
39. I am drawing here upon Varese 2011, p. 194. See also Milhaupt and West 2000, pp. 49–50; Varese 2003. On disputes over land in the Meiji period, see Brown 1993. More generally see the classic account by Mclaren (1916, pp. 72–90). I am grateful to Alison O'Connor for a discussion on this point.
40. Varese 1994, 1996 and 2001. Frye and Zhuravskaya (2001) show that Russian shopkeepers consider criminal protection as a better alternative to the one offered by the police.
41. Landesco [1929] 1968, p. 152.
42. See Gambetta 1993, p. 78.
43. For discussions of Varese (2011), see, e.g., Catino (2011), Picci (2013), Schneider and Schneider (2011), Skarbek (2012).
44. Contrary to common perception (see, e.g., Lupsha 1986, p. 44; Gambetta 1993, p. 252), Prohibition did not create the Italian Mafia. Rather, mobsters had already penetrated some key markets in the previous decade.
45. See, e.g., Nelli 1976, p. 122.
46. Varese 2010, p. 18. For a discussion of organized crime, see also Levi 1998 and Levi 2007.
47. See, e.g. the definition of extortion contained in the US Hobbs act: "The obtaining of property from another, with his consent, induced by wrongful use of actual or threatened force, violence, or fear, or under color of official right." The Hobbs Act, 18 U.S.C. §1951 (1970). For discussions, see Stern (1971–1972) and Block and Anderson (2001).
48. See the discussion in Varese 2011, p. 204fn10 and Lane 1958.
49. Schelling 1984, p. 185. See also Lane 1958, p. 402.
50. Lane 1958, p. 404.
51. Quoted in and translated by Gambetta (1988b, p. 170).
52. This story is discussed in Gambetta 1993, p. 39 and Hill 2003, p. 20.
53. Data reported in "Giustizia, Italia fanalino di coda in Europa, lentezza dei processi civili costa 96 miliardi," *Adnkronos* 14/I/2012.
54. Bonanno 1983, p. 79. See also the discussion in Lane 1942, pp. 338–9.
55. Gambetta 1988a, p. 356.
56. See, respectively, Gambetta 2009, pp. 255–56; Chu 2000, p. 71; *Independent*, November 2, 1995.
57. Gambetta 2009, p. 256. In some cases, however, film crews have entered into partnerships with "location agents" who have ensured a safe production schedule, presumably because they enjoy long-term connections with the local Mafiosi (Varese 2011).
58. Varese 1996; See also Hill 2003, p. 20.
59. See Lane 1958, p. 404; Gambetta 1993; Olson 2000.

60. Lavezzi 2008, p. 203. See also Daniele 2009. On an estimation of the presence of the Mafia in Italy, see Calderoni 2011.
61. Pinotti's study takes into consideration Apulia and Basilicata, rather than the regions where Mafias originated (Sicily, Campania, and Calabria).
62. I am grateful to Mario Lavezzi and Paolo Buonanno for an email discussion on this issue.

References

Abadinsky Howard. 1983. *The Criminal Elite: Professional and Organized Crime*. Westport, CT: Greenwood Press.

Alexander, Barbara. 1997. "The Rational Racketeer. Pasta Protection in Depression Era Chicago." Reprinted in Federico Varese, ed. 2010. *Organized Crime. Critical Concepts in Criminology*. London/New York: Routledge. Vol. III, pp. 126–52.

Arlacchi, Pino. 1993. *Men of Dishonor. Inside the Sicilian Mafia: An Account of Antonino Calderone*. New York: William Morrow and Co.

Bandiera, Oriana. 2003. "Land Reform, the Market for Protection, and the Origins of the Sicilian Mafia: Theory and Evidence." *Journal of Law, Economics, & Organization* 19(1): 218–44.

Bell, Daniel. 1953. "Crime as an American Way of Life." Reprinted in *The End of Ideology: On the Exhaustion of Political Ideas in the Fifties*. New York: Free Press, pp. 127–50.

Block, Alan A. 1983. *East Side West Side: Organizing Crime in New York 1930–1950*. London: Transaction.

Block, Walter, and Gary M. Anderson. 2001. "Blackmail, Extortion, and Exchange." *New York Law School Law Review* 44(Summer-Fall): 541–61.

Bonanno, Joseph (with Sergio Lalli). 1983. *A Man of Honour. The Autobiography of Joseph Bonanno*. New York: Simon and Schuster.

Brown, Philip. 1993. *Central Authority and Local Autonomy in the Formation of Early Modern Japan: The Case of Kaga Domain*. Stanford, CA: Stanford University Press.

Calderoni, Francesco. 2011. "Where Is the Mafia in Italy? Measuring the Presence of the Mafia across Italian Provinces." *Global Crime* 12(1): 41–69.

Campana, Paolo. 2011. "Eavesdropping on the Mob: The Functional Diversification of Mafia Activities Across Territories." *European Journal of Criminology* 8(3): 1–16.

Catino, Maurizio. 2011. "F. Varese, Mafie in Movimento. Come Il Crimine Organizzato Conquista Nuovi Territori." *Rassegna Italiana di Sociologia* 51(4): 715–718.

Chu, Yiu Kong. 2000. *The Triads as Business*. London/New York: Routledge.

Cowan, Rick (with Douglas Century). 2003. *Takedown: The Fall of the Last Mafia Empire*. New York: Berkley Books.

Daniele, Vittorio. 2009. "Organized Crime and Regional Development. A Review of the Italian Case." *Trends in Organized Crime* 12: 211–234.

Dixit, Avinash. 2011. "A Game-Theoretic Perspective on Diego Gambetta's Codes of the Underworld." *Global Crime* 12(2): 134–145.

Fiandaca, Giovanni, and Salvatore Costantino, eds. 1994. *La Mafia le Mafie*. Roma-Bari, Italy: Laterza.

Frye, Timothy, and Olga Zhuravskaya. 2001. "Rackets, Regulation, and the Rule of Law." *Journal of Law, Economics, and Organization* 16(2): 478–502.

Gambetta, Diego. 1988a. "Fragments of an Economic Theory of the Mafia." Reprinted in Federico Varese, ed. *Organized Crime. Critical Concepts in Criminology*. London/New York: Routledge. 2010. Vol. I, pp. 353–369.

Gambetta, Diego. 1988b. "Mafia: The Price of Distrust." In *Trust: Making and Breaking Cooperative Relations*, edited by Diego Gambetta. New York: Basil Blackwell, pp. 158–75.

Gambetta, Diego. 1993. *The Sicilian Mafia*. London: Harvard University Press.

Gambetta, Diego. 2009. *Codes of the Underworld*. Princeton, NJ: Princeton University Press.

Gambetta, Diego. 2011. "'The Sicilian Mafia.' Twenty Years after Publication." *Sociologica* 2. doi:10.2383/35869.

Gambetta, Diego, and Peter Reuter. 1995. "Conspiracy Among the Many: The Mafia in Legitimate Industries." In *The Economics of Organised Crime*, edited by Gianluca Fiorentini and Sam Peltzman. Cambridge: Cambridge University Press.

Graebner Anderson, Annelise. 1979. *The Business of Organized Crime*. Stanford, CA: Hoover Institution Press.

Hobbs, Dick. 2001. "The Firm: Organised Crime on a Shifting Terrain." *British Journal of Criminology* 41: 549–560.

Jacobs, James B., Coleen Friel, and Robert Raddick. 1999. *Gotham Unbound: How New York City Was Liberated from the Grip of Organized Crime*. New York: New York University Press.

Jacobs, James B. 2006. *Mobsters, Unions and the Feds. The Mafia and the American Labor Movement*. New York: New York University Press.

Landesco, John. [1929] 1968. *Organized Crime in Chicago*. Chicago/London: University of Chicago Press.

Lane, Frederic C. 1942. "The Economic Meaning of War and Protection." *Journal of Social Philosophy and Jurisprudence* 7: 254–70.

Lane, Frederic C. 1958. "Economic Consequences of Organized Violence." *Journal of Economic History* 18(4): 401–17.

Lavezzi, Mario. 2008. "Economic Structure and Vulnerability to Organised Crime: Evidence From Sicily." *Global Crime* 9: 198–220.

Levi, Mike. 1997. "Perspectives on 'Organized Crime': An Overview." *Howard Journal* 37(4): 335–45.

Levi, Mike. 2007 "Organised Crime and Terrorism." In *The Oxford Handbook of Criminology*, edited by M. Maguire, R. Morgan and R. Reiner. 4th ed. Oxford: Oxford University Press.

Lupo, Salvatore. 1996. *Storia della Mafia Dalle Origini ai Giorni Nostri*. 2nd ed. Rome: Donzelli.

Lupo, Salvatore. 2009. *History of the Mafia*. New York: Columbia University Press.

Lupsha, Peter. 1986. "Organized Crime in the United States." In *Organized Crime: A Global Perspective*, edited by Robert Kelly. Totowa, NJ: Rowman and Littlefield.

Mclaren, Walter Wallace. 1916. *A Political History of Japan During the Meiji Era 1867-1912*. London: Allen and Unwin.

Nelli, Humbert S. 1976. *The Business of Crime: Italians and Syndicate Crime in the United States*. Chicago: University of Chicago Press.

Nozick, Robert. 1974. *Anarchy, State, and Utopia*. New York: Basic Books.

Olson, Mancur. 2000. *Power and Prosperity. Outgrowing Communist and Capitalist Dictatorships*. New York: Basic Books.

Picci, Lucio. 2013. "Federico Varese: Mafias on the Move." *European Sociological Review* 29(1): 133–136.

Pinotti, Paolo. 2012. "The Economic Costs of Organized Crime: Evidence From Southern Italy." https://sites.google.com/site/paolopinotti/research.

Repetto, Thomas E. 2004. *American Mafia: A History of Its Rise to Power*. New York: Henry Holt.

Reuter, Peter. 1983. *Disorganized Crime: The Economics of the Visible Hand*. Cambridge, MA: MIT Press.

Reuter, Peter. 1984. "Racketeers as Cartel Organizers." In *Organized Crime. Critical Concepts in Criminology*, edited by Federico Varese. London/New York: Routledge, Vol. III, pp. 153–167.

Reuter, Peter. 1985. *The Organization of Illegal Markets: An Economic Analysis*. New York: United States National Institute of Justice.

Reuter, Peter. 1987. *Racketeering in Legitimate Industries: A Study in the Economics of Intimidation*. Santa Monica, CA: The RAND Corporation.

Sabetti, Filippo. [1984] 2002. *Village Politics and the Mafia in Sicily*. Montreal: McGill-Queen's University Press.

Sabetti, Filippo. 2011. "Stationary Bandits. Lessons From the Practice of Research From Sicily." *Sociologica* 2. doi:10.2383/35871.

Santoro, Marco. 2011. "Introduction. The Mafia and the Sociological Imagination." *Sociologica* 2. doi:10.2383/35868.

Skaperdas, Stergios. 2001. "The Political Economy of Organized Crime: Providing Protection When the State Does Not." *Economics of Governance* 2(3): 173–202.

Skarbek, David. 2012. "Review of Mafias on the Move: How Organized Crime Conquers New Territories, by Federico Varese." *Public Choice* 151(1–2): 405–407.

Schelling, Thomas C. 1984. What Is the Business of Organized Crime? (1971), Reprinted in *Choice and Consequence*. Cambridge, MA: Harvard University Press.

Schneider, Jane, and Peter Schneider. 2011. "The Mafia and Capitalism. An Emerging Paradigm." *Sociologica* 2. doi:10.2383/35873.

Stern, Herbert J. 1971–1972. "Prosecutions of Local Political Corruption under the Hobbs Act: The Unnecessary Distinction between Bribery and Extortion." *Seton Hall L. Rev.* 3(1):179–194.

Tilly, Charles. 1985. "War Making and State Making as Organized Crime." In *Organized Crime. Critical Concepts in Criminology*, edited by Federico Varese, Vol. I. London/New York: Routledge, pp. 334–352.

Varese, Federico. 1994. "Is Sicily the Future of Russia? Private Protection and the Emergence of the Russian Mafia." *Archives Européenes de Sociologie* 35: 224–58.

Varese, Federico. 1996. "What Is the Russian Mafia?" *Low Intensity Conflict and Law Enforcement* 5(2): 129–138.

Varese, Federico. 2001. *The Russian Mafia*. Oxford: Oxford University Press.

Varese, Federico. 2003. "Mafia." In *Concise Oxford Dictionary of Politics*, edited by Iain McLean and Alistair McMillan. Oxford: Oxford University Press.

Varese, Federico. 2006. "How Mafias Migrate: The Case of the 'Ndrangheta in Northern Italy." *Law and Society Review* 40(2): 411–44.

Varese, Federico. 2010. "What Is Organized Crime?" In *Organized Crime: Critical Concepts in Criminology*, edited by Federico Varese. London: Routledge.

Varese, Federico. 2011. *Mafias on the Move: How Organized Conquers New Territories*. Princeton, NJ: Princeton University Press.

Wang, Peng. 2011. "The Chinese Mafia: Private Protection in a Socialist Market Economy." *Global Crime* 12(4): 290–311.

CHAPTER 18

DRUG MARKETS AND
ORGANIZED CRIME

PETER REUTER[1]

I. Introduction

The markets for illegal drugs, mostly cocaine, heroin, and cannabis, probably generate, globally, more revenues than any other illegal market.[2] That same statement holds for many individual Western countries and for a small number of producer and transshipment countries. Since drug markets are so large, with some highly structured enterprises in them, it is tempting to assume that drug distribution is a major activity of organized crime, defined as broad-based and durable criminal organizations. In fact, the nature of the enterprises in drug markets varies greatly across countries, drugs, and levels of distribution in terms of their size, durability, and relationship to other criminal activities. Thus, considerable variability exists in the relationship of these criminal enterprises to organized crime. However, this depends on definition. If, as is increasingly common in Europe, organized crime is viewed as a set of profit-making criminal activities, regardless of the solidity of the organizations involved in them, drug trafficking, at least at the wholesale level, is an almost prototypical organized crime activity (e.g., SOCA, Europol, 2013). More sophisticated definitions of organized crime (e.g., Maltz 1976) exclude many small dealing organizations.

The focus of this essay will be on the upper end of the drug trade rather than on retailing, even though the latter generates most of the revenues, as discussed below. That is because the fortunes are made at those higher levels: refining and exporting in the producer countries, transshipment in the transit countries, and importing and high-level wholesaling in the consuming countries. There are no Walmarts or Starbucks in the cocaine, heroin, or cannabis markets. Retailing even the very expensive cocaine generates extremely low incomes[3] and is undertaken by generally small and ephemeral enterprises.

This essay will deal only with cannabis, cocaine, heroin, and methamphetamine, the last probably the synthetic drug generating the greatest revenues. The essay will primarily focus on the characteristics of drug markets and enterprises in them. Only at the end will the relationship to other criminal activities and to organized crime be considered. Section 1 reviews the basic features of these markets, such as the role of international trade and the low costs of production. It shows differences across drugs. For example, whereas heroin involves a lengthy international distribution chain and commercial distribution, cannabis is increasingly dominated by short chains and domestic production. The shares of total revenues going to producers and high-level distributors are different for the two drugs. Section 2 analyzes characteristics of trafficking enterprises in three producer or transit countries: Colombia, Mexico, and Tajikistan. Again, the theme is the variability, this time related to government actions. Section 3 turns to enterprise and market characteristics of high-level cocaine enterprises as the market has evolved over time in the United States and Europe.

Section 4 analyzes drug control efforts in Colombia, Mexico, and Tajikistan; it focuses on whether the intensity or nature of enforcement can account for variations in how the market and enterprises are organized. Section 5 then turns to the question of the relationship between drug production and distribution, on the one hand, and other crime and organized crime, on the other hand. The final section summarizes.

A. Sources

Though the literature on drug markets is large and growing, it focuses primarily on the retail trade rather than on the upper levels[4]. This is hardly unexpected; retailing is where the bulk of participants are found, it accounts for much of the visible violence and disorder associated with drugs, and it is much easier to study. The smaller numbers of upper-level actors invest more in protecting themselves against surveillance, and they are, in any case, less visible outside producer countries.

Desroches (2007), in a review of the literature on North America and western Europe, asserts that scarcely a dozen original research papers have been published on high-level trafficking. Research is very unevenly distributed across nations. As is often the case in empirical criminology, the United States accounts for a disproportionately large share of the total, reflecting both the greater prominence of illegal drug markets in that country as well as the relatively generous funds available for research. In western Europe, the analytic literature appears slight, though a number of descriptive studies have appeared since 1990. In the United Kingdom, there are two recent studies of importance: Pearson and Hobbs (2001) used interviews and investigative files to describe "middle markets" for drugs, while Matrix Knowledge Group (2007) used interviews with imprisoned drug dealers to describe distribution from international smuggling through wholesale distribution. Paoli (2000) collected data on drug distribution in Frankfurt and Milan, including the higher levels. Official reports provide some descriptive material but little use has been made of it.

For many countries that are important in the trade, such as Iran and Tajikistan for heroin transshipment or Morocco for cannabis exports to Europe, scarcely any research has been published.[5] This may reflect both the political sensitivity of the subject and the small size of the social science community in these countries.

II. Characteristics of Production and Distribution of Drugs

A. Production

The markets for different drugs vary in basic characteristics. Cocaine and heroin, the drugs generating the greatest harm to society, both are produced in poor countries that export the vast majority of their output. A tiny number of nations account for the vast bulk of production of coca and opium, of which heroin is a derivative. According to official estimates (e.g., US Department of State 2011; United Nations Office on Drugs and Crime 2011), Myanmar and Afghanistan have accounted for more than 80 percent of global production of opium since the mid-1980s. Since the turn of the 21st century, Afghanistan has increasingly dominated, so that in 2007 it was estimated to account for 93 percent of the total (8,200 tons out of 8,870 tons). A total of six countries account for 98 percent of world heroin production. Bolivia, Colombia, and Peru account for all coca production. The distribution of production among them has changed over time. In the 1980s, when the illegal cocaine market in the United States first emerged, it was produced primarily in Peru, Bolivia was second, and Colombia a distant third. Since the mid-1990s, this has changed markedly, with Colombia responsible for about two-thirds of total production, probably because of decreasing government control in rural areas of Colombia as well as more aggressive policies against coca production in Bolivia and Peru. Though other nations in the Andes, particularly Ecuador, are always rumored to be about to enter the coca-growing sector, none has so far done so (US Department of State 2011).

The two drugs are distributed through long chains across many countries. For heroin going from Afghanistan to Europe, ten distinct organizations may be involved in transactions from farmer to final user; transactions between separate organizations may occur in three countries between Afghanistan and the final consumer in Amsterdam.[6] The growing of poppy and coca plants takes place in poor developing countries because the law enforcement risks per unit of product are so high in Europe and North America that, even with risky smuggling, it is cheaper to produce in distant countries where land and labor are cheap and where the government imposes few costs through eradication or seizures (Paoli, Greenfield, and Reuter 2009, pp. 201–234).

This gives a distinctive hour-glass shape to the distribution of participants in the cocaine and heroin trades at various stages, as indicated in Figure 18.1. For these drugs,

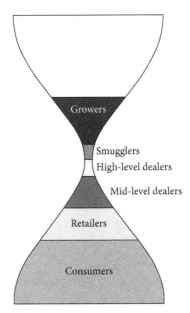

FIGURE 18.1 Numbers of participants in the cocaine and heroin production and distribution chains.

literally millions of individuals are involved, at least part-time, in the growing, harvesting, and early stage refinement of the drug, but perhaps only a few tens of thousands of individuals are involved in the smuggling sector. Retailing again involves many hundreds of thousands. The markets at different points will be influenced by that configuration.

The growing of the plants, whether of coca or poppy, is executed by small farmers acting independently. Evidence exists of complex financing ties to local money lenders in Afghanistan, which sometimes creates pressures to grow when it would not be in the farmer's own best interest. More recently, claims have also been raised of political pressures from rebel groups to grow more poppies (Mansfield 2011). In Colombia, gangs and guerrilla groups may also play a coercive role, though that is surely limited by the high mobility of the farmers in many of the growing areas. In Myanmar, the United Wa State Army (UWSA) has aggressively restricted production and even moved large numbers of farmers out of poppy-growing areas in order to limit production; this is thought to be politically rather than economically motivated, since the UWSA has pledged to eliminate opium production in the areas they control (Kramer 2007 and 2009).

Cannabis has quite a different structure. It is primarily produced domestically in the consuming countries. The United Nations Office on Drugs and Crime (UNODC) states, that in 2009, a total of 134 nations reported domestic cultivation of cannabis on their territory (United Nations Office on Drugs and Crime 2010). Though reports of large-scale production in Afghanistan occasionally appear, only Mexico and Morocco are regularly reported as having substantial export volumes. Bouchard, in a series of studies in the province of Quebec (population 7 million), has shown that it is likely that many tens of thousands of individuals are involved in aspects of cannabis production (e.g., Bouchard 2007). Since Quebec does export modest quantities to other parts of Canada and to the United States, it probably has a larger industry per capita than most places.

Synthetics present more complexity; some are produced in rich consuming countries (e.g., Ecstasy in the United Kingdom and the Netherlands in the 1990s) while others (e.g., amphetamine type stimulants, ATS) are produced in poor distant nations, such as Myanmar, for sale in Japan, Korea, and even western Europe. Methamphetamine, the only synthetic examined in detail in this essay, is produced both in Mexico for export to the United States and also in small domestic laboratories in the United States itself. The precursor chemicals are often imported clandestinely from India (US Department of Justice 2010).

From even these brief descriptions of the production conditions for the different drugs, it is clear that general statements about drug production markets are difficult to make. Coca and opium are agricultural crops with little evidence of advantages to industrialization; the technology remains primitive. Synthetic manufacturing, where economies of scale may be substantial, presents a very different set of opportunities for criminal entrepreneurs.

B. What Are the Revenues from Drug Selling and How Are They Distributed?

A staple of discussions on illegal drugs in recent years has centered on the claim of the UNODC that these markets generate total revenues of $400–500 billion globally and that the international trade is worth more than $100 billion (UNODC 2005), making it the fourth-largest international trade flow, larger, for example, than that in wine and beer. These figures seem to be substantial overstatements, and the 2011 *World Drug Report* now includes very large downward revisions of the cocaine and heroin revenues (United Nations Office on Drugs and Crime 2011).[7] Of equal interest for this essay is the distribution of the earnings across levels of the trade.

Estimates of production of illicit crops are very uncertain. Every element of the calculation (cultivation area, yield per hectare, efficiency of processing) presents its own challenge. The United Nations and the US Department of State publish separate estimates each year; these often show disturbing differences in changes year to year. These figures cannot be used to develop global revenue estimates.

The only method for producing a global estimate of drug market revenues is to sum estimates at the national level. This reflects the fact that the prices of drugs vary a great deal across countries. In the United Kingdom, heroin retailed for the equivalent of approximately $240,000 per kilogram in 2005; the comparable figure for the United States was approximately $380,000. In a country like Tajikistan, the figure might have been less than one-tenth as much. Thus, it is impossible to develop a global estimate as the product of global consumption by retail price.

Demand-side estimates start with counts of the numbers of people who consume drugs with various frequencies or intensities of use (e.g., occasional and hard core, or daily, weekly, and past year) and multiply those counts by average rates of consumption for each country. One might adjust that figure upward by some factor to account for underreporting in surveys even of legal commodities (Cook 2007).

The consumption figures generated this way look strong only relative to the supply-side estimates and not in any absolute sense. There are three main concerns:

- General population surveys miss many heavy drug users who are in treatment, in jail or prison, or in an unstable housing situation, and who are hard to locate or who are unwilling to talk about their substance use.
- Respondents are not always accurate in their reports, either because of an intention to deceive or because they have trouble recalling details.
- Available evidence is limited about the amount of drugs consumed per use-day or session.

The first concern is not insurmountable as long as a good data source of information is available about hard-to-reach populations that can complement the general population survey. ONDCP (2001) and Pudney et al. (2006) provide good examples for how this can be done with information from arrestees and treatment populations. The second concern will always be an issue—one that requires analysts to use and justify credible adjustment factors (ONDCP 2014). Finally, insights about amounts consumed can be obtained with information about expenditures and information about days of use and amount used per day, but such data are rare. Paoli, Greenfield, and Reuter (2009, Appendix B) show how little research is available on heroin consumption by addicted users. Despite the large number of surveys that inquire about marijuana prevalence, information about the amount and quality of what is typically consumed is almost nonexistent. Even seemingly minor assumptions about amount consumed (e.g., the amount of marijuana in a joint) can have major impacts on total consumption estimates (Kilmer et al. 2010).

The distribution of revenues across levels of the trade for cocaine and heroin is indicated in Table 18.1, which shows the price of a kilogram of cocaine or heroin as it moves through the system from production in Colombia (coca) or Afghanistan (poppy) to final sale in Chicago (cocaine) or London (heroin). Production accounts for a very small share of total drug revenues, perhaps as little as 1 percent; for example, the farm gate value of the coca required for a kilogram of cocaine costs less than $1,000, whereas the retail price for a gram is about $100. A larger share of revenues (perhaps 10 percent) is accounted for by smuggling out of producer countries and through transshipment countries, such as Iran, Mexico, Pakistan, Tajikistan, and Turkey.[8]

What these figures also show is that 70 to 80 percent of total revenues are generated by the last two or three transactions, as the drug goes from ounce purchases by low-level wholesalers to a fraction of a gram at the retail level.[9] No similar data are available for cannabis or methamphetamine, but it is likely that, with shorter chains from production to distribution and higher risks for the producers, a larger share goes to the cannabis grower and to the methamphetamine manufacturer.

Table 18.1 Price and Purity of Cocaine and Heroin from Production to Retail, ca. 2005

Stage	Cocaine—1 kilogram				Heroin—1 kilogram			
	Raw Price	Purity	100% Pure	Location	Raw Price	Purity	100% Pure	Location
Farm-gate	$800	100%	$800	Colombia	$900	100%	$900	Afghanistan
Export	$2,200	91%	$2,400	Colombia	$3,400	73%	$4,700	Afgn. neighbors
Import/ Wholesale (Kg.)	$14,500	76%	$19,000	Los Angeles	$10,000	58%	$17,000	Turkey
Mid-level / Wholesale (Oz)	$19,500	73%	$27,000	Los Angeles	$33,000	50%	$66,000	England & Wales
Typical retail price-Country	$78,000	64%	$122,000	United States	$105,000	44%	$239,000	United Kingdom

Source: Kilmer and Reuter (2009)

Though most of the revenues go to low-level dealers, as noted above, the fortunes are made by those at the top of the trade. For example, in 2009 *Forbes* magazine listed a major Mexican drug trafficker, Joaquin Guzman Loera, as a billionaire (*Forbes* 2011); the basis for that judgment is questionable but, no doubt, he, like the Colombian drug traffickers of the 1980s, was extremely rich.

The high share of the retail price accounted for by low-level distributors is easily explained in the standard risk compensation model used by economists. Assume that a higher level trafficker sells 1 kilogram of cocaine and has a 1 percent probability of being imprisoned for one year as a result of the transaction; the rich trafficker values a year in prison at 100,000 euros. Assume a retailer sells 1 gram of cocaine and has only a 1 in 1,000 chance of the same imprisonment; he values a year in prison at 25,000 euros. Assuming away any risk aversion, the trafficker will charge 1 euro per gram to cover the risk, while the retailer, even though he has a lower chance of being jailed and values that less highly, needs 25 euros to cover the risk associated with 1 gram. The model is highly simplified and the figures are intended to be only illustrative but the proportions are probably reasonable. The result is that, though each gram is marked up heavily at the retail level, the volumes are so low per retailer that on average each dealer has modest earnings.

III. Trafficking in Producer and Transshipment Countries

Trafficking involves distinct organizations and, again, variation is found across drugs and nations, reflecting, in part, government strategies. This is illustrated by consideration of the smuggling market in three important countries: Mexico, Colombia, and Tajikistan.

Mexico's drug market has attracted a great deal of attention since 2006 because of the extraordinary levels of violence; an estimated 11,000 drug-related homicides occurred in 2010, roughly ten times as many as in 2000 (Rios and Shirk 2011). Mexico is the source of all the major imported drugs in the United States; it is the principal foreign producer of three of them (cannabis, heroin, and methamphetamine) and the transit country for most of the cocaine. Approximately seven "cartels" were said to be operating in 2010, locked in bitter competition for specific routes (Astorga and Shirk 2010). Some of these organizations have themselves emerged from competitive killings. For example, the Beltran Leyva organization split from the Sinaloa DTO through such homicides.

This configuration of a small number of large drug trafficking organizations (DTOs) is thought to have been a characteristic of Mexico's drug markets for some decades (Astorga and Shirk 2010). What has changed is the relationship among the groups. Whereas before 2000 the long-time ruling party, the PRI, ensured generally cooperative terms among DTOs, the election of a PAN president (Vicente Fox) led to a breakdown of agreements.[10] Homicides doubled between 2000 and 2006, the end of the Fox administration. The next president, Felipe Calderón, aggressively attacked the DTOs in late 2006. A dramatic escalation in the violence ensued, now including many officials and innocent parties among the victims.

Colombia has served as the principal refiner and exporter of cocaine to the United States for 30 years, and the nation has seen a very different evolution of drug enterprises. In the 1980s, the Cali and Medellín cartels emerged as major nonstate actors with political ambitions: these groups seem to have been only loose syndicates of independent entrepreneurs who regularly collaborated but also had to compete with other, smaller Colombian smuggling enterprises (Clawson and Lee 1998). The Medellín cartel attacked the central government, seeking an agreement that it should be left alone and its leaders admitted into respectable society. Its assassination of Luis Carlos Galán, the leading presidential candidate in 1989, generated a military led crack-down against, first, the Medellín traffickers and, then, almost reflexively, against the more strategic Cali group.

After most of the leading traffickers were locked up or killed, the industry continued to operate at the same levels of throughput but in a different configuration. Since 1995, numerous smaller refining and smuggling groups have occasionally collaborated in individual shipments but no longer have political ambitions. The development of a new technology for smuggling large quantities efficiently, namely semi-submersibles,[11] has probably led to increased collaboration among them. Relations with the paramilitary and left-wing guerrilla groups have varied between cooperation and conflict. For example, the most prominent trafficking gang in 2011, Los Rastrojos, fought the Revolutionary Armed Forces of Colombia (FARC) in some areas but allied with the FARC in others (Reuter 2011)

Tajikistan, a much less well researched transshipment nation, is of interest because it presents more clearly the example of a narco-state. Paoli, Greenfield, and Reuter (2009) estimate that heroin trafficking (from Afghanistan to Russia) adds at least one-third to recorded GDP. They describe in detail the variety of organizations, large and small, that operate in the market. In the following excerpt from their analysis, I focus on the characteristics of the larger organizations that probably account for the bulk of the quantity trafficked, at least since the 1990s.

These large organized criminal groups are usually known as "criminal communities," a term inherited by most CIS countries from the Soviet penal code (see for example, Butler 1997). The most successful ones are able to deal with more than 1 ton of heroin a month; at Russian import prices, that yielded between $12 and $24 million per month in 2005.[12]

Stable and usually high-level government protection has been critical to the success of these large trafficking groups. The progress in border control and law enforcement that Tajikistan has achieved since the late 1990s—thanks to the support of international agencies and foreign donors—has facilitated the large groups' domination. By 2001, for example, a total of 12 to 13 police and custom posts could be found on the route from Khorog to Osh, a distance of only 700 to 800 kilometers. The roads from the Afghanistan border to Dushanbe are checked even more strictly. Rather than create insuperable barriers to drug transportation, this has generated large payments to border and police officials. Small-time individual smugglers are disadvantaged; apparently, there are economies of scale in corruption (Reuter 2003). This has led to some coalition of corrupted bureaucracy and drug trafficking organizations. Whereas small- to medium-sized trafficking groups rarely enjoy high-level protection, systematic collusion is the characteristic of these large enterprises.

This variation was candidly described by the Drug Control Agency of Tajikistan (DCA) (2000, pp. 17–18) in a report on the illegal drug market in Dushanbe: "The leaders of all groups have their own relations or other connections with some governmental structures or law enforcement agencies. In many cases the[se] are paid regularly definite sum[s] of money. In some large groups a leader is either a commander of military troops or law enforcement agency. In the largest groups...leader[s] have high position[s] in some governmental structure[s]."

Some of these "criminal communities" specialize in one or two phases of the heroin business and, as in the case of smaller groups, their specialization is a function of their location. However, a few large and particularly well-connected organizations involve up to a few hundred individuals, including core members and service providers, and they operate across a broad spectrum of trafficking activities, from the importation of opiates from Afghanistan up to the wholesale and, occasionally, even retail distribution of opiates in Russia and other former Soviet states.

Most of the large trafficking organizations coincide with the private armies of former civil war commanders turned career or elected public officials. As the DCA states, "there are several large organizations in Tajikistan dealing with deliver[y] of drugs. As a matter of fact they all are subject to commanders of military formations, which were formed during Tajik Civil War...some of these formations became parts of armed forces of the country; some are still under the subordination to their commanders and are illegal in their essence" (Drug Control Agency of Tajikistan 2000, p. 70; see also pp. 18 and 21–22).

The three country vignettes suggest considerable variation in the nature of smuggling enterprises and markets across different transshipment and producer countries. Surely this reflects the influence, inter alia, of the government's role. In Tajikistan, the distinction between heroin smuggling and the government may be minimal since such smuggling is substantially the most important source of earnings for corrupt officials and the political leadership. There may indeed be coordination and power to exclude others, at least other large enterprises. Heroin smuggling may provide the core criminal enterprise for gangs that are involved in other Tajikistan criminal activities. In contrast, Mexico and Colombia, despite the deep and persistent corruption of their governments, have been able to act at times very aggressively against the major drug enterprises. Since the 1990s, Colombia's market has involved high levels of cooperation among the principal traffickers without government assistance but no market power; the cooperation appears to be operational rather than strategic. When the Mexican government withdrew its at least tacit collusion, the drug traffickers there were unable to maintain their market-sharing agreements, and they have fought in a way that suggests that they believe domination is possible.

IV. High-Level Trafficking in Consumer Countries

As suggested above, the structure and characteristics of drug markets in producer and transshipment countries may be very responsive to governmental actions and inactions (Paoli, Greenfield, and Reuter 2009, pp. 201–234). In the rich consumer countries,[13] corruption seems to be less central to the business, an assertion that arouses considerable skepticism in producer countries. Corruption, like scientific hypotheses, presents a problem of epistemological asymmetry. Scientific hypotheses can only be disproved, not proven; corruption can be found but its existence never disproved. Nonetheless, US prosecutors pursue corrupt agents with considerable zeal when they find them; at the same time, the overlapping authority of enforcement agencies creates a situation in which any corrupt agent, no matter how well protected in her own department, has to be concerned with possible investigation by another agency. The market for corruption will shrink in such an environment.

Corruption is frequent but mostly not systemic in the United States, United Kingdom, and most western European nations.[14] It very rarely involves leading political figures. A different set of factors affects the nature of enterprises involved in high-level trafficking and the structure of the markets. The remainder of this section describes different types of organizations that have functioned in the cocaine market as it has evolved in the United States over the last 35 years and, more briefly, what is known about high-level European cocaine and heroin markets.

A. The Early US Cocaine Market

Adler (1985) reported observations on 65 high-level dealers and smugglers in Southern California, whom she and her husband met through contacts while in graduate school. Adler noted considerable range in the closeness and stability of relationships among participants. Some formed close and enduring partnerships that were quite exclusive; for example, one pilot was constantly being recruited by a smuggler neighbor but refused to work for him because of his loyalty to his regular smuggler employer (p. 66). Other dealers, characterized as "less reputable," existed in a network of shifting alliances.

The organizations Adler studied were micro-enterprises. Those of cocaine dealers typically consisted of only two or three people. Marijuana, because it is bulkier, required more elaborate transportation organizations. She concluded that "this is not an arena dominated by a criminal syndicate but an illicit market populated by individuals and small groups of wheeler-dealers who operate competitively and entrepreneurially" (p. 2).

Reuter and Haaga (1989) interviewed mid- to high-level US traffickers in cocaine and marijuana in the mid-1980s; the sample was recruited from low security federal prisons. They found importers who were small, opportunistic, and niche-oriented. They noted: "All one needs is a good connection and a set of reliable customers" (p. 39). Though many of those interviewed regarded themselves as part of an organization, "[m]ost of the arrangements would be better described as small partnerships, in which each partner is also involved in trading on his own account, or as long-term, but not exclusive, supplier-customer relationships" (p. 40).

Both Adler and Reuter and Haaga were describing the cocaine market in an early stage of its development. In 1978, cocaine consumption was estimated to be approximately 100 tons; by 1988, it had grown to approximately 300 tons (Everingham and Rydell 1994). Prices had plunged, the consequence of the emergence of more efficient distribution systems. It seems plausible that the generally amateur, small-scale smuggling operations described in the two studies, often involving well-educated principals with at least modestly successful legitimate careers, had been replaced by more professional and large-scale smuggling operations (see, e.g., Decker and Chapman 2008).

B. Colombian Smuggling Organizations in the United States

Fuentes (1998) has provided the most fine-grained description of the operation of the high levels of the international drug trade since the shift to large-scale smuggling; hence, we provide more detail than for other studies. He relied on transcripts from court proceedings (including extensive wiretaps) on two major organizations and lengthy interviews with five senior traffickers who have cooperated with federal agencies. These are accounts of organizations that were detected and punished. Thus, they might be atypically weak. In fact, both organizations had lasted for at least five years, while the informants had also been successful over an even longer period.

Each trafficking organization accounted for a nontrivial share of the total cocaine market in the United States. On a monthly basis, a dozen or so customers brought in loads of hundreds of kilograms; a 250-kilogram purchase at $20,000 per kilo involves a payment of $5 million. A number of multi-ton shipments arrived from Colombia; during the period August 1991 and April 1992, five shipments totaling 20 tons were warehoused by one warehouse operation.[15] In the context of a market delivering about 300 tons to final users, these are substantial quantities.

Fuentes described organizations that were durable, bureaucratic, violent, and strategic. For example, recruitment of new staff for US operations was highly systematized, with interviews by senior traffickers in Colombia and provision of collateral in the form of identification of family members who could be held hostage. It was noted: "References for prospective workers had to come from within the organization." Non-Colombians were considered higher-risk employees because it was more difficult to threaten them if they defected with money or drugs; providing familial details did help, though threats were harder to execute in the Dominican Republic than in Colombia. Recruitment was very selective. A strong preference was shown for relatives in leadership positions and cell managers were usually well educated, possessing college degrees.

Exit was allowed, provided the circumstances did not arouse suspicion that the agent had defected to the police. Colombians who were recruited by the organization in Colombia to work in the United States were issued visas that expired shortly after entry so as to limit their mobility.

The system was designed to move shipments very rapidly since inventory in the United States represented risk. Twenty-four hours was the goal for getting rid of a shipment once it had reached the destination city. Stockpiles were held in Colombia, where the enforcement risk was vastly smaller. The organizations had their own domestic transportation systems, drivers who would carry shipments of 100 kilos or more for prices ranging from $300 to $1,000 per kilo depending on the length of the trip.[16]

The scale of the organization was impressive. One large cell was estimated to have 300 workers in it, occupying at least six identifiable roles; it was estimated to have employed a total of 1,200 individuals during its lifetime. Most received modest salaries: $7,000 per month for cell manager, $2,000 for stash house sitter. Given the volume and margins for the organization, it still generated annual incomes totaling millions of dollars for the principals.[17]

Natarajan (2000) describes a similarly large organization in the New York metropolitan area. She documents one surprising phenomenon, namely that the principal US operative talked to numerous individuals; a total of 24 were identified from wiretaps, including 15 customers. This is hardly consistent with maintaining low exposure since any one of the 15 can obtain relief from lengthy prison sentences by providing information about his supplier. Perhaps what we observe here is the endgame of successful operations that become increasingly confident of their own invulnerability, which helps lead to their demise.

C. European Trafficking

Though very large seizures of cocaine and heroin continue, suggesting the existence of large traffickers, smaller trafficking entities still survive in the European market. Ruggiero and South (1995) describe opportunistic smugglers of less than a kilo of cocaine or hashish, concealing it in bicycles. Disposal of smaller quantities requires less organizational capacity; a single domestic customer may be sufficient.

It is impossible to systematically estimate what share of total European heroin imports are accounted for by large shipments, i.e., groups with the financial, organizational, and personnel capacities to assemble, purchase, ship, and distribute large quantities. Large shipments appear to account for the majority of all heroin seized, but that could reflect the higher per kilo risk associated with larger bundles.

Given that the UK cocaine market has emerged much more recently, probably around 2000, as a mass market, it is perhaps useful in this respect to also consider the study by Pearson and Hobbs (2001) of the "middle market" for cocaine in the United Kingdom as paralleling the work of Adler and of Reuter and Haaga. Pearson and Hobbs also find no evidence of large and hierarchical organizations in the cocaine trade; rather, they find evidence of networks of traders.

The most recent study is by Matrix Knowledge Group (2007), which used interviews with 222 individuals imprisoned in the United Kingdom for serious drug offenses around 2005. Since it involved dealers in at least four separate drugs and at different stages of the distribution system, from importing to retailing, the study lacks depth on any specific drug or market level. The vast majority of participants were either solo operators or they worked in small- to medium-sized enterprises. Price fixing, indicative of restricted competition, was rarely reported. Collusion, in relation to dividing up geographical areas or customers, was more common.

V. Enforcement

Illegal markets are shaped by enforcement in many respects. For example, intensive enforcement (characterized by high probability of arrest and/or long sentences conditional on conviction) provides incentives for enterprises to remain small since senior offenders will want to reduce the number of others who are potential informants against them. The many layers of the heroin and cocaine trades, from importation through retailing, represent one consequence of this configuration since it means traffickers handling large quantities of the drug will have to deal with only a small number of others; they sacrifice revenue to achieve lower risk of exposure. Cannabis dealers, facing less severe penalties, are apparently willing to work in larger groups; for example, Morselli (2001) describes a major international cannabis trafficker who at one stage of his career was working with 20 contacts.

Official estimates suggest that drug smuggling is a risky business, at least in terms of the drugs themselves. For cocaine globally, seizures[18] may be as high as 40 percent of the total (UNODC 2011). For heroin, seizure rates are lower but still substantial at 20 percent in 2010 (UNODC 2011). There is, however, no estimate of the probability of arrest specifically for high-level dealers. Sevigny and Caulkins (2004) show that most of those incarcerated in the United States are participants in distribution, but they cannot distinguish retailers from high-level traffickers.

Many seizures occur at the border and involve no offender other than the carrier, notwithstanding efforts in some countries to make "controlled deliveries" in which police follow the drugs to their final destination. Offenders carrying small amounts from one point to another across the border are called "mules." The term refers not merely to their physical roles; they also have minimal knowledge about who else is in the organization. When drugs are seized in container vessels, it can be very difficult to identify the responsible participants. Thus, though a high fraction of the quantity shipped is seized, risks to senior traffickers may be modest.

Studies of individual dealers or organizations give only a few hints about career lengths. Consider, for example, research by Fuentes (Fuentes 1998), which is particularly rich in detail. The two trafficking organizations had operated successfully within the United States for some years; one from 1983 to 1992 and the other from 1988 to 1992 at least. The head of the first organization had been convicted in 1975 and then again in 1979, but, after release in 1983, he survived for nine years without arrest. For only one other participant was a career length given; Harold Ackerman, a senior manager also involved in money laundering, was said to have operated in the United States for almost 10 years (p. 19). However, the description of the cells and the organizations generally suggested that they had operated in more or less the same form for at least a few years.

As in other illegal markets, interaction between enforcement agencies and drug traffickers and dealers is constant, most conspicuously around routes and modes of trafficking. A concentration of interdiction resources around South Florida in the early 1980s led to a shift in trafficking routes from the Caribbean to Mexico (Andreas 2000). In 2003, tough enforcement against cocaine smuggling from the Netherlands Antilles to the Amsterdam airport may have led to a shift to smuggling through West Africa to western Europe. Increased focus on smuggling in TIR trucks (Trans International Routier) in Europe may have led to more use of sea cargo for concealment.

Broader technological and social changes impinge on enforcement efforts. Ruggiero and South (1995) note that the growth of international personal mail has reduced the risk of sending small packages containing drugs through the regular international post; it is no longer a remarkable event for a household to receive a package from overseas. The universal availability of cell phones makes electronic surveillance more complicated, though not necessarily less successful once established. The same can be said for computers; they allow organizations to better control their own activities, but, once controlled and deciphered by enforcement agencies, they provide more varied and detailed information for investigation and prosecution.

Anti-money laundering controls are another component of drug enforcement specifically targeted at trafficking. While no systematic measures are available as to how much money is laundered by drug traffickers, there are two reasons to believe that control may have had a substantial effect at least on how drug traffickers conduct business. First, the absolute sums seized in a number of high-profile money laundering operations, occasionally more than $250 million (Drug Enforcement Administration 2007), constitute a nontrivial fraction of reasonable estimates of the total earnings generated by this level of trafficking. Second, there are reports that money launderers charge 5 to 10 percent for their services, a healthy tax on the revenues of high-level traffickers; given that there are many potential launderers, this may well represent a response to enforcement risk. However, an analysis by Levi and Reuter (2006) suggests that money laundering costs are such a small share of total costs of distributing drugs that even effective enforcement will not raise the retail price of drugs enough to reduce total consumption.

VI. Organized Crime and Drug Trafficking

The expansion of the drug trade in the last 40 years has presented opportunities for pre-existing criminal groups to build on their core capacities in other activities, particularly those involving illicit markets (gambling, prostitution, loansharking). One might also expect, symmetrically, that success in the drug business would lead new organizations to use their core capacities to enter other illegal markets and criminal activities. A shift in specialization by experienced offenders has taken place; for example, in Britain many drug traffickers were previously active in other criminal pursuits, including armed robbery (Dorn, Murji, and South 1992). Generally however that seems not to have happened at the organizational level. Most drug trafficking organizations remain specialized.

Particularly surprising was the minimal role of the Mafia in the United States when the cocaine market emerged in the late 1970s and early 1980s, at a time when the Mafia was still a moderately important criminal presence. Though apparently possessing some of the most important assets for this business and having had a major role in heroin smuggling during the period from 1935 to 1970, the Mafia was marginalized in cocaine trafficking. Cases involving senior Mafiosi were almost unheard of and the organizations themselves have not participated at all. This contrasts with the situation in Italy, where the Mafia, a very different organization from its US counterpart, played a significant role in heroin trafficking at least until quite recently (see, for example, Cantanzaro 1988 and Paoli 2003).

The American Mafia, as a national alliance of predominantly Italian gangs based in various cities, emerged primarily through bootlegging, though the exigencies of the gambling business also played a role in its development (Haller 1979). It was characterized by highly developed networks of systemic corruption in local law enforcement and, until about 1950 or 1960, in city politics as well. Both bootlegging and numbers banking required large numbers of agents, geographically dispersed. Using its connections with the Italian Mafia, the US Mafia imported heroin through New York City docks, utilizing control of the waterfront unions. The leaders were highly visible, as much reported on in the newspapers as prominent socialites. The names of the principal "families" were also well known throughout the nation; membership in one of these families provided an important asset for an ambitious young criminal seeking to intimidate others without investing in extensive violence himself. The individual organizations endured in recognizable form for more than half a century at least. Leaders were occasionally incarcerated but rarely for extended periods prior to the 1980s.

The assets of the Mafia families, then, included a reputation for control of contingent violence, both collective and individual; networks of agents; durability; access to capital; and control of corrupt police departments. It turned out that cocaine importing did not require these assets. Most essentially, the drug originated in Latin America, where other gangs had already established corruption relations with authorities. Moreover, the large Hispanic immigrant community in the United States was capable of providing the necessary networks and recruitment for operation. The Colombian organizations developed a reputation for violence that was comparable to, if not greater than, that of the Mafia; for this purpose, they built on the extreme violence that has characterized Colombia since the political troubles of the late 1940s (Palacios 2006). These organizations were willing to be less discriminating in their use of that violence, killing wives and children as well as principals.

Perhaps most importantly, high-level participants in the United States were at great risk from enforcement agencies. Many agencies developed sophisticated and broad investigative capabilities, creating high probabilities of arrest. If arrested, leaders were likely to serve very long sentences; the Mafia itself has largely broken down in the face of long sentences for other crimes, which have generated high-level informants. The return here was not to broad reputation but to discretion. Ostentatious display of wealth and power might be an asset in Colombia, where the corruption was systemic; it was a source of weakness in the United States, where police corruption was, by the 1980s, only opportunistic and where enforcement agencies had strong incentives and tools for apprehending leaders.

The Mafia, then, simply lacked useful assets for competing with Colombian and Mexican traffickers. But that may also explain why these drug trafficking groups have not expanded their activities to other criminal markets in the United States. Their assets are not usable in many sectors. Discretion requires that they restrict the dissemination of information about their capacities. Similarly, their workforce is predominantly from their own community, limiting their capacity to operate in the general marketplace. The contacts with corrupt authorities are limited to source countries, which play a minimal role in other smuggling, apart from illegal immigrants; in that market, protection in the importing country alone has value.

Mexican drug trafficking organizations may represent one instance of diversification into a variety of criminal activities. That certainly is a routine statement by scholars such as Luis Astorga and David Shirk (Astorga and Shirk 2010, p. 19), as well as by law enforcement authorities in Mexico. The other activities listed usually include human smuggling to the United States, extortion of businesses, and kidnapping. The first of these activities potentially uses organizational skills they already possess since drug smuggling is their core business. Extortion and kidnapping make efficient use of their reputational asset. Since the DTOs have well-known names, regularly reported in the Mexican media, a claim to the owner of a store that the threat is backed by a specific DTO will have high credibility.

This value of reputation is a contrast to the situation of Colombian and Mexican drug trafficking organizational behavior in the United States. The Colombian organizations have been in great flux over the last 20 years. Last year's Norte de Valle organization may morph into this year's Rastrojos organization. Reputations are much less well established so that it is not an important organizational asset. On the other hand, the Mexican drug trafficking organizations have committed few violent acts in the United States; their reputations are thus not established.

VII. Concluding Comments

Though for a long time it was assumed that illegal drug markets were typically monopolized, in fact, monopoly control is rare. Prior to 1980, it was widely believed that the American Mafia had dominated the major illegal markets such as those for bookmaking and loansharking and even for heroin importation into New York City until the late 1960s (e.g., Cressey 1969). Despite finding that some dealers within the United States have enormous incomes and traffic in large quantities, no researcher has found evidence, except on the most local basis (e.g., a few blocks), that a dealer organization has the ability to exclude others or to set prices,[19] the hallmarks of market power (Katz and Rosen 1994).

Even at the trafficker level, market power seems elusive. The small share of the retail price accounted for by all activities up to import is strong, but not conclusive, evidence of competition at this level.[20] The continuing decline of prices over 30 years at all levels of the market suggests that if market power ever existed, it has now been dissipated. Thus there is no level at which policymakers need be worried that tough enforcement will lead to price declines because a cartel is broken, a matter raised more than 40 years ago by Tom Schelling in his classic paper on organized crime (Schelling 1967). The explanation for the lack of market power may also be contained in Schelling's paper. Perhaps the Mafia was collecting rents on behalf of corrupt police departments that had exclusive jurisdiction and little external scrutiny; those departments are less systemically corrupt and face substantial oversight from federal investigative agencies.

This conjecture may generalize across products and countries. It may well be that, without central and effective corrupt government involvement, drug markets are likely to be fragmented and competitive. The few instances in which there are indications of market power, as in Tajikistan and perhaps Mexico prior to 2000, it is the involvement of thoroughly corrupt governments that is critical. That may also be the circumstance in which drug trafficking is no longer a specialized activity but becomes an element of organized crime.

Notes

1. School of Public Policy and Department of Criminology, University of Maryland; IZA and RAND. Doug Weiss provided helpful research assistance.
2. Note that there are no serious global estimates for any other illegal market. Nonetheless, the statement is not a contentious one.
3. For the United States, see e.g., Levitt and Venkatesh 2000 reporting on Chicago in the 1990s and Reuter, MacCoun, and Murphy 1990 reporting on Washington, DC, in 1988. For Norway, Bretteville-Jensen and Bion 2004, a study of heroin dealers in Oslo, also shows very low earnings per dealer.
4. There appear to be no comprehensive reviews of the drug retailing literature for the United States or for Europe. Important studies in the United States include: Jacobs 1999; Levitt and Venkatesh 2000; and Wendel and Curtis 2000. For the United Kingdom, McSweeney, Turnbull, and Hough 2008 provides a review.
5. Gamella and Rodrigo's (2008) description of the smuggling sector of the Moroccan hash industry provides a rare light on this sector. Raisdana and Nakhjavani (2002) describe heroin distribution in Iran.
6. For example, much of Afghanistan's heroin transits through Iran and Turkey and then is sold by the Turkish exporters in the Balkans for smuggling to a western European destination. For a detailed description of the international heroin market, see Paoli, Greenfield, and Reuter, 2009, chapter 3.
7. Kilmer and Pacula 2009 produce estimates for a number of countries that suggest that the earlier UNODC figures may have been as much as three times too high.
8. The percentage varies by drug and route. For example, Kilmer and Reuter (2009) estimate that the value added between farm-gate and import price is about 15 percent of the retail price of cocaine in the United States compared to 6 percent for heroin in the United Kingdom.
9. These are very approximate statements. Since drugs are seized at various points along the chain, a greater volume of cocaine is sold at export than at retail. However, most seizures occur very early in the system when each kilogram has a low replacement cost; thus, an adjustment for this would only slightly affect the cross-levels distribution.
10. This claim of PRI involvement in cartel agreements is a staple of the literature. I have been unable to find any English-language documentation of direct evidence for it.
11. These are small boats capable of carrying as much as 10 tons of cocaine with a very low profile that makes them hard to pick up on radar; the cocaine can be disposed of easily by opening the hatches. For a sample incident report see http://colombiareports.com/colombia-news/news/14692-colombian-forces-seize-narco-semi-submersible.html.
12. Paoli, Greenfield, and Reuter 2009 reports a kilogram price of $15,000 to $30,000. The above calculation assumes that shipments are 80 percent pure, which may be high.

13. It is useful to note once again that there is a dearth of studies of the operation of retail markets in major consuming countries that are poor, such as Iran, Pakistan, and Thailand.

14. These are time specific statements. At the time of the Knapp Commission inquiry into the New York Police Department in the early 1970s, systemic protection of heroin dealers was clearly well established (New York Knapp Commission 1973). A successor commission in the early 1990s found much less systemic corruption (Mollen et al. 1994). More recently, in the early 1990s, massive systemic corruption was found in drug enforcement in the New South Wales Police Department in Australia (Royal Commission into the NSW Police Service 1997).

15. There is an ambiguity as to whether this total was for a single organization or a confederation associated with Miguel Rodriguez-Orejuela, a principal figure in the Cali Cartel.

16. This appeared not to be so much compensation for longer time as for the number of potential police encounters.

17. This vague statement is all that can be gleaned from either Fuentes 1998 or Natarajan 2000.

18. It is not straightforward to calculate seizures as a share of total production because cocaine is often diluted close to the source and no nation regularly reports the purity of seizures.

19. The best evidence is simply the ease with which new sellers enter and the speed with which they depart. There may be rents for various capacities but certainly no power to exclude.

20. If demand is inelastic with respect to price, then a seller with market power can increase revenues and decrease costs by cutting production, until reaching a level at which the demand is elastic. Though the demand for cocaine and heroin may have elasticity greater than one with respect to final price at current levels, it is very likely that that elasticity is less than one with respect to high-level prices, though there are extreme models of price mark-up from import to trafficking that would yield a different result (see Caulkins 1990).

REFERENCES

Adler, Patricia. 1985. *Wheeling and Dealing: An Ethnography of an Upper-Level Drug Dealing and Smuggling Community*. New York: Columbia University Press.

Andreas, Peter. 2000. *Border Games: Policing the U.S.-Mexico Divide*. Ithaca, NY: Cornell University Press.

Astorga, Luis, and David Shirk. 2010. "Drug Trafficking Organizations and Counter-Drug Strategies in the US-Mexican Context." In *Shared Responsibility: US-Mexico Options for Confronting Organized Crime*, edited by David Shirk, Erik Olson, and Andrew Salee, 31–61. Washington, DC: Woodrow Wilson Center for International Scholars. http://www.wilsoncenter.org/topics/pubs/Shared%20Responsibility--Olson,%20Shirk,%20Selee.pdf.

Bouchard, Martin. 2007. "A Capture-Recapture Model to Estimate the Size of Criminal Populations and the Risks of Detection in a Marijuana Cultivation Industry." *Journal of Quantitative Criminology* 23:221–241.

Bretteville-Jensen, Anne Line, and Erik Biørn. 2004. "Do Prices Count? A Micro-econometric Study of Illicit Drug Consumption Based on Self-Reported Data." *Empirical Economics* 29(3): 673–695.

Butler, William. 1997. *Criminal Code of the Russian Federation*. London: Simmonds and Hill.

Catanzaro, Raimondo. 1988. *Men of Respect: A Social History of the Sicilian Mafia*. New York: Free Press.

Clawson, Patrick, and Renselaer Lee. 1998. *The Andean Cocaine Industry*. New York: St. Martin's.

Cook, Philip J. 2007. *Paying the Tab: The Costs and Benefits of Alcohol Control*. Princeton: Princeton University Press.

Cressey, Donald. 1969. *Theft of the Nation*. New York: Harper and Row.

Decker, Scott, and Margaret Townsend Chapman. 2008. *Drug Smugglers on Drug Smuggling: Lessons from the Inside*. Philadelphia: Temple University Press.

DesRoches, Frederick. 2007. "Research on Upper Level Drug Trafficking: A Review." *Journal of Drug Issues* 37(4): 827–844.

Dorn, Nicholas, Karim Murju, and Nigel South. 1992. *Traffickers: Drug Markets and Law Enforcement*. London: Routledge.

Drug Control Agency of Tajikistan. 2000. *The Dushanbe Illegal Drug Market*. Mimeo.

Drug Enforcement Administration. 2007. Statement by Administrator Karen P. Tandy on Two Hundred and Seven Million in Drug Money Seized in Mexico City. Press release. http://www.justice.gov/dea/pubs/pressrel/pr032007.html.

Europol. 2013. Socta 2013 EU Serious and Organised Crime Threat Assessment. https://www.europol.europa.eu/content/eu-serious-and-organised-crime-threat-assessment-socta [accessed August 6, 2013].

Everingham, Susan, and C. Peter Rydell. 1994. *The Demand for Cocaine*. Santa Monica, CA: RAND.

Forbes. 2011. "The World's Billionaires." http://www.forbes.com/wealth/billionaires.

Fuentes, J. R. 1998. "Life of a Cell: Managerial Practice and Strategy in Colombian Cocaine Distribution in the United States." PhD dissertation, City University of New York.

Gamella, Juan F., and Maris Luisa Jiménez Rodrigo. 2008. "Multinational Export-Import Ventures: Moroccan Hashish into Europe through Spain." In *A Cannabis Reader: Global Issues and Local Experiences*, edited by Sharon Rödner Sznitman, Borje Olsson, and Robin Room, 259–289. Lisbon: European Monitoring Center on Drugs and Drug Abuse.

Haller, Mark. 1979. "The Changing Structure of American Gambling in the Twentieth Century." *Journal of Social Issues* 35(3): 87–114.

Jacobs, Bruce A. 1999. *Dealing Crack: The Social World of Streetcorner Selling*. Boston: Northeastern University Press.

Katz, M. and H. Rosen. 1994. *Microeconomics*. 2nd ed. Burr Ridge, IL: Irwin.

Kilmer, Beau, Jonathan P. Caulkins, Brittany Bond, and Peter Reuter. 2010. *Reducing Drug Trafficking Revenues and Violence in Mexico: Would Legalizing Marijuana in California Help?* Occasional Paper. Santa Monica, CA: RAND. http://www.rand.org/pubs/occasional_papers/2010/RAND_OP325.pdf.

Kilmer, Beau, and R. Pacula. 2009. *Estimating the Size of the Global Drug Market: A Demand-Side Approach—Report 2*. TR-711-EC. Santa Monica, CA: RAND. http://www.rand.org/pubs/technical_reports/TR711.

Kilmer, Beau, and Peter Reuter. 2009. "Prime Numbers: Doped." *Foreign Policy* (November–December), pp. 34–35. http://www.foreignpolicy.com/articles/2009/10/19/prime_numbers_doped.

Kramer, Tom. 2007. *The United Wa State Party: Narco-Army or Ethnic Nationalist Party?* Washington, DC: East-West Center.

Kramer, Tom. 2009. *From Golden Triangle to Rubber Belt? The Future of the Opium Bans in the Kokang and Wa Regions*. TNI Drug Policy Briefing 29. Amsterdam: Transnational Institute.

Levi, Michael, and Peter Reuter. 2006. "Money Laundering: A Review of Current Controls and Their Consequences." *Crime and Justice: An Annual Review of Research* 34: 289–375.

Levitt, Steven, and Sudhira Venkatesh. 2000. "An Economic Analysis of a Drug-Selling Gang's Finances." *Quarterly Journal of Economics* 115(3): 755–789.

Maltz, Michael. 1976. "On Defining Organized Crime: Developing a Definition and a Typology." *Crime & Delinquency* 22(3): 338–346.

Mansfield, David. 2011. *Managing Concurrent and Repeated Risks: Explaining the Reductions in Opium Production in Central Helmand between 2008 and 2011*. Kabul: Afghanistan Research and Evaluation Unit. http://www.idpc.net/sites/default/files/library/Managing-concurrent-and-repeated-risks.pdf.

Matrix Knowledge Group. 2007. *The Illicit Drug Trade in the United Kingdom*. United Kingdom Home Office online report 20/07.

McSweeney, T., P. Turnbull, and M. Hough. 2008. *Tackling Drug Markets and Distribution Networks in the UK: A Review of the Recent Literature*. London: Drug Policy Commission.

Mollen, M., H. Baer Jr., H. Evans, R. C. Lankler, and H. R. Tyler Jr. 1994. Commission to Investigate Allegations of Police Corruption and the Anti-corruption Procedures of the Police Department Commission Report. New York: City of New York.

Morselli, Carlo. 2001. "Structuring Mr. Nice: Entrepreneurial Opportunities and Brokerage Positioning in the Cannabis Trade." *Crime, Law and Social Change* 35 (4):203–244.

Natarajan, Mangai. 2000. "Understanding the Structure of a Drug Trafficking Organization: A Conversational Analysis." In *Illegal Drug Markets: from Research to Policy*, edited by Mangai Natarajan and Mike Hough, 273–298. Crime Prevention Studies 11. Monsey, NY: Criminal Justice Press.

New York Knapp Commission. 1973. *The Knapp Commission Report on Police Corruption*. New York: George Braziller.

Office of National Drug Control Policy. 2001. *What America's Users Spend on Illicit Drugs, 1988–2000*. Washington, DC: Office of National Drug Control Policy.

Office of National Drug Control Policy. 2014. *What America's Users Spend on Illicit Drugs, 2000–2010*. Washington, DC: Office of National Drug Control Policy.

Palacios, Mario. 2006. *Between Legitimacy and Violence: A History of Colombia, 1875–2002*. Durham, NC: Duke University Press.

Paoli, Letizia. 2000. *Drug Markets in Frankfurt and Milan*. Freiburg, Germany: Max Planck Institute.

Paoli, Letizia. 2003 *Mafia Brotherhoods: Organized Crime, Italian Style* New York, Oxford University Press.

Paoli, Letizia, Victoria Greenfield, and Peter Reuter. 2009. *The World Heroin Market: Can Supply Be Cut?* New York: Oxford University Press.

Pearson, Geoffrey, and Dick Hobbs. 2001. *Middle Market Drug Distribution*. Home Office Research Study 227. London: UK Home Office.

Pudney, S., Badillo, C., Bryan, M., Burton, J., Conti, G. and Iacovou, M. 2006. "Estimating the Size of the UK Illicit Drug Market." In *Measuring Different Aspects of Problem Drug Use: Methodological Developments*, edited by N. Singleton, R. Murray, and L. Tinsley. London: Home Office

Raisdana, Fariborz, and Ahmad G. Nakhjavani. 2002. "The Drug Market in Iran." *Annals of the American Academy of Political and Social Science* 582:149–166.

Reuter, Peter. 2003. "The Political Economy of Drug Smuggling." In *The Political Economy of the Drug Industry*, edited by Menno Vellinga, 128–147. Gainesville: University Press of Florida.

Reuter, Peter. 2011. "Drug Smuggling Case Study: Los Rastrojos." START Center, University of Maryland.

Reuter, Peter, and John Haaga. 1989. *The Organization of High-Level Drug Markets: An Exploratory Study*. Santa Monica, CA: RAND.

Rios, Viridiana, and David Shirk. 2011. *Drug Violence in Mexico: Data and Analysis through 2010*. San Diego, CA: Transborder Institute.

Royal Commission into the NSW Police Service. 1997. *Final Report*. Vol. 1. Sydney, Australia http://www.pic.nsw.gov.au/files/reports/RCPS%20Report%20Volume%206.pdf [accessed August 6, 2013].

Ruggiero, Vincenzo, and Nigel South. 1995. *Eurodrugs: Drug Use, Markets and Trafficking in Europe*. London: Routledge.

Schelling, Thomas. 1967. "Economic Analysis of Organized Crime." In *Task Force, President's Commission on Law Enforcement and the Administration of Justice*. Washington, DC: US Government Printing Office.

SOCA (Serious and Organized Crime Agency). "Organised Crime Groups." http://www.soca.gov.uk/threats/organised-crime-groups [accessed August 6, 2013].

Sevigny, Eric, and Jonathan P. Caulkins. 2004. "Kingpins or Mules? An Analysis of Drug Offenders Incarcerated in Federal and State Prisons." *Criminology and Public Policy* 3(3): 401–434.

United Nations Office on Drugs and Crime. 2011. *World Drug Report 2011*. Vienna.

US Department of State. *Annual International Narcotics Control Strategy Report*. Washington, DC: US Department of State.

Wendel, Travis, and Ric Curtis. 2000. "The Heraldry of Heroin: 'Dope Stamps' and the Dynamics of Drug Markets in New York City." *Journal of Drug Issues* 30(2): 225–260.

CHAPTER 19

HUMAN SMUGGLING, HUMAN TRAFFICKING, AND EXPLOITATION IN THE SEX INDUSTRY

EDWARD R. KLEEMANS AND MONIKA SMIT

HUMAN trafficking is often confused with human smuggling. Both phenomena may be regarded as undesirable consequences of globalization. Smugglers as well as traffickers make use of other people's desire to improve their lives by building a better future elsewhere. Yet fundamental differences exist as well. Human *smuggling* primarily relates to illegal immigration and the violation of immigration laws. Human smugglers move people and provide a bridge between poor or dangerous countries and richer, safer ones. Some may have humanitarian motives to save political refugees or to help relatives or friends to build a new life. Others unscrupulously abuse dependent illegal immigrants by demanding high prices and providing bad or even perilous travel arrangements. Usually the relationship between smugglers and smuggled persons ends after the transport to the country of destination. In human *trafficking*, the situation is different. Human trafficking often, but not necessarily, involves border crossing. After arrival, trafficked persons must produce profit for the traffickers. Their relationships with the traffickers, or with organizations or individuals who have paid for their delivery, are longer term, victim-exploiter relationships, in which the human rights of the victim are being abused (Kelly and Regan 2000). According to the trafficking definition in the UN Protocol to Prevent, Suppress and Punish Trafficking in Persons, trafficking is the recruitment, transportation, transfer, harboring, or receipt of persons, using means such as threat or force, deception, coercion, abuse of power or of a position of vulnerability with the purpose of exploitation (UN 2000, Article 3a).

Many countries follow the aforementioned distinction between human smuggling and human trafficking in their national penal codes. However, in practice, these two phenomena can be difficult to distinguish and may be intertwined. Assisted illegal immigration may precede exploitation, as some smuggled illegal immigrants, who travel voluntarily to other countries, end up as trafficking victims in debt bondage and bad labor conditions only later on. Even the issue of mutual consent, common in human smuggling, is not always decisive in distinguishing between smuggling and trafficking (Herman 2006; van Liempt and Doomernik 2006); trafficking also usually starts with a consensual agreement between the trafficker and the future victim (Andrees 2008). When individuals have agreed to come to another country to work in the sex industry or in other sectors, their fate may not become clear until after arrival, when they are gradually forced to do work different from what they had agreed upon, or under very different circumstances than they had expected. Even then the victim may consent for various reasons, be it out of fear or because of lack of other, better options.

Exploitation of women in the sex industry is the most widely known trafficking phenomenon. It is also the prime focus of both the trafficking debate and trafficking research. It is, however, not the only manifestation of trafficking. Women, men, and children fall prey not only to exploitation in the sex industry, but also to other forms of exploitation, such as forced labor or services, slavery or practices similar to slavery, servitude, or the removal of organs. Increasing amounts of data show that other forms of trafficking, particularly trafficking for labor exploitation in private homes—as domestic servants—and in agriculture, construction, and sweatshop industries are at least as common as trafficking for sexual exploitation. Attention to these kinds of "modern slavery" is gradually increasing (Smit 2011).

The processes involved in labor trafficking differ in certain respects from the ones involved in forced prostitution, particularly in terms of the relationships between victims and offenders, characteristics of victims and offenders, the amount of force and deceit, and the exit options. Victims of labor trafficking are found in a variety of employment sectors that typically require large numbers of low-paid, flexible, seasonal workers, sometimes in difficult and dangerous conditions. The worst cases may be appalling in terms of human rights violations: Victims may experience debt bondage, withholding of identity documents, threats and abuse, reduced or no pay, excessive working hours, dangerous working conditions, poor accommodations, and discrimination (for a literature review, see Dowling, Moreton, and Wright 2007). Nevertheless, opinions vary substantially about how harsh labor conditions and restrictions on free will should be to warrant calling it "modern slavery" or "human trafficking." Due to space limitations, we will not devote more attention to trafficking for labor exploitation in this essay.

In this essay, we will discuss several topics related to human smuggling and human trafficking, with a special focus on exploitation in the sex industry. We successively elaborate upon human smuggling (section I), human trafficking for sexual exploitation (section II), policy measures and interventions (section III), and pitfalls and progress in research (section IV). Finally, we close with conclusions (section V).

I. Human Smuggling

A. Cruel Offenders and Helpless Illegal Migrants?

In the social and political debate, discussions about human trafficking tend to overemphasize images of cruel offenders and helpless victims. In Europe, public debate was fueled by the awful Dover incident in 2000, when 58 Chinese immigrants suffocated to death in a lorry while trying to reach the United Kingdom; two survivors were able to recollect this tragedy in detail. In the United States, a similar role was played with the June 1993 grounding of the *Golden Venture,* a Chinese smuggling ship, off New York City's harbor with a cargo of nearly 300 illegal immigrants. In many countries, reckless Snakeheads (Chinese human smugglers) are the common subject of daunting tales.

The reasons why these events appeal to media and politics are clear. However, such images severely misrepresent the problem and misdirect policy discussions. Human smuggling basically involves mutual consent between illegal immigrants and "smugglers," who are either family, friends, or more distant professional smugglers. People want to migrate, despite increasingly repressive Western migration regimes, for many reasons: imminent danger, discomfort, and poverty, combined with the prospect of a better life elsewhere. Next to these push factors, major pull factors are wage differences, dual labor markets in Western countries (stable, high-paying jobs combined with labor shortages for unstable, low-paying jobs), and the welfare state, particularly in Europe.

To this mainly economic perspective, Portes (1995) added the important role of migrant networks across the world, which needs to be recognized as migrants do not make isolated decisions. Social networks are important in providing information and assistance, which explains "chain migration" and collective decisions on migration by (extended) families to increase family revenues. Viewing migration this way, it is understandable that many actors—not only migrants, smugglers, family, and friends, but also employers, organizations, and some governments—may have a clear common interest in successful migration through legal or illegal means. Much illegal migration occurs through largely legal channels. Zhang (2007) reviews the ways in which several legal channels are used: entering as a legal immigrant (using forged documents); marriage fraud; the use of tourist, student, or scholar visas; and business invitations. In Europe, much attention has also been paid to the use of asylum procedures and counterfeit documents, which provides access to the welfare state (e.g., Neske and Doomernik 2006).

Two preliminary conclusions prevail. First, many more people may be involved in human smuggling than professional smugglers alone, and smuggling can be carried out entirely without involvement of professional smugglers. Second, smuggling occurs through many more channels than the most visible, which are overrepresented in the media (physical transportation of illegal immigrants by land, sea, and air). International migration may be viewed as a global business with licit and illicit aspects (Salt and Stein 1997). It involves migrants and their social networks, trying to migrate and send money home, and professional as well as amateur smugglers, who make a living out of their business. A range of actors are involved in the smuggling process, which may be divided into three stages: mobilization (country of origin), en route (transit countries), and insertion (country of destination).

B. Perpetrators

An analysis of 10 police investigations in the Netherlands into human smuggling shows that the prime suspects in these cases very often have social ties with both the countries of origin and the countries of destination (Kleemans and van de Bunt 2003; Kleemans 2007). Smugglers and clients often share the same ethnic background, and many smugglers have in the past been smuggled themselves. Smuggling networks emerge in which the organizers of (sub)routes are the major players. The prime suspects are not distant masterminds but are often involved in the day-to-day activities. The cores of these smuggling rings can be relatively small, consisting of a few people in the country of origin, in a transit country (if necessary), and in the country of destination. Many prime suspects are also closely involved in forging documents. The logistics of smuggling are far less complicated through use of forged documents: Smuggled immigrants can simply travel alone, for instance, by airplane. Without forged documents, the journey is longer, more complicated, and more uncomfortable. Additional barriers, transfers, and stops are necessary as well as reliance on local knowledge and local contacts to transfer and cater to people on the move. A longer chain also involves more complex coordination, communication, and payment schemes. Sometimes these chains are coordinated from start to finish, but in other instances clients are successively passed through the hands of groups that are only very loosely connected (see also Neske and Doomernik 2006; Zhang 2007).

C. Organized Crime?

In the literature there is a recurring debate about the amount of organization involved and the role of organized crime, particularly in smuggling Chinese (e.g., Chin 1999). Based on extensive ethnographic research, Zhang and Chin (2002) claim that Chinese human smuggling is dominated by ordinary citizens, a point also stressed in research on the US-Mexican border (Spener 2004). Familial networks and fortuitous social contacts have enabled these individuals to pool resources to smuggle human beings around the world. According to Zhang and Chin, Chinese human smuggling organizations consist of mostly peer group entrepreneurs and dyadic networks (see also Zhang and Gaylord 1996; Zhang 1997). However, much research based on law enforcement information takes a wider view of the variety of organizational structures involved (e.g. Aronowitz 2001; Schloenhardt 2001; Kleemans and van de Bunt 2003; Staring et al. 2005; Soudijn 2006). For instance, Soudijn carried out extensive research on the smuggling of Chinese immigrants, mainly through European countries into the United Kingdom, by analyzing 88 Dutch court files (1996–2003). Two conclusions diverge from what is typically found in ethnographic research. First, although many ethnic Chinese are involved, about a quarter of the suspects were not ethnic Chinese. Field interviews would miss such an observation, if they focus on Chinese smugglers and the Chinese community as they tend to do. Second, the analyzed groups within the Chinese smuggling scene take on assignments from several organizations abroad, and different alliances are continued if smuggling operations run smoothly. Rather than by central coordination, smuggling is harmonized by looser organizations through social networks. Yet, on an interpersonal level, police and court files show much more stability and cohesion as the relationships among offenders are relatively durable and consistent if no problems arise. Furthermore, large-scale smuggling groups handle a continuous flow of migrants waiting to be smuggled, which results in a need to have reliable people at hand and to construct some division of labor (Soudijn 2006).

A view of human smugglers as ruthless offenders preying on helpless victims is sometimes correct—when criminal groups are involved, violence is used, travel conditions are harsh, and prices are exorbitant. According to an ICMPD (2010) report on illegal migration, smuggling, and trafficking in Central and eastern Europe, smuggling fees range from 300 USD (smuggling of Vietnamese and Mongolian citizens from the Czech Republic to Germany) to 10,000 EUR (smuggling of Chinese citizens from China to EU countries). Zhang (2007, p. 89) states that migrants from China's southern province of Fujian typically pay 65,000 or even 70,000 US dollars each to be smuggled into the United States.

However, in general, smuggling rings, even when involving criminal groups, have a clear interest in keeping their clients satisfied as satisfied customers and their families bring in new business. In migrant communities, communication about smuggling is relatively open, and advertising by word of mouth is a common way to attract new clients. Furthermore, many migrant communities do not regard smuggling illegal immigrants as a serious offense. On the contrary, smugglers are viewed as service providers, offering the opportunity to find a better future elsewhere. Hence, the basic rationale behind human smuggling is the combined effort of immigrants, their social environment, and smugglers to circumvent immigration laws.

II. Human Trafficking for Sexual Exploitation

A. Background and Causes

Poverty is often claimed to be the root cause of trafficking in humans. Although unemployment or low earnings are among the strongest push factors (Andrees 2008), the link between poverty and trafficking is complex as is the link between poverty and migration. There is no simple correlation between the prevalence of trafficking and the Human Development Index, the Human Poverty Index, or the Gender Empowerment Measure in the 2006 UNODC trafficking in persons global report (Laczko and Danailova-Trainer 2009). The very poor usually cannot afford the investments needed to cross borders. They stay behind, become "internal migrants" (migrating from a rural to an urban area), or are caught up in internal trafficking (within a country or a region). Still, the bulk of trafficking victims originate from economically depressed and politically unstable areas in the world and the most disadvantaged social and ethnic groups in those areas (Lehti and Aromaa 2006). Some of the major countries of origin of trafficking victims have high scores on the Transparency International Corruption Perception Index (BNRM 2002). Several researchers studied the relationship between (perceived) corruption and trafficking. Studies by Lyday (2001) and Bales (2005) show a strong relationship. Studnicka (2010) studied trafficking and (perceived) corruption in Brazil. After reanalyzing a report of a parliamentary commission, he concluded that 71 percent of the cases that were investigated as trafficking cases between 1994 and 2003 involved corruption.

Personal circumstances play a role as well. A disproportionately high percentage of victims come from broken or abusive family situations. Nevertheless, in some cases, commitment to family members in need is precisely the drive to accept potentially dangerous offers abroad (see also Surtees 2008).

B. Trafficking Process

It is common to distinguish three main phases in the trafficking process: recruitment of the victim, transportation, and actual exploitation.

Much has been written about *recruitment* of victims. Several studies investigate recruitment processes, domestically and abroad. Many victims are recruited by promises of employment opportunities, often in hotel service, catering, and entertainment or as domestic workers and nannies. Most migrate willingly, and many are aware of the fact that they will work in prostitution, as was the case for the majority of trafficking victims from Central and eastern Europe in an early Dutch study (Vocks and Nijboer 1999). In fact, many were already working as prostitutes in their home countries (Agustin 2007; Janssen 2007). They do not live up to the popular, yet incomplete and one-sided image of innocent, ignorant victims. Outright abduction or selling into prostitution is often mentioned in the media, but this is rather the exception than the rule (Andrees 2008). This can also be concluded from data in the International Organization for Migration (IOM) counter-trafficking database, referring to cases assisted by IOM. In 9,646 cases (assisted during the period 1999–September 2006), only nine victims had been kidnapped, whereas 60 percent had been recruited via personal contacts. In 25 percent of these cases, the recruiters were friends, relatives, or partners. Nevertheless, outside the industrialized world, abduction and selling by relatives is more prevalent (Lehti and Aromaa 2006). A different recruitment strategy is to emotionally manipulate a victim by feigning romantic interest and the intention to form a relationship and then gradually to coerce or threaten her into prostitution. This strategy is also referred to as the "loverboy method." Not all recruitment takes place in the countries of origin. Some victims are recruited in the country of destination, after having arrived there as undocumented migrants. They are vulnerable to exploitation as they are at risk of detention and expulsion due to their illegal status.

Depending on the country of origin and the country of destination, a travel route will be chosen and travel documents will be supplied—if necessary. As was mentioned with respect to smuggled migrants, many victims of trafficking also cross borders in a legitimate way (business invitations, marriage, family reunification) by using their own passports and a tourist, student, or scholar visa (BNRM 2004). Trafficking victims often have all the required documents, one of the reasons why it is difficult to identify trafficking cases at the border (Viuhko and Jokinen 2009).

Dislocation and a high turnover are part of the prostitution business. Brothel owners are in constant need of new girls to bring in extra money. Prostitutes and pimps also travel to different locations and countries in search of new clients and profitable opportunities. A study by van Dijk (2002, reviewed in Kleemans 2007) on human trafficking in the Netherlands in the period 1997–2000, involving 521 suspects, shows that victims are bought and sold more than once, and that the turnover rate is high. Many victims report that they have worked in various cities and in various countries. In the police investigations analyzed, some victims were active in street prostitution or escort services, but most worked in brothels or in window prostitution. Forty clubs were owned by trafficking suspects, 27 clubs cooperated (the owners usually turned a blind eye), and 21 clubs were used by traffickers (the owners being unaware). People letting rooms in window prostitution were never directly involved in trafficking. They let rooms to pimps without checking on whether the prostitutes were illegal or exploited. Sometimes the girls were recruited abroad, but more often they were simply bought from other pimps or recruited domestically.

The principal means of control, next to the above-mentioned dislocation and mobility, are manipulation through perverted social relationships, close monitoring, intimidation, and outright violence. According to many studies, implied and actual violence is common and ever-present (e.g., Lehti and Aromaa 2006; Surtees 2008). However, traffickers and exploiters have started to use more subtle methods of control and are more likely to share a small part of the profits, thus discouraging victims from complaining to the authorities (US Department of State 2010). The courts are less likely to consider "soft" means of coercion as sufficient to prove coercion (International Centre for Migration Policy Development 2009). Violence and control may be integrated in complex personal relationships and (economic) dependency situations. Debt bonding is very common as recruiting expenses or travel costs have to be paid to traffickers. Traffickers tend to perpetuate this debt situation through inflated housing and living expenses and arbitrary fines for "misconduct." Close monitoring of the daily lives and earnings of the victims often accompanies this strategy. If women are sold to another pimp, the story repeats itself. Finally, particularly in cross-border trafficking, exploiting the illegal residence status of victims is a common control method; this involves confiscating passports and other identity documents as well as stoking illegal immigrants' fear of local authorities and the prospect of expulsion. The involvement of close intimate relationships in cases of exploitation offers one explanation why free will is a relative phenomenon in this context, why many victims feel reluctant to report to the authorities, why not all victims want to be "liberated," and why some, after being liberated, return to prostitution and to their exploiters.

C. Organized Crime and the Involvement of Women

Much discussed in relation to human trafficking is whether criminal groups and organized crime are involved. Forced prostitution is a profitable criminal activity that attracts several kinds of offenders, criminal groups, and criminal networks (for reviews, see Lehti and Aromaa 2006; Surtees 2008). According to the EU Organized Crime Threat Assessment (OCTA), the most active organized crime groups involved in trafficking in human beings in the European Union are Bulgarian, Nigerian, and Romanian. Groups from other Balkan countries, China, Moldova, Russia, Turkey, Ukraine, and Vietnam are also frequently reported (Europol 2009a). However, the removal and relaxation of internal border controls within the EU provided opportunities for less sophisticated, smaller or mid-level groups to operate across borders as well (Europol 2009b).

Three main forms of criminal cooperation can be distinguished (see van Dijk 2002). Solo offenders force one or more girls into prostitution. Self-supporting criminal groups control the entire process, from recruitment to prostitution, and have no established contacts with other offenders or groups involved in human trafficking; the main suspects are often in charge of brothels or sex clubs, and they rely on personal contacts to recruit and transport victims. Criminal macro networks include solo offenders and criminal groups clustered by geographical proximity, family ties, friendships, commercial circuits, or similarity in criminal activities. In trafficking networks, clusters of offenders evolve around the recruitment of victims in particular countries or areas, sometimes around transport and locations where (forced) prostitution takes place.

Women are usually viewed as victims in forced prostitution, but often they also play prominent roles as recruiters, transporters, or exploiters (Kleemans and van de Bunt 1999; Lehti and Aromaa 2006; Viuhko and Jokinen 2009; Siegel and de Blank 2010). Former victims may be used as recruiters or may be offered more favorable working conditions if they recruit replacements; relatives of male traffickers or prostitutes may be involved in monitoring and exploiting prostitutes, and some women make a career in trafficking, for example, victims of Nigerian trafficking who start recruiting or controlling other victims. Although men play a prominent role in forced prostitution, the business of prostitution is also very much a women's business. This is why women should be regarded not only as victims, but also as potential accomplices or actual traffickers. A similar point can be made about the underexposed role of women in other criminal activities, such as (Chinese) human smuggling (e.g., Soudijn 2006; Zhang, Chin, and Miller 2007).

III. Policy Measures and Interventions

A. Border Control

A traditional way to combat human trafficking is to treat it as a form of illegal migration and increase border controls, build higher fences, and target physical smuggling processes. The deficiencies of this approach are clear. For one, most human trafficking for sexual exploitation turns out to be short distance, and cross-border trafficking frequently involves victims who travel voluntarily and end up in exploitive situations later on. Another important impediment of this approach concerns the considerable negative side effects, in terms of human lives, injuries, and perilous travel conditions, as is demonstrated by research on securing the US-Mexican border (Frost 2007; Guerette 2007). The attacks of September 11, 2001, have turned US border control into a national security issue, even though all 19 terrorists involved entered the country on valid student and tourist visas (Frost 2007). Guerette (2007) shows that, since the year 2000, more than 300 migrant deaths are recorded along the US-Mexican border each year, and it is believed that many more perish but remain unfound. Nevertheless, a strong focus has been placed on additional border security measures: more fences, more surveillance, and more advanced technology. In addition, proactive harm-reduction strategies have been implemented, such as educational campaigns informing would-be migrants of the dangers of crossing in remote areas, provision of life-saving equipment and training for line agents, search and rescue operations by border search trauma and rescue teams, and lateral repatriation programs to return apprehended migrants to less hazardous places along the border. Although no overall reduction has been registered in the rate of migrant deaths since the US Border Security Initiative was created, evidence collected by Guerette seems to indicate that these last two mechanisms may have prevented some migrant deaths.

Perrin (2010) delves into the largely ignored role of transit countries in global efforts to combat trafficking in persons. According to Perrin, transit countries should pursue measures to prevent trafficking, prosecute traffickers, and protect victims. Examples are exercising due diligence in regulating the entry of foreigners in order to identify individuals at risk, checking transit documents, and providing protection to suspected trafficked persons in transit. However, enhancing cross-border detection of trafficking is easier said than done as trafficking victims often travel with legal documents, sometimes not yet knowing that they will be exploited later on, or are not willing to expose their intention to stay or work illegally in the country of destination. However, according to Perrin, in every detected trafficking case "a 'full and complete investigation' principle should apply, such that destination, transit and origin countries work to disrupt the relevant trafficking network as a whole..." (Perrin 2010, p. 24).

B. Labor Market Initiatives

Another policy line involves demand-reducing initiatives such as curbing access to the welfare state and making employers or companies responsible for contracting illegal laborers (e.g., sanctions, inspections). These initiatives may indeed reduce demand, but, at the same time, they make life much harder for illegal immigrants and their families. Engbersen, van der Leun, and De Boom (2007) point to the unintended side effects of the very effective way northern European welfare states exclude illegal immigrants from the formal economy and public services: Illegal immigrants have to participate in various informal economies or, when lacking access through social networks, engage in criminal activities.

Hence, several policy proposals focus on decriminalizing illegal immigration through labor market initiatives, such as temporary or permanent foreign worker programs or selective regularization. Whether labor market initiatives are a viable option depends very much on the local situation. Particularly in the European Union, complicating factors for such alternatives are the attractiveness of these programs for low-skilled workers (and their families), combined with an elaborate welfare state, and spillover effects to neighboring countries. Selective regularization programs have been carried out in several countries (Levinson 2005). The main bottlenecks of this approach relate to the development of objective criteria for regularization and the attractiveness of these programs for new immigrants and illegal immigrants in neighboring countries. Various international examples have shown that regularization programs are seldom a definitive solution and that implementing such programs consistently is very difficult (for a review, see Cornelius, Martin, and Hollifeld 1994). We will not elaborate on different policies for controlling immigration, but the modus operandi of human smugglers and illegal immigrants demonstrate that illegal immigration and human smuggling are closely intertwined with political asylum and immigration policies (for a review, see Guild and Minderhoud 2006).

C. Prostitution Policies

Policies on human trafficking for sexual exploitation are directly linked to the contested nature of prostitution and the different views on how authorities should deal with this ambiguous market. Over the years, prostitution policies in many countries have oscillated between harm reduction (focused on public health issues such as sexually transmitted diseases, more recently mostly HIV/AIDS) and regularization, and prohibition, and criminalization, each favored by opposing interest groups.

In many countries prostitution is de facto tolerated to some extent, though different forms of prostitution and exploitation are regulated or combated in different ways (see Munro 2006). A study commissioned by the Norwegian government compared two widely opposing policy approaches, one in Sweden (criminalization) and the other in the Netherlands (regularization) (Norwegian Ministry of Justice and the Police 2004). In Sweden, the general policy assumption is that voluntary prostitution does not exist; prostitution is viewed as a form of violence committed by men against women. The Swedes consider prostitution to be a serious social problem that inflicts damage on individuals and society. Hence, in 1999 the purchase of sexual services became punishable by law while the sale of such services was decriminalized, exempting prostitutes from prosecution. In this way, authorities hope to deter clients and generate new norms about the social unacceptability of the purchase of sexual services. Wilcox et al. (2009) reviewed the research literature on tackling the demand for prostitution. They examined 220 English-language studies from 1990 onward originating from several "key countries of interest." Although the demand for prostitution is not necessarily the same as demand for the service of trafficking victims, some of the results are interesting in this context. According to the authors, some tentative findings and promising approaches in tackling the demand for prostitution can be identified, but many strategies may lead to potentially negative consequences for prostitutes. The authors note that some of the gaps in the evidence of the effectiveness of the Swedish model include: what has happened to prostitutes who have disappeared from the street? Have levels of violence against prostitutes changed? And what has happened to the indoor market?

Meanwhile, a Swedish report was published on how the ban worked in practice and what its effects have been (Statens offentliga utredningar 2010). According to this report, street prostitution has been halved. It has increased in Denmark and Norway, and so the reduction is considered to be a direct policy result. Internet prostitution increased in all three Scandinavian countries but on a much larger scale in the neighboring countries, while the proportion of men reporting that they have purchased sexual services has decreased. However, some of these conclusions are based on comparing estimates, and the report lacks information on the methodological quality of the evaluations used or the comparison itself. Even less information is available on the effects of the ban on trafficking, but, according to the police, the ban acts as a barrier to traffickers and procurers to establish themselves in Sweden.

The Dutch authorities took a very different approach. In October 2000, after years of leniency and de facto tolerance, the general ban on brothels was lifted. The essence of this regularization approach was that, under certain conditions, making money out of voluntary prostitution by prostitutes of legal age is no longer prohibited and that brothels are legal if they comply with certain licensing conditions. At the same time, policymakers intended to crack down forcefully on unacceptable forms of prostitution, such as prostitution of minors and illegal aliens, as well as involuntary prostitution. An extensive evaluation shows that this regularization approach of location-bound prostitution (brothels, sex clubs, and window prostitution) produced some positive effects: Business owners tend to comply with licensing conditions, and the number of prostitutes without legal documents has decreased (matched by an increase in prostitutes from eastern European countries that fall within the European Economic Area). Yet, at the same time, the position of prostitutes has not improved much, and procurers are still a common phenomenon: The number of prostitutes with a pimp has not decreased (Daalder 2007). What's more, law enforcement investigations show that human trafficking still thrives behind the legal façade of regularization. The main reason for this ambiguous outcome is that the policy is focused too much on business owners, whereas we know from research that the exploitation of women is more often carried out by pimps. The legal change seems to have effectively deterred business owners from getting directly involved in human trafficking, but it has failed to address the main problem of exploitation by pimps. Prostitutes with pimps mainly work behind the windows, in the escort business, and at home.

In Finland, yet another position was taken: The law prohibits the buying of sex from a trafficking victim or from a subject of procurement. The question is whether a client will be able to know who is a victim or who is being procured. In online advertisements prostitutes and procurers sometimes declare that they are not victims and that they work independently (Viuhko and Jokinen 2009), yet, of course, this is no guarantee. The Dutch campaign "Appearances Are Deceptive," appealing to clients to call an anonymous tip line when they encounter wrongdoing, showed that some clients are willing to report on involuntary prostitution (Daalder 2007). Nevertheless, we know from a study by Di Nicola et al. (2009) that most men who buy sex are aware of trafficking and exploitation, yet this does not affect their behavior. Farley, Bindel, and Golding (2009) studied London men who buy sex in the United Kingdom. They find that 27 percent of the 103 interviewees think that they are entitled to any act they choose once they have paid, and a quarter of them believe that a prostitute cannot be raped. Furthermore, a quarter reports having encountered a woman in the sex industry whom they believe was forced, whereas only five reported their suspicions to the police. Hence, the question is not only: "is a client able to identify a victim?" but also "if so, will he act upon it?"

It looks as if prostitution policies, irrespective of their content, are not able to erase trafficking for sexual exploitation (see also International Centre for Migration Policy Development 2009). Moreover, whether they have any effect at all depends on enforcement. Involuntary prostitution—even in the regulated sector—is very difficult for inspecting authorities to detect. The same applies to prostitution of minors as it is often difficult to determine the age of young prostitutes. These hidden phenomena can be detected only by intrusive law enforcement investigations. However, besides capacity and priority problems, serious problems for mounting effective law enforcement operations are identifying abuse and the complex motives of the women involved. For a variety of reasons already mentioned, many women do not report to the police. A study on victims of trafficking demonstrates that some victims decline assistance because they want to go home—without any fuss, stigma, or repercussions—or because they want to return to work, mainly for economic reasons. It also demonstrates that several supply-driven programs and facilities, often managed by nongovernmental organizations (NGOs), are not attuned to the basic needs of these victims (Brunovskis and Surtees 2007).

IV. Research: Pitfalls and Progress

Recently, attention to the problem of human trafficking has greatly increased, and much research has been carried out into this phenomenon. Still, we do not know its exact prevalence and incidence. Estimates of the annual number of people trafficked across borders worldwide vary from 600,000 to 4 million (Lehti and Aromaa 2006). The US State Department's Trafficking in Persons Report (2006) mentions up to 17,000 victims trafficked into the United States each year. These numbers do not include US citizens trafficked within the United States. However, these estimates are questionable (US Government Accountability Office 2006). National and international data are not available, scarce, unreliable, or not comparable (e.g., Laczko 2005; Lehti and Aromaa 2006; US Government Accountability Office, 2006; Savona and Stefanizzi 2007). According to Chawla, Me, and Pichon (2009), who studied human trafficking worldwide, 14 percent of all countries have no data available at all.

One of the reasons for the lack of data is that part of the exploitation takes place in largely hidden sectors, such as the sex industry and in private households. Human trafficking is a notoriously underreported phenomenon, and traffickers and victims of trafficking are difficult to identify. As trafficking usually starts with a consensual agreement, victimization may not become apparent until after arrival at the place of destination. Pressure may be exercised by procurers, criminal networks, employers, or corrupt police or immigration officials. At the same time, trafficking is not a real priority issue everywhere or is not seen as a real problem. Farrell, McDevitt, and Fahy (2010), for example, carried out a survey among US municipal law enforcement agencies. They found that most of the leading officials did not perceive human trafficking to be a problem in their community and less than 10 percent identified human trafficking cases from 2000 to 2006.

In addition, victims of trafficking, in general, have reasons not to come forward to report what has happened to them. They are a hidden population (Tyldum and Brunovskis 2005), and so too are the perpetrators and, particularly in the sex industry, to a large extent clients as well (Di Nicola et al. 2009). Victims may not consider themselves to be victims, instead viewing themselves as migrants whose journeys went wrong, and they prefer the current exploitative situation to their original situation. They refrain from reporting to the police for many reasons, including being embarrassed, emotional attachment to the perpetrator, dependency, and fear of negative repercussions, either from their perpetrator or—because of their weak legal status—from the authorities (with expulsion as a potential outcome). Such an outcome may be viewed as the shameful ending of a failed undertaking.

Furthermore, not all research distinguishes between human smuggling and human trafficking, mingling data relating to trafficking and smuggling, and to irregular immigration as well (Bureau Nationaal Rapporteur Mensenhandel 2007). Although the UN definition on trafficking is widely shared and many states have signed and ratified the protocol (e.g., Gallagher 2006), they differ concerning the operationalization with regard to topics such as movement across borders, consent of the victim (US Government Accountability Office 2007), and the coverage of exploitation outside the sex industry. Di Nicola (2007, p. 50) refers in this respect to "the never-ending story of a definition," resulting in lack of, or incomparable data across, countries. Even within countries, governments, law enforcement agencies, and nongovernmental organizations tend to maintain their own data sets and their own reasons for defining and presenting the trafficking problem in particular ways: as not too significant a problem which they can easily control or as a significant problem that can be tackled only with large sums of money. According to Dottridge (2003), some human rights activists argue that exaggeration is not a big problem as long as attention is generated for any abuse that is occurring. However, policies and interventions based on inadequate findings may be ineffective (Kelly 2002; Dottridge 2003; Tyldum and Brunovskis 2005).

The data that do exist are most often either general estimates that are questionable due to methodological weaknesses (Cwikel and Hoban 2005; US Government Accountability Office 2006; Tyldum and Brunovskis 2005) or administrative data kept by the various authorities or organizations on the victims they assist (Laczko 2005). These data reflect the legal framework and enforcement strategies in a country rather than the actual scope of the problem (Andrees 2008). What we do know depends largely on the texts of the national penal codes. These *directly* influence which cases the police and other criminal investigation units will investigate and, subsequently, which ones will be prosecuted (and thus the "official statistics"). They also affect which cases NGOs focus upon and deal with, as far as victim assistance is concerned, as well as the focus of research.

Another deficit in trafficking research is that very little is known about the effectiveness of countertrafficking initiatives. Few of the many interventions initiated by supranational, international, and national organizations are accompanied by evaluation research (Chase and Statham 2005; Laczko 2005). The US Government Accountability Office (GAO), for example, reviewed documents of 23 US government funded anti-trafficking projects in Indonesia, Thailand, and Mexico. It revealed that 21 of the 23 projects included one or more monitoring elements, yet only 10 state how performance is measured. The majority lack a logical framework of monitoring that links activities to goals, indicators, and targets (US Government Accountability Office 2007). Preliminary results of a worldwide systematic review on interventions dealing with cross-border trafficking for the purpose of exploitation outside the sex industry yielded no randomized control trials (RCTs) nor any study rating level 3 or 4 of the Maryland Scientific Methods Scale (SMS) (pre- and post-test measure with control or comparison groups) (van der Laan et al. 2010). Many studies did not even come close to meeting these SMS criteria as they were limited to descriptions of service providers' or participants' impressions.

Despite these problems, some—modest—progress has been made (e.g., Salt 2000; Laczko and Gozdziak 2005; Savona and Stefanizzi 2007). Not so long ago only a few countries had trafficking data available. According to Vermeulen et al. (2006), who conducted a state-of-the-art study among the then 25 EU member states, Belgium and the Netherlands were the only EU countries with data sets on trafficking. Actually, the

German Federal Criminal Office and the Swedish National Crime Police had been collecting data since 1994 and 1997, respectively. In the meantime, the situation has changed. There is strong pressure to provide national trafficking data, for example, by the US government for its yearly Trafficking in Persons Report, which classifies countries in tiers according to their efforts in fighting human trafficking (US Department of State 2010). Currently most European countries supply at least some trafficking data, and there are developments that transcend the national level.

In addition, several initiatives have been launched to collect data in a uniform way. One example is the EU-funded Siamsect project, which involved the development by Ghent University in Belgium and Transcrime in Italy of a standardized EU template and collection plan for statistical information and analysis of data on missing and sexually abused children and trafficking in human beings (Vermeulen et al. 2006). However, perhaps in part due to the complexity of covering three different phenomena in one project, the Siamsect plans were not implemented, and the EU financed a different European data collection project. This project, initiated in 2007 by IOM and the Federal Ministry of the Interior of Austria, was directed at the development of guidelines for the collection of data on human trafficking. The final report contains 17 guidelines on how to collect standardized, comparable data on victims, traffickers, the trafficking process, and the criminal justice response to trafficking (Aronowitz 2009).

Yet another example is the project of the International Centre for Migration Policy Development aimed at harmonization and improved quality and reliability of data related to trafficking in persons in southeastern European countries. In the course of the project, a largely uniform data system as well as victim-centered and trafficker-centered databases were developed for, and installed in, each of the 10 participating countries/territories (Surtees 2007). A special feature of this project is the keen eye that is focused on the national situation. While the authors of the project and the accompanying handbook advocated the harmonization of data on trafficking, national needs prevailed: Data collection must respond to, and be appropriate for, the situation of each country. This way, national differences in legislation and policy are acknowledged. This increases the local utility of the data to be collected and, thus, the chance that countries/territories will, indeed, fill the databases.

In the near future, we will probably have more data on the magnitude and nature of trafficking at our disposal. In this context, the yearly worldwide US Trafficking in Persons Report should be mentioned as well. Based on information from, among others, US embassies, government officials, NGOs, international organizations, and publications, the report contains country reports with facts and figures on victims and prosecutions of perpetrators and information on the extent of government efforts to fight human trafficking. It ranks countries according to their efforts in one of three tiers: full compliance with minimum standards for the elimination of trafficking (tier 1), a "watch list" indicating no full compliance but making significant efforts (tier 2), and, finally, no full compliance and not making serious efforts (tier 3) (US Department of State 2010). The 2010 TIP Report included for the first time a ranking and full narrative on the US efforts to combat human trafficking (US Department of State 2010).

V. CONCLUSION

In this essay we focused on human smuggling and trafficking for sexual exploitation. These phenomena are frequently confused, despite the differences. Human *smuggling* primarily relates to illegal immigration and the violation of immigration laws, whereas human *trafficking* primarily relates to exploitation. Furthermore, discussions about smuggling and trafficking are often clouded by generalizations, such as the cruel smuggler and the innocent, uninformed trafficking victim lured into prostitution (e.g., Zhang 2009).

Unfortunately, the heated debates about human smuggling and human trafficking stand in contrast with the amount of sound empirical research on these issues. In the coming decade, we should find out more about the impact of different immigration policies and anti-smuggling initiatives. Opportunity-reducing initiatives against human smuggling may also have negative side effects, for example, on true political refugees, travel conditions, and prices. More research on the financial aspects of human smuggling and human trafficking might also reveal much about the profits of different actors and the social organization of these illegal activities.

The debate about tackling trafficking for the purpose of sexual exploitation tends to be particularly heated and based upon emotions and beliefs rather than facts. Weitzer (2010) describes how prohibitionist individuals and organizations, who want to abolish the sex industry as such because they regard it as universally harmful, use unjust generalizations of certain research outcomes and biased data collection methods and distort or leave out inconvenient findings to make their point. According to Weitzer, this "oppression paradigm" contributes to a mythology of prostitution that increasingly influences public policy. Much has still to be learned about the effectiveness of countertrafficking initiatives, in particular, how do different prostitution and enforcement policies affect the opportunities and restrictions of various parties, including clients, owners, operators, procurers, and prostitutes? The number of monitoring and evaluation studies in this area is rising, but still too little is known about which interventions have been the most effective in preventing human trafficking, protecting victims, and prosecuting traffickers (US Government Accountability Office 2007; van der Laan et al. 2010) and which ones are not effective or maybe even counterproductive, causing collateral damage (Dottridge 2007).

Furthermore, we need to understand why some women do not report to the authorities or why they decline assistance. Therefore, more research is needed on the complex relationships between victims and offenders. Because existing studies mainly focus on victims who have been assisted, victim profiles may be. Much can be learned from other sources, such as field interviews and law enforcement investigations. Another important area for research is the victimization of minors—boys and girls ending up in prostitution—and the roles played by their social environment. Lehti and Aromaa (2006) point out that there may be serious underreporting of human trafficking in minors. Finally, research should focus not only on victimization, but also on human agency, particularly voluntary prostitution and conditions of (in)dependency, economic motivations, women making a career in prostitution, and women who become involved in trafficking as (co-)offenders.

The contested nature of both illegal immigration and prostitution and the widely opposing views on these matters seem to block sound empirical research on human smuggling and human trafficking.

References

Andrees, Beate. 2008. "Forced Labour and Trafficking in Europe: How People Are Trapped In, Live Through and Come Out." ILO Working Paper 57. Geneva: International Labour Office.

Aronowitz, Alexis A. 2001. "Smuggling and Trafficking in Human Beings: The Phenomenon, the Markets That Drive It and the Organisations That Promote It." *European Journal on Criminal Policy and Research* 9(2): 163–195.

Aronowitz, Alexis A. 2009. *Guidelines for the Collection of Data on Trafficking in Human Beings, including Comparable Indicators.* Vienna: International Organization for Migration.

Agustin, Laura, M. 2007. *Sex at the Margins: Migration, Labour Markets and the Rescue Industry.* London: Zed.

Bales, Kevin. 2005. *Understanding Global Slavery: A Reader.* Berkeley: University of California Press.

Brunovskis, Annette, and Rebecca Surtees. 2007. *Leaving the Past Behind? When Victims of Trafficking Decline Assistance.* Oslo: Fafo. http://www.fafo.no/pub/rapp/20040/20040.pdf.

Bureau Nationaal Rapporteur Mensenhandel (BNRM). 2002. *Trafficking in Human Beings: First Report of the Dutch National Rapporteur.* The Hague: BNRM

Bureau Nationaal Rapporteur Mensenhandel (BNRM). 2004. *Trafficking in Human Beings: Third Report of the Dutch National Rapporteur.* The Hague: BNRM

Bureau Nationaal Rapporteur Mensenhandel (BNRM). 2007. *Trafficking in Human Beings: Fifth Report of the Dutch National Rapporteur.* The Hague: BNRM

Chase, Elaine, and June Statham. 2005. "Commercial and Sexual Exploitation of Children and Young People in the UK: A Review." *Child Abuse Review* 14(1): 4–25.

Chawla, Sandeep, Angela Me, and Thibault Le Pichon. 2009. *Global Report on Trafficking in Persons: Human Trafficking, a Crime That Shames Us All.* Vienna: United Nations Office on Drugs and Crime.

Chin, Ko-Lin. 1999. *Smuggled Chinese: Clandestine Immigration to the United States.* Philadelphia: Temple University Press.

Cornelius, Wayne A., Philip L. Martin, and James F. Hollifeld. 1994. *Controlling Immigration: A Global Perspective.* Stanford, CA: Stanford University Press.

Cwikel, J., and E. Hoban. 2005. "Contentious Issues in Research on Trafficked Women Working in the Sex Industry: Study Designs, Ethics and Methodology." *Journal of Sex Research* 42(4): 306–316.

Daalder, Annelies L. 2007. *Prostitution in the Netherlands since the Lifting of the Brothel Ban.* The Hague: WODC.

di Nicola, Andrea. 2007. "Researching into human trafficking: Issues and problems." In: *Human Trafficking*, edited by Maggy Lee, 49–72. Cullompton: Willan Publishing.

di Nicola, Andrea, Andrea Cauduro, Marco Lombardi, and Paolo Rospini. 2009. *Prostitution and Human Trafficking: Focus on Clients.* New York: Springer.

Dottridge, M. 2003. *Deserving Trust: Issues of Accountability for Human Rights NGOs.* Geneva: International Council on Human Rights Policy.

Dottridge, M. 2007. *Collateral Damage. The Impact of Anti-trafficking Measures on Human Rights around the World.* Bangkok: Global Alliance against Trafficking in Women.

Dowling, Samantha, Karen Moreton, and Leila Wright. 2007. *Trafficking for the Purposes of Labour Exploitation: A Literature Review.* Home Office Online Report 10/07. London: Home Office.

Engbersen, Godfried, Joanne van der Leun, and Jan de Boom. 2007. "The Fragmentation of Migration and Crime in the Netherlands." In *Crime and Justice.* Vol. 35, *Crime and Justice in the Netherlands,* edited by M. Tonry and C. Bijleveld, 389–452. Chicago: University of Chicago Press.

Europol. 2009a. *EU Organized Crime Threat Assessment.* The Hague: Europol.

Europol. 2009b *Trafficking in Human Beings in the European Union: A Europol Perspective.* http://www.europol.europa.eu./publications/serious_crime_overviews.

Farley, Melissa, Julie Bindel, and Jacqueline M. Golding. 2009. *Men Who Buy Sex. Who They Buy and What They Know.* London: Eaves/Prostitution Research and Education.

Farrell, Amy, Jack McDevitt, and Stephanie Fahy. 2010. "Where Are All the Victims? Understanding the Determinants of Official Identification of Human Trafficking Incidents." *Criminology & Public Policy* 9(2): 201–231.

Frost, Natasha. 2007. "Securing Borders and Saving Lives." *Criminology and Public Policy* 6(2): 241–244.

Gallagher, Anne T. 2006. *Human Trafficking: International Law and International Responsibility.* Utrecht: Utrecht University.

Guerette, Rob. 2007. "Immigration Policy, Border Security, and Migrant Deaths: An Impact Evaluation of Life-Saving Efforts under the Border Safety Initiative." *Criminology and Public Policy* 6(2): 245–266.

Guild, Elspeth, and P. Minderhoud, eds. 2006. *Immigration and Criminal Law in the European Union: The Legal Measures and Social Consequences of Criminal Law in Member States on Trafficking and Smuggling in Human Beings.* Leiden: Martinus Nijhoff.

Herman, Emma. 2006. "Migration as a Family Business: The Role of Personal Networks in the Mobility Phase of Migration." *International Migration* 44(4): 191–221.

International Centre for Migration Policy Development. 2010. *Yearbook on Illegal Migration, Human Smuggling and Trafficking in Central and Eastern Europe: A Survey and Analysis of Border Management and Border Apprehension.* Vienna: International Centre for Migration Policy Development.

Janssen, Marie-Louise P.C. 2007. *Reizende Sekswerkers:. Latijns-Amerikaanse Vrouwen in de Europese Prostitutie.* Apeldoorn: Het Spinhuis.

Kelly, Liz. 2002. *Journeys of Jeopardy: A Review of Research on Trafficking in Women and Children in Europe.* London: University of North London.

Kelly, Liz, and Linda Regan. 2000. *Stopping Traffic: Exploring the Extent of, and Response to, Trafficking in Women for Sexual Exploitation in the UK.* Home Office Police Research Series Paper 125. London: Home Office.

Kleemans, Edward R. 2007. "Organized Crime, Transit Crime, and Racketeering." In *Crime and Justice.* Vol. 35, *Crime and Justice in the Netherlands,* edited by M. Tonry and C. Bijleveld, 163–215. Chicago: University of Chicago Press.

Kleemans, Edward R., and Henk G. van de Bunt. 1999. "The Social Embeddedness of Organized Crime." *Transnational Organized Crime* 5(2): 19–36.

Kleemans, Edward R., and Henk G. van de Bunt. 2003. "The Social Organisation of Human Trafficking." In *Global Organized Crime: Trends and Developments*, edited by D. Siegel, H. van de Bunt, and D. Zaitch, 97–104. Boston: Kluwer Academic.

Laczko, Frank. 2005. Introduction to "Data and Research on Human Trafficking: A Global Survey." *Special Issue:International Migration* 43(1–2): 5–16.

Lackzo, Frank, and Gergana Danailova-Tranor. 2009. "Trafficking in Persons and Human Development: Towards a More Integrated Policy Response." Human Development Research Paper (HDRP) 51, no. 2009.

Laczko, Frank, and Elzbiete Gozdziak, eds. 2005. "Data and Research on Human Trafficking: A Global Survey." *Special Issue: International Migration* 43 (1–2).

Lehti, Martti, and Kauko Aromaa. 2006. "Trafficking for Sexual Exploitation." In *Crime and Justice: A Review of Research*, vol. 34, edited by M. Tonry, 133–227. Chicago: University of Chicago Press.

Levinson, Amanda. 2005. *The Regularization of Unauthorized Migrants: Literature Surveys and Country Case Studies.* Oxford: University of Oxford, Centre on Migration, Policy and Society.

Lyday, Corbin B. 2001. "The Shadow Market in Human Beings: An Anti-corruption Perspective." http://www.10iacc.org/content.phtml?documents=111&art=134.

Munro, Vanessa E. 2006. "Stopping Traffic? A Comparative Study to Responses to the Trafficking in Women for Prostitution." *British Journal of Criminology* 46: 318–33.

Neske, Matthias, and Jeroen Doomernik, eds. 2006. "Comparing Notes: Perspectives on Human Smuggling in Austria, Germany, Italy, and the Netherlands—Cluster Introduction." *International Migration* 44(4): 39–58.

Norwegian Ministry of Justice and the Police. 2004. "Purchasing Sexual Services in Sweden and the Netherlands: Legal Regulations and Experiences: An Abbreviated English Version." Report by a Working Group on the Legal Regulation of the Purchase of Sexual Services. Oslo, Norway.

Perrin, Benjamin. 2010. "Just Passing Through? International Legal Obligations and Policies of Transit Countries in Combating Trafficking in Persons." *European Journal of Criminology* 7(1): 11–27.

Portes, Alejandro. 1995. "Economic Sociology and the Sociology of Immigration: A Conceptual Overview." In *The Economic Sociology of Immigration: Essays on Networks, Ethnicity, and Entrepreneurship*, edited by A. Portes, 1–41. New York: Russell Sage.

Salt, John. 2000. "Trafficking and Human Smuggling: A European Perspective." *International Migration* 38(3): 31–56.

Salt, John, and Jeremy Stein. 1997. "Migration as a Business: The Case of Trafficking." *International Migration* 35(4): 467–489.

Savona, Ernesto U., and Sonia Stefanizzi. 2007. *Measuring Human Trafficking: Complexities and Pitfalls.* New York: Springer.

Schloenhardt, Andreas. 2001. "Trafficking in Migrants: Illegal Immigration and Organised Crime in Australia and the Pacific Region." *International Journal of Sociology of Law* 29:331–78.

Siegel, Dina, and Sylvia De Blank. 2010. "Women Who Traffic Women: The Role of Women in Human Trafficking Networks—Dutch Cases." *Global Crime* 11(4): 436–447.

Smit, Monika. 2011. "Trafficking in Human Beings for Labour Exploitation: The Case of the Netherlands." *Trends in Organized Crime* 14(2–3): 184–197.

Soudijn, Melvin. 2006. *Chinese Human Smuggling in Transit.* The Hague: Boom Juridische Uitgevers.

Spener, David. 2004. "Mexican Migrant Smuggling: A Cross-Border Cottage Industry." *Journal of International Migration and Integration* 5(3): 295–321.

Staring, Richard, Godfried Engbersen, Hans Moerland, N. de Lange, D. Verburg, E. Vermeulen, and A. Weltevrede. 2005. *De Sociale Organisatie van Mensensmokkel.* Zeist: Uitgeverij Kerckebosch.

Statens Offentliga Utredningar. 2010. *Förbud Mot Köp av Sexuel Tsjänst: En Utvärdering, 1999–2008.* http://www.regeringen.se/sb/d/108/a/149142.

Studnicka, Andrea C. S. 2010. "Corruption and Human Trafficking in Brazil: Findings from a Multi-modal Approach." *European Journal of Criminology* 7(1): 29–43.

Surtees, Rebecca. 2007. *Handbook on Anti-trafficking Data Collection in South-Eastern Europe: Developing Regional Criteria.* Vienna: ICMPD.

Surtees, Rebecca. 2008. "Traffickers and Trafficking in South and Eastern Europe: Considering the Other Side of Human Trafficking." *European Journal of Criminology* 5(1): 39–68.

Tyldum, Guri, and Annette Brunovskis. 2005. "Describing the Unobserved. Methodological Challenges in Empirical Studies on Human Trafficking." *International Migration* 43 (1–2): 17–34.

United Nations. 2000. *Protocol to Prevent, Suppress and Punish Trafficking in Persons, Especially Women and Children, Supplementing the United Nations Convention against Transnational Organized Crime.* http://www.uncjin.org/Documents/Conventions/dcatoc/final_documents_2/convention_%20traff_eng.pdf.

United Nations Office on Drugs and Crime. 2006. *Trafficking in Persons: Global Patterns.* Vienna: United Nations Office on Drugs and Crime.

United States Department of State. 2007. *Trafficking in Persons Report.* Washington, DC: US Department of State.

United States Department of State. 2010. *Trafficking in Persons Report.* Washington, DC: US Department of State.

United States Government Accountability Office. 2006. *Human Trafficking: Better Data, Strategy and Reporting Needed to Enhance US Anti-trafficking Efforts Abroad.* Report to the Chairman, Committee on the Judiciary and the Chairman, Committee on International Relations, House of Representatives. GAO-06-825.

United States Government Accountability Office. 2007. *Human Trafficking: Monitoring and Evaluation of International Projects Are Limited, but Experts Suggest Improvements.* Washington, DC: US Government Accountability Office.

van der Laan, Peter H., Monika Smit, Inge Busschers, and Pauline Aarten. 2010. *Cross-Border Trafficking in Human Beings: Prevention and Intervention Strategies for Reducing Sexual Exploitation.* Protocol at Campbell Collaboration site http://www.campbellcollaboration.org.

van Dijk, Essy. 2002. *Mensenhandel in Nederland, 1997–2000.* Zoetermeer: KLPD.

van Liempt, Ilse, and Jeroen Doomernik. 2006. "Migrant's Agency in the Smuggling Process: The Perspective of Smuggled Migrants in the Netherlands." *International Migration* 44(4): 165–190.

Vermeulen, Gert, Annelies Balcaen, Andrea di Nicola, and Andrea Cauduro. 2006. *The Siamsect Files.* Antwerp: Maklu.

Viuhko, Minna, and Anniina Jokinen. 2009. *Human Trafficking for Sexual Exploitation and Organized Procuring in Finland.* Helsinki: HEUNI.

Vocks, Judith, and Jan Nijboer. 1999. *Land van Belofte: Een Onderzoek naar Slachtoffers van Vrouwenhandel uit Centraal en Oost-Europa.* Groningen: Rijksuniversiteit Groningen.

Weitzer, Ronald. 2010. "The Mythology of Prostitution: Advocacy Research and Public Policy." *Sexuality Research and Social Policy* 7: 15–29.

Wilcox, Aidan, Kris Christmann, Michelle Rogerson, and Philip Birch. 2009. "Tackling the Demand for Prostitution: A Rapid Evidence Assessment of the Published Research Literature." Home Office Research Report 27. London: Home Office.

Zhang, Sheldon X. 1997. "Task Force Orientation and Dyadic Relations in Organized Chinese Alien Smuggling." *Journal of Contemporary Criminal Justice* 13(4): 320–330.

Zhang, Sheldon X. 2007. *Smuggling and Trafficking in Human Beings: All Roads Lead to America.* Westport, CT: Praeger.

Zhang, Sheldon X. 2009. "Beyond the "Natasha" Story: A Review and Critique of Current Research on Sex Trafficking." *Global Crime* 10(3): 178–195.

Zhang, Sheldon X., and Mark S. Gaylord. 1996. "Bound for the Golden Mountain: The Social Organization of Chinese Alien Smuggling." *Crime, Law and Social Change* 25(1): 1–16.

Zhang, Sheldon X., Ko-Lin Chin, and Jody Miller. 2007. "Women's Participation in Chinese Transnational Human Smuggling: A Gendered Market Perspective." *Criminology* 45(3): 699–733.

Zhang, Sheldon X., and Ko-Lin Chin. 2002. "Enter the Dragon: Inside Chinese Human Smuggling Organizations." *Criminology* 40(4): 737–767.

CHAPTER 20

....

ILLEGAL GAMBLING

....

TOINE SPAPENS

I. INTRODUCTION

....

This essay discusses illegal gambling and the involvement of organized criminals in this activity. Many readers will associate illegal gambling with the mafia-run casinos in Las Vegas in the 1950s and 1960s, thanks to the popular image created in Mario Puzo's novel *The Godfather* and to the films based on his book. Bear in mind, however, that these casinos were *legal*. The mafia succeeded in acquiring the necessary licenses mainly because, in the 1940s and 1950s, the authorities of the city of Las Vegas and the state of Nevada were unable, or unwilling, to screen applicants for permits. The focus of this essay, however, is not the infiltration of legal gambling by organized criminals but rather illegal gambling operations, gambling regulation, and the effects of the Internet.[1]

History teaches us that people have always been inclined to gamble, and the authorities, in their turn, have always had reasons to control this urge, stemming either from practical concerns—such as curbing gambling addiction and maintaining public order—or from religious and ideological principles (Polders 1997). Such restrictions, however, inevitably created illegal markets that organized crime groups have at times been able to dominate. The public authorities have obviously made an effort to curb illegal gambling through law enforcement. In many countries, however, they have also decriminalized all or most types of gambling, starting in the 1950s. On the one hand, regulatory regimes allow for different games of chance. On the other, restrictions are imposed on the business in order to minimize the social costs of gambling, particularly addiction problems, and to prevent criminals from obtaining operating licenses.

A largely decriminalized market, however, is still a dynamic environment, and new trends in supply or demand may affect the impact of regulatory measures.

Since the mid-1990s, the Internet has had a dramatic effect on the worldwide gambling market. The first gambling website appeared in 1995, and online gambling quickly developed into a multibillion-dollar business. The Internet not only modernized existing games of chance—it also truly globalized the gambling market. Consequently, online gambling put considerable strain on the effectiveness of common regulatory instruments. Nowadays, an operator only needs to acquire a license for online gambling in a single country to attract players from all over the world, although it may be formally illegal for it to do so in jurisdictions that prohibit Internet gambling. Many gambling websites register in countries where the authorities put little effort into screening or controlling operators. Not surprisingly, there is considerable concern about the possible involvement of criminals in online gambling for this reason and about the integrity of the games on offer. Furthermore, it is much more difficult to prevent addiction when players can access gambling websites at any given hour of the day.

Although the police and policy makers tend to automatically assume the involvement of organized crime groups in illegal gambling, criminologists have done relatively little empirical research on the topic. Nonetheless, illegal gambling has greatly influenced the discussion about organized crime. In his influential study *Theft of the Nation*, Donald Cressey based his depiction of the Italian American mafia mostly on its illegal gambling activities (Cressey 1969). Peter Reuter's landmark book *Disorganized Crime*, in which he questioned the "Cressey model" and proposed an important new approach to organized crime, was based on a study of the New York illegal gambling market in the 1960s and 1970s (Reuter 1983). On average, however, the involvement of organized crime groups in illegal gambling is underresearched, and this is particularly true of the present-day situation (see Spapens et al. 2008b; Ferentzy and Turner 2009).

The lack of research data makes it very difficult to present a systematic overview of the involvement of organized crime in illegal gambling today. On top of this, the research that is available often focuses on a local or national situation, but regulatory regimes, and thus illegal gambling markets, as well as gambling cultures may differ considerably between countries. There is, for instance, still a large illegal market for sports betting in the United States, whereas most of the member states of the European Union (EU) have now regulated bookmaking and thus greatly reduced the market for illegal operators. Bingo is an example of how differing gambling cultures may affect consumer demand. The game is quite popular in the Netherlands, and games are also run illegally (Spapens 2010), but it attracts hardly any players in Poland and Romania. Indeed, bingo venues that opened in these countries when the game was legalized soon folded because of poor business (Dzik 2009, p. 221; Lupu 2009, p. 233). It is therefore impossible to draw general conclusions about illegal gambling.

The following section offers a brief history of the various forms of gambling and their criminalization and regulation until the 1970s. Section 3 addresses current illegal gambling patterns and actors in Europe, North America, and Asia. Section 4 focuses on Internet gambling. The final section offers some brief conclusions.

II. A Brief History of Illegal Gambling

A. Gambling as a Small-Scale Vice

In many Western countries, the authorities started restricting games of chance as early as the fourteenth century. The French authorities, for example, banned specific games of chance, such as dice games, as far back as 1364 (Schotel 1905, p. 83). Elsewhere, local rulers imposed restrictions on gambling. In some jurisdictions in fourteenth-century Italy, for example, a permit was required for a particular type of game of chance that was apparently played at funerals (Polders 1997, p. 73). The reasons underlying such regulations were less ideological than practical. Gambling losses and suspected fraud often caused serious fights and breaches of the peace, which the authorities were anxious to avoid. Restrictions were usually temporary, however, because the city councils were also fully aware that games of chance, lotteries in particular, were an excellent tool to raise money for the public cause and provided a nice alternative to taxes. In 1600, for example, the Amsterdam authorities organized a lottery to fund a pension for elderly men. The aim of the oldest recorded Swedish lottery, held in Stockholm in 1699, was to raise money for the care of immigrants (Jonsson and Rönnberg 2009, p. 299).

Illegal gambling existed on a small and local scale in those days. Traveling artists, for example, offered games on city streets during markets and fairs, although mainly with the intention to con naïve locals. Although this was primarily the work of individuals, the records mention the involvement of organized gangs as well, whose members also broke into and stole property from dwellings in the countryside (Egmond 1994). People in the sixteenth and seventeenth centuries played dice or wagered in taverns, and card playing was later added to these attractions (Zumthor 1962). In the early 1700s, *casini*, from which we get the modern word "casino," were popular places in Italy for rich merchants to meet, trade, and gamble (Turner 2008, p. 41).

The eighteenth century saw another example of illegal gambling, which emerged in parallel with the new state lotteries that governments had started to organize. Lottery tickets were often expensive then, running as much as $30 in the Colonies of Great Britain in North America, for example. Agents—both legal and illegal—started to offer insurance policies guaranteeing that a winner would receive at least the cost of the ticket (Kaplan and Blount 1990, p. 265). In the Netherlands, where state lottery tickets were also expensive, players were offered the opportunity to buy a percentage of a ticket, with the wins being shared accordingly.

B. Gambling in the Era of the Industrial Revolution

From the eighteenth century on, the Industrial Revolution brought about fundamental changes in the social lives of Europeans and North Americans. Rapid urbanization was another important effect. Glasgow, for example, had 84,000 inhabitants at the beginning of the nineteenth century; this number rose to 300,000 in 1849 and to half a million by 1871. By mid-century, only 22 percent of the British population was still working in agriculture, compared with 68 percent in France (Onze Tijd 1849, pp. 238–239).

Alcohol abuse, prostitution, and gambling were endemic in the cities of the Industrial Revolution. Although gambling continued to be a local affair, it grew in scale as towns expanded in size. In 1902, the House of Lords Select Committee on Betting argued that betting was generally prevalent in the United Kingdom and that the practice of it had increased considerably, especially among the working classes (McKibbin 1979, p. 149). It was in the same period that the first Italian American crime groups emerged in New York. They controlled gambling houses and were involved in extortion and other types of crime (Critchley 2009, p. 121).

With the Industrial Revolution came new technologies that also led to a scaling up of gambling activities. The telegraph furthered off-course betting in horseracing, because it enabled punters to bet on races in cities other than their own. This new trend first took hold in the United States, and by 1904 the authorities were already prohibiting telegraph companies such as Western Union from disseminating information about horseracing (Reuter 1983, p. 15).

The vices of the nineteenth century and the resulting cost to society triggered a resurgence of Protestant moral values. From the second half of the century on, this moral crusade also led to restrictions on games of chance, particularly in the United Kingdom and the Empire, and in other countries such as the United States and the Netherlands. Between 1860 and 1930, gambling was effectively abolished in the New World (Abt, Smith, and Christiansen 1985). The descendants of the Puritans saw it as an ideologically insidious affront to the Protestant work ethic, and psychiatrists, the clergy, and some politicians condemned gambling as the road to financial ruin (Brenner 1990). On the other side of the political spectrum, the socialist and communist movements were just as strongly opposed to gambling, because of the havoc it wreaked, together with alcohol abuse, among the urban proletariat that had emerged from the Industrial Revolution.

The founding of unified national states on the European continent led to ever more effective restrictions on gambling. Independent local jurisdictions could no longer impose their own, differing, rules and regulations. The French *Code Penal*, for instance, included a nationwide ban on all games of chance (*jeux d'hasard*), except for lotteries. When the French occupied a number of European nations at the end of the eighteenth century, such as the Netherlands, they also introduced the unitary state and single penal code, including its restrictions on gambling (Spapens 2008*a*).

C. Illegal Gambling and Organized Crime

Prohibiting gambling did not make it any less attractive, however. People still felt the urge to play, and illegal gambling houses soon emerged, while off-course betting on horseracing went underground. A mere 6 months after the 1904 ban on disseminating the results of horse races in other American cities, an illegal information exchange network was set up. After the First World War, illegal bookmaking broadened to other sports, particularly to American football, baseball, and basketball (Reuter 1983, p. 15).

In the United States, illegal gambling became increasingly organized from the 1920s on. The notorious Al Capone, for example, also operated gambling dens where punters could not only bet on the horses but also play roulette, craps, and cards. Although Capone is mainly associated with bootlegging, documents recently released by the US Internal Revenue Service (IRS) reveal that his famous conviction for tax evasion actually stemmed from his illegal gambling activities (Treasury Department 1933). In 1951, the US Senate Special Committee to Investigate Organized Crime in Interstate Commerce (more popularly known as the Kefauver Committee) concluded that gambling profits had developed "into the principal support of big-time racketeering and gangsterism" after Prohibition was repealed in 1933 (Kefauver Committee 1951).

After 1918, betting on dog racing and football matches also became increasingly popular in the United Kingdom (McKibbin 1979, p. 154). In 1932, the Royal Commission on Lotteries and Betting concluded that "the streets of our towns are perambulated by bookmakers or their betting agents inviting persons to bet with them" (McKibbin 1979, p. 160). Betting had developed into a central feature of working-class leisure (Davies 1991, p. 87). In the 1920s and 1930s, crime gangs in the major cities of the United Kingdom were involved in the gambling (Murphy 1993).

One important question is to what extent "organized crime" was involved in illegal gambling activities from the 1920s on. The answer largely depends on how one defines the term. Unmistakably, a large-scale illegal gambling activity, such as a sports-betting ring or a numbers game, requires a complex, coordinated process. It involves an organization consisting of "runners" who take bets or sell tickets, "clerks" who administer wagers, and a bank or a bookmaker to calculate the odds and keep track of everything. This may easily add up to a collective of dozens of individuals working together. From a logistical viewpoint, therefore, such an operation may certainly be qualified as an organized crime group.

Other scholars, however, have argued that the term "organized crime" should apply only to syndicates that control the activities of different local organizations involved in varying types of crime (Cressey 1969). Cressey postulated that in the 1960s, the Cosa Nostra was indeed able to exert a nationwide control over the illegal gambling market in the United States. With regard to the United Kingdom, however, he thought that no single organization had reached a similar level of control, and so by his definition, organized crime did not exist in that country (Cressey 1971). Several years later, Peter Reuter questioned the existence of an overarching mafia syndicate in the United States as well, based on empirical findings in New York (Reuter 1983). Instead, the illegal gambling market in the city seemed "disorganized" and composed of numerous groups who sometimes worked together but competed for market share on other occasions.

Without further addressing the definition of organized crime, we can say that running a large-scale gambling operation for a prolonged period requires a stable and significant level of organization. The empirical evidence, albeit scarce, suggests that from the 1930s through the 1970s, serious criminals were indeed closely involved in illegal gambling operations. From the end of the Second World War, however, many countries started to decriminalize gambling, and this seems to have substantially reduced the scale of illegal betting.

III. The Present-Day Involvement of Crime Groups in Illegal Gambling

A. Europe

All the member states of the EU now allow various regulated forms of gambling (Swiss Institute of Comparative Law 2006). In the Netherlands, for example, the authorities legalized football pools in 1964, bingo, lotto, and casino gaming in 1973, and electronic gaming machines in 1986. Besides the state lottery, which was never criminalized and has been running continuously since 1762, new lotteries supporting good causes were added in the 1990s. This indeed seems to have had the intended effect of guiding customers away from illegal operations to the many legalized games on offer (Spapens 2008a, 2012). The illegal gambling activity that remains in the Netherlands can be broken down into two main categories.

First, and most important, there are still niches in the gambling market that legitimate companies are unable to fill sufficiently because of legal restrictions. One example is poker, which only Holland Casino, the monopoly operator of casino games, is permitted to offer. The demand is much higher than can be met by the 14 official casinos, however, and this opens the door to all kinds of illegally organized poker tournaments. Another example from the past were small-scale, illegal local gaming houses offering roulette and card games. These mainly attracted customers who were unable, or unwilling, to travel to one of the legal casinos. However, the authorities succeeded in closing all these venues between 1999 and 2005 by effectively applying administrative law (Spapens 2008a). Our final example is illegal commercial bingo, which is attractive because it offers much bigger cash prizes than are legally allowed (Spapens 2010).

Second, there are the illegal games played in the context of ethnic or social networks. One example concerns immigrants from the Netherlands Antilles, who sometimes prefer to play the lottery of their native country (*Wega di Number Korsou*), although the game is not legally offered in the Netherlands. Another example are illegal numbers games and sports-betting rings. Although these differ to some extent from the legal varieties, the main reason for punters to play the "black" lotto and tote appears to be that friends at the pub or coworkers are also participating and have asked them to join in (Spapens 2012).

In most cases, the individuals responsible for running illegal gambling activities have links with members of organized crime networks. Although Dutch operators are themselves sometimes actively involved in other types of serious and organized crime, gambling operations no longer appear to be a primary source of illegal income (Spapens 2008a, 2010, 2012).

I mentioned that the opportunities for organizing illegal gambling vary considerably between countries owing to differences in gambling laws and gambling cultures. For example, besides Portugal, France is the only EU country that has not authorized slot machines in public places, including "soft machines" with limited stakes and winnings (Valleur 2009, p. 73). This gives crime groups the chance to operate clandestine machines featuring video poker and other games, which are usually installed in bars (Trucy 2002, p. 164). The bartender pays out the credit points accumulated and then resets the machines to zero by means of a "knock-off" switch. Particularly in the south of France, organized crime groups reputedly control the placing of such gambling machines (Trucy 2006, p. 109). In Italy, the mafia also controls video poker centers and the placement of gambling machines in pubs. In 2000, there were approximately 800,000 video poker machines installed, with a turnover of more than €20 billion (Croce et al. 2009, p. 154).

Particularly interesting from the viewpoint of regulation are the former East Bloc countries. The socialist regimes prohibited most games of chance, but after the fall of the Iron Curtain in 1989, the new governments lifted most restrictions. In Russia, for example, gambling companies rapidly emerged, opened casinos, and placed slot machines. In 2000, there were already 2,700 gambling establishments in full operation in Russia, with 120,000 employees (Tsytarev and Gilinski 2009, p. 246). Licensing and screening were haphazard at best, and organized crime groups were believed to be heavily involved in legal gambling companies. In 2007, however, the State Duma radically decided that virtually all gambling activities should be moved to a limited number of gambling zones, mainly located in distant areas such as Siberia, the Far East, and two zones in the European part of Russia. The authorities nowadays only allow bookmakers to continue operating outside of these zones. As a result, new opportunities for illegal operators have arisen, and it is presumed that they already run hundreds of establishments housing illegal casinos and slot machines (Tsytarev and Gilinski 2009, p. 254).

The shift from a very liberalized gambling market toward stricter regulation can also be observed in other Eastern European countries, such as Poland and Romania, although to a much lesser extent than in Russia. There are no indications that new, large-scale illegal gambling operations involving organized crime groups have emerged there (Dzik 2009; Lupu 2009).

B. North America

In North America, Canada now allows most types of gambling, but the police still see illegal bookmaking and video gambling machines as a problem (Moodie 2002). In the United States, gambling laws remain restrictive. Although most states now allow lotteries and 19 states permit some form of commercial casinos, only Nevada and Oregon allow sports betting. Consequently, illegal gambling continues to be an important market for organized crime groups. The Federal Bureau of Investigation (FBI) considers bookmaking, video gambling machines, and, to a lesser extent, numbers games to be the most important types of illegal gambling on offer (Hernandez 2006).

According to the U.S. National Gambling Impact Study Commission (NGISC), approximately $80 to $380 billion of illegal sports bets were made in the United States in 1999 (NGISC 1999).[2] The Commission estimated that 92 percent of the earnings from sports betting found its way into the pockets of organized crime groups. A recent assessment by the FBI revealed that Cosa Nostra still largely controls illegal bookmaking activities in the United States (Hernandez 2006). In February 2008, for example, the Queens County police arrested 26 individuals, including the Gambino organized crime family *capo* Nicholas Corozzo, on charges of operating a highly sophisticated illegal gambling enterprise that booked nearly $10 million in wagers over a 2-year period on professional and college basketball and football, professional baseball and hockey, and other sporting events. The group had partly replaced the traditional street bookmakers with websites that punters could enter with a password in order to place their bets (*North Country Gazette* 2008).

Video gambling machines constitute another major type of illegal gambling in the United States in which the authorities also presume organized crime groups to be involved. These machines emerged in the late 1970s, when the technology of arcade games such as *Space Invaders* and *PacMan* was quickly adapted for gambling (O'Boyle 2006, p. 2). Video gambling machines may operate as modern versions of the traditional slot machines, but the technology also enabled the development of new video games such as poker and blackjack. According to the FBI, Cosa Nostra mainly controls the placing of video gambling machines, but Albanian organized crime groups are also believed to have entered the market (Hernandez 2006).

Finally, illegal lotto, better known as "The Numbers," has been available in the United States since the end of the nineteenth century (Reuter 1983, p. 45). Systematic information regarding the entire United States is not available. The Pennsylvania Crime Commission, however, investigated numbers games in Philadelphia between the 1970s and the early 1990s and found that in the 1970s, an Italian American mafia family, on the one hand, and African American operators, on the other hand, controlled the game there. The latter were active in the city's black neighborhoods. By 1999, each state had authorized an official lottery, and this seems to have reduced the illegal market, although specific ethnic groups seem to prefer their "own" numbers games. For example, when a legal state lottery was set up in Pennsylvania in the 1980s, the black population of Philadelphia preferred to keep playing the illegal lotto (Liddick 1999, p. 50). In 1990, numbers games were still popular in cities in the Northeast and Midwest, although illegal operators also offered the game in any large city with a sizeable ethnic population. The police in Florida identified 50 numbers organizations in 1988 in just a single county, all but one run by Cubans. These organizers employed some 4,500 people and handled approximately $500 million per year in wagers (Kaplan and Blount 1990, p. 266).

The police in Canada assume that illegal gambling is not a major organized crime activity nowadays; at the same time, however, it is thought to provide a steady income for crime groups from which other illicit activities can be supported (Moodie 2002, p. 7). The main illegal gambling operations are bookmaking, card dens, and video gambling machines; the police consider the latter to be the largest illicit source of income. The machines can earn up to $1,000 each per week. The crime groups involved include the Hell's Angels and Asian and Eastern European groups (Moodie 2002, p. 15).

C. Asia

Asia represents a huge gambling market, estimated at $450 billion per year in 2006. Unlike Europeans and North Americans, the Chinese do not see gambling as a vice per se but rather as an acceptable social activity and a good way to make friends and business connections. Nonetheless—or perhaps precisely because of this—most Asian governments have put heavy restrictions on gambling for a long time. In mainland China, by far the largest potential market, the lottery is the only legal type of gambling, and casino gaming, sports betting, and slot machines are all forbidden. In other Asian countries, lotteries and betting on horseracing are usually legal, but only a few permit casino gaming and sports betting. Macao, Myanmar, Singapore, and Malaysia, for example, do allow casino gaming, but the number of casinos is usually limited. Bookmaking is legal in Hong Kong and Singapore.

There is a substantial illegal market in Asia for casino gaming and sports betting. The police believe that organized crime groups are closely involved in this market, although their operations are thought to be predominantly local in scope (Finkenauer and Chin 2006, p. 56). The authorities consider the involvement of organized crime in illegal gambling a major problem in Macau, Japan, the Philippines, and Thailand and a medium priority problem in Cambodia, Taiwan, and Hong Kong (Finkenauer and Chin 2006, p. 54).

One specific problem in mainland China and Taiwan is corruption of government officials and the police in relation to illegal gambling. This specifically concerns brick and mortar gambling establishments, which are hard to hide and therefore depend on "protection" (Chin and Godson 2006, p. 19).

IV. Online Gambling

A. Internet Gambling, Crime, and Regulation Issues

The emergence of Internet gambling and its exponential growth represent one of the most significant and contentious developments in gambling over the past two decades. Although it appears to be economically significant, little is known about the Internet gambling industry, its customers, or its social and economic impacts (Jawad and Griffiths 2008). Online gambling quickly took off after the first Internet gambling operator commenced business in 1995. In 2006, statistics showed there were as many as 2,500 gambling websites operating, consisting of 1,083 online casinos, 592 sports and race books, 532 poker rooms, 224 online bingo sites, 49 skill game sites, 30 betting exchanges, 25 lottery sites, and 17 backgammon sites (Jawad and Griffiths 2008). In the same year, estimates of online gambling revenues amounted to $7.6 billion in the United States, $16 billion in the Asia Pacific region, and $6 billion in Europe (RSe Consulting 2006).

The operators of gambling websites often register in exotic countries or self-governing territories within countries. The remote gambling industry is very fluid; there are low barriers to entry and exit, and this means that operators will probably move to jurisdictions that take a laissez-faire approach to licensing if the regulatory burden in the host country becomes too onerous. In 2006, for example, Antigua hosted the most websites (537), followed by Costa Rica (474), the Kahnawake Mohawk Territory in Canada (401), and Curacao (343). The Internet has greatly reduced the effectiveness of restrictive gambling policies. It has also interfered with traditional regulatory instruments based on limiting the number of licensees and on excluding foreign operators. Understandably, the loss of control has raised concerns with the governments of countries that are the main target markets for online gambling operators.

One of their primary concerns is the risk of criminal groups owning gambling websites. It is illegal to offer online gambling facilities to the inhabitants of countries that do not allow gambling, and bona fide companies are prevented from entering the market there. Such constraints do not deter crime groups, of course. Furthermore, most jurisdictions hosting gambling websites scarcely screen the backgrounds of applicants for operating licenses, if at all. Criminals who own gambling websites can generate income with little or no risk of apprehension and prosecution. In addition, they also gain access to players' credit card and other information, which they can then use to skim the customers' bank accounts and to commit identity fraud, although there is no hard evidence that this has actually happened. More important, the games themselves can be manipulated. For example, criminal operators can adapt the gaming software to their own advantage. Even in online poker rooms, the provider can introduce a "virtual player of the house" into the game—a computer program that can manipulate the outcome at will—without the human players noticing (Spapens 2008b).

In response to the perceived risks of online gambling, the U.S. government has tried to impose restrictions but with only limited success so far. First, it tried to prosecute foreign-based suppliers of online gambling. In 1998, federal prosecutors charged 21 US citizens connected to offshore Internet gambling with violations of the Wire Act, which prohibits anyone in the business of betting or wagering from using a wire communication facility in interstate or foreign commerce to transmit bets or wagers. Only one of the indicted, who had operated from Antigua, contested the case in court and was convicted (Wohl 2009). In response, however, Antigua initiated the dispute resolution process of the World Trade Organization (WTO), believing the US sentence in this case to be in violation of the General Agreement on Trade in Services (GATS). Ultimately, the WTO ruled in favor of Antigua. The United States, however, failed to comply, and the WTO subsequently awarded Antigua the right to suspend $21 million annually.

Next, in 2006, the US government adopted the Unlawful Internet Gambling Enforcement Act (UIGEA), which prohibits the acceptance of specified forms of payment for unlawful Internet gambling by a business of betting or wagering. The Act took aim at the Achilles heel of gambling websites: the fact that payment via the Internet mostly involves banks that *do* fall under the jurisdiction of the players' country of residence. As a result, bona fide gambling websites immediately stopped taking bets from US customers. Non–publicly traded websites, however, continued to accept US players, but as of mid-2010, not one of these has been indicted under the UIGEA. In any case, Internet gambling sites can still prevent banks from recognizing transactions as gambling related—for example, by using online payment providers as intermediaries (General Accounting Office 2002, p. 21).

The attitude toward online gambling is less clear-cut in the EU. Some of the member states, such as Malta, Austria, and the United Kingdom, as well as self-governing territories such as Gibraltar and the Finnish island of Åland, allow online gambling. Others, such as the Netherlands, follow a more restrictive policy. The question is whether the principle of free movement of services within the EU should also apply to gambling operations. So far, the European Court of Justice has granted the member states considerable discretionary scope to impose restrictions on the gambling market (see Littler and Fijnaut 2007; Spapens, Littler, and Fijnaut 2008). Taking effective action against EU-based online gambling companies, however, is difficult. In 2006, a Dutch court convicted the Malta-based online gambling company Unibet for openly targeting Dutch customers, but the company simply refused to comply with the court's ruling to stop these particular activities. In October 2007, Unibets' director Peter Nylander was arrested on behalf of the French authorities for violating the French gambling law, but this, too, did not alter Unibet's policy. Obviously, taking legal action against online gambling companies based outside the EU is even more complicated, not in the least because it is often next to impossible to identify the legal and natural persons behind specific websites.

Summing up, the fact that online gambling websites operate in a legal gray area, combined with high profits and low risk of prosecution, appears to create at least some of the conditions that make an attractive illegal market for organized criminals. Unfortunately, there is no systematic information available about the actual involvement of crime groups in offshore gambling websites. A few empirical examples, however, illustrate that a lack of effective screening increases the risk of infiltration of the market by individuals of questionable integrity. The US sports-betting case described in Section 3.2 indicates that organized crime groups are certainly familiar with using the Internet for illegal gambling operations. Cases can also be cited in the Netherlands. There is, for example, evidence that a notorious Dutch drug criminal invested in an online betting company when it first began operating in the 1990s. It has since developed into one of Europe's major operators. A more recent example involves an online gambling company legally based in Malta and technically operating from Curacao but actually run by Dutchmen. Several well-known Dutch athletes have advertised for the website. Not only does the company target Dutch customers, which is illegal under Dutch law, but also players complained to the police about fraud. On the surface of things, the company that operates the website is in the hands of legitimate businesspersons. Inquiries, however, have revealed a highly complex web of suspicious business relations in the background, involving unknown investors operating from Cyprus, for example.

B. Internet Gambling Machines

One notable trend in gambling-related crime that can be attributed to the Internet is the emergence of illegal Internet gambling machines, usually found in bars, restaurants, or other establishments such as Internet cafes. These machines differ from normal electronic gaming machines, because the games are generated by a central remote system rather than within the machine itself (Turner 2008, p. 45). To the uninitiated customer, the machine is just a terminal offering access to the Internet. The bartender, however, can easily change it into a gambling machine by remote control. Technically, the terminals are highly sophisticated. They operate by means of touch screen control and accept coins as well as banknotes. Others make use of prepaid cards that can be charged with credit points beforehand. The machine adds the points won to the card, and the player may use these to play extra games or exchange them for cash.

The machines are equipped with hardware encoders offering secure communication with the main data center and with a mechanism that automatically erases all the gambling software in case the terminal is tampered with or improperly disconnected. If the police confiscate a terminal, in other words, they will find no evidence of it being a gambling machine. A recent criminal investigation in Greece revealed that the software was based on off-the-shelf Windows programs, presumably modified in Eastern Europe, whereas some of the hardware could be traced back to China (Cosmidis 2010).

Although Internet gambling machines require "local representatives" to promote and manage placing the terminals, the data center and games management can be located anywhere in the world. Consequently, it is next to impossible for the police to find and identify the core operators. Even if they do succeed in dismantling a data center, an illegal operator will have little trouble setting up shop in another place or in a different country, if necessary. There is still little if any information on who is actually running these rings of Internet gambling machines. The Greek police, however, assume that crime groups originating in Eastern Europe are involved (Cosmidis 2010).

Internet gambling machines have also sprung up in the United States. Internet sweepstakes cafes, for example, have opened all across the country. In Europe, Internet gambling machines seem to be particularly popular in Southern European countries, such as Greece, Italy, and Spain, but they can also be found in Sweden, Germany, and the Netherlands (Jonnson and Rönnberg 2009, p. 311). In the latter two countries, they are found mainly in coffee houses run and visited by Turkish immigrants and used for ille-gal betting on football matches, for example.

C. Match Fixing

The problem of match fixing has historical ties with illegal gambling, but it has become an increasing problem since the spread of sports betting via the Internet. Match fixing was particularly endemic in Asia in the 1990s. At that time, authorities in Malaysia, for example, estimated that 70 percent of the football matches were manipulated. Match-fixing scandals have led to all but four teams being banned from the Taiwanese Baseball League since 2005. Corruption is also well reported in Japanese Sumo wres-tling (Hill 2010). Corruption scandals in China caused a major loss in confidence in the integrity of domestic sporting events, and punters have switched to betting on overseas matches (Ostrov 2009). According to representatives of the Dutch Football Pool and Lotto Asscociation interviewed by the present author, Asian gamblers nowa-days wager €50 million on average on any official match, even in the lowest amateur divisions of the competition. Reporters hired by unknown betting organizations are present to give a minute-by-minute account by mobile phone of everything that hap-pens during the match.

The Internet once again triggered the further globalization of match fixing. Nowadays anyone in the world connected to the Web is able to place bets, and may therefore ben-efit from manipulating a game. The speed and detail of wagering on sports matches have also greatly increased thanks to sports-betting websites such as Betfair and Bwin. Here, patrons can place bets not only on the outcome of a match but also, for instance in foot-ball, on the exact score and on events occurring during the game, such as the first team to get a free kick. Punters may place the bets before but also after the game starts, against continuously changing odds. In addition, betting is no longer limited to a small number of top matches, as in traditional football pools but now includes a wide range of some-times obscure matches in many different countries. This considerably increases the opportunities for match fixing, because, on average, it is far easier to bribe a low-level player with a small income into throwing a game than a member of a top team.

There is considerable concern in Europe today about the integrity of football com-petitions. Bribery scandals came to light in Germany and Belgium in 2005 and 2006, the latter involving Chinese betting rings. There have also been recent allegations of match fixing related to gambling in football in the Netherlands, Finland, Portugal, Italy, Poland, Austria, the Czech Republic, Turkey, and Romania. In response, the Union of European Football Associations (UEFA) has set up its own intelligence unit to track signs of manipulation, for instance by analyzing the patterns of bets placed on specific matches (Peaker 2010).

In 2007, UEFA investigated 26 matches that it suspected of being manipulated by overseas betting syndicates, principally in Asia. The police subsequently launched an international operation coordinated by Interpol and codenamed SOGA ("Soccer and

Gambling") in China, Hong Kong, Macau, Malaysia, Singapore, Thailand, and Vietnam. Operation SOGA resulted in the arrest of 430 individuals, and the authorities shut down 272 underground gambling dens, which had an estimated turnover of $680 million. SOGA II and SOGA III followed up this operation in 2008 and 2010, respectively. SOGA II led to the arrest of 1,300 people and to the seizure of over $16 million, whereas during SOGA III the police in mainland China, Hong Kong, Macao, Malaysia, Singapore, and Thailand raided nearly 800 gambling dens, which handled more than $155 million worth of bets, and arrested more than 5,000 people. Interpol stated that illegal soccer gambling had connections to organized crime gangs, as well as links to corruption, money laundering, and prostitution.

V. Conclusion

Gambling offers a fine example of how decriminalization and regulation decreases the involvement of crime groups in an illegal services market. However, it also illustrates that regulated markets are not static and may change considerably due either to fluctuations in customer demand or technological or other trends. The boom in remote gambling has greatly reduced the effectiveness of commonly applied regulatory instruments, which rely on limiting supply and on screening operators. This and the opportunity to generate high profits with little or no risk of apprehension and prosecution make online gambling vulnerable to infiltration by organized crime. It is impossible, however, to estimate the extent to which traditional crime groups are now involved in online gambling.

Notes

1. Other gambling-related crimes include loan sharking and money laundering. For a survey of gambling and crime problems, see Spapens (2008b).
2. The Commission did not base this figure on primary research but refers to an essay written by Robert Macy instead (Macy 1999). The estimate, however, particularly the high end of it, has been continuously quoted since then.

References

Abt, V., J. Smith, and F. Christiansen. 1985. *The Business of Risk: Commercial Gambling in Mainstream America*. Lawrence: University Press of Kansas.

Brenner. R. 1990. *Gambling and Speculation. A Theory, a History and a Future of Some Human Decisions*. New York: Cambridge University Press.

Chin, K. L., and R. Godson. 2006. "Organized Crime and the Political-Criminal Nexus in China." *Trends in Organized Crime* 9(3): 5–44.

Cosmidis, E. 2010. *Illegal Gaming and New Technologies*. Paper presented at the Public Order Seminar, European Lotteries Association, March 11, 2010, Madrid.

Cressey, D. 1969. *Theft of the Nation, the Structure and Operations of Organized Crime in America*. New York: Harper and Row.

Cressey, D. 1971. *Criminal Organization: Its Elementary Forms*. London: Heinemann Educational Books.

Critchley, D. 2009. *The Origin of Organized Crime in America. The New York City Mafia, 1891-1931*. New York/London: Routledge.

Croce, M., G. Lavanco, L. Varveri and M. Fiasco. 2009. "Italy." In *Problem Gambling in Europe. Challenges, Prevention and Intervention*, edited by G. Meyer, T. Hayer, and M. Griffiths. New York: Springer, 153–171.

Davies, A. 1991. "The Police and the People. Gambling in Salford 1900–1939." *The Historical Journal* 34(1): 87–115.

Dzik, B. 2009. "Poland." In *Problem Gambling in Europe. Challenges, Prevention and Intervention*, edited by G. Meyer, T. Hayer, and M. Griffiths. New York: Springer, 219–227.

Egmond, F. *Op het verkeerde pad, Georganiseerde misdaad in de Noordelijke Nederlanden 1650-1800*. Amsterdam: Uitgeverij Bert Bakker.

Ferentzy, P., and N. Turner. 2009. "Gambling and Organized Crime–A Review of the Literature." *Journal of Gambling Issues* 23: 111–55.

Finkenauer J., and K. Chin. 2006. *Asian Transnational Organized Crime and Its Impact on the United States: Developing a Transnational Crime Research Agenda*. US Department of Justice, NCJRS. http://nij.ncjrs.gov/publications/pubs_db.asp.

General Accounting Office. 2002. *Internet Gambling: An Overview of the Issues*. GAO-03-09. http://www.gao.gov/new.items/do389.pdf.

Hernandez, D. 2006. *Cryptanalysis and Racketeering Records Unit*. Paper presented at the 13th Annual Risk Taking and Gambling Conference, Reno, NV, 2006.

Hill, D. 2010. *Viewpoint: The Murky World of Illegal Asian Gambling*. http://www.bbc.co.uk/news/world-asia-pacific-10671400.

Jawad, C., and S. Griffiths. 2008. "Preventing Problem Gambling on the Internet Through the Use of Social Responsibility Mechanisms." In *Crime, Addiction and the Regulation of Gambling*, edited by T. Spapens, A. Littler, and C. Fijnaut. Leiden/Boston: Martinus Nijhoff, 181–215.

Jonsson, J., and S. Rönnberg. 2009. "Sweden." In *Problem Gambling in Europe. Challenges, Prevention and Intervention*, edited by G. Meyer, T. Hayer, and M. Griffiths. New York: Springer, 299–315.

Kaplan, H., and W. Blount. 1990. "The Impact of the Daily Lottery on the Numbers Game: Does Legalization Make a Difference?" *Journal of Gambling Studies* 6(3): 263–74.

Kefauver Committee. 1951. *Kefauver Committee Interim Report #3, May 1 1951*. http://www.onewal.com/kef/kef3.html.

Liddick, D. 1999. *The Mob's Daily Number, Organized Crime and the Numbers Gambling Industry*. Lanham, MD: University Press of America.

Littler, A., and C. Fijnaut (eds.). 2007. *The Regulation of Gambling. European and National Perspectives*. Leiden/Boston: Martinus Nijhoff.

Lupu, V. 2009. "Romania." In *Problem Gambling in Europe. Challenges, Prevention and Intervention*, edited by G. Meyer, T. Hayer, and M. Griffiths. New York: Springer.

Macy, R. 1999. "Ban on College Sports Betting Could Costs State Books Millions." *Las Vegas Review-Journal* 4A. (May 18).

McKibbin, R. 1979. "Working-class Gambling in Britain 1880–1939." *Past & Present* 82: 147–78.

Moodie, L. 2002. *Organized Crime Section. Illegal Gambling.* Paper presented at the Gambling, Law Enforcement Systems Issues Conference, March 8, 2002. https://dspace.ucalgary.ca/bitstream/1880/47424/1/moodie.pdf.

Murphy, R. 1993. *Smash and Grab: Gangsters in the London Underworld.* London: Faber and Faber.

National Gambling Impact Study Commission. 1999. *Final Report.* http://govinfo.library.unt.edu/ngisc/reports/fullrpt.html.

North Country Gazette. 2008. *Gambino Captain, Others Busted for Sports Gambling,* 2(February).

O'Boyle, T. 2006. "The Illegal Use of Video Poker Machines by Public Bars and Private Social Clubs in Pennsylvania: It's a Rational Choice." *Journal of Economic Crime Management* 4(1): 1–26.

Peaker, G. 2010. *Fraud and Corruption in Football.* Paper presented at the Public Order Seminar, European Lotteries Association, March 11, 2010, Madrid.

Ostrov, B. 2009. "Corruption in Chinese Sport Culture." In *Corruption in International Business. The Challenge of Cultural and Legal Diversity,* edited by S. Eicher. Burlington, VT: Gower, 91–98.

Onze Tijd. 1849. *De arbeidende klassen in Engeland* [*The English Working Classes*]. Amsterdam: Uitgeverij Diederichs.

Polders, B. 1997. "Gambling in Europe: Unity in Diversity." In *Gambling: Public Policies and the Social Sciences,* edited by W. Eadington and J. Cornelius. Reno: University of Nevada, 65–100.

Reuter, P. 1983. *Disorganized Crime, Illegal Markets and the Mafia.* Cambridge, MA: The MIT Press.

RSe Consulting. 2006. *A Literature Review and Survey of Statistical Sources on Remote Gambling.* London: RSe Consulting.

Schotel, G. 1905. *Het maatschappelijk leven onzer vaderen in de zeventiende eeuw.* [*The Public Life of Our Forefathers in the 17th Century*]. Amsterdam: J.G. Strengholt's uitgeversmaatschappij N.V.

Spapens, T., A. Littler, and C. Fijnaut (eds). 2008. *Crime, Addiction and the Regulation of Gambling.* Leiden/Boston: Martinus Nijhoff.

Spapens, T. 2008a. *Joker. De aanpak van illegale casino's in Nederland.* [*Joker. The Combat Against Illegal Casinos in the Netherlands*]. The Hague: Boom Juridische Uitgevers.

Spapens, T. 2008b. "Crime Problems Related to Gambling: An Overview." In *Crime, Addiction and the Regulation of Gambling,* edited by T. Spapens, A. Littler, and C. Fijnaut. Leiden/Boston: Martinus Nijhoff, 19–54.

Spapens, T. 2010. *Valse bingo's. Illegale bingo's en de regulering van kansspelen* [*False Bingo. Illegal Bingo and the Regulation of Gambling*]. The Hague: Boom Juridische uitgevers.

Spapens, T. 2012. *Prijs! Zwarte lotto's en illegale sportweddenschappen in Nederland en het kansspeldebat in de Europese Unie* [*Winning the Prize! Illegal Numbers Games and Sports Betting in the Netherlands and the Gambling Debate in the European Union*]. The Hague: Boom Lemma uitgevers.

Swiss Institute of Comparative Law. 2006. *Study of Gambling Services in the Internal Market of the European Union, 1st part, Legal Study.* Lausanne: Swiss Institute of Comparative Law.

Treasury Department, Internal Revenue Service. 1933. *Summary Report.* (December 21, 1933). http://www.irs.gov.

Trucy, F. 2002. *Rapport d'information fait au nom de la commission des Finances, du contrôle budgétaire et des comptes économiques de la Nation (1) sur la mission sur les jeux de hasard et d'argent en France*. Paris: Sénat.

Trucy, F. 2006. *L'Évolution des Jeux de Hasard et d'Argent*. Paris: Sénat, Commission des Finances, no 58.

Tsytarev, S., and Y. Gilinsky. 2009. "Russia." In *Problem Gambling in Europe. Challenges, Prevention and Intervention*, edited by G. Meyer, T. Hayer, and M. Griffiths. New York: Springer, 243–256.

Turner, N. 2008. "Games, Gambling and Gambling Problems." In *In the Pursuit of Winning*, edited by M. Zangeneh, A. Blaszczynski, and N. Turner. New York: Springer, 33–64.

Valleur, M. 2009. "France." In *Problem Gambling in Europe. Challenges, Prevention and Intervention*, edited by G. Meyer, T. Hayer, and M. Griffiths. New York: Springer, 71–84.

Wohl, I. 2009. "The Antigua-United States Online Gambling Dispute." *Journal of International Commerce and Economics* July: 1–21.

Zumthor, P. 1962. *Het dagelijks leven in de gouden eeuw, deel II* [*Daily Life in the Golden Age, Part II*]. Antwerp/Utrecht: Het Spectrum.

CHAPTER 21

MONEY LAUNDERING

MICHAEL LEVI

I. Introduction

The hiding of income—both from lawful and from illegal activity—from governments has occurred for millennia. Meyer Lansky's claim to fame was partly his supposed skill in concealing the origins of funds used to buy real estate and legitimate businesses, including casinos that could then be used to launder further funds (Levi and Reuter 2006). The goal was not to avoid money laundering charges—since laundering was not then an offense—but to avoid tax evasion charges, which had famously brought down Al Capone, by making it difficult to trace the connection between wealth and its criminal sources.[1] So even before money laundering existed as a legal construct, efforts were being made to use illicit finance sanctions as an approach to stopping social threats, such as those generated by the prohibition of alcohol.

Laws against handling stolen property traditionally were thought of as referring only to the physical property obtained in the course of the crime. Even in those comparatively rare cases in which, as in Europe from the 18th century, attention was paid to professional receivers of stolen goods, there is no evidence that what happened afterwards to criminals' savings and reinvestments was part of the conception of serious crime control. Indeed, other than in the management of the "dangerous classes," it is questionable whether, prior to the mid-20th century, there was such a thing as an "organized crime strategy," properly construed. Laundering—an issue highlighted in the President's Commission on Organized Crime (1984)—and its control became a significant component of the war on drugs in the 1990s before it broadened to cover an ever-widening range of "threat finance" or "illicit finance," which includes financing of terrorism and nuclear proliferation as well as laundering the proceeds of corruption and tax evasion (Levi 2010). The fundamental innovation is to conscript the financial system (very broadly defined) into mandatory action and reporting (Ayling, Grabosky, and Shearer 2009), imposing the responsibility for (1) keeping suspected criminal money out, and (2) for reporting instances when they suspect that it has successfully entered—or is being inserted into—legitimate institutions. Both criminal and regulatory penalties are used to induce compliance by banks, insurance companies, pawnbrokers, and an expanding array of other businesses and professions, including, most controversially in some countries, lawyers.

In the developed world, the result has been a modest but increasing flow of criminal cases against banks and their employees for violation of these laws,[2] sometimes accompanied by regulatory fines and settlements in the tens of millions of dollars or occasionally even more. Increasingly, prosecutions are for offenses unrelated to drugs trafficking. Of the 310 US Federal money laundering prosecutions in FY 2012 (up 4.7 percent from a decade earlier), 28 percent were for drug-related laundering and 72 percent related to other offenses, of which the most prominent is tax evasion. Expressed in a different way, during FY 2011, the government obtained 0.3 drug-related and 0.7 other money laundering prosecutions for every one million people in the United States (TRAC 2012).

Although "soft law" pressures have extended these laws and institutions to developing countries, the results there have been even patchier (Chaikin and Sharman 2009; de Koker 2009: Levi 2012). The Financial Action Task Force (FATF), a collection of 34 governments, mainly countries within the Organisation for Economic Co-operation and Development (OECD), together with, the Gulf Cooperation Council and the European Commission plus eight FATF-style Regional Bodies (as of 2013)[3], has created the legislative and institutional frameworks that are now embedded in almost every nation, rich and poor. A complex collaborative system, including the International Monetary Fund and the World Bank, has monitored to date mainly formal legislative and institutional compliance with the rules; measurement of their impact on actual compliance and on levels and organization of crime is in its infancy (FATF 2013; Halliday, Levi, and Reuter 2014).

Readers might like to conduct a thought experiment on how different the levels and organization of different crimes would be if the global and national anti-money laundering regimes were not in place. What is the nature of the market for money laundering services? Who seeks to launder money and how do they locate both techniques and personnel willing to assist or who unwittingly will assist? What crimes are they involved in and in what countries? Who provides the services and what sorts of services are provided to what sorts of people?

The conclusions are readily summarized:

- There is (or ought to be) a great deal of uncertainty as to how much money is laundered or what share of criminal proceeds are laundered through the financial system rather than spent on "lifestyle" or merely stored for future use.
- The methods used for identified and proven laundering are frequently unsophisticated, except in elaborate fraud and Grand Corruption cases.
- Professional money launderers certainly exist, but they may account for a small share of all laundering (at least by volume of offenders) and seem to occupy narrow niches—it is a moot point whether or not one includes some substantial international banks in this category of professional money launderers.

- While a huge amount of data is generated by the control system, most of it is not seriously utilized for investigation and has been the subject of only modest analysis, almost nothing of which has been published.
- The system of money laundering controls has weak conceptual foundations and, though many institutions turn down customers or monitor them more intensively as a result of the legislation, the principal visible effects are (1) to allow prosecutors to occasionally add criminal charges and obtain more severe penalties, and (2) to allow regulators to impose numerically large penalties (which may be a very low percentage of the institutions' profits overall, if larger than the profits they made on the suspected transactions) for failure to implement the regulations properly.

The next section defines and describes the offense. Section III then presents examples that illustrate the variety of methods available and kinds of persons involved, along with some classifications. Section IV analyzes briefly the effects of anti-money laundering controls. Section V offers a few conclusions.

II. Defining Money Laundering in Law and Practice

Legally, money laundering refers only to concealing the proceeds of specific crimes (the "predicate" crimes). The list of predicates varies across countries, but it has gradually been extended in most nations to cover "all crimes" with a maximum sentence of at least one year of imprisonment (e.g., the European Union Third Directive of 2005)—a very low threshold. Beyond the bare-bones description of the act in terms of its intent, the question of what constitutes the act is more difficult. A standard but much critiqued description of the laundering process identifies three components: placement, layering, and integration.

> *Placement* is the process of putting illicit funds into the financial system. This may be the riskiest stage for the criminal as it is only here when there is a clear connection between the money and the crime itself.
> *Layering* is the process of moving the money through the financial system in order to further conceal the connection between the money and the crime. It is common—though no one except the offenders knows how common—to use a variety of identities, shell companies, and trusts in a number of countries to make the trail more difficult to follow.
> *Integration* is the final stage, in which the funds reenter the legitimate economy. The launderer might choose to invest the funds in real estate (sometimes also claimed to be a placement stage activity), luxury assets, or business ventures; or he or she might consume the resources with the claim—if challenged—that the funds were legitimately acquired.

Many parties can be involved in laundering, but the number can be as low as one. This insider involvement is not uncommon for large-scale financial frauds (see Levi, this publication): just as Cressey (1955) argued that all accountants *could* commit embezzlement, the perpetrator has exactly the skills required to also conceal the sources of his funds (so one might ask the control theory question "why don't more of them offend?"). At the other end of the sophistication spectrum, if drug dealers or thieves put the cash they have obtained from crime into a bank account in their own names, this is legally considered to be the offense of laundering in most common law and civil law countries. Thus, one finds many newspaper reports stating that people have been charged both with drugs trafficking and with money laundering.

Frequently, however, there is a customer for, and a supplier of, money laundering services. Once he generates a volume of business too large to spend immediately, the drug dealer or other illicit trader will need someone with other skills to launder the revenues. Both will be guilty of money laundering. It may be even more common that there are three parties: the money launderer could be an intermediary who recruits someone inside a financial institution to make the transaction and/or opens accounts to facilitate transactions.

A. Money Laundering Data Sources

Although hundreds of articles and books are available that provide reviews of legislative and regulatory responses to money laundering, and even specialist periodicals such as the *Journal of Money Laundering Control*, the empirical research literature on the phenomenon of money laundering is very slight indeed; key references from different regions are Beare and Schneider 2007; CSD 2012; van Duyne and Levi 2005; Gelemerova 2011; Levi and Reuter 2006; Matrix Research and Consulting 2007; Naylor 2004; Passas 2003; Reuter and Truman 2004; and Steinko 2012. In contrast to drug dealing, there are no ethnographic studies of money laundering, though there are individual autobiographies from prominent launderers or other insiders that give a portrait of the activity in particular places and eras (Escobar and Fisher 2010; Mazur 2009; Rijock 2012). Criminal and civil complaints in the United States and elsewhere sometimes also provide useful details, and annual reports of some Financial Intelligence Units increasingly give examples that indicate the usefulness of reports from the financial services sector (e.g. FinCEN 2013; MROS 2014; NCA 2014), though the operational successes in those cases might have happened anyway. In all these cases, it is hard to see a basis for generalizing patterns of laundering over time and place.

More might be expected from official overviews: after all, given the political, bureaucratic, regulatory, and enforcement resources devoted to combating laundering, one might hope to see some systematic analysis of the modus operandi developed by launderers. Each year the FATF (and related FATF-Style Regional Bodies such as Moneyval, which covers the 47 countries of the Council of Europe, http://www.coe.int/t/dghl/monitoring/moneyval/Typologies/Typologies_en.asp) produce oddly named

Typologies reports, which provide examples of different kinds of money laundering methods, often clustered around a particular theme, such as the use of professional intermediaries, wire transfers, etc. or the laundering of funds from particular activities, such as value-added tax frauds, or sports. However, although they have become more analytical in recent years and have moved toward "threat assessments" (FATF 2010; United Nations Office on Drugs and Crime 2011) and National Risk Assessments, it would be a mistake to think that these are based on a rigorous examination of a run of cases or of intelligence that has not reached the courts: rather, they may be the product of whatever those consulted are aware of and choose to volunteer. Enforcement agencies typically are too busy dealing with cases and processing inputs like reports from banks to systematically review what they might learn from the cases they deal with: though occasionally, deeply sanitized (and therefore often hard to visualize) reports are issued (e.g., http://www.ctif-cfi.be/website/images/EN/typo_egmont/21-100casesgb.pdf).   Increasingly, nongovernmental organizations (NGOs) such as Global Witness, Global Financial Integrity, and Transparency International—and even intergovernmental organizations (IGOs) such as the World Bank—produce hard-hitting analyses that examine high-level Grand Corruption, sometimes linked to organized crime (in the conventional sense), "blood diamonds," and other activities. (Though the quality of the underlying research and of scale/harm estimation varies.) Otherwise we must rely on what appears in the press concerning specific high-level cases, either before criminal/regulatory action or in its aftermath. The *Financial Times, Wall Street Journal, New York Times,* and—especially in transnational bribery and toxic waste cases—*The Guardian* have provided detailed and insightful coverage of some major cases; there are international groups of investigative journalists (e.g. http://www.occrp.org) whose work generates much insight into individual cases, despite defamation laws that make coverage of elite misconduct difficult.

III. Money Laundering Methods and Markets

A. Who Provides Money Laundering Services?

Money laundering has both a demand and a supply component. It takes little to create a legal basis for the offense of laundering—concealment or disposal of the proceeds of any crime, including those committed by "the launderer." Anyone engaged in business willing (for profit and/or in exchange for vice opportunities/relief from debts that are more likely during hard economic times) to run up additional revenues on their cash registers or to sell antiques, art and jewelry, or expensive automobiles (especially for cash) can help criminals conceal the proceeds of crime. This may put at risk their own businesses and assets as well as their liberty. However, if they are already on the edge financially, they may have only reputations and liberty, rather than their financial assets, to risk.

However, many money laundering cases involve more elaborate and distinct roles than the examples above. Many money launderers occupy quite narrow niches. Some, perhaps most, have only a very few customers; they will be cautious in taking on new business for fear of the downside risks, though this may depend on the predicate crimes (e.g., drugs versus tax) they service as well as on their expectations of police and prosecution strategies and regulatory regimes. Some insiders may even be blackmailed into continuing to enable laundering since they will be banned from the industry as well as perhaps prosecuted and jailed for past participation, even if they give evidence against others. This has important implications for the market for money laundering services.

John Mathewson was a US businessman who, in 1984, started a bank in the Cayman Islands that catered primarily to US tax evaders, as indicated by the flurry of convictions that emerged after he turned state's evidence (http://www.gpo.gov/fdsys/pkg/CHRG-107shrg71166/html/CHRG-107shrg71166.htm; Reuter and Truman, 2004). His customers learned about Mathewson's services through word of mouth or through advertisements at the airport on the British colony's main island, Grand Cayman. They usually came to his Guardian Bank and Trust Company offices with a letter of reference and enough cash to pay the $8,000 fees to set up and maintain the non-interest-bearing accounts. Mathewson had no prior criminal record; he had been a moderately successful small-town businessman. This, however, is an old case, and it provides little guide to current Cayman practices. More significant and recent (post-2008) are the details provided by the payments to and/or plea bargaining with banker informants in Liechtenstein, Switzerland, and the United States, and the pressure put upon UBS and other banks to reveal the identities of illegal foreign account-holders, whether their undisclosed wealth derives from licit or illicit source activities (http://www.politicsdaily.com/2010/04/26/brad-birkenfeld-tax-cheat-and-ubs-informant-doesnt-deserve-par/). In 2012, the Swiss authorities controversially issued arrest warrants against German officials who allegedly conspired with Swiss insiders to break banking secrecy.

Another case involved John Deuss, a banker with a long record of involvement in other questionable activities (e.g., busting UN sanctions against supplying oil to South Africa, defrauding the Soviet government in oil transactions), who operated a Caribbean bank that laundered money from "carousel fraud."[4] The UK authorities identified 2,500 persons involved in such fraud with accounts at that one bank. No allegations were made that Deuss had any involvement in committing the frauds themselves or that his bank laundered other kinds of criminal funds. He may simply have deduced that such frauds were unlikely to attract law enforcement interest. From media reports and this author's interviews, the banker was thought to have occupied a narrow, though lucrative, niche. In 2012, Deuss and his sister (director of Transworld Oil Computer Centrum) were each given a suspended prison sentence of six months and a fine of 375,000 euros, and the bank was fined 1.2 million euros in relation to its conduct in 2006 (http://www.amigoe.com/english/112766-fines-for-john-deuss-and-fcib).

A Russian national, Alexander Yegmenov, laundered funds for numerous Russian criminals by setting up literally thousands of shell companies in New York State, where the requirement to identify owners and directors is not (or certainly was not then) enforced (Komisar 1999). No charges were brought against the banks he used for these purposes. Indeed, American prosecutors have been extraordinarily reluctant to prosecute their own banks for money laundering, going instead after foreign-owned banks such as Mexican ones. Other than this, along with many aspects of "organized crime," there are many allegations about real estate or other business moguls acting as launderers for the underworld, but evidence is thin on the ground. Moreover, as with clients of mainstream investment firms, launderers can lose as well as gain money from their investments, for example, in real estate (van Duyne and Levi 2005; see also Unger and Ferwerda 2011). There is no reason to think that (except where they have correct inside information, e.g., about licenses for land development) criminals have any more investment skills than the average Wall Street or Swiss investment banker, though there may be more physical consequences for advisers who give the "wrong advice" to criminals!

B. How Much Money Laundering Is There?

A modern problem requires estimation of its scale so that it can be compared to other problems and so that performance measures can be developed against which to judge the efforts of those who aim to combat it. Thus, a modest number of efforts have been made to develop estimates of money laundering at the national and global levels (see Reuter and Truman 2004, chapter 2) for a review. More recently, Walker and Unger (2009) have made some highly questionable high-end guesstimates based on heroic assumptions and extrapolations; and Antonio Maria Costa, then head of the UN Office on Drugs and Crime, "said he has seen evidence that the proceeds of organised crime were 'the only liquid investment capital' available to some banks on the brink of collapse last year. He said that a majority of the $352bn (£216bn) of drugs profits was absorbed into the economic system as a result" (Syal 2009). Unfortunately, this statement contains no tested or testable evidence, so for the rest of us, it is a matter of faith or disbelief.

However, it is not clear that it is either useful or feasible to estimate the figure (see contributions to Reuter 2012). Numbers are frequently cited, with minimal documentation, becoming "facts by repetition." For example, on the basis of very modest evidence, the IMF estimated a total of $590 billion to $1.5 trillion globally in 1996 (Levi and Reuter 2006). In 2005, the United Nations cited the range of $500 billion to $1 trillion (http://www.unodc.org/unodc/en/money_laundering.html, accessed June 2, 2005). Such figures increase over time but, unlike crime rates, they never appear to fall (United Nations Office on Drugs and Crime 2011), only partly because an increasing number of predicate crimes (such as Grand Corruption) are added to them. A sustained effort between 1996 and 2000 by the FATF to produce a fully documented estimate failed. However, a few estimates of the potential demand for money laundering are regularly treated as actual money-laundering estimates.

An interesting RAND study suggested that Mexican Drug Trafficking Organizations' gross revenues (significantly more than their net profits) from moving marijuana across the border into the United States and selling it to wholesalers is likely less than $2 billion, and their preferred estimate is closer to $1.5 billion; for all drugs, the total gross estimate is $5.1 billion (Kilmer et al. 2010, 30), plus *relatively* modest further income in the low hundreds of millions from people trafficking.[5]

Even taken at face value, these numbers are only weakly related to money laundering. Even fearsome Mexican drug trafficking organizations (DTOs) have large expenses in bribes to law enforcement and politicians; and (as in the case of Irish and other paramilitaries) they have large levels of "staffing" to support, mainly in cash from cash proceeds of crimes. The dollarization of Mexico means that they do not even have currency conversion problems. In addition to such organized criminal activity, much income from selling drugs is earned by relatively disorganized offenders who use the cash to directly purchase legal goods without making use of any financial institutions. Small-time thieves earning $30,000 annually are unlikely to make use of a bank or any other means of storing or transferring value, and, although research carried out for one UK report (Matrix Research and Consulting 2007) suggests that such sums are readily attained even by high turnover "drug mules," it is impossible properly to estimate what share of these revenues will require laundering.

C. How Is Money Laundered?

The aim of laundering is to conceal the derivation of funds from crime and yet retain control over them. This involves trust of a particular person or persons—perhaps a member of one's family or ethnic/religious group—or trust of an institution, such as a bank or a money service business (MSB). The imagery of money laundering may involve cross-border transfers, but it is not clear how often this happens: logically it should depend on the risks and advantages of keeping funds within one's own jurisdiction. But sending money via institutions is not the only technique: The point is to transfer *value* by whatever means, including mispricing and mis-description of exported goods (Zdanowicz 2004) or matching those businesspeople/tourists who want dollars or euros with those who have those currencies as proceeds of crime (Passas 2003; FATF 2012). Such financial match-making can be undertaken by banks, but it can also be done by semi-legitimate networks, usually within the same ethnic or nationality group. The global trade in money is assisted by the vast sums repatriated by millions of expatriate workers around the world who send money home to their often impoverished families, making it hard to distinguish legitimate from illegitimate-source funds. The authorities have tried to regulate this market by requiring MSBs to register and to identify both the senders and the recipients of funds.

It is helpful to look at laundering techniques in terms of the problems that offenders have to confront. The laundering methods used may depend on the nature of the regime that is in place. The identification of "suspiciousness" by professionals and others with a legal responsibility to combat money laundering is often a judgment that the people and/or transactions are "out of place" for the sort of account they have and the people they purport to be. Thus, as part of the layering process, foreign students in the United Kingdom and elsewhere sometimes are approached to offer their accounts to run through transactions from "businesses," for which they are paid commission. The success of this relies on inadequate back-office monitoring of existing account holders: but in order to launder very large sums, one would need to find a lot of cooperating students. At a much higher level, if the would-be predicate offenders start out with a business that is being used as a medium for what looks like legitimate activity, then placement of funds may look unproblematic: Corporate lawyers may be keen to offer well-paid services in the construction of corporate vehicles and will not routinely suspect senior corporate staff of being major criminals. Since many frauds would be unsuccessful if they did *not* look like legitimate activity, this gives them a structural advantage over other types of offenders. We now turn to examine what is known about patterns of laundering, and, since many studies are country-specific, we will examine European evidence. (See also Beare and Schneider 2007, for a broad range of Canadian cases based on RCMP investigations.)

1. *Drugs and Laundering in Europe*

Although European research on laundering is patchy, it is more extensive than in the United States and is on a par with the Canadian work: The relative lack of American research is surprising, given the fact that the United States has been the policy leader in this field. Van Duyne and Levi (2005) review what was then known about money management by European offenders. The classification in the table below aims to map (only from cases that were final) the ways Dutch drugs perpetrators attempt to hide from government the crime-money itself or the illegal ways of acquisition. The categories are not mutually exclusive since more than one way of handling proceeds of crime may be employed in the same case and with the same money. For example, a portion of the money may be exported, part of which is subsequently brought back by means of a loan-back construction, while the expensive car is paid for in cash to be subsequently put in the name of a relative to retain effective ownership in the event of proceeds confiscation. Subsequent gangland killings in the Netherlands have targeted (previously blackmailed) wealthy real estate magnates such as Willem Endstra, who was alleged to be the banker for the underworld and whose murder in 2004 supposedly left some serious criminals uncertain of where "their" assets were (personal interviews). The issue of *how* offenders get proceeds into those property purchases is often more obscure, though some notaries have been suspected as conduits (Lankhorst and Nelen 2005).

Bearing in mind that these observations derive only from identified and proven cases, and some may have derived from an era in which it was expected that money hidden abroad was safe from the clutches of the courts, it seems plausible to interpret the evidence as follows:

- **Export of crime-money.** As observed in Table 21.1, in most cases the money was simply exported: the 31 observations, covering 17 cases, concerned €16.6 million euros that had been found in foreign bank accounts (over a time span of eight years). In four cases there was evidence of money export to foreign banks accounts,

Table 21.1 Methods of Disguising and Laundering Crime Proceeds

Forms of concealment/disguise	Frequency
Export of currency	31
Disguise of ownership	10
False justification	
Loan back	3
Payroll	2
Speculation	1
Bookkeeping	7
'Untraceable'	4

Source: Van Duyne and Levi, 2005

though either these accounts were already cleared before the police arrived or the files did not mention any figures. In the cases of Turkish or Moroccan drug entrepreneurs, this export appeared to be an obvious option, given their country of origin. Either through bureaus de change or by means of physically transporting the cash, the crime-moneys were brought safely to their home countries.

- **Disguise of ownership.** The second most frequently observed form of safeguarding assets while still being able to use them is the simple *disguise of ownership* by putting them in someone else's name. Only in a few cases was this done with any sophistication, for example, when corporate structures (legal persons) were used. The usual defects were (a) the closeness of the relationship between the nominal owner and the beneficiary, and (b) the difficulty of the nominal owners to prove actually having possessed the means to acquire the assets in the first place. Nominal owners were frequently acquaintances or relatives; some found themselves to be the involuntary owner of unknown property. For example, the mother of one middle-level Dutch cocaine trafficker, who lived only on a meager pension, was surprised to learn that she owned a villa. Also in other cases, relatives were (ab)used by putting (moveable) assets or bank accounts in their name.

  Though preexisting legal persons were used to channel drug money, few of them were actually set up for the purpose of disguising ownership. The (notable) exceptions were a British crime-entrepreneur, two Dutch cannabis traffickers, and a Turkish heroin wholesaler, all of whom invested in real estate using legal persons for the beneficial ownership. Another Dutch hash trafficker established an extensive network of legal persons to disguise the ownership of cash, bank accounts, and vehicles. These corporate constructions to *disguise* real ownership overlap with the laundering (*justification*) category discussed below: tampering with paperwork and with other evidence.

- **False justification.** From the point of view of "real" laundering, the successful *justification* (in the event of investigation) of ill-gotten moneys or assets is the core craft: providing documentary evidence that the increase in wealth, whether in terms of money, assets, or valuables, has a legitimate source. One of the methods most frequently used is the often-mentioned, well-trusted *loan-back construction*. Given the frequent references in the literature to this, it is surprising to learn that its sophistication was shallow. Van Duyne et al. described a professional provider of loan-back constructions, who designed professional loan contracts, complete with related correspondence and a real money flow of interest and repayments to the lender corporation abroad in order to imitate perfectly real loan transactions (and deduct the interest paid from tax liabilities). The loan-back provider saw to it that his clients did pay the required monthly interest and repayment. Except for one case, such professional conduct could not be observed in the cases of this study. Loan contracts were sometimes missing or the apparent "contracts" did not mention the repayment and interest terms, nor was there any record that the required demonstrable "flow back" of interest and installment payments were carried out.

In two cases, the laundering of a monthly income by means of salary payment could be observed. In one case, €75,000 euros was loaned to an independent but friendly small firm, which subsequently handed out a modest monthly salary. This laundering was not intended to justify the millions of euros in proceeds but to placate the Inland Revenue Service and create the illusion of a genuine income.

"Real" laundering by setting up *phony bookkeeping* to make the money really "white" appeared to be a craft mainly used by drug entrepreneurs who lived in the Netherlands, mimicking the sort of business they were in. For example a florist, using his horticulture as a cover for growing cannabis plants, had to obtain invoices to cover expenses as well as the income from the cannabis sales. In the cocaine traffic with Colombians, certificates of transportation of goods and accompanying phony paperwork with commodities (sugar) on the parallel market were drafted to justify the return flow of the money to Colombia. Such cover stories were easily busted by investigators.

- **The untraceability of crime profits.** This is a "default" category, consisting of supposed moneys which could not be found.

A recurrent refrain in money laundering literature and political speeches is the transnational dimension: money trails around the world through impenetrable accounts held in sunny, far away resorts. Such far-flung hideaways do exist, but how many wholesale drug entrepreneurs are customers of these facilities? Convicted British and Dutch drug wholesalers were certainly not such customers: the exotic "financial secrecy havens" rarely figured as target countries for depositing drug money (van Duyne and Levi 2005). In the Dutch case, the frequency distribution over the foreign countries clustered around *neighboring* countries, and other jurisdictions were infrequent. It seems that the Dutch drug entrepreneurs favored Belgium and Luxembourg while the Turks and Moroccans favored their own countries. A Dutch-Thai couple held bank accounts in Thailand because of the nationality of the partner. This finding contradicts the usual image of "transnational" criminals spreading their ill-gotten profits worldwide over the "bad" financial secrecy havens. Instead, it seems that the choice of banking jurisdiction is largely determined by proximity to the drug entrepreneur's "economic home." This is confirmed in later studies, e.g., van Duyne and Soudijn (2010).

Suendorf's German-language study of laundering in Germany (Suendorf 2001) contains 40 examples of money laundering in the broad juridical meaning of the word: i.e., every subsequent handling of illegal profits aimed at disguising their origins. Two cases can be considered to fall into the category of thoroughly organized money management: Organizations were established to move the crime moneys of heroin wholesalers to their respective home countries. One of them is set out below:

> The *Bosporus case* identified an extensive and complex network of money-exchange bureaus directed by an Iranian entrepreneur, who served a Kurdish heroin wholesaler. The funds were collected in various cities in Germany and carried to branches of the Iranian or associated independent bureaus. Subsequently the cash was placed in German banks and transferred to bank accounts of allied money change offices in New York. From these accounts the moneys were diverted to Dubai and—if required—back to Germany or Turkey. To fool the German police, the bureau de change submitted occasional suspicious transaction reports.

In 11 of the 40 cases there was an attempt to make an investment in the upperworld (i.e., the mainstream legitimate commercial world), though with variable success and degrees of professionalism. Most of the other examples concerned only the channeling of funds into accounts rather than full integration of suspected moneys. Overall, the sophistication and professionalism displayed was modest.

Steinko (2012) reviewed patterns of money laundering in Spain. Drug trafficking is the predicate offense in more than 90 percent of the cases analyzed. However, the most important criminal proceeds are those generated by cases of "urban planning–related corruption," which have a major environmental and social impact. A total of 60 percent of the proceeds of crime known about were laundered through the financial system. Of this, a third was through foreign banks, preferably Swiss. He noted (p. 496): "The majority of cases are technically and economically modest and have a local dimension. The few financial assets bought with illegal money show a conservative behaviour: no speculative handling of assets bought with criminal money could be detected. The analysis of the illegal non-financial assets illustrates the importance of real-estate properties and vehicles destined for regular use and, somewhat less importantly, for the acquisition of houses and luxury cars for conspicuous consumption. The main objective of money launderers is regular and conspicuous consumption and to obtain an income through the renting of property."

The well-researched threat assessment by the CSD (2012, pp. 63–65) noted that most Bulgarian organized criminals did have licit businesses—more so than in other European studies—and that, in 2010, investment of funds of illicit origin was mainly focused on four distinctive sectors: (1) trade (including dealing in real estate property)—31 percent; (2) construction—27 percent; (3) gambling—18 percent, and (4) tourism—10 percent. "The majority of the complex money laundering schemes involve notaries, accountants, lawyers, and financial experts. In larger criminal groups bosses

Table 21.1 Uses of Profits by UK Drug Dealers

Use of profit	Often	Sometimes	Never	Non-response	Total
Profits spent on lifestyle	68	2	5	29	104
Profits reinvested in drug tafficking	48	1	7	48	104
Profits invested in property or other assets	25	12	29	38	104
Profits laundered through legitimate businesses	19	2	39	44	104
Profits spent on drug habit	17	11	10	66	104
Profits sent overseas	8	8	48	40	104

may assign the control of such operations to particular persons. There are no specialist money launderers who provide money-laundering services to other criminals."

Imprisoned human traffickers in the United Kingdom stated that transferring money abroad was not difficult, and it seems reasonable to infer that unconvicted ones found it even easier. The proceeds from facilitation of the trafficking were often returned to the home country, where land and property were then bought. Facilitators based in the United Kingdom kept the bulk of the money there for disposable income and for investment in property and businesses, such as shops, hotels, restaurants, and sweatshops.

Finally, a British interview-based study of drugs dealers suggests the following pattern of expenditure and laundering (Matrix Research and Consultancy 2007 p. 39; see Table 21.1):

> Some dealers stressed that they "did not do anything flashy with their earnings," e.g. "just spending the money on the kids...and paying the mortgage" (p. 39). The information collected pointed to unsophisticated money laundering techniques with a tendency to use friends and family, for example by investing in their businesses or bank accounts. One interviewee reported establishing a fraudulent painting and decorating business and buying winning betting slips that he cashed at betting shops across the country.

One freelance hauler involved in the drugs trade reported that his boss would specifically identify a firm in financial trouble but who still had regular consignments coming into the country. He then went round and offered them a part of a deal so he could use their legitimate consignment as a front to enable a drugs importation. One might expect such willingness to mix legitimate and illegitimate trade (and confidence to make corrupt offers) to have become more frequent during the economic crises of 2007–present; however, the evidence base is not good enough to test this.

The danger (not avoided by van Duyne and Levi 2005) of this sort of analysis is that, although it throws some appropriately skeptical light on official claims and popular assumptions about money laundering sophistication, it rests upon those cases successfully dealt with by the authorities. It, therefore, excludes those cases that are problematic to prosecute, whether in Europe, Mexico, or "failed states" elsewhere. What the studies show is that much variation exists internationally in patterns of laundering and in the markets for laundering services, which do not appear to be dominated by hierarchical "Mr. Bigs" or, indeed, by criminal masterminds generally. However, the skills involved in getting massive sums in VAT and other frauds to disappear beyond the reach of well trained forensic accountants tells us something about the sophistication of *some* launderers and about the opacity of the world of international finance, despite the efforts that have been made to increase transparency and mutual legal assistance.

D. Corruption and Money Laundering

Money-laundering controls have also come to be seen as an important tool for dealing with corruption, particularly in developing countries (Levi et al. 2007; Chaikin and Sharman 2009; Global Witness, 2009, 2012). The recovery of illicitly acquired assets is one of the central motifs of the UN Convention against Corruption of 2005. The range of activities and the ways in which wealth transfers are effected illustrate some of the difficulties in using anti-laundering money (AML) measures to punish corruption. While Grand Corruption is identified with notorious dictators and their "cronies," many other forms of corruption are not insubstantial. Large bribes are paid to border or internal law enforcement officials, to judicial officers, or to those who control them not to proceed against criminals or their goods: The latter can be illegal (like narcotics increasingly trafficked through from Latin America via West Africa), counterfeit (software and other intellectual property, alcohol, medicines, cigarettes, tobacco), or legal but untaxed smuggled dutiable genuine goods. Corruption can arise in any area of procurement. But no formal bribes in the form of direct transfer of cash or bank transfer need take place, making the identification of the offense, proof of corruption (and laundering), and appropriate sanctions nearly impossible. Sometimes it is simply understood that, if people want to do business in a particular town or country, they have to buy or sell via businesses or professionals whom they know to be connected to elites, criminals, or both. In a sense, this is invisible organized crime.

Value transfers need not take place via electronic funds transfer or other banking methods: They may involve false invoicing, the purchase of goods and services knowingly at inflated prices (such as flowers regularly supplied by the Japanese Yakuza—author interviews, 1998), or more convoluted chains of agreements that rely on family relationships and minimize direct financial flows in the short term. Nonetheless, money laundering is an important correlate of corruption, embezzlement, and other serious crimes for gain.[6] This may mean that the assets are being expatriated illicitly or, when the procurements are large enough, placed by the companies paying the bribes, perhaps via "commission payments" to intermediaries. It is common for falsified documentation—the overpricing or even invention of services—to be used. Again, payments do not occur in the country where the briber and bribed originate, but they go offshore. Unlike proceeds of crimes, such as drug trafficking, that result in cash payments, many corrupt transactions are not easy to arrange through informal value transfer systems. They are more suited to formal systems, at least in instances where the corrupted persons wish to place their assets overseas.

Although Switzerland historically was the destination of choice for many plundered assets—having the desirable combination of honest safe-keeping, political stability, and ethical neutrality toward the sources of funds—there is no longer any reason to suppose that it is the destination of choice for corrupt assets nowadays. Indeed, the activism of the Swiss authorities might be regarded as a deterrent, though large forfeitures there remain quite rare.

IV. Anti-money Laundering (AML) Measures and Their Effectiveness

AML measures were first developed at a national level, in the United States and the United Kingdom in the mid-1980s (though bulk cash deposit Currency Transaction Reporting was introduced as early as 1970 in the United States). Since that time, by a combination of imitation, political peer pressure, and technical assistance, the world has witnessed an extraordinary growth in efforts to control crime for gain (and latterly, terrorism) via measures to identify, freeze, and confiscate the proceeds of crime nationally and transnationally. [7] From its beginnings in the War on Drugs, this has become an attempt to deal with the crime-facilitating consequences of the "dark side of globalization," i.e., core policy to open up money flows via the liberalization of currency restrictions and marketization in developing countries, including former Communist societies. Stripping "proceeds of crime" from offenders, both by criminal and, increasingly, by civil process, is politically popular and has a positive demonstration effect in local communities in that it is aimed at encouraging the public to see that crime does not pay. It is expected a priori to inhibit criminal careers of individuals and "organized crime groups" by restricting their abilities to save and to integrate their funds, which remain at risk. Moreover, many on the political left who would ordinarily be civil libertarians see pro-transparency AML activities as mechanisms to reduce the kleptocracy/Grand Corruption that has damaged central and eastern European countries as well as much of Africa, Asia, and South America, hence, the passage of the UN Convention against Corruption (2005), to match the previous UN Vienna

Drugs Convention (1988) and the UN Transnational Organised Crime Convention (2002).

More and more entities and professions are being brought into the AML network. Banks must train their staff and report suspicions with procedures that are fairly standard worldwide, throughout the EU, under the 2001, 2005, and 2013 European Directives. In the EU, accountants, art and car dealers, casinos and jewelers, lawyers and notaries are required to identify clients and report them to the authorities if their transactions are in cash over €15,000 euros or are deemed "suspicious" (Levi et al. 2007; EC 3rd and 4th money-laundering directives; Unger et al. 2014). Few such reports would have been made without the threat of criminal and regulatory sanctions. One useful way of conceptualizing the issue is as a global crime risk management exercise that seeks to conscript as unpaid deputy sheriffs foreign governments and those parts of the private sector that seem unwilling to volunteer for social responsibility to combat dirty money (Favarel-Garrigues et al. 2008). Many former communist European countries—having rejected all-knowing invasive states—find themselves pressured into establishing central databases for financial transfers and sharing data on these reports across the EU.

In 2009, the total number of all Suspicious Activity Reports (SARs) filed by US financial institutions was 1.52 million (FinCEN 2013)—half of them from banks—while Currency Transaction Report (CTR) filings of large cash deposits, whether suspected or not of originating from crime, are ten times greater. From a few informal tip-offs from bankers to police in 1986, the number of SARs filed in the United Kingdom rose to 20,000 in 2000 and then to 316,527 in 2013 (NCA 2014). Upon receipt, SARs are logged into the UKFIU internal SARs database (known as ELMER) and are made available to Law Enforcement Agencies (LEAs) for investigation. There are approximately 1.38 million SARs on ELMER. All SARs which populate the database are subject to immediate checks, including those previously entered into the system where new information may change the nature of a previous SAR—a frequent occurrence. SARs are retained on ELMER for a period of six years or until proven not to be linked to crime.

Reporting in the UK and elsewhere is uneven, focussed on large banks, one large money transmitter, and one gaming firm: about half of all SARs are submitted by four firms and 20 reporters submitted 75 percent of all SARs. Significant increases have occurred throughout the 47 countries of the Council of Europe (wider than the EU), reflecting the increased training and number of bodies covered by anti-laundering legislation, plus political pressures of the EU *acquis communautaire*—the detailed criteria with which countries must comply before they are admitted to the EU.

Nonetheless, the totals still vary enormously between countries: by contrast with the very large US and UK figures, the number of reports made in 2012 for suspicion of money laundering in Switzerland hit an all-time high of 1,585 (double that in 2009), with the value of assets implicated being 3.12 billion Swiss francs (approximately US$3.33 billion at the 2013 exchange rate). The banking sector accounted for two-thirds of all reports. Fraud accounted for a third of all suspected predicate crimes with embezzlement and corruption accounting for a further 21 percent.

What are the implications of this? At first sight, the data suggest the Swiss authorities are doing little about money laundering. However, a suspicious transaction report has much graver consequences in Switzerland. When an account is reported as suspicious there, it is *automatically* frozen for up to five days pending investigation of whether or not a formal criminal investigation should be opened, placing a premium on having few ill-founded suspicions. If 1 million Americans and a quarter million Britons had their accounts frozen, there would be a significant outcry and vastly increased investigative resources would be needed to process the reports within a few days! Takats (2006) has developed a model that suggests the government can be flooded with paperwork and rendered less effective by an overly broad reporting system.

One way of looking at the impact of AML laws is to examine the famous 1983 Brinks' Mat gold bullion robbery at London's Heathrow Airport, which netted around $52 million in gold. This happened before any money laundering legislation was in effect in the United Kingdom, and the gold was largely smelted down and used to make jewelry, leading to sudden very large increases in the business turnover of one suspect, funds from whose business were withdrawn in cash to such an extent that the regional Bank of England branch ran out of £50 notes with which to supply the local bank branch. Yet no one made any report to the authorities, nor was anyone obliged to do so (Levi 2007). That very probably would not happen now.

What other kinds of effects of AML can we deduce? Levi and Reuter (2006) reviewed the evidence of impact of AML to that date, and they have concluded that there has been little crime suppression to date, nor—given the poor quality and vast range of estimates of proceeds from drugs, for example—is it plausible that we would be able to detect any effects and separate them from error. As for the impact of AML on improving criminal justice performance, the few analytical studies carried out show that this has been very modest to date. The extent to which this is attributable to low resource investment and to poor communications between public and private sectors, especially cross-border, remains to be determined. No one knows what the total number of *persons* subjected to extra financial surveillance is in Europe (EU and beyond), but it is a significant feature in the policing landscape, even though scarce financial investigation resources mean that relatively little is done about many of the reports that are received.

AML regimes might have two other benefits in addition to controlling crime: improving the efficiency of the system or catching offenders who otherwise would escape. Cuéllar agrees that such regimes might have improved efficiency in drug control and in reducing a few related criminal activities, but he argues that they have failed in catching offenders. The principal use to which the US AML regime has been put has been to increase the penalties with which prosecutors can threaten predicate offenders (Levi and Reuter 2006). The regime has had little success in apprehending professional money launderers or high-level criminals. In Europe, some activity has been undertaken against professionals such as lawyers as well as against bankers—though more by regulatory than criminal sanctions—but the extent to which this has incapacitated crime networks, reduced the variety of their offending, or reduced the scale of their growth as "criminal organizations" remains unknown and largely unanalyzed (van Duyne and Levi 2005;

Nelen 2004). There are limits in the extent to which the police (or, for that matter, bankers) can pursue the rationale behind suspected transactions without interviewing suspects. However, greater attention to who really owns and controls (beneficially owns) assets (FATF 2013) should logically help with asset recovery compared with post-arrest or even post-charge financial investigations that were commonplace before. In this sense, AML has an influence on law enforcement methodologies, from drugs to Grand Corruption. Thus, in the UK regime, investigators can require those convicted of serious and organized crimes to file annual financial reports and can place monitoring orders on suspected offenders' accounts that prospectively allows them to track funds movements. They can also require forfeiture of cash over £1,000 inland as well as at borders unless the suspect can convince the court that the funds were legitimately acquired. This introduces a conviction-to-grave process of financial self-reporting by offenders in which provable lying by them introduces extra risks.

In many respects, the policy transfer process in AML and anti-corruption efforts—assisted by foreign aid for particular developments and economic sanctions for non-cooperation—has been a major success. Nevertheless, (a) the goal of affecting the organization and levels of serious crimes has been displaced in practice by the more readily observable goal of enhancing and standardizing rules and systems; (b) the critical evaluation of what countries actually do with their expensively acquired suspicious transaction report data remains in its infancy; and (c) the punishment for poor AML performance, though apparently similar internationally, in practice has focused more sharply upon smaller and weaker jurisdictions than upon the major nations and upon minor rather than "too big to be prosecuted" banks, raising questions about the equity of the process (Sharman 2011; Halliday, Levi, and Reuter 2014). The mechanisms that facilitate laundering are intricately linked to those that enable wealthy corporations and individuals to hide their assets from public knowledge and—a separate issue—to minimize the taxes that they are obliged to pay (Blum et al. 1998; Godefroy and Lascoumes 2007; Sharman 2011; Shaxson 2011). However, it remains a fact that in wider Europe, out of the billions of euros obtained and then in part saved from crimes annually, far less than €1 billion is confiscated (Matrix Insight 2009), and—for all their successes in individual cases—the shift to civil forfeiture independent of prosecution in the United Kingdom and in the Irish Republic has hitherto had only a modest impact on this, especially net of the costs of investigation, court action, and asset management (Harvey 2008; National Audit Office 2013; Public Accounts Committee 2007). What has happened to these unconfiscated billions over the decades? What social harm do they do, and where?

How should the effectiveness of the AML regime be assessed? Money laundering itself is only the intermediate target; the true target is, instead, the volume of predicate crimes, perhaps weighted in terms of their harmfulness. Reduction in the volume of the money laundered is not a conceptually strong measure of the effectiveness of the regime; subtler outcome measures, which have yet to be developed, are needed. Levi and Reuter (2006) examine in detail the problem of finding such measures to reduce crimes other than terrorism and bribery/kleptocracy since the bulk of AML activities have been devoted to such criminal activities as drugs, other illegal markets, and white-collar crimes.

In terms of crime control, the AML regime may generate two other benefits. First, part of the social appeal of proceeds of crime confiscation is the public satisfaction that offenders are denied the fruits of crime (see Kilchling, this publication). Seizure of funds generates revenue for the government, and the incarceration of those who conspire to make the profits of crime appear legitimate punishes senior offenders. The seizures attack the negative role models offered by offenders living "high on the hog." Research in Europe finds ample illustrations of law enforcement officers stressing the pain that asset confiscation brings to offenders in absolute terms and compared with at least European levels of imprisonment (Levi and Osofsky 1995; Nelen 2004):[8] though plausible, this has not been independently verified on a large sample of offenders, nor is it clear how it impacts upon the willingness of these or other offenders to commit crimes in the future. Given the stakes that financial and legal professionals have in maintaining their employment and licensure, they may be relatively deterrable (Lankhorst and Nelen 2005; Middleton and Levi 2005), that is, unless they are being blackmailed/threatened or unless they/their firms are at serious risk of going bust anyway, modest expected risks of apprehension and punishment may be enough to discourage many from participating. In some instances the only way to apprehend those principal offenders who separate themselves from the predicate offenses is to convict them of money-laundering offenses associated with predicate crimes that have been committed by others. Such cases aim to show that the law with respect to a wide range of predicate crimes applies to everyone.

However, it is also important to think about what the AML system does *not* impact on. Since scrutiny of sources of criminal earnings for low earners is limited, it is probably only criminal incomes of more than perhaps $30,000 to 50,000 annually that create a need for concealing the source of the revenues. Thus, unless the AML processes stop all bigger league criminals from importing drugs or committing frauds, most offending by volume will be unaffected. However, it seems unlikely that laundering is such a scarce skill that incarcerating a few hundred will have a major impact on availability. The rise of artificial tanning and nail parlors in the United Kingdom is an illustration of cash-hiding self-laundering potential, especially since tax agencies do not profit from, and are not set up to investigate, overreporting of taxable income. Although professional money launderers certainly exist, they are surprisingly infrequent in reported cases.

This is important for both policy and research purposes. The rationale behind the current AML regime is based, in part, on the implicit assumption that the regime provides tools to apprehend and punish a set of actors who provide a critical service for the commission of certain kinds of crime and who were previously beyond the reach of the law—an assumption that makes the market model a useful heuristic device for analyzing the effects of laws and programs. However, if money laundering is mostly done by predicate offenders or by nonspecialized confederates, then the regime accomplishes much less. For research purposes, the prominence of the amateur launderer implies that the market-model concept is a strained analogy since most laundering is done by amateurs who are not regular players.

In short, AML performance measures are difficult to develop, since they would have to link the AML actions to changes in the predicate crimes: This is hard enough in the case of drugs, on which evidence is best, though one might expect bank detections to be better for frauds. High-level dealers, the only ones who need money laundering services, account for no more than 25 percent of total drug revenues (Levi and Reuter 2006). Assume that in the current regime money launderers charge customers approximately 10 percent of the amount laundered. Now assume that an improved system raised the price for money laundering services by half, to 15 percent. The result would be an increase in the price of drugs of only 1.25 percent, far too small to be picked up by existing monitoring systems. This is not an argument that money-laundering controls are not effective or cost-effective, but only that their success cannot be empirically assessed by examining prices and quantities in drug markets.

It is generally agreed that data generated by the AML system must be better used. Greater skilled commitment to financial investigation and adjudication is likely to improve criminal justice and disruption yields, whatever effect this may have on levels of offending of different kinds. There are many individual cases in which SARs have added to (or, more rarely, stimulated) investigations and proceeds of crime recoveries (Gold and Levi 1994; Fleming 2005; NCA 2013; SOCA 2012; see also Harvey 2008).

The paucity of cases against stand-alone launderers and investigations that have their origin in money laundering information supports the criticism that the AML regime has brought in few new offenders. No systematic data are available on the origins of cases against major criminals such as principal drug dealers and so it is impossible to tell whether more of them are being captured through money laundering laws and investigations. Furthermore, where heads of state or their families are involved in Grand Corruption (including embezzlement and, sometimes, illicit trafficking and other major organized crimes), it is far from obvious to whom either domestic or foreign institutions should report without fear of retaliation or who has sufficient motivation to take serious action. In this respect, the national Financial Intelligence Unit model, like most national crime investigation and prosecution models, breaks down when confronted with key elites, even where they have no formal immunity for acts performed in office (Levi 2012).[9]

Finally, whatever the gains from money-laundering controls, a variety of costs also need to be considered. Reuter and Truman (2004) offer a very rough estimate of $7 billion for the costs of the US AML regime in 2003. That figure includes costs to the government ($3 billion), the private sector ($3 billion, and the general public $1 billion). However, it does not include two potentially important cost elements: the effect on the international competitive position of business sectors subject to AML rules or the costs of errors. There has been a rise in demand for Money Laundering Reporting Officers—who must by law be appointed in every regulated institution, though they do not have to be exclusively devoted to that role—and escalating use of expensive software that tries to identify "suspicious transactions" on the basis of pattern analysis.

V. Concluding Remarks

Money laundering, though a traditional activity, is a very modern crime, created by the late-20th-century state to enlist the financial sector (and, later, many other sectors) in its pursuit of the proceeds of crime and deterrence of career criminality, particularly transnational crime. Undoubtedly, many billions of dollars are laundered, but whether that is 1 percent or 10 percent of GDP in developed economies is very much a matter of guesswork.

Money is laundered in many ways by offenders of very different kinds. It is, indeed, one of the few activities that connect Al Qaeda, Colombian drug dealers, Credit Suisse, and Enron officers. There are many different techniques for laundering, involving both the most respectable and the most marginal of institutions. Given the commitment of state authority, co-opted financial institutions and the violation of individual privacy to the pursuit of money laundering, it would be worthwhile learning a great deal more about laundering itself than we currently know.

A broad and intrusive set of controls have been erected to prevent money laundering. In addition to their considerable financial and privacy costs, these controls have potentially large unintended effects. For example, international banks have, at times, made it difficult for money service businesses (MSBs) to wire remittances of immigrant workers back to their home countries—or even handle MSBs' accounts—because they fear that bank regulators will monitor them more closely for possible money laundering violations, and that they might be penalized themselves if the MSBs do launder proceeds of crime or finance terrorism. The AML requirements of extensive documentation before opening an account can thus reduce the access of poor persons to the financial system. The methodology for evaluating countries' performance at AML has been reformed from 2013 to shift it toward a risk-based approach based on an analysis of the money-laundering problems in each society. Showing that the system generates substantial crime or corruption control benefits ought to be high on the agenda of the relevant policy-making community.

Notes

1. Mark Haller provided helpful clarifying comments on this matter.
2. In March 2010, Wachovia settled what was then the biggest action brought to date under the US Bank Secrecy Act of 1970 (http://www.justice.gov/usao/fls/PressReleases/2010/100317-02. html). It paid federal authorities $110m in forfeiture, for allowing a huge volume of transactions later proved to be connected to drug smuggling and a $50m fine for failing to monitor cash used to ship 22 tons of cocaine despite being warned by one of its money-laundering reporting officers. The Deferred Prosecution Agreement placed Wachovia on probation for one year, and it was later taken over by Wells Fargo. In 2012, HSBC agreed to pay a fine of $1.9 billion for a large volume of money-laundering offenses connected to drugs and other crimes (Senate 2012); while it escaped prosecution, the bank was subject to major reforms of its anti-laundering efforts worldwide (http://www.justice.gov/opa/pr/2012/December/12-crm-1478.html). Prosecutions of other banks have followed.

3. Some 27 international and regional organizations—including the IMF, UN, and World Bank—are associate members or observers of the FATF and participate in its work. See http://www.fatf-gafi.org/pages/aboutus/membersandobservers/

4. The scheme takes advantage of the fact that value added tax (VAT) is rebated if the item is exported to another country. Sales are made to dummy foreign corporations and rebates are then fraudulently claimed, while companies owing the VAT to the national tax authorities typically go "bust" and cannot pay their bills. The difficulty is often proving the connection between the companies/managers, since they claim to be independent of each other. See FATF (2007) for a description of the scheme. This is a far from trivial phenomenon, costing several billion dollars' worth of losses annually and forcing a restatement of the UK balance of payments (Levi et al. 2007): The fact that relatively little is known about what happens to the money is, therefore, interesting in itself.

5. It is important to focus on *gross* revenues because estimating *net* revenues requires information about what DTOs pay to produce or purchase the drugs, and data are far too poor to permit this properly.

6. Often, such acts could be labeled as corruption, embezzlement, *and* theft since the terms are not mutually exclusive.

7. For a sound legal and institutional history of these changes, see Gilmore 2011. For a more socio-legal history, see Levi 2007 and Alldridge 2008.

8. These are supported by interviews with UK law enforcement personnel, 2002–2005.

9. This is not uniquely a problem for the countries of the South, especially Africa: Scandals engulfed Prime Minister Berlusconi (Italy) and President Chirac (France) while in office, as well as—at a more modest level—former German chancellor Kohl. Many of these scandals involve campaign finance in both the wealthier nations as well as some poorer countries.

REFERENCES

Alldridge, Peter. 2008. "Money Laundering and Globalization." *Journal of Law and Society* 35(4): 437–463.

Ayling, Julie, Peter Grabosky, and Clifford Shearing. 2009. *Lengthening the Arms of the Law.* Cambridge: Cambridge University Press.

Beare, Margaret, and Stephen Schneider. 2007. *Money Laundering in Canada: Chasing Dirty and Dangerous Dollars.* Toronto: University of Toronto Press.

Blum, Jack, Michael Levi, Tom Naylor, and Phil Williams. 1998. *Financial Havens, Banking Secrecy and Money-Laundering.* Issue 8, UNDCP Technical Series, UN document V.98–55024. New York: United Nations.

Chaikin, David, and Jason Sharman. 2009. *Corruption and Money Laundering: A Symbiotic Relationship.* London: Palgrave.

Cressey, Donald. 1955. *Other People's Money.* New York: Free Press.

CSD. 2012. *Serious and Organised Crime Threat Assessment, 2010–11.* Sofia, Bulgaria: Center for the Study of Democracy.

de Koker, Louis. 2009. "Identifying and Managing Low Money Laundering Risk: Perspectives on FATF's Risk-Based Guidance." *Journal of Financial Crime* 16 (4): 334–352.

Escobar, Roberto, and David Fisher. 2010. *The Accountant's Story: Inside the Violent World of the Medellin Cartel.* New York: Grand Central.

FATF (Financial Action Task Force). Annual. *Report on Money Laundering Typologies.* Paris: Financial Action Task Force.

FATF. 2007. *Laundering the Proceeds of VAT Carousel Fraud.* Paris: FATF. http://www.fatf-gafi. org/media/fatf/documents/reports/Trade_Based_ML_APGReport.pdf.

FATF. 2010. *Global Money Laundering & Terrorist Financing Threat Assessment.* Paris: Organisation for Economic Co-operation and Development.

FATF. 2012. APG Typology Report on *Trade Based Money Laundering.* Paris: FATF. http://www. fatf-gafi.org/media/fatf/documents/reports/Trade_Based_ML_APGReport.pdf.

FATF. 2013. *Methodology for Assessing Technical Compliance with the FATF Recommendations and the Effectiveness of AML/CFT systems.* Paris: Organisation for Economic Co-operation and Development.

Favarel-Garrigues, Gilles, Thierry Godefroy, and Pierre Lascoumes. 2008. "Sentinels in the Banking Industry: Private Actors and the Fight against Money Laundering in France." *British Journal of Criminology* 48(1): 1–19.

FinCEN. 2013. *The SAR Activity Review—By the Numbers*, Issue 18. Washington, DC: US Treasury.

Fleming, Matthew. 2005. *UK Law Enforcement Agency Use and Management of Suspicious Activity Reports: Towards Determining the Value of the Regime.* http://www.ucl.ac.uk/scs/ downloads/research-reports/fleming-LEA-SARS

Gelemerova, Liliya. 2011. *The Anti-Money Laundering System in the Context of Globalisation: A Pantopticon Built on Quicksand?* Oisterwijk: Wolf Legal.

Gilmore, William. 2011. *Dirty Money: The Evolution of International Measures to Counter Money Laundering and the Financing of Terrorism.* 4th ed. Strasbourg: Council of Europe.

Global Witness. 2009. *Undue Diligence: How Banks Do Business with Corrupt Regimes.* London: Global Witness.

Global Witness. 2012. *Grave Secrecy.* London: Global Witness.

Godefroy, Thierry, and Pierre Lascoumes. 2007. *Capitalisme Clandestine.* Paris: Decouverte.

Gold, Michael, and Michael Levi. 1994. *Money-Laundering in the UK: An Appraisal of Suspicion-Based Reporting.* London: Police Foundation.

Halliday, Terence C., Michael Levi, and Peter Reuter. 2014. *Global Surveillance of Dirty Money: Assessing Assessments of Regimes to Control Money-Laundering and Combat the Financing of Terrorism.* Chicago: American Bar Foundation.

Harvey, Jackie. 2008. "Just How Effective Is Money Laundering Legislation?" *Security Journal*, 189–211.

Kilmer, Beau, Jonathan P. Caulkins, Brittany M. Bond, and Peter H. Reuter. 2010. *Reducing Drug Trafficking Revenues and Violence in Mexico: Would Legalizing Marijuana in California Help?* Santa Monica, CA: RAND.

Komisar, Lucy. 1999. "Russian Cons and New York Banks." *Village Voice* (December 7).

Lankhorst, Francien, and Hans Nelen. 2005. "Professional Services and Organised Crime in the Netherlands." *Crime, Law and Social Change* 42(2–3): 163–188.

Levi, Michael. 2007. "Pecunia non olet? The Control of Money-Laundering Revisited." In *The Organised Crime Community,* edited by F. Bovenkerk and M. Levi, 161–182. New York: Springer.

Levi, Michael. 2010. "Combating the Financing of Terrorism: A History and Assessment of the Control of 'Threat Finance.'" *British Journal of Criminology Special Issue Terrorism: Criminological Perspectives* 50 (4): 650–669.

Levi, Michael. 2012. "How Well Do Anti–money Laundering Controls Work in Developing Countries?" In *Draining Development? Controlling Illicit Flows from Developing Countries,* edited by Peter Reuter, 373–414. Washington DC: World Bank Press.

Levi, Michael, and Lisa Osofsky. 1995. *Investigating, Seizing and Confiscating the Proceeds of Crime.* Police Research Group Paper 61. London: Home Office.

Levi, Michael, and Peter Reuter. 2006. "Money Laundering: A Review of Current Controls and Their Consequences." *Crime and Justice: An Annual Review of Research* 34: 289–375.

Matrix Research and Consultancy. 2007. *The Illicit Drug Trade in the United Kingdom.* 2d ed. London: Home Office. Online Report 20/07. http://webarchive.nationalarchives.gov. uk/20110220105210/rds.homeoffice.gov.uk/rds/pdfs07/rdsolr2007.pdf.

Matrix Insight. 2009. *Assessing the Effectiveness of EU Member States' Practices in the Identification, Tracing, Freezing and Confiscation of Criminal Assets.* Brussels: European Commission.

Mazur, Robert. 2009. *The Infiltrator: My Secret Life Inside the Dirty Banks behind Pablo Escobar's Medellín Cartel.* New York: Little, Brown.

Middleton, David, and Michael Levi. 2005. "The Role of Solicitors in Facilitating 'Organized Crime': Situational Crime Opportunities and Their Regulation." *Crime, Law & Social Change* 42(2–3): 123–161.

MROS. 2014. *Report 2013: Annual Report by the Money Laundering Reporting Office Switzerland MROS.* Bern: Federal Office of Police, Swiss Federation.

National Audit Office. 2013. *Confiscation Orders.* London: National Audit Office.

Naylor, R. Tom. 2004. *Wages of Crime.* Ithaca, NY: Cornell University Press.

NCA. 2014. *Suspicious Activity Reports (SARs) Annual Report 2013.* London: National Crime Agency.

Nelen, Hans. 2004. "Hit Them Where It Hurts Most? The Proceeds-of-Crime Approach in the Netherlands." *Crime, Law and Social Change* 41:517–534.

Passas, Nikos. 2003. *Informal Value Transfer Systems, Terrorism and Money Laundering.* www. ncjrs.gov/pdffiles1/nij/grants/208301.pdf.

President's Commission on Organized Crime. 1984. *The Cash Connection: Organized Crime, Financial Institutions, and Money Laundering.* Interim Report to the President and the Attorney General. Washington, DC: US Government Printing Office. https://www.ncjrs. gov/pdffiles1/Digitization/166517NCJRS.pdf.

Public Accounts Committee. 2007. *Assets Recovery Agency: Report.* London: Public Accounts Committee. http://www.publications.parliament.uk/pa/cm200607/cmselect/ cmpubacc/391/391.pdf

Reuter, Peter, and Edwin M. Truman. 2004. *Chasing Dirty Money.* Washington, DC: Institute for International Economics.

Rijock, Kenneth. 2012. *The Laundry Man.* New York: Viking.

Sharman, Jason. 2011. *The Money Laundry.* Princeton, NJ: Princeton University Press.

Shaxson, Norman. 2011. *Treasure Islands.* London: Bodley Head.

Serious Organised Crime Agency (SOCA). 2012. *The Suspicious Activity Reports Regime Annual Report 2011.* London: Serious Organised Crime Agency.

Steinko, Armando Fernández. 2012. "Financial Channels of Money Laundering in Spain." *British Journal of Criminology* 52: 908–931.

Suendorf, Ulrike. 2001. *Geldwäsche: Eine kriminologische Untersuchung.* Neuwied, Germany: Luchterhand.

Syal, Rajeev. 2009. "Drug Money Saved Banks in Global Crisis, Claims UN Advisor." *The Observer* (December 13). http://www.guardian.co.uk/global/2009/dec/13/drug-money-banks-saved-un-cfief-claims.

Takats, Elod. 2006. "A Theory of 'Crying Wolf': The Economics of Money Laundering Enforcement." International Monetary Fund Working Papers.Washington, DC: International Monetary Fund.

Transational Records Access Clearinghouse. 2012. *Federal Money Laundering Enforcement Efforts Lag.* Transactional Records Access Clearinghouse, Syracuse University. http://trac.syr.edu/tracreports/crim/303/.

Unger, Brigitte, and Joras Ferwerda. 2011. *Money Laundering in the Real Estate Sector: Suspicious Properties.* Cheltenham, UK: Edward Elgar.

Unger, Brigitte, Joras Ferwerda, Melissa van den Broek, and Ioana Deleanu. 2014. *The Economic and Legal Effectiveness of the European Union's Anti-Money Laundering Policy.* Cheltenham: Edward Elgar.

United Nations Office for Drugs and Crime (UNODC). 2011. *Estimating Illicit Financial Flows Resulting from Drug Trafficking and Other Transnational Organized Crimes.* Vienna: United Nations Office for Drugs and Crime.

US Department of State. 2003. *International Narcotics Control Strategy Report.* Washington, DC: Department of State.

US Senate. 2012. *US Vulnerabilities to Money Laundering, Drugs, and Terrorist Financing: HSBC Case History.* Washington, DC: Permanent Subcommittee on Investigations, US Senate.

van Duyne, Petrus C., and Michael Levi. 2005. *Drugs and Money: Managing the Drug Trade and Crime-Money in Europe.* Abingdon, UK: Routledge.

van Duyne, Petrus, and Melvin Soudijn. 2010. "Crime-Money in the Financial System: What We Fear and What We Know." In *Transnational Criminology Manual.* Vol. 2, edited by M. Herzog-Evens, Nijmegen: Wolf Legal.

Walker, John, and Brigitte Unger. 2009. "Measuring Global Money Laundering: 'The Walker Gravity Model.'" *Review of Law & Economics* 5(2): 821–853.

Zdanowicz, John. 2004. "Detecting Money Laundering and Terrorist Financing via Data Mining." *Communications of the ACM* 47(3): 53–55.

CHAPTER 22

....

ARMS TRAFFICKING

....

ANDREW FEINSTEIN AND PAUL HOLDEN

I. INTRODUCTION AND LITERATURE REVIEW

This essay examines arms trafficking and the organized manner in which this criminal activity takes place. The essay is organized as follows: section II provides a quick typography of the arms trade, identifying two "worlds" that the trade inhabits—the formal trade and the shadow world of illicit and clandestine deals. Section III identifies the main methods by which arms trafficking has been criminalized to date. It is important to note, here, that arms dealing only becomes trafficking if transactions are conducted that violate national or international law. Section IV focuses on two notorious arms traffickers—Viktor Bout and Leonid Minin—to illustrate points raised in earlier sections. Section V provides a brief discussion of how arm traffickers are able to find collaborators in many key areas, notably in the intelligence and black-ops communities. Section VI looks at the success (or lack thereof) in tracking, arresting, and prosecuting arms traffickers to date. The final section addresses the prospects for whether arms trafficking can be effectively brought under control.

While much has previously been written about the global arms trade in the academic literature, few books or middle-size to long pieces have been written about the trade in the past 25 years. The most comprehensive study of the trade and arms trafficking is Anthony Sampson's definitive *The Arms Bazaar*, which was first published in 1977 (Sampson 1977). *The Arms Bazaar* was a global best-seller and did much to publicize the more controversial aspects of the arms trade. As such, it served as an inspiration and guide for *The Shadow World: Inside the Global Arms Trade*, published by one of the essay authors (Andrew Feinstein) in 2011. *The Shadow World* is the first global study of the arms trade and weapons trafficking since *The Arms Bazaar*. Much of this essay draws from material included in *The Shadow World* or discovered during the research process. Additional material was also drawn from an article written by Andrew Feinstein, Paul

Holden, and Barnaby Pace published by the Stockholm International Peace Research Institute (Feinstein, Holden, and Pace 2011).

This is not to suggest that the arms trade is entirely uncovered by academic analysis. Special mention should be made of the Stockholm International Peace Research Institute (SIPRI), which publishes an annual yearbook on the arms trade as well as other subject specific reports, and Amnesty International, which publishes well-researched reports about weapons trafficking. Nevertheless, due to the relative paucity of academic focus on arms trafficking, the following essay is drawn largely from contemporaneous media reportage, relevant United Nations (UN) reports on the monitoring of arms embargoes, documents emanating from court proceedings, and primary resource material that was gathered during the research for *The Shadow World*.

II. A Typography of the Arms Trade

Global defense spending is substantial. In 2010, for example, an estimated $1.62 trillion was dedicated to military expenditure, of which over $700 billion was spent by the United States alone (SIPRI 2011).[1] This is equal to 2.6 percent of global domestic product and equals roughly $235 for every person on the planet. Expenditure on conventional armaments constitutes only a small portion of this total: an estimated $60 billion per year (Roeber 2005).[2]

The arms trade is home to a range of activities stretching from legitimate government-to-government contracts to arms trafficking involving nonstate actors in some of the world's least developed countries. While arms industry executives are often keen to emphasize the difference between the two realities, there is substantial evidence to suggest the existence of a continuum of unethical behavior and illegality that characterizes the arms trade in all its manifestations to varying degrees. There are, in effect, two worlds, each interlinked and involving players that move from one reality to another.

The first world is the "respectable" world of state-sanctioned government-to-government contracts. Usually this involves the production, sale, and distribution of larger conventional weapons such as aircraft and naval systems, although there is also a robust trade in small arms and ammunition to both governments and individual end users. Unfortunately, this world is not without its own problems. In particular, the formal and legitimate trade is often inflected with bribery and corruption.[3]

This is clear in the example of BAE Systems, the second largest defense manufacturer in the world. BAE admitted, during criminal proceedings with the US Departments of Justice and State in 2010 and 2011, that it had created a sophisticated network of "consultants" and "advisors" who were paid roughly £135 million in thousands of transactions via a highly secretive mechanism based in the British Virgin Islands (US Department of Justice 2010). BAE Systems acknowledged that the payments were made "even though in certain situations there was a high probability that part of the payments would be used in order to ensure that BAES was favoured in the foreign government decisions regarding the sales of defence articles" (US Department of Justice 2010).

What we call the "Shadow World" is constituted by deals conducted in the "gray" and "black markets." Deals in the "gray market" are undertaken by individuals associated with (or directly employed by) state security and intelligence agencies. While some of these trades are not illegal, they are undertaken in secret as exposure may have political ramifications. Gray market deals often involve the illegal sale and distribution of weapons to embargoed parties. Perhaps the best known example of this form of trade is the Iran-Contra scandal, in which the United States secretly sold weapons to the Iranian government in anticipation of a deal to release American hostages. Part of the proceeds of the sales were used to fund the Nicaraguan Contras, a rebel group whose funding by US intelligence and security agencies was specifically prohibited by Congress (see Walsh 1997). The "black market," meanwhile, consists of deals that are illegal in conception and execution and are usually undertaken by arms dealers in a manner that violate international conventions and embargoes. Arms trafficking is predominantly the preserve of the "shadow world," although it must be acknowledged that actors in this world can and do work in aid of the formal trade.

Arms trafficking can be defined as the sale and/or distribution of military matériel in violation of national and international law or binding international conventions and agreements. While some legislation allows for prosecution for arms trafficking, it is useful to acknowledge that arms trafficking involves a repertoire of offenses depending on the nature of the deal undertaken. Most typically, as we describe in more detail next, arms trafficking can and usually does involve the following crimes:

- Fraud (falsifying permits, bills of landing, end-user certificates, and cargo manifests, among other documents)
- Corruption (bribes paid to warlords and other actors to secure business or, in more unique scenarios, bribes flowing in the opposite direction)
- Theft (where arms are procured from producers or military agencies without their knowledge or permission, usually facilitated by collusive and corrupt employees)
- Money laundering (where the true nature of illegal payments made and received by the trafficker is disguised and reintroduced into the formal banking system)
- Intimidation, assault, or murder (usually in instances where officials or other individuals attempt to obstruct the progress of a deal)

As this suggests, arms trafficking is a relatively sophisticated crime, especially when arms are delivered across large distances by air or sea in violation of international monitoring. As such, arms trafficking relies on the input and collusion of a large number of individuals operating in a coordinated manner, suggesting that it should be considered a form of organized crime. Activities of members of arms trafficking organizations would range from acting as middlemen or go-betweens between the arms producer and the buyer; pilots or captains employed to transport cargo by air or sea; individuals responsible for money laundering and the securing of forged documents; collusive state employees willing to provide such documents or other forms of assistance (including nonenforcement of mandated duties); and "muscle" provided to protect the organization from nonpayment or other threats.

III. Criminalization

Although it might sound tautologous, the trade in arms only becomes arms trafficking, by definition, when such trade is specifically outlawed by national legislation or international agreement. Thus, deals that may be considered unethical and make use of criminal elements are not considered arms trafficking unless that activity has been specifically criminalized.

The criminalization of arms trafficking takes two prominent forms in the international arena. The first—and the one with the longest historical roots—is country-specific embargoes put in place by individual governments. These are often, but not always, implemented by means of overarching legislation that allows governments to identify prohibited recipients in terms of the founding legislation, as well as seek the prosecution and conviction of offenders.

One of the best known pieces of such legislation is the Arms Export Controls Act (AECA). Passed in the United States in 1976, it served to integrate a series of disparate laws that spoke to the issue of controlling arms exports (US Department of State 2012b). The Act "provides the authority to control the export of defense articles and services, and charges the President to exercise this authority" (US Department of State 2012b). Chapters and sub-chapters can be added to the US legal code identifying companies or recipients who are forbidden from importing US defense equipment: one such example is a sub-chapter outlining comprehensive sanctions against Iran. The law often operates in conjunction with the International Traffic in Arms Regulations (ITAR) that is frequently updated by the US government (US Department of State 2012a).

The Act mandates the State Department's Directorate of Defense Trade Controls (DDTC) to regulate arms export (GAO 2005). In order to export arms, the state or any private manufacturer or reseller has to apply for a license that permits the export of equipment. If the deal for which a license has been applied does not meet the criteria and sub-chapters included within the AECA and/or ITAR, the issuing of the license is to be denied. If, however, the company or individual who has been denied the license continues with the transaction, they are guilty of violating the AECA and/or ITAR and can be prosecuted and sanctions imposed as determined by the AECA. In addition, if an individual or company that exports arms from the United States without seeking a license in terms of AECA and/or ITAR, they are considered in violation of both acts and can be prosecuted accordingly.[4] According to ITAR, any individual or company who violates the provisions of the regulations "shall upon conviction be fined for each violation not more than $1,000,000 or imprisoned not more than 20 years, or both."[5]

The second form of criminalization is regional and international agreements that prohibit the export of defense articles to individual companies or armed groups. The most notable of such agreements are mandatory UN arms embargoes. These are brought into force by means of resolutions issued by the UN Security Council. UN member countries are expected to integrate such resolutions into their national legislation so that law enforcement activities can be undertaken by the relevant national body—this is necessary as the UN has no criminal enforcement mechanisms and relies on individual governments to prosecute individuals or companies that violate the terms of the UN arms embargoes.

The use of mandatory UN arms embargoes was limited until the fall of the Berlin Wall, partially due to the fact that the Cold War and the use of vetoes by permanent members of the UN Security Council (UNSC) often led to deadlock and disagreement. Only two mandatory UN arms embargoes were put into effect before 1990: UNSC Resolution 232, which placed a mandatory arms embargo on Rhodesia between 1966 and 1979 (UNSC 1966), and UNSC Resolution 418, which placed a mandatory arms embargo on apartheid South Africa between 1977 and 1994 (UNSC 1977).

Since 1990, however, there has been a veritable explosion of UN arms embargoes. Between 1990 and 2006, for example, the UNSC agreed to 27 mandatory arms embargoes and 2 additional voluntary embargoes (Fruchart et al. 2007, p. xiii). Currently,[6] there are 13 active mandatory UN arms embargoes in place.

It should be noted that the other notable arms embargo mechanism—mandatory embargoes for European Union (EU) members—currently has additional embargoes in place against countries and parties. Those currently[7] under EU arms embargoes that are not under UN embargoes are Belarus, China, Guinea, Myanmar (Burma), South Sudan, Syria, and Zimbabwe (Table 22.1).[8]

IV. Two Traffickers in the Post–Cold War Era: Viktor Bout and Leonid Minin

Viktor Bout is perhaps the best known modern arms trafficker. Bout was born in the small town of Dushanbe in the USSR in 1963 (Daly 2008). He was remarkably proficient at languages and enrolled in the Soviet Union's Military Institute of Foreign Languages (Bout 2009). By the time the Berlin Wall fell, he was fluent in six languages.

Bout was masterful in taking advantage of the chaos into which the post–Cold War Soviet militaries were plunged by rapid transition. In 1991, he moved into the field of air freighting, acquiring hulking transport planes on the cheap from Soviet army officials looking to cash in during the tumult of the early 1990s (Farah and Braun 2007, pp. 32–36). His first purchase was three transport aircraft for the meager sum of $40,000 each (Farah and Braun 2007). Due to the fact that Russian officials often declared planes as scrap—despite being fully operational—to raise funds for themselves,

Table 22.1 Mandatory UN Arms Embargoes

Target Party/Country	Date Imposed	Establishing Document
Al-Qaeda and associated individuals	January 16 2002	UNSCR 1390
Taliban	January 16 2002	UNSCR 1390
Cote d'Ivoire	November 15 2004	UNSCR 1572
Democratic Republic of Congo (nongovernment forces only)	July 23 2003	UNSCR 1493
Eritrea	December 23 2009	UNSCR 1907
Iraq (nongovernment forces since 2004)	August 6 1990	UNSCR 661
Iran	December 23 2006	UNSCR 1737
Lebanon (nongovernment forces only)	August 11 2006	UNSCR 1701
Liberia (nongovernment forces since 2009)	November 19 1992	UNSCR 778
Libya	February 26 2011	UNSCR 1970
North Korea	October 14 2006	UNSCR 1718
Somalia	January 23 1992	UNSCR 733
Sudan (Darfur region)	July 30 2004	UNSCR 1556

Source: Extrapolated from the Stockholm International Peace Research Institute Arms Embargo Database. www.sipri.org/databases/embargoes.

Bout was able to grow his fleet to 50 planes (Coalition for International Justice 2005, pp. 16–22).

By 1992, Bout had entered the world of arms dealing. His first client was the Northern Alliance, which had taken power in Afghanistan following the USSR's withdrawal (Farah and Braun 2007, p. 45). In 1996, Bout's pilots were captured by Taliban fighters, and he was forced to negotiate their release. His negotiation skills seemed to impress the Taliban, for whom Bout began delivering arms. Using his base in Sharjah in the United Arab Emirates, Bout was responsible for delivering an estimated $50 million worth of arms to the insurgents (Farah and Braun 2006).

But Bout's most lucrative market was to be Africa. Between 1994 and 1998, he won $325 million worth of contracts to supply the Angolan government air force. At the very same time, Bout was supplying the Angolan government's main civil war opponent, UNITA. Bout's planes made 37 deliveries of weapons to UNITA from Bulgarian arms suppliers (Bowcott and Norton-Taylor 2000; see also UNSC 2000a). UNITA, at the time, was subject to a UN arms embargo.

In 2000 and 2001, Bout supplied perhaps his most notorious client—Charles Taylor, the warlord-president of Liberia. Liberia had been subject to a UN arms embargo since 1992. Taylor's military endeavors were notoriously violent and included supporting the brutal Revolutionary United Front (RUF) in neighboring Sierra Leone, which rose to international infamy through the use of child soldiers known as "Small Boy Units" (Gberie 2005).

Bout was able to ply his trade by establishing convoluted front companies and aircraft registries. His planes were registered in various semi-failed states that allowed him to effectively evade detection. One such registry was Liberia itself, where Bout's business partner, Sanjivan Ruprah, was appointed by Taylor as the "Global Civil Aviation agent worldwide for the Liberian Civil Aviation Register" (UNSC 2000b). And Bout was always able to rely on pliant officials to provide him documents that were necessary for ferrying weapons to the world's most dangerous inflicts.

Bout sourced most of his weapons from the Ukraine—a go-to state for any arms trafficker who needed weapons without facing questions. In 1992, Ukraine's stockpile of weapons was valued at $89 billion. Over the next 6 years, an estimated $32 billion worth of arms, ammunition, and sophisticated weapons systems were stolen and resold (Traynor 2001). One parliamentary investigation into the thefts eventually ground to a halt in 1998 after producing 17 volumes of evidence (Traynor 2001).

Bout went underground from 2001 on as he was pursued by numerous law enforcement agencies around the world. Much of his success in evading capture was due to his closeness to more than one country's intelligence and security structures, as we discuss in more detail later.

Bout can be considered a typical post–Cold War arms trafficker, displaying many defining features of the illegal trade in arms. First, he was able to establish complex front companies and aircraft registration schemes. The latter was due to the opaque and disorganized nature of many aircraft registries in less-developed countries. Second, Bout was able to source a considerable amount of weapons from the old Eastern Bloc, which after 1990 became the primary source of cheap stockpiled weapons for many arms dealers. Third, he had a truly global reach due to both his aircraft infrastructure and the globalized nature of the arms trade.

Another notable—and typical—arms trafficker to emerge in the last decade is Leonid Minin. Minin was born in Odessa, Ukraine, in 1947. First operating under the name Leonid Bluvstein, Minin moved to Israel and then to a more permanent location in the town of Norvenich, near Koln in West Germany (Comando Generale dell'Arma dei Carabinieri 1996). It is unclear what Minin did to secure his finances in the 1970s and 1980s, but by the early 1990s he had come to the attention of investigators in Italy and elsewhere. In 1992, for example, Russian police investigated him for involvement in smuggling art works and antiques (Comando Generale dell'Arma dei Carabinieri 1996). In 1997, he was arrested on charges of drug possession, after which he was denied entry into Monaco, where he had established numerous enterprises (Comando Generale dell'Arma dei Carabinieri 1996).

According to a Russian criminal intelligence investigation, Minin had by the mid-1990s become a major player in organized crime and mafia circles in Ukraine, which controlled, among other things, the export of oil and natural gas. It was reported that by early 1990, 67 percent of all oil exports from Odessa (the country's main oil refining and exporting port) was controlled by the Odessa *Neftemafija* (oil mafia) (Comando Generale dell'Arma dei Carabinieri 1996).[9] The Russian investigation determined that Minin was "one of the most important" members of the *Neftemafija* as his companies, Galaxy and Limad, were central to the trade. The mafia members who fell under Minin were also "involved in international arms and drug trafficking, money laundering, extortion and other offences" (Comando Generale dell'Arma dei Carabinieri 1996).

In 1998, Minin left Ukraine after rumors circulated that individuals with Russian mafia associations had ordered his assassination (Monza Public Prosecutor's Office 2001). After a chance meeting during a stay in Ibiza, Minin agreed to go into business with Fernando Robleda, a Spanish businessman involved in logging in Liberia (Monza Public Prosecutor's Office 2001). The Ukrainian, after flying to Liberia to meet Taylor (and allegedly offering arms and bribes to the president for additional forestry concessions [Central Examining Court 2000, 2002; Monza Public Prosecutor's Office 2001]), became a director in Exotic Tropical Timber Enterprises (ETTE 1998). Over the next few years, Minin would make a decent profit from logging activities in Liberia, despite international approbation about abuses in the Liberian timber industry. Minin conducted his first delivery of armaments only a week after convincing Taylor to sign over additional concessions to ETTE. Minin apparently sourced the weapons from Ukraine and had them ferried to Niger (UNSC 2000b, p. 35, para 2011). From the Niger town of Niamey, Minin oversaw the transport of 68 tons of ammunition and arms in his own BAC-11 personal jet. Once unloaded, the weapons were transported across the Liberian border by Taylor's forces into the hands of the RUF (UNSC 2000b).

In 1999, Minin conducted two further deals. The first was typical of many arms trafficking transactions. Minin had sourced 715 boxes of ammunition, cartridge powder, antitank missiles, RPG launchers, and missiles from the Ukrainian state arms manufacturer, *Ukrspetsexport* (Isenberg 2004). An end-user certificate was provided, fraudulently, by the Ministry of Defence in Burkina Faso indicating that the weapons were to be used by the Burkina Faso government (Amnesty International 2006). Once the weapons landed in Burkina Faso aboard an Antonov 124, a portion of the arms were transported to the town of Bobo Dissoulou, where they were transferred on to Liberia by Minin. For supplying the end-user certificate, the Burkina Faso government retained a share of the weapons (Amnesty International 2006).

Minin was eventually arrested while staying in a hotel in Italy in 2000. The police had been called after somebody who was also resident at the hotel reported a ruckus from Minin's room. When the police entered the room, they found him comatose, surrounded by drugs, diamonds, money, and four prostitutes. It was only after the police searched his effects and discovered a panoply of documents that they realized they had stumbled on a major arms trafficker.

Minin was, like Bout, a variation of the typical post–Cold War arms dealer. Like the Russian, Minin was able to source considerable amounts of weapons (and transportation) from former Soviet states (notably Ukraine). And, like Bout, he was easily able to procure fraudulent documentation to give a legitimate sheen to his activities. Unlike Bout, however, Minin was also involved in natural resource exploitation: an activity that has also marked the post-1990 period. Many arms traffickers are either directly involved in smuggling both arms and minerals for their clients or are paid in funds raised by militias who have seized control over such resources. In the Democratic Republic of Congo, for example, nongovernment forces have used their access to arms to seize control over lucrative diamond mines (UNSC 2002a). The militias use forced labor to extract the diamonds, which are then sold on the international black market (UNSC 2002a). The funds that are raised in this way are used to purchase additional arms to carry on their part of the war. Arms trafficking and mineral smuggling thus become part of a self-supporting system: a criminal and devastating vicious circle.

V. Protectors and Collaborators

Successful arms trafficking deals are only possible due to the involvement and collusion of numerous actors, four of whom are the most prominent. The first of these collusive protagonists is the security establishments (in particular the intelligence and "black-ops" divisions) of many countries. These security entities serve a number of functions, including, but not limited to, providing market information as to prospective clients, sourcing weapons from surplus stock for use by arms traffickers, and, perhaps most importantly, providing protection from prosecution and conviction. In return, they get gray deals done and, on occasion, information.

Many intelligence and security agencies in the developed world have made use of arms traffickers for deals that may be illegal and certainly unpalatable if publicly linked to the organizing state. The case of Victor Bout is instructive. In 2002, Belgium, which had investigated Bout for years, issued an Interpol "red notice" demanding his arrest by Interpol members. In late February 2002, firm intelligence was provided to Belgian and European authorities (operating under Operation Bloodstone) that Bout was due to fly from Moldova to Athens aboard his personal plane. Operation Bloodstone operatives planned to arrest him as he landed in Athens (Farah and Braun 2007, pp. 102–203). When Bout's flight departed, British field agents sent an encrypted message stating that the "asset" was en route. Minutes later the plane disappeared from radar, reappearing 90 minutes later far off course. When the plane eventually landed in Athens, Bout was nowhere to be found. One European investigator claimed that Bout's evasion could only have been achieved with US complicity (perhaps in anticipation that Bout could provide useful intelligence on his erstwhile clients, the Taliban): "There were only two intelligence services that could have decrypted the British transmission in so short a time. The Russians and the Americans. And we know for sure it was not the Russians" (Farah and Braun 2007, p. 203). Bout eventually settled in Russia, where he was portrayed as the victim of a US conspiracy by powerful political players and protected from extradition.

Another example with a longer historical pedigree is that of Gerhard Mertins. A decorated former Nazi (Silverstein 2000, p. 111), Mertins became a figure of ill repute when his company, Merex, engaged in a number of shady deals. Merex had been propelled into business at the behest of Gehlen Org, the German postwar intelligence agency that would eventually morph into the official intelligence agency of West Germany, the BND (Ascherson 1972). Gehlen Org was staffed with a number of prominent ex-Nazis with whom Mertins was familiar.

In 1966, Mertins arranged a deal to sell surplus German F-86 aircraft to Pakistan, then under a NATO embargo due to tensions between Pakistan and India. When the details of the deal were leaked to the media, Mertins faced considerable criticism in his new homes of Switzerland and America. Remarkably, it later emerged during legal proceedings that Mertins' Pakistan deal had originally been approved and arranged by German intelligence (*Spiegel* 1975, 1987; Silverstein 2000, p. 120).

Nevertheless, US congressional hearings were constituted to investigate the deal. At the same time, the FBI investigated whether Mertins and his company should be declared "foreign agents" as he was working for the German government. However, it emerged that Mertins had been working closely with US Army Intelligence, which intervened to prevent Mertins being listed publicly as an agent as it could "jeopardize his continued use" (Silverstein 2000, pp. 123 and 130). Mertins thus had both been prompted to go into business as an arms trafficker and had his identity protected by two of the most powerful intelligence communities in the developed world.

The second prominent collaborator is organized crime, in particular those elements of organized crime involved in international smuggling. Smuggling by its nature involves the transport of goods in a manner that evades detection. Arms traffickers can, if need be, turn to existing smuggling networks to assist in transporting weapons. In addition, organized crime networks often possess sophisticated means of laundering funds raised from illicit activity, helping arms traffickers both reinject their earnings into the formal economy and raise "clean" money for further arms purchases.

A good example of the link among arms trafficking, organized crime, and the secretive world of intelligence is that of International Business Consult (IBC). IBC was a multifunctional front company set up in 1992 by Roger D'Onofrio and Michele Papa (Regione Carabinieri Campania 1995). D'Onofrio held joint US-Italian citizenship and was widely considered to be a CIA agent who had retired from service by the late 1980s. Michele Papa, meanwhile, a lawyer based in Catania, had made his name by acting as a semi-official representative for Libya in Italy (Magnuson, Thomas, and Ogden 1980; *Le Monde* 1984). In the late 1970s, Papa became a household name after it emerged that he had tapped up Billy Carter, the brother of then US President Jimmy Carter, to provide lobbying services for Libya in Washington. Carter was so aggressive in his lobbying efforts that he was forced to register as an agent of the Libyan government. When it was discovered that Billy had been given a loan of $220,000 from Libya, it prompted fierce disapproval, coming to be characterized as "Billygate" in the United States (Magnuson, Thomas, and Ogden 1980).

In 1992, D'Onofrio traveled to Liberia, where he met with Charles Taylor and suggested to him that IBC could be of service. To cement the relationship, Taylor and the RUF warlord Ibrahim Bah were given 50 percent of the shares in IBC (Regione Carabinieri Campania 1995; Republic of Liberia 2009, para. 113–115). IBC was soon involved in smuggling diamonds out of Liberia at Taylor's request, as well as importing weapons for the RUF and Taylor's forces.

To assist in turning diamonds into money that could be used to purchase weapons, IBC turned to Dennis Anthony Moorby, who ran a company by the name of Swift International Services in Canada.[10] Moorby, who was incidentally named by German authorities as an agent of Gerhard Mertin's Merex, was suspected by Italian and Canadian police services of being a prominent money launderer for the infamous Gotti family and the Gambino clan (Regione Carabinieri Campania 1998, p. 308). In one deal, IBC made use of the diamond money laundered by Moorby to purchase arms from the Bulgarian company Kintex. Using existing smuggling networks, the weapons were transported into Liberia disguised as a load of oranges and olives.

The third collusive group is the formal arms trade. Arms traffickers are all too easily able to source weapons from producers who are considered to be "legitimate" defense enterprises. In certain instances, there is no distinction between production and trafficking: individuals have been known to wear both "hats." Heinrich Thomet is one such individual. In 1991, Thomet entered into business with Karl Brugger to form Brugger and Thomet (B&T) Switzerland.[11] B&T won licenses to produce a range of weapons and act as a sales arm for companies in need. Thomet eventually sold his shares in the company. More recently, he has been accused of smuggling arms into and out of Zimbabwe and was once under investigation by US authorities, who suspected him of transporting weapons from Serbia to Iraq (Lawson 2011). Thomet is currently on the US State Department's Defense Trade Controls watch-list and has relocated to Montenegro.

In addition, arms traffickers and brokers are frequently employed by members of the formal defense trade to act as a conduit into markets where less salubrious sales methods are expected and delivered. This provides arms traffickers both an extra stream of income and a further entry into the cozy environment populated by the defense industry and government security agencies. John Bredenkamp and BAE, Viktor Bout and Joe der Hovsepian and US contractors are examples of this practice (Feinstein 2011).

The last collusive group is the global banking system and, in particular, banks and company registries operating in offshore tax havens. These havens provide the necessary secrecy for arms traffickers to launder funds and disguise their activities. In addition, they provide a firewall that often presents an insurmountable obstacle for investigating authorities as traffickers develop a web of obscure and misleading company structures around the world. Indeed, the existence of offshore tax havens, and the failure of banks to properly disclose suspected criminal activity, is perhaps the primary reason why so few arms traffickers are ever successfully arrested and convicted.

VI. A SHOCKING TRACK RECORD: LAW ENFORCEMENT AND EVASION

Despite the high-profile nature of the arms trade and the infamy of notable arms traffickers, the track record of law enforcement is exceptionally poor. This is particularly clear with reference to mandatory UN arms embargoes. Despite around 502 violations of embargoes being tracked and reported by UN monitoring teams, only two cases have ever come to court, with one successful conviction to date.[12]

Law enforcement officials who seek to prosecute arms trafficking face an uphill battle for a number of reasons, three of which are most notable. The primary difficulty is that of jurisdiction, which frequently prevents national governments from prosecuting their own nationals as the criminal activity has occurred abroad. The case of Leonid Minin is illustrative. As we saw, Minin was arrested in 2000 in a seedy hotel in Italy in possession of hundreds of incriminating documents that detailed his deals in Liberia. After being successfully prosecuted for drug possession, Minin's prosecutor, Walter Mapelli, turned to the arms trafficking charges, for which he had mountains of evidence: enough to have Minin retained in pretrial detention.

However, in 2002 Minin successfully appealed to have the pretrial detention overturned (Amnesty International 2006, pp. 60–63). The matter was appealed all the way to Italy's highest court, which ruled that the Italian court had no jurisdiction over the matter. Minin was not Italian (despite living there for years), no negotiations had taken place in Italy, and the arms had not transited the country. The UN arms embargo against Liberia did not suffice as a framework for prosecution, indicative of how some countries often fail to integrate mandatory UN arms embargoes into their national legislation (Amnesty International 2006). Mapelli complained, after losing his final appeal, that "jurisdiction is one step behind criminality today, because criminality is operating globally and continues to do so all the more. Whereas each state is very jealous of its own sovereignty and its own prerogatives within its borders, the consequence of this is that each state only sees one little segment of the whole business" (Brunwasser 2002).

The second problem is that the close relationship between many arms traffickers and state intelligence networks helps to protect the traffickers despite overwhelming evidence that may be presented against them. In Viktor Bout's case, for example, he was able to evade arrest for close to a decade, first via suspected US interference and, later, through the protection provided by Russian political players. Bout was only arrested when he was lured out of his protective shell by a sophisticated international sting launched by the US Drug Enforcement Administration (DEA), whose agents arrested Bout in Thailand in 2008 (Tatty 2008). It is assumed he was no longer useful to the United States, and the DEA was keen to show success in the ubiquitous "War on Terror."

Even this prosecution faced hurdles, despite the substantial resources available to the DEA. Bout appealed against an extradition request filed by US authorities who wanted to prosecute the trafficker for agreeing to supply weapons to the Columbian rebel group FARC. In this, Bout was loudly supported by leading members of the Russian political elite, leading the presiding judge to worry aloud about political interference (Bangkok Criminal Court 2009). After the first extradition request was refused by the Thai judge (on the basis that Thailand did not recognize FARC as a terrorist group), a second extradition request was duly filed (Bangkok Criminal Court 2009). It was only in 2011, in highly controversial circumstances, that Bout was finally extradited to the United States, where he was swiftly convicted on the charges presented. And where it was conveniently overlooked that he had undertaken flights into Baghdad on behalf of the US Department of Defense and defense contractors between 2003 and 2005, when the Interpol warrant was active (Farah and Braun 2007).

The last problem is a simple one: arms trafficking most often takes place in situations of war or imminent conflict and has, especially since the fall of the Berlin Wall, been most profitable in failed or semi-failed states. In situations of such chaos and disruption, detecting arms traffickers (especially if they are using sophisticated evasion techniques) is difficult. In severe cases, the number of violations is so overwhelming that it can promote a sense of inertia. Take this paragraph from a 2002 UN report on the arms embargo in Somalia that virtually admits defeat in the face of a tide of arms traffickers: "There have been numerous and regular violations—by individuals, factions and political leaders, local and regional administrators and outside state actors. In fact, the violations are so numerous that any attempt to document all of the activities would be pointless" (UNSC 2002b).

Taken together, jurisdictional issues, the difficulties in gathering evidence, and the protection afforded arms traffickers by national security agencies make the prosecution and conviction of arms traffickers exceptionally rare phenomenon.

VII. PROSPECTS AND PREDICTIONS

The medium- and long-term prospects for a reduction in arms trafficking are slim. Many of the problems identified here remain unresolved: jurisdictional issues are still an obstacle, as is the existence of tax havens and complicit banks. In addition, security and intelligence agencies throughout the world have not provided any indication that they will reduce their reliance on "black-ops" and counterinsurgency. Equally important is the fact that many of the conflicts that survived and thrived on the back of arms trafficking remain alive and devastating: conflict in the DRC, for example, provides a virtual free-for-all for arms traffickers due to the fact that warring parties have almost untrammeled access to rich mineral resources.

Arms trade activists pinned much hope on the creation of a strong international Arms Trade Treaty (ATT). However, after extended negotiations at the United Nations, the treaty that was finally adopted by the General Assembly in April of 2013 is extremely weak. It addresses some of the issues that facilitate rampant weapons trafficking while ignoring others, including corruption. Fatally, the treaty contains no enforcement mechanisms whatsoever. Therefore, a country could ratify the treaty and do absolutely nothing to apply or enforce it. In fact, in at least one instance, a country has proposed weakening their arms export requirements to conform to the treaty.

But perhaps the biggest problem facing those who wish to reduce arms trafficking is the fact that the world is simply awash in weapons. In many African countries, for example, a massive surplus of easily available arms means that setting up in business as an arms trafficker takes little more than motivation and a sense of moral ambiguity. In countries such as Somalia, open-air arms markets have proliferated, where anybody can purchase powerful weapons for paltry sums. In nearby Sudan, decades of conflict has meant that virtually every adult male has access to some form of small arms. Thus, even if the export of weapons from the developed world is stridently curbed, arms traffickers will still have ready access to their stock in trade. Such is the legacy of a world in which arms traffickers have operated with near total impunity for decades.

Notes

1. "World military spending reached $1.6 trillion in 2010, biggest increase in South America, fall in Europe according to new SIPRI data." http://www.sipri.org/media/pressreleases/2011/milex.
2. This figure varies considerably from year to year; the trade in small arms is worth approximately $4 billion a year and has an impact far beyond this monetary value because small and light weapons are easy to use and maintain and are abundantly available (Stohl and Grillot 2009).
3. For a detailed discussion of corruption in the global arms trade, see Feinstein, Holden, and Pace (2011).
4. 22 USC 2778—Control of Arms Exports and Imports. http://www.law.cornell.edu/uscode/text/22/2778.
5. See Act mentioned in previous note, paragraph C.
6. As of March 2012.
7. As of March 2012.
8. Extrapolated from the Stockholm International Peace Research Institute Arms Embargo Database. http://www.sipri.org/databases/embargoes.
9. Note that this is also variously spelled as Naftna Mafija.
10. "Agreement No. 002A Between Swift International Business Services Canada Inc. (Montreal), Battisto Elmo (Milan) and IBC International Business Consult (Monrovia)," undated; "Agreement No. 002A Between Swift International Business Services Canada Inc. (Montreal), Battisto Elmo (Milan) and IBC International Business Consult (Monrovia)," February 25, 1994 (signed Dennis Moorby, Battisto Elmo and Dr. Rudolf Meroni); "Agreement No. 001A Between Swift International Business Services Canada Inc. (Montreal), Battisto Elmo (Milan) and IBC International Business Consult (Monrovia)," March 2, 1994, signed Dennis Moorby, Battisto Elmo, Dr. Rudolf Meroni and Carlo Galeazzi. Documents gathered and collated by Italian police under auspices of the "Cheque to Cheque" investigation.
11. http://www.bt-ag.ch/index.php.
12. Discussion with Professor James Stewart, former appeals counsel, Office of the Prosecutor, International Criminal Tribunal for the former Yugoslavia, and leading academician in the area of corporate responsibility for international crimes.

References

Amnesty International. 2006. "*Dead on Time—Arms Transportation, Brokering and the Threat to Human Rights.*" ACT30/08/20006. (August). pp. 60–6.. London: Amnesty International.

Ascherson, N. 1972. "The Arms Export Control Act." "Our Man in Pullach." *New York Review of Books.* (June 1). http://pmddtc.state.gov/regulations_laws/aeca.html.

Bangkok Criminal Court. 2009. "Judgment: Offense Against Act on Extradition in the Matter Between The Public Prosecutor (Thailand) and Mr. Viktor Bout." (August 11). Black Case No. 3/2551. https://reportingproject.net/PeopleOfInterest/documents/Viktor%20 Anatolyevich_Bout,_Charges_850.pdf

Bout, V. 2009. "Times Topics." *New York Times*. (August 11).

Bowcott, O., and R. Norton-Taylor. 2000. "Victor Bout: Africa's Merchant of Death." *Guardian (UK)* (December 23).

Brunwasser, M. 2002. "Leonid Efimovich Minin: From Ukraine, A New Kind of Arms Trafficker." PBS/Frontline World Investigative Series: Sierra Leone Gun Runners. (May 2002). http://www.pbs.org/frontlineworld/stories/sierraleone/minin.html.

Central Examining Court. 2000. Statement of Fernando Robleda. Madrid. (June 6).

Central Examining Court. 2002. Interrogation of Vadim Semov. Madrid. (April 25).

Coalition for International Justice. 2005. "Following Taylor's Money: A Path of War and Destruction." Washington DC: Coalition for International Justice.

Comando Generale dell'Arma dei Carabinieri. 1996. "Minin Leonid Efimovic." Annesso "1." Roma: Ufficio Criminalitá Organizzata (March 17).

Daly, J. 2008. "The Deadly Convenience of Viktor Bout." *ISN ETH Zurich*. (June 24).

Exotic Tropical Timber Enterprises. 1998. Minutes of the Meeting of the Board of Directors. Hotel Africa. (December 10).

Farah, D. and Braun, S. 2006. "The Merchant of Death." *Foreign Policy*. (October 10).

Farah, D. and Braun, S. 2007. *Merchant of Death*. New Jersey: Wiley.

Feinstein, A. 2011. *The Shadow World: Inside the Global Arms Trade*. London: Hamish Hamilton.

Feinstein, A., Holden, P., and Pace, B. 2011. "Corruption and the Arms Trade: Sins of Commission." In *SIPRI Yearbook: 2011*. Oxford: Oxford University Press.

Fruchart, D., Holtom, P., Wezeman, S., Strandow, D. and Wallensteen, P. 2007. *United Nations Arms Embargoes: Their Impact on Arms Flows and Target Behaviour*. Stockholm and Uppsala, Sweden: SIPRI and Uppsala University.

Gberie, L. 2005. *A Dirty War in West Africa*. London: Hurst.

Isenberg, D. 2004. "Anatomy of Two Arms Dealers." *Asia Times*. (June 19).

Lawson, G. 2011. "Arms and the Dudes." *Rolling Stone*. (March 31).

Magnuson, E., Thomas, E. and Ogden, C. 1980. "The Burden of Billy." *Time* (US). (August 4).

Monza Public Prosecutor's Office. 2001. Interrogation of Leonid Minin. (July 8 and September 11).

Regione Carabinieri Campania. 1995. Interrogation of Roger D'Onofrio. (December 6).

Regione Carabinieri Campania. 1998. "Informativa di Reato Relativa all'operazione "Cheque to Cheque." June 30.

Republic of Liberia Truth and Reconciliation Commission. 2009. *Economic Crimes and the Conflict: Exploitation and Abuse* 2009. Volume III (Appendices). http://trcofliberia.org/resources/reports/final/volume-three-3_layout-1.pdf.

Roeber, J. 2005. "Hard-wired for Corruption." *Prospect*. (August 28).

Sampson, A. 1977. *The Arms Bazaar*. New York: Viking.

Semo, M. 1984. "In Italy: A Subtle Mixture of Intimidation and Seduction." *Le Monde*. (April 22–23).

Silverstein, K. 2000. *Private Warriors*. New York: Verso, p. 111.

Stockholm International Peace Research Institute (SIPRI). 2011. In *SIPRI Yearbook: 2011*. Oxford: Oxford University Press.

Stohl, R., and Grillot, S. 2009. *The International Arms Trade*. Cambridge, MA: Polity Press.

Tatty, S. 2008. "Taking Down Arms Dealer Viktor Bout." *Men's Journal.* (December 12).

Traynor, I. 2001. "The International Dealers in Death." *The Guardian.* (July 9).

UN Security Council. 1966. "Resolution 232 (1966) of 16 December 1966, 16 December, S/RES/232 (1966)." http://www.unhcr.org/refworld/docid/3b00f23414.html.

UN Security Council. 1977. "Resolution 418 (1977) Adopted by the Security Council at its 2046th meeting, on 4 November 1977, S/RES/418 (1977)." http://www.unhcr.org/refworld/docid/3b00f16e30.htm.

UN Security Council. 2000a. "Final Report of the Monitoring Mechanism on Angola Sanctions." (December 21, 2000, S/2000/1225).

UN Security Council. 2000b. "Report of the Panel of Experts Appointed Pursuant to Security Council Resolution 1306 (2000), para. 19, in Relation to Sierra Leone." (December, S/2000/1195, para. 225).

UN Security Council. 2002a. "Final Report of the Panel of Experts on the Illegal Exploitation of Natural Resources and Other Forms of Wealth in the Democratic Republic of Congo." (S/2002/1146).

UN Security Council. 2002b. "Report of the Panel of Experts on Somalia Pursuant to Security Council Resolution 1425 (2002)." (S/2003/223).

US Department of Justice. 2010. "Statement of Offence" in the matter of the United States of America v. BAE Systems plc, Violation: Title 18, United States Code, Section 371 (conspiracy), United States District Court for the District of Columbia.

US Department of State. 2012a. International Traffic in Arms Regulations 2011. http://pmddtc.state.gov/regulations_laws/itar_official.html.

US Department of State. 2012b. Arms Export Control Act. http://pmddtc.state.gov/regulations_laws/aeca.html

US Government Accounting Office (GAO). 2005. "Defense Trade: Arms Export Control System in the post-9/11 Environment." Report to the Chairman, Committee of International Relations, House of Representatives, GAO-05-234, Appendix I. Washington, DC: United States Government Accountability Office.

Walsh, L. 1997 *Firewall: The Iran-Contra Conspiracy and Cover-up.* New York: Norton.

1975. "Fall Merex: Rechtsbruch durch Tarnung." *Der Spiegel.* (December 22).

1987. "*Prozente fur Pfadfinder.*" (March 23).

CHAPTER 23

ORGANIZED FRAUD

MICHAEL LEVI[1]

"Some will rob you with a six-gun, And some with a fountain pen."

Woody Guthrie, *Pretty Boy Floyd*

I. INTRODUCTION

THIS essay deals with the extent and organization of fraud, which is commonly regarded as a significant proportion of the total proceeds of crime, at least in advanced economies. It generates illicit income next only to drugs trafficking if not exceeding it in value (Europol 2011, 2013; Levi & Burrows 2008; Levi et al. 2013; Mills et al. 2013; SOCA 2010). For the United Kingdom alone (where the most serious efforts to measure fraud have taken place), the latest reasoned official estimate is £52 billion (NFA 2013), far larger than the costs of (a) the nonfraud component of street and household crimes and (b) total estimated "organized crime" (Dubourg & Prichard 2009; Mills et al. 2013). Of this, "the NFA's estimate of fraud perpetrated by organised criminals is cautiously £18.9 billion. This includes £8.9 billion of £24 billion of fraud identified to have an organised crime element, along with an additional £9.9 billion estimated to be lost to OCG [Organised Crime Group] fraud" (NFA 2013: 10).[2]

Fraud comes in many forms, directly victimizing all ages and socioeconomic groups, including individual and corporate elites, and governments (Levi & Burrows 2008; Levi 2011; NFA 2013). Unfortunately, for this global text, there have not been similar cost studies elsewhere, though in some countries such as Australia and the United States, "identity fraud" has been measured by corporate and individual victimization surveys, not always clearly or consistently (ABS 2008; Baum 2007; Harrell & Langton, 2013; NFA 2010, 2011, 2013). Global corporate fraud victimization surveys have become increasingly widespread since the mid-1980s (Bussman & Werle 2006; Ernst & Young 2011; Kroll 2013; Levi 1987; PWC 2009, 2011), though these surveys seldom tell us much about the *organization* of fraud or about *non*-corporate victims. Forensic consultancies' analyses of their cases are interesting (KPMG 2007) but are usually biased toward larger cases because clients seldom pay them to investigate smaller ones, and this unintentionally overstates the proportion of fraud that involve insiders as sole or collusive principals. This is less true of the data provided by the Association of Certified Fraud Examiners, but their global report (biased, like their membership, toward North America) still shows that the vast majority of average and total fraud losses were the result of senior management acts; 87 percent of occupational fraudsters had never been charged or convicted of a fraud-related offense, and only 5.6 percent (slightly more in earlier years) had prior convictions, with about the same again having prior charges but not convictions (ACFE 2012). This suggests that they mostly were not "organized criminals" in the normal sense of that term.

Some common offenses against individuals—like payment card fraud and many identity fraud—are also fraud against financial institutions, which normally have to reimburse their customers. Other individuals (at least in the developed world) are entitled to official compensation for fraud only if the financial services institution that goes bust or is found responsible is regulated by the state. (Although, especially in the United States, victims and regulators can and often do sue through the civil courts, including for civil racketeering, where triple damages are obtainable.)

Most corporate and individual surveys indicate that fraud has been rising, though variably in different parts of the world. Ernst & Young (2011) reports that the rise has been much greater in Latin America and western Europe than elsewhere. Kroll (2013) reports that 70 percent of companies surveyed globally had been victims of fraud in the previous year, a rise from the previous year. Information theft, loss, or attack was the first or second most common (though not the most costly) sort of economic crime against business (Kroll 2010, 2013), a *motif* echoed by Detica (2011: 2), who heroically estimated that cybercrimes cost the United Kingdom £27 billion per annum, of which the theft of intellectual property from UK businesses was estimated at £9.2 billion per annum. (See Anderson et al., 2012, for an alternative, grounded analysis of e-Crime costs, which leaves out the costs of intellectual property hacking because no one currently has any defensible idea of its costs.[3]) Note, however, that retail-level intellectual property crime includes the copying of products that may be bought knowing they are not authentic, so there may be no *deception*. Technically, this can be organized crime but not organized *fraud*. The only section of the report that mentioned organized crime was in contamination of the supply chain in energy, construction, and transport sectors, rather than fraud. However, readers should note that business corruption is often a form of fraud, if it leads to inferior work/price padding/environmental hazards.

In an attempt to examine the impact of organized crime on crimes against business, the British government looked at business perceptions of the cause of its losses. Respondents to the Commercial Victimisation Survey who had experienced crime in the past year were asked whether they thought that the most recent incident of each crime type experienced was carried out by a loosely knit group, an organized group of criminals, or someone working alone. Respondent perceptions of this varied considerably by the type of crime, though except where offenders were identified, it seems plausible that these judgments were commonsense inferences from the nature of the activities rather than a reflection of actual knowledge. In the most recent incidents of thefts of vehicles, around half respondents thought that the offense was carried out by an organized group of criminals. Just over a quarter thought an organized group of criminals committed the latest incidents of burglary and theft from vehicles. Rightly or wrongly, the crime types least likely to be thought to have been carried out by an organized group of criminals were thefts (3 percent) and fraud by employees (0 percent) (Home Office, 2013).

Why include fraud in a handbook of organized crime? The relationship between fraud, organized crime, and white collar crime is a conceptually complex one. When Sutherland (1945) wrote his classic presidential address for the American Sociological Association toward the end of the Second World War, "White-collar crime *is* organized crime," he was pointing to the "organizedness" of the crimes committed by the otherwise legitimate corporations he had researched as well as, perhaps, appropriating some of the demonization that historically attaches to the "organized crime" label.[4] Later theorists such as Shapiro (1990), arguing that the focus on offender status was too confusing, redefined white collar crimes as crimes of deception or as breaches of agent-principal trust. Pushed to its limits, this would mean that all white collar crimes are organized fraud (though of course, not all organized crimes are fraud).[5] However, whatever the definitional complexities, it is now recognized that fraud is an important and growing component of what organized crime networks and hierarchies do. This essay will first explore some of these linkages, then go on to discuss some sorts of fraud in greater detail and discuss briefly the kinds of measures that are taken against fraud and what we know about their effects. To date, these issues have received modest government attention and research funding, so our knowledge is very patchy in general and in specific countries. Indeed, a key aspect that differentiates some fraud from other property crimes is that it involves no need for direct interaction between offenders and victims/consumers, and they may never be in the same countries at the same time.

II. The Link between Fraud and "Organized Crime"

Unlike most forms of conventionally defined organized crime, where the forensic proof problem may be linking the suspect to the agreed-on criminal activity—especially where more junior network/hierarchy members are unwilling to give evidence or are not credible witnesses—there can be a genuine legal dispute about whether particular commercial conduct was "fraud" and, especially, about whether top managers knew about it. Indeed, the criminalization of acts such as insider trading, price-fixing, and transnational bribery, and the imposition of corporate criminal liability, may themselves be the subject of social controversy and intensive lobbying. But this legal ambiguity seldom applies in the volume fraud area (such as the duplication of identities for credit fraud or the use of stolen payment cards), where people operating a business use false identities and disappear, or where there are other clear indicators of "bad faith" and little credible innocent explanation. In practice, "organized fraud" can be a shorthand phrase for fraud committed by career criminals rather than by respectable people: the very mindset that Sutherland was seeking to undermine in his analogy but which remains a powerful folk image because implicit in the threat imagery of "organized crime" is that everything an "organized criminal" does threatens "legitimate society" (whereas, by omission, whatever those who are *not* organized criminals—or terrorists—do is *less* threatening to society). Hence, the regular references are made to organized criminals "infiltrating" or "corrupting" commerce.

We have already set out why asking what proportion of frauds is "organized crime" might not be an intelligent question. What people usually mean is "are people who do 'normal' working-class crimes like drugs trafficking and robbery or extortion now doing fraud?" This does not have a universal answer. In countries such as Bulgaria and Russia, and parts of the Balkans, partly because of fear of retaliation for "unauthorized" criminal or legitimate business action, there is an intermingling between fraud, corruption, politics, and what is conventionally viewed as "organized crime" (CSD 2012; Glenny 2008; Rawlinson 2010). By contrast, in the United Kingdom, this is not the case, though almost two thirds of identified organized crime groups whose primary activity is fraud are also involved in other crimes (author interviews 2010). Such cross-criminality may be one factor in why the police are aware of the participants and have classified them as members of organized crime groups. Data from the long-running Dutch Organized Crime Monitor reveal not just the importance of fraud in organized crime careers but also the presence of a large proportion of late adult-onset fraud and money-laundering offenders in the serious crime community (van Koppen 2013; van Koppen et al. 2010a, 2010b).

The National Fraud Authority (NFA 2010) provided data on only two areas in which it has "organized fraud costs": a £348 million figure from the Insurance Fraud Bureau (IFB) in relation to staged motor accidents (based on strong software linked network data) and the harder-to-validate "criminal attack" figure—£5 billion—representing a third of the total tax fraud figure (NFA 2010: 15). About £1 in every £10 of Britain's exports in 2006 was linked to organized Value Added Tax carousel fraud, but costs and scale have declined substantially since in response to tighter scrutiny of businesses registering for VAT and several major prosecutions, and the adjustment of EU VAT rules in response to the major losses that have now shifted to other European nations (Levi et al. 2013).

It seems likely that most of the £59.7 million in reported losses from online banking fraud in 2009 (£39.6 million in 2012) was the result of "organized crime." Such groups may also be involved in cyberextortion and commercial espionage, which are not included by Financial Action Fraud UK (2013). In a similar logic, a significant proportion of the *estimated* (and disputed by parts of the industry) £1 billion of mortgage fraud (NFA 2010: 25) will have been committed by at least networks, if not tighter groups, comprising mortgage brokers, valuers, lawyers, and property investors, as well as some dishonest staff working for financial institutions and mortgage applicants. In the United

States, mortgage origination fraud has been linked both to traditional "organized crime groups" and to specialized fraud networks, as well as to elites who recklessly (and in the view of some, intentionally) parceled in fact fraudulent "subprime" mortgages into credit derivatives called collateralized debt obligations and sold them on to other corporations, which lost fortunes unless they sold them on in turn before "the music stopped" in the Global Financial Crisis. After this and the "bailout" of many global banks, taxpayers in many countries ended up as the indirect victims of such corporate recklessness, though the multi–billion dollar *civil* settlements extracted from bankers such as JP Morgan in 2013—who did not admit fraud—will go a small part of the way toward offsetting these losses.

The analytical and research literature on fraud is quite sparse, reflecting its marginal status within government constructs of "the crime problem," which in turn affects research funding, and also the relative inaccessibility of fraud networks to outsiders. (For good resources, see Karstedt & Farrall 2006; Levi 2008c, 2011; Nelken 2012; Simpson & Weisburd 2009.) The settings for fraud both influence and reflect networks, in the context of fraud opportunities and "capable guardians," in the classical routine activities and situational opportunity models. This is set out in Box 23.1.

Box 23.1 The Organization of Fraud: A Process Model

1. See a situation as a "financial crime opportunity"

2. Obtain whatever finance is needed for the crime

3. Find people willing and able to offend (if this is necessary for the fraud contemplated) and who are controllable and reliable

4. Obtain any equipment/data needed to offend

5. Carry out offenses in domestic and/or overseas locations with or without physical presence in jurisdiction(s). This will usually involve manipulating—with varied degrees of complexity, technology and interpersonal communication skills—victims' perceptions of "what is happening"

6. Minimize immediate enforcement/operational risks. Especially if planning to repeat fraud, neutralize law enforcement by technical skill, by corruption, and/or by legal arbitrage, using legal obstacles to enforcement operations and prosecutions which vary between jurisdictions

7. Convert, where necessary (e.g. where goods rather than money are obtained on credit), the fruits of crime into money or other usable assets

8. Spend as much of the proceeds as you want

9. Find people and places willing to store those proceeds you wish to retain (and perhaps conceal their origin—see the money laundering chapter in this volume)

10. Decide which jurisdiction(s) offers the optimal balance between social/physical comfort and the risk of asset forfeiture/criminal justice sanctions. Indifference in any one State or sub-state arena may suffice to neutralize an investigation, and staffing inadequacies as well as corruption may be the cause of official inaction.

A. Organizing Fraud

When analyzing the dynamics of particular crimes and/or criminal careers, these procedural elements can be broken down further into much more concrete steps, sometimes referred to as "scripts" (Morselli 2009; Morselli & Roy 2008). There is also a personality dimension: some seek opportunities to defraud and look for facilitators like accountants or lawyers; whereas others just take what comes opportunistically. Those who are connected to "organized crime" may already have in place all the steps as part of their ongoing "criminal enterprise." Criminal finance, some or all criminal personnel, or the "tools of crime" (from nontransparent special purpose vehicle companies to anonymous prepaid debit cards) may come from or go to another country, constituting "transnational" crimes; or else remain within one country, constituting "national" or even regional crimes in federal jurisdictions like Australia, the United States, and, to a lesser extent, Germany.[6] In the case of fraud, offenders may start with differential access to local, national, or international resources, but the exploitation of interstate and international regulatory and criminal justice asymmetries—such as different levels of enforcement in the states or countries in which the fraudsters operate—represents a positive advantage for fraud compared with most other property crimes.

Applying the sort of script found in Box 23.1, fraudsters seek potential victims for their schemes and develop techniques for getting them to part with their money voluntarily. In some cases, they or others may revictimize the same people by offering (for a fee) to help them get back the money they have lost. Another characteristic difference is that the offender and victim do not ever have to be in the same place at the same time. Some such offenses involve face-to-face contact throughout or at some stage; others are done wholly remotely, like lottery, eBay, and many romance scams. (For a good review of "419 fraud," so called after section 419 of the Nigerian criminal code, see Schoenmakers et al. 2009.)

Choice of offender or victim location is determined by a range of factors (e.g., the large number of relatively wealthy but still anxious elderly people in Florida or the southeast of England), though many consumer frauds can be plotted at the other end of the world (see, e.g., Holtfreter et al. 2005, 2008). In the larger cases, professional intermediaries and bank accounts are necessary components in presenting a plausible front and in obtaining and laundering the funds; in others, cash may be wired via money service bureaus (like Western Union) or by "underground banking" (Passas 2005) to foreign or domestic locations, despite anti–money laundering provisions that require plausible customer identification.

As with embezzlers (Cressey 1955), existing businesspeople find it easy to transfer funds out of the company and/or to commit bankruptcy fraud: this is one reason why they do not need to be part of "organized crime."[7] Their key practical problem is organizing the escape from criminal sanctions and from civil remedies by creditors. The corporations can be substantive and real, or they can be mere fronts or shells for the perpetration of fraud. But people can also commit fraud against companies and the government as outsiders or from more junior positions. Fraud permits a variety of offender organizational permutations, from Mafia-type associations to sole or small group offending.

As for the persistence of crime techniques over time, this varies depending on the countermeasures taken by potential preventers in industry, the regulatory sector, and, to a lesser extent, criminal justice. Those businesses that during the 1960s and 1970s deceived their creditors as to the reasons for increasing their orders on credit, on the basis that they needed them to supply their expanding "mail order" trade, would now do the same on the basis that they have a booming Internet-based sales business, especially prior to consumer spending peaks such as Christmas (Levi 2008a). In the era of the credit card, dishonest merchants might pass large quantities of (i) fake or (ii) genuine (but on stolen card) transactions through their commercial accounts, claim (as is normal with traders) advance reimbursement from merchant acquirer card companies, and then disappear before the card issuer, merchant acquirer, or cardholder realizes that there has been a fraud at all.[8] Payment cards were rare during the 1970s, but fraudsters can now use payment card numbers skimmed from unsuspecting cardholders to order hundreds of computers on the Internet from different suppliers, have them delivered to "drop addresses" in any credible country, and then forwarded to addresses elsewhere for resale. All of this occurs before the cardholder becomes aware that there is anything wrong, unless the card issuer or card scheme has picked these up proactively as "unusual transactions" and alerted the customer. This and other cyberfraud techniques reflect a comparative criminal advantage arising from the combination of high technological skills and high motivation due to poor opportunities in their home countries. There are also large-scale credit card and loan "bust-outs" using stolen identities to obtain goods and money. Although these are often referred to as "identity theft," they are more accurately referred to as identity duplication, since the original person is not deprived of their existing identity. These illustrations show that behavior of victims-to-be and "capable guardians" has to be considered as part of the organization of crime (see Reyns 2013, for a good account in relation to online crimes).

A priori, it would appear that different skill sets and statuses will be needed to commit different sorts of fraud offenses. People who occupy senior posts in financial services have to pass "fit and proper person" tests involving the absence of a criminal record and, perhaps, financial probity and competence checks. One possibility for "underworld" offenders is to obtain cooperation from or to put pressure on people in respectable positions in order to use them as tools of fraud. Therefore, one port of entry is to "do a deal" with existing brokers, as the younger members of New York Mafia families did with some Russian American brokers during the 1990s, against the advice of their elders who thought it too dangerous to move outside "the family" whom they could control via ties of mutual obligation (Diih 2005). Such intergenerational tensions are part of the response to declining market position for traditional "organized crime," eroded as it was by the undercover infiltration and electronic surveillance, followed by prosecutions under the Racketeer Influenced Corrupt Organization (RICO) legislation. The Italian American Mafiosi chose Russian American brokers because they judged that people of that background were more likely than others to find an approach from "the Mob" attractive. As with Nigerian scams, Russians' reputation for corruptibility generates more criminal offers from other people than would be the case in Finland, New

Zealand, or Norway, for example, which rank highly on the Transparency International index of perceived noncorruptibility (TI 2013).

To illuminate such issues, we must first consider what sorts of networks are needed for different offenses and the extent to which their contacts and skill sets enable them to commit a variety of fraud (and nonfraud) offenses. For price-fixing cartels, for example, what is needed is an ability to pose as a legitimate bidder (which usually will require them to have experience in a relevant area of business) *and* trust between "repeat players" that if they overbid for contracts, the winner this time will overbid later to enable them to win: as with the Madoff Ponzi scheme, walls of secrecy and silence in the social environment of the plotters are crucial elements (Van de Bunt 2010). In more competitive markets, the alternative may be corruption of the contract-giver, perhaps even at the specification stage where the "specification" can be devised in order to give one party an in-built advantage. Cartels use their own corporate and individual identities for contracts (though not necessarily for the many secret meetings that precede the bids; see Eichenwald 2001, for a marvelously rich account, and Harding 2007) and would seldom need any false corporate fronts for money laundering purposes since no illicit money changes hands, but bribe-payers might need some false or genuine trading fronts in order to channel payments to the corrupt public official or private sector beneficiary, to create some distance between themselves and both individual and corporate liability.

Sometimes what is needed for the accomplishment of fraud is compliant people who do not ask critical questions: this was the case with "rogue trader" Nick Leeson and Barings Bank (Leeson 1997). Some corporate fraudsters—such as the late Robert Maxwell (Bower 2008) and the chiefs of Enron (McLean and Elkind 2004)—appoint staff on much higher-than-normal market salaries to ensure their loyalty or willful blindness when facing alternative employment on much lower salaries. In this sense, the Enron staff resembled those whose conduct was analyzed by Cohen (2001) in *States of Denial* and the older literature on "techniques of neutralization." Rogue trader Jerome Kerviel of French bank Société Générale may have had an occasional accomplice (as was alleged at his criminal trial in 2010 in Paris, leading to his imprisonment—see Kerviel 2010) but managed to rack up trading losses of billions in 2007 without the aid of an "organized crime group." taking advantage of weaknesses in supervision that later led to the resignation of some senior management. All of this should be borne in mind when thinking about fraud and organized networks: there may be no need for conscious coconspirators, depending on the chain of authority within large corporate or governmental settings and their competence. What some offenders are able to do is simply to deploy the range of global corporate mechanisms available in a free enterprise society where there are (perhaps tautologically) insufficient "capable guardians" to stop them misusing the disguises offered by the corporate form or the authority and power of a corporate role. The extent to which these opportunities will be reduced by 2013 G8 and G20 initiatives to require identification of "beneficial owners" of corporations remains a matter for speculation at the present time.

As the Enron indictments showed (McLean & Elkind 2004), there were plenty of accountants, bankers, and lawyers as well as some senior management willing to participate in criminal or marginal operations. But they had nothing to do with any criminal subcultures as conventionally defined. Likewise, the many white collar crime studies on the savings and loans "failures" (Black 2014; Calavita & Pontell 1993) on accounting fraud (Tillman & Indergaard 2005, 2007a, 2007b), and on fraud associated with the global financial crisis (Deflem 2011) emphasize—sometimes overemphasize—elite networks rather than socioeconomically marginal firms (Shapiro 1981) or gangsters. However, there is no logical reason why all three sets of organizational form cannot be involved in fraud and money laundering.

III. Identity Frauds and Telemarketing Scams

By contrast with notable criminal and marginal entrepreneurs operating under their own personal names discussed earlier (though sometimes using many corporate and trust vehicles), other fraud may depend on false identities—wholly fictitious or "borrowed" from real people—either for their commission or for the laundering process. Thus, a senior executive or junior in the finance department might create a company or an individual to receive payments, otherwise resting on their ability to make transfers without question: how elaborate the rest of the process is depends on how anxious they are to avoid suspicion and conviction. If the aim is to flee, then they may need false identities and that would usually involve others who can supply them consciously. If the aim is to stay and deceive, then it may involve others able to create a smokescreen of activities.

People other than insiders selling financial products need to find targets to approach and develop persuasive methods of getting them to part with funds. One way of doing so is to pretend to be someone else who *is* creditworthy. In the past a simple method was to steal someone's credit card and (in the absence of photos on cards) to look sufficiently plausible that a normally ill-motivated (in)capable guardian (in routine activities terminology) such as a shop assistant would sell goods to them or—a stiffer but still possible test—give them money at a bank counter. When Chip and PIN were introduced, this became much harder in the United Kingdom and in some terminals overseas, and the locus of fraud shifted to technological efforts to capture both, or to the use of cards and duplicate cards abroad, with UK-issued card losses overseas doubling between 2006 and 2007, after remaining fairly stable or falling over the previous six years. Since then they have dropped markedly.[9] Chip and PIN necessitated a change in the organization of fraud to greater internationalization of conspirators: electronic details copied from cards (a particular specialty of Sri Lankans working in UK petrol stations) could be sent to confederates abroad.[10] Though this process of internationalization had started before, it accelerated as a result of the improvement of protection against fraud on lost and stolen cards (Levi 2008b). Likewise, the cruder forms of bankruptcy fraud in which new companies were created by people using false names and paid for the first few orders before accelerating credit massively, selling the goods off and disappearing, were frustrated by enhancements in commercial credit control and pattern analysis, necessitating either wider transnational fraud or "less organized" fraud in the sense of fewer scammers operating in tandem (Levi 2008a, 2008c). A key point here is the interaction between changes in the technology and organization of crime prevention and changes in the levels and organization of fraud. (See McIntosh 1971, for an influential early exercise along these lines.) Alternatively, "identity thieves" can try to bypass the control systems by applying for new credit facilities in the names of their victims, using a variety of techniques to get around the change of address (easier in highly mobile societies like the United States) or even diverting the victim's mail to their own address for a period.[11] In the United States, losses attributable to identity theft rose from $13.2 billion in 2010 to $21 billion in 2013 (http://www.statisticbrain.com/identity-theft-fraud-statistics/). In the United Kingdom, *card* fraud attributable to identity theft have fluctuated, reaching a peak of £47.4 million in 2008 and were £32.1 million in 2012.

The contemporary equivalents of "The Sting" are (1) "boiler room" operators, who telephone investors with tips on "fabulous" shares that turn out to be worthless and impossible to sell. In one recent case (author interview with police), they worked in a room with a tape continuously playing in the background to simulate a busy stock brokerage; and (2) the "419" advance fee fraudsters who may hire or "borrow" official rooms when they know that the legitimate users are away to use as props in their stings. In some investment scams involving wines and spirits or ostrich farms, the operators do have some real products on show but vastly fewer than those "purchased" by the victims.

How do they find their targets? This can be done through random dialing of telephone directory entries; through share registers of public companies; through perusal of advertisements in personal columns, articles about wealthy people in the media; and through the use/purchase of existing "sucker lists" (which, except for serial fraudsters reusing their old lists, is the only method that would *require* contact with other offenders, nowadays via the Dark Web and its trust mechanisms as well as in person). Shover et al. (2003) note that fraudulent firms employ sales agents who work from lists purchased from any of dozens of businesses that compile and sell information on consumer behavior and preferences. My interviews with investigators in several countries (2008) suggest that exchanges of "mooch lists" are extensive and rapid—once someone has subscribed to one lottery or other product by Internet, mail, or telephone, they soon experience allied scam "offers" from other fraudsters, suggesting that there is a sufficiently broad scope for fraudsters to be noncompetitive.

Holtfreter et al. (2008) showed that although the fraudsters may cast their nets at random, the financial behavior of consumers was key to whether they became victims. In high-level corporate misconduct, however, "victims" may think that they are dealing with reputable businesspeople as normal investments.

How are telemarketing fraudsters organized? Some fraudulent telemarketing organizations consist of only two or three persons who operate in a community for only a few days or weeks before moving on. These "rip and tear" operators depend on the months-long lapse between the time they begin operating and the time law enforcement and consumer protection agencies become aware of and target them. Somewhat larger "boiler rooms" feature extensive telephone banks and large numbers of sales agents telephoning people on purchased lists or past "sucker lists," offering them great opportunities to be on the inside of a great scheme. Larger telemarketing operations commonly take on the characteristics of formal organizations, with hierarchies, a division of labor, graduated pay, and advancement opportunities. Those who are ill suited to cold call selling or cannot neutralize any guilt they feel at tactics simply leave the business.

Unlike the cons described by Maurer (2000, originally 1940)—which are pure artifices and therefore must hire willing conspirators—the investment scams can hire junior personnel through advertisements and agencies who may be quite ignorant of (or turn a blind eye to) the true rationale of the business. Only the originators may be active criminals. Some telephone salespeople may be experienced multiscam participants (Shover et al. 2003; Stevenson 1998), but others may simply have the ethical blindness of commission-based income-generators. This mindset is little different from financial services industry "mis-selling" of pension plans and of payment protection insurance, which led to payments of billions of pounds in compensation by British firms. Some criminal telemarketers interviewed by Shover et al. (2003) got a "high" from overcoming customer reluctance (see Katz 1990 and Levi 2008a, for the emotional rewards from crime commission). Such generic persuasion techniques are discussed by Cialdini (2007); a particular subset of online interpersonal persuasive techniques is the romance scam, the dynamics of which have been well researched by Whitty (2013) in the United Kingdom.

What factors influence the choice of venue for boiler rooms and their modus operandi? Boiler rooms are commonly based abroad (e.g., in recent years, in Spain, where police interest is low but telecommunications facilities are good) and never seek authorization by regulators, as is legally required for all investment services. If the fraudsters have sufficient nerve, they can seek to become regulated in one European Union (EU) country and obtain a "passport" to operate in another under EU single market regulations, using that as a base for fraud and making it difficult for local regulators to intervene to close them down. In all of these cases, what the boiler room is really selling is Great Expectations.

The growth in cross-border consumer fraud operations can be illustrated by data from the United States. (No equivalent data are yet available for the United Kingdom.) During 2009, the U.S. multiagency Consumer Sentinel, which acts as a one-stop shop for complaints, received over 1.3 million complaints, rising to 2 million in 2012, just over half of which were of fraud and almost a fifth of identity theft (Federal Trade Commission 2011, 2013a). Just over half reported the complaint to the police and a report was taken; a third made no report to the police. In 2012, American consumers reported fraud losses of over $12 million to companies located in Canada, and losses of over $182 million against companies located in other foreign countries (Federal Trade Commission 2013b). Almost by definition, all of these were "organized fraud" but, without knowing how many people were involved, not all may have been organized crime in the UN Palermo Convention sense.

In a longer work it would be possible to draw parallels, in terms of the dynamics between setting and criminal act, in relation to a broader range of identity and other fraud: for example application fraud and insurance fraud. If we take mortgage fraud, for example, fraud typically takes two forms: customers lying about their own means—that is, exaggerating their income—and/or falsifying documents, such as creating fake pay slips that show they earn an amount large enough to justify the mortgage they need, even if it is a multiple of their real income. This can be done simply by printing fake pay slips, if necessary on a color printer. Self-certificated mortgages (at higher interest rates) were allowed to cater for the increasing number of self-employed persons who could not produce genuine pay slips. One incentive for mortgage introducers is that they are paid commission; one incentive for lenders is that they have sales targets to hit and performance bonuses to get, and nonpayment usually comes much later. In some cases, the borrower is told there is no way they are going to get the mortgage they want with their income, and that they should leave that part of the mortgage application form blank. After they have gone, the broker inserts the false income. In the United States particularly, there have been widespread scandals relating to commission-hungry brokers lying to purchasers about the affordability of mortgages, which they discover only when the initial low rates expire add cite. In other cases, the would-be purchaser colludes with the broker. In other cases still, the broker (or lawyer) purchases the properties for themselves as beneficial owner, using the names and real or fictitious income details of clients. In a rising market, where there is demand (for example from students) for rental properties, fraudulent purchasers see little downside risk. In some cases, valuers specially selected by lenders are aware that the lenders need to lend, and try to give the valuation required to enable the mortgage to be granted: this is especially so where all the parties' desires are in the same direction (author interviews with surveyors 1980s and 2008). However when the market turns, as it did in 2007 (and earlier in the United States), these fraud are shaken out as people cannot keep up with repayments. (See Nguyen & Pontell, 2010, for a stimulating discussion of the phenomenon in the United States, which had more modest dynamics in Europe, though European banks—and later European taxpayers—ended up suffering because they purchased derivatives based on these nonperforming loans.)

IV. Control Efforts against Organized Frauds

There is insufficient space to discuss the varied industry, regulatory, and criminal justice measures taken against fraud worldwide. Some aspects of business self-regulation have been integrated earlier into discussions of fraud trends. Creditors in highly competitive industries are reluctant to share details about their fraud losses with other firms and are afraid that publicity may make them more attractive to other fraudsters (author interviews with companies, 2008–2010). Sharing information via third parties such as credit reference agencies, payment card schemes and not-for-profit industry bodies is highly developed in the United Kingdom and represents one route to reducing risk, provided that data protection legislation allows it. (Data protection rules are variable within the European Union and around the globe.) These third parties—some of which operate internationally, like Visa, MasterCard, and some anticounterfeiting bodies—might be viewed as "capable guardians," but what they may see or construct out of their partly automated analytical methods are *suspicions* of fraud rather than undisputed crimes that they have witnessed. Expensive manual analysis is needed to supplement these automated alerts.

Electronic tracking of the financial and other geolocation footprints on individual adults are quite pervasive (especially in the United Kingdom and North America, far less so in Asian, Africa, Eastern Europe, or even parts of Western Europe), and attempts to side-step these controls on identity thefts and identity "cloning" are a key battleground against fraud today. Licit and illicit migration flows generate particular difficulties and asymmetries in the validation of credit histories. For example the birth registers and other personal identifiers are absent from centralized records in many African and Asian countries, so cannot readily be checked, and certainly not electronically. Even addresses in Africa are usually postbox numbers rather than physically identifiable dwellings. Many of the features of late modernity on which "identity validation" rests are not uniformly available.

Around the world, fraud connected with organized crime may be dealt with by specialized bodies such as the *Directione Nazionale Anti Mafia* in Italy rather than by the ordinary detectives or the *Guardia di Finanza*; in the United Kingdom, they may be divided among the 43 constabulary forces, the national "lead force" for economic crime—the City of London police—and the National Crime Agency). Specialist prosecutors in the Crown Prosecution Service or the Serious Fraud Office will then handle the prosecution aspects *if it comes to that*. In the United States, racketeering legislation may be used against organized crime–connected fraud. The politics of the financial crisis have led some FBI resources to be returned to white collar crime units from counterterrorism and to a more aggressive attitude by the Department of Justice. In countries where there is no legal requirement to prosecute, administrative disruptions such as closure of the businesses allegedly run by "organized crime" may be pursued instead and civil recovery of assets attempted outside conviction (see Kilchling, this volume). In Europe, there are also specialized bodies such as OLAF (the Organisation for the Struggle Against Fraud) that investigate fraud against the European Union but have no powers of arrest or direct prosecution and seek to energize often reluctant national fraud prosecutors to take on the cases they develop (Levi 2011; Quirke 2010; Xanthaki 2010; White 2010).

Criminal justice actions against fraud are typically low key and modestly resourced, except where the fraud are "signal crimes" like pension fund fraud and Madoff-like Ponzi schemes that outrage the media, politicians, and the public. Even then, coordination between different public and private sector bodies may be poor (Doig & Levi 2009; Levi 2010), and politicians may be wary of unleashing generalized hostility toward financial institutions to whose prosperity they feel bound. Many "organized crime" investigations are resource intensive and involve intrusive surveillance, but these tend to be employed to deal with fraud only where the targets are seen to be morally undeserving generally. Where their social standing is more ambiguous or even elite, there are countervailing attempts to discredit investigations, as former Italian Prime Minister Berlusconi has consistently done against the Milanese and other investigative judges from the *tangentopoli* and *mani pulite* period of the early 1990s onward, even after his final conviction and expulsion from Parliament in 2013.

V. Conclusions

Globalization of fraud is affected by settings, with their rich and varied opportunities (reflecting patterns of business, consumer and investment activities), the abilities of would-be perpetrators to recognize and act upon those opportunities (the "crime scripts" perspective), and their interactions with controls including law enforcement and formal regulation (touched only lightly upon here). Constructs of "organized crime" should be (and are becoming) less obsessed with the structure of groups than with what people need from the largely illicit and largely licit worlds to go about the business of fraud. In other words, analysis of "organized-ness" is becoming decentered and reunderstood as much in terms of settings as in terms of the acts themselves.

Such observations or claims about the contested and shifting nature of analysis over time complicate the already difficult question of whether fraud "itself" has changed over the years (Levi 2008a, 2012, 2013; Shover & Grabosky 2010). It seems reasonable to reflect on two "historical" questions:

1. In what respects has fraudulent activity changed, in terms of the sorts of techniques and organization that are or can be used, in relation to the efforts made (intentionally or not) to prevent fraud?
2. In what respects has the world of fraud changed and what would the sort of people with the sort of skill sets/networks who committed fraud in the 1960s and 1970s have contemplated doing today?

In relation to the first question, although the basic techniques used by fraudsters in the 1960s are still available today, especially against those investors and trade creditors who make only modest enquiries, the professionalization of investor protection and credit management, and media articles/programs on savings and investment makes the commission of such fraud harder. e-Commerce, the growth of lightweight, high value electronic products, and the technology of rapid delivery anywhere in the world have cut down decision times and opened up domestic and foreign markets to fraudsters. At the high end of insolvency fraud, however, it seems doubtful whether the more skillful abuses of insolvency by those who, for example, establish beneficially owned corporate fronts offshore and then create artificial debts to them which enable them to vote in friendly liquidators or administrators, are any harder to commit or are any more likely to be punished today than they were 30 years earlier. Formal social control—the police and criminal courts—has not been particularly interested in fraud beyond the more visibly harmful "widows and orphans" cases, though 2010–2014 saw a growth of investigative interest in insider trading and in global rate-fixing (LIBOR, FOREX) by major international banks rather than by organized criminals as conventionally understood.

There has been a growth in "civil recovery" regimes, applying financial investigation and asset forfeiture (irrespective of criminal conviction) to supplement the postconviction confiscation remedies that have replaced the criminal bankruptcy orders. However even if they have substantial savings rather than spending "their" proceeds as they went along (like the high-spending bankruptcy and telemarketing fraudsters interviewed by Levi, 2008a, and by Shover et al., 2003) few fraudsters are high profile career criminals of a seriousness level that would interest major Organized Crime Task Forces. This question is connected to the second.

What forms of fraud constitute a "rational choice" depends on the confidence, skills and contact set of any given individual offenders. The presence or absence of "crime networks" known to and trusted by the willing offender makes a difference to "crime capacitation": an issue often neglected in individualized explanations of involvement in crime. Choice of crime type might also be affected by age. Kleemans (2013) and colleagues have used data from the Dutch Organised Crime Monitor to stress late onset fraud and other offending. Those offenders who were in their 50s and over might not be attracted toward the technological challenges of cyberactivities, and—except via close encounters on porn sites, in night clubs, or in prisons—the age gap might apply to co-criminality as it does to other feature of contemporary life. So today's new generation fraudsters might gravitate toward more "teckie" forms of fraud, whereas if they were in late career, it might seem too risky to adapt in unfamiliar territory unless they can find someone younger to collaborate with. This is a general proposition about the relationship between age and risk-taking/innovation. Some fraudsters display a remarkable aptitude for creativity and constant testing out of commercial systems and private individuals for signs of weakness. This focus on "criminal transferrable skills"—the set of aptitudes including social networking that individual/sets of offenders have—concentrates our attention on offender creativity, energy and social networking skills in finding co-offenders (or "turning" nonoffenders into co-offenders) and in adapting techniques: many offenders (and nonoffenders) lack one or all of these qualities.

Objectively, there are far more opportunities for disintermediated crime in late modernity than in the postwar decades. With only modest sophistication, the Internet and social constructions of what is normal have made it easier for foreign natural and legal persons to defraud consumers and suppliers, for example via counterfeited or cloned payment cards. Fraudsters could be involved in the theft of personal data from garbage ("bin raiding") or by hacking into data storage facilities; or account manipulation by insiders, whether in call centers or elsewhere. (The offshoring of call centers led to periodic media alarm stories about blackmail and corruption in India: but it is nonsensical to think that this cannot happen in the developed West, with badly paid, high turnover staff ratios. Indeed, there may be tougher regimes in Indian call centers—staff searches and prohibitions on mobile phones—than might be allowed in Europe.) Rings of staged accidents with claims for hard-to-falsify personal injuries would be within the skill set of some (once they worked out what to do), as would organized benefit fraud and—especially—the sale of counterfeit products, whose quality digital technology has done so much to improve, despite the best efforts of the anticounterfeiting coalitions. For the more adventurous, scams can involve some currently fashionable musical or sporting events, or a social cause such as "renewable energy." One may expect some future scams involving "new products" such as carbon trading. The underlying concepts were available to investors at the time of the Dutch Tulipmania in the 1630s or the British South Sea Bubble in the 1720s, but some investors in each subsequent generation and/or country have to learn the lessons for themselves. Arguably, as evidenced by declining savings ratios and the willingness to borrow against the legal security of homes in the United Kingdom and elsewhere, there has been a step change in people's expectations of steady state or rising affluence, and resistance to personal financial decline. When times get hard, people may take more risks to avoid downward socioeconomic mobility, and this offers opportunities to fraudsters. At a policy level, this means that a focus on "regulating" rather than on "eliminating" fraud is sensible: what constitutes an acceptable level of fraud may depend on who the victims are, how much they can afford it, and the collateral damage caused. But it may also depend on who is committing it, and however ill-defined and ill-theorized, the focus on the harm of "organized crime" means that where they identify fraud as associated with very bad people, those frauds may receive a higher priority than they would otherwise do. In this sense, as Levi (2008a) argued, for fraudsters, "small is beautiful"; or large can be beautiful (to criminals) unless it evokes serious fears of economic harm and consumes few enough resources that the authorities can readily cope to counteract it. Despite the decline in crime rates in the developing world, few countries have transformed their policing to adjust to the demands of combating economic crimes, whether they are committed by "organized crime" or by those who avoid the taint of violence and remain outside the intelligence-led policing radar.

Notes

1. Professor of Criminology, School of Social Sciences, Cardiff University. Contact details Levi@Cardiff.ac.uk. The author is grateful for the ESRC Professorial Fellowship RES-051-27-0208 under whose auspices some of the research used in this chapter was conducted.
2. The NFA (2013: 32-22) notes:
   "In October 2012 analysis of the organised crime group mapping (OCGM) data held by the National Fraud Intelligence Bureau (NFIB) suggested that of the OCGs known to the authorities and considered to be nationally significant, 67 percent are involved with fraud as a crime category (with 85 percent involved in specialist money laundering, 77 percent

drugs and 67 percent violent crime). The analysis also confirmed that there are 7,503 OCGs considered to be active in the UK. Of these, 1,365 are linked to some form of fraudulent activity. Counter-fraud professionals believe these figures significantly under-represent the true involvement of OCGs in fraud.

OCGs that are assessed to be involved in fraud are linked to mortgage fraud, tax fraud, benefit fraud, identity theft, payment card crime and insurance fraud. One-quarter (25 percent) of these OCGs have realised group assets of more than £1 million, but these are not exclusively from fraud.

OCGs linked to fraud have been identified and are being managed by law enforcement agencies in every region of the country. Fraud is a transnational crime and 462 OCGs are assessed to have some form of international link, be this through their geographical base or through the reach of their criminal activities.

The NFA estimate of fraud perpetrated by organised criminals has been refreshed. The methodology uses existing estimates of fraud loss, and calculates the proportion that might be attributable to OCGs by fraud type. These estimates derive from consultation with industry experts and law enforcement and are based on management assumptions and judgements; to provide an illustrative indication of loss. Fraud loss because of organised crime activity now stands at £8.9 billion of the £24 billion that can be mapped through fraud loss type to organised groups. Areas of loss captured include tax and benefits fraud; retail banking, insurance, mortgage, telecommunications and mass-marketing fraud (see individual estimates in 'Fraud by type' section).

It is not yet possible to identify the level of OCG activity against every fraud type or victim. Although, if it is assumed that the 37 percent loss for the above identifiable fraud estimate is reflective of fraud losses due to organised crime in the rest of our fraud loss estimate, an additional £9.9 billion might be lost to fraud. This could tentatively equate to a total fraud loss of £18.9 billion."

3. Even sophisticated denial of service blackmail attempts against corporations can be carried out by teenagers in their bedrooms acting alone, though organizing bank accounts and laundering may require cooperation.

4. Even though the potentially demonizing effect of his later book was arguably diminished by the substantial cuts in corporate names and other components he had to make to please Indiana University trustees and their corporate donors: an interesting message for our times (Sutherland, 1985).

5. Esoterically inclined readers may note that according to the UN Transnational Organised Crime Convention, one needs three or more people acting together for some time to constitute organized crime, so not all well-organized fraud are organized crime!

6. Consider this in relation to the UK and the European National Intelligence Model, in which level 1 refers to crimes within a police force area, level 2 to crimes within the United Kingdom but involving more than one force area, and level 3 refers to international crimes (Maguire & John, 2006). Does the mere fact that money is transferred overseas or credit cards are used fraudulently overseas make them level 3 crimes? In the United States, crimes against nearly all financial institutions are federal offenses because they are federally insured and the "wires" cross state lines but, bizarrely, the FBI regularly reports on burglaries and robberies against banks but less regularly on fraud against them.

7. Prearranging outlets for fraudulently obtained (and stolen) goods is important for optimal organized crime. I interviewed one offender who would have had difficulty in disposing of a truckload of yoghurt had he not been arrested before he dealt with the dilemma. One

nineteenth-century British-located German fraudster obtained from Germany a gross (144) of artificial glass eyes, which he was unable to sell, and in the end, he had to dispose of for the price of the postage it cost to obtain them (Levi, 2008a).

8. Unless the purchases on "borrowed" card data are picked up by the sophisticated electronic systems used by the card issuers in some countries that model customer transaction patterns and contact customers proactively if there are transactions that do not fit their profiles.

9. Between 2002 and 2012, "card not present" losses on UK-issued cards where the buyer and seller were not in the same place rose from 26 percent (£110.1 million) to 63 percent (£245.8 million) of all card fraud losses, with a record high of £328.4 million in 2008. E-Commerce card fraud rose from £28 million in 2002 to 140.2 million in 2012; in 2008, when e-commerce fraud was at its peak, it cost an estimated £181.7 million. Online card fraud spending in 2008 was £41 billion. In 2012 card spending was £68 billion, up 66 percent on 2008, while e-commerce fraud dropped 23 percent over the same period. Online banking fraud reported to UK Cards rose from £12.2 million in 2004 to £39.6 million in 2012, with its peak to date in 2009 (UK Cards Association, 2013).

10. Hence, there is some connection between payment card fraud and the financing of the Tamil Tigers (LTTE), at least before their military defeat in 2009, but what proportion even of Sri Lankan card fraud went to finance terrorism rather than to sustain impoverished people or make some foreigners wealthy remains unknown—another example of the loose conceptualization of the link between organized crime and terrorism.

11. For interesting research studies of identity theft—a more heterogeneous term than the phrase might suggest—see Copes and Vieraitis 2007, 2008, 2012; Copes et al. 2013; and Holt and Turner 2013.

REFERENCES

ABS. (2008). Personal Fraud in Australia. Canberra: Australian Bureau of Statistics. http://www.ausstats.abs.gov.au/Ausstats/subscriber.nsf/0/866E0EF22EFC4608CA2574740015D234/$File/45280_2007.pdf.

ACFE. (2012). Report to the Nations on Occupational Fraud and Abuse. Austin: Association of Certified Fraud Examiners.

Anderson, Ross, Chris Barton, Rainer Bohme, Richard Clayton, Michel J. G. van Eeten, Michael Levi, Tyler Moore, and Stefan Savage. (2012). "Measuring the Cost of Cybercrime." http://weis2012.econinfosec.org/papers/Anderson_WEIS2012.pdf.

Baum, Katrina. (2007). Identity Theft 2005. Washington, DC: Bureau of Justice Statistics. http://www.ojp.usdoj.gov/bjs/pub/pdf/ito5.pdf.

Black, William. (2014). The Best Way to Rob a Bank Is to Own One. Updated edition. Austin: University of Texas Press.

Bower, Tom. (2008). Maxwell: The Final Verdict. London: Harper Collins.

Bussman, Kai, and Markus Werle. (2006). "Addressing Crime in Companies: First Findings from a Global Survey of Economic Crime." British Journal of Criminology 46(6): 1128–1144.

Calavita, Kitty, and Henry Pontell. (1993). "Savings and Loan Fraud as Organized Crime: Toward a Conceptual Typology of Corporate Illegality." Criminology 31(4): 519–548.

Cialdini, Robert. (2007). Influence: The Psychology of Persuasion, 2nd ed. New York: HarperCollins.

Cohen, Stan. (2001). States of Denial. Cambridge: Polity.

Copes, Heith, and Lynne Vieraitis. (2007). "Identity Theft: Assessing Offenders' Strategies and Perceptions of Risk." Technical Report for National Institute of Justice. NCJ 219122. NIJ Grant No. 2005-IJ-CX-0012.

Copes, Heith, and Lynne M. Vieraitis. (2008). "Stealing Identities: The Risks, Rewards and Strategies of Identity Theft." In Perspectives on Identity Theft, edited by Megan McNally and Graham Newman. New York: Criminal Justice Press.

Copes, Heith, and Lynne M. Vieraitis. (2012). Identity Thieves: Motives and Methods. Boston: UPNE.

Copes, Heith, Lynne M. Vieraitis, Stephanie M. Cardwell, and Arthur Vasquez. (2013). "Accounting for Identity Theft: The Roles of Lifestyle and Enactment." Journal of Contemporary Criminal Justice 29(3): 351–368.

Cressey, Don. (1955). Other People's Money. New York: Free Press.

CSD. (2012). Serious and Organised Crime Threat Assessment 2010–2011. Sofia: Center for the Study of Democracy.

Deflem, Mathieu (ed.). (2011). Economic Crisis and Crime, Sociology of Crime, Law, and Deviance, Volume 16. Bingley: Emerald.

Detica. (2011). The Cost of Cyber Crime. London: Detica and the Cabinet Office.

Diih, Sorle. (2005). Unpublished Ph.D. thesis, Cardiff University, Cardiff.

Doig, Alan, and Michael Levi. (2009). "Inter-agency Work and the UK Public Sector Investigation of Fraud, 1996–2006: Joined up Rhetoric and Disjointed Reality." Policing and Society 19(3): 199–215.

Dubourg, Richard, and Stephen Prichard (eds.). (2009). Organised Crime: Revenues, Economic and Social Costs, and Criminal Assets Available for Seizure. London: Home Office.

Eichenwald, Kurt. (2001). The Informant: A True Story. New York: Doubleday.

Ernst & Young. (2011). Driving Ethical Growth—New Markets, New Challenges: 11th Global Fraud Survey. London: Ernst & Young.

Europol. (2011). EU Organized Crime Threat Assessment: OCTA 2011. The Hague: Europol.

Europol. (2013). EU Serious and Organized Crime Threat Assessment: SOCTA 2013. The Hague: Europol.

Federal Trade Commission. (2011). The Consumer Sentinel Network Databook for January-December 2010. http://www.ftc.gov/sentinel/reports/sentinel-annual-reports/sentinel-cy2010.pdf.

Federal Trade Commission. (2013a). The Consumer Sentinel Network Databook for January-December 2012. http://www.ftc.gov/sentinel/reports/sentinel-annual-reports/sentinel-cy2012.pdf.

Federal Trade Commission. (2013b). Cross-Border Fraud Complaints January-December 2012. Chicago: Federal Trade Commission.

Financial Fraud Action UK. (2013). Fraud: The Facts 2012. London: Financial Fraud Action UK.

Glenny, Misha. (2008). McMafia. London: Bodley Head.

Harding, Chris. (2007). Criminal Enterprise: Individuals, Organisations and Criminal Responsibility. Cullompton: Willan.

Harrell, Erika, and Lynn Langton. (2013). Victims of Identity Theft, 2012. Washington, DC: Bureau of Justice Statistics.

Holt, Thomas J., and Michael G. Turner. (2012). "Examining Risks and Protective Factors of On-Line Identity Theft." Deviant Behavior 33(4): 308–323.

Holtfreter, Kristy, Shanna Van Slyke, and Thomas Blomberg. (2005). "Sociolegal Change in Consumer Fraud: From Victim-Offender Interactions to Global Networks." Crime, Law and Social Change 44(3): 251–275.

Holtfreter, Kristy, Michael Reisig, and Travis Pratt. (2008). "Low Self-control, Routine Activities and Fraud Victimization." *Criminology* 46(1): 189–220.

Home Office. (2013). Crime against Businesses: Headline Findings from the 2012 Commercial Victimisation Survey. London: Home Office.

Karstedt, Suzanne, and Stephen Farrall. (2006). "The Moral Economy of Everyday Crime: Markets, Consumers and Citizens." *British Journal of Criminology* 46(6): 1011–1036.

Katz, Jack. (1990). Seductions of Crime. New York: Basic Books.

Kerviel, Jérôme. (2010). L'engrenage: Mémoires d'un trader. Paris: Flammarion.

Kleemans, Edward. (2013). "Organized Crime and the Visible Hand: A Theoretical Critique on the Economic Analysis of Organized Crime." *Criminology and Criminal Justice* 13(5): 615–629.

Van Koppen, Mere V. (2013). Pathways into Organized Crime: Criminal Opportunities and Adult-onset Offending. Amsterdam: Vrije Universiteit.

Van Koppen, Mere V., Christian. J. de Poot, and Arjan. A. J. Blokland. (2010a). "Comparing Criminal Careers of Organized Crime Offenders and General Offenders." *European Journal of Criminology* 7(5): 356–374.

Van Koppen, Mere V., Christian J. de Poot, Edward R. Kleemans, and Paul Nieuwbeerta. (2010b). "Criminal Trajectories in Organized Crime." *British Journal of Criminology* 50(1): 102–123.

KPMG. (2007). Profile of a Fraudster 2007. London: KPMG.

Kroll. (2010). Global Fraud Report. London: Kroll Consulting.

Kroll. (2013). 2013/2014 Global Fraud Report. London: Kroll Consulting.

Leeson, Nick. (1997). Rogue Trader. London: Time Warner.

Levi, Julia. (2011). "Olaf: A View from Inside." *Amicus Curiae* 85(Spring): 17–19.

Levi, Michael. (1987). Regulating Fraud: White-Collar Crime and the Criminal Process. London: Routledge.

Levi, Michael. (2008a). The Phantom Capitalists: the Organisation and Control of Long-Firm Fraud, 2nd edition. Aldershot: Ashgate.

Levi, Michael. (2008b). "Combating Identity and Other Forms of Payment Fraud in the UK: An Analytical History." In Perspectives on Identity Theft, edited by Megan McNally and Graham Newman. Monsey, NJ: Criminal Justice Press.

Levi, Michael. (2008c). " 'Organised Fraud': Unpacking Research on Networks and Organisation." *Criminology and Criminal Justice* 8(4): 389–420.

Levi, Michael. (2010). "Public and Private Policing of Financial Crimes: the Struggle for Co-ordination." *Journal of Criminal Justice and Security* 12(4): 343–357.

Levi, Michael. (2011). "Assessing the Costs of Fraud." In The SAGE Handbook of Criminological Research Methods, edited by David Gadd, Susanne Karstedt, and Steven Messner. London: Sage.

Levi, Michael. (2012). "The Organization of Serious Crimes." In The Oxford Handbook of Criminology, edited by Mike Maguire, Rod Morgan, and Robert Reiner, 5th edition. Oxford: Oxford University Press.

Levi, Michael. (2013). "Financial Crimes and the Global Financial Crisis." In Human Dimensions in Organised Crime, Money Laundering and Corruption, edited by Petrus van Duyne, Jackie Harvey, Georgios A. Antonopoulos, Klaus von Lampe, Almir Maljevic, and Jon Spencer, pp. 201–228. Oisterwijk: Wolf Legal Publishers.

Levi, Michael, and John Burrows. (2008). "Measuring the Impact of Fraud: A Conceptual and Empirical Journey." *British Journal of Criminology* 48(3): 293–318.

Levi, Michael, Martin Innes, Peter Reuter, and Rajeev Gundur. (2013). The Economic, Financial & Social Impacts of Organised Crime in the EU. Luxembourg: CRIM Committee, European Parliament. http://www.europarl.europa.eu/committees/en/crim/studies.html#.

Maguire, Mike, and Tim John. (2006). "Intelligence Led Policing, Managerialism and Community Engagement: Competing Priorities and the Role of the National Intelligence Model in the UK." *Policing and Society* 16(1): 67–85.

Maurer, David. (2000). The Big Con. London: Arrow.

McIntosh, Mary. (1971). "Changes in the Organization of Thieving." In Images of Deviance, edited by Stan Cohen. London: Penguin.

McLean, Bethany, and Peter Elkind. (2004). The Smartest Guys in the Room: The Amazing Rise and Scandalous Fall of Enron. London: Portfolio.

Mills, Hannah, Sara Skodbo, and Peter Blyth. (2013). Understanding Organised Crime: Estimating the Scale and the Social and Economic Costs, Research Report 73. London: Home Office.

Morselli, Carlo. (2009). Inside Criminal Networks. New York: Springer.

Morselli, Carlo, and Julie Roy. (2008). "Brokerage Qualifications in Ringing Operations." *Criminology* 46(1): 71–98.

Nelken, David. (2012). "White-collar Crime." In The Oxford Handbook of Criminology, edited by Mike Maguire, Rod Morgan, and Robert Reiner, 5th edition. Oxford: Oxford University Press.

NFA. (2010). Annual Fraud Indicator. London: National Fraud Authority.

NFA. (2011). Annual Fraud Indicator. London: National Fraud Authority.

NFA. (2013). Annual Fraud Indicator. London: National Fraud Authority.

Nguyen, Tomson H., and Henry Pontell. (2010). "Mortgage Origination Fraud and the Global Economic Crisis: A Criminological Analysis." *Criminology & Public Policy* 9(3): 591–612.

Passas, Nikos. (2005). Informal Value Transfer Systems, Terrorism and Money Laundering. http:// www.ncjrs.org/pdffiles1/nij/grants/208301.pdf.

PWC. (2009). Global Economic Crime Survey. London: PriceWaterhouse Coopers.

PWC. (2011). Global Economic Crime Survey. London: PriceWaterhouse Coopers.

Quirke, Brendan. (2010). "Fighting EU Fraud: Why Do We Make It Difficult for Ourselves." *Journal of Financial Crime* 17(1): 61–80.

Rawlinson, Patricia. (2010). From Fear to Fraternity: A Russian Tale of Crime, Economy and Modernity. London: Pluto.

Reyns, Bradford W. (2013). "Online Routines and Identity Theft Victimization Further Expanding Routine Activity Theory beyond Direct-Contact Offenses." *Journal of Research in Crime and Delinquency* 50(2): 216–238.

Schoenmakers, Yvette, Edo de Vries Robbé, and Anton van Wijk. (2009). Mountains of Gold: An Exploratory Research on Nigerian 419-Fraud. Amsterdam: SWP.

Shapiro, Susan P. (1981). *Thinking About White Collar Crime: Matters of Conceptualization and Research*. Washington, D.C.: National Institute of Justice.

Shapiro, Susan. (1990). "Collaring the Crime, Not the Criminal: Reconsidering the Concept of White-Collar Crime." *American Sociological Review* 55(3): 346–365.

Shover, Neal, Glenn S. Coffey, and Dick Hobbs. (2003). "Crime on the Line: Telemarketing and the Changing Nature of Professional Crime." *British Journal of Criminology* 43(3): 489–505.

Shover, Neal, and Peter Grabosky. (2010). "White-collar Crime and the Great Recession." *Criminology & Public Policy* 9(1): 429–434.

Simpson, Sally, and David Weisburd (eds.). (2009). The Criminology of White-Collar Crime. New York: Springer.

SOCA. (2010). The UK Threat Assessment of Organized Crime 2009/10. London: Serious and Organized Crime Agency.

Stevenson, Robert. (1998). The Boiler Room and Other Telephone Sales Scams. *Urbana*: University of Illinois Press.

Sutherland, Edwin. (1945). "Is 'White Collar Crime' Crime?" *American Sociological Review* 10(2): 132–139.

Sutherland, Edwin. (1985). White-Collar Crime: The Uncut Version. Princeton: Yale University Press.

TI. (2013). Corruption Perceptions Index 2013. Berlin: Transparency International.

Tillman, Robert, and Michael Indergaard. (2005). Pump and Dump: The Rancid Rules of the New Economy. New Brunswick: Rutgers University Press.

Tillman, Robert, and Michael Indergaard. (2007a). "Corporate Corruption in the New Economy." In International Handbook of White-Collar and Corporate Crime, edited by Henry Pontell and Gilbert Geis. New York: Springer.

Tillman, Robert, and Michael Indergaard. (2007b). Control Overrides in Financial Statement Fraud: A Report for the Institute of Fraud Prevention. http://www.theifp.org/research%20grants/tillman%20final%20report_revised_mac-orginal-EDITED.pdf.

UK Cards Association. (2013). Fraud: the Facts 2010. London: UK Cards Association.

Van de Bunt, Henk. (2010). "Walls of Secrecy and Silence: The Madoff Case and Cartels in the Construction Industry." *Criminology and Public Policy* 9(3): 435–453.

White, Simone. (2010). "EU Anti-fraud Enforcement: Overcoming Obstacles," *Journal of Financial Crime* 17(1): 81–99.

Whitty, Monica T. (2013). "The Scammers Persuasive Techniques Model: Development of a Stage Model to Explain the Online Dating Romance Scam." *British Journal of Criminology* 53(4): 665–684.

Xanthaki, Helen. (2010). "What Is EU Fraud? And Can OLAF Really Combat It?" *Journal of Financial Crime* 17(1): 133–151.

CHAPTER 24

··

CYBERCRIME

··

KIM-KWANG RAYMOND CHOO AND PETER GRABOSKY

I. INTRODUCTION

Computers and network-based systems lie at the heart of critical infrastructures around the world, particularly in the technologically advanced countries (National Infrastructure Advisory Council 2004). This is hardly surprising as the proliferation of information and communications technologies (ICT) and connectivity of the Internet in today's digital age open the door to increased productivity, faster communication capabilities, and immeasurable convenience. This creates not only benefits for the community, but also risks of criminal exploitation.

Digital technology has empowered ordinary individuals as never before. A person acting alone can communicate with millions of people, instantly and at negligible cost. Sole individuals are now able to penetrate and disrupt major governmental systems and prominent retailing sites. Organizations too have been greatly empowered by digital technology, for better and for worse.

This essay looks at the exploitation of digital technology in furtherance of organized crime. It first addresses the concept of criminal organization and suggests the desirability of a more expansive construction to accommodate the evolution and diversification of organizational forms in the modern era. It then looks at three types of organized crime groups: (1) traditional organized crime groups, which make use of ICT to enhance their terrestrial criminal activities; (2) organized cybercrime groups, which operate exclusively online; and (3) organized groups of ideologically and politically motivated individuals, who make use of ICT to facilitate their criminal conduct. The essay notes emerging trends in organized cybercrime and concludes with a few suggestions for the prevention and control of organized crime in the digital age.

Although it would be pleasing to be able to cite comprehensive statistics on patterns and trends in organized cybercrime, this remains an elusive goal. Much cybercrime is unreported. Some is even undetected. Of those offenses that do come to the attention of authorities, the organizational circumstances of the perpetrator (or perpetrators) is often unknown. Those official statistics that do exist often relate to the substantive offense rather than the technologies by which it was committed. One may say with confidence that the increasing pervasiveness of digital technologies means that they will continue to be exploited for criminal purposes by organizations both terrestrial and virtual.

II. ORGANIZATIONS

A. Morphology

Legitimate organizations look very different today from the way they appeared a century ago (if indeed they existed that long in the past and have survived). What were once vertically integrated organizations have shed functions, preferring to "contract out" specific tasks to specialist service providers rather than deliver everything using in-house resources. In recent years, the term *virtual organization* has been coined to refer to networked entities, in general, or to those organizations that outsource a significant amount of activity (Tapscott and Williams 2006).

When scholars and law enforcement officials think of organized crime, they instinctively think about stereotypical organizations committing certain types of crime. The classic monolithic, pyramidal organization, such as the Yakuza, triads, or the Italian mafia, engaged in extortion or in the delivery of illicit services come immediately to mind. While a few criminal organizations still fit the classic monolithic, hierarchical, formal model, analysts began well over a decade ago to observe emerging variations (Halstead 1998). Much organized criminal activity began to be recognized as the collective work of loose coalitions of groups, collaborating with each other from time to time to achieve certain objectives. A case discussed below illustrates the franchise-like operations of an organized crime family in the United States, where peripheral associates manage teams of ordinary criminals and pass a percentage of their "take" to formal ("made") family members. Indeed, today the term *network* has become more familiar than *family* to describe organized crime (Williams 2001). Such networks are involved in activities as "traditional" as extortion and drug trafficking and as contemporary as software piracy, credit card fraud, and online child exploitation (Choo, Smith, and McCusker 2007; Choo 2009).

There remain aspects of organizational life in cyberspace that resemble the terrestrial world. In some cases, small groups of youth engage in online activity much as they would on the street; "hanging out" and showing off to each other. While much adolescent behavior in either setting is an innocent manifestation of youthful exuberance, some is not so innocent. Youth congregate in cyberspace, as they do on the street, for illicit fun and for illegal profit. Their organizational structure resembles more that of kids "messing around" in physical space than that of an organized crime group.

Other aspects are different. Organizations in cyberspace may involve repeated and intense interactions among people who have never met each other in person. Moreover, they may be situated almost anywhere on the surface of the earth. Drug newsgroups attract people interested in the manufacture of synthetic illicit drugs (Schneider 2003). To the extent that these relationships become institutionalized, new organizational forms are created. Contact made in IRC chatrooms between people who have never met each other (and may never meet each other) in physical space can evolve into hacker groups, piracy or "warez" groups, or child pornography rings (Holt 2007).

B. Longevity

The lifecycle of organizations has also become more varied. Some organizations are stable and enduring, such as the Vatican or Oxford University. Others transform themselves, adapting to dramatically changing circumstances. The Singapore Police Force of today is substantially different from the Singapore Police Force of 1819. Some organizations have come into existence only recently to exploit a new opportunity. Google, Inc. was first incorporated as recently as 1998. Other organizations are short-lived, coming into existence for a particular purpose and then disbanding. Consider the Beijing Organizing Committee for the Olympic Games (BOCOG) that was established to oversee the 2008 Olympic Games in Beijing. It exists no longer. Some organizations are extremely short-lived. One of the more recent manifestations of the evanescent organization is swarming, i.e., "the unexpected gathering of large numbers of people in particular public locales" (White 2006). The communications processes that underlie such gatherings need not involve high technology; rather, word of mouth can suffice. But one can easily appreciate how swarming can be facilitated by the Internet or by digital telephony. In Australia, recent years have seen the use of text messages to make plans for group sexual assaults and race riots (Morton 2004; Perry 2005). Iranian dissidents used social networking technologies to organize protests against President Mahmoud Ahmadinejad in 2009 (LaFraniere and Ansfield 2010).

More recently, social media played a significant role in organizing the uprisings in Egypt and Tunisia that led to the overthrow of their authoritarian regimes. Social networking sites such as Facebook enabled strategic communications regarding the timing and location of protest activity. Media such as YouTube were used to transmit a picture of brutal police repression, locally and throughout the world, in avoiding state censorship (Preston 2011). Social media were also used in coordinating the riots that took place across the United Kingdom in August 2011. The BlackBerry messaging service was used to encourage looting and to arrange the time and location of gatherings. This prompted the British government to explore the development and imposition of controls over the technology (Pfanner 2011).

III. Organized Crime Groups

The definition of "organized criminal group" from Article 2 of the UN Convention on Transnational Organized Crime is adopted in this essay:

> a group having at least three members, taking some action in concert (i.e. together or in some co-ordinated manner) for the purpose of committing a 'serious crime' and for the purpose of obtaining a financial or other benefit. The group must have some internal organization or structure, and exist for some period of time before or after the actual commission of the offence(s) involved.

Whether the changes in organizational life noted above will result in more ephemeral collectivities to be deemed criminal organizations remains to be seen. It has even been suggested that a single individual who succeeds in building a network of compromised computers (a robot network or "botnet")[1] is creating a new form of criminal organization (Chang 2012).

A. Traditional Organized Criminal Groups

Organized crime is not a new phenomenon. It preceded, and then accompanied, the rise of the modern state. Pursuit of financial gain has always been the driving force behind traditional organized crime, although the desire for power, respect, comradeship, and adventure also figure prominently in the motivational mix.

However, the nature of organizational life is changing for criminal organizations no less than for legitimate ones. Monolithic, hierarchical, formal organizations still exist, but organizational form is becoming increasingly diverse. So too are the activities in which criminal organizations engage. To a significant extent, these trends are the products of rapid developments in information and communications technology (ICT), as traditional organized criminal groups have recognized the value of leveraging ICT to facilitate or enhance the commission of crimes. Examples include: using ICT to facilitate drug trafficking; to traffic in corporate secrets and identity information; to commit extortion, frauds, and scams online; to launder money using online payment systems; and to distribute illegal materials over the Internet. Of course, criminal organizations, like their legitimate counterparts, also use digital technology for routine incidental purposes, such as record keeping and communication.

Examples of traditional organized criminal groups involved in cybercrime include the highly structured and global criminal syndicates such as the Asian triads and Japanese Yakuza, whose criminal activities have been known to include computer software piracy and credit card forgery and fraud (Organisation for Economic Co-operation and Development 2007). Commentators have also suggested that traditional organized crime groups (e.g., outlaw motorcycle gangs) use online resources, such as social networking sites, to perform background checks on potential and new members (Douglis 2010) and to promote themselves to impressionable young people.

Traditional organized criminal groups from eastern Europe have also been known to carry out extortion from online gambling and pornography websites by threatening to carry out denial-of-service attacks using botnets (Choo 2007). In recent years, organized criminal groups have been reported to recruit "a new generation of high-flying cybercriminals using tactics which echo those employed by the KGB to recruit operatives at the height of the cold war" (McAfee 2006, p. 2). This should come as no surprise to long-time political observers. In countries such as Russia, the lack of economic and employment opportunities have forced many highly educated individuals with advanced computer and programming skills to work in the cyber underground.

In its 2008 threat assessment, the Serious Organised Crime Agency in the United Kingdom warned that traditional organized criminal groups are also "increasingly using false and stolen identities to commit non-fiscal frauds" (Serious Organised Crime Agency 2008, p. 9). For example in May 2009, 11 defendants, alleged to be members of a "crew" working in Florida for an associate of the New York–based Bonnano crime family, were charged with various offenses, including the illegal manufacture of fraudulent checks and fraud in connection with access devices. The group included one individual with a background in computing who accessed databases with a view toward identifying potential extortion victims. He also used his computing skills in the production of counterfeit checks.[2] In Japan, conventional criminal groups also provide venture capital for technicians specializing in hacking and fraud (Tokyo Reporter 2009). Another case involved a large and diverse conspiracy among members of the Gambino crime family alleged to have engaged in fabrication of false bar code labels and credit cards. One member of the conspiracy, who worked for a chain of home improvement stores, had access to the requisite technology (US Department of Justice 2010). A third example involved other associates of the Bonnano family who were active in the telecommunications industry and who were implicated in a scheme of fraudulent billing of telephone accounts.[3]

In October 2011, 111 individuals from five different criminal groups were indicted by local authorities in New York City for a range of offenses related to identity theft, credit card forgery, and fraud. A number of the accused were also allegedly involved in a range of terrestrial offenses, including burglary and robbery. It was alleged that the groups obtained credit card details from skimming (for example, by complicit restaurant employees) or from Internet suppliers through illegal websites. Counterfeit credit cards were then manufactured, and teams of shoppers deployed to purchase high-end merchandise, some of which was sold online by fences (Queens County District Attorney 2011).

Traditional organized crime groups (and organized cybercrime groups described in the next section) have also been known to hire money mules in the money laundering process. Money mules are individuals hired by organized criminals to perform international wire fraud or to purchase prepaid cards, and then to mail or ship prepaid cards out of the country without regulators being aware (Choo 2008, footnote 14). As Choo,

Kim-Kwang Raymond, Russell G Smith, and Rob McCusker (2009, p. xxi) point out, "[o]rganised operations that make use of conventional technology-enabled crime methodologies, such as financial scams or piracy, will also increase as the use of networked computers for criminal purposes develops."

In rare cases, criminal organizations may engage the services of former law enforcement officers with a degree of technological expertise. One former FBI agent accessed the bureau's database and alerted two suspects that they were targets of an investigation (US Department of Justice 2005).

B. Organized Cybercriminal Groups

Another category of organized criminal group consists of like-minded individuals who usually know each other only online, but who are involved in an organizational structure working collectively toward a common goal because the Internet makes it far easier to meet and plan activities. Although the objective is usually pursuit of financial gain, it can include other criminal goals such as producing and disseminating child pornography and related materials. For example, in 2007 more than 700 suspects associated with the UK-based Internet chatroom, "Kids, the Light of Our Lives," were arrested worldwide (Child Exploitation and Online Protection 2007).

Another example relates to software piracy. "Drink or Die" was a group of information technology specialists who obtained copies of software and other digital products, stripped them of their copyright protection, and posted them to hundreds of Internet sites around the world. Prior to their collaboration in furtherance of piracy, none had significant criminal backgrounds. Members were located in a number of countries, including the United States, the United Kingdom, and Australia; most of their interactions occurred in cyberspace rather than on the ground. In December 2001, the simultaneous execution of 58 search warrants brought an end to the conspiracy. One of the members, an Australian, had never set foot in the United States, although he was eventually extradited, convicted, and imprisoned there (Urbas 2006).

C. Ideologically and Politically Motivated Cybercrime Groups

Prior to September 11, 2001, terrorism and organized crime were usually considered separate entities because they did not share the same motivating factor. The primary objective of organized crime is money. By contrast, terrorist organizations have political goals. In recent years, however, a convergence between terrorism and organized crime has been noted. The variety of ways in which digital technology may be used in furtherance of terrorism include communications, intelligence, propaganda and psychological warfare, recruitment, and training (Thomas 2003). Conventional criminal organizations have a great deal of expertise to offer terrorist groups. Crimes commonly associated with organized criminal groups (e.g., scam and fraud schemes, identity and immigration crimes, and the counterfeit of goods) are also precursor crimes used by terrorist groups to raise funds (Sanderson 2004).

Some terrorists engage in cybercrime to acquire resources with which to finance their operations, especially since formal funds transfers have come under increasing scrutiny from anti–money laundering authorities. Imam Samudra, convicted architect of the 2002 Bali bombings, reportedly called upon his followers to commit credit card fraud (Sipress 2004). The Tamil Tigers are alleged to have engaged in credit card fraud to support their operations (Hutchinson and O' Malley 2007).

Others seek to harass or threaten an adversary. Originally, this took the form of "mail bombing" in which thousands of emails were directed at a target in an effort to degrade the system. In May 1999, the White House website was overloaded with "visits" following the bombing of the Chinese embassy in Belgrade (National Infrastructure Protection Center 2001). Today, botnets are used for such a purpose, as was the case in the 2007 denial of service attacks against Estonian servers (Landler and Markoff 2007).

A 2006 report (IDSS 2006) highlighted the proliferation of jihad-oriented sites in Southeast Asia, which facilitate radicalization among the Muslim community in the region. Eight thousand websites espousing radical ideologies, such as hosting hate and terrorism contents, are reportedly identified in a more recent report by the Wiesenthal Center's Digital Terror and Hate 2.0 (Simon Wiesenthal Center 2008). Such sites target the digital generation—the young and the Internet-aware—particularly within the Muslim community. The latter, with a shallow understanding of Islam, may be vulnerable to the seductive propaganda posted on such sites and forums.

In 2007, Singapore's Internal Security Department investigated Internet-driven radicalization cases involving Singaporeans attracted to terrorist and radical ideas on the Internet (Kor 2007). More recently, in April 2010, a full-time national serviceman in the army was arrested in Singapore under that nation's Internal Security Act. According to the media release from the Ministry of Home Affairs, it was alleged that the accused began searching for jihadist propaganda online while he was a student in one of Singapore's local educational institutions. Over time, the accused became deeply radicalized by the materials he found online and convinced that it was his religious duty to undertake terrorist activities. The accused allegedly went online in search of information on bomb-making, and he produced and posted a video glorifying suicide bombing before being arrested (Ministry of Home Affairs, Singapore 2010). This case and others around the world illustrate some of the ways in which terrorists can exploit the Internet and new media channels (e.g., social networking sites) for criminal purposes.

D. State-Organized Cybercrime

When a government or large commercial network comes under cyber attack, it is not immediately apparent whether the source of the attack is a skillful teenager, an organized crime group, or a nation-state. In fact, it may involve two or more of these. Governments do not always use civil servants to perform their "dirty work." They may turn a blind eye to illegality that is seen as serving state interests. They may offer tacit, or even active, encouragement to cyber criminals.

A number of prominent attacks, the origins of which remain obscure, have occurred in recent years. The cyber attacks against government servers in Estonia in April 2007 apparently sought to intimidate the Estonian government and its people for having relocated a Soviet-era memorial to fallen Russian soldiers. It has been suggested that criminal organizations played a significant role in the attacks; the degree to which the Russian government was complicit remains unclear (Landler and Markoff 2007).

In March 2009, it was revealed that a number of computer systems serving the Dalai Lama's Tibetan exile centers around the world had been penetrated by a sophisticated surveillance system. The scale of the surveillance activity, which was traced to three sites in China as well as to a webhosting service in Southern California, seemed to indicate government activity. It was suggested the work may have involved patriotic hackers who were associated with, but independent of, the state.[4] The Chinese government dismissed the suggestion that it was involved in the surveillance (Markoff 2009; Munk Centre 2009). Cybercriminals can make use of various technologies, including launching a cyber attack from proxy servers in third countries to conceal their identity. Definitive attribution of the source(s) of any cyber attack is no easy task and can be very time consuming. It largely depends on the technical expertise of perpetrators and several other factors, including the jurisdiction from which they operate. State-sponsored cyber attacks are no longer fiction, but the question remains: "How does one determine whether an attack is criminal or an act of cyber war?"

In January 2010, Google announced that it had become the target of a sophisticated and coordinated attack, apparently originating in China, that resulted in the accessing of Gmail accounts, including those of Chinese human rights activists. The Chinese government denied responsibility. More broadly, the US government, assisted by the telecommunications industry, engaged in widespread illegal interception of telecommunications traffic during the George W. Bush administration (Bamford 2008).

In 2010, it became apparent that a worm malware referred to as "Stuxnet" had disrupted centrifuges essential to uranium enrichment processes in Iran. Analysis of Stuxnet suggested that the malware was designed to reprogram the ICS "by modifying code on programmable logic controllers (PLCs) to make them work in a manner the attacker intended and to hide those changes from the operator of the equipment" and the malware consisted of "[several] zero-day exploits, a Windows rootkit, the first ever PLC rootkit, antivirus evasion techniques, complex process injection and hooking code, network infection routines, peer-to-peer updates, and a command and control interface" (Falliere, Murchu, and Chien 2010, pp. 1–2). The degree of sophistication of the code, the knowledge of Siemens control systems necessary for its development, the need for testing and refinement of the worm, and the challenge of its ultimate insertion in relevant Iranian computer systems suggest that it was the work of state actors, subsequently reported to be the United States and Israel (Markoff 2010, 2011; Sanger 2012).

In 2011, South Korean authorities accused China-based North Korean hackers of infiltrating online gaming sites. After establishing robot accounts and using automated software, the players allegedly accumulated gaming points and exchanged them for cash. A percentage of the proceeds was reportedly retained by the players and the remainder transferred to North Korea (Choe 2011).

Cybercrime, in general, and organized cybercrime, in particular, are following two basic trends: sophistication and commercialization.

E. Sophistication

Technology does not stand still, and those who seek to make best use of it, for purposes legitimate or otherwise, must keep abreast of the latest developments. The trajectory is a long one from using commercial off-the-shelf (COTS) technology to scan and duplicate $50 notes to the industrial-sized operations for the manufacture of pirated DVDs.

Viruses and worms once took days to spread around the globe. They now take minutes to do so. Malicious code can be designed to look for openings and, once it invades a target computer, to cover its own tracks (Thompson 2004; Markoff and Vance 2010); it can also be designed to allow remote control of a computer, enabling the intruder to activate audio and video recording features and to capture the information contained therein (Markoff 2009). The scope and complexity of the attack against the Dali Lama's systems appears to be without precedent, as does the domestic electronic surveillance practiced by the US government. The "Stuxnet" worm that infected Iranian nuclear facilities in 2010 was precisely calibrated and apparently the work of a skilled team of programmers (Broad and Sanger 2010). On a more modest level, participants in an international stock fraud conspiracy (discussed below) used special software to conceal the origin of their Spam emails and to circumvent their recipients' Spam filters. (US Department of Justice 2009a).

F. Commercialization

At the dawn of the digital age, much computer crime took place for fun rather than for profit. The distribution of illicit images of children occurred in the context of a barter economy. Other computer criminals were motivated by the intellectual challenge, by adventure, or by rebellious spirit rather than by mercenary considerations. Practitioners of digital piracy gave products away rather than selling them. Virus writers regarded their activity as an art form rather than as a way to make a living. Today, the services of accomplished hackers are available for hire; a criminal group can rent robot networks for use in spamming, denial of service attacks, or extortion, and digital piracy has become big business. Additional categories of financially motivated cybercrimes include:

Computer or network intrusions such as hacking and unauthorized access to obtain sensitive information. For example, in 1994, A Russian named Vladimir Levin obtained access to the servers of Citibank in the United States. He was able to impersonate legitimate Citibank account holders and began to transfer funds from their accounts to new accounts opened by his accomplices around the world. The fraud was detected, and the accomplices were arrested when they attempted to withdraw the money (Smith, Grabosky, and Urbas 2004, p. 51).

In August 2008, 11 individuals (including three US citizens, one from Estonia, three from Ukraine, two from the People's Republic of China, one from Belarus, and one with unknown place of origin) were charged with numerous crimes, including conspiracy, computer intrusion, fraud, and identity theft. It was alleged that the group members were involved in the hacking of nine major US retailers and the theft and sale of more than 40 million credit and debit card numbers. These numbers were used to withdraw tens of thousands of dollars from ATMs (US Department of Justice 2008).

Phishing: Internet scams frequently use unsolicited messages purporting to originate from a legitimate source to deceive individuals or organizations into disclosing their financial and/or personal identity information. This information can then be used to commit or facilitate crimes such as fraud, identity theft, and stealing of sensitive information (e.g., banking credentials or trade secrets). Several researchers and security practitioners have also noted the involvement of organized crime groups in phishing scams. A large conspiracy involving 38 individuals in Romania and the United States obtained credit card details through phishing. They then used these details in the counterfeiting of credit cards (US Federal Bureau of Investigation 2008a, 2008b).

Spam is unsolicited commercial email intended to persuade recipients to buy products, legitimate or otherwise. Spam may also be used to spread false rumors about stocks traded on stock exchanges around the world. In November 2009, four men were sentenced in the United States for their participation in an international stock fraud scheme. They purchased thinly traded shares and then used mass emails to spread false rumors about the shares likely increase in price. When the price of the shares increased, the conspirators sold their holdings for a profit (US Department of Justice 2009a).

Malware creation and dissemination: Malware, also known as malicious software, is designed to install itself on a computer without the computer owner's informed consent, particularly if it does so in a way that may compromise the security of the computer. Malware includes Trojans, viruses, and worms. The 2008 UK Threat Assessment report noted that "most new malware is designed to steal financial data (such as credit card details, bank account details, passwords, PIN numbers) as a precursor to various frauds and other deceptions" (SOCA 2008, p. 9). In 2009, Albert Gonzalez, a resident of Miami, Florida, pleaded guilty to controlling a number of servers and granting access to other hackers with the knowledge that they would use their access to store malware and then attack corporate victims. Their ultimate objective appears to have been theft of credit card details. Gonzalez used multiple antivirus programs to test the quality of his malware (US Department of Justice 2009b).

Internet frauds and scams are limited only by the imagination of prospective criminals. Offenses of this type include Nigerian advance fee frauds (also known as 419 scams), online auction frauds, and identity and credit card frauds. Fraudulent investment solicitations are greatly facilitated by digital technology. In 2004, four men pleaded guilty to fraud concerning an Internet-based Ponzi scheme involving 15,000 investors and USD$60 million in investments (US Department of Justice 2004).

G. Countries Involved in Contemporary Cybercrime

Organized cybercrime is a global phenomenon. Those countries that strictly regulate online access (such as Burma) host fewer offenders and have fewer victims. Countries with many persons skilled in information technology, but which offer fewer opportunities for legitimate enrichment (such as Russia), have many offenders. Affluent nations with high individual and corporate connectivity, and with a vibrant e-commerce sector (such as the United States, the United Kingdom, and the countries of continental western Europe), will have more victims. The world's two most populous nations, China and India, are experiencing increasing affluence and digital connectivity; their prominence in cybercrime is likely to increase commensurately.

IV. Responding to Organized Cybercriminal Activities

As the Internet and other forms of information and communications technologies continue to advance, the opportunities for cybercriminal activities will increase. At the same time, the resources and skills of most law enforcement agencies will remain limited. This gap will require an adroit combination of warnings, reassurance, and strategic targeting of the most serious cyber threats. Sovereign states have their own priorities. Authorities in the United States are particularly attentive to online child pornography, theft of (US-owned) intellectual property, and attempts to compromise US government and commercial systems. By contrast, law enforcement in the People's Republic of China is more concerned about comments critical of government policy, including statements advocating Tibetan and Taiwanese independence.

We have noted that cybercrime can be committed by individuals or groups alike as easily from across the globe as from across town. And some organizations themselves transcend national borders. As is the case with terrestrial transnational organized crime, the effective control of transnational cybercrime requires a degree of cooperation between countries. The foundation for this cooperation requires a degree of legislative uniformity, common priorities, and adequate investigative capacity.

A. Self-Defense

Regardless of whether or not the perpetrator is organized, the first line of defense against cybercrime is self-defense. Just as is the case in the terrestrial world, people with assets to protect should safeguard them. At the most basic level, parents should exercise a degree of supervision over their children's use of digital technology to reduce the likelihood of their becoming victims or offenders. Ordinary users should invest in an appropriate level of security software, safeguard their PIN numbers, and avoid unsolicited overtures from suspect sources. Large organizations that may be vulnerable to attack should have a security system in place commensurate with the assets that they need to protect. Fortunately, enormous incentives are in place for commercial actors to contribute to cyberspace security. Untold riches await those who can design systems that are easy to use but difficult to exploit for criminal purposes.

B. Capacity Building

Jurisdictions need the legislative and enforcement capacity to respond to cybercrime as it continues to evolve. Because cyber attacks can originate from almost anywhere and can be routed through numerous jurisdictions en route to their target, it is in the interest of all nations that those on the disadvantaged side of the digital divide have the resources to allow cooperation with their better endowed counterparts. Unfortunately, this is easier said than done. The poorest nations cannot afford to pay their police much less establish high-tech crime squads.

Essential to successful interdiction of cross-national organized cybercrime are three factors, namely (1) legislative harmony, (2) a framework of law enforcement cooperation, and (3) the capacity to investigate and, if necessary, to prosecute. The first steps in this direction were taken by the G-8 and by the Council of Europe, whose cybercrime convention has served as a legislative and policy model for a number of non-European nations, including Australia and Japan. The UN Convention against Transnational Crime provides a further framework.

Not all of the world's nations are equally enthusiastic about the Council of Europe Cybercrime Convention, however. Those who were not involved in the laborious work of drafting the convention may feel a lack of "ownership." Others, recalling the history of European imperialism, may harbor suspicions of policies emanating from Europe. Alternative protocols have thus been proposed with a view toward obtaining the imprimatur of the United Nations (Schjolberg and Ghernaouti-Helie 2009).

C. Public/Private Cooperation

In years past, police in many countries would portray themselves as omniscient, omnicompetent, and omnipresent. This posture of invincibility was central to their strategy of public reassurance. More recently, police have conceded that the volume of cyber-crime exceeds their capacity to control it on their own. Thus, they have sought to form partnerships with a variety of nonstate actors.

This is entirely appropriate as a great deal of knowledge about cybercrime and its control resides outside of the public sector. The information security industry, for example, commands vast expertise. Software and entertainment industries are often very knowledgeable about the risks they face and about where these risks originate. Large corporations such as Microsoft provide training programs for law enforcement agencies around the world, and they offer monetary rewards for information leading to the identification of virus writers.

D. International Cooperation

Organized cybercrime has proven to be a daunting challenge for law enforcement but not an insurmountable one. One could cite a number of successful investigations, not only within a given jurisdiction, but also investigations of cross-national criminal activity involving law enforcement agencies from many countries. A number of cross-national investigations of organized cybercrime groups have been successful. Among many others, these include the case involving the arrest of two Romanian citizens on an Interpol warrant. Both defendants were extradited to the United States and were charged each with one count of conspiracy to commit fraud in connection with access devices, one count of conspiracy to commit bank fraud, and one count of aggravated identity theft. It was alleged that both defendants and five other Romanian citizens participated in an Internet phishing scheme that victimized individuals, financial institutions, and companies (US Federal Bureau of Investigation 2009).

E. Cyber Security Research

Although networks and software breaches often attract most of the media's attention when it comes to cybersecurity, hardware is similarly vulnerable. A hardware breach can be more difficult to detect and, hence, defend against than a network or software intrusion. The challenge for the public and private sectors is to design technologies that are robust in the sense that their legitimate use is minimally constrained but their illegitimate use is prevented or discouraged (Grabosky 2007). A need exists, arguably, for more research to be funded to find ways to mitigate existing and new cybersecurity risks.

Governments are wise to invest significantly in education, science, and R&D. Doing so would enable information security researchers to play a more significant role in designing state-of-the-art cryptographic software and hardware that can be deployed in an online environment. Of course, criminals are also able to develop and use technologies in furtherance of their own objectives. The future of organized cybercrime seems likely to be characterized by a continuing technological "arms race."

V. Conclusion

Few today would challenge the assertion that the era of globalization has been accompanied by an increase in transnational organized crime. Digital technology has empowered traditional criminal organizations, dramatically increasing the ease with which they can commit offenses such as fraud and extortion. It has also enabled the emergence of entirely new crime groups and entirely new crime types, such as online piracy and vandalism. It is likely that, as digital technology becomes more pervasive, its use as an instrument and as a target of organized crime will become increasingly common. Every new technology, and every new application, will be potentially vulnerable to criminal exploitation. It is also likely that new organizational forms will emerge to combat cybercrime. These forms could entail increasingly integrated international and public/private partnerships. Indeed, Susan Brenner has suggested that, one day, the response to cybercrime may be the responsibility of a private multinational body (Brenner, 2002). This may sound farfetched, but it is no more farfetched than was the idea of cybercrime itself a generation ago.

Notes

1. A botnet ("robot network") is a network of individual computers infected with bot malware. These compromised computers are also known as zombies or zombie computers. The zombies, under the control of the botnet controller, can then be used as remote attack tools to facilitate the sending of spam, hosting of phishing websites, distribution of malware, and mounting denial of service attacks. Building botnets requires minimal levels of expertise (Ianelli and Hackworth 2005). A brief two-step overview on how to build a botnet is outlined in Choo (2007).
2. http://www.justice.gov/usao/fls/PressReleases/Attachments/090521-02.Indictment.pdf.
3. http://www.justice.gov/usao/nye/vw/PendingCases/CR-03-304_Indictment_S6-_US_v_SALVATORE_LOCASCIO.pdf.
4. Among the many classified US government documents published by Wikileaks in November 2010 were allegations that the Chinese government orchestrated a systematic campaign of computer intrusions, including "government operatives, private security experts," and specially recruited "internet outlaws" (Shane and Lehren 2010).

References

Bamford, James. 2008. *The Shadow Factory: The Ultra-secret NSA from 9/11 to the Eavesdropping on America.* New York: Doubleday.

Brenner, S. W. 2002. "Organized Cybercrime? How Cyberspace May Affect the Structure of Criminal Relationships." *North Carolina Journal of Law & Technology* 4(1):1–50.

Broad, William J., and David E. Sanger. 2010. "Worm Was Perfect for Sabotaging Centrifuges." *New York Times* (November 18). http://www.nytimes.com/2010/11/19/world/middleeast/19stuxnet.html?pagewanted=2&emc=eta1

Chang, Yao Chung. 2012. *Cybercrime in the Greater China Region: Regulatory Responses and Crime Prevention Across the Taiwan Strait.* Cheltenham: Edward Elgar

Child Exploitation and Online Protection. 2007. "Global Online Child Abuse Network Smashed - CEOP lead international operation into UK based paedophile ring." CEOP (June 18) http://www.ceop.police.uk/Media-Centre/Press-releases/2007/Global-Online-Child-Abuse-Network-Smashed/

Choe, Sanh Hun. 2011. "Seoul Warns of Latest North Korean Threat: An Army of Online Gaming Hackers." *New York Times* (August 4). http://www.nytimes.com/2011/08/05/world/asia/05korea.html?_r=1&scp=1&sq=north%20korea%20hackers&st=cse

Choo, Kim-Kwang Raymond. 2007. "Zombies and Botnets." *Trends and Issues in Crime and Criminal Justice* 333:1–6. http://www.aic.gov.au/publications/current%20series/tandi/321-340/tandi333.aspx

Choo, Kim-Kwang Raymond. 2008. "Organised Crime Groups in Cyberspace: A Typology." *Trends in Organized Crime* 11(3): 270–95.

Choo, Kim-Kwang Raymond. 2009. *Online Child Grooming: A Literature Review on the Misuse of Social Networking Sites for Grooming Children for Sexual Offences.* Research and Public Policy 103. Canberra: Australian Institute of Criminology. http://www.aic.gov.au/publications/current%20series/rpp/100-120/rpp103.aspx

Choo, Kim-Kwang Raymond, Russell G Smith, and Rob McCusker. 2009. *Future Directions in Technology-Enabled Crime: 2007–09.* Research and Public Policy 78. Canberra: Australian Institute of Criminology. http://www.aic.gov.au/publications/current%20series/rpp/61-80/rpp78.aspx

Douglis, Fred. 2010. "Closing the Open (Face) Book." *IEEE Internet Computing* (September–October): 4–6.

Falliere N., L. O. Murchu, and E. Chien. 2010. *W32.Stuxnet Dossier: Version 1.3* (November 2010). Cupertino, CA: Symantec.

Grabosky, Peter. 2007. "The Internet, Technology, and Organized Crime." *Asian Journal of Criminology* 2(2): 145–161.

Halstead, Boronia. 1998. "The Use of Models in the Analysis of Organized Crime and Development of Policy." *Transnational Organized Crime* 4(1): 1–24.

Holt, Thomas J. 2007. "Subcultural Evolution? Examining the Influence of On- and Off-Line Experiences on Deviant Subcultures." *Deviant Behavior* 28:171–198.

Hutchinson, S., and P. O'Malley. 2007. "A Crime-Terror Nexus? Thinking on Some of the Links between Terrorism and Criminality." *Studies in Conflict & Terrorism*, 30(12): 1095–1107.

Ianelli N., and A. Hackworth. 2005. *Botnets as a Vehicle for Online Crime.* Pittsburgh, PA: CERT Coordination Center.

Institute of Defence and Strategic Studies (IDSS). 2006. *Proceedings of the International Conference on Terrorism in Southeast Asia: The Threat and Response.* http://www.rsis.edu.sg/publications/conference_reports/NEW%20TerrorismSEAConference05.pdf

Kor, Kor Bian. 2007. "S'pore's diy Terror: Who Is This Man." *The New Paper* (Singapore) (June 10).

LaFraniere, Sharon, and Jonathan Ansfield. 2010. "China Alarmed by Threat to Security from Cyberattacks." *New York Times* (February 11). http://www.nytimes.com/2010/02/12/world/asia/12cyberchina.html?emc=eta1

Landler, Mark, and John Markoff. 2007. Digital Fears Emerge after Data Siege in Estonia." *New York Times* (May 29). http://www.nytimes.com/2007/05/29/technology/29estonia. html

Markoff, John. 2009. "Tracking Cyberspies through the Web Wilderness." *New York Times* (May 29). http://www.nytimes.com/2009/05/12/science/12cyber.html?scp=106&sq=dalai+ lama&st=nyt

Markoff, John. 2010. "A Silent Attack, but Not a Subtle One." *New York Times* (September 26). http://www.nytimes.com/2010/09/27/technology/27virus.html?scp=5&sq=stuxnet&st=cse

Markoff, John. 2011. "Malware Aimed at Iran Hit Five Sites, Report Says." *New York Times* (February 11). http://www.nytimes.com/2011/02/13/science/13stuxnet.html?scp=3&sq= stuxnet&st=cse

Markoff, John, and Ashlee Vance. 2010. "Fearing Hackers Who Leave No Trace." *New York Times* (January 19). http://www.nytimes.com/2010/01/20/technology/20code. html?scp=4&sq=markoff&st=nyt

McAfee. 2006. *Virtual Criminology Report: Organised Crime and the Internet*. Santa Clara, CA: McAfee.

McCusker, Rob. 2006. "Transnational Organised Cyber Crime: Distinguishing Threat from Reality." *Crime, Law and Social Change* 46(4–5): 257–273.

Ministry of Home Affairs, Singapore (MHA). 2010. "Detention, Imposition of Restriction Orders and Release under the Internal Security Act, July 06, 2010." *Media release* (July 6). http://www.singaporeunited.sg/cep/index.php/web/Our-News/Detention-Imposition-O f-Restriction-Orders-And-Release-Under-The-Internal-Security-Act

Morton, Tom. 2004. "Mutating Mobiles." Background Briefing, ABC Radio National (April 25). http://www.abc.net.au/radionational/programs/backgroundbriefing/mutating-mobiles/34 08828#transcript

Munk Centre for International Studies. 2009. "Tracking GhostNet: Investigating a *Cyber Espionage* Network." Toronto: Munk Centre. http://www.nartv.org/mirror/ghostnet.pdf

National Infrastructure Advisory Council (NIAC). 2004. *Prioritizing Cyber Vulnerabilities*. http://www.dhs.gov/xlibrary/assets/niac/NIAC_CyberVulnerabilitiesPaper_Feb05.pdf

National Infrastructure Protection Center 2001. *Cyber Protests: The Threat to the U.S. Information Infrastructure*. National Infrastructure Protection Center, Washington. http:// www.au.af.mil/au/awc/awcgate/nipc/cyberprotests.htm

Organisation for Economic Co-operation and Development (OECD). 2007. *The Economic Impact of Counterfeiting and Piracy*. Paris: Organisation for Economic Co-operation and Development. http://www.oecd.org/dataoecd/11/38/38704571.pdf

Perry, Michael. 2005. "Sydney Violence Fueled by Race, Ignorance and Youth." *New York Times* (December 15). http://www.redorbit.com/modules/news/tools.php?tool=print&id=330837

Pfanner, Eric. 2011. "Cameron Exploring Crackdown on Social Media after Riots." *New York Times* (August 11). http://www.nytimes.com/2011/08/12/world/europe/12iht-social12.html? scp=1&sq=social+media+london+riots&st=nyt

Preston, Jennifer. 2011. "Movement Began with Outrage and a Facebook Page That Gave It an Outlet." *New York Times* (February 5). http://www.nytimes.com/2011/02/06/world/ middleeast/06face.html?pagewanted=1&sq=socialmediaegypt&st=cse&scp=2

Queens County District Attorney. 2011. "111 Individuals Charged in Massive International Identity Theft and Counterfeit Credit Card Operation Based in Queens." *Media release* (October 7). http://www.queensda.org/newpressreleases/2011/october/op%20swiper_ credit%20card_id%20fraud_10_07_2011_ind.pdf

Sanderson, Thomas. 2004. "Transnational Terror and Organized Crime: Blurring the Lines." *SAIS Review* 24(1): 49–61.

Sanger, David. 2012. *Confront and Conceal: Obama's Secret Wars and Surprising Use of American Power.* New York: Crown.

Schjolberg, Stein, and Solange Ghernaouti-Helie. 2009. *A Global Protocol on Cybersecurity and Cybercrime.* Oslo: Cybercrimedata.

Schneider, Jacqueline L. 2003. "Hiding in Plain Sight: An Exploration of the Activities of a Drugs Newsgroup." *Howard Journal of Criminal Justice* 42(4): 372–389.

Serious Organised Crime Agency (SOCA). 2008. *The United Kingdom Threat Assessment of Serious Organised Crime.* London: Serious Organised Crime Agency.

Shane, Scott, and Andrew W. Lehren. 2010. "Cables Obtained by WikiLeaks Shine Light into Secret Diplomatic Channels." *New York Times* (November 28). http://www.nytimes.com/2010/11/29/world/29cables.html?hp

Simon Wiesenthal Center. 2008. *iReport: Online Terror + Hate: The First Decade.* http://www.wiesenthal.com/atf/cf/%7BDFD2AAC1-2ADE-428A-9263-35234229D8D8%7D/IREPORT.PDF

Sipress, A. 2004. "An Indonesian's Prison Memoir Takes Holy War into Cyberspace: In Sign of New Threat, Militant Offers Tips on Credit Card Fraud." *Washington Post* (December 14). http://msl1.mit.edu/furdlog/docs/washpost/2004-12-14_washpost_jihadis_online.pdf

Smith, Russell G., Peter Grabosky, and Greg Urbas. 2004. *Cyber Criminals on Trial.* Cambridge: Cambridge University Press.

Tapscott, Don, and Anthony D. Williams. 2006. *Wikinomics: How Mass Collaboration Changes Everything.* London: Atlantic.

Thomas, T. L. 2003. "Al Qaeda and the Internet: The Danger of 'Cyberplanning.'" *Parameters* 33(1): 112–123. http://www.iwar.org.uk/cyberterror/resources/cyberplanning/al-qaeda.htm

Thompson, Clive. 2004. "The Virus Underground." *New York Times Magazine* (February 8). http://www.nytimes.com/2004/02/08/magazine/the-virus-underground.html

Tokyo Reporter. 2009. "On the 'Tokyo Vice' Beat with Jake Adelstein." (October 27). http://www.tokyoreporter.com/2009/10/27/on-the-tokyo-vice-beat-with-jake-adelstein/

Urbas, Gregor. 2006. "Cross-National Investigation and Prosecution of Intellectual Property Crimes: The Example of 'Operation Buccaneer.'" *Crime Law and Social Change* 46(4–5): 207–221.

US Department of Justice. 2004. "Fourth Defendant in Massive Internet Scam Pleads Guilty to Fraud and Money Laundering Charges Case Involves $60 Million in Investments by 15,000 Investors." *Media release* (November 18). http://www.justice.gov/criminal/cybercrime/press-releases/2004/nordickPlea_triwest.htm

US Department of Justice. 2005. "Former FBI Agent Pleads Guilty to Obstruction of Justice." *Media release* (June 23). http://www.justice.gov/usao/nye/pr/2005/2005jun23.html

US Department of Justice. 2008a. "Retail Hacking Ring Charged for Stealing and Distributing Credit and Debit Card Numbers from Major US Retailers." *Media release* (August 5). http://www.justice.gov/opa/pr/2008/August/08-ag-689.html

US Department of Justice. 2008b. "38 Individuals in US and Romania Charged in Two Related Cases of Computer Fraud Involving International Organized Crime: International Law Enforcement Cooperation Leads to Disruption of Organized Crime Ring Operating in US and Romania." *Media release* (May 19). http://www.justice.gov/opa/pr/2008/May/08_odag_434.html

US Department of Justice. 2009a. "Detroit Spammer and Three Co-conspirators Sentenced for Multi-million Dollar E-mail Stock Fraud Scheme." *Media release* (November 23). http://www.justice.gov/opa/pr/2009/November/09-crm-1275.html

US Department of Justice. 2009b. "Major International Hacker Pleads Guilty for Massive Attack on US Retail and Banking Networks." *Media release* (December 29). http://www.justice.gov/opa/pr/2009/December/09-crm-1389.html

US Department of Justice. 2010. "High Ranking Crime Family Soldier Pleads Guilty to Racketeering Charge." *Media release* (January 5). http://www.justice.gov/usao/nj/Press/files/pdffiles/2010/mer00105%20rel.pdf

US Federal Bureau of Investigation. 2008. "Gone Phishing: Global Ring Gets Rather Slick." (May). http://www.fbi.gov/page2/may08/phishing_052008.html

US Federal Bureau of Investigation. 2009. "Two Romanian Citizens Extradited to the United States to Face Charges Related to Alleged Phishing Scheme." *Media release.* (September 29). http://www.fbi.gov/newhaven/press-releases/2009/nh092909.htm

White, Rob. 2006. "Swarming and the Social Dynamics of Group Violence." *Trends and Issues in Crime and Criminal Justice* 326:1–6.

Williams, Phil. 2001. "Transnational Criminal Networks." In *Networks and Netwars,* edited by John Arquilla and David Ronfeldt. Santa Monica, CA: RAND Corporation, 61–97.

CHAPTER 25

....

THE ILLEGAL EXPLOITATION OF NATURAL RESOURCES

....

TIM BOEKHOUT VAN SOLINGE

I. INTRODUCTION

....

Natural resource exploitation is a mostly unexplored field of study for criminologists. There is, however, good reason to include natural resources in (organized) crime studies as they represent a lucrative illegal source of revenues for criminal, as well as militant and rebel, organizations. The extraction and trade in such resources can be considered an organized crime activity, if a broad definition of organized crime is accepted (see "Organized Crime: A Contested Concept"). The policy emphasis on conventional illegal goods such as illicit drugs draws attention away from these other, lesser-known sources of illegal revenues. The case of the Taliban in Pakistan well exemplifies this neglect. While drugs are often assumed to be the main commodities funding this movement, natural resources such as timber, emeralds, and other gemstones were for several years, until well into 2009, very important, if not the predominant, sources of income for this organization (Yusufzai and Wilkonson 2009; Khan 2010; Rodriguez 2010).

The term "natural resources" refers to materials or substances such as minerals, forests, water, and fertile land that occur in nature and can be used for economic gain (*New Oxford Dictionary* 2007). Natural resources cover a wide spectrum, and obviously not all are discussed here. This contribution focuses on some of the planet's richest natural resources, tropical rainforests, and some of the natural resources found there. In all of the presented cases, a substantial part of the natural resource exploitation is illegal.[1]

In the economic and natural resources literature, "resource curse" is a well-known expression. It refers to the fact that resource-rich countries on average experience less development than do countries without those resources: lower economic growth rates, lower levels of human development, and more inequality and poverty (Sachs and Warner 2001; Kolstad and Søreide 2009, p. 214). Having many natural resources thus paradoxically appears detrimental to a country's economic development. There is also evidence, especially for African countries, that an abundance of natural resources is the single most important factor determining whether a country experiences civil war (Collier and Hoeffler 1998, 2002).

This contribution gives a new, or additional, meaning to the concept of "resource curse." The presence of natural resources, in particular in forested tropical regions with low population density and weak governance, not only makes it likely that a resource-rich country or area will perform relatively poorly in economic terms but also makes that country vulnerable for criminal activities such as illegal natural resource exploitation, corruption, collusion, and, in some cases, (systematic) violence. In this way, the resource curse is a crime curse, too: the presence of many natural resources correlates with crime and violence.

Corruption is the main reason why resource-rich countries perform poorly economically (Kolstad and Søreide 2009, p. 214). Corruption also plays an important facilitating role in illegal logging practices (FAO and ITTO 2005; Koyuncu and Yilmaz 2009; Miller 2011). However, the fact that corruption is prevalent in illegal logging and other (illegal) natural resource exploitations does not necessarily mean that organized crime is involved. How can we, then, characterize the activities and actors (including individuals, organizations, and networks) that are involved in the (illegal) exploitation of natural resources, and is it justified to label them as organized crime? These are the two core questions this chapter aims to answer.

These research questions lead to a number of subquestions about the phenomenon of illegal resource exploitation of tropical rainforests, as well as about the actors involved, their revenues, and the policies adopted to control natural resource exploitation. What is illegal or otherwise harmful about resource exploitation, who are the actors involved, and to which extent are they organized? Also, what is known about the markets, their mechanisms, and the revenues? Finally, what are the policies with regard to (illegal) resource exploitation?

To answer these questions, this essay presents several case studies of (illegal) resource exploitation and trafficking. All are located in tropical regions and concern economically developing or emerging countries. With the partial exception of one case (Liberian timber), the natural resource exploitation is illegal. The first case (section 3) discusses the large-scale illegal timber exploitation in Indonesia. This is followed by section 4, on resource exploitation of the rainforests in West Africa (Sierra Leone and Liberia) and Central Africa (the Democratic Republic of Congo). The final case study (section 5) is about resource exploitation in Amazonia, the rainforest around the Amazon River in South America. In such a way, all three of the planet's largest tropical rainforests are discussed in this chapter—ranked in size respectively: the rainforests of Amazonia (mainly Brazil), the rainforest in Central Africa (mainly DR Congo), and the rainforests of Southeast Asia (mainly Indonesia).[2] All three are also equatorial rainforests, the planet's most biodiverse areas. Before discussing the case studies, section 2 positions the theme of tropical deforestation within the realm of criminology and explains why it is relevant to include non-Western and environmental subjects such as tropical deforestation in criminological research.

Various data and methods were used for the writing of this essay. Some data were gathered by the author via qualitative methods, such as interviews, observations, and ethnographic fieldwork.[3] Most data, however, derive from written sources: scientific publications, press articles, and nongovernment organization (NGO) reports. NGOs such as the Environmental Investigation Agency (EIA) have produced valuable and impressive reports on illegal resource exploitation, such as the criminal networks involved in the large-scale illegal logging of, for example, Indonesia's rainforests (EIA and Telapak 2004, 2005, 2006, 2010). More generally, NGOs have devoted much more attention to illegal resource exploitation than criminologists and law enforcement agencies. This not only means that they often have more specialized knowledge about these illegal activities and the players involved but also means that they show themselves, more so than the official enforcement agencies, to be vanguards of the environment and environmental laws and regulations.

II. The Globalization and Greening of Criminology

Criminological journals, handbooks, and conferences show that criminology devotes relatively little attention to harms and crimes outside the Western world. Criminology's Western or "Northern" bias (Olmo 1984; Nelken 1994; Agozino 2003) means it is dominated by Western research themes, usually based on crime priorities of Western governments and their law enforcement agencies, and also framed in their language, as Hulsman (1986) in particular and other critical criminologists after him have shown.

From a global perspective, it would be logical to also pay attention to the harms and crimes outside the Western world. It can be argued that most victims of (organized) crime live there, not in the West. However, in "Southern" developing and emerging countries with relatively weaker governments and rule of law, not many criminologists are around and, if they are, investigating illegal activities in which the economically, politically, or militarily powerful may be involved is more difficult and dangerous than in the West. Still, from the perspective of international victimization in this globalized age, it would be fair to abandon the limited, Western bias and address crime issues on all continents.

Criminological publications and conferences generally play little attention to environmental harms and crimes. These are often considered more environmental than criminal issues and investigating them generally has a lower status among criminologists and law enforcers than investigating the traditional vices and crimes. Green crimes are often considered "soft" crimes, less harmful and leading to fewer victims than the traditional, "real" predatory crimes. Exceptions are environmental crimes in corporate crime studies (Huisman 2010) and waste disposal in organized crime studies, because of the involvement of the American and Italian mafias and Japanese Yakuza (Block and Scarpitti 1985; Hill 2003; Ruggiero 1996; Ruggiero and South 2010).[4]

Criminology, however, is rapidly becoming more international and globalized (Marshal, Ineke Haen, and Kristiina Kangaspunta. 2006, p. 7). Criminology is also becoming greener, as is shown by the rapid growth of one of its youngest branches, green criminology. It takes environmental harm as an explicit perspective, extends the concept of victimization beyond humans, and has introduced concepts like ecological justice (White 2008). Green criminology handbooks have appeared (Beirne and South 2007, Sollund 2008, White 2010); criminology conferences now have panels on green criminology; and in 2011, the journal *Green Criminology* saw light. This essay on tropical deforestation fits into both trends, by focusing on green harms and crimes in non-Western countries.

On a global scale, the logging of tropical rainforests occurs at a speed of several football fields per minute. Until the first years of this century, deforestation in some countries with large tropical rainforests such as Brazil and Indonesia occurred at such a scale that areas corresponding to a quarter to a half of the Netherlands, Switzerland, or Taiwan were logged in one single year.[5] Although deforestation decreased in both tropical countries in the last few years (Lawson and MacFaul 2010), large areas of tropical rainforests continue to be—partly or mostly illegally—logged or burnt.[6]

Illegal logging is widely perceived to be a more serious issue in tropical countries (ITTO 2009, p. 6). A substantial part of the tropical timber that is on the market involves illegal timber. Until only a few years ago, it was a common estimate that about half of the tropical timber on the European and Western markets was of illegal origin (Friends of the Earth 2001; Jaakko Pöyry Consulting 2005). Over the years, however, illegal logging has received much attention by NGOs, international policy makers, and the media. This has resulted, since 2002, in a significant reduction by an estimated 22 percent of illegal logging in some major tropical timber–exporting countries (Lawson and MacFaul 2010, p. 102). This progress, however, does not negate the fact that a substantial part of logging in tropical rainforests remains illegal. For example, while illegal logging in Indonesia was halved since 2006 (from 80 percent to 40 percent of all logging), an illegal share of 40 percent remains substantial (p. 94). In 2009, more than 100 million cubic meters of illegal timber were still being felled worldwide. These illegal logs, laid end to end, would encircle the globe more than 10 times (pp. 102–3).[7]

Illegal logging and, more generally, illegal deforestation have recently entered the realm of organized crime studies (Boekhout van Solinge 2008a), after groundwork was laid down by NGOs: EIA and Telapak (2004, 2005, 2006, 2010), Friends of the Earth (2001), Global Witness (2002), Greenpeace (2001, 2005), and WWF Mexico (2004). Also, academicians from the fields of anthropology, biology, forestry, and geography have published articles about illegal logging.[8] Surprisingly, considering the fact that it clearly concerns an illegal activity, publications in criminological journals or handbooks are hard to find. Numerous well-documented reports and articles thus exist on illegal logging but rarely from a criminological point of view. In a recent, well-documented overview study on illegal logging by the British think-tank Chatham House, the term "criminal" is hardly used and the terms "criminal organizations," "criminal networks," and "organized crime" are not mentioned at all—only "timber mafia" appears once in a footnote (Lawson and MacFaul 2010).

Logging and deforestation are illegal when forest areas are exploited without (governmental) permits or when permits are not respected (FAO and ITTO 2005; MacAllister 1992). Timber products that result from illegal logging practices are logically also illegal.

The value and criminogenic potential of tropical timber are often underestimated. Some hardwoods are so expensive that they are priced in liters. One tree may be worth thousands of euros. For example, the ultimate retail value of one mahogany tree, once turned into furniture, is over US$250,000 (London and Kelly 2007, p. 138). The annual worldwide sales of forest products are estimated at US$1 trillion (Khatchadourian 2008), whereas the illegal timber market is a multibillion-dollar business. The World Bank (2005) estimated that governments were losing US$5 billion in tax revenues as a result of illegal logging.

The harm perspective that is common in green criminology (see Beirne and South 2007) can be easily applied to deforestation, and especially to the (illegal) logging of tropical rainforests. Deforestation studies by NGOs, as well as the few existing criminological publications (Boekhout van Solinge 2008a, 2008b, 2008c, 2010a, 2010b) show there is nothing soft about these crimes. First, as will become clearer from the case studies, tropical deforestation is closely related to the use of violence against forest inhabitants or against environmentalists and human rights activists. Among the victims, indigenous populations are strongly overrepresented, which includes humanity's oldest societies of hunter-gatherers, whose populations are dwindling. The world's last remaining so-called uncontacted tribes, estimated at around 100 and living in the rainforests of the Amazon and New Guinea (Middleton 2007), are particularly threatened (Boekhout van Solinge 2010b). Indigenous people are, however, not the only human victims of deforestation. It is a misconception that all tropical rainforests are mostly inhabited by indigenous people. In the Brazilian Amazon, for example, indigenous populations (some 500,000 people) represent only 2.5 percent of the total human population in that area.[9]

Second, the green criminological perspective used here implies that victims are not exclusively humans. Tropical rainforests are the Earth's most biodiverse places. They cover about 6 percent of the land surface but contain more than half of the known species and organisms. They are, however, "also the leading abattoirs of extinction, shattered into fragments that are then being severely adulterated or erased one by one" (Wilson 2002, p. 59). Tropical deforestation directly leads to the extinction of animal and plant species, which strongly contributes to the current extinction crisis, which may develop into a new mass extinction.[10] The Red List of the World Conservation Union (IUCN) shows that a quarter of the assessed species are currently threatened with extinction. As the biodiversity decline is considered a serious problem, UN Conventions on Biodiversity (CBD) have been adopted. The UN declared 2010 as the International Year of Biodiversity, but a *Science* publication that year showed that biodiversity continued to decline, with increasing risks of species becoming extinct (Butchart et al. 2010).

The animals genetically closest to humans, the great apes, are also seriously threatened with extinction by deforestation. All great apes—chimpanzee, bonobo, gorilla, and orangutan—live in tropical, mainly equatorial rainforests. Contributing to their near extinction in the wild is wildlife trade and poaching (for bush meat), both of which are stimulated by deforestation (Boekhout van Solinge 2008*b*, 2008*c*).

Third, many, if not all, humans, and particularly future generations, may potentially become victims of tropical deforestation as it accounts for 17 percent of global carbon emissions, more than all forms of transport combined (IPCC 2007, p. 5; Tollefson 2007). It now seems to be scientifically established knowledge, partly due to the UN's Intergovernmental Panel on Climate Change (IPCC), that deforestation contributes to greenhouse gasses and climate change.[11]

III. Timber Syndicates in Equatorial Asia

Asia's largest rainforests are found in and around Indonesia, famously described by Alfred Wallace in *The Malay Archipelago: The Land of the Orangutan, and the Bird of Paradise* (1869). Forests that in Wallace's time were dense and immense have considerably shrunk or disappeared. Most of Java's forests have disappeared, and Sumatra's and Borneo's lowlands have largely been deforested.[12] The Moluccas, the former Spice Islands, also suffer from illegal logging.[13] More recent is the illegal logging on the only remaining large island that has not yet been subjected to widespread deforestation: New Guinea.[14]

The large-scale logging of Indonesia's forests started in the 1970s when logging concessions were given to foreign (mostly Japanese) companies. It increased further during the 1980s and 1990s and stimulated economic liberalization (Tsing 2005), the fall of the Suharto regime in 1998 (Nellemann et al. 2007, p. 21), and the policy of decentralization and regional autonomy since 2001 (Boekhout van Solinge 2008*c*). Combined with prevalent corruption, it resulted in some 80 percent of all logging being illegal (Nellemann 2007; Boekhout van Solinge 2008*c*).

Between 1985 and 1997, Indonesia's national forest cover loss was 1.9 percent per year, with some areas such as Sumatra and Kalimantan having forest losses of 2.5 percent per year (Wicke et al. 2011, p. 200). In the 30 years between 1975 and 2005, Indonesia's forest cover decreased from 130 million hectares to 91 million hectares (Wicke et al. 2011). This corresponds to a total deforestation of 390,000 km^2, an area larger than Germany, and an average annual deforestation of 13,000 km^2, an area slightly smaller than Northern Ireland. This made Indonesia's forest-clearing rate among the highest in the world (Hansen et al. 2009).

The main causes for deforestation in Indonesia have been logging for timber, mining, palm oil, and—less known—paper. The world's two largest paper pulp factories, owned by APP and RAPP, are, however, found on the island of Sumatra. Both companies have been accused, mainly by NGOs, of also logging illegally.[15] The logging of rainforest by paper companies has led to friction between the national police, who have confiscated hundreds of thousands of cubic meters of wood from paper companies RAPP and IKPP because of their alleged illegality, and the Ministry of Forestry, who have stated that the logging was legal.[16]

The different Indonesian elites—economic, military, and political—have prof-ited most from (illegal) deforestation. These elites regularly overlap: some politicians own logging companies, which facilitates corruption and collusion. Complicating the Indonesian case further is the major role of the army, which owns many commercial companies, including timber companies.[17]

Tsing (2005) gave a detailed account of the Indonesian deforestation disaster. It has led to conflicts between loggers and villagers and between villages and fueled ethnic conflicts. She described how economic liberalization made the lines between public, private, and criminal exploitation unclear. Also, the "slippage back and forth between military and private enterprise" and the "fluidity between public and private" made it difficult to distinguish between domestic, foreign, and government ownership. The mil-itary, of course, has the advantage of having "the muscle to make the best deals" (Tsing 2005, pp. 34–7). It has created an "authoritarian lawlessness that made resources free for those who could take them," while "violence became key to ownership" (Tsing 2005, pp. 67–8).

Not only the army but also the police are involved in illegal logging, although in a less structural way than the army. In 2005, in Indonesian Borneo, hundreds of trucks with illegal meranti timber from Betung Kerihun National Park were trafficked daily to Malaysian Borneo (Sarawak).[18] A new police chief was appointed—after his predecessor was fired for being involved in timber smuggling—who had arrested some Malaysians working for a Chinese Malaysian timber baron. Despite the arrest, anyone traveling in the border area saw that trafficking continued, with illegal logs stacked up high or made into rafts, waiting for border crossing. The police chief explained the low level of law enforcement as being due to the lack of equipment such as four-wheel drive vehicles. Ironically, several confiscated Malaysian four-wheel drive vehicles were stationed at the police station. The scale of the smuggling was so massive that corruption or collusion seems likely.[19]

EIA and the Indonesian NGO Telapak (2005) have revealed some of the syndicates involved in timber trafficking from Papua. Merbau timber was illegally logged with the involvement of the Indonesian military, while brokers and banks in Jakarta, Singapore, and Hong Kong facilitated monthly timber shipments of some 300,000 cubic meters to China, where the timber was processed and consequently exported worldwide (mainly for flooring in Western countries). Chinese Malaysians coordinated the trafficking and arranged for Malaysian documents. It partly explains why for years, several millions of cubic meters of "Malaysian timber are from unknown sources" (Lawson and MacFaul 2010, p. 96). Collusion facilitates it, because, just like in Indonesia, Malaysia's economic and political elites overlap (Jomo et al. 2004, p. 211).

The EIA/Telapak 2006 study prompted Indonesian President Yudhoyono to send army troops to Papua for a crackdown on forestry officials, army personnel, military police, Malaysian financiers, and timber traders. Increased national awareness and (international) attention, led by more law enforcement, reduced illegal logging by half, from 80 to 40 percent of all logging (Lawson and MacFaul 2010, p. 94). A new EIA/ Telapak study (2010), however, showed that few of the (illegal) timber entrepreneurs involved or coordinating illegal logging were caught and that even fewer were sanctioned. In 2010, President Yudhoyono reacted to the poor performance of the judicial system toward illegal logging—which, according to a 2005 estimate, resulted in US$2 billion in lost resources annually. He consequently ordered the newly created Taskforce for the Eradication of Judicial Mafia to examine suspicious verdicts in illegal logging cases (p. 3). Surveyed international timber experts considered corruption—particularly among the judiciary—to be the most important aspect of illegal logging in Indonesia (Lawson and MacFaul 2010, pp. 43, 86).

IV. Plunder in Equatorial and West Africa

In Africa, natural resource exploitation and trade have a long history, with caravan routes transporting gold from West Africa. Later, European colonizers named some countries after exploited resources, such as Côte d'Ivoire and Gold Coast, today's Ghana.

Africa has remained rich in natural resources: precious metals and stones like gold and diamonds, metals and minerals like copper, cobalt, and, increasingly, coltan, which is used in laptops and cell phones. More than anywhere else, natural resource exploitation is connected to armed conflicts. Over the past decades, it has made Africa the most war-hit continent and the main destination of "small" arms like Kalashnikovs (IANSA et al. 2007; Naím 2007, p. 55).

The country that best shows the relationship between armed conflict and illegal resource exploitation is the Democratic Republic of Congo. Its conflict officially ended in 2003, but in some areas, especially in Eastern Congo, it still continues. This war is sometimes referred to as the African World War, because it involved eight countries and resulted in over 5 million casualties, the largest human loss since World War II. It also resulted in the largest United Nations (UN) interventions in the world, involving nearly 20,000 soldiers from over 40 countries (French 2009). These UN interventions, however, could not prevent states, rebels, criminals, companies, and businessmen from becoming involved in plundering DR Congo's natural resources and wildlife, thereby sustaining the conflict. The UN Expert Panel on the Illegal Exploitation of Natural Resources in DR Congo labeled this conflict therefore as a "self-financing war" (UNSC 2001, p. 27). Former US Secretary of State Hillary Clinton describes the ongoing conflict in Eastern DR Congo as "driven by exploitation of natural resources."[20]

Diamonds were the best-known natural resource being exploited illegally during the Congo war. It led to a new expression, "conflict diamonds," or diamonds originating in areas controlled by forces fighting the legitimate and internationally recognized government of the relevant country (UNSC 2000, p. 26).[21] Other commodities that were exploited illegally in DR Congo were cassiterite (a mineral), coltan (a metallic mineral), gold, niobium (a metal), timber, and tree bark from prunus Africana, which is used in medicine for prostate treatment (UNSC 2001, pp. 8–12). The Congo UN Expert Panel wrote that government structures were "the engines of this systemic and systematic exploitation" (UNSC 2001, p. 3). For example, while neighboring Rwanda and Uganda do not produce diamonds, they suddenly started exporting them during the conflict.

Although Rwanda's authorities stated that Rwanda has no diamond production, it exported rough diamonds at an average annual value of over US$1 million (UNSC 2001, p. 25). Rwanda's official production figures also showed irregular patterns for cassiterite, coltan, and gold. The UN Expert Panel considered it "revealing" that the production increases coincided with the presence of Rwandan troops in DR Congo (pp. 24–5).

Rwanda also exported much coltan—and continues to do so—from DR Congo, which permitted its army to sustain its presence in DR Congo (UNSC 2001, p. 30). As French (2009) explained, Rwanda sought control of Eastern Congo in order to have "continued access to the Congo's economic wealth" such as the abundance of natural resources like coltan. Rwanda's coltan exports rose nearly tenfold between 1999 and 2001, surpassing revenues from the country's main traditional exports: tea and coffee (UNSC 2001). It is sometimes argued that today's gold rush is over coltan (Viner 2011, p. 36), which is essential for today's digital economy, being used in mobile phones and laptops. The demand for it is almost infinite, and DR Congo has one of the largest world reserves.[22]

Uganda, although not a producer of diamonds, also started exporting rough diamonds from the moment it occupied eastern DR Congo in 1997 (UNSC 2001, pp. 18–21).[23] In addition, its gold exports were "consistently greater" than its production and increased during Uganda's partial occupation of DR Congo (pp. 19–20). Similar sudden increases in Uganda's exports were seen in cassiterite, timber, and coffee. Uganda's illegal practices were known and essentially stimulated by the World Bank, which praised Uganda's economic performances and presented it as a success (p. 39). The UN Expert Panel noted that the World Bank "was informed about a significant increase in gold and diamond exports from a country that produces very little of these minerals or exports quantities of gold that it could not produce" (p. 38).

In DR Congo, army commanders and businesspeople formed "criminal cartels" with "ramifications and connections worldwide" (UNSC 2001, pp. 3, 38, 41). Planes owned by (in)famous arms trader Victor Bout transported coltan and other resources. Businesswoman Aziza Kulsum Gulamali—who just like Bout holds several passports and was previously involved in arms, gold, ivory, and cigarette trafficking—was another important coltan trader. The rebel group RCD-Goma appointed her a general manager of a conglomerate of four companies, which obtained the monopoly for the commercialization and export of coltan from RCD-Goma–controlled territories (UNSC 2001, pp. 18–9). Banks in Brussels and New York facilitated financial transactions.

Timber was also extracted illegally. Schemes of international timber companies allowed for the certification of timber that was "characterized by unlawfulness and illegality" (UNSC 2001, p. 10). The timber was exported to Asian, European, and North American countries via Burundi, Rwanda, and Tanzania.

Not only governmental crimes, defined by Friedrichs (2010, p. 128) as "the whole range of crimes committed in a governmental context," but also corporate crime, illegal acts committed by legal corporations, was—and still is—prevalent in Congo's illegal natural resource exploitation. The UN Expert Panel mentioned the opportunistic behavior of private companies vital for the conflict and named them as "the engine of the conflict" (UNSC 2001, p. 42).[24]

A very different and much lesser-known type of illegal natural resource exploitation in Congo concerns charcoal. In Africa, charcoal from timber is the main cooking fuel. In 2007, a family of rare gorillas, famous as a tourist attraction, was murdered in the Virunga Reserve in DR Congo, Africa's oldest national park and a World Heritage Site.[25] While it was first assumed rebels were responsible, it later turned out that a powerful criminal charcoal network was responsible. The murder was a response to the enforcement by Virunga park rangers against charcoal trafficking from the Virunga Reserve. The illicit charcoal trade is estimated at $30 million annually (Jenkins 2008). As the rare gorillas are the main reason for park rangers' presence, the gorillas were apparently seen as a hindrance to illegal charcoal exploitation.

Two better-known African cases of natural resource exploitation concern conflict diamonds from Sierra Leone and conflict timber from Liberia (Boekhout van Solinge 2008a).[26] During Sierra Leone's bloody civil war (1992–2002), diamond extraction, estimated at $25 to $75 million annually (UNSC 2000, p. 17), allowed rebels of the Revolutionary United Front (RUF) to buy weapons. The RUF rebels mostly obtained their weapons from neighboring Liberia, which was ruled by former warlord Charles Taylor. Most arms were imported from Eastern Europe by (in)famous arms traffickers Leonid Minin and the previously mentioned Victor Bout. Lebanese businessmen dominated the diamond trade from Sierra Leone, just like in DR Congo (UNSC 2001, p. 16). Of the over 40 different diamond dealers in Sierra Leone, most of them were Lebanese (UNSC 2000, p. 18). The wealthy Lebanese businessman Talal El Ndine was described as a key player, bringing foreign businessmen and investors to Liberia to "collaborate with the regime in legitimate business activities as well as in weapons and illicit diamonds" (UNSC 2000, p. 37).

Liberia, in the meantime, was exporting unrealistically large quantities of diamonds, much of them to Belgium (Antwerp), Europe's main diamond center. In 1998, for example, Liberia's official diamond exports totaled 8,000 carats, valued at $800,000. "In the same year, Belgium recorded imports from Liberia by 26 companies, totalling 2.56 million carats, valued at US$217 million." (UNSC 2000, p. 37) One company alone imported 168,456 carats, valued at $87 million, more than the highest estimates of Liberia's production capacity, which do not exceed 150,000 carats per year (UNSC 2000, p. 24). Belgium also recorded substantial diamond imports from the Gambia, which does not produce diamonds at all. Significantly, many prominent diamond exporters from Sierra Leone were also exporters of diamonds from the Gambia (UNSC 2001, p. 18). The UN Expert Panel noted that the Gambia had become a "mini-Antwerp," with "reputable companies simply buying what is available on the open market" (UNSC 2000, p. 26).

As it became obvious that many of the diamonds in Liberia actually came from Sierra Leone, the UN Security Council implemented diamond sanctions against Liberia in 2001. The recommendation of the UN Expert Panel to also ban Liberian timber—believed to facilitate arms trafficking—was not followed as China and France, the main destinations of Liberian timber, objected in the Security Council (Beaumont 2001).

With diamonds being banned, timber became Liberia's main source of revenue. In 2000, Taylor had adapted the law, allowing him to exploit strategic commodities such as Liberia's rainforest, the largest in West Africa (Global Witness 2001). Taylor's brother was a member of the Forestry Development Authority (FDA), as was Dutch timber baron Kouwenhoven and the previously mentioned Lebanese diamond trader El Ndine. International arms trafficker Minin was another key figure in Liberia's timber industry (UNSC 2000, p. 37).

Liberia's rainforest was being exploited at a much faster pace than before. Timber extraction and exports peaked at 1 to 1.3 million cubic meters per annum, with a value of approximately US$100 million (Shearman 2009, p. 5). It rapidly reduced the size of West Africa's largest rainforest and one of the planet's biological hotspots (Wilson 2002, p. 215). NGOs' protests and requests to ban the trade in Liberian "conflict timber" were in vain, as the timber exploitation was legal, being approved by the Liberian FDA. In the meantime, Liberian timber brought Kouwenhoven millions, and in 2002, he entered the ranks of the 500 wealthiest Dutch (Boekhout van Solinge 2004, 2008b). Kouwenhoven was later indicted in the Netherlands for using his timber business for the trafficking of weapons. This court case is, however, after several appeals, still pending.[27]

During 2001 and 2002, the number of press and NGO reports about the link between Liberian timber and arms trade increased (Boekhout van Solinge 2008b). In 2003, the UN Security Council did implement timber sanctions against Liberia.[28] It drained Liberia's main source of revenue, and one month later Taylor resigned and fled the country. The US intelligence community "absolutely put the fall of Taylor on the timber sanctions" (Khatchadourian 2008).

V. "Pirate Cows" and Violence in Equatorial America

Like Africa, America has a history of resource exploitation, with countries being named after resources, such as Argentina (silver) and Brazil (Brazil wood). After Spanish conquistadores robbed the Incas and Aztecs of their gold—which pirates and privateers consequently tried to intercept at sea,[29] the gold quest for El Dorado drove them into the Amazon interior. El Dorado was never found, but the Amazon's natural resources have nevertheless continuously attracted outsiders. In the industrial nineteenth century, there was a run on rubber, also leading to the (in)famous biopiracy case of 1876, when 70,000 rubber seeds were smuggled out of the Brazilian Amazon.[30]

Today, natural resource exploitation in the Amazon usually implies deforestation, be it for bauxite, gold, iron, oil, timber, or land conversion.[31] Large-scale deforestation in the Brazilian Amazon started in the 1970s, when the military government wished to open up the "undeveloped" Amazon Rainforest (London and Kelly 2007). Some 20 percent of the entire Amazon has today been deforested; 80 percent of the total deforestation in the Amazon Rainforest has taken place in Brazil, which has two-thirds of the Amazon within its borders (Malhi et al. 2008; Verweij et al. 2009). Between 1988 and 2006, the annual deforestation rate in the Brazilian Amazon averaged 18,100 km². It peaked in 2004 with 27,400 km², before gradually decreasing to some 11,000 km² in 2007 (Malhi et al. 2008, p. 169).

The creation of cattle ranches has been responsible for around 70 percent of deforestation in the Brazilian Amazon (Malhi et al. 2008, p. 169). In the Brazilian Amazon, there are 70 million cows, almost three times the number of people living there. In Brazil as a whole, cows also outnumber humans (200 million versus 190 million). Until 10 years ago, Amazon beef was primarily sold in the region, but it is now exported worldwide.[32] Brazilian beef exports increased fivefold between 1997 and 2003, which made Brazil the world's main beef and leather exporter. Four-fifths of the growth has come from within the Amazon (Pearce 2004).

As many of the cattle in the Amazon are grazing on illegally deforested rainforest, they are locally called "pirate cows." The problem of illegal deforestation for cattle is being increasingly acknowledged. In 2009, the new federal prosecutor in Brazil's state of Pará started a campaign to promote "legal meat," by demanding guarantees of legality for meat and by increasing enforcement against cattle farmers involved in illegal deforestation.[33]

Next to cattle, a second important driver of Amazonian deforestation is soy cultivation. Brazil has become the world's second-largest soy producer (after the United States), producing over a quarter of the world's production in 2010.[34] The soybeans are mostly exported and used as cattle food in Europe and China. Much of the increase in soy production comes from the Amazon (London and Kelly 2007, p. 169).

In the Brazilian Amazon, a substantial part of all deforestation is illegal. Greenpeace in the Amazon, using satellite data, estimates that between 60 percent and 80 percent of all deforestation in the Brazilian Amazon is illegal. Land grabbing has become "a way of life in the Amazon" (London and Kelly 2007, p. 151).[35] Land titles are often falsified or land officials are bribed to change titles. Even in cases in which the land is owned or leased legally, Brazil's federal laws mandate that a maximum of 20 percent is deforested for agricultural purposes, but landholders often deforest more (London and Kelly 2007, p. 159; Boekhout van Solinge 2010b, p. 271).

A structural problem with law enforcement in the Amazon is the remoteness of the areas and low population densities, which makes governmental presence generally low. A governmental official might have to travel days if he wants to intervene against, for example, illegal logging, where he would have to "confront armed loggers all too ready to threaten him with violence or, more benignly, ready to offer a bribe" (London and Kelly 2007, p. 151).

The low governmental presence is illustrated by the still-existing slave-like working conditions that particularly occur in the Amazon on some of the cattle ranches (and also on farms growing sugarcane for ethanol production). It is a form of slavery or forced labor of workers who are kept in debt bondage and who have armed guards preventing them from leaving (Breton 2003). A special governmental task force raids farms and businesses and frees several thousand workers every year, but an estimated 25,000 Brazilians continue to toil in debt slavery conditions (Phillips 2009).[36]

In Latin America, with a history of latifundia, the Weberian ideal type of nation-states having the monopoly on violence does not exist in all territories of states (Koonings and Kruijt 2004). In rural areas, large landowners traditionally have a great deal of power, sometimes with their own "hired guns." Landowners, loggers, miners, and prospectors may see forest communities or environmentalists as a hindrance to their plans. It is not uncommon that they are threatened, chased away, or killed (Loureiro 2001; Greenpeace International 2003; CIMI 2009; CPT 2009).

A famous murder case occurred in 1988, when rubber tapper and environmentalist Chico Mendes was killed by the son of a rancher (Mendes 1989). Mendes' murder led to worldwide attention and concern over tropical deforestation. Another murder attracting international attention was that of 73-year-old American nun Dorothy Stang in 2005 in Brazil's Pará state. As a protector of the poor and the rainforest, she had made enemies among loggers and ranchers and was receiving death threats. In this case as well, a rancher was behind the murder. In 2011, a prominent married couple of rainforest activists were murdered, also in Pará. They had been on a hit list for a long time but were refused police protection. The double murder was widely reported in the international press, as it occurred on the day that the Brazilian House of Representatives voted for a new Forest Act, allowing for more deforestation (Phillips 2011).

While these murders received international attention, deforestation in the Amazon has led to numerous unreported cases of violence. Before Mendes' murder, only 10 people had ever been brought to court for around 1,000 murders that occurred in the Amazon in the 1980s (Phillips 2008). In Pará state alone, the Pastoral Land Commission CPT estimated that 475 activists were murdered between 1996 and 2001 (London and Kelly 2007, p. 139). CPT revealed in 2008 that at least 260 people were living "under the threat of murder because of their fight against a coalition of loggers, farmers and cattle ranchers" (Phillips 2008). Environmentalists also face danger. Tellingly, the head of Greenpeace Amazon travels with bodyguards, and Greenpeace's office in the Amazon (in the city of Manaus) has a sophisticated security entrance.

Indigenous communities are strongly overrepresented among the victims, as they live in the rainforests that others wish to exploit and because they are often found at the bottom of "society" (CIMI 2009). The small and rapidly decreasing number of so-called uncontacted tribes are particularly threatened. One of the reasons that they avoid contact with Western civilization seems to be that they have been attacked by ranchers or loggers.[37]

While land conversion for cattle and soy is responsible for most deforestation in the Amazon, the harvesting of tropical timber often is the first step in the deforestation process. One tree can be worth thousands of dollars or euros, which can pay for the first cuts into the forest: a trail for trucks and bulldozers and later farmers (London and Kelly 2007, p. 139). In the Brazilian Amazon, the timber business has the reputation of being dirty and dangerous, with rampant illegal activity and widespread violence against those resisting logging.[38] It is generally assumed that illegal logging represents around 70 percent of all harvested timber in the Brazilian Amazon (Lawson and MacFaul 2010, p. 84). Although in itself Brazil has a sophisticated Amazon surveillance system—using satellites, radar, and 900 monitoring posts on the ground—that which is observed from the air is rarely enforced on the ground (London and Kelly 2007, pp. 71–3). Moreover, there are also other ways to circumvent surveillance, such as by changing or arranging paperwork by corrupting officials.[39]

More sophisticated methods also exist. In 2008, it was discovered that hackers changed data in the governmental timber-tracking database, allowing 107 logging companies to falsify and "legalize" 1.7 million cubic meters of illegal logs from Pará state (Lawson and MacFaul 2010, p. 43). A federal prosecutor is suing those companies for about $833 million, and 202 people are facing prosecution (Greenemeier 2008).

Although law enforcement in the Amazon still is limited, it is increasing, partly due to increased involvement of the generally not corrupt federal police and prosecutors—compared with the more corruption-prone state law enforcers, in particular the military police. The number of fines for illegal timber increased eightfold between 2003 and 2007, but only 2.5 percent of these were successfully collected, and seizures still only represent 5 percent of the estimated illegal production (Lawson and MacFaul 2010, p. 15).

Illegal deforestation in the Brazilian Amazon obviously means corporate crimes occur, often committed by timber companies and cattle and soy farmers. The power of large landholders and the violence that is committed on their behalf in remote areas with low governmental control show similarities with the mafia prototype of nineteenth-century Sicily (Blok 2008, p. 7). Just like in nineteenth-century Sicily, the state control over the use of violence is low and has been to some extent replaced by a dominant class of large (absentee) landholders or men acting on their behalf.[40]

VI. Discussion and Conclusion: Natural Resources and Organized Crime

This essay included cases studies on resource exploitation in the rainforests of several resource-rich tropical countries—Indonesia, DR Congo, Sierra Leone, Liberia, and Brazil. In all of the described regions, the concept of "resource curse" in its traditional sense adapts well. Despite their wealth in natural resources, they are known as economically underdeveloped.[41]

In the discussed case studies, the resource curse is also a crime curse. Almost all of the natural resource exploitation described thus far has been mostly or completely illegal.

Moreover, this illegal exploitation is related to a variety of other illegal acts, varying from corruption and collusion to systematic violence. In the one case where the resource exploitation was legal—timber from Liberia—this was because the former president Charles Taylor, currently condemned for war crimes, legalized Liberia's natural resource exploitation.

The resource curse literature mentions corruption as the main reason why resource-rich countries perform relatively poorly in economic terms (Kolstad and Søreide 2009). The literature further suggests that countries are more likely to suffer the resource curse when they have poor institutions—such as those governing the private sector by the rule of law and institutions that hold politicians accountable for using public resources (ibid., p. 217).

All of the discussed countries or regions in the case studies indeed perform poorly with regard to the presence and functioning of those institutions. Corruption often facilitates illegal exploitation practices, but the findings of this essay suggest that corruption is not a necessary condition for the appropriation and sometimes blatant plundering of a country's or region's natural resources. The institutions that could potentially limit the illegal and harmful exploitation of natural resources are sometimes (virtually) absent, such as in some remote areas of tropical rainforests. Even for the marketing and export of illegally exploited natural resources, corruption is not always a necessary condition. In many cases, illegally exploited products such as timber, diamonds, coltan, meat, and soy can be sold without much hindrance on the international market as apparently legal products. The lack of institutional control thus exists not only on the supply side but also on the demand side and in the transit phase.[42] The absence of institutional requirements and control on the demand side, combined with the lack of transparency in products' chains of custody, result in illegally exploited natural resources being easily sold internationally in a seemingly legal way. People with high (nonsustainable) consumption patterns—in other terms, large ecological footprints[43] —are in a way, often unknowingly, accomplices of these crimes and harms.

The players who are involved in the exploitation activities described in this chapter form a wide spectrum. In Indonesia, the economic, political, and military elites are involved. These elites often overlap, which blurs the distinctions between private, public, and criminal exploitations (Tsing 2005). Other players involved are corrupt officials from the forestry sector and judiciary, Chinese Malaysian businessmen, brokers, banks, and international logging companies.

In Sierra Leone, diamonds were extracted in rebel-controlled territories, and many of them were traded through neighboring Liberia, Gambia, or other West African countries—facilitated by government officials, businessmen (especially Lebanese), and diamond companies in Belgium, which served as an important, albeit not exclusive, destination. The timber in neighboring Liberia was harvested legally, but quite a number of the players in Liberia's timber industry were, according to the UN Expert Panel (UNSC 2000, p. 13), also involved in other illegal activities, with large amounts of the proceeds being used to pay for extrabudgetary activities, including weapons acquisition.

In DR Congo, a large variety of players were, and still are, involved in the exploitation of its natural wealth: armies, rebel groups, state officials, corporations, legal and illegal entrepreneurs, and, in a way, the World Bank, which has played a facilitating and stimulating role by praising Uganda's (illicit) economic performances. The UN Expert Panel (UNSC 2001) explicitly mentioned states and corporations as the engines of illegal exploitation.

In the Brazilian Amazon, "agricultural crimes" occur.[44] It is common that large landowners illegally appropriate public land (land grabbing). In many cases, this is done by "buying" or forging documents with the help of corrupt officials. In other cases, the land is just "taken," and if necessary, accompanied by the use of violence. The many murders that have been committed in this context generally do not seem to be individual acts but are in a way orchestrated and organized, being preceded by death threats from loggers and especially ranchers forming coalitions. Many cattle ranches have been created on illegally deforested land, while on some remote farms even modern slavery exists. The timber business in the Amazon is characterized by much illegal logging, corruption, and violence.

To what extent is it justified to label the different illegal activities in this chapter as organized crime? Using the UN definition of organized crime,[45] the described criminal networks easily fit into that definition. While the current UN definition of organized crime remains somewhat general and does not necessarily imply victims, an earlier UN definition emphasized the use of threats and violence,[46] which corresponds with many of the case studies.

A more useful scientific definition of organized crime is given by Alan A. Block (1983, p. vii), who emphasizes that "organized crime is a social system and a social world. The system is composed of relationships binding professional criminals, politicians, law enforcers, and various entrepreneurs." Block's definition better covers the discussed illegal resource exploitation. The term "social systems" and "social world" refer to the more systematic collaborations between a large variety of actors, from the underworld, as well as from the economic and political "upperworld."

The case studies have shown that many types of relations exist between the actors involved, with overlapping and collusion between legal and illegal entrepreneurs, corporations, traditional criminals, as well as state actors and agencies.[47] In some cases, such as in West and Central Africa, where there was governmental involvement, the natural resource exploitation can be considered as state crimes as Green and Ward (2004) defined them—state organizational deviance involving the violation of human rights. But these African cases, as well as the Indonesian and Brazilian cases, also showed that many legal entrepreneurs and businesses are involved in the exploitation or trade of natural resources that are mostly exploited illegally. It confirms Ruggiero's (1996) argument that the difference between corporate crime and organized crime is difficult to define. Moreover, the Indonesian and African cases showed that corporate crime and governmental crime are not completely distinct categories either. The African cases further illustrated that some activities could be labeled as political crimes (Passas 2002, p. 17), considering that some of the actors were not primarily motivated by financial gain but by political motives. The analysis of Passas (2002, p. 22) on the many interfaces between the underworld and the upperworld probably best fits the natural resources exploitation of this essay. By emphasizing the symbiotic relationships that are formed between legal and illegal actors, Passas blurs the whole distinction between underworld and upperworld.

What the different case studies of this chapter mostly show is that the traditional distinctions between corporate crime, governmental or state crime, and organized crime do not always hold. They appear too rigid for the variety of relationships and collaborations between legal and illegal actors that are profiting from natural resource exploitation. As such, natural resource exploitation is a good case in point where the traditional criminological distinctions and categorizations do not apply. As most criminological theory is still based on Western societies and concepts, it should also be expanded and revised to understand and explain the natural resource exploitation activities in vast and remote areas of Southern, tropical countries.

Notes

1. Important natural resources that are mostly exploited legally, such as oil, gas, diamonds, and gold—although (organized) crime is involved—are not discussed. Nor is discussed the illegal trade in wildlife and wildlife products, valued over US$ 10 billion (Elliot 2009, p. 61), in which organized crime is also involved—e.g., Russian Mafia in caviar, and Chinese Triads in animal parts for Traditional Chinese Medicine. Naylor (2004) however states that the illegal wildlife market is dominated by the same actors as those operating in the legal market.

2. The world's largest forest, in Russian Siberia, which is not included in this essay, also suffers severely from illegal logging. Khatchadourian (2008) described the large-scale illegal logging in Siberia and that several murders were committed related to illegal logging. This essay, however, focuses on deforestation in tropical countries, where illegal logging generally is more prevalent and where the human and nonhuman victims are more numerous, considering the higher human populations and higher biodiversity in tropical rainforests.

3. Some ethnographic findings and impressions can be found in the footnotes, mainly based on visits and research in Indonesia and especially Brazil.

4. There is also a North–South dimension, with waste being exported to Southern countries, which only sometimes gets international attention. For example, in 2006, 500 tons of toxic waste from a tanker of Transfigura, a Swiss trading company headquartered in the Netherlands, was dumped at different sites in Abidjan, Côte d'Ivoire. Over 100,000 residents sought medical treatment and at least 15 died (Faber 2009, p. 101).

5. The sizes of the Netherlands, Switzerland, and Taiwan are, respectively, around 37,000 km^2, 41,000 km^2, and 36,000 km^2. In the 1990s, the annual deforestation rate in the Brazilian Amazon was around 20,000 km^2. In Indonesia, the annual deforestation during this decade averaged 10,000 km^2. An annual deforestation of 10,000 km^2 corresponds to 5,479 football fields per day, 228 per hour, or 3.8 per minute.

6. Tropical rainforests normally cannot burn easily, for the simple reason that they are too humid. At the end of the dry season, however, forest fires do occur. In the Amazon, these fires are often caused by ranchers, creating farmland for cattle (see further). In recent years,

Indonesia's rainforests suffered several times from extended dry periods, such as in 1997 and 2006, apparently related to the El Nino effect (Nellemann et al. 2007, p. 31; Makmur 2009), which led to enormous forest fires, which were a regional problem (smog) and also global problem (large carbon releases).

7. Based on an average 50-cm-diameter log; 100 million cubic meters of logs would stretch 510,000 km, while the circumference of the Earth at the equator is just over 40,000 km (Lawson and MacFaul 2010, p. 103).

8. A search in any large academic library shows that articles on illegal logging have been published in many scientific journals: *Conservation and Society, Environmental Management, Forest Ecology and Management, Forest Policy and Economics, Journal of Environment and Development, The Journal of Developing Areas, Journal of Southeast Asian Studies, Madagascar Conservation and Development, Remote Sensing of Environment, Society and Natural Resources, World Development*, and more. Also, less specialized journals like *The Economist* and *New Scientist* have published articles about illegal logging.

9. In the 2000 census, some 700,000 Brazilians classified themselves as indigenous, 0.4percent of the Brazilian population. A majority of them live in the Amazon (see IBGE, the Brazilian Institute of Geography and Statistics: http://www.ibge.gov.br). IBGE estimates that around 1500, when the Europeans arrived, the indigenous population on the territory that now is Brazil numbered between 1 and 5 million.

10. Today's extinction crisis is sometimes called the sixth extinction (see Leakey and Lewin 1996). The current extinction rates are unprecedented and much higher than the fifth extinction of 65 million years ago, when the dinosaurs also became extinct. The causes of the current extinction are pollution, hunting/fishing, the introduction of species, fragmentation of landscapes, climate change, and, primarily, habitat destruction. Much literature exists on the subject, but it is well summarized in the documentary series *The State of the Plane*t by David Attenborough (2004).

11. Unlike the image that is portrayed in media (as if climate change and its relation with increased carbon emissions are still matters of strong scientific debate), there exists quite a strong scientific consensus that carbon emissions have strongly increased since the industrial age and that it is increasingly likely that this is causing climate change. See the reports of IPCC (http://www.ipcc.ch), or for a more accessible overview, see Flannery (2007). For an explanation for the difference in perception between scientific specialists and the general public, see Oreskes and Conway (2010).

12. Borneo is, after New Guinea, the world's second-largest tropical island and is divided among three states. The major part is composed of Kalimatan, a region of Indonesia. A minor part is composed of East Malaysia, the provinces Sarawak and Sabah. A small part is composed of the sultanate of Brunei.

13. Illegal deforestation regularly involves violence. I was told and shown pictures of a victim on the island of Ceram who, after resisting illegal logging on his family land, was beheaded with a chain saw. The renowned orangutan protector Willie Smits has made so many enemies with his work that he sleeps at many different places, as he told me in Jakarta in 2005.

14. Indonesia's Papua province is the western half of New Guinea; the eastern side is the country Papua New Guinea.

15. WWF Indonesia (2004) accused APP, one of the world's largest paper companies, which is owned by the Indonesian conglomerate Sinar Mas Group, of logging in protected reserves. Since 2008, an increasing number of corporations have stopped buying paper from APP (see Monbiot 2010). In 2010, after a Greenpeace report stated that APP is responsible for

the destruction of rainforests, including the Bikut Tigapuluh forest, one of the last refuges for the Sumatran tigers and orangutans, French supermarket multinational Carrefour announced that it would stop buying APP paper. Greenpeace did not state that the logging was illegal (Deutsch 2010). In 2008, RAPP, the other paper giant, which is owned by Indonesian billionaire Sukanto Tanoto, sued the Indonesian newspaper *Koran Tempo* for defamation after it published articles about RAPP logging illegally. Judges ordered the newspaper to pay damages to RAPP and to publish extensive apologies (Wisnu 2008).

16. Part of the friction seems to be that a Forestry Law (No. 49/1999) conflicts with an Environmental Law (No. 23/1997). In 2007, the Indonesian House of Representatives held hearings on the logging by or for paper pulp factories, but the hearing with RAPP was cancelled as the company was seen as being uncooperative. See Sijabat (2007).

17. The Indonesian army (TNI) is only partly funded by the Indonesian state and earns much of its income through army-owned commercial companies, including logging and timber (processing) businesses. While it is a governmental policy goal for TNI to no longer own commercial businesses, these reforms have proceeded slowly (see, e.g., Saragih 2011).

18. It is potentially dangerous to investigate illegal logging in the field. In 2005, when the head of an NGO office in Borneo's interior invited me to witness timber trafficking from Indonesia to Malaysia, he insisted that I have a good cover story and would not present myself as a criminologist. He presented me to a soldier, who originated from a forest community, who told me that his superiors were involved in illegal logging.

19. While the new police chief wanted to give me the impression of being a good law enforcer (also by showing me the detained Malaysians), Indonesian environmentalists who had "checked him out" later told me they suspected his hands were not clean either. The arrest of the Malaysians might have been symbolic or a way to neutralize competitors.

20. Hillary Clinton stated this after visiting DR Congo in 2009 (French 2009). Different media reports suggest that this description was still valid in 2011 (see Hochschild 2011; Viner 2011).

21. The "conflict diamonds" phenomenon led to the implementation of a stricter policy, the Kimberley Process Certification Scheme. Although an improvement, it still lacks independent monitoring, and in practice the supposed distinction between legal and illegal diamonds does not exist, as Siegel showed (2008, 2009).

22. Sources differ about DR Congo's percentage of the world's total coltan reserves. Some sources say DR Congo has 80 percent of Africa's reserves, other sources say it has 80 percent of the world's reserves, while some sources put it at 60 percent of the world's reserves or less. The sources seem to agree that DR Congo has one of the world's main coltan reserves.

23. In the first year of occupation, 1997, Uganda's rough diamond exports were valued at $198,000, but in the following years, it quickly rose to between $1 million and $2 million (UNSC 2001, p. 21).

24. Annex I of the report of the UN Expert Panel lists many of these companies. Almost a third of them are found in Belgium, the former colonizer of DR Congo and (after World War I) also of Burundi and Rwanda, which implies that many (trade) connections still exist. Companies from the Netherlands are also well represented. Other European companies are based in Germany, the United Kingdom, and Switzerland. See UNSC (2001, pp. 46–7).

25. Approximately 680 remain of this mountain gorilla species, and more than half of them (380) live in the Virunga mountains. See the section on mountain gorillas in the Red List of (critically) endangered species of the World Conservation Union IUCN: http://www.iucnredlist.org/apps/redlist/details/39994/0. A television documentary (shown by National Geographic and CNN) was made about the murder of the gorilla family.

26. While "conflict diamonds" was the term coined in UN reports, the media increasingly started using the term "blood diamonds," perhaps influenced by the popular Hollywood film *Blood Diamond* (2006) about Sierra Leone. The court case against former Liberian President Charles Taylor, indicted for war crimes by the UN Special Court for Sierra Leone (UNSL), received much media attention in 2010, when top model Naomi Campbell was summoned to testify, as she apparently received a "blood diamond" from Charles Taylor. The UNSL was set up jointly by the government of Sierra Leone and the United Nations. In 2012, the UNSL sentenced Charles Taylor to 50 years in jail. See the website of the SPSL: http://www.sc-sl.org.

27. In 2006, Kouwenhoven was convicted and sentenced to 8 years' imprisonment for weapons trafficking, but after an appeal (of both the defendant and prosecutor), he was found not guilty in 2008. The prosecutor appealed again, and in 2010, the Dutch High Court overturned the Appeal Court's decision—stating that two anonymous witnesses should be heard, which the Appeal Court had refused—and sent the case back to the Appeal Court. See the decision of the High Court in the Netherlands (code BK8132, 08/01322).

28. As was decided by the United Nations Security Council Resolution 1478 of 2003, the already existing ban on diamond exports from Liberia was extended to timber as well. Resolution 1343 of 2001 against Liberia had already installed a weapons embargo, measures against the export of rough diamonds and travel restrictions on senior government members. For an overview, see: http://www.un.org/Docs/sc/committees/Liberia2/LiberiaSelEng.htm.

29. In modern terms, privateers could be considered as state-sponsored organized crime: raiding and robbing ships with the permission of a government. Chambliss (1989) labels it state-organized crime.

30. The Englishman Henry Wickham smuggled 70,000 rubber seeds from the Brazilian Amazon to London, from where they were taken to tropical Asia. This broke the Amazon's monopoly on high-quality rubber—increasingly in demand during industrialization—and led to the economic demise of the Amazon and, to some extent, Brazil (Grandin 2010, p. 26). Brazilians dubbed Wickham "the prince of thieves" and "executioner of Amazonas," as "his theft is hardly defensible in international law" (Jackson 2008, p. 191). With the help of the British consul, Wickham misled Brazilian customs officials by forging documents and declaring that his load contained delicate specimens for Queen Victoria's botanical gardens (Jackson 2008). Wickham's rubber theft is considered as the classic case of biopiracy, which is the appropriation, without payment, of indigenous biological (often biomedical) knowledge and genes. As Wickham operated for the British Empire, his rubber theft can be considered as a governmental crime. Tropical plants are an important source for medicine, and they continue being objects of biopiracy, today mainly as targets of the pharmaceutical industry, which also patents (parts of) plants (see South 2007). Biopiracy today could be categorized as corporate crime. The profits can run in the millions or billions (London and Kelly 2007, p. 249).

31. The Amazon's soil is poor in nutrients but rich in (precious) metals. The practice of gold prospecting is old and well-known. Less known is that world's largest iron mine is also found in the Amazon. Over the last years, bauxite mining (for aluminium) has increased greatly. For example, in Jurutí, in Pará state, where bauxite is found at a depth of 12 meters, the US aluminium company Alcoa is clearing rainforest, which has led to conflicts with rainforest inhabitants (Boekhout van Solinge 2010b, p. 271).

32. The European Union is the largest importer of Brazilian beef, followed by Chile, Egypt, the United States, Saudi Arabia, and Russia (Pearce 2004). Some of the beef is exported and sold in tins.

33. See the website on legal meat (*carne legal*) of the Federal Prosecutor's Office: http://www.carnelegal.mpf.gov.br/, where it is stated that in 2009, Pará was the "champion state" regarding illegal deforestation in the Amazon region. Some Brazilians I met were wondering how long the prosecutor was going to stay in office or stay alive, considering the large (commercial) interests he is challenging in Pará, known for its lawlessness and violence.

34. The website soystats (http://www.soystats.com) shows that in 2010, Brazil produced 27 percent of the world's soybeans, 70 million metric tons. The United States produces 90.6 million metric tons (35 percent).

35. If the subject of deforestation and land grabbing ("grilagem" in Portuguese) is discussed in the Amazon with an independent lawyer, journalist, intellectual, or academic specialist, he or she will almost certainly explain that most of the land grabbing in the Amazon is illegal. As various lawyers explained to me in Santarém (such as at UFOPA university in Santarém, in 2010 and 2011), farmers and loggers commonly take (grab) public land illegally. New landholders just take the land, or they show some "bought" paperwork to the sometimes illiterate forest communities. Armed (ex) law enforcers—hired for the job—or gunmen may accompany them.

36. The documentary *Bound by Promises: Contemporary Slavery in Rural Brazil* (Beatriz Affonso 2009) shows that year, more than 25,000 rural workers are enslaved by landowners, mostly in the Amazon region. See also *BBC News* of June 26, 2010 (Hernandez 2010).

37. The (western) Amazon is the world's main area of "uncontacted" small tribes of hunter-gatherers—estimated at around 50. The second most important area is the island of New Guinea. In both equatorial forests, most deforestation is illegal. See Boekhout van Solinge (2010*b*).

38. Any visitor will notice when addressing the subject in the Amazon. In the Brazilian media the term "timber mafia" is commonly used, which seems to refer to large-scale timber trafficking networks that often make use of corruption, collusion, and violence.

39. A timber trader I once met in Germany told me, after a long talk, that he had been trading illegal timber. On paper, the timber came from different Brazilian states, but in reality it was from Pará state. A timber trader I met in Pará explained that he tried to get legal timber, but that some 30 percent of his timber was still of suspicious origin. He allowed me to join a business meeting with a colleague in which they discussed the problem of the mayor delaying paper work—presumably with the intent to be paid.

40. In some cases of the large landholders in the Amazon, they are absentee landholders, coming from southern Brazil or the southern Amazon (such as Mato Grosso state), where they live part or most of the time. They resemble the absentee landlords of nineteenth-century Sicily, who lived mostly in the city (Palermo) and trusted the management to *Mafiosi*, middlemen or power brokers.

41. While Brazil is not a developing country but an emerging economy, Brazil's North Region, where the Amazon Rainforest is found, is one of Brazil's economically less-developed areas.

42. While researching illegal logging and timber, I was told several times by Dutch policy makers that it was not possible to do anything against illegal timber as WTO free trade rules would not allow this. I suspect that this nonsensical argument originates from the corporate timber lobby. On several occasions, I heard corporate representatives saying the same.

43. The concept of ecological footprint refers to the average amount of productive land and shallow sea that a human is using. If everyone were to have a European lifestyle, this would require between two and three planets. A North American lifestyle for everyone would require five planets (Wilson 2002, p. 23).

44. As crime in cities is sometimes described as urban crime, the term "rural crime," or more specifically "agricultural crime" may denote well the types of crime that occur in the process of and with the objective of agricultural production. "Cattle crime" may also be an appropriate term, as most (illegal) deforestation in the Brazilian Amazon occurs in order to create cattle farms.

45. The United Nations Convention against Transnational Organized Crime (2000) defines an organized criminal group as "a structured group of three or more persons, existing for a period of time and acting in concert with the aim of committing one or more serious crimes or offences established in accordance with this Convention, in order to obtain, directly or indirectly, a financial or other material benefit" (United Nations General Assembly 2000).

46. "The term organized crime usually refers to large-scale and complex criminal activities carried out by tightly or loosely organized associations and aimed at the establishment, supply and exploitation of illegal markets at the expense of society. Such operations are generally carried out with a ruthless disregard of the law, and often involve offences against the person, including threats, intimidation and physical violence" (United Nations 1990, p. 5).

47. With thanks to my colleague Damián Zaitch for sharing his ideas with me on the various criminological concepts and how they could apply to this field of research.

REFERENCES

Agozino, Biko. 2003. *Counter-Colonial Criminology. A Critique of Imperialist Reason,* London: Pluto Press.

Attenborough, David. 2004. *The State of the Planet* (series of documentaries). London: BBC.

Beaumont, Peter. 2001. "How a Tyrant's 'Logs Of War' Bring Terror to West Africa." *The Observer* 27. (May 2001).

Beirne, Piers, and Nigel South, eds. 2007. *Issues in Green Criminology. Confronting Harms Against Environments, Humanity and Other Animals.* Devon, UK: Willan.

Boekhout van Solinge, Tim. 2004. "De Handel in Illegaal Tropisch Hardhout." In *Discretie in het Strafrecht,* edited by M. Miranda Boone, Renée S.B. Kool, Caroline M. Pelser, and Tim Boekhout van Solinge. The Hague: Boom Legal Publishers.

Block, Alan. 1983. *East Side-West Side: Organizing Crime in New York 1930–1950,* 2nd ed. New Brunswick, NJ: Transaction.

Block, Alan A., and Frank R. Scarpitti. 1985. *Poisoning for Profit: The Mafia and Toxic Waste in America.* New York: William Morrow.

Blok, Anton. 2008. "Reflections on the Sicilian Mafia: Peripheries and Their Impact on Centres." In *Organized Crime. Culture, Markets and Policies,* edited by Dina Siegel and Hans Nelen. New York: Springer.

Boekhout van Solinge, Tim. 2008a. "Eco-Crime: The Tropical Timber Trade." In *Organized Crime. Culture, Markets and Policies,* edited by Dina Siegel and Hans Nelen. New York: Springer.

Boekhout van Solinge, Tim. 2008b. "Crime, Conflicts and Ecology in Africa." In *Global Harms. Ecological Crime and Speciesism,* edited by Ragnhild Sollund. New York: Nova.

Boekhout van Solinge, Tim. 2008c. "The Land of the Orangutan and Bird of Paradise Under Threat." In *Global Harms. Ecological Crime and Speciesism,* edited by Ragnhild Sollund. New York: Nova.

Boekhout van Solinge, Tim. 2010a. "Equatorial Deforestation as a Harmful Practice and Criminological Issue." In *Global Environmental Harm. Criminological Perspectives,* edited by Rob White. Devon, UK: Willan.

Boekhout van Solinge, Tim. 2010b. "Deforestation Crimes and Conflicts in the Amazon." *Critical Criminology* 18(4): 263–77.

Breton, Binka Le. 2003. *Trapped. Modern-Day Slavery in the Brazilian Amazon*. Sterling, VA: Kumarian Press.

Butchart, Stuart H.M. et al. 2010. "Global Diversity: Indicators of Recent Declines." *Science* 328(5982): 1164–8.

Chambliss, W. J. 1989. "State-Organized Crime." *Criminology* 27(2): 183–208.

CIMI ≛ Conselho Indigenista Missionário. 2009. *Violência contra os Povos Indígenas no Brasil*. Brasilia: CIMI.

Collier, P., and A. Hoeffler. 1998. "On Economic Causes of Civil War." *Oxford Economic Papers* 50: 563–73.

Collier, P., and A. Hoeffler. 2002. *Greed and Grievance in Civil War*. Oxford: Centre for Study of African Economies, Oxford University Press. Working Paper 2001–2002.

CPT ≛ Comissão Pastoral de Terra. 2009. *Conflitos no Campo Brasil 2008*. Goiâna, Brazil: CPT.

Deutsch, Anthony. 2010. "Greenpeace Fires Salvo Over Indonesian Paper Producer." *The Financial Times* (Jakarta). (July 6).

EIA and Telapak. 2004. *Profiting from Plunder: How Malaysia Smuggles Endangered Wood*. London: EIA.

EIA and Telapak. 2005. *The Last Frontier. Illegal Logging in Papua and China's Massive Timber Theft*. London: EIA.

EIA and Telapak. 2006. *Behind the Veneer: How Indonesia's Last Rainforests Are Being Felled for Flooring*. London: EIA.

EIA and Telapak. 2010. *Rogue Traders: The Murky Business of Merbau Timber Smuggling in Indonesia*. London: EIA.

Elliot, Lorraine. 2009. "Combating Transnational Environmental Crime: 'Joined Up' Thinking About Transnational Networks." In *Eco-Crime and Justice. Essays on Environmental Crime*, edited by Kristiina Kangaspunta and Ineke Haen Marshal. Turin, Italy: UNICRI.

Faber, Daniel. 2009. "Capitalising on Environmental Crime: A Case Study of the USA. Polluter-Industrial Complex in the Age of Globalization." In *Eco-Crime and Justice. Essays on Environmental Crime*, edited by Kristiina Kangaspunta and Ineke Haen Marshal. Turin, Italy: UNICRI.

Flannery, Tim. 2007. *The Weather Makers. Our Changing Climate and What It Means for Life on Earth*. London: Penguin.

French, Howard W. 2009. "Kagame's Hidden War in the Congo." *The New York Review of Books*. (September 24).

Friedrichs, David O. 2010. *Trusted Criminals. White Collar Crime in Contemporary Society*, 4th ed. Belmont, CA: Wadsworth.

Friends of the Earth. 2001. *European League Table of Imports of Illegal Tropical Timber*. London: Friends of the Earth.

FAO ≛ Food and Agriculture Organization of the United Nations and ITTO ≛ International Tropical Timber Organization. 2005. *Best Practices for Improving Law Compliance in the Forestry Sector*. Rome: FAO.

Grandin, Greg. 2010. *Fordlandia. The Rise and Fall of Henry's Ford Forgotten Jungle City*. London: Icon Books.

Green, Penny, and Ward, Penny. 2004. *State Crime. Governments, Violence and Corruption*. London: Pluto Press.

Global Witness. 2001. *The Role of Liberia's Logging Industry on National and Regional Insecurity. Update May 2001*. London: Global Witness.

Global Witness. 2002. *The Logs of War: The Timber Trade and Armed Conflict*. London: Global Witness.

Greenemeier, Larry. 2008. "Hackers Help Loggers Illegally Strip Trees From the Amazon." *The Scientific American Newsblog*. (December 16, 2008). http://www.scientificamerican.com/blog/.

Greenpeace. 2001. *Logs of War. The Relationship Between the Timber Sector and the Destruction of the Forests of Liberia*. Madrid: Greenpeace.

Greenpeace. 2005. *Danzer Group Involved in Bribery, Illegal Logging, Dealings With Blacklisted Arms Trafficker and Suspected of Forgery*. Amsterdam: Greenpeace Forest Crime File.

Greenpeace International. 2003. *State of Conflict. An Investigation Into the Landgrabbers, Loggers and Lawless Frontiers in Pará State, Amazon*. Amsterdam: Greenpeace International.

Hansen, M., S. Stehman, P. Potapov, B. Arunarwati, F. Stolle, and K. Pittman. 2009. "Quantifying Changes in the Rates of Forest Clearing in Indonesia from 1990 to 2005 Using Remotely Sensed Data Sets." *Environmental Research Letters* 4(3): 034001.

Hernandez, Vladimir. 2010. "Forced Labour Clouds Boom in Brazil's Amazon." *BBC News*. (June 26, 2010). (http://www.bbc.co.uk/news/10230766).

Hill, Peter B.E. 2003. *The Japanese Mafia: Yakuza, Law, and the State*. New York: Oxford University Press.

Hochschild, Adam. 2011. "Africa Abandoned." *The New York Times*. (April 3).

Huisman, Wim. 2010. *Business as Usual? Corporate Involvement in International Crimes*. The Hague: Eleven International.

Hulsman, Louk H. G. 1986. "Critical Criminology and the Concept of Crime." *Contemporary Crises* 10: 63–80.

IANSA ≟ International Action Network on Small Arms, Oxfam International and Saferworld. 2007. *Africa's Missing Billions. International Arms Flow and the Cost of Conflict*. London: IANSA.

IPCC ≟ Intergovernmental Panel on Climate Change. 2007. *Climate Change 2007. Summary for Policy Makers*. Geneva: IPCC.

ITTO ≟ International Tropical Timber Trade Organisation. 2009. *Annual Review and Assessment of the World Timber Situation*. Yokohama, Japan: ITTO.

Jaakko Pöyry Consulting. 2005. *Overview of Illegal Logging. Report Prepared for the Australian Department of Agriculture, Fisheries, and Forestry*. Melbourne: Jaakko Pöyry Consulting.

Jackson, Joe. 2008. *The Thief at the End of the World: Rubber, Power, and the Seeds of Empire*. New York: Viking.

Jenkins, Mark. 2008. "Who Murdered the Virunga Gorillas?" *National Geographic Magazine*. (July).

Jomo, K. S., Y. T. Chang, K. J. Khoo, et al. 2004. *Deforesting Malaysia. Political Economy and Social Ecology of Agricultural Expansion and Commercial Logging*. London/New York: ZED.

Khan, Amir Mohammad. 2010. "'Timber Mafia' Made Flood Worse." *Al Jazeera*. (August 17).

Khatchadourian, Raffi. 2008. "The Stolen Forests. Inside the Covert War on Illegal Logging." *The New Yorker*. (October 6).

Kolstad, Ivar, and Tina Søreide. 2009. "Corruption in Natural Resource Management: Implications for Policy Makers." *Resources Policy* 34: 214–26.

Koonings, Kees, and Dirk Kruijt. 2004. *Armed Actors. Organized Violence and State Failure in Latin America*. London/New York: Zed Books.

Koyuncu, Cuneyt, and Rasim Yilmaz. 2009. "The Impact of Corruption on Deforestation: A Cross-Country Evidence." *The Journal of Developing Areas* 42(2): 213–22.

Olmo, Rosa Del. 1984. *América Latina y su Criminologia*. Mexico City: Siglo Veintiuno.

Lawson, Sam, and Larry MacFaul. 2010. *Illegal Logging and Related Trade. Indicators of the Global Response*. London: Chatham House.

Leakey, Richard E., and Roger Lewin. 1996. *The Sixth Extinction. Patterns of Life and the Future of Humankind*. London: Weidenfeld & Nicolson.

London, Mark, and Brian Kelly. 2007. *The Last Forest. The Amazon in the Age of Globalisation*. New York: Random House.

Loureiro, Violeta Refkalefsky. 2001. *Estado, Bandidos E Heróis. Utopia e luta na Amazônia*, 2nd ed. Belém, Brazil: Cejup.

MacAllister, Debra J. 1992. *Illegal Timber Trade: Asia-Pacific*. Cambridge, UK: Traffic International.

Marshal, Ineke Haen, and Kristiina Kangaspunta. 2006. "Introduction." In *Eco-Crime and Justice. Essays on Environmental Crime*, edited by Kristiina Kangaspunta and Ineke Haen Marshal. Turin, Italy: UNICRI.

Malhi, Yadvinder, J. Timmons Roberts, Richard A. Betts, Timothy J. Killeen, Wenhong Li, and Carlos A. Nobre. 2008. "Climate Change, Deforestation, and the Fate of the Amazon." *Science* 319(5860): 169–92.

Mendes, Chico. 1989. *Fight for the Forest. Chico Mendes in His Own Words*. London: Latin America Bureau.

Middleton, Lucy. 2007. "The Last Place on Earth...to Make Contact With Civilization." *New Scientist* 194(2608): 37.

Miller, Michael J. 2011. "Persistent Illegal Logging in Costa Rica: The Role of Corruption Among Forestry Officials." *The Journal of Environment Development* 20(1): 50–68.

Monbiot, George. 2010. "The Sumatran Rainforest Faces Destruction. And Now One of the Biggest Logging Companies Has Hired a Former Green Activist to Justify Its Actions." *The Guardian*. (December 2).

Naím, Moisés. 2007. *Illicit. How Smugglers, Traffickers, and Copycats Are Hijacking the Global Economy*. London: Arrow.

Naylor, R.T. 2004. "The Underworld of Ivory." *Crime, Law and Social Change* 42: 261–95.

Nelken, David. 1994. "Reflexive Criminology?" In *The Futures of Criminology*, edited by David Nelken. London: Sage.

Nellemann, C., Miles, L., Kaltenborn, B. P., Virtue, M., and Ahlenius, H. (eds). 2007. *The Last Stand of the Orangutan—State of Emergency: Illegal Logging, Fire and Palm Oil in Indonesia's National Parks*. UNEP United Nations Environment Programme. Arendal (Norway): UNEP/GRID.

New Oxford Dictionary. 2007. "Apple (computer)."

Oreskes, Naomi, and Erik M. Conway. 2010. *Merchants of Doubt: How a Handful of Scientists Obscured the Truth on Issues from Tobacco Smoke to Global Warming*. New York: Bloomsbury.

Passas, Nikos. 2002. "Cross-Border Crime and the Interface Between Legal and Illegal Actors." In *Upperworld and Underworld in Cross-Border Crime*, edited by Petrus C. van Duijne, Klaus van Lampe, and Nikos Passas. Nijmegen: Wolf Legal.

Pearce, Fred. 2004. "Brazil's Beef Trade Wrecks Rainforest." *New Scientist* 182(2442): 14–5.

Phillips, Tom. 2008. "Hundreds of Brazil's Eco-Warriors at Risk of Assassination." *The Guardian*. (December 22).

Phillips, Tom. 2009. "Brazilian Taskforce Frees More Than 4,500 Slaves After Record Number of Raids on Remote Farms." *The Guardian*. (January 2).

Phillips, Tom. 2011. "Amazon Rainforest Activist Shot Dead." *The Guardian*. (May 24).

Rodriguez, Alex. 2010. "Pakistan Flood Crisis Blamed Partly on Deforestation." *Los Angeles Times*. (October 13).

Ruggiero, Vincenzo. 1996. *Organized and Corporate Crime in Europe: Offers That Can't Be Refused*. Aldershot, UK: Dartmouth.

Ruggiero, Vincenzo, and Nigel South. 2010. "Criminology and Dirty Collar Crime." *Critical Criminology* 18: 251–62.

Sachs, J. D., and A. M. Warner. 2001. "The Curse of Natural Resources." *European Economic Review* 45: 827–38.

Saragih, Bagus B. T. 2011. "TNI Blasted for Not Handing Over Businesses." *The Jakarta Post*. (March 12).

Shearman, P. L. 2009. *An Assessment of Liberian Forest Area, Dynamics, FDA Concession Plans, and Their Relevance to Revenue Projections*, Washington, DC: Rights and Resources.

Siegel, Dina. 2008. "Diamonds and Organized Crime: The Case of Antwerp." In *Organized Crime. Culture, Markets and Policies*, edited by Dina Siegel and Hans Nelen. New York: Springer.

Siegel, Dina. 2009. *The Mazzel Ritual. Culture, Customs and Crime in the Diamond Trade*. New York: Springer.

Sijabat, Ridwan Max. 2007. "Illegal Logging: Torn Between Environment, Business." *The Jakarta Post*. (October 16).

Sollund, Ragnhild. ed. 2008. *Global Harms. Ecological Crime and Speciesism*. New York: Nova.

South, Nigel. 2007. "The 'Corporate Colonisation of Nature': Bio-prospecting, Bio-piracy and the Development of Green Criminology," In *Issues in Green Criminology. Confronting Harms Against Environments, Humanity and Other Animals*, edited by Piers Beirne and Nigel South. Devon, UK: Willan.

Tollefson, Jeff. 2007. "Deforestation on the Agenda at Climate Meeting?" *Nature* 450(7170):590–1.

Tsing, Anna Lowenhaupt. 2005. *Friction. An Ethnography of Global Connection*. Princeton, NJ: Princeton University Press.

United Nations. 1990. *Eighth United Nations Congress on the Prevention of Crime and the Treatment of Offenders, Havana, Cuba 27 August to 7 September 1990*. United Nations: A/Conf.144/7, 26 July 1990. New York: UN.

United Nations General Assembly. 2000. *United Nations Convention Against Transnational Organized Crime*. New York: United Nations General Assembly Resolution 55/25 of 15 November 2000.

UNSC—United Nations Security Council. 2000. *Report of the Panel of Experts Appointed to Security Council Resolution 1306 (2000), Paragraph 19, in Relation to Sierra Leone*, Report S/2000/1195. New York: UN.

UNSC—United Nations Security Council. 2001. *Report by the Panel of Experts on the Illegal Exploitation of Natural Resources and Other Forms of Wealth of the Democratic Republic of Congo*. Report S/2001/357. New York: UN.

Verweij, Pita, Marieke Schouten, Pieter van Beukering, Jorge Triana, Kim van der Leeuw, and Sebastiaan Hess. 2009. *Keeping the Amazon Forests Standing: A Matter of Values*. Zeist: WWF Netherlands.

Viner, Katharine. 2011. "Brick by Brick: Eastern Congo Is the Rape Capital of the World and the Worst Place on Earth to Be a Woman." *The Guardian*. (April 9).

Yusufzai, Ashfaq, and Isambard Wilkonson. 2009. "Taliban Jihad Against West Funded by Emeralds From Pakistan." *Sunday Telegraph*. (April 4).

Wallace, Alfred R. 1869. *The Malay Peninsula. The Land of the Orangutan, and the Bird or Paradise: A Narrative of Travel With Studies of Man and Nature*. London: Macmillan.

White, Rob. 2008. *Crimes Against Nature. Environmental Criminology and Ecological Justice.* Devon, UK: Willan.

White, Rob, ed. 2010. *Global Environmental Harm. Criminological Perspectives.* Devon, UK: Willan.

Wicke, Birka, Richard Sikkema, Veroniks Dornburg, and André Faaij. 2011. "Exploring Land Use Changes and the Role of Palm Oil Production in Indonesia and Malaysia." *Land Use Policy* 28: 193–206.

Wilson, Edward O. 2002. *The Future of Life.* New York: Vintage.

Wisnu, Andra. 2008. "Tempo Loses Legal Battle to RAPP." *The Jakarta Post.* (July 4).

World Bank. 2005. *Europe and Northern Asia FLEG, Questions and Answers.* Washington, DC: World Bank.

WWF Indonesia. 2004. *App Buys Illegal Wood From Proposed Tesso Nillo National Park. Monitoring of Illegal Logging Operations in Riau, Sumatra.* Jakarta: WWF Indonesia.

WWF Mexico. 2004. *Illegal Logging and Its Impact in the Monarch Butterfly Biosphere Reserve.* Mexico City: WWF Mexico.

PART IV

POLICIES TO
CONTROL
ORGANIZED CRIME

CHAPTER 26

ORGANIZED CRIME CONTROL IN THE UNITED STATES OF AMERICA

JAMES B. JACOBS AND
ELIZABETH DONDLINGER WYMAN

In the United States, the Federal Bureau of Investigation (FBI) and the Department of Justice[1] (DOJ) have carried out a very active and successful organized crime control offensive since the early 1970s. The traditional Italian-American organized crime families (known as the Mafia, La Cosa Nostra (LCN), or simply "the mob") have been severely weakened and, in some cities, eliminated. Many other less-well-organized crime groups have also been greatly weakened or even eradicated.

The federal investigative and prosecutorial agencies have the legal tools and expertise to effectively combat organized crime groups. Nevertheless, organizational commitment and resources cannot always be assured. Looking back, it is impressive that organized crime control remained a top federal law enforcement priority for more than 30 years. However, the very success of the organized crime control effort diminished the seriousness of the problem in comparison to other crime control priorities (such as terrorism, white collar crime, identity theft, and computer hacking). In addition, depending on one's definition, "organized crime" encompasses many different criminal groups. How to prioritize the importance of these groups for allocating law enforcement resources is not obvious. This essay explains the organization of the US organized crime control effort, the legal tools that have made the anti-organized crime campaign successful, and future challenges facing organized crime control.

I. WHAT COUNTS AS ORGANIZED CRIME?

As Patrick J. Ryan (1994) has pointed out, law enforcement groups define their own targets and thus "define the subject matter of their efforts and that becomes the subject matter of the history of [organized crime in America]." Beginning in the early 1970s, the FBI and DOJ more or less equated "organized crime" with Italian-American "crime families." This made sense because the Italian-American crime families, known as Cosa Nostra or LCN, had long been the most visible, prominent, sophisticated, and powerful crime groups in the United States (Abadinsky 2010; Roth 2009; Raab 2005; Dash 2009). The FBI identified 23 LCN crime families in 19 cities; each city had one crime family except New York City, which was home to five families. It is our view that the LCN crime families operated autonomously, although some law enforcement officials and analysts see more coordination than we do.

The federal government has directed its organized crime control efforts mostly, but not exclusively, against these LCN crime families. However, if "organized crime" is defined more broadly, hundreds of groups could be labeled "organized crime." (For instance, the Congressional Research Service (2010) has recently identified Russian, Asian, Balkan, Middle Eastern, and African crime groups.) Congress has played an important role in defining and prioritizing organized crime threats by convening high-profile hearings on LCN and sometimes other groups (Jacobs and Mullin 2003). However, two presidential commissions focused exclusively on the Italian-American LCN groups (President's Commission on Law Enforcement and the Administration of Justice 1967; President's Commission on Organized Crime 1986). While the LCN crime families have been the most long-lasting, sophisticated, and powerful organized crime group in the United States, for empirical, logical, and political reasons it is not possible to define organized crime as solely an Italian-American phenomenon (Maltz 1976). The FBI's official definition, for example, defines "organized crime" as

> any group having some manner of a formalized structure and whose primary objective is to obtain money through illegal activities. Such groups maintain their position through the use of actual or threatened violence, corrupt public officials, graft, or extortion, and generally have a significant impact on the people in their locales, region, or the country as a whole (Federal Bureau of Investigation 2010).[2]

This definition would include hundreds of other groups, including Irish, Russian, Chinese, Israeli, and Albanian groups, as well as bikers clubs, street gangs, and drug traffickers. The larger the number of groups defined as organized crime, the less successful the federal anti-organized crime program looks. The FBI and DOJ do not have the resources to investigate and build strong cases against all these groups; if limited federal organized crime control resources are dispersed over dozens or scores of different groups, the resources available for use against the most important organized crime groups would necessarily be diminished.

II. Federal, State, and Local Elements of the Anti-organized Crime "Program"

The FBI and the DOJ have been the most important government agencies in defining and combating organized crime. (While the FBI is part of the US Department of

Justice, it operates more or less autonomously.) For reasons that are still unclear, J. Edgar Hoover, who served as FBI director from 1924 until his death in 1972, did not believe that organized crime should be an FBI priority, preferring to keep the FBI focused on communist and other "subversive" threats. After Hoover's death, the FBI reinvented itself as a modern law enforcement agency. Italian-American organized crime became its number one priority (Jacobs, Worthington, and Panarella 1994). In the early 1980s, in New York City alone, 350 FBI agents worked with more than 100 New York City Police Department officers on LCN investigations (Bonavolonta and Duffy 1996). The FBI's organized crime control program remained a top priority until the 9-11-2001 terrorist attacks on the World Trade Center and Pentagon. Then the FBI substantially shifted resources and attention to counterterrorism.

DOJ's Organized Crime and Racketeering Section (OCRS), located at DOJ headquarters in Washington, DC, has provided important leadership for the organized crime control program. In the 1970s, OCRS formed and directly supervised special anti-organized crime strike forces in key cities around the country. These strike forces, working with the FBI, carried out many extraordinary investigations and prosecutions, but the 93 US Attorneys (one for each federal judicial district) were never happy about their independence. In the 1980s, the strike forces were taken away from OCRS and integrated with the US Attorneys' offices in their respective jurisdictions (Mollenhoff 1972).

Each US Attorney's office has a unit that focuses on organized crime plus one or more other crime problems, such as terrorism, violent street crime, or drug trafficking. For example, the Southern District of New York's US Attorney's office has an "Organized Crime and Terrorism Unit," while the Central District of California's US Attorney's office has an "Organized Crime and Drug Task Force Section" as well as a "Violent and Organized Crimes Section." The FBI has its own organized crime control program, which focuses on LCN, drug trafficking organizations, and other organized crime threats. As federal investigators and prosecutors combine organize crime control with other criminal control priorities, the attack on organized crime could be diluted.

Other federal agencies also play a role in organized crime control. For instance, the Drug Enforcement Administration (DEA) focuses on major drug trafficking groups. The Internal Revenue Service (IRS) has prepared criminal cases against organized crime figures who fail to pay their taxes. The Office of Labor Racketeering (OLR) in the Inspector General's Office of the US Department of Labor plays an important role in investigating LCN's infiltration and exploitation of labor unions (Office of Inspector General 2009; Jacobs 2006). In addition, to combat drug trafficking organizations, Organized Crime Drug Enforcement Task Forces, created in 1982, combined the resources and expertise of the Drug Enforcement Administration; the Bureau of Immigration and Customs Enforcement; the Bureau of Alcohol, Tobacco, Firearms, and Explosives; the US Marshals Service; and the Coast Guard (US Drug Enforcement Administration 2010).

Some state and local police and prosecutorial offices have also played important roles in attacking organized crime. For example, the New York City Police Department (the nation's largest) has long had an organized crime bureau, and New York State since 1970 has had an "Organized Crime Task Force" with statewide jurisdiction. A few of the largest county district attorneys' offices have units that focus on prosecuting organized crime groups. For example, the Manhattan DA's office has both a Rackets Bureau and a Construction Industry Strike Force/Labor Racketeering Unit (CISF/LRU), and the Los Angeles County DA's office includes an Organized Crime Division.

Coordinating the investigations of numerous federal law enforcement agencies is a constant challenge. Even more daunting is the challenge of coordinating federal investigations with scores of state and local law enforcement investigations. The National Council on Organized Crime, created in 1970, and the National Organized Crime Planning Council, created in 1976, are permanent coordinating bodies. Beginning in the 1970s, federal, state, and local law enforcement agencies created joint task forces to promote coordination (Jacobs, Worthington, and Panarella 1994). Of course, at any given time there are innumerable important informal relationships between the personnel of different agencies, such as the FBI and the New York City Police Department.

A. Political Support and Independence

To be successful, an organized crime control program needs political support; it cannot succeed in the face of high-level political opposition and interference. Historically, the Italian-American organized crime families successfully neutralized law enforcement efforts by corrupting local politicians, police officials and prosecutors. Thus, a politically independent and high-integrity FBI and Department of Justice[3] were essential for a successful organized crime control program. The FBI's political independence has been reinforced by the independent status of the FBI director, who, after J. Edgar Hoover, is appointed by the president with the advice and consent of Congress, to a 10-year nonrenewable term.[4]

The US organized crime control effort has waxed and waned depending upon the president and attorney general. For example, it flourished under President John F. Kennedy and Attorney General Robert F. Kennedy in the early 1960s and deteriorated under President Lyndon Johnson and Attorney General Ramsey Clark in the next administration. It once again flourished under President Ronald Reagan in the 1980s and Attorney General William French Smith and Deputy Associate Attorney General Rudolph Giuliani. (As US Attorney in New York City from 1983 to 1988, Giuliani brought many of the most important organized crime prosecutions in US history.) In 1983, Reagan established the Presidential Commission on Organized Crime, which, from 1983 to 1986, examined the state of organized crime and organized crime control. In addition, throughout the 1980s Congress kept the spotlight on organized crime with high visibility public hearings (see Jacobs and Mullin 2003). The Senate Permanent Subcommittee on Investigations' hearings in the 1980s illuminated LCN's role in providing illicit goods and services as well as its infiltration of unions, companies, and whole industries (US Senate 1988; Jacobs and Mullin 2003).

III. INVESTIGATIVE POWERS
AND STRATEGIES

The most important strategies for investigating organized crime groups are electronic surveillance, informants, and undercover policing.

A. Electronic Surveillance

Since the mid-1970s, the FBI has been heavily involved in gathering intelligence information on organized crime groups. Initially, it sought to identify and map the members, hierarchy, criminal activities, and business operations of each LCN family. Electronic surveillance was vital to this effort. In the 1960s, the FBI extensively used telephone intercepts (wiretaps) against LCN, but evidence obtained by electronic eavesdropping was not admissible at federal trials.

The Omnibus Crime Control and Safe Streets Act of 1968 brought electronic surveillance out of the shadows and placed it under a transparent regulatory regime supervised by federal judges (see American Bar Association 1999). Title III of that Act permits both wiretapping and "bugging" (electronic eavesdropping by means of surreptitious amplifying devices) pursuant to a court-issued warrant and a number of statutory restrictions (Electronic Communications Privacy Act 2006). To obtain a warrant, a prosecutor must persuade a judge that there is probable cause to believe that the communications device or premises on which they seek to eavesdrop is being used for criminal purposes and that traditional investigative methods have failed.[5] A judicial warrant is limited to 30 days (renewable for an additional 30 days). The agents have to "minimize" the privacy intrusion, by ceasing to eavesdrop on conversations unrelated to criminal activity (Electronic Communications Privacy Act 2006).

The FBI, and a few state and local police agencies, planted listening devices in LCN members' homes, offices, social clubs, and automobiles. For example, they managed to place a bug in Gambino crime family boss Paul Castellano's kitchen; in Genovese crime family underboss (second in command) Anthony Salerno's East Harlem's Palma Boys Social Club; in Gambino crime family boss John Gotti's Ravenite Social Club and in the apartment above the club where Gotti held his most important discussions; in acting Colombo crime family boss Tommy DiBella's home; in the Colombo family's Maniac Club; and in the Casa Storta Restaurant where Colombo crime family underboss Gennaro Langella conducted family business (Jacobs and Gouldin 1999). The New York State Organized Crime Task Force planted a bug in Lucchese family capo Salvatore Avellino's car (Jacobs and Gouldin 1999). The FBI even obtained a judge's permission to plant a listening device in Philadelphia crime boss John Stanfa's lawyer's office (Jacobs and Gouldin 1999). LCN members and associates could not safely transact business out of doors because of FBI devices that amplify and record conversations on the street or in a park. Extensive video surveillance enabled investigators to map criminal networks and prosecutors to prove conspiracies.[6]

As technology evolved, Congress extended the scope of the lawful electronic surveillance regime so that, if agents have probable cause, they can eavesdrop on cell phones, computers, email, and Internet-based telephone services (Electronic Communications Privacy Act 2006; Communications Assistance for Law Enforcement Act 1994; USA PATRIOT Act 2001; FISA Amendments Act of 2008; American Council on Education v. FCC, 451 F.3d 226 [2006]). The Communications Assistance For Law Enforcement Act of 1994 required telecommunications carriers and manufacturers of telecommunications equipment to modify and design equipment, facilities, and services to ensure that there are built-in surveillance capabilities, allowing federal agencies, with a search warrant, to monitor all telephone, broadband Internet, and VOIP traffic in real-time. Subsequently, the FBI unsuccessfully lobbied for "back-door access" to commercial encryption technology (Froomkin 1998).

B. Informants and the Witness Security Program

Extensive use of informants is another hallmark of US organized crime control. Under US law, court approval is not needed to recruit and utilize informants, many of whom are themselves involved in criminal activity. Law enforcement agencies have the discretion to recruit and even pay informants. However, finding and recruiting informants who have inside knowledge about an LCN crime family's operations presents special problems. For one thing, the LCN families demand adherence to the code of *omertà*, or silence. For another thing, members and nonmembers fear that, if their cooperation is revealed, they will be killed. Nevertheless, the FBI has been able to recruit some very productive informants. One of the most famous was Jackie Presser, a top figure (and eventually president) of the International Brotherhood of Teamsters, the largest private sector union in the United States. Providing assistance to the FBI was advantageous to Presser because, in return, the FBI made a number of his legal problems disappear. In addition, he was able to eliminate union rivals by providing the FBI information about their criminal activities (Neff 1989).

LCN's code of *omertà* began to break down in the late 1970s. Dozens of organized crime members and associates agreed to cooperate with federal prosecutors in exchange for lesser sentences, even if this required testifying openly in criminal trials involving their former colleagues. (Under US criminal procedure, trial witnesses cannot remain anonymous.) Salvatore Gravano, the underboss (second in command) in the Gambino crime family was one of the most famous LCN cooperating witnesses. While Gravano admitted to participating in 19 murders, the prosecutors deemed his testimony against crime family boss John Gotti and other LCN leaders so important that they agreed to recommend that Gravano serve only a five-year prison term in exchange for his assistance (Maas 1997). In 2004, Joseph Massino, boss of the Bonanno crime family became a government informant and provided information leading to the conviction of numerous organized crime figures.

The Witness Security Program (WSP) has contributed significantly to the successful recruitment of cooperating witnesses. Established by the 1970 Organized Crime Control Act, the WSP protects witnesses in pretrial detention, while incarcerated after trial, and after release. It can relocate protected witnesses and provide individuals with new homes, identities, and jobs (Earley and Shur 2002). The WSP has been extremely successful, albeit expensive. Approximately 18,000 witnesses and family members have entered the WSP since 1971 (US Marshals Service 2010).

Prosecutorial flexibility is another important feature of US organized crime control and of US criminal procedure generally. Unlike in many other countries, US prosecutors have broad, unreviewable discretion to make deals with potential witnesses. Considering the severe prison sentences faced by many prosecuted LCN members, a prosecutor's offer of a shorter prison term in exchange for information or testimony is very tempting.

Formal cooperation agreements between prosecutors and cooperating witnesses are intended to lessen the risk of false testimony. The cooperating witness signs a document fully disclosing his past crimes and states that, if the witness testifies fully and truthfully, the prosecutor will recommend that the judge render a reduced sentence; however, the actual sentence is the judge's decision. The "deal" does not become final until the witness finishes testifying, sometimes in multiple trials. The prosecutor has sole discretion to determine whether the witness has testified fully and truthfully. If the prosecutor believes that the witness has not done so, she may void the deal; the witness could then go to trial or plead guilty. In a trial at which a cooperating witness testifies, the cooperation agreement is made known to the judge and jury. Nevertheless, defendants understandably feel prejudiced when faced with incriminating evidence from witnesses who depend on prosecutors for a recommendation of sentencing leniency.

C. Undercover Policing

The FBI and other investigative agencies have discretion to infiltrate crime groups with covert agents who hope to obtain first-hand intelligence information and evidence of particular crimes. Unlike some other countries, court approval is not needed for undercover operations. In at least two extraordinary instances, FBI agents, operating with false identities, were able to penetrate LCN families and, over the course of several years, obtain extremely valuable evidence. Joseph Pistone's (aka Donnie Brascoe) success in the 1970s was unprecedented. By hanging around bars and clubs frequented by LCN members and associates, Pistone eventually gained the trust of LCN members. After six years undercover, he nearly became a member of the Bonanno crime family, just before it became necessary for him to break his cover (Jacobs, Worthington, and Panarella 1994). The evidence he gathered during those years played an important role in several Cosa Nostra trials, including the "commission case" (Pistone and Woodley 1987).

In the 2000s, FBI agent Jack Garcia infiltrated NYC's Gambino crime family. From 2003 to 2005, Garcia shared with Gambino members and associates the profits from supposed stolen property schemes. He developed a close relationship with Greg DePalma, a *caporegime* (lieutenant) in the crime family (Garcia and Levin 2008). Garcia's testimony helped to secure DePalma's conviction for racketeering and a 12-year prison sentence (Keteyian 2008).

IV. Procedural and Substantive Criminal Laws

1. Pretrial Detention

The 1984 Bail Reform Act allows defendants to be kept in pretrial detention if a federal judge determines that "no condition or combination of conditions will reasonably assure the appearance of the person as required and the safety of any other person and the community" (18 U.S.C. § 3142(e)(1)). In one case, Genovese crime family boss Anthony Salerno was indicted on 29 racketeering counts. Witnesses at Salerno's pretrial detention hearing testified that he personally took part in two murder conspiracies; intercepted conversations indicated that he had also been part of a number of other conspiracies to commit violent crimes. In ordering that Salerno be held in pretrial detention without bail, the federal district court judge said, "When business as usual involves threats, beatings, and murder, the present danger such people pose in the community is self-evident." The US Supreme Court upheld the lower court's decision and the constitutionality of the statute on the ground that pretrial detention is a "regulatory" scheme that does not constitute punishment before trial. (United States v. Salerno, 481 U.S. 739 [1987]).

A. Conspiracy Law

The United States does not criminalize mere membership in an organized criminal group, but aggressive use of conspiracy and racketeering laws comes close to achieving the same result. The federal conspiracy law prohibits two or more people from "conspiring to commit any offense against the United States," where at least one person performs "any act to effect the object of the conspiracy" (18 U.S.C. § 371). The essence of a conspiracy is an agreement to commit a crime. The agreement does not have to be explicit. It can be proved by snippets of intercepted conversations, video surveillance, and related conduct. Once a conspiracy has been proven, each coconspirator is guilty of every crime committed by every coconspirator in furtherance of that conspiracy. Because coconspirators are considered agents of one another, incriminating hearsay statements by a coconspirator inculpating another coconspirator are admissible as evidence.

B. RICO

A presidential crime commission and congressional hearings in the late 1960s sounded a warning about the threat of organized crime, especially its infiltration of the legitimate economy. In response, the 1970 Racketeer Influenced and Corrupt Organizations (RICO) Act provided federal investigators and prosecutors with an even more powerful anti-organized crime weapon than tradition conspiracy law (Blakey 2006). RICO makes it a federal crime to (1) use the proceeds of a pattern of racketeering activity or collection of an unlawful debt to acquire an interest in any enterprise; (2) acquire an interest in any enterprise by commission of a pattern of criminal activity or collection of an unlawful debt; (3) participate in conducting the affairs of an enterprise through a pattern of racketeering activity and collection of an unlawful debt; (4) conspire to commit each of the three substantive RICO offenses (18 U.S.C. § 1962). An enterprise may be either a legitimate organization or a group of individuals "associated in fact" (18 U.S.C. § 1961). A "pattern of racketeering activity" means the commission, within a 10-year period, of at least two of a long list of federal offenses or their state equivalents (18 U.S.C. 1961).[7]

In passing RICO, Congress clearly had in mind the specter of LCN families using dirty money to buy their way into a legitimate business, using extortion, fraud, or other criminal conduct to take over a legitimate business, or, once in control of a legitimate business, using criminal tactics to further that business's interests (Lynch 1987a; Lynch 1987b; Blakey and Gettings 1980). However, nothing in the wording of RICO limits its use to situations involving the take over or operation of a lawful business. Could the leaders and members of an organized crime group be guilty of a RICO offense by participating in the affairs of their organized crime group (an association in fact) through the commission of two or more crimes in furtherance of that group's money-making goals? After the Supreme Court approved this interpretation of the law in a watershed decision, United States v. Turkette, 452 U.S. 576 (1981), DOJ was able to use RICO essentially to convict individuals for being active members of an LCN crime family (Lynch 1987a; Lynch 1987b).

RICO provides federal prosecutors a number of advantages. First, it provides federal jurisdiction over cases previously beyond the reach of federal criminal law. The federal government may not prosecute an individual for violating a state law, but it may use RICO to prosecute an individual for violations of state criminal law if the crimes constitute a pattern of racketeering activity. Second, RICO allows the government to bring a case against many individuals (members of a crime family) at the same time if they participated in the affairs of the same criminal enterprise (the crime family). The need to prove the existence of an enterprise and a pattern of criminal activity allows the government to introduce evidence of the entire history of the LCN family (i.e., the enterprise) and the full range of that crime family's criminal activities. A third advantage for prosecutors is that a RICO prosecution permits introduction of evidence relating to multiple crimes and criminal schemes, not normally permitted to be charged in a single criminal trial; this might lead jurors to believe that the defendants must be guilty of *something*. For instance, evidence of the relationships between the defendants may be admissible because it is relevant to proving the existence of an enterprise. Previous convictions that would not otherwise be admissible may be allowed if they relate to the enterprise's activities (United States v. Minicone, 960 F.2d 1099 [1992]; Gunnigle 2006). In other words, RICO allows the government creative license to present evidence, otherwise inadmissible, as long as it is relevant to proving an element of the RICO offense. Fourth, RICO prosecutions allow the government to use FBI agents as expert witnesses to offer evidence of the organized crime family's (enterprise's) structure, hierarchy, rules, and criminal activities (Bryan 2003; US Department of Justice 2000). Fifth, RICO violations are punishable by very heavy sentences: up to 20 years imprisonment for each substantive offense, plus 20 years if convicted of conspiracy to violate one of the substantive RICO offenses. A RICO defendant can also be sentenced for the predicate offenses that constituted the pattern of racketeering activity and for the substantive offenses committed by each coconspirator in furtherance of the RICO conspiracy. In short, a RICO defendant almost always faces life imprisonment. In addition, RICO requires the convicted defendant to forfeit to the government the proceeds of his criminal activity. And the judge can also impose heavy fines, up to twice the amount of the defendant's illicit gains (United States v. Cagnina, 697 F.2d 915 [1983]; United States v. West, 877 F.2d 281[1989]; United States v. Marino, 277 F.3d 11[2002]; United States v. Boylan, 620 F.2d 359 [1980]; United States v. Sutton, 700 F.2d 1078 [1983]; United States v. Truglio, 731 F.2d 1123 [1984]). These financial penalties are meant to strip RICO defendants of all their unlawful assets and weaken the financial base of their organizations.

These government-friendly characteristics of RICO law have led prosecutors to use RICO in nearly all organized crime cases (Jacobs, Worthington, and Panarella 1994). For instance, the US Attorneys for both the Eastern and Southern Districts of New York brought charges against leaders of each New York City crime family in the "family RICO" cases. In the "commission case," Rudy Giuliani, the US Attorney for the Southern District of New York, charged four LCN bosses with participating in an organized crime commission through a pattern of racketeering activity (Jacobs, Friel, and Radick 1999).

C. Civil RICO Provisions

In addition to creating four criminal offenses, RICO includes a civil remedy that allows the government to sue individuals and groups to prevent future RICO violations. This has proved to be a very powerful remedy for combating LCN's influence in labor unions. The first such case, in 1982, was brought against the International Brotherhood of Teamsters (IBT) Local 560 in New Jersey (United States v. Local 560, International Brotherhood of Teamsters, 581 F.Supp. 279 [1984]). It resulted in the court's appointing a trustee to run and reform the union; that trusteeship lasted 10 years. In 1988, the government brought a civil RICO lawsuit against the entire IBT, the largest US private sector union (1.5 million members). (Jacobs 2011). The defendants were the union's general executive board and the leaders of the New York City LCN families. The government alleged that the union officers allowed LCN to exploit the union and its benefit funds in exchange for LCN's support for the union's ruling clique. The case was settled in 1989, the parties agreeing that there should be no taint of organized crime influence in the union. The agreement authorized the court to appoint officers to enforce the settlement by investigating and eliminating corruption and racketeering within the union and by supervising free and fair elections of union officers. The court-appointed officers are still at work after more than 20 years. They have expelled more than 500 officers and members from the union and have conducted five free and fair elections of international officers (Jacobs and Cooperman 2011). Similar lawsuits have been successfully brought against 20 other local and national unions.

V. The Difficulty of Evaluating the Success of the Organized Crime Control Program

Evaluating success in fighting organized crime is very difficult. We do not have good measures of the strength or profitability of organized crime groups. While the consensus among knowledgeable observers is that the Italian-American LCN organized crime families have been significantly weakened throughout the United States and fully dismantled in some cities (Blakey 2009), it is not possible to empirically verify this perception. Moreover, no consensus exists about the current strength of hundreds of non-LCN organized crime groups[8] or even about how organized crime should be defined.

The best information about organized crime is probably held in FBI intelligence files, which obviously are not shared with evaluators. Even if they were, we could not be confident that FBI assessments are accurate. On the one hand, FBI investigators might be consciously or unconsciously biased in favor of seeing organized crime groups as larger and more important than they really are (for example, to justify maintaining or enhancing the agency's budget or allocation of resources to organized crime control). On the other hand, they might be biased in underestimating the current strength of organized crime groups due to overestimating the success of their efforts.

Evaluators could attempt to assess success by counting the number of LCN-related indictments or defendants each year. But that number obviously depends upon the resources that are devoted to organized crime control. Since the 9-11-2001 attacks, the FBI has vastly increased its counterterror operations at the expense of organized crime and other priorities. In addition, even if resources were held constant, counting the number of organized crime indictments or defendants would not be satisfactory. All indictments are not equally important. Some involve the most powerful organized crime figures or multimillion dollar crimes, while others are far less significant. Some follow up previous prosecutions, while others break new ground.

Perhaps organized crime members themselves would be the best sources of information? Dozens of LCN members have become cooperating witnesses, providing detailed information about their former crime families. But how much confidence could we have in these cooperating witnesses' assessments? An LCN member does not necessarily know how powerful his own group really is, much less how powerful other groups are. He may boastfully exaggerate his crime family's importance or contrariwise downplay its influence to flatter FBI investigators and DOJ investigators or to protect his former colleagues and their operations.

However, to conclude that nothing can be done to determine the status of organized crime would be unduly pessimistic. One possible means of gathering accurate information would be to create an independent commission that would be charged with making city-by-city assessments of organized crime strength and activities on an annual or biennial basis. In addition, we ought not to disregard the uniform agreement among law enforcement officers that the LCN families have been severely weakened. It seems unlikely that all observers are wrong. Still, it would be wise to be cautious about prematurely declaring victory and to remember that LCN has been very resilient in the past. A resurgence is not impossible.

A. Challenges for the Future

The biggest future challenges for US organized crime control efforts are resources and focus. Since 9-11-2001, the FBI has significantly shifted resources away from organized crime control and to counterterrorism. That priority shift will likely persist for many years. In addition, among non-counterterrorism priorities, many crime problems now compete for attention, including corporate crime, environmental crime, computer crime, drug trafficking, and human trafficking. Moreover, organized crime control will be able to claim fewer resources if decision-makers perceive that past expenditures have significantly reduced the magnitude of the problem.

As long as LCN was almost universally perceived as the most serious organized crime threat, there was no resistance to focusing the organized crime control effort on the LCN families. These families also could be readily identified on account of their names, high visibility, and geographical specialization. Beyond LCN, agreement is lacking on how criminal groups should be prioritized and which groups warrant the attention of federal law enforcement agencies. There are hundreds, perhaps thousands, of small, medium, and large groups, whose participants engage in criminal activities. These include bikers' groups, street gangs, Russian cliques, Chinese triads, Jamaican posses, South American drug cartels, Israeli amphetamine trafficking groups, and a great many others. The FBI and federal prosecutors cannot target more than a few at a time. The emergence of the Central American MS-13 gang in many states, including California and New York, led to the creation of a federal MS-13 task force (Connell 2005). But similar task forces cannot be set up to target more than a few gangs and gang-like organizations. The DOJ has recently discussed merging the OCRS with its Gangs Unit (Palazollo 2010). This shift, however, represents more of a movement *away* from single-minded concentration on Italian-American organized crime families than a movement *toward* focus on a small number of the most dangerous groups. Reasonable people will differ on which groups constitute the biggest threats and on which groups FBI, DOJ, and other federal law enforcement targeting can have the most effect for the least expenditure of resources.

In the future, much of the responsibility for organized crime control will necessarily fall on state and local police and prosecutors. Building up the capacity of statewide enforcement agencies, like New York State's Organized Crime Task Force, would be a major step forward, as most police and prosecution offices are small and cannot themselves marshal the resources to properly address organized crime groups. The federal law enforcement agencies will need to play a consulting and coordinating role, providing financial and material assistance where and when necessary.

Notes

1. The Department of Justice, headed by the US Attorney General, is the cabinet department in charge of enforcing federal laws. Most of the DOJ's prosecutors are placed in 93 US Attorneys' offices, located throughout the United States. But there is also a substantial cadre of prosecutors in "Main Justice," the DOJ's Washington, DC, headquarters. One of Main Justice's units is the "Organized Crime and Racketeering Section," which helps to define organized crime priorities and provide assistance to the US Attorneys' offices. The DOJ also contains several law enforcement agencies, including the FBI. However, the FBI operates quite independently.

2. Many experts and scholars have also offered definitions. The President's Commission on Organized Crime in 1986 identified several key characteristics of an organized crime group: "continuity, structure, membership, criminality, violence, and a common purpose of profit or power" (President's Commission on Organized Crime 1986). Sociologist Michael Maltz's definition is even broader: cooperation between two or more individuals to commit crimes, where those crimes are intended to gain economic or political power (Maltz 1976).

3. The George W. Bush administration's firing of some US Attorneys for political reasons was a striking and harshly criticized exception to the independence of the DOJ (Johnston and Lipton 2007).

4. Even though the FBI has been largely scandal-free, there have been exceptions. Two Boston scandals rocked the law enforcement community in the 2000s, one in which an FBI agent was convicted in 2002 of aiding a gangster who has appeared on the FBI's "Ten Most Wanted" list; in another in 2003 an agent was indicted for helping set up a mob hit on a businessman (O'Neill 2000; Collins 2003). In addition, a retired FBI supervisor in New York City was indicted in 2007 for helping an LCN informant commit multiple murders in the 1980s and 1990s; however, that case was later dismissed (Brick 2007). For the most part, however, the FBI's successes have been due, in part, to its political independence and culture of integrity.

5. The DOJ reports every year on the number of eavesdropping applications and almost all are granted. For example, in 2008, there were 1,891 applications and 1,891 authorizations (Administrative Office of the United States Courts 2008).

6. A number of courts have held that, while Title III does not on its face extend to video surveillance, its provisions apply by analogy (United States v. Torres, 75 F.2d 875 [1984]; United
   States v. Koyomejian, 970 F.2d 536 [1992]).
7. There are two other federal racketeering statutes: 18 U.S.C. § 1955 (prohibiting illegal gambling businesses) and 18 U.S.C. § 1959 (prohibiting violent crimes in aid of racketeering
   activity).
8. However, there also seems to be a consensus that Chinese organized crime in New York
   City is also in decline (Feuer 2010).

References

Abadinsky, H. 2010. *Organized Crime*. Belmont, CA: Wadsworth.

Administrative Office of the United States Courts. 2008. "2008 Wiretap Report." Washington,
DC: Administrative Office of the United States Courts.

American Bar Association. 1999. *ABA Standards for Criminal Justice Electronic Surveillance,
Third Edition, Section B: Technologically Assisted Physical Surveillance*. Washington,
DC: American Bar Association.

Blakey, G. 2006. "RICO: The Genesis of an Idea." *Trends in Organized Crime 9*:8–34.

Blakey, G. 2009. "Organized Crime: The Rise and Fall of the Mob." Notre Dame Law School.

Blakey, G., and B. Gettings. 1980. "Racketeer Influenced and Corrupt Organizations (RICO):
Basic Concepts—Criminal and Civil Remedies." *Temple Law Quarterly 53*:1009–1048.

Bonavolonta, J., and B. Duffy. 1996. *The Good Guys: How We Turned the FBI 'Round—And
Finally Broke the Mob*. New York: Simon & Schuster.

Brick, Michael. 2007. "Ex-FBI Agent's Trial Fizzles, As Does Witness." *New York Times*
(November 1).

Bryan, T. et al. 2003. "Racketeer Influenced and Corrupt Organizations," *American Criminal
Law Review 40*: 987–1040.

Collins, D. 2003. "Ex-FBI Agent Charged in Mob Hit." *CBS News*.

Communications Assistance for Law Enforcement Act, 47 USC §1001-1010 (2).

Congressional Research Service. 2010. *Organized Crime in the United States: Trends and Issues
for Congress*. Washington, DC: Congressional Research Service.

Connell, R. 2005. "MS-13: An International Franchise." *Los Angeles Times* (December 26).

Dash, M. 2009. *The First Family: Terror, Extortion, Revenge, Murder, and the Birth of the
American Mafia*. New York: Random House.

Earley, P., and G. Shur. 2002. *WITSEC: Inside the Federal Witness Protection Program*.
New York: Bantam.

Electronic Communications Privacy Act, 18 U.S.C. §§2510-22 (2006).

Federal Bureau of Investigation. 2010. "Organized Crime: Glossary." http://www.fbi.gov/hq/
cid/orgcrime/glossary.htm.

Feuer, A. 2010. "The Last of the Asian Godfathers." *New York Times* (April 18).

FISA Amendments Act of 2008 (2008), *Pub.L. 110-261*.

Froomkin, D. 1998. "Deciphering Encryption." *Washington Post Online*.

Garcia, J., and M. Levin. 2008. *Making Jack Falcone: An Undercover FBI Agent Takes Down a
Mafia Family*. New York: Touchstone.

Gunnigle, J. 2006. "'Birds of a Feather' RICO: Tying Partners in Crime Together." *Syracuse
Journal of International Law and Commerce 25*:41–106.

Jacobs, J. 2006. *Mobsters, Unions, and Fed: The Mafia and the American Labor Movement*. New York: New York University Press.

Jacobs, J. and K. Cooperman. 2011. *Breaking the Devil's Pact: The Battle to Free the Teamsters Union from the Mob*. New York: New York University Press.

Jacobs, J., C. Friel, and R. Radick. 1999. *Gotham Unbound: How New York City Was Liberated from the Grip of Organized Crime*. New York: New York University Press.

Jacobs, J., and Gouldin, L. 1999. "Cosa Nostra: The Final Chapter." *Crime and Justice* 25:129–189.

Jacobs, J., and E. Mullin. 2003. "Congress' Role in the Defeat of Organized Crime." *Criminal Law Bulletin* 39:269–312.

Jacobs, J., J. Worthington, and C. Panarella. 1994. *Busting the Mob: United States v. Cosa Nostra*. New York: New York University Press.

Johnston, D., and E. Lipton. 2007. "White House Said to Prompt Firing of Prosecutors." *New York Times* (March 31).

Keteyian, A. 2008. "The Fed Who Infiltrated the Mob." *CBS News*.

Lynch, G. 1987a. "The Crime of Being a Criminal, Parts I & II." *Columbia Law Review* 87: 661–764.

Lynch, G. 1987b. "The Crime of Being a Criminal, Parts III & IV." *Columbia Law Review* 87: 920–984.

Maas, P. 1997. *Underboss: Sammy the Bull Gravano's Story of Life in the Mafia*. New York: HarperCollins.

Maltz, M. 1976. "On Defining 'Organized Crime': The Development of a Definition and a Typology." *Crime and Delinquency* 22:338–346.

Mollenhoff, C. 1972. *Strike Force: Organized Crime and the Government*. Englewood Cliffs, NJ: Prentice Hall.

Neff, J. 1989. *Mobbed Up: Jackie Presser's High Wire Life in the Teamsters, the Mafia, and the FBI*. New York: Atlantic Monthly Press.

Office of Inspector General for US Department of Labor. 2009. "Semiannual Report to Congress, Volume 62." Washington DC: Office of Inspector General.

O'Neill, G. 2000. *Black Mass: The True Story of an Unholy Alliance between the FBI and the Irish Mob*. New York: Public Affairs.

Palazollo, J. 2010. "Breuer Mulling Merger of Gang Unit and Organized Crime Section." *Main Justice* (February 17), http://www.mainjustice.com/2010/02/17/breuer-mulling-merger-of-organized-crime-and-gang-sections/.

Pistone, J., and R. Woodley. 1987. *Donnie Brasco: My Undercover Life in the Mafia*. New York: Signet.

President's Commission on Law Enforcement and the Administration of Justice. 1967. *Task Force Report on Organized Crime*. Washington, DC: US Government Printing Office.

President's Commission on Organized Crime. 1986. *The Impact: Organized Crime Today*. Washington, DC: US Government Printing Office.

Raab, Selwyn. 2005. *The Five Families: The Rise, Decline, and Resurgence of America's Most Powerful Mafia Empires*. New York: St. Martin's.

Racketeer Influenced and Corrupt Organizations Act, 18 U.S.C. § 1961.

Racketeer Influenced and Corrupt Organizations Act, 18 U.S.C. § 1962.

Roth, Mitchel P. 2009. *Organized Crime*. Upper Saddle River, NJ: Prentice Hall.

Ryan, P. 1994. "A History of Organized Crime Control: Federal Strike Forces." In *Handbook of Organized Crime in America*, edited by R. Kelly, K. Chin, and R. Schatzberg, 333–58. Westport, CT: Greenwood.

United States v. Salerno, 481 U.S. 739 (1987).

US Department of Justice, Criminal Division. 2000. *Racketeer Influenced and Corrupt Organizations Act: A Manual for Federal Prosecutors.* Washington, DC: US Department of Justice.

US Drug Enforcement Administration. 2010. "Organized Crime Drug Enforcement Task Forces," http://www.justice.gov/criminal/taskforces/ocdetf.html.

US Marshals Service. 2010. "Facts and Figures," http://www.usmarshals.gov/duties/factsheets/index.html.

US Senate Permanent Subcommittee on Investigations of the Committee on Governmental Affairs. 1988. *Twenty-Five Years after Valachi, 100th Congress, 2d Sess.* Washington, DC: U.S. Government Printing Office.

USA Patriot Act. 2001. *PUB.L. 107-56.*

Violent Crimes in AID of Racketeering Activity, 18 U.S.C. § 1959.

CHAPTER 27

U.S. ORGANIZED CRIME CONTROL POLICIES EXPORTED ABROAD

MARGARET BEARE AND MICHAEL WOODIWISS

I. INTRODUCTION

ON a weekend in late January 2011, newspapers around the world heralded the "biggest Mafia round-up" ever as U.S. officials arrested over 120 alleged mobsters (Raab 2011). There had been major mob arrests previously, and each wave of arrests served to confirm the effectiveness of the U.S. response to organized crime and served to highlight the potential threat posed to society from one specific form of organized crime—the structured, membership-based mafia families. The impact of U.S. organized crime policies on foreign jurisdictions is undeniable and highly controversial. In this essay, we argue that the American view of organized crime and the responses to those threats have become the international responses. In some cases the international community has sought out the advice and expertise of the United States in countering their domestic crime problems, but in many matters greater pressures have been exerted in the quest to "harmonize" enforcement ideas around the globe—with the United States providing the "standard." Further, as the reoccurring mobster sweeps suggest, structural conditions that promote or at least facilitate organized crime remain in place and receive inadequate attention.

There is a difference between the view of the United States as offering a model for combating organized crime that is merely imitated by foreign jurisdictions, versus a deliberate strategy on behalf of the United States to encourage, pressure, or coerce international jurisdictions to comply. The rhetoric takes on a moral tone with the United States needing to provide the leadership. In 1997, Senator John Kerry wrote about the need for the globalized world to harmonize their policies and practices with the United States taking the lead:

Just as it is abundantly clear that America cannot go it alone against global crime and terrorism, it is equally obvious that only America has the power and prestige to champion that cause, forge the alliances, lead the crusade. We've done it twice before—in World War II and in the fifty-year struggle against communism. And we must do it a third time, and for the same reasons as before, so that those who would impose their will through deception and violence are vanquished and defanged (Kerry 1997, p. 193).

Speaking in support of the 2000 United Nations Convention against Transnational Organized Crime (U.N.TOC) to a United States congressional committee, Samuel Witten, a legal advisor at the State Department, noted that the United States could comply with the Convention's criminalization obligations without the need for new laws. "The value of these Convention provisions for the United States," he argued, "is that they oblige other countries that have been slower to react legislatively to the threat of transnational organized crime to adopt new criminal laws in harmony with ours" (Andreas and Nadelmann, p. 173). Witten, like Kerry, was illuminating an aspect of a process that Ethan Nadelmann has described as the "Americanisation of International Law Enforcement." "The modern era of international law enforcement," he elaborated is "one in which U.S. criminal justice priorities and U.S. models of criminalization and criminal investigation have been exported abroad."

Foreign governments have responded to U.S. pressures, inducements, and examples by enacting new criminal laws regarding drug trafficking, money laundering, insider trading, and organized crime and by changing financial and corporate secrecy laws as well as their codes of criminal procedure to better accommodate U.S. requests for assistance. Foreign police have adopted U.S. investigative techniques, and foreign courts and legislatures have followed with the requisite legal authorizations. And foreign governments have devoted substantial police and even military resources to curtailing illicit drug production and trafficking... By and large, the United States has provided the models, and other governments have done the accommodating.... (Nadelmann 1993, p. 470)

Nadelmann's claim has been substantiated by, for example, studies of organized crime control policies implemented in Italy, the Netherlands, Germany, France, Spain, the United Kingdom, Denmark, the Czech Republic, Poland, Switzerland, Albania, and Russia. American practices and precedents have strongly influenced remarkably similar changes in all these countries including institutional reforms, such as the creation of new, more centralized, policing agencies, and laws addressing the use of informers and wiretaps, plus laws that make criminal association an offense (Fijnaut and Paoli 2005, pp. 625–1042; La Spina 2012, this volume). The political rhetoric and crime journalism that has accompanied these changes often showed clear American influences, as illustrated by the headline and first sentence of the UK *Guardian* newspaper's announcement of the establishment of the Serious and Organised Crime Agency (SOCA) by British Prime Minister Tony Blair in 2006: "Blair launches FBI-style crime agency" followed by "Tony Blair said today that Britain's new FBI-style crime squad would make 'life hell' for the 'Mr Bigs' of organized crime" (*Guardian* 3 April 2006). Similar claims were made at the launch of the next "British FBI," which is now called the National Crime Agency, in October 2013.

One increasingly visible indication of U.S. success in exporting its organized crime control policies is the increasing ubiquity of organized crime control training programs. The FBI and other American law enforcement institutions pioneered these programs in the 1970s and have since trained thousands of officers not only from America but also from all over the world. In 1995 under President Bill Clinton, the United States set up International Law Enforcement Academies (ILEAs) in numerous locales including Budapest, Hungary; Bangkok, Thailand; Gaborone, Botswana; and Roswell, New Mexico, where police are trained in enforcement techniques involving crimes such as drugs, trafficking in people, and, more recently, cybercrime, including pornography and terrorism.

Once drugs and other forms of organized crime became linked to "national security," the training offered by the United States shifted somewhat. The 2008 U.S. federal budget included $16.5 million to fund an ILEA in El Salvador, with satellite operations in Peru. The objective has been to train an average of 1,500 police officers, judges, prosecutors, and other law enforcement officials throughout Latin America per year in "counterterrorism techniques." This focus on security and anti-terrorism issues, rather than more general police training in drug control, brought with it controversy regarding what was actually being taught. Salvadorans refer to the ILEA as a new "School of the Americas" (SOA) for police—and are aware of the controversial history to some of these training programs.

SOA atrocities came to light with *Washington Post* reporter Dana Priest's discovery, in September 1996, of SOA torture training manuals, and later with the acquisition by the founder of SOA Watch, Father Roy Bourgeois, of a previously classified list of SOA graduates, many of whom were recognized as leaders of death squads and notorious counterinsurgency groups (Community in Solidarity with the People of El Salvador, 2007).

The number of foreign officers receiving training has been doubling each couple of years—in 1999, 5,047 students from 173 countries gained training at these academies, and by 2002, that number had reached 10,115 (King and Ray 2000, p. 404). In addition to training administered in the foreign jurisdictions, many more police and other enforcement officials travel to the United States for training. Quoting Nadelmann: "The U.S. had extended its law enforcement reach by improving the way other countries do business. The success of the U.S. Drug Enforcement Administration (DEA) internationally, particularly in Europe, is attributed to the 'Americanization' of foreign drug enforcement" (Nadelmann 1993, p. 247). As of February 2010, the Federal Bureau of Investigation (FBI) had offices in 70 cities overseas and the DEA had offices in almost 90 (Bayley and Nixon 2010, p. 7).

Although, as Andreas and Nadelmann demonstrate, there has also been a "Europeanization of International Crime Control," in recent decades, there is no doubt that the United States has done most to set the international agenda on the analysis and control of drugs, organized crime and transnational organized crime (Andreas and Nadelmann 2006, pp. 237–41). "Major international agreements, that the United States played an instrumental role in creating," they write "have built on and reinforced each other and provided models for future agreements" (p. 245).

A thorough examination of this Americanization process and the extent to which U.S. legislative and institutional practices have been copied abroad is beyond the scope of this essay, we will, however, trace the significant part the American effort to export a global drug prohibition regime played in the export of organized crime control policies, before more closely examining the process as it played out in Canada. This essay concludes with a brief account of the export of administrative approaches to organized crime. It therefore traces the route by which the U.S. model became the international model and briefly examines with what consequences.

II. From International Drug Control to Transnational Organized Crime Control

A. Exporting Drug Prohibition

The process of exporting of American organized crime control policies followed closely that of exporting American drug control policies and, as we shall see in this first section, the process of Americanization began more than a century ago. The origins of American efforts against the use of certain types of drugs can be dated to the late nineteenth century, when missionaries wrote exaggerated and alarmist reports on the devastation caused by opiate addiction amongst people in China (Newman 1995). In response to these and other claims that tended to focus on the behavior of foreigners or racial minorities at home, American campaigners helped shape an international drug control system under the auspices of the League of Nations before the Second World War and at the end of the war were even better placed to shape the drug control policies of the United Nations (Musto 1987; Taylor 1969).

As Bewley-Taylor and others have documented, American influence, primarily represented by Commissioner Harry Anslinger and his Federal Bureau of Narcotics (FBN), permeated the personnel of the postwar U.N. drug control bureaucracy and ensured that the United States had a considerable impact on the creation and implementation of international drug control legislation. American influence lay behind, for example, the 1953 Protocol for Limiting and Regulating the Cultivation of the Poppy Plant, the Production of International and Wholesale Trade in and Use of Opium. The protocol empowered a U.N. agency to employ certain supervisory and enforcement measures, such as requests for information, proposals for remedial measures, and sometimes the imposition of an embargo on the importation or exportation of opium, or both. In other words it was an attempt to control opium at source. Although this aim had been incorporated in earlier drug control agreements, no working machinery had been provided for enforcement. "Some sort of international watchdog was necessary to keep the recalcitrant nations in line," Anslinger wrote at the time, "The Protocol signed today will help close these gaps" (Bewley-Taylor 2001, pp. 92–93). The American response to both drugs and organized crime has since been consistently about closing gaps in national and international control mechanisms (pp. 54–101).

At the same time as the United States was working though the League of Nations and the United Nations to influence the direction of international drug control policies, U.S. officials were also assuring that individual nations pursued drug control policies in harmony with their own. In 1929 Canada, our case study to be examined later, led the way by modeling its Narcotic Control Act on the American 1914 Harrison Act, with severe criminal prohibitions aimed at illicit trafficking (King 1972, p. 14). In the immediate aftermath of the Second World War the American authorities worked to Americanize the drug control policies of the defeated Axis powers, Germany, Japan, and Italy (Bewley-Taylor 2001, pp. 63–64). Federal Bureau of Narcotics (FBN) agents in the 1940s and 1950s, as Ethan Nadelmann has narrated, became "briefcase agents"— "Constantly on the go, they maintained contact with high-level police throughout Europe and the Middle-East, developed informants, pressured local police and their governments to do more against drug trafficking" (Nadlemann 1993, p. 133).

They met resistance from political officials by countering with threats. As Rome-based FBN agent Charles Siragusa recalled in his memoir, *The Trail of the Poppy: Behind the Mask of the Mafia* (1966),

> The police overseas almost always worked willingly with us. It was their superiors in the governments who were sometimes unhappy that we had entered their countries. Most of the time, though, I found that the casual mention of the possibility of shutting off our foreign-aid programs, dropped in the proper quarters, brought grudging permission for our operations almost immediately (p. 212).

Anslinger, Siragusa, and other FBN agents made the Mafia and, in particular, New York gangster, Charles "Lucky" Luciano, central to the international trade in drugs which was thought erroneously to have its hub in Italy. When a major heroin ring was broken up in San Francisco in 1952, for example, the FBN told the *New York Times* and other newspapers that "Luciano was behind it" and "was controlling all drug smuggling from Italy." Similar claims were repeatedly made and never questioned (Bernstein 2002, p. 118). Building on these unsubstantiated claims, media outlets consistently portrayed the multitude of drug markets as highly centralized "mafia" structured operations that posed a direct "national security" threat to America and later "international security threat" to the whole world. In the popular crime literature of the 1980s and 1990s, these claims were recycled as "historical background" to the evolving international organized crime problem. Claire Sterling, one of the best-selling and influential crime writers, for example, claimed that Luciano "understood the laws of supply and demand, the benefits of scale, the advantages of a transcontinental operation joining raw material procurement to manufacturing to transport and marketing. He was the seminal force behind what became the biggest commercial enterprise in the world: the multinational heroin conglomerate" (Sterling 1900, p. 100). Luciano's better biographers have shown these claims to be nonsensical (Newark 2010; Scaduto 1976). Properly researched studies have shown that most notions about centralized control of drug markets are built on flimsy foundations. "Monopoly control is rare" and "market power seems elusive," according to Peter Reuter's summary, based on the scholarly literature on drug markets (Reuter 2000, p. 320).

While the 1953 U.N. Opium Protocol was thought to have been a good start in the direction of complete international drug control, Harry Anslinger and his supporters felt that the U.N. 1961 Single Convention did not build on this. John E. Ingersoll, Director of the Bureau of Narcotics and Dangerous Drugs (BNDD)[1], was sent to a special session of the U.N. Commission on Narcotic Drugs (CND) in the autumn 1970. His brief was to point out the perceived weaknesses and initiate the first part of a United Nations plan, which, in Ingersoll's words "could develop into an effective worldwide program" (Ingersoll 1970). The Convention's primary weakness, according to the American delegation, was the fact that it rested "essentially upon faithful cooperation by all parties in the context of their national decision rather than upon effective international measures." The United States thus decided that the Single Convention had to be amended to "curb and, eventually prevent entirely" the illicit drug traffic. The proposed amendments had two basic objectives: first "to establish enforceable controls and appropriate international machinery to assure compliance, and, second, to provide inducements to Parties to perform faithfully all their treaty obligations." The flip side of "inducements for compliance" is "negative sanctions for failing to meet obligations"—a strategy that runs through the United States led developments toward harmonization. Ingersoll's delegation bluntly told the U.N's Division of Narcotic Drugs (DND) that it

> will be expected to pursue their present activities more vigorously but will have to assume new and important responsibilities." These new responsibilities were to include "a capacity for the planning and implementing of technical assistance programs to assist countries.... in the establishment and improvement of national drug control administrations and enforcement machinery, the training of personnel required for these services..." (Commission on Narcotic Drugs 1970).

Thus, the long-term effort to "direct" the international communities' response to drugs became U.S. formal policy. To institutionalize the process of exporting drug control policies, the Bureau of International Narcotic Matters (INM) was created in 1978 in the State Department. INM existed first and foremost as a "policy shop," representing America in international dealing with drugs, with the DEA and other drug enforcement agencies. It also helped organize crop eradication and other anti-drug measures and prepare the annual International Narcotics Control Strategy Report on global drug production, traffic, and what it terms "drug abuse." This report and the drug control certification process that INM managed from the late 1980s decided whether other countries were taking measures in line with prohibition policies. Essentially, the INM helped manage the effort to harmonize other countries' drug control policies along American lines. U.S. drug control policy was held up as a model for other countries to follow.

All the INM's work continues to the present day but in the early 1990s its remit was expanded to include money laundering, arms or other contraband, human trafficking and other forms of transnational crime. Accordingly in 1995 its name was changed to the Bureau of International Narcotics and Law Enforcement (INL). Today, the INL's main task is to work toward the implementation of America's International Crime Control Strategy. It developed this with other agencies in 1998 "as a roadmap for a coordinated, effective, long-term attack on international crime." In the pursuit of this aim American diplomats work incessantly through multilateral and bilateral forums to define what the INL calls "global norms for effective criminal laws" which are in effect American norms. The INL also "actively" encourages "foreign governments to enact and enforce laws based on these norms" (U.S. State Department 2011).

American diplomacy's most significant success during the 1980s was the negotiation of the United Nations Convention against Illicit Traffic in Narcotics and Psychotropic Substances in 1988. In the same year that the U.S. Congress reported on widespread increases in the production, manufacture, and traffic of illicit drugs, U.N. member states undertook moves to strengthen international legislation against drug trafficking. David Stewart, assistant legal advisor to the State Department and a member of the U.S. delegation to the International Conference where the convention was adopted noted that: "The U.S. participated actively in the negotiation of the Convention, and many of its provisions reflect legal approaches and devices already found in U.S. law." (Stewart 1990, p. 387). The Convention, which is essentially an instrument of international criminal law, has at its core Article 3; "Offences and Sanctions." As the U.N. Commentary to the Convention notes, the treaty deviates from the earlier drug conventions by requiring Parties to "legislate as necessary to establish a modern criminal code of criminal offences relating to various aspects of illicit trafficking and ensure that such activities are dealt with as serious offences by each state's judiciary and prosecutorial authorities (United Nations 1998, p. 48). As such the 1988 Convention significantly extended the scope of measures against trafficking, introduced provisions to control money laundering and seize the assets of drug traffickers, to allow for extradition of major traffickers and improved legal co-operation between countries. The Convention can be seen as a significant stage in the internationalization of American drug prohibition policies and remains an impediment for any country wishing to pursue alternative drug control policies.

B. Exporting Transnational Organized Crime Control

The convention came into force at the same time as the international community was beginning to make its responses to the forces of globalization and the collapse of the Soviet Union. Journalists and television documentary makers were also finding ways to update their organized crime formulas. Of these, the aforementioned Claire Sterling, did most to popularize and internationalize three themes that permeated the popular literature: organized crime groups as giant multinational corporations of crime, organized crime as an international security threat, and the need for "best practice," usually American, organized crime control techniques to be applied by police forces across the globe. In 1994 her book *Thieves' World: The Threat of the New Global Network of Organized Crime* (published in the UK as *Crime Without Frontiers)* developed these themes and illustrated the shift from the total preoccupation with the Italian Mafia to the view that similarly structured criminal groups were forming a global partnership—Sicilian and American Mafias, Colombian drug cartels, Chinese Triads and Japanese Yakuza had joined with the Russian Mafia to mount a full-scale attack on Russia and Europe to plunder both. "America" she emphasized, "was the first to realize the futility of trying to cope on its own. It has been urging other nations for years to work together on drugs, money laundering, counterfeiting, fraud—to perceive modern organized crime to be the planetary phenomenon it is" (Sterling 1994, 251).

In 1994 the United Nations held the World Ministerial Conference on Organized Transnational Crime in Naples and demonstrated that ideas that had no empirical support dominated international discourse on organized crime at the highest levels. United Nations Secretary-General Boutros Boutros-Ghali, set the tone of the conference with his opening address. Organized crime, he began, "has become a world phenomenon. In Europe, in Asia, in Africa and in America, the forces of darkness are at work and no society is spared...." It "scoffs at frontiers," he continued, "and becomes a universal force." Traditional crime organizations have, in a very short time, succeeded in adapting to the new international context to become veritable crime multinationals. It "undermines the very foundations of the international democratic order. Transnational crime poisons the business climate, corrupts political leaders and undermines human rights. It weakens the effectiveness and credibility of institutions and thus undermines democratic life" (U.N. 1994. Quoted in Woodiwiss and Hobbs 2009, p. 117). Boutros-Ghali concluded with what was already becoming a familiar call to international co-operative action.

It is clear from studies of the background to this conference that it represented a coincidence of interests between the United States, the member states of the European Union and the internal politics of the U.N. itself (Elvins 2003). It provided an international forum for a global conspiracy theory of organized crime that reflected the views of Sterling and her sources mainly from the American intelligence and law enforcement community. Many speakers at Naples implicitly or explicitly emphasized the success of U.S.-approved organized crime control strategies.

The main result of the conference was to put the elaboration of the United Nations Convention against Transnational Organized Crime (U.N.TOC) at the center of discussion. This process culminated in December 2000, when representatives of more than a hundred countries met in Palermo, Sicily to sign up to the Convention in principle, and 23 September 2003 when it came into force, having been ratified by the required number of states. Nations that have ratified the U.N.TOC Convention have committed themselves to the type of American measures deemed to be effective in combating organized crime by the U.N.

Having successfully internationalized their approach to organized crime, Washington, via the U.N.TOC Convention, also hoped to strengthen the global drug prohibition regime. This was implied when an attachment to a draft of the convention put the "illicit traffic in narcotic drugs or psychotropic substances and money-laundering," as defined in the 1988 U.N. convention, at the top of its list of serious crimes (United Nations, General Assembly 1999, pp. 52–3).

The following Canadian case study focuses on the export of the Racketeering and Corrupt Organizations (RICO) Statute, Currency Transaction Reporting and Criminal Associations Legislation, and illustrates ways in which international amendments and other formal and informal mechanisms effected major changes in the policing and criminal justice systems of sovereign nations.

III. Canada as a Case Study

Canada and U.S. share a long border so it is understandable that the influence of the US on Canada might be greater than elsewhere—however evidence as we have described reveals that the influence is in fact global. Each major inquiry or legislative thrust in the US had wide repercussions internationally. In many cases, key Canadians have played a role in spreading the US preferred responses to transnational crime. Evidence reveals that Canada's Colonel Clement Sharman was a very significant ally of Anslinger and helped him dominate the early years of UN drug control policy—culminating in the various anti-drug conventions. In 1988, the then Assistant Commissioner of the RCMP Rodney Stamler, played a major role in the discussions that led to the creation of the 1988 UN Convention Against Illicit Traffic in Narcotic Drugs and Psychotropic Substances (Beare 1996, p. 147). These transitions away from traditional domestic law and domestically framed policies and procedures and into an environment of internationally negotiated agreements were not made without evidence of a tension that continues until today. Canada wishes on one hand to cooperate internationally and yet also to "maintain itself in the highly insular, sovereign camp, bound by jurisdictional entanglement" (Currie 1998). Perhaps more currently this tension relates in part to the *Charter of Rights and Freedoms* which serves to protect the "rights" of Canadians, rights that may not be protected elsewhere. With specific reference to the impact on Canada, we examine in this section three key anti-organized crime enforcement tools, which were either "born in the USA" or advanced by the US.

The development of legislation, policies, and police practices in the US became the model that the US preferred for Canada. The 1967 US President's Crime Commission Task Force on Organized Crime served as an early alert to Canadians as well as Americans of the various threats from organized crime. US definitions and US perceptions of what and who were the organized criminals directly influenced Canadian media, politicians, and academics. While at the end of 1963, Metropolitan Toronto Police testified that organized crime had "decreased greatly in the last three years" and was described as "50-100% better" (Ontario Police Commission Inquiry 1964, p. 70), by 1967 the media had adopted organized crime as a priority issue. This prioritizing of organized crime by the media relied heavily on the credibility of U.S. "experts" whose concern regarding the infiltration of criminal investment into legitimate businesses was packaged for Canadian consumption (Beare & Naylor 1999):

- A visit to Toronto by Professor Charles A. Rogovin, advisor to President Johnson on organized crime, resulted in the following headline in the *Toronto Star* "Crime Said Moving In On Business" (March 15, 1967, 9).
- Ralph Salerno, another of the "group of 6" U.S. organized crime experts spoke to the Quebec Royal Commission and was quoted by the *Toronto Star* as predicting that Expo/67, being held in Montreal, would provide a good opportunity for organized crime (April 21, 1967, 39).
- The *Toronto Star* informed the public that the mafia had completed a "feasibility study" on Yorkville in Toronto in order to determine whether they ought to take over marijuana trafficking in the village (Oct. 4, 1967, 1).

Most alarming to Canadians was the message that the criminals who were moving into Canada were in fact an extension of US crime families. As part of the Ontario Police Commission Inquiry on Organized Crime, a team from Toronto, including the Chief of Police for Metropolitan Toronto, travelled to Washington to question Joseph Valachi, a prominent Mafia turncoat, regarding comments he had made to the 1967 US President's Crime Commission linking Buffalo N.Y. mobsters to Toronto. Specific links were drawn between local criminals and the New York crime families. While never gaining the notoriety of the 1957 Apalachin meeting of crime families, a number of US racketeers from Detroit were claimed to have met at the James Bay Goose Club in northern Canada on September 30, 1958—either for a hunting party or for more sinister purposes such as a meeting to discuss plans for US mafia members to move into Canada (*The Sun* 1961). The RCMP accepted the latter explanation and the media headlines announced: "Big US Crime Spreading here, police brass warn" (*Toronto Star* August 1967 p. A1). The stage was set—now Canada had to respond to this perception of a growing criminal invasion from over the border. Whether the threat was as great, and whether the nature of the threat was as it was portrayed, are separate questions. The threat became identical to the mafia-type depiction of organized crime within the US.

Three key responses to organized crime—RICO, Currency Transaction Reporting mechanisms (CTRs), and Criminal Associations Legislation—can be traced directly to a deliberate initiative by the United States to export to Canada and to the wider international community these specific policies, legislation, and bureaucratic machinery.

C. RICO *Comes to Canada*

Despite the enactment of the Omnibus Crime Control and Safe Streets Act of 1968 to combat organized criminals, the US federal government still believed that they lacked adequate tools to combat criminal *organizations*. Title IX of the Organized Crime Control Act of 1970 created the Racketeer Influenced and Corrupt Organizations Act

(RICO)[2], which is considered by many to be the single most important piece of organized crime legislation enacted (Jacobs 2006). RICO has become one of the dominant tools used in organized crime prosecutions within the United States. The arrests of Mafia figures are claimed to have been accomplished in large part due to wiretaps and informants—and the lengthy sentences that can be received from a RICO conviction are claimed to have weakened the legendary vow of *omertà* or code of silence (Bonavolonta and Duffy 1997; Volkman 1999; Griffin and Denevi 2002; Kaplan 2001).

Although it was seldom used until the early 1980s, by the end of that decade it was serving as the model for "fighting organized crime" internationally. Four factors lead to the international spread of this approach—first were the extremely successful mob movies followed by some widely publicized success with the RICO trials against the U.S. crime families. A third factor was the success of the U.S. in informing the international community that foreign jurisdictions were not immune and were at risk of being entwined in the "octopus" of global organized crime, deemed to be based largely on illicit drug profits. The fourth factor was the wide publicity given to the amount of money that countries could gain from the seizure and forfeiture of criminal proceeds, and under civil forfeiture to provide restitution/compensation to the victims.

Making the criminal pay, while victims, governments, and police departments gained, became the mantra. Each of these four above mentioned factors played upon Canada and led to the creation in 1989 of the Proceeds of Crime Legislation and the more recent legislation that followed to target money launderers and suspected terrorists. Once a country took that first step toward mimicking aspects of the US RICO model, other amendments followed in turn, as threats shifted from drugs, to organized crime more generally, and later to add the threat of terrorism to the mix. While some procedural aspects of RICO were rejected due mainly to differences in the two Federal justice systems—the shared focus became "going after criminal proceeds" and lengthened sentences. The route that led to this legislation reveals considerable direct US involvement.

During the 1980s, Canada actively sought out the experiences of the U.S. officials including the key U.S. RICO drafter, Robert Blakey. Professor Robert Blakey was invited to Ottawa twice (1982 and 1983) to advise on the creation of a "made-in-Canada" version of anti-organized crime legislation. At one of these meetings, Blakey was accompanied by Steven Zimmerman, Office of Chief Counsel for the DEA, Brian Murtagh, Acting Attorney-in-Charge of the U.S. Organized Crime Strike Force 18,[3] and Stephen Horn, member of the American Bar Association Committee on the prosecution and defense of RICO cases. Six months later a second workshop was held—this time with U.S. and U.K. officials—and again with Robert Blakey[4] (Canada 1982 & 1983). These meetings were part of a larger Federal-Provincial Enterprise Crime Working Group that was studying the status of organized crime and organized crime enforcement and legislation in Canada. The result was the 1983 *Enterprise Crime Study Report* (Canada 1983). This report found that Canadian legislation was deficient in two ways: it focused on single criminal transactions by single criminals rather than the activities of groups of criminals (such as the crime families within the United States) and also the existing forfeiture provisions were too restrictive.

Before most other countries had forfeiture laws to enable the seizing of proceeds from organized criminals, the U.S. was actively seizing these illicit proceeds and equally actively sharing the booty directly with, not only its own police forces, but also making offers to share with its foreign enforcement colleagues who were involved in the various joint-force investigations—while knowing at the time that Canadian legislation would not allow this sharing to occur. The inability of the Canadian police to capitalize on these offers caused much debate within Canada and intense lobbying by Canadian police forces. The apparent success of the U.S. proceeds of crime forfeiture program and an enthusiasm for sharing these riches with foreign police agencies served to encourage the Canadian police to demand the same access to their seized assets and a sharing protocol with foreign jurisdictions. By 1998, the United States was pursuing what they themselves called "an aggressive program to strengthen asset forfeiture and sharing regimes." By that date Canada, Switzerland, Jersey and the United Kingdom had each shared forfeited assets with the United States (U.S. State Dept. 1998 International Narcotics Control Strategy Report).

If an additional catalyst was needed to propel Canada toward new legislation the Pinto case served that role (Canada. Royal Bank of Canada v. Bourque et al). A Columbian businessman—also described as a member of Colombian parliament—was arrested by the FBI in 1983 for his part in a massive $40 million U.S. conspiracy to launder money. A small portion of this money, approximately $600,000 U.S., had been deposited into an account under the name Agropecuria Patasia Ltd. at the Royal Bank in Montreal. Under the existing Canadian legislation only tangible and portable money or property derived from crime could be seized by authorities. Money that was mingled in a bank account was deemed to be "intangible" (*Gazette* 1985). According to Mr. Justice Lamer, the bank account could be seized if there was a victim, but drugs were considered to be a victimless crime. This case was mainly a U.S. case with numerous U.S. criminals—and yet it served to provide Canadian police with the incentive to demand the same tools enjoyed by the U.S. officials and to be able to share in the seized illicit proceeds. Likewise it drew U.S. attention to what they perceived to be weaknesses within the Canadian legislation.

In addition to criminal forfeiture, RICO allows for the state or private victims to sue civilly to recoup "treble" damages (i.e., the defendant must pay to the plaintiff three times the amount of damages that have been determined by a court). The civil asset forfeiture provisions of RICO focuses on property, not people and therefore no person need be actually charged (U.S. GAO Report 1998). In the opinion of the critics, the quest for criminal proceeds by law enforcement in the United States had turned into an enterprise that took precedent over any objective of pursuing justice (Levy 1996, p. 153; Cheh 1994 p. 4). Michael Zeldin,[5] former Director of the Justice Department's Asset Forfeiture office states:

> We had a situation in which the desire to deposit money into the asset forfeiture fund became the reason for being of forfeiture, eclipsing in certain measures the desire to effect fair enforcement of the laws (Taifa Nkechi 1994).

This was one aspect of the U.S. model that was rejected by Canadian officials who feared that if police forces were to gain directly from the forfeiture of criminal proceeds, there would too great of an incentive for this policy to bias the prioritizing of criminal investigations and to hamper the collaboration across jurisdictions. Easy, quick forfeitures rather than the lengthy but possibly more serious investigations and a "competition" for seizures were the concerns. To date Canada has rejected, at the federal level, both civil forfeiture and also the policy in the United States of returning forfeited proceeds directly to police forces. However, seven Canadian provinces have civil forfeiture legislation—British Columbia, Alberta, Saskatchewan, Manitoba, Ontario, New Brunswick and Nova Scotia (Krane 2010).

There is no doubt however that the RICO model had a major impact on legislative changes in Canada and that Canada, like many other countries, used it from which to extract concepts around which domestic legislation could then be shaped (Gastrow 2002, p. 22). In relation to the RICO legacy, the Canadian 1989 Proceeds of Crime Legislation created a distinct criminal offense for possession of the proceeds of crime and money laundering. The legislation allowed for much broader criminal forfeiture than was previously available under the Canadian Criminal Code. Police could now seize, restrain, and forfeit assets—both tangible and intangible that were derived from various criminal and drug offenses. Originally the legislation applied to only 24 offenses that were deemed to be "enterprise crimes" plus designated drug offenses. That list has since been expanded to include virtually all indictable offenses and more recently even some additional offenses that are seen to be associated with the activities of criminal organizations. However, even this expanded list was deemed to be too limited.

In August 2010 the federal government publically announced new regulations that designated several "signature activities" of criminal groups as being "serious offences." Before these changes (which were made on July 13th by order-in-council), the criminal acts perpetrated by criminal organizations had to meet the definition of "serious offence" as described under subsection 467.1(1) of the Criminal Code. However, the government's concern was that some criminal activities of so-called criminal organizations failed to meet this criterion because the offenses were not "indictable offences punishable by sentences of five years or more." In those cases the police and prosecutors could not use the many special procedures available in organized crime investigations and prosecutions in areas such as peace bonds, bail, wiretaps, proceeds of crime and parole eligibility (Stratton 2010). The "signature activities" include the following gambling related offenses:

- Keeping a common gaming or betting house.
- Betting, pool-selling, and bookmaking.
- Committing offenses in relation to lotteries and games of chance.
- Cheating while playing a game or in holding the stakes for a game or in betting.
- Keeping a common bawdy-house.
- Various offenses in the Controlled Drugs and Substances Act relating to the trafficking, importing, exporting or production of certain drugs. (CBC News 2010)

D. Currency Transaction Reporting (CTR)

While RICO was beginning to prove itself to be effective against the traditional Mafia families and therefore one could imagine other jurisdictions evaluating this degree of success, the United States had other components that they argued required universal harmonization. The enforcement focus had moved "up" from targeting customers, to distributors, to the higher level "king pins" and eventually landed on the money. The U.S. Bank Secrecy Act (1970)—also known as the Currency and Foreign Transactions Reporting Act—required financial institutions in the United States to assist the government in fighting money laundering. This Act established requirements for record keeping and reporting by private individuals, banks and other financial institutions. With "winning the war on drugs" as a priority, the Bush (Sr.) administration turned to a new type of law enforcement agency. The United States established their Financial Crimes Enforcement Network (FinCEN) in April 1990 by Treasury Order Number 105–08 (Grabbe 1995, pp. 33–44). Its original mission was to provide a government-wide, multi-source intelligence and analytical network to support the detection, investigation, and prosecution of domestic and international money laundering and other financial crimes. The 1984 U.S. Presidential Commission on Organized Crime had declared "money laundering to be the lifeblood of organized crime." In 1988 a "confidential" but much quoted report by the RCMP and the DEA detailed how millions of dollars of drug money was crossing the U.S.–Canada border annually. This unverified and already dated report was leaked to the public and served to support the U.S. complaints that the international community—including Canada—was letting the United States down in their fight against money laundering (Beare and Schneider 2007, p. 9). This criticism from the United States continued through the 1990s.

While U.S. pressure on Canada has at times been intense, a direct confrontation occurred when the United States listed Canada among the 21 "highest priority countries" deemed to be major money laundering countries. No empirical data offered publically to justify this classified list and the U.S. Treasury refused to make public the full list to the U.S. General Accounting Office's Money Laundering subcommittee. However, Ottawa was informed of their place on the list and the follow-up meeting with U.S. officials confirmed this listing. The Kerry Amendment (Section 4702 of P.L. 100–690) to the Anti-Drug Abuse Act of 1988 mandated that foreign nations must require financial institutions to report deposits of U.S. $10,000 or greater, and that mechanisms be established to make this information available to U.S. law enforcement officials. Basically countries were being told to replicate the U.S. Currency Transaction Reporting (Tracking) (CTR) System. Upon failure to do so, sanctions are to be imposed against non-cooperative countries (U.S. GAO 1991). Headed by the Senator Kerry Commission, by November 1990, the United States had "made formal approaches" to 18 countries that the United States considered to be of prime concern. According to the 1991 GAO Report on Money Laundering, when approached by U.S. officials, "no country had declined to discuss implementation of section 4702." In Senator Kerry's own words:

> I insisted that U.S. laws require major money laundering countries to adopt laws similar to ours on reporting currency, or to face sanctions if they didn't…the Clinton administration is taking the Kerry Agreement idea one step further—advising what President Clinton calls "egregious money laundering centers" that if they don't change their ways, the United States will…make these centers feel our pain. (Senator John Kerry 1997, p. 152)

During 1989, a delegation led by Salvatore Martoche, then Assistant Secretary of the Treasury for Enforcement in Washington[6] came to Ottawa to "encourage" the Canadian officials to adopt a U.S. style currency reporting system or at least meet the requirements of the U.S. government in some other manner. Martoche made it clear that the language of the Kerry Amendment was designed to establish parallel systems to those in place in the United States—with the backup threat that failure to do so would result in a country being denied access to the U.S. currency clearing system.

An interesting debate appears in the 1991 GAO *Money Laundering Report* as to whether or not bullying countries to conform was the most effective method in order to secure compliance with these U.S. laws. Initially Treasury appears to have taken the view that it is "not necessary to threaten countries with sanctions" and that a "heavy handed approach by the United States may work against obtaining currency reporting information." By 1990 however, Treasury is described as having "taken a more positive view" of the clout that is to be found in section 4702 (U.S. GAO 1991, p. 58).

In a 1998 report from the U.S. Bureau for International Narcotics and Law Enforcement Affairs, Canada was again designated as of "primary concern" for international money laundering—falling alphabetically between Burma and the Cayman Islands (U.S. State Dept. 1998). These U.S. rankings were of course met with opposition from those countries listed, especially since the United States itself had been involved in a number of high profile laundering cases. On the basis of research carried out by John Walker, the United States was the "#1" country for being both the origin for dirty money and the destination of laundered money (Walker 2000; Beare & Schneider 2007, p. 70).

At this stage, Canada had no equivalent body to FinCEN. Canada's response to the challenge of making financial transactions more accountable had been an enhanced "record keeping requirement" involving the retaining of bank records, supported by a voluntary suspicious-transaction reporting to police, and the "good practices/know your customer" approach to banking, rather than a mandatory reporting system (Beare 1996). This Canadian model did not involve mandatory reporting and there was no centralized mechanism into which transaction reports were to flow.

Amid the pressure to duplicate the U.S. system, Canadian officials attempted to determine the actual gains from the U.S. CTR system. U.S. officials had claimed that it alerted law enforcement officials to cases that had previously been unknown to them (i.e. "rang bells"), rather than merely revealing the presence of additional illicit proceeds during on-going investigations. Canadian Department of Justice officials were supplied with a list of U.S. cases as proof of their claims—however, their trip down to FinCEN revealed that in every case the actual investigation had been prompted by alternative sources of evidence. These findings were confirmed by Michael Levi's UK-based research:

> Overall, despite being sincerely believed in by their adherents, it is arguable that in the context of the United States, where there are many banks and where cash transactions reports are made on paper, currency-reporting requirements are an example of an over-trumpeted intelligence methodology, since except in targeted investigations, the system has neither the capacity to input the data rapidly (within six months) nor the capacity of putting the information to sound operational use. (Levi 1991)

The U.S. system is now fully computerized and is again claimed to be an essential tool in the fight against money laundering. In May 1994, its mission was broadened to include regulatory responsibilities and therefore "created a single anti-money laundering agency that could combine regulatory, intelligence, and enforcement missions" (Pike 1998). Arguably from an originally false set of claims, internationally a massive "industry" has evolved that now includes the creation of the international Financial Action Task Force (FATF),[7] with the regional FATF offices, and the Egmont Group, which consists of a network of Financial Intelligence Units (FIUs) such as the original U.S. FinCEN body. In 2008 the permanent headquarters of the secretariat of the Egmont Group was opened in Toronto Canada and as of 2010 the president of Egmont announced that there were 120 FIUs from around the globe as members of their network:

> This reflects the ever-increasing global commitment to work together across borders and regions in the exchange of financial information and intelligence, to fight ML and TF activities. (Egmont group 2010)

Driven by the work of the United States and the Financial Action Task Force (FATF), the "required" uniform standard now requires mandatory reporting of suspicious transactions and reporting of large transactions. Canadian legislation and policies are now in compliance with the demand of the international community—and with the United States. Canadian legislation moved progressively through the following pieces of legislation—each broadening and deepening the attached powers for surveillance and policing specific to anti-money laundering. Bill C-22 Proceeds of Crime Money Laundering Act was enacted in 2000 and was amended one year later to include terrorist financing (PCMLTFA).[8]

It is impossible to separate the influence of the United States from the influence of the FATF—in many ways the FATF gave the United States an international voice. Canadian legislation reflects their combined power to exert direct influence on Canadian policy making. As concluded by the FATF Canadian Evaluations of 1997 and 2008 (FATF 2008) Canada was one of the last of the G8 countries to have mandatory "currency transaction reporting" for large and/or suspicious financial transactions and was considered to be tardy in establishing a financial intelligence unit (FIU). Canada basically had to enact this legislation. This legislation[9] made mandatory the reporting of suspicious transactions, created a cross-border reporting requirement, and also created FINTRAC (Financial Transactions Reports Analysis Centre of Canada). Six years later, PCMLTFA was amended a second time with Bill C-25 (An Act to amend the Proceeds of Crime (Money Laundering) and Terrorist Financing Act and the Income Tax Act and to make a consequential amendment to another Act). This 2006 amendment to the PCMLTFA broadened the record-keeping and reporting measures applicable to financial institutions and intermediaries (Canada 2006). Under this legislation, money services, businesses and foreign exchange dealers had to register, and it allows FINTRAC to disclose additional information to law enforcement and intelligence agencies. In addition to other enhancements, the legislation broadened the ability of Canadian agencies to share information with their foreign counterparts.

The international demand for compliance with money laundering laws has moved forward with incredible speed—but with what consequences we do not know (Beare & Schneider 2007). Valsamis Mitsilegas describes the process by which money laundering counter-measures evolved toward greater "harmonization" in Europe:

> Through its association with transnational organized crime, it was perceived to threaten interests ranging from human life to the social fabric per se and state stability and sovereignty. The use of credit and financial institutions for money laundering purposes on the other hand, added to these categories the threat to the soundness and stability of the financial system as a whole. (Mitsilegas 2000)

The disaster of 9/11 and the sweeping of terrorism into the mandate of the Financial Action Task Force (FATF), culminated in a lifetime mandate for that organization. If the FATF was at all concerned about obtaining a renewed lease on its mandate, by October 31, 2001 (post 9/11) its future was assured. FATF issued new international standards to combat terrorist financing in addition to their original preoccupation over money laundering. The core work of the FATF since its creation in 1989 has been to combat money laundering (40 Recommendations), and since 2001, terrorist financing (9 Recommendations, FATF 2008–2012). This focus on money laundering is now over 20 years old and the FATF has become increasingly aggressive in the measures to enforce harmonization of anti-aundering strategies. What had begun as peer-evaluative, consensus-building exercise became a black-listing regime under the year-long FATF presidency by the United States. The former United States Treasury Undersecretary for Enforcement, Ronald K. Noble, became the FATF President for its seventh round during 1995–1996. A list of "Non-Cooperative Countries or Territories" (NCCTs) is now compiled and maintained by the FATF with the threat that "counter measures" in the form of negative sanctions could be directed against such countries. The 2011 list includes ten countries with "deficiencies" in their anti-laundering and anti-terrorist procedures, and an additional two countries (Iran and the Democratic People's Republic of Korea) where the FATF is calling for member countries to apply "counter-measures" to further encourage compliance (FATF Public Statement—28 October 2011).

Intensive anti-money laundering campaigns, multi-national agreements and diverse political pressures to conform, harmonize, and sanction have at best produced unverifiable compliance results. The rhetorical hype could not have been greater—likewise, the massive money laundering related cases involving negligence and/or corruption within financial banking institutions could also not have been greater. Banks in countries around the world have been found implicated in schemes and scams—including the major banks in major cities. In some laundering cases the most prestigious banks, rather than the smaller "off-shore" so-called havens, have played a prominent role. One example would be the estimated $7 billion to $15 billion of Russian Capital flight laundered through the Bank of New York between 1996–1999 (Beare & Schneider 2007, pp. 224–228). But the United States is not alone. A June 2011 report from the UK Financial Services Authority (FSA) suggests:

> Britain's banks, large and small, have done little to mend their ways since findings 10 years ago that 15 City firms played a central role in laundering up to $1.3bn of funds linked to former Nigerian dictator Sani Abacha. Those firms received nothing more than a private censure. Leaks later revealed that among those to have done at least some business with the Abacha regime were Barclays, HSBC, NatWest, and the London branches of Deutsche Bank and Commerzbank (Bowers 2011).

Obviously some cases have been successful and some sophisticated launderers have been prosecuted. As one enforcement tool among many, the strategy has merit. The danger lies in the exuberant expectations that overcome concerns for rights and protections of citizens. False promises and fraudulent claims are also of concern. The 2010 WikiLeaks revealed government cables sent by Secretary of State Hillary Clinton and senior State Department officials, which indicate that in contrast to the U.S. insistence that the harmonized measures to control money laundering and terrorist financing are essential and are having success, the truth appears to be less positive. The cables catalog a list of laundering methods that are being used that are in no way impacted by the measures that have been put in place under all of our anti-laundering legislation and policies (Lichtblau & Schmitt 2010).

E. Criminal Associations Legislation

When countries were beginning to appreciate the loose criminal networks and the blurring of legitimate and illegitimate operations, and the appreciation of "harms" not captured by traditional organized crime—the international community moved to criminalize "criminal associations" and proceed along what critics might argue to be the well-worn path that depicted organized criminals as distinguishable "bad guys" in a capitalistic sea of "good guys." Nations that ratified the 2000 United Nations Convention against Transnational Organized Crime (U.N.TOC) committed themselves to the type of measures deemed to be effective in combating organized crime—to criminalize the conduct of "organized criminal groups." This works best of course when the criminal operations resemble a more traditional mafia-type or gang structure rather than the fluid networks of the more sophisticated operations or the even more elusive ad hoc connections that are made and unmade almost spontaneously.

As already mentioned, all of the components of the U.S. anti-organized crime strategy can be found to be replicated in this U.N. Convention. One of the key requirements of those who ratified the U.N. Convention was to pass legislation to criminalize four separate specific crimes. Article 5 of this Convention outlines what countries are agreeing to in terms of the "criminalization of participation in an organized criminal group" and it specifies the terminology that described the criminal acts of participation, facilitating in, counseling, and/or the actual commission of crime involving an organized criminal group.

A contradiction appears in the series of U.N. responses to organized crime and now replicated by the western governments. In 2002, a U.N. report emphasized the diversity in the various organized crime operations. Based on an international survey, their report presented five typologies—that is, different structures and different methods of operation (United Nations. U.N.CICP 2002). Rather than rigid organized crime families and structures, organized crime in some jurisdictions, and for some criminal markets, was found to consist of loose, networks with fluid involvement of participants rather than "members" as such. And yet, during the same period of time the U.N. Convention follows a very different approach and serves to encourage harmonization on matters pertaining to transnational organized crime as understood along the more traditional structured approach.

Canada ratified this Convention in May 2002 and new Canadian legislation was proclaimed in January of that same year. In Canada, Bill C-95, known as the anti-gang legislation, introduced into Canadian law the notion of "Participation in a Criminal Organization" as a triggering mechanism for additional powers for the justice system and enhanced sanctions for the convicted. Bill C-95 was followed by Bill C-24 in 2002 (An Act to Amend the Criminal Code (Organized Crime and Law Enforcement). Bill C-24 serves as a confirmation of the government's commitment to the "membership" perspective. The new legislation (C-24) brought Canada more in line with the United Nations Convention Against Transnational Organized Crime (U.N.TOC) and, more in harmony with the U.S. approach to "the threat of transnational organized crime."

IV. THE EXAMPLE NOT FOLLOWED: ADMINISTRATIVE APPROACHES

"Bernard Madoff says banks and funds were 'complicit' in $90bn fraud" (Rushe 2011).
"111 charged in Medicare scams worth $225 million" (Kennedy 2011).

"Guns to Mexico flowing like drugs to the other direction" (Schachter 2010).

"Mexico's 'war next door' linked directly to the United States: Federal Authorities say traffickers are now entrenched in 270 American cities" (Potter 2010).

If proof were needed, these recent headlines, along with the many that accompanied the mafia arrests noted at the beginning of this essay, indicate that organized criminal activity is still damaging and destructive in the United States after more than 40 years of organized crime control. There is no doubt that U.S. federal and local police and prosecutors, using the RICO statute and other organized crime control powers, did well to put serious criminals such as Tony Salerno, Tony Corallo, and John Gotti and hundreds of other American Mafiosi behind bars (Lynch 1987; Blumenstein 2009), and that adaptations of RICO, in particular, have had their own successes in many other countries. However, as a neglected aspect of the New York Mafia story shows, had effective regulatory structures existed before the 1990s many of these gangsters would not have been able to exert such control over sections of the city's economic life in the first place. Imaginative U.S. administrative solutions to organized crime—at least as part of the anti-organized crime strategies—may be what the world should be copying.

In 1987 New York State Governor Mario Cuomo began to address the city's organized crime problems by setting up the Construction Industry Strike Force (CISF), which included state and local prosecutors, detectives, and accountants. The strike force not only initiated a large number of criminal prosecutions against Mafiosi, but it usefully deployed the insights gained from these cases and made significant proposals across a broad front in a serious effort to purge the industry of organized crime. Examples, noted by Cyrille Fijnaut, included the proposal to establish a special anticorruption bureau in the construction industry, the appointment—at the cost of the big construction companies—of special inspectors to audit major projects for compliance with building regulations, and in the case of noncompliance to report this to the appropriate administrative and justice authorities (Fijnaut 2002, p. 17).

Perhaps the anti-organized crime model that ought to be exported is the monitoring mechanism that is referred to as an Independent Private-Sector Inspector General (IPSIG) oversight system. Within the United States, an IPSIG is an independent, private sector firm with legal, auditing, investigative, and loss prevention skills, that is employed by an organization (voluntarily or by compulsory process) to ensure compliance with relevant law and regulations and to deter, prevent, uncover, and report unethical and illegal conduct by, within and against the organization provide sources. IPSIGs attempt to solve the dilemma of what can be done if organized criminals have entered into or gained control or influence over legitimate businesses or organizations that employ large numbers of legitimate workers and supply necessary services. The organizations cannot be closed down—and yet the organized criminal influence must be eliminated. In some cases the criminality might mean a loss of dollars but in situations regarding borders and ports there are significant security considerations. The IPSIG process was in operation most prominently at Ground Zero following 9/11. Knowing that the clean-up would turn into a corrupt, fraudulent, money grab by mostly everyone with access to the clean-up resources (including actual organized criminals), Mayor Giuliani's officials selected four accounting firms (IPSIGs) to monitor the clean-up by overseeing the construction work in each of four quarters. A fifth firm, KPMG, carried out standard auditing responsibilities at the site. The Integrity Monitors reported to the Department of Investigation forming an additional layer of oversight (Lupkin and Lewandowski 2005, pp. 6–19).

In Canada suggestions have been made for an embedded auditor—a system whereby a court would order that government regulatory inspectors be placed within a convicted corporation to monitor compliance for a period of time (Archibald, Jull, Roach 2004). In the United States the auditors are private companies that are paid by the corporation or operation that is being monitored. Whichever model is used, the idea is based on a recognition that criminals look for every opportunity to corrupt officials and to criminally infiltrate businesses and vulnerable businesses and services will be exploited.

In June 1996 Mayor Rudolph Giuliani supported the New York City Council's decision to create the Trade Waste Commission (TWC) with the explicit goal of eliminating mafia-connected waste-hauling companies. The TWC was structured as a regulatory agency with a law enforcement agenda. Its executive officers, attorneys, monitors, and police detectives were recruited for their experience in related investigations and prosecutions. As well as checking for mobster involvement in waste-hauling companies, the TWC also sought to strengthen the customers' position by setting maximum rates, regulating contract duration and keeping customers informed of their rights (Jacobs & Gouldin 1999, pp. 175–6). By the late 1990s customers were paying between 30 and 40 percent less to have their waste removed. Historically, the gangsters who owned and operated New York waste companies had set their own rates, retained contracts through force and observed very few customer rights! Other local initiatives addressed problems that the city's corrupt political infrastructure had left to fester for decades. The city's regulatory and licensing powers, for example, were used to attempt to limit the control over the Fulton Fish Market of gangster-dominated unloading companies (Woodiwiss 2005, pp. 81–2).

The European nation most influenced by the New York administrative approach to organized crime control has been the Netherlands. Dutch policy makers, particularly those who attended the influential Dutch-American Conference on Organized Crime in The Hague in 1990, were concerned about organized crime activity within the legal economy and became convinced that a control effort based solely on a police repressive approach would be inadequate and needed to be supplemented by an approach involving various agencies in local governments (Fijnaut and Jacobs 1991; vi). In 2003 largely as a result of this new perception of the organized crime problem, the Netherlands passed the BIBOB Act (Bevordering Integriteitsbeorde-lingen door het Openbaar Bestuur— Ensuring Integrity of Decisions by Public Administration). This act and other measures require the Dutch police to perform new warning and advisory tasks, involving using information from their criminal investigations to alert other public and private agencies and thus allowing for a more "joined up" approach to organized crime control. There are problems with this approach such as the quality of police information, interorganizational relations, and cultural differences, and these will need to be faced but they are a step toward limiting the damage of organized crime (Terpstra 2012).

Despite the clear benefit to the people of New York, the United States government has not championed the use of broad administrative alternatives in its foreign policy. Putting checks and balances on business activity, whether this is organized by public or private bodies or by a combination of both, does seem to hold out some prospect of successfully curtailing the opportunities for successful organized criminal activity in legal markets so long as the administrative process is transparent and those involved are accountable. However, there remains little prospect of successfully combating organized crime in illegal markets such as drugs as long as the global prohibition model perpetuates a "one-size-fits-all" approach.

V. Conclusion

The verdict of America's Wickersham Commission investigation of organized crime in 1931 still applies: "Intelligent action requires knowledge not, as in too many cases, a mere redoubling of effort in the absence of adequate information and a definite plan" (Smith 1991, pp. 149–151). As we have seen, much more than a redoubling of effort has occurred since Wickersham, involving indeed a multiplication and internationalization of effort, with little impact made on the extent of organized criminal activity overall. More fully effective organized crime control policies would need to be based on more rigorously researched foundations than mafia mythologies spread by Harry Anslinger and other Cold War warriors. Properly conducted research, however, may turn up some unpalatable realities, particularly about the war on drugs. It may be found, to quote Henry Barrett Chamberlin writing at the beginning of the 1930s when the counterproductive effects of alcohol prohibition were clear to most, that "some of the very best intentions of American idealists have supplied the pavement for the hell of organized crime" (Chamberlin 1931 & 1932). In contrast, enforceable laws and a broader administrative approach may prove to deliver some measureable impact in the international effort to control organized crime.

Notes

1. The Bureau of Narcotics and Dangerous Drugs was the successor agency to the FBN which had to be abolished in 1968 after a scandal revealed endemic corruption including the protection of drug traffickers within the agency.
2. RICO is codified at 18 U.S.C. § 1961–1968. See also *Organized Crime in the United States: Trends and Issues for Congress* by Kristin M. Finklea, December 22, 2010. http://www.fas.org/sgp/crs/misc/R40525.pdf
3. The United States Strike Force was created in the late 1960s for the purpose of finding and stopping illegal racketeering. It was formed in a congressional effort led by Robert

Kennedy. See U.S. General Accounting Office. 1989. Report to the Chairman, Permanent Subcommittee on Investigations Committee on Governmental Affairs—Issues Regarding Strike Forces. http://archive.gao.gov/d25t7/138558.pdf

4. Canada 1982 and 1983. Unpublished Reparative Sanctions Workshops June 1982 and January 1983. Ottawa.

5. As quoted in the *New York Times* (May 31, 1993, p.1), Zeldin accused his successor, Cary Copeland, of putting the maximization of seized funds ahead of good law enforcement. Zeldin characterized his Department's orders as saying "Forfeit, Forfeit, Forfeit. Get Money, Get Money, Get Money."

6. From 1988 to 1990, Martoche served as an Assistant Secretary of the Treasury overseeing law enforcement under President Reagan and President George H. W. Bush.

7. Quoting from their site, "The Financial Action Task Force (FATF) is an inter-governmental body whose purpose is the development and promotion of national and international policies to combat money laundering and terrorist financing. The FATF is therefore a 'policy-making body' that works to generate the necessary political will to bring about legislative and regulatory reforms in these areas." http://www.fatf-gafi.org/pages/0,2987,en_32250379_32235720_1_1_1_1,00.html

8. Amended *The Act to Facilitate Combating the Laundering of Proceeds of Crime.* Post 9/11, this piece of legislation was changed to *Proceeds of Crime (Money Laundering) and Terrorist Financing Act in 2001).*

9. 36th parliament, 2nd Session, Edited Hansard, No.79, Wednesday April 5, 2000 [1525–1725] and No. 80 Thursday April 6, 2000 [1110–1250].

References

Andreas, Peter and Ethan Nadelmann. 2006. *Policing the Globe: Criminalization and Crime Control in International Relations.* Oxford: Oxford University Press.

Archibald, Justice Todd L., Jull, Kenneth E., and Roach, Kent W., 2004. Regulatory and Corporate Liability: From Due Diligence to Risk Management, Aurora: Canada Law Book. Chapter 12.

Bayley, David and Christine Nixon. 2010. *The Changing Environment for Policing, 1985–2008. New Perspectives in Policing.* Washington, DC: National Institute of Justice, Harvard Kennedy School, Program in Criminal Justice Policy and Management.

Beare, Margaret, 1996. *Criminal Conspiracies: Organized Crime in Canada.* Scarborough: Nelson Canada.

Beare, Margaret and Thomas Naylor. 1999. *Major Issues Relating to Organized Crime: Within the Context of Economic Relationships.* Ottawa: Law Commission of Canada. https://www.ncjrs.gov/nathanson/organized.html.

Beare, Margaret and Steven Schneider. 2007. *Money Laundering in Canada.* Toronto: University of Toronto Press.

Bernstein, Lee. 2002. *The Greatest Menace: Organized Crime in Cold War America.* Amherst: University of Massachusetts Press.

Bewley-Taylor, David, 2002. *The United States and International Drug Control, 1909–1997.* London: Continuum.

Blumenstein, Matthew. 2009. "RICO Overreach: How the Federal Government's Escalating Offensive against Gangs Has Run Afoul of the Constitution." *Vanderbilt Law Review* 62(1): 211–238.

Bonavolonta, Jules and Brian Duffy. 1997. *The Good Guys: How We Turned the FBI Round and Finally Broke the Mob*. New York: Pocket Books.

Bowers, Simon. 2011, "British Banks Ignore Money-Laundering Rules, Says FSA." *The Guardian*, Wednesday 22 June 2011 20.16 BST. http://www.guardian.co.uk/business/2011/jun/22/uk-ba nks-ignore-money-laundering-rules-says-fsa.

Canada. 1983. *Enterprise Crime Study Report*, June 10. Ottawa: Department of Justice.

Canada. 1984. *Royal Bank of Canada v. Bourque et al.* [1984] 38 c.r. (3d) 363 (Pinto Case).

Canada. 2006. *Working Together to Combat Organized Crime: A Public Report on Actions under the National Agenda to Combat Organized Crime*. Ottawa: Public Safety Canada. http://www.publicsafety.gc.ca/prg/le/oc/_fl/ogcrime06_e.pdf.

CBC News. 2010. "Organized Crime Law Changes Unveiled." Last updated August 4, 2010. http://www.cbc.ca/news/politics/organized-crime-law-changes-unveiled-1.910802.

Chamberlin, Henry Barrett. 1931–1932. "Some Observations Concerning Organized Crime." *Journal of Criminal Law and Criminology* 22(5): 652–670.

Cheh, Mary M. 1994. "Can Something This Easy, Quick and Profitable Also be Fair." *New York Law School Law Review* 39(1–2): 1–48.

Commission on Narcotic Drugs. 1970. Preliminary U.S. Proposals, Talking Paper, Special Session, Geneva, September 25 to October 3, Egil Krogh Files, Box 31, Folder: International Trafficking—U.N. Commission, Box 31, WHCF, Nixon Presidential Materials Staff, National Archives.

Community in Solidarity with the People of El Salvador. 2007. "Exporting U.S. 'Criminal Justice' to Latin America." *Upside Down World*, June 14. http://www.projectcensored.org/top-stories/articles/4-ilea-is-the-us-restarting-dirty-wars-in-latin-america/.

Currie, Robert. 1998. "Peace and Public Order: International Mutual Legal Assistance 'The Canadian Way.'" *Dalhousie Journal of Legal Studies*, 7: 91–124.

Egmont Group of Financial Intelligence Units. 2010. E-Newsletter, December. http://www.egmontgroup.org/news-and-events/news/2010/12/23/egmont-newsletter-december-2010.

Elvins, Martin. 2003. "Europe's Response to Transnational Organised Crime." In Adam Edwards and Peter Gill (eds.), *Transnational Organised Crime: Perspectives on Global Security*. London: Routledge.

Fijnaut, Cyrille (ed.). 2002. *The Administrative Approach to (Organised) Crime in Amsterdam*. Amsterdam: Public Order and Safety Department, City of Amsterdam.

Fijnaut, Cyrille and James Jacobs (eds). 1991. *Organized Crime and Its Containment*. Deventer: Kluwer Law and Taxation.

Fijnaut, Cyrille and Letizia Paoli (eds.). 2005. *Organized Crime in Europe: Concepts, Patterns and Control Policies in the European Union and Beyond*. Dordrecht: Springer, Kluwer.

Financial Action Task Force. 2008. *Evaluation Canada 2008*, February 29. http://www.fatf-gafi.org/dataoecd/5/3/40323928.pdf.

Financial Action Task Force. *Revised Mandate 2008–2012*. http://www.fatf-gafi.org/dataoecd/3/32/40433653.pdf.

Financial Action Task Force. 2011. *Public Statement*, 28 October. http://rbidocs.rbi.org.in/rdocs/content/PDFs/FATS090212.pdf.

Gastrow, Peter. 2002. "The Origin of the Convention." In Hans-Jorg Albrecht and Cyrille Fijnaut (eds.), *The Containment of Transnational Organized Crime: Comments on the U.N. Convention of December 2000*. Strafrecht: Max-Planck-Institute fur auslandisches und internationals.

Gazette, Montreal. 1985. "Top Court Vetoes RCMP Appeal on Right to Seize Bank Accounts," May 14. http://news.google.com/newspapers?nid=1946&dat=19850514&id=A4YoAAAAIB AJ&sjid=2KUFAAAAIBAJ&pg=1629,1757374.

Grabbe, J. Orlin. 1995. "The Money Laundromat." *Liberty* 9(2): 33–44. http://www.virtualschool. edu/mon/ElectronicProperty/MoneyLaundromat.

Griffin, Joe and Don Denevi. 2002. *Mob Nemesis: How the FBI Crippled Organized Crime.* Amherst: Prometheus Books.

Guardian. 2006. "Blair Launches FBI-style Crime Agency," 3 April.

Ingersoll, John. 1970. Commission on Narcotic Drugs, Special Session, Geneva, September 25 to October 3, Preliminary U.S. Proposals, Talking Paper, Egil Krogh Files, Box 31, Folder: International Trafficking—U.N. Commission, Box 31, WHCF, Nixon Presidential Materials Staff, National Archives.

Jacobs, James B. and Lauryn P. Gouldin. 1999. "Cosa Nostra—The Final Chapter." In Michael Tonry (ed.), *Crime and Justice: A Review of Research,* Vol. 25. Chicago: University of Chicago Press.

Jacobs, James B. 2006. *Mobsters, Unions, and Feds.* New York University Press. NY.

Kaplan, David E. 2001. "Getting It Right: The FBI and the Mob." *U.S. News and World Report,* June 18.

Kennedy, Kelli. 2011. "111 Charged in Medicare Scams Worth $225 Million." *New York Post,* February 17. http://www.nypost.com/p/news/national/charged_in_medicare_scams_worth_zaEAiDzFwbVOxfAKWRQPcL.

Kerry, Senator John. 1997. *The New War: The Web of Crime That Threatens America's Security.* New York: Simon & Schuster.

King, Leslie E. and Judson M. Ray. 2000. "Developing Transnational Law Enforcement Cooperation: The FBI Training Initiatives." *Journal of Contemporary Criminal Justice* 16(4): 386–408.

King, Rufus. 1972. *The Drug Hang-Up: America's Fifty Year Folly.* New York: W.W. Norton.

Krane, Joshua Alan. 2010. *Forfeited: Civil Forfeiture and the Canadian Constitution.* LLM Thesis, University of Toronto, Toronto. https://tspace.library.utoronto.ca/bitstream/1807/25734/3/Krane_Joshua_A_201011_LLM_thesis.pdf.

La Spina, Antonio. 2012. "The Fight against the Italian Mafia." Details forthcoming.

Levi, Michael. 1991. *Customer Confidentiality, Money Laundering, and Police Bank Relationships: English Law and Practise in a Global Environment.* London: Police Foundation.

Levy, Leonard. 1996. *A License to Steal.* Chapel Hill: University of North Carolina Press.

Lichtblau, Eric and Eric Schmitt. 2010. "Cash Flow to Terrorists Evades U.S. Efforts." *New York Times,* December 5. http://www.nytimes.com/2010/12/06/world/middleeast/06wikileaks-financing.html?_r=1&ref=world.

Lupkin, Stanley N. and Edgar J. Lewandowski. 2005. "Independent Private Sector Inspectors General: Privately Funded Overseers of the Public Integrity." *NYLitigator* 10(1): 6–19.

Lynch, Gerald E. 1987. "RICO: The Crime of Being a Criminal." *Columbia Law Review* 87(4): 661–764.

Mitsilegas, Valsamis. 2000. *Money Laundering Counter-measures in the European Union: A New Paradigm of Security Governance versus Fundamental Legal Principles.* PhD Thesis, University of Edinburgh, Edinburgh.

Musto, David. 1987. *The American Disease: Origin of Narcotic Control.* New York: Oxford University Press.

Nadelmann, Ethan. 1993. *Cops across Borders: The Internationalization of U.S. Criminal Law Enforcement.* University Park: Pennsylvania State University Press.

Newark, Tim. 2010. *Lucky Luciano: The Real and Fake Gangster.* New York: St Martin's Press.

Newman, R. K. 1995. "Opium Smoking in Late Imperial China: A Reconsideration." *Modern Asian Studies* 29(4): 765–794.

Nkechi, Taifa. 1994. "Civil Forfeiture vs. Civil Liberties." *New York Law School Law Review* 39(1–2): 95–115.

Ontario. 1964. *Report of the Ontario Police Commission on Organized Crime*, Judge Bruce Macdonald, Chairman. January. Ottawa: Queen's Printer.

Pike, John. 1998. *FINCEN History*. http://www.fas.org/irp/agency/ustreas/fincen/history.htm.

Potter, Mark. 2010. "Mexico's 'War Next Door' Linked Directly to the United States: Federal Authorities Say Traffickers Are Now Entrenched in 270 American Cities." *NBC News*, December 13. http://www.msnbc.msn.com/id/39812764/ns/world_news-americas/.

Raab, Selwyn. 2011. "Omertà May Be Dead; the Mafia Isn't." *New York Times*, January 23.

Reuter, Peter. 2000. "Connecting Drug Policy and Research on Drug Markets." In Mangai Natarajan and J. M. Hough (eds.), *Illegal Drug Markets: From Research to Prevention Policy, Crime Prevention Studies*, Vol. 11. Monsey: Criminal Justice Press.

Rushe, Dominic. 2011. "Bernard Madoff Says Banks and Funds Were 'Complicit' in $90bn Fraud." *The Guardian*, February 16. http://www.guardian.co.uk/business/2011/feb/16/bernard-madoff-says-banks-complicit-in-fraud?INTCMP=SRCH.

Scaduto, Tony. 1976. *Lucky Luciano*. London, Sphere.

Schachter, Abbe Wisse. 2010. "Guns to Mexico Flowing Like Drugs to the Other Direction." *New York Post*, November 10. http://www.nypost.com/p/blogs/capitol/guns_to_mexico_flowing_like_drugs_EjSaH97muLwMrA1TIstxuM.

Siragusa, Charles. 1966. *The Trail of the Poppy: Behind the Mask of the Mafia*. Englewood Cliffs: Prentice Hall.

Smith, Dwight C. 1991. "Wickersham to Sutherland to Katzenbach: Evolving an 'Official' Definition for Organized Crime." *Crime, Law and Social Change* 16(2): 135–154.

Sterling, Claire. 1990. *The Mafia: The Long Reach of the International Sicilian Mafia*. London: Grafton.

Sterling, Claire. 1994. *Thieves' World: The Threat of the New Global Network of Organized Crime*. New York: Simon & Schuster.

Stewart, David P. 1990. "Internationalizing the War on Drugs: The U.N. Convention against Illicit Traffic in Narcotic Drugs and Psychotropic Substances." *Denver Journal of International Law and Policy* 18(3): 387–404.

Stratton, Terry. 2010. "Government of Canada Enacts New Regulations to help Fight Organized Crime." *Stratton*, August 4. http://www.terrystratton.ca/EN/manitobans%E2%80%99_corner/government_of_canada_enacts_new_regulations_to_help_fight_organized_crime//.

Taylor, Arnold H. 1969. *American Diplomacy and the Narcotics Traffic, 1900–1939*. Durham, NC: Duke University Press.

Terpstra, Jan. 2012. "The Warning and Advisory Task of the Police: Forging a Link between Police Information and Multi-Agency Partnerships." *Policing* 6(1): 67–75.

The Sun. 1961. "Grid Men Named in Crime Expose," December 1. http://quixoticjoust.blogspot.com/2012/02/canadian-organized-cr ime-and-florida.html.

Toronto Star. August 10, 1967. "Big U.S. Crime Spreading Here, Police Brass Warn," p. A1.

Toronto Star. March 15, 1967. "Crime Said Moving In On Business," p. 9.

Toronto Star. April 21, 1967. "Expo Would Provide a Good Opportunity for Organized Crime," p. 39.

Toronto Star. October 4, 1967. "Feasibility Study of Yorkville—Mafia," p. 1.

United Nations. 1998. "Commentary on the United Nations Convention against Illicit Traffic in Narcotic Drugs and Psychotropic Substances, Vienna, 20 December 1988." New York: UN.

United Nations, General Assembly. 1999. *Revised Draft United Nations Convention against Transnational Organized Crime*, Ad Hoc Committee on the Elaboration of a Convention against Transnational Organized Crime (A/AC.254/4/Rev4), July 19.

United Nations. 2000. Convention against Transnational Organized Crime Convention. U.N. Office for Drug Control and Crime Prevention. http://www.unodc.org/documents/treaties/U.N.TOC/Publications/TOC%20Convention/TOCebook-e.pdf.

United Nations, U.N.CICP. 2002. Assessing Transnational Organized Crime: Results of a Pilot Survey of 40 Selected Transnational Organized Criminal Groups in 16 Countries. Vienna: Crime Reduction and Analysis Branch Centre for International Crime Prevention, United Nations Office.

U.S. General Accounting Office. 1989. *Issues Regarding Strike Forces*. Report to the Chairman, Permanent Subcommittee on Investigations Committee on Governmental Affairs. http://archive.gao.gov/d25t7/138558.pdf.

U.S. General Accounting Office. 1991. *Money Laundering: The U.S. Government in Responding to the Problem*. Report to the Chairman, Subcommittee on Terrorism, Narcotics and International Operations, Committee on Foreign Relations, U.S. Senate. http://archive.gao.gov/d20t9/143917.pdf.

U.S. General Accounting Office. 1998. *State Laws and Procedures Affecting Drug Trafficking Control: A National Overview*. National Governors' Association et al. GAO Report HR-99-1 January, pp. 73–77.

U.S. President's Commission on Organized Crime. 1984. *The Cash Connection: Organized Crime, Financial Institutions and Money Laundering*. Interim Report to the President and the Attorney General, May 7.

U.S. State Department. 1998. *International Narcotics Control Strategy Report*. Bureau for International Narcotics and Law Enforcement Affairs, February 26, 1999.

U.S. State Department. 2011. Information on the Bureau for International and Law Enforcement Affairs. http://www.state.gov/p/inl/.

Volkman, Ernest. 1999. Gangbusters: The Destruction of America's Last Great Mafia Dynasty. New York: Avon Books.

Walker, John. 2000. *Modelling Global Money Laundering Flows: Some Findings*, October 10. http://www.johnwalkercrimetrendsanalysis.com.au/ ML%20method.htm.

Woodiwiss, Michael. 2005. *Gangster Capitalism: The United States and the Global Rise of Organized Crime*. London: Constable.

Woodiwiss, Michael and Dick Hobbs. 2009. "Organized Evil and the Atlantic Alliance: Moral Panics and the Rhetoric of Organized Crime Policing in America and Britain." *British Journal of Criminology* 49(1): 106–128.

CHAPTER 28

··

EUROPEAN UNION ORGANIZED CRIME CONTROL POLICIES

··

CYRILLE FIJNAUT

I. INTRODUCTION

IT is not true that organized crime came to be identified as one of Europe's larger problems only after the establishment of the European Union (EU) in 1992 (marked by the signing of the Treaty on European Union, usually referred to as the Maastricht Treaty). Italy is a case in point; since the first half of the 19th century, many authors have described the various groups that make up the Italian Mafia as a form of organized crime (see, for example, the works of C. Lombroso, Fijnaut 2009a). Although countries such as Germany, the Netherlands, and the United Kingdom do not have Italy's lengthy history in this respect, since the 1970s authors there have increasingly stressed the need to focus more on organized crime in these countries (Clarke 1980; Sielaff 1983; Schulz 1983; Dellow 1987; Schuster 1987; Bossard 1988; Fijnaut et al. 1998, pp. 7–13).

We should also not forget that, as far back as 1973, the Council of Europe (CoE) commissioned a study by A. Mack and H. J. Kerner on the "crime industry" in Europe (Mack and Kerner 1975). Even then, it seems, organized crime was considered a problem transcending the borders of the separate states of Europe; consequently, it was also regarded as a problem demanding a certain level of concerted action on the part of those states. The fact that the European Union was involved in various ways in combatting organized crime from its inception was, thus, the next step in an ongoing development rather than the starting point of an entirely new one.

Even so, after the establishment of the European Union, the fight against organized crime steadily became a more important and widely discussed agenda item in the policy of the EU and its member states. The EU's policy in this domain is, therefore, largely cumulative in nature; but, it is also so all-encompassing that it has become almost impossible to chart (Scherrer, Mégie, and Mitsilegas 2009). On the one hand, the difficulty is that the relevant policy has been defined in a succession of overall policy plans, and that it has also fanned out into many separate problem areas such as drug trafficking, the weapons trade, and human trafficking (e.g. for drug trafficking, see Friedrichs 2008, pp. 171–178; Chatwin 2011). On the other hand, the problem is that, since the EU's founding, policy with regard to the fight against organized crime has been linked with its overall constitutional evolution and to the policy it has pursued since that time in a variety of areas beyond that of organized crime in the narrow sense. One good example is the EU's counterterrorism policy (Friedrichs 2008, pp. 58–86; Ryder 2009).

That the EU's policy on organized crime is interwoven with its overall constitutional evolution can be seen in the fact that both the Maastricht Treaty and the follow-up treaty—the Treaty of Amsterdam, which introduced considerable changes to Title VI of the Treaty on European Union concerning Justice and Home Affairs— regarded the fight against organized crime as an issue to be tackled mainly under the Third Pillar of the EU, i.e., the intergovernmental pillar. Here, it is the member states—and not the supranational institutions of the European Community (e.g. the European Commission and the Court of Justice in Luxembourg, operating under the First Pillar)—that have almost exclusive authority to act pursuant to the unanimity and other principles (Regan 2000; Denza 2002). In the Treaty of Lisbon (which was signed in 2007 after the draft Constitutional Treaty fiasco and which became effective on December 1, 2009), the fight against organized crime was transferred to what had until then been referred to as the First Pillar. Within the new constitutional framework established in the amended Treaty on the Functioning of the European Union, it is considered a shared responsibility of the EU and its member states.[1] The strongest indication that the fight against organized crime is interwoven with the union's policy in other domains is the EU's increasing interference in the foreign policies of its member states. More specifically, it can be seen in the policy on games of chance pursued by the various EU institutions (Littler et al. 2011).

Given the above, it is impossible to describe the EU's policy on organized crime in any great detail in just a few pages (Fijnaut and Paoli 2004, pp. 239–259). This essay, therefore, offers a mere overview of the European Union's overall policy in this area. It begins by outlining how the EU's policy on organized crime first came about and how the EU attempted to master the problem prior to the Treaty of Lisbon in 2007. This gives the reader a basic understanding of the groundwork for the EU's current policy. It then looks in greater detail at how that policy has evolved since the Lisbon Treaty entered into force and at the main points of that policy as it stands today, based on the agreements made during the Hungarian presidency (January–June 2011).[2]

II. The Groundwork for the Current Policy

A. Piecemeal Engineering until the Maastricht Treaty

1. Consequences of Completing the Internal Market

Article K.1.9., Title VI, of the Maastricht Treaty concerns police cooperation in the European Union. The text of this article clearly demonstrates that, while not referring literally to preventing and combating "organized crime," those drafting the treaty had certainly considered how to deal with offenses that are now almost automatically categorized as such, i.e., "unlawful drug trafficking and other serious forms of international crime." The question of how to tackle these problems was raised in 1984–1985, when plans to complete the European Community's internal market before January 1, 1993, came up for discussion. The answer can be broken down into three parts (Fijnaut 1999).

To begin with, the answer was provided in the 1990 convention implementing the Schengen Agreement of June 14, 1985, between the countries of the Benelux Union, West Germany, and France on the gradual abolition of checks at their common borders. The Schengen Agreement and its implementing convention not only eased police and judicial cooperation between the member states, but also made it possible to improve information-sharing between law enforcement authorities, for example by means of the Schengen Information System (Fijnaut 1992, pp. 89–118).

Second, the answer was given in the Council directive adopted by the member states of the European Community in 1991—complementing the CoE's 1990 Convention on Laundering, Search, Seizure and Confiscation of the Proceeds from Crime—to prevent their financial systems from being abused by organized criminals for money-laundering purposes. The directive obliged member states not only to adopt legislation imposing criminal sanctions on money laundering, but also to ensure that their financial institutions would register and report unusual and suspect transactions to the competent authorities (Quillen 1991).[3]

Third, the answer was provided by the Convention based on Article K.3 of the Treaty on European Union on the Establishment of a European Police Office (Europol), signed by the EU member states in 1995 after lengthy and arduous discussion. The convention does not itself refer to organized crime but only (in Article 2.1.) to "unlawful drug trafficking and other serious forms of international crime where there are factual indications that an organized criminal structure is involved."[4] It is otherwise in the documents produced by the working group set up in 1991 to prepare the establishment of Europol (at the urging of Germany within the context of TREVI, the counterterrorism network founded by the member states of the European Community in 1975), which make no bones about Europol being meant to combat "illegal drug trafficking and international organised crime" (Fijnaut 1992, pp. 100–103).

2. *Fear of the Italian Mafia and the Fall of the Iron Curtain*

The difference in the way the convention and the working group's documents define Europol's mission is subtle (in terms of substance) but nevertheless extremely meaningful. It demonstrates that, around 1990, the term *organized crime* had not yet gained credence throughout the European Union. That changed rapidly after prosecuting magistrates Giovanni Falcone and Paolo Borsellini were murdered in Italy (on May 23, 1992, and July 19, 1992, respectively) (Jamieson 1993). Their murders forced a breakthrough in this regard. Following a special meeting on September 7, 1992, between the German and Italian ministers of home affairs concerning strategies to combat Italian organized crime in Europe, the European ministers of justice and home affairs met on September 18 in Brussels and set up the Ad Hoc Working Group on International Organised Crime. The group was given six months to produce a set of specific recommendations. It is by no means unusual that these ministers regarded the Italian Mafia as a particularly serious threat to the European Union; Falcone had delivered a lecture in Germany shortly before his murder in which he warned that the unification of the European Community into a single market would undoubtedly help the Italian Mafia spread its tentacles beyond Italy (Falcone 1992).

We should also not forget that, at the time, it was not only researchers and police officials, but also members of the European Parliament who felt that the collapse of the Soviet Union could well lead to an increase in organized crime in western Europe (Ulber 1992; Joutsen 1993; Flormann 1994; Dunn 1996). A report published in October 1993, drawn up by H. Salisch on behalf of the Committee on Civil Liberties and Internal Affairs and concerning the relationship between commonplace offenses and organized crime in urban areas, emphasized that the disappearance of the Iron Curtain would undoubtedly allow East European criminal organizations to extend their operations to the territory of the European Community (European Parliament 1993). Another report published by the same committee a few months later (January 1994) stated in no uncertain terms that the activities of Mafia-type groups operating in East European countries would increase the threat of organized crime in the European Union. Because it would be beyond the capacity of the individual member states to combat international organized crime effectively, this report also argued that the European Community should take responsibility in this matter (European Parliament 1994).

A further point of note is that, in about 1990 at the time of the collapse of the Iron Curtain, the United States repeatedly warned that the completion of the internal market in the European Community would leave the door wide open to the expansion of organized crime within its territory without provision for a parallel increase in the powers of the police and judiciary to combat it. In a lecture delivered at a meeting of German police commissioners in 1990, a prominent official with the Federal Bureau of Investigation (FBI) stated that if the European Community member states did not quickly come up with a joint strategy for the problems of organized crime, they would not be able to master these problems in the longer term (Baker 1990; Martens 1991).

American commentators were not alone in their assessment of the situation; their views were shared by French authors, for example (Borricand 1992).

It is not surprising, then, that in May 1993 the aforementioned ad hoc working group presented a set of recommendations to the relevant ministers of the member states concerning not only the Italian Mafia, but also the problem of organized crime in general.[5] Nevertheless, the definition of organized crime put forward in its report was heavily influenced by the generally accepted image of the Italian Mafia. According to the working group, this type of crime was committed by criminal groups that were organized hierarchically; operated on both the legitimate and black markets; ran cross-border operations; attempted to influence politics, the media, and the economy; sought, when necessary, to control certain territories; had the financial resources necessary to procure the necessary infrastructure and expertise; and were prepared to use violence and corruption to achieve their goals.

The working group's recommendations included improving judicial cooperation by ratifying the conventions of the Council of Europe, agreeing on a common definition of organized crime, achieving a certain measure of harmony in special investigative powers, and arranging exchanges of prosecutors and judges. The group also addressed the need to improve law enforcement cooperation. It suggested, among other recommendations, that Europol and researchers should analyze organized crime, that cross-border police cooperation should be intensified, and that police and customs should cooperate more closely. The working group also urged other international forums to draw attention to the fight against international organized crime.

3. The Role of the Berlin Declaration

The latter recommendation met with some success early on, during a conference organized in Berlin on September 8, 1994. At this event, the ministers of justice and home affairs of the member states of the European Union met with their counterparts from several Central and East European countries to discuss a long list of measures intended to improve cooperation between their countries in combating organized crime, for example, by arranging exchanges of liaison officers, the cross-border use of such investigative methods as observation and controlled delivery, and the provision of technical assistance in criminal investigation and prosecution. They also agreed that they would defend recommendations in line with their own Berlin Declaration on Increased Cooperation in Combatting Drug Crime and Organized Crime at a United Nations conference in Naples later that year (November 1994).[6]

It goes without saying that the recommendations incorporated into the Berlin Declaration could not be acted on immediately. The same can naturally also be said for recommendations issued in May 1993 by the Ad Hoc Working Group on International Organised Crime. Generally speaking, they were not recommendations that the member states could take action on immediately. The single exception was the recommendation concerning the collection of data on organized crime in the member states. As a guideline for data collection, an assessment mechanism was provided that the member states were to use for the first time in 1995 to obtain an accurate picture of the scale of, and trends in, organized crime in 1994. The definition of organized crime adopted in this context matched closely the definition given previously by the working group.[7]

B. Under the Banner of the Treaty of Amsterdam

1. *En Route to a Programmed Approach*

Whereas the Maastricht Treaty did not give explicit instructions for controlling international organized crime at the EU level, the Treaty of Amsterdam provided a fairly detailed frame of reference within the context of the Third Pillar (which it had overhauled entirely so as to transform the territory of the union into an "area of freedom, security and justice") for policymaking in this domain. Articles 29 *et seq.* of the Treaty on European Union as amended by the Treaty of Amsterdam not only stated that police and judicial cooperation would focus explicitly on combating "crime, organised or otherwise," but also carved out new opportunities for improving cooperation in this respect. It is, of course, no surprise that these opportunities mirrored the recommendations put forward in the Ad Hoc Committee's report and the Berlin Declaration, with respect to both closer police and judicial cooperation and mutual approximation of criminal sanctions (Carrapico 2010).

We should also not disregard the fact that at the Dublin Summit of December 13 and 14, 1996, the European Council adopted the Irish presidency's proposal to set up a High Level Group of Officials that was to draft a "comprehensive action plan" to combat organized crime by April 1997 (the proposal followed the murder of Irish journalist Veronica Guerin, who was gunned down in Dublin in November 1996 in retribution for her investigations into organized crime in the city). After all, after completing its work in April 1997, the working group sent a letter to the chairman of the Intergovernmental Conference preparing the Treaty of Amsterdam urging him to include its main recommendations in the text of the Treaty. The final version of the Action Plan to Combat Organized Crime was not published until August 15, 1997.[8] Based on this Action Plan, the fight against organized crime was, and would obviously remain, the responsibility of the member states. It was simply accepted that the fight would consequently not be as effective as one would have hoped (Solomon 1994–1995). The European Parliament naturally regretted that the plan was not more firmly embedded in the structures of the First Pillar, the European Community. According to a parliamentary committee, this would have made actual implementation of the plan much more likely (European Parliament 1997; Nilsson 1998).

The plan was based on the idea that controlling organized crime would require the member states to integrate prevention, investigation, and prosecution. In line with this basic idea, it called for more expert analysis of such crime, in particular by Europol, and it asked the member states to actually implement the instruments available to them to combat it. The plan then went on to define "political guidelines." These included harmonizing laws that could contribute to the fight against organized crime, concluding negotiations for a convention on mutual assistance in criminal matters, defining a pre-accession pact on cooperation against crime with the candidate countries of Central and eastern Europe, and establishing a multidisciplinary working party on organized crime within the Council to develop policies to coordinate the fight against organized crime. Finally, the plan set out a detailed action plan of 30 different recommendations, with specific target dates for each one. The recommendations were not limited to questions covered previously in the plan, such as defining the mechanisms for data analysis on organized crime and the speedy ratification of CoE conventions on mutual legal assistance; they also proposed new initiatives, for example, to intensify the fight against corruption, screen businesses before allowing them to participate in tender procedures, and shield vulnerable professionals, such as notaries and lawyers, from the influence of organized crime.

This is not the place to discuss how many of the recommendations summarized in this Action Plan were actually put into practice. Some of them were certainly adopted. For example, in 1997 Europol conducted its first large-scale analysis of organized crime in the EU, the 1997 EU Situation Report on Organised Crime: Report to the European Parliament.[9] The Falcone Programme, which was meant to promote exchanges and cooperation between the officials responsible for combating organized crime, was launched in 1998.[10] In the same year, the EU member states and candidate countries in Central and eastern Europe signed the Pre-Accession Pact on Organised Crime. [11] In addition, the member states also adopted a Joint Action Plan in the same year, based on Article K.3 of the Maastricht Treaty, in which they undertook to make the participation "in a criminal organisation in the Member States of the European Union" a criminal act. Article 1 provided the following definition of a criminal organization: "a structured association, established over a period of time, of more than two persons, acting in concert with a view to committing offences which are punishable by deprivation of liberty or a detention order of a maximum of at least four years or a more serious penalty, whether such offences are an end in themselves or a means of obtaining benefits and, where appropriate, of improperly influencing the operation of public authorities."[12] This very open-ended, general definition differs considerably from the description of a criminal organization given in the 1993 report.

In view of these actions, it is not surprising that internal progress reports filed in December 1998 and 1999 claimed that considerable progress had been made and that notable successes had been recorded in implementing the Action Plan.[13]

2. *The Main Outlines of the Tampere Programme*

The progress report referred to above also mentions that the Council, at the request of the European Parliament, had adopted a resolution on December 3–4, 1998, concerning the prevention of organized crime "with reference to the establishment of a comprehensive strategy for combating it." This resolution ended by asking the member states, Europol, and the European Commission to produce a comprehensive report regarding such prevention.[14] This was evidently not an easy task. Indeed, it took until June 1999 for the first version of the report to be compiled by the incoming Finnish presidency

(June–December 1999). It bore the title *The Prevention and Control of Organised Crime: A European Union Strategy for the Beginning of the New Millennium.*[15] As the title indicates, the report covered not only the prevention of organized crime, but also all possible measures for controlling it, i.e., strengthening the collection and analysis of data on organized crime, strengthening partnerships between the criminal justice system and civil society, developing measures intended to prevent the penetration of organized crime into the public and legitimate private sectors, strengthening Europol, increasing the effectiveness of special investigative means, and strengthening cooperation between law enforcement and judicial authorities within and outside the European Union.

This draft version was, however, superseded by the decisions taken during the special European Council of Tampere organized in October 1999 by the Finnish presidency. The purpose of the special council was to convert the innovations that the Treaty of Amsterdam had introduced in the Treaty on European Union into practical policy measures.[16] With respect to the EU's fight against organized crime, the Tampere Programme emphasized the following points:

- increasing cooperation in cross-border areas, for example by setting up joint investigative teams;
- setting up Eurojust (a multinational European team of national prosecutors, magistrates, or police officers, the counterpart of Europol) and a Task Force of European Chiefs of Police;
- founding a European Police College;
- defining a European strategy against drugs for the 2000–2004 period;
- setting up Financial Intelligence Units meant to improve information-sharing on money laundering;
- integrating justice and home affairs policy into foreign policy.

In November 1999, some of these points were incorporated into the final version of the above-mentioned report on the prevention and control of organized crime in the European Union. The relevant points included the application of criminal sanctions in a limited number of relevant sectors, for example, drug trafficking, trafficking in human beings, environmental crime and financial crime; measures making the fight against illegal immigration a priority of operational cooperation between the member states; and measures enabling the member states to establish joint investigative teams assisted by Europol. The report was published in May 2000.[17] We should not lose sight of the fact that the European Parliament generally approved the report, although it expressed frustration in not being involved in its revision. In its July 2001 resolution concerning the report, the European Parliament's key criticism was that the attention given to individual recommendations in the Action Plan only reflected the urgency of securing an effective containment of organized crime, but also obscured the priorities in such a policy. As the European Parliament saw it, maximum priority ought to be given to tracing, freezing, seizing, and confiscating the proceeds of crime and combating money laundering because, it added, the strength of criminal organizations lay precisely in their having huge financial and economic resources at their disposal.[18]

It should be obvious that a significant number of recommendations made in the new, overall Action Plan were indeed implemented in the early years of this century. An evaluation dated June 30, 2003, states that "the majority of the recommendations have been carried out, and considerable progress has been achieved in most areas covered."[19] These included the recommendations intended to strengthen cross-border cooperation in combating organized crime, such as the EU Convention of 2000 on mutual legal assistance in criminal matters, the founding of Eurojust, and the setting up of a network of Financial Intelligence Units. However, the evaluation also highlighted the work that still needed to be done, for example, scientific research on organized crime in Europe, the screening of persons and businesses to prevent organized crime from infiltrating the public sector, and witness protection.

Of particular note is that the Tampere Programme's recommendation that justice and home affairs policy should be more closely linked to the EU's foreign policy did not remain an idle promise; in the years thereafter, that recommendation took the shape of the Justice and Home Affairs External Relations Multi-presidency Programmes. It also received a major boost in December 2003 with the official introduction of the European Union Security Strategy, which included the fight against organized crime as one of its priorities. As the relevant document states in the plainest of terms: "Europe is a prime target for organised crime. This internal threat to our security has an important external dimension: cross-border trafficking in drugs, women, illegal immigrants and weapons accounts for a large part of the activities of criminal gangs." This particular definition has multiple implications, for example, that Europe also exports all kinds of serious and organized crime, and that imports of organized crime into Europe imply the existence of markets for illegal goods and services there (Fijnaut 2008). More telling was the fact that this approach to the problem made it even more important to combine the fight against organized crime by means of a foreign policy that replaced piecemeal fashion approach taken since the early 1990s. Indeed, it was so important that the EU had, in effect, approved a basic policy principle first adopted by the US government back in the 1960s, that is, "the first line of defence will often be abroad" (Keukeleire and MacNaughtan 2008, pp. 57–65, 230–240; Monar 2010).[20]

Finally, we should not lose sight of the fact that the EU had become a party to the United Nations Convention against Transnational Organised Crime, signed in Palermo in 2000.[21] This convention gave the EU's aim of incorporating the fight against organized crime into its foreign policy a basis in international law (Rijken and Kronenberger 2001).

3. The Main Outlines of the Hague Programme

The evaluations of the Tampere Programme carried out in 2003 and 2004 showed that, although much progress had been made, much remained to be done to ensure that policy and its practical implementation kept pace with the nature and scale of, and the trends in, organized crime in the EU member states (Fijnaut 2004).[22] The approach chosen in 2005 in the new Hague Programme: Strengthening Freedom, Security and Justice in the European Union was not merely a response to the evaluations of the Tampere Programme, but also based on the structure and content of the rejected draft Constitutional Treaty discussed earlier.[23] Although the fight against organized crime was not a major separate theme in this program, it did set out numerous measures that could easily be related to that issue, such as the introduction of a "principle of availability" that would encourage cross-border information-sharing between law enforcement and judicial authorities and measures encouraging the member states to make greater use of Europol and Eurojust. Examples of measures copied from the draft Constitutional Treaty included those inviting the Council to set up a Committee on Internal Security and to organize a joint meeting every six months between the chairpersons of all the relevant consultative bodies in order to gain practical experience with coordination.

However, the action plan adopted by the Council and the Commission in the summer of 2005 to implement the Hague Programme devoted a considerable number of pages specifically to the fight against organized crime.[24] The action plan included a whole list of recommendations, ranging from improving the knowledge of organized and serious crime to measures to prevent such crime (cooperation with businesses, anti-corruption measures) and control it, for example, through greater efforts to seize and confiscate criminal assets, closer coordination in tackling such problems as human trafficking, and further application of criminal sanctions. The underlying principle for these action points was a communication published by the Commission in June 2005 entitled *Developing a Strategic Concept on Tackling Organised Crime*.[25] This document had already indicated that it would not be easy to develop a comprehensive strategy, given the complexity of the very concept of organized crime. Any policy in this area would almost certainly come down to efforts to "integrate the different tools and measures...taken at local, national and EU level and fill identified gaps." In line with this, the aim was to "ensure effective cooperation between all relevant actors."

The most important overall outcome of the Hague Programme was the Council Framework Decision of October 24, 2008, "on the fight against organised crime."[26] Pursuant to this decision, the member states are obliged to take measures ensuring that certain types of conduct related to a criminal organization are regarded as offenses (for example, active participation in the organization's criminal activities), that those offenses are punishable, and that a legal person held liable for such offenses is punishable by law. The decision also provides for arrangements with respect to jurisdiction in cross-border cases and the coordination of prosecution. In addition to this general decision, the main aim of which is to promote cross-border cooperation in combating organized crime, various special policy programs were drawn up between 2005 and 2009 (with a view to implementing the Hague Programme) focusing on cybercrime, human trafficking, and the drug problem (Calderoni 2010).

The Commission's evaluation of the Hague Programme (published in June 2009) lists these and other initiatives but does not indicate the Commission's views in each specific case. Instead, its assessment can be found in the general text of the evaluation document. Certain passages of this text make clear that, at the time, the Commission considered that considerable advances had been made toward realizing many of the ambitions of the Hague Programme, and that most of its specific measures had been adopted. However, it also considered that progress had been quite uneven because the European Parliament, the Court of Justice, and the Commission itself had not been empowered to implement the program equally across the board. As a result, practical progress had fallen behind what had been officially agreed, and, to the extent that the program had been implemented, it was difficult to evaluate as member states were not formally compelled to report to the Commission on implementation.[27] It is naturally no surprise that the Commission took the opportunity to express its disappointment about the rejection of the Constitutional Treaty and to pin its hopes on the Treaty of Lisbon. The latter, which amends the 1957 Treaty Establishing the European Community (now referred to as the Treaty on the Functioning of the European Union), gave rise to an EU in which promoting an "area of freedom, security and justice" has become the joint responsibility of the EU and its member states (Article 4.2.h).

III. UNDER THE BANNER OF THE TREATY OF LISBON

A. Main Differences from the Treaty of Amsterdam

The fact that the main responsibility for the "area of freedom, security and justice" is no longer solely allocated to the member states but constitutes a shared responsibility between those member states and the European Union has many repercussions. This constitutional change in the relationship between the two sides first of all means that decision making in this domain in the European Council and the Council of the European Union is no longer dominated by the member states. Since the Treaty of Lisbon entered into force on December 1, 2009, the European Commission and the European Parliament have participated wholeheartedly in such decision making, and they will be joined by the Court of Justice in several years. Equally important is that member states are no longer required to take decisions by unanimity; with a few exceptions, resolutions are now adopted by majority.

It is also important to point out the far-reaching changes in the role that the EU institutions play when it comes to developing, implementing, and evaluating policy in the domain in question. Pursuant to Article 68, the European Council is now competent to produce "strategic guidelines for legislative and operational planning within the area of freedom, security and justice." Article 71 further provides for a Standing Committee (COSI) in the Council "in order to ensure that operational cooperation on internal security is promoted and strengthened within the Union . . . .

[I]t shall facilitate coordination of the action of the Member States' competent authorities." And what is equally significant is that Article 70 more or less obliges the member states to cooperate with the Commission in conducting an "objective and impartial evaluation of the implementation of the Union policies... by Member States' authorities," within a framework determined by the Council. All these provisions demonstrate that the EU is no longer limited to simply developing policy programs in the area of freedom, security, and justice, but it is now also authorized to stipulate how such programs are to be carried out by the member states and will, moreover, check whether they are, in fact, being implemented and how such implementation is being carried out.

Finally, note that this does not mean that the member states have relinquished any autonomy when it comes to internal security. As Article 72 clearly states: "This Title shall not affect the exercise of the responsibilities incumbent upon Member States with regard to the maintenance of law and order and the safeguarding of internal security." It is, therefore, obvious that the Treaty of Lisbon, like its predecessors, will not transform Europol into an executive police service that can conduct criminal investigations in the territory of the European Union at will (Article 88) and that the founding of an executive body such as the European Public Prosecutor's Office within the context of Eurojust, although described in Article 86, has so far not been forthcoming given the fact of considerable resistance.

B. Key Outlines of the Stockholm Programme

The policy program that hinges on the Treaty of Lisbon—similar to the way the Tampere Programme hinged on the Treaty of Amsterdam and the Hague Programme on the draft Constitutional Treaty—is the Stockholm Programme, adopted by the European Council on December 1, 2009. This program devotes considerable attention to controlling all possible forms of cross-border crime and, consequently, to the basic principles and forms of police and judicial cooperation between the member states (Fijnaut 2009b; Gless 2010). Much of the focus is on the fight against serious and, in particular, cross-border organized crime. Indeed, sections 4.1 to 4.5 are devoted more or less exclusively to this problem and include the following notable points.

To begin with, the European Council and the Commission should define a comprehensive Internal Security Strategy (ISS) based on clarifying the division of tasks between the European Union and the member states, respect for fundamental rights, stringent cooperation between the union agencies, a focus on improving preventive action, and the usefulness of regional cooperation. The ISS should also take into account the external security strategy developed by the union as well as other union policies, in particular those concerning the internal market. Developing and implementing the ISS should become one of the priority tasks of COSI. By now, this strategy has been not only described on paper, but also adopted by the Commission as an action program (November 2010).[28]

Second, the Stockholm Programme points out the need to develop a "common culture" in law enforcement, and, in particular, to create a multifunctional and properly balanced EU Information Management Strategy. This means that in this strategy operational interests must be weighed against the strict protection of personal data.

Third, the program attaches great importance to cross-border law enforcement cooperation between the member states, in particular, in border regions. Europol and Eurojust should be involved as much as possible in cross-border operational cooperation, and the union should promote Joint Police and Customs Centres, including through financing programs.

Fourth, the program states that organized crime is becoming ever more globalized, and that it is, hence, increasingly important that law enforcement possess the ability to work effectively across borders and jurisdictions: "The fight against these criminal phenomena will involve systematic exchange of information, widespread use of European agencies and investigative tools and, where necessary, the development of common investigative and prevention techniques and increased cooperation with third countries." No specifics are provided in the Stockholm Programme; instead, the details are to be set out in two further initiatives. The first calls on the Council and the Commission to "adopt an organised crime strategy, within the framework of the Internal Security Strategy." The second calls on the Council and the Commission to "set its priorities in crime policy by identifying the types of crime against which it will deploy the tools it has developed, while continuing to use the Organised Crime Threat Assessment Report (OCTA) and its regional versions." With regard to these priorities, the text immediately adds that the European Council considers the following types of crime as deserving special priority in the years to come: trafficking in human beings, sexual exploitation of children, cybercrime, drugs, and economic crime and corruption. The text also indicates, for each type of crime, what must be done to tackle these problems, including legislation, operational cooperation within and outside the EU, protection of victims, informing citizens, financial investigations, and so on.

Fifth, the program also points out the importance of controlling serious, organized crime by taking administrative measures and promoting the necessary cooperation between administrative authorities. "The awareness of the links between local crime and organised crime and its complex cross-border dimensions is increasing," according to the text. This represents a breakthrough in the EU's policy. Both the Tampere Programme and the Hague Programme show that, until recently, the EU mainly pursued a policy of repression—in the criminal law sense—with respect to organized crime. Starting with the 1997 Action Plan, EU policymakers have continuously stressed the importance of prevention in the fight against organized crime, but what they actually meant by prevention remained relatively vague. That lack of specificity is accounted for by the fact that the fight against serious crime was, and often still is, regarded by circles in Brussels as a matter best dealt with by the police, the public prosecutions services, and the tax authorities. The idea that the national authorities, and in particular local authorities, can and must play a key role in preventing and suppressing organized crime is one that has only recently found credence in such circles, specifically owing to pressure by the Netherlands (van Daele et al. 2010, pp. 60–66, 459–480).

Indeed, it was back in the early 1990s that the Netherlands and Germany first began to consider that organized crime could be tackled through administrative measures in both illegal markets and legal sectors, for example, the property market (Kube 1990; Sieber and Bögel 1993; Fijnaut 2001). Many of these ideas—at least those being discussed in the Netherlands—were based on the policy adopted by authorities in New York City, which combined criminal investigations with administrative measures interfering with La Cosa Nostra's control of legitimate markets such as those in the food and waste industries (Fijnaut and Jacobs 1991; Fijnaut 2010).

Evidence that the administrative approach to organized crime has gained credence in the EU can be found in the fact that the relevant Council working group has not only made efforts to clarify what that approach could mean in practical terms, but also has raised the subject at conferences (Ministerie van Binnenlandse Zaken 2008). This explains why this approach has been included in the table of contents of the reference book currently being compiled by a COSI project group entitled *Complementary Approaches and Actions to Prevent and Combat Organised Crime—A Collection of Good Practice Examples from EU Member States*. Unfortunately, the text of the reference book has so far remained classified.[29]

C. Policy for the Years Ahead

The program adopted by the Hungarian presidency of the Council of the European Union (January 1 to June 30, 2011) made the fight against organized crime a key priority. Arguing that organized crime forms a serious threat to security of the European Union's citizens, the Hungarian presidency asserted that "increasing the efficiency of fight against organized crime will be one of its priorities" and that—in line with the Internal Security Strategy—it would "continue with the implementation of the recently adopted policy cycle, which provides for increased coherence in operational cooperation."[30]

The idea of implementing a policy cycle that would improve the coherence, direction, consistency, and transparency of the fight against organized crime in the EU was embraced by COSI on October 5, 2010. That will certainly come as no surprise, as an "organized crime strategy" had already been put forward as one of the recommendations of the Stockholm Programme.[31] In this case, COSI has established a "policy cycle" consisting of four steps:

- policy development on the basis of a European Union Serious and Organised Crime Threat Assessment (EU SOCTA);
- identification of a limited number of priorities, both regional and pan-European. For each of the priorities a Multi-annual Strategic Plan (MASP) is to be developed in order to achieve a multidisciplinary, integrated and integral approach to effectively address the prioritized threats;

- implementation of annual Operational Action Plans (OAP) that need to be aligned with the strategic goals that have been determined in the MASP;
- at the end of the policy cycle, a thorough evaluation of the progress made, serving as input for the next policy cycle.

The relevant document goes on to say that the normal policy cycle is four years, but that, on the basis of Europol's OCTA of 2011, an initial reduced two-year policy cycle could be implemented (2011–2013). The first full four-year cycle will thus cover the 2013–2017 period.

To get started on the initial "half" cycle, COSI is instructed in the document to submit conclusions to the Council to decide on the priorities for the 2011–2013 period. The member states are called upon to support all phases of the cycle, to integrate the actions developed within the European policy cycle into their national planning, and to allocate dedicated resources to support a common EU approach. The Commission is called upon to develop, together with the experts of the relevant EU agencies and member states, a MASP for each priority and a mechanism to evaluate the implementation of OAPs.

On June 9 and 10, 2011, the Justice and Home Affairs Council defined the priorities for the fight against organized crime in the 2011–2013 period. These are to:

- weaken the capacity of organized crime groups active or based in West Africa to traffic cocaine and heroin to and within the EU;
- mitigate the role of the western Balkans as a logistical center for organized crime groups;
- reduce the production and distribution in the EU of synthetic drugs;
- combat all forms of trafficking in human beings and human smuggling by targeting the organized crime groups conducting such criminal activities;
- reduce the general capabilities of mobile (itinerant) organized crime groups to engage in criminal activities;
- step up the fight against cybercrime and the criminal misuse of the Internet.

COSI is then instructed not only to coordinate, support, monitor, and evaluate OAPs for each priority, but also to ensure "consistency in the implementation of operational actions necessary... including effective cooperation between relevant national authorities and between EU agencies." COSI must also see to it that these priorities are taken into account in the European Union's external policy.

IV. CONCLUSION

Our account of the EU's overall policy on organized crime describes how, over the course of 20 years, that policy evolved from a somewhat vague unease shared by the member states about the potential impact of organized crime on the internal market of the European Union into a comprehensive and coherent set of statutory, institutional, operational, and technical measures for which the member states and the EU institutions bear joint responsibility, both in defining such measures and in implementing them. It goes without saying that this evolution only became possible after the necessary scope was created by introducing relevant far-reaching changes in the constitutional structure of the European Union. The steps currently being taken under the banner of the Treaty of Lisbon would have been unthinkable under the terms of the Maastricht Treaty.

The question is naturally asked: why were such changes introduced in the first place? Part of the answer lies in the fact that the policymaking institutions of the EU have consistently identified organized crime as a genuine threat to the union, supported by Europol's analyses. The evaluation of these analyses lies beyond the remit of this text. However, it would be advisable to subject these analyses to critical and continuous assessment, given their impact on policymaking. Fortunately, many more opportunities to do so exist today than 20 years ago. Both the individual member states and the European Union have access to many more resources relevant for this purpose than in the past. Equally important, there are now more researchers in the individual member states who take an interest in the problem of organized crime. That makes it easier to set up multinational research groups than it was a number of years ago. Even so, any assessment remains difficult for a variety of reasons (Zoutendijk 2010).

It has become even more important to monitor the situation continuously because the EU's policy in this area increasingly "interferes" in the way the law enforcement and justice systems are organized not only in the member states, but also—through the Union's foreign policy—in non-EU countries, both in Europe and in other parts of the world. Organized crime may well pose a threat to the EU and its citizens, but the policy that is being adopted in response also poses a threat, so to speak, to the sovereignty of the union's member states. After all, they will increasingly be obliged (or will oblige themselves, whether or not that is readily apparent) to amend not only their laws on important points, but also the way key public services, such as the police, public prosecution services, tax authorities, and local government, are organized and operate, thereby altering the justice system as a whole.

That need not be problematical—certainly not if the nature and scale of, and the trends in, organized crime require such changes in the view of the governments and parliaments of the countries in question. However, what must be realized is that, for all these measures to be effective and efficient in actual practice, an outstanding level of coordination, if not integration, will be required. Inevitably, this means that their implementation will automatically take the fight against organized crime to the supranational level in the operational and, perhaps, institutional sense. If that is a positive change and also what we want, then there is no problem. But we must by no means neglect to ask what form such supranationalization will, can, or should take. To answer this question, we must not only chart trends in organized crime itself, but also examine the impact of policymaking on both organized crime and on the way the member states are organized and operate in this area. Otherwise, policy developed and implemented to combat organized crime in the EU will be simply a leap in the dark. Everything possible must be done to avoid this, for example, though it is difficult in this domain, by conducting thorough and scientifically grounded research (Castle 2008; Gabor 2003; Levi and Maguire 2004).

Notes

1. See http://www.consilium.europa.eu/treaty-of-lisbon.aspx?lang=en.
2. See also in this connection: Scherrer, Mégie and Mitsilegas (2009).
3. Council of the European Union. Council Directive…on Prevention of the Use of the Financial System for the Purpose of Money Laundering. *Official Journal*, L 166/77-83, 28.6.1991.
4. Council of the European Union. Convention…on the Establishment of a European Police Office (Europol Convention). *Official Journal*, C 316/1-32, 27.11.1995.
5. Ad Hoc Working Group on International Organized Crime. *Report to Interior and Justice Ministers*. Kolding, 6-7.5.1993 (unpublished).
6. Council of the European Union. *EU: Berlin Declaration on Increased Cooperation in Combating Drug Crime and Organized Crime*. Berlin: Pres/94/182, Rapid, 30.9.1994. Concerning the Naples conference, see Williams and Savona (1996).
7. Council of the European Union. *Establishing a Mechanism for the Collection and Systematic Analysis of Information on International Organised Crime*. Brussels: no. 12247/1/94, ENFOPOL 161, 28.1.1995.
8. Council of the European Union. Action Plan to Combat Organized Crime. *Official Journal*, C 251/1-18, 18.8.1997. The working group's letter to the Intergovernmental Conference was appended to the Action Plan.
9. The report was published by Europol during the Austrian Presidency (The Hague, File No. 2530-34r1).
10. *Official Journal*, L 99/8-12, 31.3.1998.
11. *Official Journal*, C 220/1-5, 15.7.1998.
12. *Official Journal*, L 351/1-3, 29.12.1998.
13. Council of the European Union. *Progress Report to the European Council (meeting in Vienna) on the Combating of Organised Crime*. Brussels: no. 11571/4/98, CRIMORG 141, 4.12.1998; Council of the European Union. *Finalisation and Evaluation of the Action Plan on Organised Crime*. Brussels: no. 9917/3/99, CRIMORG 96, 12.11.1999.
14. *Official Journal*, C 408/1-4, 29.12.1998.
15. Council of the European Union. *The Prevention and Control of Organised Crime: a European Union Strategy for the Beginning of the New Millennium*. Brussels: no. 9423/99, CRIMORG 80, 21.6.1999.
16. See http://www.consilium.europa.eu/summits.
17. *Official Journal*, C 124/1-33, 3.5.2000.
18. *Official Journal*, C 146/113-16, 17.5.2001.
19. Council of the European Union. *Report on Measures and Steps Taken with Regard to the Implementation of the Recommendations of the European Union Strategy for the Beginning of the New Millennium on Prevention and Control of Organised Crime*. Brussels: no. 10925/03, CRIMORG 49, 30.06.2003.
20. The *European Security Strategy* can be found on the website of the European Council (http://www.consilium.europa.eu/eeas/security-defence/european-security-strategy.aspx?lang=en).

21. *Official Journal*, L 261/69, 6.8.2004.
22. Commission of the European Communities, *Area of Freedom, Security and Justice: Assessment of the Tampere Programme and Future Orientations*, Brussels, COM (2004) 401, 2.6.2004.
23. *Official Journal*, C 53/1-14, 3.3.2005.
24. *Official Journal*, C 198/1-22, 12.8.2005.
25. Commission of the European Communities, *Developing a Strategic Concept on Tackling Organised Crime*, Brussels, COM (2005) 232, 2.6.2005.
26. *Official Journal*, L 300/42- 45, 11.11.2008.
27. Commission of the European Communities, *Justice, Freedom and Security in Europe since 2005: an Evaluation of the Hague Programme and Action Plan*, Brussels, COM (2009), 263, 10.6.2009.
28. European Commission, *The European Internal Security Strategy in Action: Five Steps Towards a More Secure Europe.* Brussels, COM(2010) 673, 22.11.2010.
29. The relevant document (10899/11, 30.5.2011) can be found in the Council's archives but cannot be viewed by outsiders. For an outline of the reference book, see the Terms of Reference document of November 30, 2010, drawn up by the COSI Project Group "Organised Crime."
30. *The Programme of the Hungarian Presidency of the Council of the European Union.* Brussels, 2011, p. 24.
31. Council of the European Union. *Draft Council Conclusions on the Creation and Implementation of a EU Policy Cycle for Organised and Serious Crime.* Brussels: no. 15358/10, COSI 69, 25.10.2010.

REFERENCES

Baker, William. 1990. "Organized Crime in the United States: A Warning for Europe?" Unpublished manuscript.

Borricand, Jacques. 1992. "Crime organisé et coopération européenne." *Revue internationale de criminologie et de police technique* 45(4): 445–454.

Bossard, André. 1988. "La criminalité transfrontalière multidisciplinaire." *Revue de science criminelle et de droit pénal comparé* 40(4): 756–765.

Calderoni, Francesco. 2010. *Organized Crime Legislation in the European Union: Harmonization and Approximation of Criminal Law, National Legislations and the EU Framework Decision on the Fight against Organized Crime.* Heidelberg, Germany: Springer.

Carrapico, Helena. 2010. "The Evolution of the European Union's Understanding of Organized Crime and Its Embedment in EU Discourse." In *Defining and Defying Organized Crime: Discourse, Perceptions and Reality,* edited by Felia Allum, Francesco Longo, Daniela Irrera, and Panos Kostakos, 43–54. London: Routledge.

Castle, Allan. 2008. "Measuring the Impact of Law Enforcement on Organized Crime." *Trends in Organized Crime* 11(2): 135–156.

Chatwin, Caroline. 2011. *Drug Policy Harmonization and the European Union.* Basingstoke, UK: Palgrave.

Clarke, Michael. 1980. "Syndicated Crime in Britain." *Contemporary Crises* 4(4): 403–420.

Dellow, John. 1987. "Organized Crime." *Police Journal* 60(3): 200–204.

Denza, Eileen. 2002. *The Intergovernmental Pillars of the European Union.* Oxford: Oxford University Press.

Dunn, Guy. 1996. "Major Mafia Gangs in Russia." *Transnational Organized Crime* 2(2–3): 63–87.

European Parliament. 1993. *Mass Crime in Urban Areas and Its Links with Organized Crime.* Brussels, A3-289/93, PE 2005.509, 14.10.1993.

European Parliament. 1994. *Criminal Activities in Europe.* Brussels, A3-033/94, PE 207.498, 27.1.1994.

European Parliament. 1997. *Report on the Proposal for an Action Plan to Combat Organized Crime.* Brussels, A4-0333/97, PE 223.427, 29.10.1997.

Falcone, Giovanni. 1992. "La criminalité organisée: Un problème mondial." *Revue internationale de criminologie et de oolice technique* 45(4): 391–398.

Flormann, Willi. 1994. "Die Russen-Mafia auf dem Weg nach Westen?!" *Der Kriminalist* 45(9): 411–416.

Friedrichs, Jörg. 2008. *Fighting Drugs and Terrorism: Europe and International Police Cooperation.* London: Routledge.

Fijnaut, Cyrille. 1992. "Naar een Gemeenschappelijke' Regeling van de Politiële Samenwerking en de Justitiële Rechtshulp." In *Schengen: Proeftuin voor de Europese Gemeenschap?* edited by Cyrille Fijnaut, Jules Stuyck, and Peter Wytinck, 89–118. Antwerp: Kluwer Rechtswetenschappen.

Fijnaut, Cyrille. 1999. "Judicial Cooperation and Organized Crime in the European Union." In *International Law and The Hague's 750th Anniversary*, edited by Wybo Heere, 9–14. The Hague: T.M.C. Asser Press.

Fijnaut, Cyrille, ed. 2001. *The Administrative Approach to (Organised) Crime in Amsterdam.* Amsterdam: City of Amsterdam.

Fijnaut, Cyrille. 2004. "Police Co-operation and the Area of Freedom, Security and Justice." In *Europe's Area of Freedom, Security and Justice*, edited by Nigel Walker, 242–282. Oxford: Oxford University Press.

Fijnaut, Cyrille. 2008. "The Lack of Coherence between Internal and External Security Policies of the European Union." In *The Viability of Human Security*, edited by Monica den Boer and Jaap de Wildt, 97–108. Amsterdam: Amsterdam University Press.

Fijnaut, Cyrille. 2009a. "Lombroso's Kijk op de Italiaanse Maffia." *Justitiële Verkenningen* 35(3): 47–58.

Fijnaut, Cyrille. 2009b. "Het Voorstel voor het Stockholm Programma: Een Gebrekkige Stimulans voor de Discussie over de Verdere Ontwikkeling van de Politiële en Justitiële Samenwerking in de Europese Unie." *Panopticon* 30(6): 3–21.

Fijnaut, Cyrille. 2010. "The Introduction of the New York Double Strategy to Control Organised Crime in the Netherlands and the European Union." *European Journal of Crime, Criminal Law and Criminal Justice* 18(4): 43–65.

Fijnaut, Cyrille, Frank Bovenkerk, Gerben Bruinsma, and Henk van de Bunt. 1998. *Organized Crime in the Netherlands.* The Hague: Kluwer Law International.

Fijnaut, Cyrille, and James Jacobs, eds. 1991. *Organized Crime and Its Containment: A Transatlantic Initiative.* Deventer: Kluwer Law and Taxation.

Fijnaut, Cyrille, and Letizia Paoli, eds. 2004. *Organized Crime in Europe: Concepts, Patterns and Control Policies in the European Union and Beyond.* Dordrecht: Springer.

Gabor, Thomas. 2003. *Assessing the Effectiveness of Organized Crime Control Strategies: A Review of the Literature.* Ottawa: Department of Justice.

Gless, Sabine. 2010. "Police and Judicial Cooperation between the European Union Member States: Results and Prospects." In *The Future of Police and Judicial Cooperation in the European*

Union, edited by Cyrille Fijnaut and Jannemieke Ouwerkerk, 25–48. Leiden: Martinus Nijhoff.

Jamieson, Alison. 1993. "Giovanni Falcone: In Memoriam." *Studies in Conflict and Terrorism* 16(4): 303–313.

Joutsen, Matti. 1993. "The Potential for the Growth of Organized Crime in Central and Eastern Europe." *European Journal on Criminal Policy and Research* 1(3): 77–86.

Keukeleire, Stephan, and Jennifer MacNaughtan. 2008. *The Foreign Policy of the European Union*. Hampshire: Palgrave Macmillan.

Kube, Edwin. 1990. "Organisierte Kriminalität: Die Logistik als Präventionsansatz." *Kriminalistik* 46(12): 629–634.

Levi, Michael, and Mike Maguire. 2004. "Reducing and Preventing Organised Crime: an Evidence-based Critique." *Crime, Law and Social Change* 41(5): 397–469.

Littler, Alan, Nele Hoeckx, Cyrille Fijnaut, and Alain-Laurent Verbeke, eds. 2011. *In the Shadow of Luxembourg: EU and National Developments in the Regulation of Gambling*. Leiden: Martinus Nijhoff.

Mack, John and Hans-Jürgen Kerner. 1975. *The Crime Industry*. Farnborough, UK: Saxon House.

Martens, Frederick. 1991. "Transnational Enterprise Crime and the Elimination of Borders." *International Journal of Comparative and Applied Criminal Justice* 15(1): 101–07.

Ministerie van Binnenlandse Zaken. 2008. *Administrative Measures to Combat Organised Crime: EU Seminar Report, Amsterdam, March 13–14, 2008*. The Hague: Ministerie van Binnenlandse Zaken.

Monar, Jörg. 2010. "The Integration of Police and Judicial Cooperation in Criminal Matters into EU External Relations: Achievements and Problems." In *The Future of Police and Judicial Cooperation in the European Union*, edited by Cyrille Fijnaut and Jannemieke Ouwerkerk, 49–72. Leiden: Martinus Nijhoff.

Nilsson, Hans. 1998. "Cooperation in Justice and Home Affairs." In *Crime sans Frontières: International and European Legal Approaches*, edited by Peter Cullen and William Gilmore, 116–123. Edinburgh: Edinburgh University Press.

Quillen, Jeffrey. 1991. "The International Attack on Money Laundering: European Initiatives." *Duke Journal of Comparative and International Law* 2(1): 213–240.

Regan, Eugene, ed. 2000. *The New Third Pillar: Cooperation against Crime in the European Union*. Dublin: Institute of European Affairs.

Rijken, Conny, and Vincent Kronenberger. 2001. "The United Nations Convention against Transnational Organised Crime and the European Union." In *The EU and the International Legal Order: Discord or Harmony?*, edited by Vincent Kronenberger, 481–518. The Hague: T.M.C. Asser.

Ryder, Chris. 2009. "Organised Crime and Racketeering in Northern Ireland." In *Combating Terrorism in Northern Ireland*, edited by James Dingley, 128–136. London: Routledge.

Scherrer, Amandine, Antoine Mégie, and Valsamis Mitsilegas. 2009. *The EU Role in Fighting Transnational Organised Crime*. Brussels: European Parliament.

Schulz, Heinz. 1983. "Bekämpfung der Organisierten Kriminalität." *Der Kriminalist* 34(9): 385–387.

Schuster, Leo. 1987. "Die Unterwelt des Freihandels: Organisierte Kriminalität: Herausforderung für die nächsten Jahre." *Kriminalistik* 43(3): 163–164.

Sieber, Ulrich, and Marion Bögel. 1993. *Logistik der Organisierten Kriminalität*. Wiesbaden: Bundeskriminalamt.

Sielaff, Wolfgang. 1983. "Bis zur Bestechnung leitender Polizeibeamter." *Kriminalistik* 39(8–9): 417–422.

Solomon, Joel. 1994–1995. "Forming a More Secure Union: The Growing Problem of Organized Crime in Europe as a Challenge to National Sovereignty." *Dickinson Journal of International Law* 12(13): 623–648.

Ulber, Gerhard. 1992. "Europa—Paradies für Kriminelle?" *Kriminalistik* 48(2): 81–92.

van Daele, Dirk, Tijs Kooijmans, Benny van der Vorm, Kelly Verbist, and Cyrille Fijnaut. 2010. *De Bestuurlijke Aanpak van Georganiseerde Criminaliteit in Nederland en België.* Antwerp: Intersentia.

Williams, Phil, and Ernesto Savona, eds. 1996. *The United Nations and Transnational Organized Crime.* London: Frank Cass.

Zoutendijk, Andries. 2010. "Organized Crime Threats Assessments: A Critical Review." *Crime, Law and Social Change* 54(1): 63–86.

CHAPTER 29

THE FIGHT AGAINST THE ITALIAN MAFIA

ANTONIO LA SPINA

I. INTRODUCTION

COSA Nostra, the 'Ndrangheta, and the Camorra were born and have their "headquarters" in Italy, where they exert a negative influence on politics, civil society, and the economic underdevelopment in the Mezzogiorno. At the same time, however, in the past 30 years, Italian policies against the Mafia have developed steadily and are now deemed an example of "best practice" all over the world (for a comprehensive overview of organized crime control policies in Europe see Fijnaut and Paoli 2004).

Some of the most relevant anti-Mafia legislation was adopted as a result of specific events, such as homicides and attacks of criminal organizations against the state. Statute 575/1965 regarding the forced banishment of mafiosi far from their hometowns and other provisions against the Mafia were adopted after the "Ciaculli massacre" in Palermo. Statute 646/1982 (the so-called Rognoni-La Torre law) was passed after the murders of the member of parliament La Torre and of the general Dalla Chiesa. A law aimed at inducing entrepreneurs to cooperate with police forces and to refuse to pay the "pizzo" (protection money) was enacted when the businessman Libero Grassi was killed. Further homicides of judges and policemen—including the Capaci and the via D'Amelio massacres in which Giovanni Falcone and Paolo Borsellino were killed—were related to other measures such as the decree-law 306/1992 (the so-called Falcone decree, dealing with trials and police action in anti-Mafia fight).

In the past 15 years, anti-Mafia measures have no longer been reactions to such events. Nowadays, the declared trend is toward increasing efforts, creating a "system" of anti-Mafia measures and instruments, and defining it as a distinctive subsector of security policies. A very recent example is the "Extraordinary Plan Against the Mafia" (statute 136, approved unanimously, with one abstention, by the Italian Parliament in

August 2010).[1] Contemporary Italian public debate is generally attentive to security issues. From 1992 on, the fight against the Mafia has gained more specific attention, which endures over time.

In this essay, I discuss the different types of measures taken against the Mafia in Italy and the institutions founded to coordinate this fight and will provide an overview of the effects of anti-Mafia policies. Section 1 will deal with the many anti-Mafia measures that *directly* address and repress criminals and their organizations, followed in section 2 by measures that (through means other than criminal law) instead address the citizenry, entrepreneurs, other types of white-collar workers, public administration, and only *indirectly* the Mafia itself. Section 3 will review the public institutions involved in the fight against the Mafia. In conclusion, I will evaluate the overall efficacy of anti-Mafia policies.[2]

II. Policy Instruments Directly Addressing Mafia Crimes

Direct policy instruments are aimed at discovering and punishing those who acted or may act in a certain way and at inhibiting them from performing or repeating such actions. I will now briefly review the most important elements of such policy instruments.

A. Criminal Offenses

Especially in the 1980s and the 1990s, some important innovations in the field of criminal law were launched. The Rognoni-La Torre law introduced a new crime, that of criminal association of Mafia type—article 416-bis in the Criminal Code (CC). A criminal association is deemed a Mafia type when its members "use the power of intimidation of the associative bond, as well as the condition of subjugation and the conspiracy of silence ensuing therefrom, to commit crimes, to take directly or indirectly the management or in any way the control of businesses, to obtain the granting of authorizations, tenders and public services, to create unfair profits or advantages for themselves or others, or to prevent or obstruct the free exercise of voting rights, or to obtain votes for themselves or others during elections." The mere fact of belonging to such an organization (described in factual terms, from a sociological perspective, which the law incorporates) is in itself a crime (Ingroia 1993).

The Mafia considered here is not only the Sicilian Cosa Nostra. Also, other criminal organizations, such as the Camorra (Di Gennaro and La Spina 2010), the 'Ndrangheta, and the Mafias from abroad, were subsequently included in explicit terms. In 1992, another specific crime was also foreseen (through a modification of the CC) concerning the exchange of money for votes, offered by Mafia members to elected offi-cials. Prosecutors and judges have also used the concept of "concorso esterno" in the crime described in article 416-bis (i.e., the external participation in the criminal organi-zation by people who are not members in a strict sense). This judicial construction was applied to prosecute "white collar" criminals such as professionals, entrepreneurs, and politicians (Visconti 2003).

B. Investigative Powers and Preventive Measures

Mafia-type organizations exploit their threatening power to manage illicit trafficking, exact unlawful profits from economic actors, and control private economic activities as well as administrative and political decisions. The Rognoni-La Torre law, by reform-ing the previous statute 575/1965, granted the public prosecutor and the police chief at district level relevant powers to investigate the standard of living, income, and assets of suspected Mafiosi, their families, and employees. Such investigations can be based on the statements of Mafia defectors (the so-called *pentiti*) or, even more frequently, on the tapping of conversations between Mafia members, their relatives, and their strawmen. The police as well as the public prosecutor can exercise not only powers aiming to bring defendants to court but also powers of a preventive kind (i.e., aiming to hinder the com-mission of Mafia crimes that have not happened yet). These powers include interception of communications (through wiretapping or by other means), proposals of precau-tionary forced residence or assets seizure, covert operations carried out by undercover agents, search of entire buildings, and utilization of information offered by intelligence services. Preventive actions are proposed by the police force or by the public prosecutor and decided by the judicial authority.

C. Asset-Related Preventive Measures

Assets that appear to stem from criminal activities are those whose value is dispropor-tionate in comparison with the official income of the accused person. The seizure can take place immediately, long before the conclusion of the often lengthy financial and asset-related inquiries. Any kind of assets can be seized (buildings, country estates, firms, shares, and so on). The preventive action against the assets is separated from the judicial process focused on ascertaining individual criminal responsibilities. Such an approach is rather unique in the Western world. Seized assets, especially when they are firms, are not easy to manage, because once they are entrusted to an administrator nom-inated by the court, their market value may collapse (but this is not always the case). Some recent legislation (statutes 125/2008, 94/2009, 50/2010, 136/2010) has expanded the possibility to "chase" the assets of a Mafioso even after his death (by targeting his heirs), or when he uses strawmen, or when his assets are abroad. In addition, the prob-lems of innocent third parties are addressed.

D. Suspicious Financial Transactions and Money Laundering

Other regulations (among these the legislative decree 153/1997) deal with suspicious financial transactions and money laundering. The attempt to obscure that an amount of money, goods, or other valuable utility has an illicit origin can be connected both to typical Mafia activities (such as extortion or drug trafficking) and to ordinary crime not related to Mafia activities. Police officers can also act as infiltrating agents and simulate money laundering, to discover the various ramifications of Mafia associations. The object of investigation, therefore, is now the transaction, and no longer the person. The role of banks and financial brokers is much more relevant than it used to be, insofar as they are obliged to keep a register of all transactions exceeding a certain amount. Suspicious transactions (e.g., multiple operations made by the same person or by his relatives or employees) must now be reported to the Bank of Italy to detect those that may be linked with Mafia organizations. According to recent pieces of legislation (one is the legislative decree 231/2007), many categories of professionals must report suspicious transactions.

E. Witnesses

"Witnesses of justice" may be private witnesses or victims, or even, and much more significantly, people who were formerly involved in the Mafia (the so-called *pentiti*) who then decided, usually once they are in jail, to abandon it and to cooperate with public prosecutors and policemen. The use of witnesses involves several complex questions. First, these people and their relatives are in danger of retaliation. Therefore, the law envisaged that the same public prosecutor who deals with the witness (and is also in charge of judging the witness' reliability and the significance of his/her contribution) proposes a protection program to an ad hoc central commission. The program is then managed by a central protection service. Such programs involve furnishing witnesses and their relatives with a new place of residence, new identity documents, and in some cases financial assistance. If the witness is an offender, she or he may also be held in custody according to a special and very favorable regime (including the possibility of benefiting from the various "alternatives" to jail) and obtain substantial penalty reductions. Precautions are taken when the witness is heard by the prosecutor and during the trial (for a balanced assessment of the Italian system's strengths and weaknesses, see Allum and Fyfe 2008).

Statute 45/2001 revised the matter, with several aims and questions in mind: the promotion of the cooperation of witnesses outside the Mafia; the need for witnesses to disclose those assets that they have earned illicitly, so as to make their statements more credible; the necessity of a cross-examination of such statements during the trial; the necessity that the witnesses serve a minimum amount of the penalties to which they are sentenced; and the avoidance of coordinated statements between them and other witnesses or other people interested. In addition, the law restricted the practice of making "statements in installments," given that it was often the case that after one or even more years since their initial "repentance," some witnesses sometimes "remembered" that it would have been appropriate to accuse persons that they had not mentioned at all in their previous statements. Therefore, after the reform, witnesses are supposed to declare what they know only in the 6 months following their decision to cooperate.

Several decisions of the Court of Cassation recognized as valid and sufficient evidence the "cross-confirmation" of the depositions of different witnesses (among many others, see Cass. n. 256, 1/4/1992, or n. 554, 24/6/1992; Minna 1995). Article 195 of the Code of Criminal Procedure admits a *de relato* (or hearsay) declaration, that is information not based on what witnesses say they have directly experienced but rather based on statements allegedly made in the past to them by people who are now perhaps deceased, ill, or missing (Cass. n. 35412, 24/9/2007; n. 11100, 12/5/2008; n. 10580, 10/3/2009).

F. Mafia Trials

Procedural rules concerning the treatment of Mafia crimes in court were modified so as to allow trials with hundreds of defendants, the most effective use of the evidence available, its circulation between connected trials, and the protection of those pieces of information that should remain secret. The reasons expressed by a court to justify a given sentence in a given trial can serve as evidence in other trials. The participation of defendants in hearings can also take place in a "virtual" way, through multiperson video conferences, while they stay in their maximum security prisons (but in separate rooms, so as to make communication between them impossible). Statute 63/2001 (the so-called fair trial legislation, which also required a constitutional amendment) introduced some general innovations that are also important in Mafia trials. One is about the intricate case of the "witness-defendant" (which typically occurs when the witness is a *pentito*). In the past many, *pentiti* had the opportunity to accuse somebody as a witness, at the same time refusing to answer embarrassing questions during the cross-examination, because this was supposed to be allowed by the defendant's right to remain silent. The new law stated that when the witness-defendant makes a statement only implicating somebody else, he will be warned that he will be treated as a simple witness with regard to such statements, with all the connected obligations and responsibilities. Statute 63/2001 also restricted the possibility of connections between trials, favoring instead distinct, less complex, and hopefully swifter criminal lawsuits. Furthermore, it rendered the depositions given to the public prosecutor or to the police useless (apart from giving grounds to evaluate the witness' reliability), if these are not confirmed in hearing. Many judges and public prosecutors have criticized this provision, especially with regard to Mafia-related lawsuits, where witnesses can be frightened by possible retaliation. Especially when the prosecution's case is based on the depositions of "pure" witnesses, there is a strong probability that such statements will not be repeated in the hearing. Second, the new provisions require much more cumbersome proceedings, because they force the public prosecutor to put his cards on the table earlier to allow cross-examination, especially with regard to defendants' statements concerning other persons or regarding witness-defendants. A possible consequence of the "fair trial" legislation, however, is that of inducing prosecutors to rely on "objective" evidence, obtained through wiretapping, videotaping, satellite, and so on.

G. Penalties and Incarceration Regime

The penalties and the imprisonment regime for Mafia members are severe. Offenders sentenced for the crime of Mafia association (article 416-bis CC) cannot benefit at all from measures that allow for treatments that are "alternatives" to detention. Furthermore, contacts between prisoners and the outside world are restricted and strictly checked, to prevent such people from communicating with each other and thereby continuing to exert their influence in the organization, as was the case with some bosses until the seventies. A special incarceration regime has been selectively applied since 1992 to the most dangerous and prominent Mafiosi. In 2002 this special treatment was confirmed and made permanent. Statute 94/2009 made it even more severe.

III. INSTRUMENTS ADDRESSING CIVIL SOCIETY, PUBLIC ADMINISTRATION, AND— INDIRECTLY—THE MAFIA

The instruments treated so far in § 1 are "direct" and belong to criminal substantive and procedural law. Other policies are of a more indirect kind, insofar as they try to promote a "culture of legality" and the reaction of civil society against the Mafia, or to render public administration and public activities more impermeable to it, or to strengthen the capabilities and performance of police forces. To use a metaphor: Direct instruments are intended to capture and punish "fishes". Indirect ones are instead aimed at draining the water in which these particular kinds of "fish" swim or simply creating systematic hindrances to their typical behavior[3].

A. Promoting the Resistance of Entrepreneurs Against Racketeers

After the murder of the entrepreneur Grassi, who had publicly announced his choice to refuse to pay the protection racket, a decree-law was adopted (419/1991, converted into statute 172/1992). It was aimed at restoring various kinds of costs incurred by people who resist the protection racket. In the same years several anti-racket associations were created between small and medium firms. Statute 44/1999 then reformed the 1991 act.

It increased the amount of benefits granted to victims of racketeers by extending the types of reimbursable damages as well as covering the entire amount paid, made their payment swifter and more reliable, involved the associations in its management, eased the obligations of cooperation between victims and investigators, and created an ad hoc anti-racket commissioner, who is also responsible for coordinating actions against usury. The organizations of entrepreneurs are acting in the same direction. In 2007, the Sicilian branch of Confindustria began by asserting that members who pay the "pizzo" shall be expelled from the organization. More recently, the national Confindustria also adopted a similar, but somewhat different, internal rule, according to which members who are victims of extortion must report it, but will be expelled only if they are involved in criminal proceedings.

In some trials, entrepreneurs who had been victims of extortion were deemed guilty of having abetted Mafia members, because they had not reported the extortion[4].

B. Public Tenders

The sector of public works and procurements is one of those in which the Mafia traditionally either tries to determine the winners, by organizing "queues" of firms, or (more frequently nowadays) asks the firm, after the completion of the process, to pay sums of money, subcontract various projects, buy raw materials from certain sellers, employ certain people, and so on. Some recent provisions are devoted to counteracting this, among other things by allowing prefects to order inspections in building yards (statute 94/2009), by increasing the penalties for those who disturb public procurements, by creating single central offices for public contracts at the regional level, by requiring the traceability of financial fluxes, and by monitoring employees and truck drivers (statute 136/2010). Entrepreneurs who have been victims of extortion (either by Mafiosi or by civil servants) but failed to report it shall be excluded from public tenders (statute 94/2009; for a critical assessment, Militello and Siracusa [2010]).

Firms or individuals dealing with the public sector (because they ask for public aid or bid for public contracts) are requested to exhibit an "anti-Mafia certificate," which means not only that they have not been deemed guilty of Mafia-related lawbreaking, but also that they have not been subject to the preventive measures. One of the "books" of the new anti-Mafia code (written by the executive according to the delegation in statute 136/2010) is devoted to such documentation. Among other things, there will be a single national database, and several additional actors involved with a firm which has won a public bid (such as the works manager or the auditors) will now have to get this certification.

C. Mafia Infiltration in Local Public Institutions

Presidents of regions and provinces or mayors can be suspended, while provincial and municipal councils can be suspended or dissolved in cases when a connection between such local administrators and Mafiosi can be shown. These regulations were directed at political personnel, while an appropriate treatment of the compulsory transfer or expulsion of civil servants colluding with the Mafia was lacking. The recent statute 94/2009 states that the control exerted by the prefecture must focus on civil servants as well. These can be suspended or assigned to another office or task.

D. Strengthening the Effectiveness of Police Operations

EU cohesion policies aim at reducing the imbalances between the most developed European areas and those whose per capita gross domestic product is below 75% of the community average. The four Italian regions which still exhibit the most worrying economic backwardness are exactly those in which Mafia presence is strongest. The second Community Support Framework (1994–1999) for Italy included a National Operational Program (PON) called "Security and Development for the Mezzogiorno" (SDM). Such programs have also been present in the third and fourth period of EU funding connected to cohesion policy (2000–2006; 2007–2013, each with an endowment of more than 1.1 billion euros). The global objective is to generate and stabilize in the Mezzogiorno security standards equal to or at least near to those that can be found in the rest of the country. More specific objectives were, among others, investment in the use of new technologies, the inducement of swifter responses and decisions by police forces and the courts, the diffusion of a culture of legality, a closer involvement of civil society, special technologies for the protection of environmental and cultural resources, and social and economic development at the local level. The performance of such programs is well above the average of EU cohesion policies, when implemented according to the Italian style.

E. Spreading a Culture of Legality

In many cases subnational and local public institutions are acting to support the spreading of collective movements against the Mafia, as well as to sensitize the younger generations. "Legality protocols" (also known as "legality agreements") include the prefect, the police forces, the social partners, and other grassroots actors. Such parties commit themselves to cooperate to guarantee better security and legality in given areas. For instance, local as well as national police corps intensify their activities, state organs support this with extraordinary programs and aid, firms declare themselves open to controls and inspections when they implement public works, and so on. Such actions can also receive financial support by the above-mentioned PON. Local governments or civic associations can obtain confiscated buildings or land. Some of them use such resources to produce economic goods or services. Finally, we have several important examples of grassroots movements (such as Addiopizzo and Libero Futuro in Sicily, or Ammazzateci tutti in Calabria) that experiment and try to diffuse innovative approaches in the civic fight against the Mafia (such as the concept of "critical consumption," which involves informing consumers which suppliers oppose the protection racket). We also have several centers or foundations named after eminent people murdered by the Mafia. Some of these centers and foundations perform a large amount of initiatives with schools, universities, and actors of civil society, so as to spread the opposition to Mafia-type crime and to enrich its academic understanding.

IV. INSTITUTIONS

Apart from the Ministries of the Interior and Justice, and the various police forces, in the Italian state we find a number of public bodies whose task is specifically related to the fight against the Mafia. According to Giovanni Falcone (Falcone and Padovani 1993, chap. IV), Cosa Nostra is a pervasive and unitary phenomenon, systematically capable of transcending individual offences, investigations, and criminal lawsuits. Territorial Commissions and the so-called Cupola were created to discuss strategic decisions and to settle disputes. They were subsequently dismantled under the impact of state repression. More recently there have been unsuccessful attempts to recreate them in Sicily.[5] Recent investigations show that also in Calabria there is something similar to a Commission.[6]

However, a Mafia-type criminal organization (such as Cosa Nostra or the 'Ndrangheta) is not a "multinational of crime" (although the media and a certain stream of literature insist on such a picture), because their coordinating bodies are not the executive boards of a corporation and only have limited powers (Paoli 2003). Falcone pled for the establishment of a national office of prosecution, as well as for a national police force specifically devoted to it and able to face its international dimension as well. His dream was finally realized after his death in 1992.

The National Anti-Mafia Directorate (Direzione Nazionale Antimafia—DNA) was created in 1991. It coordinates the district-level Anti-Mafia Directorates (DDAs), but does not have (contrary to Falcone's idea) an autonomous power to initiate criminal lawsuits. The DNA can obtain information, including on the existence of an offence (which frequently happens with statements made by witnesses). The DNA also summons frequent meetings with the DDAs, so as to homogenize interpretations and ways of behaving (this happened, for instance, with the new regulations introduced by statute 45/2001 concerning witnesses). The DNA prosecutor cooperates with other prosecutors in Mafia-related investigations, resolves possible conflicts concerning the way these are carried out, and undertakes those preliminary investigations started at the DDA level, if the general directives are not respected or if the co-ordination is not effectively realized. The DNA is a contact point in international judicial relations. It has a Public Tenders Service, and there is also an agreement with the Authority for the Supervision of Public Works, so that they are able to elaborate various "indicators of anomaly" to detect Mafia infiltrations. The DNA also participates in the Committee for Financial Security, to explore financial transfers. Some of the powers of the DNA Chief Prosecutor have been increased by statutes 125/2008, 94/2009, 99/2009, 50/2010, and 136/2010.

The Anti-Mafia Investigative Directorate (Direzione investigativa antimafia—DIA) was created in 1991 with the aim of unifying the action of all the police forces involved in the fight against the Mafia. This was not an easy task. There were difficulties of communication and co-ordination, even in the field of intelligence activities. After almost two decades of operation, it can be said that several steps have been taken towards this goal.

According to statute 410/1991, the DIA's mission is "to carry out, in coordinated manner, intelligence activities targeting organized crime and to conduct investigation exclusively concerning the Mafia and Mafia-related matters. DIA intelligence activities focus on the structures of criminal organizations, their national and international connections, their objectives and modes of action as well as upon any other Mafia criminal activities, including extortion." Therefore, the DIA is supposed to engage in coordinated intelligence efforts, focusing on the whole Mafia phenomenon and on criminal subjects, rather than on single crimes, at the same time pursuing its investigational activity at an international level. The DIA acts in fields such as the monitoring of tenders and public works (with an ad hoc Central Monitoring Authority, focused on major investments), suspicious transactions, and proposal of preventive measures. It will administer the above-mentioned single national database for anti-Mafia certifications. The DIA is headed by a director, selected among the highest-ranking officers of the law enforcement agencies. The Department has three branches: preventive investigations (central intelligence unit, collecting and analyzing information), criminal investigations (planning of investigative activities and coordinating police operations), and international investigation relations. The DIA is also a member of the most important international police networks.

An important institution was, and to a certain extent still is, the Parliamentary Inter-chambers Committee for the Inquiry into the Phenomenon of the Mafia (and other similar criminal associations). It oversees the implementation of statute 646/1982, other related legislation, and parliamentary indications; formulates proposals to improve existing legislation; reports to the Parliament about the results of its operations; and conducts studies and inquiries to ascertain the evolution of the Mafia. In this respect it acts with the same powers and the same limitations of judicial authority.

A Central Commission and a Central Protection Service manage protection programs for the security of witnesses of justice and their families. Operational Units for Protection exist at the local level.

As I already mentioned, statute 44/1999 created within the Ministry of Interior the position of commissioner for coordinating antiracket and antiusury initiatives. Two solidarity funds correspondingly exist, for the victims of extortion and for the victims of usury. The Commissioner chairs a Solidarity Committee, which provides for the redress of the damages suffered by both kinds of victims.

Statute 512/1999 instituted, within the Ministry of Interior, a commissioner for co-ordinating the solidarity initiatives for the victims of Mafia-related offences which have already been the subjects of judicial decisions, a solidarity committee, and ad hoc solidarity fund, with the aim of easing the payment of the amounts due.

There is also a "Fondo unico giustizia" (Unified Fund for Justice), amounting to 2.2 billion euros as of August 2011, financed both with cash seized from Mafia members and revenues from confiscated assets, which provides additional resources for the judicial system.

Confiscated real estate assets belonging to Mafia members must be devolved to the state, so that they can remain at its disposal or be assigned to the municipalities. These can administer the assets directly or instead assign them without charge to private non-profit bodies. Decree-law 4/2010 created the long-awaited National Agency for Seized and Forfeited Goods, with its main seat in Reggio Calabria. Given the inherent difficulties in the management of such goods and the delays in their assignment, many of them used to remain not assigned and left to deteriorate over time. This specialized agency is meant to overcome such delays and inefficiencies, by intervening during the whole "life-cycle" of the goods, from the seizure by the judiciary until the final assignment, which takes place with the assistance of experts and interest groups. The establishment of the Agency has the potential to become a turning point.

V. A Tentative Assessment of Italian Anti-Mafia Policy

According to a DIA estimate, at the end of 1996 the number of members of the four Italian main Mafia-type associations (Cosa Nostra, Camorra, 'Ndrangheta, Sacra Corona Unita) was 20,857, while in December 1995 it was believed to be 20,200 (quoted in Svimez 1997, p. 457). Those figures have possibly been rounded downwards. The Ministry of Interior [2006, pp. 432,6] reported that in the years between 1992 and 2006 a total of 2,998 fugitives were arrested in Italy (Table 29.1). If we also consider people arrested abroad, the total increases to 3,650. Almost all of them belong to Mafia-type organized crime. Of course there were many other arrested people who were not fugitives.

The numbers peaked in 1993–1995 in Sicily (after the Capaci and via D'Amelio massacres) and 1998–1999 in Campania. Situation-specific conditions most likely played a significant role, perhaps more so than the government in office (otherwise we should conclude that the drop in years 2001–2006 is to be ascribed to this).

In a press conference held on August 15, 2011, the Interior Minister Maroni stated that 8,885 Mafiosi (including 32 of the most dangerous fugitives) were captured in the period between May 2008 and June 2011.[7] We must again consider that not all of these people were fugitives when they were arrested.

The data concerning incarcerations are also interesting, because they should represent the situation in a more complete way. On June 30, 2011, according to the statistics of the Department of Penitentiary Administration,[8] a total of 6,319 persons (of whom 119 were women and 76 were foreigners) were in jail in connection with the crime of Mafia-type association foreseen by article 416-bis CC. For comparison, they were 2,130

Table 29.1 Fugitives Arrested in Italy, According to the Region in Which the Arrest Was Made 1992–2006

	1992	1993	1994	1995	1996	1997	1998	1999	2000	2001	2002	2003	2004	2005	2006	Total
Calabria	29	47	34	59	66	34	68	48	37	38	41	25	24	22	26	598
Campania	24	30	44	43	49	33	102	107	77	61	47	35	46	42	31	771
Emilia Romagna	0	5	2	8	6	1	5	7	8	4	7	3	5	5	1	67
Lazio	7	20	23	17	30	13	32	16	19	10	15	18	6	5	9	240
Lombardia	2	14	23	15	16	15	14	20	11	18	10	10	10	7	4	189
Piemonte	3	9	7	5	4	2	7	9	7	7	5	2	7	2	3	79
Puglia	12	22	20	20	18	21	21	18	24	17	8	11	9	7	6	234
Sicilia	12	69	71	90	56	39	46	33	28	22	20	24	20	13	14	557
Other regions	10	14	17	22	22	7	20	23	30	24	15	22	21	11	6	264
Total Italy	99	230	241	279	267	165	315	281	241	201	169	150	146	114	100	2,998

Source: Ministry of Interior 2007, p. 434.

such inmates in 1992, 3,340 in 1993, 3,997 in 1994, and 5,295 in 2002. The number of persons subjected to the special incarceration regime (article 41-bis of the penitentiary law) was 681 in August 2010; in comparison, there were 498 in 1992, 659 in 2003, 577 in 2005, and 526 in 2006. Not all of them were charged under article 416-bis.[9] The DIA (2011, p. 14 ff.) report for the second half of 2010 clearly shows the characteristics of the 2,401 people arrested or charged in the whole of 2010, having been deemed guilty under article 416-bis CC. Let us suppose, for the sake of argument, that today the number of members of Mafia-type organizations is between 25,000 and 30,000. These figures say that on the one hand we are still far away from having all the affiliates in jail, but also that the probability of being imprisoned is now very high and has grown in recent years. From the point of view of a person who is considering whether to become or remain a member, such a fact cannot be without consequence. Furthermore, the fact that all these people are in jail imposes a huge economic cost on Mafia organizations, which have to pay for lawyers and give financial assistance to the families of arrested persons.

Large and powerful criminal organizations, with many members, should also be fought by means of appropriate weapons with regard to the procedural side. "Maxi-trials" (as we already hinted at sub § 1) appear to be the obvious consequence of this. Nevertheless, for many years, they met with obstacles and criticisms. The first maxi-trial, held in Catanzaro in 1969, ended with almost all the defendants being acquitted (107 of 114). After the approval of the Rognoni-La Torre law (article 416-bis CC), new opportunities arose. A new maxi-trial was held in Palermo between February 1986 and December 1987 with 474 defendants (of whom 119 were fugitives at that time); 360 of them were convicted, with 19 life sentences. A special *aula bunker* was built to accommodate the sessions of the trial. After several ups and downs, the decisions taken by the Palermo court mostly survived the appeals brought against them at the various levels of the judicial order, so that the "Buscetta theorem" eventually received confirmation. Another important maxi-trial, held in Manhattan from October 1985 to March 1987, was the so-called Pizza Connection Trial. This was closely connected to the Palermo maxi-trial. Many defendants belonged to Sicilian families, and some of the *pentiti* heard (such as Tommaso Buscetta and Salvatore Contorno) were also crucial in the proceedings in Palermo (Stille 1995; Jamieson 2000). Maxi-trials then became frequent and widely accepted, also with regard to other criminal organizations. The "Spartacus Trial," held against the Casalesi camorrists, lasted 10 years (from 1998 to 2008) and ended with severe penalties against the most prominent bosses (16 of them were sentenced to life). Also in Calabria, especially in the last 3 years, we find a number of maxi-trials, with hundreds of defendants, which received little media coverage and therefore are not widely known. Among them are the "Galassia," "Heracles," "Omnia," "Operazione Ultimo Atto," "Drug off," and "Skhoder" (concerning also many Albanian defendants) trials.

Another unmistakable indicator of effectiveness has to do with the seizures and forfeitures of the proceeds of crime. Some data are impressive.[10] According to a report of the Government's Extraordinary Commissioner (quoted in Svimez 2001, p. 910), the number of confiscated assets as of 2000 was 5,809 (of which 2,785 were immovable, 2,800 movable, as well as 224 firms), but only 1,161 of these had been appraised at that time (for a total value of approximately 140 million euros), and only 480 had been assigned to the entitled subjects (the state, the municipalities, and some nonprofit organizations). In November 2009, the Extraordinary Commissioner reported that the number of immovable forfeited assets was 8,933, and the number of such firms was 1,185 (Maruccia 2009). At the already-quoted press conference on August 15, 2011, the Interior Minister declared that between May 2008 and June 2011, 41,381 goods were seized (for an amount of 18,561 million euros) and 7,654 forfeited (for an amount of 4,192 million euros). The National Agency for Seized and Forfeited Goods reports that on July 1, 2011, the total number of immovable assets confiscated amounted to 10,125, while the number of confiscated firms was 1,427.[11]

As far as witnesses are concerned, from 1997 on, there has been a decrease in their number. In 1996 there were 1,214. This decreased to 1,028 in 1997, and there were 1,119 in 2003. Then there was a further decrease of the total number, reaching 800 in 2007. When statute 45/2001 was passed, many judges feared that it would cause a further decrease in new collaborations, as well as a lower profile of the new *pentiti*. Actually, a remarkable reduction of the amount of witnesses took place *before* the new statute (in 1997, as previously said), because the Central Commission adopted stricter criteria for the admission of new witnesses. This means that the criteria were probably too lenient before 1997, allowing for the admission of many "witnesses" who may not have been genuine. With the new statute in force, there have been, just to quote a couple of examples, 117 new *pentiti* admitted in 2003 and 105 in 2005.[12] Again, the fact that their number has decreased in comparison to the years before 1997 is a result of the new criteria adopted. At the same time, however, a strong incentive to collaborate is given by the special incarceration regime, which, as it has been said, is now permanent and stricter than it used to be. Also, in very recent times there have been several important, although sometimes debatable, cases of collaboration (including people who were not Mafia members, like the son of Vito Ciancimino).

Also of interest are criminal statistics concerning Mafia-related offences. In the South, Mafia-related homicides underwent, first in Sicily, a steady and strong reduction after a peak in 1991 (Ministry of Interior 2007, p. 112 ff.; Svimez 2010, p. 494 ff.; Svimez 2011, p. 888 ff.). In Sicily, we find 28 Mafia homicides in 1985 (and 116 in Campania in the same year). But the number rose to 253 in Sicily and 232 in Campania in 1991. In 1995, there were 88 in Sicily and 113 in Campania; in 2001, 20 in Sicily and 57 in Campania; and in 2008, 12 in Sicily and 59 in Campania. Overall, we observe that in the past 15 years, some Mafia-related crimes have tended to fall in the South and to grow in North Central Italy. In this specific respect, the difference between the two parts of the country is lessening (DPS 2005, 2010).

In qualitative terms, there are many important symptoms showing that the different mafias are being weakened and possibly destroyed by state action (Maffei and Merzagora Betsos 2007; DIA 2009; 2011). Several police operations have produced hundreds of arrests each. Under the leadership of Bernardo Provenzano, Cosa Nostra had chosen a strategy of invisibility, communications reduced to a minimum, moderation in extortion claims, and strict selection of members. Since he was captured, the organization does not seem capable of recovery. Especially in the area of Palermo, the organization is in crisis because of the arrests of all prominent bosses and the huge seizures of the proceeds of crime. With regard to the Neapolitan Camorra, a number of people have been arrested as well, including the most important bosses. We also have a number of relevant "pentiti" and many seizures of assets. Today the 'Ndrangheta is perhaps the richest criminal organization, because of its drug-trafficking activities and its ability to expand itself in the richest Italian regions of the North, as well as internationally. The 'Ndrangheta did not use to be vulnerable to informants, because its affiliates are typically linked by strict family ties to one another. Despite this, in recent times many members and bosses have been arrested, and significant amounts of assets have been seized. That is why some of the judges who are leading such an acceleration in law enforcement action have been recently threatened. This is not a sign of strength, but rather of anxiety.

The various Mafia-type criminal organizations are political organizations in themselves and are used to maintaining relationships with the ruling elites of the official state. This was already evident after the unification of Italy. Under Fascist rule the Mafia underwent repression, up to a certain point, and was not relevant from the electoral point of view, given the character of that political regime. When the republic was created, criminal organizations became much more salient for their capacity to mobilize consent. At the same time, they were interested in influencing the different powers of the state. Many white collar workers in politics and public administration (and in some occasions also among the members of "repressive apparatuses") have been investigated because of such cooperative relationships. Some well-known trials (such as the one against the former Prime Minister Giulio Andreotti) ended up with acquittals (although in this case the final decision asserted that that he was guilty during the seventies, but not punishable because the crime fell under the statute of limitations). In more recent times there have been cases in which important politicians (among them a former president of the Sicilian region) were convicted with a final verdict. Apparently then, given the effectiveness of investigations and judicial actions, members of the Italian political class should now be strongly discouraged from cooperating with Mafia-type organizations. Nevertheless, a recent review made by the Anti-Mafia Parliamentary Committee has shown that at least 45 people who had been already convicted of crimes which should have prevented them from running for office, in fact stood for the administrative elections in 2010. Of these, at least 11 were elected.[13] Even today, therefore, it is not always the case that a politician who appears to have had dealings with *mafiosi* (on the basis of evidence evaluated by the judiciary) is forced to retire from public life by his fellow party members and by public opinion.

On the one hand, it cannot be denied anymore that in the field treated here repression has become more and more effective. The same cannot be said for indirect policies, which are intended to promote the rebellion of the so-called civil society against the Mafias. What was just said with regard to politicians is already discouraging. It must be said that the success of indirect policies is more difficult to quantify, if we compare them to direct measures. Education to legality produces an impact in the long term, and it is not easy to separate it from the effects of many other causes. We have seen before (§ 2) that new associations have emerged, and that new codes of conduct have been adopted. The Southern society or, better, the Italian society as a whole has to mobilize. The anti-Mafia fight should not be left to judges and policemen only.

VI. Conclusion

Are all these good intentions producing the hoped results? We should distinguish between a general and final objective and a more immediate one. The first one has to do with the development of Southern Italy, blocked, among other things, by the very endemic presence of the Mafias. It is clear to all that such underdevelopment is still there. However, as I have just said, the Mafias are only *one* of its factors involved (besides administrative inefficiency, clientelism, ineffective development policies, weak legality and so on). *The* unmistakable sign of success of indirect policies is the increase in reports against racketeers. Let us have a look at these data. In the Mezzogiorno as a whole (Eurispes 2009, p. 633 ff.; Svimez 2011, p. 888 ff.) after a peak at the beginning of the nineties, complaints of fire or bomb attacks have begun to diminish, remarkably so after 2004. We find 134 of them in Campania, 108 in Apulia, 211 in Calabria, and 200 in Sicily in 1985. The number rose to 667 in Apulia, 691 in Calabria, and 479 in Sicily in 1991 (while in Campania there were 89 in the same year). There were 60 in Campania, 208 in Apulia, 400 in Calabria and 237 in Sicily in 1995. In 2001, reports numbered 103 in Campania, 208 in Apulia, 311 in Calabria and 323 in Sicily. But in 2005 we find only 67 complaints in Campania, 68 in Apulia, 30 in Calabria, and 38 in Sicily. The figures were roughly the same in 2008. No doubt criminal organizations of Mafia type still want to keep exploiting many economic activities in these regions, but perhaps they fear ever more state repression (which is easily attracted by those visible acts). At the same time, however, reports of extortions appear to be growing, albeit very slowly. A fire or an explosion is difficult to hide. This compels victims, in a sense, to report these crimes to the police. In contrast, extortion can happen in the shadows, silently. Therefore, the small number of reports when extortion is concerned is not a sign of success. In this phase, a successful anti-Mafia fight should produce a sharp increase in reports of the latter kind, but this is still not the case. Nevertheless (Svimez 2011, p. 888 ss.), we see that the number of reported extortions in 1985 was 388 in Campania, 141 in Apulia, 83 in Calabria, and 189 in Sicily. In the following years there was a steady increase, especially after the 1992 massacres. In 2008 we find 1201 cases in Campania, 618 in Apulia, 343 in Calabria, and 697 in Sicily. Furthermore, in the same year 434 complaints were registered in Piedmont, 813 in Lombardy, 423 in Emilia Romagna, and 585 in Lazio. This means that, as it is now well known, some criminal organizations (the 'Ndrangheta more than the others) have expanded to Northern regions and are now rooted there. In any case, reporting of extortions has increased everywhere, but not as much as it should. A proper evaluation of the effectiveness of an anti-Mafia fight would require much more space, data, and reflection. What I have presented so far is a partial and initial evaluation, which shows us the great strides forward that have been already made and are in the making, as well as the areas in which much is still to be done.

Notes

1. This law delegates the executive to enact an anti-Mafia "Code." Some critical remarks on the law can be found in Balsamo [2010]. The first version of the "Code" was drafted, devoting most of the space to preventive measures and anti-Mafia documentation. There was also a section regarding the crime of Mafia-type association and other substantive provisions. This was deemed unsatisfactory by the community of specialists and therefore retired by the executive. With regard to other faults, there is a commitment to adopt a "corrective" law. All these are signs of haste, to say the least. See *Osservazioni al Codice antimafia*, numero monografico di 'A Sud d'Europa', Centro studi Pio La Torre, Anno 5, n.25, 4 luglio 2011, http://www.piolatorre.it/asudeuropa/rivista.asp?id=185.
2. For a former and wider analysis of the topics treated in this chapter see La Spina 2004.
3. Space constraints prevent me from articulating the distinction between direct and indirect instruments, which does not coincide with that between criminal and non-criminal law. For instance, the regulations about "pentiti" are actually in between: on the one hand, they are administered by the judiciary and the law enforcement apparatus; on the other, they aim to induce a desired behavior through a reward. Secondly, some aspects of criminal law have a "social" effect in their symbolic and preventive dimension. Conversely, legislation concerning fields such as anti-racketeering or public works also has implications for criminal law (La Spina 2008).
4. Also in this case there is a mix of direct repression (addressed to a victim of racketeers) and willingness to promote a cooperative attitude, to hit criminal organizations indirectly.
5. Such an attempt turned into a bitter defeat for the organization, thanks to the "Perseus" operation.   http://www.timesonline.co.uk/tol/news/world/europe/article5358034.ece; http://www.theaustralian.com.au/news/arrests-crush-sicilian-mafia-revival/story-e6frg6to-1111118343755;http://www.streetgangs.com/billboard/viewtopic.php?f=91&t=42649
6. http://www.time.com/time/world/article/0,8599,2003598,00.html;   http://dailycaller.com/2010/07/13/major-anti-crime-sweep-in-italy/;   http://articles.cnn.com/2011-03-08/world/italy.crime.syndicate_1_ndrangheta-calabria-region-crackdown?_s=PM:WORLD
7. See the file 0472_1106_Lotta_alla_mafia.ppt giugno 2011 at http://www.interno.it/mininterno/export/sites/default/it/sezioni/sala_stampa/dossier/.
8. http://www.giustizia.it/giustizia/it/mg_1_14_1.wpfacetNode_1=0_2&facetNode_2=1_5_2 8&previsiousPage=mg_1_14&contentId=SST653129, read 15 August 2011.
9. The data can be found in: http://www.giustizia.it/resources/cms/documents/Andamento_41bis_11.8.2010.pdf. With regard to the August 2010 figure, 584 out of 681 were in jail as a result of article 416-bis. The fact that some Mafia members are in prison because they are accused or convicted of crimes other than those that fall under article 416-bis might explain, albeit only partially, the inconsistency between the data given by the Interior Minister (8,885 Mafiosi captured between May 2008 and June 2011) and those given by the Department of Penitentiary Administration of the Ministry of Justice (6,319

people in jail by June 2011 as a result of article 416-bis, which obviously should include all the people convicted or arrested in the previous years and still in jail).

Public debates focused instead on who is entitled to claim credit for such recent successes (the executive, the police forces, or the judiciary). On the one hand, there is a clear tendency toward an increase in the effectiveness of anti-Mafia fight. This has to do with better technologies, policemen and prosecutors who become more and more skilled, together with the significant efforts of the executive branch of government. On the other hand, the recent peak in arrests is also related, among other things, to a new wave in the fight against the 'Ndrangheta, which is related to a turnover in the judicial personnel. The 'Ndrangheta reacted by trying to intimidate the prosecutors (see http://www.guardian.co.uk/world/2010/oct/05/ndrangheta-bazooka-found-reggio-calabria; http://www.lifeinitaly.com/news/en/43940; http://archiviostorico.corriere.it/2010/agosto/27/avvertimento_locali_che_seguono_palermitani_co_8_100827033.shtml). It must be noted that the majority supporting the executive, whose minister claimed the above-cited successes, is more or less the same which voted against the utilization of wiretapped conversations in the trial against a former secretary of state, Cosentino, accused of having relationships with Camorrists. This same group has also avoided dissolving some local councils infected by Mafias (http://mafiatoday.com/tag/nicola-cosentino/; http://www.adnkronos.com/IGN/Aki/English/Politics/Italy-Prosecutors-seeks-subpoeana-in-ex-ministers-mafia-trial_311918740949.html).

10. Although there is again a need for coordinating the different sources.

11. http://www.benisequestraticonfiscati.it/AgenziaNazionale/beniConfiscati/Beni_sequestrati_confiscati.html.

12. The most recent report of the Central Protection Service available on the Internet dates back to 2007: http://www.interno.it/mininterno/export/sites/default/it/assets/files/16/0761_SCP_Relazione_2_sem_2007.pdf.

13. http://www.corriere.it/cronache/11_febbraio_10/commissione-antimafia-politici-impresentabili_70b4ded0-355f-11e0-8090-00144f486ba6.shtml

References

Allum, Felia and Nick Fyfe. 2008. "Developments in State Witness Protection Programmes: The Italian Experience in an International Comparative Perspective." *Policing. A Journal of Policy and Practice* 2(1): 92–102.

Balsamo, Antonio 2010. "Verso il Codice Antimafia." In Di Gennaro, Giacomo and Antonio La Spina (Eds.). *I costi dell'illegalità. Camorra ed estorsioni in Campania*. Bologna, Italy: Mulino.

Di Gennaro, Giacomo and Antonio La Spina (Eds.). 2010. *I costi dell'illegalità. Camorra ed estorsioni in Campania*. Bologna, Italy: Mulino.

Dipartimento per lo Sviluppo e la Coesione Economica. 2005. "Rapporto Annuale 2004." http://www.dps.mef.gov.it/rapporto_annuale_2004.asp.

Dipartimento per lo Sviluppo e la Coesione Economica. 2010. "Rapporto Annuale 2009." http://www.dps.mef.gov.it/rapporto_annuale_2009.asp.

Direzione Investigativa Antimafia (DIA). 2009. "Relazione del Ministro dell'interno al Parlamento sull'attività svolta e sui risultati conseguiti dalla Direzione investigativa antimafia, gennaio-giugno." http://www.interno.it/dip_ps/dia/.

Eurispes (Istituto di studi politici, economici e sociali). 2009. *Rapporto Italia 2009.* Roma: Eurilink.

Falcone, Giovanni and Marcelle Padovani. 1993. *Men of Honour: The Truth About the Mafia.* London: Warner.

Fijnaut, Cyrille, and Paoli, Letizia (eds.) 2004. *Organised Crime in Europe: Conceptions, Patterns, and Policies in the European Union and Beyond.* Dordrecht: Springer.

Ingroia, Antonio 1993. *L'associazione di Tipo Mafioso.* Milano: Giuffrè.

Jamieson, Alison 2000. *The Antimafia: Italy's Fight Against Organized Crime.* London: Macmillan.

La Spina, Antonio. 2004. "The Paradox of Effectiveness: Growth, Institutionalization and Evaluation of Anti-Mafia Policies in Italy." In Fijnaut, Cyrille and Paoli, Letizia (eds.). *Organised Crime in Europe: Conceptions, Patterns, and Policies in the European Union and Beyond.* Dordrecht: Springer

La Spina, Antonio. 2008. "Recent Anti-Mafia Strategies: The Italian Experience." In Dina Siegel and Hans Nelen (eds.). *Organized Crime. Culture, Markets and Policies.* New York: Springer.

Maffei, Stefano, and Isabella Merzagora Betsos. 2007. "Crime and Criminal Policy in Italy: Tradition and Modernity in a Troubled Country." *European Journal of Criminology* 4: 461–482.

Maruccia, Antonio. 2009. "Relazione Annuale del Commissario Straordinario del Governo." http://www.beniconfiscati.gov.it/media/134592/relazione%20annuale%202009.pdf.

Militello, Vincenzo, and Licia Siracusa. 2010. "L'obbligo di Denuncia a Carico dell'Imprenditore Estorto fra Vecchi e Nuovi Paradigmi Sanzionatori." In Di Gennaro and La Spina (eds.).

Ministry of Interior. 2007. "Rapporto sulla Criminalità in Italia." http://www.interno.it/mininterno/export/sites/default/assets/files/14/0900_rapporto_criminalita.pdf.

Minna, Rosario 1995. *La Mafia in Cassazione.* Scandicci (Florence), Italy: La Nuova Italia.

Paoli, Letizia 2003. *Mafia Brotherhoods: Organized Crime, Italian Style.* New York: Oxford University Press.

Stille, Alexander 1995. *Excellent Cadavers. The Mafia and the Death of the First Italian Republic.* New York: Vintage.

Svimez (Associazione per lo sviluppo dell'industria nel Mezzogiorno). 1997. *Rapporto 1997 sull'Economia del Mezzogiorno.* Bologna, Italy: Mulino.

Svimez. 2001. *Rapporto 2001 sull'Economia del Mezzogiorno.* Bologna, Italy: Mulino.

Svimez. 2010. *Rapporto 2010 sull'Economia del Mezzogiorno.* Bologna, Italy: Mulino.

Svimez. 2011. *150 Anni di Statistiche Italiane: Nord e Sud 1861-2011.* Bologna, Italy: Mulino.

Visconti, Costantino 2003. *Contiguità alla Mafia e Responsabilità Penale.* Torino, Italy: Giappichelli.

CHAPTER 30

....

ORGANIZED CRIME CONTROL IN AUSTRALIA AND NEW ZEALAND

....

JULIE AYLING AND RODERIC BROADHURST

I. INTRODUCTION

....

ON March 22, 2009, a brawl erupted at Sydney domestic airline terminal between two outlaw motorcycle gangs (OMCGs), the Hells Angels and Comancheros, during which a participant was stabbed and bludgeoned to death with a metal bollard in front of travelers. A few days later, his brother, a Hells Angel who had also participated in the mêlée, was shot and seriously wounded outside his home. The extraordinary open violence at the airport was the subject of intense media attention already attracted by longstanding tensions between the Hells Angels and Comancheros and incidents of armed conflict between rival OMCGs the Bandidos and Notorious.

The public spectacle of this murder constituted a turning point in Australia's approach to OMCGs. It was the trigger for changing a measured inquiry into controversial new laws on serious and organized crime passed in South Australia in 2008 into the rapid adoption of laws similar to those in South Australia in three other Australian jurisdictions, with others foreshadowing such laws. The premier of New South Wales reflected public alarm when he announced new legislative measures to address the OMCG problem the following day: "I was sickened by this brazen attack. Violence of this nature particularly in front of families and children is nothing short of disgusting" (Welch 2009). Although the additional police powers (discussed later) were widely criticized, bipartisan political support enabled them to be rushed into law.[1] It was also a catalyst for a wider debate about organized crime in Australia and hastened the adoption of a nationally coordinated approach between each of Australia's nine jurisdictions (composed of six states, two territories, and the federal jurisdiction) to combat organized crime.

OMCG feuds over honor and drug territories have been more or less continuous since OMCGs first became attracted to the lucrative profits involved in the drug trafficking business in the late 1960s/1970s. Occasionally, this rivalry has become public, most notoriously in the 1984 Milperra Massacre. The massacre, sparked by the Bandidos' break from the Comancheros in the early 1980s, led to a gun battle involving about 60 gang members in a hotel car park in Sydney's west. The confrontation resulted in the gunshot deaths of four Comancheros, two Bandidos, and a 14-year old female bystander; 20 others were wounded by gunfire. Forty-three people were charged with murder and other offenses, and the trial was one of Australia's largest criminal cases (Harvey and Simpson 1989). As a result, changes in New South Wales (NSW) firearms laws were made, but the legacy of that event has persisted. In 2007, another OMCG (the Nomads) affiliated with the Comancheros defected to the Bandidos, leading to tit-for-tat drive-by shootings and fire-bombings. The NSW police sought to curtail the fighting by creating the Operation Ranmore Task Force (Kennedy 2007), which then arrested 340 gang members and affiliates. Continuing that approach to the present, Strike Force Raptor was put in place in response to the Sydney airport murder. Raptor had arrested over 700 OMCG members and affiliates as of April 2010 (Jacobsen and Kontominas 2010).

Like NSW, South Australia, Western Australia, and Queensland have also faced consistent OMCG problems. In Victoria, the notoriety of OMCGs have been overshadowed by the Melbourne underworld, made up of a number of criminal groups involved in the illicit drug trade, protection, illegal gambling, prostitution, and armed robbery. Recent violence has been associated with particular families such as the Moran family in the city's west (whose origins relate to Irish waterside workers and the Painters and Dockers Union—see later) and the Williams family. Other groups have origins associated with the Calabrian 'Ndrangheta's protection of the fresh food industry, such as the Carlton crew. Gangs such as the Sunshine Crew and the Radev gang also continue to be active (Illingworth 2008; Silvester and Rule 2010).[2] All of these groups are associated with the notorious "gangland murders" of some 36 criminals and their associates between 1998 and 2010, some of which took place in public.

In New Zealand, both youth and adult gangs are a growing criminal problem. The death of a 2-year-old girl in her Wanganui (North Island) home in May 2007, the result of a drive-by shooting that was part of a feud between the two main patched non-OMCG gangs, Black Power and the Mongrel Mob, threw the spotlight on these gangs and their participation in organized criminal activities. It resulted in new responses to organized crime, including the development of an organized crime strategy and a number of legislative and institutional changes.

While Australia and New Zealand face many of the same organized crime problems, they have approached them in different ways. For both countries, the illicit market in drugs is the primary challenge. Heroin is imported from South East Asia and Afghanistan, cocaine (not yet a big problem in New Zealand) mainly from South America, and ecstasy and other amphetamine-type substances from Europe, with precursor chemicals sourced from China and India for the domestic production of amphetamines, particularly methamphetamine (often sold in the form of "ice"). Compared with North America and Europe, the street price of illicit drugs is high, perhaps reflecting the small market and the limited number of criminal players. An emerging trend is the transhipment of methamphetamine through some Pacific islands and the discovery of methamphetamine super-laboratories in the Pacific region (Burnet Institute 2010). Cannabis is usually domestically grown and remains the most widely used drug in both countries.

The international laundering of the proceeds of drug importation and trafficking as well as of other serious crimes is complemented by identity theft, extortion, and fraud. Violence and the threat of violence have also been hallmarks of some organized crime groups' activities. Financial crime, cybercrime, and trafficking in firearms and people continue to increase. In New Zealand, the extraction and smuggling of pāua shell (Ministry of Justice 2008), and in Australia, of abalone and shark fins (Putt and Anderson 2007), constitute lucrative markets for organized crime.[3]

In Australia, with a population of around 22 million, the cost of organized crime is estimated at AUD10 to 15 billion per annum. This figure represents losses to business and taxation revenues, and expenditures on law enforcement and regulatory efforts to counter organized crime as well as on managing consequential social harms (Australian Government 2009). The Australian Crime Commission (ACC) suggests that a significant proportion of the proceeds of organized crime are sent offshore (Outram 2009). In New Zealand, with a population of around 4 million, the overall cost of organized crime activity is not clear, but the methamphetamine market alone is estimated to be worth more than NZD1 billion (Ministry of Justice 2008). However, by world standards, Australia's and New Zealand's problems with organized crime are moderate. Van Dijk's (2007) organized crime index uses indicators such as perceptions about organized crime, unsolved homicides, high-level corruption, money laundering, and the extent of the black economy to place both Australia and New Zealand very low on the index. Yet, in both countries, organized crime is perceived to be a growing threat in need of a vigorous and coordinated response.

This essay begins by briefly outlining significant organized crime groups in Australia and New Zealand and explores the institutional and legislative arrangements that have been put in place in each jurisdiction to deal with the organized crime problem. The essay also considers the ways in which Australia and New Zealand have addressed transnational crime through cooperative arrangements, particularly within the Asia-Pacific. Finally, we consider briefly some of the impacts of the measures that have been adopted to fight organized crime in Australia and New Zealand and conclude with a few thoughts about future directions.

II. Organized Crime Groups

Organized crime has long been established in Australia, but the significance of different organized criminal groups varies between jurisdictions, as do policy and legislative responses. The Sydney "razor" gangs of the 1920s are the best known of the early organized criminals. They arose in response to the prohibition of prostitution and the sale of cocaine by chemists as well as the "sly grog" boom that followed the six o'clock closing of public bars. However, since the late nineteenth century, NSW, Victoria, and Queensland have hosted gangs of Australian criminals now described by law enforcement as the "East Coast criminal milieu." These Anglo-Celtic Australians were joined by other criminal groups who came as migrants after the second World War and were accordingly categorized by their ethnicity—for example, the Calabrian mafia, Russian mafia, Vietnamese, Chinese, Colombian, and Middle Eastern organized crime groups.[4] Each of these groups has been regarded as usually specializing in a limited number of criminal activities. The growing role of OMCGs in organized crime has also been identified in recent decades. Australia has approximately 39 OMCGs with around 3,300 patched members; some of these OMCGs have links to overseas OMCGs (Australian Crime Commission 2009).

As elsewhere, a shift has been detected away from strongly hierarchical crime groups based on ethnicity, place, or activity toward more flexible, entrepreneurial groups that are open to instrumental associations across ethnicities and that operate in multiple criminal markets and across jurisdictions. Sometimes, these networks are temporary partnerships between individuals or groups for the specific purpose of taking advantage of criminal opportunities as they arise (Parliamentary Joint Committee on the Australian Crime Commission 2009). OMCGs, for instance, have begun to include members of non-Caucasian origins, particularly Lebanese and Pacific Islanders, and to do criminal business with groups such as Chinese organized crime.

Similarly, New Zealand's organized crime is increasingly characterized by loose networks rather than structured groups. Once regarded as separate groups, ethnic gangs such as Black Power and the Mongrel Mob, OMCGs and Asian organized crime are becoming more fluid, less ethnically distinct, and more likely to collaborate with each other (Ministry of Justice 2008). OMCGs, for example, are known to distribute drugs and precursors imported by Asian criminal groups. Over the past 10 years, an increasing number of New Zealand's criminal groups have developed overseas links. As in Australia, criminal groups in New Zealand vary in strength and form, but the single jurisdiction makes mobilizing law enforcement against them a simpler matter than in Australia.

III. Institutional Arrangements

Each of Australia's nine jurisdictions has its own policies, laws, and institutions for dealing with the activities and impacts of organized crime. Historical events have shaped the institutions created to deal with organized crime. The Woodward Royal Commission into Drug Trafficking (1977–1979) in NSW investigated the links between those involved in drug production and distribution (primarily the Italian mafia) and the NSW police. The Commission made 89 recommendations for legal, administrative, and law enforcement reform, including the sharing of information between agencies concerned with the drug trade and between Australian jurisdictions, as well as with international agencies and other countries. At the federal level, the Royal Commission on the Activities of the Federated Ship Painters and Dockers Union (1980–1984), known as the Costigan Royal Commission, examined the criminal activities and organized crime connections of the union, and its findings resulted in the establishment of the National Crime Authority in 1984. Links between corrupt police and organized criminal interests have also been extensively investigated in different states at various times (e.g., the Fitzgerald Inquiry in Queensland [1987–1989], the Wood Royal Commission in New South Wales [1994–1997], the Kennedy Royal Commission into Police in Western Australia [2002–2004]), and these have led to the establishment in most Australian states of institutions empowered to scrutinize police, tackle corruption, and investigate suspicious activities.

In 2003, the Australian Crime Commission (ACC) replaced the National Crime Authority and two other federal agencies—the Australian Bureau of Criminal Intelligence and the Office of Strategic Crime Assessments. The ACC has a unique governance model: its board is composed of all the territory and state police commissioners and the commissioner of the Australian Federal Police (AFP), as well as the heads of relevant Commonwealth agencies such as the Attorney-General's Department, Australian Customs and Border Protection Service, the Australian Securities and Investments Commission, the Australian Tax Office, and the Australian Security Intelligence Organisation. In addition, the ACC has a responsible Minister and a dedicated Parliamentary Joint Committee to oversee its activities. Several functions are entrusted to the ACC, including monitoring and forecasting trends in organized crime in Australia, conducting investigations with coercive powers of questioning and mandatory document production, and providing a coordinating role for the nine jurisdictions and many agencies responsible for suppressing organized crime. Task forces and targeted operations are undertaken as required in relation to specific illicit markets and criminal groups. OMCGs have been a particular focus for the ACC in recent years. One innovation, announced in July 2010, is the creation of a Criminal Intelligence Fusion Centre within the ACC that brings together all the ACC usual partner agencies as well as the Department of Immigration and Citizenship, Centrelink,[5] and the Australian Transaction Reports and Analysis Centre (AUSTRAC) to work on criminal intelligence analysis with a particular emphasis on identifying high-risk cash flows, criminal groups, and patterns of crime (McClelland and O'Connor 2010).

Two other national institutions are noteworthy. AUSTRAC is Australia's anti–money laundering and counterterrorism financing regulator and specialist financial intelligence unit. Established in 1989, it supervises industry compliance with relevant legislation and analyzes the financial transaction reports submitted by businesses, disseminating the financial intelligence obtained to its partner agencies to assist them in their investigations. It also leads Australia's role in the international Financial Action Task Force on Money Laundering (FATF). A second agency, CRIMTRAC, was established by the Australian government in 2000 as a technology-development agency, aimed at generating national approaches to information sharing between law enforcement agencies, such as criminal record, fingerprint, and DNA databases.

New Zealand's institutional response to organized crime is more recent and less complex. Reflected in its unitary government and first placing in Transparency International's Corruption Perceptions Index (TI-CPI) since 2006,[6] New Zealand has had fewer concerns over corruption, either in the police or the government generally. The Organised and Financial Crime Agency (OFCANZ) was established in July 2008 as a semiautonomous unit within the New Zealand Police. Its mission is to combat national and transnational organized crime through multiagency action. To this end, it works with agencies such as the National Intelligence Centre (part of the New Zealand Police), the Ministry of Justice, the Serious Fraud Office, the Inland Revenue, the Customs Service, the Ministry of Social Development, and the Department of Internal Affairs to mount targeted operations against identified targets, explore prevention options, and build intelligence. Its first operation, completed in October 2009 (Taskforce Abyss), resulted in the arrest of a number of members of the Tribesmen Motorcycle Gang and their associates for selling, supplying, and manufacturing methamphetamine. Given its relatively recent creation, it will take time before the impact of OFCANZ's presence on organized crime will be felt.

New Zealand is also a member of FATF, an intergovernmental body (sponsored by the Organisation of Economic Co-operation and Development [OECD]) whose purpose is to develop and promote national and international standards of best practice on anti–money laundering and the combating of terrorist financing (AML/CFT). Following FATF reviews of Australia's and New Zealand's AML/CFT regimes in 2005 and 2009, respectively, both countries are considering revisions to their anti–money laundering and counterterrorist laws to ensure full compliance with FATF recommendations. Regulatory obligations for some financial agencies and related businesses and professions are likely to be introduced or expanded. Both countries are also members of the Asia/Pacific Group on Money Laundering (APG), an international organization consisting of 40 member countries and jurisdictions in the Asia-Pacific region.[7] APG conducts mutual evaluations (sometimes jointly with other organizations such as FATF and the World Bank) to determine the extent that members comply with international standards and provides support through the coordination of technical assistance and training.

IV. STRATEGIC RESPONSES TO ORGANIZED CRIME

The founding of OFCANZ reflected a policy shift by the New Zealand government following the public outcry over the death of the child in the Wanganui shooting noted above. Among the proposed measures was the development of an organized crime strategy and changes to the law (discussed later). The strategy has four components: *community* (building community resilience and empowerment through engagement), *prevention* (strengthening collaborative approaches to prevention), *intelligence* (improving the gathering, secure sharing, and effective use of information), and *enforcement* (ensuring optimal disruption, investigation, and prosecution of organized criminal activity). A collaborative approach is essential to this policy, but New Zealand faces the same challenges as others of building trust within and between agencies and finding a balance between effectively sharing information, ensuring security, and maintaining individual privacy.

Organized crime strategy has primarily been the responsibility of the states and territories in Australia. Under the Australian Constitution, general criminal law and laws of criminal procedure are the responsibility of the states and territories, and the Commonwealth (federal) government does not have a specific legislative mandate over crime. Its power to legislate on the topic of organized crime derives from its other legislative powers, primarily those with respect to trade and commerce between the states, defense, international affairs, taxation, customs, and the environment. Hence, while some states (such as Victoria) have had organized crime strategies for some time, there was until recently no overall national framework. The Commonwealth developed a strategic framework and legislation to implement it after then Prime Minister Kevin Rudd delivered Australia's inaugural National Security Statement (NSS) on December 4, 2008. This declared officially for the first time that transnational crime is a security threat to the nation, foreshadowed clarification of the role of the Commonwealth in combating serious and organized crime, and enhanced coordination among Commonwealth agencies (National Security Statement 2008).

As noted, the murder at Sydney airport provided an additional impetus toward a national approach to organized crime. On April 16, 2009, some 3 weeks after the incident, the Standing Committee of Attorneys-General (SCAG) resolved that "organised crime is a national issue requiring a nationally coordinated response by all jurisdictions" (Standing Committee of Attorneys-General 2009). SCAG observed that the Commonwealth was already developing a strategic framework and agreed that the states and territories should consider the introduction of specific legislative measures to combat organized crime where they had not already done so. These included enhanced powers for police with respect to coercive questioning, controlled operations, the use of assumed identities, witness protection, employment of surveillance devices, and asset confiscation, as well as cross border investigative powers. SCAG also agreed on the desirability of introducing an offense of consorting "or similar provisions that prevent a person associating with another person who is involved in organised criminal activity as an individual or through an organisation" (Standing Committee of Attorneys-General 2009). A key aspect of the national response was full cross-jurisdictional cooperation and coordination of law enforcement against organized crime.

The Commonwealth Organised Crime Strategic Framework that followed on November 25, 2009, also stressed that the adoption of a whole-of-government response was essential for addressing organized crime. Key elements of the framework included the development of biennial threat assessments and response plans under the leadership of the ACC, as well as implementation of multiagency responses through task forces and working groups to address policy and legislative changes. The framework also called for the development of new capabilities, among them intelligence generation and sharing, the ability to target the criminal economy, and partnerships between the state, industry, and the community to prevent the infiltration of organized crime. International and domestic partnerships are also regarded as crucial. The implementation of the framework's criminal intelligence fusion capability is, as discussed earlier, well under way, while other innovations are still in the process of implementation and their success is yet to be assessed.

V. COOPERATIVE RESPONSES TO TRANSNATIONAL ORGANIZED CRIME

In May 2010, the governments of Australia and New Zealand strengthened commitments to combating transnational crime through greater information and technology sharing and cooperative partnerships by signing a joint declaration with Canada, the United States, and Great Britain (McClelland 2010). In practical terms, Australia works through the AFP to address transnational organized crime at a strategic and operational level. The AFP's International Liaison Officer Network is its primary tool. This has expanded from a few posts at the AFP's inception in 1979 to 85 international liaison officers (LOs) in 30 countries in 2010. The primary role of the LO is to foster collaboration and intelligence sharing with the host-country's law enforcement and government agencies over criminal matters (e.g., mutual assistance requests). An AFP officer has also been seconded to the United Nations Office on Drugs and Crime (UNODC) Regional Centre for East Asia and the Pacific in Bangkok.

Another of the AFP's international roles is capacity building. For example, three times a year, the AFP undertakes a senior training course (the Management of Serious Crime [MOSC] program) in Canberra,[8] Singapore, and Semarang in Indonesia. The aim of MOSC is to build both knowledge and networks. International participants are funded by the AFP's Law Enforcement Cooperation Program (LECP). The LECP also supports other initiatives, particularly in the areas of illicit drugs and people trafficking, with a focus on the Asia-Pacific region. This includes training courses for regional law enforcement officials, the provision of infrastructure and equipment for police organizations in developing countries, and funding and assistance for crime teams in Thailand, Cambodia, and Colombia. The Pacific Transnational Crime Network and the Pacific Transnational Crime Coordination Centre are LECP initiatives that support Pacific law enforcement agencies. The AFP also engages with the ASEAN Chiefs of Police Conference (ASEANAPOL) in its capacity as a dialogue partner (since 2008) to develop and implement sustainable strategies to strengthen regional cooperation on transnational crime. Under the mantle of ASEANAPOL, the AFP has been able to negotiate bilateral training initiatives. For example, the AFP proposed and then facilitated a training course on human trafficking investigations held as part of the Joint ASEAN Senior Police Officers Course in Brunei in April 2009.

Similarly, but on a smaller scale, New Zealand Police also work to ensure stability in the Pacific region. Both Australian and New Zealand police perform peace-keeping roles in the region (e.g., the Regional Assistance Mission to Solomon Islands [RAMSI]). Part of that work has involved building the operational capacity of local police agencies. Both the strengthening of law enforcement capabilities and the elimination of corruption are essential to combating the growth of organized crime in the region, given the proclivity of criminals to exploit the power vacuums that often develop as states emerge from periods of conflict (Dupont et al 2003).

VI. LEGISLATIVE RESPONSES TO ORGANIZED CRIME

There are a number of ways laws can tackle organized crime. Laws can target individuals on the basis of their participation in organized crime groups or, alternately, the groups themselves can be targeted by focusing on their activities, their objectives, their impacts, and/or their structures (Ayling 2011). Laws also provide police and other law enforcement agencies with specific powers to investigate and act on their findings. Australia and New Zealand have used a combination of these legislative tactics.

Both Australia and New Zealand are parties to the 2001 United Nations Convention against Transnational Organized Crime (UNTOC), which came into effect in July 2003 and obliges signatories to criminalize serious crime "where the offence is transnational in nature and involves an organized criminal group" (Article 3.1.). However, neither has adopted the UNTOC's definition of "organized criminal group" in their legislation.[9] Where UNTOC refers to such a group as being composed of at least three people, one Australian definition of "serious and organised crime" requires a minimum of only two offenders (section 4 of the Australian Crime Commission Act 2002). Where UNTOC refers to the direct or indirect acquisition of material or other benefits as the aim of organized criminal groups, New Zealand defines these groups by reference to their objective or one of their objectives being the obtaining of material benefits from serious offenses punishable by at least 4 years' imprisonment *or* the commission of serious violent offenses.

New Zealand, like Canada, introduced laws to specifically target criminal organizations in 1997. In 2002, New Zealand criminalized participation in an "organised criminal group" (s.98A of the Crimes Act 1961), but the number of prosecutions was low. The section was amended in 2009 as part of the government's programme on organized crime, doubling the penalty from 5 to 10 years' imprisonment and altering the wording to "enable the use of additional investigative techniques (interceptions) which will improve the ability of police to prosecute this offence successfully" (Ministry of Justice

2008). This provision does not require the commission of any substantive offense and participation is not defined. However, for a person to be liable for the offense, his or her participation in the group must involve knowledge that three or more people in the group share the common objective of obtaining material benefits from offenses punishable by at least 4 years' imprisonment or of committing serious violence offenses, whether or not the person also shares that objective. The person must also know that his or her conduct contributes to the occurrence of criminal activity or be reckless as whether that conduct may so contribute. It is irrelevant to the definition of an "organised criminal group" whether some of the people in it are subordinates or employees of others, whether only some of them are involved in the planning, arrangement, or execution of its activities or that its membership changes from time to time.

Part 3A, Division 5, of the NSW Crimes Act 1900, enacted in 2007, is closely modelled on the New Zealand provision and has been used successfully against criminal groups. Section 93T criminalizes the commission of acts such as assault and damage to property when done with an intention to participate in a criminal group, and the penalties imposed are correspondingly higher than when done without that intention. In 2010, the Australian Capital Territory also inserted a new Part 6A in its Crimes Act 1900 criminalizing participation in a criminal group.

There are many offenses on the statute books in Australia and New Zealand that involve preparation for and facilitation of criminal activities that may be organized crime (conspiracy laws, aiding and abetting, accessory before and after the fact, possession of and dealings with stolen property, and so on) and that directly target organized crime (corruption offenses and money laundering, for example) and public violence (assault, homicide, and so on). In addition, there is provision for the confiscation of the proceeds of crime in every Australian jurisdiction[10] and in New Zealand. In the past 10 years, many Australian jurisdictions have also moved to introduce unexplained wealth laws, beginning with Western Australia in 2000 and followed by the Northern Territory (2003), Queensland (2009), the Commonwealth (2009), and South Australia (2009). New Zealand does not have unexplained wealth laws. Such laws place the onus on individuals whose total wealth appears to be greater than the income they can have lawfully acquired to establish that their wealth has been obtained legally. There is no requirement on the state applying for an unexplained wealth declaration to prove that the person has engaged in serious criminal activity. Court-ordered restraint or freezing of assets may take place while the courts are considering this question. Forfeiture of those assets may occur when their owner cannot discharge the onus and the court makes a declaration. The detailed workings of the provisions of unexplained wealth statutes vary between jurisdictions. Together with civil forfeiture laws, these laws have been successfully used to seize substantial assets from suspected organized criminals (Bartels 2010a) but they have also attracted criticism for offending fundamental common law and human rights principles (Roth 2010).

These new measures, together with a wide array of criminal investigation powers relating to undercover and controlled operations, telecommunications interception, coercive questioning, and search and seizure, have provided the basis for

Table 30.1 Tools for combating serious organized crime – Australian jurisdictions and New Zealand (as at July 2011)

	Search warrants	Telecomms interception	Controlled operations	Assumed identities	Witness protection	Surveillance devices	Coercive powers[1]	Control orders	Anti-fortification	Proceeds of crime	Unexplained wealth
Cth	Y	Y	Y	Y	Y	Y	Y	Y[2]	N	Y	Y
NSW	Y	Y	Y	Y	Y	Y	Y	Y[3]	Y	Y	Y
Vic	Y	Y	Y	Y	Y	Y	Y	N	N	Y	N
Qld	Y	Y	Y	Y	Y	Y	Y	Y	Y	Y	Y[4]
WA	Y	Y	Y	Y	Y	Y	Y	N	Y	Y	Y
SA	Y	Y	Y	Y	Y	Y	N	Y[5]	Y	Y	Y
Tas	Y	N[7]	Y	Y	Y	Y	N	N	Y	Y[6]	N
ACT	Y	Y	Y	Y	Y	Y	N	N	N	Y	N
NT	Y	Y	Y	Y[8]	Y	Y	N	Y	Y	Y	Y
NZ	Y	Y	Y[9]	Y[9]	Y	Y[9]	Y[10]	N	Y	Y	N

This table is based on a table in the Australian Government Attorney-General's Department's December 2009 Answers to Questions on Notice to the Parliamentary Joint Committee on the Australian Crime Commission's Inquiry into the legislative arrangements to outlaw serious and organized crime groups. It has been revised by the authors to bring it up to date and clarify some points.

1. Coercive powers are contained in the *Australian Crime Commission Act 2002* and the mirror ACC legislation of the States and Territories. Additionally, legislation in New South Wales, Victoria, Queensland and Western Australia gives certain state agencies coercive powers in relation to serious and organized crime.

2. A person can be subject to a control order if the order substantially assists in preventing a terrorist attack or if the person has trained with a listed terrorist organisation. There are no control orders in relation to organized crime.

3. The *Crimes (Criminal Organisations Control) Act 2009* (NSW) was held unconstitutional by the High Court of Australia in the case of *Wainohu v New South Wales* [2011] HCA 24 (23 June 2011).

4. Queensland's laws do not include provision for unexplained wealth orders, but do create a statutory presumption that the unexplained portion of a person's wealth is derived from illegal activity, subject to a finding that the person engages in "serious crime-related activity" and to proof of unexplained wealth. The onus is on the respondent to rebut that presumption (Bartels 2010a).

5. Section 14(1) of the *Serious and Organised Crime (Control) Act 2008* (SA) dealing with control orders was held invalid by the High Court of Australia in the case of *South Australia v Totani Et Anor.* [2010] HCA 39 (11 November 2010).

6. There are no civil confiscation provisions in Tasmania – criminal forfeiture only.

7. There is no ACT specific legislation. The Commonwealth legislation applies in the ACT to offences committed against the Commonwealth.

8. As far as the authors can ascertain, the use of assumed identities by police officers is limited to the context of the Territory Witness Protection Program.

9. Currently, work by New Zealand's undercover officers has little statutory backing, and the provisions that do exist are found in a number of different pieces of legislation. The *Search and Surveillance Bill*, when enacted, will give the police powers of search and surveillance with and without warrant (depending on the circumstances) and put the legal status of covert police operations on a firmer legal footing.

10. The Serious Fraud Office has the power to demand documents and information to be produced and questions to be answered in relation to serious or complex fraud offences. The *Search and Surveillance Bill* provides for the Police Commissioner to apply to a court for an examination order in a business or a non-business context, and for police to apply to an issuing officer (a person entitled to issue search warrants) for an order to produce documents.

Abbreviations: Cth – Commonwealth; NSW – New South Wales; Vic – Victoria; Qld – Queensland; WA – Western Australia; SA – South Australia; Tas – Tasmania; ACT – Australian Capital Territory; NT – Northern Territory; NZ – New Zealand.

several successful police operations against organized criminals involved in violence and drug offenses. These include the innovative combined operations approach of the Purana Task Force in Victoria that investigated gangland killings in Melbourne, Strike Force Raptor and Operation Ranmore in New South Wales, and Operation Avatar in South Australia that focused on the Finks OMCG before being replaced by the Crime Gangs Taskforce in 2008. In New Zealand, investigative techniques such as covert surveillance or undercover operations have had limited statutory backing, resulting in little guidance on their parameters and inadequate legal protections for the officers involved. New Zealand Police requested the government to consider, in the interests of transparency and certainty, the provision of a more comprehensive statutory regime, similar to those in several overseas jurisdictions, and proposed its inclusion in the new Policing Act enacted in 2008. The New Zealand Law Reform Commission conducted a review, and a new Search and Surveillance Bill was introduced in 2008 that sought to place law enforcement operations on a firmer legal footing. After further enhancement in July 2009, the legislation was delayed. A revised bill may be introduced in late 2010. In the meantime New Zealand police officers continue to rely on common law powers, piecemeal legal provisions (such as provisions of the Evidence Act 2006 dealing with witness anonymity), and nonlegal arrangements with other government agencies. While many effective operations have been conducted on this basis, the police are eagerly anticipating passage of the new legislation.[11] Table 30.1 summarizes police powers to combat organized crime in Australia and New Zealand.

Despite the apparent success of existing investigative powers and general criminal laws against organized criminals, issues about how best to control organized crime have continued to evoke debate. In March 2008, the effectiveness of legislative efforts to disrupt and dismantle serious and organized crime groups was referred to the Parliamentary Joint Committee on the Australian Crime Commission (PJC-ACC). The August 17, 2009, PJC-ACC's report commented on the need for Australia to take "a holistic and coordinated approach," particularly by coordinating across jurisdictions. It highlighted the valuable role of the confiscation of criminal assets in depriving criminals of both motivation and resources to continue their criminal activities. The advocacy of a national approach by the Committee, as well as in the SCAG resolutions of April 2009, resulted in the passage of two new laws by the federal parliament: the Crimes Legislation Amendment (Serious and Organised Crime) Act 2010 and the Crimes Legislation Amendment (Serious and Organised Crime) Act (No. 2) 2010. These laws criminalize participation in criminal organizations,[12] ranging from associating in support of the commission of offenses up to directing the activities of such an organization, and include escalating penalties for increasing degrees of participation, much like the Canadian legislative model. They also provide significant enhancements of interception and surveillance powers and of the legal protection of witnesses and of agents involved in undercover and/or controlled operations. Unexplained wealth provisions on a national level are included. These laws go some way toward creating an Australian law on organized crime.

At the state/territory level, the approach has been different. One impetus for the PJC-ACC inquiry was the introduction in February 2008 by the parliament of South Australia of the Serious and Organised Crime (Control) Act 2008 (the SA Act). That statute was passed in September 2008. It is clear from the state parliamentary debates that the main objective was to tackle the problem of OMCGs rather than organized crime groups more generally. The laws, however, were cast in broad terms that cover any criminal group. This model has cascaded through a number of other Australian jurisdictions. Ten days after the Sydney airport incident, NSW enacted the Crimes (Criminal Organisations Control) Act 2009 (the NSW Act). In October 2009, the Northern Territory enacted the Serious Crime Control Act 2009. Queensland followed suit in December 2009 with the Criminal Organisation Act 2009. Western Australia plans to put a bill before Parliament in 2010. Victoria, Tasmania, and the Australian Capital Territory have so far declined to put similar legislation forward.[13]

Briefly, and with some degree of oversimplification, this legislative model contains two main steps. The first is the declaration of an organization either by the attorney-general (in South Australia) or by a court or judge (in the other states).[14] A declaration can be made if the maker is satisfied that the organization's members associate for the purpose of organizing, planning, facilitating, supporting, or engaging in serious criminal activity and the organization itself represents a risk to public safety and order. A declaration is of no prohibitive force of itself. It does not outlaw the organization, nor does it have any effect on the organization, its property or affairs (Mr. Justice Bleby in *Totani & Anor v The State of South Australia* [2009] SASC 301, para 39).

A declaration does, however, pave the way for the second step: the making of control orders by a court on the basis of such a declaration. A control order can be made in relation to a member of a declared organization. "Member" is defined broadly and includes a person who identifies as belonging, or is treated as belonging, to the organization, and in some cases, a person who associates with a member. In making an order, the court is to have regard to information put to the court by the Police Commissioner, which may relate, among other things, to the person's criminal record, their history of behaviour and their associations with others who engage or may engage in serious criminal activity. This information need not be of a standard that would meet the requirements of evidence in a criminal trial; for example, it could be hearsay. Action must be taken by the judge or court to maintain the confidentiality of any of this information that is classified as criminal intelligence, through, for instance, hearings *in camera* or even absent the parties. Control orders may do a number of things—primarily, they proscribe association and communication among members of declared organizations. Depending on the jurisdiction, they may also prohibit the controlled person from having certain items in his possession or from being on or in the vicinity of certain premises, from recruiting or attempting to recruit others into the organization, or from engaging in or applying for an authority to engage in certain occupations. The breach of a control order, a civil instrument, carries a criminal penalty of up to 5 years' imprisonment. Orders remain in force until revoked.

Unlawful associations provisions were not unknown in Australia and New Zealand prior to the current flurry of legislative activity. Consorting laws that prohibited associations with reputed criminals, prostitutes, and persons with no apparent means of support were introduced in New Zealand in 1901 and in a number of Australian states in the 1920s and 1930s (Steel 2003).[15] Similarly, nonassociation and place restriction orders have been used in some jurisdictions (the Northern Territory and NSW) to prevent offenders from being placed in vulnerable positions where they are more likely to reoffend. However, in contrast to the new control orders, these latter orders apply only to individuals convicted of serious offenses, are of limited duration and carry a far less onerous penalty for breach.

Australia's terrorism laws (based on the UK terrorism legislative regime) were a useful model for the new organized crime laws.[16] The Commonwealth's Criminal Code was amended in 2002 to enable regulations to be made listing an organization as a terrorist organization. It became an offense to be a member of a terrorist organization and to associate with a member of a terrorist organization on two or more occasions. In 2005, further amendments enabled a court to impose control orders that impose prohibitions and restrictions on suspected terrorists, including limiting their movements and communications. Loughnan (2009, p. 464) suggests that, in providing the model for the new organized crime laws in Australia, these laws "have become the archetypal offences in the criminal corpus."

Mention might also be made of civil approaches to dealing with organized crime. Anti-fortification laws that allow police to apply for court orders requiring the demolition or modification of heavily fortified premises (such as OMCG clubhouses) are found in New Zealand and are common in Australian state jurisdictions. In South Australia, under the Development Act 1993 applications for developments that may involve the creation of fortifications must be referred to the Police Commissioner for assessment. The relevant planning authority must refuse an application if the Commissioner assesses it as an application solely for fortifications. There are also civil means of dealing with the visible menace of organized crime. In New Zealand, for example, the Wanganui District Council (Prohibition of Gang Insignia) Act 2007, which came into force in September 2009, bans the display of gang insignia in specified places designated by the Council's bylaw. Breach attracts a hefty fine. Gang insignia covers any representation that denotes membership of, affiliation with or support for a gang, including clothing. In a similar vein, in NSW, license conditions require that licensees of licensed premises ban members of specified OMCGs from entering any of 53 establishments while wearing club colors and accessories. The license conditions have been welcomed by licensees because it gives them "a rule to stand behind when refusing access" to the bedecked bikies (Fife-Yeomans 2009). In many jurisdictions, the character of certain individuals may preclude them from holding a liquor license or influence their right of entry to licensed premises. For example, in South Australia barring orders have been used to prevent members of the Finks OMCG from allegedly distributing illicit drugs in licensed premises.[17] In NSW, controlled members of declared organizations are ineligible to hold a liquor license and the fitness of others to hold such a license may be tainted by close association with members of declared organizations.[18]

VII. Some Considerations on the Impact of Measures Against Organized Crime

There was fierce opposition to the New Zealand Wanganui "patch" law and to the new organized crime laws introduced in various Australian states. A legal challenge to the validity of the Wanganui bylaw in December 2009 in the District Court was unsuccessful, but on July 30, 2010, a new action was lodged in the New Zealand High Court by a member of the Hells Angels which successfully argued that the bylaw went beyond the scope of the Act, which contemplated a limited geographic application for the bylaw to make it consistent with the Bill of Rights Act 1990. Whanganui police[19] reported that they believe the bylaw was acting as an effective deterrent to gang activity, with the result that an overt gang presence was much less noticeable on the streets (New Zealand Police 2010). Thirteen prosecutions for breach of the bylaw occurred between September 2009 and May 2010, and prosecutions then declined.

An attempt to use the 2008 South Australian declaration/control order laws against members of the Finks Motorcycle Club in 2009 resulted in a legal challenge by two of the controlled persons. In September 2009, the South Australian Supreme Court in the *Totani* case[20] held part of the SA Act invalid on constitutional grounds (relating to impairment of judicial integrity). All Australian state governments (other than Tasmania and the Australian Capital Territory) and the Commonwealth government supported South Australia in its appeal to the High Court of Australia, but the appeal was ultimately dismissed.[21] Despite the uncertainty at the time over the status of these types of laws, an application was lodged by NSW Police in July 2010 for a declaration of the Hells Angels Motorcycle Club by the NSW Supreme Court under the NSW Act. The application and the Act itself were challenged in the High Court on constitutional grounds by the Hells Angels, and in June 2011 the Act was held invalid on constitutional grounds (again, relating to incompatibility with the integrity of the court).[22] Both the South Australian and New South Wales governments are considering redrafting their respective laws.

These new Australian laws have been subject to harsh criticism by civil libertarians, lawyers, academics, and other commentators (see, for example, Cowdery 2009; Gray 2009; Loughnan 2009, Bronitt and McSherry 2010). The NSW Director of Public Prosecutions, an independent public official, described the NSW Act as "... another giant leap backward for human rights and the separation of powers—in short, the rule of law in NSW" (Cowdery 2009). One of the main issues is the targeting of individuals on the basis not of their offenses but rather of their status as members or associates of a (legal) organization (Loughnan 2009). In a similar way to terrorism laws, these laws are raising issues about the appropriate balance between individual liberty and state security. Another important issue is the openness of these laws to misuse by targeting organizations that are simply unpalatable to authorities rather than clearly engaged in criminal activity (Cowdery 2009). A third issue is the use of criminal intelligence against individuals who, because of its sensitivity, may be unable to access it and so defend themselves against allegations contained therein (Gray 2009). To deal with this issue, the Queensland government provided, in its legislation, for the appointment of a Criminal Organisations Public Interest Monitor, who is able to check and test the information put to the court and make submissions about its appropriateness and validity.

An unintended side effect of the new organized crime laws has been that many OMCGs who have been traditional enemies have been banding together to fight the laws under the umbrella of United Motorcycle Councils in several states. These organizations are mounting forceful public relations campaigns and planning legal challenges to the new laws. However, it is still too early to assess the likely overall effectiveness of these laws. One might speculate that, as this legislative model relies on declaring criminal organizations such as OMCGs that have clearly defined boundaries and names, the laws are likely to be of limited effectiveness in tackling more covert and less stable criminal groups or in dealing with associations between group members and criminal individuals outside the group.

VIII. Conclusion

Both Australia and New Zealand are stable democratic nations with low levels of corruption and, by international standards, relatively low levels of organized criminal activity. Policing agencies, however, are convinced that organized crime is an increasing threat to public order in both countries. Incidents of public violence have been a key driver in focusing attention on this issue. As a result, organized crime has been elevated to a national security threat, and new strategies, laws, and institutions have been developed, that emphasize cooperative and coordinated ways of working together on a whole-of-government basis both at state and federal levels in Australia. The best solution may be to introduce a national uniform organized crime law, bringing all Australian law enforcement agencies (including the courts and prosecutors) together under a single code.

Public anxiety over violent incidents, generated at least partly by sensationalist media coverage, and the ensuing political rhetoric have led in Australia to what many commentators regard as an overreaction: rushed state and territory laws having draconian and sometimes unintended impacts, which raise questions about the appropriate balance between public safety and reassurance and the protection of individual liberties and maintenance of a strong rule of law. The work already done by successive governments on the scope of the organized crime problem in Australia and New Zealand needs to be continued by assessing the capabilities and limitations of existing laws and exploring alternative models from other jurisdictions. Only a better understanding of the macro networks, the crime groups and the business processes of organized crime will lead to the emergence of effective measures of suppression and reduce the demand for exceptional and sometimes undemocratic responses.

IX. Addendum

This addendum (written in 2013) outlines some of major changes to law and policy in both countries since July 2011, when the chapter was last revised.

A. New Zealand

In August 2011, the New Zealand Government issued a policy document, "Strengthening New Zealand's Resistance to Organised Crime: An all-of-Government Response." It proposed a range of legislative and operational improvements to existing strategies, relating to reducing the misuse of legal arrangements such as companies and trusts, preventing bribery and corruption, disrupting identity crime, enhancing investigations of cybercrime, improving anti–money laundering and crime proceeds recovery measures, and enhancing information sharing and mutual legal assistance arrangements. The response is to be implemented over 3 years, with outcomes and a renewed response developed in the fourth year.

The New Zealand Search and Surveillance Act, enacted in 2012, expands police powers and regulates their exercise. It includes provisions relating to warrantless powers of entry and search, computer searches, and surveillance and interception. The Act specifically seeks to temper law enforcement and investigation powers with human rights values, while ensuring those powers encompass new technologies and that investigative tools are adequate for law enforcement needs (s.5). The statute passed by a small margin (61 to 57) through the Parliament, being opposed by all but the government. Police welcomed clarification of their powers. However, some commentators criticized the legislation as heralding a police state, highlighting privacy concerns and arguing that the legislation gives too many government agencies surveillance opportunities.

A new Wanganui patch bylaw was drafted in 2012, and public consultation took place. In May 2013, a proposal for a new national law, the Prohibition of Gang Insignia in Government Premises Bill, was read for the second time in the New Zealand parliament. The Bill makes it an offense to wear a gang patch on government premises, including schools, kindergartens, and police stations. It has not yet passed into law. In the light of the Bill's existence, the Wanganui bylaw was put on hold.

B. Australia

A spate of drive-by shootings in NSW in early 2012 involving OMCG members, and continuing violence by OMCGs on Queensland's Gold Coast in which bystanders have been injured, have increased the pressure on governments to deal with organized crime and OMCGs in particular.

The main Australian response since mid-2011 has been in the legislative and judicial arenas. Both South Australia and NSW redrafted their laws to take account of the High Court's decisions referred to in the chapter. The Northern Territory also amended its laws. In 2012, Western Australia and Victoria passed similar laws (Criminal Organisation Control Act 2012 [WA] and Criminal Organisations Control Act 2012 [Vic.]). Also in 2012, following an application to the courts by the Queensland government for a declaration that the Finks MC was a criminal organization, a legal action was taken in the High Court challenging that state's legislation. In March 2013, the Queensland legislation was declared constitutionally valid (*Assistant Commissioner Michael James Condon v Pompano Pty Ltd* [2013] HCA 7). The declaration application against the Finks is currently proceeding. An outcome of the latest High Court decision is that NSW has amended its legislation to bring it into line with the Queensland Act, and South Australia is also proceeding to do so.

NOTES

1. Mr Barry O'Farrell, Leader of the the NSW Opposition stated in the chamber: "I would have no problems if you put all the gang members in two rooms and allow them to shoot themselves to death, Mr Speaker, I would have no problems with that at all" (Cornwall 2009); "We need resolve, not simply to lock up these bikie gang criminals, but to break them up completely" (Welch 2009).

2. Personal communication with second author by Melbourne anonymous "underworld" figure.

3. Abalone is an edible gastropod mollusk. *Pāua* is the Māori name for abalone. Abalone is also known as ear-shells, sea ears, muttonfish or muttonshells, ormer (in the UK), perlemoen, and venus's-ears (in South Africa). Abalone is very popular in Chinese and Japanese cooking. In China, in particular, it is regarded as a luxury item suitable for serving on special occasions. Abalone/*pāua* has an iridescent mother-of-pearl shell that is used to make jewellery and other decorative items. Both Australia and New Zealand impose strict bag and size limits on abalone removals, but poaching, particularly of undersized specimens, remains a huge problem.

4. Grabosky (1977, p. 393) noted the presence of the Camorra among the small Italian-Australian community in Sydney in the 1920s and 1930s. Criminal association laws were introduced in NSW in the 1920s to suppress the violence associated with the razor gangs.

5. Centrelink is the agency responsible for the management of social security payments in Australia.

6. New Zealand placed second in TI-CPI in 2004 and 2005.

7. The APG is just one of a number of FATF-style regional bodies which all have similar roles.

8. Participants include senior Australian law enforcement officers, members of international police services and members of government investigative agencies such as the Australian Customs and Border Protection Service, the Australian Taxation Office, and the Australian Securities and Investments Commission.

9. The Convention establishes several offense categories: participation in an organized criminal group, money laundering, corruption, and obstruction of justice as well as protocols

in respect to trafficking in women and children, illicit manufacturing and trafficking in firearms, and smuggling of migrants. Serious crime is defined broadly (conduct attracting punishment of 4 or more years' imprisonment) and an organized criminal group is defined in Article 2(a) as *"a structured group of three or more persons, existing for a period of time and acting in concert with the aim of committing one or more serious crimes or offences established in accordance with the convention, in order to obtain, directly or indirectly, a financial or other material benefit."* A "structured group" refers [Article 2(c)] to one that is not "randomly formed for the immediate commission of an offence," and such groups need not have formally defined roles or continuity of membership.

10. Tasmania's confiscation scheme does not include civil forfeiture. Thus a conviction or abscondment after charge is required before the criminally derived assets can be confiscated by the state (Bartels 2010c).

11. We are indebted to Hamish McCardle of New Zealand Police for much of the information concerning New Zealand contained in this paragraph.

12. An organization for this purpose consists of two or more persons, consistent with the definition of "serious and organised crime" in the *Australian Crime Commission Act* 2002 cited earlier.

13. There are a number of reasons for this. Tasmania, as an island, suffers very little from OMCG activities or organized crime in general (Parliamentary Joint Committee on the Australian Crime Commission 2009). Similarly, "[t]he ACT, as a small jurisdiction with a small population base, is unlikely to experience serious organised crime groups and activities to the degree and frequency of some of the other larger jurisdictions" (Australian Capital Territory Government 2009). Victoria has taken the view that it already has in place effective and comprehensive strategies and legislation to deal with organized crime (Bartels 2010b). Furthermore, both the Australian Capital Territory and Victoria have human rights instruments that are likely to create obstacles to enforcing a legislative model of the kind enacted in the other states.

14. In Queensland, the court declares the organization as a criminal organization. In all other jurisdictions with this type of legislation, the organization is simply declared.

15. Many of these laws remain on state statute books today, but their restricted application and lack of reference to modern communications methods make them of limited use in tackling organized criminal groups. Thus when South Australia enacted its 2008 legislation, along with its control order scheme it substituted a new consorting law for the old, including in its Act a provision making it an offense punishable by up to 5 years' imprisonment for *any* person (subject to specified exceptions) to associate with a member of a declared criminal organization or the subject of a control order on not less than 6 occasions in a 12 month period.

16. Hong Kong anti-triad laws may also have been influential in crafting the SA Act: personal communication, Stephen Pallaras QC, South Australian Director of Public Prosecutions, October 2008.

17. Personal communication, Mr A. Harrison, Assistant Commissioner of Police, South Australia, November 2009, March 2010. Banning orders, barring orders and exclusion notices imposed by or on application of the police are common in a number of states under relevant liquor licensing legislation. See for example, ss.125A and 125B of the Liquor Licensing Act 1997 (South Australia).

18. See ss. 40 and 45 of the Liquor Act 2007 (New South Wales).

19. *Whanganui* can be spelled either with or without the "h". In deference to the name's Māori origins, Crown agencies such as the police use the "h", but the town's name is generally spelled without it.

20. *Totani & Anor v The State of South Australia* [2009] SASC 301.
21. *South Australia v Totani* [2010] HCA 39 (11 November 2010).
22. *Wainohu v New South Wales* [2011] HCA 24 (23 June 2011).

References

Australian Capital Territory Government. June 2009. *Government Report to the ACT Legislative Assembly: Serious Organised Crime Groups and Activities*. Canberra: Australian Capital Territory Government.

Australian Crime Commission. March 23, 2009. "How Serious Is the Threat Posed by Outlaw Motorcycle Gangs? Frequently Asked Media Questions." http://www.crimecommission.gov.au/media/faq/org_crime.htm.

Australian Government. 2009. *Commonwealth Organised Crime Strategic Framework*. Canberra: Commonwealth of Australia.

Ayling, Julie. 2011. "Criminalizing Organizations: Towards Deliberative Lawmaking." *Law & Policy* 33(2): 149-178.

Bartels, Lorana. 2010a. "Unexplained Wealth Laws in Australia." *Trends and Issues in Crime and Criminal Justice* 395. (July 2010). Canberra: Australian Institute of Criminology.

Bartels, Lorana. 2010b. "The Status of Laws on Outlaw Motorcycle Gangs in Australia." *Research in Practice Report* 2, 2nd ed. Canberra: Criminology Research Council, Australian Institute of Criminology.

Bartels, Lorana. 2010c. "A Review of Confiscation Schemes in Australia." *AIC Reports: Technical and Background Paper 36*. Canberra: Australian Institute of Criminology.

Bronitt, Simon, and Bernadette McSherry. 2010. *Principles of Criminal Law*, 3rd ed. Rozelle, NSW: Thomson Reuters.

Burnet Institute. 2010. *Situational Analysis of Drug and Alcohol Issues and Responses in the Pacific 2008-09*. Canberra: Australian National Council on Drugs.

Cornwall, Deborah. 2009. "New Bikie Laws an Attack on Civil Liberties." *Lateline* (April 2). http://www.abc.net.au/lateline/content/2008/s2533733.htm.

Cowdery, Nicholas. 2009. Comments on Organisation/Association Legislation—"Bikie Gangs." (May, updated November). http://www.odpp.nsw.gov.au/speeches/speeches.html.

Dupont, Benoît., Peter Grabosky, and Clifford Shearing. 2003. "The Governance of Security in Weak and Failing States." *Criminal Justice* 3: 331–349.

Fife-Yeomans, Janet. 2009. "Pubs, Clubs Ban Bikies' Colours," *The Daily Telegraph*. (November 7). http://www.dailytelegraph.com.au/news/pubs-clubs-ban-bikies-colours/story-e6freuy9-1225795176272.

Grabosky, Peter N. 1977. *Sydney in Ferment: Crime, Dissent and Official Reaction 1788 to 1973*. Canberra: Australian National University Press.

Gray, Anthony. 2009. "Australian 'Bikie' Laws in the Absence of an Express Bill of Rights." *Journal of International Commercial Law and Technology* 4(4): 274–286.

Harvey, Sandra, and Simpson, Lindsay. 1989. *Brothers in Arms: The Inside Story of Two Bikie Gangs*. Sydney: Allen and Unwin.

Illingworth, Simon. 2008. *Filthy Rat*. Fremantle, WA: Fontaine Press.

Jacobsen, Geesche, and Belinda Kontominas. 2010. "Hells Angels Challenge Anti-Bikie Laws in Court." *Sydney Morning Herald*. (July 23). http://www.smh.com.au/nsw/hells-angels-challenge-antibikie-laws-in-court-20100722-10mzz.html.

Kennedy, Les. 2007. "Police Fear Milperra Massacre Could Be Repeated." *Sydney Morning Herald.* (May 9). http://www.smh.com.au/news/national/police-fear-milperra-massacre-c ould-be-repeated/2007/05/08/1178390312304.html.

Loughnan, Arlie. 2009. "The Legislation We Had to Have? The Crimes (Criminal Organisations Control) Act 2009 (NSW)." *Current Issues in Criminal Justice* 20(3): 457–465.

McClelland, Robert. 2010. "Media Release—International Declaration to Combat Organised Crime." (May 1, 2010). http://robertmcclelland.com.au/2010/05/01/international-declaration-to-combat-organised-crime/.

McClelland, Robert, and Brendan O'Connor. 2010. "Joint Media Release—Launch of Criminal Intelligence Fusion Centre." (July 13, 2010). http://www.ministerhomeaf-fairs.gov.au/www/ministers/oconnor.nsf/Page/MediaReleases_2010_ThirdQuarter _13July2010-LaunchofCriminal IntelligenceFusionCentre.

Ministry of Justice. 2008. *The Programme of Action for Organised Crime and the Organised Crime Strategy for 2008-2009.* Wellington: New Zealand Ministry of Justice.

National Security Statement. 2008. "The First National Security Statement to the Australian Parliament." Address by the Prime Minister of Australia The Hon. Kevin Rudd MP. (December 4).http://www.royalcommission.vic.gov.au/getdoc/596cc5ff-8a33-47eb-8d4a-9205131ebddo/TEN.004.002.0437.pdf.

New Zealand Police. 2010. "Policing Fact Sheet: Wanganui District Council (Prohibition of Gang Insignia) Act 2009." http://www.police.govt.nz/wanganui-district-council-prohibition-g ang-insignia-act-2009.

Outram, Michael. 2009. "A Collaborative Approach to Fighting Serious Organised Crime in Australia." Presentation to the AIPIO Conference Navigating Uncertainty, Canberra. (July 28–30). http://www.docstoc.com/docs/32452810/A-collaborative-approach-to-fighting-serious-organised-crime-in.

Parliamentary Joint Committee on the Australian Crime Commission. 2009. *Inquiry Into the Legislative Arrangements to Outlaw Serious and Organised Crime Groups.* August. Canberra: Commonwealth of Australia.

Putt, Judy, and Katherine Anderson. 2007. "A National Study of Crime in the Australian Fishing Industry." *Research and Public Policy Series No. 76.* Canberra: Australian Institute of Criminology.

Roth, Lenny. 2010. "The Criminal Assets Recovery Amendment (Unexplained Wealth) Bill 2010." *NSW Parliamentary Library Research Service e-brief.* (August 2010). Sydney: New South Wales Parliament. http://www.parliament.nsw.gov.au/prod/parlment/publications. nsf/key/TheCriminalAssetsRecoveryAmendment(UnexplainedWealth)Bill20100/$File/ Unexplained+wealth.pdf.

Silvester, John, and Andrew Rule. 2010. *Underbelly: The Gangland War.* Melbourne: Floradale.

Standing Committee of Attorneys-General. 2009. "Communiqué 16-17 April 2009." http:// www.scag.gov.au/lawlink/scag/ll_scag.nsf/pages/scag_meetingoutcomes.

Steel, Alex. 2003. "Consorting in New South Wales: Substantive Offence or Police Power?" *University of New South Wales Law Journal* 26(3): 567–602.

Van Dijk, Jan. 2007. "Mafia Markers: Assessing Organized Crime and Its Impact Upon Societies." *Trends in Organized Crime* 10: 39–56.

Welch, Dylan. 2009. "Hells Angel Killed in Airport." *The Age* (March 23). http://www.theage. com.au/national/hells-angel-killed-in-airport-attack-20090322-950m.html.

CHAPTER 31

....

ORGANIZED CRIME "CONTROL"
IN ASIA

Experiences from India, China,
and the Golden Triangle

....

RODERIC BROADHURST AND NICHOLAS FARRELLY

I. INTRODUCTION

....

ASIA covers a vast area and includes more than half the globe's population. Its largest countries, China and India, are the two most populous in the world. This mega-region is host to major religions (Islam, Buddhism, Hinduism, and Christianity) but also includes socialist market states, with explicitly secular orientations, like China and Vietnam. The South Asian "subcontinent," with its population of 1.5 billion, has more people living below the poverty line than any other region in the world. In contrast, the average income of the 1.3 billion people in China has risen rapidly. This has also created significant inequality from province to province and between urban and rural areas. Parts of Southeast Asia (where 10 countries share 590 million people) are still impoverished, with Cambodia, Laos, and Myanmar (Burma) rated among the poorest in the world. Taken as a whole, Asia has some of the world's fastest growing economies but also presents extremes of inequality and destitution that are often ineffectively mitigated by government policies. Such inequalities help generate many forms of crime alongside the related problems of poor governance and corruption.

In recent decades, this vast Asian region has, in general terms, experienced the same globalizing trends and rapid trade liberalization as the rest of the world. But while trade has created a climate of interdependence, the sheer diversity of interests and the persistence of traditional antagonisms have not been contained by regional governance mechanisms to the same extent as they have been in Europe. For instance, the South Asian Association for Regional Cooperation (SAARC) has not yet proved to be an effective multilateral mechanism for cooperation against cross-border criminal activities (Gordon 2009).[1] The Association of South East Asian Nations (ASEAN) has been more active but has also generally failed to keep pace with regional crime developments.[2] In West and Southwest Asia and, to some extent, Central Asia, there is an absence of multilateral efforts to suppress transnational organized crime.[3] The result is increasing cross-border criminal opportunity but no commensurate rise in regional governance and law enforcement capacity.

Given the vast scope of the Asian mega-region, in this essay we are compelled to confine our discussion of the response to organized crime to India and China (including Hong Kong and Macau) and to ASEAN, with a specific focus there on the subregion known as the "Golden Triangle." In doing so, we are conscious that we neglect some important countries and subregions where organized crime co-mingles with separatism and terrorism (such as the southern Philippines, West Papua, Aceh, Cambodia, North Korea, and southern Thailand). Also, the Japanese *yakuza* or *boryukudan* ("violent ones"), although active throughout parts of Asia and the Pacific, are not addressed in this essay because the essay by Hill provides an account of them.

Instead, we focus on the responses to organized crime in India, China, and the Golden Triangle. Our goal is to explain how countermeasures against organized crime fit into wider debates about law enforcement, public order, and security. We are also concerned with the perceptions/nature of criminal activity in the subregions that we examine. We find that, by-and-large, strategies for control of organized crime receive significant attention at both national and regional levels, albeit with mixed results (see Ganapathy and Broadhurst 2008). This discussion is followed by an analysis of the regional and multilateral responses to organized crime focusing, most particularly, on the more developed initiatives emerging from ASEAN. We conclude with an assessment of the prospects for effective measures against organized crime in the highly complex Asian mega-region and describe some of the persistent challenges that effective transnational law enforcement will face.

II. INDIA: ORGANIZED CRIME AND THE STATE RESPONSE

Criminal groups have a long history in India; perhaps the best known were the *thuggee*, whose practices included rituals associated with the cult of the Hindu goddess of destruction, Kali. The thuggee modus operandi was the murder (strangulation) and robbery of travelers after deceitful attachment to their caravans. It is from these groups that the English word "thug" is derived. Thuggee operated from at least the seventeenth century but were eventually suppressed by the British from the 1830s on, after they established a specialist police agency, the "Thuggee and Dacoity Department," whose combination of intelligence capacities, dissemination of knowledge about thuggee techniques and tactics, extensive powers of arrest, and use of informants (former thugs or "approvers" who gave evidence against the stranglers[4]) helped break up the larger groups (Dash 2005). These police actions coincided with the rise of modern transportation that reduced the opportunities for attacks on slow-moving caravans. Although thuggee were motivated not by religion but by poverty, the use of rituals associated with Kali helped reinforce codes of silence and bonds of fraternity. One of the legacies of their suppression was the Criminal Tribes Act of 1876, which recognized the secret nature of these groups but also unfairly criminalized entire communities (Bayley 1969, pp. 110–11; Dash 2005, pp. 280–81).[5]

India has, however, continued to experience significant levels of organized criminality. Dacoits, or rural bandits, operated freely until recent times in the Chambai region and in parts of Madhya Pradesh and Uttar Pradesh (Sarkar and Tiwari 2001), among others. Caste, place, and religion continue to determine the nature of India's urban criminal or "goondas" networks, and many criminal gangs are caste based (Thilgaraj and Gandhirajan 2007). Poverty, as in the past, is a major cause of crime, and widespread corruption arises partly from the low wages of police and other officials.[6] As a result, crime is also greatly underrecorded. Even before India's 1991 market reforms and trade liberalization—which generated many opportunities to manipulate foreign currency exchange through *hawala* (informal networks of lenders and brokers)—criminal gangs had become more identifiably urban in character. Despite attempts to strengthen anti–money laundering law enforcement, *hawala* provides the major means for tax evasion and the laundering of criminal and terrorist funds. Mumbai, along with Karachi and Dubai, are considered the key centers (Gordon 2010).

Turning again to history, after the police reforms of 1903, the obsolete Thuggee and Dacoity Department was replaced by the Department of Criminal Intelligence, which took on special and "political" crimes as part of the new imperial Indian Police Service (IPS) (Dodwell 1932, pp. 372–3). At that time, radical and costly police reform was considered one of the "most urgent needs of Indian administration" (Lord Curzon cited in Dodwell 1932, p. 372). They proved almost impossible to implement in any consistent fashion, and although "Independence brought revolutionary changes in the political structure of government, it brought none of any consequence to the structure of police administration" (Bayley 1969, p. 51). The IPS continued after India became independent as one of the few national, thus "all India," services. The IPS provides the leadership of the police services across the country and has among its principal duties the suppression of offences associated with organized crime and insurgency.

The IPS has been subjected to Supreme Court criticism, and there is currently a concerted effort to reform the IPS and modernize police forces throughout India (India Ministry of Home Affairs 2010). Gordon (2010) notes the generally unprofessional condition of police institutions but also indicates that a flurry of legislative and administrative reform has been recently stimulated in part by the poor response to India's "9/11"—the Mumbai attacks of "26/11" 2008—and by other pressing issues of security and counterinsurgency. However, the 1861 British colonial-era Police Act, which provided for the original paramilitary model of policing, remains the basic approach and contributes to the poor standards and absence of community policing traditions (Bayley 1969, p. 49). The system of justice inherited from the British has also resulted in an overburdened and inefficient legal system in India that has led to amendments to the criminal law authorizing some forms of plea-bargaining and the creation of "fast-track" courts (Gordon 2010; India Ministry of Interior 2010).

A. Scale and Activities

Organized crime in India and South Asia more generally may be characterized by its diversity of activities (from illicit drugs to counterfeit medicinal products), capture of elements of government (*"goondas raj"*), and convergence with terrorism or longstanding insurgencies in particular states and border regions. India's Maoist insurgency, for example, which was responsible for 908 deaths in 2009 alone, also presents a serious criminal and security problem in some states. Combating this and other insurgency groups absorbs a substantial proportion of funds allocated to modernize the police (Ministry of Home Affairs 2010). The most serious terrorist attack before the "26/11" (2008) event was the 1993 Mumbai bombings where over 200 people were killed. This attack allegedly involved Dawood Ibrahim's "D Company" crime network,[7] which bribed police and customs officials to allow importation of explosives (Rollins, Wyler and Rosen 2010). "D Company" supposedly typified the "new India" with members coming from all religions and a range of castes, but its activities led to the breakaway of Muslim members and subsequent murderous rivalry between them and the Hindu members of "D Company" (Gordon 2010).

Extensive smuggling networks, which are vectors of transnational crime, developed under India's formerly high trade tariff regime. Criminal groups now concentrate on human trafficking, smuggling of arms, and explosives and illicit drugs. India and Pakistan are transit and destination countries for illicit drugs from Southeast and Southwest Asia. The United Nations Office on Drugs and Crime (UNODC) estimates for India are dated and exclude female users, but surveys suggest 0.7 percent of males are opiate users (mostly opium, not heroin). The region has developed a significant domestic addiction problem with estimates of between 1.39 and 3.31 million opiate users in South Asia (pp. 153–154).[8] "Tribal" minorities located on the India–Myanmar border are engaged in the opium trade, and precursor chemicals for the production of heroin and amphetamines flow back to Southeast and Southwest Asia from India (UNODC 2010). Other important transnational crimes include intellectual property theft, money laundering, and cybercrime. Because of India's rapidly growing online presence (Internet penetration is 7 percent, or around 80 million users), it is an emerging site of cybercrime and intellectual property crime. Large numbers of women from poorer countries like Nepal and Bangladesh are also trafficked to work in the sex industry or in sweat shops and domestic service throughout the region. Despite a massive program of frontier fencing (India Ministry of Interior 2010), explosives and weapons are smuggled across the porous India–Nepal border, and even the more secure Pakistan–India border has many smuggling routes (Gordon 2010).

B. Responses

India is a complex federal system comprising 26 states and a federal government in New Delhi.[9] That federal government has until recently played a minor role in the suppression of crime. There is no national law on organized crime although the Prevention of Terrorism Act (POTA) introduced in 2002 has been applied to crime groups who may be connected to terrorist groups, and the National Investigations Act (2008) may provide for a wider role for the IPS. Nevertheless, some states, notably Maharashtra, have enacted laws that address both organized crime and terrorism. The Maharashtra Control of Organized Crime Act (MCOCA) was introduced in 1999 to curb the growth of organized crime, particularly the role of several well-organized crime groups active in Mumbai, India's commercial capital. The key event that led to the introduction of MCOCA was the shooting of popular movie and music producer Gulshan Kumar in 1997. He had apparently refused to pay the usual protection required by organized crime for participating in the lucrative film industry based in Mumbai.[10] Kumar was one of several leading "Bollywood" entrepreneurs to be murdered between 1994 and 2001 (Sarkar and Tiwari 2001).

The premise of the MCOCA was that existing measures to suppress organized crime were inadequate and thus created special courts to administer "a special law with stringent and deterrent provisions including in certain circumstances power to intercept wire, electronic or oral communication to control the menace of organised crime."[11] The preface also makes it clear that "in recent years [there have been] criminal activities like murders of tycoons related to the film industry as well by builders, extortion of money from businessmen." Among the many additional powers is the admission of uncorroborated confessions. Bail is not available to anyone accused of having committed an offence under the MCOCA. The MCOCA defines organized crime as any continuing unlawful activity by an individual, singly or jointly, either as member of an organized crime syndicate or on behalf of such a syndicate by use of violence or threat of violence or intimidation or coercion, or other unlawful means with the objective of obtaining benefit, profit, or advantage or promoting insurgency. Other states have enacted very similar laws to the MCOCA, such as Uttar Pradesh (2007), Andhra Pradesh (2001–2004[12]), and Karnataka (2001). However, an equally tough version introduced by Gujarat in 2003 had been repeatedly held up at the federal level and was ultimately passed in July 2009 following amendments that limited the extension of powers of detention, denial of bail, and the admission of uncorroborated confessions.

While MCOCA-style anti–organized crime laws have been controversial, many states have long had laws that attempt to suppress "goondas" and mafia-like activities. The Tamil Nadu Law of 1982 for "Prevention of Dangerous Activities of Boot Leggers, Drug Offences, Forrest Offenders, Goondas, Immoral Traffic Offender, Slum-grabbers, and

Video Pirates Act" represents a typical example augmented recently by enhanced punishment for organized criminals. Thilgaraj and Gandhirajan (2007) describe the main crime groups in Chennai as forming mercenary gangs (i.e., protection, election intimidation, assassination, kidnap, extortion, and land acquisition), robbery and dacoit gangs, theft gangs, and those involved in activities associated with financial fraud. They note the infiltration of the political system via election rigging is inevitable because of the use of criminal gangs to intimidate voters and officials. They also outline the measures introduced in Tamil Nadu to suppress organized crime, and these include special police units, communications intercepts, witness protection, limited powers for confiscation of tainted wealth, and the use of fast track courts. They argue that a symbiosis between police, politicians, and the "goondas" presents a major challenge that requires the attention of the federal government and greater cooperation across states and at the international level (Thilgaraj and Gandhirajan 2007, pp. 210–11, 216). It is for this reason that efforts to tackle organized crime have often proved ineffective. In the short term, powerful figures are often immune to official sanction.

III. "BLACK" SOCIETIES AND GREATER CHINA

The recent reemergence of criminal gangs (*bang*) and the expansion of triads[13] in the People's Republic of China (PRC) have occurred in the context of rapid modernization, socioeconomic change, and globalization. Socialist market reforms and economic development provided attractive illicit opportunities that have encouraged the revival of different forms of organized crime than once flourished in pre-communist China. The uncertainties of the transition from austere communism to capitalism help to induce the reinvention of criminal groups usually known as "black" societies. Between 1979 and 1997, such gangs gradually reemerged, especially in the form of Hong Kong and Macau triads in Shenzhen and other triad-like groups in Taiwan (Zhang 2009; Chiu 2010).[14] During the first government "hard strike" campaigns in the 1980s, the term "black society" returned to the official discourse of crime control (Liu and Wu 2002).[15]

For Chinese law enforcement agencies, organizations with the "character of black society" are a special type of crime group, and they can be distinguished by their attachment to a particular locality and the use of violence and command complexity, but they may not resemble organized crime groups as found elsewhere (Zhang 2010). The main distinguishing feature is an element of official protection ("umbrella") and adoption of a legal business form (Liu and Wu 2002). "Black" societies have sometimes captured local authorities and challenged the authority of Public Security Bureau and People's Court officials. The growth of these organized crime groups heightened concerns about the influence of foreign criminals and has hastened the need to foster mutual assistance with foreign police services.

A. Evolution and Activities of "Triads" or "Black" Societies

The violent subculture of triads originated in the vigorous market competition of the 19th and early twentieth centuries over waterfront labor, and competition over the lucrative (illicit) opium trade. Because triad societies often had a patriotic and ritualistic element, the distinction between contemporary "black" societies and the pre-war and earlier triads or secret societies is important and a degree of overlap and ambiguity between triad/black society, illicit business and "organized crime" is inherent. In largely immigrant societies, such as Hong Kong and other coastal cities with large "floating" populations, black societies represent a type of social capital that compensates for weak family and clan affiliations. Black societies are not exclusively criminal but are secret brotherhoods (usually with a master-disciple form) that become loose cartels bound by social as well as economic ties. The scale and activities of black societies have now also changed and moved beyond traditional predatory street crime, vice, extortion, and drug dealing predicated on violence to embrace diverse "gray" business activities that include trafficking, copyright, Internet, and financial service crimes (Yam 2001b).

Triads are sometimes depicted as a worldwide network that uses connections among overseas Chinese for drug and human trafficking (Lintner 2003). Zhang and Chin (2003) have argued that triads have been in decline among overseas Chinese and are skeptical about the existence of global networks of triads (see also Yam 2001b, pp. 28–9). They argue, in the case of human trafficking, this is because of a "structural deficiency" that arises from a strong common culture and tradition that provide discipline in a local context but also limit their capacity to develop strong transnational networks. Later, they note the growth of Chinese crime groups in both local and transnational illicit activity (Zhang and Chin 2008). Xia (2008) sees this as a combination of indigenous growth and the return of the triads especially in Guangdong and other coastal provinces (see also Zhao and Li 2010).[16]

B. Response

Concern about the role of criminal societies has a long history, and anti-triad laws prohibiting membership in Hong Kong, for example, date back to 1845. The law had been "cast wide . . . to enable triad type activities to be stamped out" (*HKSAR v Chan Yuet Ching*) and triads have long been regarded as a criminal conspiracy. Suppression of corruption and bribery among police had been a priority in Hong Kong, and a series of scandals involving corrupt officers led to political intervention and the establishment of the Independent Commission Against Corruption (ICAC) in 1974 with powers to compel witnesses and to examine unexplained wealth. This severed the symbiotic link between the police and triads. Hostility toward the potential organized crime–police symbiotic relationship and crime syndicates, whether triad related or not, has been sustained in Hong Kong. For example, the Drug Trafficking (Recovery of Proceeds) Ordinance of 1989, the Organised and Serious

Crimes Ordinance (OSCO) of 1994, and later amendments and statutes granted law enforcement agencies further powers to investigate and prosecute patterns of unlawful activities associated with organized crime. These measures have not been copied in the rest of China, partly due to the difference in legal traditions.

Subsection 2(1) of the Hong Kong (SAR) Organized and Serious Crimes Ordinance defines "organized crime" as a Schedule 1[17] offence that (a) is connected with the activities of a particular triad society; (b) is related to the activities of two or more persons associated together solely or partly for the purpose of committing two or more acts, each of which is a Schedule 1 offence and involves substantial planning and organization; or (c) is committed by two or more persons, involves substantial planning and organization and involves (i) loss of the life of any person, or a substantial risk of such a loss; (ii) serious bodily or psychological harm to any person, or a substantial risk of such harm; or (iii) serious loss of liberty of any person. In Macau, organized crime is defined as "associations or secret societies" constituted for the purpose of obtaining illegal advantages. The definition also requires that the "existence of the association is manifested in an accord, agreement or in other ways" aimed at committing one or more specified crime types.[18] To prove the existence of a secret society, it need not have a clear hierarchy or places to meet or, indeed, to meet regularly or have written rules of formation and profit sharing.

In the PRC, a "criminal group" or "syndicate" refers to any relatively stable criminal organization that is composed of more than three persons for the purpose of jointly committing a crime (Article 26, PRC Criminal Law 1997). Organizations with the "character of a black society" or of a "gangland nature" are redefined in the 2011 revisions to Article 294 as part of the broad reforms included in the 8th Amendments to the PRC Criminal Law. Among the changes was the criminalization of the bribery of foreign officials (Article 164) and, in the context of the contaminated milk scandals, clearer definitions and enhanced punishments for those involved in bogus drugs and food adulteration (Articles 141–144). In the revised criminal law, such criminal organizations will be more formal than a criminal group with positions for a leader, mid-level organizers, and core members as well as ordinary or affiliate members: all may be subject to punishment for breach of internal rules. They are also profit oriented but have a stable income derived by providing illegal drugs or goods, extortion, and receiving protection fees from legal business. They routinely use violence or threats to extort or manipulate a market or business or elements of society. Finally, officials are implicated to provide protection through the use of bribery, threats, or induction, or a member may be placed into a government agency to provide an "umbrella" (see the People's Supreme Court, "Explanation of Questions Related to Judging Cases of Organizations with Character of Black Society," issued in 2000 and cited in Zhang 2010[19]). In response, central government investigative teams have been deployed to assist city and county Public Security Bureau officers deal with local organized crime groups.

The revised Article 294 (1997 Criminal Law as amended in 2011) holds ringleaders criminally responsible for actual offenses committed and enhances their punishment including the forfeiture of property, punishes overseas crime groups who recruit members in the PRC, and punishes state functionaries involved. It defines activities of an "organization of the character of a black society" as

(1) A relatively stable criminal organization is formed with a relatively large number of members, and there are specific organizers or leaders and basically fixed core members.

(2) Economic interests are gained by organized illegal or criminal activities or other means, and it has certain financial strength to support its activities.

(3) By violence, threat or other means, it commits organized illegal or criminal activities many times to do evil, bully and cruelly injure or kill people.

(4) It dominates a certain area by committing illegal or criminal activities or taking advantage of the harboring or connivance by the state functionaries, forming an illegal control or significant influence in a certain area or sector, which seriously disrupts the economic and social order.[20]

A key countermeasure in mainland China has also been to promote anticorruption efforts. In the context of modernization, and increasing corruption, "hard-strike" anti-crime programs have not proved to be effective in curbing the growth of organized crime (Zhang & Chin 2008; Trevaskes 2010). Police and prosecutors are also restrained by the absence of forfeiture of property laws, inadequate unexplained wealth pro-visions, or laws that punish those who are members of overseas gangs (Zhang 2010). The need to demonstrate that the criminal group has an organizational structure and can enforce rules on its members, combined with the limited capacity of many Public Security Bureau units, and the absence of Hong Kong–style conspiracy laws are key limitations in the suppression of black societies. Efforts in China to curtail corrup-tion and reduce organized crime will be crucial and need to be guided by greater clar-ity in the PRC criminal law and transparency in the oversight role of all levels of the Chinese Communist Party. The costs of internal public order have rapidly grown, and the legitimacy of the police will depend increasingly on their efforts to curb organized crime (Social Development Research Group 2010). While China's domestic laws comply in part with the United Nations Convention against Transnational Organized Crime's (UNTOCC[21]), Lewis (2007) notes that legal reforms are not driven by a fear of trans-national organized crime alone but also by internal security, revenue protection, and, threats from "separatists." It is those other "organized" threats to stability that have been the subject of the most consistent official attention.

IV. The Golden Triangle: Flows and Politics

Another key area within the Asian mega-region, which in fact sits between India and China, has come to be known as the Golden Triangle (e.g., Lyttleton 2004). Arguably the most notorious Asian borderland with respect to organized criminal activities, this is the area where the northeastern portion of Myanmar meets northern Thailand,

northern Laos, and the peripheral zones of southwest China. It is ethnically, linguisti-
cally, culturally, and politically complex, with long histories of war, trade, and migration. During the twentieth century, it developed a reputation as a key site for the global
narcotics trade (McCoy 1972; Belanger 1989; Renard 1996; Chin 2009). This trade was
made possible by the generally lawless character of parts of this mountainous region and
by the almost permanent conditions of civil conflict that defined its post–World War II
history (Yawnghwe 1993). The trigger for the massive growth in opium and the heroin
trade was the influx of the Chinese Nationalist 13th Army under General Li Mi in 1949
into the border areas, pushed out by the victorious Communist troops. Under General
Li's command, a tax on opium was raised in Wa and Shan areas as a means of supporting
his army.

By the 1960s, the remnants of this force and their merchant allies accounted for 90 percent of the international heroin business.[22] Among the many so-called narco-armies
that emerged were various Shan militias (the most prominent among these was the
Mong Tai Army of Sino-Shan warlord Khun Sa), Communist Party of Burma splinter
groups (including the United Wa State Army and the Eastern Shan State Army), and
then other opportunistic ethnic and political movements that have maximized opportunities for narcotics production and trafficking. The Thai government opium monopoly also benefited the various military administrations after the Second World War,
although the sale of opium was banned in 1959.

In previous decades, the bulk of the drugs trafficked from this region were derived
from the local opium crop, and the Heroin No. 4 that was produced contributed significantly to global narcotics flows. However, since the late 1990s, the opium and heroin trades have largely been replaced by the market for amphetamine-type stimulants
(ATS). Initially as a Southeast Asian regional problem, but now trafficked far more
widely into parts of South and East Asia, and to Western countries, the pills produced
in Golden Triangle laboratories have helped to define a new era of illegal drug production; some have even described it as an "epidemic" (McKetin et al. 2008). UNODC
estimates of ATS consumption in the Southeast and East Asian region is thought to
be driven by at least 3.43 million but as many as 20.6 million users—many more users
compared with the estimates for opiate users at between 2.83 and 5.06 million users
(UN 2010, pp. 153, 214–15).

In Thailand, the pills are widely known as *ya ba* (or "crazy medicine") and were the
subject of former Prime Minister Thaksin Shinawatra's 2003 "war on drugs." That official
effort to disrupt the drug trade was predicated on perceptions of a national crisis. It led
to around 3,000 extrajudicial killings.[23] Other countries have similarly confronted the
problems that come from large quantities of relatively cheap pills, marketed, in most
cases, to youthful populations with sufficient disposable income to use regularly. In the
Thai case, the vanguard of amphetamine consumers was in the trucking, fishing, and
construction industries. The capacity of laborers to work hard, for very long periods of
time, ensured that an early vernacular term for the drug was *ya kayan* ("industriousness
medicine"). This was followed by a period when the pills were popularly known as *ya
ma* ("horse medicine") because they could provide animal-like strength and resilience.

Most of the drugs that have flowed into Thailand have been produced by minority ethnic groups in the northeast part of Myanmar, particularly in the Shan state. This region has long borders with China, Laos, and Thailand, and there are countless ways that large quantities of drugs can be moved across the national frontiers. Convoys of heavily armed troops carrying such drugs have now become part of local economic and political mythology.

Arguably the most important of the groups associated with this trade is the Wa (see Chin 2009). The Wa speak a Mon-Khmer language but have become increasingly Sinified as their towns in their mountain strongholds have been encouraged to take advantage of the commercial opportunities that China offers.[24] The United Wa State Army is the most important of their armed groups, and since the late 1980s it has operated under a ceasefire agreement with the Myanmar military. One outcome of that ceasefire has been increased opportunities for trade, including of narcotics. In Thailand, the idea that the *wa daeng* ("red Wa") are crucial to the regional organized crime system/network has gained significant acceptance at both popular and official levels. These Wa criminal groups do not operate in isolation, and their connections with Chinese, Lao, Thai, African, and other organized crime syndicates remain the subject of speculation.

Such speculation indicates that for students of organized crime, this region is enduringly problematic. With the exception of major studies by McCoy (1972) and Chin (2009), there has been little concerted academic scrutiny of criminal activities in the region. It has fallen to international and national counter-narcotics agencies, and a plethora of nongovernment organizations, to help develop a fuller picture of the historical evolution and contemporary character of organized crime. What is striking about these organized criminal groups is the significant, long-term links, with local insurgencies, international criminal syndicates, and elements of the local and national bureaucracies as well as politics. Eradication efforts have, therefore, proved to be less successful than the enormous investment in both counter-opium and counter-amphetamine operations would normally indicate. For many in Thailand, Myanmar (Burma), and Laos, but also in other regional transshipment and funding hubs, the Golden Triangle has remained a profitable and flexible subregion for illicit "gray" businesses.

A. Evolution and Activities

As the nature of the regional economy has changed, we should also bear in mind that the Golden Triangle is no longer defined by the narcotics trade alone. Complementary trade in weapons, chemicals, timber, and people are all part of this very significant evolution, which has also seen great expansion of gambling across the region, particularly in areas that are easily accessible to Thai and Chinese, who cannot legally gamble on their home soil. In other ways, the economic clout of Thailand and China has led to a situation where the Golden Triangle is being constantly reconfigured in response to the consumer demands, and the political priorities, of these countries. For instance, during the late 1990s until around 2005, heavy investment in casinos along the China–Burma border led to large towns with economies almost entirely founded on gambling. These towns have recently encountered economic difficulties as Chinese tolerance for gaming (especially outside Macau) has cooled as a result of anxieties about tax evasion and money laundering. Difficulties with visas and access have meant that some of the major gambling centers, like Mong La in Burma's Shan State, are struggling to survive with much more modest flows of gaming tourists (mostly from Thailand). Some have also sought to provide technological innovations with, for example, Internet gambling.

Two other organized crime businesses also deserve close attention: guns and people.

First, the trade in weapons is key to the criminal enterprises that have managed to survive in the Golden Triangle. There was a time when weapons from the wars in Indo-China, and especially in Cambodia, would easily find their way to the Golden Triangle usually having been trucked across Thailand. The regional arms market has developed since then and the significant incomes of many criminal and rebel groups have meant that weapons can be brought from other sources. Thailand's gun laws are also weak with many handguns imported on fake import licenses; over 400 000 were estimated to have arrived in the country between 1995 and 2001 (Sittapong Tanyapongpruch 2001, p. 602).

Second, it is the trade in people (what the Thais call "*kan kha manut*") that often capitalizes on the misery that has accompanied the dislocations of those who have lived alongside war in the Golden Triangle for generations. The lack of economic and other opportunities in Myanmar have also encouraged many to attempt to flee their circumstances there. While most of these migrants are not trafficked by criminal organizations and, rather, find their way from the border to Thailand, or Malaysia, using a range of brokers and other networks, there are still some who find themselves trafficked into conditions of grave exploitation and abuse, especially as prostitutes (see Farrelly 2012). In the cases of both weapons and people trafficking, the role of organized crime is opaque and is distorted by the analytical inclination to look for simple explanations. In the case of the Golden Triangle, there is a complex interaction of ethnic, political, economic, cultural, and criminal dynamics that have led to the current situation. It is a situation that has proved difficult for law enforcement agencies to adequately police.

B. Subregional Response

The response to the interrelated criminal activities that occur in the Golden Triangle was first, and most publically, associated with the United States and Thai government efforts to pacify Thailand's northern frontier. In the 1960s and 1970s, a cocktail of communist insurgency, ethnic sentiment, and narcotics income led to a dangerous period for Thailand. On Thai soil, a range of counter-narcotics programs were implemented, most of which sought to remove the incentives for production and provide alternative income opportunities. Many of these activities were publicized in ways that attributed successes to the direct interventions of members of the Thai royal family, particularly King Bhumibol Adulyadej. Such policies had only minor effect on the various, usually transnational, organized criminal groups that were profiting from the trade. As political and economic conditions changed, they tended to survive, and even prosper, with new sources of income and new ways of exploiting the peculiar configuration of lawlessness and opportunity that still exists, particularly in northeast Burma.

Thailand, Burma, and Laos have all developed laws that could, if fully enforced, serve to disrupt criminal activities in the Golden Triangle. Thailand, as an example, has the Measures for the Suppression of Offenders in Offences Relating to Narcotics Act 1991, a Money Laundering Control Act 1999, and the Anti-Trafficking in Persons Act 2008. Similarly, Burma has a portfolio of relevant laws and seeks to implement them with the oversight of officials from the United Nations Office of Drugs and Crime (UNODC). In all cases, the public presentation of the fight against organized crime has been given significant attention. However, the challenge is that for all of the governments, but particularly in Burma, there are substantial capacity constraints, which are sometimes partnered with poor interagency coordination and a reputed unwillingness to interdict drug supply routes or curtail the lucrative payoffs associated with the drug trade.

Formal responses from the relevant governments have been inadequately enforced, and challenges to the major criminal groups (e.g., the Thai godfathers known as *jao pho*, ethnic Chinese–Thai organized crime, and the "red Wa") are often sporadic and disjointed. As far as we can discern, few Southeast Asian countries, despite being signatories of the UNTOCC, have explicit and comprehensive laws to target organized crime.[25] Widespread corruption among the police and other agencies is still reported in all of these countries. Nonetheless, the law in these countries provides harsh punishment for those participating in organized crime if convictions are made. Thailand resumed carrying out the death penalty for convicted drug traffickers, including those dealing in amphetamines in July 2009 (Amnesty International 2009). In the past, such tough policies have had limited effect on drug abuse and organized trafficking networks (Sittapong Tanyapongpruch 2001). One of the problems is that groups that may, for instance, become criminalized in Thailand will usually enjoy sanctuary elsewhere. The same dynamic often occurs for those criminal groups that are most problematic in the eyes of the Myanmar authorities; they make their homes in Thailand. Such a situation is complicated by the lack of any legal consensus about which groups are most dangerous and how they can be best identified, managed, and prosecuted.

Thailand, finally, has the usual tools to enable it to tackle the tainted wealth of organized criminals through forfeiture and anti–money laundering laws as well as providing for witness protection in 2003, expanded mutual legal assistance, and other measures. Unfortunately, political instability and competing law enforcement agencies have undermined some of the benefit of these reforms. In this sense, the legal mechanisms for dealing with organized criminal groups in the Golden Triangle are far less important than the political and economic considerations that have kept organized crime in business. It is also relevant that many organized criminals seem to find mainland Southeast Asia an enduringly attractive home. Ease of access, inexpensive global transport and communication links, and a "relaxed" lifestyle may contribute to the attraction of the Golden Triangle and adjacent areas for transnational crime. ASEAN, in concert with

China and the United States, has failed to take on the challenges of establishing a viable economic and civil society capable of negating the narco-businesses that have been part of the Golden Triangle economy for so long.

V. Regional Responses to Organized Crime

This discussion of the Golden Triangle should lead us to consider how the forces of globalization and their sociopolitical and economic impacts have provided impetus to view organized crime not only as a domestic social problem but also as a "transnational" global threat. This new interest in transnational forms of organized crime has also been connected to the increased concern (especially since the terrorist attacks of September 11 2001) about potential interactions with terrorism as well as risks posed by "failed" states. Multilateral responses to law enforcement have become increasingly important in order to improve the effectiveness of mutual legal assistance to address both longstanding (e.g., narcotics trafficking) and newer (e.g., cybercrime) international, cross-border crimes.

Like the European Union and Council of Europe, ASEAN has sought to coordinate the response to nontraditional security concerns such as transnational crime and counter terrorism. Unlike the situation in Europe, institutional reform and integration of cross-border agencies in the policing sector have not followed. Dorn and Levi (2008) provide an example of such differences in their comparative assessment of the anti–money laundering and antiterrorist finance policies in Asian and European countries. Their account considers the different nuances of Asian and European policy practices regarding illegal timber logging, "informal" fund transfers, and terrorism. It is apparent that differences in policy priorities occur because in Asia, economic and financial issues dominate, while European authorities emphasize political dialogue around issues of security and human rights. Economic development has often been prioritized by Asian governments and can trump concerns about illicit trade. A lack of concrete action in respect to many problems, including maritime piracy, illegal drugs, and terrorism, has generated criticism of ASEAN's lack of progress on nontraditional security threats. ASEAN's intent is that over time these issues will be managed through a more integrated framework for cross-jurisdictional cooperation. There are also competing concerns about other human security issues such as pandemics and environmental hazards (ASEAN Secretariat 2006).

Nevertheless, there has been progress. Throughout ASEAN, the appointment of police liaison officers to consular posts, 24/7 contacts for senior designated officers, exchange programs, enhanced protection for courts and police who faced retaliation by transnational criminal organizations, and the sharing of criminal intelligence are no longer novel developments. But they are also inconsistent across the region as a whole. General efforts to improve information sharing (e.g., a regional database, typology studies, networking), joint police operations, mutual legal assistance (e.g., the integrity of travel documents and control over the movement of persons of interest and the harmonization of laws criminalizing transnational crimes), institutional capacity building (a Centre for Combating Transnational Crime), and training are being discussed. However, Emmers (2003) has argued that the "securitization" of transnational crime in ASEAN in the mid-1990s context may have made the development of cooperative arrangements in policing more difficult and limited action to dialogue.

ASEAN has since the mid-1990s begun to establish multilateral measures to improve the law enforcement cooperation of member states and to work more closely with the ASEAN + 3 (China, South Korea, and Japan) and ASEAN + 6 (includes South Korea, Australia, and New Zealand) cohorts. In respect to ASEAN, the 1997 and 1998 Manila *Declaration on the Prevention and Control of Transnational Crime*, the 1999 Yangon *Plan of Action to Combat Transnational Crime*, and the 2004 Vientiane *Declaration Against Trafficking in Persons Particularly Women and Children* provide for dialogue and joint action. ASEAN in 2004 entered into cooperative arrangements with China to enhance law enforcement capacity and address "such non-traditional security issues as trafficking in illegal drugs, people smuggling including trafficking in woman and children, sea piracy, terrorism, arms smuggling, money laundering, international economic crime and cybercrime."[26]

At the November 2009 7th ASEAN Ministerial Meeting on Transnational Crime (AMMTC), held in Siem Reap, Cambodia, a revised ASEAN-China Memorandum of Understanding on "Cooperation in the Field of Non-traditional Security Issues" was concluded, and the first ASEAN Plus China Ministerial Meeting on Transnational Crime (1st AMMTC + China) was held in November 2009.[27] Joint efforts are coordinated through the framework of the ASEAN AMMTC supported by meetings of the relevant senior officials (SOMTC) who are tasked with developing 5-year plans and coordination with other ASEAN senior officials responsible for "drug matters" and the meetings of ASEANAPOL (Chiefs of National Police) and heads of customs and immigration. Following the 29th ASEAN Chiefs of National Police (ASEANAPOL) meeting, the establishment of a permanent ASEANAPOL secretariat commencing in January 2010 was agreed.[28] The "Work Plan on Combating Illicit Drug Production, Trafficking, and Use" (2009–2015) was adopted by the 7th AMMTC and reflects the worthy but ambitious vision of a "drug-free" region by 2015. Several objectives are noted in the AMMTC's general action plan and include the development of a regional countermeasures strategy, greater cooperation among police, prosecutors, and judges,[29] enhanced coordination among ASEAN itself; a strengthened ability to counter "sophisticated" transnational crime, and bilateral and multilateral treaties on mutual legal assistance and extradition (ASEAN Plan of Action to Combat Transnational Crime, n.d. 2010).

Such transnational cooperation and the role of agencies such as Interpol and the UNODC are important because they help create the necessary climate to bring about a universal jurisdiction for many serious crimes. A key development was the UNTOCC adopted in 2000 and ratified in September 2003 by 135 countries, including China, India, Japan, and all other Asian countries (except North Korea). An additional protocol addressing human smuggling[30] had also been adopted; however, fewer countries have ratified the protocol dealing with firearms smuggling.

VI. Conclusion

Policies for controlling organized crime in the Asian mega-region are underdeveloped compared with some other parts of the world. For global law enforcement, this is worrisome because as the weight of economic and demographic influence shifts to Asia, many countries are struggling to enforce their current laws, and regionwide initiatives are underdeveloped. Furthermore, the overlap between terrorist and crime networks seems more problematic in many parts of Asia as noted in the example of India, where the convergence of crime and terrorism is observed.[31] The absence of a central response from India's government may lead to further problems given the limited capacities of the Indian police. India's muted engagement with major mega-regional bodies such as ASEAN suggest that a useful pan-Asian structure capable of addressing threats such as transnational organized crime is far from materializing. Reform of the policing services and the development of effective courts and anticorruption regimes (as found in Hong Kong, Singapore) will be essential.

Capacity building, strengthened mutual legal assistance, and other recommended measures have yet to be developed in some countries, and the emergence of a concerted regional response is essential—such that SAARC and ASEAN (including the "plus three") embrace a wider vision of their respective roles in crime control. The current approach by government across Asia may be expressed by the Chinese idiom "if the water is too clean the fish will have nothing to eat." Keeping the water dirty has sometimes been considered pragmatic and forward-looking. This sums up the policy dilemma faced by China, India, Thailand, Burma, and other countries in curbing the endemic corruption that contributes to the poor performance of government in providing effective control of organized crime (although some analysts, are more optimistic).

It is obviously foreseeable that some of the areas where organized crime has flourished could now be brought under fuller control by the central governments that seek to manage them. Nonetheless, the longstanding pattern of inadequate law enforcement and weak governance of criminal matters lead us to conclude on a less optimistic note. In this regard, we echo a Philippines scholar who suggested with respect to terrorism that, Asian "[g]overnments have placed more importance on their sovereignty than on their efficacy in defeating a common enemy/threat" (Cruz 2008, pp. 13–14). In areas such as the Golden Triangle, but even in Hong Kong and Macau, the persistence of organized crime has a way of confounding law enforcement models for its eradication. The globalized economy rewards nimble and flexible economic actors, and Asian organized crime groups have come to exemplify these characteristics even, or perhaps especially, when they are not undertaking explicitly criminal activities. It is through the blurring of different forms of economic and political action that these groups have survived for so long. Our anticipation is that the future of crime in Asia will continue to fertilize the criminal groups that have come to make "thug," "triad," and "Golden Triangle" notable parts of the international language of criminal organization.

NOTES

1. SAARC has eight members: Afghanistan, Bangladesh, Bhutan, India, Maldives, Nepal, Pakistan, and Sri Lanka. There are a number of areas where it promotes security cooperation including counterterrorism and counternarcotics.
2. ASEAN was established in 1967 with the signing of the 'Bangkok Declaration' by Indonesia, Malaysia, Philippines, Singapore, and Thailand. These countries were later joined by Brunei Darussalam (1984), Vietnam (1995), Laos and Myanmar (1997), and Cambodia (1999), to make up the current ten member states.
3. The Shanghai Cooperation Organisation (SCO) may, however, emerge to play an increasing role in the mitigation of nontraditional security threats, such as transnational organized crime, in central Asia. It was founded in 2001 with Kazakhstan, China, Kyrgyzstan, Russia, Tajikistan, and Uzbekistan as members. Pakistan, India, Mongolia, and Iran are observers.
4. The term 'approver' is still used today for offenders who inform on their co-offenders.
5. A revisionist view of the Thuggee suggests that their prevalence and danger were exaggerated by the colonial authorities in order to extend British hegemony; however, there is little doubt that in the times of turmoil and change of the early nineteenth century, they presented considerable danger.
6. Transparency International's Corruption Perception Index 2009 identfied India, like China, as a country exposed to bribery and corruption. However, for context the index ranks Afghanistan at 179 (second worst in the world), Nepal at 143, and Pakistan and Bangladesh at 139. These South Asian countries are considerably higher than India at 84 and China at 79. Hong Kong, by contrast, is ranked 12 (http://www.transparency.org/policy_research/surveys_indices/cpi/2009/cpi_2009_table).
7. Dawood Ibrahim is South Asia's most notorious criminal figure and is allegedly behind a range of crimes, including terrorist activities. His whereabouts are currently unknown.
8. Estimates of the prevalence of amphetamine-type stimulants are not available for India.
9. Twenty-three official languages are recognized in India.
10. His religious and political connections may have also had a role in his assassination. Kumar's music empire had grown as a result of his effective marketing of cover versions of popular songs that exploited the loopholes in the legal definition of copyright theft in India—this likely made him enemies among established singers and music producers who could turn to the Mumbai underworld for retaliation.
11. Statement of objects and reasons: Maharashtra Control of Organized Crime Act, 1999 (Maharashtra Act No. 30 of 1999).
12. The Act was to operate for 3 years and ceased at the end of 2004.
13. It was Hong Kong–style triads rather than the Shanghai 'green gang' (*ching bang*) that have expanded into the mainland because they tended to be more egalitarian and formerly enjoyed the haven provided by operating from British Hong Kong.

14. For example, economic development in Shenzhen Special Economic Zone (SEZ) and many coastal cities attracted millions of rural migrants from all over China. The emerging market economy created a market for protection and corruption. Shenzhen was a focal point of Hong Kong and Taiwanese triads because of a demand for illicit services, and drug smuggling.

15. They cite the vice president of the standing committee of the People's Congress on 'Explanation of Criminal Code Amendment' of 1997 as stating that there was no significant or typical 'black society organization' in China but 'organizations with the character of a black society' did exist and Article 294 referred to those 'organizations of black society' that are outside China and that try to induct Chinese citizens into their organizations.

16. Zhao and Li (2010) examined 64 cases relating to organized crime in Hong Kong and concluded that there was a trend to regionalization rather than internationalization (i.e., organized crime activities had expanded from Hong Kong to mainland China). The presence of triads in international cases was rare, and they argued that since the transfer of Hong Kong to the control of the PRC, it has declined.

17. Schedule 1 offences include the common law offences of murder, kidnapping, false imprisonment and conspiracy to pervert the course of justice, and certain statutory offences in respect to drugs, money laundering, and so on (for details, see Chapter 455, laws of Hong Kong, or Yam 2001*a*).

18. See Article 1(1), Organized Crime Law 1997: the list contains offences commonly associated with organized crime including homicide, offences against the person, abduction and kidnapping, rape, trafficking in persons, extortion, exploitation of the prostitution of others, loan sharking, robbery, illegal immigration, illegal gambling, trafficking in fauna, artifacts, explosives and firearms, document and credit card fraud, and corruption.

19. The Standing Committee of the National People's Congress (NPC) issued a further interpretation in 2002 that clarified and reiterated the four criteria in the earlier guidance on 'the character of a black society' as prescribed in Article 294 but appeared to make optional the involvement of officials (personal communication and translation, Lena Zhong and Wing Lo, October 2010). These interpretation were the basis for the comprehensive amendments to Article 294 of the PRC Criminal Law (Amendment (VIII) to the Criminal Law of the PRC, as adopted at the nineteenth meeting of the Standing Committee of the Eleventh NPC of the PRC on February 25, 2011, and came into effect on May 1, 2011.

20. Unofficial translation as provided by the College for Criminal Law Science of Beijing Normal University 2011, courtesy of Lu Jianping.

21. The PRC makes a reservation with regard to Article 35, paragraph 2 of the Convention and is not bound to refer disputes to the International Court—a reservation made by many countries, including the United States.

22. This 'lost army' formed an irregular border force known as the Yunnan People's Anticommunist Volunteer Army supported by the United States Central Intelligence Agency, but it was also the genesis of the opium/heroin business (McCoy 1972).

23. Since the coup of September 2006, deposed former Prime Minister Thaksin's government has been lambasted by its political opponents for the human rights abuses committed during the "war on drugs." However, Thaksin enjoyed remarkable popular support for these policies, support that was shared across almost all segments of Thai society. There remains contention about the final death toll from this period, and it is likely that a final figure will never be agreed (see Tassanai et al. 2005, p. 116, for useful details).

24. In fact, this is a pattern that is replicated in many of China's border areas. The combination of relative legal impunity and economic opportunity has created hotspots for crime.
25. The former British colonies (Singapore, Malaysia, and Brunei) have versions of the Hong Kong style antisocieties (antitriad) laws, but a suite of legal measures aimed at disrupting enterprise crime, racketeering, money laundering, and capable of addressing tainted wealth and corruption and providing witness protection are yet in place. An overview of legislation in the Asia-Pacific notes the absence of specific antiorganized crime laws in Indonesia, Thailand, Vietnam, and Cambodia but notes a US-style antiracketeering bill has been under consideration in the Philippines (see Schloenhardt 2009).
26. Article 1 of the 'MOU Between the Governments of the Member Countries of the Association of Southeast Asian Nations and the Government of the People's Republic of China on Cooperation in the Field of Non-Traditional Issues', Bangkok, Thailand, January 10, 2004.
27. The eighth ASEAN AMMTC was held in Bali in October 2011.
28. See the Joint Communiqué of the 29th ASEAN Chiefs of Police Conference, Ha Noi, May 13–15, 2009.
29. Another objective that seldom receives attention is to encourage the rehabilitation of perpetrators of such crimes.
30. ASEAN has also undertaken to develop a regional convention on trafficking in persons and the Bali Process to combat people smuggling is a new multilateral mechanism designed to address this major cross-border crime.
31. The link between crime and terror is often circumstantial, but terrorists may use crime to raise funds needed to support their goals (Findlay 2008).

References

Amnesty International. 2009. "Thailand: Resumption of Executions a Backwards Step." London: Amnesty International. (August 26). http://www.amnesty.org/en/library/info/ASA39/006/2009/en.

ASEAN Secretariat 2006. "ASEAN Regional Security: The Threats Facing It and the Way Forward." ASEAN Secretariat's Information Paper distributed at the OSCE-Thailand Conference on Challenges to Global Security: From Poverty to Pandemic. (April 25–26, 2006). Bangkok. http://www.aseansec.org/18394.htm.

ASEAN. "Plan of Action to Combat Transnational Crime." 2010. http://www.aseansec.org/documents/DocSeriesOnTC.pdf.

Bayley, David H. 1969. *The Police and Political Development in India*. Princeton, NJ: Princeton University Press.

Belanger, Francis W. 1989. *Drugs, the US, and Khun Sa*. Bangkok: Duang Kamol.

Chin, Ko-Lin. 2009. *The Golden Triangle: Inside Southeast Asia's Drug Trade*. Ithaca, NY: Cornell University Press.

Chiu, Ge-pin. 2010. "Review on Organisation With Character of Black Society in China in the Past 60 Years." *Crime Investigation* 1: 6–9 [in Chinese].

College for Criminal Law Science, Beijing Normal University. 2011. "Symposium on Amendment (VIII) to the Criminal Law of the People's Republic of China," March 5, 2011, Beijing. http://www.criminallawbnu.cn/english/showpage.asp?channelid=100&pkid=325.

Cruz, Francisco N. 2008. "Combating Transnational Terrorism in Southeast Asia the ASEAN Way." Philippine Institute for Political Violence and Terrorism Research, Manila.

Dash, Mike. 2005. *Thug: The True Story of India's Murderous Cult*. London: Granta Books.

Dorn, Nicholas and Michael Levi 2008. "East Meets West In Anti-Money Laundering and Anti-Terrorist Finance: Policy Dialogue and Differentiation on Security, the Timber Trade and 'Alternative' Banking." *Asian Journal of Criminology* 3(1): pp. 91–110.

Dodwell, H. H. 1932. *The Cambridge History of India. Volume VI: The Indian Empire 1858–1918*. Cambridge: Cambridge University Press

Emmers, R. 2003. "ASEAN and the Securitization of Transnational Crime." *The Pacific Review* 16(3): pp. 419–438

Farrelly, N. 2012. "Exploitation and Escape: Journeys Across the Burma-Thailand frontier." In *Labour Migration and Human Trafficking in Southeast Asia: Critical Perspectives*, edited by M. Forde, L. Lyons, and W. van Schendel. Oxford: Routledge.

Findlay, M. 2008. "Global Terror and Organised Crime: Symbiotic or Synonymous." *Asian Journal of Criminology* 3: 75–89.

Ganapathy, N., and R. Broadhurst. 2008. "Organized Crime in Asia: A Review of Problems and Progress." *Asian Journal of Criminology* 3(1): 1–12.

Gordon, Sandy. 2009. "Regionalism and Cross-Border Cooperation Against Crime and Terrorism in the Asia-Pacific." *Security Challenges* 5(4): 75–102.

Gordon, Sandy. 2010. *India's Unfinished Security Revolution*. New Delhi: Institute for Defence Studies and Analyses.

India Ministry of Home Affairs. 2010. *Annual Report 2009–2010*. http://www.mha.nic.in/uniquepage.asp?Id_Pk=288.

Lewis, Margaret. 2007. "China's Implementation of the United Nations Convention Against Transnational Organized Crime." *Asian Journal of Criminology* 2(2): 179–96.

Lintner, Bertil. 2003. *Blood Brothers: The Criminal Underworld of Asia*. New York: Palgrave Macmillan.

Liu, Xian-quan, and Wu Yun-feng. 2002. "Discussion on Defining Organisation With Characters of Black Society (I)." *Crime Investigation* 1: 22–28.

Liu, Xian-quan, and Wu Yun-feng. 2002. "Discussion on Defining Organisation With Characters of Black Society (II)." *Crime Investigation* 2:25–28.

Lyttleton, C. 2004. "Relative Pleasures: Drugs, Development and Modern Dependencies in Asia's Golden Triangle." *Development and Change* 34(5): 909–35.

McCoy, A. 1972. *The Politics of Heroin in South Vietnam*. New York: Harper Colophon Books.

McKetin R., N. Kozel, J. Douglas, R. Ali, B. Vicknasingam, J. Lund and J.-H. Li. 2008. "The Rise of Methamphetamine in Southeast and East Asia." *Drug and Alcohol Review* 27:220–28.

Renard, Ronald D. 1996. *The Burmese Connection: Illegal Drugs and the Making of the Golden Triangle*. Boulder, CO: L. Rienner.

Rollins, John, Liana Sun, Wyler, and Seth Rosen. 2010. *International Terrorism and Transnational Crime: Security Threats, U.S. Policy, and Considerations for Congress*. United States Congressional Research Service.

Schloenhardt, Andreas. 2009. "Palermo on the Pacific Rim: Organised Crime Offences in the Asia Pacific Region." UNODC, Regional Centre for East Asia and the Pacific. (August 2009). http://www.unodc.org/documents/eastasiaandpacific//2009/08/Palermo/Schloenhardt_Palermo_in_the_Pacific_07_Final_UNODC_2009.pdf.

Sittapong Tanyapongpruch. 2001. "Transnational Crime in Thailand." UNAFEI, 119th International Training Course, Resource Materials no. 59, UNAFEI, Fuchu,Tokyo. http://www.unafei.or.jp/english/pdf/PDF_rms/no59/ch31.pdf.

Social Development Research Group, Tsinghua University Department of Sociology. 2010. "New Thinking on Stability Maintenance: Long-Term Social Stability via Institutionalised Expression of Interests." *Southern Weekend* (April 14). http://www.infzm.com/content/43853 [original in Chinese; trans. David Kelly http://chinaelectionsblog.net].

Sumita, Sarkar, and Arvind Tiwari. 2001. "Combating Organised Crime: A Case Study of Mumbai City." Paper presented at the All India Criminology Conference, National Institute of Criminology and Forensic Science, Ministry of Home Affairs, Government of India, New Delhi, November 1–3, 2001. http://www.satp.org/satporgtp/publication/faultlines/volume12/Article5.htm.

Thilgaraj and Gandhirajan 2007. "Organized Crime in the City of Chennai." Broadhurst R, and N. Ganapathy, eds. *Organized Crime in Asia*, 28–29 June 2007, symposium proceedings. Singapore. pp 193–217.

Trevaskes, S. 2010. *Policing Serious Crime in China: From 'Strike Hard' to 'Kill Fewer.'* London: Routledge.

UNODC. 2010. *The Globalization of Crime: A Transnational Organized Crime Threat Assessment.* Vienna: UNODC.

United Nations. 2010. *World Drug Report 2009.* Vienna: UNODC. http://www.unodc.org/unodc/en/data-and-analysis/WDR-2010.html.

Xia, M. 2008. "Organizational Formations of Organized Crime in China: Perspectives From the State, Markets, and Networks." *Journal of Contemporary China* 17(54): 1–23.

Yam, Tat-wing. 2001a. "Fighting Hong Kong Organised Crime, the Organised and Serious Crime Ordinance." Resource Materials Series no. 58, UNAFEI, Fuchu Tokoyo, pp. 14–26. http://www.unafei.or.jp/english/pdf/PDF_rms/no58/58-03.pdf.

Yam, Tat-wing. 2001b. "Triads." Resource Materials Series no. 58, UNAFEI, Fuchu Tokoyo, pp. 27–39. http://www.unafei.or.jp/english/pdf/PDF_rms/no58/58-03.pdf.

Yawnghwe, Chao-Tzang. 1993. "The Political Economy of the Opium Trade: Implications for Shan State." *Journal of Contemporary Asia* 23(3): 306–326

Zhang, Sheldon X., and Ko-lin Chin. 2003. "The Declining Significance of Triad Societies in Transnational Illegal Activities—A Structural Deficiency Perspective." *British Journal of Criminology* 43(3): 469–88.

Zhang, Sheldon X., and Ko-lin Chin. 2008. "Snakeheads, Mules, and Protective Umbrellas: A Review of Current Research on Chinese Organized Crime." *Crime, Law and Social Change* 50(3): 177–95.

Zhang, Tien-hong. 2010. "Analysis on Organisation With Character of Black Society." *Criminology Journal* 2: 204–19 [in Chinese].

Zhang, Yuan-huang. 2009. "Rethinking on the Notion and Development of Organised Crime in China." *Renmin University Law Review* 1: 219–29 [in Chinese].

Zhao, Guo-ling, and Li Qiang. 2010. "Analysis on the Organised Crime in Hong Kong." *Chinese Criminal Science* 4: 96–109 [in Chinese].

CHAPTER 32

FINANCE-ORIENTED STRATEGIES OF ORGANIZED CRIME CONTROL

MICHAEL KILCHLING

I. INTRODUCTION

"CRIME should not pay." This traditional aim of crime control has gained new attention, particularly since the rise of organized crime policies in the United States in the late 1980s and the subsequent adoption of such policies in most parts of the world by the early 1990s. In the decades before, the aim had been more or less buried as a consequence of the rehabilitative paradigm in Western societies. For a long time, criminal policy was predominantly characterized by the idea of penal intervention as a (positive) treatment for individuals. Even in jurisdictions in which medieval roots of confiscation had survived, such as the *confiscation générale* in France, these provisions had lost their relevance and were more or less neglected in court practice. Judicial attention was mostly concentrated on the fair and adequate punishment of individual offenders, whereas the extent of profit obtained through a particular crime was considered as a sentencing criterion at best, be it as an aggravating factor or in other ways. Beyond this, the issue was of little interest, neither in the micro perspective of prosecutors or judges in their every day routine nor in the macro perspective by criminal policy. The whereabouts of proceeds derived from crime was normally seen as a matter of private law, and responsibility lay with the victims who had to sue the offender (post criminal conviction) by means of a private claim. Advanced strategies and instruments, such as asset recovery and recovery assistance in favor of (individual) victims, that today accompany seizure and confiscation, were more or less unknown.

It is certainly not just by coincidence that the development of proceeds-oriented crime control goes hand in hand with the about-face in penal doctrine that nowadays seeks to introduce, or reintroduce, direct criminal responsibility of legal entities. In a corporate context, the focus on financial intervention is even more obvious than in the catalogue of sanctions, or measures, to be imposed on natural persons. Nevertheless, in the specific context of organized crime, the concept of proceeds-oriented crime control significantly differs from the traditional perspective of confiscation as mirrored in our initial reference. As a means for tackling organized crime specifically, confiscation policies are based on a totally different concept and implemented through new and very specific strategies and instruments. With regard to its particular preventive element, proceeds-oriented crime control mainly addresses organizations (criminal as well as legal) no matter who supports or operates them from behind the scenes—persons or legal bodies, or perhaps both.

Ironically, forms of confiscation that had primarily been used as a politically motivated weapon in many penal codes of the communist states of the former Eastern bloc were just about to be abolished (as a signal of the new rule-of-law era to start at the beginning of the 1990s) when their promotion by the United States and other international actors as "the" new and promising tool in the fight against organized crime emerged. Based on a set of continuously growing international treaties and agreements, governments were forced into reintroducing instruments that had just been disqualified as legal wrongs of the old system (see Plywaczewski and Filipkowski 2004; Krajewski 2005). This was particularly true for those countries interested in joining the European Union, which, out of its own political interests, was (and still is) one of the key promoters of organized crime-related confiscation policies.

II. The Purpose of Finance-related Strategies of Organized Crime Control

Whereas confiscation has sometimes been promoted by policymakers, namely in the United Kingdom, as the "new big idea" that characterizes 21st-century crime control policies (Friedman 2003. p. 1), the concept appears more as part of a traditional rationale of criminal law in continental Europe, at least in major jurisdictions such as France and Germany. In these countries we find, for example, traditional instruments such as the *confiscation générale,*[1] that can be translated as total confiscation (Kletzlen and Godefroy 1997, p. 273) based on which criminals who had fallen from grace could be deprived of all their wealth in both pre-revolutionary and post-revolutionary France (see Ehrhard 1934). In jurisdictions such as Germany the various versions of the criminal code have provided for detailed regulations on forfeiture since 1871; although replaced by a completely revised system in 1969, the basic principles of the 19th century still prevail (see Eser 1969, 1993). In either case, the term "crime should not pay" did not necessarily have such an explicit finance-related or economically focused meaning than the one that finally emerged in the context of organized crime control.

What makes confiscation so particularly attractive in the context of organized crime control? Finance-related strategies of crime control have their origin in a conceptual framework presented in a 1986 report by the [US] President's Commission on Organized Crime.[2] Only two years later, the concept was internationally acknowledged and adopted by the UN Vienna Convention, which clearly emphasized that:

> [illicit drug trafficking] generates large financial profits and wealth enabling transnational criminal organizations to penetrate, contaminate and corrupt the structures of government, legitimate commercial and financial business, and society at all its levels (recital, quoted from the 1988 Vienna Convention).[3]

This narrow, purely drug-related approach was rapidly widened and developed into a general concept for the tackling of all organized crime. The 1990 Council of Europe Convention therefore promotes:

> .....confiscation as a modern and effective method of fighting all kinds of serious
> .....crime (recital, quoted from the 1990 Strasbourg Convention).[4]

Later on, the 1990 Convention was replaced and widened in scope by the 2005 Warsaw Convention,[5] which also dealt with the financing of terrorism. As a result of the permanent enlargement of its scope, confiscation developed to become a major tool with regard to any kind of "acquisitive criminality" (HMCPSI 2004). Whereas, in the past, the penal price that had to be paid for crime commission was a loss of personal liberty—be it in terms of physical liberty or, since the second half of the 20th century more and more also in terms of financial freedom—the focus is now on the rescission of illegal financial transactions, mostly as an additional legal consequence. Based on the concept of organized crime as rational crime (Albrecht 1998, 2002), the strategy is a purely economic, or business-oriented, one, based on criminological rational choice theories: The prospect of state-enforced removal of probable financial gain shall prevent engagement in organized crime.

In its 1997 Action Plan to Combat Organised Crime, the Council of the European Union clearly stressed that "the major driving force behind organised crime is the pursuit of financial gain."[6] Wolfgang Hetzer, a consultant at the EU's Anti-fraud Office (OLAF), highlighted this basic characteristic in almost metaphoric terms: The greed for profit is organized crime's "raison d'être" (1999, p. 148). Taking the profit out of crime (Levi 1997) is therefore considered to be the most consequent policy strategy in this area. In the international arena, this approach was initially emphasised in the Vienna Convention, where the signatory states declared that they are:

> [...] determined to deprive persons engaged in illicit traffic of the proceeds of their criminal activities and thereby eliminate their main incentive for so doing (recital, quoted from the 1988 Vienna Convention).[7]

Not enough, in the specific context of organized crime, confiscation has more than the "regular"—individually and generally—deterrent function. In addition to the purpose of neutralizing the main incentive of crime, i.e., the greed for illegal profit, it has further preventive purposes, aiming at removing the capital for future—illegal and legal (or apparently legal)—investment activities of organized crime groups, as well as at protecting the legitimate economy from corruption and infiltration.

Furthermore, in targeting groups, organizations, and organized crime as a whole, the analysis and consideration of the organizational perspective adds another significant aspect here. Since individuals can be easily replaced by other individuals, individual prosecution in traditional terms is not likely to achieve the above-mentioned deterrent and preventive aims. In light of this fact, it can be supposed that a double strategy, combining, on the one hand, traditional prosecution—focusing on the treatment of individuals (*in personam*)—and, on the other hand, proceeds-oriented measures (*in rem*), will provide a more significant impact. The leading argument is that traditional responses such as imprisonment and fines alone are ineffective; the better alternative is to attack the property (rather than persons). This is true, regardless of the actual shape of the organizational structures; it applies in the case of a more loosely connected group, a strictly hierarchical organization, or a co-operative criminal network (for more details, see Paoli in this publication).

It is this explicit link between the two elements that defines modern finance-related strategies of crime control. The recovery of the proceeds is, therefore, considered to be one of the crucial aspects of target-oriented organized crime policies (Levi and Osofski 1995; Bodnar 2003). The approach was adopted in many parts of the world, including by the European Union. Its Millennium Strategy provides an extra chapter on "tracing, freezing, seizing and confiscating the proceeds of crime,"[8] which resulted in a variety of policy initiatives. Before the entry into force of the Lisbon Treaty, this was clearly the most frequently addressed former Third Pillar area and has seen the highest number of binding legal acts to be implemented by the member states.[9] The message is always the same:

> In order to be effective [...], any attempt to prevent and combat such crime must focus on tracing, freezing, seizing and confiscating the proceeds from crime (quoted from recital no. 1, EU Framework Decision 2005/212/JHA).[10]

The keywords referred to in the headings of these instruments are, like the titles of the 1990 Strasbourg Convention and the 2005 Warsaw Convention, a perfect summary of the different elements of the confiscation strategy that will be addressed in the following section.

III. The Concept of Finance-Related Crime Control

The concept of finance-related crime control consists of three major elements: (1) the tracing of assets, (2) their provisional blocking (freezing, seizing), and (3) their final removal or recovery (forfeiture, confiscation).[11]

Obviously, the concept represents a fundamental change to traditional prosecution systems, above all for the continental systems of Europe. Besides the previously outlined broadening of the purpose and scope of criminal intervention based on economic concepts, the proceeds-oriented approach has also significantly realigned the routine of investigations in terms of both substance and technique. In addition to traditional evidence gathering, specialized investigators—located either in police or in prosecution departments or in dedicated agencies such as the Irish Criminal Assets Bureau (CAB) or the Serious Organised Crime Agency (SOCA)[12]—explicitly focus on collecting all available information about assets, their origin and movement. In relevant cases, such financial investigations complement the regular steps of enquiry and seek to reach two further, mainly investigative aims[13]:

- to trace back the money flows in order to gather information—and evidence—on the organizational and personal background of a case, in particular, to clear up interpersonal relations/connections, gather information about the group structure, and identify possible further participants; and
- to compile a comprehensive picture of the financial background of suspects, including their legal property, in order to prepare the way for the broadest possible seizure and recovery of assets (which in many countries can involve legitimate assets of suspects as well).[14]

Van Duyne and Levi (1999) are right in referring to these investigative aims as being of a strategic and tactical character. To implement this approach to criminal investigations, the "new" offense of money laundering was created.[15] In technical terms, the statutory offense is the material anchoring point for proactive financial as well as other investigative measures. From a doctrinal perspective, it is an offense type that has no real criminal substance. It appears more as an auxiliary offense and serves as a kind of materialized instrument of investigation (Pieth 1995, 1998). A look into the British Proceeds of Crime Act 2002[16] provides an obvious insight into the special character of money laundering as an auxiliary offense: Of its 462 main sections, only one small part at the end deals with money laundering (Part 7: sections 327 to 340). The systematics behind this structure clearly indicates that confiscation is the main subject matter; the crime of money laundering is only a means to support it. Similar conclusions can be drawn from the design of the 1990 Strasbourg Convention and the 2005 Warsaw Convention, which likewise address confiscation first. The most consistent approach to money laundering has been taken in jurisdictions such as Switzerland, where it has been defined as conduct that aims to frustrate successful confiscation.[17] From an analytical point of view, this combination of offense-related "classical" investigations with finance-related investigations based on money laundering legislation can be understood as a second double strategy of the finance-related strategy of crime control.

Technically speaking, two types of financial investigations exist: embedded and independent. Embedded—or dependent—investigations have a concrete offense as their starting point; police use information to examine the extent and whereabouts of an offense's proceeds. In accordance with the character of the whole process, this type of financial investigation is reactive. In contrast, independent financial investigations are initiated in reaction to a suspicious transaction report. This type of investigation is proactive in character, and it proceeds from the asset(s) in search of the related crime. In theory, the pro-active approach is the prototype of the money laundering concept. However, regarding the Money Laundering Control Act, evaluation of money laundering cases in Germany has shown that only a handful of all cases that resulted in a money laundering charge and court conviction had their investigative origin in a suspicious transaction report.[18] In other words, it is very difficult to identify and determine crimes from which suspicious assets are really derived as long as police have no clue concerning the real origin of the assets. Therefore, the concept of financial investigations tends to be much more successful in the classical, reactive form.

Last but not least, the success of finance-related crime control depends on a third double strategy. The prospect of successful seizure and recovery is dependant on the capacity of investigative agencies to take advantage of asset-related information and evidence that have been generated by the private business sector. Based on administrative money laundering legislation, financial institutions and other businesses in the regulated sector are subject to extensive record-keeping requirements. Leaning on related FATF recommendations, the EU forces its member states to retain all financial records for at least five years.[19] Once a suspicion occurs, all data that has been "non-suspiciously" stored has to be transferred from the private record-keepers (which are the legal owners of the data) to state authorities. Most business sectors, including all relevant legal-, tax-, and business-related service and advisory professions, are now included in the administrative money laundering control regime.

All these aspects underline the rationale of money laundering control that has been designed and implemented to recover the proceeds of crime. For further details on money laundering policies, see Levi, Money Laundering (in this publication).

IV. International Instruments Promoting Finance-related Crime Control

As already noted, finance-related crime control was actively promoted and introduced at an international level. States—foremost among them the United States—and international organizations, spearheaded by the United Nations (UN), the Organization of American States (OAS), the Council of Europe and the European Union (EU) and supported by expert commissions such as the Financial Action Task Force and its related regional suborganizations[20] and others[21] (the democratic legitimacy of which may appear questionable), exercised considerable political pressure to implement these principles worldwide (Pieth 1998, p. 160). Within the EU, the significance of finance-related crime control is even higher as the legally nonbinding FATF recommendations are regularly transformed into directives that have to be mandatorily implemented by the member states.[22] Further binding legal acts of the EU address the issue of confiscation[23] in an effort to streamline the very different national provisions.[24] These political initiatives have been supported by further recommendations and the drafting of model legislation.[25]

The 1988 Vienna Convention[26] enshrined a narrow and limited scope with regard to drug trafficking, which was widened in the following years in the 1990 Strasbourg Convention[27] and the 2000 Palermo Convention[28] to cover all kinds of organized and transnational organized crime and, with the 2005 Warsaw Convention,[29] to include the financing of terrorism. Further extensions were initiated by the FATF; these mainly introduced finance-related supervision and intervention to combat corruption[30] and, more recently, even proliferation.[31]

All international instruments provide some basic principles and general rules for the implementation and improvement of national confiscation regimes. In sum, contracting parties have, in particular, to comply with the following principles:

- Confiscation shall address proceeds derived from drug crime and other serious crimes. The range of offences for which the confiscation regime shall apply is as wide as possible. States can either provide a list of specified offences (catalogue principle; in its appendix, the 2005 Warsaw Convention lists the most recent minimum number of such offences)[32] or regulate the application of confiscation more generally, i.e., on the basis of a maximum penalty of more than one year or a minimum penalty of more than six months (threshold principle).
- Confiscation shall include property into which proceeds have been transformed or converted, including laundered property, property acquired from legitimate sources or legitimate property to the extent that such property has been intermingled with illegal proceeds, and income or other benefits derived from proceeds as well as from property into which proceeds of crime have been transformed or converted or from property with which proceeds of crime have been intermingled.
- Recovery shall not be limited to the different types of proceeds and their probable replacement values. States shall always provide for the general possibility of value confiscation, enabling the competent authorities to confiscate legal assets to the extent that their value corresponds to that of the (direct or indirect) illegal gain.
- Confiscation shall include drugs, if they were the object of the crime, and materials, equipment and other instrumentalities.
- EU member states (only) are, in addition, required to provide for some form of extended confiscation powers, on the basis of which proceeds presumably derived from alleged crimes other than those for which a person has been found guilty, can be taken away, too.[33]
- To facilitate the enforcement of eventual future confiscation, authorities shall be equipped with the necessary powers to identify, trace, freeze, or seize the proceeds,

assets, or other property liable to confiscation. Seizure shall be enforced as quickly as possible.

- Investigative powers shall include access to bank, financial, or commercial records. These powers shall not be restricted on the grounds of bank secrecy. This rule, stipulated first in the 1988 Vienna Convention and repeated in the 2000 Palermo Convention, marked the end of century-old bank diligence traditions.

- With regard to the transnational character of organized crime, recovery shall apply globally. Therefore, all conventions emphasize the importance of mutual assistance and cooperation. Based on the 2005 Warsaw Convention, public prosecutors and other judicial authorities of the 47 member states of the Council of Europe are explicitly allowed to communicate directly with each other[34] in money laundering and recovery matters. For the member states of the European Union, such communication is regulated in detail and facilitated through the introduction of a uniform template to be used for direct requests.[35]

- Amongst EU member states, the principle of mutual recognition and enforcement of seizure[36] and confiscation[37] orders applies. Accordingly, all orders issued by the competent authorities of another member state have to be executed without further examination in terms of the facts and legal prerequisites of the original order. Recognition and execution can be refused only on the basis of a limited catalogue of grounds, such as, e.g., the principle of *ne bis in idem*, ineligibility, immunity, and additional post-decision facts that are of central relevance from the requested state's perspective.[38]

In addition to these mandatory elements, some further points of consideration are addressed internationally. These include, e.g., possibilities on how to extend the group of persons liable for confiscation. Exemplifying their own national law, Denmark launched during its EU presidency of 2003 an initiative to introduce an EU-wide rule according to which legal persons under the control of the offender or his or her close relatives should be held liable for confiscation, too.[39] The final document, however, provides only that states "may consider" implementing such an amendment.[40] A proposed general extension of liability to all spouses and cohabitees was rejected by the Council and never entered the final document. The Council also rejected the Danish suggestion to introduce a reversal with respect to the burden of proof. From the outset, this has clearly been one of the most controversial points in international recovery discussions as it touches on fundamental national legal principles and delineates the dividing line between continental and common law legal traditions. Therefore, all relevant international texts are carefully worded in this respect. Whereas the 1988 Vienna Convention encourages states to consider reversing the onus of proof regarding the lawful origin of alleged proceeds or other property liable to confiscation,[41] later treaties, such as the 2000 Palermo Convention, hold off from a formal reversal of the burden of proof, suggesting instead that national legislatures may consider requiring that an offender "demonstrate" the lawful origin of the funds or assets in question. The 2005 Warsaw Convention adopted this approach: It applied the usual mandatory terminology (states "shall" introduce) but commented that such steps are conditional on whether such a rule is consistent with the principles of domestic law and the nature of the judicial or other proceedings. Besides the major common law jurisdictions that provide for a true reversal in the onus of proof, several civil law jurisdictions have introduced at least some form of responsibility on the offender to explain the source of their assets, thus alleviating regular standards of proof for the prosecution when the offender remains silent about the asset's origin. These changes will be addressed in more detail in the following section.

V. Different Models and Instruments of Confiscation

Despite the fact that recovery policies have been framed by an impressive number of detailed international standards (see previous section), a great variety of distinct approaches, models and rules can still be found in the national legal systems. This is due both to the profound differences that exist among criminal justice systems, which have a much longer tradition than other areas such as civil or administrative law, and to the fact that criminal law belongs to a core area that, together with constitutional law, defines the shape of a legal system. Further disparities depend on the history of confiscation legislation in a given jurisdiction. On the one hand, there are countries in which confiscation has been a traditional part of the *penal acquis*. In these systems, the question as to whether, in which way, and to what extent existing provisions should be amended depends on principal considerations concerning what is consistent or not with the system and its underlying doctrine. This is typically the case in civil law jurisdictions where reforms often go along with judicial interventions that limit the space of action, often with explicit reference to constitutional principles. On the other hand, there exist other legal systems, particularly in common law jurisdictions, which are much less bound by traditions and doctrines. Legislation in England and Wales is a very good example. A review shows evident parallels with the rise and progress of international legal texts.[42] With its focus on income generated from drug trafficking, the Drug Trafficking Offences Act of 1986 (DTOA) opened the way for the implementation of the new strategy, followed by the Drug Trafficking Act of 1994 (DTA) and the Proceeds of Crime Act of 2002 (PCA), amended by the Serious Organised Crime and Police Act 2005 (SOCPA) and the Serious Crime Act 2007; all legislative steps taken reflect the growth and development in international confiscation policies.

In the last two decades, most countries have amended their laws in order to facilitate seizure and confiscation of proceeds illegally obtained or suspected to derive from an illegal origin. From a comparative perspective, systems vary significantly in many respects and are still far from being compatible. Confiscation regimes can be penal, civil, administrative, or preventive. Sometimes, different types of confiscation run parallel in a country to the extent that, at the same time, penal and civil or penal and preventive confiscation is available. Besides their basic legal character, recovery regimes differ with regard to the standards of evidence that have to be met and the range of confiscation measures available. Further aspects—that unfortunately cannot be discussed in detail here[43]—include whether confiscation is mandatory or optional, how its extent is defined and calculated, if there are maximum limits, and to what extent third parties, in particular bona fide third parties, are liable for confiscation.

With regard to the legal character of the various confiscation rules, two basic systems can be distinguished: On the one hand, regulations of a sanction/reaction-based character in the broadest sense and, on the other hand, those with a preventive character. In those legal systems that have regulated confiscation within the context of criminal reactions, two main differences may be further distinguished. Only a few countries understand confiscation to be a criminal penalty or sanction. The penal character is most unambiguous in France. The judge has the option to impose confiscation as an additional or even as the (only) prime sanction. In the latter alternative, confiscation then becomes quasi the substitute prime sanction and, as such, can even replace a prison sentence.[44] In most other legal systems, however, the penal character—or rather, the repressive focus—of the confiscation regimes is, in contrast, more restrained. It mostly appears as a supplementary consequence or measure. The common denominator in those systems is that their punitive character is denied. At most, certain penal side effects are conceded.

Regulations with an explicitly nonpunitive function are dominant in the common law jurisdictions and in Italy. In particular, in the United States, the United Kingdom, and Ireland civil forfeiture is exclusively understood to be an intervention *in rem*, which does not explicitly inculpate the owner or other persons concerned.[45] A similar understanding applies with regard to the Mafia-related preventive measures (*misure di prevenzione*) in Italy.[46] As distinct from the regulations in the United States, United Kingdom, and Ireland, this *patrimonial* instrument is not designed according to principles of civil procedure but rather as a preventive confiscation regime. The purpose is to strip the Mafia of its assets; the individual person is of secondary interest, if at all. With its customs fine (*amende douanière*), France has implemented an additional track with administrative character that clearly has a recovery function as well. However, although the instrument is clearly located outside the penal system, the European Court of Human Rights[47] considers it as a penal measure since it can be enforced by means of imprisonment for contempt of court, which, unlike imprisonment in default, has no redemption effect that would eliminate the debt. The United Kingdom also makes this drastic variant of enforcement available.

As mentioned earlier, one of the major points of political and academic discussion concerns the relevant evidentiary standards provided for confiscation. Despite these controversies, only a few countries to date are, without any exception, sticking to the "classic" criminal law principles of evidence. Besides the major common law jurisdictions that provide for a true reversal in the onus of proof, a number of civil law jurisdictions have introduced some type of evidentiary relief regarding the burden of proof on the side of the confiscating state—even those with a penal confiscation regime. Either the standard (or measure) of proof of the illegal origin has been relaxed under certain conditions—e.g., "balance of probabilities" instead of "beyond reasonable doubt"—or some forms of responsibility have been placed on the offenders' side requiring him or her to explain[48] (or demonstrate[49] or certify[50]) the source of their assets, thus alleviating the regular standards of proof for the state in case the offender remains silent about the origin. Switzerland has a unique approach under which assets of offenders found guilty for participating in a criminal organization are legally presumed to belong to that organization unless the contrary is proven by the offender.[51]

A kind of factual legislative presumption with a reversal in the burden of proof is also the basis for the lifestyle approach that was first introduced in the United Kingdom with respect to narcotics.[52] Under this law, the illegal origin of all forms of income of offenders with a flamboyant lifestyle, including presents, for the period six years before the conviction is presumed, unless its legal origin has been proven otherwise. An even more drastic variant is provided in the French Penal Code: Drug dealers, procurers, and terrorists who fail to justify the origin of their lifestyle are not only liable to confiscation, but also, simultaneously, their failure to justify constitutes a criminal offense of its own.[53] Interestingly, a similar provision introduced in Italy in 1992 was found unconstitutional in 1994.[54]

In addition to all these strategies that, in a wider sense, address (or manipulate?) rules of evidence, the basis for recovery can also be broadened by alleviating requirements for the accessory connection between the assets and the crimes from which they derive. This can be achieved through extended confiscation. Based on the 2005 Framework Decision, all EU member states are required to provide some form of extended confiscation. These instruments aim to grasp at additional assets that, although they are not the subject of the crime for which a person has been charged and found guilty, are presumed to derive from other, probable, crimes. In concrete terms, three different models have been provided between which the national legislatures can choose.[55] The first alternative provides that such extended confiscation should be possible when the court, based on specific facts, is fully convinced that the property in question has been derived from criminal activities of the convicted person. The German provision on extended forfeiture[56] has been the role model for this clause. Similar to the Austrian regulations,[57] legislators can limit the extension to income generated in a certain time period. The second European alternative suggests limiting extended confiscation to situations in which the court is fully convinced that the assets in question are derived from similar criminal activities of the convicted person—a rule that more or less reflects the Dutch approach to extended confiscation.[58] The third alternative reflects the British lifestyle approach, according to which property that is disproportionate in value to the lawful income of a convicted person can be removed once the court is fully convinced that the property in question has been derived from further criminal activity of the convicted person.

This leads to consideration of a final issue that focuses on the general "range" of confiscation, that is, to what extent should the offender and his or her property be liable for confiscation? Should recovery have its focus on the—original—illegal assets only, or should the state also have access to other sources? In most of the jurisdictions, the latter principle applies, although in different forms. Some jurisdictions provide for value confiscation as an alternative, i.e., as an additional option in case the original property has been moved abroad or is not available for other, legal or factual, reasons. Sometimes, however, recovery is generally ordered and executed in the form of a payment order. In these cases, it appears as a type of monetary penalty, which does not have the symbolic character of confiscating specific, namely illegally obtained assets, even if the economic effect is, of course, the same. Regardless which of the principles is applied, value confiscation has three significant advantages:

- concealment, displacement, or destruction of assets is made irrelevant,
- the ability to grasp *legal property* is made possible, and
- it is easier and faster, and thus saves investigative resources.

The variety of concepts, models, and instruments is also a factor that makes comparative evaluation of its effectiveness rather difficult. So far, scientific research has not provided reliable findings on whether specific instruments and types of legislation bring significantly better results than others. This is not surprising since the systems are so complex that it would require considering a vast number of variables and further context factors. Available statistics and research so far indicate that application in terms of the frequency of confiscation orders and the value of assets recovered is, on the whole, increasing. This suggests that each system has its particular strengths and weaknesses (Savona and Vettori 2001; Kilchling 2002; Vettori 2006).

VI. CRITIQUES AND CONTROVERSIES

Since its initial emergence, the finance-related strategy of crime control has been the subject of diverse academic and political critiques. One reason for this is certainly the political origin of the concept and the way in which it has been driven forward at an international level. Some authors in Europe called it nothing less than an "Americanisation of justice" (Arzt 1996). What has to be considered, too, is the fact that the approach is an important part of international organized crime control policies. As Fijnaut and Paoli (2004, p. 1038) rightly noted, these policies have by definition always been controversial. Moreover, the recovery regime in itself is, intentionally, the most "draconian" (Millington and Sutherland Williams 2010, p. 4, quoting from a court case) component. It is likely that some of the provisions would have been unacceptable under current standards of human rights, had they not explicitly focused on the threat of organized crime. It was, for example, the explicit reference to the danger emanating from Mafia activities and structures to the public system that led the European Court of Human Rights to rule that the preventive confiscation regime of Italy is barely admissible.[59]

In principle, two types of controversies can be identified: Broad criticism, aimed at the concept as a whole, and specific criticism, aimed at problems of implementation and execution.

In some jurisdictions it is indeed the concept of asset confiscation that raises fundamental questions, in particular whether the entire property of a person can be subject to a recovery action. In some countries, such as Argentina, Belgium, and Mexico, general confiscation of property is constitutionally prohibited as a kind of unusual or extreme penalty. These and most other jurisdictions, however, allow for court-ordered confiscation of assets that are related, in one way or another, to concrete criminal behavior. In addition, in countries such as Germany, there exist explicit rulings by the Constitutional Court according to which income derived from crime is principally excluded from the fundamental right to protection of property.[60] Interestingly, the German legislature introduced a special form of criminal penalty for offenders involved in organized crime that had many characteristics of general confiscation.[61] However, for a variety of reasons, in particular its unlimited extent, this provision was declared unconstitutional in 2002; the Constitutional Court held that total confiscation of a person's assets is arbitrary and a breach of both the principle of guilt and the principle of predictability.[62]

Other controversies address issues arising from the execution practice. Such concerns are of explicit relevance in systems that are more aggressive than others. A vivid discussion in this regard can, for example, be followed in consulting US research with regard to civil forfeiture. Tonry (1997) reported several cases of abuse of confiscation powers in which suspects who were never charged or found guilty were nevertheless stripped of all their wealth, often by local authorities. Besides general problems of police discrimination, the practice that local authorities can also directly benefit from asset recovery can be seen as a false incentive. For Levy (1996) the civil confiscation regime of the United States is nothing less than a "license to steal." In judgments such as *Austin v. the United States*[63] judicial control seeks to counterbalance excessive application.

However, even without such direct incentives, broadly designed regulations for seizure and confiscation can cause problems. Some cases from the German court practice perfectly illustrate this problem. In recent years, courts carefully defined the (legally unsubstantiated) scope and limits of provisional seizure. In 2006, the Constitutional Court prohibited the unlimited, "haphazard," freezing of assets without a sufficient evidential basis. In a case in which the total assets of a defendant (about €28 million) were seized, the court held that the principle of proportionality had been violated although—what is rather typical following the rule that seizure should be initiated as quickly as possible once investigations have been started—it was not yet clear whether the person would be charged or if confiscation would be ordered (and, if so, to what extent).[64] In another case, the entire sum of a person's bank accounts, amounting to €2.17 million, was seized. The case was later dismissed in return for payment of a fine of €500; unsurprisingly, this seizure was declared unconstitutional, too.[65]

VII. Future Perspectives: New Areas, Aggravated Instruments

From today's perspective, the clear focus of international confiscation policies on organized crime has slowly faded away. They can be sensibly applied in other areas, such as corruption or business and economic crime. However, in other areas, such as the financing of terrorism where rational choice concepts do not apply, adaption does not promise any added value. It is not plausible to expect that the confiscation of a terrorist's actual property may prevent any future attack. On the contrary, the political context of counterterrorism policies may even disqualify the approach. Nevertheless, aggravated instruments such as the worldwide freezing of all assets of individuals suspected to be in contact with terrorist groups based on name lists issued by the UN and EU[66]—which neither have an explicit legal basis nor provide for sufficient options for legal review— continue to gain in importance. Unlike the recovery measures that focus on organized crime, these are clearly political measures.

Another approach to further intensify recovery indirectly is to tax away illegal assets.[67] The primary intention behind this so-called Al Capone approach is to force criminals to pay tax on their illegal income as well. What makes this concept additionally attractive is that, with the necessary declarations, tax authorities could gather financial information that could be used in criminal investigations as well. However, serious concerns about such an approach exist. Indeed, the barriers between criminal investigation and taxation become blurred when tax authorities have to be informed about any relevant information gathered in the context of financial investigations by police and vice versa. In addition, some jurisdictions provide for aggravated rules for confiscation in the case of tax crime. In Germany, for example, the Penal Code provides that, in the case of professional (organized) tax fraud, not only the evaded taxes become the subject of the money laundering crime, but also the money or assets themselves; thus, everything is subject to confiscation.[68]

In the near future, a further strengthening of the concept can be expected. Review and amendment of the confiscation legislation is one of the priorities of the European Commission under the Stockholm Programme 2010–2014. In addition, a new directive on aggravated confiscation measures will soon be launched. It will require that member states improve their legislation in order to establish a comprehensive system for seizing, freezing, managing, and confiscating criminal assets.[69]

VIII. Conclusion

This essay has shown that the shape of confiscation has dramatically changed since the traditional metaphor "crime should not pay" first emerged. With the development of organized crime control policies, the concept of a finance-related strategy of crime control, forfeiture, and confiscation has been transformed. Initially a rather vague moral concept that was more cardinal than practical, it has since become a much more functional and targeted instrument to neutralize the incentive to engage in organized criminal activities. However, once implemented and established, it has encroached, together with money laundering control, on an array of additional areas of crime.[70] It is no longer a principle of criminal law but a tool of criminal policy. From this perspective it has to be seen as a logical, and forceful, part of the postmodern culture of control (Garland 2001).

This transformation becomes clear and even more obvious in light of its adoption in the counterterrorism field. Here, the measures were actually transformed into a real kind of weapon. The freezing of assets that are under suspicion draws obvious parallels with political measures that have been implemented by the European Union and sometimes even the United Nations against enemy regimes, such as the former Taliban regime, Belarus, Iran, Liberia, Myanmar, North Korea, or, recently, Syria. As a kind of universal measure, they have lost any connection to (organized) crime and, indeed, to criminal law at all.

It is, therefore, of little surprise, and perhaps to fittingly complete the picture, to note that even the International Criminal Court in The Hague can now order forfeiture as a sanction against those found guilty of genocide or other crimes for which it has jurisdiction.[71]

NOTES

1. Some rudiments can still be found in articles 213-1 and 222-49 of the Code pénale.
2. President's Commission on Organized Crime. *America's Habit: Drug Abuse, Drug Trafficking, and Organized Crime.* Washington, DC: President's Commission on Organized Crime,1986.   http://books.google.de/books?id=QcLZf3XU_mAC&printsec=frontcover &hl-de&source=gbs_ge_summary_r&cad=0#v=onepage&q&f-;false
3. UN Convention against Illicit Traffic in Narcotic Drugs and Psychotropic Substances.
4. European Convention on Laundering, Search, Seizure and Confiscation of the Proceeds from Crime of November 8, 1990.
5. Council of Europe Convention on Laundering, Search, Seizure and Confiscation of the Proceeds from Crime and on the Financing of Terrorism of May 16, 2005.
6. Council Action Plan to Combat Organised Crime of April 28, 1997 (97/C 251/01), O.J. C 251/1.
7. UN Convention against Illicit Traffic in Narcotic Drugs and Psychotropic Substances.
8. The Prevention and Control of Organised Crime: A European Strategy for the Beginning of the New Millennium (2000/C 124/01), O.J. C 124/1.
9. See section IV.
10. Council Framework Decision 2005/212/JHA of February 24, 2005 on Confiscation of Crime-Related Proceeds, Instrumentalities and Property, O.J. L 68/49.
11. Terminology differs between jurisdictions and instruments. For the purpose of this essay, provisional measures are referred to as "seizure" (considering that in Europe "freezing" is mainly used to refer to the freezing of suspicious terrorist assets; see below, section VII), and final measures or orders as "confiscation" (considering that "forfeiture" is mainly used as a synonym in US terminology, whereas the British and the German systems, for example, strictly differentiate between the two).
12. SOCA is the successor of the former British Assets Recovery Agency (ARA), which was abolished by the Serious Crime Act 2007.
13. For further details, see Madinger and Zalopany 1999, pp. 121 et seq.
14. For more details, see section V.

15. For critical remarks, see Pieth 1998.
16. http://www.legislation.gov.uk/ukpga/2002/29/contents
17. Cf. article 305*bis* of the Swiss Penal Code.
18. In only 7 out of 78 cases evaluated by the Max Planck Institute were investigations initially based on a suspicious transaction report, according to the Money Laundering Control Act. In all other cases, the successful conviction for money laundering was based on evidence obtained through embedded financial investigations from the predicate offense that led to the assets. For further details, see Kilchling 2002.
19. Cf. article 30 s. 3 of the Third EU Money Laundering Directive 2005/60/EC of 26.10.2005, O.J. L 309/15.
20. In particular, the Asia/Pacific Group, the Financial Action Task Force of South America (GAFUSUD), the Middle East and North Africa Financial Action Task Force (MENAFATF), the Inter-Governmental Action Group against Money Laundering in West Africa (GIABA), and the Caribbean Financial Action Task Force (CFATF).
21. In particular, the Council of Europe Committee of Experts on the Evaluation of Anti-money Laundering Measures and the Financing of Terrorism (MONEYVAL), or the Egmont Group of Financial Intelligence Units.
22. [First] Directive 91/308/EEC of June 10, 1991, on prevention of the use of the financial system for the purpose of money laundering, O.J. L 166/77; [second] Directive 2001/97/EC of December 4, 2001, amending Council Directive 91/308/EEC on prevention of the use of the financial system for the purpose of money laundering, O.J. L 344/76; [third] Directive 2005/60/EC of October 26, 2005, on the prevention of the use of the financial system for the purpose of money laundering and terrorist financing, O.J. L 309/15. A fourth directive is under preparation.
23. Joint Action 98/699/JHA of December 3, 1998, on money laundering, the identification, tracing, freezing, seizing, and confiscation of instrumentalities and the proceeds from crime, O.J. L 333/1; Framework Decision 2001/500/JHA of June 26, 2001, on money laundering, the identification, tracing, freezing, seizing, and confiscation of instrumentalities and the proceeds of crime, O.J. L 182/1; Framework Decision 2005/212/JHA of February 24, 2005, on Confiscation of Crime-Related Proceeds, Instrumentalities and Property, O.J. L 68/49.
24. See section V.
25. Cf. the 1995 Model Legislation by UNDCP and the 2005 Model Legislation jointly published by the UNODC and the IMF, http://www.imf.org/external/np/leg/amlcft/eng/pdf/amlml05.pdf; similar activities were initiated by the World Bank. More relevant links are provided on the related IMF website at http://www.imf.org/external/np/leg/amlcft/eng/aml4.htm
26. See above, note 3.
27. See above, note 4.
28. UN Convention against Transnational Organized Crime of November 15, 2000.
29. See above, note 5.
30. Introduced through recommendation no. 6 of the 2003 version of the 40 Recommendations.
31. Compare the 2012 version of the [40] FATF Recommendations (http://www.fatf-gafi.org).
32. The list requires exertion of confiscation at least for the following crimes: (a) participation in an organized criminal group and racketeering; (b) terrorism, including financing of terrorism; (c) trafficking in human beings and migrant smuggling; (d) sexual exploitation, including sexual exploitation of children; (e) illicit trafficking in narcotic drugs and

psychotropic substances; (f) illicit arms trafficking; (g) illicit trafficking in stolen and other goods; (h) corruption and bribery; (i) fraud; (j) counterfeiting currency; (k) counterfeiting and piracy of products; (l) environmental crime; (m) murder, grievous bodily injury; (n) kidnapping, illegal restraint, and hostage-taking; (o) robbery or theft; (p) smuggling; (q) extortion; (r) forgery; (s) piracy; and (t) insider trading and market manipulation.

33. Framework Decision 2005/212/JHA (see note 23). For more details, see section V.

34. Cf. article 34 of the 2005 Convention (see above, note 5).

35. See below, notes 36 and 37.

36. Framework Decision 2003/577/JHA of July 22, 2003, on the execution in the European Union of orders freezing property or evidence, O.J. L 196/45.

37. Framework Decision 2006/783/JHA of October 6, 2006, on the application of the principle of mutual recognition to confiscation orders, O.J. L. 328/59.

38. Cf. article 8 of Framework Decision 2006/783/JHA.

39. Initiative of the Kingdom of Denmark with a view to the adoption of a Council Framework Decision on Confiscation of Crime-related Proceeds, Instrumentalities and Property (2002/C 184/03), O.J. C 184/3.

40. Cf. article 3 s. 3 of the Framework Decision 2005/212/JHA (see above, note 23).

41. Cf. article 5 s. 7 of the Vienna Convention (see above, note 3): "[Parties] may consider ensuring that the onus of proof be reversed [...]."

42. For more details, see Friedmann 2003, pp. 5 et seq., Millington and Sutherland Williams 2010, pp. 2 et seq.

43. For more details, see Kilchling 1997; Savona and Vettori 2001; Vettori 2006.

44. Cf. article 131-21 of the French Penal Code. Under article 222-49 it can be ordered additionally. For more details, see Matsopoulou 1995; Kletzlen and Godefroy 1997.

45. For more details, see Gallant 2005.

46. Article 416*bis* of the Italian Penal Code and article 12*sexies* of Law no. 501/1994. For more details, see Vettori 2006.

47. Judgment of 08/06/1995 (*Jamil* case), Series A, Vol. 317.

48. Cf. article 76a of the Danish Penal Code.

49. Cf. article 20 ss. 2 and 3 of the Austrian Penal Code.

50. Cf. article 12*sexies* of Law no. 501/1994.

51. Cf. article 72 of the Swiss Penal Code.

52. Cf. article 2 (3) Drug Trafficking Offences Act (DTOA) 1994.

53. Cf. articles 222-39-1, 225-6, 421-2-3 of the French Penal Code.

54. Constitutional Court, ruling of February 17, 1994, nullifying article 12*quinquies* of Law no. 356/92.

55. Cf. article 3 s. 2 of Framework Decision 2005/212/JHA, see above, note 10.

56. Cf. article 73d of the German Penal Code.

57. Cf. article 20 ss. 2 and 3 of the Austrian Penal Code.

58. Cf. article 36e s.2 of the Dutch Penal Code.

59. Judgments of February 22, 1994 (*Raimondo* case), Series A, Vol. 281, pp. 21 et seq.

60. BVerfG, 2 BvR 564/95 of 14.01.2004 with reference to an earlier ruling of 12.12.1967.

61. The so-called asset penalty (Vermögensstrafe) according to article 43a of the German Penal Code had provided that offenders could be punished by confiscation limited by the total of their assets.

62. BVerfG, 794/95 of 20.03.2002.

63. *Austin v. United States*, 113 S. Ct. 2801 (1993); for more details, see Tonry 1997.

64. BVerfG, 2 BvR 820/06 of 29.05.2006.
65. BVerfG, 2 BvR 1012/02 of 05.05.2004.
66. A variety of different lists exist. See, for example, EU Council Regulation (EC) 881/2002 of May 27, 2002, imposing certain specific restrictive measures directed against certain persons and entities associated with the Al-Qaida network, O.J. L 139/9 (title redrafted through Council Regulation (EU) 754/2011 of August 1, 2011, O.J. L 199/23).
67. For more details, see Alldridge 2003.
68. Cf. article 261 s. 1.3 and s. 7 of the German Penal Code.
69. European Commission, The EU Internal Security Strategy in Action: Five Steps towards a More Secure Europe. COM(2010) 673 final of 22.11.2010.
70. With the 2012 relaunch, the scope of the FATF recommendations (previously FATF 40+9) was extended to also combat the proliferation of weapons of mass destruction (http://www.fatf-gafi.org).
71. Cf. article 77 of the Rome Statute.

References

Albrecht, H.-J. 1998. "Organisierte Kriminalität: Theoretische Erklärungen und empirische Befunde." In *Organisierte Kriminalität und Verfassungsstaat*, edited by H.-J. Albrecht, 1–40. Heidelberg, Germany: Müller.

Albrecht, H.-J. 2002. "The UN Transnational Crime Convention: An Introduction." In *The Containment of Transnational Organized Crime*, edited by H.-J. Albrecht and C. Fijnaut, 1–18. Freiburg: Ed. Iuscrim.

Alldridge, P. 2003. *Money Laundering Law: Forfeiture, Confiscation, Civil Recovery, Criminal Laundering and Taxation of the Proceeds of Crime*. Oxford: Hart.

Arzt, G. 1996. "Amerikanisierung der Gerechtigkeit." In *Festschrift für Otto Triffterer zum 65. Geburtstag*, edited by K. Schmoller, 527–549. New York: Springer.

Bodnar, A. 2003. "Criminal Confiscation." In *Asset Recovery: Criminal Confiscation and Civil Recovery*, edited by I. Smith and T. Owen, 176–234. London: LexisNexis.

Ehrhard, F. 1934. *La confiscation générale en droit français moderne*. Paris: Recueil Sirey.

Eser, A. 1969. *Die strafrechtlichen Sanktionen gegen das Eigentum*. Tübingen, Germany: Mohr.

Eser, A. 1993. "Neue Wege der Gewinnabschöpfung." In *Beiträge zur Rechtswissenschaft. Festschrift für Walter Stree und Johannes Wessels zum 70. Geburtstag*, edited by W. Küper and J. Wessels, 883–853. Heidelberg, Germany: C. F. Müller.

Friedman, D. 2003. "Asset Recovery: An Overview." In *Asset Recovery: Criminal Confiscation and Civil Recovery*, edited by I. Smith and T. Owen, 1–32. London: LexisNexis.

Fijnaut, C., and L. Paoli. 2004. "Comparative Synthesis of Part III." In *Organised Crime in Europe: Concepts, Patterns and Control Policies in the European Union and Beyond*, edited by C. Fijnaut and L. Paoli, 1035–1041. Dordrecht: Springer.

Gallant, M. M. 2005. *Money Laundering and the Proceeds of Crime: Economic Crime and Civil Remedies*. Cheltenham, UK: E. Elgar.

Garland, D. 2001. *The Culture of Control: Crime and Social Order in Contemporary Society*. Oxford: Oxford University Press.

Hetzer, W. 1999. Finanzbehörden im Kampf gegen Geldwäsche und organisierte Kriminalität. *Juristische Rundschau*: 141–148.

HM Crown Prosecution Service Inspectorate (HMCPSI) 2004. *Payback Time: Joint Review of Asset Recovery since the Proceeds of Crime Act 2002*, http://www.hmcpsi.gov.uk/documents/reports/CJJI_THM/BOTJ/PaybackTIme_Rep_Nov04.pdf

Kilchling, M. 1997. "Comparative Perspectives on Forfeiture Legislation in Europe and the United States." *European Journal on Crime, Criminal Law and Criminal Justice* 5(3): 342–361. (thematic issue on money laundering and confiscation)

Kilchling, M. 2001. "Tracing, Seizing and Confiscating Proceeds from Corruption (and Other Illegal Conduct) within or outside the Criminal Justice System." *European Journal on Crime, Criminal Law and Criminal Justice* 9(4): 264–280.

Kilchling, M., ed. 2002. *Die Praxis der Gewinnabschöpfung in Europa.* Freiburg: Ed. Iuscrim.

Kletzlen, A., and T. Godefroy. 1997. "Confiscation and Anti-money-laundering Regulations under French Law." *European Journal on Crime, Criminal Law and Criminal Justice* 5(3): 273–280. (thematic issue on money laundering and confiscation)

Krajewski, K. 2005. "Systems of Penal Sanctions and their Development in Western and Central Europe: Convergence or Divergence?" In *The Third German-Hungarian Colloquium on Penal Law and Criminology,* edited by F. Irk and H.-J. Albrecht, 47–64. Miskolc, Hungary: Bíbor Kladó.

Levi, M. 1997. "Taking the Profit Out of Crime: The UK Experience." *European Journal on Crime, Criminal Law and Criminal Justice* 5(3): 228–239. (thematic issue on money laundering and confiscation)

Levi, M., and L. Osofsky. 1995. "The End of the Money Trail: Confiscating the Proceeds of Crime." In *Butterworths International Guide to Money Laundering: Law and Practice,* edited by R. Parlour, 301–316. London: Butterworths.

Levy, L. 1996. *A License to Steal: The Forfeiture of Property.* Chapel Hill: University of North Carolina Press.

Madinger, J., and S. Zalopany. 1999. *Money Laundering: A Guide for Criminal Investigators.* Boca Raton, FL: CRC Press.

Matsopoulou, H. 1995. "La confiscation spéciale dans le nouveau code pénal." *Revue de Science criminelle et de Droit pénal compare:* 301–317.

Millington, T., and M. Southerland Williams. 2010. *The Proceeds of Crime.* 3d ed. Oxford: Oxford University Press.

Pieth, M. 1995. "Das zweite Paket gegen das organisierte Verbrechen." *Schweizerische Zeitschrift für Strafrecht* 113: 225–239.

Pieth, M. 1998. "The Prevention of Money Laundering: A Comparative Analysis." *European Journal of Crime, Criminal Law and Criminal Justice* 6: 159–168.

Plywaczewski, E., and W. Filipkowski. 2004. "The Development of Organised Crime Policies in Poland: From Socialist Regime to 'Rechtsstaat.'" In *Organised Crime in Europe: Concepts, Patterns and Control Policies in the European Union and Beyond,* edited by C. Fijnaut and L. Paoli, 899–930. Dordrecht: Springer.

Savona, E., and B. Vettori. 2001. *The Seizure and Confiscation of the Proceeds from Crime in the European Union Member States: What Works, What Does Not and What Is Promising.* Transcrime Report no. 1. Trento, Italy.

Tonry, M. 1997. "Forfeiture Laws, Practices and Controversies in the US." *European Journal on Crime, Criminal Law and Criminal Justice* 5(3): 294–307. (thematic issue on money laundering and confiscation)

van Duyne, P., and M. Levi. 1999. "Criminal Financial Investigations: A Strategic and Tactical Approach in the European Dimension." In *Global Organized Crime and International Security,* edited by E. Viano, 139–156. Aldershot, UK: Ashgate.

Vettori, B. 2006. *Tough on Criminal Wealth: Exploring the Practice of Proceeds from Crime Confiscation in the EU.* Dordrecht: Springer.

INDEX

Printed in the USA
CPSIA information can be obtained
at www.ICGtesting.com
BVHW020725060823
668156BV00004B/3

9 780190 947323